Quilters' Travel Companion

8th Edition 2004 - 2006

Published by:

chalet PUBLISHING
32 Grand Avenue
Manitou Springs, CO 80829
(719) 685-5041

Edited by:
Audrey Swales Anderson
& Thomas Culp

Check out our website:
www.chalet-publishing.com
E-mail:
info@chalet-publishing.com
Fax: (719) 685-2347

Chalet Publishing
is the Home of
the *Quilters' Travel Companion*

With all our love,
this book is dedicated to
Audrey's husband, Marlow and
Tom's wife, Rona.
Thank you for your hours of
assistance and support.

Thanks for your help, Ruth O'Riley

Illustrations from Clip Art:
Winter Weather & Garden Party
by Rebecca Carter,
Countryside Collection & Four Seasons
by Kathy Distefano Griffiths
From My Hands to Warm Your Heart
by Lori Gardner
All Occasions & Everyday by Annette Ward
At The Cabin by Leeré Aldrich
and Whimsy for all Seasons by Jeff Goddsell
Distributed by Provo Crafts, Salt Lake City

How to Use this Guide

General Purpose: Whenever you're away from home be sure to take your *Quilters' Travel Companion* (QTC). You never know when you might have an opportunity to check out a shop. This guide includes featured listings for over 2000 quilt shops in the United States and Canada and even one in the Bahamas. Lots of customers have told us that they have the shops sign their book along the way--great fun!

Layout of the Book: The shop listings are organized by state. We provide a state map which will enable you to tell at a glance where each of the featured shops is located. The number on the state map will also be found in the shop listing.

In addition, for each state we include a listing of other shops located in that state. A phone number is included for these shops. Please call before venturing there as our information on these shops is not as good as for the featured shops. We have made every effort for the information in this book to be up-to-date and accurate. Unfortunately shops do move, change hours, or go out of business; so if you want to be sure before you go a phone call might be prudent.

All the 'featured shops' information was correct when published. Also note that many new telephone area codes have been added across the country and many more new ones are planned.

Send us Info: We've tried hard to include every shop in the country, but we're sure that we've missed some. If you know of one we've missed drop us a note or call us at (719) 685-5041, Fax: (719) 685-2347 email--info@chalet-publishing.com or visit our website at: www.chalet-publishing.com.

Plan your Trips: There are two basic ways we see you using our 'Travel Companion'.

You will have to use commercial maps in conjunction with our state maps. We are just trying to provide general locations.

1) Whenever you're traveling on business or vacation check out your route and see what shops you may be close to. The state maps should give you an idea if you'll be in the vicinity of a store. Then if you have time or can make time give yourself a break and STOP !

Since beginning these guides in 1992, I have certainly realized that I used to drive right by shops on my travels, but not stop because I didn't realize they were close.

2) Or go WILD and take a few days with family or friends and plan a whole trip going from shop to shop. Many shops are in historic / tourist places so your trip just may lead you into an unexpected adventure. Either way, enjoy exploring all the great shops scattered across this country. We would be grateful if you'd tell them that QTC got you there.

New treatment of the Guilds: Once again the guilds are included in this edition. We hope you have fun visiting some other clubs. We get all our information about guilds from the shops or folks using the 'Travel Companion'.

We know not all addresses are complete, but this is all we have been given. If you need more information about a guild, please try contacting a shop in that area.

Map Conventions used in the QTC:

a) Our state maps only include major roads; please use our maps in conjunction with commercial maps.

b) All maps are oriented with North at the top.

c) The shops are marked either by a square with the street address inside (i.e. 100) or by a star ☆

* = traffic light	■ =Business or landmark
┼┼┼┼┼┼┼┼ = Railroad	A Gray line or area = water
Dashed line = state border	● = City

Chalet Publishing's mascot, Max.

www.chalet-publishing.com

CONTENTS

U.S.A. Shops

Bahamian Shop

Canadian Shops

Have a Great Trip

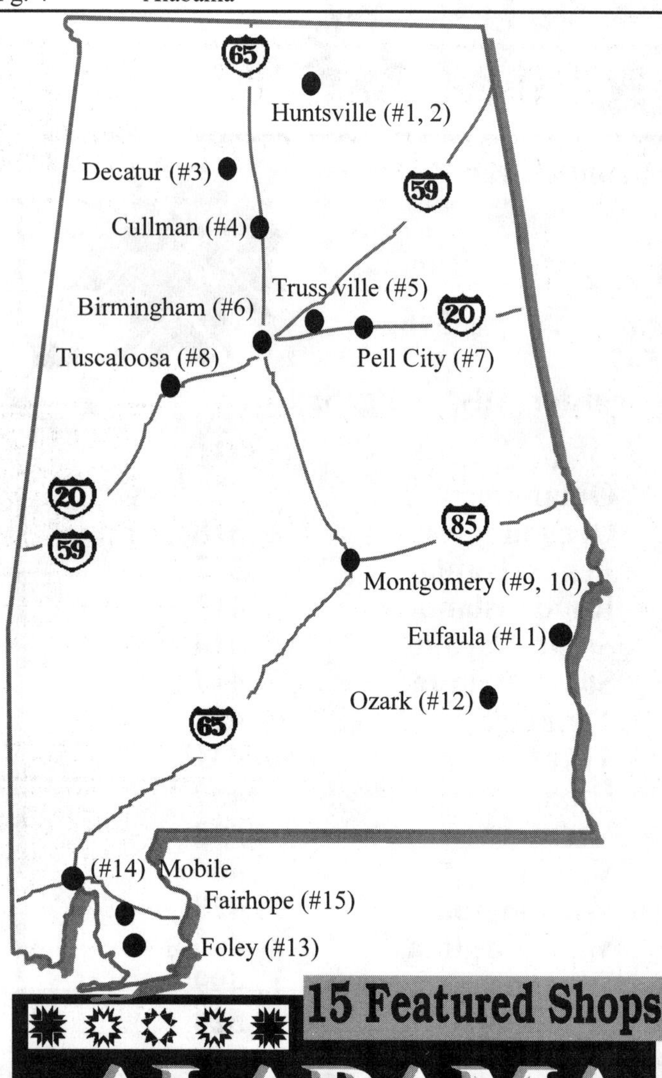

15 Featured Shops

ALABAMA

Huntsville, AL #1

603 Humes Avenue 35801
(256) 533-3886
patchesand@knology.net
Visit our Web Site at:
www.patches&stitches.com
Owner: Linda Worley
Est: 1978 2500 sq.ft.

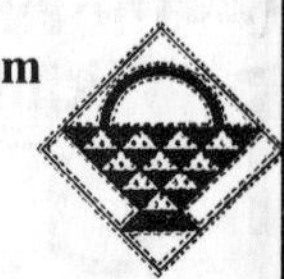

**Mon - Fri 9:30 - 5:30
Thur til 6
Sat 9:30-4:30**

Toll Free # 1-877-SHE-SEWS
Complete line of quilt supplies; also cross-stitch and needlepoint. Extensive Fibers. Mail order.

We are located in one of Huntsville's Historic Mill Villages. Call for directions if you can't find us. We are off of Andrew Jackson behind the CVS Pharmacy.

Huntsville, AL #2

**Mon - Fri 10 - 5
Sat 10 - 4**

Lydia's

518 Madison St. 35801
(256) 536-9700 Est: 1992
E-Mail: Lydiashsv@aol.com
Web Site: www.Lydias.com
Owners: Michael & Mary Penton 3000 sq.ft.

Quilting & Heirloom Sewing Classes & Supplies
Husqvarna Viking Sewing Machines
2 Blocks from Downtown Historic District.

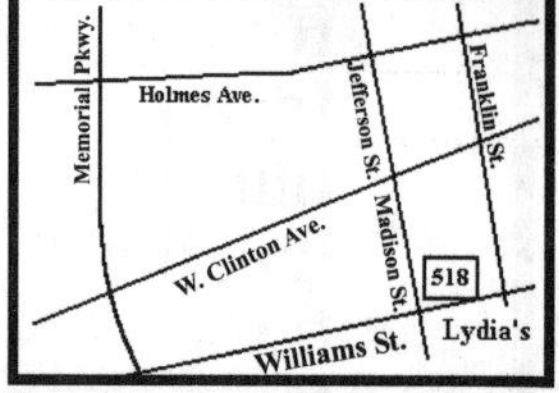

Decatur, AL #3

**Mon - Fri 10 - 5
Sat 10 - 4**

Crafty Bear Quilt Shop

2208 Danville Rd. S.W. 35601
(256) 351-0420 Est: 1988
E-Mail: cbearshop@mindspring.com
Owner: Helen DeButy 2500 sq.ft.

Cotton Fabrics, books, patterns, supplies, and lots of classes. The friendliest quilt shop for service, inspiration and sharing of ideas.

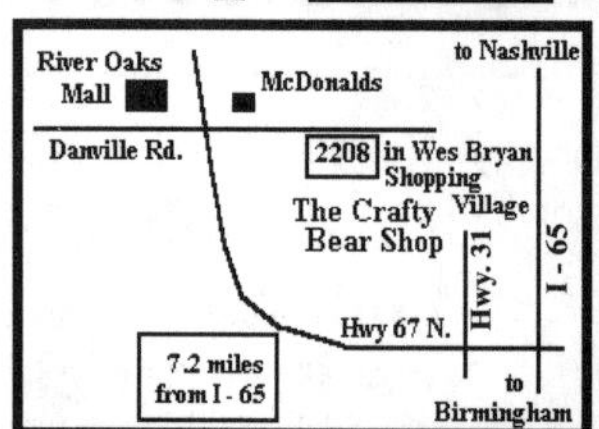

Cullman, AL #4

Mon - Sat 10 - 5

Quilts In The District

103 1st Ave. NE, Suite 100 35055
(256) 734-1005
quiltsindistrict@bellsouth.net
Owners: Becky & Dewey Hanks
Est: 2004 2500 sq.ft. 1000 bolts
Newest Shop in Area! Basic, specialty and reproduction fabrics. Latest books, notions. Beginning to intermediate classes! Great teachers, customer service!

Trussville, AL #5

Heart to Heart Quilt Shop

1110 N. Chalkville Rd. 35173
(205) 661-0537 Fax: (205) 661-9497
E-Mail: h2hquilt@earthlink.net Est: 1998
Web Site: www.hearttoheartquiltshop.com
Owners: Terry Cates & Cindy Wilson 2500 sq.ft.

Mon- Sat 9 - 5 Tues 9 - 8

Located in Valley View Shopping Center.
Newest Designer 100% cotton Fabrics, Books, Notions, Patterns, Classes. Helpful, friendly staff.

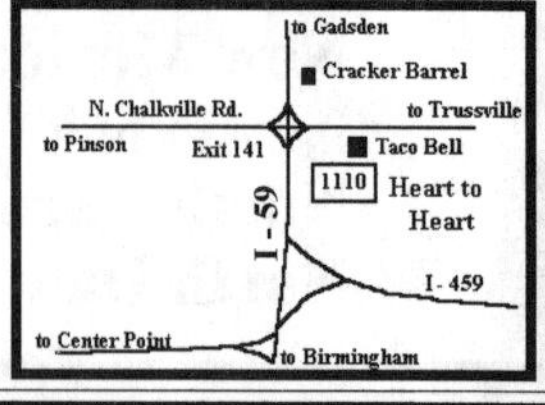

Birmingham, AL #6

Quiltmaker's Workshop

A Quilter's Quilt Shop

1930 Edwards Lake Rd. #132 35235
(205 6[illegible]1-9780
Owner: Annie Woods

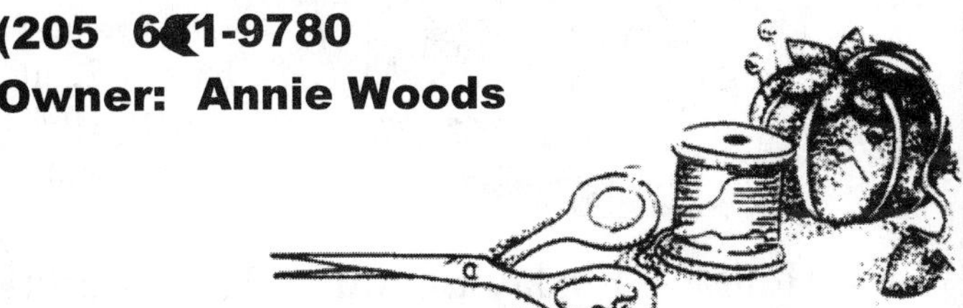

Serving the Greater Birmingham Area since 1994

Mon - Sat
10 - 5
Thur til 8

I - 59
Exit 32
Edwards Lake Rd.
1930
Valley Ctr.
Hampton Inn
I - 459
Quiltmaker's Workshop
I - 20
to Atlanta

Over 3000 bolts of the latest cotton fabrics
Great Books
Patterns
Notions
Gadgets
Gifts

Friendly service and free advice
Classes for all levels.

Pell City, AL #7

Mon - Fri 10 - 6
Sat 9 - 5

Heart N Home Quilts

1605 Martin St. S, Suite 1 (Hwy. 231) 35128
(205) 814-0063
heartnhome@coosahs.net
www.heartnhomequilts.com
Owner: Kathy Kirby

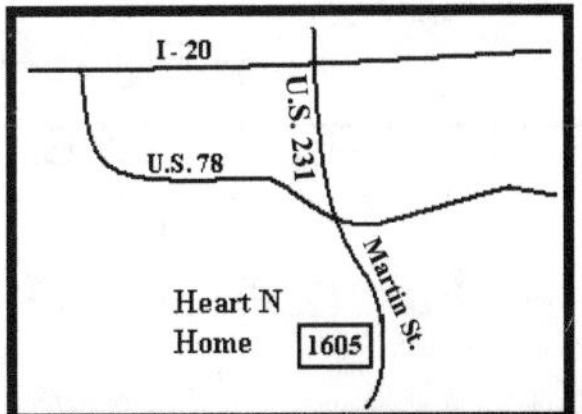

Quality 100% cotton fabrics, books, notions & quilting supplies. Classes for ages 10 & up. Friendly, personal service. Janome sales & service. Kathy is a certified *Quilt in a Day* Inst.

Tuscaloosa, AL #8

Mon - Fri 10 - 5
Sat 10 - 3

Carolina Lily Quilt Shop

2120 7th St. 35401
(205) 349-8899
Owner: Joy W. Robertson
Est: 1997
carolinalily@earthlink.net

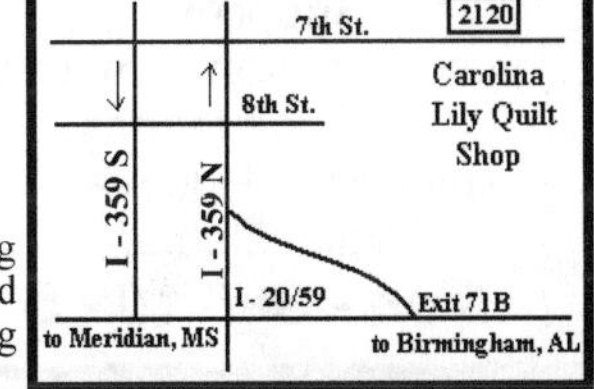

100% cotton fabrics from all leading manufacturers, books, patterns, frames and quilting notions. Classes and machine quilting also available.

Montgomery, AL #9

Mon - Fri 9 - 4
Sat by Appt.

Rose of Sharon

Mulberry District
1721 W. 2nd St. 36106
(334) 281-9775 Est: 1994
Owner: Sharon Wilson

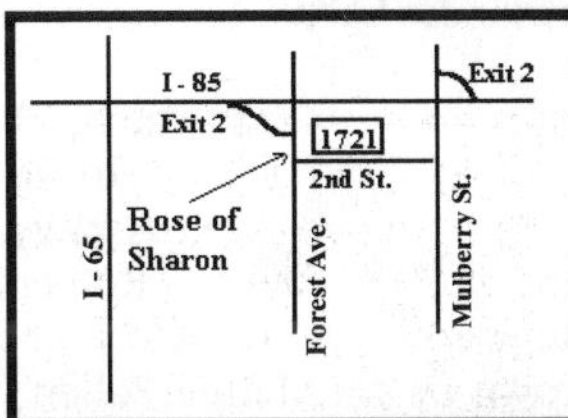

100% cotton fabrics, thread, stencils, notions and quilted items for sale. Hand guided machine quilting by Susan Moseley.

Montgomery, AL #10

Mon - Fri 9:30 - 5
Sat 9:30 - 3

Kudzu Blossom Quilt Shop

3666-E Debby Dr. 36111
(334) 288-8108
Owner: Janice Jarrett
Est: 1997 1500 sq.ft.

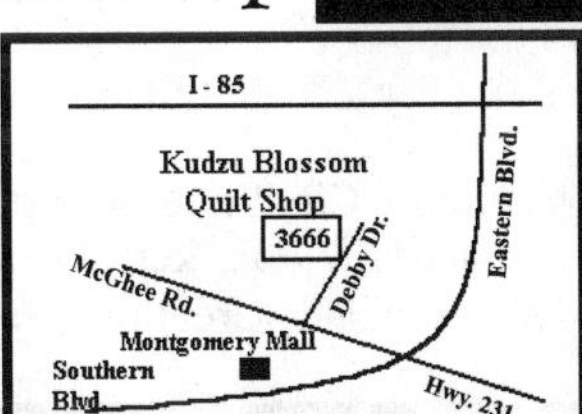

A wonderful shop to meet all your quilting needs. Lots of great fabrics, books, patterns, and quilting supplies.

Eufaula, AL #11

Tues - Fri 10 - 5:30
Sat 10 - 4

Eufaula's Quilt-N-Sew

131 E. Broad St. 36027
(334) 688-1870 Fax: (334) 687-1022
dhardin@veriqik.com
Est: 2001 3000 sq.ft. 3000+ Bolts

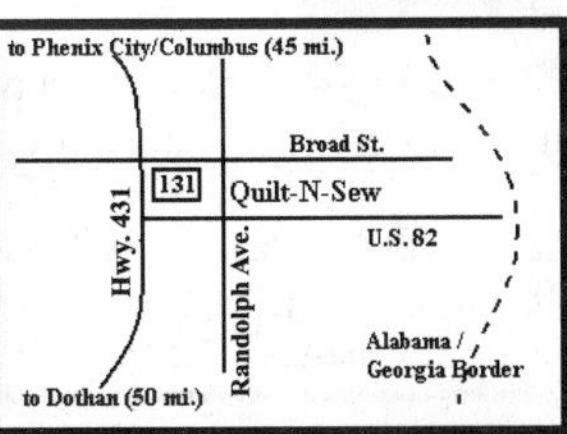

Downtown in beautiful, historic Eufaula. Many fabrics, sewing & quilting notions, patterns, trims, buttons, books.
Long-arm machine quilting done on site.

Ozark, AL #12

Mon - Sat 9:30 - 5

Front Porch Quilt Shoppe

199 N Hwy. 231 36360
(334) 445-3521
Owner: Melanie Simpson
Est: 1999

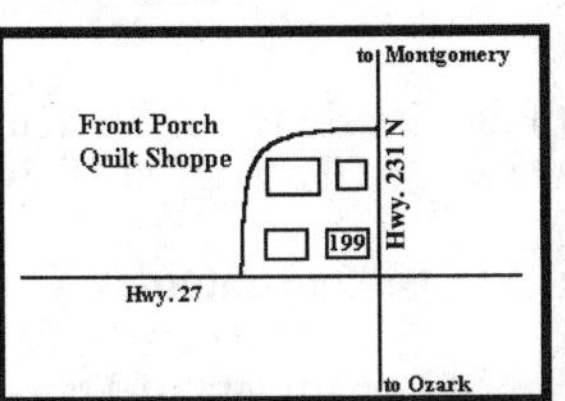

This charming shop is located in Deloney's Verandas. "Where quilters gather" for fabric - books - patterns - notions - classes and fun.

Foley, AL #13

Mon - Sat 10 - 5
Thur til 7

Lacy's Quilt Studio

"Continuing the Art of Quilt Making Into the Next Generation"

904 N. McKenzie St. (Hwy. 59) 36535
(251) 943-4302 Fax: Same
Email: lacy@lacysquiltstudio.com
Website: www.lacysquiltstudio.com
Owner: Lacy Peturis

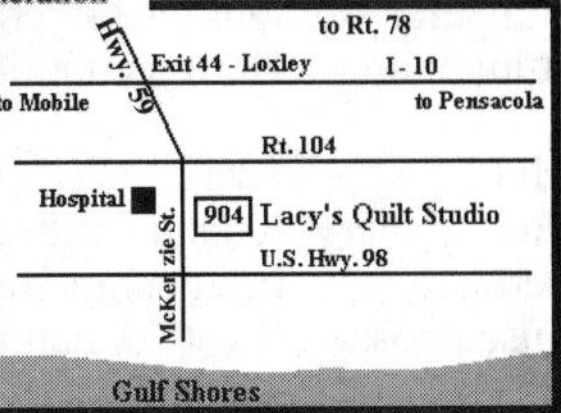

Lacy's Quilt Studio carries the finest 100% cotton fabrics, along with the newest quilt books, patterns and notions.

5763 Airport Blvd. Mobile, Al 36608
(251) 343-8270
Fax: (251) 343-8390 nnworks5763@aol.com

WWW.NOSTALGICNEEDLE.COM

Mobile, AL #14

Quilting and Heirloom Sewing Fabrics and Supplies.
Patterns, notions, imported laces and fabrics.
Authorized Husqvarna Viking Dealer.
Mon - Sat 10 - 5

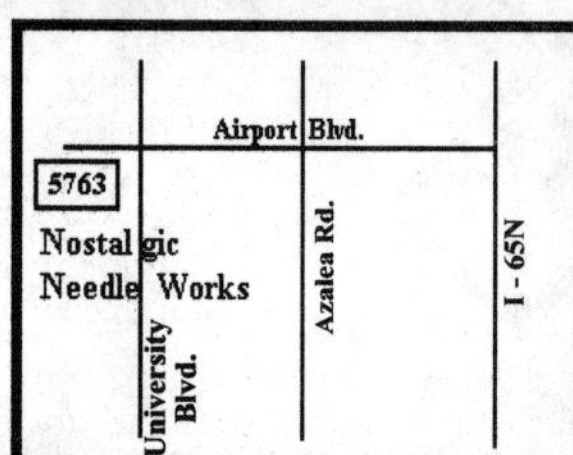

Bears & Quilting By The Bay

212 1/2 Fairhope Ave.
36532
(251) 928-8989
Fax: Same
Owner: Nancy Scott
Est: 1994
2000 sq.ft.

Store Hours: Monday-Saturday 10:00 - 5:00

Your one stop shopping for bears, fabrics, quilting books, notions, kits, BOM's and quilting classes.

Over 2,500 bolts of fabrics and more arriving daily. Lots of new books and old time favorites and many different BOM's (block of the month) to choose from.

All bear lovers and fabricholics welcome !!
e-mail: nancy@bearsandquilting.com
www.bearsandquilting.com

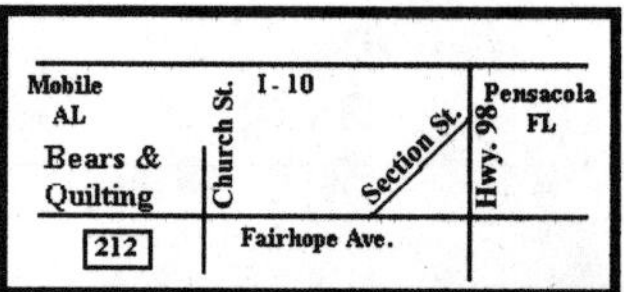

I - 10, Exit 35A 7.5 miles to "Welcome to Fairhope" veer to right will become Section St. 4th traffic light turn right onto Fairhope Ave. Store located on left hand side, 1/2 block past Church St.

Fairhope, AL #15

Other Shops in Alabama: *We suggest calling first*

Alberta	Gee's Bend Quilters Collective, 14570 County Rd 29	334-573-2323
Albertville	Memory Lane Quilts, 115 E. Main St., PO Box 1663	256-891-8928
Alexander City	Midtown Fabrics & Crafts, 26 Main St.	205-234-2394
Anniston	Cloth Patch, 2120 Noble St.	205-237-9972
Athens	Hickory House Gift Shoppe & Antique Mall, 23101 Hwy. 72 E	205-232-9860
Athens	Quilt to Remember, 27344 Elkins Rd	256-233-2585
Auburn	Kid's Kloset, 555 Opelika Rd	334-821-7781
Brownsboro	Martha Pullen Co., 149 Old Big Cove Rd	800-547-4176
Daphine	Noel's Southern Quilts, 30725 Cemetary Rd	251-621-2920
Decatur	Quilts & More, 1310 Church St NE	256-355-1886
Dothan	J&J's Quilts & Things, 14 Leon Dr	334-794-8025
Elkmont	Heart of Dixie Quilt Shop, 23640 Highway 99	256-232-0508
Foley	Quilt Connection, 21188 Miflin Rd.	334-943-4641
Gulf Shores	Sea Quilt Shoppe, 22131 Cotton Creek	251-968-7327
Killen	Calico Rose Quilt Shop, 1367 Hwy 72	256-757-7600
Millbrook	Path Less Traveled, 4531 Bibb Dr	334-290-2992
Mobile	L.M.L.L., 551Grand Bay-Wilmer Rd S	334-649-2639
Mobile	Fabric Works, 5441 Hwy. 90 W.	334-666-0285
Opelika	Opelika Sewing Center, 3305 Pepperell Pkwy	334-749-9522
Pelham	Harry's Southern Textiles, 2775 Hwy. 31 S	205-664-1811
Pell City	Southern Comfort Quilts, 2715 Stemley Bridge Rd	205-338-7311
Rainbow City	Stitchin Post, 3805 Rainbow Dr.	256-442-0933
Russellville	Parker's Discount Hwy., 24 E	205-332-4539
Wetumpka	Creations Galore, 105 E. Main	334-567-6096

Alabama Guilds:

Athens	Athens Piecemakers Quilt Guild	Meets: 1st Thursday 7 p.m., First Christian Church, basement
Birmingham	Birmingham Quilters Guild	
Decatur	Quilt Lover's Guild, 2208 Danville Rd. SW, 35601	Meets: 1st Tuesday 7pm. at Crafty Bear Quilt Shop
Enterprise	Enterprising Quilters, P.O. Box 310328, 36331	Meets: 1st & 3rd Thursdays at 7pm, Citizens Bank Comm. Room
Florence	Shoals Piecemakers Quilt Guild	
Hartselle	Quilter Lovers' GuildHartselle Library, 35640	
Huntsville	Heritage Quilters of Huntsville, 35824	Meets: 3rd Thursday 7 p.m. at Faith Presbyterian Church, corner Whitesburg Dr. & Airport Rd.
Mobile	Azalea City Quilters Guild	Meets: 2nd Tuesday at 10:30 a.m. at United Methodist Church
Montgomery	Kudzu Quilter's Guild, 3933 Croydon Rd., 36109	
Pell City	Friendship Quilters, 1605 Martin St. So. Suite 1, 35128	Meets: 2nd Saturday @ 10am at Pell City Recreation Center
Tuscaloosa	West Alabama Quilters Guild, P.O. Box 020059, 35401	Meets: 2nd Saturday at 9:30 a.m. at Department of Transportation, 1000 28th Avenue

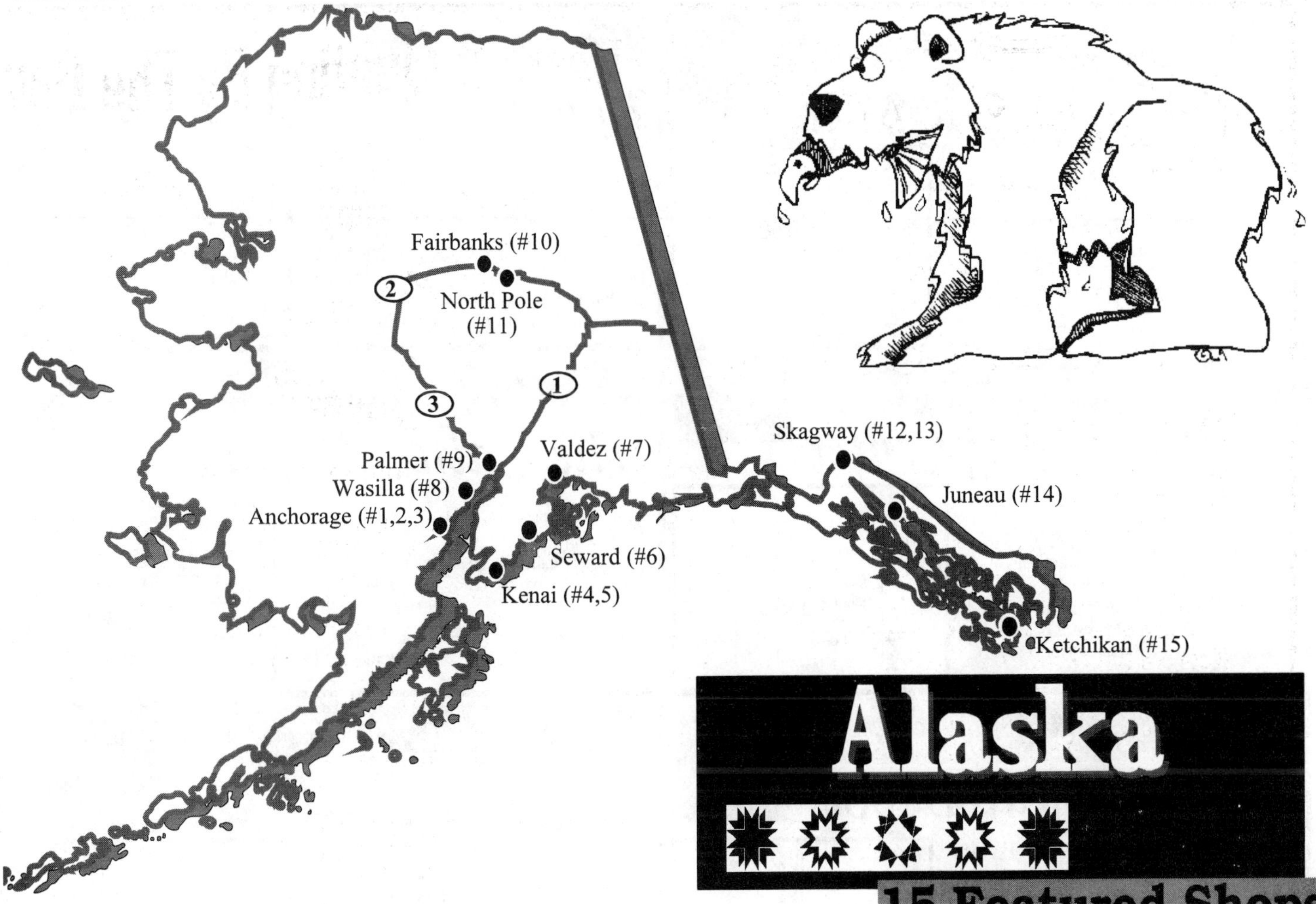

Fairbanks (#10)
North Pole (#11)
Palmer (#9)
Wasilla (#8)
Anchorage (#1,2,3)
Valdez (#7)
Seward (#6)
Kenai (#4,5)
Skagway (#12,13)
Juneau (#14)
Ketchikan (#15)

Alaska

15 Featured Shops

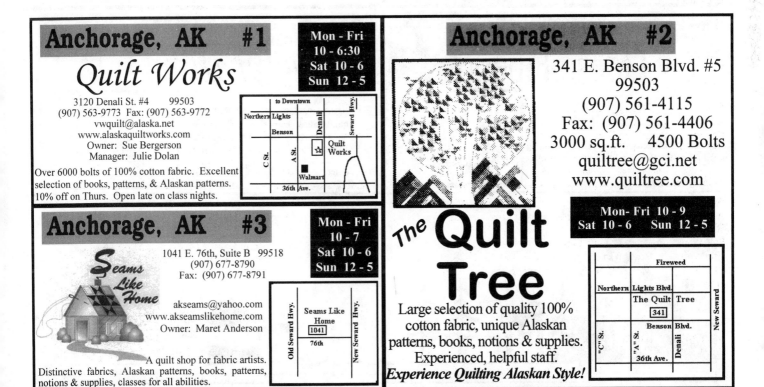

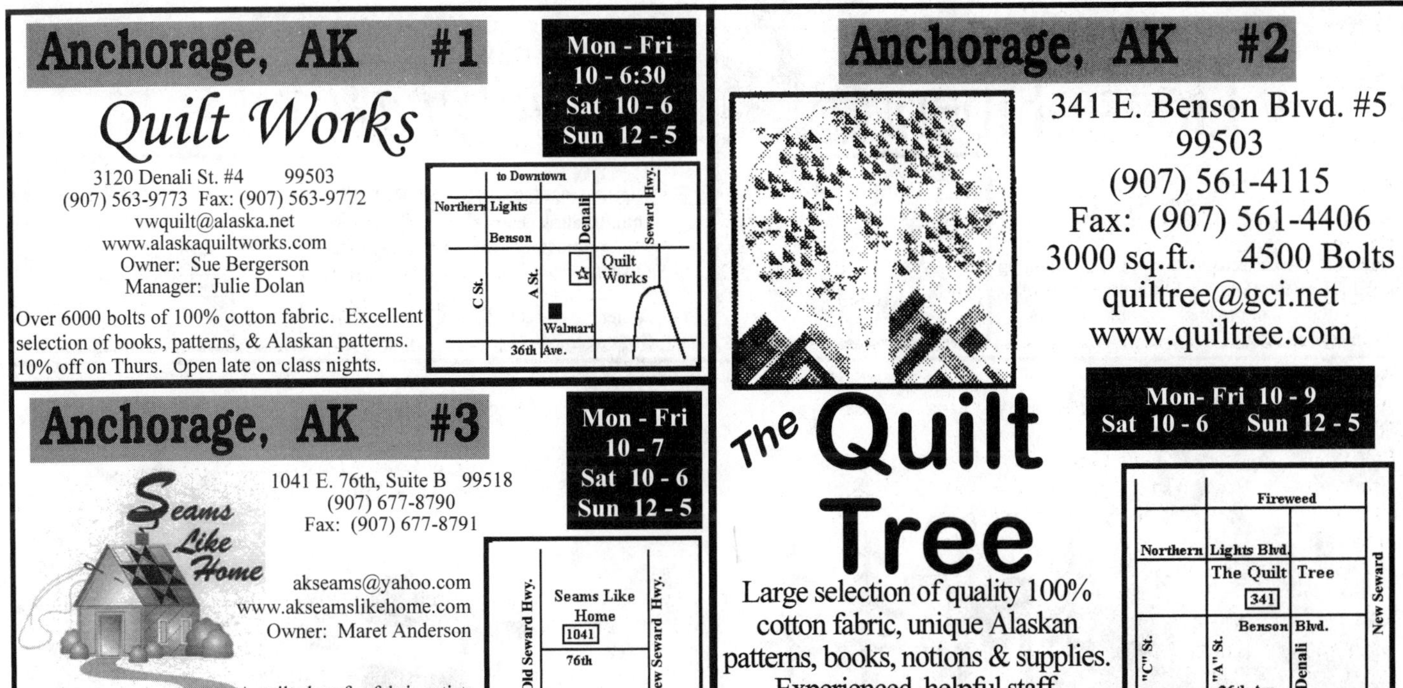

Anchorage, AK #1
Quilt Works
Mon - Fri 10 - 6:30
Sat 10 - 6
Sun 12 - 5
3120 Denali St. #4 99503
(907) 563-9773 Fax: (907) 563-9772
vwquilt@alaska.net
www.alaskaquiltworks.com
Owner: Sue Bergerson
Manager: Julie Dolan
Over 6000 bolts of 100% cotton fabric. Excellent selection of books, patterns, & Alaskan patterns. 10% off on Thurs. Open late on class nights.
to Downtown
Northern Lights
Benson
Denali
Seward Hwy.
C St.
A St.
Quilt Works
Walmart
36th Ave.
Anchorage, AK #2
341 E. Benson Blvd. #5
99503
(907) 561-4115
Fax: (907) 561-4406
3000 sq.ft. 4500 Bolts
quiltree@gci.net
www.quiltree.com
Mon- Fri 10 - 9
Sat 10 - 6 Sun 12 - 5
The Quilt Tree
Large selection of quality 100% cotton fabric, unique Alaskan patterns, books, notions & supplies. Experienced, helpful staff.
Experience Quilting Alaskan Style!
Fireweed
Northern Lights Blvd.
The Quilt Tree
341
Benson Blvd.
"C" St.
"A" St.
Denali
36th Ave.
New Seward
Anchorage, AK #3
Mon - Fri 10 - 7
Sat 10 - 6
Sun 12 - 5
Seams Like Home
1041 E. 76th, Suite B 99518
(907) 677-8790
Fax: (907) 677-8791
akseams@yahoo.com
www.akseamslikehome.com
Owner: Maret Anderson
A quilt shop for fabric artists. Distinctive fabrics, Alaskan patterns, books, patterns, notions & supplies, classes for all abilities.
Old Seward Hwy.
Seams Like Home
1041
76th
New Seward Hwy.

Kenai, AK #4

Mon - Fri 10 - 6
Sat 10 - 5

Quilt Kits Alaska

49926 Douglas Ln. 99611
(907) 776-8858
www.quiltkitsalaska.com
Owner: Terry DiBetta

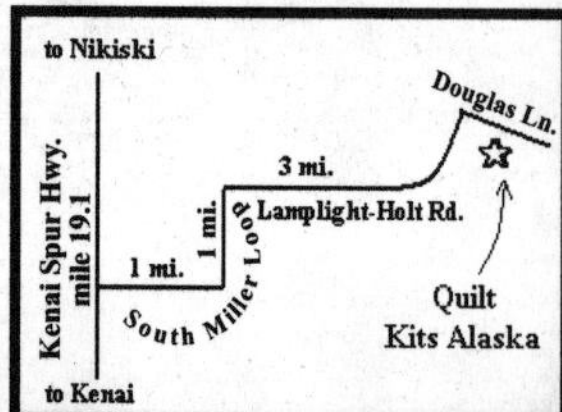

Quilt Kits - Quilting Fabrics (including 500+ Batiks) - Classes - Alaskan Patterns - Books
Sewing Space Available
Beautiful Lake Front Setting.
Motorhome Turn Around Space.

Kenai, AK #5

Mon - Sat 9 - 6
Sun 1 - 4

Kenai Fabric Center

115 N. Willow 99611
(907) 283-4595 Fax: (907) 283-5609
Est: 1970 6000+ Bolts

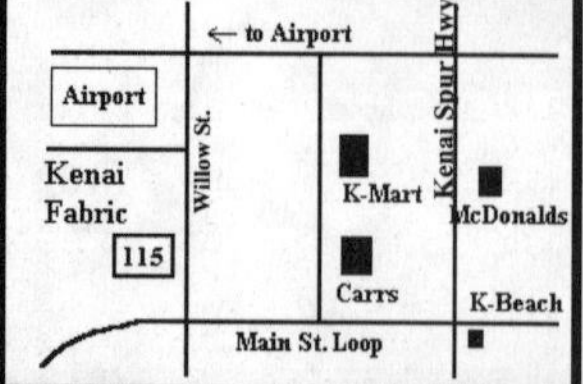

Quilting Fabrics & Classes, & Outerwear fabrics, Husqvarna/Viking & White Sewing Machines & Sergers, Notions, Yarns, Books, Family-owned.

Seward, AK #6

Mon - Sat 10 - 6

Seward Sewing Center

216 4th Ave. 99664
(907) 224-7647 Fax: (907) 224-7648
Est: 2000 880 sq.ft. 700 Bolts

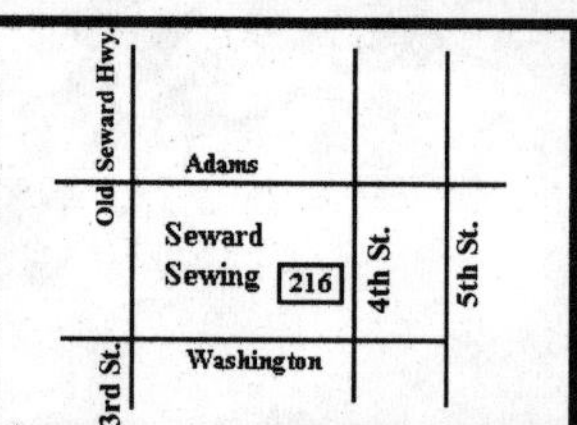

Best prices on the Kenai Peninsula. A good variety of "Alaska" fabrics. Located in historic downtown Seward. Come see us.

Valdez, AK #7

Mon - Sat 10 - 5:30

The Calico Whale

354 Fairbanks Dr. 99686
(907) 835-4263 Fax: (907) 835-5263
calicowhale@alaska.com
Owner: Trudy Koszarek
Est: 1995 1500 sq.ft.

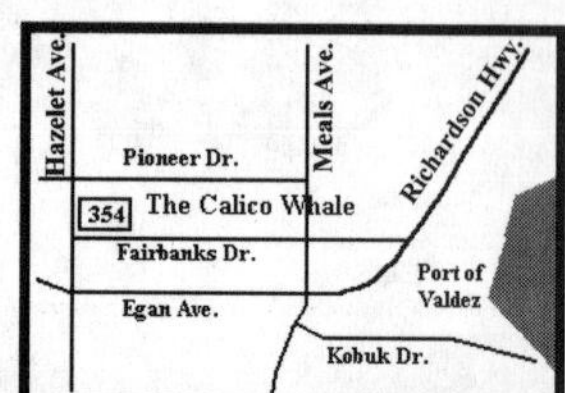

Good selection fabrics, books, patterns, quilting supplies, needlework and local handmade gifts.

Wasilla, AK #8

Mon - Fri 10 - 6
Sat 10 - 5

Sylvia's Quilt Depot

1261 S. Seward Meridian Pkwy. #J 99654
Across from Wal-Mart
(907) 376-6468 Fax: (907) 376-6403
sylviasquilt@gci.net
www.sylviasquiltdepot.com
1000 Bolts including many Batiks

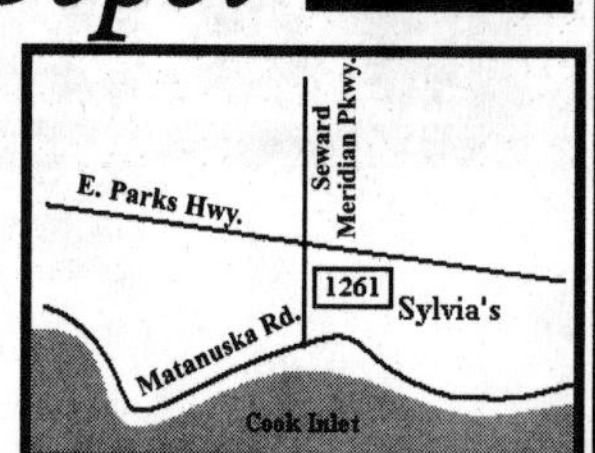

All who enter are friends and we would love to say "Hello". We offer many fabrics, kits, patterns & books.

Palmer, AK #9

Mon - Fri 10 - 6
Sat 10 - 5
Sun 1 - 5

Just Sew

579 S. Alaska 99645
(907) 745-3649
Owners: Jim & Cheri Cooper
2400 sq.ft.

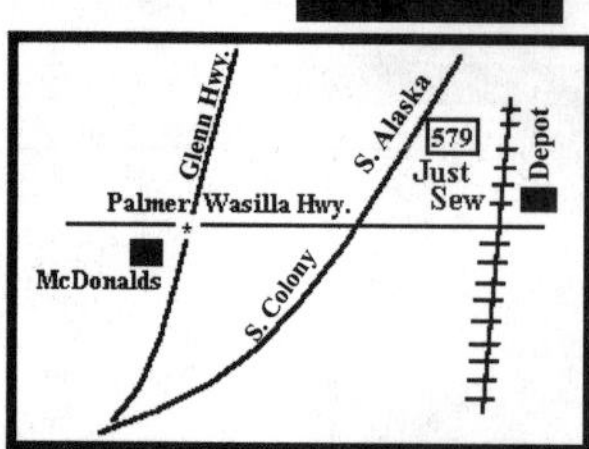

All your quilting and needlework supplies. 100% cottons, books, patterns, notions, cross-stitch supplies, yarn, and lots more!

Fairbanks, AK #10

Mon 12 - 7
Tues - Sat 9:30 - 6
Sun 12 - 5

Snow Goose Fibers

1875 University Ave. 99709
(907) 474-8118
snogoose@eagle.ptialaska.net
www.snogoose.com

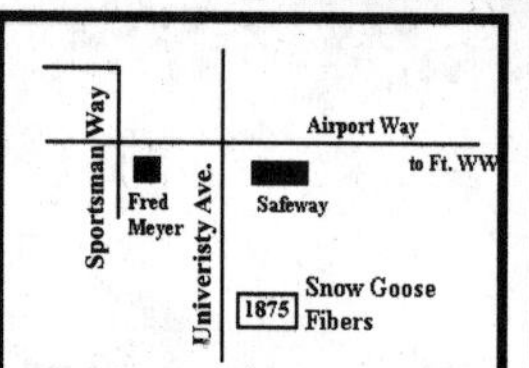

Wonderful Alaskan Kits, Patterns, Fabric featuring our wildlife. Beautiful New Store; 4000 bolts of 100% cottons. Call or email for summer hours! Don't miss this shop!

North Pole, AK #11

Mon - Sat 10 - 6

The Quilting Trail

3136 Dyke Rd. 99705
(907) 488-8091
qtrail@alaska.com
www.quiltingtrail.com
Owner: Marie Noah

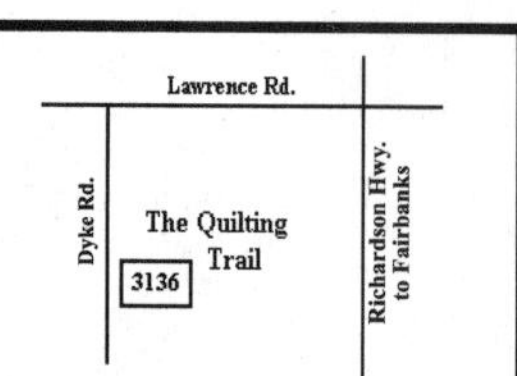

Pfaff Dealer, Over 1200 Bolts of Fabric, Yarn, Quilting Supplies & Alaskan Gifts.

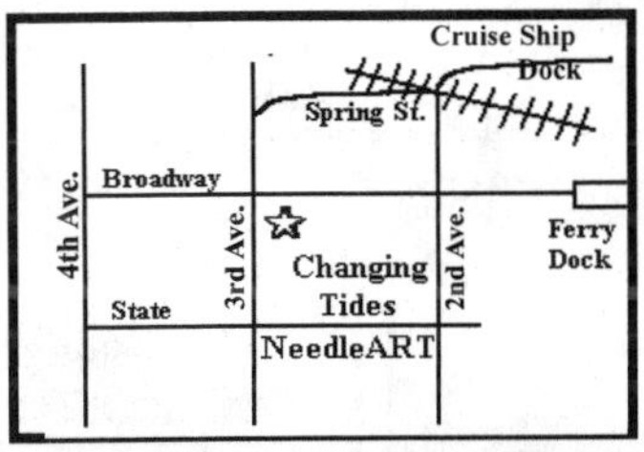

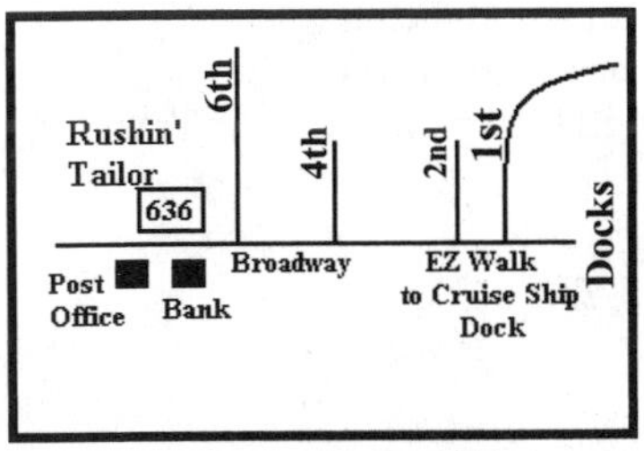

Juneau, AK #14

Mon - Fri 10 - 6
Sat 10-5 Sun 12-5
Closed Sun
June, July, Aug

RainTree Quilting

9131 Glacier Hwy. #7 99801
9 miles from cruise ship dock
(907) 789-7900 Fax: (907) 789-1940
sew@raintreequilting.com
www.raintreequilting.com

Over 1500 bolts of 100% cotton fabrics. Large selection of books, patterns, notions. Alaskan fabrics and patterns. Bernina Dealer.

Ketchikan, AK #15

Silver Thimble Fabric Shoppe

5 Salmon Landing #204 99901
(907) 225-5422
Owner: Betty T. Gale Est: 1984

Available: Quilting fabrics, supplies, Alaskan patterns and sewing machines.

Other Shops in Alaska: *We suggest calling first*

Anchorage	Amish Shop, 320 W 5th Ave	907-277-1185
Anchorage	Three Sisters Fabric Boutique, 1120 Huffman #10	907-345-8041
Cordova	Forget-Me-Not Fabrics, P.O. Box 1109	907-424-3656
Cordova	Calico Corner, P.O. Box 320	907-424-3285
Craig	Attic Treasures Quilt Shop, 1 Easy St.	907-826-2535
Fairbanks	Quilts Unlimited, 1918 Jack St.	907-452-1918
Glenallen	Alora's Quilt Shop, Mile 187 Glenn Hwy., PO Box 758	907-822-5833
Haines	Seams Like Yesterday, 221 3rd Ave. N, P.O. Box 1167	907-766-2265
Homer	Seams To Be, 1103 Ocean Dr	907-235-6555
Kodiak	The Stitchery, P.O. Box 3809	907-486-5580
Palmer	PM Quilting, PO Box 1692	907-746-2525
Petersburg	Island Bound Quilting, P.O. Box 358	907-772-3249
Petersburg	Fabric Basket, 314 Sandy Beach Rd., P.O. Box 1636	907-772-4576
Sitka Calico	Cross Stitch, 231 Lincoln St.	907-747-5122
Sitka Abby's	Reflection, 231 Lincoln St.	907-747-3510
Skagway	Dirce Ann's, 412 8th Ave., P.O. Box 284	907-983-2376
Skagway	Crocus Creek Quilts, P.O. Box 37	867-668-7699
Soldotna	Robin Place Fabrics, 105 Robin Pl.	907-262-5438
Tok	Design Genie Fabrics & Gifts, 1313 1/2 Alaska Hwy.	907-883-2501
Wrangell	Haystack, 1002 Case Ave	907-874-3648

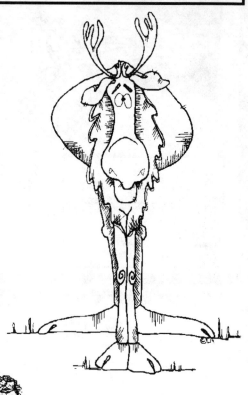

Alaska Guilds:

Anchorage	Anchorage Log Cabin Quilt Guild, P.O. Box 202582, 99520	Meets: Thursdays at 10 a.m. or 1st and 3rd Thursday at 7 p.m. Lutheran Church, 15th & Cordova, Anchorage
Anchorage	Christian Stitchin, 99504	
Bethel	Kozy Kusko Quilters Box 126 99559	
Big Lake	North Star Guild P.O. Box 520973 99652	Meets: Tuesdays 10 a.m. to 5 p.m. at the Mid Valley Senior Ctr
Cordova	Cordova Northwest Quilt Guild Box 1995 99574	
Craig	Craig Quilters Box 142 99921	
Dillingham	Tundra Patchwork Quilter's Guild, P.O. Box 347, 99576	Meets: 3rd Saturday (Oct. thru May) H. S. Home Ec Room
Fairbanks	Cabin Fever Quilters Guild, P.O. Box 83608, 99708	Meets: 3rd Tuesday at Fairbanks Lutheran Church
Juneau	Capital City Quilters, P.O. Box 35036, 99803	Meets: 4th Monday @ 7pm at Yacht Club Room @ Wildflower Court
Ketchikan	Rainy Day Quilters, P.O. Box 1256, 99928	Meets: 4th Tuesday at First Lutheran Church
Kodiak	Kodiak Bear Paw Quilters, Box 3856, 99615	Meets: 2nd Sunday various locations
Palmer	Valley Quilter's Guild, P.O. Box 2582, 99645	Meets: 1st Thursday (except Aug.) 6:30 p.m. at Palmer Train Depot
Petersburg	Petersburg Quilters, Box 217, 99833	
Sitka	Ocean Waves Quilters, Box 1771, 99835	
Soldotna	Redoubt Quilters Guild, P.O. Box 2992, 99669	Meets: Thursday 10 a.m.
Tok	Tok Quilters, Box 229, 99928	
Valdez	Valdez Artist Guild, P.O. Box 1401, 99686	

ARIZONA

36 Featured Shops

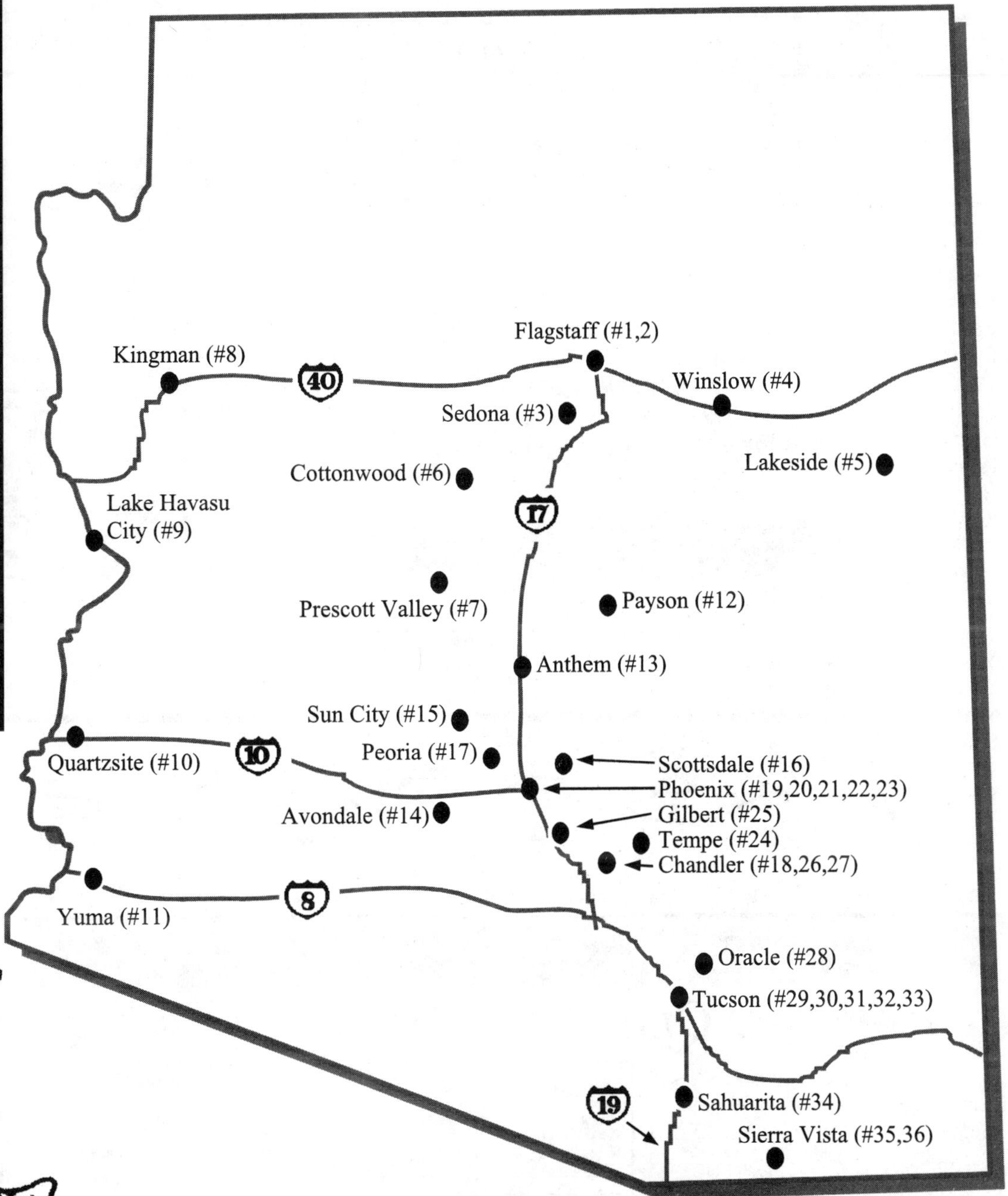

Flagstaff (#1,2)
Kingman (#8)
40
Winslow (#4)
Sedona (#3)
Lakeside (#5)
Cottonwood (#6)
Lake Havasu City (#9)
17
Prescott Valley (#7)
Payson (#12)
Anthem (#13)
Sun City (#15)
Quartzsite (#10)
10
Peoria (#17)
Scottsdale (#16)
Phoenix (#19,20,21,22,23)
Avondale (#14)
Gilbert (#25)
Tempe (#24)
Chandler (#18,26,27)
8
Yuma (#11)
Oracle (#28)
Tucson (#29,30,31,32,33)
19
Sahuarita (#34)
Sierra Vista (#35,36)

Flagstaff, AZ #1

Mon - Sat 9 - 5:30

Odegaard's Sewing Center

19 W. Aspen 86001
(520) 774-2331 In AZ (800) 360-2331
Fax: (520) 774-4668
Bernina, Pfaff, Viking, Singer

Large selection of 100% Cotton Fabrics, Quilting Books & Patterns. Southwest Fabrics and Notions.

U.S. 180 Humphreys
Beaver
Aspen
19
Odegaard's
Route 66

Flagstaff, AZ #2

Mon - Sat 10 - 5 Sun 1 - 4

Pine Country Quilts

1800 S. Milton Rd., #13 86001
(928) 779-2194 Green Tree Village
Owner: Shelly & Keith Breunig
Est: 1985 1300 sq.ft. 1000 Bolts

Fabrics, books, and notions for the traditional and contemporary quilter. Pure quilting fun on the way to the Grand Canyon!

to Flagstaff & Grand Canyon
University Dr.
Pine Country
Green Tree Village Shp. Ctr.
Forest Meadows Dr.
Milton Rd.
I - 40
to CA
Exit 195
to NM
I - 17
to Phoenix

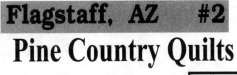

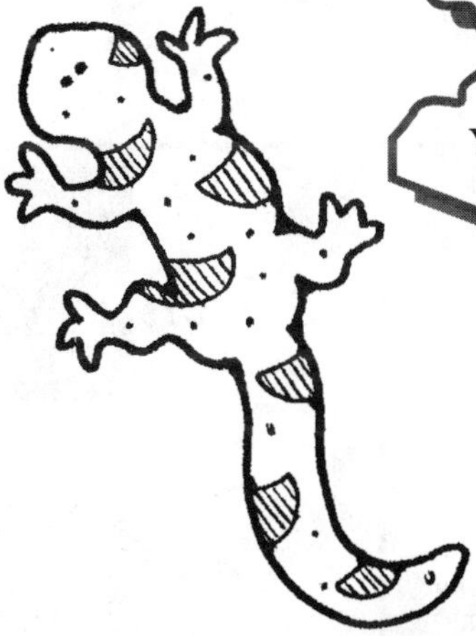

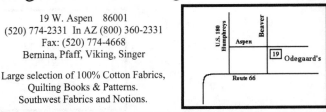

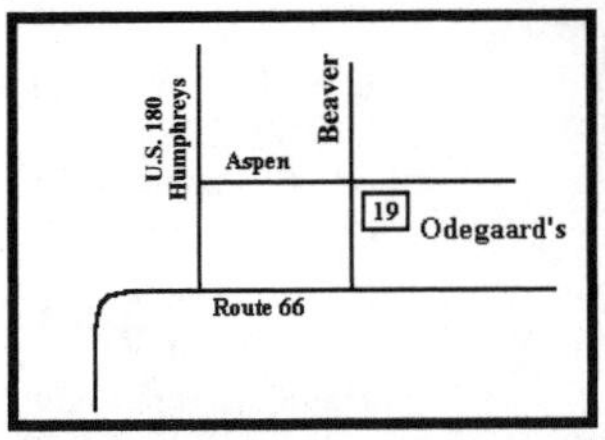

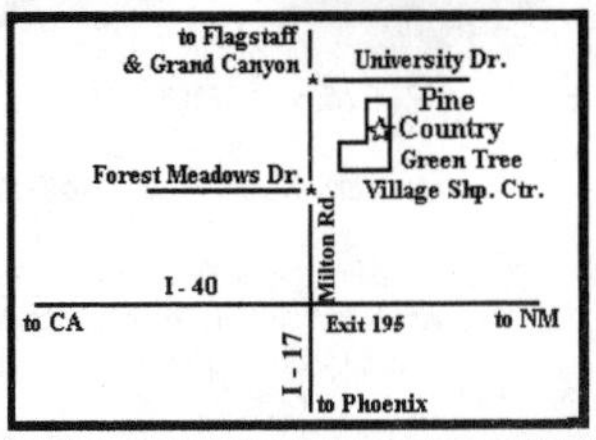

Not only do we have beautiful fabrics, we also have beautiful views! We've added a Quilters' Gallery with artwork and traditional & antique quilts. Come Visit!

The Quilter's Store & Gallery

Quilting Supplies — Classes — 100% Cotton Fabrics
Personalized Instruction Available

(928) 282-2057
Marge Elson, Proprietor
3075 West Highway 89A 86336

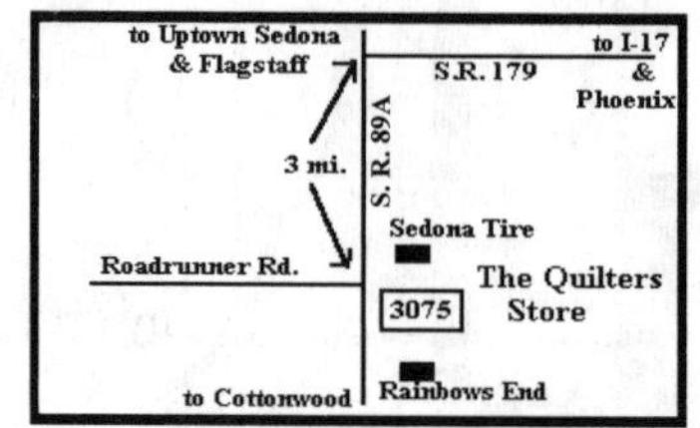

Sedona, AZ #3

Monday - Friday: 9 a.m. - 5 p.m.
Saturday: 9 a.m. - 4 p.m. **Sunday**: 12 p.m. - 4 p.m.

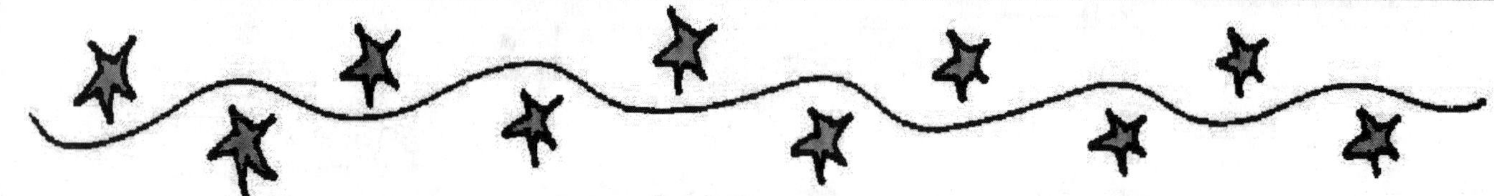

Winslow, AZ #4

Mon - Sat 10 - 5:30

Canyon Rose Quilt Company

212 W. First St. 86047
(928) 289-2800 Fax: (928) 289-0259
carol@canyonrosequiltcompany.com
Owner: Carol Patton
Est: 2002 1400 sq.ft. 1500 Bolts

We are located in a restored 1890's home on the original main street in downtown Winslow.

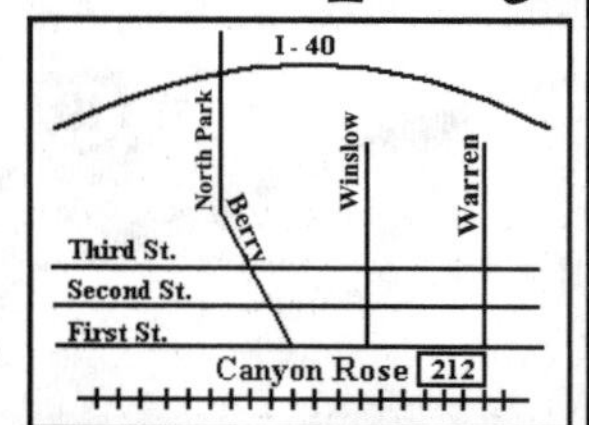

Lakeside, AZ #5

May - Oct Mon - Sat 10 - 5
Nov - April Tues - Sat 10 - 4

Bear Hollow Quilters Den

4237 W. White Mountain Blvd.
Mailing: P.O. Box 9, Pinetop, 85935
(928) 368-2886
www.quiltersden.com
Est: 1997 1800 sq.ft. 2000+ Bolts

Complete Quilt Store. Fabrics, Notions, Books & Patterns. In store long arm quilting. Fun and Friendly. Pine Needles Patterns, Fossil Ferns, Batiks, Flannels, Thimbleberries.

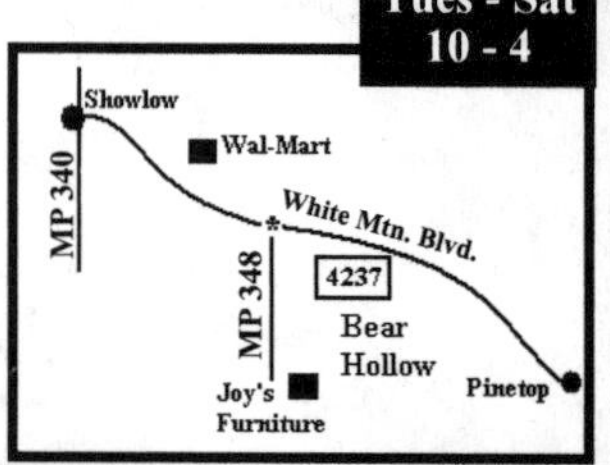

Cottonwood, AZ #6

Mon - Fri 9 - 5
Sat 9 - 4

Quilter's Quarters

1675 E. Cottonwood St. #G 86326
(928) 634-8161
Owner: Mary Beth Groseta

Service with a smile!
Lots of great fabrics, notions, kits & books.
Antique Quilts & Tops & Linens.
Gift Items!

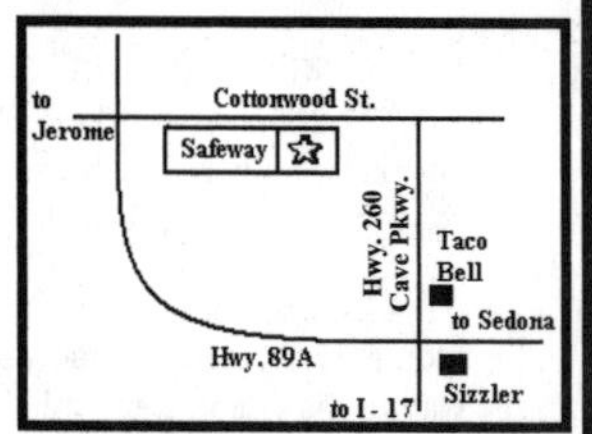

Prescott Valley, AZ #7

Mon - Fri 9 - 5
Sat 9 - 4

A Quilter's Dream

8732 E. Hwy. 69 86314
(928) 772-0864
Owner: Sherrill Short

Beautiful 100% Cotton Fabrics. Great Selections of Books, Patterns & Notions. Unique Gifts. Classes for all Levels of Quilting.

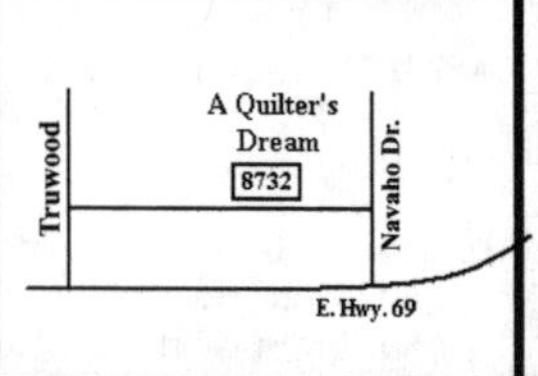

Kingman, AZ #8

Connie's Quilter's Hide-A-Way

308 E. Beale St. 86401
(928) 753-9095
ckett@citlink.net

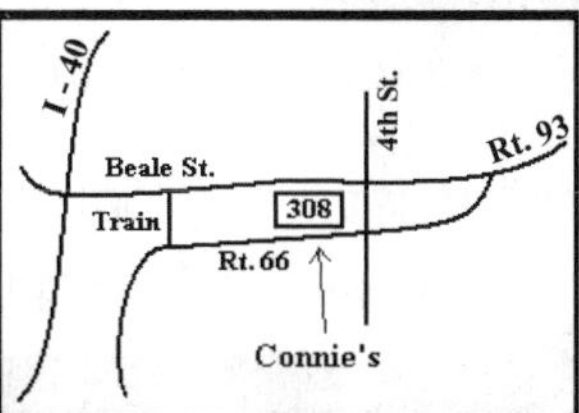

A small, friendly quilt shop with high quality fabrics and a variety of classes. Located one short block from Historic Route 66.

Lake Havasu City, AZ #9

Mon - Fri
9 - 5
Sat 9 - 4

Sew What?

2876 Sweetwater Ave. #2 (Right off Hwy. 95) 86406
(928) 453-4040 Fax: (928) 453-3023
SewWhatJK@aol.com
Owner: Jeanette Kennedy
Est: 1995 4000 Bolts

Largest selection of fabrics, books, patterns, & quilting supplies on the Colorado River and the American Home of the London Bridge.

Quartzsite, AZ #10

Mon - Sat
9 - 5
Closed May thru Aug

Desert Fabric

185 Washington Ave 85346
(520) 927-7447 Fax: (928) 927-3416
E-Mail: jbarc@tds.net
1400 sq. ft. 1100+ Bolts

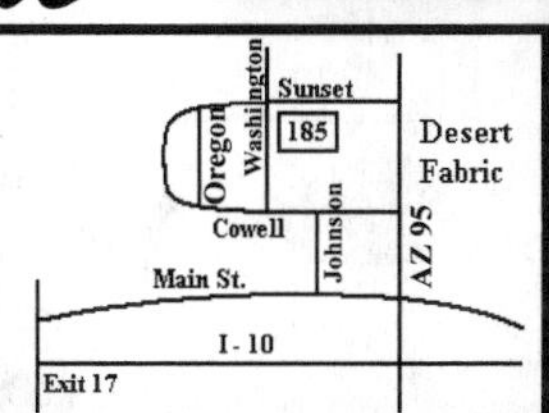

Quality fabric selection to satisfy any quilters taste. Excellent selection of southwest prints to remember your Arizona visit.

Yuma, AZ #11

Mon 9 - 9
Tues - Sat 9 - 5
Sun 11-4 Oct-March

102 E. 3rd St. 85364
(928) 376-0911
Est: 1997
Owner: Wanda Hinkhouse
quiltwand@prodigy.net
www.quiltandsewhouse.com
Husqvarna VIKING and Bernina dealer.
10% Discount if you show your Guild card before purchase.

Payson, AZ #12

Mon - Sat
9 - 5

904 N. Beeline, Suite E 85541
(928) 468-6360 Fax: (928) 474-9550
Est: 2001 4500 sq.ft. 2000 Bolts

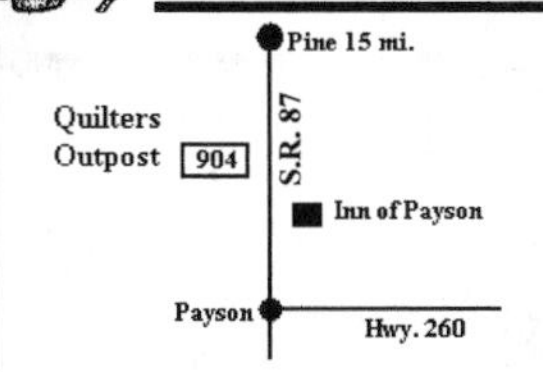

Fabrics, Books, Patterns, Notions, Silk Ribbon, Yarns and Specialty Threads. Horn Furniture. PFAFF Sewing Machines.

felicity fabrics

10am-6pm Mon-Sat
10am-9pm Thursday

a celebration of quilting

Anthem, AZ #13

- Fabric
- Patterns
- Quilt Kits
- Books
- Classes
- Notions

42101 N 41st Dr, Suite140
Anthem, AZ 85086
1 block west of I-17, exit 229,
3 blocks south of Anthem Way.

623-551-2580
1-866-551-2580
www.felicityfabrics.com

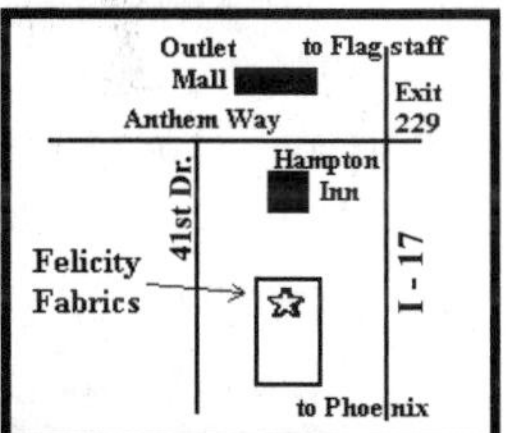

felicity (fə lis′ ə tē) n. something causing happiness or satisfaction; the quality or state of being happy.

14

COTTON FIELDS Quilt & Knit

www.cottonfieldsquiltknit.com

Full service quilt & knit:
1800 bolts of fabric, yarn, books, patterns, notions, classes.
Est: 2003
Fax: (623) 535-1462
info@cottonfieldsquiltknit.com
Owner: Mary McElvain

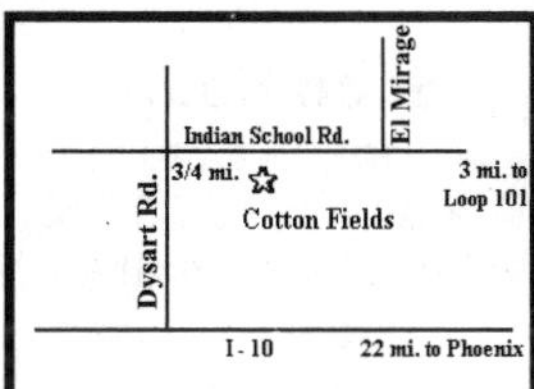

A shop like no other!

Hours
Mon - Sat 9:30 - 5:30
Thurs 'til 9:00

12409 W. Indian School Rd. A105
Avondale, AZ 85323
ph:(623) 535-1200

Sun City, AZ #15

Mon - Fri
9:30 - 5
Wed til 7
Sat 9:30 - 4
Sun 12 - 4

Sun Valley Quilts

Inspiration ~ Imagination ~ Creativity!

9857 W. Bell Rd. 85351
(623) 972-2091 Fax: (623) 972-6085
sunvalleyquilts@aol.com
www.sunvalleyquilts.com
Owner: Dawn S. Maher
Est: 2001 3000 sq.ft. 3000+ Bolts

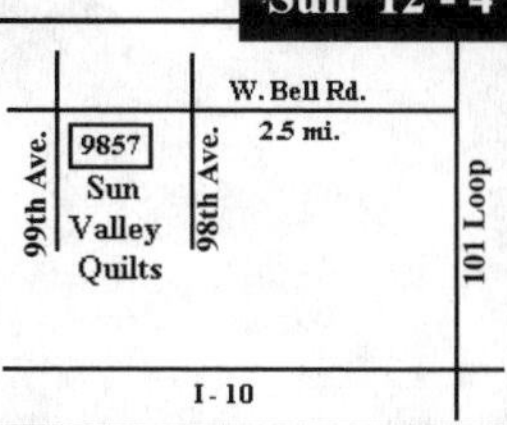

Largest fabric selection in West Valley! Books, notions, gifts & more. Bernina Dealer.

4219 E. Indian School Road, Suite 103
Phoenix, AZ 85018
Phone: 602 553-8350 Fax: 602 381-8805
www.berninaconnection.com
bcreative@berninaconnection.com
Open Mon-Sat 9:30-5:30 Tue 9:30-9:00
Closed Sun

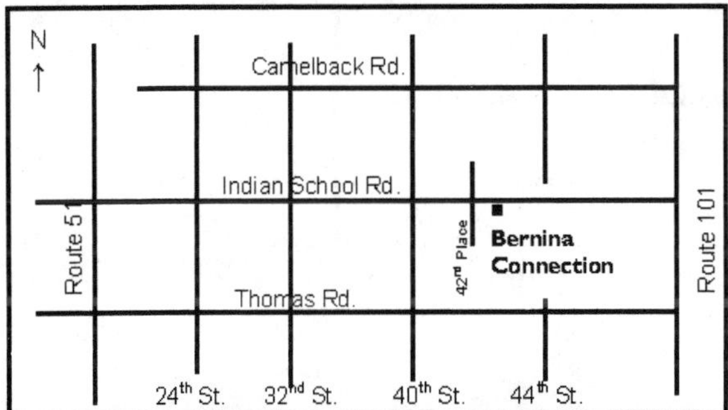

Phoenix, AZ #22

Fabulous Fabrics for Quilting and Garments!
Full Line of Kaffe Fassett Fabric!
Batiks in Cotton and Rayon!
Fun Flannels!
Our Technicians Repair All Makes & Models of Sewing Machines and Bernina Sergers!
Notions Books Patterns Kits!
Over
600 styles of Buttons!
Embellishment Necessities!
Valdani Thread 35 wt hand dyed variegated!
Complete line of AURIfil & Mettler Thread!
All colors of Isacord Embroidery Thread!
Quilting, Garment & Sewing Classes!
Bernina Machine Mastery Classes!
Fun and Friendly Clubs!

Nothing Sews Like A Bernina. Nothing.
BERNINA®

Connect With The Best at The Bernina Connection!

QuiltZ

...Your Quilting Destination

8,000 sq. ft. of Inspiration
Over 4,000 Bolts
Owner: Darleen Ros

Check for our COLOR OF THE MONTH 20% off Every month a Different color.

20% OFF
ALL BOOKS! ALL THE TIME!

QuiltZ Hours:
Mon--Sat 10 to 5
Sunday 12 to 4
(closed Sundays in Summer)

Come visit our specialty departments:

* Simply Southwest
* Batik Beauties
* Fantastic Florals
* Vintage 30's
* Basically Bright
* Flannel Fun
* Christmas Corner (year round)

and *much, much* more!

Each of these depatments is full of FABRIC, PATTERNS, GIFTS & IDEAS
Come see for yourself!

QuiltZ
13825 N. 32nd St.
Phoenix, AZ 85032
(602) 482-4141
www.QuiltzAz.com
Email quiltz@quiltzaz.com

Easy Freeway Access!

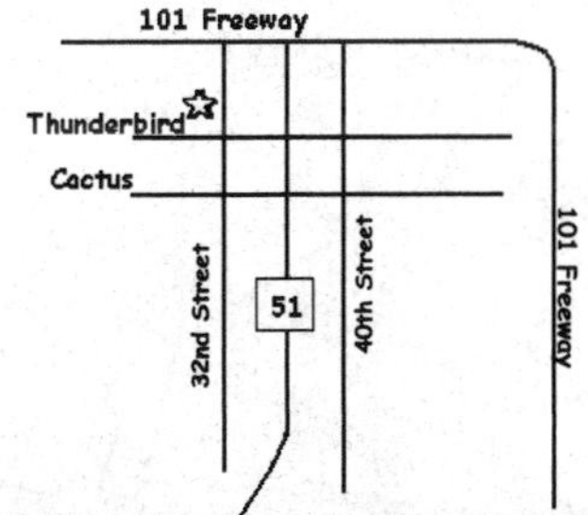

Phoenix, AZ #23

Est: 1982

Tempe, AZ #24

the Quilter's Ranch

1030 E. Baseline Road #178 85283
(In Lake Country Village Shopping Center)
(480) 838-8350

Friendly, knowledgeable staff
Cozy and inviting environment
From batiks to southwest to homespuns;
something for everyone!

quiltersranch@juno.com

Mon - Sat 9:30 - 5:30
Thurs til 9 Sun 12 - 4

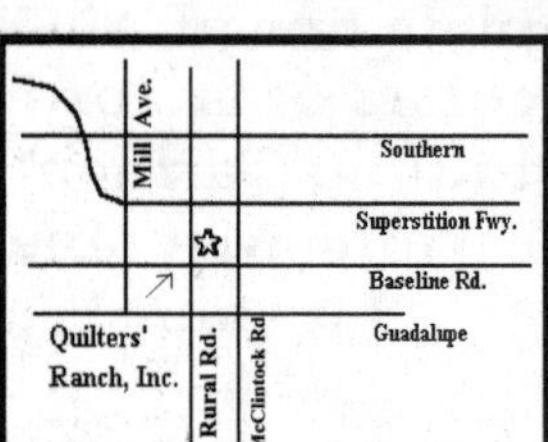

Owner: Susan Visotsky

Gilbert, AZ #25

On The QT Quilt Shop

Mon - Fri 9:30 - 6
Thur til 8
Sat 9:30 - 5

207 N. Gilbert, Suite 113 85234
(480) 558-5020 Fax: (480) 558-5021
ontheqt1@cox.net
Owner: Jean Kramer

Everything you need for your quilts. Fabrics, notions, thread, embellishments, kits, patterns, books, magazines and more. We have a wide range of embellishments for crazy quilting. Beads - Funky fibers - Charms - Ribbons

Hwy. 60
Baseline
Guadalupe
Gilbert Rd.
207 On The QT
Cullumber

Chandler, AZ #26

Mon - Fri 10 - 6
Thur til 8
Sat 10 - 5
Labor to Mem Sun 12 - 4

1949 W. Ray Rd. #38 85224
(480) 857-3443 Fax: (480) 857-6945
CuttingEdgeQ@aol.com
Est: 2001

Cutting Edge QUILTWORKS

Premium Quality Fabric for Quilters. Take Ray Rd. Exit from I - 10 or 101. East on Ray to Dobson (SE corner)

I - 10
Ray Rd.
Hwy. 101
Dobson
1949 Cutting Edge

Zoe's Trunk

Chandler, AZ #27

Owners: Mary Lucille and Gwyn Chamberlain

2986 North Alma School Rd., Suite 4
Chandler, AZ 85224
480-857-4833
quilts@zoestrunk.com
Est: 2000 3500+ Bolts

www.zoestrunk.com

Monday thru Saturday 9:30 - 5:30
Tues & Thurs till 7:30

A Place to set your creativity free!
Fabric, books and classes for all your quiltmaking adventures.
Wool, patterns, classes and kits for rug hooking and penny rugs.
The Valley's largest selection of batiks, brights, flannels, 1930's & 18th Century reproduction fabrics
Hand-dyed wools
Kits available - we would be happy to customize one for <u>you</u>
Mail order available - just call, email or write

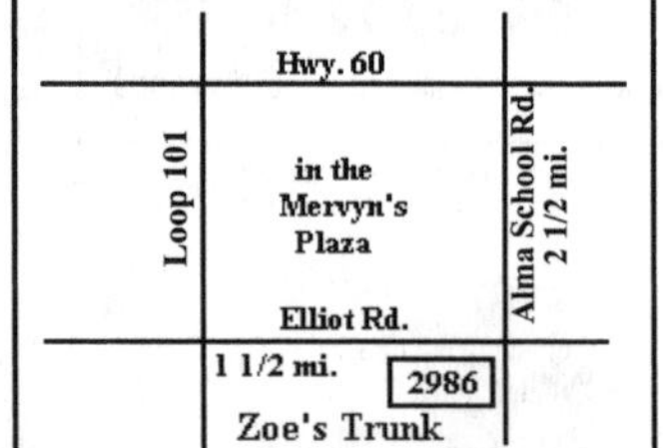

Visit these Restaurants in the area to get more energy for shopping at Zoe's Neighbors, Crackers & Co., Burrito Express, & Garcia's

Purr-fect Quilters Cottage

Fabric Gifts
Notions Fudge

1575 W. American Ave. Oracle, AZ 85623
(520) 896-2414
quilters@theriver.com
Est: 2001 2100 sq.ft. 2000 Bolts

We are a friendly shop with great tasting fudge. We have a selection of gifts, books, notions, patterns and of course a wonderful selection of fabric! Come in and visit us.
We love show and tell

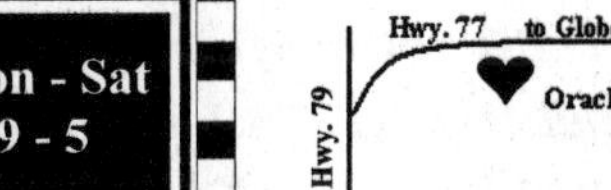

Mon - Sat 10 - 5

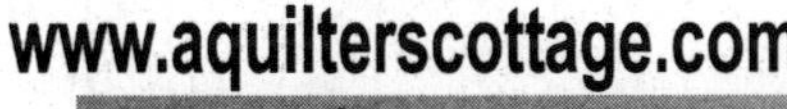

Oracle, AZ #28

Tucson, AZ #29

Mon - Sat 9 - 5

Bernina Sewing Center

4500 E. Speedway #39 85712
(520) 795-7786 Est: 1976
bernina@mindspring.com
www.mindspring.com/~bernina

quilting cottons * heirloom laces & embroideries
* books * threads * classes *
* Bernina Sales & Service *

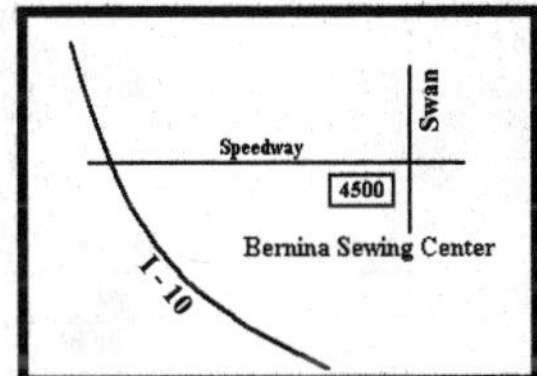

Tucson, AZ #30

Mon - Fri 9:30 - 5
Sat 9:30 - 4:30

Cactus Quilt Shop

6482 N. Oracle Rd.
Plaza Del Oro Shopping Center
In The NE Corner - Under the Clock
(520) 498-4698
Fax: (520) 498-4708
www.cactusquiltshop.com
Owner: Nancy Landon
Est: 1997 1890 sq.ft. 3000 plus Bolts

Everything for the Quilter Plus Treasures.

We specialize in reproduction fabrics--largest collection in the South West!
And don't miss our Kitty Corner.

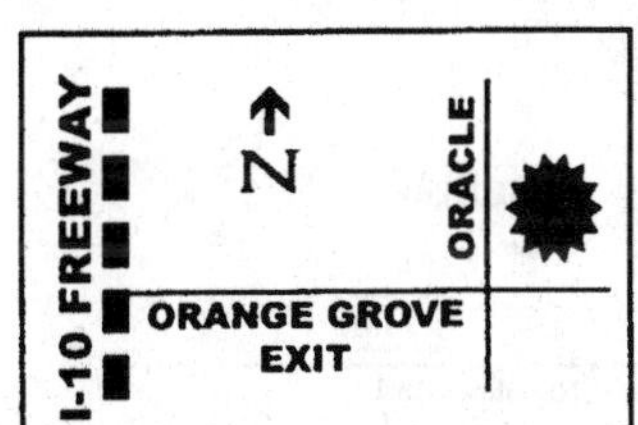

Tucson, AZ #31

- Owners Welcoming You -
Joelee Furrier and Julia Spalla

We provide an extensive variety of fabrics, hand-dyed wools, classes and supplies all in a beautiful and comfortable atmosphere. Our friendly and knowledgeable staff is trained and ready to serve you!

5648 East Broadway Boulevard
Tucson, Arizona 85711
520-514-7000

Monday thru Friday 10 am to 6 pm
Tuesday - open late - 8 pm
Saturday 10 am to 5 pm

www.bellaquiltworks.com

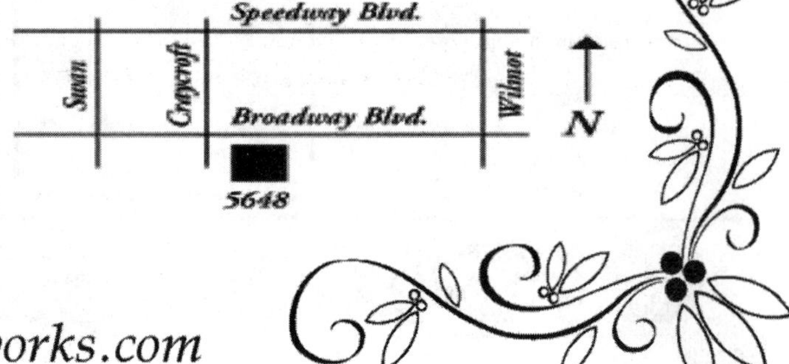

Thimbleweed Quilts

Mon - Sat
10 - 5

Over 2,000 bolts of fabric. Lots of kits, Block of the Month's, Patterns and Classes. Professional machine quilting available on a Gammill machine.

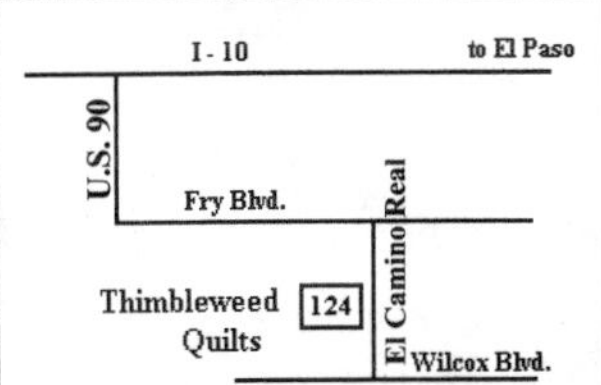

124 El Camino Real
85635
(520) 458-3221
Owner: Pat Boeck
Est: 2001

Sierra Vista, AZ #35

Sierra Vista, AZ #36

The Squirrel's Nest

Quilting & Beyond

Mon - Fri
10 - 5
Sat 9 - 4

530 Bartow Dr. 85635
(520) 417-1070 Fax: (520) 417-1061
info@fibernuts.com
Est: 1990 3200 sq. ft. 4000 bolts
www.fibernuts.com

If you like color, you will love our selection of fabric. Large oriental collection and something for everyone.

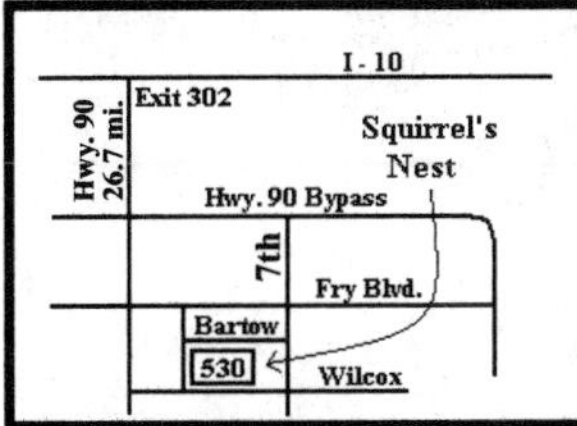

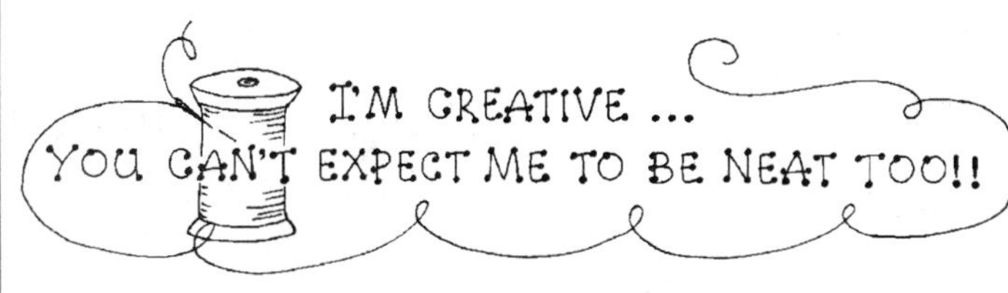

Other Shops in Arizona: *We suggest calling first*

Ajo	Bee Patch, 1161 W. Snyder Rd.	520-387-7765
Benson	Cozy Quilt Shop, 256 W 5th St	520-586-7514
Bullhead City	Sew Wild Fabrics, 3712 Hwy 95 #4	928-704-4948
Chandler	Joyce Nelson Retail, 1363 W Cindy St	480-456-5104
Flagstaff	Rosamond's, 6090 E. Robles Rd.	520-527-4658
Gilbert	Patchwork Pieces Quilt Co., 1250 N. Sailors Way	480-545-7096
Glendale	Heart Strings, 7157 N. 58th Dr.	623-937-3713
Glendale	Country Home Quilting, 7604 N 59th Ave	623-842-4756
Goodyear	I Quilt For You, 14880 W Amelia Ave	623-547-2815
Green Valley	Hearts and Hands, 110 E. Dubal Rd.	520-399-2050
Green Valley	Quilts 4 U, 219 W Calle De Las Trendos	520-625-1400
Mesa	Sally's Fabrics, 2647 W. Baseline Rd.	602-839-0154
Mesa	Sally's Fabrics, 1235 E. Main St.	480-833-7201
Mesa	Kachina Woodworks, 555 E Ivy Rd	480-964-2013
Mesa	Bernina Southwest Sewing, 7143 E. Southern Ave. #135	480-964-8914
Peoria	Quilters' Bee, 7549 W Cactus Rd	623-334-9359
Phoenix	The Quilted Apple, 3043 N. 24th St.	602-956-0904
Phoenix	Quilters Paradise, 3639 W. Juniper Ave.	602-993-2590
Prescott Valley	Bernina & Sew Much More, 2517 N. Great Western Dr.	928-772-3454
Scottsdale	Sew from the Heart, 9180 E. Indian Bend Rd. #F4	480-998-8886
Springerville	Crazy Quilt Shoppe & Gifts, 310 E. Main, P.O. Box 299	928-333-2739
Sun City	Quiltery, 10757 Grand Ave	623-815-7341
Tempe	Quilt Kits & More, 2436 E. Balboa Dr.	480-897-3430
Tucson	Quilters Bee, 3860 N. El Moraga Dr.	520-743-0391
Yuma	Quilting Bee, 2370 W. 32nd St.	520-726-3000
Yuma	Abby's Attic, 2575 W 24th St	928-314-4240
Yuma	Cactus Creek Quilting, 11805 S. Fortuna Rd. Ste A-1	928-345-9390

Arizona Guilds:

Cottonwood	Quail Country Quilters	Meets: 2nd & 4th Thursday at VFW Hall
Green Valley	North of the Border Quilters, 85614	Meets: 1st & 3rd Thursday 9:45 a.m. at M & L Bank, 270 W. Continental Rd.
Lakeside	Card Trick Quilters, 159 W. White Mtn. Blvd., 85901	Meets: 3rd Thursday 6 p.m. at The Bent Needle
Phoenix	Phoenix Arizona Quilter's Assoc., P.O. Box 30074, 85046	
Phoenix	Arizona Quilters Guild, 85071	
Prescott	Thumb Butte Quilters,	Meets: 2nd Monday at Prescott Christian Church
Prescott	Mountain Top Quilters, P.O. Box 12961, 86304	
Prescott Valley	Lonesome Valley Quilt Guild, 8944 Sommer, 86314	Meets: 1st Monday @ 6:30 pm Prescott Valley United Methodist
Scottsdale	Delightful Quilters, 8230 E. Raintree Dr., 85260	Meets: Last Thursday 10 a.m. at Quilters Delight
Somerton	Desert Lilies Quilt Guild, 2775 W. Co. 18th St., 85350	Meets: Every Thurs. 10 a.m. at Sheriff's Posse Bldg, Yuma
Tucson	Tucson Quilter's Guild, P.O. Box 14454, 85732	Meets: 2nd Wed. at 9:00 a.m. St. Francis Cabrini Hall, 3201 E. Predidio
Yuma	T.A.S. of Yuma 102 E. 3rd St., 85364	Meets: 1st & 3rd Friday 9 a.m. at Quilt & Sew House

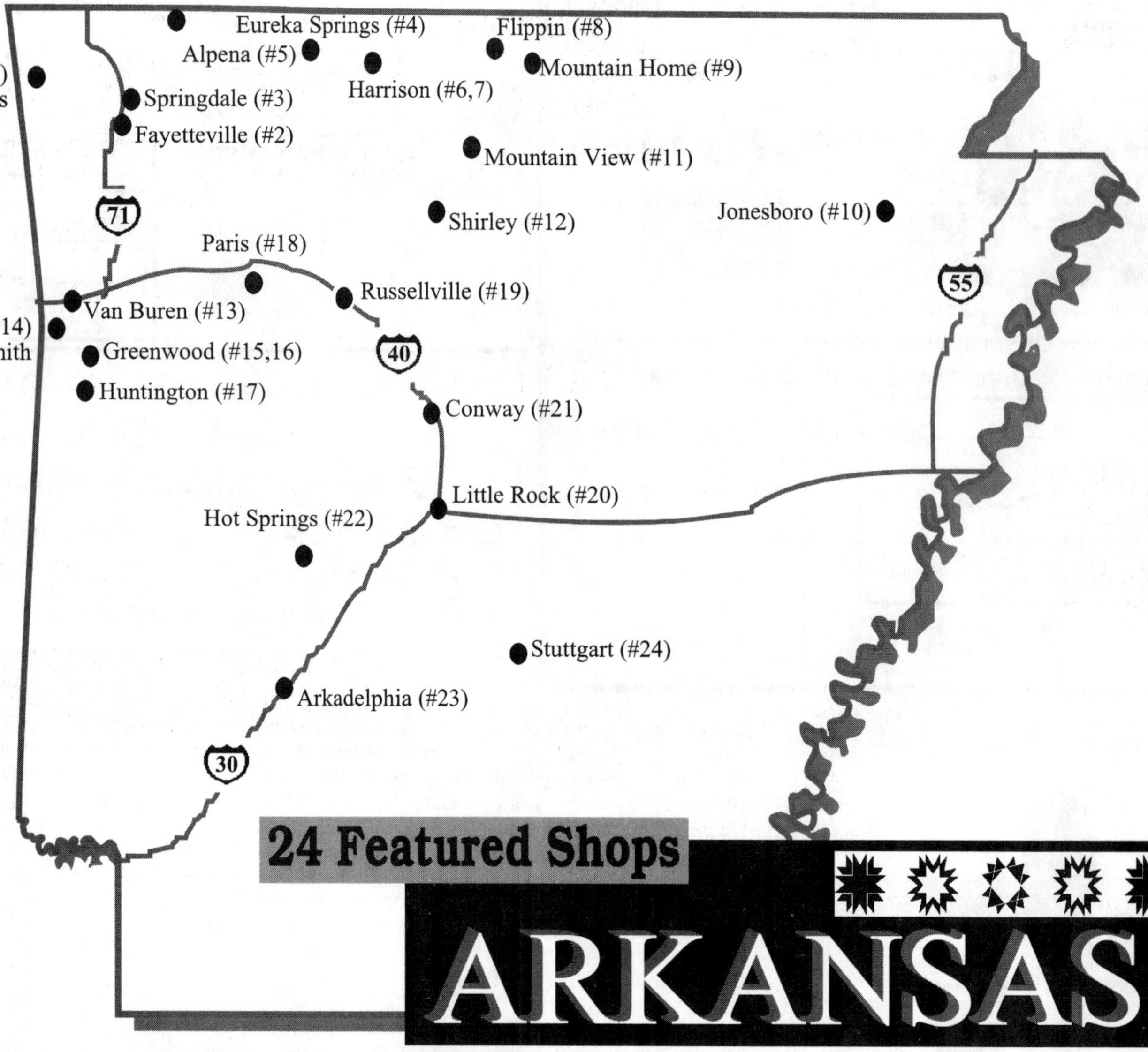

Eureka Springs (#4)
Flippin (#8)
Alpena (#5)
Mountain Home (#9)
Siloam (#1) Springs
Springdale (#3)
Harrison (#6,7)
Fayetteville (#2)
Mountain View (#11)
71
Shirley (#12)
Jonesboro (#10)
Paris (#18)
55
Russellville (#19)
Van Buren (#13)
Fort (#14) Smith
Greenwood (#15,16)
40
Huntington (#17)
Conway (#21)
Little Rock (#20)
Hot Springs (#22)
Stuttgart (#24)
Arkadelphia (#23)
30

24 Featured Shops

ARKANSAS

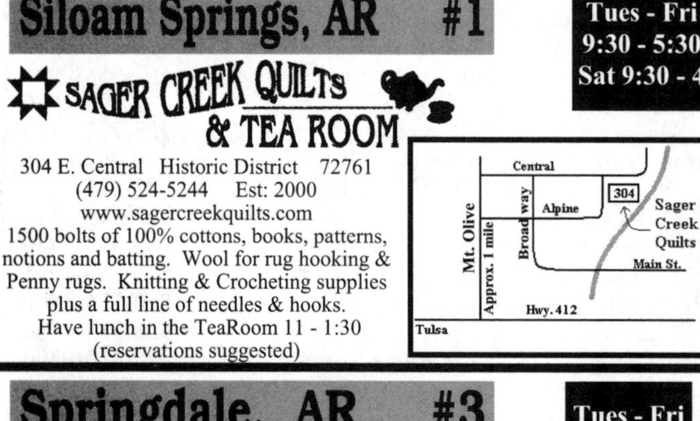

Siloam Springs, AR #1

Tues - Fri 9:30 - 5:30
Sat 9:30 - 4

SAGER CREEK QUILTS & TEA ROOM

304 E. Central Historic District 72761
(479) 524-5244 Est: 2000
www.sagercreekquilts.com
1500 bolts of 100% cottons, books, patterns, notions and batting. Wool for rug hooking & Penny rugs. Knitting & Crocheting supplies plus a full line of needles & hooks.
Have lunch in the TeaRoom 11 - 1:30 (reservations suggested)

Central
304
Sager Creek Quilts
Alpine
Broadway
Mt. Olive
Approx. 1 mile
Main St.
Hwy. 412
Tulsa

Springdale, AR #3

Tues - Fri 10 - 4
Sat 10 - 3

The Quilting Barn

3366 Elm Springs Rd. 72762
(479) 756-0589
quiltingbarnetc@cox-internet.com
Owner: Lila Rostenberg, Jane Whittle, & Darlene Szabo Est: 1993

800 Bolts of 100% cotton fabric. Lots of patterns, books & notions. Homespuns, 1930's & 1800's reproduction pieces.

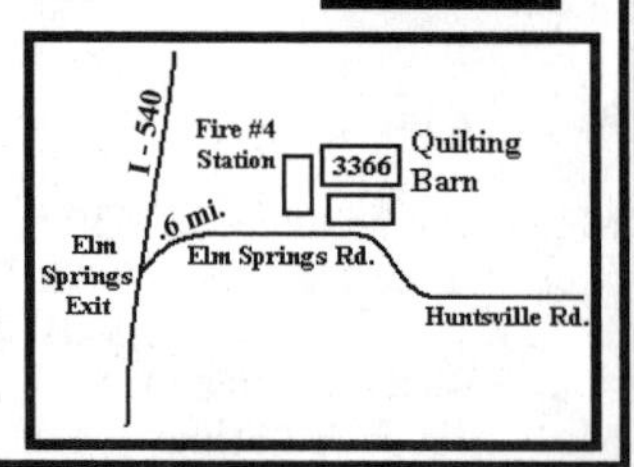

SPINNING STAR FABRICS

1422 N. College 72701
(479) 443-2243
Fax: (479) 443-2236

Fayetteville, AR #2

- 100% Cotton Prints for Quilting & Apparel
- Buttons, Lace & Trims
- Linens, Silks, Organically Grown Cotton

& Heirloom Fabrics

- Notions, Tools & Patterns
- Classes for All Ages & Skill

Mon - Sat 9 - 6
Thur til 9

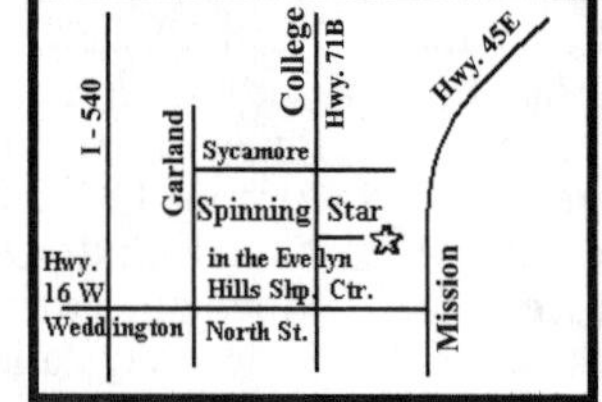

www.spinning starfabrics.com
spinstarfab@aol.com

Eureka Springs, AR #4

Warren Electronics & Digital Quiltz

36 Hwy. 23 S 72632
(479) 253-9049 Est: 1995
E-Mail: warren@ipa.net
Owners: John & Martha Ann Warren

Inspiration for Quilters through high quality cotton fabrics. We demonstrate computer design software in our shop. Tourists welcome & appreciated

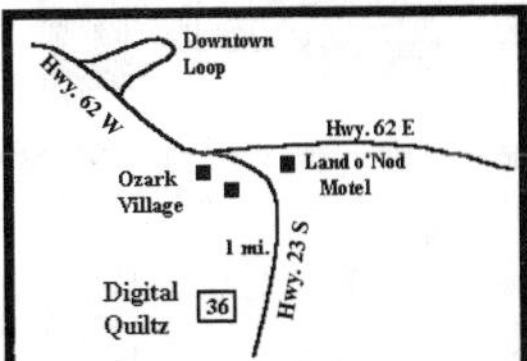

Alpena, AR #5

Mon - Sat
9 - 5

BJ's RAG BARN

307 E. Elm St. 72611
(870) 437-2325
Owner:
Teresa Wymore
Est: 1973
2400 sq.ft.

Fabrics & Handcrafts. Lace - 10¢ Yard.
We now have Quilts. Frames & Threads.
Country Accents.

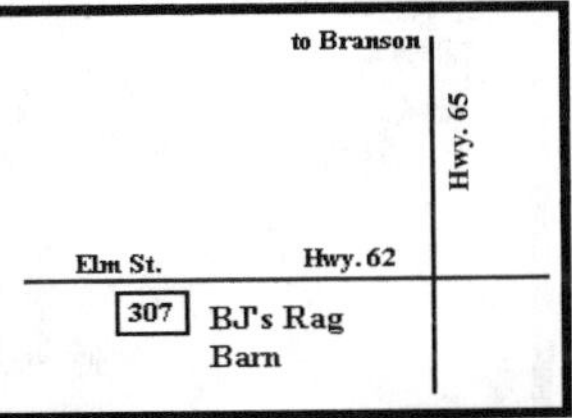

Harrison, AR #6

Daily
9 - 5

Heart Quilt Shop

8874 Hwy. 62 West 72601
870-437-5400
Brian & Trena Johnson

We make all kinds of quilts: Moose, Deer, Eagles, Birds, Angels, Tractors, Horses, Fishing, Trains, Lighthouses and Reversable Ones. We also have traditional Quilts: Lone Star, Double Wedding Ring, Log Cabin, Christmas Tree Skirts, Angels, Quilted Angels. Stop by and get a Free Quilt Pattern

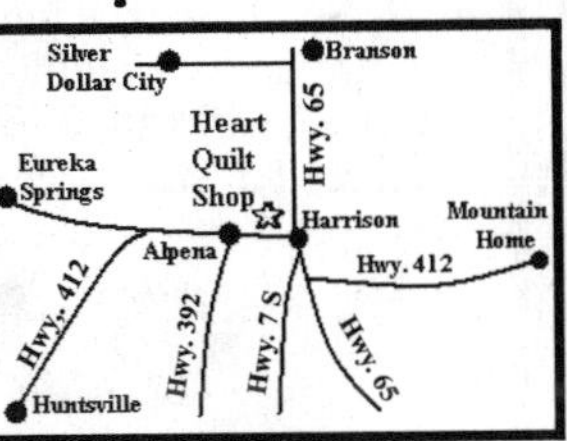

Harrison, AR #7

Country Corner Quilt Shop

We Meet All Your Quilting Needs!

10872 Hwy. 392
Harrison, AR 72601
870-437-2299
E-mail: QuiltShop@eritter.net
Est: 1986 4000+ Bolts

Arkansas' Largest Independently Owned Quilt Shop

Mon - Sat 8 - 5

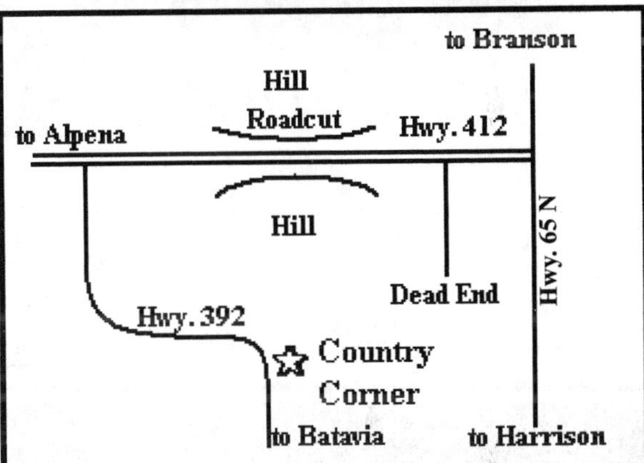

4000 BOLTS OF FABRIC * 100% COTTON
CHOSEN WITH THE QUILTER IN MIND

PATTERNS & BOOKS GALORE
STENCILS SULKY THREAD NOTIONS

CLASSES
BLOCK OF THE MONTH PATTERNS AND KITS

HAND GUIDED MACHINE QUILTING
WE DO QUALITY CUSTOM WORK IN OUR SHOP TO FIT YOUR SPECIFIC NEEDS.
STOP BY AND WATCH US WORK.

SALES, SERVICE AND INSTRUCTION ON NOLTING LONG ARM QUILTING MACHINES AND SIMPLICITY HOME SEWING MACHINES AND SERGERS.

Flippin, AR #8

CURIOSITY SHOP

9084 HWY 62 E
FLIPPIN AR 72634
870-453-5300
jeffross@southshore.com
Owners: Jeff & Paula Ross

Body Shop
Curiosity Shop
9084
Hwy. 62 / 412
Silzell Feed Stop
Hwy. 101

QUALITY MACHINE QUILTING AT AFFORDABLE PRICES

FOR A PRICE LIST AND PATTERN SHEET SEND LSASE TO THE ABOVE ADDRESS

We have a large selection of
Fabrics (1200+ bolts) 100+ bolts of Thimbleberries
Books ~ patterns ~ notions
Hours 9am to 5pm Monday thru Saturday

Wall to Wall Samples & Quilts for Sale

Tues - Fri 9:30 - 5
Sat 9:30 - 3

Full Service Quilting Shop!

Fabric, Books, Patterns, Notions. Class schedule available on the internet with free pattern at www.remembermequiltshop.com Babylock, Bernina and Elna sewing machines sales & repairs. In an historic 2-story rock house built in 1908 with a new classroom.

Remember Me Quilt Shop

914 S. Main 72653 (870) 425-7670
rememberme@cox_internet.com

P&B, Hoffman, Monarch, Moda, RJR, South Seas, Kings Road. Embroidery headquarters, classes, software machines, thread & stabilizers etc.

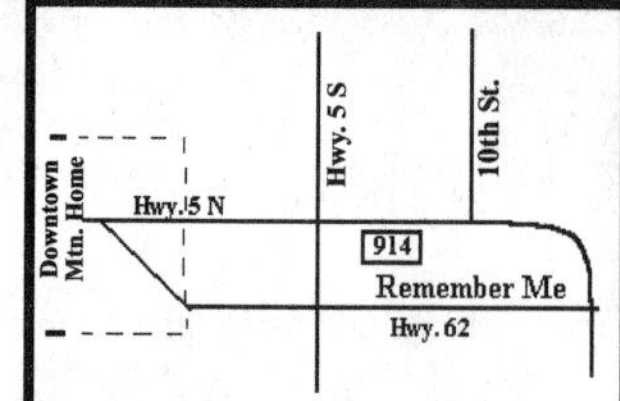

Mountain Home, AR #9

Jonesboro, AR #10

Tues - Fri 10 - 5:30
Sat 10 - 4
Mon by Appt.

Quilters Corner

2010 Wilkins 72401
(870) 931-1138 Est: 1996
padavis@cox-internet.com
Owners: Leonard & Ann Davis

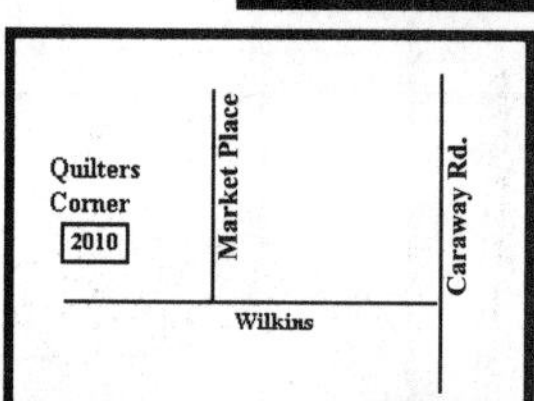

Fabrics, Notions, Books & Patterns. Machine Quilting. Classes for beginners and advanced. Friendly Service and a great place to visit.

Mountain View, AR #11

Mon - Sat 9 - 5

The Quilting Bee

212 W. Main St., P.O. Box 2360 72560
(870) 269-9302
ddhigg@mvtel.net Est: 2002
Owners: Daphne Higginbotham
& Brenda Goodwin 600+ Bolts
Located in the "Ozark Folk Music Capital of the World". 2000 sq.ft. of Fabrics, Notions, Books, Gifts & Good Times!

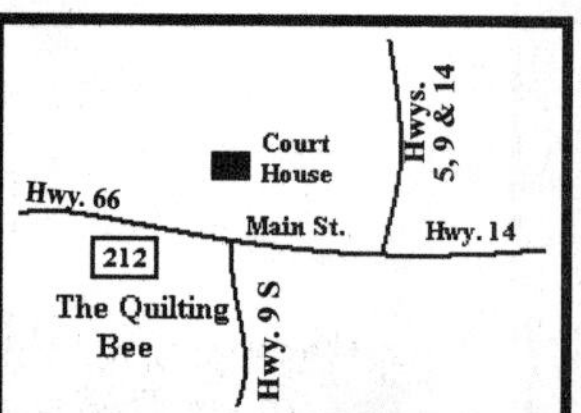

Shirley, AR #12

Tues - Fri 10 - 5:30
Sat 10 - 2

Quilt In Time

15509 Hwy. 16 East 72153
(501) 723-4448
pjallen@hypertech.net
www.pattiallen.net
Owner: Patti Allen Est: 2003
Quality fabric including hand-dyed, notions and quilting classes. Custom long-arm quilting a specialty. Additional hours by appointment, call ahead!

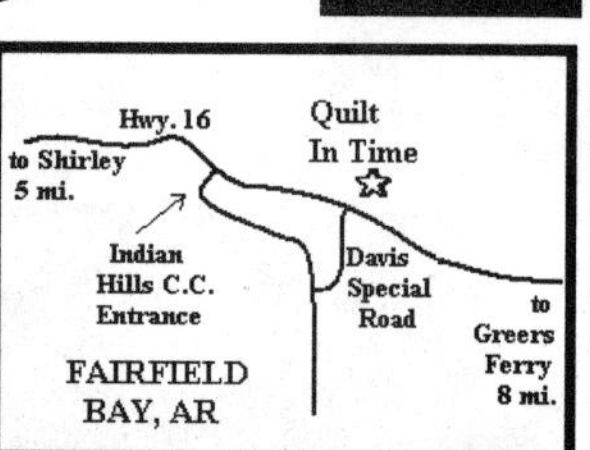

Historic Van Buren, AR #13

Mon - Sat 9:30 - 5

Olde Towne Quilt Shoppe

703 Main St. 72956
(479) 474-6378
www.thequiltshoppe.com
Est: 1997
Owner: Yolanda Mullins
Where family heirlooms are created. Fabrics, Notions, Patterns. Custom quilts & home décor.

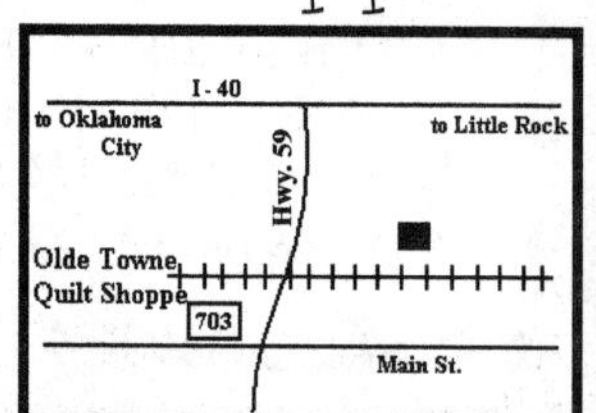

Fort Smith, AR #14

Mon - Sat 10 - 6

Bernina Outpost, Inc.

2909 Old Greenwood Rd. Ste 3 72903
(479) 649-9188
berninaoutpost@sbcglobal.net
Owner: Lynne M. Sbanotto
Est: 2002 1400 sq.ft. 500 bolts

Bernina Outpost, Inc. sells quality Bernina sewing and embroidery machines. Moda & Benartex fabrics, quilting supplies and books.

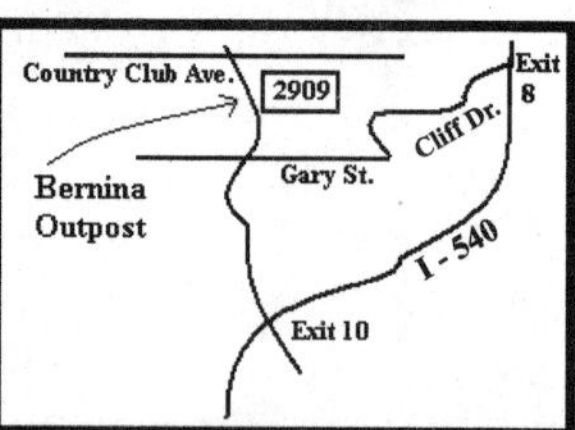

Greenwood, AR #15

Mon - Fri 10 - 4 Sat 10 - 3

Main Street Fabric

20 N. Main, P.O. Box 908 72936
(479) 996-7349
Owner: Oleta Kennedy
Est: 1990
1600 sq.ft. 1600 Bolts

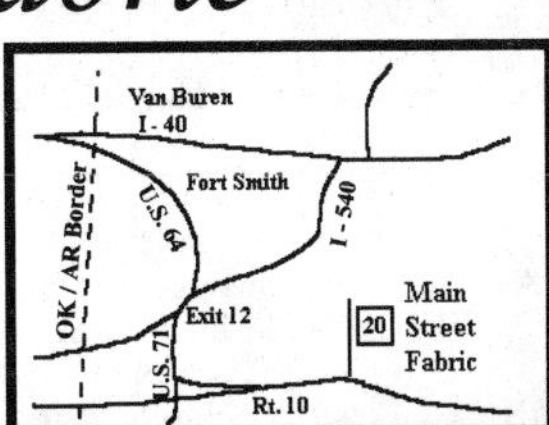

Great selection of 100% Cotton Fabric, Books, Patterns, Notions, Supplies. Classes Avail. Approximately 10 miles south of Exit 12

Greenwood, AR #16

Mon - Sat 8 - 5

Crooked Creek Quilts

1736-A West Center 72936
(479) 996-5808
billlove@valuelinx.net
Est: 1995 1000 sq.ft.

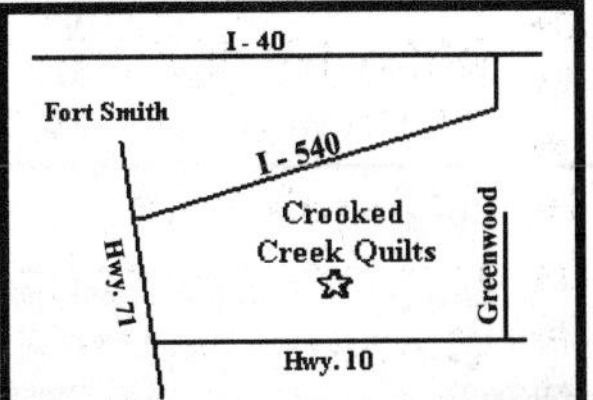

We do classes in piecing and applique.
Custom machine quilting.
14 miles south of Fort Smith and one mile on Hwy. 10 spur East.

Huntington, AR #17

Wed & Sat 9:30 - 5

MAMA'S LOG HOUSE

3715 E. Clarks Chapel Rd.
72940
(479) 928-1600 or
(479) 883-0254 Est: 1982
mamaslog@valuelinx.net
www.mamasloghousequiltshop.com

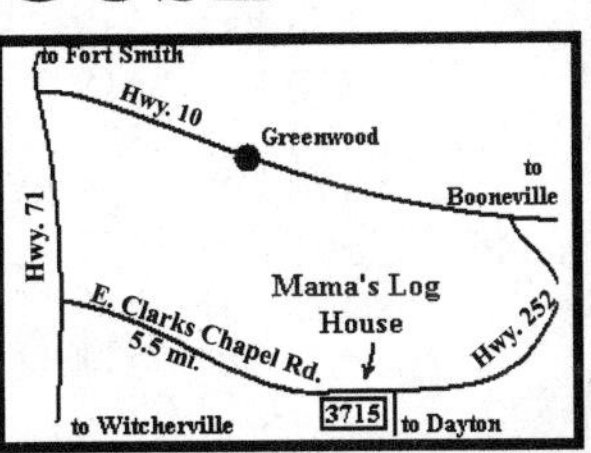

Quilting Supplies - Crafts - Split Oak Baskets 100% Cotton Fabric

Paris, AR #18

Tues - Fri 10 - 5:30 Sat 10 - 4

Neu-Country

116 W. Church St. 72855
(479) 963-1079 Fax: Same
neu63@cswnet.com
Owners: Dottie & Ray Neumeier
Est: 2002 500+ bolts

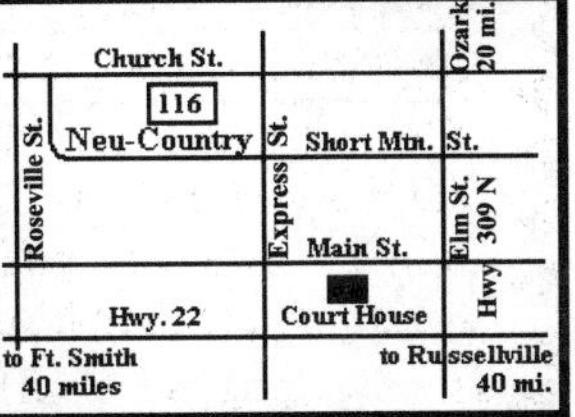

"That Little Quilt Shop in Paris"
Quilting Fabrics and supplies, Thimbleberries, RJR, Hoffman and more. Long-arm Quilting.

Russellville, AR #19

Mon - Fri 10 - 5 Sat 9 - 4

DONNA'S SEW 'N QUILT

1610 S. Arkansas Ave. 72801
(479) 967-9591 Fax: Same
www.donnassewnquilt.com
Est: 1995 1000+ Bolts

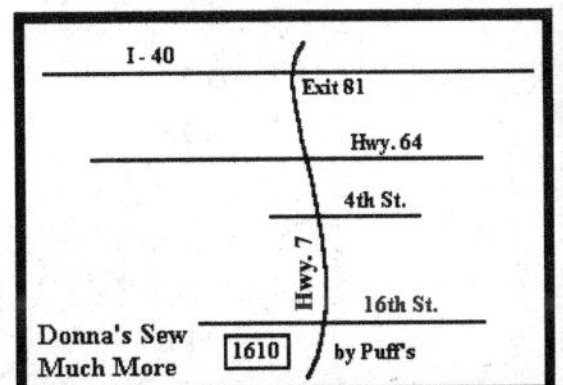

The River Valley's place for quilters to learn, quilt, and have fun and get the finest available for their quilting needs. Husqvarna Viking Dealer.

Conway, AR #21

Mon - Sat 10 - 5

Expressive Quilting

2455 Washington Ave. # 103 72032
(501) 505-8376 Fax: (501) 505-8366
cawd45@expressivequilting.com
www.expressivequilting.com
Est: 2002 1500 sq.ft.
Dedicated to the Art of Quilting
100% premium cotton fabrics - Books - Notions - Patterns - Classes
SuperQuilter and HandiHandles dealer.

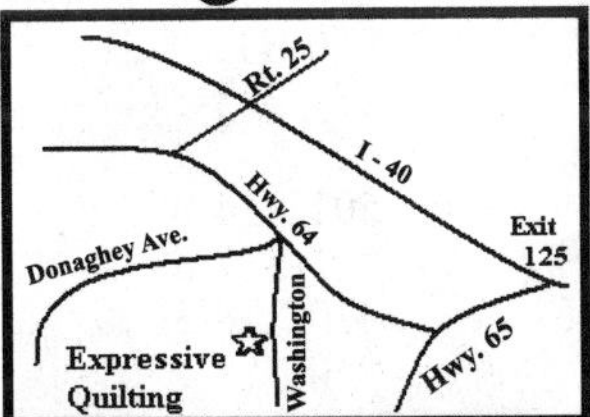

Hot Springs, AR #22

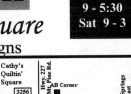

Mon - Fri 9 - 5:30 Sat 9 - 3

Cathy's Quiltin' Square
& Monogrammin' Designs

3256 Albert Pike 71913
Est: 1999
(501) 760-6099
Owner: Cathy Anderson
3600 sq.ft. 1200 Bolts
Catalog $12.95

Quilt Fabric, Patterns, Books, Notions, Custom Machine Quilting, & Embroidery

The Stitchin' Post

Little Rock, AR #20

10301 Rodney Parham Rd.
(In Breckenridge Village)
Little Rock, AR 72227
(501) 227-0288
Est: 1972 3600 sq.ft.

Mon - Fri 10 - 5:30 Sat 10 - 5

VIKING Husqvarna

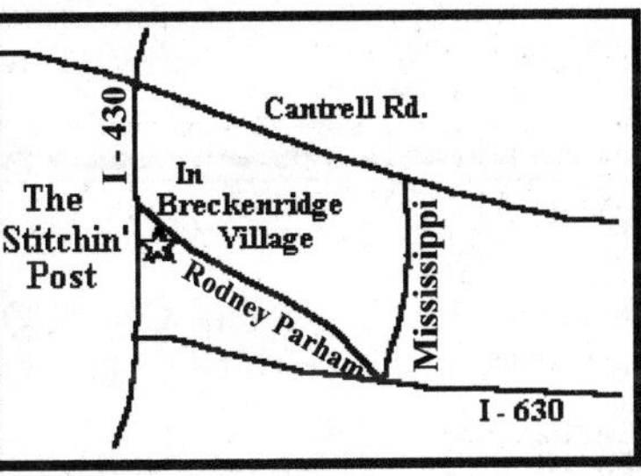

Serving quilters for over 30 years.
Domestic and imported cottons.
Quilting supplies and classes.

Arkadelphia, AR #23

Tues - Sat 9:30 - 5:30

Churn Dash Quilts

2901 Pine St. 71923
(870) 230-8401 Fax: (870) 230-8408
bfgilbert@iocc.com
Owner: Barbara Gilbert
Est: 2002 1400 sq.ft. 600 Bolts

Specializing in high quality machine quilting. Fabulous fabrics, books, patterns and notions. Wide variety of classes.

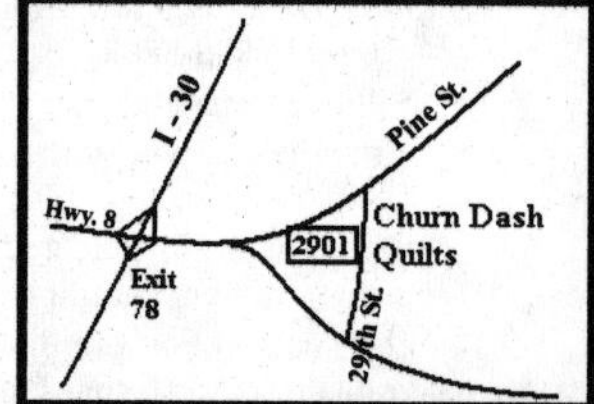

Stuttgart, AR #24

Mon - Fri 9:30 - 5 Sat 10 - 2

The French Seam

2014 S. Main St. 72160
(870) 673-8156 Fax: (870) 673-6280
luv2sew@frenchseam.com

Authorized Bernina dealer. Quilting, heirloom, silk ribbon, fashion fabric and notions. Machine embroidery supplies Machine repair.

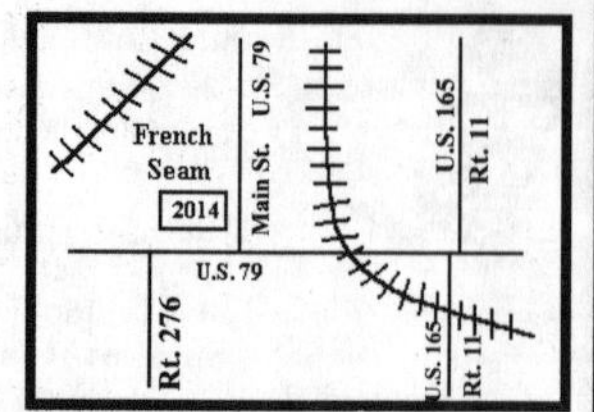

Other Shops in Arkansas: *We suggest calling first*

Ash Flat	Homestead Stitches, HC 67, Box 256	870-994-2033
Batesville	The Fabric Connection, 151 W. Main St. PO Box 2313	870-793-2405
Blytheville	Village Shoppe, 5221 Southside Dr	870-532-4144
Camp	Quilts & Things, R.R. #1, Box 573	870-895-2518
Cave City	Quilt Rack, 1094 Hwy 230	870-283-5351
Cave City	Kuntry Korner, 1044 N Main St	870-283-5900
Clarksville	Linda's Machine Quilting, 332 County Road 3461	501-331-4957
Dover	Stitches Etc., 9958 S.R. 7 N	501-331-3656
Dover	Bear Bluff Quilts, 28958 SR 7 N	501-331-3511
Eureka Springs	The Cotton Patch Quilts, 1 Center St.	479-253-9894
Eureka Springs	Vicky's Too, 2039B E. Van Buren	479-253-7889
Eureka Springs	Honeysuckle Rose Quilts & Gifts, 1 Spring St.	479-253-5148
Eureka Springs	The Gingham Goose, P.O. Box 2186	479-253-9141
Eureka Springs	The Quilt Shop, 2 Center St.	479-253-2093
Eureka Springs	Treasures from the Pacific, 435 W. Van Buren	479-253-8681
Eureka Springs	Ozark Mountain Quilts, 33 Spring St	479-253-6033
Fort Smith	Heirlooms Quilt Shop II, 1415 N. 38th	501-782-6839
Harrison	Sewing Place, 1065 Zinc Rd.	870-743-6739
Hebie Springs	Quilting Fabric & Sew Much More, 2233 Hwy 25B	501-362-2206
Hot Springs	Quilt Land, 218 Central Ave	501-623-0219
Hot Springs	Log Cabin Crafts, 450 S. Rogers Rd.	501-767-6624
Hot Springs	Daisy Patch, 111 Murray Hill Pl.	501-362-8988
Marshall	In Stitches, 108 Nome St	870-448-3123
Maysville	Tapestry Garden, 24318 Coats Rd	501-291-4257
Mountain Home	Quilters Home, 62 Bellwood Ln	870-481-5880
N Little Rock	Sew Much More, 4004 John F Kennedy Blvd	501-753-6050
Omaha	Quilting Bee, 24790 U.S. Hwy. 65 N	501-426-5466
Paragould	Hillcrest Quilt Shop, 8802 Hwy 412 W	501-236-1988
Pea Ridge	Country House Quilting, 16324 N. Hwy 94	501-451-8978
Pelsor	Country Palace Ozark Crafts, HC 30 Box 108	870-294-5366
Pelsor	Nellie's Craft Shop, HC 30 Box 102	870-294-5317
Pleasant Grove	Trails End Quilting, 494 Ford Ln	870-652-3727
Rogers	S&D Stitches, 6412 W Southgate Rd	479-273-5112
Russellville	Hancock Fabrics of Russellville, 1408 S. Arkansas	
Sherwood	Blossom Quiltworks, 114 Country Club Rd.	501-834-8800
Sherwood	Jubilee Quilted Creations, 1800 E Keihl Ave	501-835-3939
Sulphur Springs	Quilt Corner, 110 S. Hibler Ave. P.O. Box 280	479-298-3006
Yellville	Fabric Heaven Warehouse, 11125 Hwy. 14 N	870-453-2361

Arkansas Guilds:

Benton	Saline County Quilters Guild, 224 W. South St., 72015
Eureka Springs	Eureka! Quilters Guild, 90 Grand Ave., 72632 Meets: 2nd & 4th Wednesday 1 p.m. at the Lone Star Church Bldg., Hwy. 23 South
Fort Smith	Belle Point Quilters' Guild, P.O. Box 3853, 72913 Meets: 4th Monday 7 p.m. at East Side Baptist Church
Huntington	Dayton Quilting Society, 3715 E. Clarks Chapel Rd., 72940 Meets: 2nd & 4th Saturday at Mama's Log House
Little Rock	Arkansas Quilters Guild, 4219 Sugar Maple Ln., 72212
Mountain Home	Hill 'n Hollow Quilters Guild, P.O. Box 140, 72653 Meets: 1st Friday 9:30 a.m. at Redeemer Lutheran Church
Prescott	Hope Quilter's Guild, 624 Cale Rd., 71857
Rogers	Quilter's United in Learning Together, P.O. Box 164, 72757 Meets: 4th Thursday 7pm at Wesley United Methodist Church, Springdale

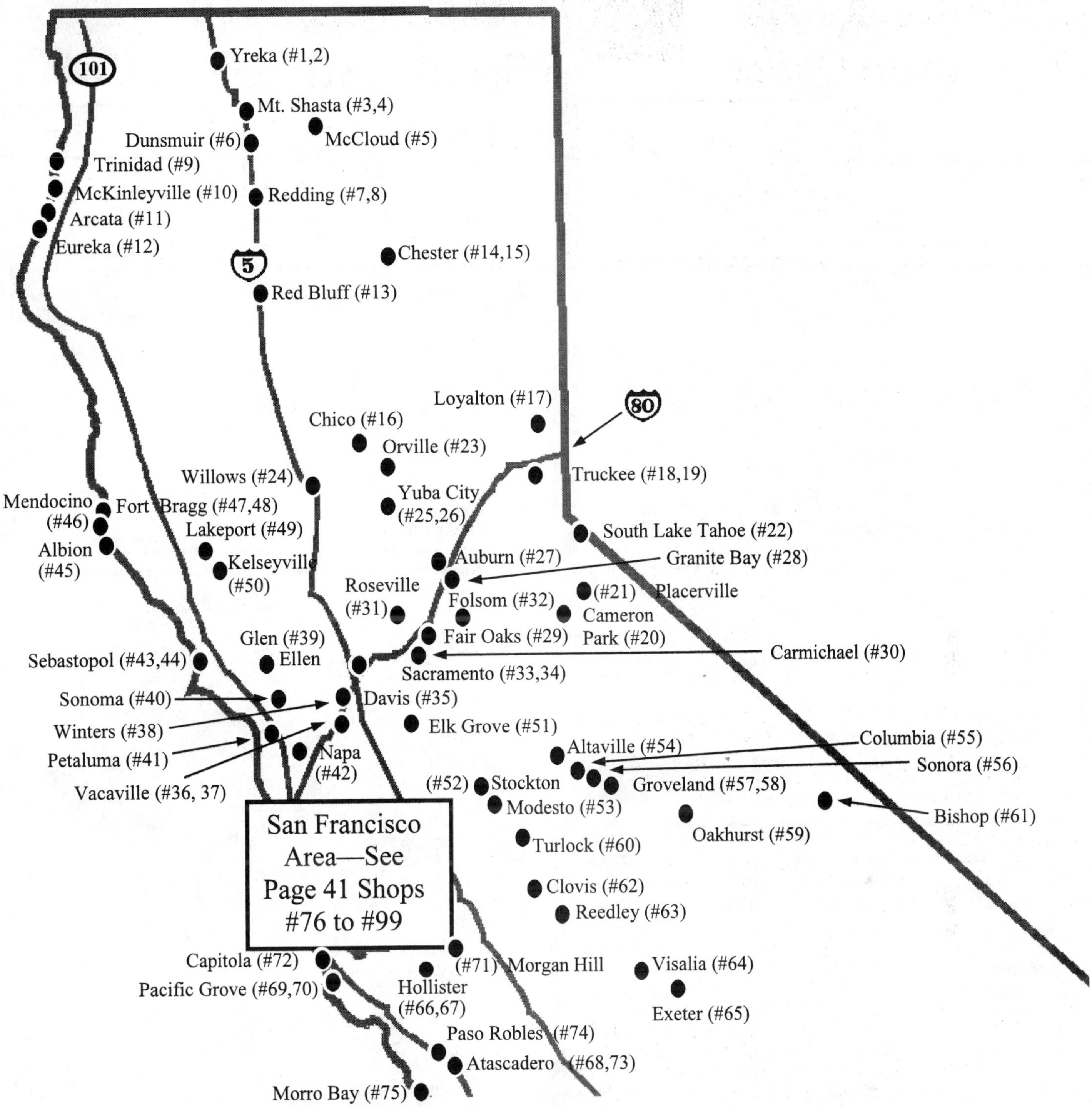

101
Yreka (#1,2)
Mt. Shasta (#3,4)
McCloud (#5)
Dunsmuir (#6)
Trinidad (#9)
McKinleyville (#10)
Redding (#7,8)
Arcata (#11)
Eureka (#12)
5
Chester (#14,15)
Red Bluff (#13)
Loyalton (#17)
80
Chico (#16)
Orville (#23)
Willows (#24)
Truckee (#18,19)
Yuba City (#25,26)
Mendocino (#46)
Fort Bragg (#47,48)
Lakeport (#49)
South Lake Tahoe (#22)
Albion (#45)
Kelseyville (#50)
Auburn (#27)
Granite Bay (#28)
Roseville (#31)
Folsom (#32)
(#21) Placerville
Cameron Park (#20)
Glen (#39) Ellen
Fair Oaks (#29)
Sebastopol (#43,44)
Carmichael (#30)
Sacramento (#33,34)
Sonoma (#40)
Davis (#35)
Winters (#38)
Elk Grove (#51)
Petaluma (#41)
Napa (#42)
Altaville (#54)
Columbia (#55)
Sonora (#56)
Vacaville (#36, 37)
(#52) Stockton
Groveland (#57,58)
Modesto (#53)
Bishop (#61)
Oakhurst (#59)
Turlock (#60)

San Francisco Area—See Page 41 Shops #76 to #99

Clovis (#62)
Reedley (#63)
Capitola (#72)
(#71) Morgan Hill
Visalia (#64)
Pacific Grove (#69,70)
Hollister (#66,67)
Exeter (#65)
Paso Robles (#74)
Atascadero (#68,73)
Morro Bay (#75)

For Southern California See Page 46 Shops #100 thru #167

723 S. Broadway 96097
(530) 842-5549 Fax: (530) 842-2646
janelson@tco.net
Owners: John and Nancy Nelson

Yreka, CA #1

FABRIC, Notions, Books, Patterns and Classes.
Handcrafted Quilt Racks, Frames, Ladders and Quilting Accessories.
Great Parking and Accessibility.

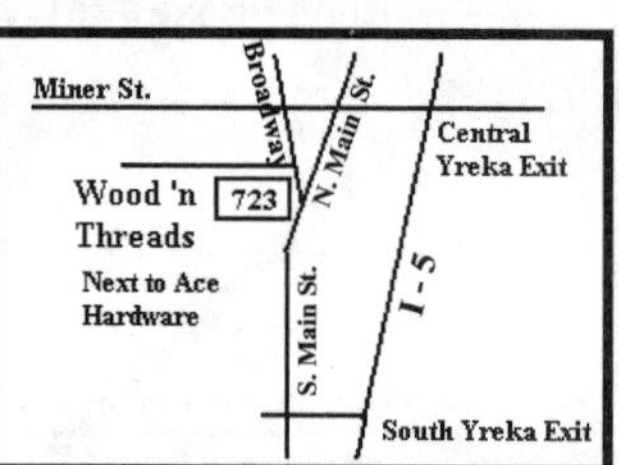

Mon - Sat 10 - 5

Yreka, CA #2

Mon - Fri 10 - 5
Sat 10 - 4

Wooden Spools

304 N. Main St. 96097
(530) 842-4562

woodenspools@webtv.net

Fabric — Notions — Books
Custom Machine quilting service.

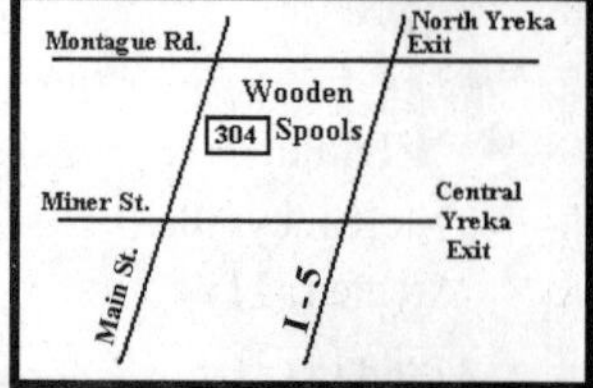

Mt. Shasta, CA #3

Mon - Sat
10 - 5
Some Sundays

Weston's
Quilting and Crafts

414 Chestnut St. 96067
(530) 926-4021
Owner: Michaela Weston
Est: 1968 1900 sq.ft.

Fabric - Yarns - Needle Arts
Serving you for over 35 years

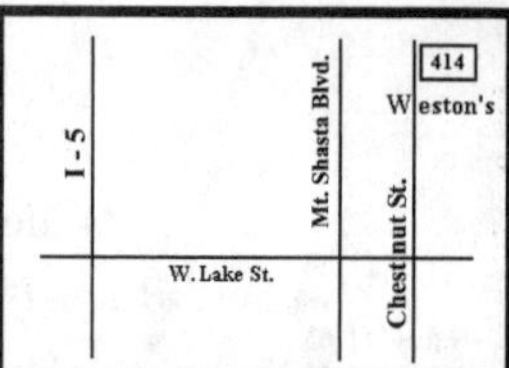

412 S. Mt. Shasta Blvd. 96067
(530) 926-0768 Fax: (530) 926-4908
sewunique1@hotmail.com

Designer fabric, quilting supplies, books and gifts.
Classes and Quilting Retreats.
Call for newsletter.
Fun, Friendly Store.
Janome Dealer.

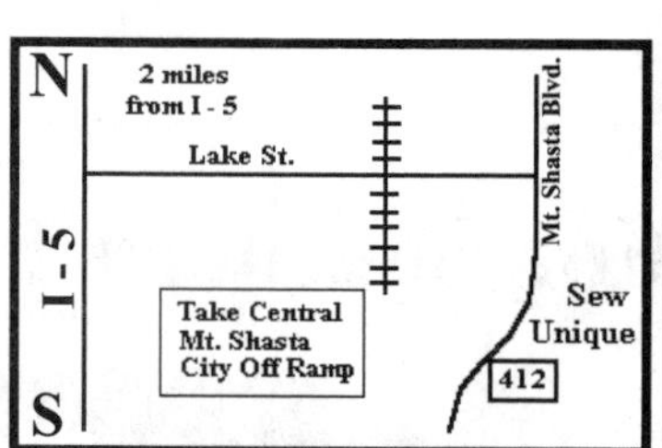

Mon - Sat 10 - 5
Closed Mon
Nov. - April

Mt. Shasta, CA #4

McCloud, CA #5

Mon - Sat
10 - 5

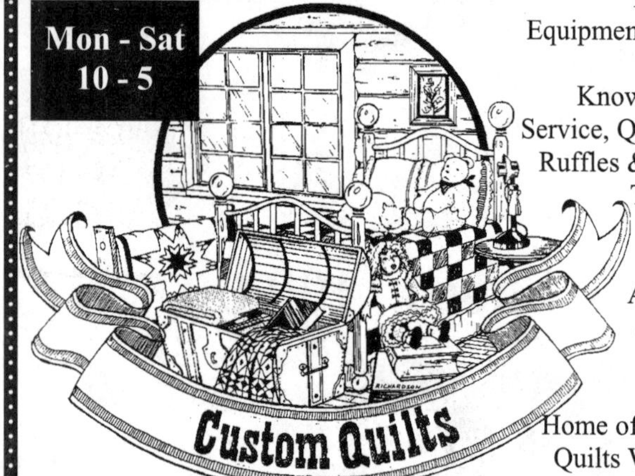

Fabulous Fabric, Quilting Books, Patterns & Equipment, Classes, Friendly, Knowledgeable Service, Quilts, Dust Ruffles & Window Treatment, Wedding Attire, Alterations & Custom Machine Quilting
Home of McCloud Quilts Weekends.

Custom Quilts

207 Quincy Ave.
McCloud, CA 96057-0347
530-964-2500
quiltldy@snowcrest.net
Open Some Sundays in Summer

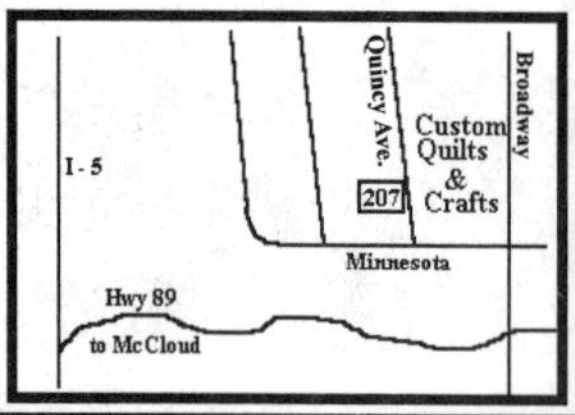

I-5
Quincy Ave.
Custom Quilts & Crafts
207
Broadway
Minnesota
Hwy 89 to McCloud

Dunsmuir, CA #6

5853 Sacramento Ave. 96025
(530) 235-4519
E-Mail: FabricTrain@Finestplanet.com
Web Site: www.thefabrictrain.com
Owners: Bill & Ann Sanford

Jan 1st thru March 1st
10 am to 4 pm
March thru December
10 am to 5 pm
Closed Sunday & Monday

Full Service Fabric Store.
Large selection of Hoffman, Moda, Northcott, & Flannels, David Textiles & Fleece.

Located in historic Dunsmuir. "The Railroad Town"

to Mt. Shasta 8 miles
Pine St.
I-5
Dunsmuir Exit
Dunsmuir Ave.
The Fabric Train
5853
Sacramento Ave.
Railroad Yard
to Redding 45 miles

Redding, CA #7

Mon - Fri
9 - 5:30
Sat 10 - 5

Sew What

2473 Athens Ave. 96001
(530) 242-0177
www.sewwhatquilts.com
Owner: Lori Orlando
Est: 2002 1800 sq.ft.
Over 2500 bolts specializing in Brights & Batiks. Notions, Books, & Patterns, Friendly, helpful Staff. Located in the Cypress Shopping Center

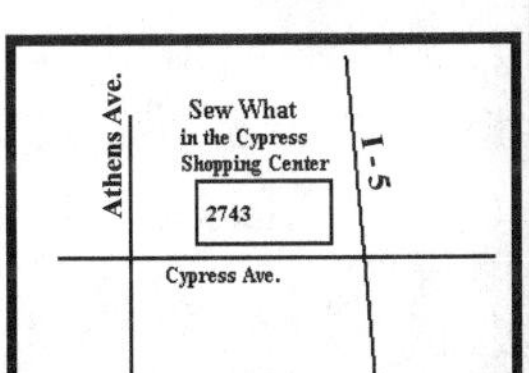

Redding, CA #8

Mon - Sat
9:30 - 6
Sun 11 - 5

Decor Fabrics

961 Dana Dr. 96003
(530) 221-8313 Fax: (530) 221-8387
Owners: Fred & Judy Zerull
Est: 1965 12000 sq.ft.

Specializing in quilting cottons, books & Patterns, upholstery & drapery fabrics, yarns & art needlework, art supplies and a frame shop.

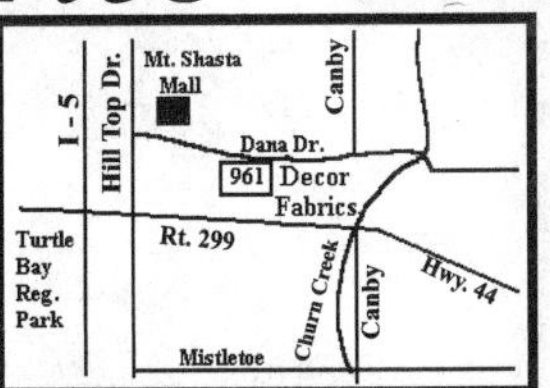

Trinidad, CA #9

Ocean Wave Quilts

529 Trinity St. 95570
(707) 677-3770 Fax: (707) 677-3795
Owner: Sandi Globus
Est: 1994 800 sq.ft. 1000 Bolts

Open 6 days
9:30 - 5:30
Closed Tues

A unique shop containing fabulous fabrics, books and notions located in a historic fishing village nestled between redwoods and beaches.

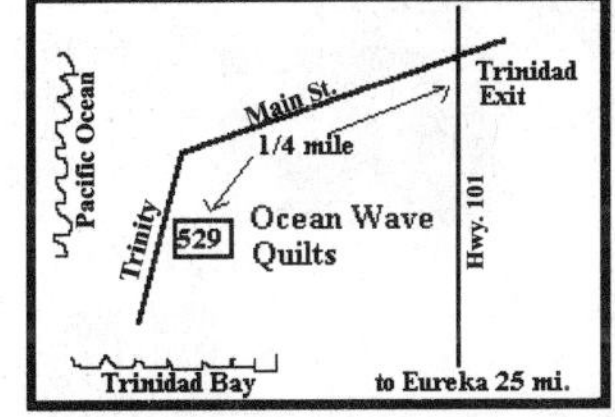

McKinleyville, CA #10

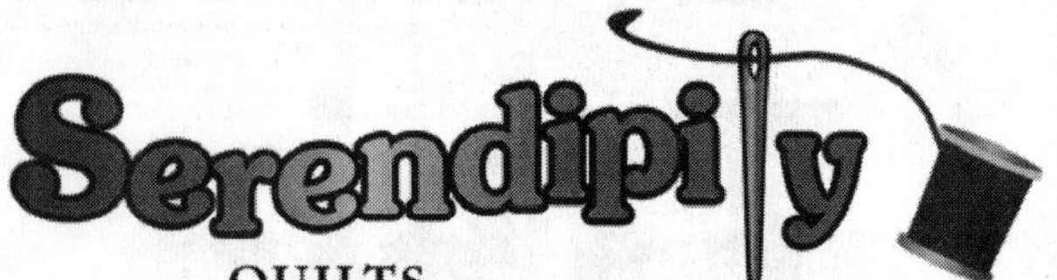

QUILTS

1977 Central Ave.
McKinleyville, CA 95519
Www,serendipityquilts.com
PH: (707) 839-9015 FAX: (707) 839-9016

Open 7 days a Week
Mon - Sat 10 am-5:30 pm, Sunday, Noon-4 pm
3000+ Bolts 2800 sq.ft.

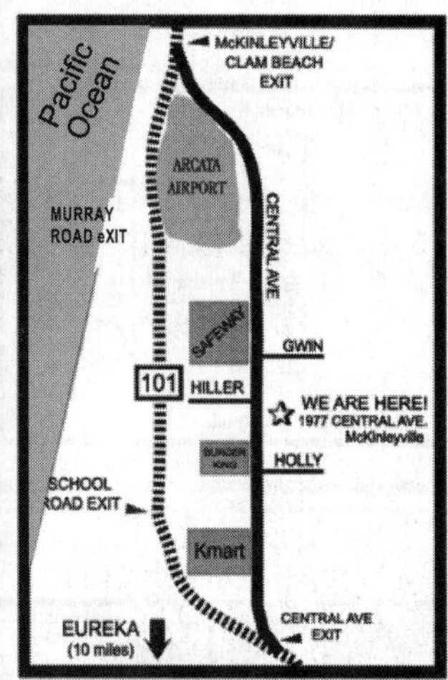

- SPECIALIZING IN FLANNELS!
- Kits Available
- Classes - All Levels
- Books & Patterns
- Notions
- Gifts

Arcata, CA #11

Tues - Sat 11 - 6
Sundays 12 - 5
Spring & Summer

Daisy Drygoods

959 "H" St. 95521
(707) 822-1893
daisy@humboldt1.com
daisydrygoods.net Est: 2001
Owners: Mary Anderson & Anne Hitt 2600 sq.ft.

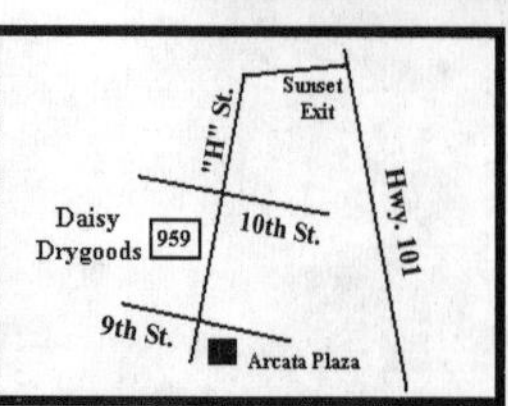

Antique & collectible sewing and fashion items including feedsacks, quilts, chenilles, buttons, cigarette silks and lace. An art quilter's paradise!

301 W. Harris St. Eureka, CA 95503
(707) 444-9662 Fax: (707) 443-6649
www.scottiedogquilts.com
ScottieDogQuilts@aol.com
Owner: BrendaLou Scott

Mon 10 - 9
Tues - Fri 10 - 5:30
Sat 10 - 4

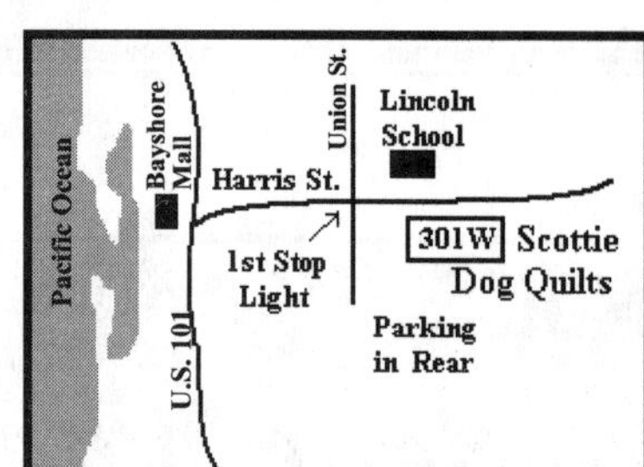

Wonderful selection of 100% Cotton Fabrics.
Full line of Patterns, Books, Notions & Gifts.
Classes and Retreats for beginning through advanced quilters.

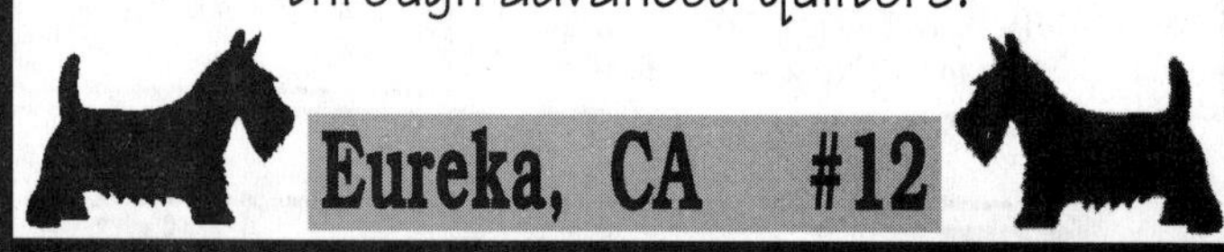

Eureka, CA #12

Red Bluff, CA #13

In Stitches

Tues - Sat 10 - 5

208 Elm St. 96080
(530) 529-1436
institches@snowcrest.net
Est: 2001 1400 sq.ft.

1300+ bolts of 100% cotton from leading fabric manufacturers. Patterns, books, kits, gifts and collectibles. 10% discount to guild members.

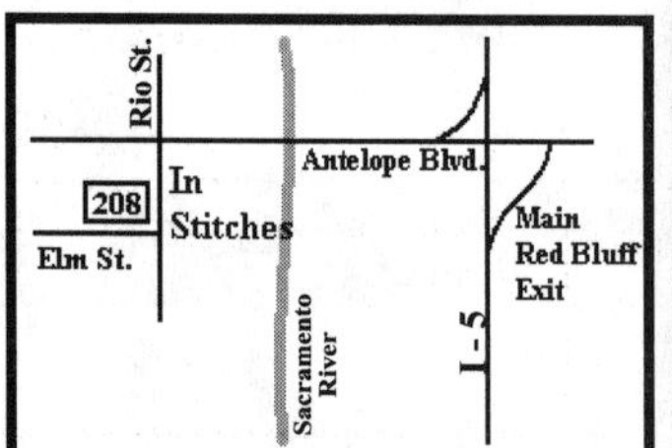

Chester, CA #14

Oct 1 - April 30
Mon - Sat 10 - 5
May 1 - Sept 30
Mon - Sat 10 - 5
Sun 12 - 4

135 Main St. #6E
P.O. Box 546
96020
Est: 1992
1500 sq.ft.
3000 Bolts

Owners: Jennifer & Sharon Paine
(530) 258-3901

Fabric, Notions, Specialty Yarns, X-stitch, Dyes, and Silk Ribbon. We're next to beautiful Mt. Lassen and Lake Almanor. Classes Offered

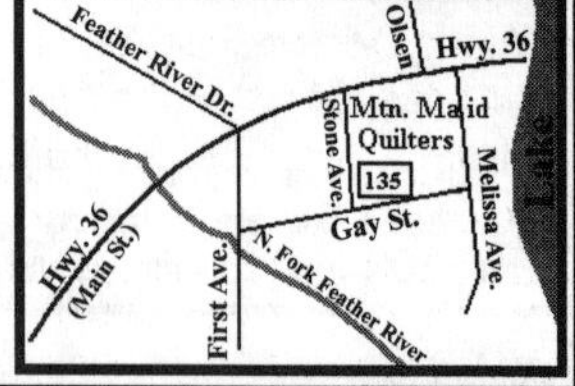

Chester, CA #15

Mon - Fri 9 - 5:30
Sat 9 - 5

Paper Stuff

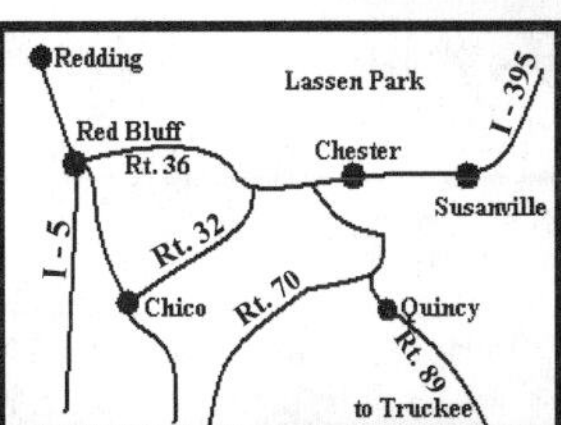

425 Main St., P.O. Box 679 96020
(530) 258-3966 Fax: (530) 258-2565
Owner: Lynn Wistos Est: 1999

Located on Main Street next to Chester True Value. High Quality Fabrics - Over 2000 Bolts of 100% Cotton

Chico, CA #16

Mon - Sat 10 - 5:30
Sun 11 - 4

Honey Run Quilters

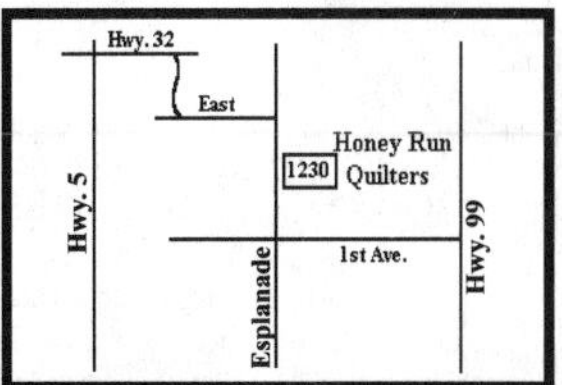

1230 Esplanade 95926
(530) 342-5464
Owner: Sharon Berg

The latest in fabrics, books, patterns & notions. Friendly, knowledgeable service. Good Parking. Coffee's always on!

Loyalton, CA #17

Mon & Tues 10 - 3
Wed - Sat 10 - 5

Happy Heart Quilts and Collectibles

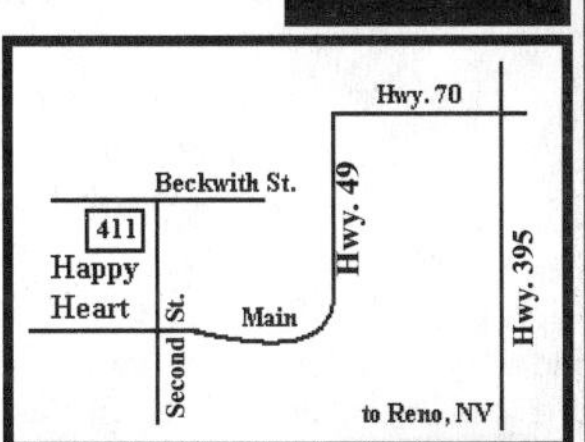

411 Second St. #B 96118
(530) 993-4025
Est: 2003
This cozy small town shop features 100% cotton fabrics, notions, books, gifts and collectibles. Located 42 miles north of Reno, NV

Truckee, CA #18

Mon - Sat 10 - 5:30
Sun 12 - 4

Truckee Fabrics

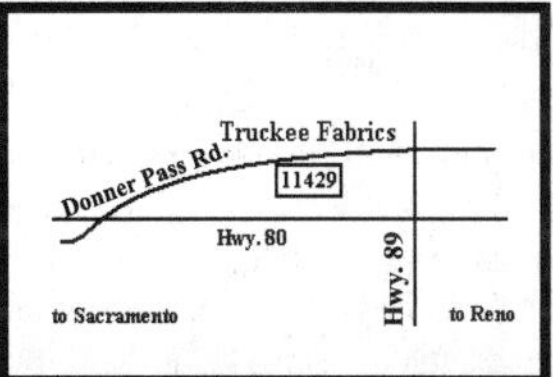

11429 Donner Pass Rd. 96161
(530) 582 - 8618
2000 + Bolts

Over 2000 Bolts of Cotton Fabrics including Flannels and Mountain Theme Prints. A large Selection of the Latest Books and Notions.

Truckee, CA #19

Mon - Sat 9:30 - 5:30
Sun 10 - 4

DONNA'S Stitchery

12219 Business Park Dr. #12 96161
(530) 587-6708

Est: 1979

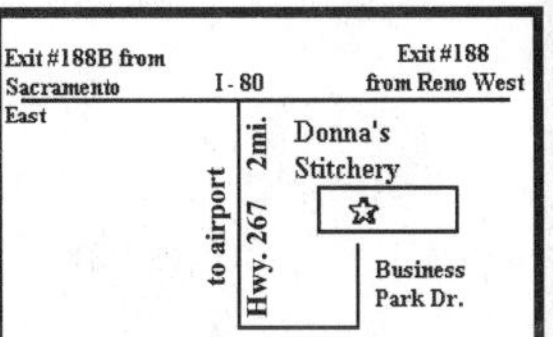

Books & Notions
100% cotton fabrics specializing in orientals, batiks, flannels and mountain theme prints.

Cameron Park, CA #20

HIGH SIERRA QUILTERS

ON THE ROAD TO SOUTH LAKE TAHOE

2,700 sq.ft. shop 3,300+ bolts of 100% cottons

Great selection of cottons, flannel and batiks from major manufacturers, quilting supplies, full line of quilting notions, books, patterns, classes, gift items & more.

In the Bel Aire Shopping Center, Hwy. 50 at Cameron Park Dr., 30 miles east of Sacramento

3450 Palmer Drive, #8, Cameron Park, CA 95682
Phone 530-677-9990 Fax 530-677-9992
Owners: Linda Van Dyke & Doug Hodder

Mon - Fri 10 - 5:30 Sat 10 - 5 Sun 12 - 4

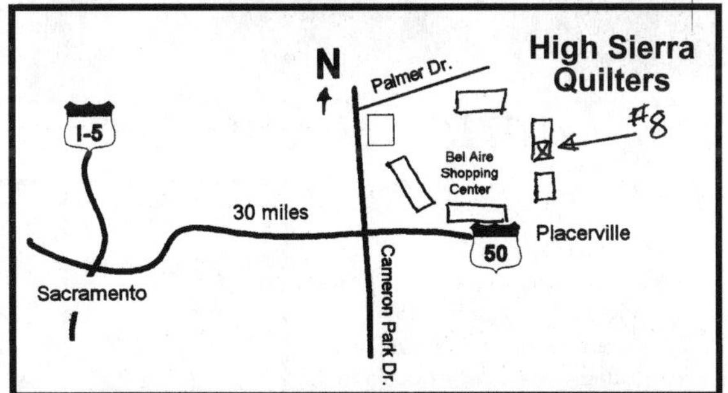

Placerville, CA #21

Mon-Fri 10-6
Sat 10-5
Sun 12-4

Singing Dog Quilt Works

656 Main Street (Across from Thompsons Toyota)
Placerville, CA 95667
(530) 622-7396
info@singingdogquiltworks.com
www.singingdogquiltworks.com

Small town service, big city selection!
We pride ourselves on catering to your creative spirit!
Over 3,000 bolts of natural fiber fabrics!
Viking Dealer Sales & Service
Notions, Books, Patterns, Classes, Machine Embroidery and Mores!
Est. 2001

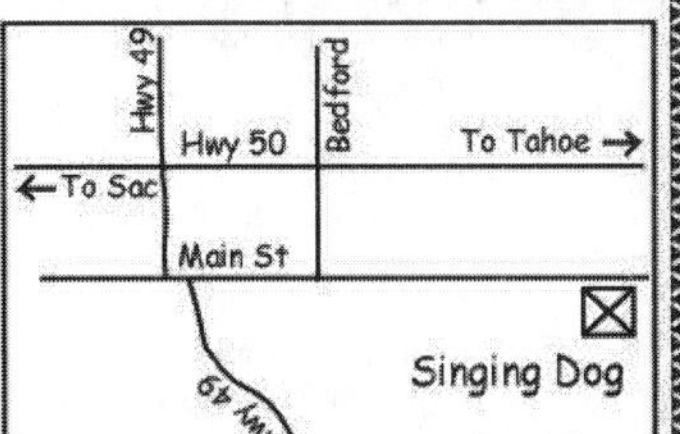

South Lake Tahoe, CA #22

Everyday 10 - 6

Quilting Tahoe

2264 Lake Tahoe Blvd. #7 96150
(800) 476-9065 or
(530) 544-9797
quiltingtahoe@aol.com
www.quiltingtahoe.net
Owners: Penny & Bill Burroughts
Est: 2003 900 sq.ft. 900 Bolts

Quality fabrics from top manufacturers. Backgrounds and blenders are a specialty, textures too. Classes - see our website.

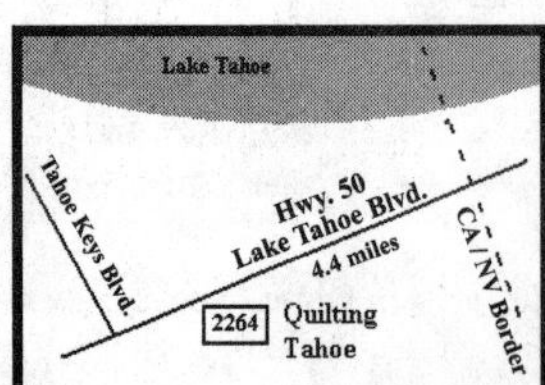

Oroville, CA #23

Tues - Fri 10 - 5 Sat 10 - 1

Mary Jane's Quilt Shop

2330 Lincoln St., Suite 3 95966
(530) 533-0401
Owners: Rich & Mary Jane Jasek
Est: 2003 600 sq.ft.

Small intimate shop run by husband & wife. 100% cotton fabrics from top companies, books, notions. Classes too.

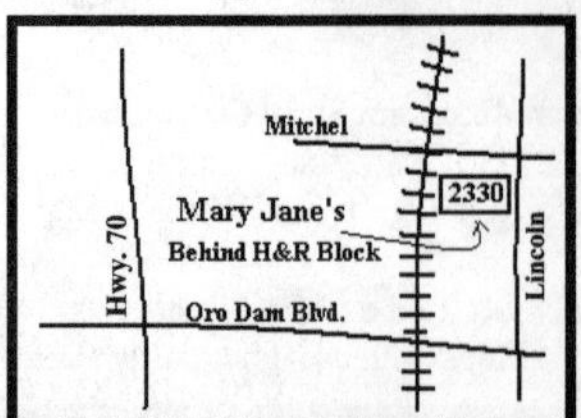

Willows, CA #24

Tues - Fri 10 - 5 Sat 12 - 4

Quilt Corral

201 N. Tehama St. 95988
(530) 934-8116

Full service quilt shop.
Notions, books & Patterns. A room of Flannels & Homespuns. Lots of cowboy material, 30's reproductions. Great gifts & Italian Charms

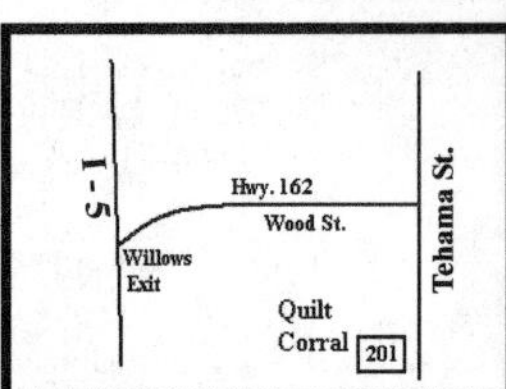

Yuba City, CA #25

Mon - Sat 10 - 6

Jomama's Quilts

624 Plumas St. 95991
(530) 790-0616
jomamas@sbcglobal.net

High quality quilting fabrics, patterns, books and notions. Hand smocked infant and toddler dresses. Located in downtown Yuba City.

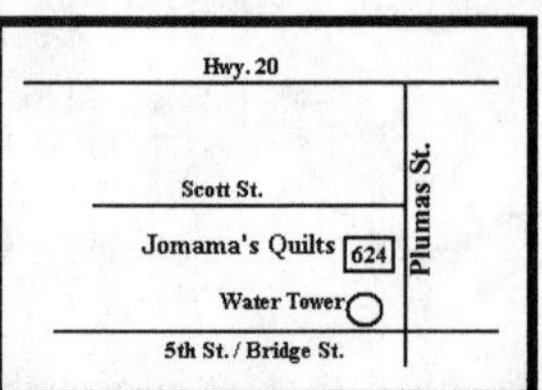

Yuba City, CA #26

Mon - Sat 10 - 5

My Favorite Quilt Shop

229 Clark Ave., Hillcrest Plaza 95991
(530) 673-7720
Owner: Sandy Ferrari
Est: 1978 900 sq.ft. 700 Bolts

Large variety of awesome quilts in stock.
Or we'll make yours to order!

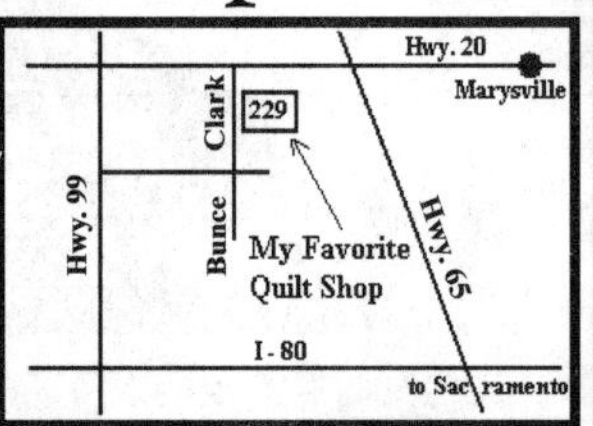

Your Northern California Destination Quilt Shop!
Featuring a wide variety of top quality cotton fabrics, books, tools and notions; an extensive calendar of classes; and a friendly, knowledgable staff. www.cabinfeverquiltshoppe.con

Hours: M - F 9:30 - 6, Saturday 9:30 - 4, Sunday 10-3

Directions:
From I-80 east, exit at Elm Ave. Left onto Elm, right on High St., left on Cleveland, right on Lincoln Way.

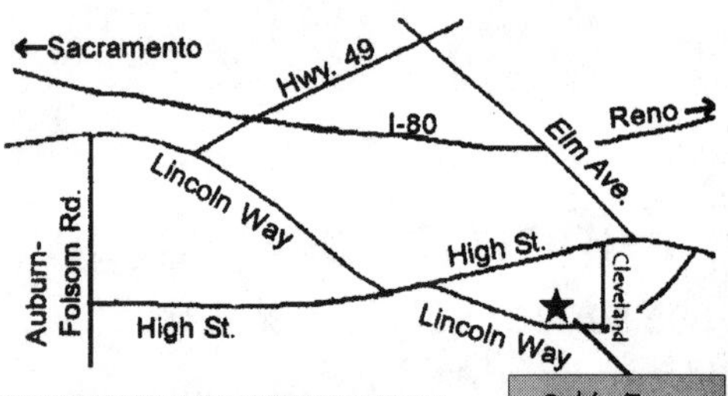

Auburn, CA #27

Granite Bay, CA #28

Tues - Fri 10 - 5:30 Sat 10 - 4

8683 Auburn-Folsom Rd. 95746
(916) 791-6228 Fax: Same
thecocqshop@surewest.net
2000 sq.ft.
1600 bolts

You just can't miss this beautiful quilt shop! Batiks, Moda, SSI, RJR, Northcott, Erlanger, P&B, Troy, Flannels and lots more.
www.thecocqshop.com

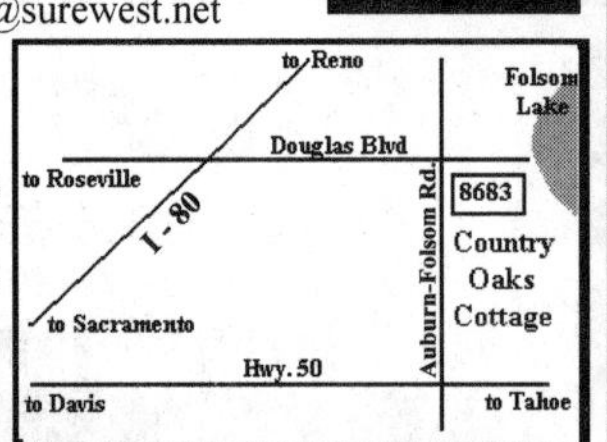

Fair Oaks, CA #29

Mon - Sat 9 - 5

Tayo's Fabrics & Quilts

10127 Fair Oaks Blvd. 95628
(916) 967-5479
info@tayosfabrics.com
www.tayosfabrics.com
Owner: Shenna Mealey Est: 1983

Fabrics, books, patterns & notions for traditional & contemporary quilting, cloth dolls, wearable art & fashion sewing. Felted wool, crazy quilting supplies. Classes. Personal & friendly service.

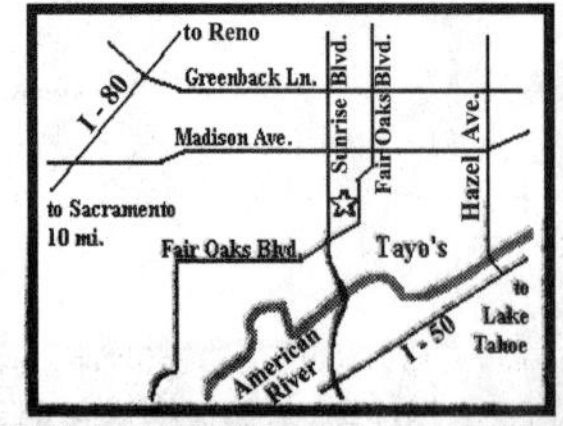

Carmichael, CA #30

Mon - Fri 9 - 9 Sat 9 - 7

Beverly's Fabrics

6456 Fair Oaks Blvd. (at Marconi Ave.)
(916) 486-8374 95608
Fax: (916) 486-1730
www.beverly'sfabric.com

We cater to Quilters! High Quality Fabrics from Top Companies! Lots of Notions, Books, Classes. Very Friendly, Helpful customer service.

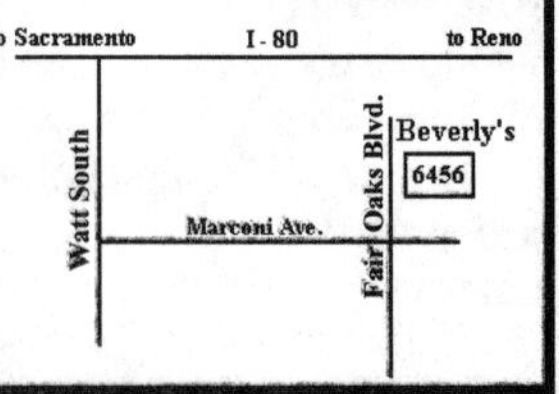

Largest Selection of Patterns in Northern California

Roseville, CA #31

The Stitching Station

1000 Sunrise Ave. 95661
(916) 773-0296 Fax: (916) 773-0294
Owner: Sandra Satnowski
Est: 1989 2400 sq.ft.

If you're a quilter, you've heard about The Stitching Station. We have the most unique array of Quilting supplies in the Sacramento area, with a large selection of show quality quilts and doll models on display.

Mon - Fri 10 - 6 Sat 10 - 5:30

Fabric, Books, Supplies, Notions, Doll Patterns, Quilting Classes. Large selection of 30's reproduction fabrics and a great collection of Homespuns.

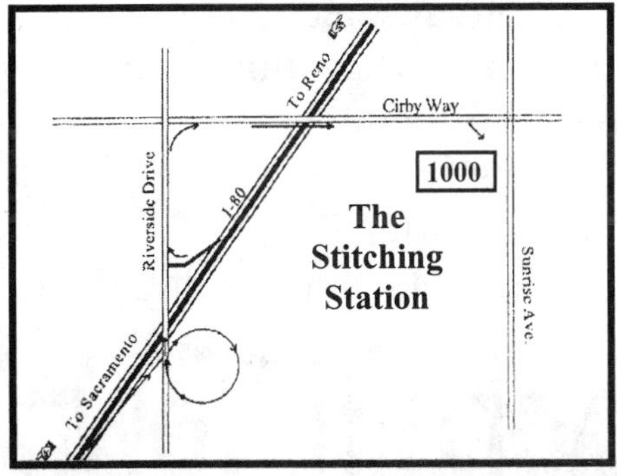

From Sacramento: Take I - 80 east (towards Reno) to the first Roseville exit, Riverside Dr./Auburn Blvd. Follow the signs to Riverside Dr. (pass through the underpass, circle around and cross over the freeway). Turn right again at the second stoplight, Cirby Way. Follow Cirby Way approximately 1 mile, and turn right just before Sunrise Ave. The Stitching Station is on the right.

From Reno: Take I - 80 west (towards Sacramento) to the Riverside Dr. off-ramp. Turn right onto Riverside. Turn right again at the first stoplight, Cirby Way. Follow Cirby Way approximately 1 mile, and turn right just before Sunrise Ave. The Stitching Station is on the right.

Folsom, CA #32

LIBERTY STAR QUILTS

- Large selection of the finest quality 100% cotton fabrics
- Wool and wool felt
- Books and Patterns
- Notions
- Stitchery
- Kits
- Gift Items

Monday - Saturday 10:00 am - 5:30 pm

Mail Order Available
Conveniently located 4 miles N of U.S. 50

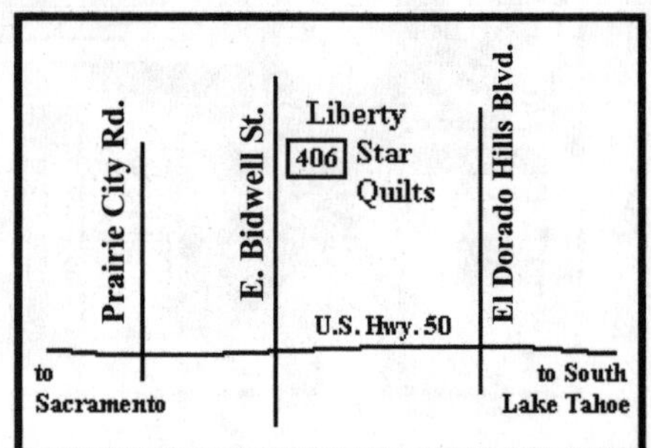

406 E. Bidwell St., P.O. Box 517
Folsom, CA 95630
(916) 983-6747

Est: 2004 1500 sq. ft. 2000+ bolts

Material Girls

Sacramento, CA #33

2617 Alta Arden Expressway 95825
(916) 485-4252 Fax: (916) 485-4272
Owner: Terri Lanning
Est: 1997 3500 sq.ft.
4500 Bolts
www.matgirls.com

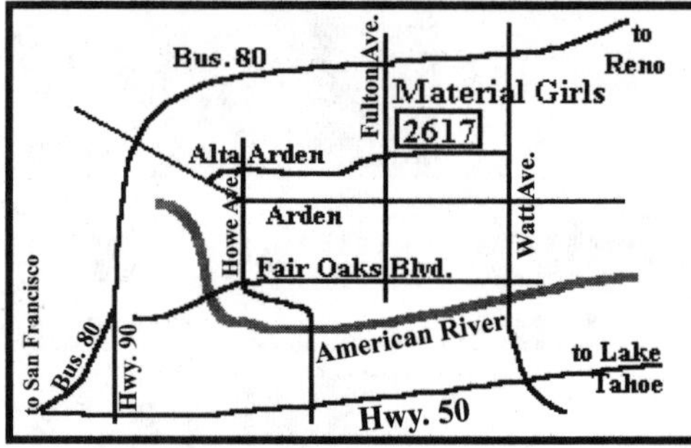

Mon - Sat 10 - 6
Sunday 12 - 4

A great selection of :

- Quality 100% cotton fabric
- Books & Patterns
- Notions
- Classes Offered
- Quilting Machine on Premises.

QUILT SHOP

"Friendliest Shop in Town"

Quilters' Corner, Inc.

Sacramento, CA #34

9792 B. Business Park Dr., Sacramento, CA 95827
(916) 366-6136 Fax: (916) 366-6105
E-Mail: quilterscorner@rcip.com

Sacramento's newest quilt shop.

Over 3,000 sq.ft. of fabrics, books, patterns, notions, and gifts. We have Thimbleberries Club, Quiltsitter Circle and Jan Patek Girl Gang.

Mon - Fri 10 - 6
Sat 10 - 4 Sun 12 - 4

www.quilterscornersac.com

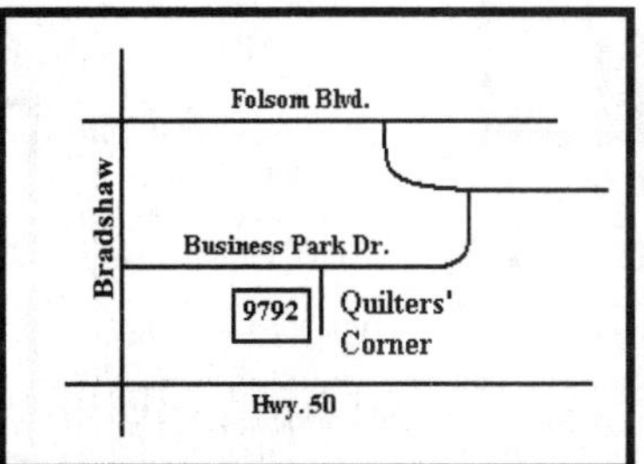

Take Hwy. 50 to Bradshaw Rd., We are north of the Freeway. Turn on Business Park Dr. About 1/2 mi. turn into Driveway 9792 (Across from Marsh's Carpets)

Davis, CA #35

Mon 10 - 8
Tues - Fri 10 - 5:30
Sat 10 - 5
Sun 11 - 5

Pincushion Boutique

2827 Spafford St. 95616
(530) 758-3488 or (800) 758-3488
sweettrt@pacbell.net
www.sweettreat.com
Owner: Beth Murphy
Est: 1977 5000 sq.ft.
3000 Bolts + 10,000 fabrics in 1/2 yd. Cuts.
Home of Sweet Treat™.
Helpful quilters on staff.
Mail Order & Sweet Treat™ Subscription.

Covell Blvd.
Pole Line
5th St.
Pena
2827
Pincushion Boutique
Spafford St.
2nd St.
Mace Blvd.
to S.F. I - 80 to Sacramento

Vacaville, CA #36

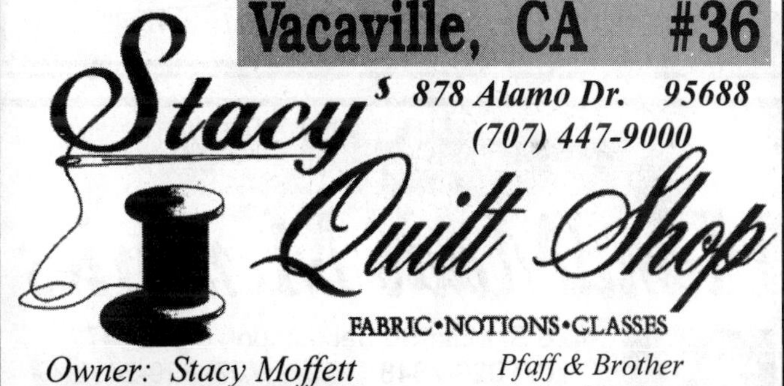

878 Alamo Dr. 95688
(707) 447-9000

Owner: Stacy Moffett

Pfaff & Brother Sewing Machines
In-house service all makes.

Mon - Fri 10 - 6
Sat 10 - 5 Sun 11 - 4

All cotton fabrics, books, notions and classes. Full line of Kona Cotton solids. Original patterns from our home town teachers.

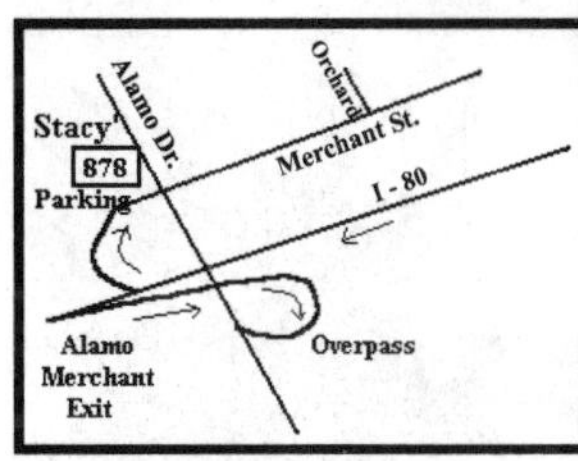

From Sacramento, exit Merchant St.
From San Francisco, exit Alamo Dr.

Vacaville, CA #37

Hours by Appt.

The Unique Spool

407 Corte Majorca 95688
(707) 448-1538
www.uniquespool.com
Owner: Roberta Dent

African, animal, Australian fabrics plus domestic prints, ethnic quilt patterns, puppet patterns & more.

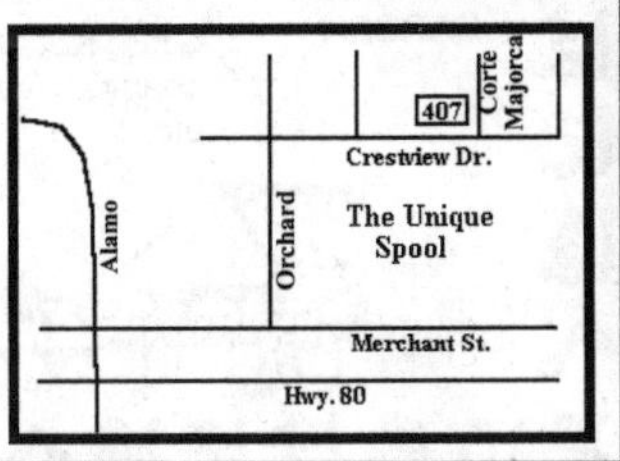

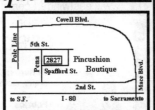

Winters, CA #38

Mon - Sat 10 - 4:30 Fri til 9 Sun 10 - 3

Cloth Carousel & Quiltworks

9 Main St. 95694
(530) 795-2580
Owner: Laurie A. Sengo & Diane Salera
Est: 1995

Specializing in service. 1200 bolts, notions, books, classes. We offer quality custom machine quilting. Eleven miles North of Vacaville off I - 505.

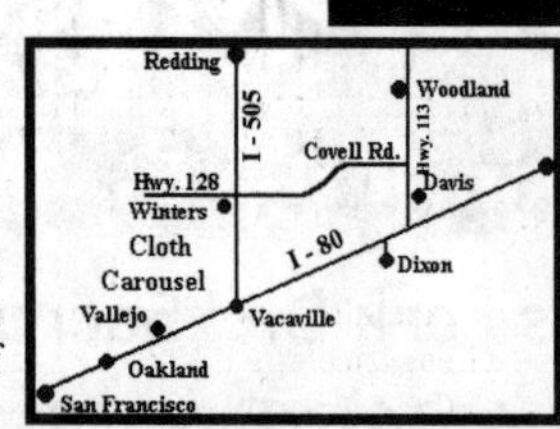

Glen Ellen, CA #39

Open Daily 10 - 5 Closed Mon

Quilted Cottage

13875 Sonoma Hwy.
(Hwy. 12) 95442
(707) 938-3650 Fax: Same
thingsbydi@msn.com
Owner: Diana Nissim

Located in the peaceful country of Sonoma County. Everything for the quilter: books, notions, classes, gifts, wool, wool felt, and 1000 bolts of cotton fabric

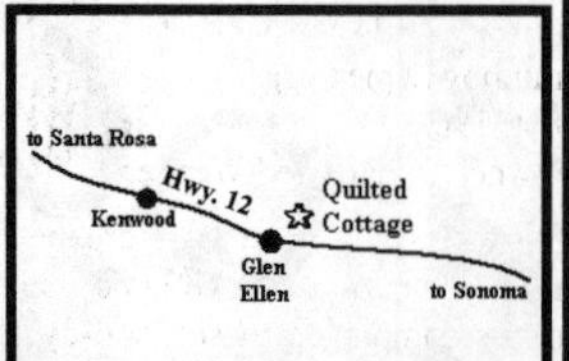

Sonoma, CA #40

Mon - Fri 9:30 - 6 Sat 10 - 5:30 Sun 11 - 4

201 W. Napa St. #14
Sonoma Mkt.Pl. 95476
(707) 996-3515
Est: 1963 2600 sq.ft.
4000 Bolts
We do Mail Orders & Invite Fabric Requests.

Complete line of quilting fabrics, books, patterns and notions. Hoffman, RJR, VIP, Kona & Many Unusual Fabrics.

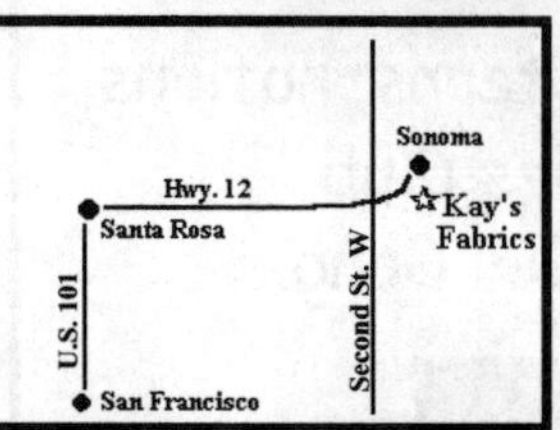

Petaluma, CA #41

Mon - Sat 10 - 5:30 Sun 12 - 4

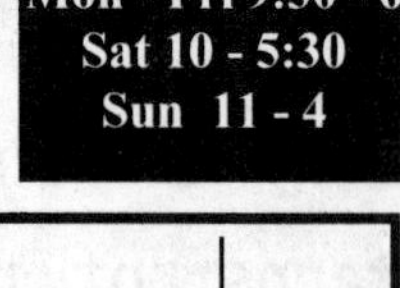

200 G St. 94952
(707) 763-0945
angels@QuiltedAngel.com
www.QuiltedAngel.com
Owner: Susie Ernst
Est: 1991 3600 sq.ft. 4000+ Bolts

A "destination" Quilt Store. Fabrics from all major suppliers, books (800 titles), notions, patterns & classes.

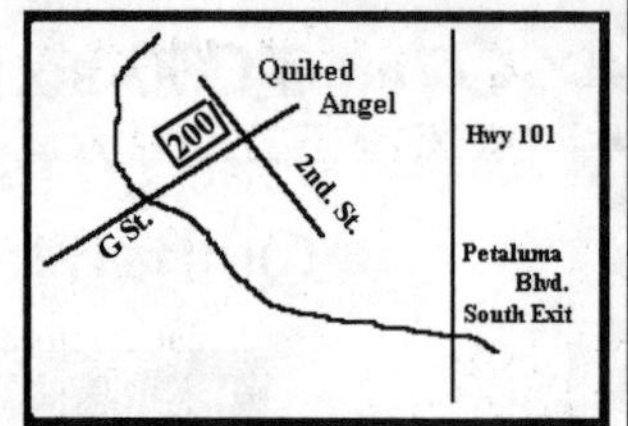

Napa, CA #42

Mon - Fri 10 - 5 Tues til 7 Sat 10 - 3

QUILTMAKER

1275 Napa Town Center 94559
(707) 252-6793 Fax: (707) 252-3552
Owners: Diane Massey-Todd & Nancy Eberlin
Est: 1996 1500 sq.ft. 3000+ bolts

Quiltmaker says it all! We are all things quilting! The best in quilt classes, tools, books and fabrics.

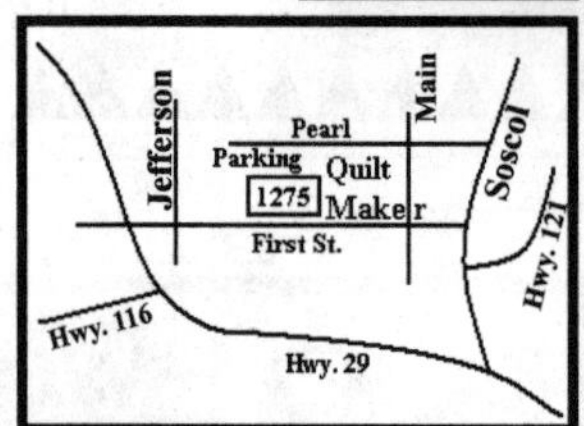

いろはにほへといろはにほへといろはにほへといろはにほへといろはにほへといろはにほへと

Sebastopol, CA #43

Eastwind Art

(707) 829-3536

P.O. Box 811
Sebastopol. CA 95473
Eastwindart811@sbcglobal.net
www.eastwindart.com

Owner:
Joanne Newcomb
Established 1973

SPECIALTY: JAPAN

VISIT OUR JAPANESE GARDEN

Patterns: Japanese crafts, clothing, quilts.

Fabrics: Japanese cotton prints, kimono scraps.

Sashiko: Needles, thread, stencils, indigo fabric.

Books: Japanese designs, sashiko, reference.

Gifts: Note cards, charms, maneki neko, etc.

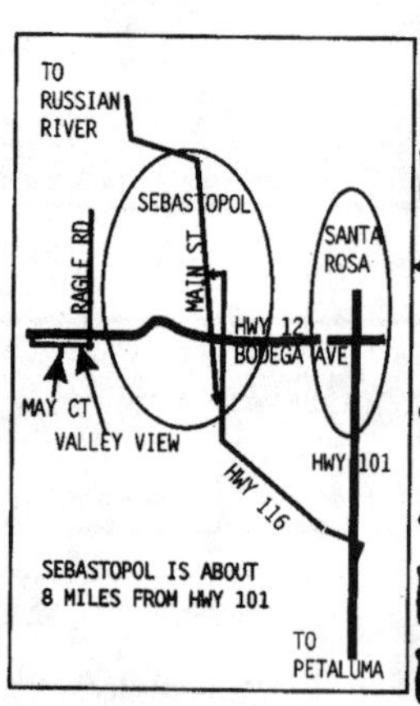

といろはにほへといろはにほへと

Sebastopol, CA #44

HandMade Memories

Mon - Fri 10 - 6 Sat 10 - 5

428 S. Main St. Sebastopol, CA 95472
(707) 829-7648 Fax: (707) 829-2492
Fabric@sonic.net
Owners: Nancy & Karla Samples
Est: 2003 2500 sq.ft. 3000 bolts

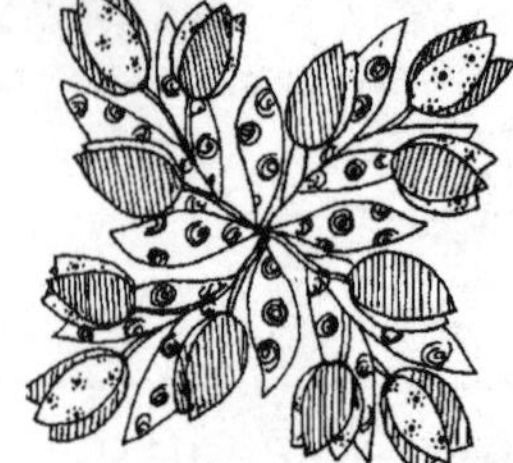

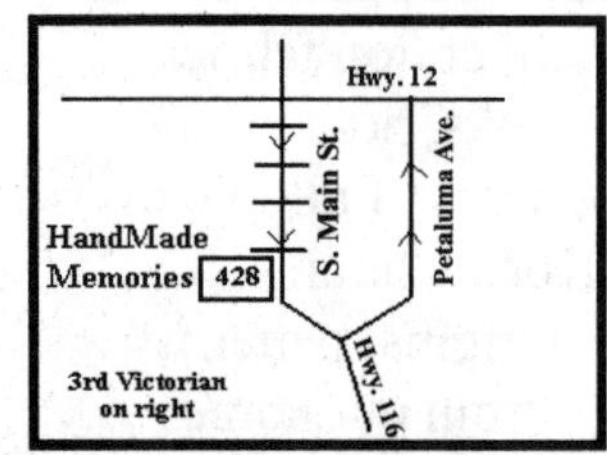

This Victorian home, circa 1875, has become a Quilter & Scrapbooker's dream. 3000+ bolts of 100% cottons, batiks, flannels, & novelty prints. All the notions & books to go with. Also everything you need for scrapbooking & card making.

Albion, CA #45

Phone for Appointment

Rainbow Resource Co.

P.O. Box 222 95410
(707) 937-0431
rainbow@mcn.org
Est: 1969
Owner: Charlene Younker

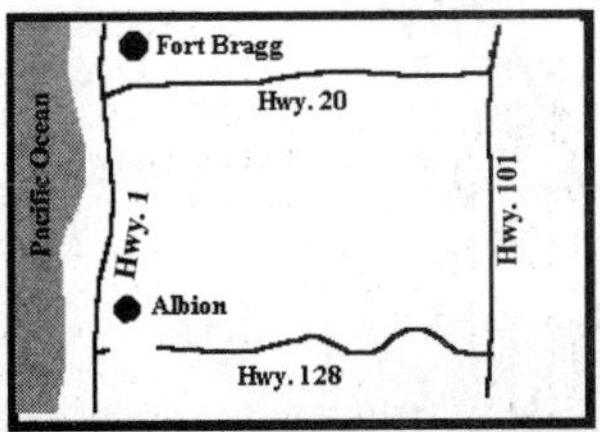

My own line of hand silk-screened fabric for quilters, along with related fabrics from various companies. Also hand-dyed rick rack & other items. Unusual Buttons, & Fun Stuff.

Mendocino, CA #46

Daily 10 - 5:30

45270 Main St., P.O. Box 1692 95460
(707) 937-4201 oceanq@mcn.org
www.oceanquiltsmendocino.com Est: 1999
Great selection of finished Quilts.
Gifts for quilters and folk art.

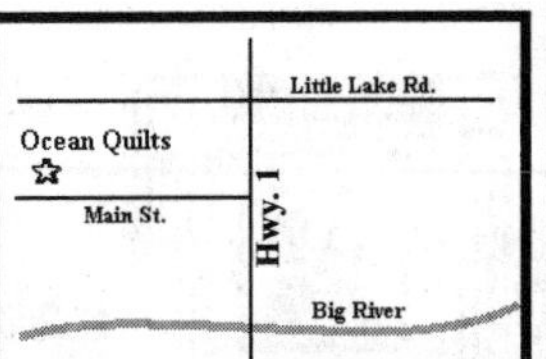

Fort Bragg, CA #47

Open Daily

FABRIC Indulgence & Art Supply

544 S. Main St. 95437
(707) 964-6365 Fax: (707) 964-6365
Est: 2000 3000 sq.ft. 3000 Bolts

lunarain@mcn.org
Owners: Erin Severi & Tabitha Korhummel
Fine fabrics, notions, books, patterns, natural fibers, dyes, silk painting supplies & inspiration.

Mendocino 10 mi.
Dowtown Fort Bragg
Hwy. 1
S. Main
Noyo Bridge
544
Fabric Indulgence
Hwy. 20

Fort Bragg, CA #48

Mon - Fri 9:30 - 5
Sat 10 - 4:30

Sew'n Sew Fabrics

320 N. Franklin St. 95437
(707) 964-4152
Fax: (707) 964-7046
Owner: Nancy Lamphear

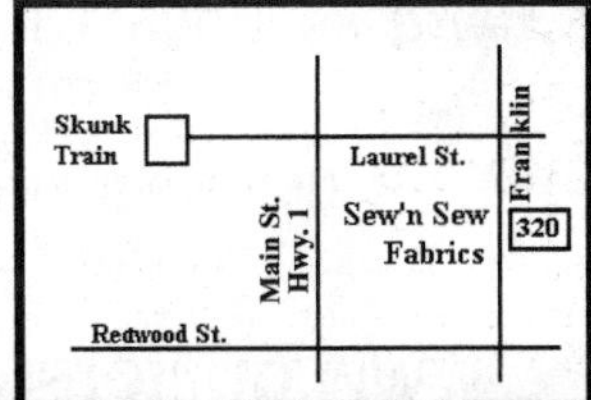

New Location. Lots of classes. A large colorful collection of Quilting Fabrics and a great selection of books & patterns.
Husband Friendly.

Lakeport, CA #49

Tues - Sat 10 - 4

Kerrie's Quilting

1853 N. High St. 95453
(707) 263-8555
Owner: Harry & Kerrie Hershey

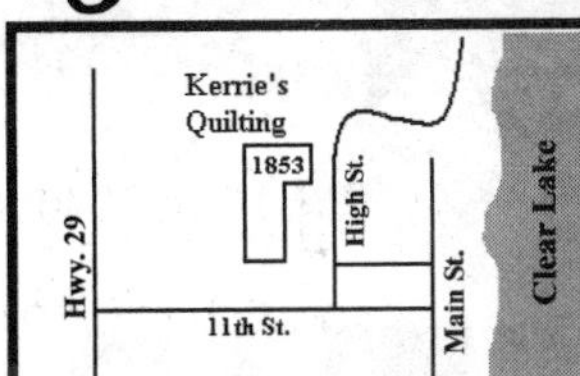

A friendly, small town shop at the lake. Cotton fabrics, books, notions, classes & retreats. Authorized Elna dealer.

Kelseyville, CA #50

Quilted Treasures

www.quilted-treasures.com

3925 Main St., P.O. Box 1189 95451
(707) 279-0324 Fax: (707) 279-4430
Anne Barquist, President

Thousands of premium cotton fabrics
Flannel is our specialty: 100's to choose from
Batiks, ikats, silk, rayons, and fleece
Home deco, fashions
Patterns and books
Quilts on display

1 hour from Hwy. 5
45 min. from Hwy. 101

Mon - Fri 10 - 5:30 Sat 10 - 4

For all your Quilting needs!

Elk Grove, CA #51

Country Sewing Center

9639 E. Stockton Blvd. 95624
(916) 685-8500
E-Mail: cntrysew@elkgrove.net
Visit our Web-Site: www.elkgrove.net/csc
Owners: Susan & Bill Zimlich
Est: 1993 2400 sq.ft. 3000+ Bolts

Mon - Fri 10 - 6
Sat 10 - 5

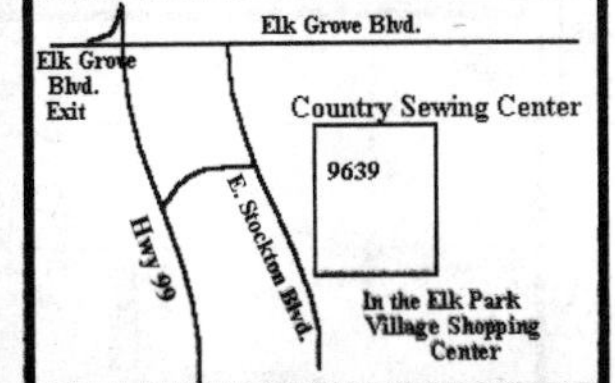

Great selection of 100% cotton fabrics, books & notions.
Friendly, small-town service.
Elk Grove exit from 99 or I - 5 then East.

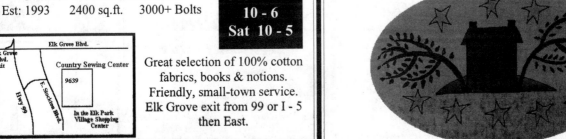

Stockton, CA #52

QUILTERS QUARTERS

1517 N. Lincoln St. 95204
(209) 462-0161
Stockton's only Quilt Shop

Fabric, Classes & Supplies for the Contemporary Quilter

Over 3,000 bolts in a small space
150 Kona Cotton solids always in stock,
Batiks, Brights, Kaffee Fasset Stripes & Homespun Plaids

quiltersquarters@comcast.net
Owner: Debbie Chase

www.quiltersquarters-stkn.com

Reg Hours:
Mon, Tue, Thurs, Fri 10 - 6,
Wed 1 - 7,
Sat 10 - 4

Located at Harding Way & Lincoln St.

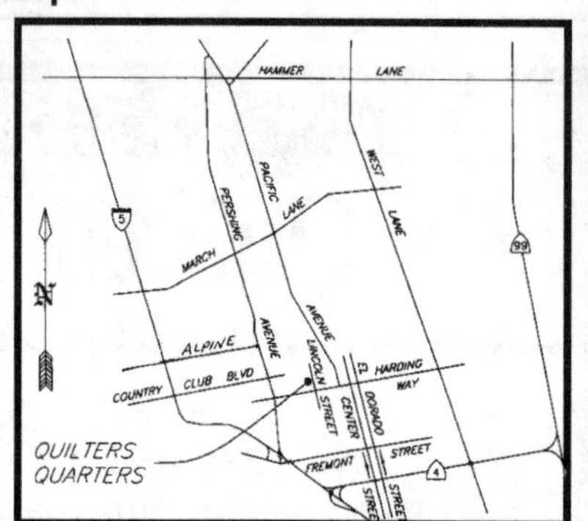

Modesto, CA #53

Mon - Fri 9:30 - 5:30
Sat 10 - 5
Sun 12 - 4

R. Lily Stem Quilts

909 W. Roseburg Ave. Suite B 95350
(209) 577-1919 Fax: (209) 577-1412
Owner: Marilyn Nelson
Est: 1986 3200 sq.ft.

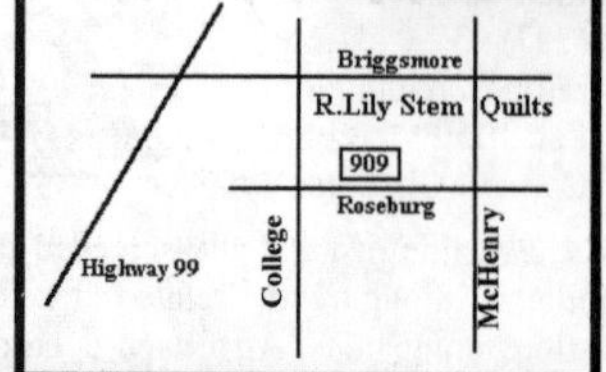

Fabulous fabrics, books, patterns, classes and great service ! 10,000 bolts of Fabric.

Altaville, CA #54

The Country Cloth Shop

457 S. Main St. P.O. Box 868
"Angels Camp" 95221
(209) 736-4998

Fax: (209) 736-9519
E-Mail: ccshop @goldrush.com
Owners:
Ginger & Chuck Duffy
Est: 1980 1600 sq.ft.

Mon - Sat 10 - 5

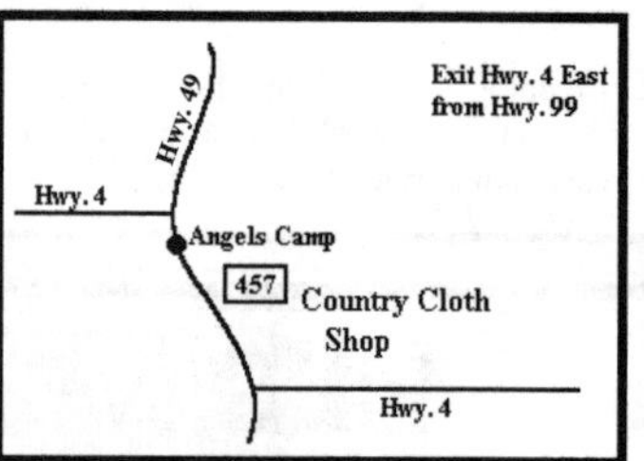

Authorized Bernina Dealer
Located in historic Angels Camp in the Mother Lode foothills.
Good selection of fabrics, books, patterns & threads.

COLUMBIA STATE HISTORIC PARK

Largest selection in Northern California of 19th Century historic reproduction fabrics! Plus books, patterns, kits for your traditional quilting projects. A unique shopping experience in a restored Gold Rush building.

Columbia, CA #55

www.columbiacalifornia.com

22735 Main St.,
P.O. Box 425 95310
209-533-1849

7 Days a Week 10 - 5

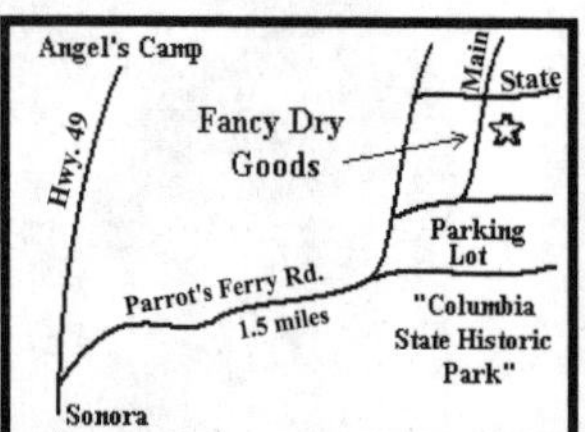

Sonora, CA #56

Mon - Fri 10 - 5
Sat 10 - 4

Sew Country
Quilts & Fabrics

19060 Standard Rd. #5 95370
(209) 533-5015
Sewcountry@bigvalley.net
Owner: Kathy Azebedo Est: 2003
Full line of top quality quilting fabrics. Over 250 bolts of Flannel, 110 bolts of Batiks. Large selection of Books, Patterns, Notions & Classes.

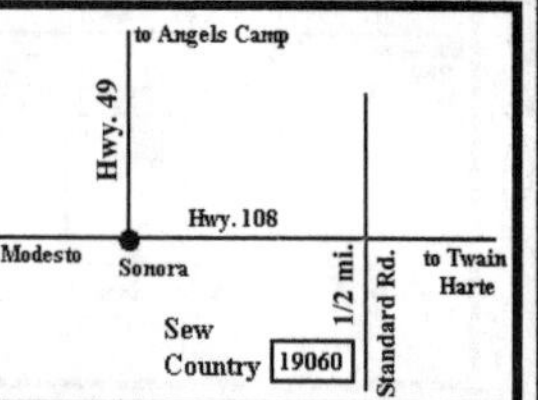

Groveland, CA #57

Mon - Sat 10 - 4

Bunny Rose & Co.

18757 Back St., P.O. Box 1063
(209) 962-5702 95321
bunnyrose@goldrush.com
Owner: Bunny Kite

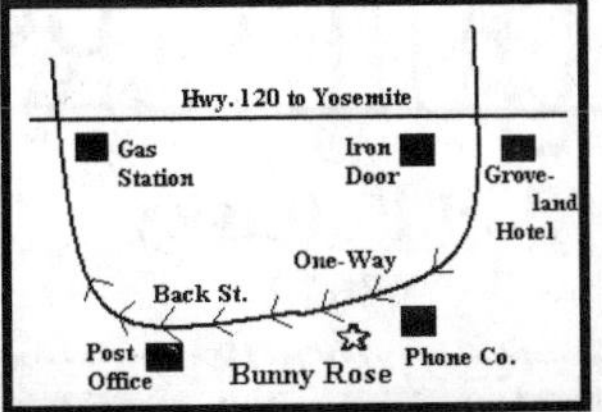

Specializing in quilting fabrics, notions & books. Come visit on your way to Yosemite.

Groveland, CA #58

Mon, Tues, Thurs, Fri 9 - 3 Sat 9 - 2

Nana's Quiltin' Place

18727 Hwy. 120, P.O. Box 302 95321
(209) 962-0944
nanasqp@sonnet.com
Owner: Sandy Smith Est: 2000

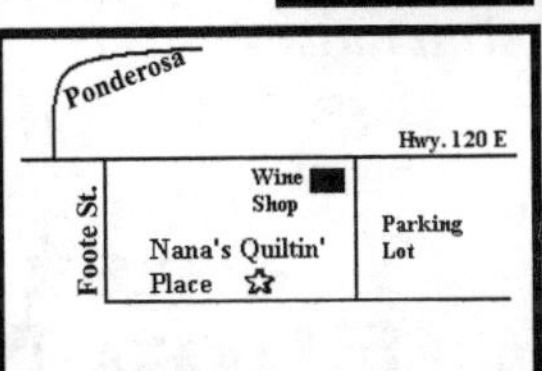

After your quilt is made let Nana's do the quilting & binding. Enjoy a visit to Yosemite while you're here.

Oakhurst, CA #59

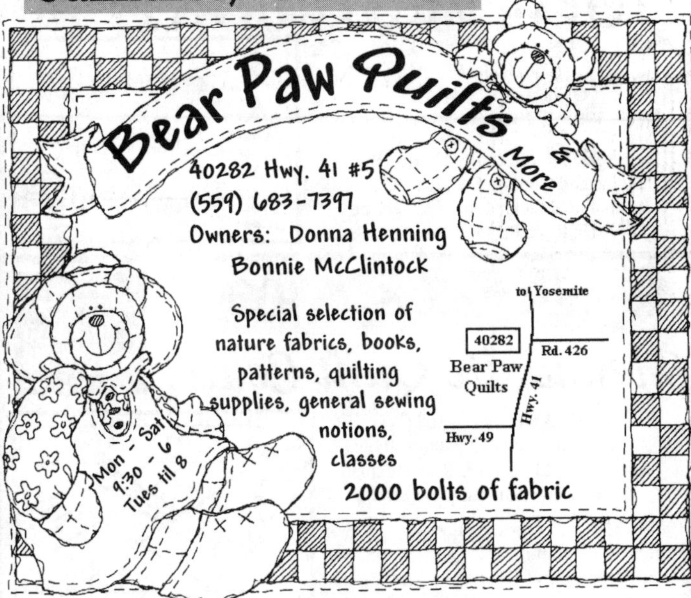

Turlock, CA #60

625 E. Main St.
Turlock, CA 95380
(209) 632-3225

E-mail: clothandquilts@charter.net
Fax: (209) 632-3354
Est: 2001 3900 sq.ft.
Owners: Cindy Kooistra, Debbie Sanders, & Margaret Labno

Mon - Sat 9:30 - 5:30

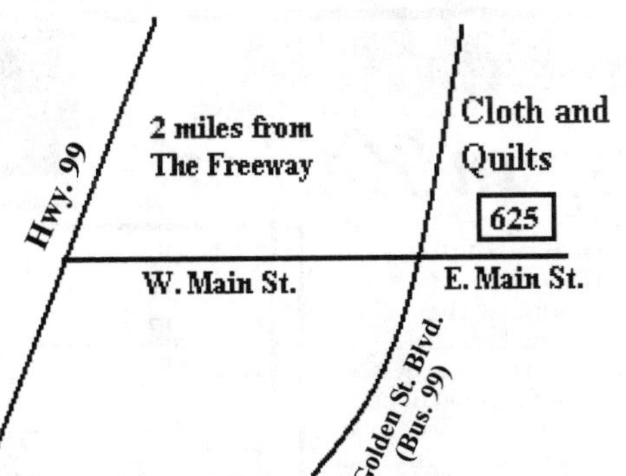

Your One Stop Quilt Shop!

Over 4200 Bolts of Fabrics, Books, Patterns and Notions.

If we don't have it, we will try to get it.

Classes Available

Bishop, CA #61

Mon - Sat 10 - 5:30

Sew It Seams

124 N. Main St. 93514
(760) 873-5635
Owner: Nancy Wood
Est: 1995 2200 sq.ft. 1100 Bolts

Large Selection of Quality Fabric. Books, Patterns and Quilting Supplies. Classes Available. Machine Sales & Service. Friendly & Personal Service.

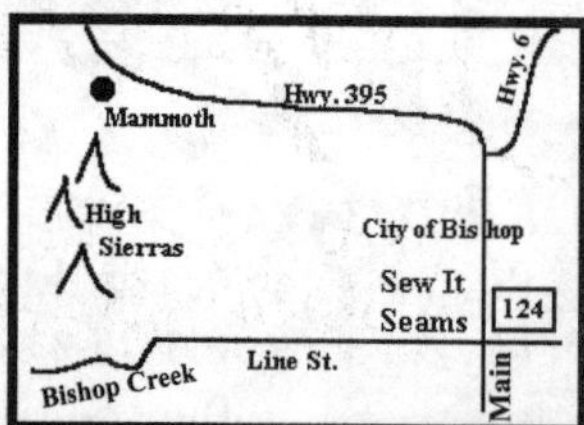

Reedley, CA #63

Mon - Fri 9:30 - 4:30 Sat 10 - 4

Mennonite Quilt Center

1012 "G" St. 93654
(209) 638-3560 2500 sq.ft.
Mgr: Mary Elizondo & Ruth Buxman & Kathleen Heinrichs 450 Bolts

100% Cotton Fabrics, notions, Books, Patterns, & Battings. Quilters on site Monday mornings. Quilt show year around. Tours Avail.

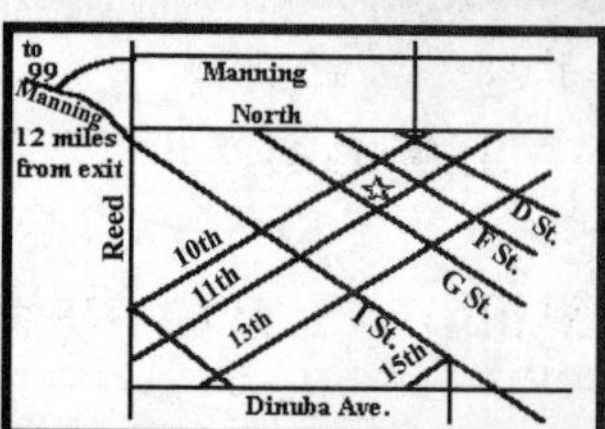

Visalia, CA #64

Mon - Fri 9:30 - 5:30 Thur til 7 Sat 9:30 - 4:30

Thimble Towne

400 W. Caldwell Ave. #F 93277
(559) 627-5778
Est: 2000
thimbletowne@aol.com
Owner: Kathy & Stu Veltkamp

100% cotton fabrics; books and patterns galore; mail order welcome; newsletter; classes Bernina Sewing Machines

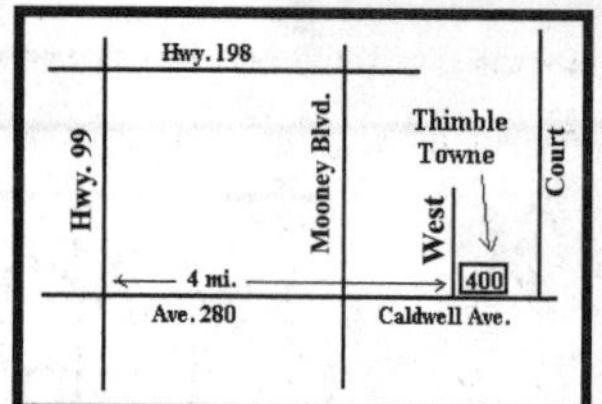

Clovis, CA #62

QUILTERS' PARADISE

339 Pollasky
93612
(559) 297-7817
Fax: 297-0838
qpshop@aol.com
Owners:
Kathy Beechinor
Colette Belt
Barbara Pontius
Est: 1978
5000 sq.ft.

- Helpful, friendly service
- Great selection of newest Fabrics, Books, Patterns & Notions
- Customized Kits & Fabric Paks & Original Patterns
- Reproduction fabrics & hand dyed wools with Projects & Kits
- Block of the Months
- New merchandise arriving daily
- Mail orders & Special orders welcome
- Visa & Mastercard

Just What the Shop Name Says!!

Mon - Fri 10 - 6
Sat 10 - 5
Sun 12 - 4

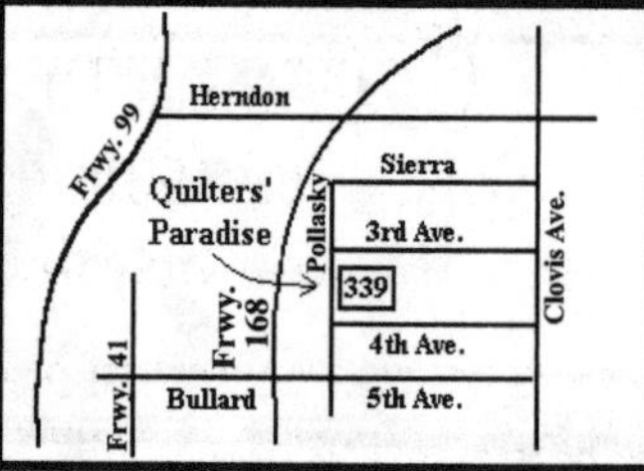

www.quilters-paradise.com

The QUILT STORE

Downtown Exeter * 2500+ Bolts

Fabric * Classes * Supplies * Gifts
On Site Machine Quilting

Exeter, CA #65

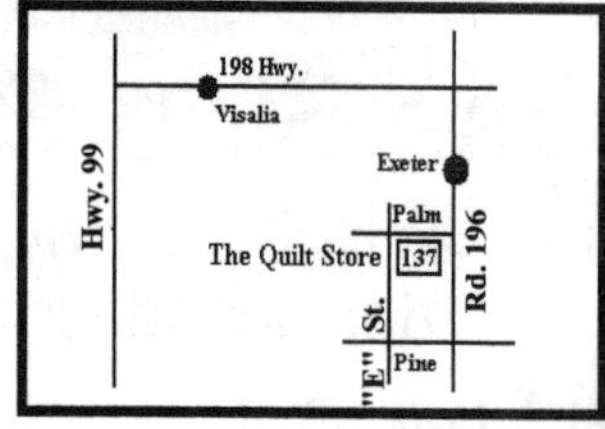

137 North E Street / Exeter, CA 93221 / (559) 594-4450
Monday - Friday 10 - 5 / Thursday 10 - 8 / Saturday 10 - 4

Hollister, CA #66

Mon - Fri 10 - 6 Sat 10 - 4

Creative Friends Craft Supplies

191 San Felipe Rd. #M1 95023
(831) 636-7773 Fax: (831) 636-1965
www.creativefriends.net
Owners: Karen Coatsworth & Mary Lundquist

We carry a large selection of fabrics, notions, books, patterns, and some yarns. We specialize in personal service.

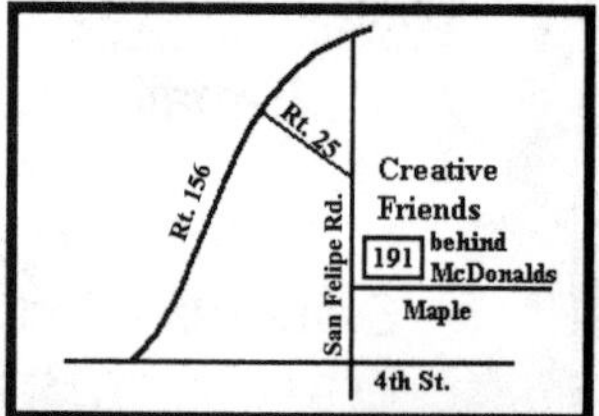

Hollister, CA #67

Tues 10 - 7 Wed - Fri 10 - 5 Sat 10 - 4

Homespun Harbor

1709-L Airline Hwy. 95023
(831) 630-9438
Homespunharbor@aol.com
www.homespunharbor.com
Owners: Ghleanna & Dennis Reeves
Est: 1993 1700 sq.ft. 2800 Bolts
The Aloha spirit moved from Honolulu to Hollister in 2003. Many Batiks, Asian and Tropical prints plus many others.

to San Jose
Hwy. 25
San Felipe St.
McCray
Noah Rd.
Hwy. 101
San Benito St.
Homspun Harbor
1709
Hwy. 156
Union Rd.
Airline Hwy.
to Salinas

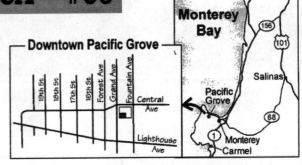

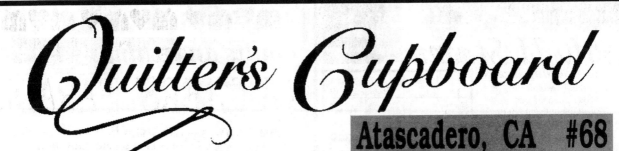

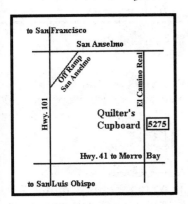

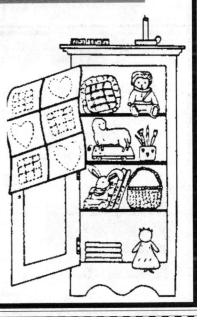

Pacific Grove, CA #70

Mon - Sat 10 - 5:30
Sun 10:30 - 4

The Hand Maden

"For All Your Sewing Needs"

620 Lighthouse Ave. at 17th
(831) 373-5353
thm@redshift.com
Owners: Jeanne & Jim Graham

Extensive fabric selection for quilters & wearable artists. Books, Patterns, Notions, Buttons and Sew Much More. Husqvarna Viking Machines.

The Hand Maden 620 17th 16th Forest Central Ave. to Monterey Lighthouse to Hwys. 68 & 1

Morgan Hill, CA #71

Mon - Fri 10 - 5
Sat 10 - 4

Quilts and Things

16985 Monterey St. #312G 95037
(408) 776-8438 Fax: Same
quiltclass@aol.com

Located between the San Francisco and Monterey Bay Areas, Quilt and Things is a cozy shop filled with must-have fabrics. We have 1,800 bolts of fine quality cotton fabric.

to San Jose Dunne Ave. Quilts and Things Monterey St. Hwy. 101 Tenant Ave.

Capitola, CA #72

1475 41st Ave. #A1, Capitola, CA 95010
(831) 462-3930 Fax: (831) 462-9403
Owner: Sam Ridino Est: 1979
Free Schedule of Classes "Sewing by the Sea"

Mon - Fri 10 - 7
Saturday 10 - 6
Sunday 11 - 5

Hwy. 1 Soquel Dr. Clares St. Capitola Mall 41st Ave. Capitola Rd. 38th Ave. Cabrillo Sewing 1475

Home to over 3,000 bolts of quality quilting fabric, as well as the latest in books, notions, quilting supplies and classes.

Atascadero, CA #73

Sew Fun

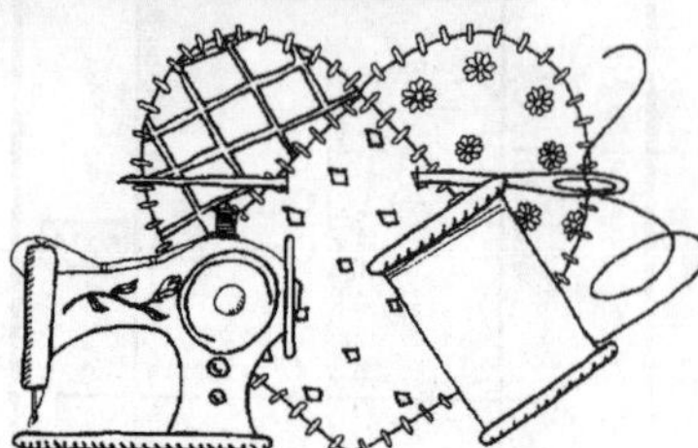

8775 El Camino Real 93422 (805) 462-9739
Owner: Lynn Barksdale Est: 1996 3200 sq.ft.
Lynn@atsewfun.com

Mon - Fri 10 - 6
Sat 10 - 5 Sun 12 - 5

www.atsewfun.com

Complete Quilt Shop.
4000+ bolts of cotton fabrics - Batiks, Brights, Orientals, Flannels and much more. Vast selection of books, notions, gift items, and patterns. Friendly and helpful staff. Janome Sewing Machine Dealer.

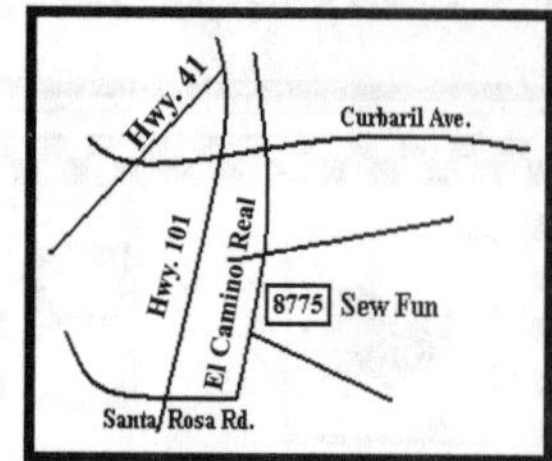

Paso Robles, CA #74

Tues - Sat 10 - 5

The Quiltery

715 24th #V (Upper Level) 93446
(805) 227-4561
Owner: Sherline Lockhart
Est: 1999 800 sq.ft. 900 Bolts

Over 900 bolts: Maywood, Timeless Treasure, etc. $5 yd. Everyday! In house long arm machine quilting - 10 yrs. of experience and always Friendly Service.

The Cotton Ball

Named one of the top 10 Quilt Shops In North America by Better Homes & Gardens Quilt Sampler Magazine

475 Morro Bay Blvd., Morro Bay, CA 93442
www.thecottonball.com 1.800.895.7402
805.772.2646 Fax: 805.772.6357
cottonball@thegrid.net
Owner: Judi Appell Est: 1969 7000 Sq.ft.

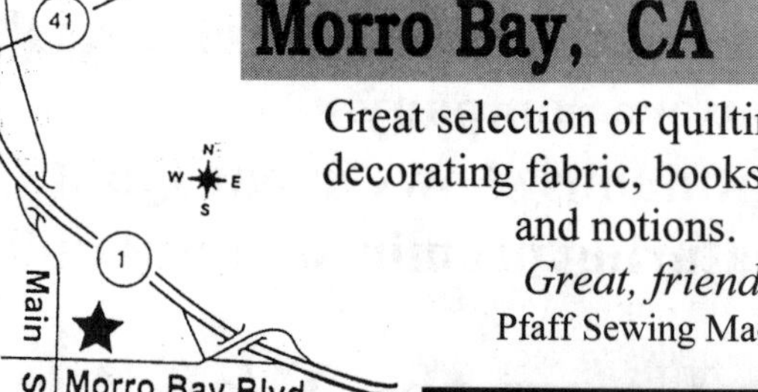

Morro Bay, CA #75

Great selection of quilting fabric, decorating fabric, books, patterns and notions.

Great, friendly service!

Pfaff Sewing Machine Dealer

Mon - Sat 10 - 5 Sun 12 - 4

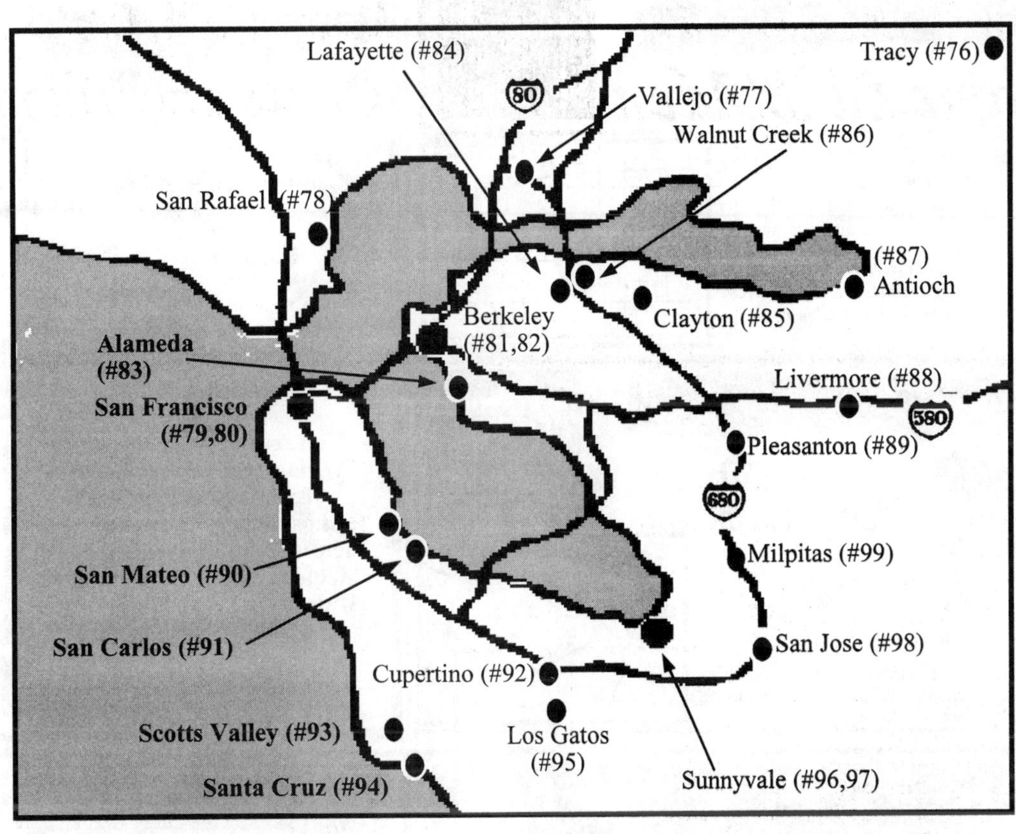

24 Featured Shops **Shops #76 - 99**

"A Fabric Store and Sew Much More . . . . "

Sew Many Quilts

71 E 10th Street, Tracy, CA 95376
(209) 836-5426 Fax: (209) 836-5584
Owner: Colette Lenoir Est: 2001 2000 sq. ft.

Tracy, CA #76

Located in the historic downtown section of Tracy, California; Sew Many Quilts carries over 3000 bolts of 100% cotton fabrics for quilting and other sewing and craft projects. This is a full service quilting store featuring a complete line of notions, decorative buttons, beads and embellishments, books and patterns, quilt-theme jewelry and gifts. The shop specializes in fabrics from other parts of the world. Come and see the "International Room" showcasing Australian, Hawaiian, African, Native American and Asian fabrics as well as African mudcloth and African and Indonesian Batiks. You will find many specialty fabrics like shimmers and pearlescents for art quilting, hand painted Batik panels and Hand-dyes, as well as vintage silk kimono cloth kits and shortcut packages. Stop in and pick up a class schedule. Beginning to advanced quilting classes are offered with guest lectures and quilt trunk shows to keep you up to date on the newest trends.

Tues, Thurs, Fri 10 - 5
Wed & Sat 10 - 7
Mon 11 - 2 Sun 12 - 4

to 580 Bay Area
11th St.
to 5 Stockton Manteca Modesto
Tracy Inn
Sew Many Quilts 71
Central
10th St.

"Your Quilting Link Between the East Bay and the Central Valley"

Vallejo, CA #77

Mon 11 - 8
Thur & Fri 11 - 5:30
Sat 10 - 5
Sun 11 - 5

Seams Like Art

318 Georgia St. 94590
(707) 647-1222
Owner: Sandy Hager Est: 2002
3000 sq.ft. Too many Bolts to Count

Two blocks from San Francisco/Vallejo Ferry in Oldtown Vallejo. 100% Cotton Fabrics, Notions, Books, Patterns, Classes, A Fun Shop!

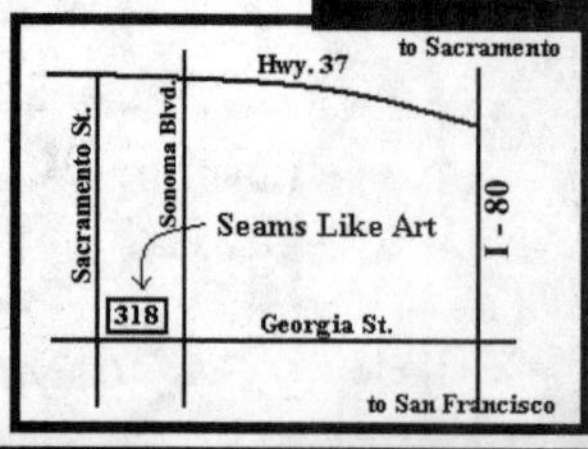

Pumpkin Seed Quilts & Textiles

1414 - 4th St. San Rafael, CA 94901
(415) 453-4758 Fax: (415) 453-4768
Owner: Jennifer Una McCoy
Est: 2001 1800 sq.ft. 2500 Bolts

T, W, F 10 - 6 Th 10 - 9 Sat 10 - 5 Sun 12 - 5

Full service quilt shop with classroom and gallery. Exciting "downtown" atmosphere with friendly and helpful staff. Fabric favorites include: batiks, asian, brights, K. Fassett, reproductions and over 200 solids.

Pumpkin Seed
to Santa Rose
1414
4th St.
"E" St.
"D" St.
Hwy. 101
to San Francisco

San Rafael, CA #78

San Francisco, CA #79

Black Cat QUILTS

2608 Ocean Ave. 94132
(415) 337-1355 Fax: (415) 337-1383
www.blackcatquilts.com
Owner: Gretchen G. Nelson
Est: 1996 1500 sq.ft.

The only store in San Francisco devoted exclusively to meeting your quiltmaking needs. Featuring fabrics, books, patterns, notions & classes.

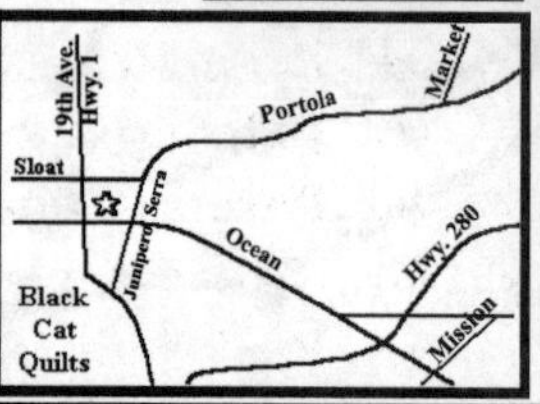

San Francisco, CA #80

Mon - Fri 10 - 6
Sat 10 - 5:30
Sun 12 - 5

Mendels Far~Out Fabrics

1556 Haight St. 94117
(415) 621-1287 sales@mendels.com
www.mendels.com
Owner: Bette Mosias 3900 sq.ft.

Lots of wonderful cotton fabrics, unusual ethnic - large selection textile dyes, paints, great buttons, trims and an art supply store.

Clayton St.
Mendels Far-Out Fabrics
Ashbury St.
1556
Haight St.

Berkeley, CA #81

Mon - Fri 10 - 6:30
Sat 10 - 6
Sun 11 - 5:30

Stonemountain & Daughter Fabrics

2518 Shattuck Ave. 94704
(866) 4SEW-FUN (510) 845-6106
www.stonemountainfabric.com
Owners: Suzan & Bob Steinberg Est: 1981
6000 sq.ft. Thousands of Bolts

Huge Selection of Quality, Unique Cottons at affordable prices! Ethnic, Quilting & Basic Cottons. Wools, Silks, Rayons, & Linens also Available.

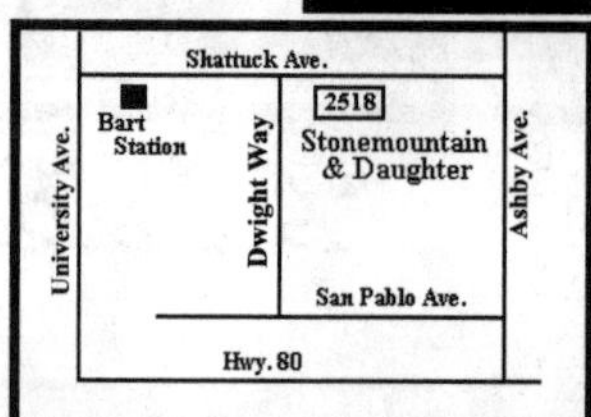

Berkeley, CA #82

Mon - Sat 10 - 6
Sun 12 - 4

New Pieces

1597 & 1605 Solano Ave. 94707
(510) 527-6779 Fax: (510) 527-9344
sharona@newpieces.com
www.newpieces.com
Est: 1984 2800 sq.ft. 3000 Bolts

Contemporary Art Quilt & Doll Shop and Gallery. Commission quilts, quilt service, long arm quilting, & workshops.

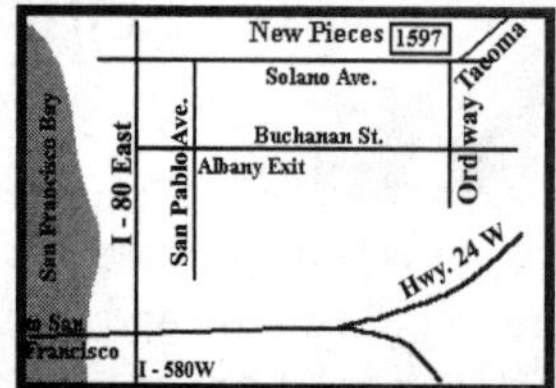

Alameda, CA #83

Tues - Sat 10 - 6
Thur til 9
Sun 12 - 5

Quilt Fans

1716 Lincoln Ave. 94501
(510) 749-6717
Owner: Cathy Rodriguez

Fan-tastic quilt fabric and supplies for quilt fan-ciers. 100% cottons, batiks, wool felt, patterns, books and notions. Classes too!

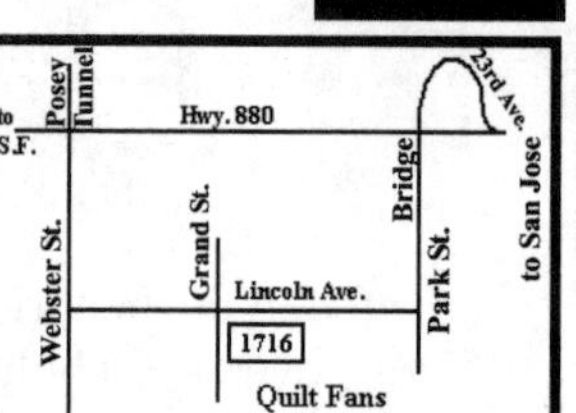

Lafayette, CA #84

Mon - Sat 9:30 - 5:30
Thur til 9
Sun 12 - 5

The Cotton Patch

1025 Brown Avenue 94549
(925) 284-1177 Est: 1978
www.quiltusa.com
and www.quiltusa.yahoo.com
Proprietor: Carolie Hensley

Cotton prints, solids, batiks, oriental fabrics. 800 book titles, gifts, notions, etc. Bernina Dealer.

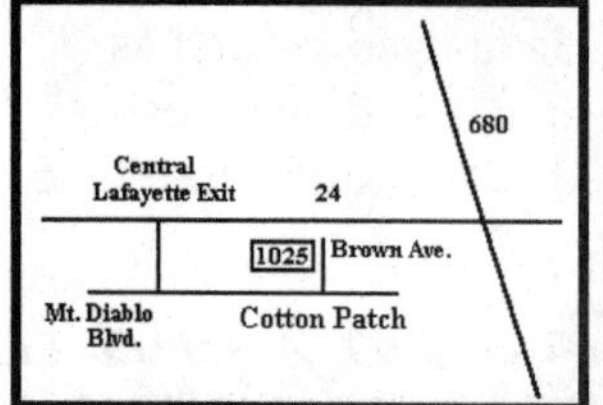

Clayton, CA #85

Tues - Sat 10 - 6

Cottontales

6200 Center St. Suite J 94517
(925) 673-0742 Fax: (925) 673-0749
donna@cottontales.com
www.cottontales.com
Est: 2000 1150 sq.ft. 2000 bolts

Fine Cotton Fabrics, Quilting Notions, Patterns, Books and Gift Items. In Historic Old Clayton, with Wooden Sidewalks and Fine Restaurants.

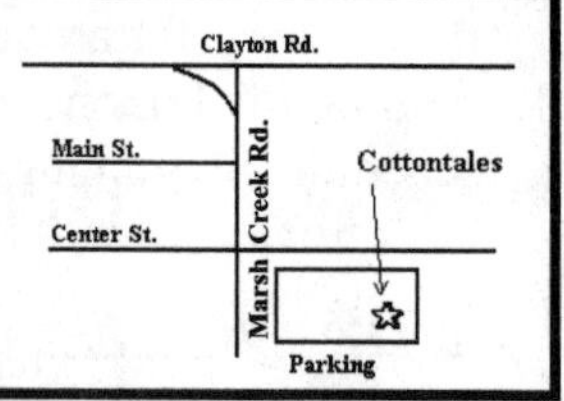

Walnut Creek, CA #86

Thimble Creek

1536 Newell Ave.
94596
(925) 946-9970
Owners:
Roxie & Joe Wood
Est: 1994 6000 sq.ft.
6000 Bolts

Wonderful quilts on display in a spacious, friendly atmosphere. Great selection of books, patterns, notions, fabric & classes !

Mon - Fri
9:30 - 5:30
Tues & Thur
til 8
Sat 9:30 - 5
Sun 12 - 4

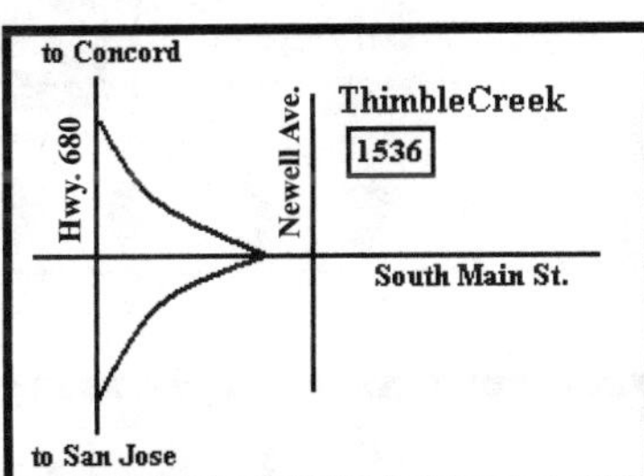

www.thimblecreek.com

The Quilting Queens

720 West 2nd Street 94509
(925) 9-QUILTS (978-4587)
E-Mail: TheQuilting
Queens@prodigy.net
Fax: (925) 756-2445
Owners: Bernie & Alexandra
Est: 2001 1550 sq.ft. 4000 bolts

We Are A Full Service Quilting Store.

- Friendly, knowledgeable & helpful staff
- Fabric galore & more arriving daily
- Patterns, books, notions & supplies
- Classes for all levels
- Professional custom machine quilting
- Visa & Master Card welcome

Antioch, CA #87

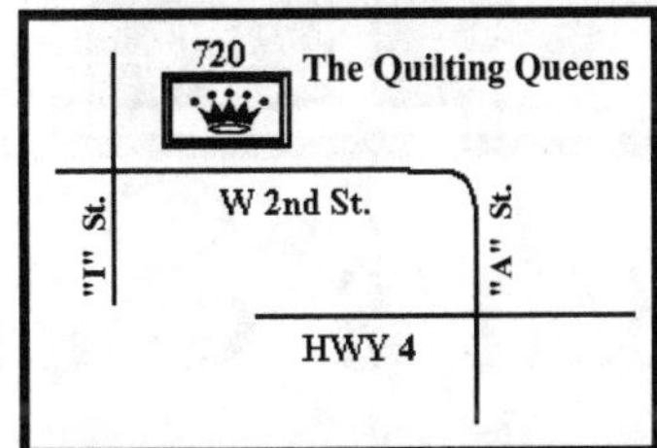

Mon - Sat
10 - 5:30

2033 Railroad Ave.
Livermore, CA 94551
(925) 371-7064

Hwy. 580 / Railroad Ave. / 2033 In Between Stitches / L St. / Livermore Ave. / First St.

IN BETWEEN STITCHES
QUILT & GIFT STORE

Mon - Fri
10 - 5:30
Sat 10 - 5
Sun 10 - 3

Fax:
(925) 371-7065
Est: 2002

A place where friendships grow

www.inbetweenstitches.com

Livermore, CA #88

The Village Quilt Shop

Mon - Fri
10 - 6
Sat 10 - 5
Sun 12 - 4

Welcome to our Quilt Shop.

We offer a large selection of 100% cotton Fabrics, notions, books, patterns and classes, beginning to advanced.

1989 "F" Santa Rita Rd., 94566
(925) 462-9340
Fax: (925) 462-4135
Owner: Tammy MacLean
Est: 1981 2400 sq.ft. 2000+ Bolts
thevillagequiltshop@att.net
www.TheVillageQuiltShop.net

Village Quilt Shop
Pleasanton

Pleasanton, CA #89

San Mateo, CA #90

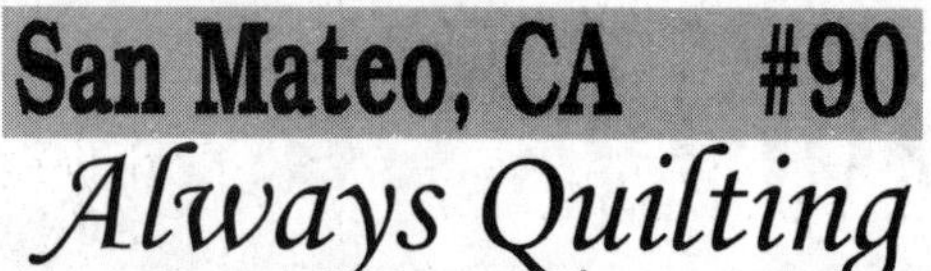

Mon - Fri 10 - 4
Sun 1 - 4
Sat by Appt.

1660 S. Amphlett Blvd., Suite 112 94402
(650) 458-8580 Fax: (650) 349-3248
info@alwaysquilting online.com
www.alwaysquiltingonline.com
Owners: Kit Morse & Julie McAuliffe
Est: 2003 2300 sq.ft. 2000+ bolts

Visit our friendly shop located in the Bayshore Corporate Center.

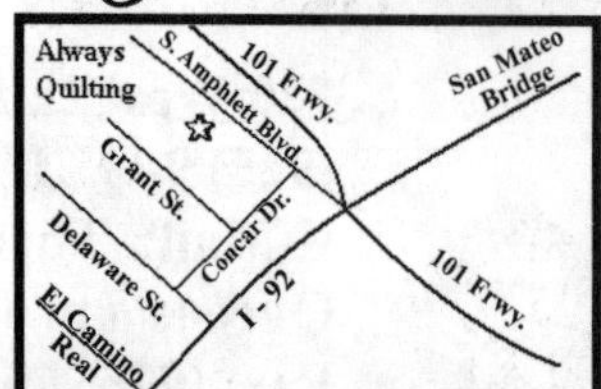

San Carlos, CA #91

The Laurel Leaf

Mon - Sat
10 - 5

648 Laurel Street 94070
(650) 591-6790
Owner: Julie Murphy
Est: 1983 2200 sq.ft.

100% Cotton Fabric, Books, Patterns, Quilting Supplies, Classes.
10 Min. South of San Francisco Airport

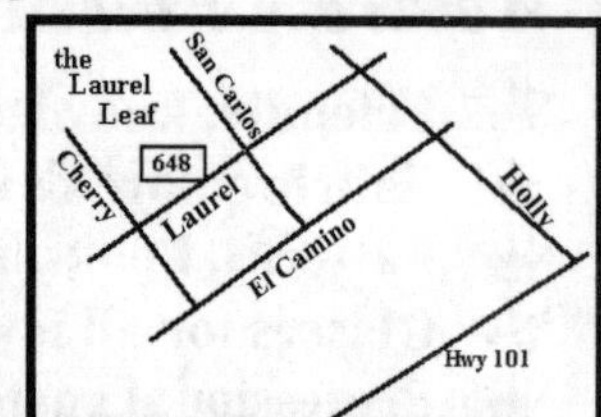

Whiffle Tree Quilts

10261 S. DeAnza Blvd. 95014
(408) 255-5270
www.whiffletreequilts.com
Owner: Louise Horkey
Est: 1982 1280 sq.ft.

Mon - Fri 9:30 - 6
Thur til 8
Sat 9:30 - 5
2nd Sun 12 - 4

Cupertino, CA #92

A terrific store full of fabric, patterns, & notions & books. The user-Friendly quilt shop in the heart of Silicon Valley!

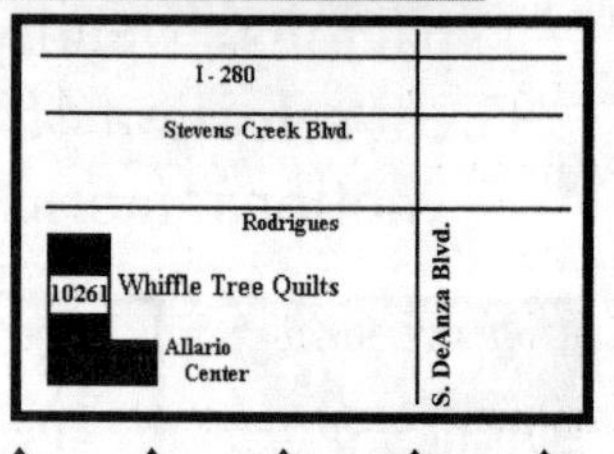

Judy's Sewing Center

222 G Mt. Hermon Rd. 95066
(831) 440-1050 Fax: (831) 440-1709
JHSewing@aol.com
Owner: Judy Hollaway Est: 1997 2500 sq.ft.

Scotts Valley, CA #93

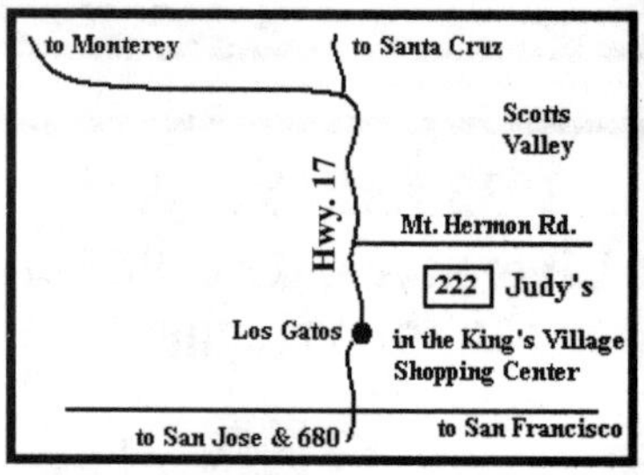

Mon - Sat
10 - 6
Sun 12 - 5

to Monterey
to Santa Cruz
Scotts Valley
Hwy. 17
Mt. Hermon Rd.
222 Judy's
Los Gatos
in the King's Village Shopping Center
to San Jose & 680
to San Francisco

Judy's Sewing Center has something for everyone. Visit our quilt shop which offers over 3,500 bolts of the finest quality cotton fabrics, Books, Patterns, Notions, & Lots of Classes. Call ahead to see if there is a class for you. We also offer group classes.

Judy's Husqvarna Viking Store carries a complete line of Husqvarna Viking Sewing Machines and Sergers, Koala Cabinets, Horn Cabinets & multiformat Embroidery designs & monograms.

Judy's Home Décor offers a wonderful selection of Fabrics, Lamps, Pictures, Pillows and Kitchen linens...

www.judyssewingcenter.com

ALL THE FABRIC YOU NEVER KNEW YOU NEEDED

Imagination Meets Inspiration!

A new, exciting shop featuring a diverse palette of ethnic, eclectic, and worldly fabrics appealing to the quilter! Color, pattern, and textures of unusual variety including standards you know and love. First class service, advice, and community. Come for the day and enjoy the local color of the Pleasure Point area of Santa Cruz; we're four blocks from the Pacific Ocean! Sample our local coffeehouse and eateries as well as the shopping convenience of the Capitola Mall on 41st Avenue.

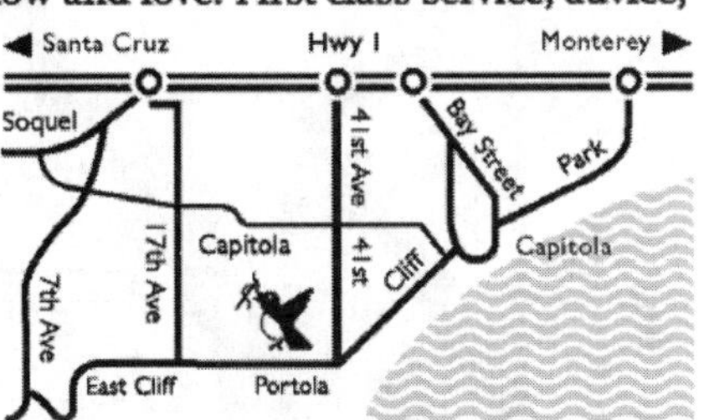

ROUND ROBIN FABRICS

3703 Portola Drive
Santa Cruz, CA 95062
Monday - Saturday
10 AM - 5 PM
831.476.8722

#94

Visit us on the web!
www.roundrobinfabrics.com

Los Gatos, CA #95

Mon 10 - 4
Tues - Fri 10 - 6
Sat & Sun
11 - 5

Natural Expressions of Los Gatos

326 N. Santa Cruz Ave. 95030
(408) 354-5330 Fax: (408) 354-5750
www.naturalexpressionsofLosGatos.com
Est: 2003 1500 sq.ft. 2300 Bolts

The source for all of your quilting and beading needs. Huge selection of fabric and beads.

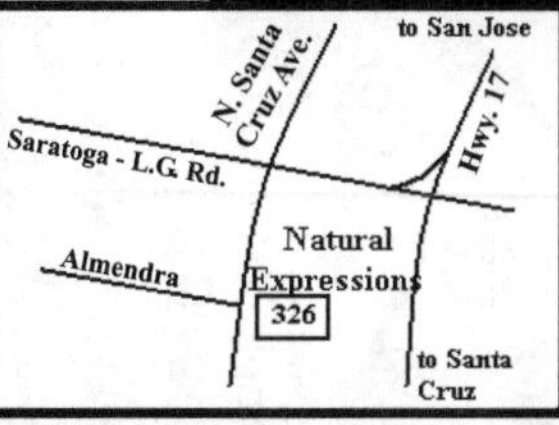

1326 S. Mary Ave., Sunnyvale, CA 94087
♥(408) 735-9830♥www.thegranaryquilts.com

Sunnyvale, CA #96

Your Friendly Neighborhood Quilt Shop!

- ♥ 100% Cotton Fabrics
- ♥ Quilting Supplies
- ♥ Books & Patterns
- ♥ Gifts for Quilters
- ♥ Notions
- ♥ Classes

Owner: Paula Ivers

Shop Hours:
Mon, Wed-Sat 10am - 6pm
Tues 10am - 8pm
Last Sunday 10am - 4pm
Of the Month

Easy Freeway Access!

Sunnyvale, CA #97

Mon - Fri
10 - 6
Sat 10 - 5

Carolea's Knitche

586 South Murphy Ave. 94086
(408) 736-2800
Owner: Carolea Peterson
Est: 1973 1400 sq.ft.

The very latest in Hoffman, Alex Henry, Jinny Beyer, Kaufman, Tony Wentzel, Gutcheon . . . Mail orders welcome.

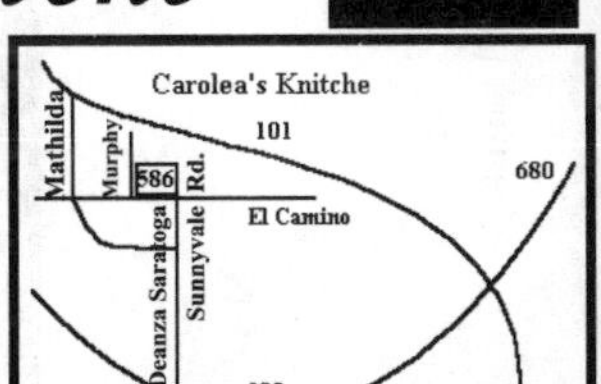

San Jose, CA #98

Tues - Sun 10 - 5
Thur til 8

San Jose Museum of Quilts & Textiles

110 Paseo de San Antonio 95112
(408) 971-0323 Fax: (408) 971-7226
www.sjquiltmuseum.org
Est: 1977
Non-profit Public Benefit Museum

Regularly changing exhibits of Quilts and Textiles. Museum Store has extensive assortment of books on quilting.

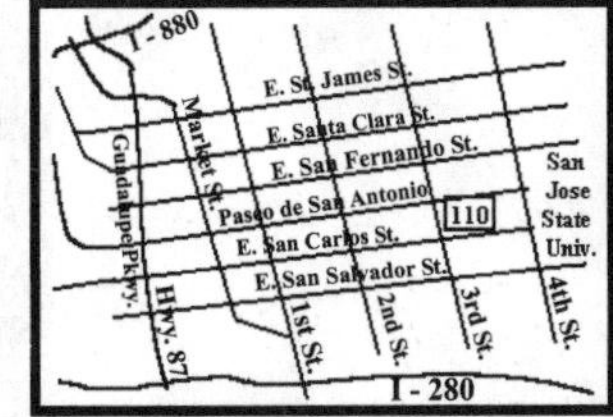

Milpitas, CA #99

Mon - Fri
10 - 7
Thur til 9
Sat 10 - 5
Sun 11 - 5

Fabrics 'n' Fun

10 S. Abbott Ave., Suite A 95035
(408) 946-3860 Fax: (408) 946-3844
lillian@fabricsnfun.com
www.fabricsnfun.com
Owner: Lillian Sienknecht 3300 sq.ft.
Colorful fabrics, wonderful books, patterns, notions, samples, great classes, knowledgeable helpful staff. A fun place to visit. Everything for the quilter's resources. PFAFF & Brother sewing machines

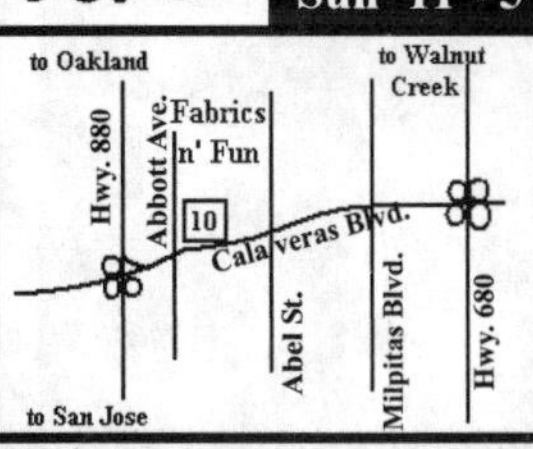

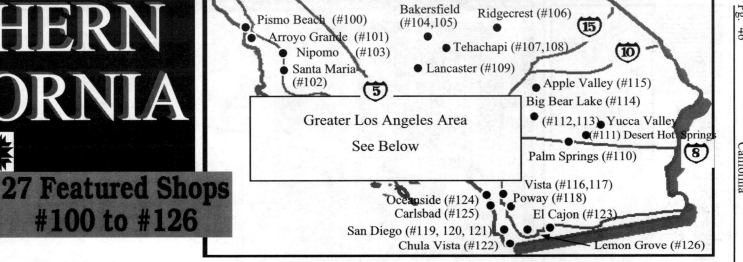

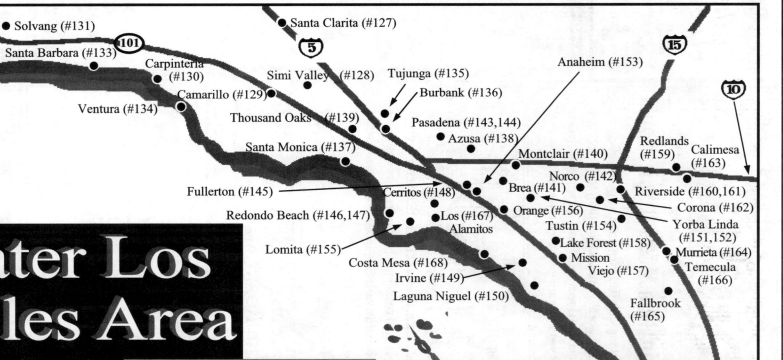

Pismo Beach (#100)
Arroyo Grande (#101)
Nipomo (#103)
Santa Maria (#102)
Bakersfield (#104,105)
Ridgecrest (#106)
Tehachapi (#107,108)
Lancaster (#109)
Apple Valley (#115)
Big Bear Lake (#114)
(#112,113) Yucca Valley
(#111) Desert Hot Springs
Palm Springs (#110)
Greater Los Angeles Area
See Below
Vista (#116,117)
Poway (#118)
Oceanside (#124)
Carlsbad (#125)
El Cajon (#123)
San Diego (#119, 120, 121)
Chula Vista (#122)
Lemon Grove (#126)
15
10
5
8

Greater Los Angeles Area

41Featured Shops #127 to #168

Buellton (#132)
Solvang (#131)
Santa Clarita (#127)
Santa Barbara (#133)
Carpinteria (#130)
Simi Valley (#128)
Tujunga (#135)
Burbank (#136)
Anaheim (#153)
Camarillo (#129)
Ventura (#134)
Thousand Oaks (#139)
Pasadena (#143,144)
Azusa (#138)
Redlands (#159)
Calimesa (#163)
Santa Monica (#137)
Montclair (#140)
Norco (#142)
Fullerton (#145)
Cerritos (#148)
Brea (#141)
Riverside (#160,161)
Corona (#162)
Redondo Beach (#146,147)
Los Alamitos (#167)
Orange (#156)
Yorba Linda (#151,152)
Tustin (#154)
Lomita (#155)
Lake Forest (#158)
Murrieta (#164)
Mission Viejo (#157)
Temecula (#166)
Costa Mesa (#168)
Irvine (#149)
Laguna Niguel (#150)
Fallbrook (#165)
101
5
15
10

Quiltin' Cousins

330 Pomeroy 93449
(805) 773-4988
Owners: Shawn Lombardo & Gerri Kautz

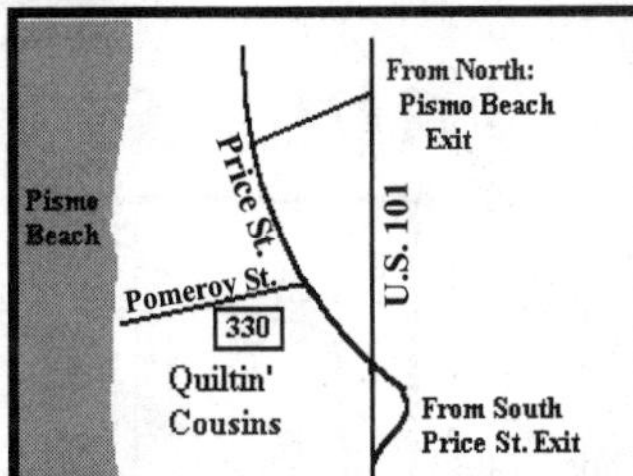

Tues - Fri 10 - 5
Sat 10 - 4

The "cousins" will greet you with their knowledge and friendly inspiration. Fabric, books, notions, patterns, gifts and classes.

Pismo Beach, CA #100

Creative Patches House

Patricia Hughes

Est: 1997

(805) 929-3704
136 A North Thompson Rd.
Nipomo, CA 93444
Fax: (805) 929-3857
patti@creativepatches.com
www.creativepatches.com

Mon - Sat 10 - 5

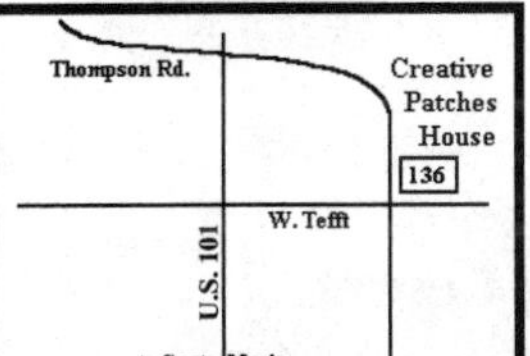

....A Unique Quilt Shop....
....Fantastic Class Room....
Largest Selection of Books & Notions on the Central Coast
Over 2000 Bolts of 100% Cotton Fabrics
Bernina & Janome Sales & Service

Nipomo, CA #103

Also Visit "Janeels Ribbon Works" Jan Lee (Owner) featuring Brazilian & Silk Embroidery

Arroyo Grande, CA #101

Mon - Sat 10 - 5
Sun 12 - 4

The Quilt Attic

106 Bridge St. 93420
(805) 474-0717
TheQuiltAttic@aol.com
Website: www.quiltspot.com
Est: 1998 2000 sq.ft.

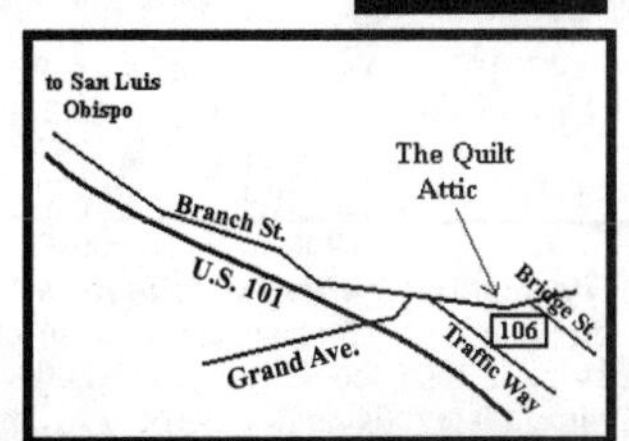

Cotton fabrics, books, patterns, notions, gifts and classes for quilters. We have Computer Software to design your quilts.

Santa Maria, CA #102

Sophie Ann's Quilts

Mon - Fri 10 - 5
Sat 10 - 4

1765 - B South Broadway 93454
(805) 925-1888
Owner: Helga Trampush
Est: 1986 950 sq.ft.

Stowell
Broadway
Newlove
101 Freeway
1765
Sophie Ann's Quilts
Betteravia

Finest in contemporary and traditional fabrics. Bolts of 100% Cotton Fabric, books, notions, classes and always friendly Service !

Bakersfield, CA #104

STRAWBERRY PATCHES

6439 Ming Ave. #C,
Bakersfield, CA 93309
(661) 835-1738 Fax: (661) 835-0406
Owner: Suzanne Zingg Est:1985 2500 sq.ft.

www.strawberry-patches.com

Voted one of America's Top Ten quilt shops by American Patchwork & Quilting Magazine. Selection, Service, Smiles.

Authorized BERNINA Dealer

Mon - Fri 10 - 5:30
Sat 10 - 5

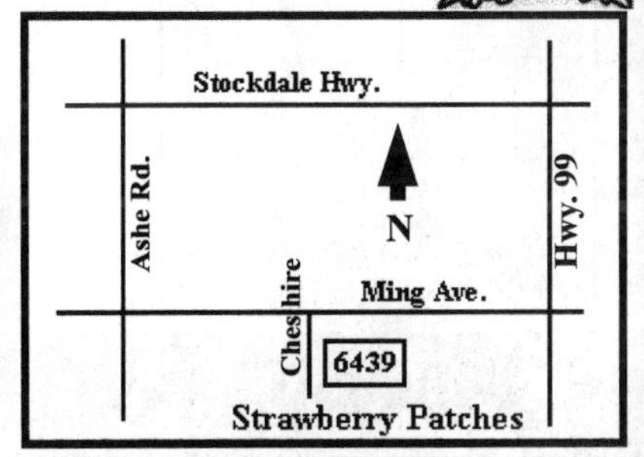

Bakersfield, CA #105

Mon - Sat 9 - 6

To Quilt 'n Sew

2701 Calloway Dr., Suite 414 93312
(661) 589-8863 Fax: (661) 587-3974
2quilt@etcrier.net
Owner: Robin Laiblin
Est: 2000 1900 sq.ft. 2000+ Bolts

"The happiest quilting store in Kern County"

Complete quilt store specializing in customer service. 200+ book titles and 200+ distinct Quilting stencils and patterns. Classes for beginners to advanced.

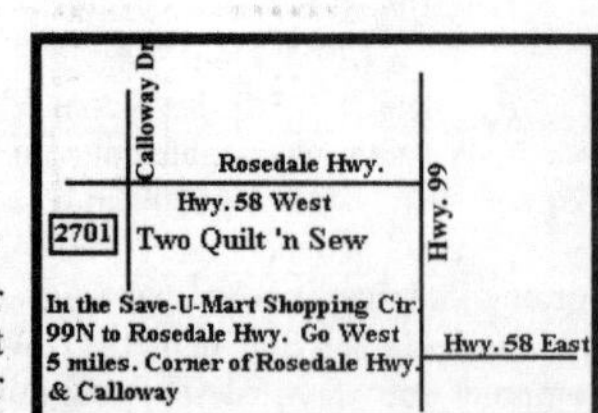

Ridgecrest, CA #106

Mon - Sat 10 - 3
Mon & Tues 7 - 9 pm

Quilted Heart & Home

425 E. Ridgecrest Blvd. 93555
(760) 371-1116
quiltedheart@ridgenet.net
Owners: Cindy and Jerry
Est: 1995 1600 sq.ft. 2500+ bolts

A cute, friendly store stuffed to the brim with fabrics, notions and patterns.

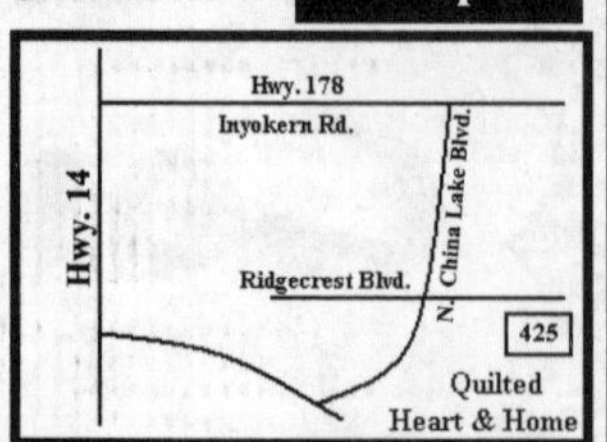

Tehachapi, CA #107

Tues - Fri 9:30 - 3:30
Sat 10 - 3

* 5 Heart Quilts & Fabric *

Est: 1993
1900 sq.ft.
1600 Bolts

104 W. Tehachapi Blvd.
(661) 822-8709 93561
Owner: Claudia Blodget - Lye

A Quilters Heaven with all of the Colors - 100% Cotton, Hoffman, Alex. Henry, Northcott, Benartex, Books, Notions and Classes - For Your Needs.

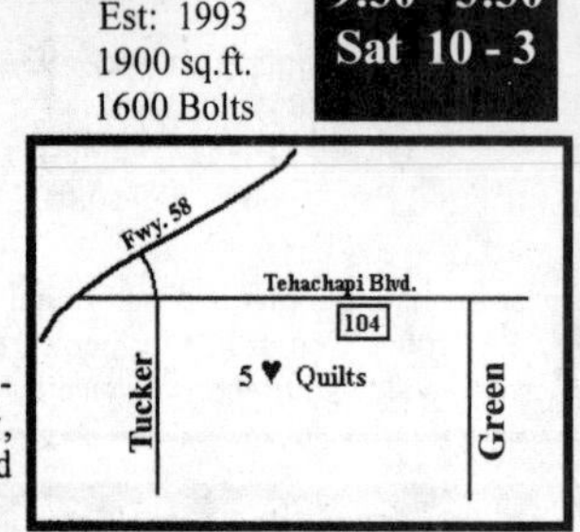

Tehachapi, CA #108

Mon 12 - 5
Tues - Fri 9 - 5
Sat 10 - 4

Debbie's Fabrics

208 S. Mill St. 93561
(661) 823-7114
Owner: Debbie Szydlowski
Est: 2000 1200 sq.ft.
1100+ Bolts

Great prices on quilt shop quality fabrics from RJR, Moda, SSI, P&B, Benartex, etc. Old fashioned, friendly staff.

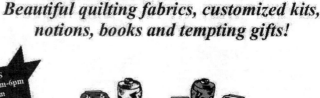

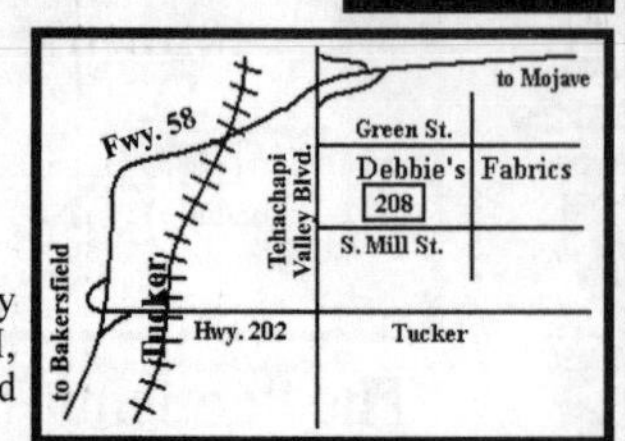

Bolts in the Bathtub

The Antelope Valley's favorite quilt and gift shoppe.
You'll find classes for all skill levels.
Beautiful quilting fabrics, customized kits, notions, books and tempting gifts!

BERNINA Authorized Dealer

Your Sewing Room away from Home

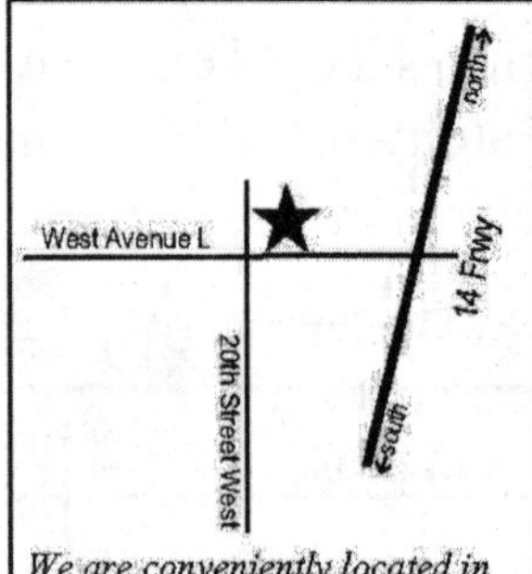

We are conveniently located in Lancaster, California. Exit Avenue L off of the 14 Freeway, head west. Go ½ mile to the Ralph's Shopping Center on right.

STORE HOURS
Tues.-Thurs.-Fri. 10am-6pm
Wed. 10am-8pm
Sat. 10am-5pm
Sun. 12pm-5pm

A BERNINA Sewing & Quilting Center
A Quilt and Gift Shoppe
1945 West Avenue L, Lancaster, California 93534
Tel (661) 945-5541

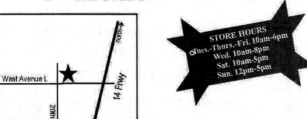

Lancaster, CA #109

Sign up to receive our newsletter Notes from the Bathtub at www.boltsinthebathtub.com or email: info@boltsinthebathtub.com

#110

Creative Expressions of Palm Springs

1111 South Palm Canyon Drive
Palm Springs, CA 92264
Tel: 760-327-2587
Fax: 760-322-2319
www.creativeexpressionsps.com
vmgonzales@AOL.com

All your Quilting needs:

Bali Batiks ▪ Novelties ▪ Solids ▪ Prints ▪ Reproductions

Notions — Patterns — Books — Threads — Embellishments

3,000+ bolts of high-quality, 100% cotton fabrics

All your Beading needs:

Exquisite ▪ Exotic ▪ Ethnic ▪ Contemporary

Beads from around the world — Seed Beads — Semi-Precious Stones — African Trade Beads — Crystals — Sterling Silver — Books — and much more

Fast, Friendly, Professional Service provided by our excellent staff.

Mon - Sat 9 - 5, Sun 12 - 5 Sept - June

Classes available in quiltmaking, beaded jewelry, wearable art, and more. Call for a free class schedule.

We are about 11.7 miles from I-10 when taking Palm Springs/ Hwy. 111 exit.

We are about 8.5 miles from I-10 when taking the Ramon exit.

Hwy. 111 becomes Palm Canyon Dr. after you enter the City of Palm Springs.

We share a building with Club Liquors. Parking is in the rear.

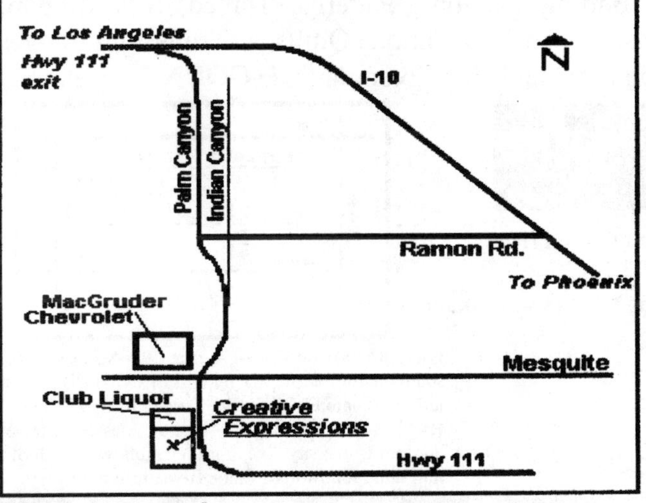

Map not to scale

Desert Hot Springs, CA #111

Mon - Sat 9:30 - 5 Sun 12 - 5

Fabric Fools

14080 Palm Dr., Suite B 92240
(760) 251-7560 Fax: (760) 251-7561
calibonn@aol.com
Owner: Bonnie Scott, Foolish Proprietor
Est: 2003 3000 sq.ft.

A new sale each month.
Only the best quality of over 2000 bolts.
Spacious & bright. A real treat!

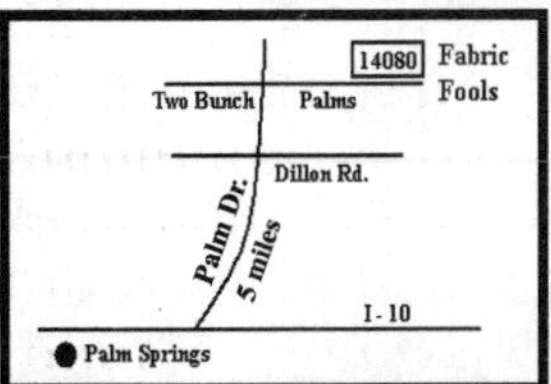

Yucca Valley, CA #112

Mon - Sat 9 - 4

Stitchin & Quiltin

57353-A 29 Palms Hwy. 92284
(760) 365-1744
Owner: Loreli Hagedorn

Quilting Supplies.
Free Classes with purchase of Materials.
Sewing Machine Repairs

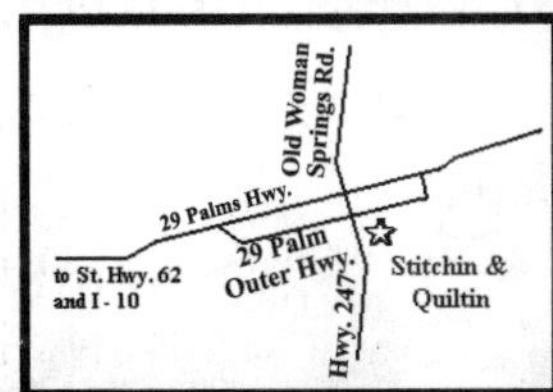

Yucca Valley, CA #113

Donna's Country Store

55879 29 Palms Hwy. 92284
(760) 365-0577
Fax: (760) 369-2237
Owner: Donna Wightman
Est: 1992

Mon - Sat 10 - 5:30 Sun 10 - 4

2800 bolts of quilting Fabric, Books, Notions and classes. For your gift needs we carry Boyd Bears, and Candles.

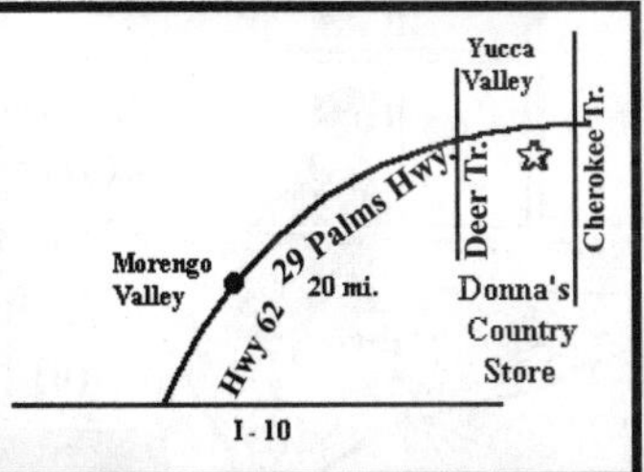

Big Bear Lake, CA #114

Mon - Sat 11 - 5 Closed Wed Summer Sundays 11 - 3

The Patchwork Peddler

582 Paine Rd. 92315
(909) 878-4629
Fax: (909) 878-4729
candace@bbv.net
Owner: Candace Wright - Wilkerson

A Shop for Quilters
Fine Fabrics — Notions — Patterns
Classes — Specializing in Beginning Quilting

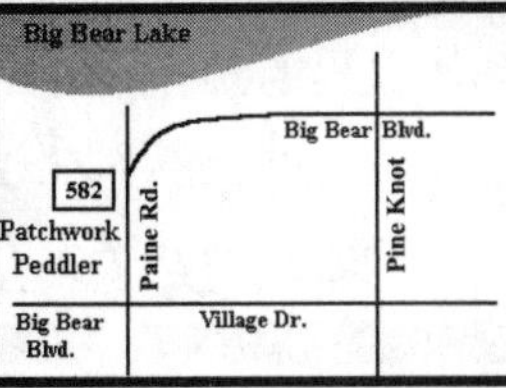

Apple Valley, CA #115

Mon - Sat 10 - 5

Cozy Quilt'n

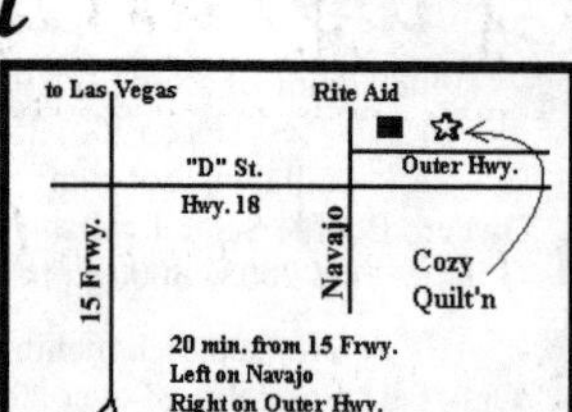

21810 Hwy. 18 #9 92307
(760) 240-7778 Fax: (760) 240-7738
Owner: Sue Tumbleson
Est: 2002 1100 sq.ft. 1200+ bolts

Anniversary "Quilt's on Parade" - an Outdoor Display of Quilts made in our Classes - is held in Late May, call for dates.

Vista, CA #116

Mon - Fri 10 - 5:30 Sat 10 - 4

Fat Quarters Quilt Shop

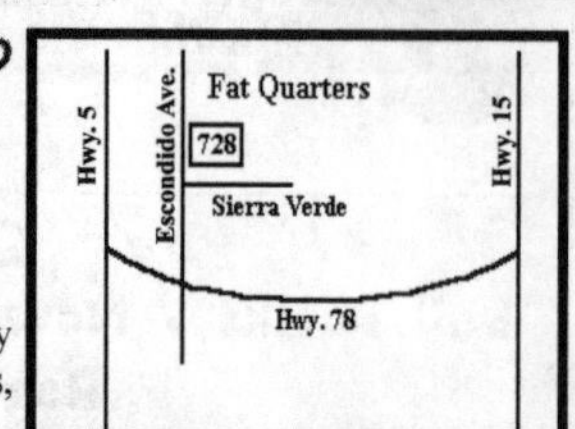

728 Escondido Ave. 92084
(760) 758-8308
www.fatquartersquiltshop.com
Owners: Kelly & Mary Sullivan

Charming house filled with primitive country quilts. Lots of fabrics, quilting supplies, gifts, antiques & friendly people.

Vista, CA #117

Mon - Sat 10 - 5

Sew Special Fabrics

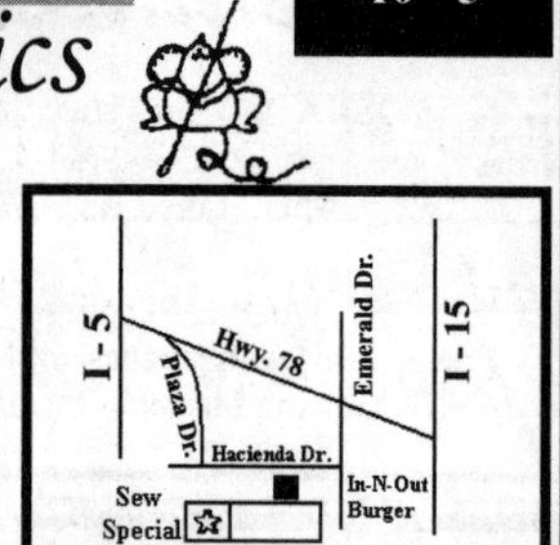

2020 Hacienda Dr., Suite P 92081
(760) 940-0363 Fax: (760) 431-6846
Orders: (888) 940-0663
sewspecial@adelphia.net
www.sewspecialfabrics.com
Owner: Wendy Mathews
Est: 1982
1800 sq.ft. 2000+ Bolts

Heirloom Sewing and Quilting
Fine fabrics & laces. Classes.

Poway, CA #118

Mon, Fri Sat 10 - 5 Tues, Wed Thur 10 - 7

Amidon Quiltworks

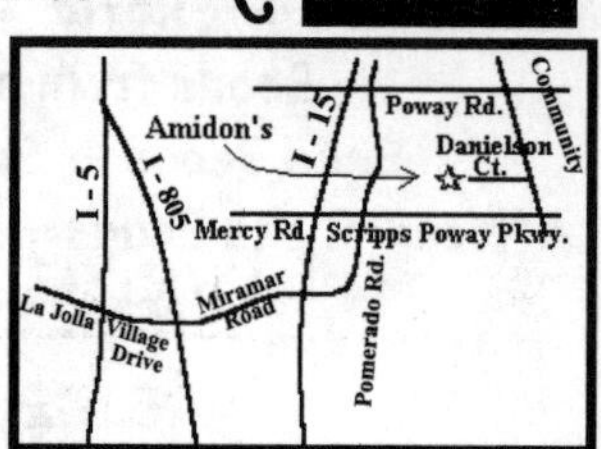

12625 Danielson Ct. #111
92064
(858) 486-0696
Fax: (858) 486-1618
www.amidonquiltworks.com
Owner: Nancy Amidon
Est: 1994 3800 sq.ft. 5000 Bolts

A full service quilt shop carrying fabrics, books, patterns, notions and gifts.
Mail Order Available.

San Diego, CA #119

Rosie's Calico Cupboard

7151 El Cajon Blvd. Suite 'F' 92115 (619) 697-5758
Fax: (619) 465-8298 E-Mail: rozgonzalez@cox.net
Web Site: www.rosiescalicocupboard.com

Offering over 4900 sq.ft. (stocked to the brim) with over **18,000** bolts of **First Quality** 100% Cotton Prints, plus Books, Batting, Notions, Patterns, Thread, Silk Ribbon, Quilting & Crafting related gift items, New & Old Antique Quilts, a 'Trunk Full of over 500 lbs of Buttons', plus much, much more and all at Everyday **DISCOUNT** prices.

Monday - Friday 9 - 5 Wednesday til 8
Saturday 8 - 5 Sunday 11 - 5

- Well stocked sale rack with values from 25 to 75% off suggested Retail Prices.
- New stock arriving daily.
- 1100 sq.ft. Classroom with a full calendar or Quilting & Crafting Classes year round.
- Mail Orders and Special Orders Welcome
- Visa, MC, Discover, American Express, ATM Cards Accepted

A Full Service Quilt Shop
Catering to Quilters and Crafters Since 1983

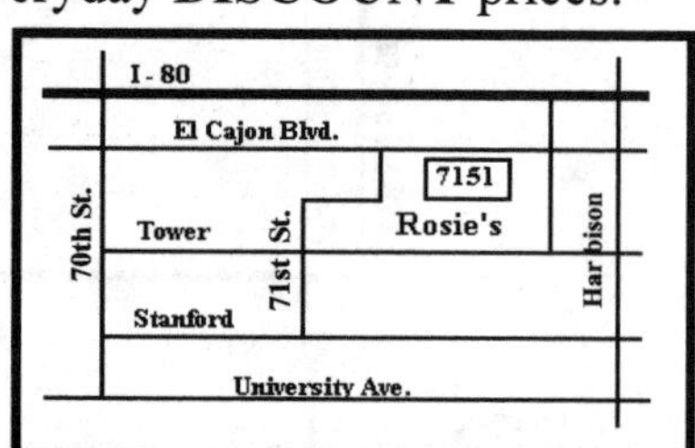

Hwy. 8 (East or West) — take 70th St. exit, travel south on 70th St. for 1/2 mile to El Cajon Blvd., turn left (east) onto El Cajon Blvd., travel for 1 1/2 blocks.
Hwy. 94 (East or West) — take the Mass. exit, travel north to University Ave., turn left, follow to 70th St., turn right, follow to El Cajon Blvd., turn right.

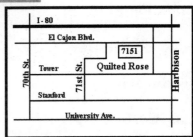

San Diego, CA #121

Hand-loomed Cottons from Guatemala & India, African Prints, Batiks, Ethnic Braids, Cuna Indian Molas, Unique Assortment of Printed Cottons.

Mon - Fri 10 - 6
Closed Sat Sun 11 - 3

6364 El Cajon Blvd.
92115
(619) 286-4364
Est: 1974
1200 sq.ft. 5000 Bolts

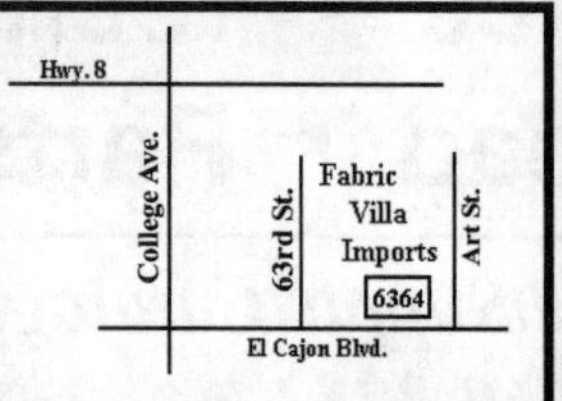

BERNINA • BERNINA • BERNINA • BERNINA • BERNINA

Chula Vista, CA #122

Quilters' Choice

"Authorized Bernina Dealer"
417 Third Avenue 91910
(619) 425-2545
E-Mail: Quilterschoice@hotmail.com
www.QuiltersChoice.com
Owner: Kathy Schaeffer

Visit Quilters' Choice - You won't be disappointed. Ask for your free gift with purchase.

Great selection of fabric, notions, books, classes and lots of inspiration.

Our friendly, knowledgeable staff is here to serve you.

Mon - Fri 10 - 7
Sat 10 - 5 Sun 12 - 4

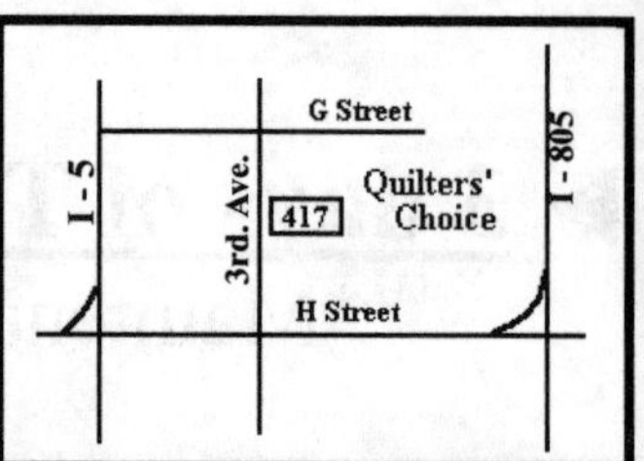

El Cajon, CA #123

12 min from downtown San Diego

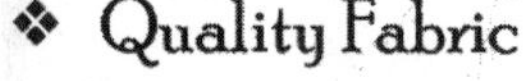

Cozy Quilt Shop

2940 Jamacha Rd, Ste H
El Cajon, CA 92019
619-670-0652 www.cozyquilt.com

- Quality Fabric
- Notions
- Inspiration
- Books and Patterns
- Friendly Staff
- Classes for all Levels

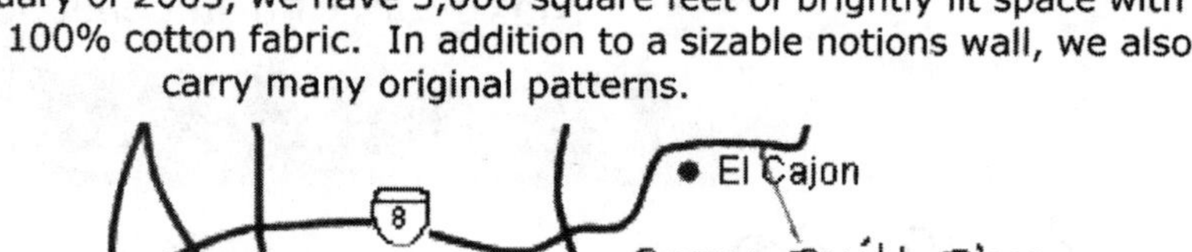
Established in January of 2003, we have 3,000 square feet of brightly lit space with over 2600 bolts of 100% cotton fabric. In addition to a sizable notions wall, we also carry many original patterns.

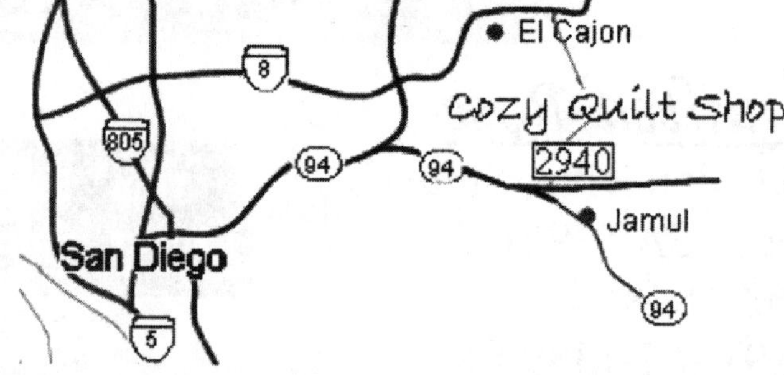

From San Diego: 94 East. Stay on 94 until it turns from freeway to city street (Do not be tempted to take 125 or turn left at Jamacha Blvd). Left at the stop light of Cuyamaca College Drive West. (Target, TGI Fridays and Staples will be on your right.) Left into parking lot. Next to ERoma Day Spa.
From East County: I-8 to Second Street exit. Go South. Second Street Turns into Jamacha Rd. We are about 3 miles from the freeway on your right.

Mon–Sat 9:30-5:30
Thu til 6:30
Sun noon–4pm

SEW MUCH BETTER

1824-A Oceanside Blvd. 92054
(Boney's Center — one block east of I - 5)
760-433-5151

Owners:
Larry & Mary Danielson

30 miles North of San Diego
5 miles North of Legoland
60 miles South of Disneyland

Oceanside, CA #124

Mon - Sat 9:30 - 5:00

QUILTING FABRIC 2000+ BOLTS 100% Cotton Fabrics
Hoffman, Batiks, Benartex, Kona Bay, South Seas, RJR, P&B, others
Quilting classes. Books, Patterns, Notions, Antique Quilts

Home of: ***EASY QUILTER***
(Free Motion Quilt Frame)

www.easyquilter.com

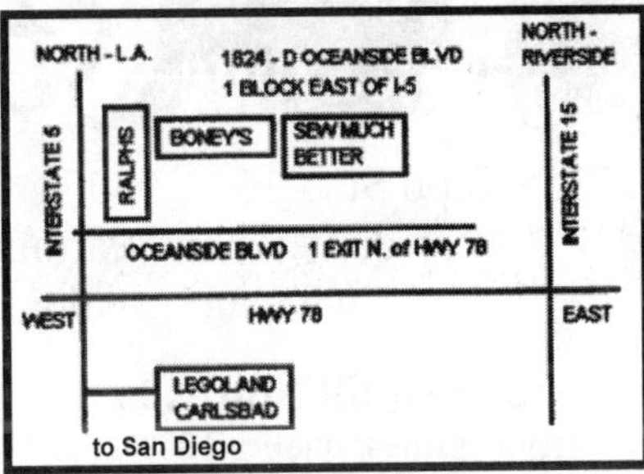

QUILTING & ARTISAN CENTER

Carlsbad, CA #125

AUTHORIZED JANOME SEWING MACHINE DEALERS

Friendly experienced staff make you feel at home! Cozy Cottage fully stocked with a large assortment of books, patterns, notions, tools, mats — everything a quilter needs. Great collection of 100% cottons and batiks. Classes offered every day.

2801-A Roosevelt St. 92008
(760) 720-7397 **Fax: (760) 720-7627**

www.sowingsisters.com

Mon - Sat 9 - 5
Sun 9 - 3

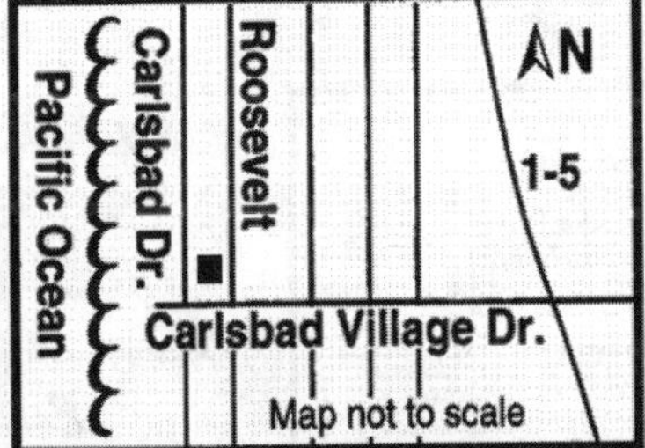

Lemon Grove, CA #126

Tues - Fri 9 - 4
Sat 10 - 6

Ethnic Quilts & Fabrics

2607-09 Lemon Grove Ave. 91945
(619) 461-0783
enbriggs@aol.com
www.ethnicquilts-fabrics.com
Est: 1999 1400 sq.ft.

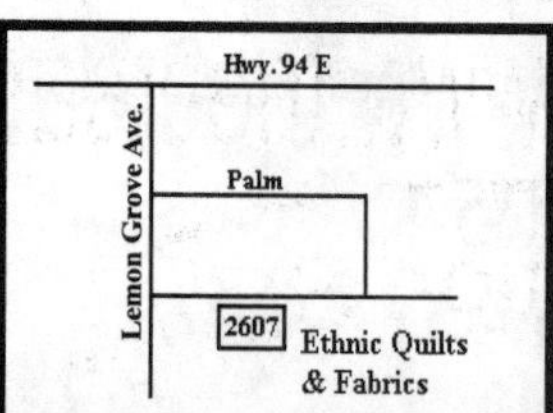

Beautiful African Fabric and Custom Machine Quilting Available.

Simi Valley, CA #128

Owner:
Linda Patton

Quilt Station

2355 Tapo St . #16 93063 (805) 584-6915
quiltstation@earthlink.net
www.quiltstation.com

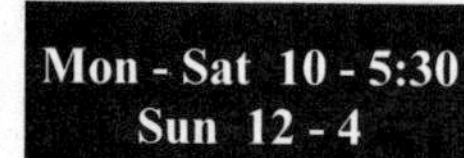

A Complete quilt Store . . .
We carry the finest quality 100% Cotton Fabrics in prints and solids. A complete line of Books, Patterns and Notions to round out your quilting needs along with gift items for your Quilting Friends. We offer a wide variety of classes for all levels of quilters. Our friendly staff is here to help you.

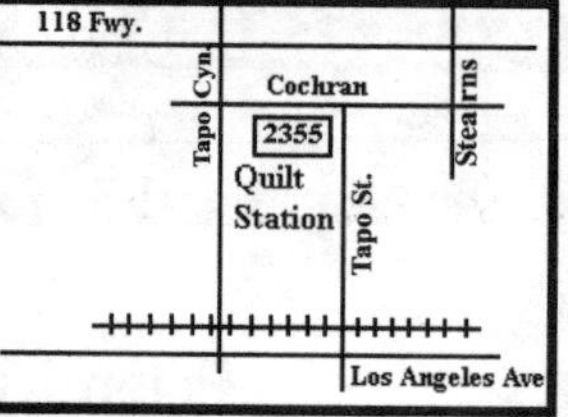

The Treasure Hunt

Folk Art ♥ Gifts
Special Treasures
Greeting Cards
Collectibles
Good Times

Fabric ♥ Quilting
Stenciling ♥ Painting
Knitting ♥ Crochet
Country Crafts
Floral Designs
Needlework

Mon - Sat 10 - 5
Sun 11 - 4

Pacific Ocean — Linden Ave. — 919 — Maple Ave. — The Treasure Hunt — Carpinteria Ave. — 101 Freeway — Casitas Pass Rd.

919 Maple Ave.
93013
(805) 684-3360
Owner: Roxanne Barbieri
Est: 1982

Carpinteria, CA #130

Loving Stitches
QUILT SHOPPE

Mon - Sat
10 - 5

21515 Soledad Canyon Rd. #110
Santa Clarita, CA 91350
(661) 254-1296

We will be moving at the end of 2004, please call for the new address and directions.

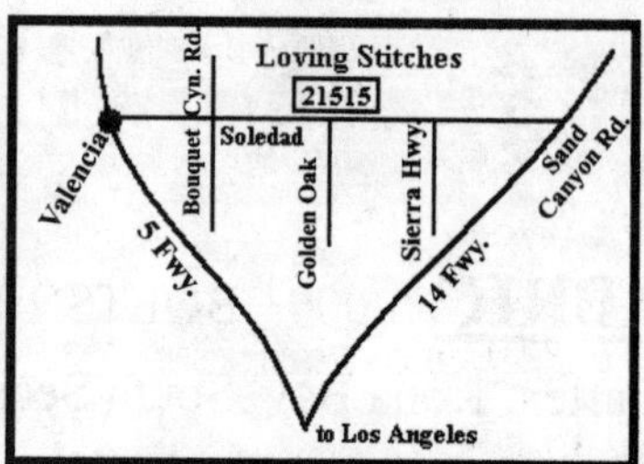

Over 3000 bolts of fabric. A large selection of Orientals, 30's Reproductions, Flannels, and Batiks. We are also a Thimbleberries Club Shop and carry a large selection of Thimbleberry Fabrics.

Santa Clarita, CA #127

Camarillo, CA #129

2117 Pickwick Drive
93010
(805) 445-8875
www.stitcherz.com
Janet & Jaye Killian, owners

Mon. - Sat. 10-5:30

Stitcherz has a friendly, knowledgeable staff; a large selection of quality 100% cotton fabrics; quilting books, supplies, & notions. We love felted wool and Thimbleberries, too!

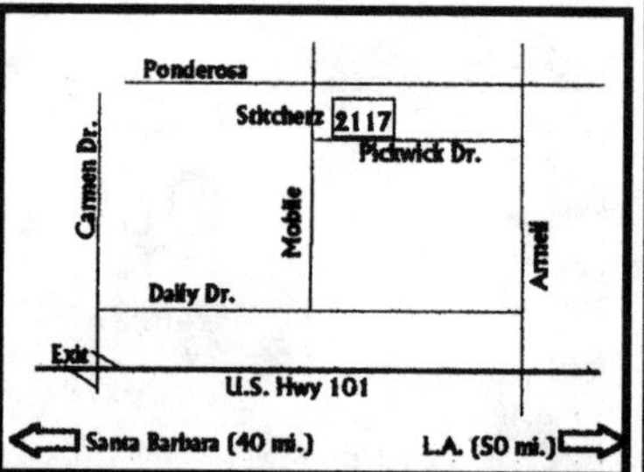

Solvang, CA #131

Mon - Sat
9 - 5:30
Sun 9 - 5

Rasmussen's Solvang

1697 Copenhagen Dr. 93463
(805) 688-6636 Fax: (805) 688-2847
info@rasmussenssolvang.com

We offer a large selection of quilting fabric, patterns, and books; as well as needlework and knitting supplies. We welcome phone and mail orders.

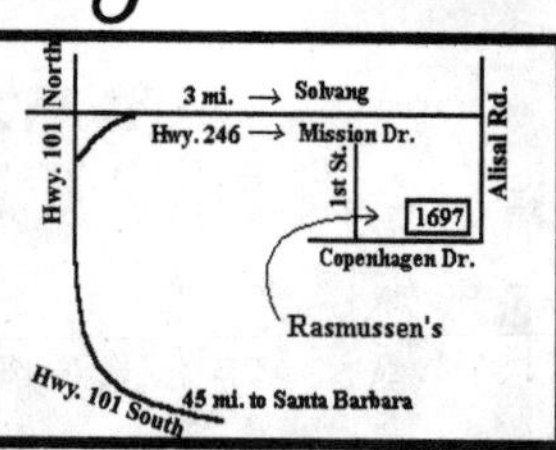

Buellton, CA #132
www.thecreationstation.com
252 E. Hwy. 246, Unit A
Buellton, CA 93427
(805) 693-0174
The Creation Station
FABRIC
& Quilt Shop
Wed - Sat
10 - 5
Sun 10 - 4
Fax: (805) 693-0164
Est: 2002 2800 sq.ft.
Owners: Dawn & Patrick Farrier
All fabric $5.00 per yard!
Unique selection of 100% cotton
& flannel fabrics amidst
our fun & funky nostalgic setting
HWY 246
To Lompoc
To Solvang
101 FWY
Albertson's Plaza
Burger King
Car Dealer
Creation Station
Antonio's Pizza
Steve's Tires
Mon - Fri
10 - 6
Sat 10 - 5
Blue Island Quilts
"Looking for the Unusual?"
Santa Barbara ►
◄ Goleta
101
Patterson
Magnolia Center
Hollister
• Fabrics - carefully selected, top quality cottons including tropical, asian, australian, batik & one-of-a-kind
• Patterns - our own original designs as well as the mainland's best selection of Hawaiian Quilt patterns
• Books, notions, specialty items & gifts
Santa Barbara, CA #133
5140 Hollister Avenue, Santa Barbara, CA 93111
805 683-0112

Ventura, CA #134

Tues - Sat 10 - 6
Sun 11 - 4

Quilt Ventura

4572 Telephone Rd.
Suite 908 93003
(805) 658-9800
www.quiltventura.com
Owner: Joey Strait

Delighting quilters with contemporary fabrics, books, notions and awesome classes!

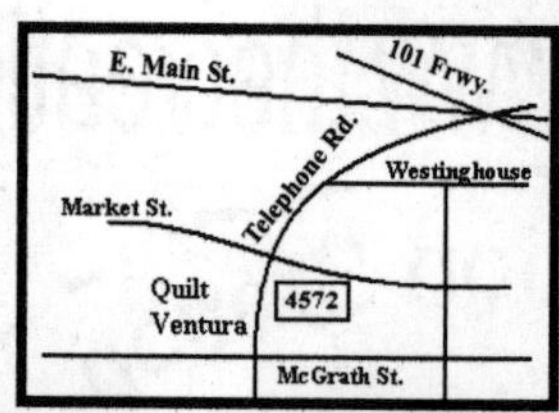

Tujunga, CA #135

Mon - Fri 9:30 - 7
Sat 9:30 - 6

Patchwork Penguin

6540 Foothill Blvd., Suite B104 91042
(818) 352-7300 Fax: (818) 352-3544
thequiltingnut@patchworkpenguin.com
www.patchworkpenguin.com
Owner: Crissa DuCharme
New Quilt & Yarn Shop

Quality fabrics, yarns, gifts and classes and Fabulous Customer Service. 10% everyday on regular priced merchandise.

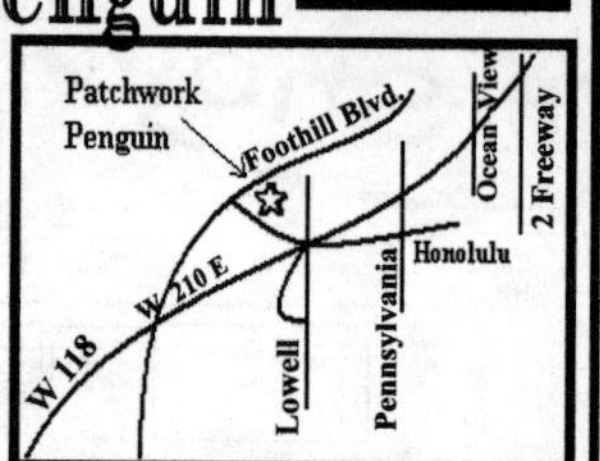

For the Finest in Quilting in Southern California, Sewing Arts Center features 3000 bolts of extraordinary quilting fabrics, including 600 batiks, bunches of brights, and beautiful Asian textiles.

Extensive Selection of Threads, Buttons, Beads & Notions.
And yes, we've got over 100 classes per quarter !
In addition to providing custom long arm quilting services, we are Southern California's Husqvarna Viking and BERNINA Specialists.

Reliable Repairs on All Makes and Models.

NEW LOCATION !
3330 Pico Blvd.
Santa Monica, CA 90405
(1/2 block east of Our former location)
Telephone: 310-450-4300
NEW HOURS !
Mon-Sat, 10-6:30 PM;
Sun, 11-5 PM
Visit us on line at:
www.sewingartscenter.com

Now Carrying Bernina, too!

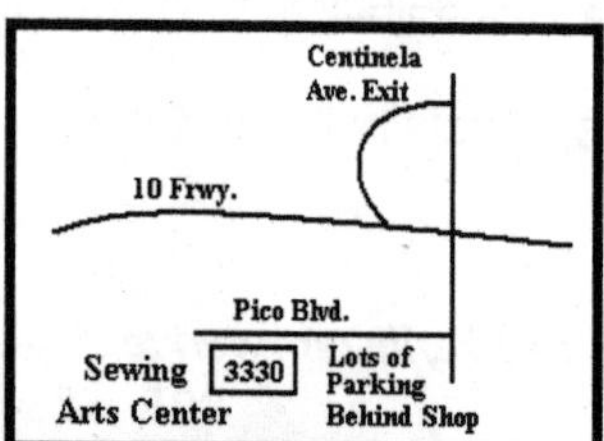

Santa Monica, CA #137

Q is for Quilts

Burbank, CA

Over 6,000 bolts of fabric

Large selections of

- Batiks
- Flannels
- Orientals
- 30's
- Colors
- Novelties

Mon - Fri 10 - 6
Sat 10 - 5
Sun 12 - 4

Helpful smiling faces
And
A wide variety of classes!

620 S Glenoaks Blvd.
Burbank, California
(818) 567-0267
www.qisforquilts.com

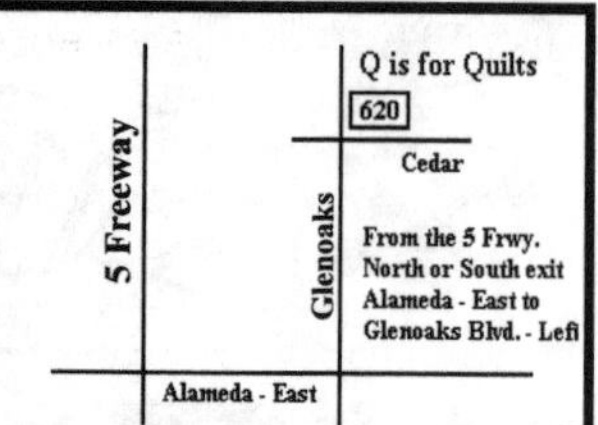

Burbank, CA #136

ESTHER'S TREASURES

"For Such A time As This"

Quilters are always our special guests! We feature "Kharisma" Heirloom Qualtiy Quilts, quilted Batik vests, handcrafted dolls and "Clayworks" collectibles. "Kharisma" Heirloom Quality Quilts are special...each stitch a loving expression of beauty and taste...a must see for the expert quilter and a wonderful addition to your quilt collection. Whimsical, cozy, simple treasure quilts also available.

625 N. Azusa Ave. 91702
(626) 969-6070 Fax: Same
Estherstreasures@msn.com
www.estherstreasures.com
Vera E. Amrull
Est: 2003 1300 sq.ft.
Mon - Fri 11-6, Sat 10-7

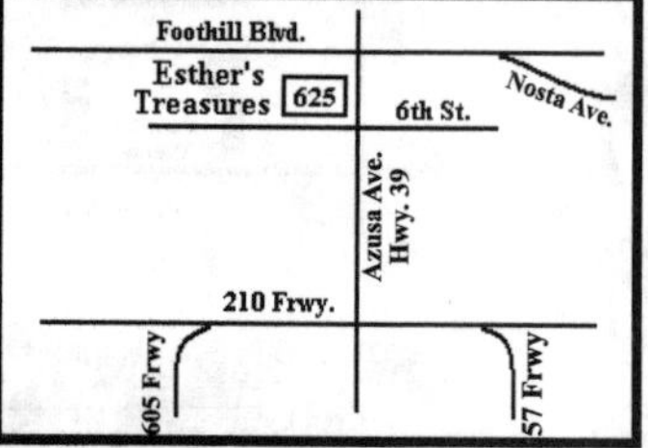

"a place of women for women networking in outreach"

Azusa, CA #138

Thousand Oaks, CA #139

Mon - Thur 10 - 6
Fri & Sat 10 - 5
Sun 12 - 4

Mary's Quilt Inn

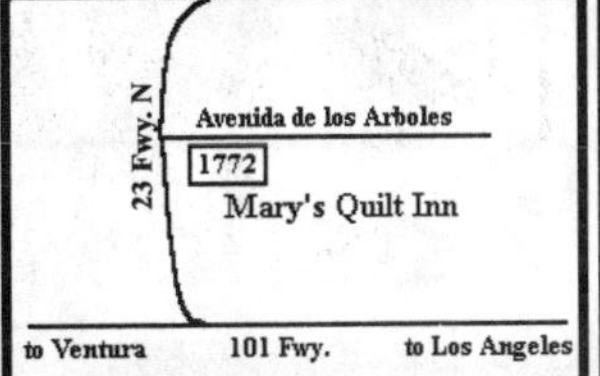

1772 Avenida de los Arboles #E 91362
(805) 241-0061 Owner: Mary Freeman
Est: 1978 1575 sq.ft. 1250+ Bolts

We offer a large variety of fabrics, classes, quilting supplies, books & patterns.

Brea, CA #141

Cozy Cottage Fabrics

Mon - Thur 10-8, Fri & Sat 10-5, Sun 12-4

We offer a large selection of quilting fabrics, software, books, notions, patterns and classes. You'll love our wide selection of 1930's reproductions, batiks, flannels and novelty fabrics. We also carry wool rug hooking supplies. and a wide variety of gifts.

740 N. Brea Blvd. 92821
(714) 529-2999
www.cozycottagefabrics.com
Info@cozycottagefabrics.com
Owner: Kris Giannetti
Est: 2003 2000 sq.ft.

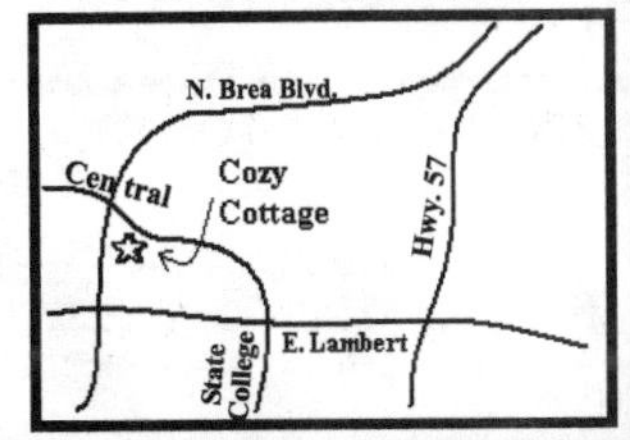

Norco, CA #142

The Tattered Rabbit Quilt Shop

Visit us online or stop by and see our completely unique display of quality 100% cotton fabrics and quilting supplies. We carry all your favorite manufacturers: Hoffman, Moda, Benartex, Michael Miller, Timeless Treasures, South Seas & many others.

Mon - Fri 11 - 6 Sat 10 - 4

1660 Hamner Ave., Suite 16
Norco, CA 92860
(909) 278-9108
Fax: (909) 278-9073
4fabric@tatteredrabbit.com
www.tatteredrabbit.com
Owners: Noel & Martha Hardcastle

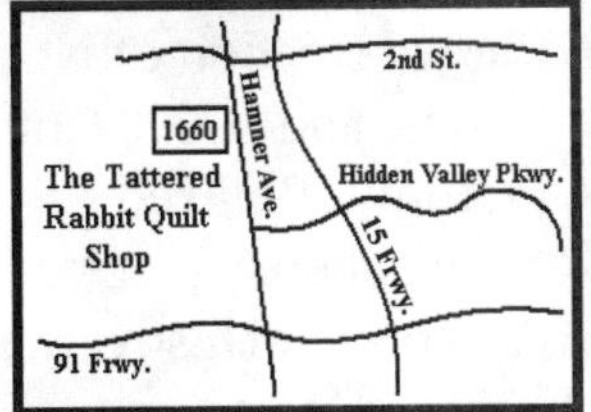

"A Hare Better Than Other Quilt shops"

Montclair, CA #140

"Your Idea Place"

500 Books
Gifts for Quilters
Notions and Supplies
Classes for all Skill Levels
4,000 Bolts of Cotton Fabric
Over 1,000 Doll, Critter & Quilt Patterns
Featured in Quilt Sampler Magazine

(909) 985-9000
Mon - Sat 10 - 5
Sun 12 - 3

Note: There are *"two"* Arrow Highways

210 Fwy
Foothill Blvd.
N
(The wrong) Arrow
Arrow Hwy.
8th St.
57 Fwy
I-10
Central
Mountain
I-15

5436D Arrow Hwy., ✷ Montclair CA 91763
www.thefabricpatch.com

A Quilter's Dream

...if you love to quilt or love a quilter.

150 N. San Gabriel Blvd., Suite 500 91107

Mon - Sat 10 - 5:30
Sun 12 - 4

(626) 744-2779

Visit us on-line for convenient at home shopping at: www.aquiltersdream.com

We are known for our Fabric Packs, Kits, Batiks, Flannels and other beautiful 100% cottons.

Pasadena, CA #143

I - 210
Walnut St.
150
Quilter's Dream
Huntington Dr.
San Gabriel
Rosemead
Enter on Walnut
I - 10

Pasadena, CA #144

Mon - Fri 9:30 - 7
Sat 9:30 - 6
Sun 12 - 5

Bearly Stitchin Sewing Center

2245 E. Colorado Blvd. A-106 91107
(626) 796-2118 Fax: (626) 796-3966
E-Mail: bstitchin@earthlink.net
Est: 1986 3100 sq.ft. 2000 Bolts

Complete selection of 100% cotton fabrics. Bernina and Husqvarna Viking sewing machines, books, notions, machine accessories and cabinets.

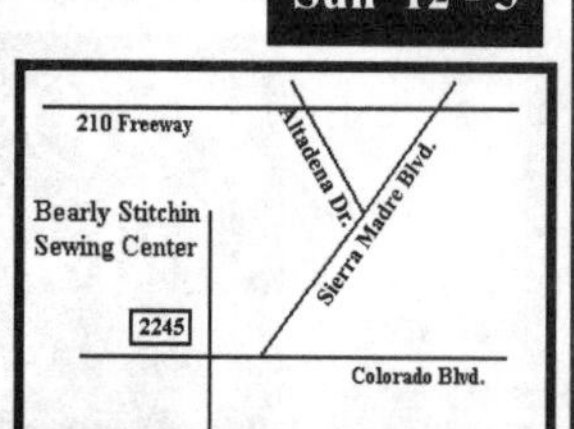

Fullerton, CA #145

Mon - Thur 9:30 - 7
Fri & Sat 9:30 - 5

The Quilt Cupboard

1335 E. Chapman Ave. 92831
(714) 526-5911 Fax: (714) 526-5922
sheri@thequiltcupboard.net
www.thequiltcupboard.net
Owner: Sheri Siedentop
Est: 2003 1400 sq.ft. 1500+ Bolts
Be welcomed by our friendly and knowledgeable staff. Shop for the newest fabrics, books, patterns, notions, kits, classes and gifts

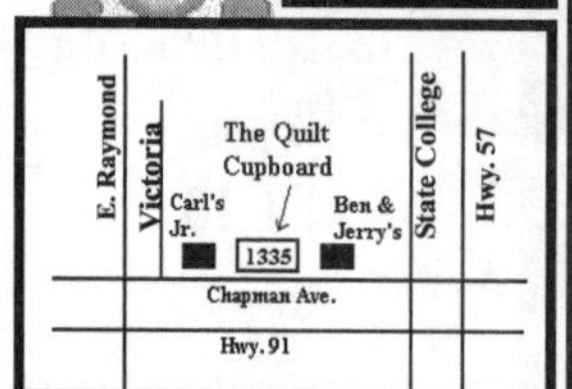

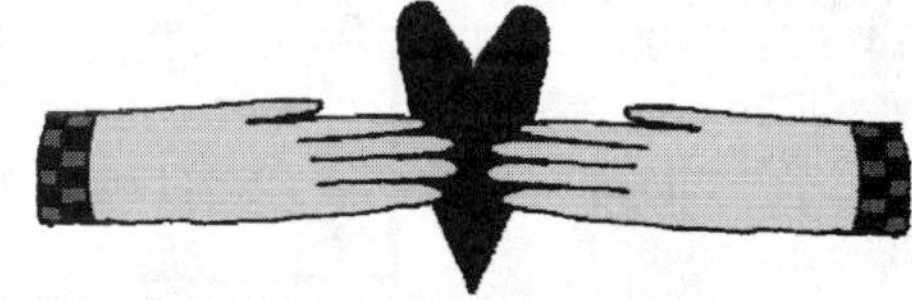

Redondo Beach, CA #146

Luella's Quilt Basket

1512 Aviation Blvd. 90278
(310) 798-1282
luellas@verizon.net
Owner: Luella Fournell
Est: 1988 1400 sq.ft.

Mon - Sat 10 - 6

- Large selection of Notions, Books, and 100% Cottons
- Friendly, Relaxed Atmosphere
- Authorized Husqvarna Viking Dealer

Rosecrans Blvd.
Sepulveda Blvd.
Aviation
405 Fwy.
Artesia Blvd.
1512
Luella's Quilt Basket

www.luellas.com

FRESH FABRIC ARRIVING DAILY

Redondo Beach, CA #147

-Hoffman
-Alexander Henry
-P & B
-Moda
-Timeless Treasures
Hawaiian & Tropical Prints
Flannel Prints & Novelties
Exquisite Decorator Fabrics
Bridal & Special Occasion

~ Since 1959 ~

THE COTTON SHOP
FINE FABRICS

1922 Artesia Blvd Redondo Beach, CA 90278

Open Mon-Thurs 10-7 Fri-Sat 10-6 Sun 11-5 Visa Mastercard American Express Discover

(310) 376-3518

TALL MOUSE

Arts, Crafts & Custom Framing

Crafts. Discover life's little pleasures.

The **Tall Mouse Quilt Shoppe** has a large assortment of the finest 100% cotton fabrics, complete quilting supplies, notions, books and patterns. PLUS cross-stitch, ribbons, buttons, beads, stencils and a complete scrapbook department with die-cut machines are only just a few of the perks to the Tall Mouse shopping experience . Classes are also offered throughout the year.

Yorba Linda **#151**
17506 Yorba Linda Blvd.
714-996-0101

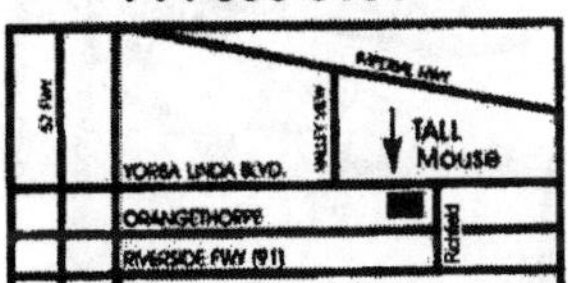

Laguna Niguel **#150**
23932 Aliso Creek
949-360-5777

Cerritos **#148**
13233 South St.
562-865-0800

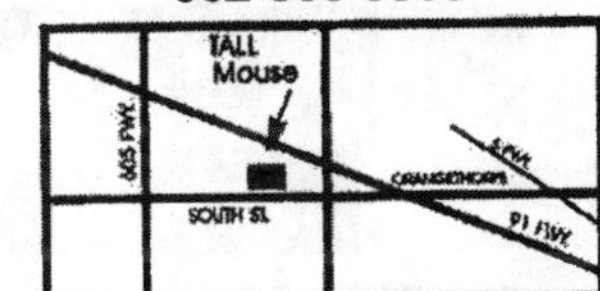

Irvine **#149**
5695 Alton Pkwy.
949-551-3300

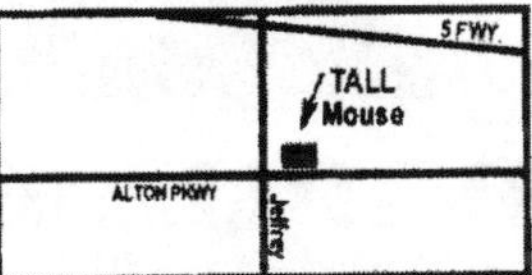

Family Owned & Operated for 38 YEARS!

Vistit us at www.tallmouse.com

Tall Mouse is Your Family Place for Creativity!

OPEN 7 DAYS
Mon. - Fri. 9:00am-9:00pm
Sat. 9:00am-6:00pm
Sun. 10:00am-6:00pm

Yorba Linda, CA #152

Mon - Sat 9:30 - 5:00
Sun 11:30 - 3:30

4825-D Valley View Ave. 92886
(714) 993-3091 Fax: (714) 993-2316
calicohws@aol.com
www.calicohouse.homestead.com
Owners: Jane, Janice, Cari
Est: 1981 1500+ Bolts

Complete Quilt Shop.
Books, Fabrics, Notions, Classes.

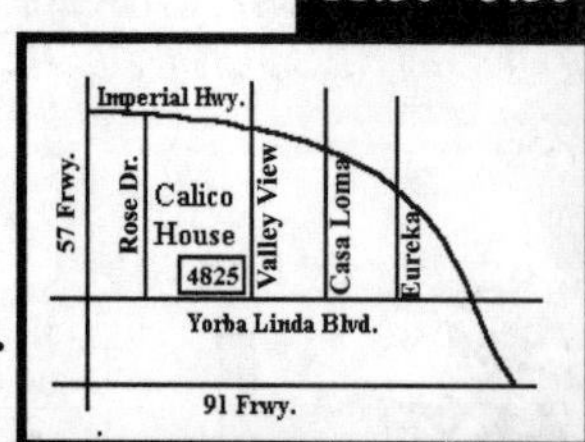

Tustin, CA #154

Flying Geese Fabric

A Quilter's Shop & More

307 El Camino Real
Tustin, CA 92780
(714) 544-9349
www.flyinggeesefabric.com

...in the heart of Old Towne Tustin with tree lined streets, cozy tea houses and quaint antique shops...

GREAT CLASSES AVAILABLE
- Beginner and Intermediate Quilting
- Hand and Machine Quilting
- Hand and Machine Applique
- Beginner and Intermediate Sewing
- Clothing Classes
- Children's Sewing (ages 7 - 17)

BETHANY SERVICE PROJECT
2nd and 4th Friday Mornings

Mon & Wed 10 - 7 Tues & Thur 10 - 6
Fri & Sat 10 - 5

Lomita, CA #155

TREADLEART

Tues - Thur 10 - 6
Fri & Sat 10 - 5
Sun 12 - 5

25834 Narbonne Ave. 90717
(310) 534-8372 Fax: Same
treadleart@treadleart.com
www.treadleart.com
Owner: Janet Stocker Est: 1978
7000 sq.ft. 5000 Bolts

Supplies for all your sewing, quilting and embroidery needs. Fabric, books, patterns, rulers, cutters, sewing machines and accessories. Tour groups Welcome.

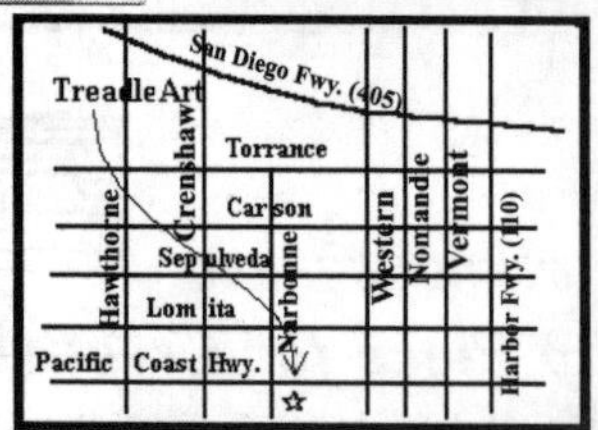

Anaheim, CA #153

Timeless Quilts™

(714) 520-5304
www.timelessquilts.com

Timeless Quilts has moved to its new location in another beautifully restored 1920's craftsman home. It too begs you to "come on in" as you approach it from Lincoln Ave. The beautifully landscaped grounds set the stage for an equally eye-catching interior. The shop's visual charm is only the surface... once in the shop you will find a large array of fabric, quilt kits, quilt supplies, notions and "above & beyond" customer service.

Shop Hours:
Tues. - Sat.
10am - 5pm

Sunday
Noon - 4pm

Shop and Classroom are Handicapped Accessible.

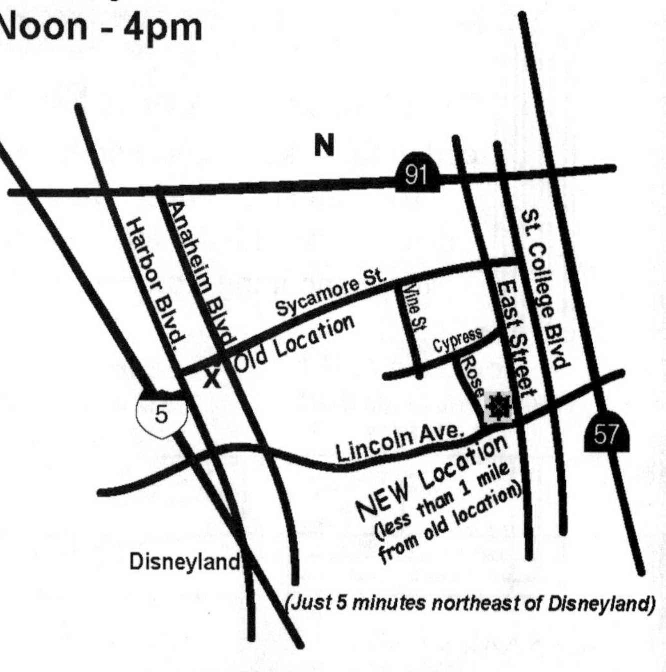

1155 E. Lincoln Ave.
Anaheim, CA 92805
(Corner of Lincoln Ave. & East St.)

Leah's Fabric Gallery

FOR QUALITY, SELECTION & SERVICE

since 1969

JANOME Quilting & Embroidery Machines

Leah's for Quilting:

400+ Book titles · 250+ patterns · 4000+ bolts of quality cotton fabric
Extensive selection of quilting and embroidery supplies
Unique gift items · Great classes with outstanding teachers

Convenient Store Hours

Mon-Fri	10 AM — 8 PM
Sat	10 AM — 6 PM
Sun	Noon — 5 PM

Friendly & Knowledgeable Sales Staff

2 Great Locations

e-mail: lfg4quilting@usa.net

★ **Leah's in Mission Viejo**
Corner of Avery & Marguerite Pkwy
28641 Marguerite Pkwy
Mission Viejo, Ca. 92692
(949) 364-6372
4 miles N of Mission San Juan Capistrano

♥ **Leah's in Orange**
W of Tustin Ave on Katella
1321 E. Katella Ave.
Orange, Ca. 92867
(714) 639-3245
4.7 miles EAST of Disneyland

Mission Viejo, CA #157

Orange, CA #156

REMEMBER: At Leah's, Guild Members always receive a 10% discount on all purchases. **Excludes sale merchandise**

Material Possessions Quilt Shop

22600-C Lambert St., Suite 905
Lake Forest, Ca 92630
949-586-3418 fax 949-586-7125
Sewing Center 949-586-2655
www.quilt@quiltessentials.com email quilt@quiltessentials.com

- Established 1995–9,500 sq. ft.
- 6,000 bolts of 100% cotton fabric
- All major fabric manufacturers
- Specializing in ethnic fabrics
- Hand dyed & marbled fabrics
- Hundreds of books & patterns
- Silk, vintage, and decorative ribbons
- Beginning to advanced quilting, needle art, and doll classes.
- Quilt Sampler Magazine

Lake Forest, CA #158

Bernina® Authorized Sales & Service

How to find us: Traveling from Interstate 5 or 405 take Bake Pkwy exit. Turn east toward the mountains. Travel to the third light and turn right on Muirlands. Turn right on Aspan. We are the fifth building on the right, facing Aspan. We are located in an industrial park. The number on the building is 22600-C.

Hours

Mon.- Sat. 10:00 AM - 5:30 PM Wed. 10:00 AM - 9:00 PM Closed Sunday

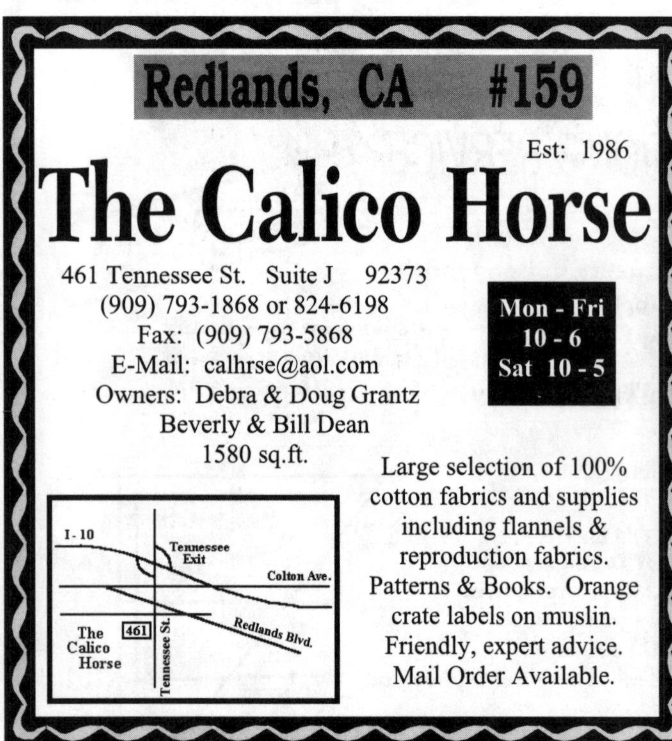

Riverside, CA #160

Pieceful Threads

Sewing Center

10191 Magnolia Ave.
Riverside, CA 92503
(909) 353-8983
Fax: (909) 353-8985
info@piecefulthreads.com
3400 sq.ft. 1500+ Bolts

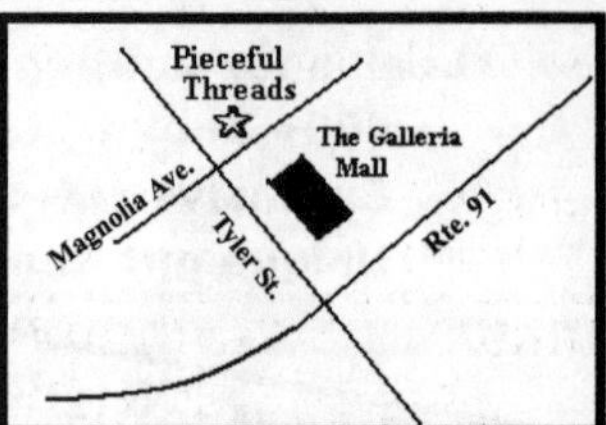

Large selection of 100% cotton fabrics - batiks, flannels, depression, repro, brights, novelties. Great selection of books, patterns, notions, supplies, classes, trunk shows. Viking / White dealer. Specialize in machine embroidery too.

Mon - Fri 10 - 7 Sat 10 - 5
Sun 12 - 5 (Closed Sun July & Aug)

www.piecefulthreads.com

Riverside, CA #161

THE QUILTERS COCOON

"Your Full Service Quilt Shop"
10250 Indiana Ave., Riverside, CA 92503
909-351-0346
thequilter@quilterscocoon.com
www.quilterscocoon.com

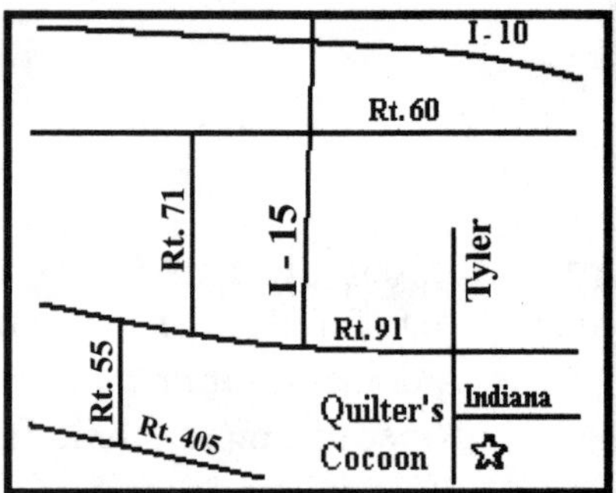

Mon - Sat 10:00 - 5:00
Thur 10:00 - 8:00 Sun 11:00- 4:00

Largest Quilt shop in the Inland Empire. Conveniently located right off the 91 frwy. in Riverside.

Known for our friendly and personal service set in a warm and welcoming atmosphere.

Offering: Fabrics, Notions, Gadgets, Books, Patterns, Batting and Gifts

Three classrooms offering a wide variety of classes for beginners to advanced quilters.
UFO workshops & more.

Machine quilting services done on the premises using a long-arm Gammill.

Corona, CA #162

Tues - Sat 10 - 5

Stars & Scraps Quilt Shop

2175 Sampson Ave. #121 92879
(909) 737-3959
starsandscraps@aol.com
Owner: Sharon Yeager Est: 2002

2400 sq.ft. with 1200+ bolts. Notions, books & patterns. We are a Primitive Country Shop. Williraye dealer. Classes too.

91 Frwy.
I - 15
Stars & Scraps Quilt Shop
2175
McKinley
Sampson Ave.

Calimesa, CA #163

Everything Nice

1007 Calimesa Blvd., # J
Calimesa, CA 92320
909-795-2778
Owners: Judy DeBoer & Cathy Brown
Est: 1999 2000 sq.ft.

A really fun Quilt Shop featuring a unique selection of fun 100% cotton fabrics. Books, patterns, magazines and notions. Authorized Elna and Babylock dealers.

in the Crown Village Shp. Ctr.
Everything Nice
1007
Ave. "L"
Exit County Line Rd.
Exit Calimesa Blvd.
to Redlands
10 Frwy.
to Palm Springs

Mon 10 - 8
Tues - Fri 10 - 6
Sat 10 - 3
Closed Sun

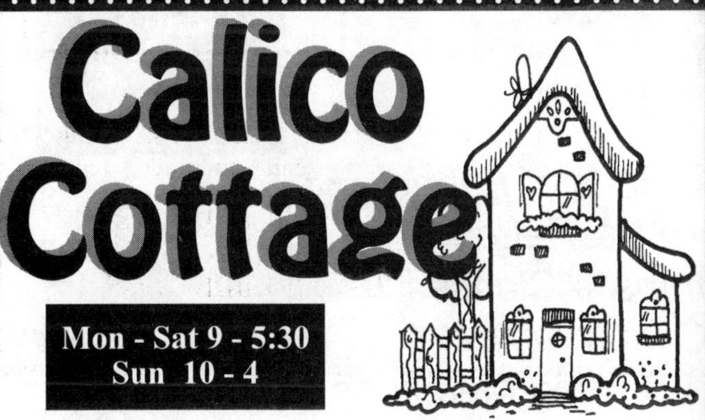

Mon - Sat 9 - 5:30
Sun 10 - 4

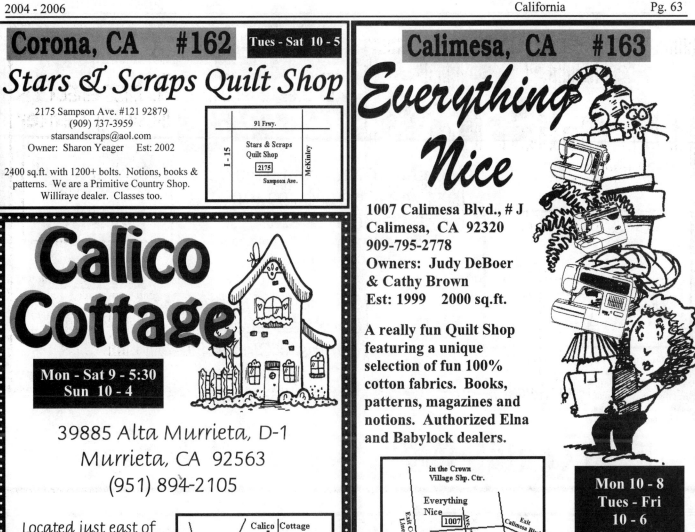

39885 Alta Murrieta, D-1
Murrieta, CA 92563
(951) 894-2105

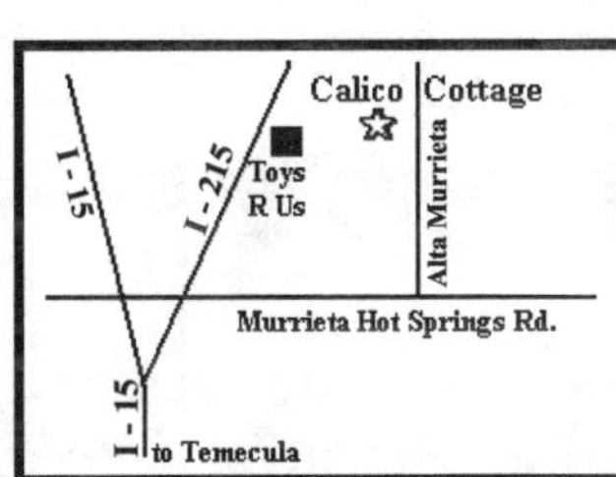

Located just east of the 215 in the Murrieta Town Center, directly across from Toys R Us.
Over 1000 bolts of premium cottons; books, patterns, notions and classes.

Fax: (909) 894-2105
Owners: Ellen French & Debra Andrews
Est: 2003 2026 sq.ft.
1100+ Bolts

Murrieta, CA #164

Happiness is finishing a quilt!

Sharon Walters — Owner

Mon - Sat 9:30 - 4:30

129 S. Vine St 92028
(760) 723-3060
Est: 1990 800 sq.ft.
1500 Bolts

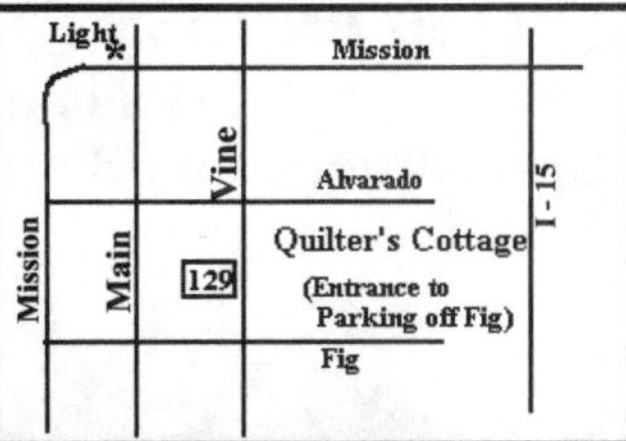

Fallbrook, CA #165

28780 Old Town Front St. #D2
(951) 693-3213 92590
Fax: (951) 693-3216
Website: www.woerthstitching.com
Owner: Aileen Woerth

Mon - Sat 9:30 - 5:30
Sun 10:30 - 4

I - 15
Front
Ynez Rd.
Woerth Stitching
Santiago Rd.
Front

3500 Bolts of Fabric
Books & Patterns
Notions & Classes
Gifts & Quilts
Bernina Sewing Machines

From Interstate 15, exit Hwy. 79 South and proceed West approximately 7/10 of a mile. Make a right turn into South Creek Mall, the first driveway north of the Harley Davidson dealer, and proceed East. We are in Suite D-2 and we face the freeway.

Temecula, CA #166

Bunney Hutch Quilt N' Sew

4478 Cerritos Avenue
Los Alamitos 90720
(714) 226-9647
Fax: (714) 226-9649

91 FWY
CARSON
WARDLOW
SPRING
WILLOW
605 FWY
NORWALK
LOS ALAMITOS BLVD
BLOOMFIELD
LINCOLN
BALL
CERRITOS
KATELLA
LEXINGTON
DENNI
VALLEY VIEW
405 FWY

www.bunneyhutch.com jm@bunneyhutch.com
Owners: Jean-Marie Bunney-Lytton and Jerry Lytton

- *Janome Sewing Machines Sales & Service*
- *Koala Cabinets*
- *HandiQuilter Sale & Accessories*

Los Alamitos, CA #167

On-site sewing machine service of all makes & models.
Custom sewing furniture & wood products.

"Hop on In . . ." Over 4000 bolts. We offer the finest quality books, notions and 100% cotton fabrics in a friendly, relaxed atmosphere with old-fashioned personal service. Specializing in Batiks, flannel, Oriental, landscape and 'flavors'. We have a wonderful teaching staff and offer a variety of classes. We love beginners. Many original designs taught by our instructors.

Mail Orders Welcome Visa, MC, American Express

Mon - Fri 10 - 9 Sat 10 - 6 Sun 11 - 5

Other Shops in California: *We suggest calling first*

Albany Quilted Fish, 968 San Pablo Ave 510-526-1642
Albion The Quilt Complex, 30701 Middle Ridge 707-937-0739
Aliso Viejo The Cotton Boutique, 15 Oak View Dr 949-362-9961
Aliso Viejo The Cotton Boutique, 27101 Aliso Creek Road 949-362-6646
Alpine Kat's Cottage, 2526 Alpine Blvd. 619-445-2877
Alturas Nana's Quilts, 110 E 1st St 530-233-2602
Anderson Carol's Quilt Shop, 17456 Flowers Ln. 530-357-2575
Arcata Fabric Temptations, 942 `G' St. 707-822-7782
Arroyo Grande Chameleon Fabric, 107 Nelson St. 805-481-4104
Avalon Catalina Crafters, 115 Sumner Ave. 310-510-3590
Benicia Nancy's Needleworks, 335 Viewmont St 707-745-3625
Berkeley Ninepatch, 2001 Hopkins St. 510-527-1700
Blocksburg In Stitches, P.O. Box 257 707-926-0306
Bonsall A.H. Mercantile Co., PO Box 1354 760-726-3355
Brentwood Pine Needle Quilts, 1135 2nd St. Ste C 925-516-7782
Bridgeport Hampton House, 261 Main St. 760-932-9138
Camarillo Baron's Fabric, 379 Carmen Dr. 805-482-9848
Cambria Pine Tree Patchworks, 815 Main St 805-927-3869
Campbell Golden State Sewing, 2435 S. Winchester 408-866-1181
Carmichael A Stitch In Time, 4415 Rollingrock Way 916-966-3400
Chico Nana's Quilt Co., 828 Cairgrove Ct 530-345-6720
Clayton Cottontales, 6200 Center St. #J 925-673-0742
Clovis Sew Kwik Quilter, 2555 Clovis Ave 559-348-0853
Compton Becerra Quilting, 3221 N. Alameda St. 310-638-7141
Crescent City Heavenly Stitches, 1981 Northcrest 707-465-3565
Delhi The Quilting Depot, PO Box 661 209-833-6622
Escondido Baker's Sewing Center, 112 N Kalmia St 760-745-4140
Escondido Quilter's Paradise, 2253 E. Valley Pkwy. 760-738-9677
Etna Wooden Spools, 538 Main St 530-467-5633
Exeter Annie Hand Crafted Gifts, 179 E Pine St 559-584-0034
Fair Oaks Jeanette's Fabrics, 11045 Fair Oaks Blvd 916-482-1899
Fairfax Rainbow Fabrics, 50 Bolinas Rd. 415-459-5100
Ferndale Itsy Bitsy Quilt Shop, 606 Main Street 707-786-9002
Folsom Meissner Sewing Maching Co., 1013 Riley 916-984-7071
Fortuna All Washed Up, 685 Spring St 707-725-9773
Fountain Valley Jenny's Fabrics, 8984 Warner Ave 714-894-2202
Fremont Quilting Bee Sewing Center, 39161 Farwell 510-494-9040
Fresno Sierra Craft, 1131 N De Wolf 559-251-9320
Galt Creative Quilts, 10393 Twin Cities Rd 209-745-0633
Garden Grove Bear's Quilt Shop, 9706 Chapman Ave 714-590-9209
Gilroy Nimble Thimble, 55 W. 6th St. 408-842-6501
Goleta Finely Quilted, 58 La Calera Way 805-967-5011
Granada Hills Patchwork N' Things, 12355 Jolette 818-360-2828
Gridley Camellia's Quilts, 180 Vermont St #A 530-846-3325
Healdsburg Fabrications, 118 Matheson St. 707-433-6243
Hillister Timber & Textiles, 898 San Benito St 831-637-3955
Inyokern Quilted Patches, 300 Mark Ct. 760-377-5378
Julian Julian Yarn Basket, 2122 Main St. 760-765-0849
La Habra Calico Corner Quilt Shop, 2094 W LaHabra 562-694-3384
La Mesa Save Nine Quilting, 4679 68th St. 619-644-1445
La Mesa The Country Loft, 4685 Date Ave. 619-466-5411
Lafayette Patchwork Plus, 3 Burr Ct 925-283-0294
Laguna Beach Klassic Creations, 157 Canyon Acres 949-494-7966
Lake Elsinore Ironside Cottage, 671 Acacia St 909-471-2741
Lake Forest Penache, 24611 Shadowfax Dr. 949-768-5979
Lakewood Conerstone Quilt Shop, 6138 Faust Ave 562-630-0330
Lancaster Stitch Peddler, 42921 cinema Ave 661-951-0663
Lancaster Cozy Quilts, 42555 32nd St. W 805-945-1207
Live Oak Quilt Co., 8656 Kent Ave 530-695-1793
Los Angeles F & S Fabrics, 10654 W Pico Blvd 310-475-1637
Lucerne Valley Hilltop Quilt Shop, 8555 Aliento Rd 760-248-9639
Magalia Seams To B, 14543 Grinnell Ct. 530-873-2670
Manhattan Beach Once Upon a Quilt, 312 Manhattan Beach Blvd. 310-379-1264
Manteca Horsefeathers Quilt Shop, 1360 1/2 E Yosemite Av 209-823-1633
McKinleyville Redwood Quilting Studio, 1805 Central 707-839-5566
Modesto Helens Yardage, 1331 Crows Landing Rd 209-526-0903
Montrose Quilt 'n' Things, Inc., 2411 Honolulu Ave 818-957-2287
Mountain View Eddie's Quilting Bee, 264 Castro St. 650-969-1714
Mountain View Buttons & Bolts Factory Outlet, 264 Castro St. 650-965-9712
Newbury Park The Quilters' Studio, 1090 Lawrence Dr. #101 805-480-3550

Newman Pins & Needles Fabric & Quilt Shoppe, 934 Fresno St 209-862-3274
North Hollywood Tilt & Quilt, 12836 Waddell St. 818-508-6898
North San Juan Small Patches, P.O. Box 329 530-292-1159
Oakland Poppy Fabric, 5151 Broadway 510-655-5151
Oceanside Prairie Canyon Quilts, 1824 Oceanside Blvd 760-439-6507
Oroville Mary Jane's Quilt Shop, 3884 Hilldale Ave 530-538-8086
Oxnard Fabric Well, 3075 Saviers Rd. 805-486-7826
Paradise Debbie's Quilt Shop, 6455 Skyway 530-877-8458
Pico Rivera S & J Quilts, 7860 Paramount Blvd. 310-942-7784
Placerville Pine Tree Fabrics, 1462 Broadway 530-626-0445
Porterville Busy B's Boutique, 375 N Main St #B 559-782-3067
Poway Silver Creek Quilting, 14655 Deerwood St. 858-679-6980
Poway Pickled Pieces, 13879 Carriage Rd 858-513-9123
Quincy Quincy Emporium, 535 Lawrence 530-283-0716
Redding Sew Simple, 3001 Bechelli Ln. 916-246-9310
Redwood City Adams Notion & Yardage, 2090 Brdwy 415-366-1711
Ridgecrest Casa Java Roasting Co., 972 N. Norma St. 760-446-5282
Riverside Wimsies, 4175 Wayne Ct. 909-687-2462
Roseville Meissner Sewing Machine, 1850 Douglas 916-786-3630
Sacramento Meissner Sewing Machine, 8771 Elk Grove 916-686-1108
Sacramento Meissner Sewing Machine, 2417 Cormorant 916-920-2121
Sacramento Electric Texture, 972 Robertson Way 916-492-2111
San Clemente Nine Patch, 1501 Avenida Hacienda 949-361-9145
San Diego Once Upon A Quilt, 4594 30th St 619-563-4164
San Diego Kojo, 9654 Siempre Viva Rd. #1 714-841-5656
San Jose Born to Quilt, 1685 Branham Lane #254 408-445-2641
San Jose Going to Pieces, 1375 Blossom Hill Rd. 408-723-4133
San Juan Bautisto Heavenly Quilting & Supplies, 340 Merrill Rd 831-623-4680
San Luis Obispo Betty's Fabrics, 1229 Carmel St. 805-543-1990
San Pedro Quilt Sails, 1312 W. 37th 310-548-7094
San Rafael Beverly Fabrics & Crafts, 836 4th Street 415-256-8121
Santa Ana Unique Quilting, 1969 Ritchey St 714-258-0311
Santa Ana Quilting Possibilities, 2207 S. Grand Ave 714-546-9949
Santa Barbara Craft Essentials, 187 S. Turnpike Rd. 805-681-3115
Santa Cruz Hart's Fabric Center, 1620 Seabright 408-423-5434
Santa Maria Betty's Fabrics, 1627 S. Broadway, 805-922-2181
Santa Marie Santa Maria Sewing, 709 E Main St. #D 805-922-1784
Santa Monica Bay Cities Sewing Arts Center, 3306 Pico Blvd 310-560-4300
Santa Paula Brownie's Basement, 866 E. Main St. 805-525-4556
Solvang Quilt Shoppe, 1693 Mission Dr #A102 805-693-0124
Solvang Quilts Galore, 1582 Copenhagen Dr 805-693-1028
Sonora Willow Creek Quilts, 13775 Mono Way 209-532-1869
Soquel Beverly Fabrics, 100 Cotton Lane 831-475-2851
Tahoe City Patchwork Mountain, 163 Roundridge 530-581-2566
Temecula Amish Touch, 27452 Jefferson Ave #7A 909-699-3399
Torrance AAA Sewing, Fabrics, 3770 Sepulveda Blvd 310-791-1190
Tracy Quilts by Rita, 1741 Summertime Ct. 209-833-6240
Twain Harte Twain Harte Pharmacy, 18711 Tiffeni 209-586-3225
Ukiah Sharin Stitches & Strokes, 202 S. State St 707-462-7397
Ukiah Sharon's Sew N Vac, 202 S. State St. 707-964-6226
Upper Lake Gracious Ladies, 9479 Main St. 707-275-2307
Vacaville Cowtown Quilters, 631 Harvard Ave. 707-448-8656
Valencia Quilted Heart, 24201 Valencia Blvd. #1371 805-255-0771
Vallejo Pieced on Earth Quilts, 336 Georgia St 707-644-6768
Ventura Fabrictown, USA, 2686 E Main St 805-643-3434
Walnut Creek Home Town Quilting, 230 Summit Rd 925-939-8728
Weaverville Stitch Witchery, 1310 Nugget Ln. 916-623-6891
Woodland Hills The Quilt Emporium, 4918 Topanga Canyon Blvd. 818-704-8238
Yorba Linda Cranberry Quiltworks, 3960 Prospect Ave. #M 714-223-1701
Yucca Valley Quilting Between Friends, 7379 Hopi Tr 760-365-4519

California Guilds:

Albany East Bay Heritage Quilters, P.O. Box 6223, 94706 Meets: Last Monday except July & Dec. @ 7pm at First Unitarian Church Hall in Kensington
Antioch Delta Quilters, P.O. Box 154, 94509
Aptos Pajaro Valley Quilt Assoc, P.O. Box 1412, 95003
Arnold Independence Hall Quilters, P.O. Box 842, 95223
Arroyo Grande South County Quilt Guild, P.O. Box 656, 93421
Auburn Foothill Quilters Guild, P.O. Box 5653, 95604
Bakersfield Cotton Patch Quilters, P.O. Box 9944, 93389
Benicia Carquinez Strait Quilters, P.O. Box 1101, 94510
Big Bear Lake Busy Bear Quilt Guild, 92315
Bishop The Calico Quilter's--Nite Owls, 1335 Rocking W. Dr., 93514 Meets: Last Thursday 6:30 p.m. at The Fabric Store
Brawley Desert Quilters Guild, 410 W. C St., 92227
Bryn Mawr Citrus Belt Quilters , 92318
Camarillo Camarillo Quilters Assoc. P.O. Box 347, 93011-0347 Meets: 2nd Tuesday (except Aug.) 9:30 a.m. at Orchid Bldg., 816 Camarillo Springs Rd.
Campbell Santa Clara Valley Quilt Assoc., P.O. Box 792, 95009
Canoga Park Valley Quiltmakers Guild, P.O. Box 589, 91305
Chester Chester Piece Makers, P.O. Box 1702, 96020 Meets: 2nd Monday 7 p.m. at Memorial Hall, Gay St.
Chico Anne's Star Quilt Guild, P.O. Box 4318, 95927
Chino Hills LA Quiltmakers Guild, 16167 Augusta Dr., 91709
Clear Lake Clear Lake Quilters Guild, 95422
Colusa Pacific Flyway Quilters, 1974 Wescott Road, 95932
Copperopolis The Bluegrass Quilters, P.O. Box 273, 95228 Meets: at Bluegrass music festivals
Corona Inland Empire Quilt Guild, P.O. Box 2232, 92878 Meets: 2nd & 4th Monday 6:45pm at Corona Sr. Center Corner of 10th & Belle
Crestline Dogwood Quilters, P.O. Box 3, 92325 Meets: First Saturday 9:30 at St. Richards Episcopal in Skyforth
Danville Diablo Valley Quilt Guild, P.O. Box 1884, 94526
Diamond Springs Gold Bug Quilters, 95619
Downieville Mountain Star Quilters, P.O. Box 647, 95936
El Cajon Sunshine Quilters, P.O. Box 20483, 92022
Elk Grove Elk Grove Quilters Guild, P.O. Box 1413, 95759 Meets: 3rd Thursday 7 p.m. at Elk Grove High School
Eureka Redwood Empire Quilters Guild, P.O. Box 5071, 95501
Fairfield North Wind Quilters, P.O. Box 2891, 94533
Fallbrook Fallbrook Quilters Guild, P.O. Box 1704, 92028 Meets: 6:30 at Fallbrook Community Center
Folsom Folsom Quilt & Fiber Guild, P.O. Box 626, 95630
Fremont Piecemakers Quilt Guild, P.O. Box 2051, 94536
Fresno San Jaquin Valley Quilt Guild, P.O. Box 5532, 93755
Garden Grove Orange Grove Quilters Guild, P.O. Box 453, 92842 Meets: 2nd Wednesday at 9:30 a.m. at United Methodist Church
Glendale Glendale Quilt Guild, P.O. Box 5366 91201
Grass Valley Pine Tree Quilt Guild, P.O. Box 3133 95945
Hayfork Log Cabin Quilters, P.O. Box 1359 96041
Hemet Valley Quilters, P.O. Box 2534, 92545
Hillsboro Wonder Woman Quilt Guild, 231 E. Main St., 97123 Meets: 3rd Monday 6:30 p.m. at Cloth & More
Huntington Beach Hens & Chickens Quilt Fellowship, PO Box 2748, 92647 Meets: 2nd Saturday @ 9am at Golden West College Community Center
Idyllwild Mountain Quilters, P.O. Box 603, 92349
Indio Coachella Valley Quilt Guild, 43-761 Towne St., 92201
Irvine Flying Geese Quilters, P.O. Box 292, 92604 Meets: 2nd Monday at 6:45 p.m. at Trinity United Presbyterian Church
La Habra Friendship Square Quilt Guild, P.O. Box 681, 90633 Meets: 3rd Monday @ 6:15 at East Whittier United Methodist Church
Lancaster Antelope Valley Quilt Association, P.O. Box 4107, 93534

Lodi Tokay Stitch-N-Quilt Guild, P.O. Box 1838 95241 Meets: 3rd Thursday @ 6:30pm at UCC Church
Lompoc Quilter's Etc. P.O. Box 2507, 93438 Meets: 4th Thursday
Long Beach Quilters By The Sea, PO Box 7613 90807 Meets: 2nd Thursday @ 7pm at Christ Lutheran Church
Los Angeles ADA Quilt Guild, 90010
Los Banos Westside Quilters Guild, 1019 Walnut Wood Court 93635
Los Osos Bear Valley Quilters
Loyalton Sierra Valley Guild, 411 Second St Suite B, 96118 Meets: Every Wednesday @ 6:30pm at Happy Heart Quilts & Collectibles
Lumpock Quilters Etc., P.O. Box 2507, 93438
Madera Heart of California Quilt Guild, 415 Camden Way, 93637
Manteca Manteca Quilters, P.O. Box 1558, 95336
Merced Gateway Quilters, P.O. Box 3793, 95344
Modesto Country Crossroads Guild, P.O. Box 577063, 95355
Morgan Hill Piece by Piece Quilters, 95037
Moss Beach Piecemakers By-the-Sea, P.O. Box 963, 94038 Meets: 3rd Thursday 7:30 & Last Sunday 11 a.m. at Canada Cove Mobile Home Rec. Hall, Half Moon Bay
Napa Napa Valley Quilters, P.O. Box 405, 94558
Nipomo Olde Towne Quilters of Nipomo, P.O. Box, 93444 Meets: 4th Thursday 10 a.m. & 6:30 p.m. at Creative Patches House
Norwalk Los Angeles County Quilt Guild, P.O. Box 252, 90651
Oakhurst Sierra Mountain Quilters Guild, P.O. Box 1359, 93644
Oceanside El Camino Quilt Guild, P.O. Box 1952, 92051 Meets: 2nd Thursday 9:30 a.m. at First Lutheran Church Trinity Center, 1410 Foothill Dr., Vista
Orange Orange County Quilters Guild, P.O. Box 3108, 92857 Meets: 2nd Tuesday at 6:45 p.m. at St. Joseph Center Auditorium
Oroville Oroville Piecemakers Quilt Guild, P.O. Box 1604, 95965
Pacific Grove Monterey Pen. Quilters Guild, P.O. Box 1025, 93950
Palmdale High Country Quilters, P.O. Box 900384, 93550
Palmdale Southern CA Council of Quilt Guilds, 2342 W. Avenue N.
Paradise Ridge Quilters Guild, P.O. Box 1668, 95969
Pebble Beach Northern California Quilt Club, 2935 Sloat Rd, 93953
Petaluma Petaluma Quilt Guild, P.O. Box 5334, 94955
Petaluma Quilt Guild East Bay Heritage Quilters, P.O. Box 6223, 94706
Pine Grove Sierra Gold Quilt Guild, P.O. Box 1078, 95665
Pioneertown Cactus Sew-Ables Quilt Guild, P.O. Box 317, 92268
Placentia North Cities Quilt Guild Meets: 4th Monday 7 p.m. at Placentia Presbyterian Church
Pleasant Hill Guild of Quilters of Contra Costa County, P.O. Box 23871, 94523
Pleasanton Amador Valley Quilters, P.O. Box 955, 94566
Porterville Porterville Quilters, P.O. Box 1881, 93257
Poway Friendship Quilters, P.O. Box 1174, 92074 Meets: 2nd Monday 7 p.m. at Tierra Bonita School
Red Bluff Sun Country Quilters, P.O. Box 8266, 96080 Meets: 4th Monday 7 p.m. at Community Center
Redding Redding Quilters Sew-ciety, P.O. Box 492581, 96409
Redlands Citrus Belt Quilters Meets: Last Friday
Redwood City Peninsula Quilters, P.O. Box 2423, 94064 Meets: Alternates day and night at San Mateo Garden Center
Reseda San Fernando Valley Quilt Assoc., P.O. Box 1042, 91337
Rocklin Rocklin Pioneer Quilt Guild, P.O. Box 126 95677
Rosemead Schoolhouse Quilt Guild, PO Box 356, 91770
Sacramento River City Quilters Guild, P.O. Box 15816, 95852
Sacramento Hawaiian Kapu Hui, 2617 Alta Arden Wy Meets: 1st Monday 10 a.m. at Material Girls
San Diego Seaside Quilt Guild, P.O. Box 9964, 92109
San Diego Canyon Quilters, 92192
San Francisco San Francisco Quilters Guild, P.O. Box 27002, 94127 Meets: 3rd Tuesday at 7:30 p.m. at 7777 Geary Blvd.
San Jose Peninsula Stitchery Guild, 15780 E. Alta Vista Way, 95127
San Juan Capistrano Beach Cities Quilters Guild, PO Box 322, 92693 Meets: 2nd Thursday at 6:45 p.m. at Marco Forster Middle School Cafetorium
San Luis Obispo San Luis Obispo Quilters
San Marcos North County Quilting Assoc., P.O. Box 982, 92079 Meets: 3rd Monday 6:30 p.m. at Joslyn Senior Center, 111 W. Richmar Ave.
San Rafael Marin Quilt Lovers, P.O.Box 6015, 94903
San Rafael Mt. Tam Quilt Guild, P.O. Box 6192, 94903 Meets: 2nd Tuesday 7 p.m. at Aldersgate Methodist Church. Contact: Susie Ernst (707) 763-0945
Santa Barbara Coastal Quilters Guild, P.O. Box 6341, 93106
Santa Clarita Santa Clarita Valley Quilt Guild, P.O. Box 802863, 91380
Santa Maria Santa Maria Valley Quilt Guild, P.O. Box 5075, 93456 Meets: 2nd Wednesday (Sept. - June) at St. Andrews Methodist Church
Santa Maria All-America City Quilters, PO Box 7217, 93456 Meets: 1st Wednesday @ 7pm at Maria Del Sol 1405 E Main St.
Santa Monica Santa Monica Quilt Guild, 11338 Santa Monica Blvd, 90025 Meets: 1st Wedneday 7pm at Felicia Mahood Senior Center
Santa Rosa Moonlighters, P.O. Box 6882, 65406
Santa Rosa Santa Rosa Quilt Guild, P.O. Box 9251, 95405
Santee Legacy Quilters, 9320 Lake Country Dr., 92071
Sierra Madre Wandering Foot QG, P.O. Box 9431, 91025
Signal Hill Southern California Council of Quilt Guilds, 1857 Temple Ave. #106, 90804
Simi Valley Simi Valley Quilt Guild, P.O. Box 3689, 93093 Meets: 2nd Wednesday at 7 p.m. at Senior Center
Sonoma Sonoma Valley Quilters, 1463 Mission Drive, 95476
South Lake Tahoe Tahoe Quilters, 3097 Harrison Ave. Meets: Wednesdays 9:30 a.m. & 6 p.m. at Senior Center, Hwy. 50
Standard Sierra Quilt Guild of T.C., P.O. Box 43, 95373 Meets: 2nd Monday @ 7pm at Senior Center, Sonora
Stockton Tuleburg Quilt Guild, P.O. Box 692151, 95269
Tehachapi Tehachapi Mountain Quilters, 30300 Lower Valley Rd., 93561
Temecula Valley of the Mist Quilt Guild, 27475 Ynez Rd., 92391
Templeton Almond Country Quilters, P.O. Box 538, 93465 Meets: 1st Monday at 6:30, Trinity Lutheran Church 940 Creston Rd, Paso Robles
The Sea Ranch Pacific Piecemakers' Guild
Thousand Oaks Conejo Valley Quilters, 91362 Meets: 4th Monday 6:30 p.m.
Torrance South Bay Quilters Guild, P.O. Box 6115, 90504
Truckee Truckee Quilters', 12219 Business Park Dr. #12, 96161 Meets: 2nd Tuesday @ 6:30pm at Senior Center
Truckee Bear Necessities Applique, 12219 Business Park Dr. #12, 96161 Meets: 4th Sunday @ 1pm at Donna's Stitchery
Tulare Valley Oak Quilters, P.O. Box 1093, 93275
Turlock Turlock Quilt Guild, P.O. Box 66, 95381 Meets: 2nd & 4th Monday 7pm at Cloth and Quilts
Upland Night Owl Quilters Guild, P.O. Box 5019, 91786
Vallejo Vallejo Piecemakers, P.O. Box 5515, 95381
Victorville Desert Winds Quilt Guild, P.O. Box 1989, 92392 Meets: 1st Tuesday 9 am Rick Novack Community Center 13558 Palm Street, Hesperia
West Covina T L C Quilters' Guild, 91791
Woodland Hills Afro-American Quilters, 22544 Califa, 91367
Yorba Linda North Cities Quilt Guild, P.O. Box 376, 92886 Meets: 4th Monday @ 6:45pm at Placentia Presbyterian Church
Yreka Siskiyou Country Quilter Guild Meets: 3rd Saturday of Odd numbered months @ 10:30
Yuba City Valley Quilt Guild, P.O. Box 1463, 95992
Yucca Valley Cactus Sew-Ables Quilt Guild, P.O. Box 298, 92284 Meets: 1st Monday at 9:30 a.m. (2nd Monday in September and January)

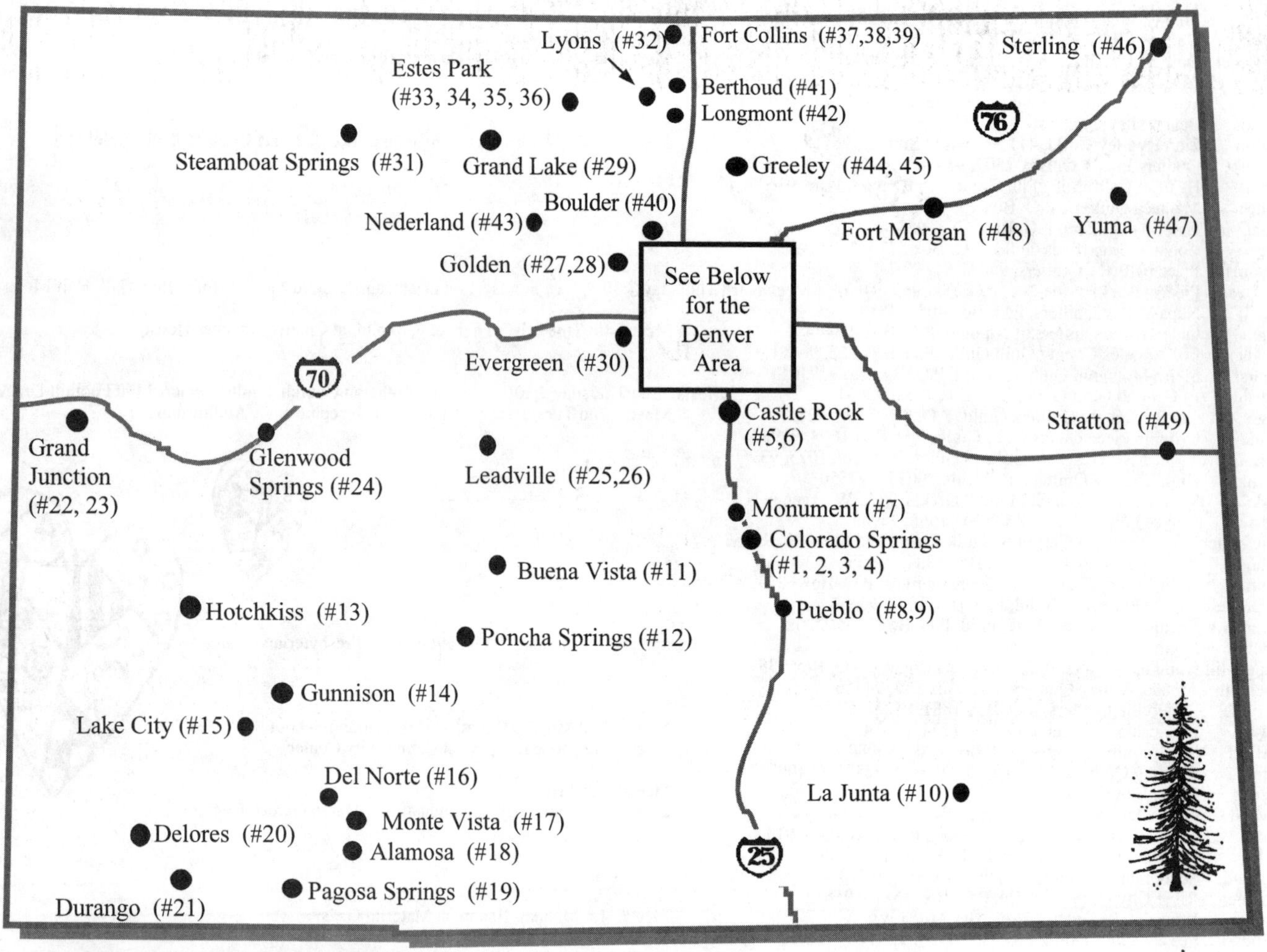

Lyons (#32)
Fort Collins (#37,38,39)
Sterling (#46)
Estes Park (#33, 34, 35, 36)
Berthoud (#41)
Longmont (#42)
76
Steamboat Springs (#31)
Grand Lake (#29)
Greeley (#44, 45)
Boulder (#40)
Nederland (#43)
Fort Morgan (#48)
Yuma (#47)
Golden (#27,28)
See Below for the Denver Area
Evergreen (#30)
70
Castle Rock (#5,6)
Stratton (#49)
Grand Junction (#22, 23)
Glenwood Springs (#24)
Leadville (#25,26)
Monument (#7)
Colorado Springs (#1, 2, 3, 4)
Buena Vista (#11)
Hotchkiss (#13)
Pueblo (#8,9)
Poncha Springs (#12)
Gunnison (#14)
Lake City (#15)
Del Norte (#16)
La Junta (#10)
Monte Vista (#17)
Delores (#20)
Alamosa (#18)
25
Durango (#21)
Pagosa Springs (#19)

59 Featured Shops

COLORADO

Lafayette (#50)
Broomfield (#51)
Westminster (#52)
70
Wheatridge (#58)
Denver (#53,57)
225
Littleton (#55,56)
Parker (#54)
470
Centennial (#59)

Colorado Springs, CO #1

Mon - Fri 10 - 5:30
Sat 9:30 - 5:30
Sun 1 - 4

LadyBugHill quilts.com

618 N. Tejon 80903
(719) 593-5949
www.ladybughillquilts.com

Fun, fabric and inspiration!
A friendly place to let your quilting imagination grow!

Unitah Ave.
Cache le Pudre
Home Lighting
Lady Bug Quilts
618
Episcopal Church
I - 25
Cascade Ave.
Nevada
Bijou
Tejon

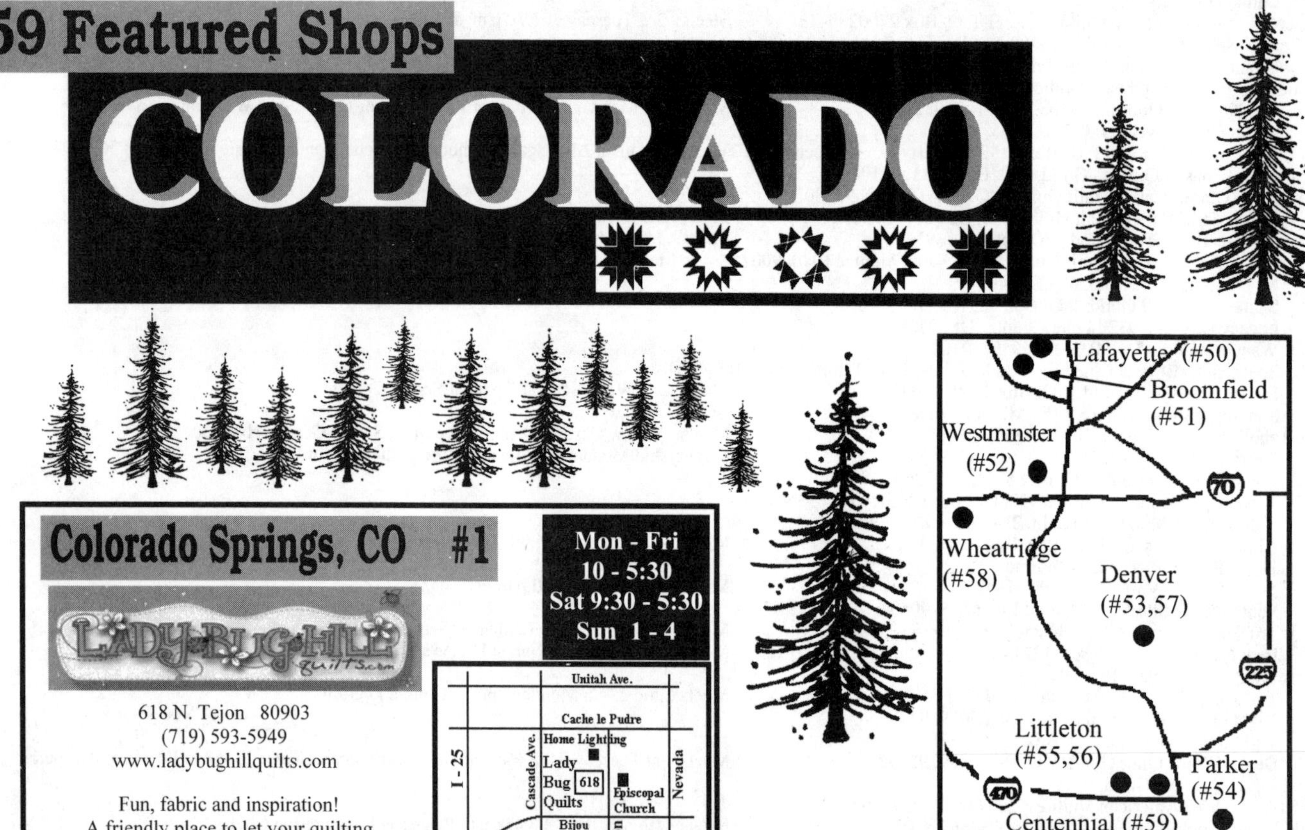

Husqvarna VIKING

RUTH'S Stitchery

www.ruthonline.net

Colorado Springs, CO #2

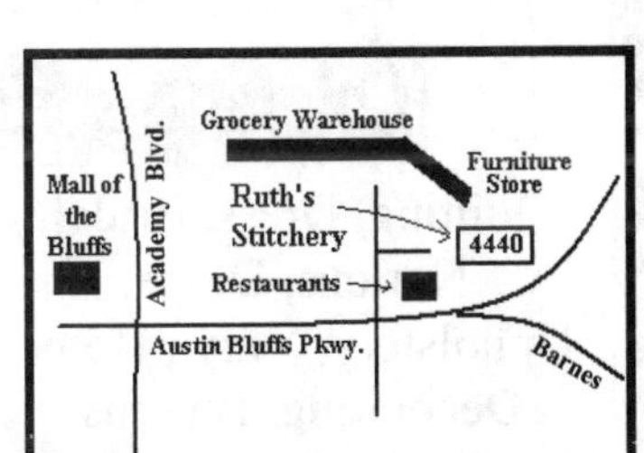

4440 Austin Bluffs Pkwy. 80918
Toll Free (888) 591-8803
(719) 591-1717 Fax: (719) 591-5356
Owner: Ruth V. Warren RStichery@aol.com
Est: 1984 7500 sq.ft. 5000 Bolts 1200 Quilt Book Titles
M/C-Visa-Discover-American Express

Mon - Sat 9 - 6 Thur til 9 Sun 12 - 5

- Hand & Machine Quilting
- Beginning to Advanced Sewing
- Counted X-Stitch / Hardanger / Tatting

Authorized Husqvarna Viking Sewing Machine / Serger Dealer and Service center for Colorado Springs area.

Fabrics
Notions
Books
Patterns
Classes

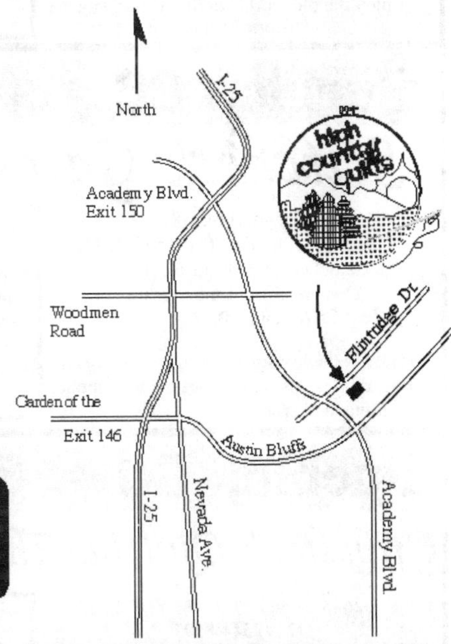

When only the best will do, think of

High Country Quilts

4771 North Academy Blvd. • Colorado Springs • CO • 80918
(719) 598-1312 • http://www.hcquilts.com • eMail: hcquilts@frii.com
Mon–Sat 9:30–6:00 • Tues 9:30–7:00 • Sun 1:00–5:00

Colorado Springs, CO #3

Mill Outlet Fabric Shop

2906 N. Prospect Street 80907
(719) 632-6296
Web Site: www.MillOutletFabric.com
Est: 1965 11000 sq. ft.

Mon 8 - 8
Tue - Sat 8 - 6

Colorado Springs, CO #4

Quilting, Dress, Bridal, Notions, Drape, Upholstery, Vinyl, Home Decorating, Buttons, Books & Batting!
Colorado's Best Selection of Fabric & Supplies!

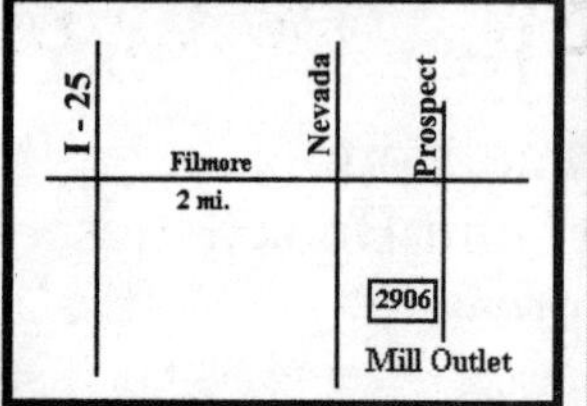

Castle Rock, CO #5

Mon - Fri 10 - 6
Thur til 7:30
Sat 10 - 5

Sew-Ciety

4714 Milestone Ln., Unit G 80104
(720) 733-8102 Fax: Same
sew-ciety@starband.net
Est: 2004 1960 sq.ft. 600+ Bolts

We carry the whole nine yards . . . .
Viking machines, Quilt Fabrics, Notions, Thread and much more.
Friendly & Fun Service!

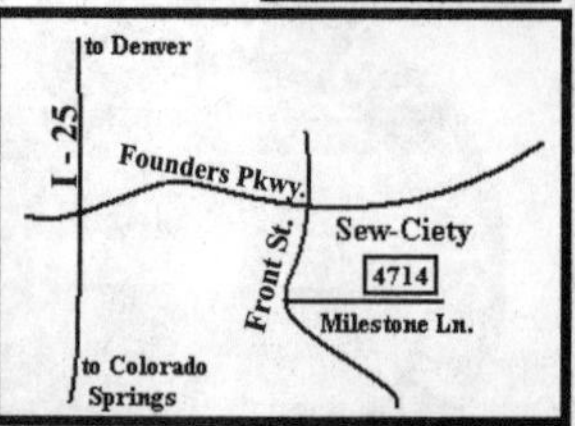

Castle Rock, CO #6

Mon - Fri 10 - 6
Sat 9 - 5
Sun 12 - 4

PLUM CREEK Quilts

981 N. Park St. 80104
(303) 663-9181
Est: 1998
Owner: Mardean Haines
www.plumcreekquilts.net

100% cotton Fabric, Books, Patterns, Notions, Classes.

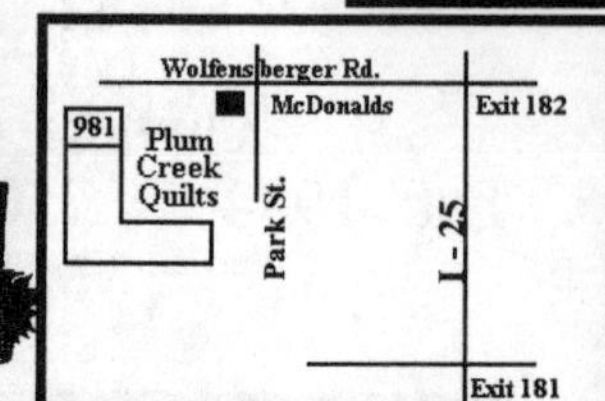

Monument, CO #7

Tues - Fri 10 - 5
Sat 10 - 2

The Quilted Cottage

341 Front St.
P.O. Box 237 80132
(719) 481-4887
Owner: Karen Hadfield
Est: 1997 1500 sq.ft.

Quality quilting fabrics & notions, quilt classes.
Enjoy the old world charm of shopping in Historic Monument Village!

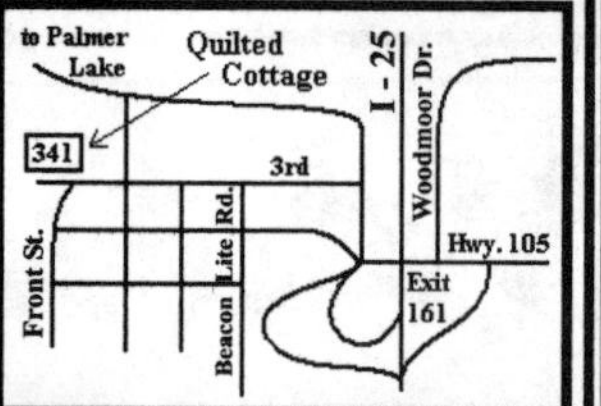

Pueblo, CO #8

Tues - Sat 10 - 5

Stitcher's Garden

319 S. Union Ave. 81003
(719) 545-3320 Fax: (719) 545-3307
stitchersgarden@msn.com
Owners: Susie Cunningham & Nancy Piazza

Located in the historic district, we feature fine cotton fabrics, patterns, books, and supplies for quilting and cross stitch.

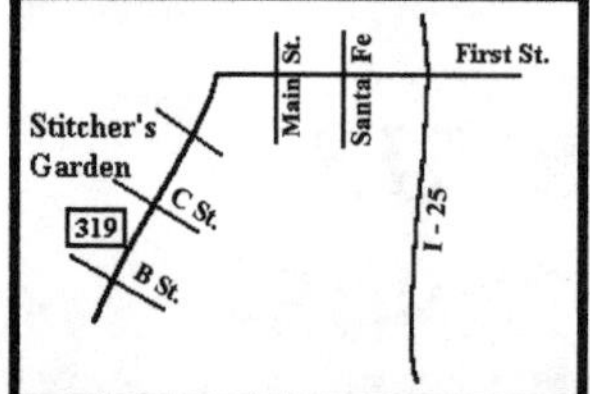

Pueblo, CO #9

Mon 12 - 5:30
Tues - Fri 10 - 5:30
Sat 10 - 5

Grandma's Quilting Threads

2648 Santa Fe Dr. #8 81006
(719) 544-8897
Owner: Kibbie Balsick
Est: 2000

Great variety of 100% cotton fabrics, books, notions, patterns and friendly service.
Classes available.

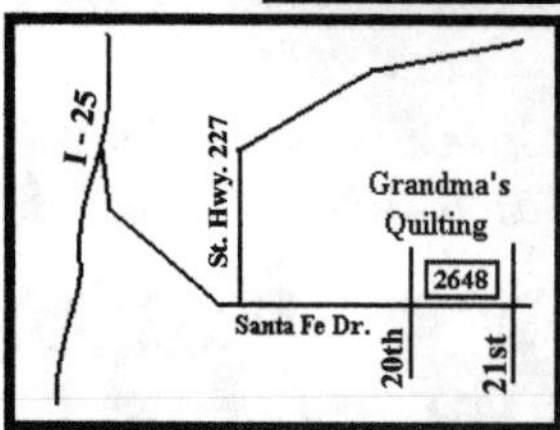

Itchin' to Stitch

Quilting Fabric & Supplies

Est: 2000

La Junta, CO #10

409 W. 3rd St. 81050
(719) 384-9050 or (888) 384-9050
Owner: Debbie Autry
www.itchintostitch.com
debbie_autry@hotmail.com

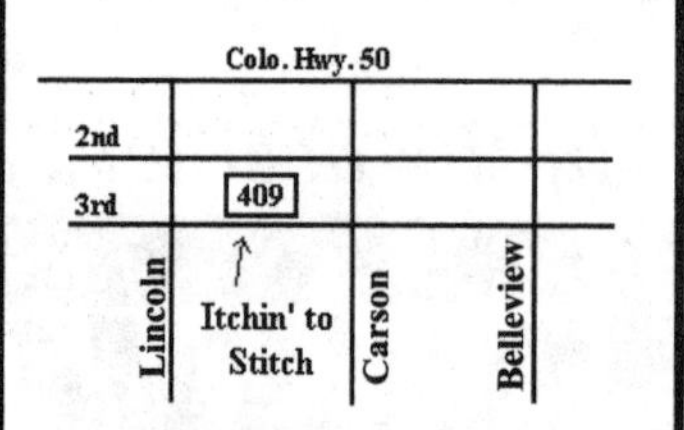

Mon - Fri 9 - 5:30
Mon til 9
Sat 9 - 4

We specialize in quality quilting fabrics, notions & classes. Friendly service always available. Stop in anytime, we enjoy meeting new people and sharing ideas.

Buena Vista, CO #11

Mon - Fri 9:30 - 5 Sat 9:30 - 3

Bev's Stitchery

202 Tabor St. P.O. Box 1773 81211
(719) 395-8780
Owner: Bev Zabloudil Est: 1977

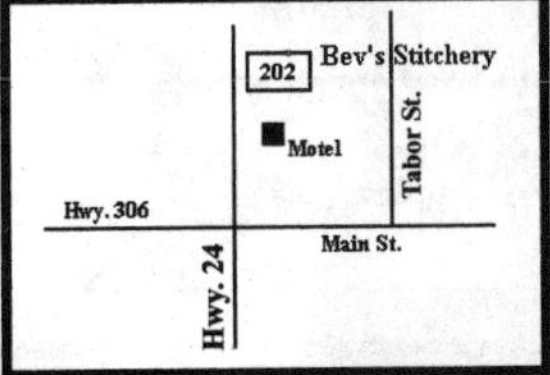

Quilting, Fabrics, Notions & Tools. Fine Needlework Supplies. Large Selection of Books. Quilting, Counted Cross-Stitch, Crochet & Knitting. Classes too!

Poncha Springs, CO #12

Mon - Sat 9:30 - 4

Quilt Studio

145 Sabeta Ave., P.O. Box 339 81242
(719) 530-9900 Fax: (719) 530-9901
mail@quilt-studio.com
www.quilt-studio.com
Owners: Fran & Jack Switzer

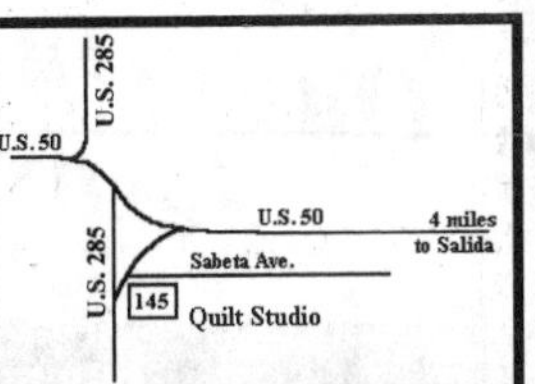

Quilt Studio is a full service shop, offering an extensive collection of fabrics, and a wide variety of notions, books, classes and machine embroidery supplies. We also carry Janome.

Hotchkiss, CO #13

Mon - Sat 9 - 5

The Quilt Patch

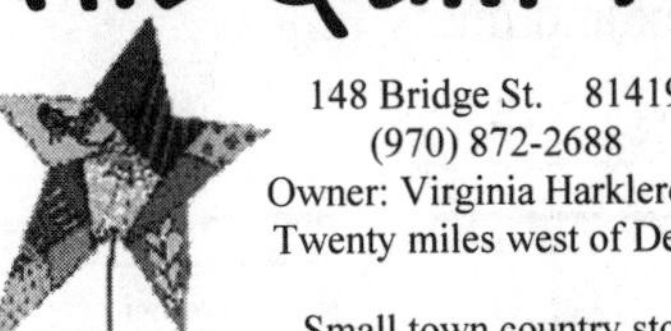

148 Bridge St. 81419
(970) 872-2688
Owner: Virginia Harkleroad
Twenty miles west of Delta

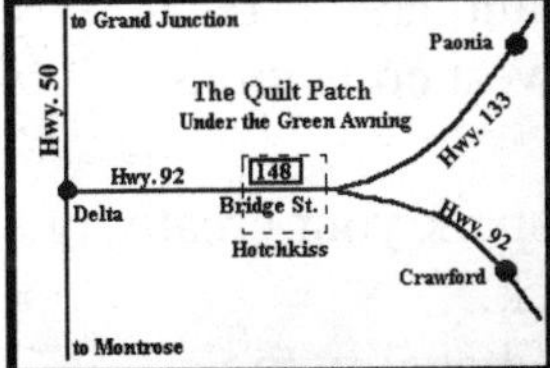

Small town country store atmosphere. Pull up a chair and visit. Over 1100 bolts.

Gunnison, CO #14

Mon - Sat Summer 9 - 5:30 Sun 12 - 4 Winter 10 - 5:30 Sun Closed

E & P Sewing Emporium

135 N. Main St. 81230
(970) 641-0474
Owner: Mary Spann
Est: 1985 2000 sq.ft.

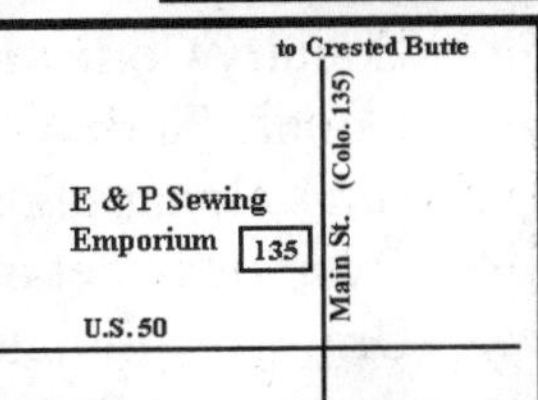

We offer Janome Sewing Machines, Quilting and Yarn Supplies and Classes. Our Quilt Festival is the last three weeks in August.

Lake City, CO #15

School Year Sat 10:30 - 5:30 Summers Tues - Sat 10:30 - 5:30

Silver Threads Quilt Shop

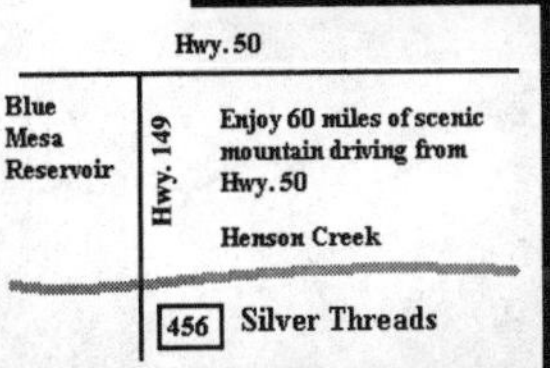

456 S. Gunnison Ave. P.O. Box 1178 81235
(970) 944-0171 Owner: Jennifer Evans
silverthreads@gunnison.com
Tiny quilt shop in an historic mountain town. Specializing in hand sewing and quilting supplies, fabrics and classes. Est: 2002

Del Norte, CO #16

Mon - Sat 10 - 5

Kathy's Fabric Trunk

16179 W. Hwy. 160 81132
(877) 873-0211
fabtrunk@fone.net
Owner: Kathy Black
Est: 2001

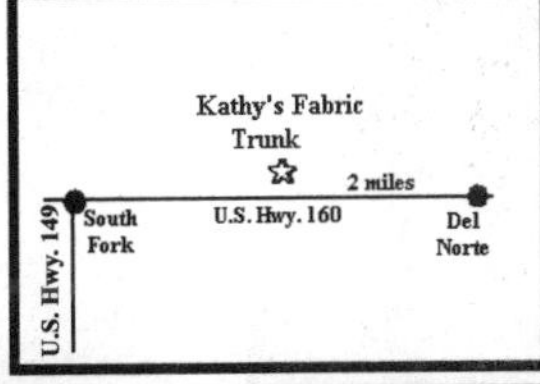

Fabrics, Patterns, Notions, Classes, Books, Floss
One day classes for busy travelers.
Come see our selection!

Monte Vista, CO #17

Mon - Fri 10 - 5 Sat 10 - 3

Shades, Quilts & Etc.

129 Adams St. 81144
(719) 852-2179 Fax: Same
jadavey@amigo.net

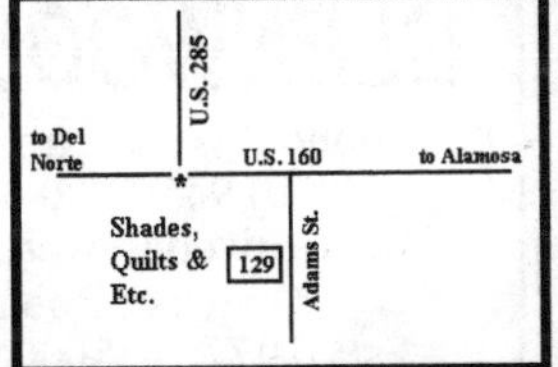

Window Covering & Quilt Shop.
Quilting Supplies including a wide selection of fabrics, notions, books & patterns. DMC Floss, Janome Sewing Machines.

Alamosa, CO #18

Mon - Fri 9:30 - 5:30 Sat 9:30 - 4

Gray Goose Fabrics

616 Main St. 81101
(719) 589-6982
Owners: Gail Mattive & Kerry Worley
2000+ Bolts 800 Books / Patterns

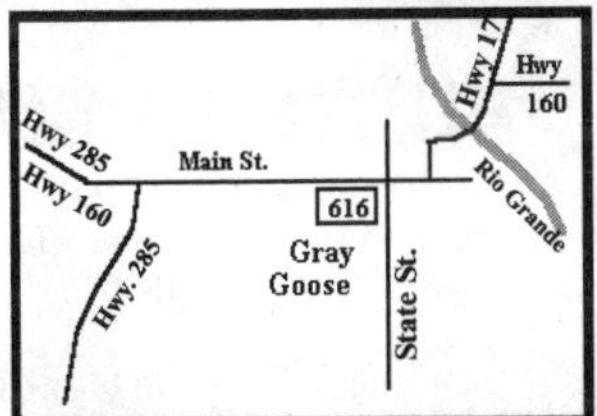

100% Cottons & quilting notions & supplies, books, and patterns.
Daytime, evening and Saturday Classes.

Pagosa Springs, CO #19

Mon - Sat 7 - 6

2435 Eagle Dr., P.O. Box 1800 81147
(970) 731-4111 Fax: (970) 731-4455
Ponderosa@pagosa.net

PONDEROSA Do it Best Home Center

www.ponderosa.doitbest.com

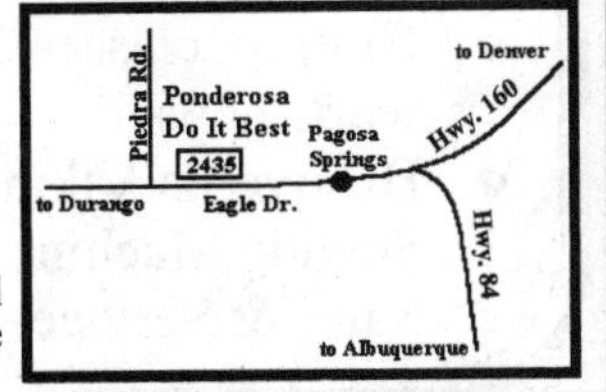

You'll be pleasantly surprised at the wonderful quilt fabrics, patterns, etc., tucked away inside our Do It Best hardware store.

Dolores, CO #20

Mon - Sat 10 - 4

Quilting & Cloth Doll Supplies

202 Railroad Ave., P.O. Box 357 81323
(970) 882-3389 Fax: (970) 892-3155
Owner: Virginia Robertson Est: 2000
1700 sq.ft. 3000 Bolts Catalog $3

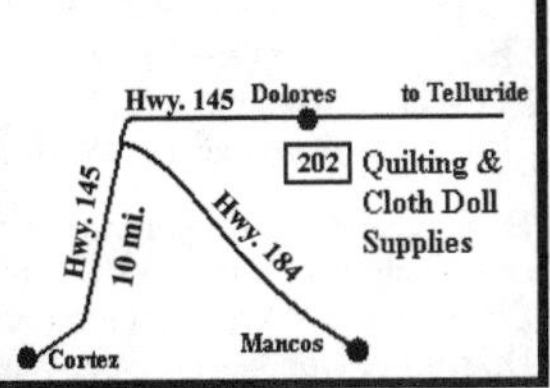

3000 bolts of wild fabrics. We consider lime green a *neutral*! Books, patterns, Virginia Robertson fabrics, classes, Pfaff & Viking Machines. Located in a log cabin in the mountains.

Durango, CO #21

"Home of Quilt Durango Festival"
First Weekend Of each April

Summer
Mon - Sat 9:30 - 6 Sun 1 - 5
Winter
Mon - Sat 10 - 5:30

600 Main Avenue--Downstairs
Durango, CO 81301
(970) 247-2582
Fax: (970) 375-0259
Owner: Pat Nicholas
Est: 1988

In the Heart of Durango Historic District.

- Over 4000 bolts of quality cotton. Complete collections by Moda, RJR, Benartex and many more
- Country Corner highlights the latest Thimbleberries and Homespuns
- Flannel Fantasy Section has 100's of bolts of the newest collections.
- Batik Bonanza features the best of Hoffman
- Over 2600 feet of ***amazing*** displays and samples to spark your creativity
- Original quilt kits. Over 300 Quilt book titles in stock.
- Free use of Bernina and Janome sewing machines and quality tools when attending our classes.

www.durangoquiltcompany.com

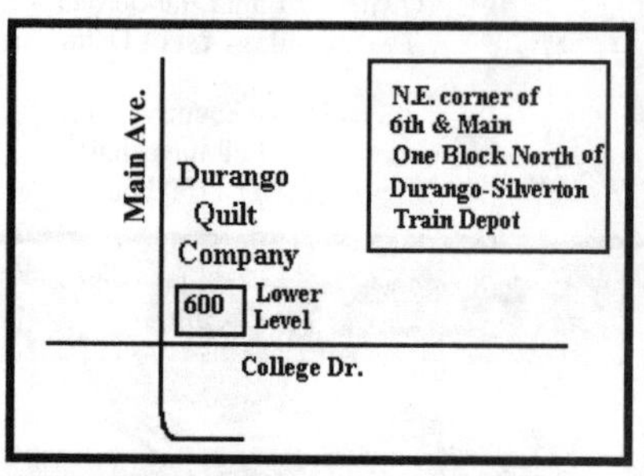

Grand Junction, CO #22

Open 7 Days a week.

Quilters' Corner, Inc.

443 Main St. 81501
Downtown Historic Grand Junction
(970) 255-8838 or (800) 255-4863

Over 3000 bolts, hundreds of books and patterns.

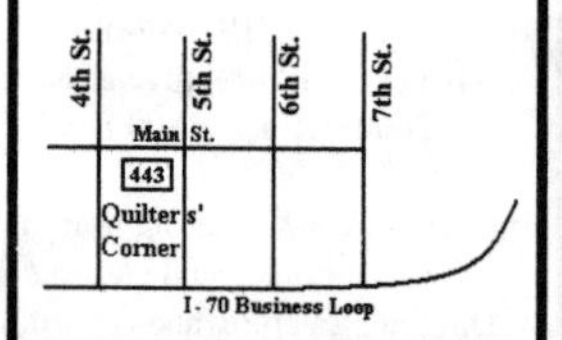

Grand Junction, CO #23

Mon - Sat 9:30 - 5:30

Hi Fashion Fabrics, Inc.

2586 Patterson Rd. 81505
(970) 242-1890 Fax: (970) 243-0360
jpvlefty@aol.com
Owners: Arlene & Jeff Vogel 18,000 sq.ft.
Est: 1965 Over 10,000 Bolts of fabric

Huge Selection of Quilting Cottons, Books, and Supplies. Complete Line of Other Fabrics: Bridal, Fashion, Outer Wear, Drapery & Upholstery, Boat Vinyl.

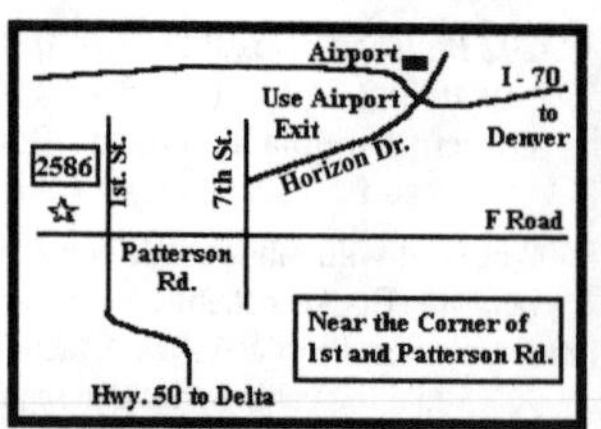

GLENWOOD SEWING CENTER

822 Grand Ave., Glenwood Springs, CO 81601
(970) 945-5900 or (800) 371-5967
glenwoodsew@compuserve.com
Owners: Bob & Sandy Boyd
Est: 1977 5000 sq.ft. 2500 Bolts

Mon - Sat 10 - 6
Sun 11 - 4

Glenwood Springs, CO #24

- Over 2,500 bolts
- Full line of books & notions
- Quilting classes & workshops
- Husqvarna Viking Sewing Machine Sales & Service.

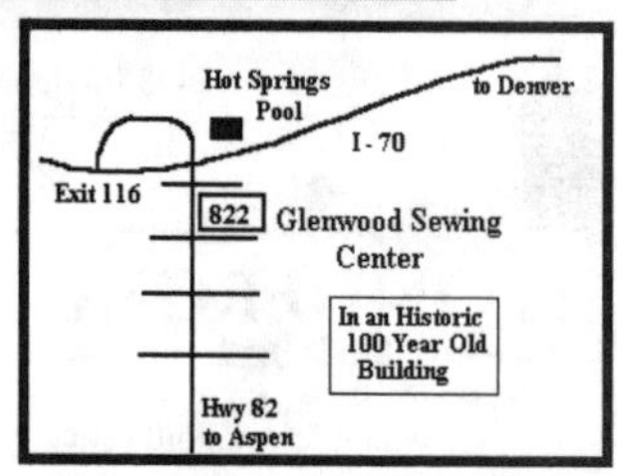

Take 1 - 70 to exit 116. First block after the bridge in downtown.

Leadville, CO #25

Hrs. Vary Please Call First

Mtn. Top Quilts

129 E. 7th St. 80461
(719) 486-3454
Owner: Gwendolyn Shepherd
Est: 1983 ccsmtq@chaffee.net

Antique quilts, old quilt blocks & tops, vintage fabrics and laces, feed sacks, buttons & embellishments, out of print quilt books, sewing collectables.

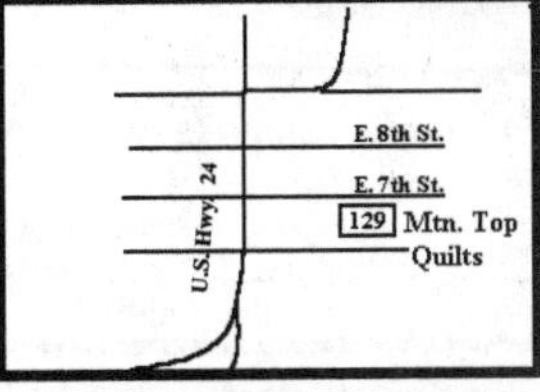

Leadville, CO #26

Mon - Sat 9 - 5

Mt. Elbert Patchwork

721 Harrison Ave. 80461
(719) 486-3243 Est: 1997
E-mail: ggg@Chaffee.net
Owner: Jane Crocker 2000 sq.ft. 2000+ Bolts

100% Cotton fabrics, notions, books, machine quilting.

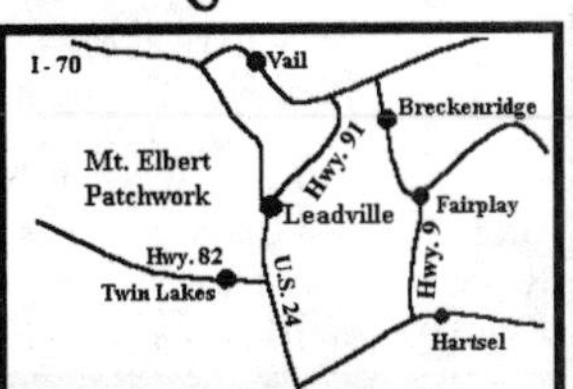

Golden, CO #27

Mon - Fri 10 - 5 Closed Weekends

Primedia Quilt Gallery

741 Corporate Circle, Suite A 80401
(303) 278-1010
Fax: (303) 277-0370

Enjoy the current quilt exhibit at the home offices of Quilter's Newsletter Magazine, Quiltmaker, and McCall's Quilting.
Free Admission.

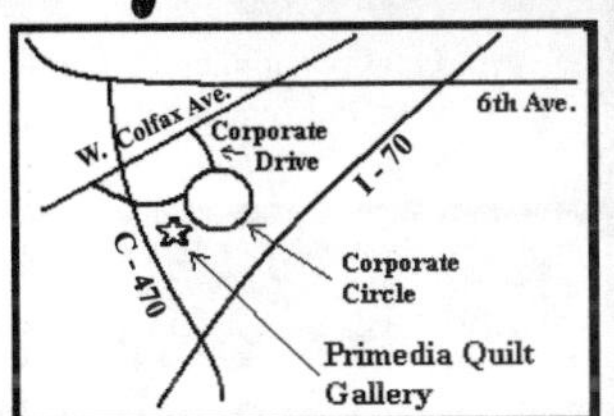

Golden, CO #28

Mon - Sat. 10 - 4

Rocky Mountain Quilt Museum

1111 Washington Ave. 80401
(303) 277-0377
Non-Profit Self Supporting Museum
www.RMQM.org
Adm: Janet E. Finley Est: 1990
Quilt Market - Gift Shop

The only Quilt Museum in the Rocky Mountains. Exhibits change 5 times a year. Send S.A.S.E. for schedule. Admission Charged

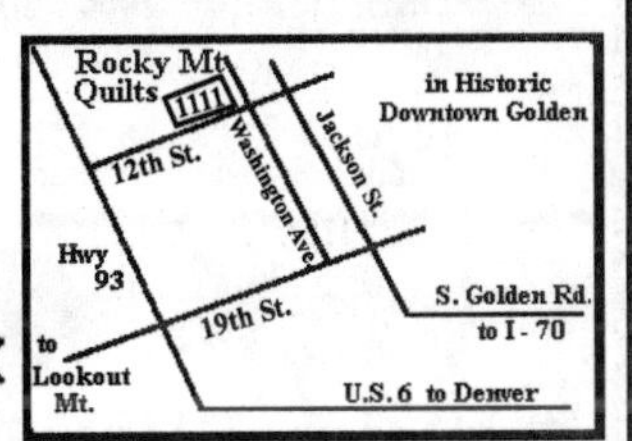

Cabin Quilts & Stitches

"A Unique Place to Shop"

For the serious quilter
Fabrics, Books, Patterns, Notions
Unique Country Gifts all in one
"Cozy" Store

908 Grand Avenue
(970) 627-3810
Grand Lake, CO 80447
Owner: Judy K. Jensen

Open Year Round

Grand Lake, CO #29

A New Store located on the Boardwalk
in beautiful Grand Lake, Colorado

Directions:
From Denver take I-70 west to U.S.40
Go North to Granby. From Granby take
U.S.34 North to Grand Lake(15 miles)
at the entrance to Rocky Mountain National Park.

Evergreen, CO #30

Mon - Sat 9:30 - 5:30 Sun 12 - 4

The Quilt Cabin

32156 S. Castle Ct. #204 80439
(303) 670-4798
Owner: Holly Engelken
Est: 1996

Great Selection Quilting Fabrics and Supplies. Reproductions, Flannels, Homespuns, and Plaids our specialty.

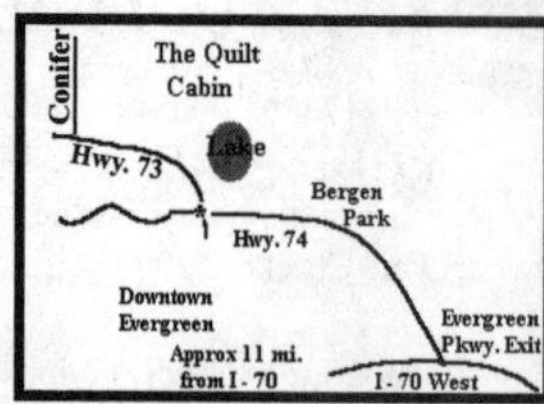

Steamboat Springs, CO #31

Mon - Sat 9:30 - 6 Sun 12 - 5

Piece by Piece

Quilting & Home Decorating

385 Anglers Dr., Suite C 80487
(970) 871-9888
Proberts@springsips.com
Owner: Millicent (Penny) Roberts

We have a great selection of fabrics and related supplies. Gifts, Classes, Machine Sales, Quilting.

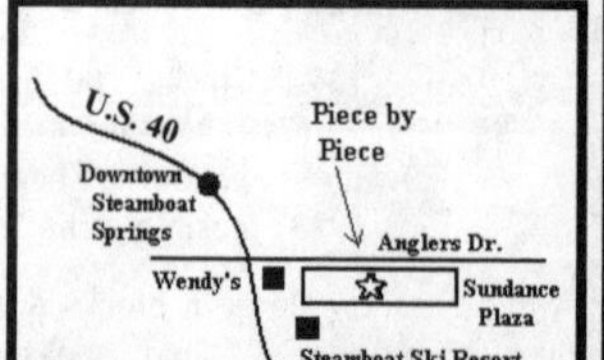

Lyons, CO #32

Mon - Sat 9:30 - 6:30 Sun 1 - 5

Quilting Hands

304 Main St., Suite C
P.O. Box 1342 80540
(303) 823-6067
Owner: Jan Rold
Est: 2000 1000 sq.ft.
3000 Bolts

Inspiration, Instruction, Fabrics, and Supplies for Quilters.

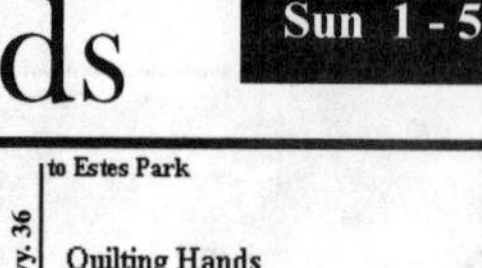

Estes Park, CO #33

Summer Open Daily 10 - 5 Winter Open Mon - Sat 10 - 5

Mountain Lady Quilt Shop Inc.

205 Park Ln., P.O. Box 436 80517
(970) 586-5330

Owner: Connie Westley
mtnladyqult@aol.com

Quality supplies for Quilters.
Custom machine and hand quilting.
Classes, mail order.

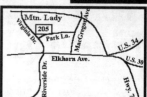

Estes Park, CO #34

Mon - Sat 10 - 5

High Country Amish Quilts

800-B Moraine Ave. 80517
(Near the South Entrance to Rocky Mtn. National Park)
(970) 577-1557
hcaq@charter.net
www.highcountryamishquilt.com

Colorado's largest selection of Amish quilts, wallhangings, pillows, rugs & table runners. Cookbooks, collectibles, teapots, angels, & other fine gifts. 1.1 miles from downtown.

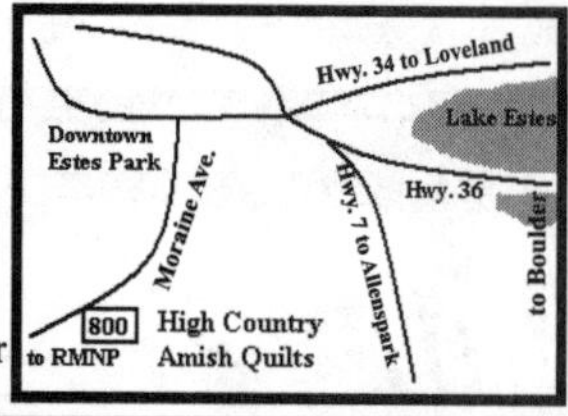

Estes Park, CO #35

Year 'round 10 - 5 Closed Wed.

242 Moraine Ave. P.O. Box 3580
(970) 586-4257 80517
Owner: Margaret McCormick
Est: 1990 1200 sq.ft.

Featuring Patterns by Colorado Designers Kits - Handmade Wooden Quilt Racks Fabrics - Christmas Projects. Largest specialty selection of Aunt Gracie's Scrap & 1930's.

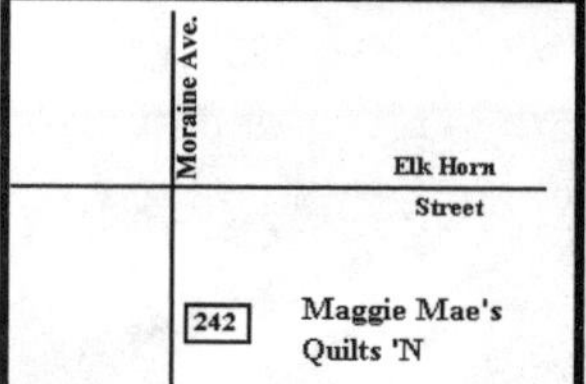

Estes Park, CO #36

Daily 10 - 5 Closed Tuesday

433 C. West Elkhorn 80517
(970) 577-7100
Owner: Judy Edwards Est: 2001
2500 sq.ft.
1000 Bolts

Lots of flannels and Lots of florals.
Large selection of gifts, candles and baskets.

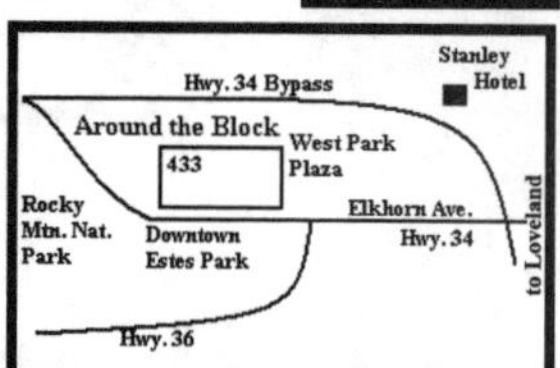

Ft. Collins, CO #38

Mon - Fri 10 - 6 Sat 10 - 5

2721 S. College Ave. 80525
(970) 223-4269 Fax: 223-4270
Quiltersgarden@frii.com
quiltersGardenshop.com
victorianCrazyQuilts.com
Owner: Susan E.H. Morehouse

Lots of Florals, Batiks and Museum Reproduction Fabrics. We carry Victorian Crazy Quilt, Silk Ribbon and Ribbonwork Supplies.

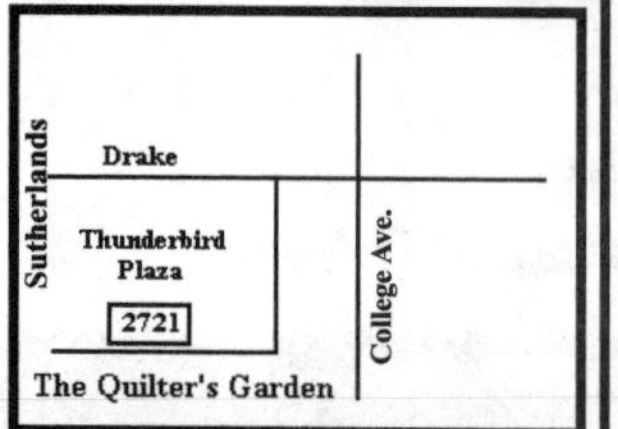

Mill Outlet Fabric Shop

2317 E. Mulberry 80521
(970) 221-0998
www.MillOutletFabric.com
Est: 1965 4000 sq. ft.

Mon - Thurs 9 - 6 Fri & Sat 9 - 5

Fort Collins, CO #37

Quilting, Dress, Bridal, Notions, Drape, Upholstery, Vinyl, Home Decorating, Buttons, Books & Batting! Colorado's Best Selection of Fabric & Supplies!

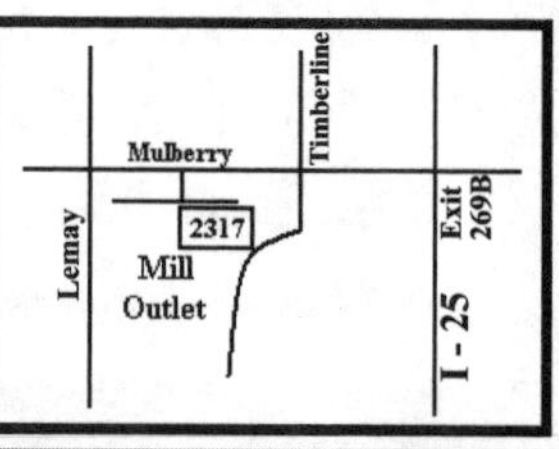

Berthoud, CO #41

Mountain Prairie Quilts

516 Mountain Ave., Berthoud CO 80513
(970) 532-3386 or (866) 532-3386
mtprairie@frii.com
www.mountainprairiequilts.com
Owner: Dana Richardson
Est: 2000 2000 sq.ft.

Mon - Fri 10 - 6
Sat 9 - 5

Quilt supplies, classes, books, 100% cotton fabrics featuring over 1800 bolts including Thimbleberries, Civil War prints, flannels, florals and much more!

We are "the Quilter Friendly Store."

Mountain Prairie Quilts
516
Mountain Ave.
Hwy. 287 to Loveland
I - 25
Hwy. 56
5.4 Miles from Exit 250

Longmont, CO #42

Mon- Sat 10 - 5:30
Mon & Thur til 7
Sun 12 - 4

The Patch Works

700 Ken Pratt Blvd. #101 80501
(303) 772-3002
Owner: Terri Miller Est: 1988
2000 sq.ft. 1600+ Bolts

Friendly atmosphere, clean bathroom, lots of fabric, books, patterns, notions.
Some one-day classes available.
Block of the Month Kits Available.

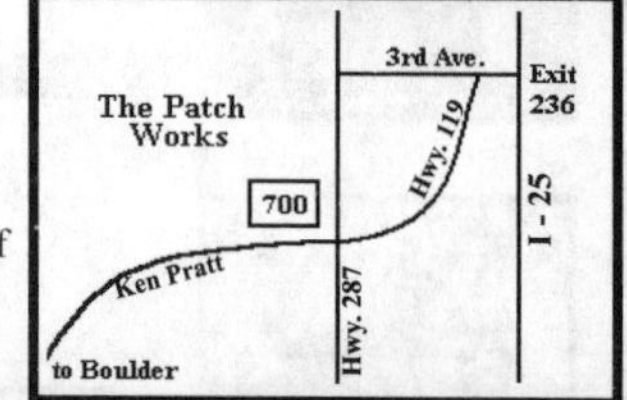

Nederland, CO #43

M, Th, F, S 11 - 5
Wed 9 - 4
Sun 11:15 - 2:30+
Tues Call Ahead

Fabric Peddlers

1 West First St. 80466-3061
(800) 670-8938 or (303) 258-0626
Fabped@peoplepc.com
www.fabricpeddlers.biz
Owner: Frances Smith
Mgr: Billie Bishop Est: 1996
Friendly Fabric store in the mountains above Boulder. Beautiful fabrics, batiks, batting, patterns, yarn & quilts. Come visit us.

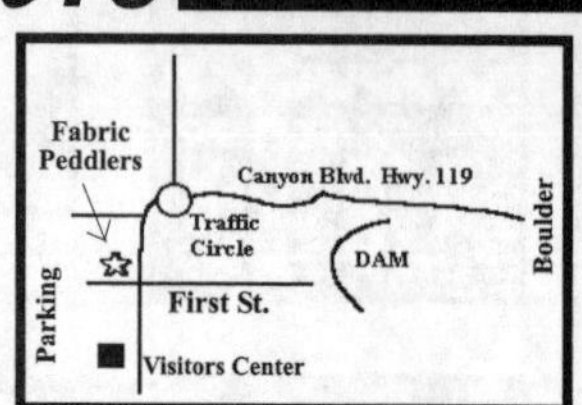

Greeley, CO #44

Mon - Fri 9:30 - 5:30
Sat 10 - 4

wild'n woolly

2308 W. 17th St. 80634
(970) 356-0335
Owner: Ruth Dixon
Est: 1978 2500 Bolts

Needlework Shop. Quilting Supplies, Hand Knitting Yarns. Needlepoint, Hardanger and Cross Stitch too!

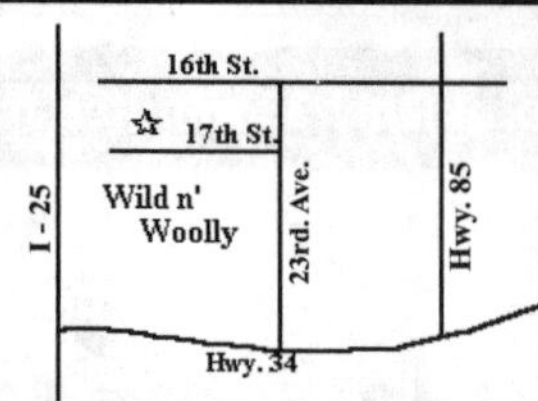

Greeley, CO #45

Mon - Fri 10 - 5:30
Sat 10 - 4

Quilter's Stash

3512 W. 10th St., #2 80634
(970) 353-6264
Fax: (970) 330-5762
Owner: Patty Winkelman
Est: 2002

Fabric, Notions, Quilt Kits, Books & Patterns, BOM

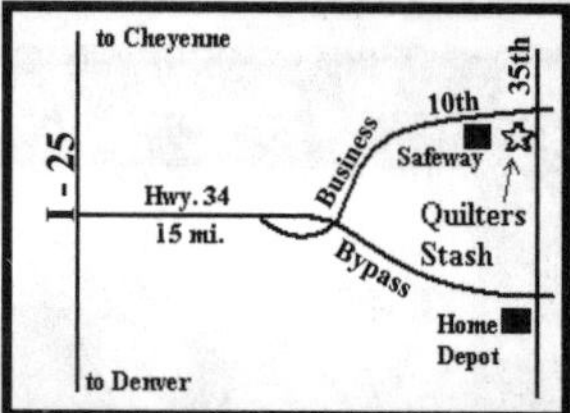

Sterling, CO #46

Mon - Sat 9 - 5:30

Quilts-N-Creations

201 Ash P.O. Box 991 80751
(970) 522-0146 Est: 1987

1000 Bolts of Printed & Solid Cottons
Bridal Headquarters for N.E. Colorado including Bridal Fabric & Trims. Tuxedo Rentals with over 70 varieties to choose from. Authorized Bernina Dealer. Custom sewing including crafts, quilts, garments or Bridal. Custom, Traditional & Heirloom Quilting.

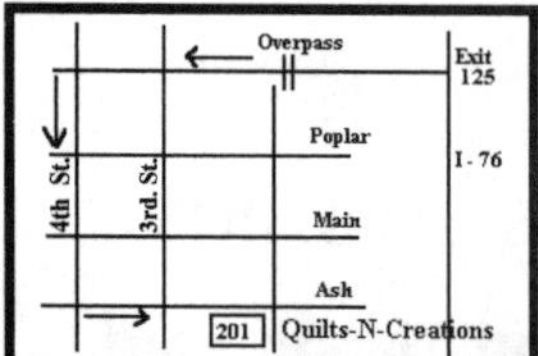

Yuma, CO #47

Tues - Fri 10 - 4
Sat 10 - 12:30

Stitches In Time

201 E. 8th Ave. 80759
(970) 848-0555 Fax: 848-3230
E-mail: junger@plains.net
Owner: Carole J. Unger
Est: 1998 700+ Bolts

A cozy quilt shop carrying 100% cotton fabrics, quilt books, patterns and notions. Classes and Machine Quilting Available.

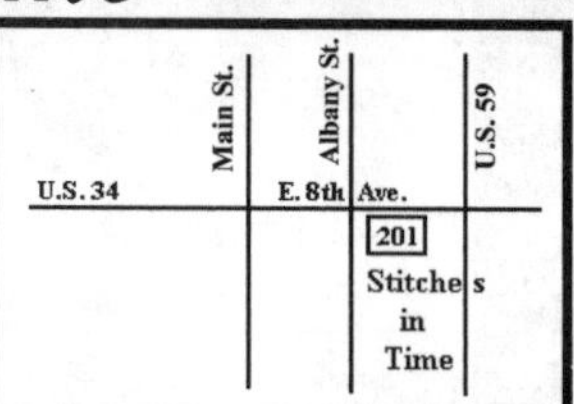

Ft. Morgan, CO #48

Mon - Sat 10 - 5

Inspirations

423 Main St. #300 80701
(970) 542-0810
Web Site: www.inspirations-quilts.com

Owners: Ginger McCafferty & Nancy Hocheder
Top quality fabrics, quilt books & patterns; kits; doll & critter patterns & many quilting supplies. You'll enjoy seeing our large selection of models.

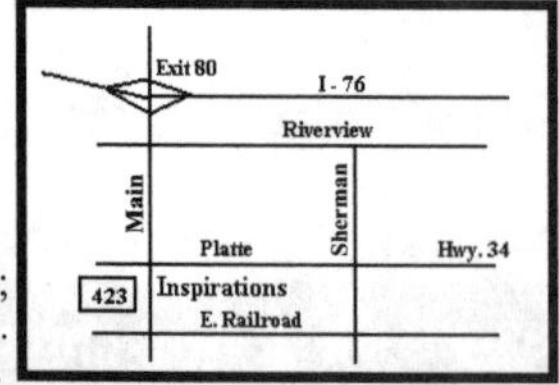

Stratton, CO #49

Tues - Sat 9:30 - 5:30

Benay's Country Quiltin'

32131 Cty. Rd. HH 80836
(970) 362-4650 Fax: (970) 348-5650
bobbenay@plainstel.com
Owner: Benay Brachtenbach
Est: 1999 500 Bolts-Great up-to-date selections
No joke - Country Quiltin' means what it says. We are in the country. Old farm house built 100 years ago. Plain but functions now as a great quilt shop. Machine quilting, classes, fabric, notions & books/patterns. Special Orders Welcome.

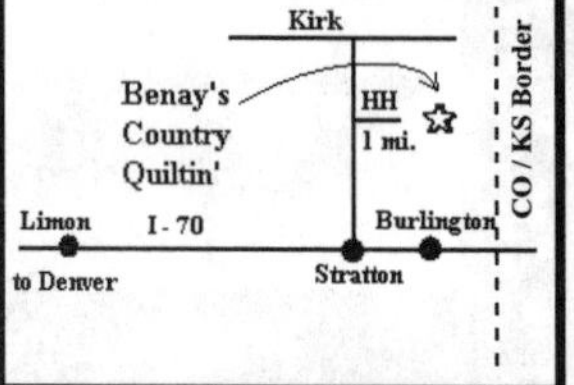

Cabin Fever Quilts & More

2695 N. Park Dr. #102 Lafayette, CO 80026
(303) 664-1877 Fax: (303) 664-1887
Owners: Kathy Lewis & Monika Koenig
Est: 1996 2500+ Bolts

cabinfever@mho.com
www.cabinfeverquilts.com

Arapahoe Rd.
Cabin Fever Quilts
North Park Dr.
Hwy. 7
I - 25
Baseline Rd.
S. Boulder Rd.
95th St. / Hwy. 42
Hwy. 287
Hwy. 36

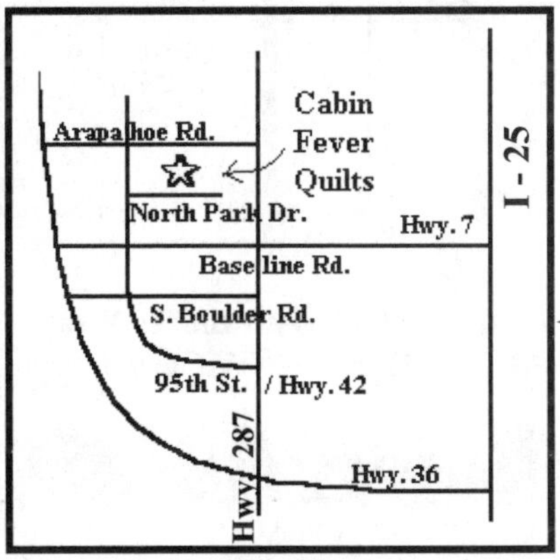

Bring in this ad for a 10% discount on Fabrics, books, notions and patterns.

Over 2500 bolts of gorgeous fabrics. Classes Galore. Books, Patterns, & Notions. Tons of Fat Quarters. Friendly, Expert Staff.

30 minutes from downtown Denver.

Mon - Fri 10 - 6
Sat 10 - 5
Sun 12 - 4

Great "homey" atmosphere. Sit by the fireplace and check out our newest books. Classes nearly every day.

Lafayette, CO #50

Mon - Fri 10-5:30
Sat 10-5
Sun 12-4

DRY CREEK QUILTS

At
Willow Run

(303) 465-2526
drycreekquilts@attglobal.net

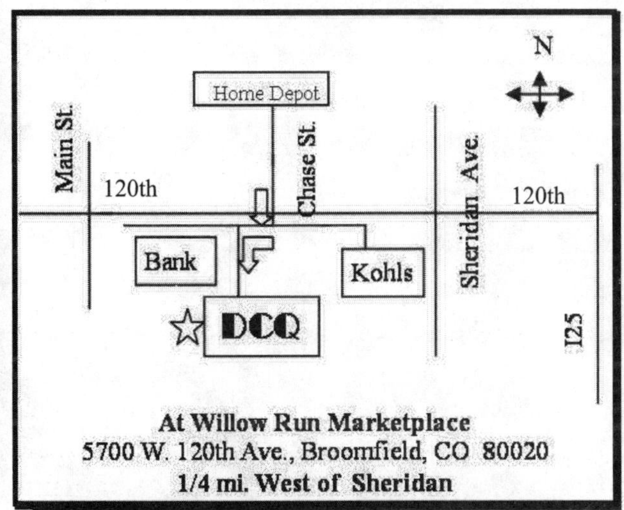

Broomfield, CO #51

4000+ Bolts

Books / Patterns

Notions / Classes

Batiks / Flannels

Brites / Florals

Let us help you put it all together!

Owners: Jo-Anne & Bruce Ginther

Tomorrow's Heirlooms

A Fine Quiltmaking Establishment

1005 W 120th, Suite 500
Westminster, CO 80234
303-457-3888
www.quiltshop.us
info@quiltshop.us

Gammill Quilting Systems

Sales, Service, Parts, Supplies, Training, and Rental

Quilting Supplies
100 % Cotton Fabric
Batiks and Brights
Templates, Notions, Tools,
Books & Patterns,
Quilt Hangers & Gifts
Thread
Machine Embroidery Supplies

Classes for the Beginner and Experienced Quilter
Hand And Machine Quilting.
Traditional, Contemporary, and Art Quilting Techniques.
Comfortable Classroom.

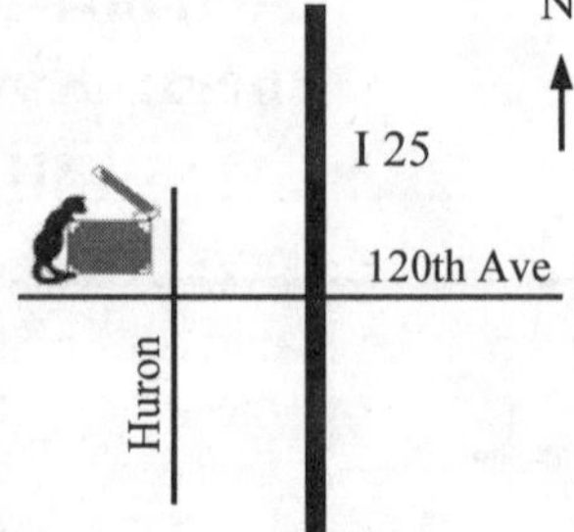

Denver

On 120th Ave Only Two Blocks West of I-25 at Huron - NW Corner

Westminster, CO #52

Mon. - Fri. 9:30 to 6:00
Saturday 9:30 to 5:00
Sunday Noon to 5:00
Open until 8:00 on Wednesday Nights

Great American Quilt Factory

Owners: Lynda Milligan & Nancy Smith

Home of Possibilities®
publishers of I'll Teach Myself and Possibilities® books

Over **5,000** bolts of cotton fabric, books, notions, and more!

Photo transfer & machine quilting services too!

Open 7 days a week!

8970 E. Hampden Ave
Denver, CO 80231
1.8 miles east of I-25 on Hampden - Exit 201
1-800-474-2665 • 303-740-6206

I-70
N
6th Ave
Peña Blvd to Airport
I-25
Colorado
Monaco
Havana
Yosemite
Hampden
I-225

www.greatamericanquilt.com

HIGH PRAIRIE QUILTS

2000+ Bolts of fabric, books, patterns, notions. Classes for everyone, from beginner to the most advanced quilter. A variety of Block of the Month quilt programs. Come visit our newly expanded, customer friendly shop. Now with over 3500 sq. ft. of quilting heaven.

Our Store Hours:
Mon - Sat 9:30 - 5:30.
Sun. 12- 4:30
Wed. evening now open till 8pm

Visit our website at
www.highprairiequilts.com

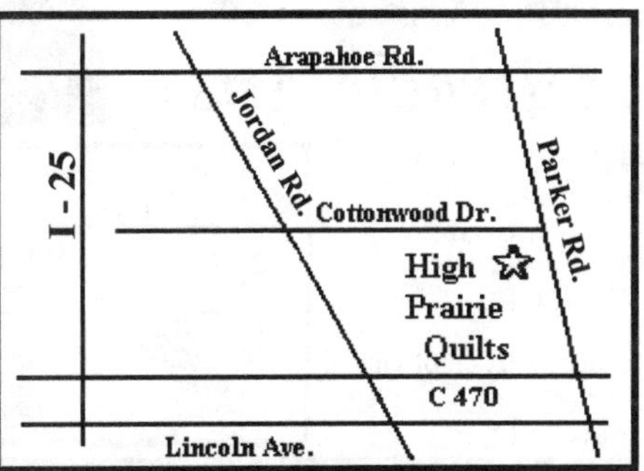

Parker, CO #54

17920 Cottonwood Dr., Parker, Colorado 80134
303- 627-0878

fabric EXPRESSIONS

A Unique Quilt Shop

Littleton, CO #55

5950 S. Platte Canyon Rd. #D12 80123
(303) 798-2556
fabricexpressions@msn.com
Owners: Toni Phillips & Juanita Simonich
Est: 1994 4200 sq.ft. 3500+ bolts

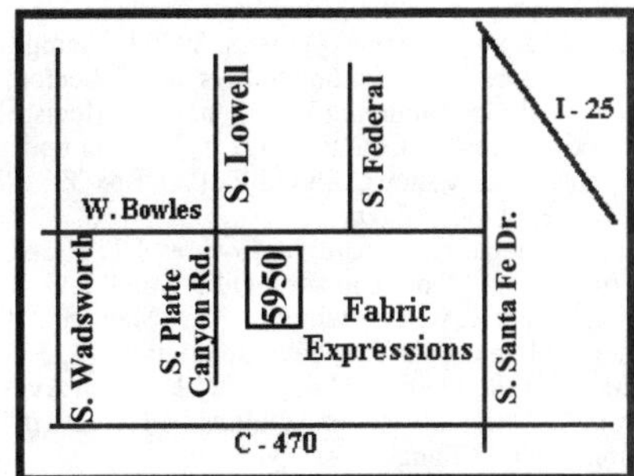

Mon - Fri
9:30 - 6
Tues til 8
Sat 10 - 5

100% Cottons! Homespuns, Flannels, Plaids, Prints, Solids. Books, Notions, Classes.
www.fabricexpressions.com

Catalog of Our Patterns SASE
Monthly Block of the Month Club

Home of "Fabric Expressions" patterns & books.

Littleton, CO #56

Mon - Wed 10 - 8
Thurs - Sat 10 - 5
Sun 12 - 4

The Creative Needle

6905 South Broadway #113 80122
(303) 794-7312
www.thecreativeneedle.com
Owner: Marge Serck
Est: 1978 3500 sq.ft. 2000 Bolts

One stop for quilting, cross-stitch, heirloom and smocking. Elna and Baby Lock machine sales and service.

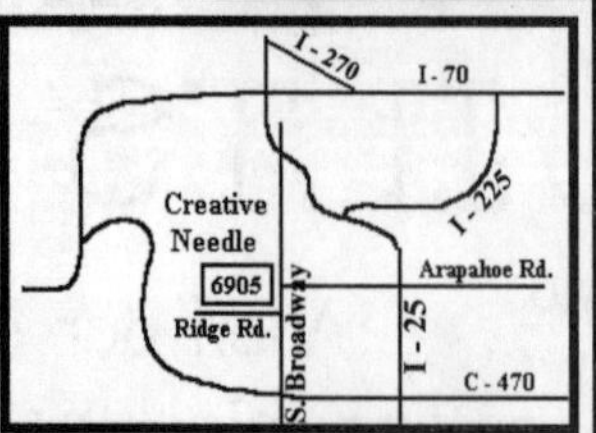

Denver, CO #57

Mon - Sat
9:30-5:30
Tues til 7:30
Sun 12 - 4

Quilts in the Attic

1025 South Gaylord St. 80209
(303) 744-8796
Est: 1972 1500 sq.ft.

Fabric - all 100% cotton - Books, Patterns, Batting, Notions, Quilting Services.
Ideas and Friendly Service. Classes.

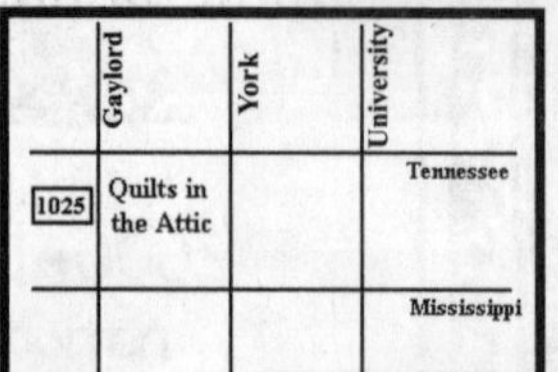

Wheatridge, CO #58

Mon - Fri
9:30 - 5
Sat 9:30 - 4

Harriet's Treadle Arts

6390 West 44th Ave. 80033
(303) 424-2742
www.harriethargrave.com
Owner: Harriet Hargrave
3600 sq.ft. Est: 1981

Over 5000 bolts - largest selection of vintage reproduction fabrics in Colorado.
Come See Us ! !

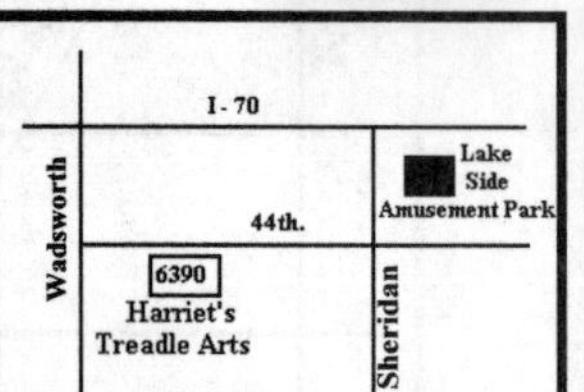

Centennial, CO #59

Mon - Sat
10 - 6
Tues til 7:30
Sun 12 - 4

Quilting up a Storm

7424 S. University, Suite D 80122
(720) 529-9659
Owner: Holly Engelken

Fabric - All 100% Cotton, Books, Patterns, Batting, Notions, Quilting Services, Classes.
Ideas and Friendly Service.

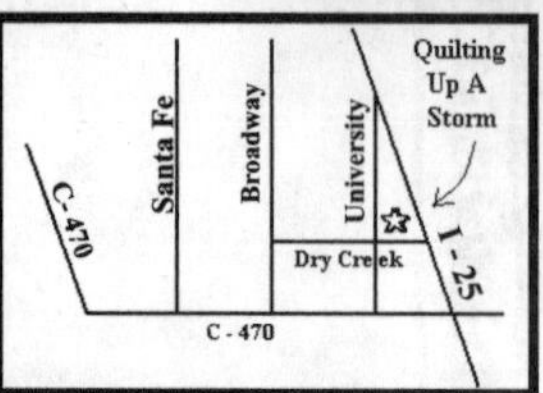

Other Shops in Colorado: *We suggest calling first*

Bayfield	The Rose Patch, 39722 U.S. Highway 160	970-884-9065
Breckenridge	Honeysuckle Rose Quilts, 211 S. Main	970-547-9654
Burlington	Prairie Quilting Co, 14080 County Rd 55	719-346-9523
Cahone	Ann Neely's Quilting Shop, 14064 Hwy. 666	970-562-4655
Cedaridge	Log Cabin Quilts, 250 S Grand Mesa Dr	970-856-3608
Colorado Springs	Spoolin' Around, 5751 North Academy Blvd	719-593-7995
Denver	D'Leas Fabric Affair, 2719 E. 3rd. Ave.	303-388-5665
Denver	Exeter River Trader, 1212 S. Broadway	303-744-7049
Durango	All for the Love of Quilts, 1474 Main Ave. #205	970-259-5566
Evergreen	Crafty Lady Quilts, 28566 Clover Ln	303-674-3126
Fort Collins	Calico Country, 4604 Terry Lake Rd.	970-493-2751
Fort Morgan	Sew & Sew Quilts, 731 State St	970-542-0144
Fort Morgan	Quilting Corner, 328 Main St.	970-867-9066
Golden	Hearts at Home, 2131 Youngfield	303-237-0811
Idaho Springs	Treadle Treasures, 1609 Miner St	303-567-2931
Indian Hills	Log Cabin Patchworks, P.O. Box 186	303-838-7343
Lafayette	Everything Quilts.com, 2528 Ginny Way	303-604-0508
Littleton	Denver Fabrics, 2777 W. Belleview Ave.	303-730-2777
Longmont	Thread Bear Quilts, 1755 1/2 Main St	720-652-9001
Longmont	Bernina Sewing Center, 1744 Collyer St	303-776-6704
Loveland	M.J.'s Quilt Shop, 265-H E. 29th St.	970-663-1300
Merino	D & J Country Antiques, PO Box 29	970-842-5813
Montrose	The Quilter's Cottage, 1425 Hawk Pkwy.	970-240-8132
Pueblo	Only Friends, 1418 Berkley Ave	719-545-6160
Rangely	Quilter's Cottage, 258 E Main St	970-675-5521
Springfield	Justa Stitchin, 965 Main St	719-523-4985
Sterling	Sew Together, 320 N. 4th	970-521-0258
Walden	Never Summer Designs, 454 1/2 Main St.	970-723-4473

Colorado Guilds:

Alamosa San Luis Valley Quilt Guild, 6750 Juniper Ln., 81101 Meets: 3rd Saturday 1:30 p.m. at Monte Vista COOP
Arvada Colorado Quilting Council, P.O. Box 2056, 80001 **Canon City** Royal Gorge Quilt Council, 1402 1/2 Sherman Ave., 81212
Aurora Aurora Piecemakers Quilt Group, 17400 E Lehigh Place Meets: 2nd Monday 7pm at Summer Valley Ranch Recreation Center
Broomfield Sew & Tell, 6470 W. 120th Ave. #D3, 80020 Meets: 2nd Friday 5 p.m. at Dry Creek Quilts
Carbondale Needle & I Quilters, 1250 Hendrick Rd, 81623 Meets: 1st Monday at Carbondale Senior Center
Castle Rock Castle Rock Quilt Club, 2301 N Woodlands Blvd Meets: 1st & 3rd Tuesday 7pm at Castle Rock Recreation Center, Senior Wing
Colorado Springs Piecing Partners, 1111 Martin Dr., 80925 **Colorado Springs** Colorado Springs Quilt Guild, P.O. Box 8069, 80907
Denver Great American Quilters, 8970 E. Hampden Ave., 80231 Meets: 1st Tuesday 7 p.m. at Great American Quilts
Denver African American Quilters and Collectors Guild, 2815 High St Meets: 3rd Saturday 10:30 at Ford-Warren Library
Denver Rocky Mountain Wa Shonaji Meets: 1st Saturday 10am at Park Hill Library **Durango** La Plata Quilter's Guild, P.O. Box 2355, 81302
Englewood Arapahoe County Quilters, 3501 Hampden Ave, 80155 Meets: 2nd Thursday at First Plymouth Congregational Church
Estes Park Estes Valley Quilt Guild, P.O. Box 3931, 80517 Meets: 2nd Wednesday 7 p.m. at Senior Center
Genesee Alpine Quilters Meets: 3rd Monday 7pm at Rockland Community Church
Glenwood Springs Quilters of the Rockies, 822 Grand Ave, 81601 Meets: 3rd Monday @ 7pm at Glenwood Sewing Center
Grand Junction Colorado West Quilt Guild, P.O. Box 393, 81501 **Littleton** Rocky Mt. Wa Shonaji
Gunnison Tursday Nite Quilters, 135 N Main, 81230 Meets: Every Tuesday 6pm at E&P Sewing Emporium
Gunnison Land of the Rainbow Quilt Guild, 1135 N. Main St., 81230 Meets: Tuesday nites 6 p.m. **Salida** Monarch Quilt Guild
Leadville Talk, Quilt and Laugh, 721 Harrison Ave, 80461 Meets: 1st Thursday 9a.m. at 721 Harrison Ave, Leadville CO
Livermore Mountain Momma Quilters, 1417 Green Mountain Dr., 80536 Meets: 2nd & 4th Mondays at 9 a.m. at Glacier View Meadows Assoc. Office
Longmont Front Range Cont. Quilters, Meets: 3rd Monday 7pm at Westminster Recreation Center
Monte Vista San Luis Valley Quilt Guild, 81144 Meets: 3rd Saturday (Except Dec.) 1:30 p.m. at Monte Vista Coop Community Room
Montrose Coumbine Quilters, 81401 Meets: 1st Saturday 9am at Library Meeting Room
Montrose Friendship Quilters of Western Colorado Meets: 4th Thursday 9am at Methodist Church
Monument The Barn Quilters Meets: 2nd & 4th Friday 9 a.m. at Woodmoor Community Center, 1691 Woodmoor Dr., downstairs
Pagosa Springs Pagosa Piecemakers Quilt Club, 1044 Park Avenue Meets: 2nd Saturday @ 10am at Mountain Heights Baptist Church
Pueblo Pride City Quilt Guild, PO Box 4204, 81003 Meets: 3rd Monday @ 8:30 am at King of Kings Lutheran Church
Pueblo Pueblo West Quilters, P.O. Box 7295, 81007 Meets: 1st Monday 7 p.m. at St. Paul the Apostle, 142 Stardust Dr.
Pueblo Calico Quilters, P.O. Box 504, 81002 Meets: 4th Tuesday @ 7pm at First Church of the Nazarene
South Fork Silver Threads Quilt Guild, P.O. Box 1, 81154 Meets: 10am alternate between Creede Baptist Church & South Fork Church of Christ
Steamboat Springs Delectable Mountain Quilter's Guild, P.O. Box 774383, 80477 Meets: 3rd Monday 6:30 p.m. at The Depot
Wheat Ridge Columbine Quilters, 6363 West 35th St Meets: 2nd Monday 7pm at Wheat Ridge Recreation Center
Yuma Yuma County Quilt Guild, 201 E. 8th Ave. Meets: 2nd Thursday 7 p.m. at Bank of Colorado Basement

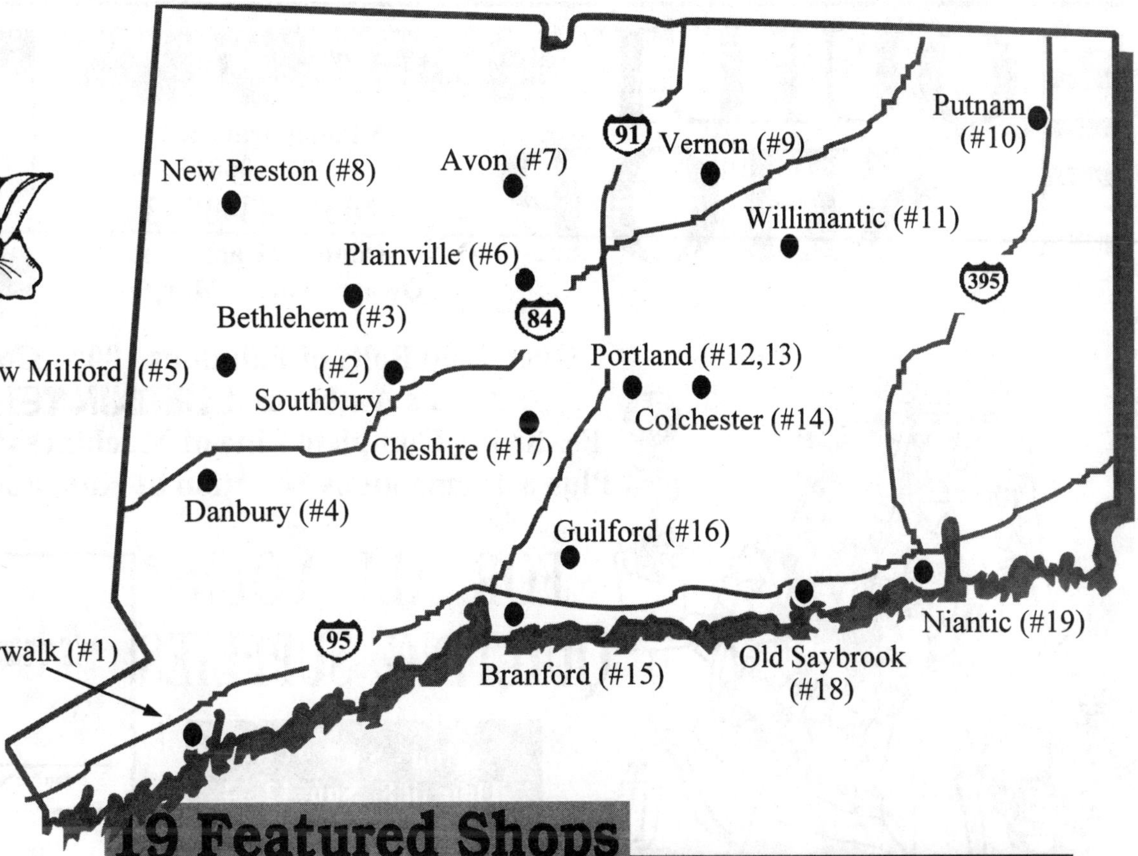

Putnam (#10)
New Preston (#8)
Avon (#7)
Vernon (#9)
Willimantic (#11)
Plainville (#6)
Bethlehem (#3)
New Milford (#5)
(#2) Southbury
Portland (#12,13)
Colchester (#14)
Cheshire (#17)
Danbury (#4)
Guilford (#16)
Norwalk (#1)
Branford (#15)
Old Saybrook (#18)
Niantic (#19)
91
84
395
95

19 Featured Shops
CONNECTICUT

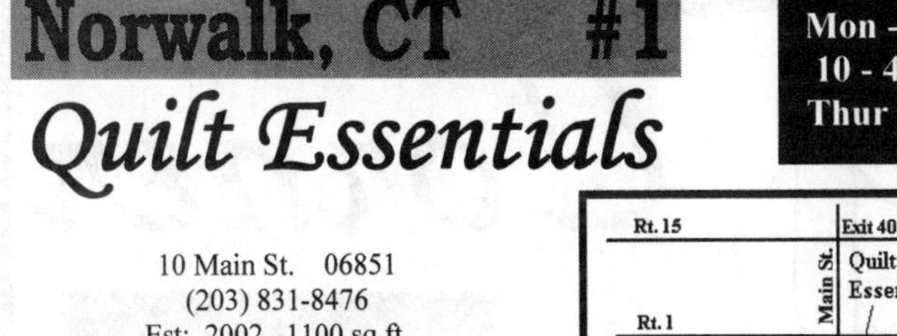

Mon - Sat
10 - 4:30
Thur til 6

10 Main St. 06851
(203) 831-8476
Est: 2002 1100 sq.ft.

2000+ bolts of 100% cottons from top manufacturers, books, notions, everything for quilting. Authorized Pfaff dealer.

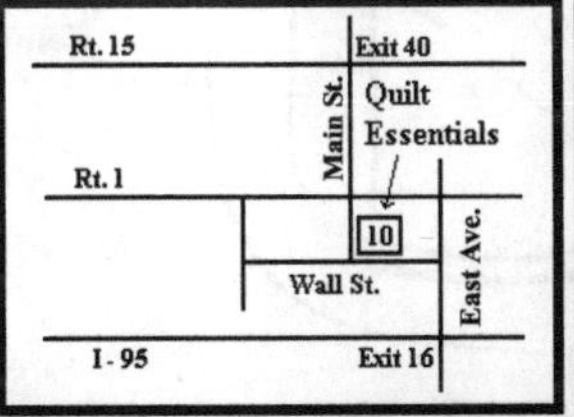

Southbury, CT #2
The Yankee Quilter

1481-6 Southford Rd. (Route 67) 06488
(203) 262-1206
Owners: Barbara & Cheryl
Est: 1989 2500+ sq.ft.

Mon - Fri 9 - 5 Thur 9 - 8 Sat 9 - 5

Area's largest selection of quilting books, patterns, & supplies. Knowledgeable, Friendly Staff, Quality Fabrics - over 3000 bolts. Classes. Gift Certificates Authorized Viking Dealer

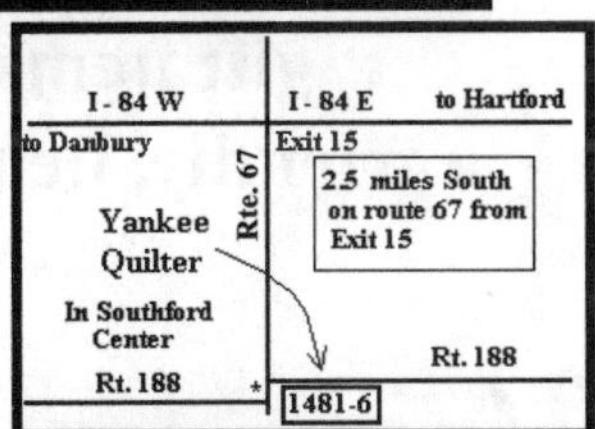

www.yankeequilter.com

Wed - Sat
10 - 5
Thur til 7
Sun 12 - 4

3 Green Hill Rd. 06751
(203) 266-6871
cmastownquiltz@msn.com
www.christmastownquilts.com
Est: 2002 1000+ Bolts

All the Expected Pleasures of a Quilt Shop, wrapped up in a Warm and Homey Atmosphere.

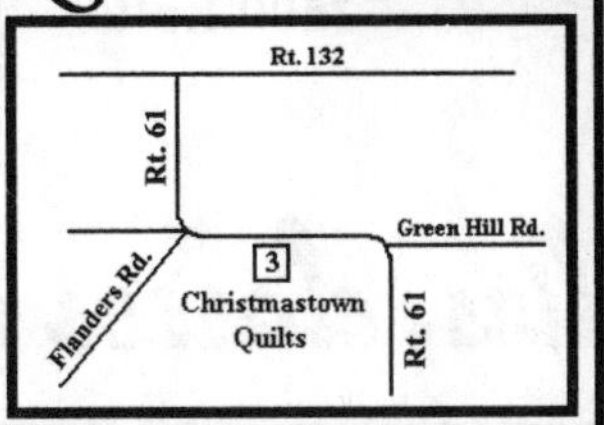

THE QUILT SHOP

Danbury, CT #4

5 Padanaram Rd.
Rt. 37 06811
(203) 743-0543
wamquilt@aol.com
Owner: Ginny Murphy

Over 2000 Bolts of Fabulous 100% Cotton Fabric.
Area's Authorized BERNINA Dealer
Featuring Complete Line of Machines & Accessories.
Plus a Tremendous Selection of Kits, Books & Classes.

FOR ALL YOUR QUILTING SUPPLIES

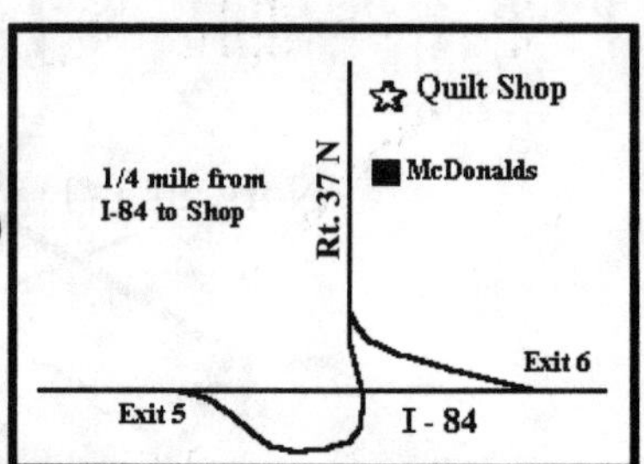

Mon - Sat 9 - 5
Thur til 8 Sun 12 - 4

"Worth The Trip"

New Milford, CT #5

Quilter's Corner

312 Danbury Rd. (Rt. 7) 06776
In The Red Barn
(860) 355-4516
Fax: (860) 355-9510
Web Site: www.quilterscorner.com

Mon - Sat 10 - 5
Wed til 8

Spacious, well lit shop filled with 100% cotton fabrics, books, patterns, notions, gift items and a friendly, helpful staff.

Owner:
Becky Frazer
Est: 1999
2300 sq.ft.
2500 Bolts

In the Red Barn Approx. 7 miles from I-84
Rt. 7
Rt. 202
New Milford
Quilter's Corner 312
Rt. 202
Rt. 7
I-84 W
Exit 7
I-84 E
Danbury, CT

Your source for fabrics supplies, classes and unique gifts.

Plainville, CT #6

Tues & Wed 4:30 - 8:30
Thur & Fri 1:30 - 8:30
Sat 10-6 Sun 1-6

The Quilting Bee, LLC
"a place to gather"

452 East St. 06062
(860) 747-3134 Fax: (860) 747-1701
diane@thequiltingbee.net
www.thequiltingbee.net
Owners: Larry & Diane Plunkett
Est: 2002 1000+ Bolts
Quality Fabric, Notions, Tools & Books for Quilters.

Rt. 372
1.5 mi.
Rt. 10
452 Quilting Bee
1.5 mi.
Rt. 84
Exit 32

Avon, CT #7

Tues - Fri 10 - 5
Sat 10 - 4

Patchwork Cottage

17 E. Main St. (Rt. 44) 06001
(860) 678-0580
Patcottage@aol.com
www.oldavonvillage.com/patchworkcottage
Owner: Patricia-Anne Barker Est: 1997

Beautiful 100% Cotton Fabrics
Books, Patterns, Notions, Classes.
Handmade Gifts.

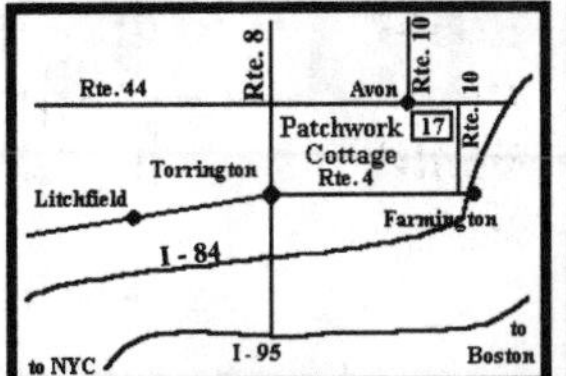

New Preston, CT #8

Common *Threads*

- 2000 Bolts of Fabric, Over 600 Book Titles
- Fat Quarters cut from Every Bolt in Stock
- Authorized Janome Dealer
- Grace Machine Quilter Dealer
- Large Class Schedule--2 Classrooms outfitted with Janome sewing machines for your use.
- Large Selection of Civil War Repro's, Homespun's, Batiks, Tone-on-Tones, Florals, Flannels and Wool.
- Gift Certificates, Notions, Patterns, Kits, Classes, and the friendliest Service.
- Gift Items
- Completed Quilts for sale

Est: 2001
Owner: Corinne Thompson

168 New Milford Tpke (Rt. 202) 06777
In the Stonemill Commons
(860) 868-2658 Fax: (860) 868-2839
commonthreads1@aol.com
www.commonthreadsquiltshop.com

Tues - Thurs 10 - 4
Fri 10 - 5:30
Sat 9 - 3
Sun 10 - 2

From Waterbury - I-84, to Rt. 8N, to Rt. 118W, to Rt. 202S
From Danbury - I - 84, to Rt. 7N, to Rt. 202 N

Quilt Gallery with an Ever Changing Display to Inspire Your Creativity

Vernon, CT #9

Mon - Fri 10 - 5
Thur til 8
Sat 10 - 4
Sun 11 - 4

Quilting By The Yard

435-O Hartford Trpk. 06066
(860) 896-1056
www.quiltingbytheyard.com
Est: 2000 2600 sq.ft. 3600 Bolts

WOW! Complete supply of quilting fabrics, books, patterns, kits, notions and classes. Spacious, well lit shop. Easy on and off I-84.

Quilting By The Yard
in Shops @ 30 Plaza
Rt. 83
Rt. 30 Hartford Trpk.
to Hartford
I - 84
Rt. 83 & 30
Exit 65 to Boston

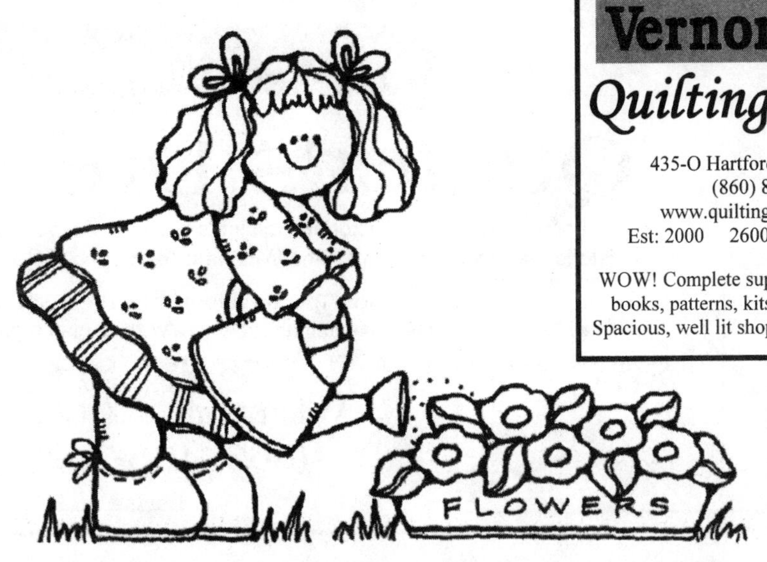

Tuffets Quilt Shop

Open 7 days a week!
Saturday - Wednesday 11 - 5
Thursday 11 - 8
Friday 11 - 9

Tuffets
151
Providence St.
Rt. 44
Exit 97
Church St.
I - 395
Kennedy Dr.
Exit 95

Over 2,000 bolts of fabric
Large selection of flannel, batik & homespun
Benartex, Marcus Bros, Maywood, Moda, P&B
RJR, Thimbleberries, Timeless Treasures

Classes for all levels, books, patterns, notions & gifts.
Fabric club and gift registry offered.

Quilts made to order.
Quilts and consignment items for sale.

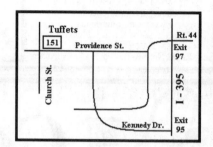

151 Providence St. 06260

860-928-5779

Putnam, CT #10

Located in the Quiet Corner of CT ~ 1/4 mile from Putnam's Antique District

Bus trips welcome ~ Please call ahead

"Everything You Need To Make Your Quilting Experience A Dream"

Nearly 4000 Bolts of Fabric

Including Hoffman, Benartex, P & B, Moda, Maywood
South Seas, Kona Bay and many more.

We Carry Tons of Books, Supplies, Patterns, Batiks, Gadgets and Quilters Tools. Sign up for our Quarterly Newsletter where you will learn more about ...

- Our Extensive Class Schedule (Over 35 - for all levels)
- Block of the Month Program (We ship anywhere!)

Quilter's Dream LLC

One of 10 featured Shops in Quilt Sampler 2000 Magazine!

Willimantic, CT #11

Quilter's Dream

Located in a lovely Victorian building situated in the downtown of an historic mill town, blocks from the Windham Textile and History Museum

Visit our Web Site at
www.quiltersdream.com
Monday - Saturday, 10 AM - 6 PM
Thursday, 10 AM - 8 PM,
Sunday, 12 Noon - 5 PM

Hartford
I-84
I-384
Rt 32
Rt 195
Rt 44
Rt 6
I-395
I-91
Rt 66
Willimantic
Rt 32
Norwich

Bus Tours Welcome* • Free Gift to All
(*Please call ahead if you wish to plan a group visit.)

1158 Main Street
Willimantic, CT 06226
(860) 456-7629

Larisa and James Key

Portland, CT #12

Hours By Appointment

Carolyn's Quilting Bee

73 Ames Hollow Rd. 06480
(860) 342-1949
Owner: Carolyn Johnson
Est: 1980

Located in the Blacksmith Shop of an 18th Century Farm.
Visitors are always welcome.

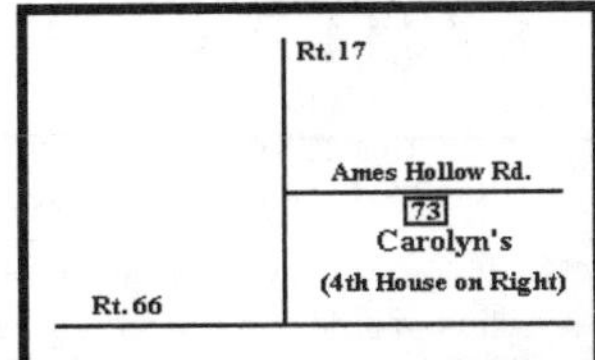

Portland, CT #13

Tues - Fri 10 - 5 Sat 10 - 3

Patches & Patchwork

216 Main St. 06480
(860) 342-4567 Fax: (860) 342-1615
pjsatpp@aol.com Est: 1980
Owner: Jane Wilk Sterry 1200 sq.ft.

We carry the unusual in fabrics. Latest books, patterns and notions. Classes. Antique quilt repair! Commission quilts. We are in our 23rd year of business!

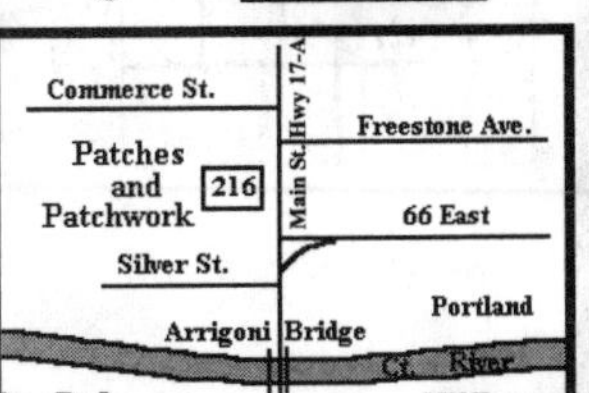

Colchester, CT #14

Mon - Fri 9 - 6 Thur til 8 Sat 9:30 - 5 Sun 10 - 5

Colchester Mill Fabrics

120 Lebanon Ave. 06415
(860) 537-2004 Fax: (860) 537-5239
cherylcmf@cs.com
Est: 1974 16,000 sq.ft.

Full Line Fabric Store specializing in Quilting Name brand fabrics, battings, books, gifts and quilting supplies.

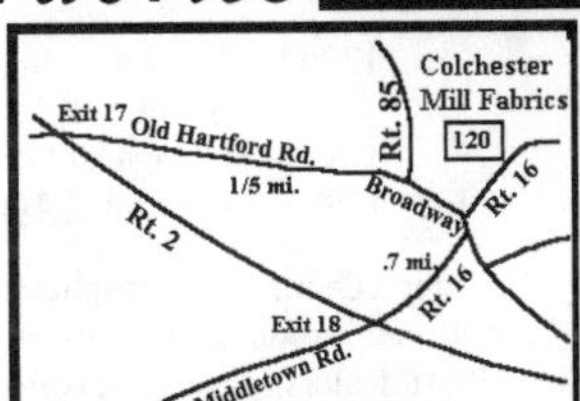

Branford, CT #15

Tues - Sat 10 - 5

Quilter's Habitat

131 Montowese St.
06405
(203) 488-2321
qhabitat@aol.com
www.quiltershabitat.com
Owner: Cher Hurney

Charming, Friendly Shop with Colorful Fabric Selection, Patterns, Books, Tools and Quilts.

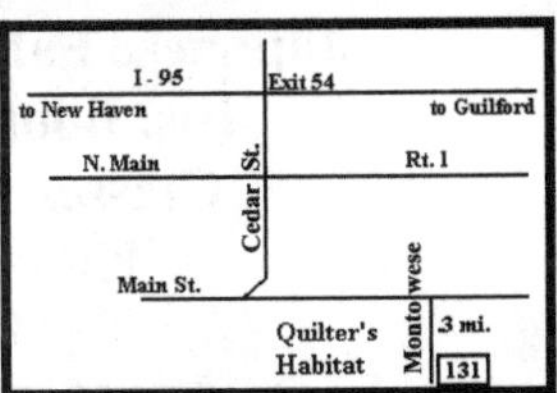

Guilford, CT #16

Calico Alley

**1310 Boston Post Rd.
Guilford, CT 06437
Strawberry Hill Plaza
(203) 458-6122
Est: 1992**

www.calicoalley.com

IT'S WORTH THE DRIVE

**2500+ Bolts of Designer Fabric & 100% Cottons, Notions, & Supplies.
Unique Block of the Month Programs—
Check them out on our Website**

TUES - FRI 10 - 5 SAT 10 - 4 SUN 12 - 4

Your Fat Quarter Headquarters 8000+ Fat Quarters

Quilt Buses Welcome by Appointment

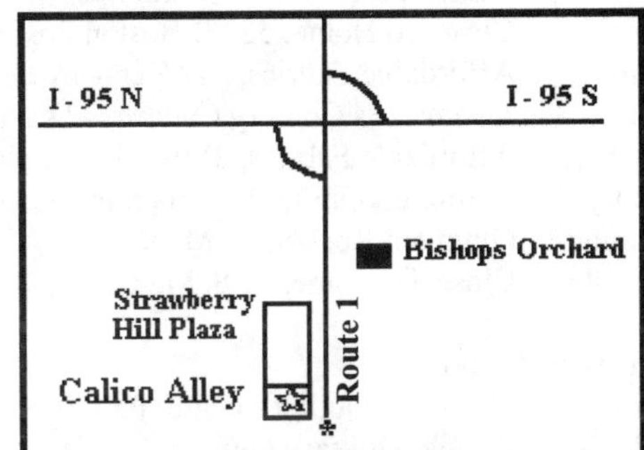

**Within minutes of Shoreline Trolley Museum & Thimble Islands
45 minutes from Mystic Seaport
60 minutes from Foxwoods Casino.
From I - 95N take Exit 57. Take a Right.**

The Watch Factory Shoppes
116 Elm Street
Cheshire, CT 06410
203 272-2443
calicoetcquilt@aol.com
www.calicoetc.com

Fabrics & Quality Quilting Supplies

For all your Quilting needs.
Over 3,600 Bolts of Fabric,
Including our wall of Balis,
Japanese Fabrics, Brights and more.
Kits, Books, Patterns, Notions
Classes with a friendly and
Knowledgeable staff.
Call for Summer Hours
New Owner - Marty Child

Cheshire, CT #17

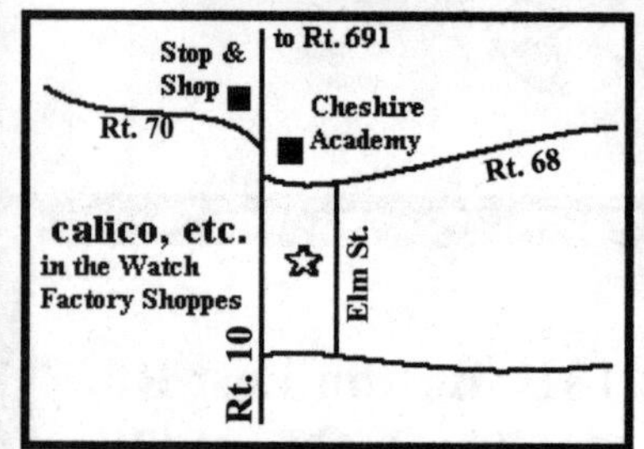

Mon & Tues 10 - 4
Wed, Fri & Sat 10 - 5
Thur 10 - 8
Sun 12 - 4

Old Saybrook, CT #18

Mon - Fri 10 - 5:30
Sat 10 - 4

Coastal Sewing Machines

27 N. Main St. 06475
(860) 388-1832
CoastalSewing@aol.com
Est: 2003 1600 sq.ft. 1500 Bolts

We offer a charming atmosphere with a great selection of product. Authorized Viking and Pfaff dealers. Easy access from I - 95.

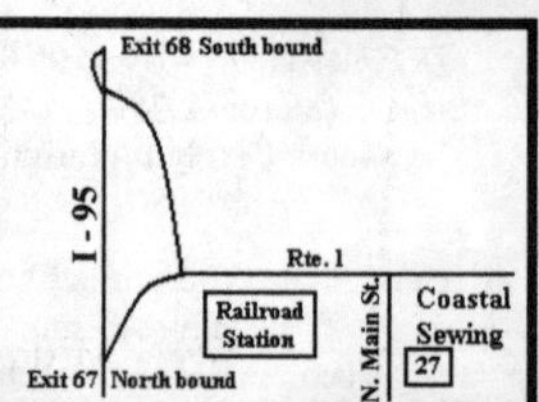

Niantic, CT #19

Mon - Fri 10 - 5:30
Sat 10 - 4

Coastal Sewing Machines

170 Flanders Rd. 06357
(860) 739-5412
CoastalSewing@aol.com
Est: 1993 2000 sq.ft. 1600 Bolts

We offer a charming atmosphere with a great selection of product. Authorized Viking and Pfaff dealers. Easy access from I - 95.

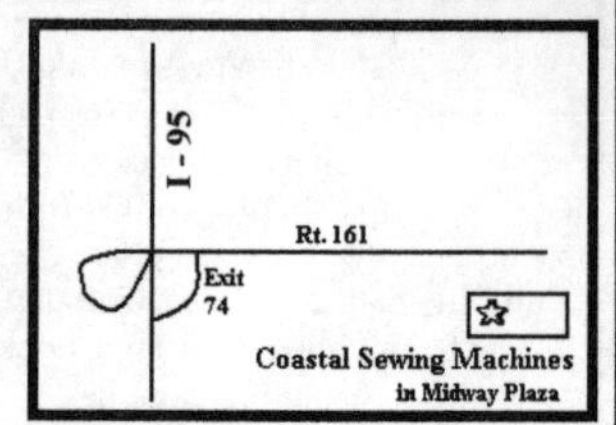

Other Shops in Connecticut: *We suggest calling first*

Bethel	Homestead Quilts, 5 Front St.	203-744-3118
Bloomfield	Wilkabee's Fabric Paradise, 8 South Barn Hill Road	860-243-8881
Bristol	Lin's Quilt Source, 162 Wanderbilt Rd	860-583-2099
Danbury	Fabric Tree, 19 Sugar Hollow Rd	203-792-5252
East Haddam	Old Lyme Village Quilts, P.O. Box 384	860-434-2602
Glastonbury	Close to Home, 2717 Main St.	860-633-0721
Orange	Close To Home, 523 B Boston Post Rd.	203-799-0828
Putnam	Affordable Fabrics, 247 Kennedy Dr.	860-928-4317
Putnam	Jeanmarie's Country Calicos, 42 Chapman St.	860-928-9382
Rocky Hill	Affordable Fabrics, 2119 Silar Deane Hwy.	860-563-7647
Simsbury	Caroline's Quilts, 542 Hopmeadow St #119	860-658-4677
Torrington	Gingham Rocker, 84 Main	860-482-9364
Unionville	Close To Home, 45 S. Main St.	860-675-4481

Connecticut Guilds:

Branford	Shoreline Quilter's Guild, P.O. Box 293, 06405	Meets: 1st Monday 7 p.m. Canoe Brook Senior Ctr, 11 Cherry Hill Rd.
Enfield	Enfield Quilter's Guild	Meets: Enfield Public Library
Hartford	Clamshell Quilt Guild, P.O. Box 3, 06385	
New London	Thames River Quilters, 06320	
Newington	Greater Hartford Quilt Guild, P.O. Box 310213, 06131	
Norwalk	Trumbull Piecemakers, 34 St. Mary's Ln., 06851	
Portland	Heart of the Valley, 06480	
Simsbury	Farmington Valley Quilters, 754 Haymeadow St., 06070	Meets: 3rd Wednesday at 7 p.m. at Eno Hall

DELAWARE

4 Featured Shops

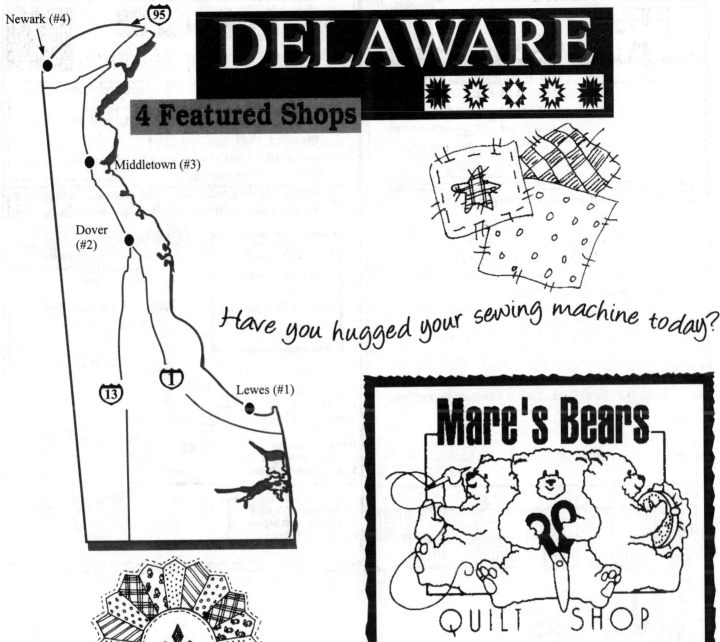

Newark (#4)

Middletown (#3)

Dover (#2)

Lewes (#1)

Have you hugged your sewing machine today?

Mare's Bears

QUILT SHOP

At the "Beacon Motel"
528 E. Savannah Rd. 19958
(302) 644-0556
www.maresbearsquiltshop.com
Owner: Maryann McFee
Est: 1995 2000 sq.ft.

Mon - Sat 10 - 5
Wed 10 - 7
Sun 12 - 4

- Fabric
- Notions
- Books & Patterns
- Classes
- Bernina Dealer

"We are located just over the drawbridge on Savannah Road @ The Beacon Motel"

Lewes, DE #1

Dover, DE #2

Shady Lane Selections

Mon, Tues, Wed 8 - 5
Fri 8 - 7
Sat 8 - 4

1121 Victory Chapel Rd. 19904
Owner: Salina Yoder
Est: 1982 2900 sq.ft. 500+ Bolts

Quilts in all sizes — We do special orders. Custom Hand Quilting. Lots of small crafts, rag rugs, etc. Fabric from Hoffman, RJR, P&B, etc.

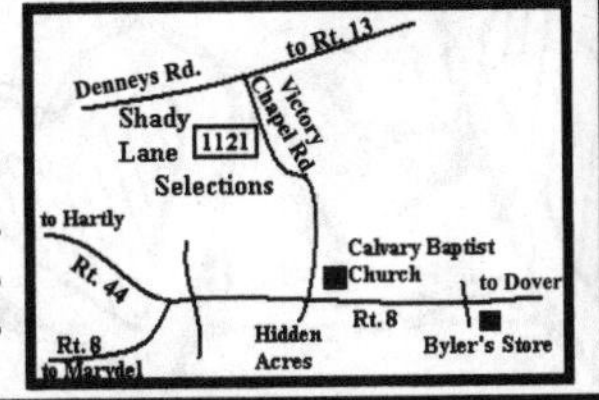

Middletown, DE #3

Wed - Fri 10 - 5
Sat 10 - 4

"Lil' Country Shoppe"

4446 Summit Bridge Rd. #7 19709
Summit Village Shoppping Center
(302) 378-5568
Lilcountryshoppe@juno.com
Est: 2002 1000 sq.ft. 1100+ Bolts
Quality 100% cottons (homespuns, brushed homespuns, flannels), Books, Patterns, Notions & Rug Hooking notions, Foundation, Hand-dyed Wool. 60 Bolts of Wool.

Newark
I-95
Rt. 896
Rt. 40
C & D Canal
Airport
Lil' 4446 Country Shoppe
Hwy. 896
Rt. 301
Middletown

Quilter's Hive

fabric classes supplies

1800 Capitol Trail, Suite 2
Newark, DE 19711
(302) 737-5699
quilthive@aol.com

2800 sq. ft. of all the fabric, gadgets and goodies that quilters love

- **over 2000 bolts of the latest 100% cotton fabrics**
- **books, patterns and notions**
- **classes frombeginning hand and machine quilting to advanced Baltimore Album- style applique**

Newark, DE #4

LOCATED AT THE CORNER OF KIRKWOOD HIGHWAY AND HARMONY ROAD

TAX FREE SHOPPING CLOSE TO I-95

HOURS

10 - 5 Monday thru Saturday

Open til 8 PM Wednesday

1 - 5 Sunday

From I-95 take Exit 3 on to Rt 273 West (towards Newark) Turn right on Harmony Road at the first traffic light Follow Harmony Road for 2.1 miles and turn left into the Calico Corners/Quilter's Hive parking lot (just before the 5th traffic light)

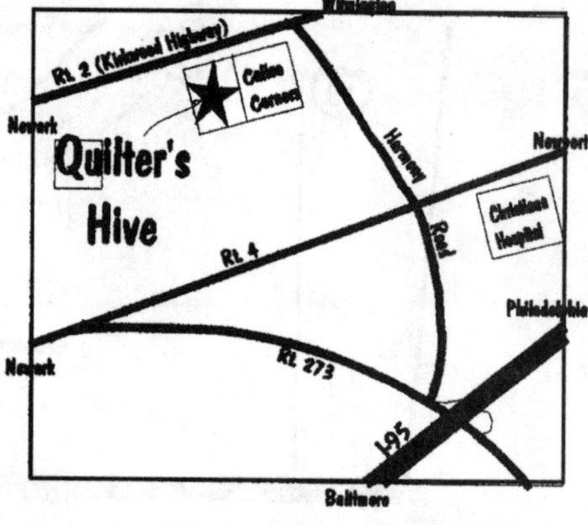

Other Shops in Delaware: *We Suggest Calling First*

Camden	Delaware Sewing Center 8 N. Main St.	302-697-2445
Dover	Delaware Sewing Centers Rodney Village Shopping Center, 1716 S Governors	302-674-9030
Laurel	Homestead Shoppe Rt. 64, Box 179	302-875-2017
Milford	Delaware Sewing Centers 235 Milford Shopping Center	302-422-9009

We didn't receive any guilds for Delaware

Shops in the District of Columbia: We suggest calling first

Washington	Daughter of Dorcas, 1109 Abbey Place NE	
Washington	Appalachian Spring, 50 Massachusetts Ave. NE	202-682-0505
Washington	Applachian Spring, 1415 Wisconsin Ave. NW	202-337-5780

Pace (#4)
Crestview (#5)
Destin (#3)
Pensacola (#1)
Panama City (#2)
Port St. Joe (#41)
10
Tallahassee (#6)
Middleburg (#8)
Lake City (#7)
Jacksonville (#9,10,11,12)
Amelia Island (#16)
(#14,15) Orange Park
Interlachen (#13)
Gainesville (#17)
Leesburg (#33)
Bunnell (#18)
Ocala (#20,21)
Crystal River (#39)
Dunnellon (#42)
Ormond Beach (#19)
Zephyrhills (#35)
Belleview (#22)
South Daytona (#23)
Hudson (#43,44)
DeLand (#24)
Port Richey (#45)
Longwood (#26)
Mount Dora (#25)
Lakeland (#54,55)
Dade City (#34)
Orlando (#27,28,32)
Cocoa (#29)
Rockledge (#37)
Holiday (#46)
Merritt Island (#36)
Dunedin (#50)
Clearwater (#48,49)
Kissimmee (#40)
Largo (#47)
Winter Haven (#56)
Tampa (#51,52)
Melbourne (#30,31)
Florida Trpk.
Parrish (#53)
Ellenton (#60)
95
Sebastian (#38)
Sebring (#57)
Sarasota (#59)
Venice (#61)
Lake Placid (#58)
Ft. Pierce (#68,69)
Port Charlotte (#62)
Port St. Lucie (#70)
Punta Gorda (#64)
Fort Myers (#63)
Coral Springs (#75)
Sanibel (#65)
75
Delray Beach (#74)
Naples (#66,67)
Royal Palm Beach (#71)
Fort Lauderdale (#72,73)
FLORIDA
76 Featured Shops
Key West (#76)

Pensacola, FL #1

Quilt Corner, located in a 100 year old house, has all of your quilting needs. We have Dazor lamps, Dovo scissors, a unique quilting frame that will fit in a motor home or closet. We have silk batts and thread. We also have Bernina and Viking machines for purchase and to use in classes. Over 4,500 bolts of quality fabrics.

9-4 Monday - Saturday, Thursdays til 8
850 439 9080
805 East Gadsden Street
Pensacola, Florida 32501

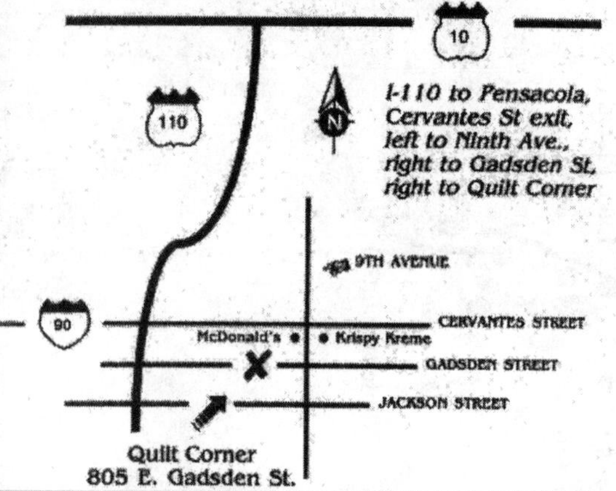

Panama City, FL #2

Quilting by the Bay

2303 Winona Drive
Panama City, FL 32405
(850) 215-7282
www.quiltingbythebay.com

A wonderful selection of fabric, books, patterns and notions. Classes for all skill levels. Friendly, knowledgeable staff.

Monday through Friday 10:00 AM to 6:00 PM
Saturday 10:00 AM to 5:00 PM

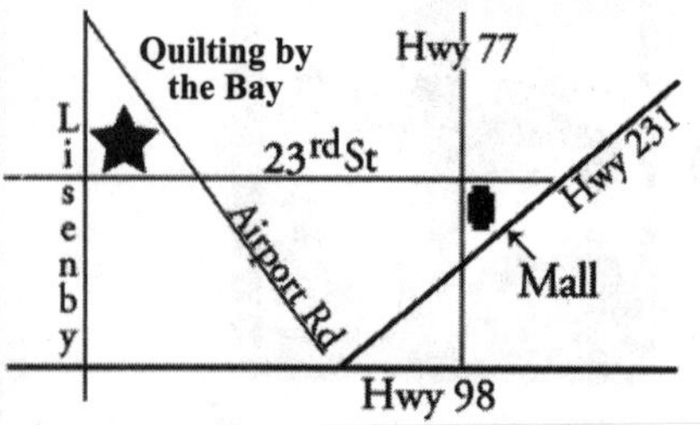

- *Just North of 23rd Street between Airport and Lisenby*
- *3 miles E of Hathaway Bridge*
- *3 miles W of PC Mall*

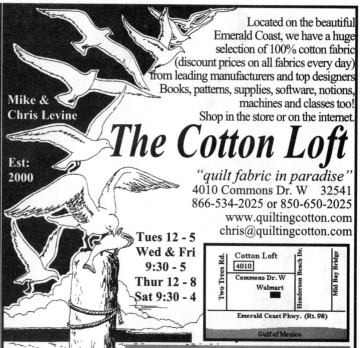

Located on the beautiful Emerald Coast, we have a huge selection of 100% cotton fabric (discount prices on all fabrics every day) from leading manufacturers and top designers Books, patterns, supplies, software, notions, machines and classes too! Shop in the store or on the internet.

Mike & Chris Levine

The Cotton Loft

Est: 2000

"quilt fabric in paradise"
4010 Commons Dr. W 32541
866-534-2025 or 850-650-2025
www.quiltingcotton.com
chris@quiltingcotton.com

Tues 12 - 5
Wed & Fri 9:30 - 5
Thur 12 - 8
Sat 9:30 - 4

Two Trees Rd.
Cotton Loft
4010
Commons Dr. W
Walmart
Henderson Beach Dr.
Mid Bay Bridge
Emerald Coast Pkwy. (Rt. 98)
Gulf of Mexico

Destin, FL #3

Pace, FL #4

Mon - Sat 9 - 5 Thur til 6

The Quilting Station

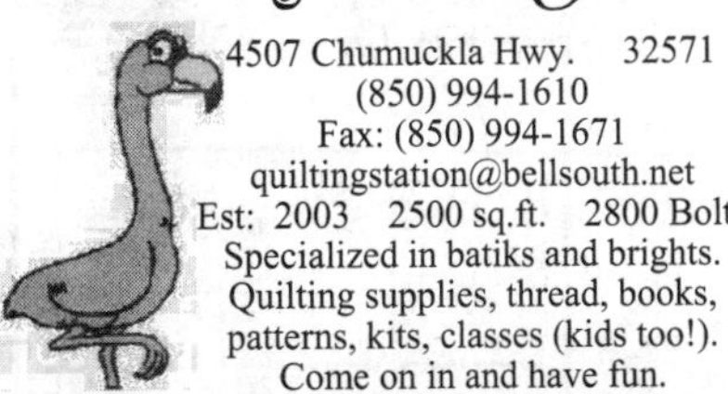

4507 Chumuckla Hwy. 32571
(850) 994-1610
Fax: (850) 994-1671
quiltingstation@bellsouth.net
Est: 2003 2500 sq.ft. 2800 Bolts
Specialized in batiks and brights.
Quilting supplies, thread, books, patterns, kits, classes (kids too!).
Come on in and have fun.

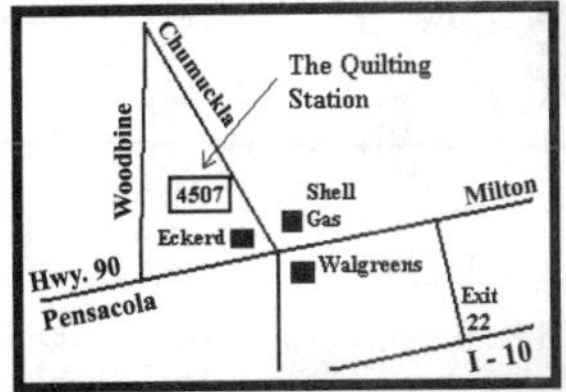

Tallahassee, FL #6

Mon - Fri 10 - 5:30 Tues 10 - 8 Sat 10 - 4:30

The Quilting PATCH

Visit Our Jacksonville Store

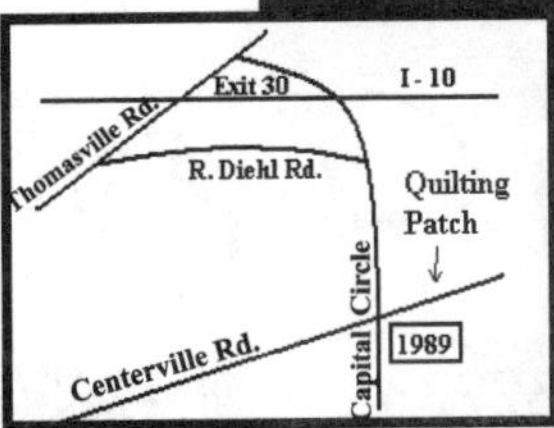

1989 Capital Circle, NE #9 32308
(850) 553-4650 Fax: (850) 553-4672
info@quiltingpatch.com
Est: 1999 3000 sq.ft. 1800 Bolts
FUN, FRIENDLY ATMOSPHERE
Top quality designer fabrics by Hoffman, Benartex, RJR, Timeless Treasures, Kona Bay, Moda, Bali, Notions, Books, Patterns, Kits, Silk Ribbon, Threads. Husqvarna Viking Machines

Margie's Nylon & Lace

Since 1971

2014 Lacey Ln. 32526 866-739-6274 (Toll Free)
(850) 682-6920 Fax: Same
margies@cyou
sew2000.com/sewwithmargies/

Bernina Janome

Largest Independent Fabric Shop in Florida's Panhandle. Classes for all interests (garments to quilting) Fabrics include Bridal, Party, Children, Knits, Quilt etc. Over 3000 bolts of fabric, over 700 book titles, quilting supplies.

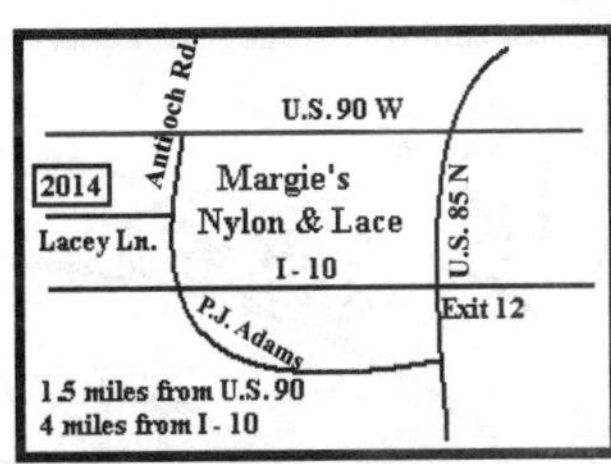

Mon - Sat 9am - 6pm

Crestview, FL #5

We are the first Little Quilt Shop in Florida

Lake City, FL #7

Creative Stitches

318 E. Duval St.
(Hwy. 90 E) 32055
(386) 754-3741
creativestitches@bellsouth.net
Fax: (386) 754-3743
Est: 2000 1800 sq.ft.
1500+ bolt

Visit our Historic Quilt House in downtown Lake City.

Husqvarna VIKING

Warm, friendly Staff.
Fabrics, Notions,
Books & Patterns.

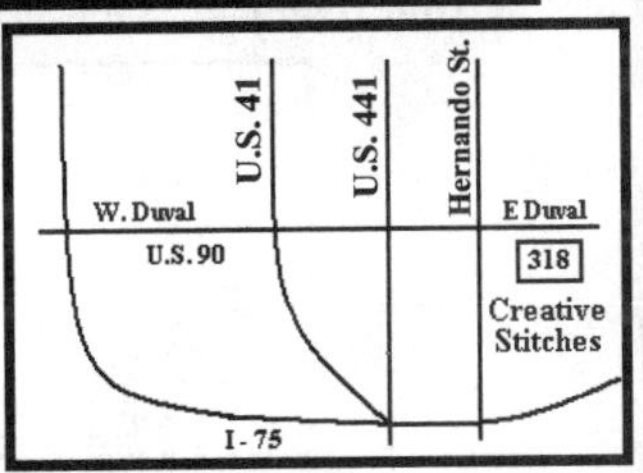

Mon - Fri 10 - 5:30 Sat 10 - 4

www.creativestitchesonline.com

LADY BUG QUILT SHOP

Tues - Fri 11 - 6 Sat 10 - 4

We are located 13.5 miles south from I-295 & Blanding Blvd. (Old Point Shopping Center). We carry 100% cotton fabric and a unique line of novelty prints. Northcott, Michael Miller, Benartex, Hoffman, Kauffman, and many other varieties. We have a great line of Batiks & Flannels. Also a wonderful line of books, patterns, and notions. We offer machine quilting. Excellent customer service. We have 2400 bolts of fabric and over 10,000 fat quarters always stocked.

2751 Blanding Blvd., #107 32068
(904) 282-2120
Flyingx@bellsouth.net
www.ladybugquiltshop.com
Est: 2001 2400+ Bolts.

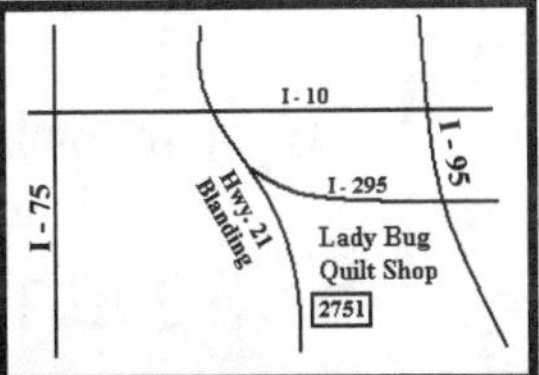

Middleburg, FL #8

Jacksonville, FL #9

Mon 10 - 8 Tues - Fri 10 - 5:30 Sat 10 - 4:30

Visit Our Tallahassee Store

4195 Southside Blvd. #102 32216
(904) 998-4554 Fax: (904) 646-5664
info@quiltingpatch.com
Est: 2003 1600 sq.ft. 1800 Bolts
FUN, FRIENDLY ATMOSPHERE
Top quality designer fabrics by Hoffman, Benartex, RJR, Timeless Treasures, Kona Bay, Moda, Bali, Notions, Books, Patterns, Kits, Silk Ribbon, Threads. Husqvarna Viking Machines

Jacksonville, FL #10

Mon - Fri 10 - 6
Sat 10 - 5

Paula's Fine Fabrics

10920 Baymeadows Rd. #14 32256
(904) 519-7705 Fax: (904) 519-1306
pjesew@aol.com
Est: 1984 3100 sq.ft.

Quilting, Clothing, Bridal & Heirloom Fabrics available. A large selection of books, notions & threads. Classes available. Authorized Bernina Dealer.

Baymeadows Rd. | I-95 | Southside Blvd. | Reedy Branch Rd. | St. Johns Bluff Rd./9A | Paula's Fine Fabrics in the Reedy Branch Shp. Center

Jacksonville, FL #11

Mon- Fri 10 - 6
Thur til 8
Sat 10 - 4

Material Things

10503-4 San Jose Blvd.
32257
(904) 260-0176
Owner: Joyce Snyder
materialthings
@bellsouth.net
Est: 1991 1575 sq.ft. 1000+ Bolts

Most beautiful selection of 100% cottons in the area. Wide variety of books, patterns, notions and classes.

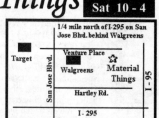

1/4 mile north of I-295 on San Jose Blvd. behind Walgreens
Target | Venture Place | Walgreens | Material Things | San Jose Blvd. | Hartley Rd. | I-95 | I-295

12

The Olde Green Cupboard

Mon - Sat 10 - 6

10950-26 San Jose Blvd., Jacksonville, FL 32223 (904) 880-6656

Picked as one of the TOP 10 Quilt Shops to visit by American Patchwork & Quilting

★Full Service Quilt Shop	★Quilting Classes	★ 2000 + Bolts of Fabric
★Longarm Quilting	★Basket Weaving Classes	★Wool & Wool Felt
★Home Decor	★ Cross-Stitch coming soon	★Primitives
★Antiques	★Furniture	★10,000 Sq. Ft
★One-of-a-Kind Items	★Samples Galore!	★Books, Patterns, Notions

I-295 to Exit 5B, San Jose Blvd South. First shopping center on your right across the street from Wal-Mart.

If you're coming to visit from out-of-town.... call ahead and we'll put on a fresh pot of coffee!

A QUILT SHOP YOU'LL NEVER FORGET!

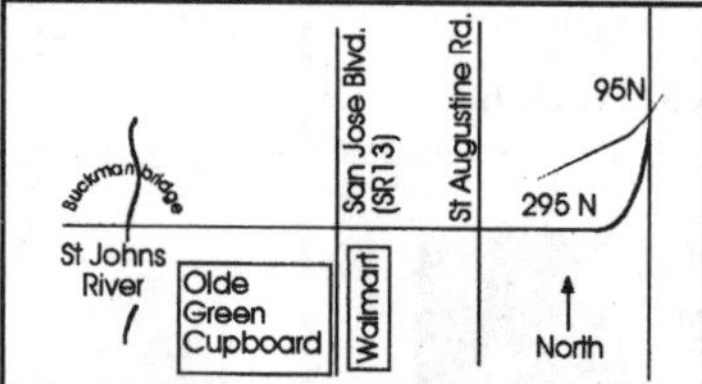

Interlachen, FL #13

Mon - Fri 10 - 5
Sat 9 - 5

Abba's Quiltery

103 Cheyenne Ave. #4 32148
(386) 684-6807

Home of the 39" Yard

Quality Quilting Fabrics, Flannels, Classes, Books, Patterns, Notions.
Present Ad for 10% Off 1st Visit

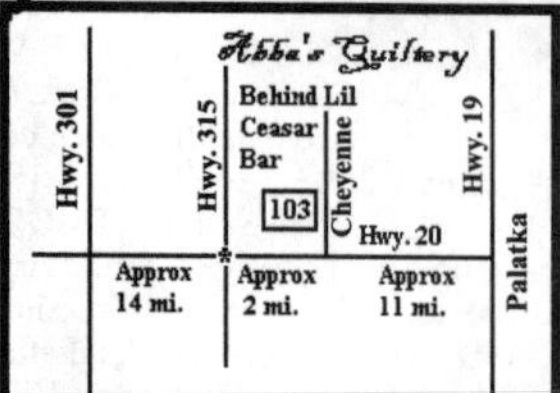

Orange Park, FL #14

Tues 10 - 8
Wed 10 - 5
Thur 12 - 8
Fri 10 - 5
Sat 10 - 4

Country Crossroads

799-3 Blanding Blvd. 32065
(904) 276-1011
TheMice@CountryCrossroad.com
www.CountryCrossroad.com
Owners: Bob & Lynn Provencher
Est: 1988 2400 sq.ft. 1000+ Bolts

"Customer Friendly" offering custom long-arm quilting, books, patterns, notions, classes. 100% cotton fabrics with emphasis on brights and novelty.

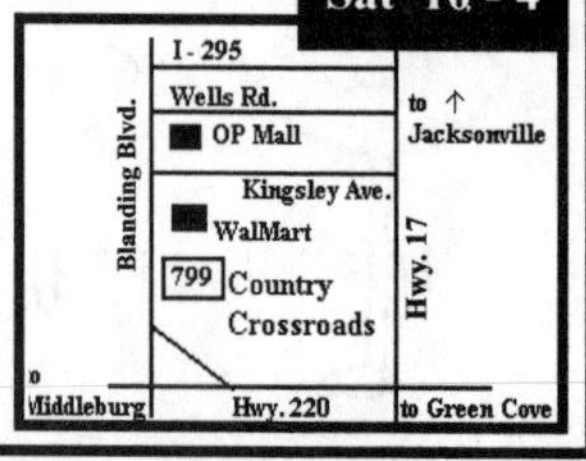

Orange Park, FL #15

Monday thru Thursday
9:00 am - 8:00 pm
Friday
9:00 am - 5:00 pm
Saturday
10:00 am - 5:00 pm

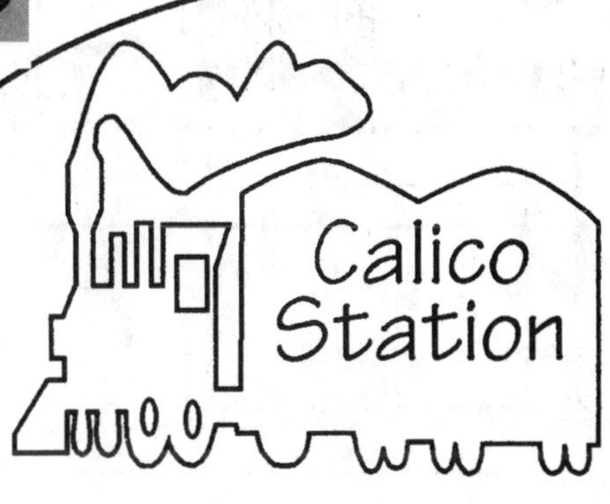

1857 Wells Road
Orange Park, Florida
32073
1-904-269-6911

Authorized Bernina Dealer

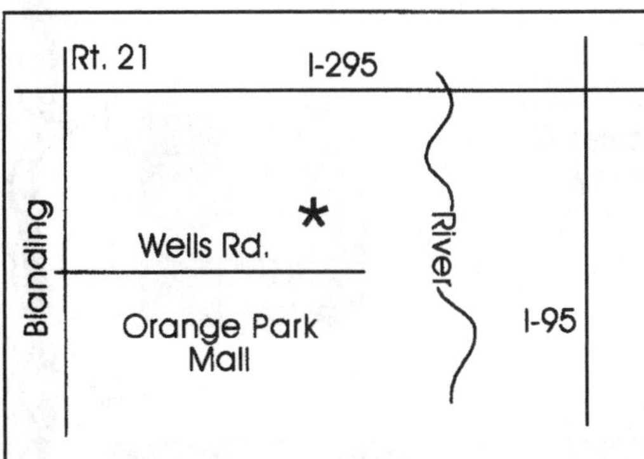

Exit Route 21 south off Interstate 295
turn left on Wells Road
turn left at the second light

Nothing Sews Like A Bernina. Nothing.

BERNINA

Over 2500 bolts of premium 100% cotton fabrics
Patterns, books, kits, threads
Long Arm quilting machine

Email: calstation1@aol.com
Website: www.calicostation.com

961687 Gateway Blvd. Suite 101-H
Amelia Island/Fernandina Beach 32034
(904) 261-9432 Fax: (904) 261-9626
Billjan599@cs.com
Owner: Jan Stokes Est: 2000

Mon - Fri
10:00 - 5:00
Sat 10:00 - 4:00
Bus Tours &
Groups Welcome

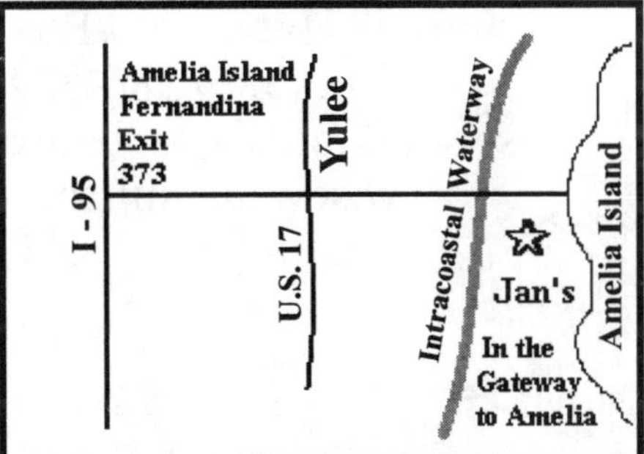

Amelia Island, FL #16

BERNINA SEWING MACHINES -- SALES & SERVICE

NORTHEAST FLORIDA'S QUILTERS PARADISE

* Over 3500 bolts of the finest 100% cotton fabrics available
* Quilting books, notions, gadgets, gizmos and gottahaves
* Great samples to inspire your creativity
* Large selection of kits
* Friendly and helpful staff

Directions: 10 min. from I-95 -- Exit 373 -- exit to the right and travel East on S.R. 200/A-1-A approximately 11 miles -- after you cross the intracoastal waterway bridge turn right into Gateway to Amelia.

Amelia Island a/k/a Fernandina Beach is a beautiful place to visit -- lots of things to see and do -- beautiful beach -- lots of golf courses -- great seafood and specialty shops.

5110 NW 34th St. 32605
(352) 372-4720 Fax: (352) 372-1222
Owner: Tammy Whisler Est: 1995 4000 sq.ft.
E-Mail: TammyWhisler@msn.com

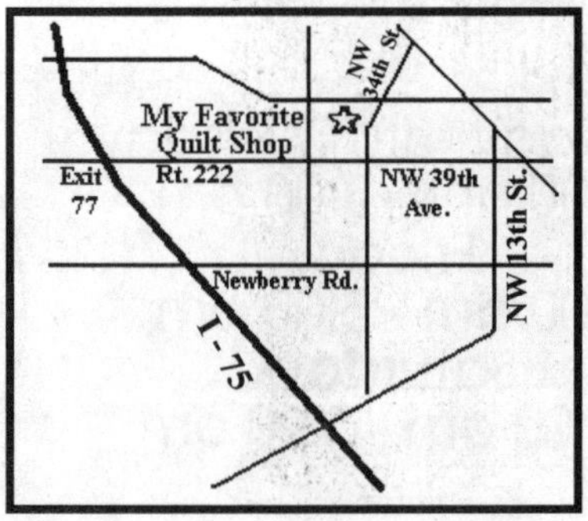

NW 34th St.
My Favorite Quilt Shop
Exit 77
Rt. 222
NW 39th Ave.
Newberry Rd.
I - 75
NW 13th St.

North Central Florida's finest Quilt Shop.
4000 sq. ft. filled with the world's Best Quilting Fabrics, Notions, Books and Patterns.
Gold Standard Bernina Dealer
E-Z on-off I - 75 Take Exit #77 (New#390)
WE LOVE QUILTERS

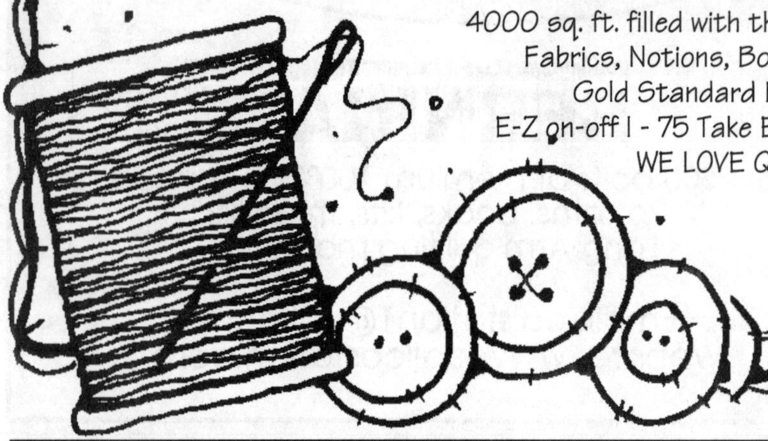

M, T, W, F 10 - 5:30
Th 12 - 8:30
Sat 10 - 4

Gainesville, FL #17

The Sew & Quilt Shop

Authorized Bernina® Dealer

(386) 586-5409
4601 E. Hwy. 100 #B6 32110
Fax (386) 586-5291
sewandquiltshop@bellsouth.net
www.sewandquiltshop.com
Est: 2001 3300 sq.ft.

Free Inspiration & Advice Always Available

Bunnell, FL #18

- 2000 bolts and growing
- Large selection of Quality 100% cotton fabrics, "Kits", gift items, books, patterns, and notions
- Professional Long-arm Machine Quilting
- Fun atmosphere with a Friendly and Knowledgeable Staff
- Quality classes and teachers
- Gift Certificates
- Bus Tours and Quilt Guilds welcome, call ahead and we'll have the coffee on!

Fabric
Books
Notions
Classes

MENTION THIS AD FOR YOUR FREE GIFT

Mon - Fri 10 - 5
Tues 10 - 8 Sat 10 - 3

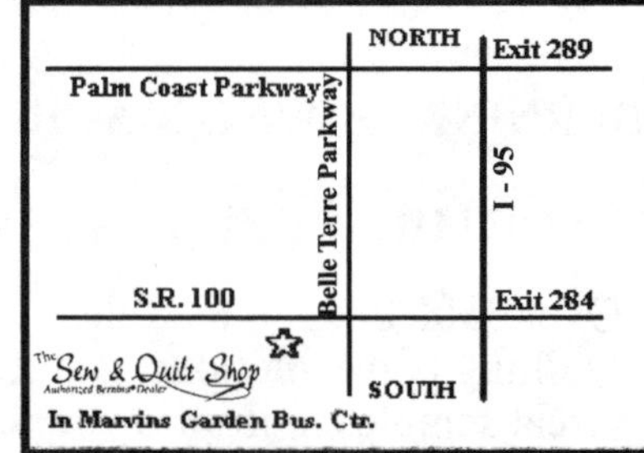

BERNINA
Bernina Sewing & Embroidery Machines & Sergers & Horn of America Cabinets.

2 miles West of I - 95,
20 miles north of Daytona Beach
20 miles South of St. Augustine

To Join our "Up-To-Date" Club, Please fill out the reverse and return to Chalet Publishing along with $8.00. For more information about the Club, please refer to the inside front cover.

QTC

Nest Quilt Shop
Sewing Machine Dealer

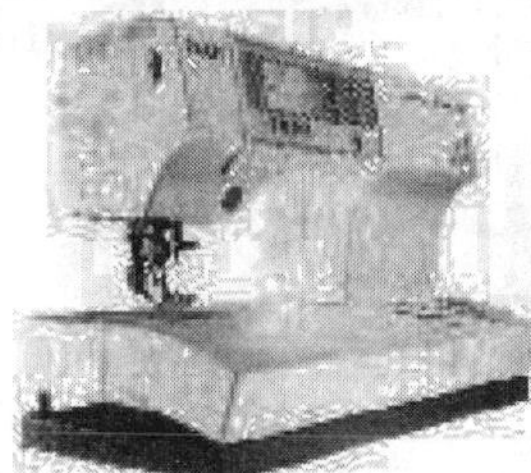

mond Beach, FL #19

ic
s

- Serger & Sewing Machines
- Long-arm Gammill rental
- Gifts & Accessories
- UFO nights

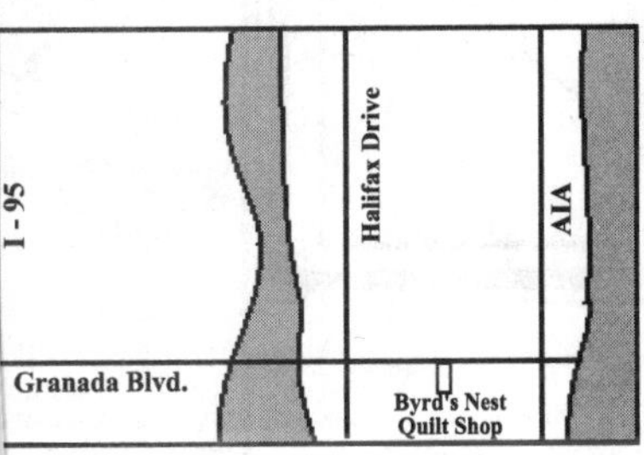

Owner of Thoroughly Modern Minis

Mon - Sat 10 - 5

h.net www.byrdsnestquiltshop.com

Whippoorwill Station
& Bernina Annex

Ocala, FL #20

3115 E. Silver Springs Blvd. 34470

(352)690-1914 E-Mail - Whip3437@aol.com

"Great friendly service"

Billie Clark - Susan Rass

"Ocala's foremost Quilt shop"

Distinctively different comes to mind when you explore our quilt shop, you will find 100% cotton and a few specialty fabrics. We have a wonderful selection of fabric for your quilt and sewing project.

Over 3,500 bolts to choose from.

Northcott.... Hoffman.... RJR..... P&B.... Moda.... Benartex.... Clothworks.... Vintage & Reproductions..... Much, Much More...

Authorized Bernina Dealer....for all your sewing machine needs........ New Classes always forming......... Call for a schedule...

Hours: Mon. - Fri. 10 - 5   Sat 10 - 3

Location may change in 2005

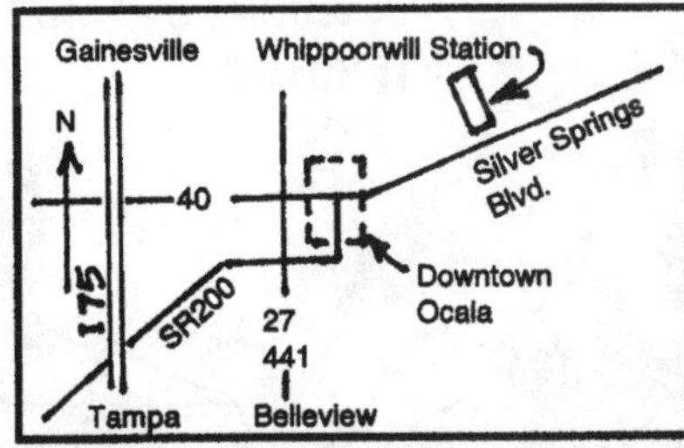

Ocala, FL #21

Peggy's Heirlooms of Tomorrow

M, W, F 9:30 - 5
T, Th til 6
Sat 9:30 - 3

7651 SW S.R. 200 #401 34476
(352) 351-8282 fax: (352) 351-3926
peggysheirlooms@aol.com
www.heirloomsoftomorrow.com
3700+ sq.ft.

Owner, Peggy Vogt, is a licensed Martha Pullen Heirloom Instructor. Enjoy the best of both worlds: "Quilting" and "Heirloom" Sewing! Featuring Thimbleberries, Northcott, Hoffman, RJR, Chanteclaire; Homespuns to Batiste!

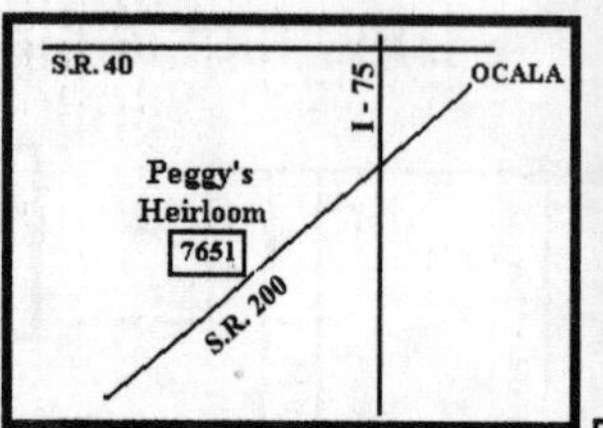

Belleview, FL #22

Mon - Fri 9 - 5
Sat 9 - 3

The Red Barn Quilt Shop

12672 South US Hwy. 301 34420
(352) 245-0332
redbarnquiltshop@webbox.com
Owner: Peggy Chiarenzelli
Mgr: Barb Andrews
Full service shop including Fabric, Supplies, Books & Patterns plus professional machine quilting.
We feature homespuns, reproductions and wools, but also carry marbles, florals and children's prints.

South Daytona, FL #23

Mon - Fri 9:30 - 4:30
Sat 9:30 - 3

Pelican Quiltworks

917 Beville Rd., Suite F 32119
(386) 761-8879
www.pelicanquiltworks.com
Owner: Michelle Ross

Quilting, Cloth Dolls & Silk Ribbon. We stock 100% Premium Quality Cotton. Fabrics and Kits for small projects. A wide variety of Books, Patterns & Cloth Doll Supplies available. Classes & Workshop offered. Several B.O.M. Programs

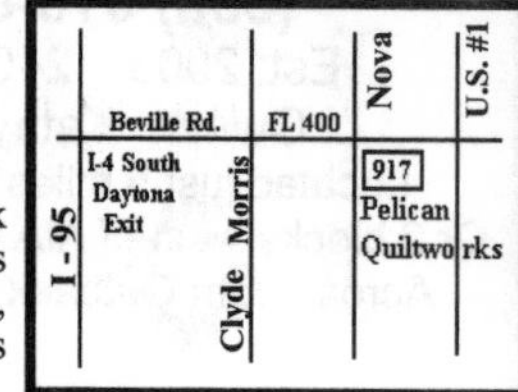

DeLand, FL #24

Quilt Shop of DeLand, Inc.

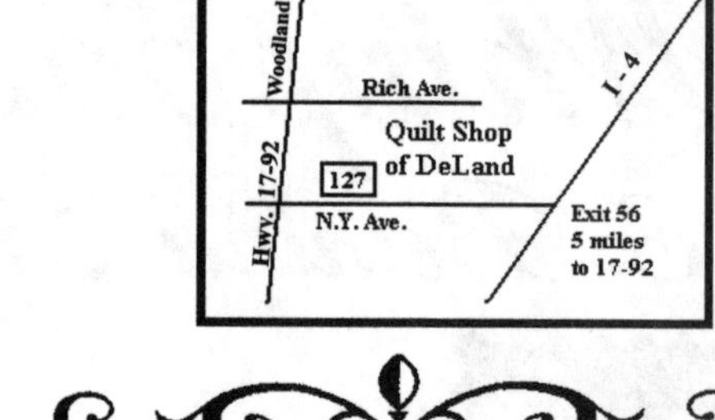

Featuring the Newest Fabrics, Patterns & Books on the Market
Located in the beautiful downtown Historic District.
And within walking distance of Stetson University

Come by for some refreshments and leisurely browse through our selection of 100% cotton fabrics.

Ask about our upcoming class schedules.

127 E. New York Ave.
DeLand, FL 32724
866-734-8782 or
386-734-8782
Owner: Judy Hansen
Est: 2001
quiltshopofdeland@hotmail.com
www.quiltshopofdeland.com

EXPERIENCE THE PERSONAL TOUCH

Mon - Sat 10 - 5

Busy Fingers

Quilt Shop, Inc.

460 N. Ronald Reagan Blvd, Suite #112
(C.R. 427) Longwood, FL 32750
(407) 767-5123
www.ourbusyfingers.com

Longwood, FL #26

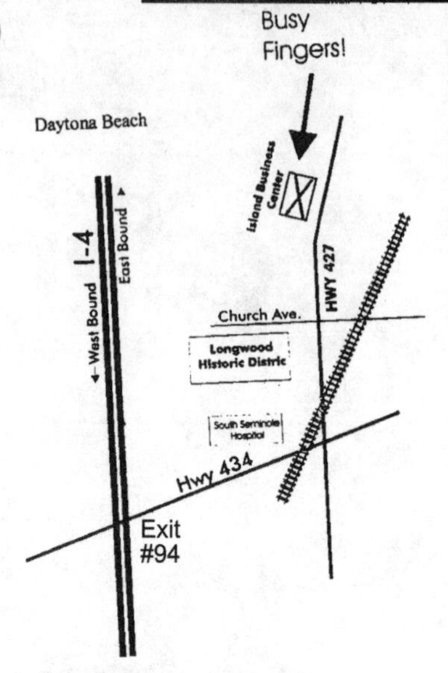

The Largest Quilt Shop in Seminole County. Located in Historic Longwood, 2.7 miles east of I - 4 off C.R. 434. Our fabrics include Hoffman, Batiks, RJR, Orientals, Maywood, Benartex, Timeless Treasures, Marcus Brothers, Kona Bay and many more. We are a Martingale Publishing Premier Shop. We offer the largest class selection in the entire Central Florida area.

Visiting Orlando ? Don't miss - - -

The Sewing Studio

FABRIC SUPERSTORE

Central Florida's Largest Selection of Quilting Fabrics

Orlando, FL #27

9605 S. Hwy. 17-92 Maitland, FL 32751
800-831-1492 407-831-6488
www.sewing.net

Mon - Fri 9:00 - 8:30
Sat 9:00 - 5:30 Sun 12 - 5

- ★Full Quilting Dept.: Fabrics, Patterns, and Books
- ★Full Line of Quilting Notions
- ★Smocking & Heirloom: Fabrics, Patterns and Plates
- ★Huge Selection of Bridal & Evening Wear Fabrics
- ★Lycra, Spandex, Stretch Velvets, Crushed Velvets
- ★Silks, Linens, Trims, Notions
- ★Buttons, Buttons, Buttons
- ★Don't Forget to Visit our Bargain Annex—Next Door!
- ★We have many 'Hard to Find' Items!

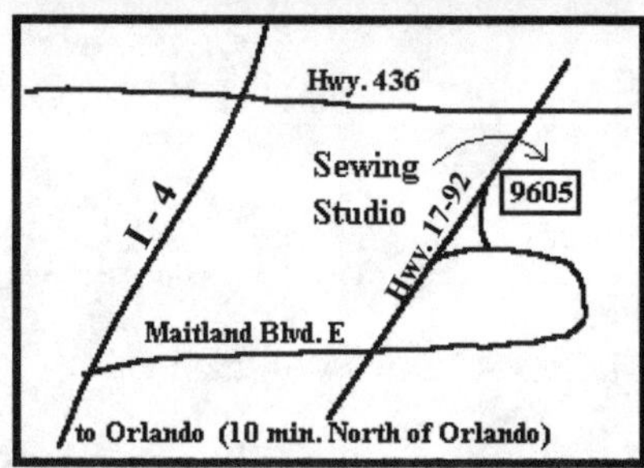

1/4 mile North of Maitland Blvd. Overpass on Hwy. 17-92

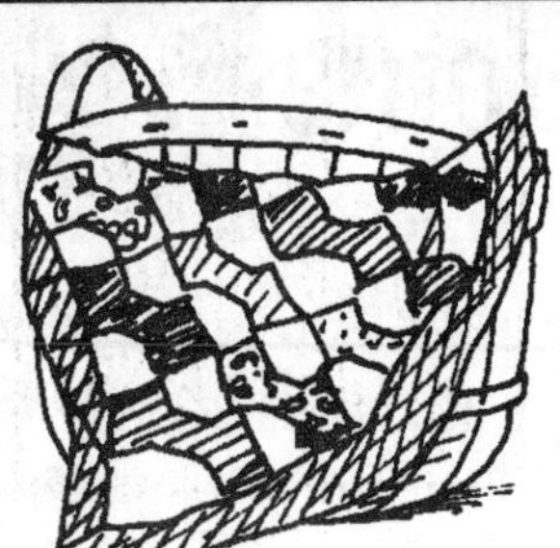

Orlando, FL #28

Sewing Gallery

407-281-0446

11921 E. Colonial Dr. (Alafaya Cummins)

info@sewandvacgallery.com 3500 sq.ft. showroom

Owners: Linda & Gabe Joseph

Mon - Fri 10 - 6
Thur til 8
Sat 10 - 4

Fabric Companies:

- Hoffman
- RJR
- South Seas
- P & B
- Benartex
- Kona Bay

Fully Stocked With:

- Fabrics
- Patterns
- Books
- Notions
- Mats
- Everything A Quilter Needs.

Factory Authorized Dealer For:

Pfaff ♦ Brother
Janome ♦ New Home ♦ Singer

We also specialize in: Bernina, Viking, Elna, White, & Babylock

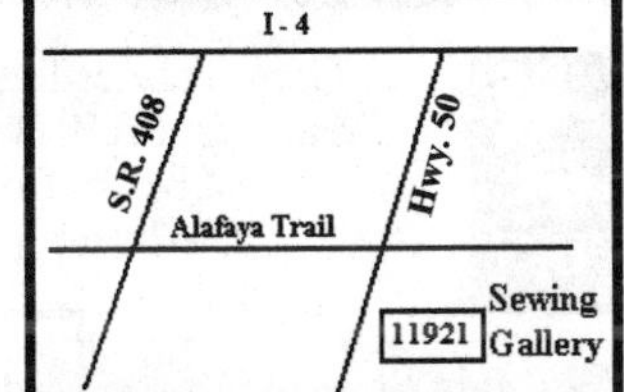

"L☺☺k"

We ship all over the World!

Quilting Folks
and Sewing Gallery

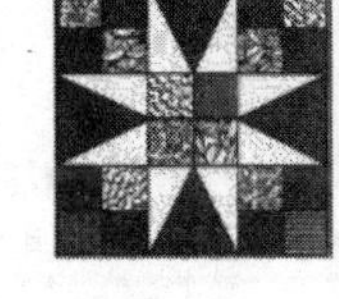

BERNINA
JANOME
PFAFF

E-Mail:
FLQuilts@aol.com

Mon - Fri 10 - 5
Sat 10 - 4

Full Line Quilt & Sew Shop
Over 2,000 Bolts of 100% Cotton Fabric
Hoffman ♥ Batiks ♥ RJR ♥ Thimbleberries
Moda ♥ South Seas ♥ Large selection of Flannel & Homespuns
And much, much more!

Cocoa, FL #29

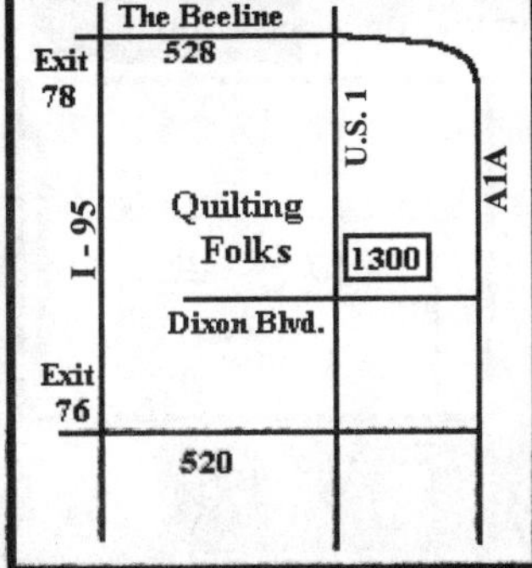

(321) 631-8601
1300 N. Cocoa Blvd.
Suite C
Cocoa, FL 32922

Owners:
Linda Joseph &
Bernadette Schecher

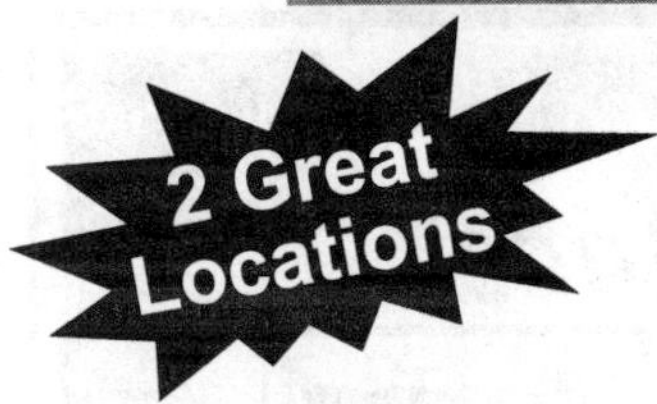

Melbourne, FL #30

(321) 253-3882
4501 N. Wickham Rd.
Melbourne, FL 32935

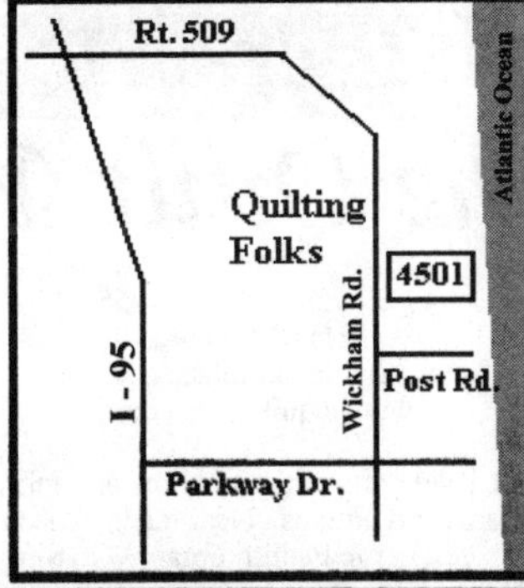

Melbourne, FL #31

Mon - Fri 9:30 - 5
Sat 9:30 - 4

Willow n Hare Quiltworks

1800 W Hibiscus Blvd #108 32901
(321) 951-7977
Owner: Susan A. Schering
Est: 2002 2000+ sq. ft.

Nestled in "The Oaks", we offer a wonderful selection of cotton fabrics, patterns, notions & classes with a friendly experienced staff.

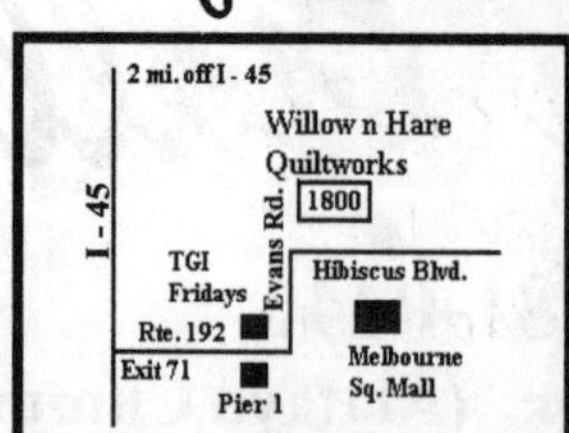

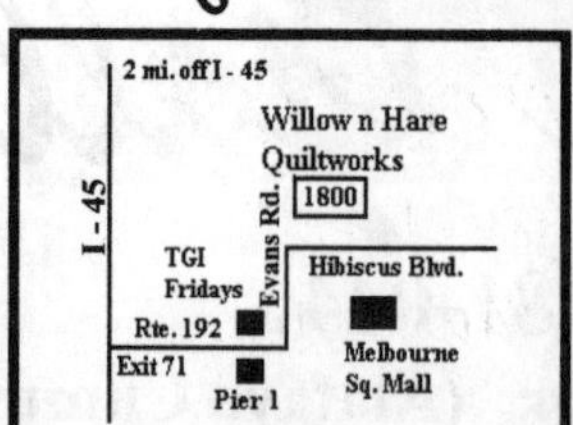

The Good Home Quilt Company

Mon - Fri 10 - 5
Sat 10 - 4

5600 W. Colonial Dr. #309 32808
(407) 523-3612 Fax: (407) 523-3613
goodhomequiltco@aol.com
Owner: Carol Crago Est: 1999 1000+ Bolts

Primitive folkart look, traditional and reproduction fabrics, patterns, books, rughooking, hand-dyed wool, stitchery and much more.

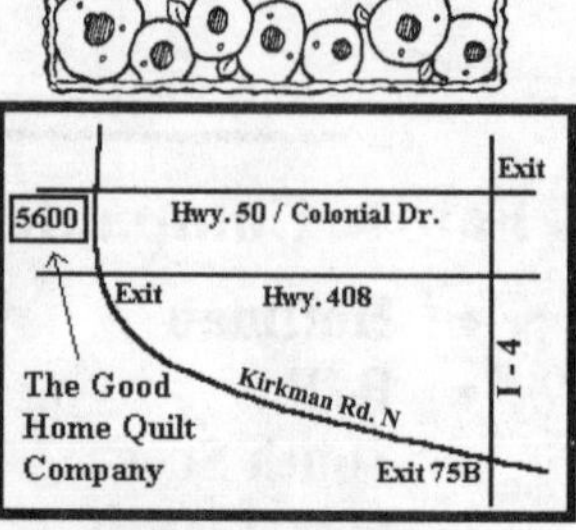

Orlando, FL #32

A QUILTER'S DREAM, INC

Leesburg, FL #33

Mon - Sat 9 - 5
Wed til 7

Great Fabrics from Hoffman, Timeless Treasures, P&B, Benartex. Stop in and see the newest books from That Patchwork Place.
"Always a friendly Smile"

703 W. Main St. 34748
(352) 728-1482
a_quilters_dream@earthlink.net
Owner: Connie Czernuch
Est: 2002
1700 sq.ft. 1000 Bolts

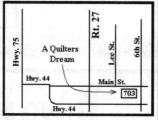

Hwy. 75
Rt. 27
A Quilters Dream
Lee St.
6th St.
Hwy. 44
Main St.
703
Hwy. 44

www.aquiltersdream.biz

Dade City, FL #34

Mon - Sat 10 - 5

Quilts on Plum Lane

14215 7th St. 33523
(352) 518-0003 Fax: (352) 518-0022
plumlaned1@cs.com
www.quiltsonplumlane.com
Owner: Donna Lillibridge
Mgr. Carol Bradshaw Est: 2003
Located in Dade City's Downtown Antique District. Large selection of Books & Patterns, notions, classes. New Brand-Name 100% Cottons, Flannels, & Batiks, Kits.

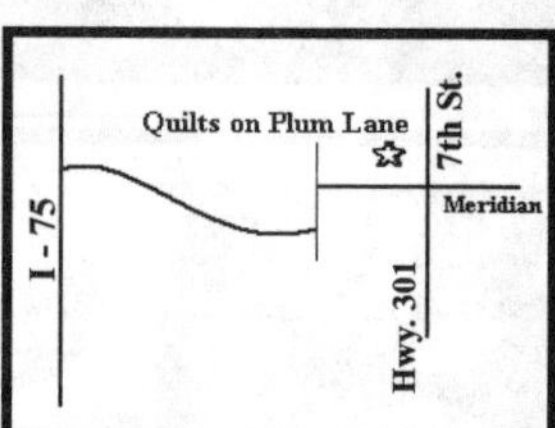

Zephyrhills, FL #35

Mon - Fri 10 - 5
Sat 10 - 3

QUILTER'S QUARTERS

4733 Allen Rd. 33541
(813) 779-2615 Fax: Same
quiltersqrtrs@verizon.net
Owner: Yvonne Pederson
Est: 2003 1000+ bolts
"The comforts of home are quilted!"
100% cotton fabric, books & patterns, sewing notions, classes & friendly, helpful service.

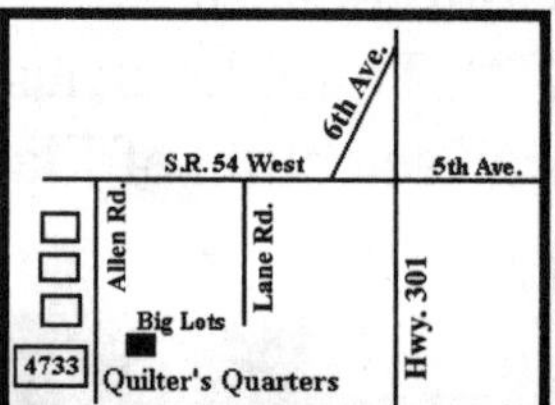

Thimbles & Thread

275 Magnolia Ave. #6 32952
(321) 456-5685
Fax: (321) 456-5774
Quilts1999@aol.com
www.thimblesandthread.com
Est: 1996 2000 sq.ft.

Mon - Sat 10 - 5
Tues & Thur 10 til 7

Books - Patterns
Notions - Classes
Mail Order - Decorative Thread
100% Cotton thread in 1200 yards and 6000 yd. spools.

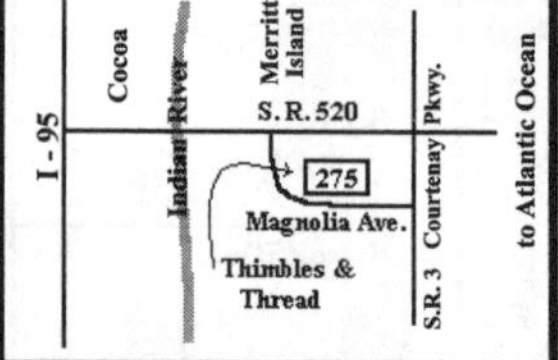

Merritt Island, FL #36

Rockledge, FL #37

Mon - Sat 10 - 5

The Quilt Place

840 Brevard Ave. 32955
(321) 632-3344
teresa@thequiltplace.com
www.thequiltplace.com

Over 1000 bolts of fabric. Lots of books, patterns and notions. Near quaint Cocoa Village. Large Pattern library. On Site Machine Quilting. Fast turn around.

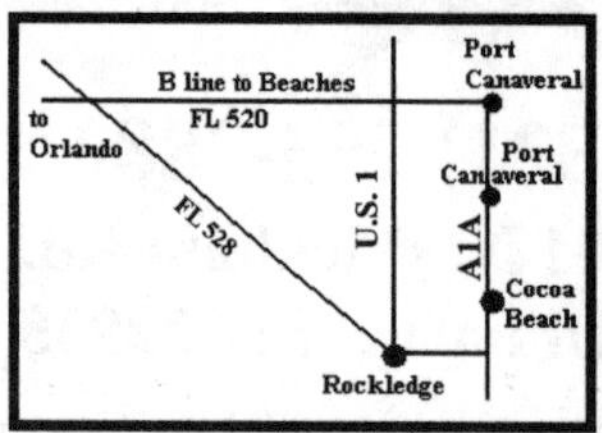

Marilou's Quilting & Sewing Center

"A Better Place to Buy"

Custom Machine Quilting, Quilting Supplies, Fabric, Books, Husqvarna Viking Sewing Machines, Sales and Service. Quilts for sale. Classes in Sewing, Embroidery & Computer.

C.R. 512
Exit 69
8 mi.
4 mi.
U.S. 1
I - 95
Marilou's 8802
C.R. 510
1/4 mile north of C.R. 510 next to Vero Beach Kampground

Sebastian, FL #38

Wabasso Plaza
8802 N U.S. Hwy 1,
Sebastian, FL 32958
(772) 589-0011
Fax: (772) 589-5682

Est: 1996

Mon - Fri 10 - 6
Sat 10 - 4

Owners: Stan Kahn & Marilou Keen
e-mail: Quilting 2125@aol.com

www.marilousquilting.com

Tomorrow's Treasures

802 N. Suncoast Blvd. (Hwy. 19) 34429 (352) 795-2600
E-Mail: sew@tampabay.rr.com Web Site: www.crquilts.com
Fax: (352) 795-0883 Est: 1998 2600 sq.ft

* Huge Classroom
* Warm & Personal Service
* Distinctive Designs
* Original Patterns
* Kits, Notions & Books
* Large Selection of Stencils
* Mail Order
* 4000 Bolts of the Finest 100% Cotton Quilting Fabrics
* Applique and Novelty Fabrics are our Specialty.
* Authorized Bernina Dealer

Fort Island Trail
1/2 mi.
Suncoast Blvd. Hwy. 19
Tomorrow's Treasures 802
Crystal River Airport

Mon - Sat 9 - 4
Tues 9 - 7
Open Sunday 1 - 4
Oct. thru April

Crystal River, FL #39

Kissimmee, FL #40

Mon - Sat 10 - 5 Tues til 9

Queen Ann's Lace

715 East Vine Street 34744
(407) 846-7998
Owners: Ginny & Tom King
Est: 1991 4500 sq.ft.
3500 Bolts of 100% Cotton
plus supplies, notions, & patterns
Everything you'll need.
Silk Ribbon Embroidery & Doll Supplies.

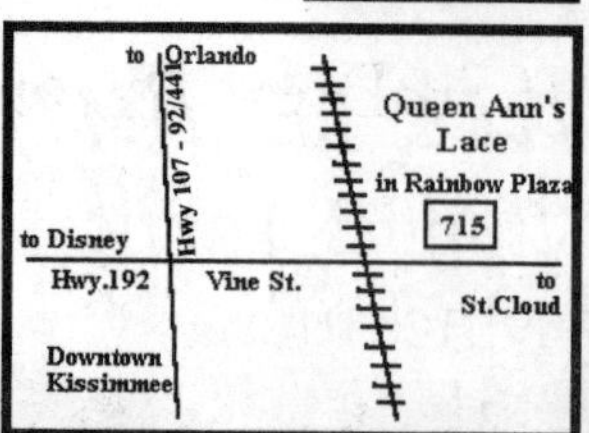

NEEDLES AND THREAD INC.

A QUILT SHOP

Port St. Joe, FL #41

Warm, Friendly family-like shop.

VON BOUINGTON
G. "SUSIE" PIPPIN

Fine Fabrics -- 100% Cotton -- Top Companies
All Notions -- Collector's Thimbles -- Books
Sewing Machines -- Embroidery

Mon - Fri 9 - 5:30 Sat 9 - 4

317 Williams Ave. 32456
(850) 227-9880
Fax: (850) 227-9846
quiltgals@gt.com.net

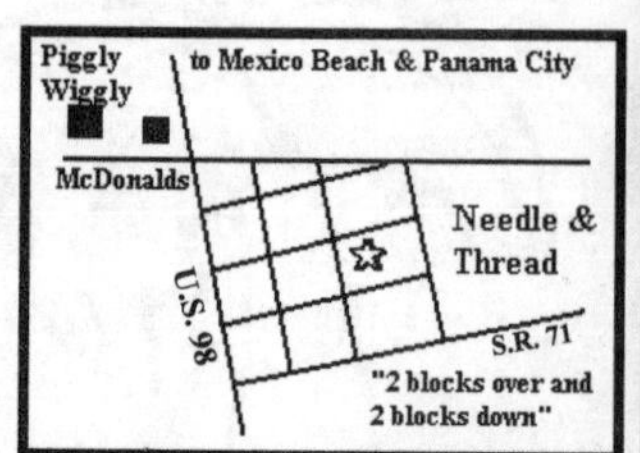

Dunnellon, FL #42

Mon - Fri 10 - 5 Sat 10 - 4

Cottonbelle Quilt Shop

20625 W. Pennsylvania 34431
(352) 489-2900 Fax: (352) 489-0050
cottonbe@bellsouth.net
www.cottonbelle.com
Owner: Nancy Eaton
Est: 2002 1500 sq.ft. 1500+ bolts
Wonderful selection of 100% cotton Fabric,
Notions, Books, Patterns & Gifts.
Rug Hooking Supplies.

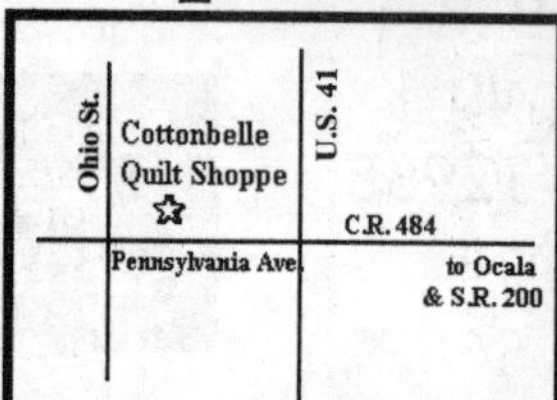

Hudson, FL #43

Tues - Sat 10 - 5 Tues, Thur, Fri 7 - 9 pm also

Quilt Til You Wilt

9609 Fulton Ave. 34667
(727) 862-6141 Fax: (727) 868-4765
pipsqeak@gte.net
Owner: Pat Wilkinson
Est: 1998 2000 sq.ft.
Professional machine quilting. Quilt & Bear making classes, Supplies for both. Over 1800 bolts of fabric!! One room of embroidery, for all your professional embroidery needs.

Cty. Line Rd.
3 miles
Quilt Til You Wilt
9609
Fulton Ave.
5 miles
New York Ave.
U.S. 19
Little Rd.
U.S. 52

Hudson, FL #44

Tues, Thur Fri 9 - 5 Wed & Sat 9 - 4

Pins & Needles Fabric & Quilt Shop

8216 State Rd. 52 34667
(727) 819-9559
viodell1@netzero.net
www.angelfire.com/fl4/pins and needles 8216
Est: 2000 1080 sq.ft. 1000+ Bolts
High quality 100% cotton fabrics, books, patterns, notions. Hand & machine quilting classes. Friendly, helpful customer service.

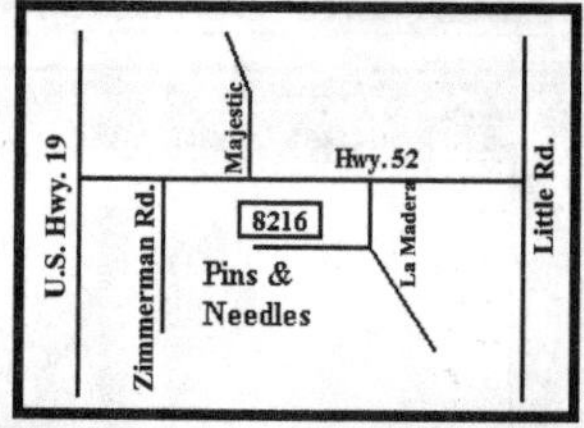

Port Richey, FL #45

Tues - Fri 9 - 5 Sat 9 - 3

A & A White's Sewing & Fabric

11720 U.S. 19 34668
(727) 697-1892
aawhitessewing@aol.com
www.sew-fabric.com
Est: 1999 1400 sq.ft. 2500+ bolts

Dealer for Pfaff, Babylock, Elna, Brother, Craftmaster, Singer, Riccar--Repairs on all Makes, Classes. Everything You Would Need For Quilting.

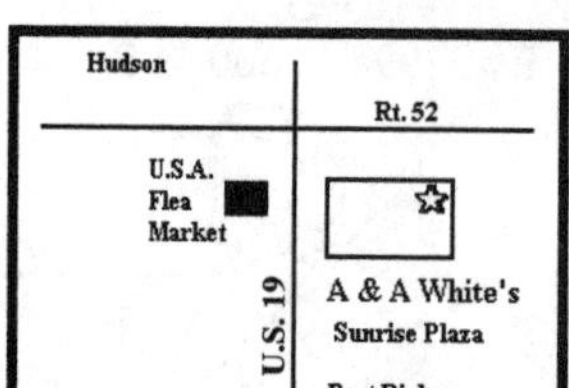

Holiday, FL #46

Mon - Fri 9 - 5 Sat 9 - 3 Sun 10 - 4

A & A White's Sewing & Fabric

2621 U.S. 19 34691
(727) 937-6510 Fax: (727) 937-6590
aawhitessewing@aol.com
www.sew-fabric.com
Est: 1979 2400 sq.ft. 3500+ bolts

Dealer for Pfaff, Babylock, Elna, Brother, Craftmaster, Singer, Riccar--Repairs on all Makes, Classes. Everything You Would Need For Quilting.

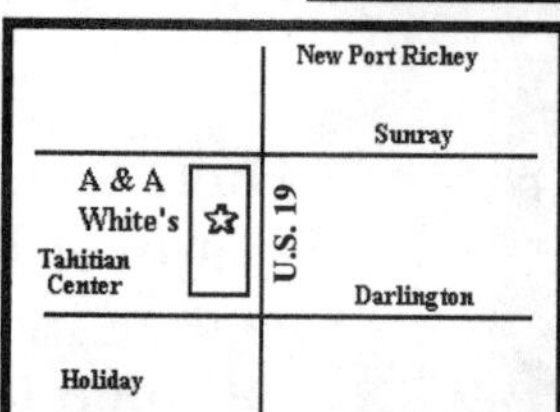

Largo, FL #47

Mon - Fri 10 - 5 Sat 10 - 4

The Quilt Stop, Inc.

7250 Ulmerton Rd. #D 33771
(727) 532-4566
QuiltStop@aol.com
www.QuiltStop.com
Owners: Michael & Cheryl Solt
Est: 1997 1200 sq.ft. 1500+ Bolts
Over 1500 Bolts of Fine Fabrics.
Notions, Books. Classes - Year Round
Friendly, knowledgeable personnel.

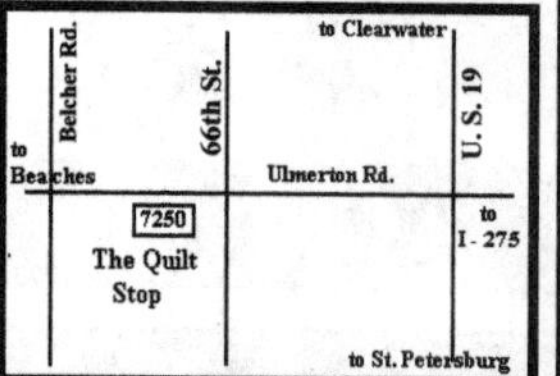

Clearwater, FL #48

Tues - Fri 10 - 4 Sat & Sun 10 - 4

A & A White's Sewing & Fabric

22095 U.S. 19 N 33765
(727) 791-6441 Fax: (727) 797-6978
aawhitessewing@aol.com
www.sew-fabric.com
Est: 2001 4000 sq.ft. 3000+ bolts

Dealer for Pfaff, Babylock, Elna, Brother, Craftmaster, Singer, Riccar--Repairs on all Makes, Classes. Everything You Would Need For Quilting.

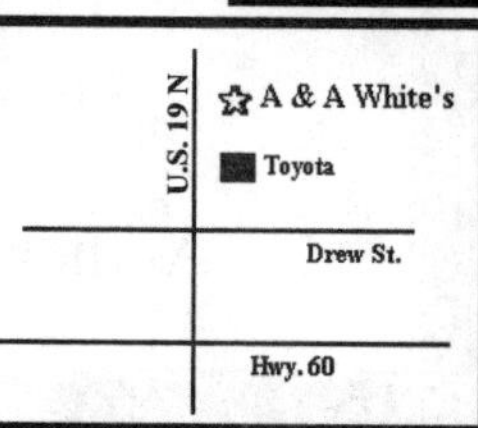

Country Quilts "N" Bears, Inc

1983 Drew Street 33765
(727) 461-4171 Est: 1986 3300 sq.ft.
Owners: Marilyn & John Humphries

Clearwater, FL #49

Country Store with a Christian Heart

A fully stocked quilt shop — 3000 bolts of cotton fabrics. Large selection of flannels. Friendly Service.

Classes in quilting, country clothing, & miniature bears. Beginner bears, advanced and limited edition Teddy Bear classes taught by Francy Gordon. Mohair, luxury plush acrylic fur, glass eyes, joints and Bear accessories available.

Mon - Fri 9 - 5
Tues til 9
Sat 9 - 4

Drew St.
1983
Country Quilts "N" Bears
Hercules
Belcher
U.S. 19
Rt. 60 (Gulf to Bay)

Dunedin, FL #50

RAINBOWS END QUILT SHOPPE

YOUR COMPLETE QUILT SHOPPE

941 BROADWAY STREET (ALT 19) 34698
(727) 733-8572 (800) 353-1928
WWW.RAINBOWS-END.COM
EST: 1982 6900 SQ.FT

LARGEST QUILT SHOP IN FLORIDA
OVER15,000 BOLTS OF COTTON FABRIC
HUNDREDS OF BOOKS, NOTIONS, PATTERNS & STENCILS
QUILT, WALLHANGING & EMBROIDERY KITS
SILK & WIRE RIBBON -- BOOKS & PATTERNS
STOP & SEE OUR LARGE COLLECTION OF SAMPLES
OF PATTERNS, BOOKS & OUR CLASSES
A PFAFF & ELNA DEALER - SALES & SERVICE

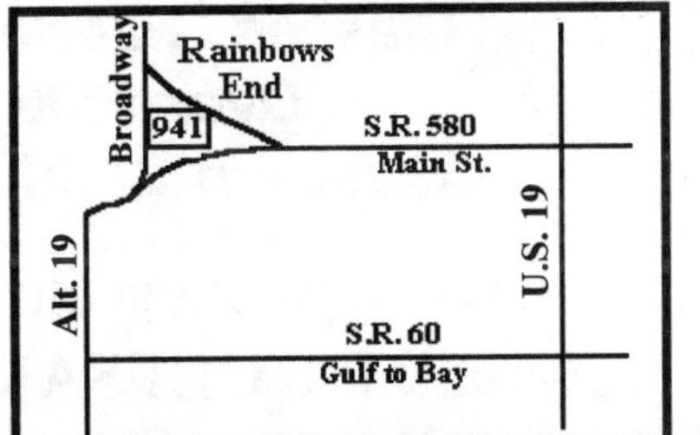

MON - SAT 10 AM-5 PM & WED 10 AM - 8 PM

Tampa, FL #51 & 52

Keep Me In Stitches

A Specialty Sewing Center

Authorized Dealers for

Janome/New Home • Baby Lock • Elna
Origins - Auto Digitizing Software

Service of all Models
Classes • Fabrics • Sewing and Quilting Supplies
Sewing Cabinets • Specialty Threads

Over 1200 Bolts of Fabric

Website: www.kmisinc.com

E-mail: Mail@kmisinc.com

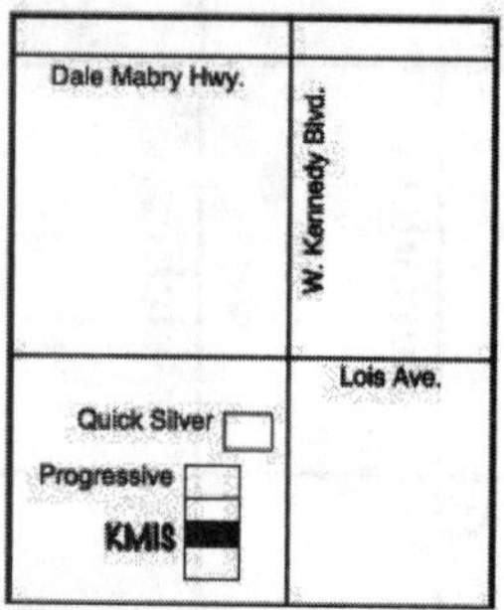

Come visit us at either of our locations.
We're the friendly quilters!

4237 West Kennedy Blvd. Tampa, FL 33609
(813) 282-1526 • Fax 282-3655

14833 North Dale Mabry Hwy. Tampa, FL 33618
(813) 908-3889 • Fax (813) 908-3898

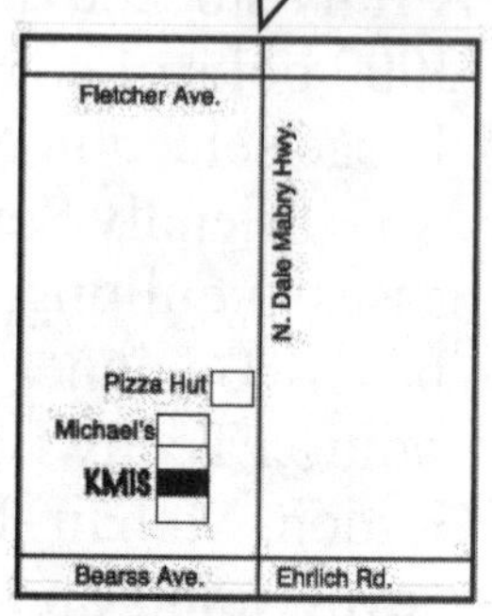

Store Hours Mon - Fri 10-6 Sat 9-4

Store Hours Mon - Sat 9-5

Parrish, FL #53

Owners: Lynn Briscoe & Lois Ankrom

8915 US 301 North, Parrish, FL 34219
Located at Parkwood Square
941.776.5669 Fax 941.776.0742

Mon - Fri 9 - 6
Sat 9 - 4

Authorized BERNINA Dealer
Classes · Fabrics · Notions
Over 4000 Bolts
Classes in Quilting & Sewing

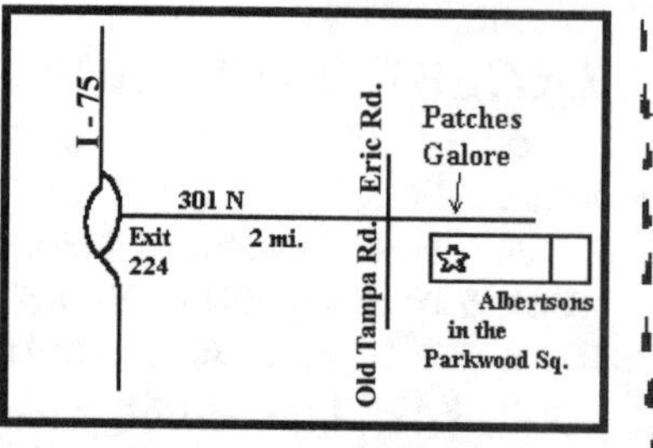

www.patchesgaloreinc.com
E-mail: PATCHESART@msn.com

Granny's Trunk

4644 Cleveland
Heights Blvd. 33813
(863) 646-0074
Fax: (863) 646-4329
Owner: Pamela Bell
1500 sq.ft.

Mon - Fri 10 - 5
Sat 10 - 4

Over 2,000 Bolts of
100% Cotton Quilt Fabrics.
Quilt books, Patterns,
Notions.
Bernina Sewing Machines.
Machine Embroidery
Supplies.

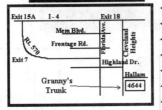

Exit 15A
I - 4
Exit 18
Mem Blvd.
Frontage Rd.
Rt. 570
Florida Ave.
Cleveland Heights
Exit 7
Highland Dr.
Hallam
Granny's Trunk
4644

Lakeland, FL #54

Winter Haven, FL #56

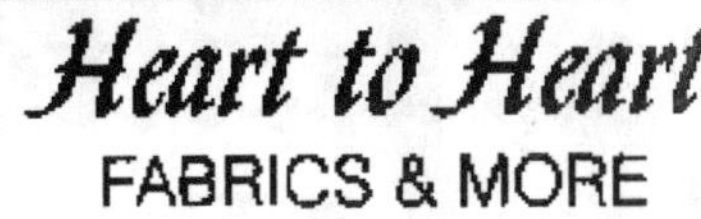

QUILTING AND SCRAPBOOK SHOP

365 5th St. SW 33880
Off Ave "C" SW between Old & New Hwy. 17
(863) 298-8185 fax: (863) 294-3685
Owners: Pat Brenchley & Patricia Roberts
Est: 2000 ♥ 4000 sq.ft.
3000+ bolts - Most $5.99 yard

Quilting & Scrapbooking Shop Specializing in 100% Cotton Fabrics, Sewing Machine Sales & Service. Acid & Lignin Free Archival Safe Papers, Stickers & Albums for Scrapbooks.

Janome
Sewing
Machines

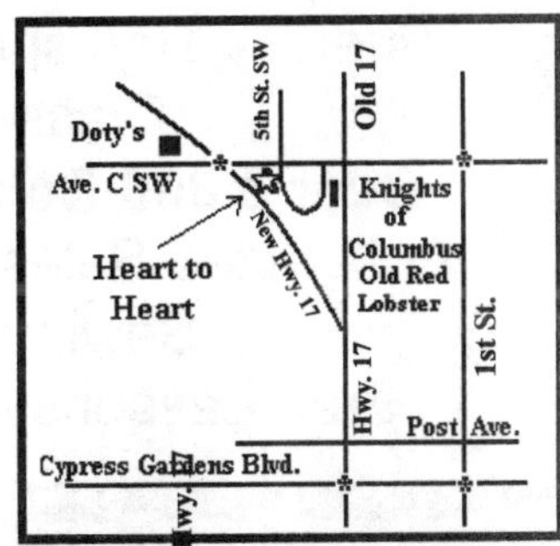

Mon - Sat 9 - 5 Tues & Fri til 8

Lakeland, FL #55

Mon - Fri
10 - 5:30
Sat 10 - 4

Patchwork Pig

228 E. Pine St. 33801
(863) 692-4774 Fax: (863) 680-9943
patchworkpig@verizon.net
Est: 2003 3000 sq.ft. 5000+ bolts

Everything for the quilter - except more time!
Over 5,000 bolts of fabric in a 1903 historic building in downtown Lakeland.

I - 4
Exit 32
Hwy. 98
Hwy. 92
Memorial Blvd.
Fla. Ave.
Patchwork Pig
Kentucky Ave.
Pine St.
228
3rd light

Sebring, FL #57

Crafty Quilters

13221 Hwy. 98 33876
(863) 655-4600 Est: 1990
E-Mail: shdee@strato.net
Owner: Dee Dee Bedard

Mon - Fri
9 - 5
Sat 9 - 3

For all your Quilting Needs.
Quilting Frames.
Classes Available.
Factory Authorized Dealer of
New Home & Janome.
Repairs on all Machines.

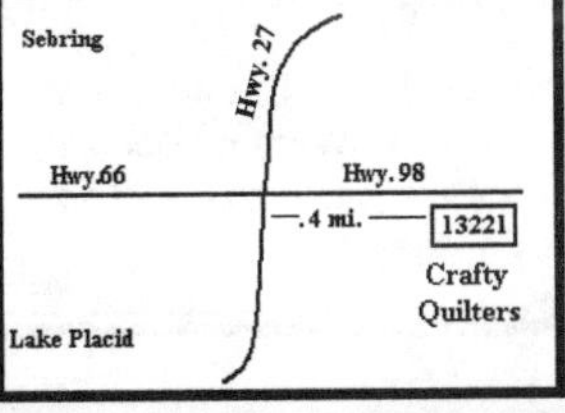

Lake Placid, FL #58

Tues - Fri
10 - 5
Sat 9 - 1

Sew-Biz

299 Interlake Blvd. 33852
(863) 699-2228 Fax: (863) 699-2272
sewbiz@htn.net
Owner: Paul & Nancy Vasilchik
Est: 1992 2400 sq. ft. 1000 Bolts.

Home of playful pets and squishy fishie and other Quilt Patterns and Books. Enjoy fellowship with fellow fabricholics.

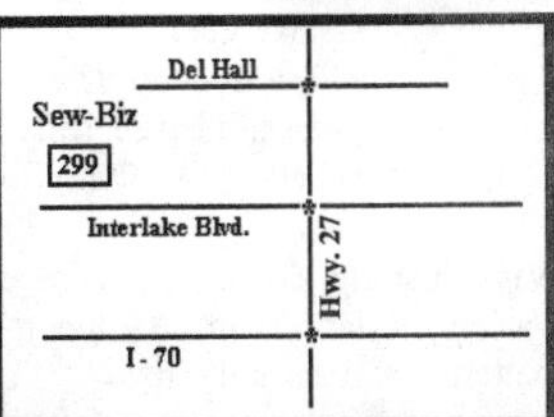

Sarasota, FL #59

Mon - Sat
10 - 5

Cotton Patch Quilt Shop

5333 N. Tamiami Tr. #103 34234
(941) 351-6677
www.cottonpatchquiltshop.com
Owner: Laura Flynn

100% cotton quilting fabrics from brights to vintage & so many wonderful fabrics in between. Providing ideas, inspiration and supplies for your quiltmaking adventures.

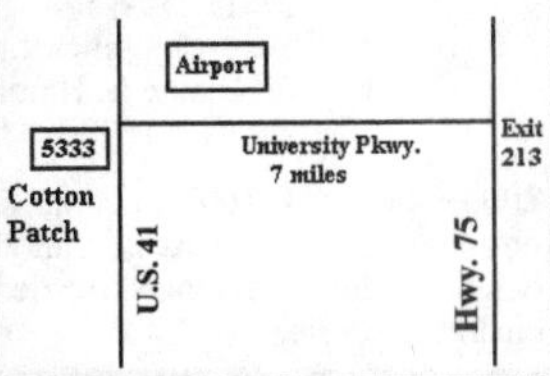

Ellenton, FL #60

2418 U.S. Hwy. 301 N 34222
(941) 729-0511 Est: 1996

Husqvarna VIKING

Mon - Sat
9:30 - 4
Summer
Tues - Sat
9:30 - 4
Or by Appt.

"Favorite Location of Quilters for over 20 Years!!"

Exceptional Fabric Selection. Knowledgeable & Friendly staff specializing in color coordination.
Classes for all Skill Levels.
Over 3,000 Bolts, Books, Notions & Patterns.
Authorized Sales & Service of Husqvarna Viking Sewing Machines & Sergers.
Free Lessons with any Machine Purchased.

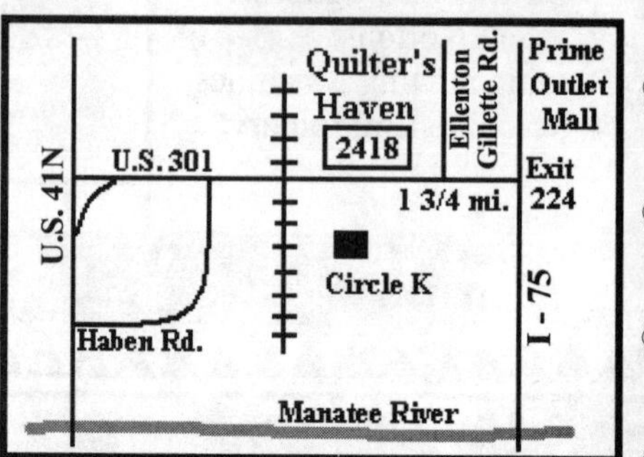

Conveniently located off I - 75, Exit 224 (Ellenton) turn right on 301 (south), go approx. 1 3/4 miles. We are on right side (north) directly across from Circle K

Venice, FL #61

Deborah's Quilt Basket

Mon - Fri
10 - 5
Sat 10 - 2
Closed Sat.
May - Sept.

337 W. Venice Ave. 34285
(941) 488-6866 Fax: Same
debsquiltbasket@aol.com
Est: 1984 2000 Bolts

Visit historic downtown Venice. See a large variety of fabrics in addition to lots of books, patterns, notions and gifts.

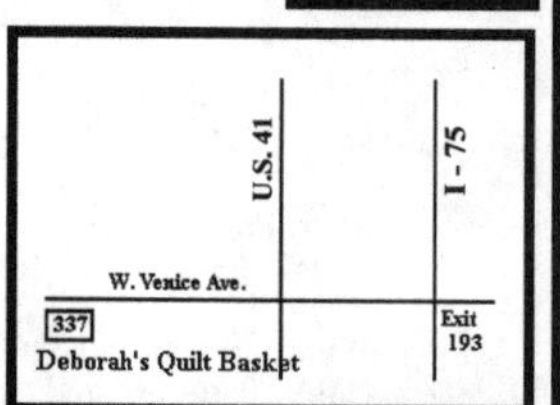

Port Charlotte, FL #62

Quilts n' More

Mon - Fri
9:30 - 5
Sat 9:30 - 4

17753 Toledo Blade Blvd #4D 33948
(941) 255-9330
quiltsnmore@comcast.net
Owner: Elaine L. Hamlin
Est: 2000 1800 sq. ft.

2000+ bolts of 100% cotton fabrics, books, notions, patterns, classes. Janome authorized dealer. Horn cabinets. Friendly, helpful customer service.

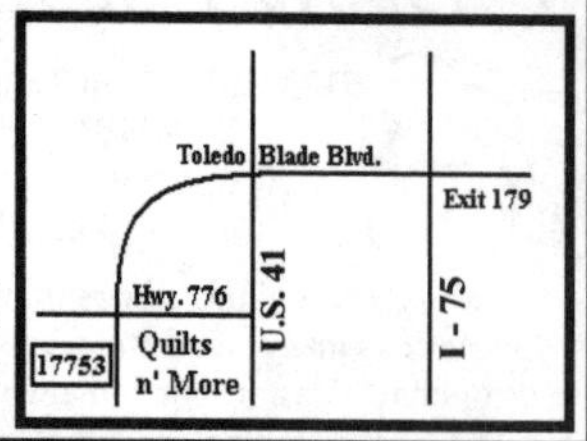

Ft. Myers, FL #63

Quilter's Corner

12717-1 McGregor, Fort Myers, Florida 33919
NE corner of College & McGregor
239-437-4555
Owner - Alice Ferriola

The most complete Quilt shop
In southwest Florida
More than 3,000 bolts of fabric
Classes, Notions, Books, Patterns

From I-75 S - exit 136 Colonial West to US 41 South to College, west to McGregor

From I-75 N - exit 131 at Daneils. West on Daniels to McGregor, then north to College.

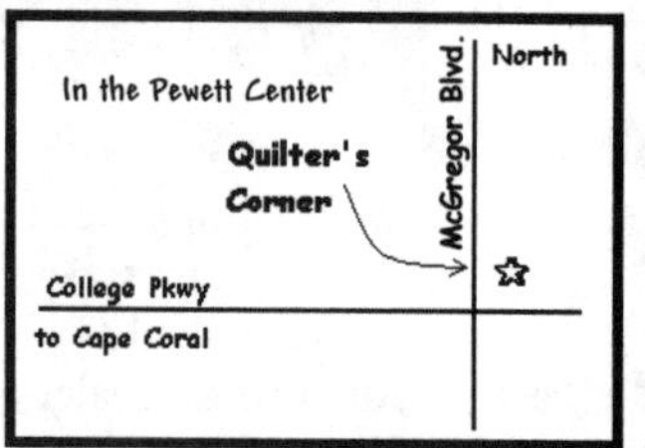

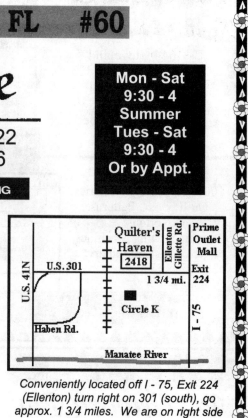

Punta Gorda, FL #64

Tues - Fri 10 - 5
Sat 10 - 3
Open Mon
11/1 - 4/30

Kountry Klub Kollectibles

149 W. Marion Ave. 33950
(941) 639-6139
Owner: Michelle Kline
Est: 1997 2200 sq.ft. 4300 bolts

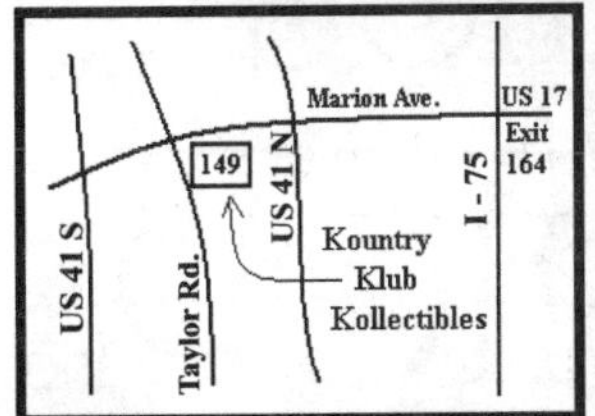

Located in historic downtown Punta Gorda. 4300 bolts of 100% cotton fabrics, notions, books, patterns and kits. Great customer service.

Sanibel, FL #65

Mon - Sat
9:30 - 5

Three Crafty Ladies, Inc.

1620 Periwinkle Way 33957
(239) 472-2893 Fax: (239) 433-9316
Craftyladies@webtv.net

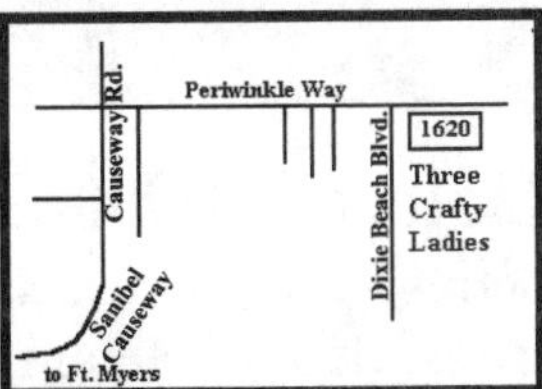

Over 2000 Quilting Fabrics featuring batiks and fish, shell, and tropical prints—including Hoffman. Quilting patterns, books and supplies.

Naples, FL #67

S. Sewing
E. Education
W. Workshops
STUDIO

2360 Immokalee Rd. 34110
(239) 598-3752 Fax: Same
Owner: Rita Decker Est: 1992 3200 sq.ft.

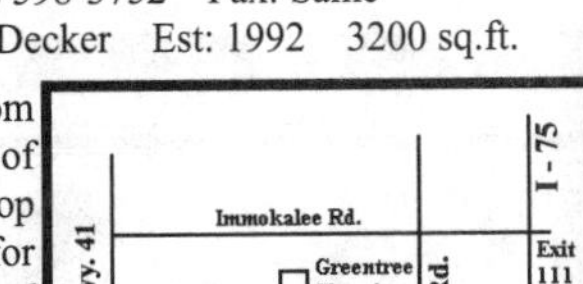

www.sewstudio.com
Unique collection of over 3000 Bolts of top quality cottons for quilting. Full line of garment construction fabrics. Notions, kits, classes. Authorized PFAFF and Singer Dealer. Rental Machines

Fort Pierce, FL #68

Mon &
Wed - Sat
9 - 5

Tomorrow's Heirlooms

1840 S. King's Hwy. 34945
(772) 461-9510
Owners: Theresa & Earle Field
2100 Bolts

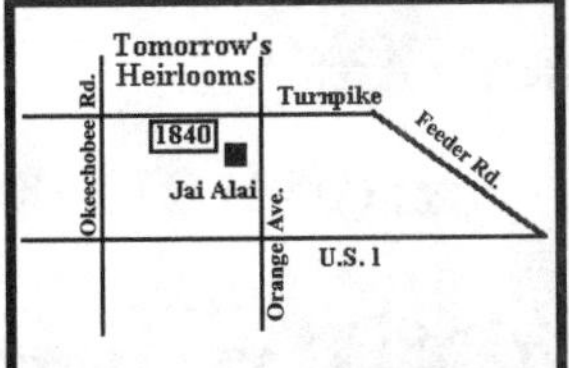

100% Cottons, Quilting Patterns, Quilting Supplies, Instruction Books.

Port St. Lucie, FL #70

Mon - Fri
9 - 5
Wed til 7
Sat 9 - 4

Keepsake Quilt Shop

10778 S. Federal Hwy. 34953
(772) 337-7728
Owner: Pamela K. Clark

Over 1000 bolts of 100% cotton fabrics by supplies including thimbleberries, RJR, Michael Miller, Hoffman, South Seas, Marcus Bros., Clothworks, Benartex and more. Books, Notions, Patterns & Classes for all levels of quilters!

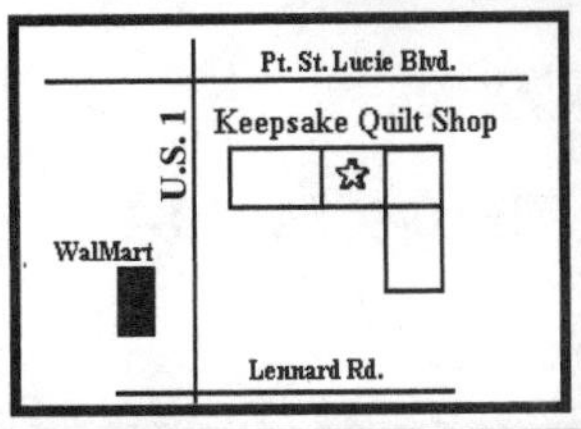

a stitch above

Yes! Everyone receives a discount
Yes! We carry a complete line of Aurifil thread
Yes! Special ordering with a smile
Yes! Free help with your quilt projects
Yes! An extraordinary line of oriental fabrics
Yes! Contemporary quilt headquarters
Yes! Tom repairs ALL machines in-house

Mon - Sat 9:30 - 5:30

Hitching Post Plaza
11514 E. Tamiami
(U.S. 41) 34113
(239) 239-1104
quiltpack@aol.com

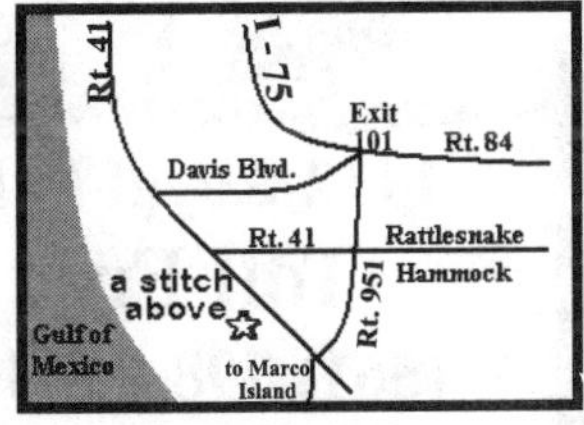

"Home of the FREE-MOTION SLIDER"

Naples, FL #66

Treasure Coast Quilt Studio

Authorized Gammill Dealer. Pfaff & White Sewing Machine Dealer. Sales & service on all machines. Wonderful selection of fabrics & classes. National teachers. Award winning longarm quilting done on-site.

Fort Pierce, FL #69

4804 S. US 1, Fort Pierce, FL 34982
772-466-1414
Owners: Rick & Tammy Mathias
Est: 2001 5000 sq.ft. 1500 Bolts

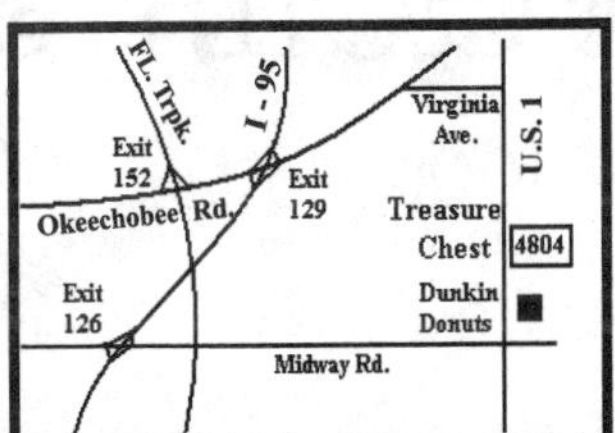

In the Del Rio Plaza

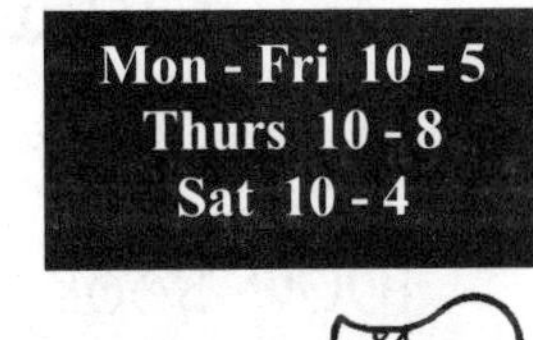

tcquiltstudio@aol.com
Website: Coming Soon

follow me to ...

Suzanne's QUILT SHOP Inc

Shop our Award Winning website since 1998
www.suzannesquilts.com

Original Owner Since 1988: Suzanne Leimer

1112 Royal Palm Beach Blvd. 33411
Toll Free (888) 798-0934
(561) 798-0934 Fax: (561) 798-3767

1112
Okechobee Blvd
Suzanne's Quilt Shop
Royal Palm Beach Blvd
S.R. 7 / 441
Turnpike
Military Trail
I - 95
Southern Blvd.
Lake Worth Rd.

6 miles West of Florida Turnpike West Palm Beach exit

Monday - Saturday 10 - 5:30
Evenings During Classes

Royal Palm Beach, FL #71

5000 Bolts of 100% Cotton Fabrics
Antique Reproductions, Aunt Grace's, Batiks, Orientals, Florals,
Thimbleberries, Debbie Mumm, Flannels, Tropicals,
Juvenile Prints, Plaids & Christmas.
Paper Foundations * Electric Quilt Software & Books
Books & Patterns for Quilts & Clothing
Quilt Planning * Classes & Private Lessons

Fort Lauderdale, FL #72

SUNSHINE SEWING COMPANY

Authorized Janome Dealer

1312 N. State Rd. 7, Margate, FL 33063
*** Fort Lauderdale Area ***
Tel: (954) 971-4810 ~ Fax: (954) 972-0035

LARGEST QUILT SHOP IN SOUTH FLORIDA

7500 Bolts of 100% Cotton Fabric ~ 1000 Batiks
1000 Book Titles ~ Classes ~ Computer Programs
Kits ~ Notions ~ Patterns

Store Hours: M,T,W,F 10-5; Th 10-9; Sat 10-4

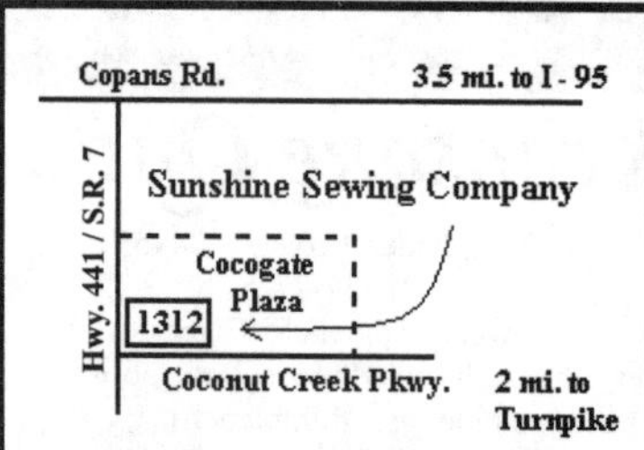

Web Site: www.sunshinesewing.com

Email: sewwithfay@aol.com

ONCE UPON A QUILT, CO.

Once Upon A Quilt
Is one of 10 shops being featured in the Fall/Winter 2004 Sampler issue of
American Patchwork & Quilting Magazine

3404 Griffin Road * Ft. Lauderdale * Florida * 33312
(954) 987-8827 * e-mail: ouaq@aol.com

We invite you to visit us in person or shop with
Us online 24/7 at...
www.onceuponaquilt.com

SHOP HOURS
9:30 - 4:30
Tuesday - Saturday

BERNINA

PFAFF
...when performance counts!

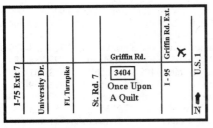

Fort Lauderdale, FL #73

2500 Bolts of 100 % Cotton Fabrics

Books * Videos * Software * Patterns
Notions * Silk & Wire edged Ribbon
Embellishments * Unique Gift Items
Classes and much more...

A Friendly Staff and a
Warm & Welcome Atmosphere

PROUD SPONSORS OF QUILT SHOW BY THE SEA
Shows on the even # Years
Next show March 2006

Visit our website
www.onceuponaquilt.com

click the Lighthouse
For up - to - date
Show information

I-75 Exit 7
University Dr.
FL Turnpike
St. Rd. 7
Griffin Rd.
3404
Once Upon A Quilt
I - 95
Griffin Rd. Ext.
U.S. 1
N

4 Miles From the Hlwd/Ft. Lauderdale Airport

Quilters Marketplace

Mon - Sat
10 - 5

Owner: Marilyn Dorwart
Est: 1987
4000 sq.ft

524 E. Atlantic Avenue 33483 (561) 243-3820
Web Site: www.quiltersmaketplace.net

I - 95
Woolbright
Atlantic Ave.
Linton
U.S. 1 South
U.S. 1 North
524
Quilters Marketplace

1200 bolts of 100% cotton including a beautiful array of tropical and Bali fabrics.
Complete Notion Dept.
Many patterns and a large selection of books.
Gifts and a Friendly Staff. Classes.

Delray Beach, FL #74

Coral Springs, FL #75

Mon - Sat 10 - 5
Sun 12 - 4

Country Stitches

11471 W. Sample Road 33065
(954) 755-2411
Owner: Gayle Boshek
Est: 1982 3200 sq.ft.

Your one stop Quilting Shoppe.
Over 3000 bolts of fabric and patterns !
You'll be glad you came !

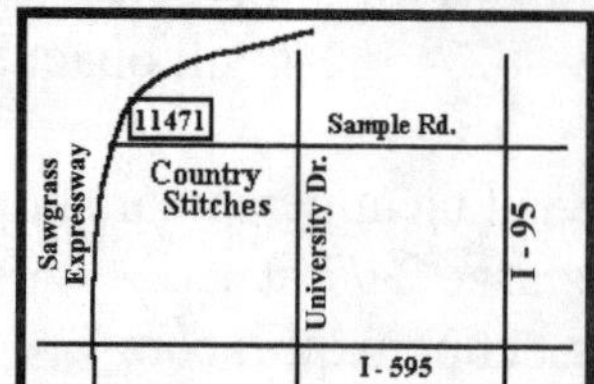

Key West, FL #76

Mon - Thur 9 - 6
Fri 9 - 4
Sat 10 - 2

Seam Shoppe

1114 Truman Ave. 33040
(305) 296-9830 Fax: (305) 296-9630
seamshoppe@aol.com
www.tropicalfabricsonline.com
Owners: Cindy & Doug Meyer Est: 1986

Quilters and Fabric Collectors ! We stock mostly tropical fabrics for fashion, quilting and upholstery including palms, batiks, florals and vintage look.

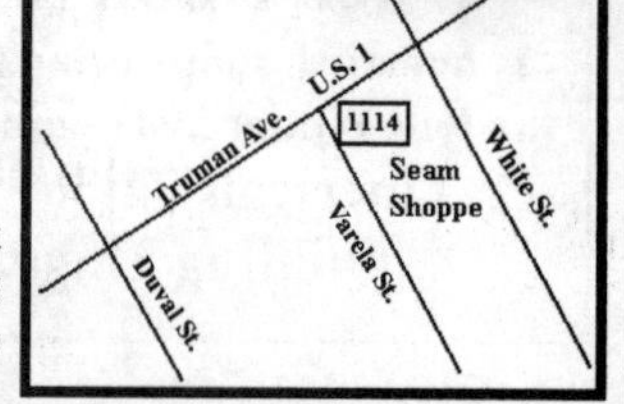

Other Shop in Florida: *We Suggest Calling First*

Big Pine Key	Samantha's, 30883 Dolgado Ln.	305-872-2235
Crestview	Granny's Attic, 337 N. Main St.	904-682-3041
Crystal River	A Stitching Place, 374 N Suncoast Blvd	352-564-0600
Davenport	Adventures in Quilts, 118 E. Bay St.	863-419-9267
Davie	Quilter's Haven, 5919 S University Dr	954-680-0199
Daytona Beach	Pieces & Patches, 1425 Tomoka Farms Rd.	904-252-5588
Delray Beach	Nanny's Attic, 124 N. Swinton Ave.	561-278-8877
Dunnellon	Mary Glendenning Quilts, 8282 SW 204th	352-489-7120
Fort Lauderdale	Silk Cotton Quilts, 2001 NW 51st St.	242-324-1073
Fort Walton Beach	Sewing Center, 913 Beal Pkwy NW	850-243-8261
Ft. Myers	Fabric Mart II, 6900 Daniels Pkwy. #15	941-482-5250
Hollywood	Ben Raymond Fabrics, 2050 Hollywood	305-927-4011
Jacksonville	Elegant Traditions, 4935 Prince Edward Rd	904-389-7821
Jacksonville	Alexa's Quilts & More, 8793 Chambore Dr.	904-641-9964
Jupiter	Quilter's Choice, 661 Maplewood Dr. #14	561-747-0525
Key West	Fabric World, 3228 N. Roosevelt Blvd.	305-294-1773
Kissimmee	Cheryl's Enchanted, 744 Country Woods	407-348-0182
Lake Placid	Quilt Shop, 23 Park Dr	863-465-3112
Lake Worth	Sew 'N Tell, 2913 29th Ln.	561-642-4710
Lakeland	Fabric Warehouse, 3030 N. Florida Ave.	863-680-1325
Leesburg	Apples Aggies Attic, 713 N. 14th St.	352-728-4445
Lehigh Acres	Gone Quilten, 1223 Homestead Rd N	239-368-2272
Miami	By The Yard, 20563 Old Cutler Rd	305-251-2451
Mt. Dora	Madison Rose Quilts & Gifts, 431 N. Donnelly	352-735-9591
North Fort Myers	Susie Q's Quilts, 4150 Hancock Bridge	941-656-2722
Orange City	Bernina Sewing Center, 840 Saxon Blvd #26	904-774-9332
Palm Bay	The Quilt Stash, 2000 Palm Bay Rd.	321-722-3306
Pendacola	The Heirloom Shop, 507 S Adams St	850-433-7780
Pensacola	A&E Fabric, 923 N New Warrington Rd	850-455-0381
Port Charles	Expert Sewing Center, 1900 Tamiami Trak,	941-766-7118
Port Orange	Moore & Moore Quilts, 2514 Guava Dr	386-761-7198
Sarasota	Alma Sue's Quilt Shop, 3667 Bahia Vista	941-330-0993
St. Petersburg	Quilting Bee, 8842 4th St. N	727-217-9042
St. Petersburg	Just Quilted, 1490 51st Ave. NE	727-521-4373
St. Petersburg	Sewing Circle Fabrics, 408 33rd Ave. N.	727-823-7391
Stuart	Tropical Quilter, 932 SE Central Pkwy	772-288-3833
Tampa	The Quilted Sampler, 4109 S. MacDill	813-831-8997
Tampa	Bernina Sewing Center, 14976 N Florida	813-969-2458
Tarpon Springs	Quilt Chest, 735 Dodecanese Blvd	727-938-6306
Trenton	Suwannee Valley Shoppe, 517 N Main	352-463-3842
Venice	Expert Sewing Center, 2067 S Tamiami Tr	941-496-8058
Winter Haven	Quilting Etc, 3879 Recker Hwy	863-292-0317
Winter Haven	A. K. Sew & Serge, 1602 Sixth Ave. S.E.	863-299-3080

◆ ◆

Florida Guilds:

Boca Raton	Gold Coast Quilter's Guild, Box 710, 33429
Boynton Beach	Boynton Library Quilters, 208 S Seacrest Blvd.
Brooksville	Brooksville Women's Club, 131 S. Main St., 34601
Coral Springs	Coral Springs Quilters Inc., 1300 Coral Springs Drive
Crystal River	Nocturnal Needlers, 802 N. Suncoast Blvd., 34429
Crystal River	Creative Quilters of Citrus County
Davie West	Broward Quilters Guild, 6500 SW 47th Street
Ft. Myers	Southwest Florida Quilters Guild, Box 2264, 33901
Gainesville	Tree City Quilters Guild, Inc., PO Box 140-698, 32614
Hollywood	Southern Stars Quilt Guild, 400 N 35th Avenue
Inverness	Citrus Friendship Quilters, 3384 S. Diamond Ave., 34452
Jacksonville	Piecemakers, P.O. Box 11996, 32239
Kissimmee	Patchers of Time, P.O. Box
Lake City	Lady of the Lake Quilters Guild, 32025
Miama	Ocean Waves Quilters, 6421 S. Mitchell Manor Circle, 33156
Miami	Ocean Waves Quilt Guild, 3801 SW 97th Avenue
Naples	Naples Quilter's Guild, P.O. Box 3055, 34106
New Smyrna	Beach Pelican Piecemakers, 32168
Niceville	Flying Needles, 32578
Ocala	Country Road Quilters, P.O. Box 4082, 34478
Orange Park	Honeybee Quilters Guild, P.O. Box 0003, 32067
Orange Park	First Coast Quilters Guild, P.O. Box 2835, 32068
Orlando	Country Stitchers, 2043 Sue Harbor Cove, 32750
Orlando	Castle Quilters, 32809
Orlando	Cabin Fever Quilter's Guild, P.O. Box 891, 32802
Palm Harbor	Largo Cracker Quilters
Pensacola	Pensacola Quilter's Guild, 32507
Plant City	Berry Patch Quilt Guild, PO Box 3221, 33563
Pompano	East Sunrise Quilt Guild, 950 S Cypress Rd
Port Richey	West Pasco Quilt Guild, P.O. Box 574, 34673
Port St. Joe	Panhandler's Piecemaker Quilt Clubm P.O. Box 522, 32457
Satellite Beach	Seaside Piecemakers, P.O. Box 2761, 32937
Silver Springs	Pine Needles Quilters, P.O. Box 535, 32688
Sparr	Possum Creek Quilters, 32091
Summerfield	Belleview Busy Bee Quilters, P.O. Box 936, 34492
Tallahassee	Quilters Unlimited of Tallahassee, P.O. Box 4324, 32315
Tampa	Quilters' Workshop of Tampa Bay, 12717 Trowbridge Ln, 33624
Venice	Venice Area Quilters Guild, 7210 Alligator Dr., 34285
West Palm Beach	Palm Beach County Quilters' Guild, P.O. Box 18276, 33416

Bradenton Manatee Patchworkers, P.O. Box 356, 34206
Meets: Thursdays 9:30am
Casselberry Central Florida Quilter's Guild, Inc., P.O. Box 180116, 32718
Meets: 4th Wednesday @ 7pm at Cypress Hall - Cypress Park
Meets: Last Tuesday at Tomorrow's Treasures Quilt Shop
Dunellen Creative Quilters of Citrus County, 7165 W. Riverbend Rd.
Meets: 2nd Monday @ 7:15pm at Davie United Methodist Church
Ft. Myers Palm Patches Quilt Guild, P.O. Box 07345, 33919
Meets: 2nd Monday 7 p.m. at Covenant Baptist Church
Meets: 3rd Monday @ 6:45pm at Hollywood Hills United Methodist Church
Jacksonville Honeybee Quilters Guild
Key Largo Florida Keys Quilters, PO Box 2781, 33037
Meets: 2nd Monday 7 p.m. at Osceola Center for the Arts.
Meets: 4th Wednesday at Southside Recreation Center

Meets: 2nd Saturday @ 9am at Olympia Heights United Methodist Church
Meets: 3rd Thursday (They are looking for a new spot, please call S.E.W. Studio)
Ocala Stitch Witches, 9020 2-C S.W. 93rd. Lane, 34481
Meets: 2nd & 4th Thursdays 10 a.m. at First Presbyterian Church, 1800 Hwy. 20 E
Meets 1st & 3rd Thursday 7 p.m.

Meets: 2nd Thursday at County Library corner of Kingsley and Plainfield.
Ormond Beach Racing Fingers Quilt Guild, 32173
Meets: 1st Thursday @ 9:30am at First Baptist Church of Pine Castle
Meets: 1st Monday 7 p.m. at Marks St. Senior Center, 99 E. Marks St.
Panama City Saint Andrews Bay Quilters Guild, P.O. Box 16225
South Miami Ocean Waves Quilt Guild, P.O. Box 43-1673, 33243
Meets: 2nd Thursday @ 6:45pm at The Winter Visitor's Center
Meets: 3rd Saturday @ 11am at Cypress Presbyterian Church
Meets: 10 am third Thursday
Meets: 2nd Thursday 7 p.m. at St. James Episcopal Church
Meets: 4th Wednesday 9:30 a.m. at Satellite Beach Civic Center
Meets: Thursdays 10 a.m.
St. Augustine St. Augustine Piecemakers
Tallahassee Sunshine State Quilters Assoc., 1113 Albritton Dr., 32301
Meets: 2nd Thursday 6:30 p.m. at Meridian Wood Church, 2870 N Meridian Rd.
Tavares Lake County Quilters Guild, P.O. Box 1065, 32778
Meets: Second Tuesday 7 p.m.
Meets: 4th Saturday @ 10am at West Palm Beach Garden Club

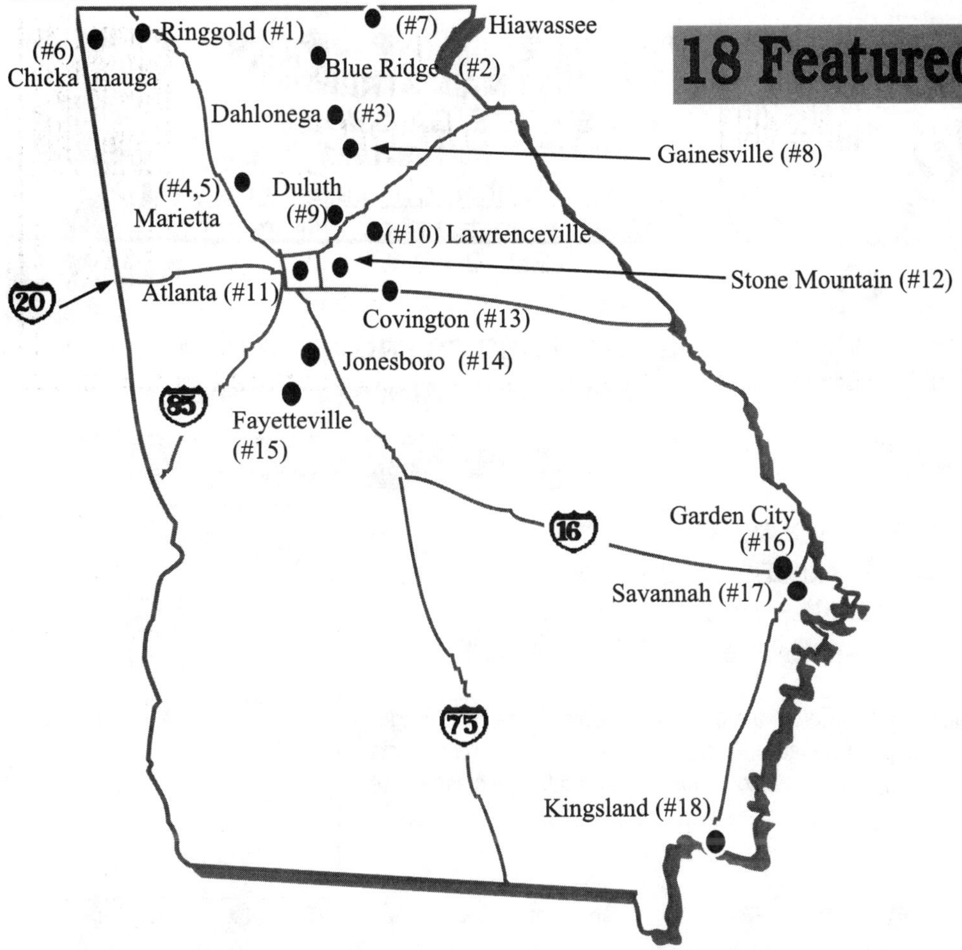

(#6) Chickamauga
Ringgold (#1)
(#7)
Hiawassee
Blue Ridge (#2)
Dahlonega (#3)
Gainesville (#8)
(#4,5) Marietta
Duluth (#9)
(#10) Lawrenceville
Stone Mountain (#12)
20
Atlanta (#11)
Covington (#13)
Jonesboro (#14)
85
Fayetteville (#15)
16
Garden City (#16)
Savannah (#17)
75
Kingsland (#18)

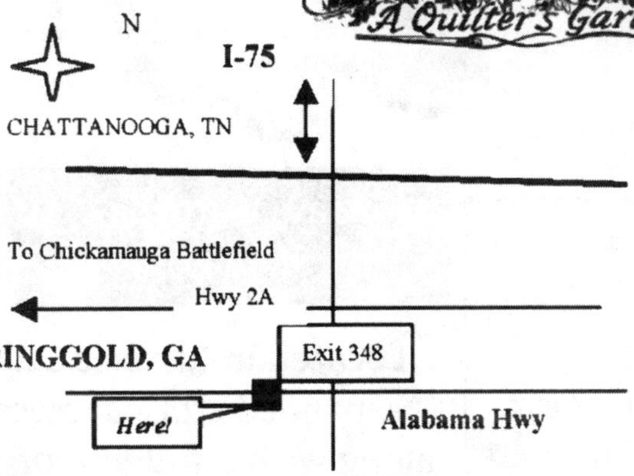

18 Featured Shops

GEORGIA

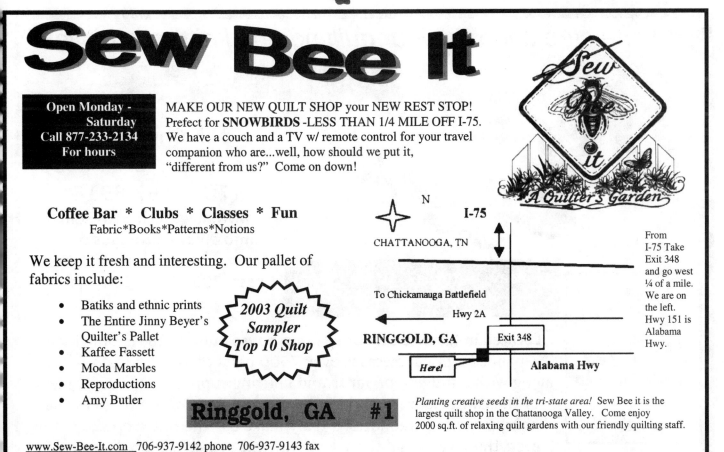

801 EAST MAIN STREET
BLUE RIDGE, GA 30513
PHONE: 706-258-1123
E-mail: mountainhollyquilters@tds.net
On the Web:www.mountainhollyquilters.com
Est. 2000

Mon - Sat
9 - 5

Winter Hrs
Jan & Feb
10 - 4

THE BEST FABRICS FROM TOP COMPANIES
SOMETHING ALWAYS ON SALE !

3000 BOLTS in 4000 + Sq.Ft.

Blue Ridge, GA #2

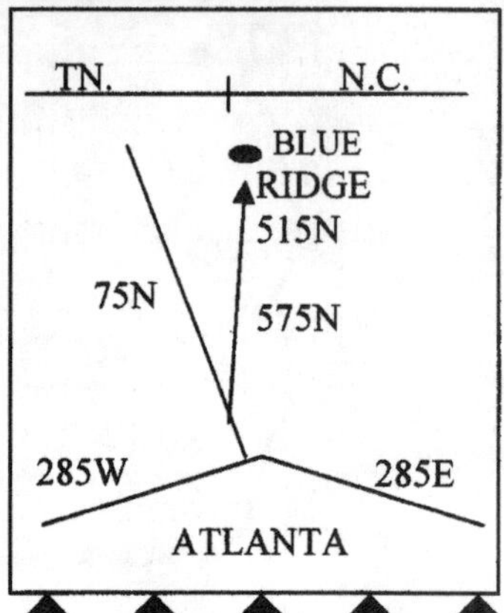

YOU WILL WANT TO SPEND HOURS IN OUR SHOP !
RELAXED ATMOSPHERE—WIDE AISLES—GREAT LIGHTING
LOUNGE & TV FOR HUSBANDS AND CHILDREN
LARGE CLASSROOM, GREAT TEACHERS & FRIENDLY STAFF.

Visit us in downtown Blue Ridge, in the beautiful North Georgia mountains. Home of the Blue Ridge Scenic Railroad , dozens of gift & antique shops, good restaurants, local theater & active arts association. " Retreat for Three", a bed and breakfast for quilters, discounts for quilters taking a class at our shop. No better town for quilters ! Plus doll and rug-hooking classes with area artists.

E-mail or call the shop for further information.

"The one stop shop for your quilting and knitting supplies."

Dahlonega, GA #3

315 Church St.
Dahlonega, GA 30533
(706) 867-8918
www.magicalthreads.com
info@magicalthreads.com
Owners: Laurelanne Hackinson
Est: 2001 5000+ sq.ft.

Monday - Saturday 10 am - 5 pm
Sunday 1 pm - 4 pm

Warwick
Town Sq.
Hwy. 60
Church St.
315
Magical Threads
Main St.
GA 400
Morrison Moore Pkwy.
I - 285
Atlanta

52 miles North of Atlanta

Located in historic Dahlonega in a house built in 1846, our newly expanded store showcases over 7500 bolts of 100% cotton fabric along with a full line of yarns and knitting supplies. Our great blend of the contemporary and the traditional, in addition to all of the books, patterns, and notions truly make us "the one stop shop" for everything you need to make your next project simply "magical".

Tiny STITCHES

2520 E. Piedmont Rd.
Suite H 30062
(770) 565-1113

New | Chastain | Exit 2 | Blackwell Rd. | Ebenezer | I - 75 | I - 575 | Bells Ferry | Canion Rd. | Sandy Plains | Barret Pkwy. | 2520 | Exit 269 | Piedmont Rd. | Tiny Stitches

Visit Georgia's Largest Quilt Shop

We are a fully stocked quilt shop
— Over 4000 bolts of cotton fabrics — over 500 book titles —
Large selection of the newest notions
Besides friendly service we have classes in quilting & clothing.

Just off I-75, Tiny Stitches is a convenient stop for the traveling Quilter. Exit 269, east onto Barrett Pkwy. This becomes E. Piedmont, we are located at 2520 E. Piedmont.

Est: 1992

We will gladly do mail order.
Visit our website: www.tinystitches.com

Mon - Sat 9:30 - 5:30

Marietta, GA #5

est. 1986

Little Quilts®

Top Ten Shop
American Patchwork
& Quilting 2004

1450-C Roswell Rd.
"Near Historic Marietta"
Phone: 770-578-6727
Fax: 770-509-9748

littlequilts@mindspring.com
www.littlequilts.com

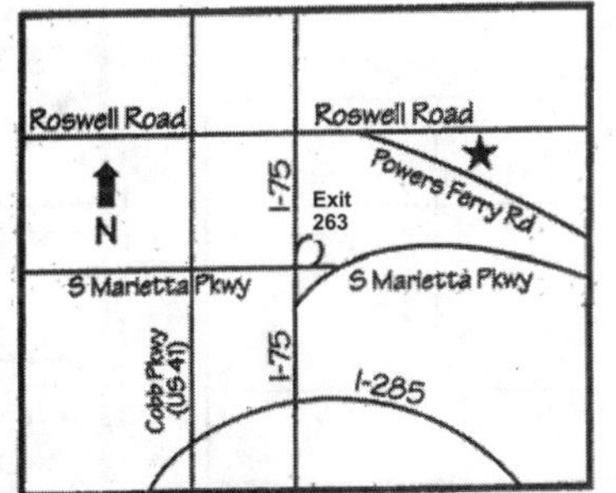

10 minutes from I-75 20 minutes N. of Atlanta

Mon - Sat 10 - 5

"Step Into Our World"

Featuring fabrics, books and patterns by Little Quilts

Our cozy shop is full of reproduction fabrics, rug hooking, stitchery, books, patterns, supplies, gifts and lots of inspiration!

Alice Berg * Mary Ellen Von Holt * Sylvia Johnson

Chickamauga, GA #6

Tues, Thur Fri & Sat 10 - 5 Wed 10 - 3

Memories & More

121 Gordon St. 30707
(706) 375-5300
Website: Coming Soon
Owner: Pamela H. Shields
Est: 1984 2000 sq.ft.

100 year old building in center of Historic District housing quilting, cross-stitch & scrapbook shop. Fabrics, Notions, Books, Gifts & Hometown Service.

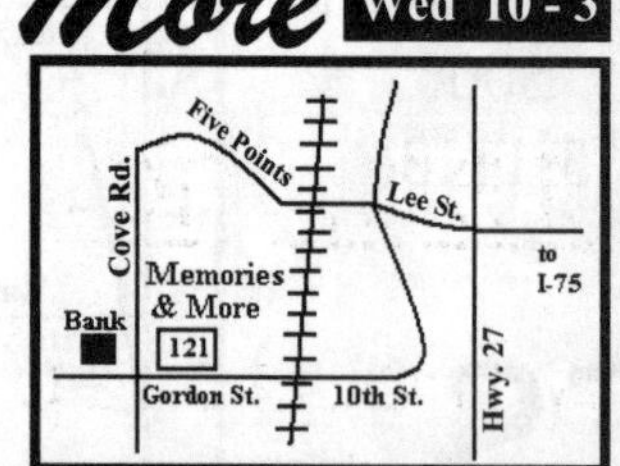

Hiawassee, GA #7

Mon - Sat 10 - 4

Log Cabin Patchworks

257 Big Sky Dr. 30546
(706) 896-7275
www.LogCabinPatchworks.com
Est: 1980 1200 sq.ft. 1500 Bolts

We specialize in Thimbleberries, Homespuns, Flannels and Reproduction fabrics.
Better Homes & Garden
Quilt Sampler Shop 2002

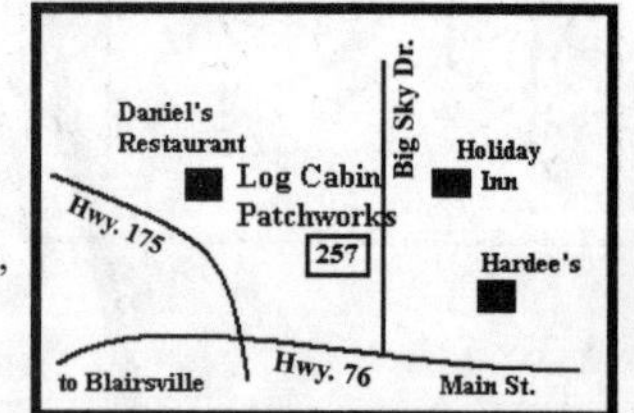

Gainesville, GA #8

Mon - Fri 10 - 5 Sat 10 - 4

Quilted Hearts Ltd.

Carrington Plaza
104 Carrington
Park Dr. 30504

(770) 536-3959 Fax: Same
Est: 1991 2500 sq.ft.
Owner: Sally Babcock

Located North of Atlanta, our shop has over 2000 Bolts of 100% cotton fabrics. We carry everything needed for quiltmaking, rug hooking, and knitting.

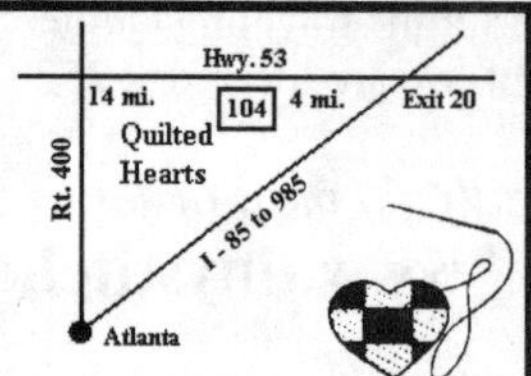

Duluth, GA #9

Mon - Sat 10 - 6

Share the Spirit Quilting & Yarn

3129 Main St. #B 30096
(678) 473-4617 Est: 2003 2100 sq.ft
berdis@bellsouth.net
www.quiltsties.com/share.htm
Owner: Diane Berdis 1800 bolts & yarn room

Fabrics, patterns, books, yarn & notions. Hwy. 120 from either direction comes directly into town. Must walk behind old buildings. Store front faces park with fountain.

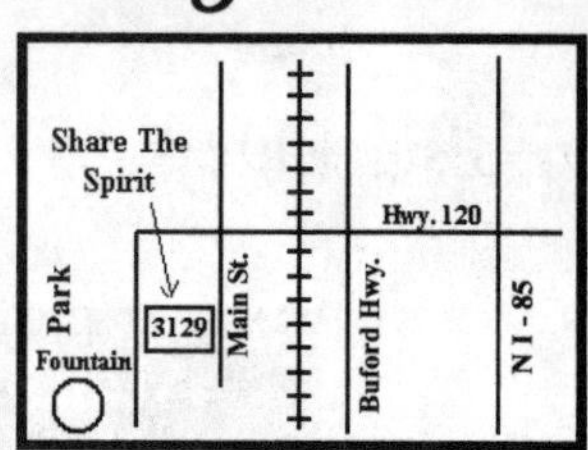

The Stitch 'N Quilt Shoppe

*Ladye Buckner * Joan Meyberg*

Est: 2002

Lawrenceville, GA #10

Thimbleberries Club

Located east of Atlanta, our shoppe has over 2,000 bolts of 100% cotton fabrics. Complete Jinny Beyer Palette, RJR, MODA, Batiks and many more.
We carry a full line of quilting notions, books & patterns.

Friendly staff always available to assist with your needs.

Long Arm Quilting Available

Shoppe Hours

Monday -- Saturday 10 am -- 6 pm, Sunday 1 pm -- 5 pm
*2070 Sugarloaf Pkwy * Lawrenceville, GA 30045*
678-985-3456
stitchnquilt@bellsouth.net

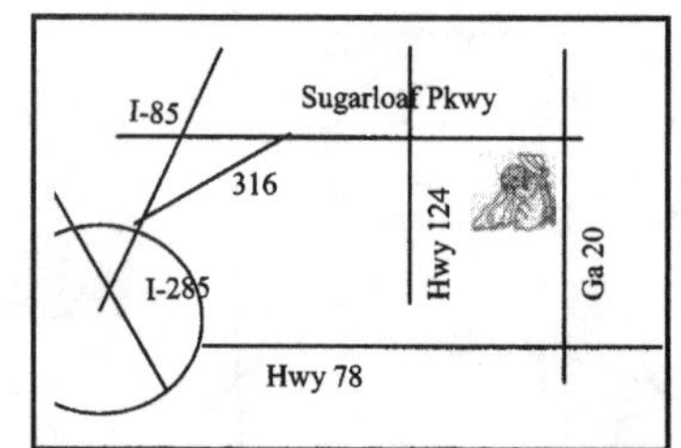

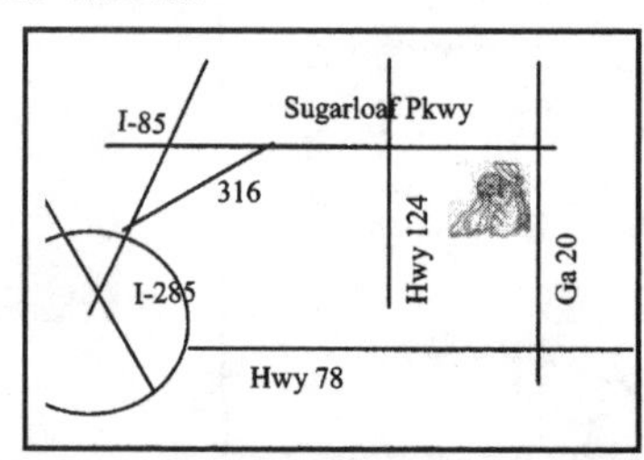

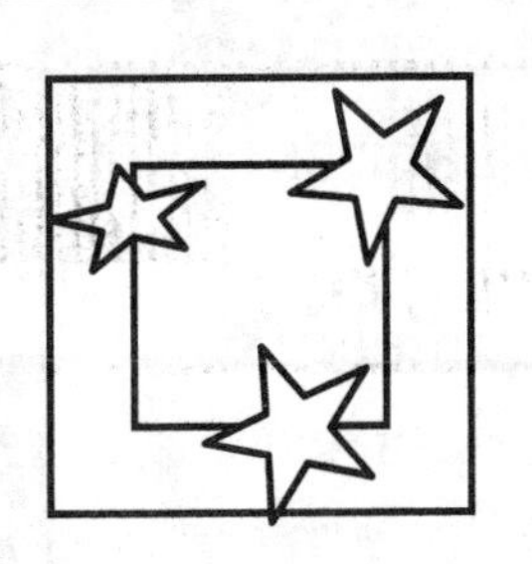

Atlanta, GA #11

404-874-7785

Intown Quilters, Inc.

Atlanta's only in-town quilt shop!!

We are located in the Emory/CDC area

Intown quilters carries an ever-growing selection of bright contemporary quilt fabrics including Alexander Henry, Kaffe Fassett, Kaufman, Benartex, Marcus Brothers, Bali Fabrications, Timeless Treasures, P & B, Timeless Treasures, Michael Miller, Northcott, Bold Over Batiks & more!

1123 Zonolite Rd. Suite 10Atlanta, Georgia 30306

Please call for directions!!

intownquilters@earthlink.com

Fax: 404-874-5531

Owner: Sarah J. Phillips

Est: 2002 1600 sq.ft. 1500 bolts and growing

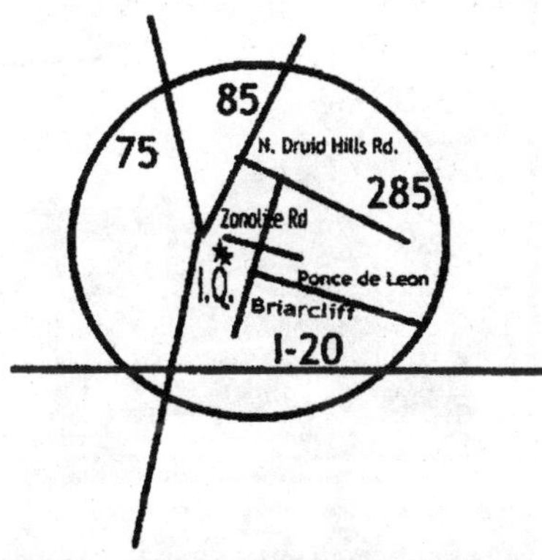

Sun 1 - 6
Tues 10 - 8
Wed - Sat 10 - 6

www.intownquilters.com

770-413-1800 • www.QuiltingEssentials.com

Quilting Essentials

A full-service quilt shop where you will find friendly and helpful staff and 3,000 bolts of quality cotton fabric.

Shop Hours:
Monday - Saturday, 10 a.m. - 6 p.m.
Sunday, 1 p.m. - 5 p.m.
Open Thursday until 9 p.m.
Open most holidays.

Stone Mountain, GA #12

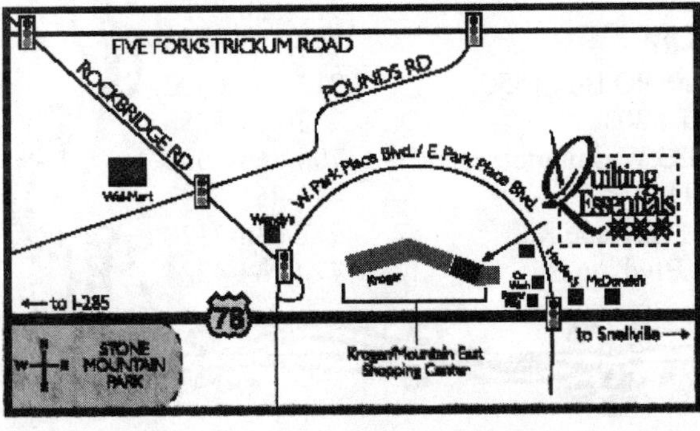

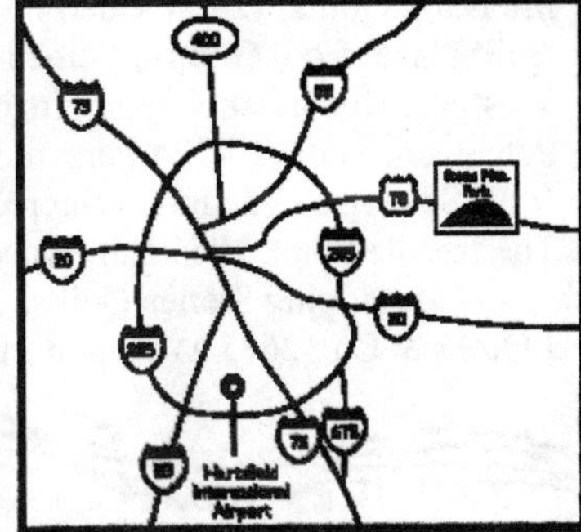

Quilting Essentials
Mountain East Shopping Center
5295 U.S. Highway 78, Suite T
Stone Mountain, GA 30087
Laurie Wragg, owner
770-413-1800

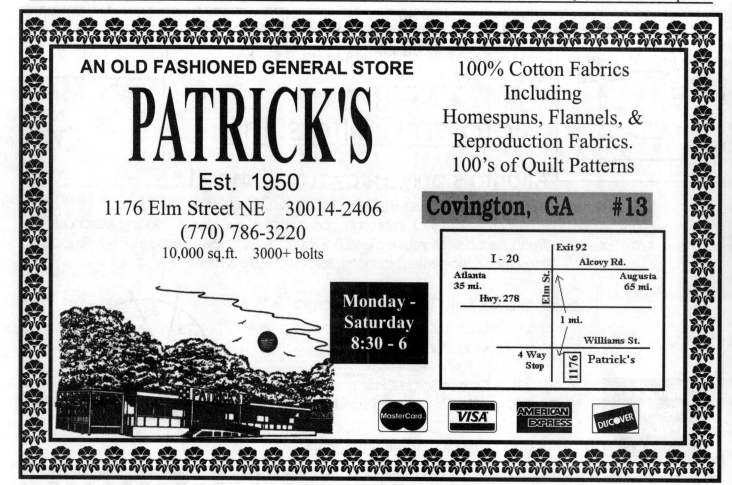

AN OLD FASHIONED GENERAL STORE

PATRICK'S

Est. 1950

1176 Elm Street NE 30014-2406

(770) 786-3220

10,000 sq.ft. 3000+ bolts

100% Cotton Fabrics
Including
Homespuns, Flannels, &
Reproduction Fabrics.
100's of Quilt Patterns

Covington, GA #13

Monday - Saturday 8:30 - 6

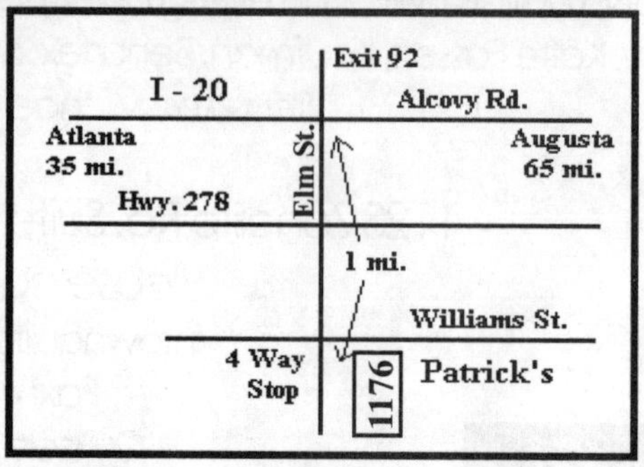

Exit 92
I - 20
Alcovy Rd.
Atlanta 35 mi.
Augusta 65 mi.
Elm St.
Hwy. 278
1 mi.
Williams St.
4 Way Stop
1176
Patrick's

MasterCard VISA AMERICAN EXPRESS DISCOVER

Other Shops in Georgia: *We suggest calling first*

Alpharetta	Southampton Quilts, 1920 Seven Seas Ct.	
Athens	Watercolor Quilts, 320 Ansley Dr	706-546-7091
Atlanta	Pintucks& Pinafores, 4300 Paces Ferry Rd SW Ste 405	770-384-1216
Augusta	Sewing Gallery, 362 Fury's Ferry Rd. #D	706-855-6479
Bainbridge	Janet's Fashion Fabrics, 124 E. Broughton St.	912-246-5674
Blairsville	Corn Crib, 101 Pat Haralson Memorial Dr. #C, PO Box 2523	706-745-3426
Blue Ridge	April Rose Quilts & Gifts, 662 E. Main St.	706-632-8494
Cleveland	The Calico Barn, 3599 Duncan Bridge Rd.	706-865-9029
Columbus	Southern Sewing Center, 2507 Manchester Expressway	706-327-1231
Cumming	Rose Arbor Quilts, 4734 Canton Hwy	770-413-8129
Dahlonega	Amber Rose Quilts & Gifts, 10 S. Chestatee St. #E	706-864-5326
Fayetteville	Sew Creative, 382 Glynn-Hood Plaza	
Jesup	Me Nan's Quilts, 129 W Cherry St	912-530-9556
Loganville	Quilt Place, 5240 Guthrie Cemetary Rd	770-787-8814
Lumpkin	Westville Historical Handicrafts, Inc., PO Box 1850	912-838-6310
Macon	Patchwork Station, 4524 Forsyth Rd. #203	912-471-8288
Martinez	Jeff's Sewing & Vacunm Center, 3833 Washington Rd #C	706-863-0090
Milledgeville	The Needle Point, 3051 Edgewood Dr.	478-453-5647
St. Simons Island	Stepping Stones Quilts, 301 Skylane Rd.	912-638-7128
Tucker	J Quilts & Co., 2615 Mountain Ind. Blvd. #6	770-934-4224

Jonesboro, GA #14

Mon - Sat 10 - 5

Quilts and Fixins

7986 N. Main St. 30236
(770) 472-0015 Fax: (770) 471-8822
fixinsj@bellsouth.net
Est: 1998 6000 Bolts
100's of samples, books, patterns, notions.
Many classes and gifts.
Exit 235 off I - 75 S. (Hwy 19&41-Tara Blvd.) Go S 3 mi, turn L onto Hwy 138. At next lite (N. Main) turn R. We're on the left.

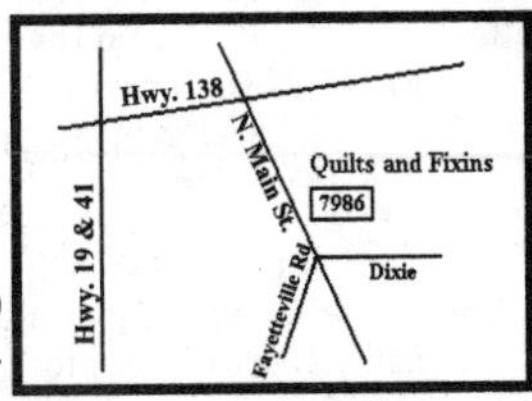

Fayetteville, GA #15

Mon - Sat 10 - 6

The Quilting Bee Shop and Gallery

485 N Jeff Davis Drive 30214
(678) 817-0602
Est: 2000 1300 sq. ft. 5000 Bolts

The Bee buzzes with 100% cotton fabric, books, patterns, & gifts. The Hive Gallery features local, & nationally known quilt artists.

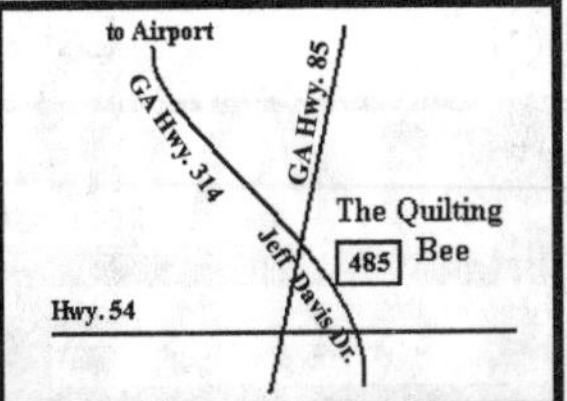

Garden City, GA #16

Mon - Fri 10 - 5 Sat 10 - 4

Sew Much More

5201 Augusta Rd. (Hwy. 21) 31408
(912) 966-5626 Fax: (912) 964-7067
bbrooks2@bellsouth.net

High Quality Quilting Fabrics and notions from all the best manufacturers (1500+ bolts). Batiks, flannels and Heirloom. Authorized Pfaff Dealer.

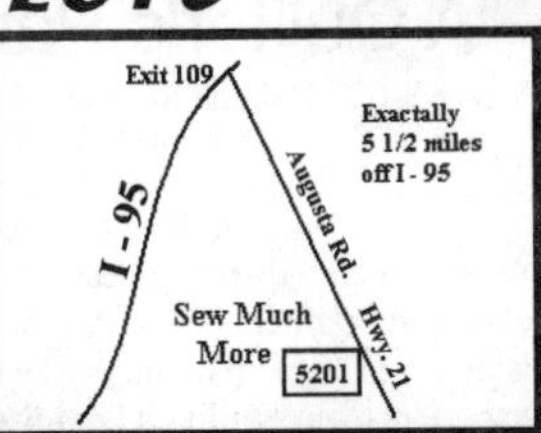

Savannah, GA #17

Mon - Fri 10 - 6 Sat 10 - 4

Colonial Quilts

11710 A Largo Dr.
(912) 925-0055
E-Mail: CQuilts11@aol.com
Savannah's Quilt Shop

Located in historic Savannah, we offer a wide array of fabric, notions, classes, books and patterns for quilting. Family owned and operated by three generations.

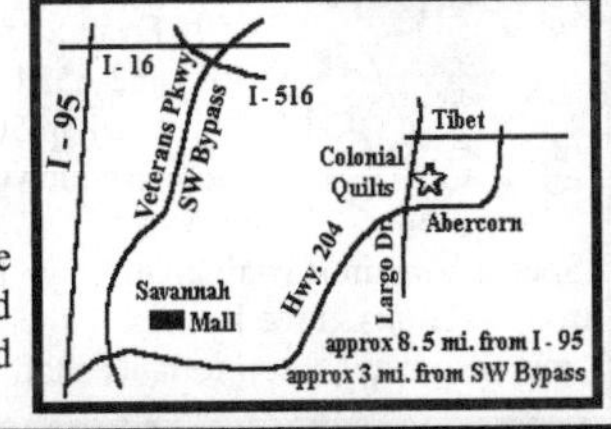

Georgia Guilds:

Athens — Cotton Patch Quilters Guild, 293 Hoyt Street, 30604
Meets: 2nd Tuesday @ 7pm at Lyndon House Arts Center Community Room

Augusta — Sew Perfect Quilters of Georgialina
Meets: 1st Thursday 10 a.m. at Lumpkin Rd. Baptist Church

Carrollton — West Georgia Quilters, 118 S White Street
Meets: 3rd Tuesday at 6:30pm, Carrollton Comm. Ctr

Clarkesville — Moutain Laurel Quilters, PO Box 1712, 30523
Meets: 3rd Thursday at 1 p.m. at Methodist Church, Washington St.

Columbus — Gala Quilters Guild, 1816 St. Elmo Dr., 31901

Covington — Cotton Boll Quilt Guild
Contact: Marilyn Titman, 270 Chestnut Rd. (770) 786-1221

Fayetteville — Quilters Guild of the Southern Crescent, P.O. Box 142061, 30214
Meets: 4th Tuesday @ 7pm Fayette Presbyterian Church

Gainesville — Hall Cty Quilt Guild, 5845 Hidden Cove, 30504

Hiawassee — Misty Mountain Quilter's Guild, P.O. Box 1144, 30546
Meets: 4th Monday 1 p.m. at Sharp Memorial Church, Young Harris

Jonesboro — N. Georgia Quilt Council, 7292 Cardif Pl., 30236

Lilburn — Cotton Club, 92 Main St., 30047
Meets: 3rd Monday 10 a.m. and 2nd Monday 7 p.m.

Marietta — Allatoona Quilters' Guild

Marietta — East Cobb Quilter's, P.O. Box 71561, 30007
Meets: Last Friday @ 9:30am St. Ann's Catholic Church

Roswell — Georgia Quilt Council, Inc., 2752 Long Lake Dr., 30075

Savannah — Calico Stitchers, P.O. Box 13414, 31416
Meets: 3rd Monday 7 p.m. at The Woods, 7564 Hodgson Memorial Dr.

Savannah — Ogeechee Quilters

Stone Mountain — Yellow Daisy Quilters, P.O. Box 1772, 30086

Valdosta — Withlacoochee Quilters Guild, 300 Woodrow Wilson Dr.
Meets: 3rd Monday 7pm at South Georgia Regional Lobrary

Kingsland, GA #18

Quality Fabrics • Notions • Classes
Quality Fabrics Starting at $5.99 per yard

Tues - Fri 11 - 5 Sat 10 - 3

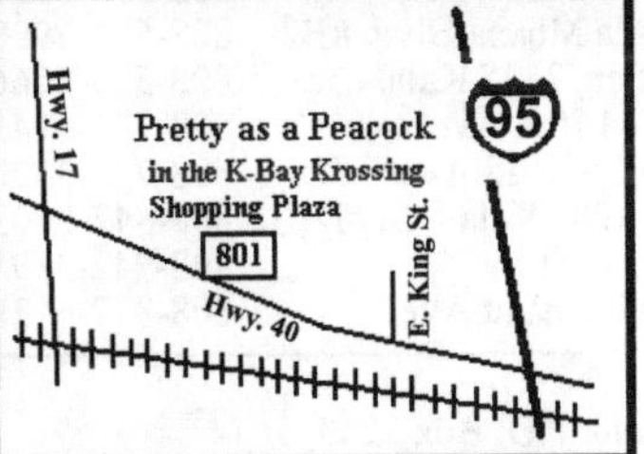

Located 1.5 miles west of I-95 (Exit 3), second exit north of Florida/Georgia line.

801 E. King Ave., Unit G (Hwy. 40)
(K-Bay Krossing Shopping Plaza)
Kingland, GA 31548
912-576-4646
prettyasapeacock@tds.net

KAUAI Lihue (#1)
OAHU
Aiea (#2)
Honolulu (#3)
MAUI
Lahaina (#4)
Kamuela (#5)
Hilo (#6)
Volcano (#7)
HAWAII

HAWAII

7 Featured Shops

Lihue, Kauai, HI #1

Mon - Sat 9 - 5

Kapaia Stitchery

P.O. Box 1327 96766
3-3561 Kuhio Hwy.
(808) 245-2281 Fax: (808) 245-1772
kapaia@gte.net
Est: 1973 Visa, MC, Discover

We Love Quilting !
The best selection of Tropicals, Batiks, & Quality 100% Cottons for Quilting.

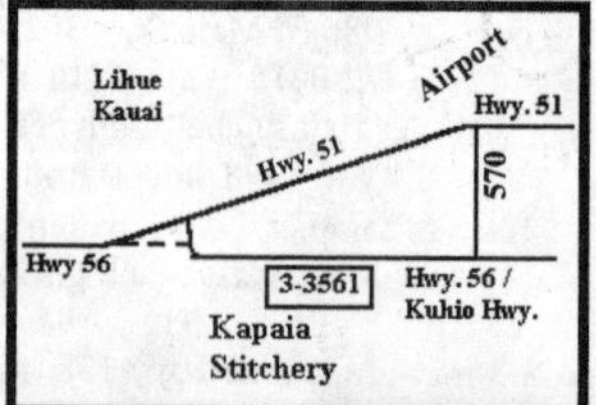

Aiea, Oahu, HI #2

**Tues - Fri 12 - 8
Sat 10 - 6**

The Quilt Hut

"A Quilter's Paradise"

98-029 Hakaha St., Suite 24 96701
(808) 486-6690
thequilthut@yahoo.com
Est: 2003 1600 sq.ft. 1000+ Bolts

A complete resource center for the truly obsessed Quilter. Whether you live on the islands or are planning a visit you must experience our Quilter's Paradise.

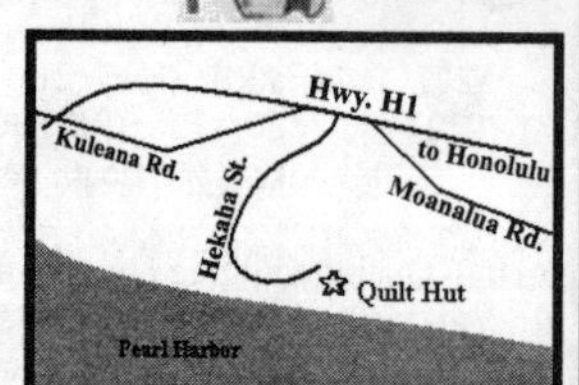

Honolulu, Oahu, HI #3

**Mon - Fri 10 - 6
Sat 10 - 4**

Kwilts 'n Koa

1126 12th Avenue 96816
(808) 735-2300 Fax: (808) 737-2300
Orders (800) 787-1855
E-Mail: KwiltsnKoa@hawaii.rr.com
Web Site: www.KwiltsnKoa.com
Owners: Kathy Tsark & Tsarkie
Catalog $10 yr.—4 issues
Est: 1991 650 sq.ft. 100+ bolts

Hawaiian quilting classes, patterns, kits / supplies; Hawaiian gifts & Koa wood.

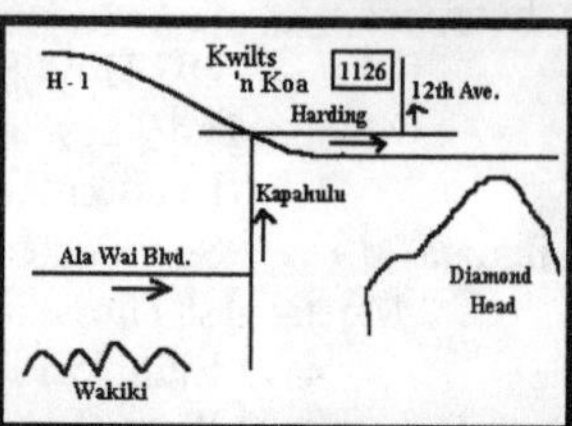

Lahaina, Maui, HI #4

**Mon - Sat 10 - 6
Sun 12 - 5**

The Needlework Shop

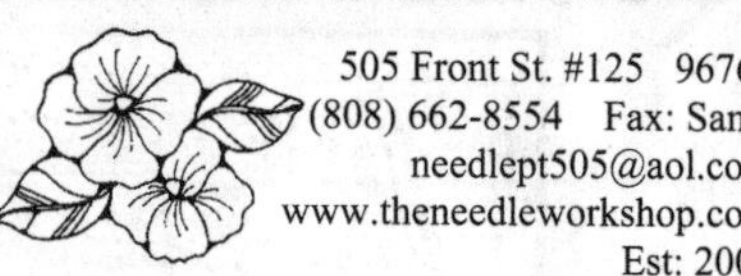

505 Front St. #125 96761
(808) 662-8554 Fax: Same
needlept505@aol.com
www.theneedleworkshop.com
Est: 2000

Specializing in Hawaiian quilting. Patterns and tropical batiks. Free lessons. Other quilt related merchandise. A comfortable shop with aloha.

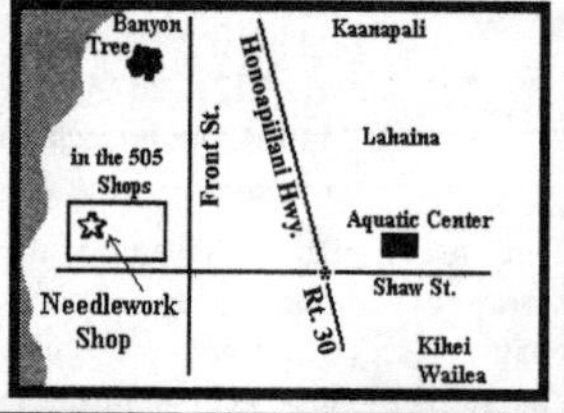

Kamuela, Hawaii, HI #5

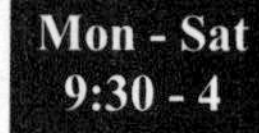

Holomua Center, P.O. Box 2631 96743
(808) 885-4482
topstitch@lava.net
Owner: Ellie Erickson Est: 1978

A fine collection of cotton fabrics including tropical prints, quilting solids, and batiks. Needlecraft supplies and Hawaiian Quilts.

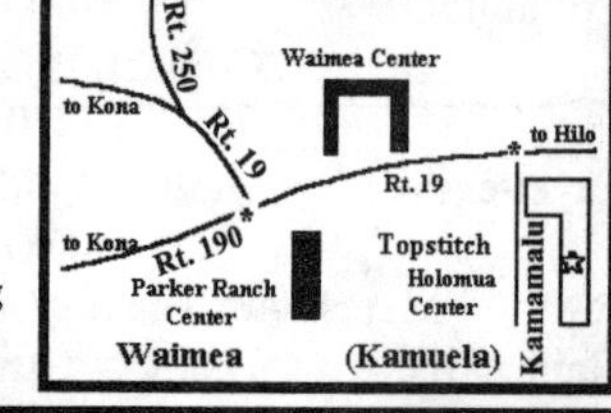

Hilo, Hawaii, HI #6

**Mon - Fri 9:30 - 5
Sat 9 - 5**

Fabric Impressions

206 Kamehameha Ave. 96720
(808) 961-4468
fabricimps@aol.com Est: 1988
Owners: Tamarra Hasselfeld & Mary Pierson

Hawaiian, Oriental and Batik fabrics, fat quarters, kits, books and patterns for quilters. Handmade in Hawaii quilts and gift items.

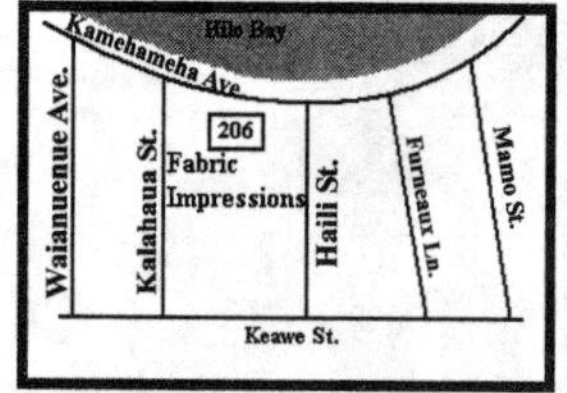

Volcano, Hawaii, HI #7

7 Days a Week 9:30 - 5:30

Kilauea Kreations

P.O. Box 959 96785
Old Volcano Hwy.
(808) 967-8090

Hawaiian Quilt Shop and local art.
Ready made to make you own.
Everything you need.
Fabric, Notions, Books, Kits

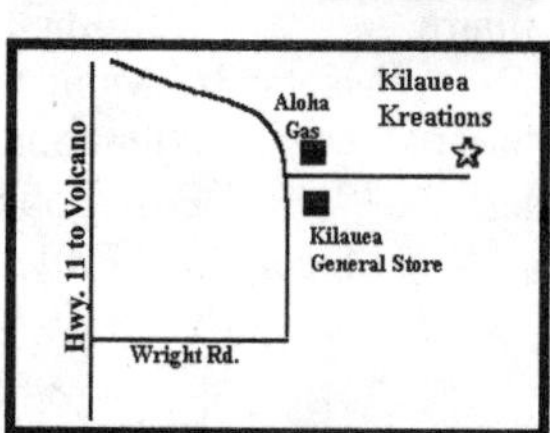
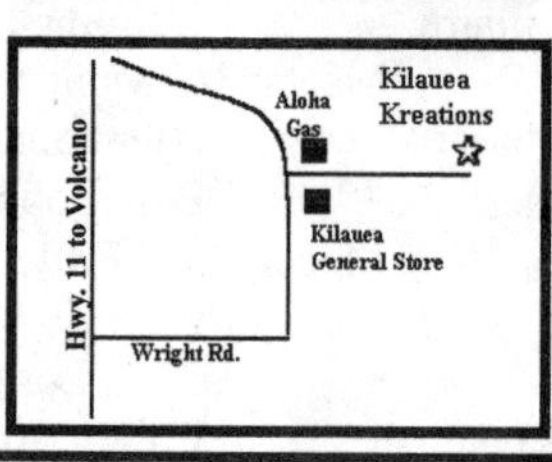

Other Shops in Hawaii: *We suggest calling first*

Aiea	Homespun Harbor, 98-029 Hekaha St. #24	808-488-5844
Honolulu	Berina of Hawaii, 320 Ward Ave. #114	808-536-6931
Honolulu	My Little Secret, 1050 Ala Moana Blvd. #B2	808-596-2990
Honolulu	Hawaiian Quilt Connection, 2525 Kalahaua	808-599-7766
Honolulu	Kaimuki Dry Goods, 1144 10th Ave.	808-734-2141
Honolulu	The Calico Cat, 1223 Koko Head Ave.	808-732-3998
Honolulu	Island Crafts & Fabrics, 1284 Kalani St #D102	808-847-0603
Honolulu	Quilts Hawaii, 2209 Young St.	808-942-3195
Kahului	Sew Special, 275 W. Kaahumanu Ave.	808-877-6128
Kailua	Fabric Gift Shoppe, 74-5599 Luhia St, Unit D5	808-329-8177
Kamuela	Upcountry Quilters. P.O. Box 2631	808-885-7666
Kapaa	Hawaii's Keepsakes, 484 Kuhio Hwy.	808-822-7963
Kealakekua	Kimura's Fabrics, P.O. Box 435	808-322-3771
Kekaha	Kauai Kwilts, 8689 Elepaio Rd.	808-337-2700
Koloa	Hawaii's Keepsakes, 1571 Poipu Rd	808-742-1288
Lahaina	Ka Honu Gift Gallery, 277 Wili Ko Pl. #40	808-661-0173
Lahaina	Quilts 'n Fabric Land, 658 Front St #134B	808-662-0951
Paia	Paia Mercantile, 2 Baldwin Ave. #B	808-579-6388
Wahiawa	The Pineapple Patch, 64-1550 Kamehameha	808-622-3494

Hawaii Guilds:

Kamuela	Mauna Kea Quilters' Guild, P.O. Box 2249, 96743	Meets: 2nd Saturday 9 a.m. at Thelma Parker Library, Waimea
Kamuela	Ka Hui Kapa Apano O'Waimea c/o Topstich, P.O. Box 2631, 96743	Meets: Last Saturday 9 a.m. at St. James Church
Maui	Maui Quilt Guild	Meets: 1st Tuesday for info call Charlene Hughes (808) 572-8864
Mililani	Hawaii Quilt Guild, 172 Kaopua Loop, 96789	
Volcano	Volcano Village Quilters, P.O. Box 959, 96785	Meets: 1st & 3rd Wednesday at Cooper Center

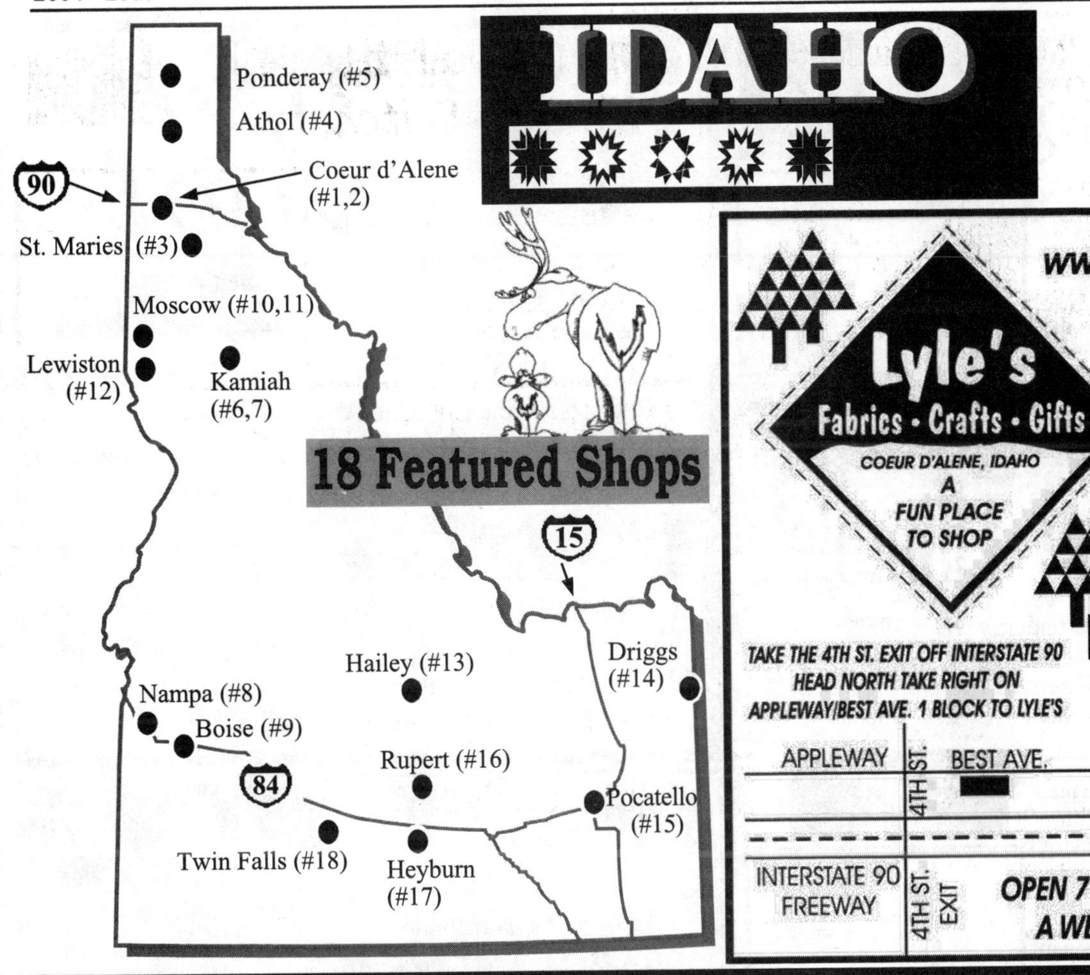

Est: 2002

Coeur d'Alene, ID #2

BEAR PAW QUILTING AND BERNINA

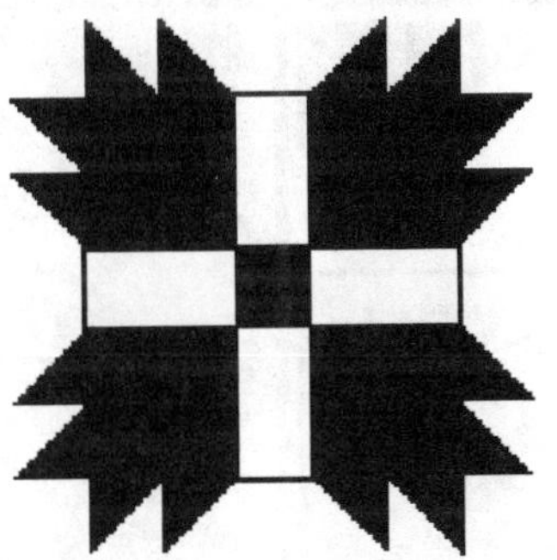

- 3000 sq. ft. of Inspiration!!

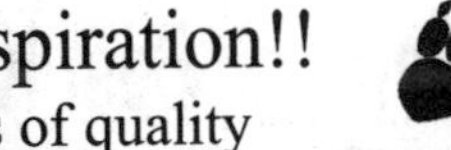

- 2500+ bolts of quality cotton fabrics
- 550 feet of color wall, blenders and backgrounds

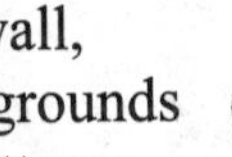

- Quilting books, patterns & notions
- Gund Bear Distributor
- Many gift ideas for quilters and friends

- Embroidery Supplies
- BERNINA Sales & Service

296 W. Sunset Ave. #30, Coeur d'Alene, ID 83815
(208) 664-1554 Fax: (208) 664-7739
bearpaw@imbris.net
www.bearpawquilting.net
Owners: Sandy Goedde & Kathryn Boss

Mon - Fri 9:30 - 6:00 Sat 10:00 - 5:00
Mem. Day to Labor Day Sun 12:00 - 4:00

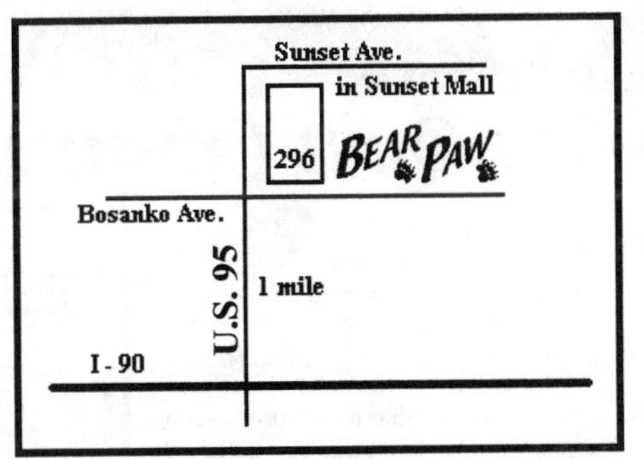

St. Maries, ID #3

Tues - Fri 10 - 6
Sat 10 - 4

Mrs. Sew-n-Sew's Quilt Shop

816 Main Ave. 83861
(208) 245-6656
info@mrs-sewnsew.com
www.mrs-sewnsew.com
Owners: Nona & Gary Davis
Est: 2000 1500 sq.ft. 1500 Bolts

Diverse selection of premium quality quilting supplies and fabrics. Books, patterns, notions as well as felted wool. Personalized, friendly service.

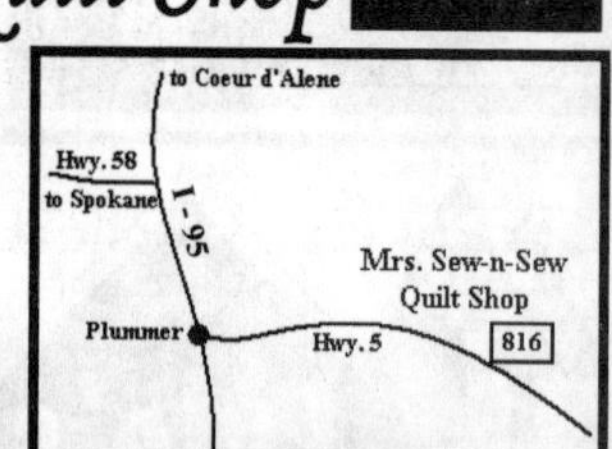

The Empty Spool

Tues - Sat 10 - 5

30404-B Hwy. 95 N,
P.O. Box 495 83801
(208) 683-3880 Est: 1993
Owners: Cindy Murray,
Karen Van Pelt
& Betsy Keifer

elna

Hwy. 54
The Empty Spool
Silverwood Theme Park
ATHOL
Hwy. 95
POST FALLS
COEUR d'ALENE
I - 90

Athol, ID #4

The friendliest shop for service, inspiration and sharing of ideas. Great selection of fabric, wonderful samples, books, patterns & notions. Fun Classes. Authorized elna dealer.

Ponderay, ID #5

Granny Thimble's

1175 Fontaine Dr., Ponderay, ID 83852
(208) 263-4875
chknlips@netw.com
Owner: Carol Kunzeman Est: 2001

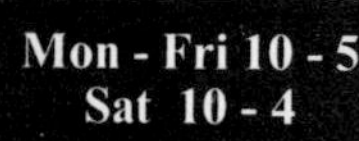

If you are looking for a quaint little place to visit that will take you back in time where life was simpler, than come visit. We have many bolts of 100% cotton fabric to choose from. We offer classes and help with all your projects and fabric needs. Come plan to sit and stay awhile and visit with us. We have the kettle on for tea and the cookies are in the oven just waiting to be shared with you!

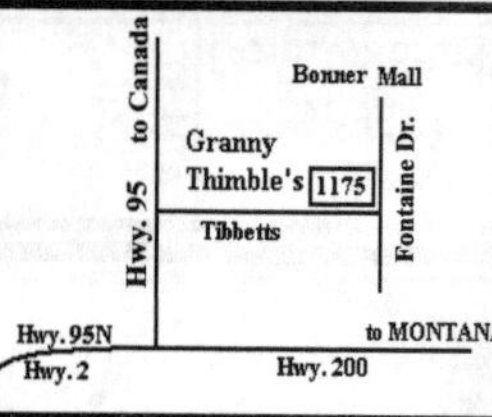

We are the Best Kept Secret in North Idaho!

Kamiah, ID #6

Mon - Sat 10 - 5
Call first for B & B

Quilt House
BED & BREAKFAST and QUILT SHOP

HC 11, Box 142 83536
Toll free 877 QUILT BB (784-5822)
(208) 935-7668 Fax: (208) 935-7686
Owner: Elaine Hutchison

Directions: After going through Kamiah, cross bridge, take immediate left. This is the Woodland Rd., follow for 12 miles past the Woodland Friends Church. (12 miles, stay left) Take all 1st lefts after the church. (2 more miles to the Quilt House) Pass the Quilt House to the driveway.

Country mountain setting, 14 miles from Kamiah. Enjoy a week-end or week long quilt retreat in a beautiful 3 story log B&B with fabulous views. Sleeps up to 14.

Kamiah, ID #7

By Appt. Only

Kamiah Kustom Kwilting

P.O. Box 278 83536
(208) 935-0884
Est: 1992
kamkuskw@camasnet.com
Owner: Joyce Anderson

A Machine Quilting Service!
Custom quilt finishing. Classes & quilting supplies available.

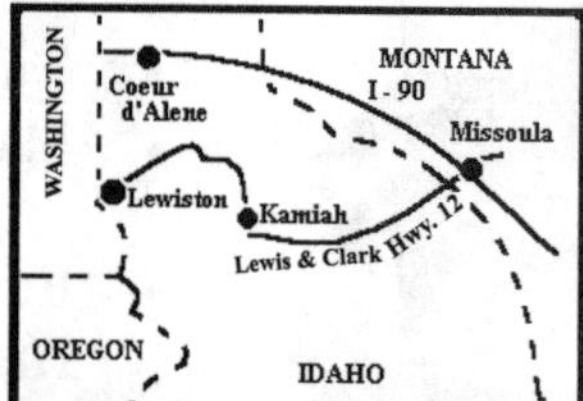

Nampa, ID #8

Mon - Fri 10 - 6
Sat 10 - 4

Material Things

509 12th Ave. Rd. 83686
(208) 461-4540

materialandmore@wmconnect.com
Owner: Rona Clement
Est: 2001 2000 sq.ft. 3000 Bolts
Friendly atmosphere, custom quilting, fabrics, books, patterns, notions, kits.
"A Quilters' Shop" We strive for great service.

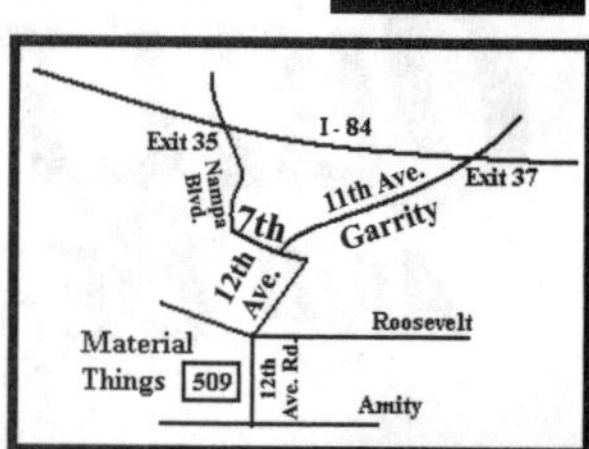

Boise, ID #9

Mon - Sat 10 - 6
Sun 12 - 5

The Quilt Crossing

5725 Fairview Avenue 83706
(208) 376-0087
qltxing@worldnet.att.net
Owner: Patty Hinkel
Est: 1987 3000 sq.ft. 2000 Bolts

Specializing in distinctive 100% cotton fabrics, classes, books, gifts & quilt / soft sculpture patterns. Bernina Sewing Machines.

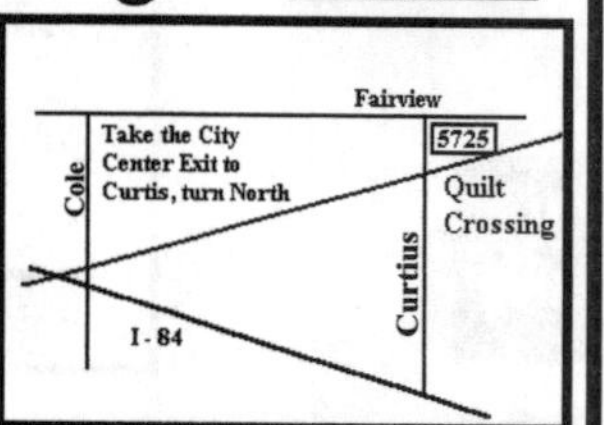

Moscow, ID #10

Mon - Sat 10 - 7
Sun 12 - 5

Quilt Something!

1420 S. Blaine St. 83843
(208) 883-4216
E-Mail: colleen@quiltsomething.com
Web Site: www.quiltsomething.com
Owner: Colleen Phillip
Est: 1996 3400 sq.ft. 2000+ Bolts
Full service shop. All major fabric houses including RJR, Benartex, Moda, Hoffman & more! Located inside mall - many restaurants nearby.

to Coeur d'Alene
Hwy. 95
Quilt Something
Eastside Market Place
to Pullman, WA
Hwy. 8
Blaine St.
Hwy. 8
to Troy
to Lewiston

2 Great Shops!

Becky's Fabrics & Bernina.... A quilt shop and more!

Becky's Fabrics & Bernina is an authorized Bernina Dealership located at two locations. The first lies in the heart of Moscow, while the second resides in the Lewiston-Clarkston Valley. Both stores stock a complete line of Bernina sewing machines, sergers and accessories and have in-store technicians available for service and repair on any Bernina machine. Becky's also stocks an assortment of quilting kits, a nice selection of books, as well as patterns and notions. Our very friendly and knowledgeable staff is always ready to assist you with your sewing machine and quilting needs. Whether you are meandering through the rolling hills of the Palouse or roaming through the deep Lewis-Clark Valley stop by and say hello.

Becky's Fabrics & Bernina
410 W. 3rd Street
Moscow, ID 83843
1-208-882-5224

bernina@moscow.com

Becky's Fabrics & Bernina
1702 21st Street
Suite 112 ~ Mall 21
Lewiston, ID 83501
1-208-743-4448

bernina@moscow.com

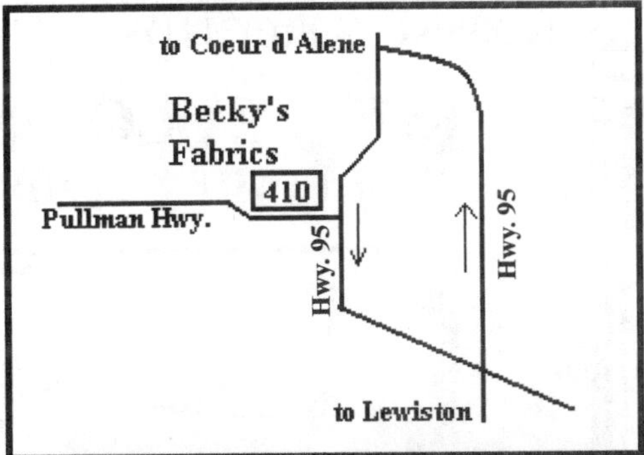

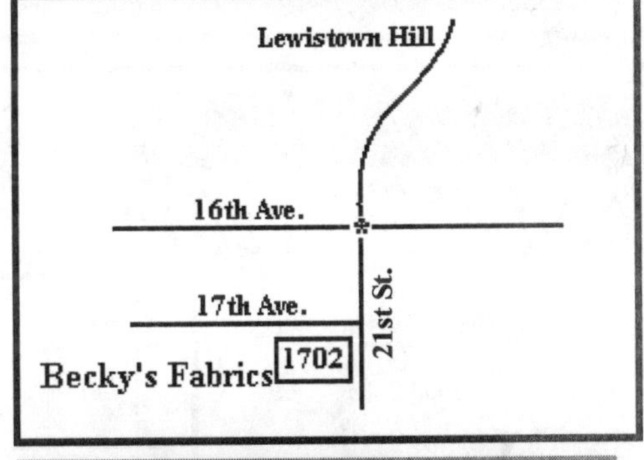

Moscow, ID #11

Lewiston, ID #12

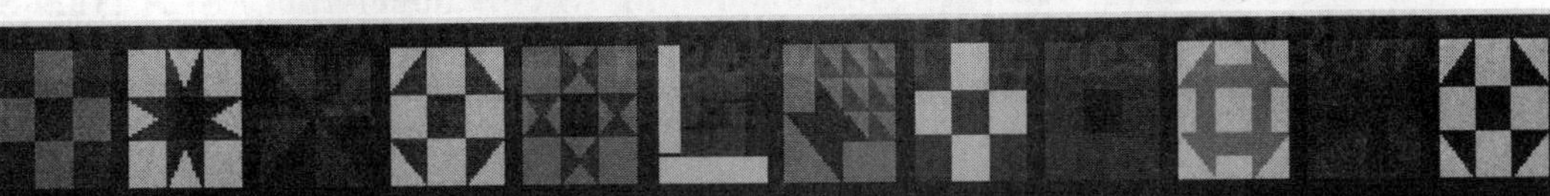

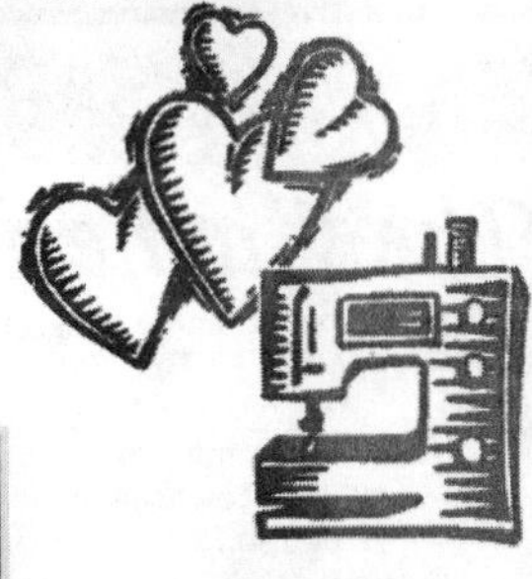

Nothing Sews Like A Bernina. Nothing.
BERNINA®

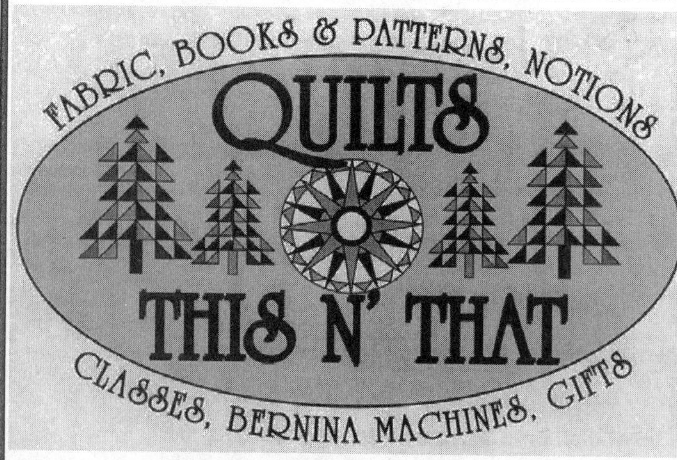

9 E. Bullion 83333
(208) 788-1331

Mon - Fri 10 - 6
Sat 10 - 5
Sun 12 - 4

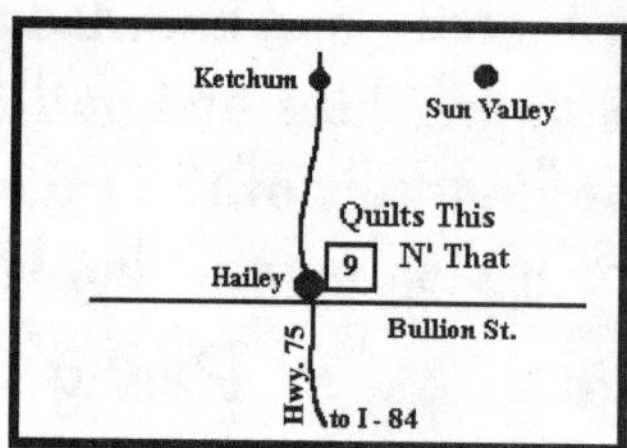

Fax: (208) 788-1868
lsullivan@sunvalley.net
Est: 1999 Over 1,000 bolts

Located in the Heart of the Scenic Wood River Valley, Just 12 miles from the famous Sun Valley Resort. We offer a unique collection of 100% Cotton Fabric from several manufacturers.

Hailey, ID #13

Driggs, ID #14

Mon - Sat
10 - 5

Wood-N-Needle

285 E. Little Ave., P.O. Box 556 83422
(208) 354-3919
Est: 2001 2000 Bolts

Main St. Hwy. 33 | 1st St. | 2nd St. | 3rd St. | Wood-N Needle 285 | Little Ave. (Ski Hill Rd.)

Large selection of 100% cotton fabrics, books, patterns and notions. Finished quilts for sale.

Rupert, ID #16

Mon - Fri
10 - 5:30
Sat 10 - 5

The Gathering Place

524 6th St. (On the Square) 83350
(208) 436-0455 Fax: (208) 436-9875
tgp@pmt.org
Coming Soon
Owners: Ron & Joyce Jensen
10,000 sq.ft. 5000+ Bolts

Idaho's largest quilt shop — 8000+ bolts of your favorite fabrics. Machine quilting. Fun Classes. Friendly Service. Country furniture, gifts & collectibles.

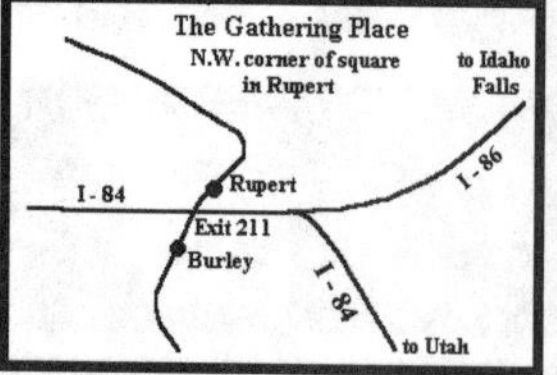

Pocatello, ID #15

Crafts & Frames

Sierra Pacific Crafts
Partners in Creativity

BENARTEX · HOFFMAN · MODA · MAYWOOD · KAUFMAN · RJR · SOUTH SEAS · MICHAEL MILLER · NORTHCOTT MONARCH · PRINCESS MIRAH · TIMELESS TREASURES

THE AREA'S FINEST QUILT SHOP

We proudly feature Quilt Patterns & Programs by: Lynette Jensen · Marti Michell · Jackie Robinson · McKenna Ryan of Pine Needles Art Quilt Kits & Many More!

Specialty Yarns by Lion Brand Yarns, Trend Setters, Paton/Bernat and more!

LARGEST SELECTION OF FLANNELS IN STOCK EVERY DAY!
- *HUGE SELECTION OF HOFFMAN BATIKS!*
- *WE SPECIALIZE IN FABRICS FOR MCKENNA RYAN'S QUILTS.*
- *LARGE SELECTION OF BOOKS, PATTERNS & NOTIONS*
- *GRACE QUILT FRAMES*

Look for our beautiful fabrics packets pre-cut and packaged for your convenience.

Stop in soon, we look forward to seeing you!

We do special orders, and we ship anywhere!

1570 YELLOWSTONE
1-877-I Quilt 2 · (208) 237-1014

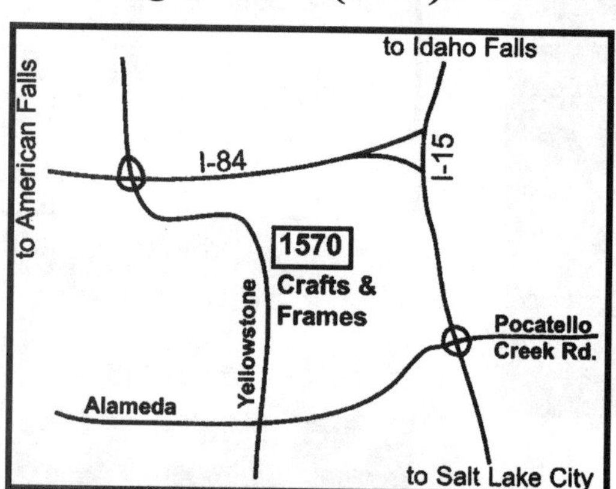

OPEN 7 DAYS A WEEK
M-F 9:30am-8pm SAT 9:30am-7pm SUN 11am-5pm
E-mail: crafts@ida.net · www.craftsnframes.com
Owner: Emma Gebo Est. 1993

Heyburn, ID #17

Mon - Sat 10 - 6
Sunday by chance or Appt. please call

Carleen's fabrics & crafts, etc.

450 21st St. 83336
(208) 679-3573
Est: 1995
Mgr: Carleen Clayville
12-1500 Bolts

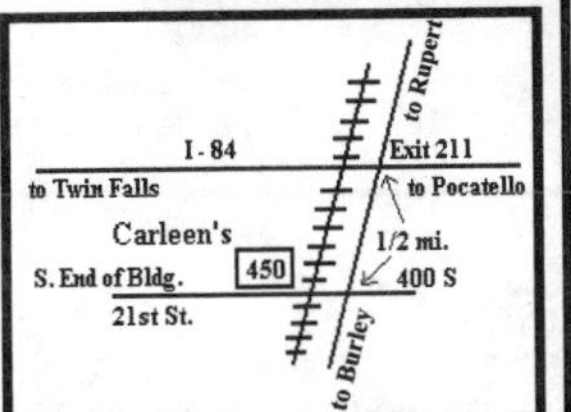

4000 sq.ft. of fabrics. Mainly Quilting Cottons. 65 - 70 shades of solids. Imported yarns, selected crafts. Bridal & better dress. Local consignment gifts & florals.
E-Mail: carleen@hereinidaho.com
Web Site: carleen.hereinidaho.com

Stitchin' Time

129 Main Ave. W
Twin Falls, ID 83301
208/735-4094
Fax 208/735-1469

Owned by
Les & Cathy Reitz

stitchintime@onewest.net
www.stitchintime.ws
In downtown, where all the unique shops are.

Mon - Thur 10 - 5:30
Fri & Sat 10 - 5

Shop in a friendly, well-lit atmosphere. 5,000 sq. ft. store with over 2,500 bolts of quality 100% cotton. Loads of quilts on display to spur your imagination. Huge selection of Books, Patterns & Notions. Professional Machine quilting available.

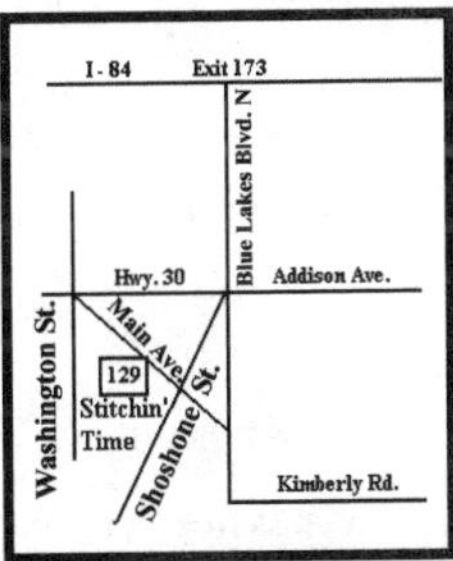

Twin Falls, ID #18

Metered Parking in front, Free Parking in back. Yes, there is a back door!

Other Shops in Idaho: *We suggest calling first*

Aberdeen Old Home Place, 2597 W 1700 S 208-397-4335
Arimo Tanner's Country Quilting, 150 Front St. 208-254-9384
Boise Quintessential Quilting, 6425 York St 208-378-8195
Boise The Country Quilter, 1002 S. Vista Ave. 208-424-3188
Boise Idaho Sewing Center, 4500 Overland Rd 208-338-0144
Bonners Ferry Gini Knits, 7225 Main St. 208-267-5921
Burley Walter Times Two, 1020 E 17th St 208-678-1317
Chubbuck Mill End Fabric, 4415 E. Burnside Ave 208-238-1388
Clarkia Joanne & Bucks Clothing Fabric & Photo P.O. Box 1133
Coldwell Cindy's Quilt Shop, 220 S 7th Ave 208-453-8228
Dalton Gardens Patterns N More, 6848 N. Government Way 208-772-7382
Eagle Seams Etc., 124 E. State St. 208-939-8227
Grace Fabulous Fabrics, P.O. Box E 208-425-3821
Grangeville Melinda's Fabrics 207 W. Main 208-983-0254
Idaho Falls Quilts 'N' Things, 1375 E. 49th N 208-524-2439
Idaho Falls Granny's Quilts, 390 N. Karey Ln. 208-522-0930
Idaho Falls Quilted Daisy, 275 Cliff St. 208-523-6395
McCall Mountan Fabrics, 123 E. Lake 208-634-8450
Meridian 2 Sisters Quilting Shoppe, 850 W. Franklin Rd. 208-887-4707
Meridian Craft Warehouse, 1160 N Eagle Rd 208-288-2039
Moscow A Quilter's Heaven, 428 West 3rd St. 208-882-6262
Orofino Lura's Fabrics, 10494 Hwy. 12 208-476-7781
Pocatello Gary's Bernina Sewing Center, 512 Yellowstone Ave 208-232-8228
Pocatello Quilt Shop, 119 S. Main 208-237-6619
Princeton In The Pines Quilt Shop, 1225 W. Hatter Creek Rd. 208-875-0011
Rexburg Porter's Craft & Frame, 19 College 208-359-0786
Rexburg The Quilt Barn, 2730 W 3800 S 208-356-6561
Rigby Abbots Variety, 120 E Main St 208-745-7738
Sandpoint Adele's Sewing Center, 516 W Oak St 208-263-9646
Soda Springs Nifty Needle, 128 S. Main 208-547-2441
Twin Falls Ann's Electric Stitchin, 129 Main Ave W 208-734-2112

Idaho Guilds:

Arco Lost River Hospital Auxillary, P.O. Box 145, 83213
Boise Twin Falls Quilt Guild, 11602 Reutzel, 83709
Boise Boise Basin Quilters, P.O. Box 2206, 83701
Burley Mt. Harrison Quilt Guild, P.O. Box 172
Caldwell Syringa Quilters Group, 15844 Wrightway Ln., 83605
Challis Bits and Pieces, P.O. Box 1082, 83226
Council Council Mountain Quilters, P.O. Box 829, 83612
Emmett Valley of Plenty Quilters, 615 E. Locust, 83617
Grangeville Sew-Ciety, 207 W. Main, 83530
Hayden North Idaho Quilters, P.O. Box 777, 83835
Heyburn Mt. Harrison Quilters, Rt. 2, Box 2150, 83336
Idaho Falls Snake River Valley Quilt Guild, 1450 Paul St., 83401
Kamiah Thimbleberries Club, HC11, Box 142, 83536
Kamiah Debbie Mumm Club, HC 11, Box 142, 83536
Kamiah Central Idaho Quilter's Guild, P.O. Box 278, 83536
Kootenai Panhandle Piecemakers, P.O. Box 39, 83840
Lewiston Seaport Quilter's Guild, P.O. Box 491, 83501
Malad Oneida Quilting Guild, 620 W 600 N, 83252
McCall Pine Needle Quilters, P.O. Box 587, 83638
Moscow Palouse Patchers, P.O. Box 9795, 83843
Nampa Nampa Friday Quilters, 210 Fay Ln., 83686
Orofino Clearwater Quilters, P.O. Box 2748, 83544
Pocatello Happy Hands Quilt Club, 40 Davis Dr., 83201
Priest River River City Rippers, 306 High St, 83856
Rupert Mt. Harrison Quilters
Sandpoint Panhandle Piecemakers, 83864
St. Maries Valley Piecemakers, 905 Main, 83861
Stanley Sawtooth Mountain Mamas, P.O. Box 33Q, 83278
Twin Falls Desert Sage Quilters, P.O. Box 812, 83301

Blackfoot Piecemakers, 9 W. River Rd., 83221
Meets: 3rd Tuesday (except July & Dec) 7 p.m. at Church of Christ, 2000 Eldorado St.
Meets: 4th Tuesday 1:30 at Trinity Lutheran Church, Rupert
Meets: Tuesday 10 a.m. at First Christian Church
Coeur d'Alene Ladies of the Lake, W 9300 Fighting Creek, 83814
Elk City Sew Help Me Quilters Meets: Last Tuesday 7 p.m.
Meets: 1st & 3rd Thursday 10 a.m. Nazareen Church, 1144 N. Washington, Emmett
Meets: Every Tuesday 7 p.m.
Meets: 4th Monday every other month starting in Jan. 6:30 p.m. Christ the King Church
Hope Clark Fork Valley Quilters, 1370 Peninsula Rd., 83836
Idaho Falls Idaho Falls Quilters, 1884 Melody Dr., 83402
Meets: 3rd Thursday 10 a.m. and 7 p.m. at Quilt House B & B Quilt Shop
Meets: 4th Thursday 10 a.m. and 7 p.m. at Quilt House B & B Quilt Shop
Meets: 1st Tuesday 6:30 p.m. at Kamiah Senior Citizens Center

Meets: 4th Monday 7 p.m. at Pautler Senior Center in Clarkston

Meets: Monday 7 p.m. (Sept - May) at McCall Public Library
Mountain Home EL-Y-HEE Quilters
Meets: Friday 1 p.m. in member's home
Meets: 2nd Thursday at Community Center

Meets: 3th Wednesday 6:30pm at Cedar Mountain Quilt Shop
Salmon Lemhi Piecemakers, Box 59, Rt. #1, 83467
Meets: 2nd Wednesday @ 6:30pm at First Lutheran Church

Meets: 2nd Thursday 7 p.m. in member's home
Weiser Thread Bears, 690 Adobe Dr., 83672

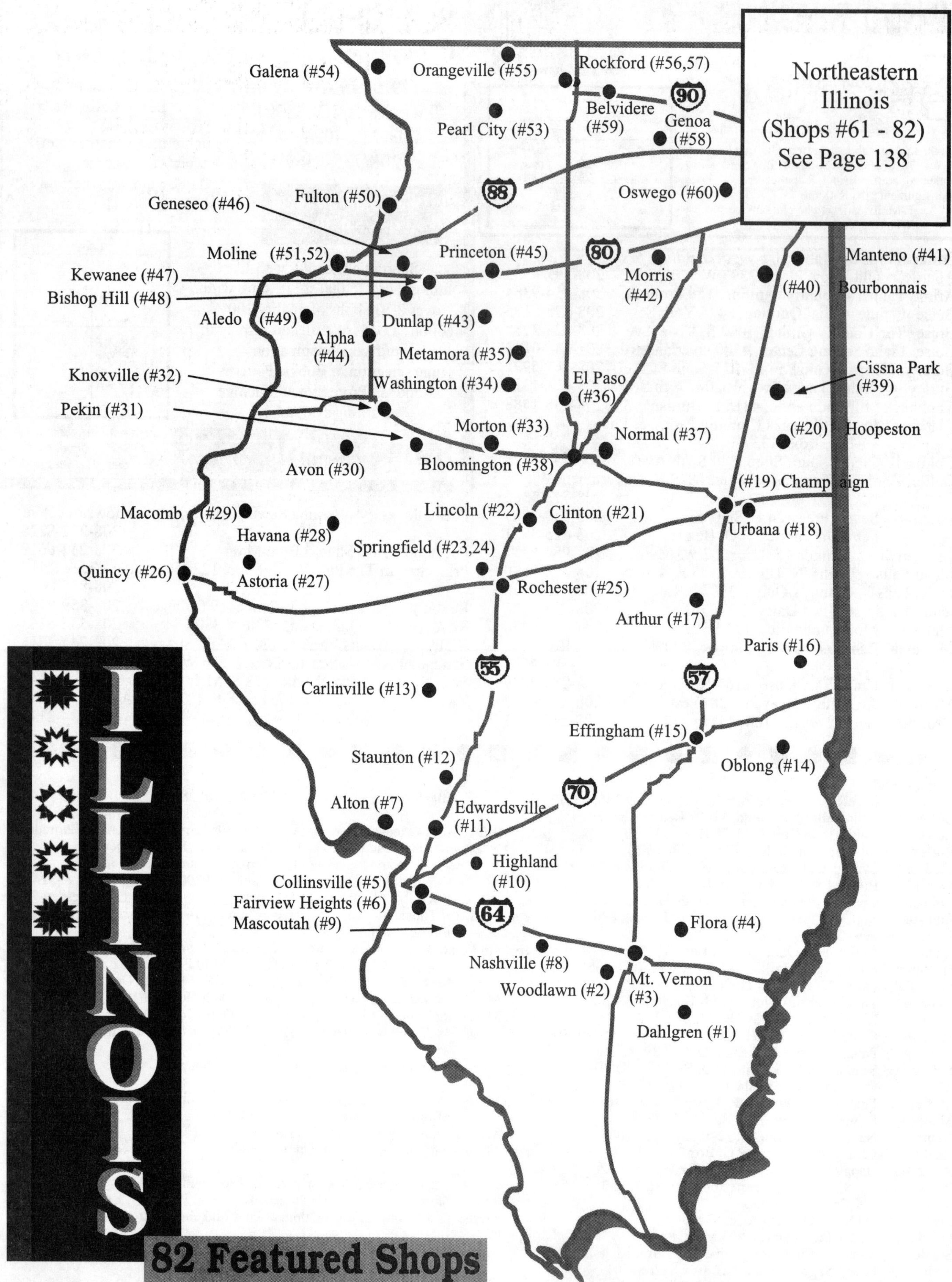

Northeastern Illinois (Shops #61 - 82) See Page 138
Galena (#54)
Orangeville (#55)
Rockford (#56,57)
90
Belvidere (#59)
Genoa (#58)
Pearl City (#53)
88
Oswego (#60)
Geneseo (#46)
Fulton (#50)
Moline (#51,52)
Princeton (#45)
80
Morris (#42)
Manteno (#41)
(#40) Bourbonnais
Kewanee (#47)
Bishop Hill (#48)
Aledo (#49)
Dunlap (#43)
Alpha (#44)
Metamora (#35)
Cissna Park (#39)
Knoxville (#32)
Washington (#34)
El Paso (#36)
Pekin (#31)
Morton (#33)
Normal (#37)
(#20) Hoopeston
Avon (#30)
Bloomington (#38)
(#19) Champaign
Macomb (#29)
Lincoln (#22)
Clinton (#21)
Havana (#28)
Urbana (#18)
Springfield (#23,24)
Quincy (#26)
Astoria (#27)
Rochester (#25)
Arthur (#17)
Paris (#16)
55
57
Carlinville (#13)
Effingham (#15)
Oblong (#14)
Staunton (#12)
70
Alton (#7)
Edwardsville (#11)
Highland (#10)
Collinsville (#5)
Fairview Heights (#6)
Mascoutah (#9)
64
Flora (#4)
Nashville (#8)
Woodlawn (#2)
Mt. Vernon (#3)
Dahlgren (#1)
ILLINOIS
82 Featured Shops

Dahlgren, IL #1

M, T, Th, F
9 - 5
Sat 9 - 3

Joyce's Country Quilts

R.R. #1, Box 54-B 62828
(618) 736-2385

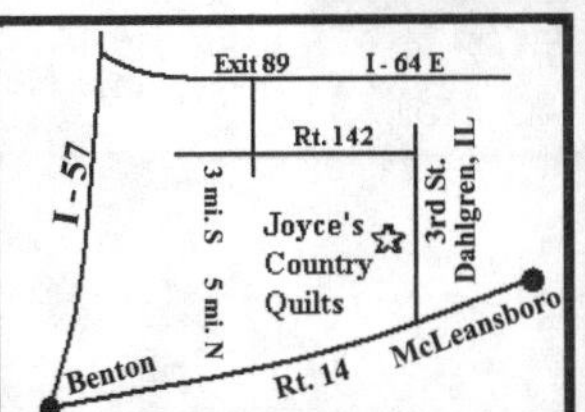

100% Cotton Fabric, Notions, Books, Hand-Quilting, Custom Quilts, Kits. A friendly country shop where everyone's welcomed!

COTTON PATCH

Mon - Sat
10 - 6
After hours
Appt. Welcomed

6194 E. Hobbes Rd. 62898
(618) 735-2483
Cottonpatch@frontiernet.net
Owner: Lynne Mears

Woodlawn, IL #2

Quality Fabric
Books, Notions
Classes

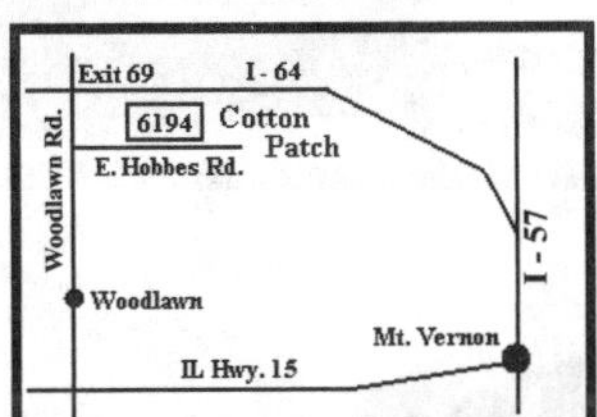

Mt. Vernon, IL #3

Mon - Fri
9:30 - 6
Sat 10 - 5

Mt. Vernon Sewing-Mart

4112 Broadway (Rt. 15) 62864
(618) 244-5856
Owner: Doug & Kathy Dial

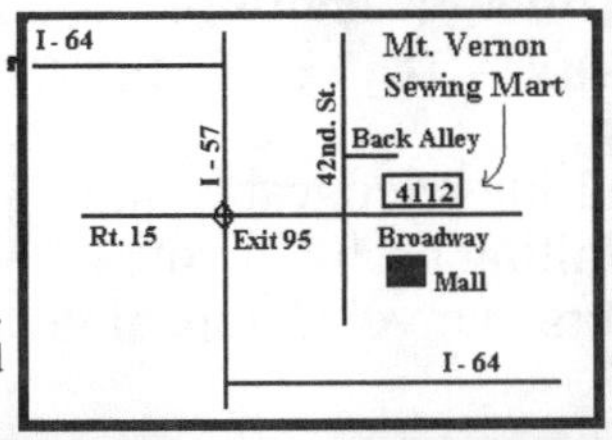

Viking & White Sewing Machines & Sergers. Fabrics, Quilting Supplies, Patterns and Books. Over 2000 sq.ft. Come and Browse.

I - 64
Mt. Vernon Sewing Mart
I - 57
42nd. St.
Back Alley
4112
Rt. 15
Exit 95
Broadway
Mall
I - 64

Flora, IL #4

Tues - Fri
9 - 5
Sat 9 - 3

Bear Paw Quilt Co.

117 W. North Ave. 62839
(618) 662-3391 Fax: Same
www.bearpawquilting.com
Est: 2002 3000 sq.ft. 2000+ Bolts

100% cotton fabrics from top companies and wool felt selected with quilters in mind. Books, patterns, notions, classes.

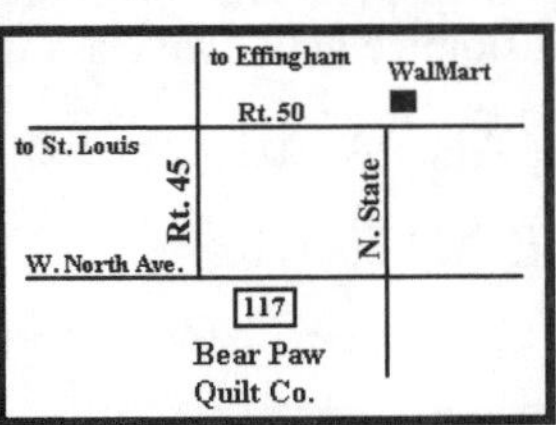

Collinsville, IL #5

110 W. Main St. 62234
(618) 345-3661
Owner: Mary Solomon
Est: 1990 4000 sq.ft.

Mon - Sat 9 - 4
Tues & Thur
til 7:30

Over 3500
Bolts of
100% Cotton Fabrics
Homespuns * Modas
Hoffmans * Batiks * RJR

BERNINA®

Bernina Sewing & Embroidery
Machines and Sergers &
Horn of America Quilting Cabinets.

Cross Patches

Only 12 min. from downtown St. Louis

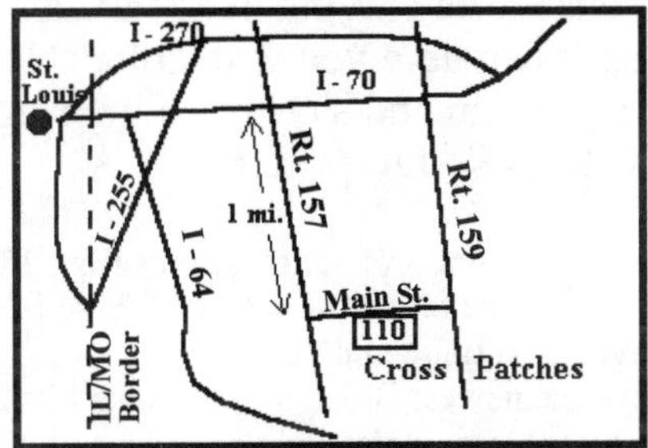

Show us this AD and we will give you a 10% (one time) discount on Fabric purchases.

Since 1903

Jackman's Fabrics

www.jackmansfabrics.com

Superstore - Fairview Heights, Illinois

Quilting • Bridal • Home Decorator Fabrics

Baby lock & elna

Sergers, Embroidery & Sewing Machines
Amazing Designs Superstore
Only 15 minutes from downtown St. Louis

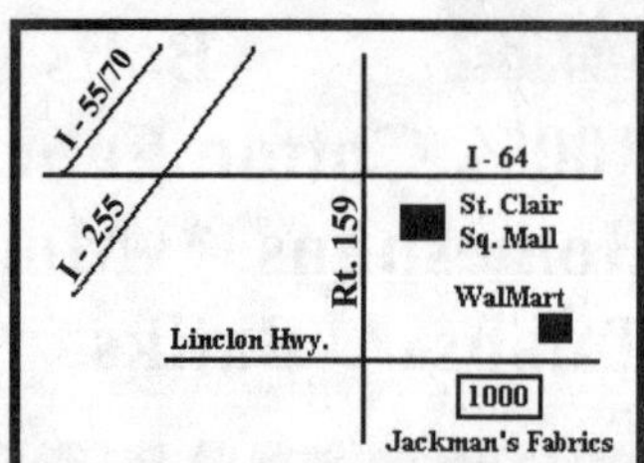

618-632-2700 • 1000 Lincoln Hwy., 62208
Mon. & Thurs. 10:00 - 9:00 • Tues., Wed., Fri. 10:00 - 6:00
Sat. 10:00 - 5:30 Sun. noon - 5:00

Fairview Heights, IL #6

Over 50,000 yards of quilting cottons!
Hoffman, Moda, Timeless Treasures, Benartex, RJR, P&B, South Seas and more . . .

Fabrics designed by Mary Engelbreit, Laurel Burch, Nancy Halvorson, Robin Pandolph, etc.

Huge collection of batiks, marbles, novelties, patterns, books, etc.

Tremendous displays! Great new ideas!

Show us this ad and you will receive a 1 time 20% discount on your entire non-sale purchase.

Alton, IL #7

PATCHWORK PLUS

Mon - Thur 9 - 5
Fri & Sat 9 - 4
Sun 12 - 4

108 W. Third St. 62002 (877) 529-9562

Fax: (618) 462-8565 E-Mail: patchplus@piasanet.com

Owner: Jan Coats Est: 1999 3600 sq.ft. 3000+ Bolts of 100% Cotton

Indulge your fabric craving in a relaxed atmosphere. Our knowledgeable and friendly staff can help you with color selection or any quilting problem you may have. Stop in and say "hello". Bring in your Quilters' Travel Companion book and receive a fat quarter free.

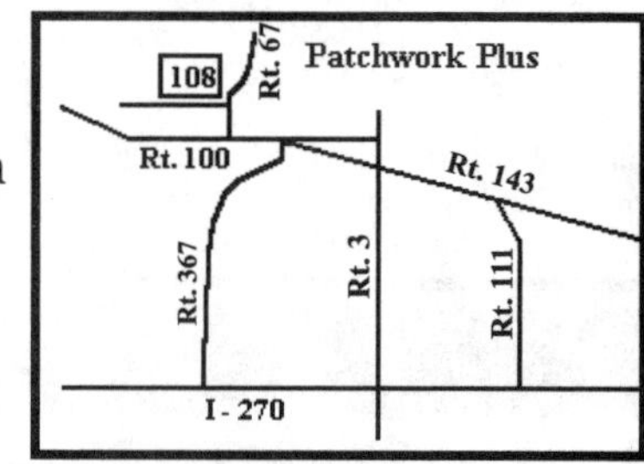

- We specialize in reproduction fabrics from 1800-1920.
  We have the largest selection of these fabrics in the St. Louis area.
- We have an Antique Quilt Club.
- We have the newest Block of the Month kits available.
- We also carry a complete line of embroidery thread including DMC and Krenik and counted cross-stitch supplies.
- We have a large classroom complete with sewing machines. Customize your own class with groups of 4 or more.

Custom Machine Quilting Also Available by:

All In Stitches—Kaye Sutton

2nd Floor of Patchwork Plus Tues - Thur 10 - 4 or by Appointment

Nashville, IL #8

Mon - Thur 8 - 5:30
Fri 8 - 6
Sat 8 - 5

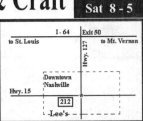

Lee's Quilting & Craft Center

212 E. St. Louis St. 62263
(618) 327-8898

Supplies for all your quilting needs. Over 1500 bolts of fabric. Over 600 quilting stencils. 114 quilt block designs to embroider.

I - 64 Exit 50
to St. Louis to Mt. Vernon
Hwy. 127
Downtown Nashville
Hwy. 15
212
Lee's

Mascoutah, IL #9

Tues 2- 6
Wed - Fri 10 - 4
Sat 10 - 2

Patchwork Corner Crafts

200 N. Jefferson St.
62258
(618) 566-2652

We have a large supply of quilting fabrics and supplies. We have pieced quilt tops, finished quilts and handmade crafts.

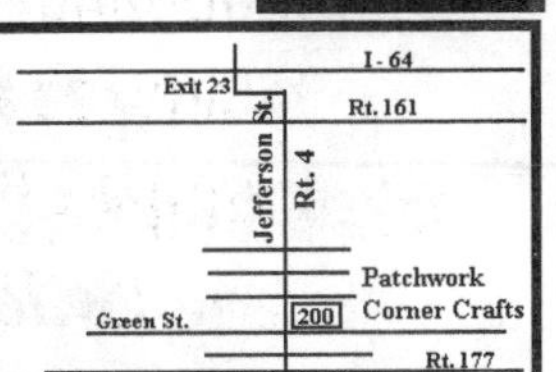

Highland, IL #10

Mon - Fri 9 - 5
Sat 9 - 4

Rosemary's Fabric & Quilts

812 Ninth St. 62249
(618) 654-5045
seifried@hometel.com
Owner: Rosemary Seifried
Est: 1988

Largest Thimbleberries Selection in St. Louis Area.
Over 3000 Bolts of Fabric.
Everything a Quilter Needs!

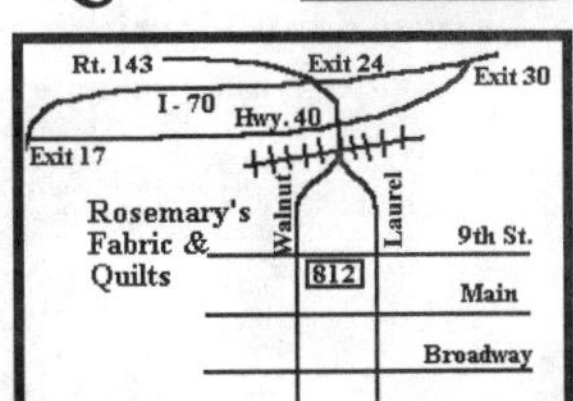

Edwardsville, IL #11

Visit our lovely shop in an historical brick home built in the 1830's where we are known for our friendliness, beautiful cotton fabrics, supplies, classes, original designs, and yes, our restroom. ***"We love being your inspiration…."***

Mon - Fri 9:30 - 5 Sat 9:30 - 4 Sun 12 - 4

1310 N. Main St. 62025
618-656-6538
thequiltedgarden@charter.net
Owner: Jenice Belling
Est: 2000 1500 Bolts

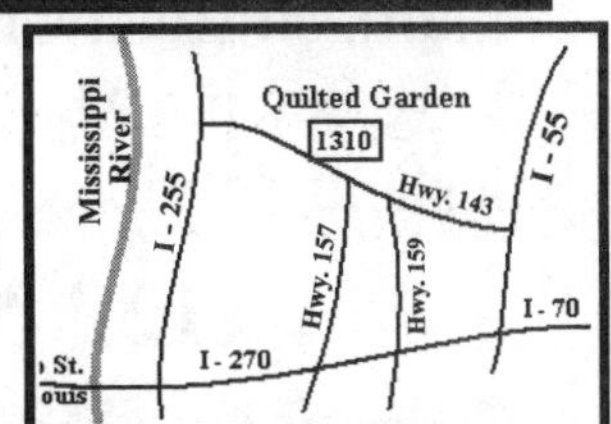

www.quiltedgarden.com

Staunton, IL #12

Tues - Sat 10 - 4

Warm N Cozy Quilts

124 E. Main St. 62088
(618) 635-5509
Warmncozy@hotmail.com
www.warmncozy.com
Owner: Debbie Chitty Est: 2002

Located in Main Street Mini Mall. Full service machine quilting. Quilts, Fabric and Notions for Sale. A friendly place for quilters.

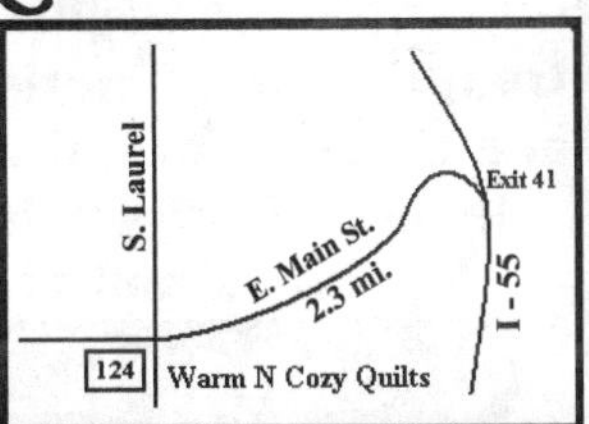

Carlinville, IL #13

Mon - Fri 9 - 4
Sat 9 - 12

The Quiltin' Shed

21887 Route 4 62626
(217) 854-3607
quiltnshed@accunet.net
Owner: Sue Ann Barto Est: 1993

Custom machine quilting. Full line quilt shop. Classes available. Embroidery blocks, thread, etc. Personal service is our specialty.

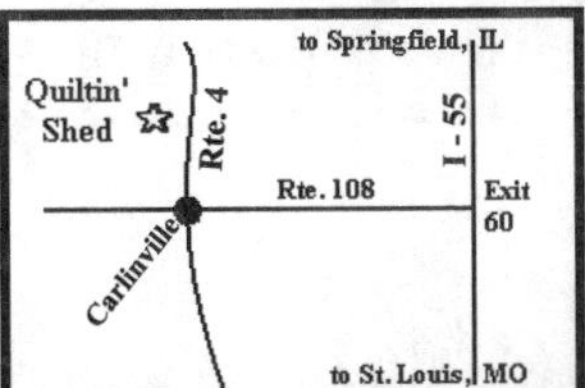

Oblong, IL #14

Mon - Sat 9 - 5
Evenings by Appt.

The Village Stitchery

108 E. Main
62449
(618) 592-4134 2400 sq.ft.
www.villagestitchery.com
Owner: Lisa Pinkston Est: 1982

Visit our unique shop which carries a complete line of fabrics and supplies for the beginning to expert quilter.

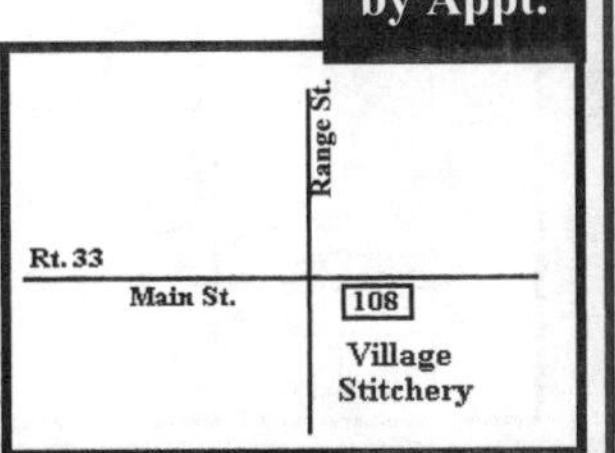

Angie's Nine Patch

Mon - Fri 9 - 5
Sat 9 - 3

Effingham, IL #15

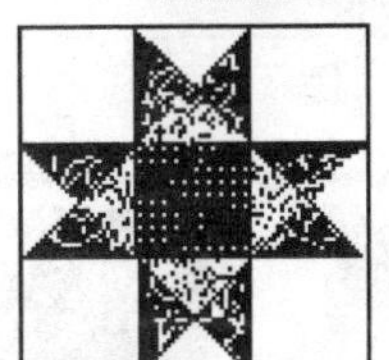

804 S. Henrietta 62401
Exit 159, turn right on Henrietta
(217) 347-9669 3000 Bolts

Large selection of fabrics, books, patterns and stamped textiles for embroidery. Notions, laces, embroidery flosses, crochet thread Low Prices.

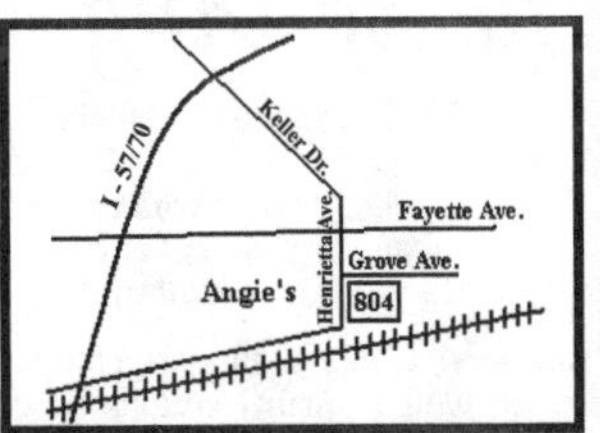

Paris, IL #16

Lori's Pins 'n Needles

(217) 465-5541
loris@comwares.net
www.lorisviking.com

Husqvarna VIKING

"Quilting Headquarters"

- Over 3000 bolts of name brand 100% cotton fabrics
- Books, patterns and quilting tools
- Large classroom area—classes and demonstrations
- Authorized Husqvarna Viking Sewing Machine Sales and Service.

Monday - Thursday 9-6
Friday 9-8
Saturday 9-5

1122 N. Main St.
P.O. Box 815 61944

Arthur, IL #17

Mon - Sat 8:30 - 5

Stitch & Sew Fabrics

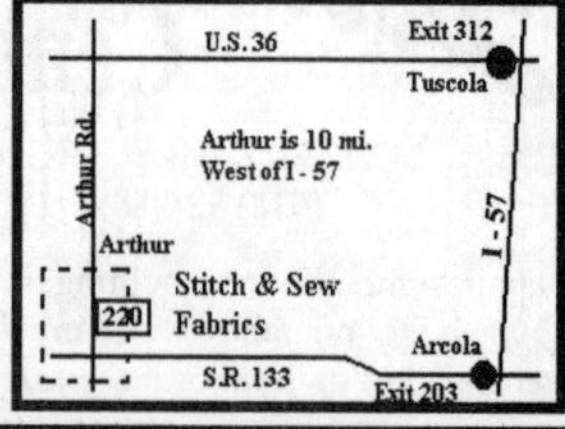

220 S. Vine St. 61911
(217) 543-2287
Fax: (217) 543-2287
Est: 1994
stitchandsew@one-eleven.net
Owners: Sam & Dorothy Herschberger
Over 2000 Bolts of cotton including Hoffman, RJR, Fashion Fabrics and more Quilting Supplies, Books, Bulk Buttons. Long Arm Quilting Available. Authorized Elna dealer.

156A Lincoln Square Mall
Urbana, IL 61801
217-328-1591
Fax: 217-328-1591
sewsassy3@yahoo.com

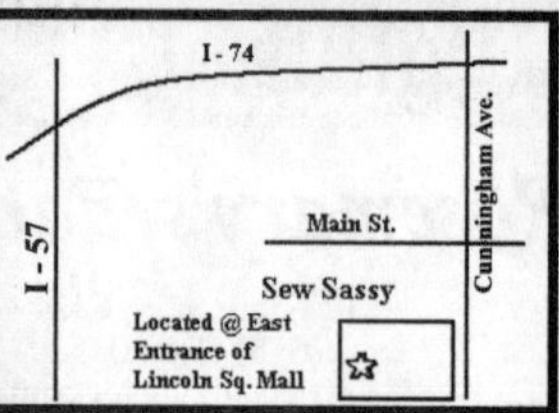

Owners: Joyce Day, Suzanne Hovey & Nancy Muncaster.

Unique fabrics, notions, patterns, and classes for quilters of all skill levels. Pfaff sewing machine sales and service.

Mon - Fri 10 - 8
Sat 10 - 6
Sun 12 - 5

Urbana, IL #18

Champaign, IL #19

Mon - Fri 10 - 7
Sat 10 - 5

B & J Sewing Center

37 E. Marketview Rd. 61820
(217) 355-6090 Fax: (217) 355-6036
bjsew2@msn.com Est: 1995
www.bjsewing.com 1500 sq.ft.
Owners: Barbara & John Marcukaitis

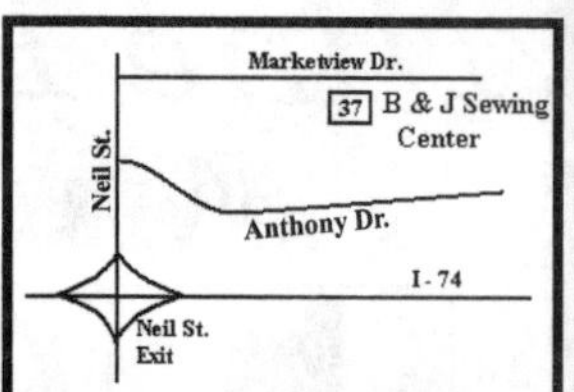

Fine 100% Cotton Fabric, Notions, Quilting Supplies, Books, Patterns, Classes. Machine Quilting of Quilts. Authorized Dealer Husqvarna Viking Sewing Machines.

Hoopeston, IL #20

Mon - Fri 9 - 5:30
Sat 9 - 3

The Sewing Boutique

222 E. Main St. 60942
(217) 283-7125 Fax: (217) 283-5580
keller@net66.com or
jbauer6@hotmail.com
Est: 1980 2200 sq.ft.

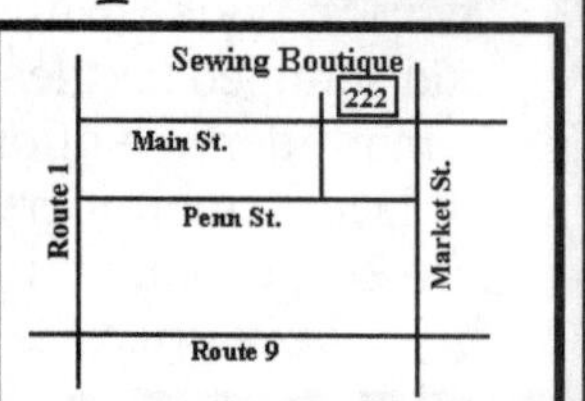

A full service fabric shop stocking fashion fabrics as well as quality cottons for quilting. Authorized Husqvarna Viking dealer. Classes Galore!

Quilters Delight

Mon & Thur 10 - 5
Tues & Wed 10 - 8
Fri 10 - 4
Sat 10 - 2

38 Clinton Plaza 61727
(217) 937-0159
Owner: Shirley Jo Monkman

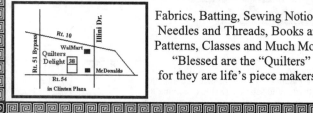

Clinton, IL #21

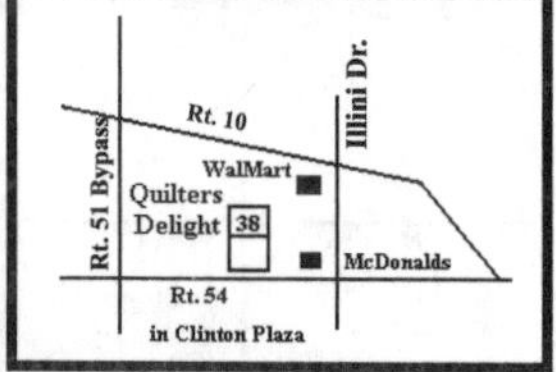

Fabrics, Batting, Sewing Notions, Needles and Threads, Books and Patterns, Classes and Much More.
"Blessed are the "Quilters" for they are life's piece makers."

Lincoln, IL #22

Sew Many Friends

127 S. Kickapoo 62656
(217) 732-4527
ivykquilts@hotmail.com
Designers: Ivy Koritz & Sue Bidwell
Est: 2000 1200 sq.ft. 700 bolts & growing

Monday thru Saturday 10 - 5

Quilting
*Sewing * Smocking*

Member of the Central Illinois Quilt Shop Hop - 3rd weekend of October

Friendly, relaxed, well-lit atmosphere.
Complete line of **supplies** for quiltmaking.
Machine quilting services available. **Classes** for hand and machine quilting and construction, smocking, and clothing construction.
Doll and clothing **patterns**. Needlework and yarn shop next door.
100% cotton fabrics from Hoffman, Moda, RJR, Maywood, SSI and more.
Bring this book in for a free fat quarter.

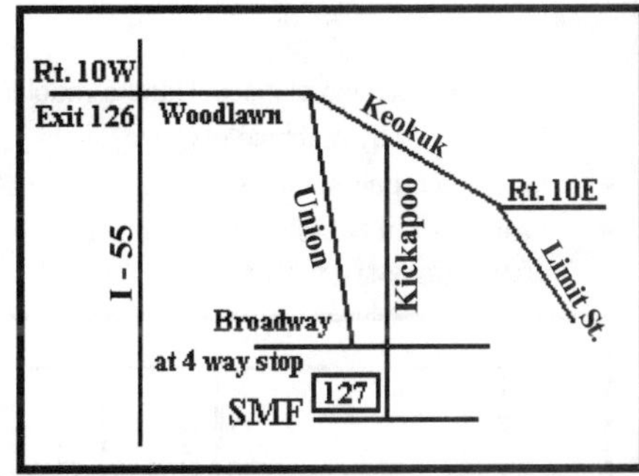

Springfield, IL #23

Mon - Fri 10 - 5
Sat 10 - 2

Sew Unique

1050 N. Grand Ave. W 62702
(217) 546-0317
Owner: Bonnie Jameson
sewunique@warpnet.net
www.sewunique.org
Est: 1998 2500 sq.ft.
Top Quality Quilting and Heirloom Fabrics and Laces. Supplies - Patterns - Books Notions - Classes. Authorized Sales & Service for Brother and Pfaff

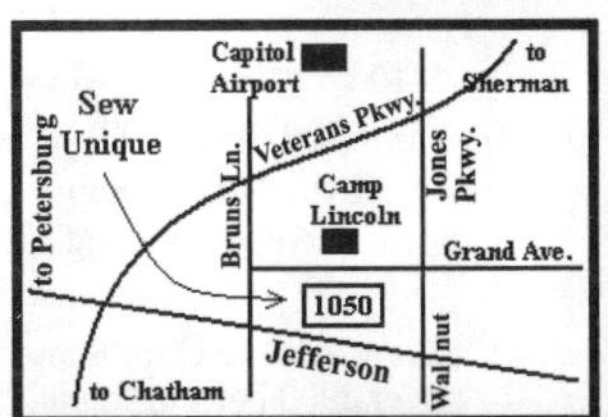

Springfield, IL #24

Mon - Fri 10 - 5:30
Tues til 8
Sat 10 - 4

CALICO HEART QUILT SHOP

2765 W. Jefferson #DD
(217) 241-1410 62702
calicoheart1@aol.com
Owner: Jane Reynolds
Est: 2003 2400 sq.ft. 2000+ Bolts

Hoffman, Moda, RJR, Timeless Treasures, Clothworks & much more. Classes, books, patterns & notions. Plus the friendliest, most helpful, knowledgeable staff around!

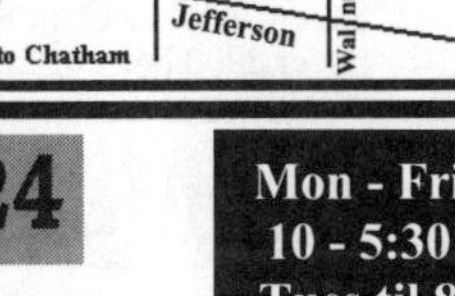

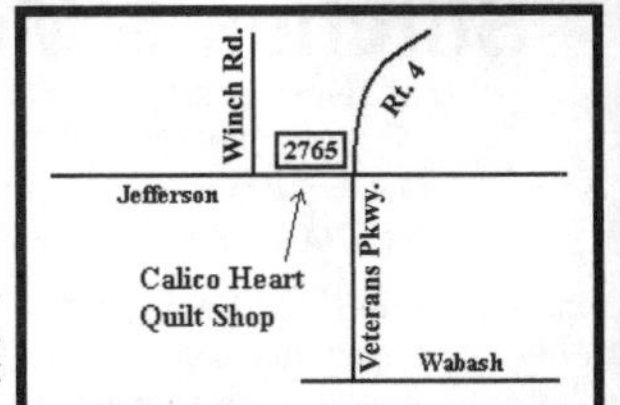

Mon - Fri 10 - 5
Thur til 8
Sat 10 - 4

peace & Applique

145 E. Main St.
P.O. Box 724 62563
Phone/Fax: (217) 498-6771
Owner: Gretchen Quistgaard & Lois Weissberg
quilter@peacenapplique.com
www.peacenapplique.com

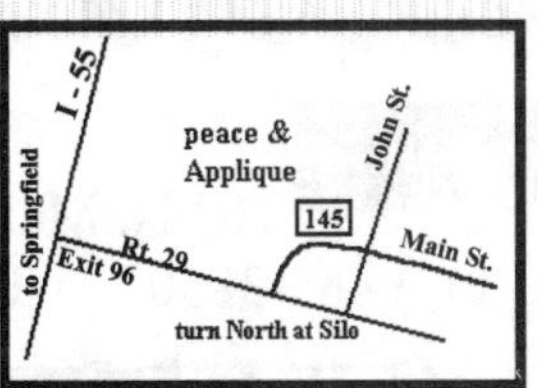

Visit our charming, newly expanded shop in an historic building with beautiful quilts hanging on the tall brick walls. Over 4000 bolts of high quality cottons including Moda, Kaufmann, Hoffman, Benartex, P&B and South Seas, with 30's, wonderful flannels, primitives and wool projects. We have books, patterns & notions, and classes for all interests & skill levels. Join us at the shop just 4 miles east of Springfield, one block north of the silo in Rochester.

Rochester, IL #25

"Every Day is a Great Day to peace & Applique"

Quilt Shop and Sewing Center

Fax: 217-223-5546

E-Mail: sew4fun@transedge.com

www.sew4fun.net

Mon, Wed, Fri 9-6
Tues, Thurs 9-8
Sat 9-4

Sewing Machines, Sergers and Embroidery Machine, Sales & Service
Authorized Husqvarna Viking & White Dealer

- 100% Cotton Fabric 2500 bolts ***Largest selection of Hoffman Batiks in the area***, Moda, Benartex, P&B Northcott and more.
- Quilting Patterns, Books & notions.
- Block of the Month- Saturday Sampler.
- Thimbleberrier Club.
- Roxanne Thimbles, Licensed Fitter.

- Sewing & quilting classes, Hand & machine.
- Embroidery by machine classes
- Machine repair services
- Free Internet Newsletter. Go to ....

www.sew4fun.net

#26

Broadway
Mall
to Macomb
Hwy 24
Sew-4-Fun
32nd
36th
I - 72
Maine St.
State St.
to Hannibal

Husqvarna VIKING

Astoria, IL #27

Tues - Fri 10 - 4:30
Sat 9 - 12

Country In The Attic Quilt & Gift Shop

111 W. Broadway, P.O. Box 23 61501
(309) 329-1376
cita2@winco.net Est: 2001

Large selection of 100% cotton fabrics, patterns, books & notions. Handcrafted & import gift items, candles, gourmet coffees, teas & cocoa.

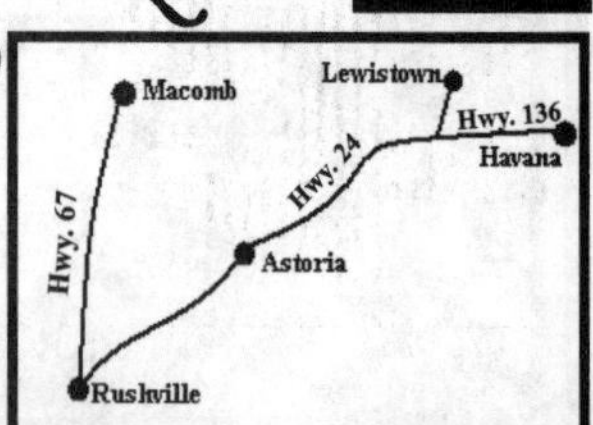

Havana, IL #28

Wed - Sat 8 - 6

Ma's Got'a Notion

106 N. Schrader St. 62644
(309) 543-6613
masgotanotion@grics.net
Owner: Sue Schaeffer
Est: 2003 1400 sq.ft.

We carry 100% cotton fabrics, patterns, books, sewing notions, crafts, primitive furniture, ready-made quilts, classes. Long arm quilting done by appointment.

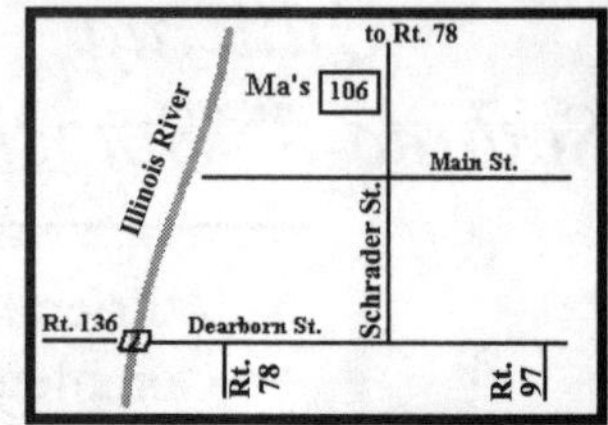

Macomb, IL #29

Mon - Fri 10 - 5
Sat 10 - 4

Piece to Peace Treasures Quilt Shop

120 N. Side Square 61455
(309) 836-5999
Fax: (309) 836-3888
Owner: Kathleen Percy
Est: 2004
3000 sq.ft.

Everything for the quilter! Cottons, Books, patterns, notions and gifts. Also available custom embroidery, screen printing and applique clothing.

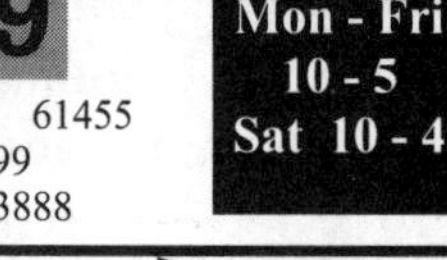
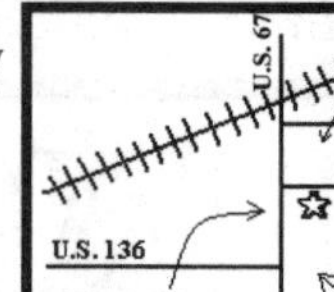

Avon, IL #30

The Clothesline Quilt Shop

Mon - Sat 10 - 5

102 N. Main, P.O. Box 122 61415
(309) 465-3850 Qultshop@avonil.net

Large selection of patterns, books, notions and 100% cotton quilt fabrics including Thimbleberries and Moda.

We also custom machine quilt with a good selection for battings.

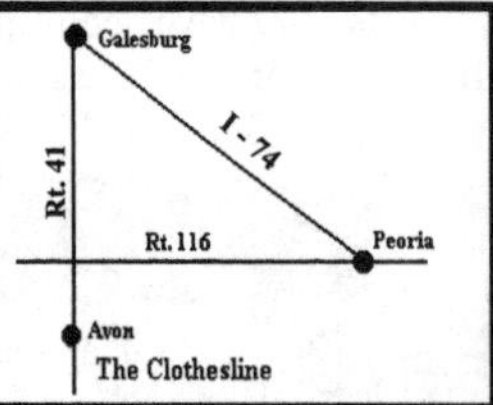

Pekin, IL #31

Mon & Fri 9:30 - 7
Tues - Thur 9:30 - 5
Sat 10 - 4

Cotton Stitches

2210 1/2 Court St. 61554
(309) 347-7399
stitches@mtco.com
www.cozycornersewing.com

Your Complete Quilt Shop!
Over 2000 bolts of fabric.

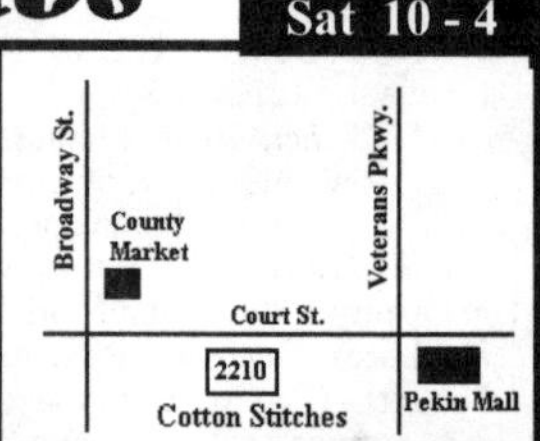

Knoxville, IL #32

Tues, Thur & Sat 10 - 5

Cabin on the Prairie Stitches & More

1581 Barefoot Rd. 61448
(309) 289-5229
Owner: Kaye Cochran
Est: 2004 800+ sq.ft.

Shop located in Log Cabin, rural setting. Quality fabric, patterns, stitchery kits, felting and more to fit your stitching needs.

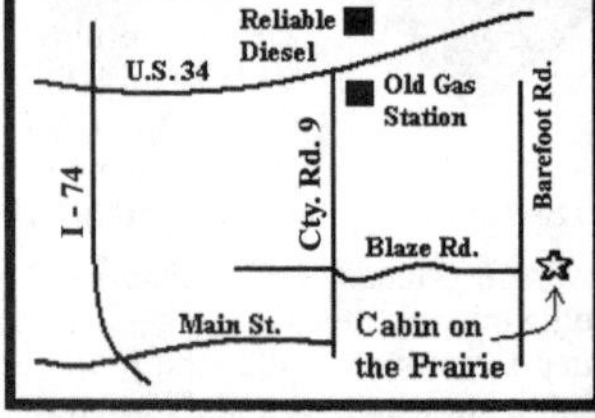

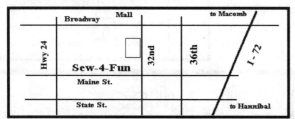

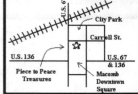

Metamora, IL #35

Mon & Fri 9:30 - 6
Tues - Thur 9:30 - 5
Sat 10 - 4

Cozy Corner Quilts & Sewing Center

101 W. Partridge St.
P.O. Box 409 61548
(309) 367-9303
Fax: (309) 367-9632
www.cozycornersewing.com

Your Complete Quilt Shop!
Over 2000 bolts of fabric.

Cozy Corner
101
Partridge
Menard
Parking
Rt. 116
to Roanoke
to Peoria

El Paso, IL #36

Tues 10 - 7
Wed - Sat 10 - 5

Karla's Country Quilt Shop

37 W. Front St. 61738
(309) 527-8458
Owner: Karla R. Uphoff

100% cotton fabric, books, notions & gifts. Small town friendly with big town selection. Comfortable seating for non-quilters. Play area for children. Just 20 miles north of Bloomington/Normal and I-74 and I-55.

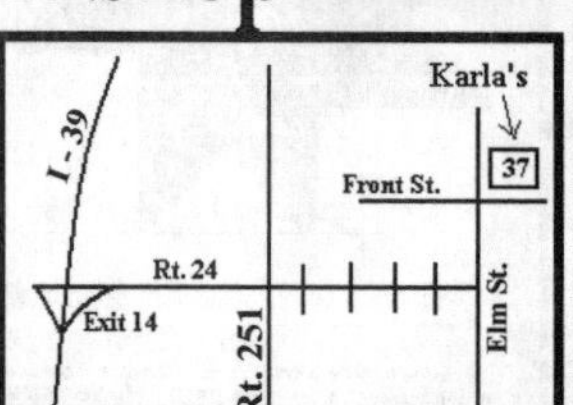

Normal, IL #37

Mon - Fri 9:30 - 6
Sat 9:30 - 5
Sun 12 - 4

Sewing Studio

1503 E. College, Suite C 61761
(309) 452-7313
Owners: Margaret Couch
Est: 1983 2600 sq.ft.

Quality quilting and fashion fabrics. Quilting & sewing classes, books. Quilting & heirloom supplies & notions. Bernina / Viking / White Dealer

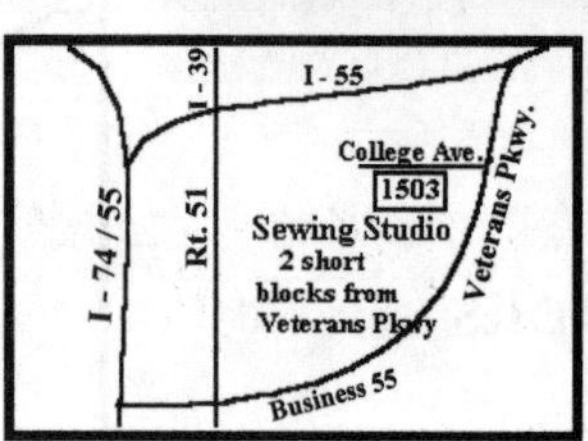

Bloomington, IL #38

Mon - Fri 10 - 5
Sat 10 - 4
Sun 12 - 4

The Treadle

2101 Eastland 61704
(309) 662-1733

Over 10000 Bolts of Calicos, Batiks, Homespuns and Flannels. Largest selection of Quilt Books and Patterns in Central Illinois.

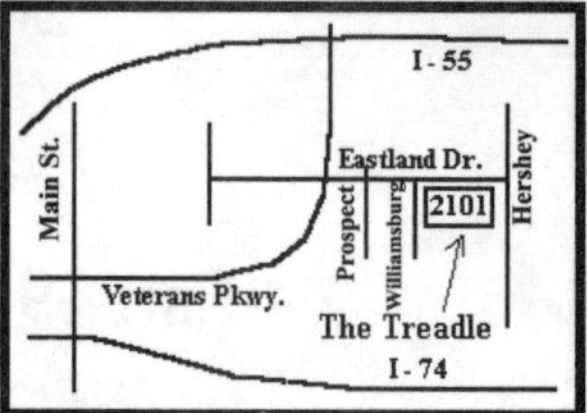

Prairieland Quilts

New, larger store with over 3,000 bolts of fabric, large selection of books, patterns, and supplies. Janome sewing machine sales and service; machine and hand quilting service available; home of QuiltersWarehouse.com serving the world with an online catalog of over 3,500 quilt books and patterns.

Mon - Fri 9 - 4
Sat 9 - 3

JANOME

101 N. 2nd. St. (Rt.49) 60924
(815) 457-2867
www.prairielandquilts.com
Owner: Suzanne Bruns Est: 1993

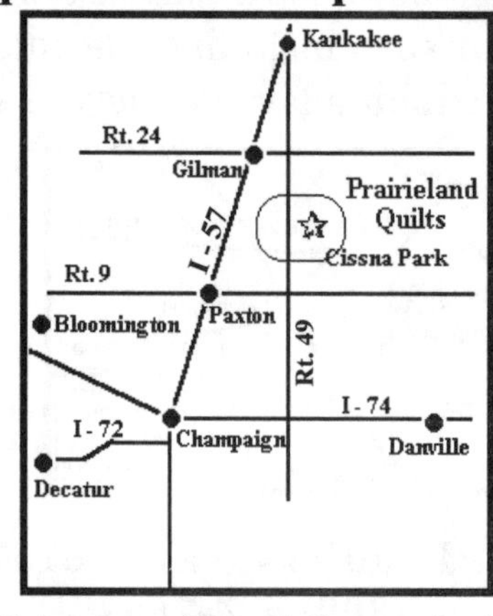

Bring your 'Travel Companion' with you and receive a one time 10% discount on your purchase.

Cissna Park, IL #39

Bourbonnais, IL #40

Mon - Fri 9 - 6
Sat 9 - 4

B & J Sewing Center

616 S. Main St. 60914
(815) 937-9955 Fax: (815) 937-9566
bjsew@TheRamp.net Est: 1994
www.bjsewing.com 3000 sq.ft.
Owners: Barbara & John Marcukaitis

Fine 100% Cotton Fabric, Notions, Quilting Supplies, Books, Patterns, Classes. Machine Quilting of Quilts. Authorized Dealer Husqvarna Viking Sewing Machines.

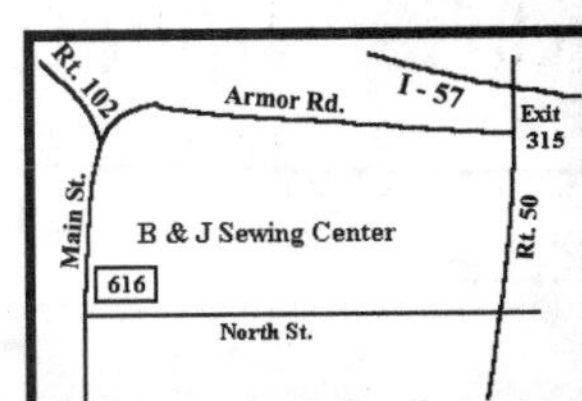

Manteno, IL #41

Mon - Fri 10 - 5
Thur til 8
Sat 10 - 3

Just Between Friends

Quilt Shoppe, Inc.

19 W. Division St. 60950
(815) 468-6050 Fax: (815) 468-6051
Owners: Jan Behm & Linda Michalek
Est: 1999 1200 sq.ft. 1000+ Bolts

Latest books, patterns, notions, fabric including large selection of Thimbleberries. Pfaff sewing machines. Friendly, personal service. 45 miles south of Chicago.

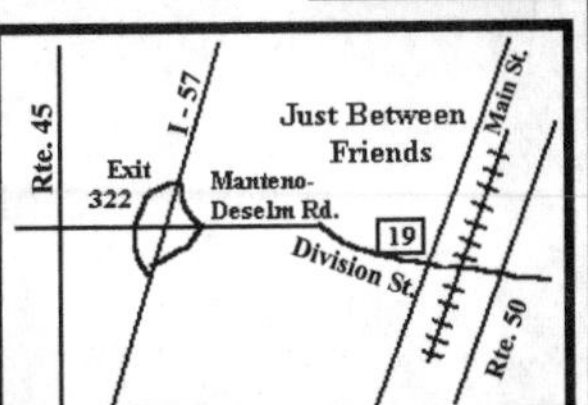

THE FABRIC CENTER

"A SEWING MACHINE SUPERSTORE"

A Quilters Dream

301 Liberty St. 60450 (815) 942-5715
fabctr@uti.com
Owner: Lonnie Booker
in nostalgic downtown

Morris, IL #42

- *Over 4,000 bolts of cotton fabric (discounted 20% off everyday)*
- *Largest selection of Hoffman fabrics in IL*
- *Also featuring Debbie Mumm, Moda, RJR, Concord, Timeless Treasures, Michael Miller, Kona, Benartex, Hi-Fashion, Springs, Kaufman, P&B & more.*
- *Quilting notions, stencils, patterns and books and quilting frames.*
- *Brother & Janome New Home Dealer.*

Quilting Classes Avail. Year Round

Mon - Wed 9 - 5:30
Thur 9 - 7
Fri 9 - 5:30
Sat 9 - 5

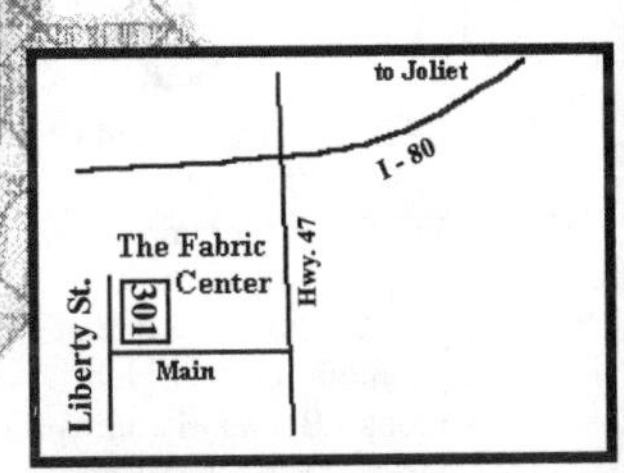

Quilt & Sew Dreams

(309) 243-9067
"Lake of the Woods Plaza"
12200 N. Brentfield Dr. 61525
quilt@npoint.net Est: 1998

Mon 10 - 8 Tues - Fri 10 - 5 Sat 10 - 4

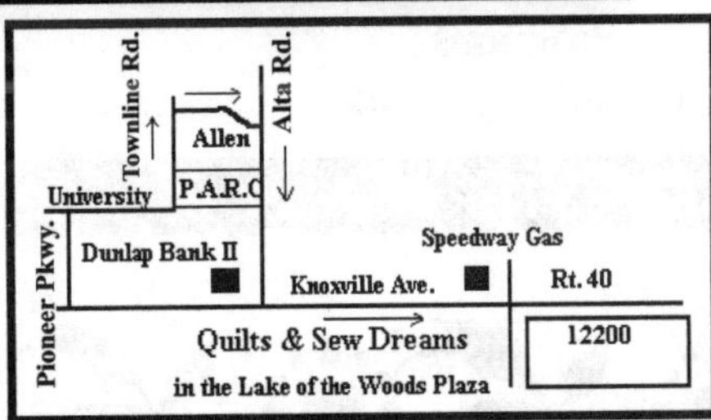

Just North of Peoria on Rte. 40./Knoxville Ave.

Dunlap, IL #43

Full Service Quilt Shop Husqvarna/Viking & White Dealership. Cozy Atmosphere with Friendly, Knowledgeable staff. Quality Cottons, Supplies, Service, Education & Inspiration.
Lots of display samples to delight & inspire.
Largest thread selection in the area.
Eclectic mix of fabrics with fat quarters galore!
Professional Machine Quilting Service

Husqvarna VIKING

Blessed are the Piecemakers

Alpha, IL #44

Thurs & Fri 11 - 4
Or by Appt.

Country Designs

210 S. 2nd St., P.O. Box 96 61413
(309) 629-9201 or (309) 334-2725
Fax: (309) 629-3201
Owners: Edna Mahalovich & Vicki Blender
Est: 2004 1000 sq.ft.

Long-arm machine quilting - weaving & other fine creations. We will quilt your quilt or will do custom work. √ Us Out!!

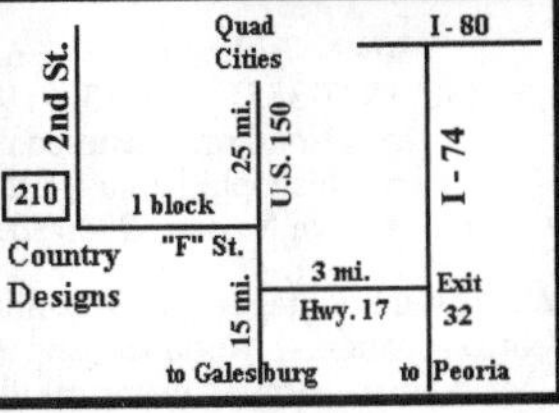

Princeton, IL #45

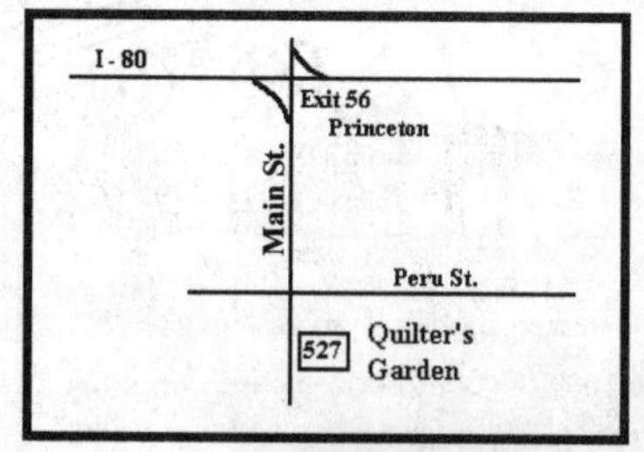

527 S. Main St. 61356
(815) 879-3739 (87 - WE - SEW)
quiltersgarden@yahoo.com Fax: (815) 879-3739
Owners: Beth Rosene & Carol Keller
Est: 2000 1700 sq.ft.

Quilter's Garden

Stroll our garden of quality fabrics, patterns, books and notions. Over 2000 bolts of 100% cotton fabrics including Batiks Cotton flannels, Moda Marbles and Thimbleberries.
Classes at all skill levels.
Machine quilting
Block of the Month Programs
Free parking in back

Bed and Breakfast sewing retreat center "Stairway to Stitchin" is available.
Home of zany quilt guild program, "A Visit from Aunt Sewsie."
Call or e-mail for details.

Geneseo, IL #46

Mon - Fri
10 - 5
Sat 10 - 4

Quilt Quarters

137 S. State St., Room 101 61254
(309) 944-2693 Est: 1992
quiltqtr@hotmail.com
Owners: Mike & Janette Dwyer

Satisfying Quilters and their needs. Come in and browse our fabric, patterns, books and inspiration. We are right above The Cellar in the Geneseo House "First floor, right door"

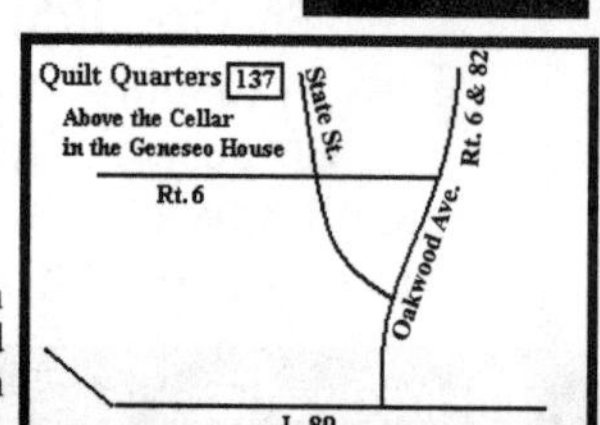

Kewanee, IL #47

Tues - Fri
10:30 - 5
Sat 9 - 5
Sun 12 - 4

The Quilt Box

109 E. Third St. 61443
(309) 854-9000 Est: 2003
QuiltBox@theramp.net

We cater to Quilters! Full line of 100% cotton fabrics, wool felt.
Notions - Books - Patterns
Floss - Gifts - Classes

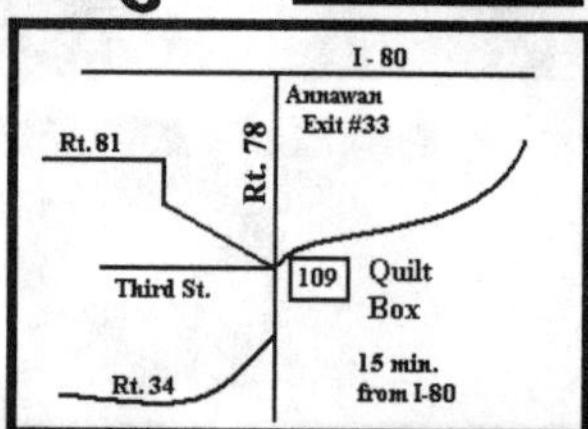

Bishop Hill, IL #48

7 Day a Week
10 - 5
April - Dec.

Village Smithy

309 N. Bishop Hill St. 61419
(309) 927-3851 Fax: (309) 937-5438
nelsonfarm@geneseo.net
www.bishophill.com Est: 1984
Owner: Marilyn Nelson 2900 sq.ft. 800 Bolts

We feature vintage quilts, quilting supplies, fabrics, patterns, Antiques and Collectibles. Located in a charming historical village.

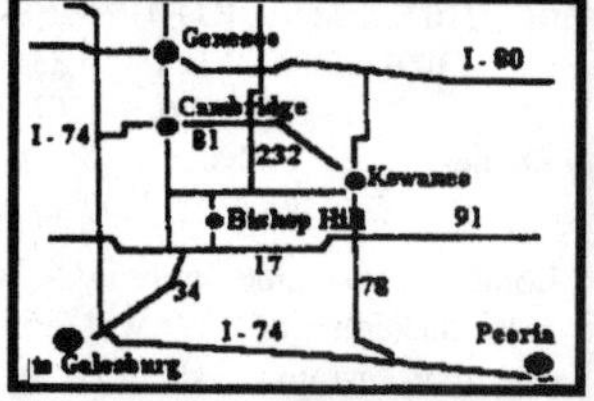

Aledo, IL #49

Mon - Fri
9 - 5
Sat 9 - 3

Farmer's Daughter Quilt Shop

100 S. College Ave. 61231
(309) 582-5858
farmersdaughterquilts
@hotmail.com
Owner: Dawn Lloyd
Est: 2002 900 sq.ft. 600 Bolts

Large selection of fine 100% cotton fabrics, books & patterns. Machine quilting and classes available.

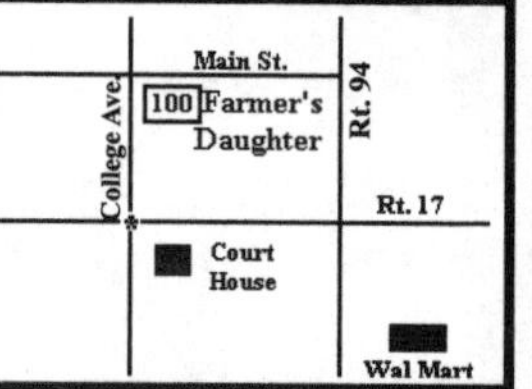

Fulton, IL #50

Featured in the American Patchwork & Quilting Shop Sampler 1998.

Over 2000 Bolts of Fabric, Notions, Books, Patterns, Stencils, Machine Quilting, Classes.

Now featuring the Antique Loft with antiques, fine oak furniture and Sleepy Eye Pottery.

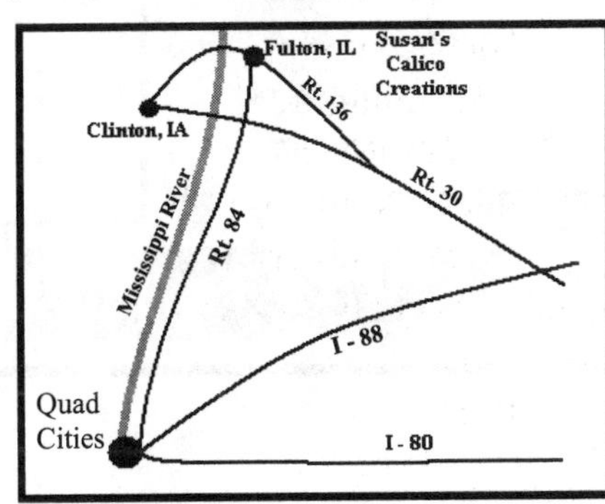

1108 4th St. Fulton, IL 61252
(815) 589-2221

Hours: Tues - Sat 10 - 5
Thurs 10 - 8 Sunday 12 - 4

www.atcalicocreations.com

Owner: Susan May
Est: 1986 8,000 sq.ft.

Moline, IL #51

The Quilt Basket

M, T, Th, F 9:30 - 5
Wed 9:30 - 9
Sat 9:30 - 4

2521 53rd St. 61265
(309) 764-1346
Owner: Ann Filiatreau
Est: 2002

Machine quilting, 100% Cotton Fabric, large selection of Flannels, Notions, Books, Patterns, Quilt Classes. Hand made wood items by local craftsmen.

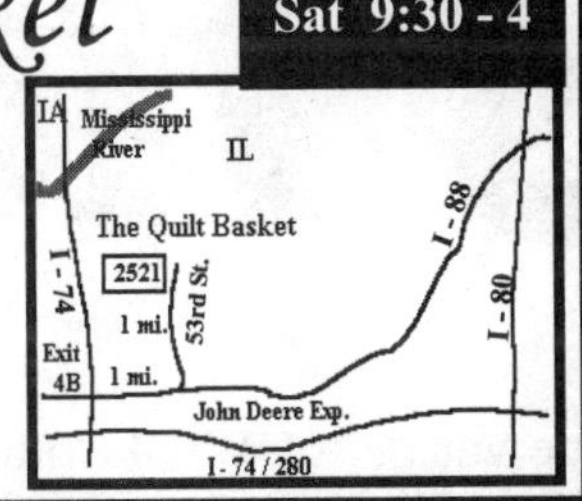

Pearl City, IL #53

Sew many Antiques

Mon - Fri 11 - 7
Sat 10 - 5
Sun 11 - 5

140 - 160 S. Main St., P.O. Box 55
(815) 443-2211 61062
sewmanya@aeroinc.net
www.sewmanyantiques.com
Owners: Jill & Dave Kempel and Vicki & Dave Olsen
Est: 1992 4300 sq.ft. 2000+ Bolts
Filled with over 2000 bolts of fabric, patterns, books, gifts, and antiques. We offer classes, retreats & always a friendly welcome.

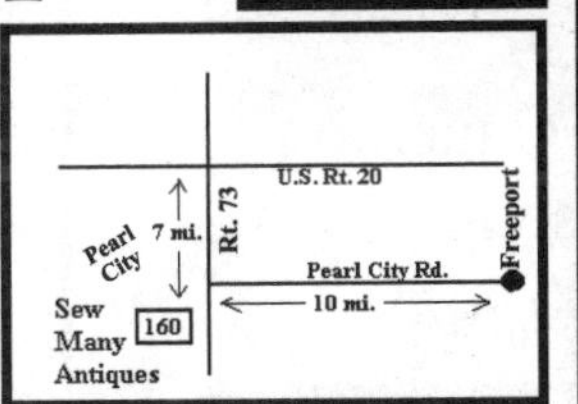

Moline, IL #52

Mon - Fri 10 - 5
Sat 10 - 2
Call Ahead for Special Appt.

4000+ bolts 100% cotton. Large assortment of Thimbleberries, Hoffman, Kaufman & Moda. Books, Patterns, Notions.

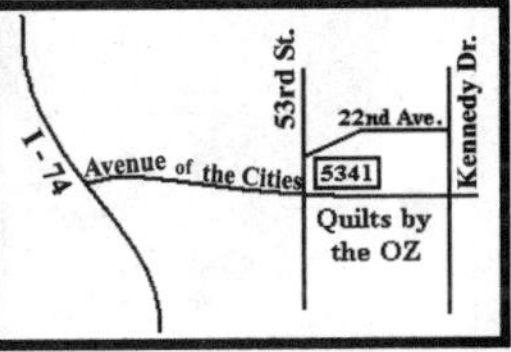

5341 Avenue of the Cities
(Enter from 22nd Ave.) 61265
(309) 762-9673 or
(800) 735-9673
quiltoz@mchsi.com
Owner: Harlene Rivelli
Est: 1987 2400 sq.ft.

From I-74: Go East to 53rd St. North (L) 1 block to 22nd Ave. East (R) to 2nd driveway, right again.

Phat ¼'s offers over 1000 bolts of fabric, thread, books, patterns, notions and of course Pretty Hot And Tempting Quarters.

Mon - Wed 10 - 5 Thurs 10 - 8
Fri & Sat 10 - 6 Sun 11 - 3

303 S. Commerce
Galena, IL 61036
815-776-0034
Est: 2004 850 sq.ft.
pqquilting@aol.com
www.phatquartersquilting.com

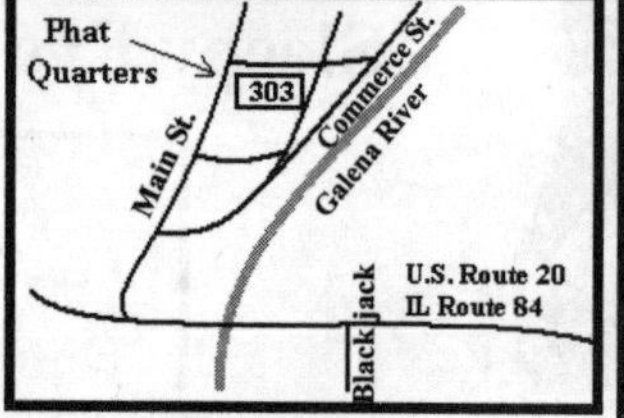

Galena, IL #54

Orangeville, IL #55

Uniquely Yours Quilt Shop

Highway 26 N 61060
(815) 789-4344
Cell Phone (608) 558-5158
gene.haffele@monroe.k12.wi.us
Owner: Sandy & Gene Haffele
Est: 1990 6000+ Bolts

Mon - Sat 9 - 5
Thur 9 - 8

New shop located in the lower level of our new home.
Over 2100 square feet of high quality 100% cotton fabric.
Large selection of books, patterns & quilt supplies.
Country location, country charm, friendly, helpful staff.

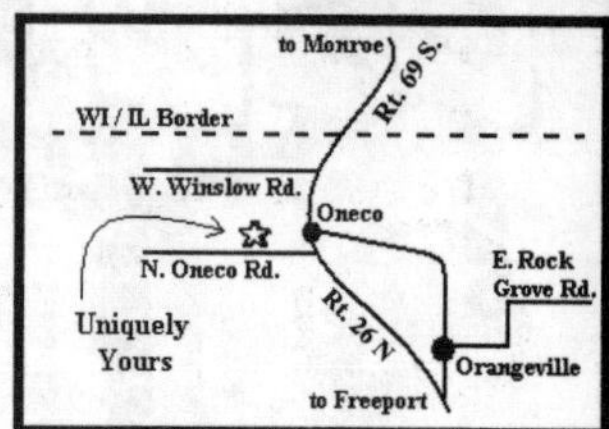

Largest selection of Fabric in Stateline Area.

Rockford, IL #56

Quilter's Haven

Quilter's Haven carries a wide variety of 100% cotton fabrics (numbering 3000+), books, and patterns. In addition we carry supplies for rug hookers. We offer a unique combination of classes and have several samples to inspire you! Friendly, individual attention is what we are known for.

4616 E. State St. 61108
(815) 227-1659
Owners: Stephanie Gauerke
& Cathy Johnson
Est: 1995 1200 sq.ft.

Mon - Sat 10 - 4 Wed til 7

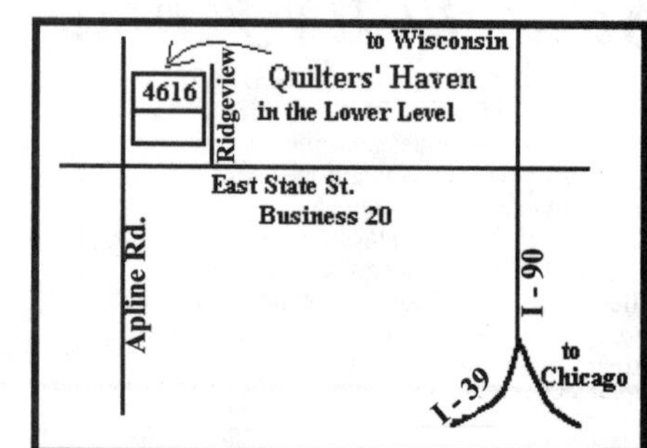

Rockford, IL #57

6903 Harrison Ave. 61108
Toll Free: 877-548-4555 815-397-5160
Fax: 815-399-5025
E-Mail: farmquilts@aol.com
Web Site: www.quiltersgeneralstore.com
Owner: Jan Ragaller

Mon - Sat 10 - 5
Sun 12 - 4

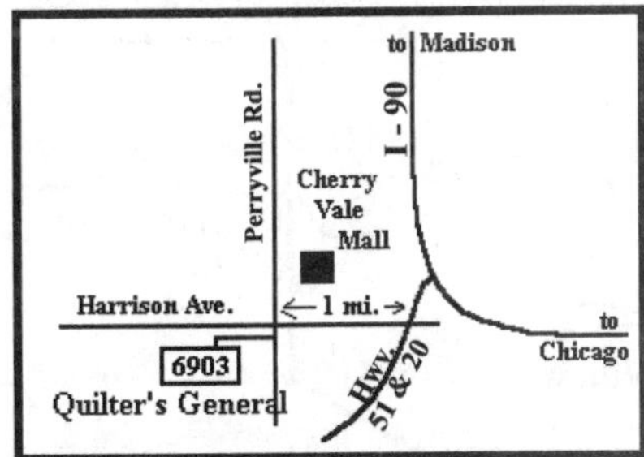

QUILTER'S GENERAL STORE INC.

"Featured in American Patchwork and Quilting "Sampler 2001"

This "country in the city" shop boasts 2000+ bolts of cotton fabric, books, patterns, notions and a friendly, helpful staff of quilters. Located in a beautiful 1875 farm house. Classes for all levels. Newsletter and special orders upon request.

Mon - Fri 10 - 5
Sat 10 - 3

1200+ Bolts of beautiful fabrics...A Warm, cozy shop where you come in a customer and leave a friend. Come see our quilts on the ceilings and walls and our 20 gallon tub of buttons.

Cottage Quilts

438 W. Main St. 60135
(815) 784-2190
Cottage-Quilts-Genoa
@hotmail.com
Head Baa Baa: Kathy Pulley
Est: 2003 650 sq.ft.

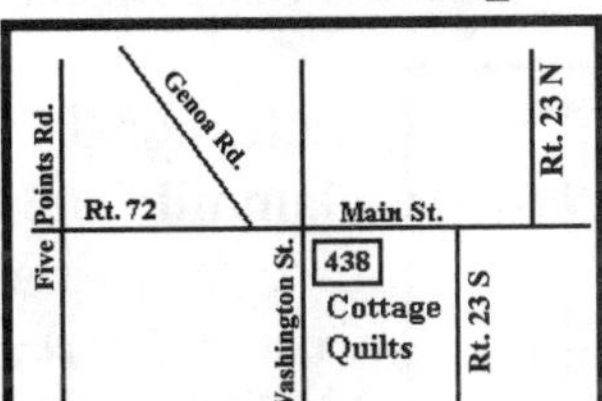

Genoa, IL #58

Belvidere, IL #59

Tues - Sat 10 - 5

All My Stitches

407 South State St. 61008
(815) 547-1099
AllMyStitches1@aol.com
Owner: Cindy Davison
Est: 2001 1200 sq.ft.

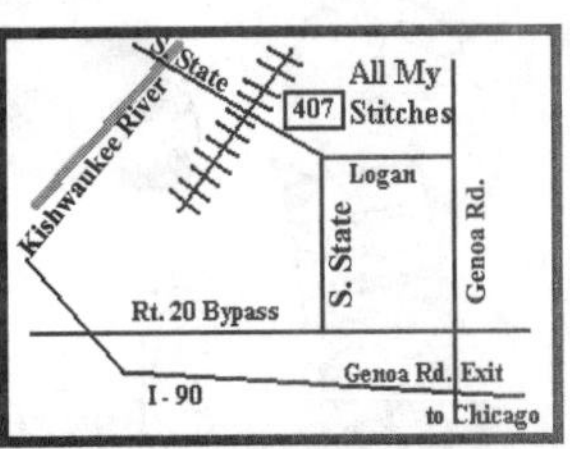

Collections of 100% cotton solids and prints from all the best manufacturers. Books, patterns, notions & classes. Husqvarna Viking dealer.

Oswego, IL #60

Mon - Sat 10 - 5
Tues & Thur til 8

Prairie Stitches Quilt Shoppe

4775 Rt. 71 60545
(630) 554-9701 Fax: (630) 554-9758
PrairieStitches@comcast.net
Owners: Cindy Sansale & Kim Nimtz
Est: 2002 1200 sq.ft.

A shop with a friendly, relaxed atmosphere carrying your favorite fabrics, including reproduction lines. Also wool & rug hooking supplies

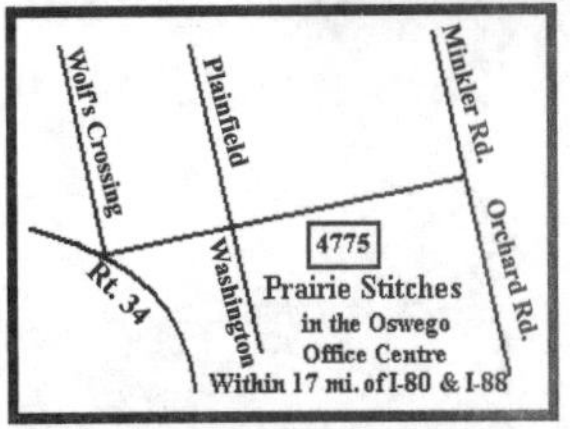

Northeastern Illinois Area

Shops #61 - 82

22 Featured Shops

Sunshine and Shadow

Quilt Shoppe

1241 N. Green St. 60050
815-759-6900
Owner: Terri LaDuke
Est: 1991 2000 + Bolts

McHenry, IL #61

Over 2000 bolts of quality fabrics. Large selection of books and patterns. Classes. Authorized PFAFF dealer. Machine Repairs.

Mon - Sat 10 - 4
Sun 12 - 4

Libertyville, IL #62

Sewing Source

1429 Peterson Rd. (Rt. 137)
(847) 223-9009
Fax: (847) 223-8818 debbiesews@aol.com
www.sewsource.com
Owner: Debbie Tomec
Est: 1995 1800 sq. ft. 1500 Bolts

HOURS:
Mon - Fri 10 - 6
Sat 10 - 4
Or by Appt.

We sell Quilting and Embroidery Machines.
Horn cabinets
A full line of Quilting Fabrics
Over 200 Books and Patterns
Classes Available

Repairs on all makes of Sewing Machines & Scissor Sharpening by Joe.

Professional Quilting on a **Gammil Long-Arm by L.A. Machine Quilting**: Custom Work, Discounts, Mail Order Available.
(Reasonable Prices)

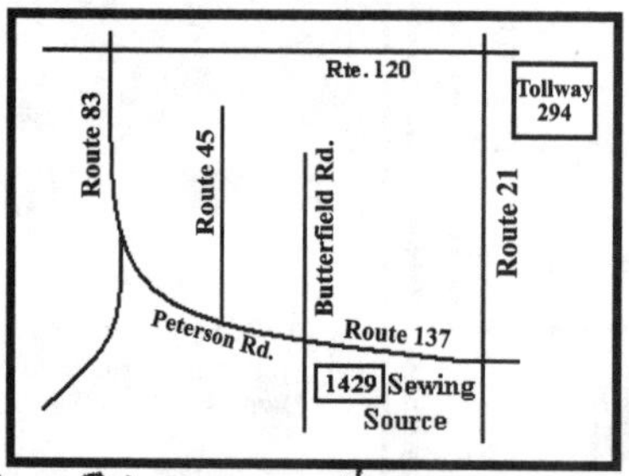

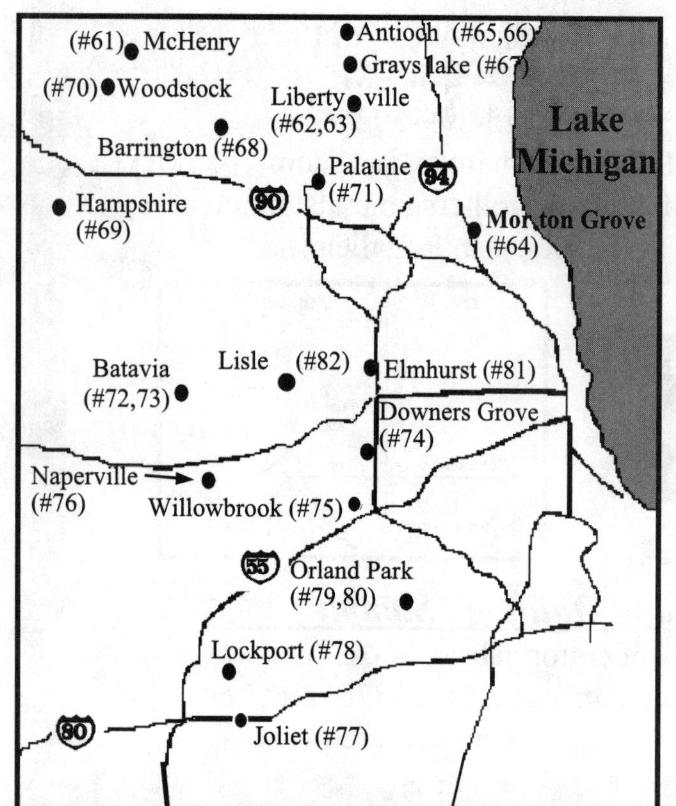

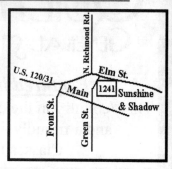

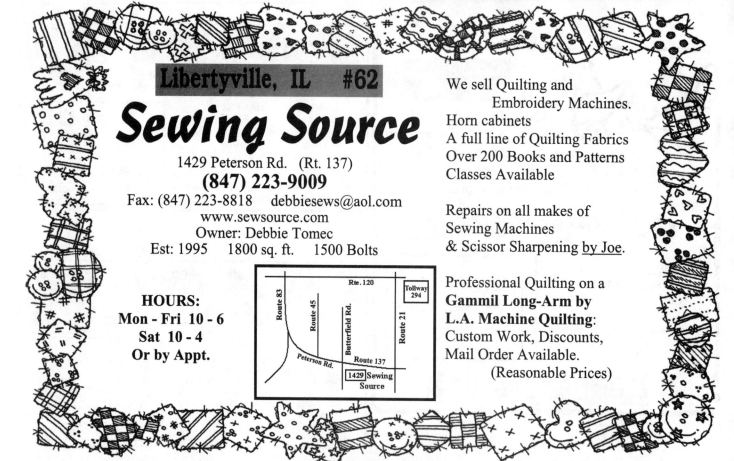

Libertyville, IL #63

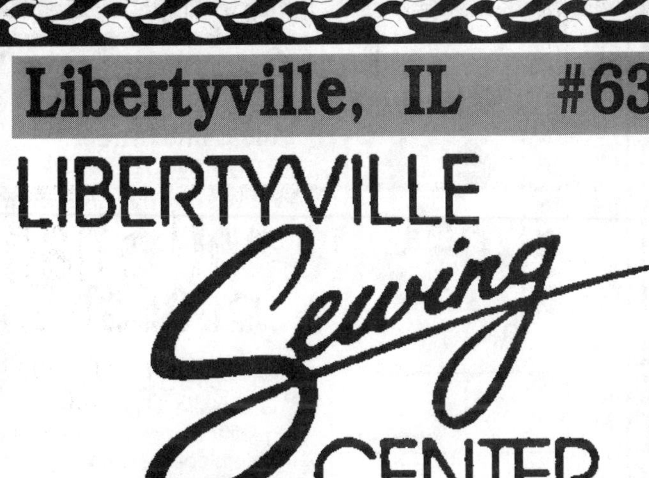

Mon - Thur
9 - 9
Fri & Sat
9 - 5

Large Selection of :
- Calicos featuring Hoffman.
- Quilting Supplies.
- Buttons
- Threads
- Sales & Service -All Makes & Models

baby lock

Nothing Sews Like A Bernina. Nothing.
BERNINA

brother

The Quilter's Dream Sewing Center 2080

326 Peterson Rd. 60048
(Brookside Shp. Ctr.)
(847) 367-0820
Est: 1982 5400 sq.ft.
Owners: Linda & Rick Mosier
E-Mail: Libertysew@aol.com
www.libertyvillesewing.com

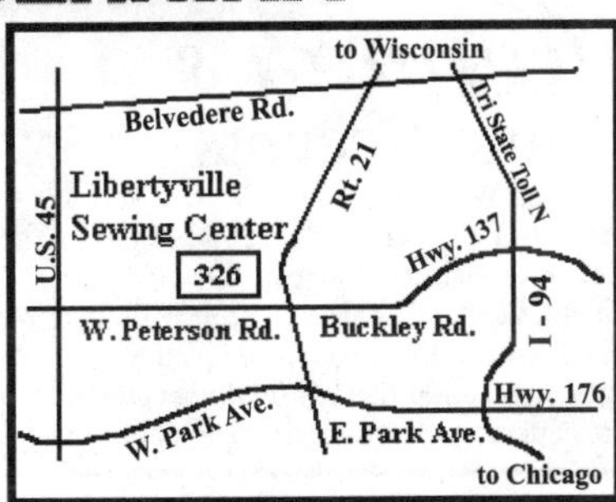

Exit Hwy. 137 from North or South
Exit Hwy. 21 from North only
Exit Hwy. 176 from South only

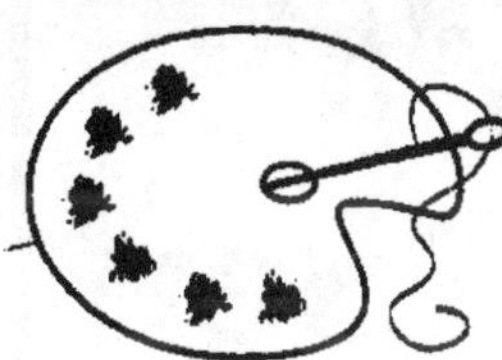

QUILTER'S PALETTE

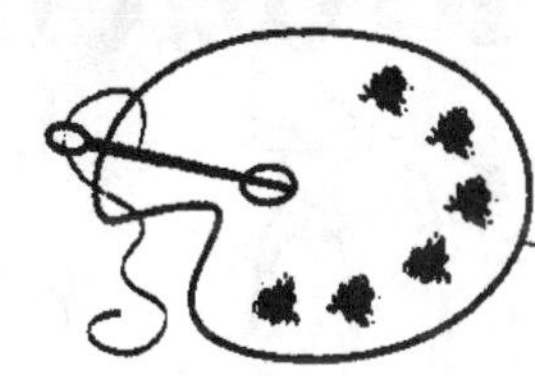

6737 W. Dempster
Morton Grove, IL 60053
Phone: 847 . 663 . 8957
E-mail: qpalette@ameritech.net
4000 sq.ft. 4800+ bolts
Owner: Sharron Evans

Dempster
Prairie View Shopping Plaza
Golf
Waukegan Rd.
6737
Quilter's Palette

*** Over 4,000 square feet of fabrics, * quilting and doll supplies.**

*** Many brands including Moda, Hoffman* Batiks and 30's reproduction fabrics**

*** Quilting Books & Supplies ***

*** The Newest notions, latest techniques, * exhilarating classes and much, much more!**

Sun 12 - 4 Mon & Thurs 10 - 8 pm Tues, Wed, Fri & Sat 10 - 5

Morton Grove, IL #64

Inspirations Everywhere!

Antioch, IL #65

Mon - Sat 10 - 5

Quilter's Dream, Inc.

384 Lake St. 60002
(847) 395-1459
Owners: Wendy Maston & Robin Kessell
Est: 1994 4000 sq.ft.

We carry the finest in quilting supplies and fabrics. We also offer long-arm quilting and custom quilts. We are an authorized ELNA & Brother Dealer.

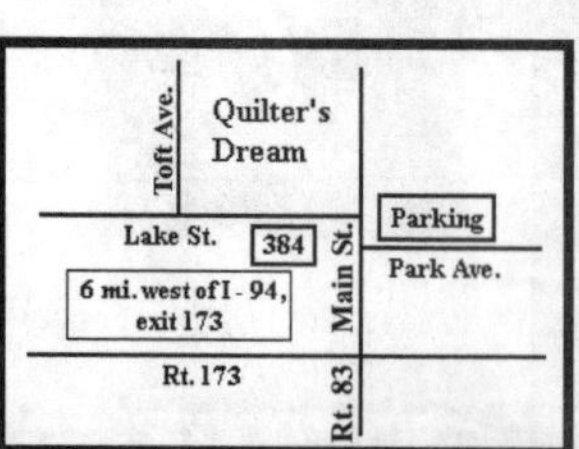

Antioch, IL #66

Mon - Fri 9 - 8
Sat 9 - 6
Sun 10 - 5

Hannah's Home Accents®

455 W. Lake St. 60002
(888) 784-6638 Fax: (847) 395-3391
info@hannahs.com Est: 1961
www.hannahs.com 5000 sq.ft. 2500+ Bolts
High quality fabrics from top companies.
Very large collection of flannels, quilting cottons, books, patterns and notions for the quilter.

Hwy. 50
to Milwaukee
Hannah's 455
Lake St.
Hwy. 83
Hwy. 45
I - 94
Toll Rd.
Rt. 173
Hwy. 59
to Chicago

Grayslake, IL #67

SHOO FLY FABRICS & SUCH QUILTS

146 Center Street
Grayslake, IL 60030
www.shooflyquilts.com
847-548-4967

Mon. - Fri. 11:00-5:00
Sat. 10:00-5:00

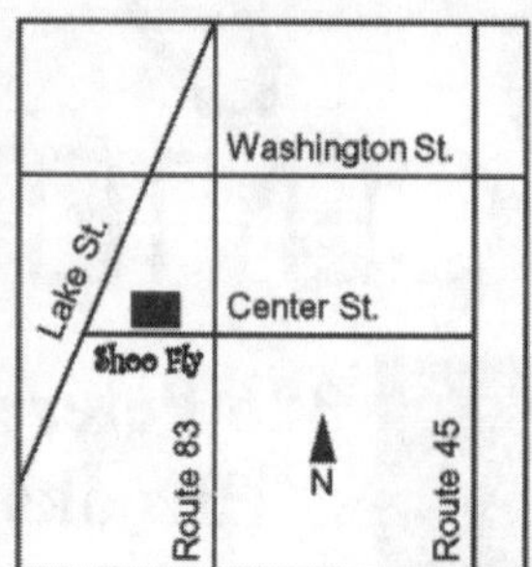

Located in historic downtown Grayslake, Illinois. High quality fabrics featuring Moda, Thimbleberries, and reproduction prints. Patterns, books, notions, and unique gift items are beatifully displayed among antiques and our two working fireplaces. Classes and quilting services available. Husbands and children welcome.

Barrington, IL #68

A Touch of Amish

130 Applebee St. 60010
(847) 381-0900
(888) 5-QUILTS (578-4587)
Owner: Lynn Rice
Est: 1986 2500 sq.ft.

Tues - Sat 10 - 4

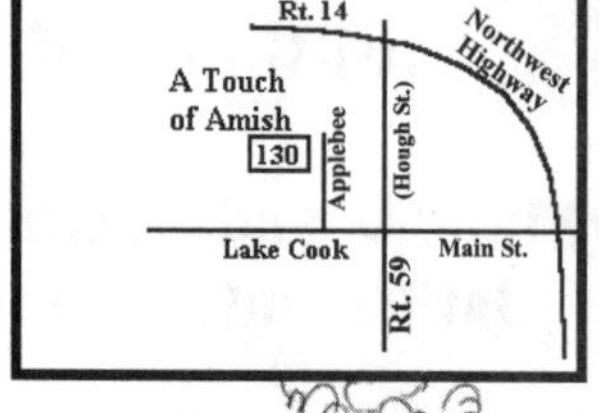

Wonderful fabrics, books, patterns, custom quilting, free weekly demonstrations, and always great service.

Visit us at:
www.atouchofamish.com

Hampshire, IL #69

Judy's Quilt 'n' Sew

Where Good Things Begin....

290 South State St
Hampshire, IL 60140
(847) 683-4739

2700 Bolts of Fabric

Kits, classes, books, patterns and notions. Pfaff Sales and Service

www.FriendshipStar.com

10-5 Mon-Fri, 10 to 3:30 Sat & 12 to 3 Sun

Woodstock, IL #70

Mon - Fri 10 - 4:30
Sat 10 - 4

Woodstock Quilts, Inc.

216 S. Seminary 60098
(815) 338-1212
Owner: Debbie Best Est: 2002

Fabric, Quilting Supplies.
2 Blocks East of the
Historical Woodstock Square

You Stitch Love Into Every Quilt,
Choose Your Fabric With Love

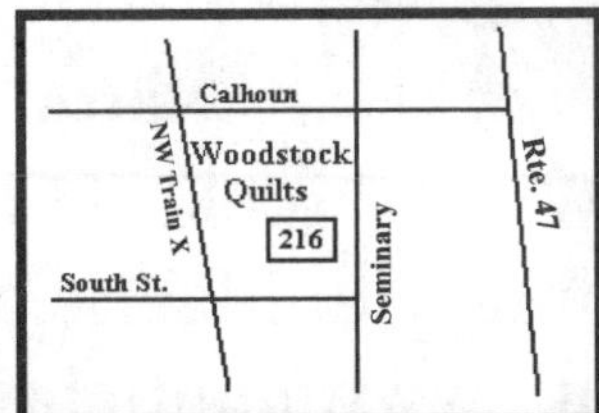

Palatine, IL #71

Prints Charming II, Ltd.

Mon - Sat
10 - 5
T & Th til 8
Sun 12 - 4

Thousands of beautiful fabrics, challenging classes, newest notions, patterns & books, and friendly, competent staff. Only 5 minutes from Woodfield Shopping Area.

1905 S. Plum Grove Rd.
Palatine, IL 60067
(847) 202-5602
Fax: (847) 202-5604
E-Mail: pc2quilts
@mindspring.com
Owner: Barbara Hutton
Est: 1999 3000 sq.ft.

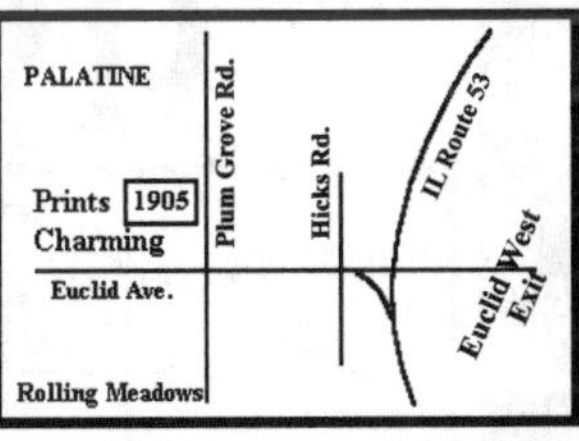

www.printscharmingii.com

Batavia, IL #72

QBU
Prairie Shop

1911 W. Wilson Street
Batavia, IL 60510
630-406-0237
www.qbuprairieshop.com
Owner: Karen Lukac

Purveyors of fine quality quilting cottons, Notions, books, beads and other goods for the Discriminating fiber artist and jewelry artisan.
Over 3200 bolts of fabric & hundreds of beads from around the world!

Quilting & beading classes offered for all levels (Thurs, evenings & weekends too)!
Send a SASE and we will be happy to send you A schedule of our classes or check our website!

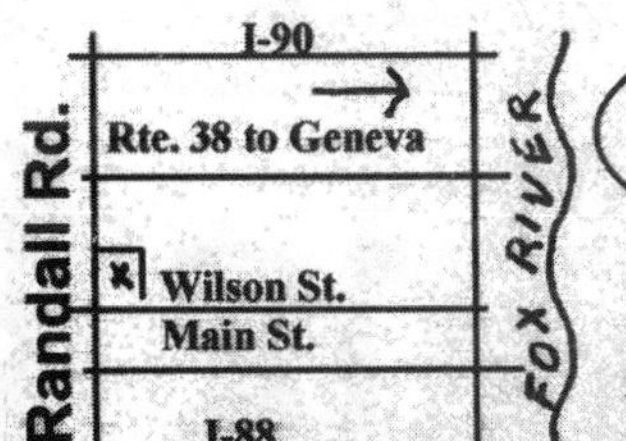

Mondays-Fridays 10 to 5
Thursdays 10 to 8
Sat. 10 to 4; Sun. 12 to 4

We are located at the NE corner of Randall & Wilson next to the Ace!

Batavia, IL #73

Windmill City Quilts

Owner:
Tammy Rice

Always something On sale!

- ♥ Uniquely packaged fabric collections
- ♥ Quilt Kits Galore
- ♥ Books and patterns
- ♥ Classes
- ♥ 2,400 Sq Ft
- ♥ 5,000+ Bolts
- ♥ Notions

Plenty of Parking. Comfy chair for Hubby

Mon, Wed, Fri, Sat 10 - 5
Tues & Thur 10 - 8 Sun 12 - 4

On the Fox River
Near Corner of Wilson & 25
Below Nonna's Restaurant

3 Webster Street
Batavia, IL 60510

(630) 482-2984
Fax: (630) 482-2985

needlinaround@wcquilts.com
www.wcquilts.com

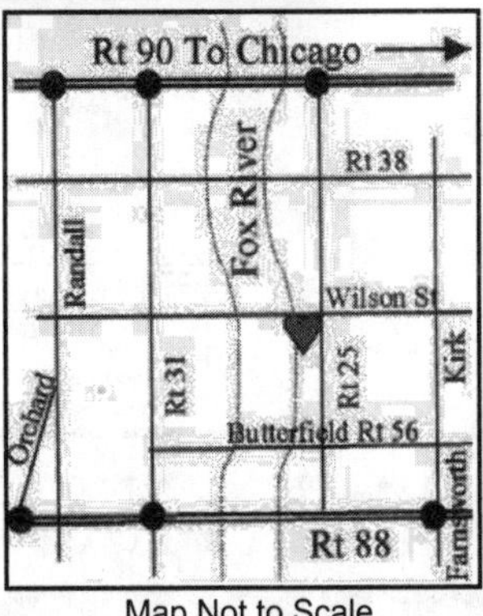

Map Not to Scale

Downers Grove, IL #74

Tues, Wed, Fri 10 - 5
Thur 10 - 9
Sat 10 - 3

The Quilt Basket

1012 Curtiss St. 60515
(630) 515-8820 Fax: (630) 724-1160
qltbasket@sbcglobal.net
www.thequiltbasket.com
Owner: Renee Wright
Est: 1998 1200 sq.ft. 1200+ Bolts

Fabrics, Classes, Books & Notions. Friendly Staff, Personal Service with years of quilting experience. Visit us for all your quilting needs.

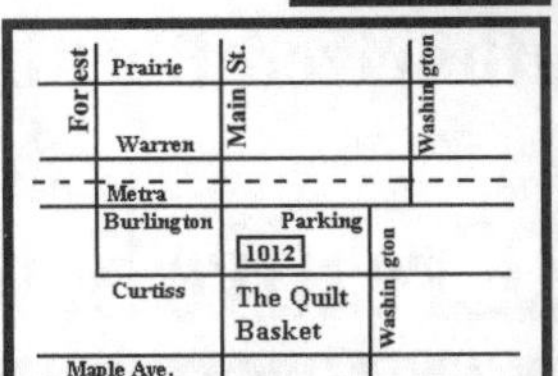

Willowbrook, IL #75

7237 Kingery Rd. (Rt. 83), Willowbrook, IL 60527
630.321.9051 E-Mail: info@quiltfabric.com
Visit us for online shopping at: www.quiltfabric.com

quiltfabric.com

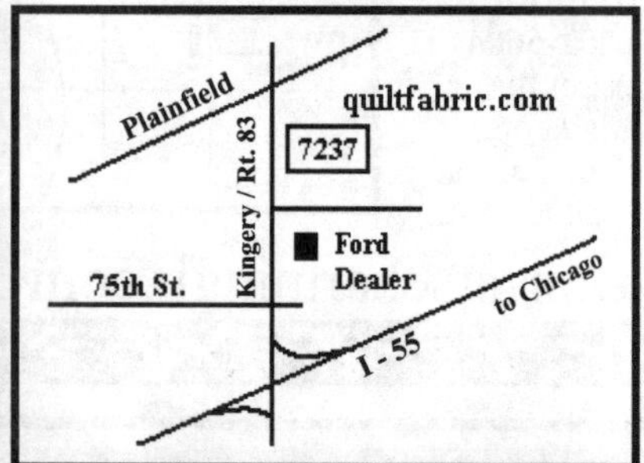

Tues & Wed
9:30 - 5:30
Thur 9:30 - 8
Fri & Sat
9:30 - 4:30
Sun 12:30 - 4

Come in for some inspiration!
Bright, friendly atmosphere.
Kits, models, top quality fabrics,
patterns, books and notions.
PFAFF authorized dealer.
Can't get here in person?
Shop online at our off-price store.

Naperville, IL #76

790 Royal St. George Dr. #119
(630) 420-7050 60563
snssew@aol.com
Owners: Beryl & Sarah Coulson
Est: 1981 7300 sq.ft.

Mon - Sat
10 - 5
Tues &
Thur til 9

Stitches N' Stuffing

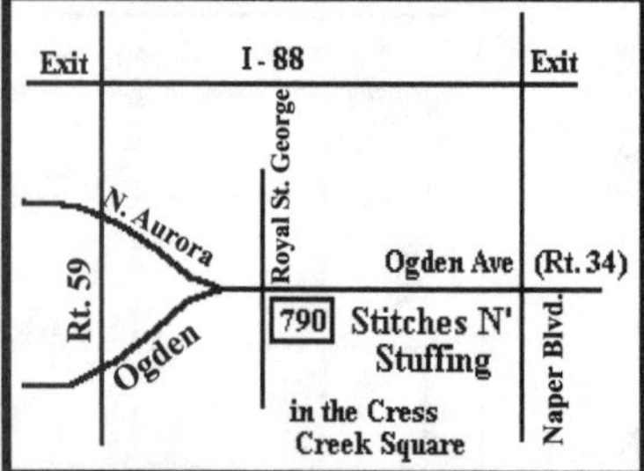

Facing Ogden Ave (Rt. 34) In the Cress Creek Square

www.stitchesnstuffing.com

4000+ Cotton Fabrics & Homespuns.
Patterns, Books, Notions & Cross - Stitch
Authorized Bernina sales/service

Stitches-N-Stuffing and Bernina...Creative Sewing at Its BEST!

Joliet, IL #77

Roberts Sewing Center

www.AQuiltersParadise.com

of cotton fabric
highest quality—lowest prices

We're expanding to 12,000 sq.ft.

2011 S. Weber Rd. 60435
(815) 729-1600
Owner: Ken Roberts Est: 1930
Bus Tours - Please Call Ahead - 800-273-9111

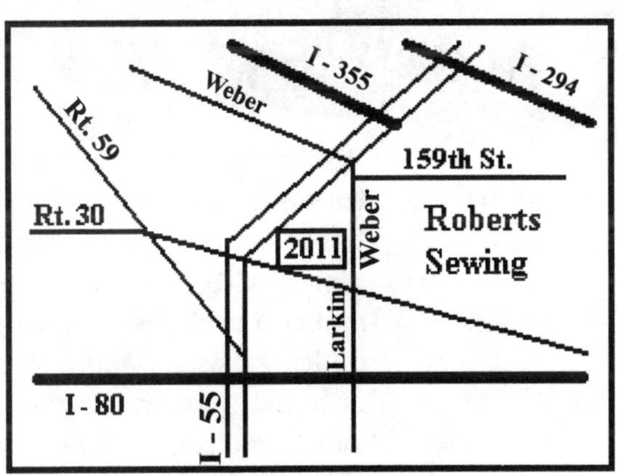

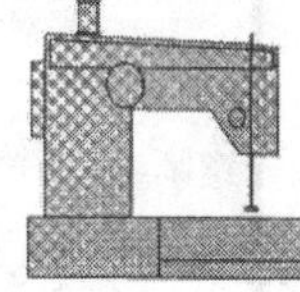

The Lowest Prices in Illinois
Pfaff - - Viking
Home & Industrial Machines

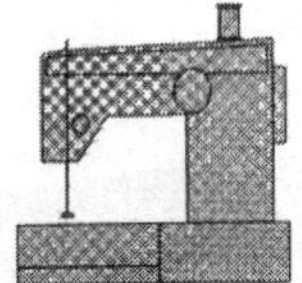

Mon - Sat 9:30 - 5:30 Tues & Thur 9:30 - 7:00

Lockport, IL #78

Thimbles

Mon - Fri 10 - 5
Thur til 7
Sat 10 - 4
Sun 12 - 4

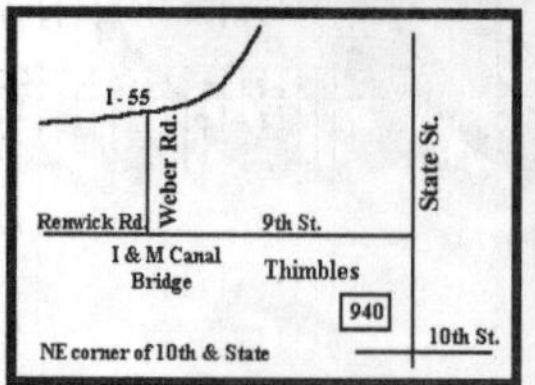

940 S. State St. 60441
(815) 836-8735 Fax: (815) 836-8174
thimblesquilts@sbcglobal.net

Located on Lockport's Historic State St.
1500 Bolts Fabric, Books, Patterns,
Notions & Classes.

Quilters' Cotton Co.

Orland Park, IL #79

Est: 1988
qcc3c@aol.com
Owners:
Laura Kincaid
& Clayton
Kincaid

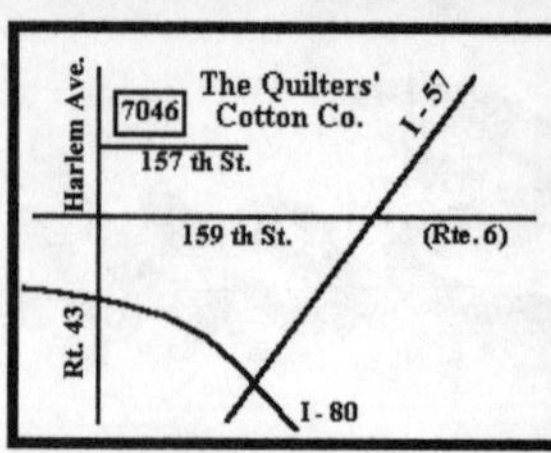

2500+ Bolts of 100% Cottons — Moda, Benartex, P&B, RJR, Hoffman, Kaufman, Marcus Brothers, Homespuns, Flannels. 250+ Books, 150+ Pattern Companies, Great selection of notions, classes. Authorized Pfaff sewing machine dealer.

www.quilters-cotton.com
7046 West 157th St. 60462
(708) 614-7744

Mon 12-8, Tues 10-5
Wed 10-8, Thur 10-5
Fri 10-5, Sat 10-4

Threadneedle Street
"The Road to Creativity"

We are located in Historic Old Orland in a yellow Victorian house. We carry a substantial selection of 100% cotton fabric, high-quality quilting supplies, clear and comprehensive sewing and quilting classes, and a large selection of books, patterns and kits. We provide knowledgeable service to our customers and are known for our helpful and friendly atmosphere. When you're in the area, this is a quilt shop stop not to be missed.

Store Hours

Mon, Wed, Fri & Sat
10am to 5pm

Tues & Thur
10am to 8pm

Sunday
Noon to 4pm

See you soon!
Nancy, Jeanne, Char & Jo

Creative Treasures
Annual Outdoor Quilt Show
Saturday of Labor Day Weekend

9925 W. 143rd Street
Orland Park, Illinois 60462
Phone: (708) 403-8490
E-mail: TNSTREET@aol.com

QUILTER'S TAKE THEIR FEET TO THREADNEEDLE STREET

Authorized
Elna
&
SIMPLICITY
Sewing
Machine
Dealer

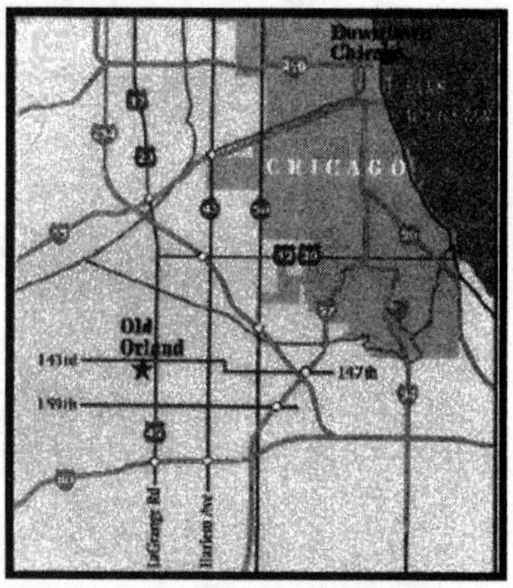

Orland Park, IL #80

Fabrics etc.2

446 N. York Road
Elmhurst, IL 60126
630-279-1482
www.fabricsetc2.com

You'll find wonderful samples to inspire you and many kits to entice you. Our diverse fabric selection and talented, friendly staff are here to help you create fabulous quilts. Over 175 classes & workshops per year. Sewing Machine Rental available for in classroom use by travelers.

Authorized Dealer:
Babylock, Elna, Janome, Horn
Full line of machines, sergers & accessories. On site sewing machine service & repairs.

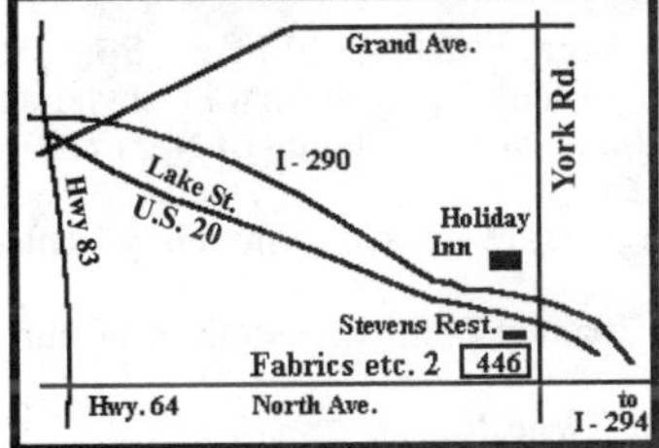

Mon - Sat 10 - 5
Thur 10 - 8

20 min. from downtown Chicago
Exit 290 at York Rd.
1 block south on York

✦Finest 100% Cotton Fabrics ✦ Numerous Flannels & Batiks
✦ Books ✦ Notions ✦ Patterns ✦ Kits ✦ Fat Quarters
✦ Clubs ✦ Classes ✦ Block of the Month

New Owner: **MARY FORTE**
Bus Tours by appointment please.

Elmhurst, IL #81

Follow Your Heart.

You can find us with a map but something Inside will also know the way. Our shop is filled with fabric that calls to you, inspires and rewards you for making the trip. So come and touch...see...discover us!

PIECEFUL HEART FABRICS

- Over 4,000 bolts of pure heaven
- Books, Patterns, Classes and lots of fresh ideas.
- Hours:
Mon & Thurs 10-8
Tues, Wed, Fri 10-5
Sat 10-4 Sun 12-4

2723 Maple Ave. Lisle, IL 60532
(630) 718-0112
(1/2 Block East of Naper Blvd.)

Lisle, IL #82

Other Shops in Illinois: *We suggest calling first*

Altamont Quilts & More, 95 Main St 618-483-5629
Alton All in Stitches, 108 W. 3rd St. 618-462-1738
Arthur Millers Dry Goods, 175 E 50 N
Arthur Quilts & Crafts R.R. 1 Box 185A 217-543-2702
Arthur The Calico Workshop, 228 S. Vine 217-543-2312
Barrington Finn's Fabrics, 113 North Cook 708-381-5020
Benton J & J Fabric, 9093 Aden St. 618-439-6033
Bushnell Country Stitches, 413 W Mani St 309-772-3885
Carpentersville Quiltmaster Inc., 1 S. Winconsin 708-426-6741
Carpentersville Grist Mill Ends, 39 E. Main St. 847-426-6455
Carthage Blue Moose, 64 S Madison St 217-357-3933
Champaign Londa's Sewing, 404 S. Duncan Rd. 217-352-2378
Crete Just Between Friends, 219 Milburn 708-672-5641
Crystal Lake Fabric Shop, 21 N. Williams 815-459-2084
Edwardsville Edwardsville Sewing Center, 110 N. Main St. 618-656-4272
Effingham Calico Shoppe, 1108 N. Merchant St. 217-342-6628
Fox River Grove Window Box Gardens, 38 Manchester Ct. 847-516-2496
Geneva The Quilted Fox, 416 W. State St. 630-232-4888
Homer Glen Golden Oak Quilting, 14101 S Golden Oak Dr 708-301-5005
Hutsonville Apple Blossom Quilt Shop, St. Rte. 1 618-563-4388
Jerseyville Cillas Attic, 701 W Exchange St 618-498-7820
Lemont That Thread Shop, P.O. Box 325 708-301-3172
Macomb Aunt Kitty's Quilts, 121 N. Scotland St. 309-833-3907
Mattoon Fabrics N' More Inc., 817 S. 19th St. 217-234-4700
Milford Dixie Cloth Shop, 130 E. Jones 815-889-5349
Moline Always In Stitches, 1413 16th Ave 309-757-0017
Mt. Zion Stewart's Sewing Machines, Inc., 415 N. St. Hwy. 121 217-864-6142
Naperville Needles, 2960 Artesian Rd #144 630-904-0500
Normal Something Sew Special, 1003 Gregory St 309-452-7330
Odin Mary's Vogue Shop, 105 Green US Hwy 50 618-775-8371
Olney Quilts & Clutter, 713 W. Main St. 618-395-0114
Oregon Stitches In Time, 201 N 3rd St #15 815-732-4599
Pecatonica Country Gate Quilting, 520 Mani St 815-239-9142
Pittsfield The Pin Cushion, 510 N. Jackson St. 217-285-6923
Princeton Old Times--Quilter Heaven, 954 N. Main St. 815-872-9841
Princeton All Things Quilted, 630 Timber Ridge Rd 815-875-1296
Quincy Jean Lyle, P.O. Box 289 217-222-8910
Rantoul Needle & I, 801 Arends Blvd. 217-892-2638
Rockford Gingerbread & Calico, 4125 Charles St. 815-399-5194
Roscoe Home & Hearth Inc., 5496 Elevator Rd. 815-623-5353
Springfield The Quilted Ones, 2001 Barberry Dr.
Tinley Park Sew Creative, 6787 159th St. 708-429-6056
Towanda Bolines at Indian Creek, 6 Pepperwood Ct. 888-214-3819
West Frankfort Calico Country Sewing Ctr., 310 S. Logan St. 618-932-2992
Wheaton Craftique/Never Enough Knitting, 121 N. Main St. 630-221-1007
Yates City Out Of The Closet, 106 E Main St 309-358-1488

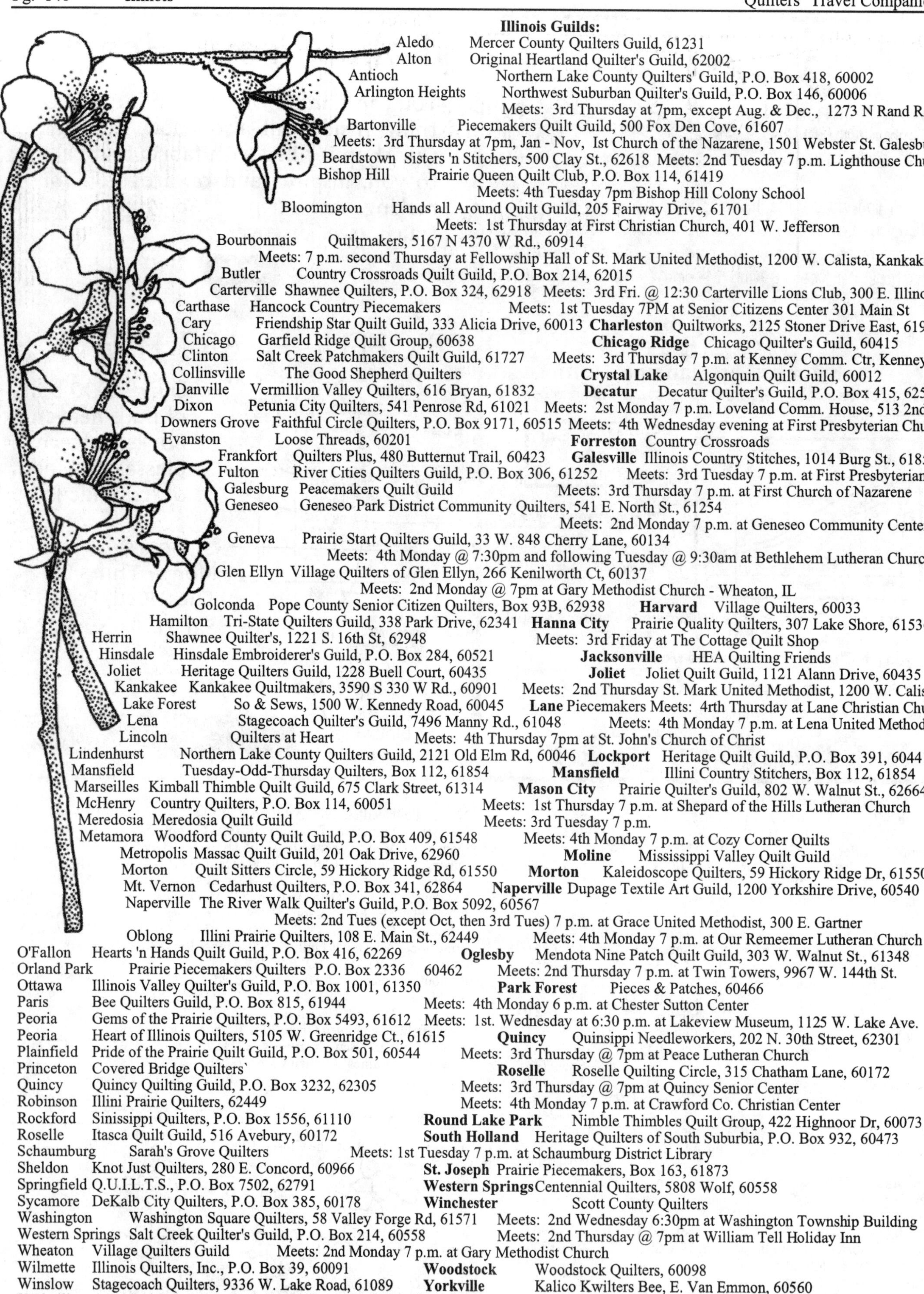

Illinois Guilds:

Aledo Mercer County Quilters Guild, 61231
Alton Original Heartland Quilter's Guild, 62002
Antioch Northern Lake County Quilters' Guild, P.O. Box 418, 60002
Arlington Heights Northwest Suburban Quilter's Guild, P.O. Box 146, 60006
Meets: 3rd Thursday at 7pm, except Aug. & Dec., 1273 N Rand Rd
Bartonville Piecemakers Quilt Guild, 500 Fox Den Cove, 61607
Meets: 3rd Thursday at 7pm, Jan - Nov, Ist Church of the Nazarene, 1501 Webster St. Galesburg
Beardstown Sisters 'n Stitchers, 500 Clay St., 62618 Meets: 2nd Tuesday 7 p.m. Lighthouse Church
Bishop Hill Prairie Queen Quilt Club, P.O. Box 114, 61419
Meets: 4th Tuesday 7pm Bishop Hill Colony School
Bloomington Hands all Around Quilt Guild, 205 Fairway Drive, 61701
Meets: 1st Thursday at First Christian Church, 401 W. Jefferson
Bourbonnais Quiltmakers, 5167 N 4370 W Rd., 60914
Meets: 7 p.m. second Thursday at Fellowship Hall of St. Mark United Methodist, 1200 W. Calista, Kankakee
Butler Country Crossroads Quilt Guild, P.O. Box 214, 62015
Carterville Shawnee Quilters, P.O. Box 324, 62918 Meets: 3rd Fri. @ 12:30 Carterville Lions Club, 300 E. Illinois
Carthase Hancock Country Piecemakers Meets: 1st Tuesday 7PM at Senior Citizens Center 301 Main St
Cary Friendship Star Quilt Guild, 333 Alicia Drive, 60013
Chicago Garfield Ridge Quilt Group, 60638
Clinton Salt Creek Patchmakers Quilt Guild, 61727
Collinsville The Good Shepherd Quilters
Danville Vermillion Valley Quilters, 616 Bryan, 61832
Dixon Petunia City Quilters, 541 Penrose Rd, 61021 Meets: 2st Monday 7 p.m. Loveland Comm. House, 513 2nd St.
Downers Grove Faithful Circle Quilters, P.O. Box 9171, 60515 Meets: 4th Wednesday evening at First Presbyterian Church
Evanston Loose Threads, 60201
Frankfort Quilters Plus, 480 Butternut Trail, 60423
Fulton River Cities Quilters Guild, P.O. Box 306, 61252
Galesburg Peacemakers Quilt Guild
Geneseo Geneseo Park District Community Quilters, 541 E. North St., 61254
Meets: 2nd Monday 7 p.m. at Geneseo Community Center
Geneva Prairie Start Quilters Guild, 33 W. 848 Cherry Lane, 60134
Meets: 4th Monday @ 7:30pm and following Tuesday @ 9:30am at Bethlehem Lutheran Church
Glen Ellyn Village Quilters of Glen Ellyn, 266 Kenilworth Ct, 60137
Meets: 2nd Monday @ 7pm at Gary Methodist Church - Wheaton, IL
Golconda Pope County Senior Citizen Quilters, Box 93B, 62938
Hamilton Tri-State Quilters Guild, 338 Park Drive, 62341
Herrin Shawnee Quilter's, 1221 S. 16th St, 62948
Hinsdale Hinsdale Embroiderer's Guild, P.O. Box 284, 60521
Joliet Heritage Quilters Guild, 1228 Buell Court, 60435
Kankakee Kankakee Quiltmakers, 3590 S 330 W Rd., 60901
Lake Forest So & Sews, 1500 W. Kennedy Road, 60045
Lena Stagecoach Quilter's Guild, 7496 Manny Rd., 61048
Lincoln Quilters at Heart Meets: 4th Thursday 7pm at St. John's Church of Christ
Lindenhurst Northern Lake County Quilters Guild, 2121 Old Elm Rd, 60046
Mansfield Tuesday-Odd-Thursday Quilters, Box 112, 61854
Marseilles Kimball Thimble Quilt Guild, 675 Clark Street, 61314
McHenry Country Quilters, P.O. Box 114, 60051
Meredosia Meredosia Quilt Guild
Metamora Woodford County Quilt Guild, P.O. Box 409, 61548
Metropolis Massac Quilt Guild, 201 Oak Drive, 62960
Morton Quilt Sitters Circle, 59 Hickory Ridge Rd, 61550
Mt. Vernon Cedarhust Quilters, P.O. Box 341, 62864
Naperville The River Walk Quilter's Guild, P.O. Box 5092, 60567
Meets: 2nd Tues (except Oct, then 3rd Tues) 7 p.m. at Grace United Methodist, 300 E. Gartner
Oblong Illini Prairie Quilters, 108 E. Main St., 62449
O'Fallon Hearts 'n Hands Quilt Guild, P.O. Box 416, 62269
Orland Park Prairie Piecemakers Quilters P.O. Box 2336 60462
Ottawa Illinois Valley Quilter's Guild, P.O. Box 1001, 61350
Paris Bee Quilters Guild, P.O. Box 815, 61944 Meets: 4th Monday 6 p.m. at Chester Sutton Center
Peoria Gems of the Prairie Quilters, P.O. Box 5493, 61612 Meets: 1st. Wednesday at 6:30 p.m. at Lakeview Museum, 1125 W. Lake Ave.
Peoria Heart of Illinois Quilters, 5105 W. Greenridge Ct., 61615
Plainfield Pride of the Prairie Quilt Guild, P.O. Box 501, 60544 Meets: 3rd Thursday @ 7pm at Peace Lutheran Church
Princeton Covered Bridge Quilters`
Quincy Quincy Quilting Guild, P.O. Box 3232, 62305 Meets: 3rd Thursday @ 7pm at Quincy Senior Center
Robinson Illini Prairie Quilters, 62449 Meets: 4th Monday 7 p.m. at Crawford Co. Christian Center
Rockford Sinissippi Quilters, P.O. Box 1556, 61110
Roselle Itasca Quilt Guild, 516 Avebury, 60172
Schaumburg Sarah's Grove Quilters Meets: 1st Tuesday 7 p.m. at Schaumburg District Library
Sheldon Knot Just Quilters, 280 E. Concord, 60966
Springfield Q.U.I.L.T.S., P.O. Box 7502, 62791
Sycamore DeKalb City Quilters, P.O. Box 385, 60178
Washington Washington Square Quilters, 58 Valley Forge Rd, 61571 Meets: 2nd Wednesday 6:30pm at Washington Township Building
Western Springs Salt Creek Quilter's Guild, P.O. Box 214, 60558 Meets: 2nd Thursday @ 7pm at William Tell Holiday Inn
Wheaton Village Quilters Guild Meets: 2nd Monday 7 p.m. at Gary Methodist Church
Wilmette Illinois Quilters, Inc., P.O. Box 39, 60091
Winslow Stagecoach Quilters, 9336 W. Lake Road, 61089
Yorkville Prairie Point Quilt Guild, 9103 Ament Road, 60560

Charleston Quiltworks, 2125 Stoner Drive East, 61920
Chicago Ridge Chicago Quilter's Guild, 60415
Meets: 3rd Thursday 7 p.m. at Kenney Comm. Ctr, Kenney, IL
Crystal Lake Algonquin Quilt Guild, 60012
Decatur Decatur Quilter's Guild, P.O. Box 415, 62525
Forreston Country Crossroads
Galesville Illinois Country Stitches, 1014 Burg St., 61854
Meets: 3rd Tuesday 7 p.m. at First Presbyterian
Meets: 3rd Thursday 7 p.m. at First Church of Nazarene
Harvard Village Quilters, 60033
Hanna City Prairie Quality Quilters, 307 Lake Shore, 61536
Meets: 3rd Friday at The Cottage Quilt Shop
Jacksonville HEA Quilting Friends
Joliet Joliet Quilt Guild, 1121 Alann Drive, 60435
Meets: 2nd Thursday St. Mark United Methodist, 1200 W. Calista
Lane Piecemakers Meets: 4rth Thursday at Lane Christian Church
Meets: 4th Monday 7 p.m. at Lena United Methodist
Lockport Heritage Quilt Guild, P.O. Box 391, 60441
Mansfield Illini Country Stitchers, Box 112, 61854
Mason City Prairie Quilter's Guild, 802 W. Walnut St., 62664
Meets: 1st Thursday 7 p.m. at Shepard of the Hills Lutheran Church
Meets: 3rd Tuesday 7 p.m.
Meets: 4th Monday 7 p.m. at Cozy Corner Quilts
Moline Mississippi Valley Quilt Guild
Morton Kaleidoscope Quilters, 59 Hickory Ridge Dr, 61550
Naperville Dupage Textile Art Guild, 1200 Yorkshire Drive, 60540
Meets: 4th Monday 7 p.m. at Our Remeemer Lutheran Church
Oglesby Mendota Nine Patch Quilt Guild, 303 W. Walnut St., 61348
Meets: 2nd Thursday 7 p.m. at Twin Towers, 9967 W. 144th St.
Park Forest Pieces & Patches, 60466
Quincy Quinsippi Needleworkers, 202 N. 30th Street, 62301
Roselle Roselle Quilting Circle, 315 Chatham Lane, 60172
Round Lake Park Nimble Thimbles Quilt Group, 422 Highnoor Dr, 60073
South Holland Heritage Quilters of South Suburbia, P.O. Box 932, 60473
St. Joseph Prairie Piecemakers, Box 163, 61873
Western Springs Centennial Quilters, 5808 Wolf, 60558
Winchester Scott County Quilters
Woodstock Woodstock Quilters, 60098
Yorkville Kalico Kwilters Bee, E. Van Emmon, 60560

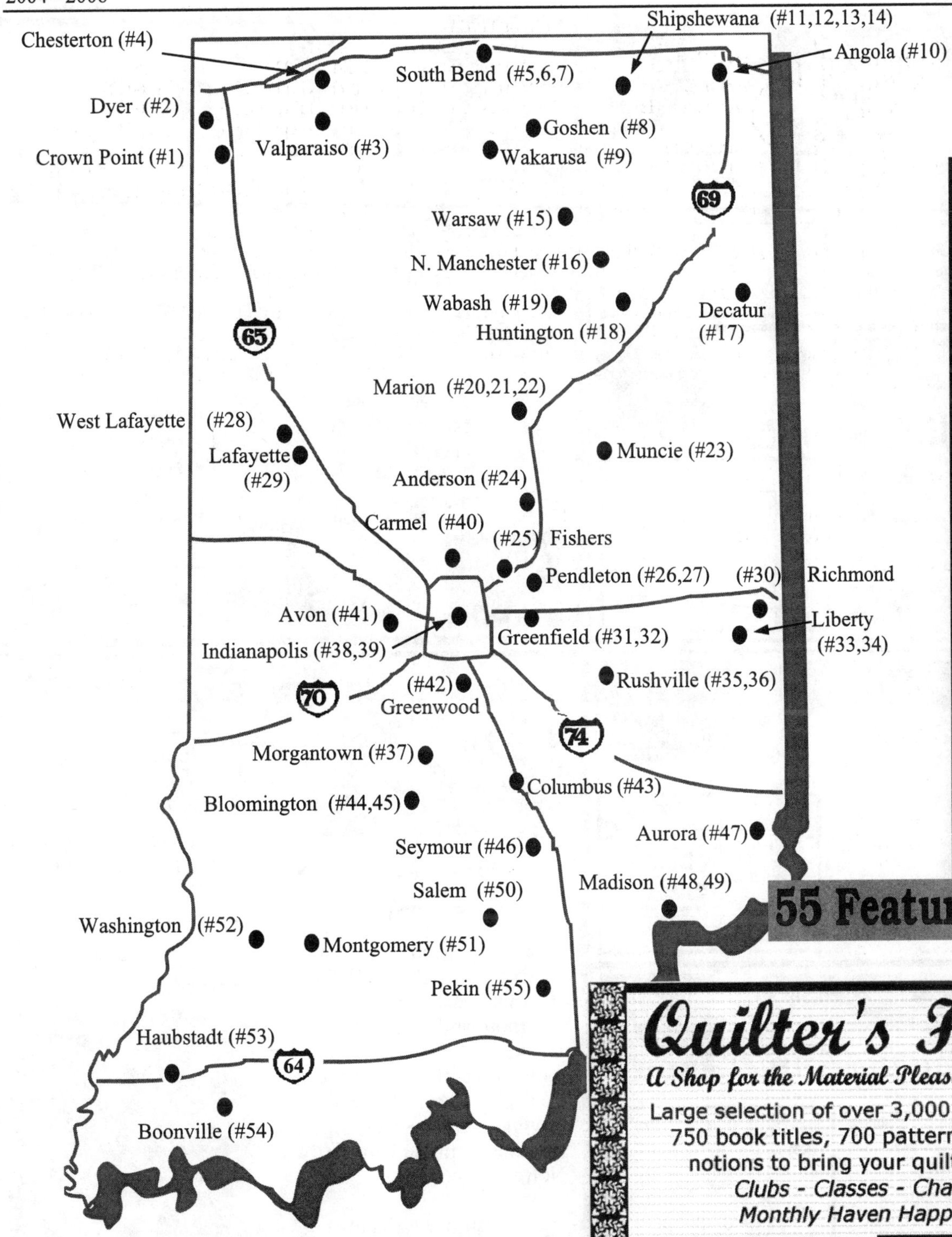

Shipshewana (#11,12,13,14)
Chesterton (#4)
Angola (#10)
South Bend (#5,6,7)
Dyer (#2)
Goshen (#8)
Crown Point (#1)
Valparaiso (#3)
Wakarusa (#9)
Warsaw (#15)
N. Manchester (#16)
Wabash (#19)
Decatur (#17)
Huntington (#18)
Marion (#20,21,22)
West Lafayette (#28)
Lafayette (#29)
Muncie (#23)
Anderson (#24)
Carmel (#40)
(#25) Fishers
Pendleton (#26,27)
(#30) Richmond
Avon (#41)
Liberty (#33,34)
Indianapolis (#38,39)
Greenfield (#31,32)
(#42) Greenwood
Rushville (#35,36)
Morgantown (#37)
Columbus (#43)
Bloomington (#44,45)
Aurora (#47)
Seymour (#46)
Salem (#50)
Madison (#48,49)
Washington (#52)
Montgomery (#51)
Pekin (#55)
Haubstadt (#53)
Boonville (#54)

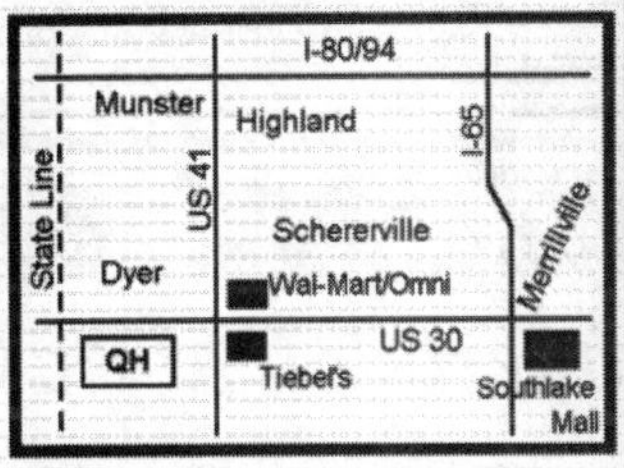

INDIANA

55 Featured Shops

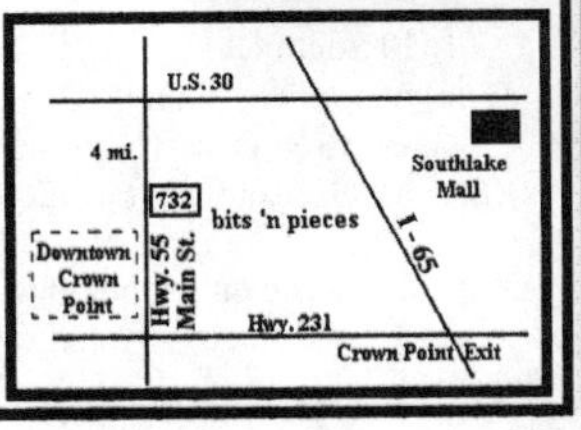

Valparaiso, IN #3

Mon - Fri 10 - 5:30
Thur til 7
Sat 10 - 3

Needle & Thread

60 W. Jefferson 46383
(219) 462-4300 Est: 1990
Owner: Marlene Rock 1500 sq.ft.
2300 Bolts Free Newsletter

Visit our old Victorian house filled with everything for quilting. We also carry supplies for cross stitch, tatting, & silk ribbon embroidery. Classes.

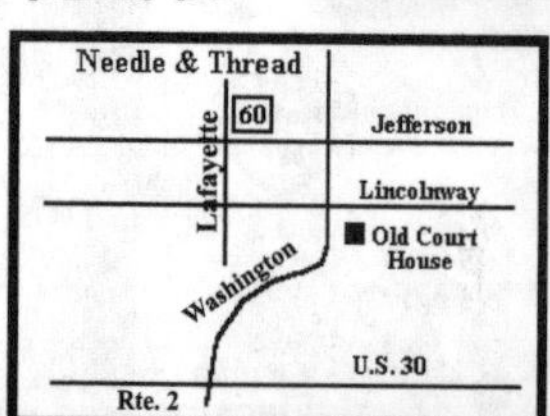

Crazy Eighths

Fabric, Friendship & Fun !!

Easy exit from I-94 or Indiana Toll Road
Hwy. 49 to Chesterton - West on Indian Boundary Rd.
In the Subway Plaza.

374B Indian Boundary Rd.
Chesterton, IN 46304
(219) 929-4511
crazy.eighths@verizon.net
www.crazyeighths.com
Owner: Ellen Maxwell
Est: 2002

- Cozy quilt shop with friendly service
- Sure to inspire your creativity
- Always something on sale

Tues - Fri 10 - 5
Sat 10 - 3

Chesterton, IN #4

South Bend, IN #5

Mon - Sat 10 - 6
Thur til 8

Stitch 'N Time Fabrics

2305 Miami St. 46614
(574) 234-4314 Est: 1993
Fax: (574) 968-4314
stitchntime1@aol.com
www.stitchntimefabrics.com 4000+ Bolts
Owner: Valerie Strycker 3800 sq.ft.
Large Selection of Notions, Books & Patterns.
Singer & Pfaff sewing machines.
Service of all makes. Classes.

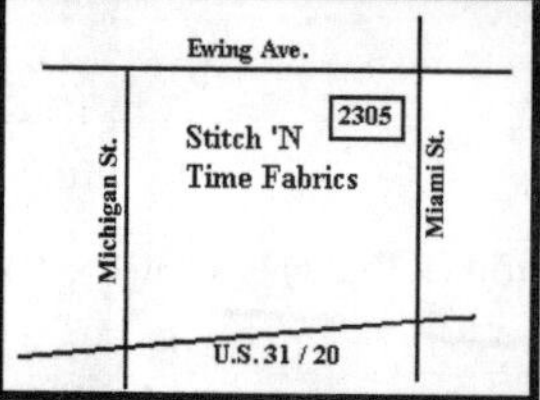

South Bend, IN #6

Mon - Sat 10 - 5
Or By Appt.

Heckaman's Quilts & Yarns

63028 U.S. 31 South 46614
(574) 291-3918

Quilts for Sale. Custom Orders Welcome
Let us Quilt your Heirlooms by Hand or Machine.
Beautiful Yarns. Ashford Spinning Wheels.
Rug Hooking Supplies

South Bend, IN #7

Erica's

©Erica

1320 N. Ironwood Dr.
South Bend, IN 46615
574-233-3112

Monday, Tuesday
Wednesday & Friday
9:30-5:30
Thursday 9:30-8:30
Saturday 9:00-4:00
Sunday 12:00-4:00

Fabrics by: Moda, Mumm's the Word, Teresa Kogut, Cheri Strole, JRJ, P&B, Thimbleberries, Benartex, Hoffman, Balis, AE Nathan, and more and more fabrics. Books, patterns, tools and more tools. Lots of samples and fabric packs. Bernina and Viking sewing machines and sergers. Minutes from the University of Notre Dame.

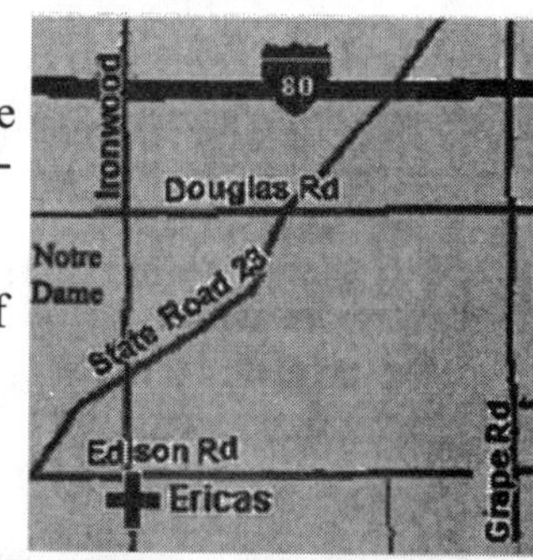

Visit our website at
www.ericas.com

Goshen, IN #8

Mon - Fri 9 - 5:30
Sat 9 - 4

Meredith's Sewing Corner

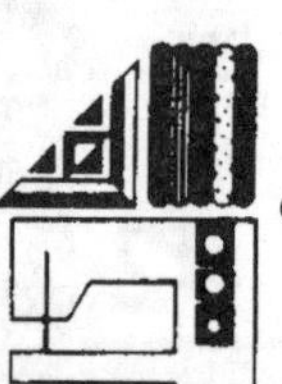

712 W. Lincoln Ave. 46526
(574) 533-3414

6000 square feet a full fabric store, needle crafts and Bernina Sewing Machines. Wonderful displays. Great prices.

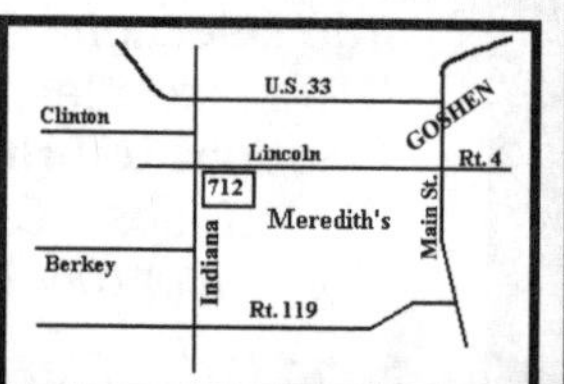

Wakarusa, IN #9

Mon 9 - 7
Tues - Fri 9 - 5
Sat 9 - 2

Jeanette's Fabric Boutique

105 S Elkhart St., P.O. Box 511 46573
(574) 862-4207 Fax: (574) 862-1637
jeanette@galaxyinternet.net
www.jeanettesfabric.com
Owner: Jeanette Prenkert
Est: 1981 2500 sq. ft. 2000+ Bolts

Large selection quilting fabrics; many classes; personal help anytime; authorized Janome and Baby Lock dealer; unique store in a small town.

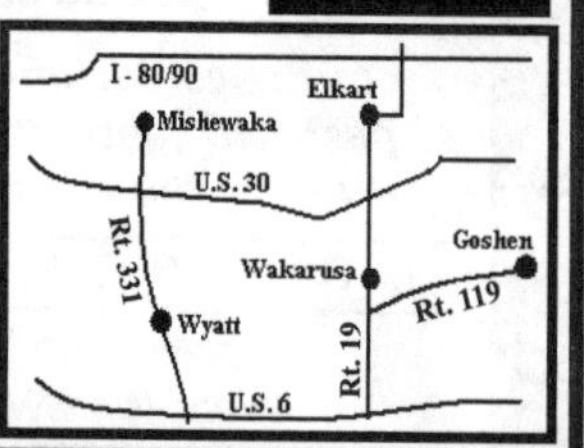

Angola, IN #10

Mon - Fri 9 - 5
Sat 9 - 4

Sewing Sewlutions

1650 South Old U.S. 27 46703
(260) 665-6948 Fax: (260) 624-2356
www.sewingsewlutions.com
Est: 1999 2600 sq.ft. 1200 Bolts

Your full service quilt store in the Indiana Lake Country. Stop by and say "hi".

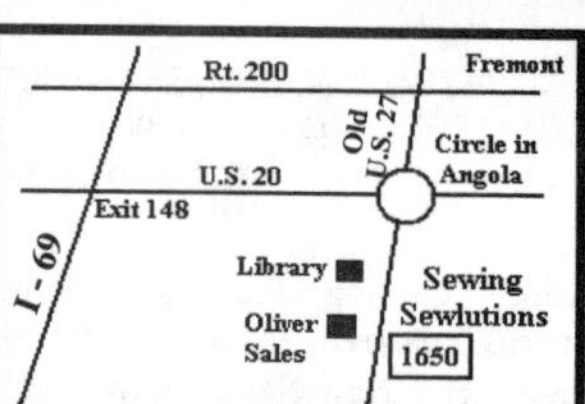

Shipshewana, IN #11

"FIND THE BASIC AND THE UNUSUAL!"

- **OVER 12,000 BOLTS OF FABRIC with over 4,000 bolts of quilting type fabrics.** Brands include: Hoffman, Benartex, Concord, P & B, Marcus Bros., Peter Pan, Bali, Moda, RJR, V-I-P, Springs, Chanteclaire, hand dyed fabrics, homespuns, quilter's flannel and many more!
- **FASHION, BRIDAL AND HOME DECORATING FABRIC** (including Waverly, John Wolf & Robert Kauffman)
- **SILK, VELVET, WOOL, LINEN, DENIM, CALICO, AND MANY HARD-TO-FIND FABRICS**
- **QUILTING SUPPLIES AND BOOKS, PATTERNS, SEWING NOTIONS, TRIMS AND ACCESSORIES**

Visit a family tradition that still places friendly service,

Open: 8:00 AM - 5:30 PM
Monday - Saturday, Closed Sunday
Will Mail Order Credit Cards Accepted.

YODER'S SHOPPING CENTER
P.O. BOX 245, State Road 5
Shipshewana, IN 46565
(260) 768-4887
www.yoderdepartmentstore.com
fabrics@shipshewana.com

I - 94
Exit 107 I - 80/90 Exit 121
Hwy. 120
Ind. 13 Ind. 5 Ind. 9 I - 69
Yoder Dept. Store
Ship. Auction
Hwy. 20

Shipshewana, IN #12

Lolly's Fabrics & Quilts

Huge selection of 100% cotton quilting fabrics, notions, books, Batiks, flannels; quilts & wallhangings quilted by our local Amish ladies.
There is *only* one Shipshewana!

Sales: Feb. 5, 2005
6-9am Annual Pajama Sale

DAILY April - Dec 9 - 5
Jan - March 10 - 4

Due to a fire we are temporarily located at 305 E. Main at the North entrance of Wells Fargo Bank

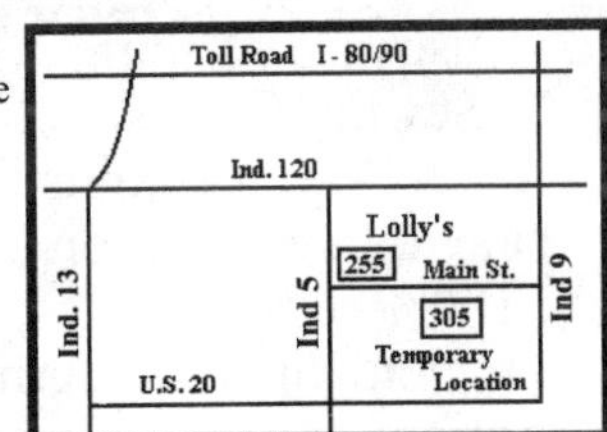

P.O. Box 277, 255 E. Main St. 46565
260/768-4703 Fax: 260/768-7304
Elsie@lollys.com www.lollys.com

Shipshewana, IN #13

Mon - Sat 9:30 - 5
Winter Hrs. Vary

Rebecca Haarer Folk Arts and Antiques

165 Morton St. 46565
(260) 768-4787
Owner: Rebecca Haarer
Est: 1971 Free Brochure

Antique Quilts, Quilt Tops, Quilt Blocks and Fabric. Amish Quilts, Dolls, Rockers and Stencils. Amish Quilt Lectures.

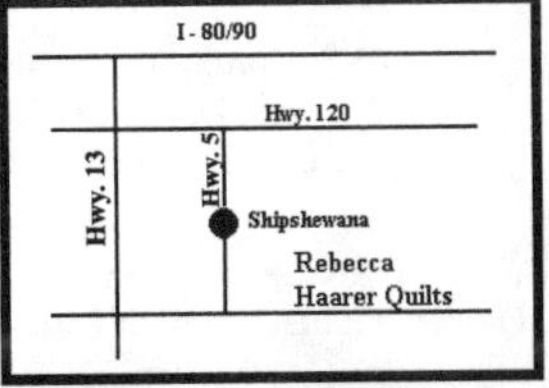

Shipshewana, IN #14

Mon - Fri 8 - 5
Sat 8 - 3

Spector's Store

305 S. Van Buren (Ind. 5)
P.O. Box 347 46565
(260) 768-4439

Full line of Fabric and Notions, Quilt and Craft Supplies. Hand stitched, Quilted items. Wallhangings and Quilts. Excellent values on Solid and Printed Fabrics.

I - 94
Exit 107 I - 80/90 Exit 121
Hwy 120
Ind. 13 Ind 9 I - 69
Spector's Store
305
Ship. Auction
Ind 5 U.S. 20

Warsaw, IN #15

Mon - Thur 9 - 5:30
Fri 9 - 6:30
Sat 9 - 4

Lowery Sewing & Vacuum Center

707 E. Winona Ave. 46580
(574) 267-8631 Fax: (574) 267-8161
sales@lowerysewing.com
www.lowerysewing.com
Est: 1948 7500 sq.ft. 3000+ Bolts

Large selection of fabrics, notions, books, & patterns. Janome sales & service. Full service, friendly help. We sell only the best.

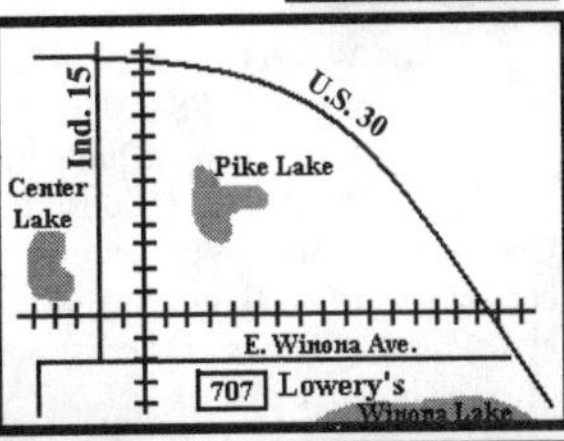

N. Manchester, IN #16

Tues - Fri 10 - 5
Sat 10 - 3

The Creative Stitch Quilt Shop

229 E. Main St. 46962
(260) 982-1080
creativestitch@kconline.com
Owner: Linda Cearbaugh

A full service quilt shop featuring quality quilting fabrics, wool-felt, notions, kits, books and patterns. We offer friendly service, quality custom long-arm machine quilting and a wide range of classes for all skill levels.

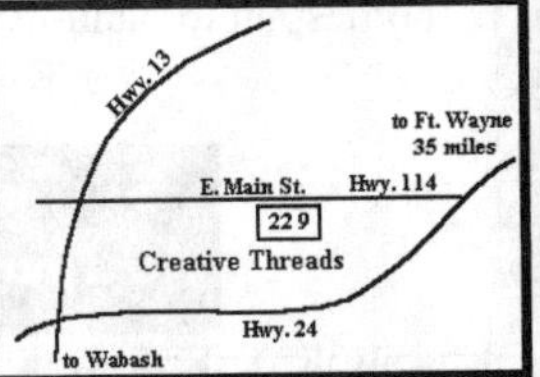

Decatur, IN #17

Mon - Fri 10 - 5
Sat 9 - 12

Country Creations

5342 N 400 W 46733
(260) 547-4535
fabrics2@onlyinternet.net
Owners: Bev and Gene Weber
Est: 1998 3000 sq.ft.

Cotton for quilting, supplies, books, patterns, classes.
Custom long-arm quilting

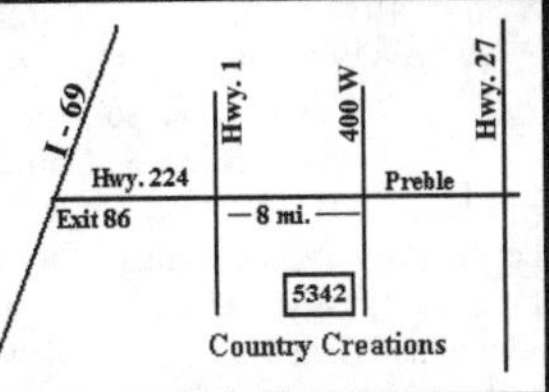

The Sewing Basket
and Quilt Shoppe

517 N. Jefferson St. 46750
(260) 359-0777
Fax: (260) 359-0277
thesewingbasket_shoppe
@hotmail.com
Est: 2003
2000 sq.ft. 1200 Bolts

Husqvarna-Viking Sewing Center.
New & Antique quilts for sale, Large selection of 100% cotton fabrics, complete line of patterns, notions, classes & best selection of books.

Mon - Fri 9 - 7 Sat 10 - 5

N. Jefferson St. | IN 9 | U.S. 24 | W. Park Dr. | 517 Sewing Basket | Broadway | Downtown Huntington | Hwy. 224 | S. Jefferson | St. Rd. 5

Huntington, IN #18

Wabash, IN #19

Mon - Fri 10 - 5:30 Sat 10 - 5

Nancy J's Fabrics

1604 South Wabash 46992
Toll Free (866) 563-3505 Est: 1980
Owners: Nancy Jacoby & Miriam Peebles

The latest & greatest Fabrics. Books and Patterns for quiltmaking.
Plan to spend a day in Historic Wabash!

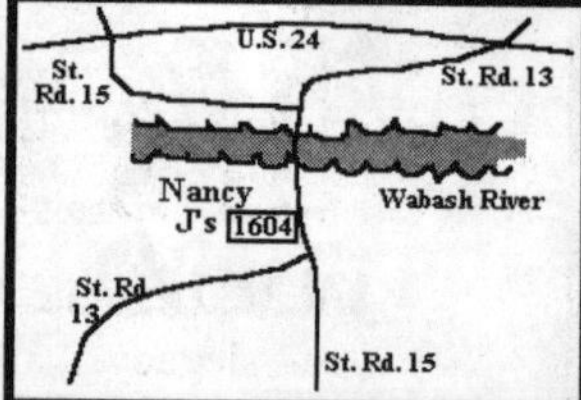

Marion, IN #20

Mon - Fri 10 - 6 Closed Wed & Sun Sat 10 - 3

Sew Biz

"Where Sewing Is Exciting"
3722 South Western Ave. 46953
(800) 500-3830 or (765) 674-6001
Fax: (765) 674-5992 Est: 1983
sewbiz@comteck.com
www.sewbizmarion.com
Owner: Donelle McAdams 5000 sq.ft.

Viking & White Dealer. 100% cottons, books, patterns, classes, dolls, bears, bunnies, etc. A place to share ideas and get inspired.

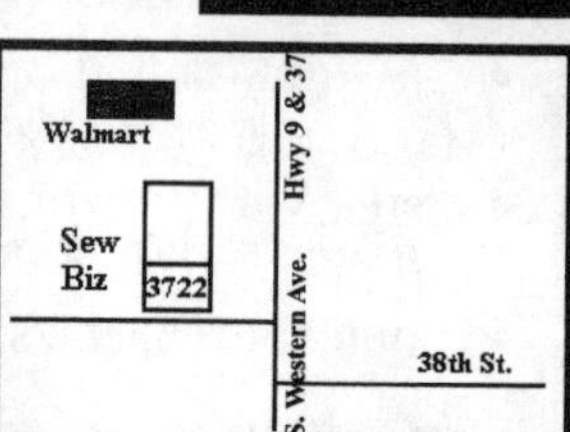

Marion, IN #21

Mon - Fri 10 - 5 Sat 10 - 2

Sunshine Fabrics

303 S. Norton Ave. 46952
(765) 664-8832 or (888) 664-8832
Est: 1997 2000 sq.ft.

Fabrics, Books, Patterns and Notions for the Quilter. Quilter's Hall of Fame located in Marion.

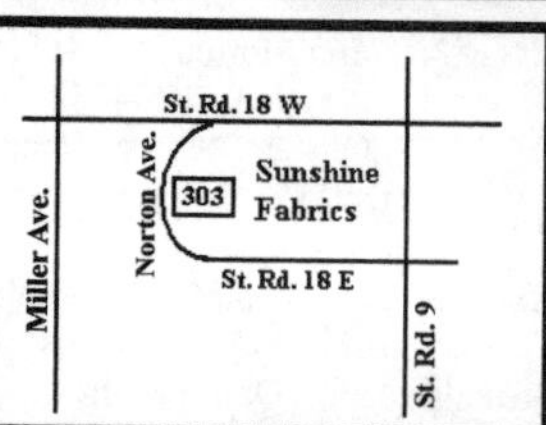

Marion, IN #22

Please Call First

The Quilters Hall of Fame

926 S. Washington, P.O. Box 681 46952
(765) 664-9333 Fax: Same

Annual Celebration featuring quilt shows, lectures, workshops and more. Third weekend in July! Call for schedule.
Renovation of Marie Webster Home is nearing completion. Plan to open in 2004
Web Site: www.quiltershalloffame.org
E-mail: quilters@comteck.com

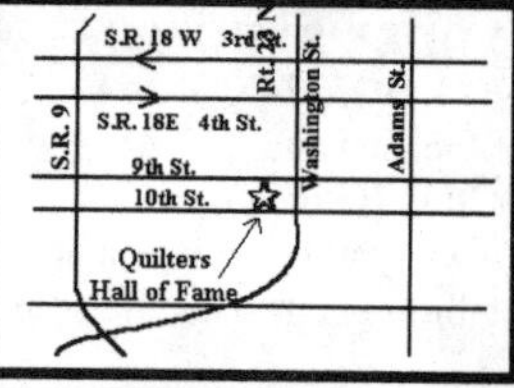

Muncie, IN #23

Mon - Fri 10 - 5 Closed Wed. & Sun Sat 10 - 4

Quilters' Toy Box

804 W. McGalliard 47303
(765) 288-7316
Owner: Tanya Dumpert
Est: 2002 1500 Bolts

One stop quilt shop, embracing 100% cotton fabrics (with an emphasis on batiks and flannels), books, patterns, notions, and offering creative classes.

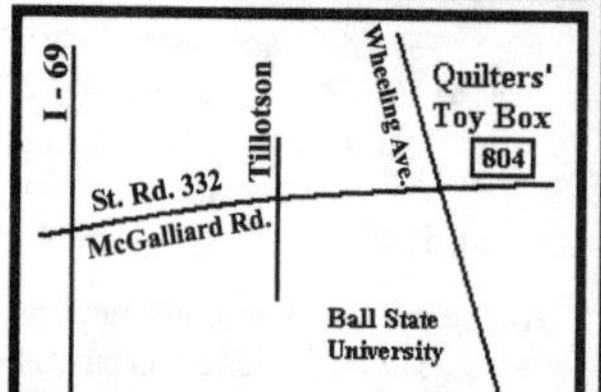

Anderson, IN #24

Tues - Sat 10 - 5

The Quilt Shoppe

1013 N. Broadway 46012
(765) 620-2139 Fax: (765) 649-2311
donnernay@aol.com
Owner: Dawn R. Cornell
Est: 2004 3000 sq.ft. 2500 bolts

The most up-to-date high quality fabrics from Moda, RJR, P&B. Uniquely packaged kits & collections, Gifts, antiques and a fun, feeling good environment to visit again and again.

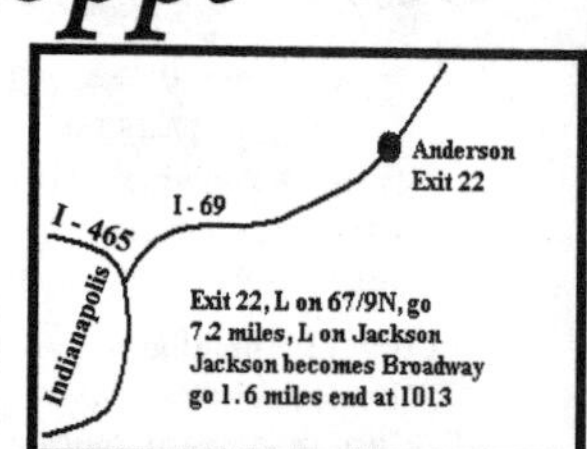

Quiltmakers

11854 Allisonville Rd. 46038
(317) 585-5825
Fax: (317) 585-5826
shopquiltmakers@aol.com
www.shopquiltmakers.com
Est: 1999 2400 sq.ft. 2000 Bolts

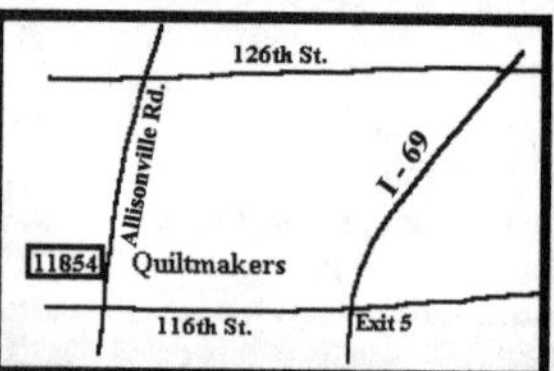

Fishers, IN #25

Find the latest fabrics from traditional to contemporary, homespun to hand-dyed here! Books, patterns and notions. Knowledgeable Staff.

Mon - Sat 10 - 5 Thur til 8:30 Sun 1- 4

Pendleton, IN #26

Ruth's Legacy, Ltd.

104 W. High St. 46064
ruthslegacy@aol.com
(765) 778-2488 Est: 1996 2700 sq.ft.

Mon - Sat 10 - 5
Sun 1 - 5

The very latest fabrics from Hoffman, Michael Miller, Kona Bay, Hi-Fashion & more. Classes, Patterns, Notions & Friendly Service. Over 35 different cat prints. Large selection of Batiks. Long-arm Machine Quilting Service available. Distinctive Gifts & Collectibles such as Just the Right Shoe, Lee Middleton Dolls and A.I. Root candles plus Carol Wilson greeting cards.

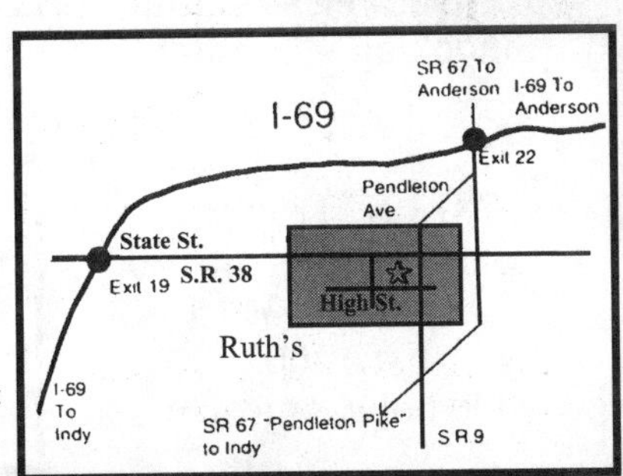

Needles in a Quilt

132 W. State St. (Hwy. 38)
Pendleton, IN 46064
(765) 778-7936
soglesp@aol.com
Owner: Sandy Ogle
2400 sq.ft. 2000 bolts

Mon - Sat 10 - 5
First Tues & Wed 10 - 8

Fabric Lines: Thimbleberries, Debbie Mumm, Moda, P&B, Marcus Brothers, Homespuns, Flannels, Reproduction, South Seas.
Full Line Quilting Supplies & Classes
Clubs: Quilt In A Day
Thimbleberries
Moda

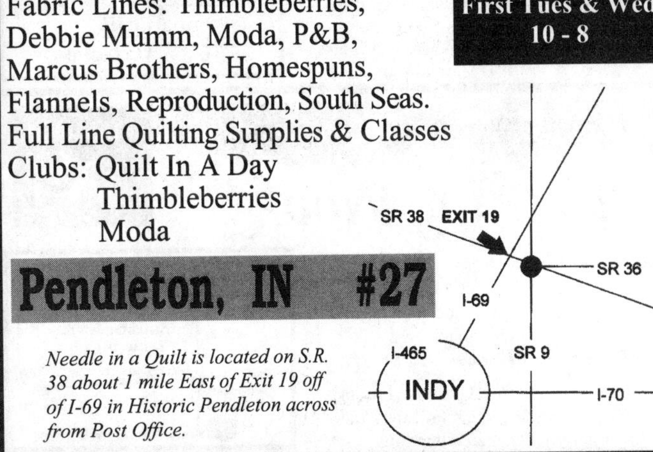

Pendleton, IN #27

Needle in a Quilt is located on S.R. 38 about 1 mile East of Exit 19 off of I-69 in Historic Pendleton across from Post Office.

West Lafayette, IN #28

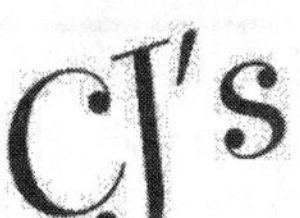

Quilt Shop

500 Sagamore Pkwy. W 47906
(765) 497-1769
cjs-quiltshop@att.net
Owner: C J Hurst

Mon - Fri 10 - 6
Thur til 8 Sat 9 - 5

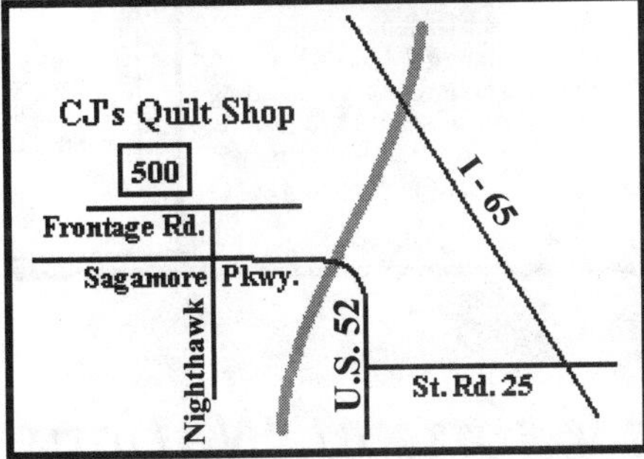

Full line of quilting fabrics and notions
Custom long-arm machine quilting services. Authorized Janome dealer.
Always helpful, friendly advice!

Quilter's Harvest

2307 State Road 25 West 47909
(765) 474-2057 Est: 1999 4000 sq.ft.
www.quiltersharvestonline.com
Owners: Karen Lõser & Stephen James

Quality 100% Cotton Fabrics
Quilting Supplies
Books & Patterns
Classes on quilting & wearable art
Block of the Months

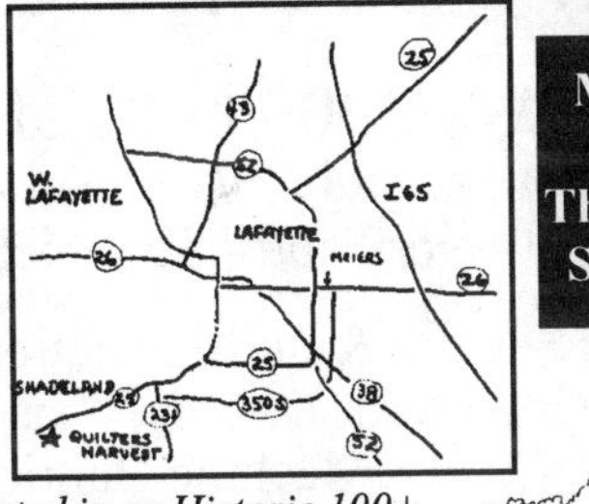

Mon - Sat 10 - 5
Thur til 7:30
Sun 12 - 4

Quilter's Harvest is located in an Historic 100+ year old brick Church, complete with a white picket fence & a beautiful stained glass window in the loft.

Lafayette, IN #29

Richmond, IN #30

Mon - Fri 9 - 5
Sat 9 - 3

The Side Door

3430 E. Main St. 47374
(765) 962-7678
thenook@myvine.com
www.stitchingnook.com
Owner: Diana Bruns Est: 2003

100% Cotton Fabrics, Quilting Notions, Classes, Machine Sales, and Friendly Personal Attention.

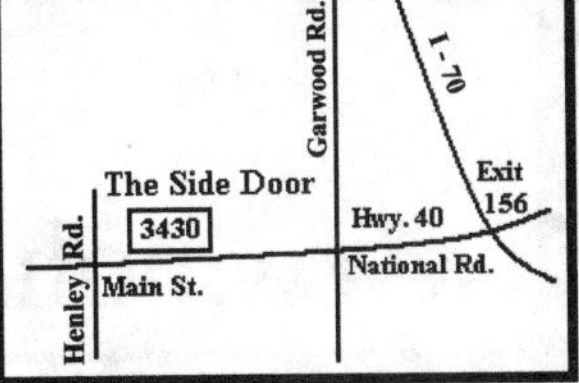

Greenfield, IN #31

Mon - Fri 10 - 6
Sat 10 - 4

9 PATCH

A Quilter's Paradise
1712 Melody Lane 46140
(317) 468-0699
www.9patch.com
High Quality fabrics from top manufacturers
Notions, Books, Patterns, Classes. Koala Sewing Cabinets
Jasmine Quilting Frames.
"Where Heirlooms Begin"

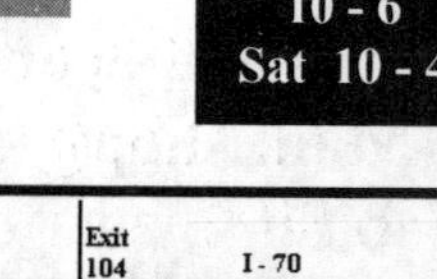

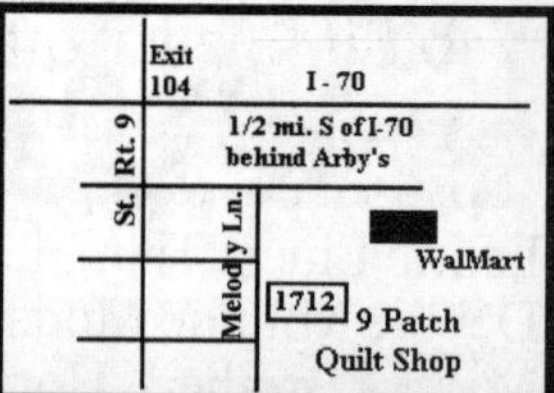

Greenfield, IN #32

Zig-Zag Corner
Quilts & Baskets

T, W, F 10 - 5 Th 10 - 12 Sat 10 - 4

Supplies and classes for:
Quilting -- Tatting -- Basket Weaving
Smocking -- Embroidery -- Heirloom Sewing
www.zigzagcorner.com

7872 N. Troy Rd.
Greenfield, IN 46140
(317) 326-3115
Est: 2002
1000 bolts & growing

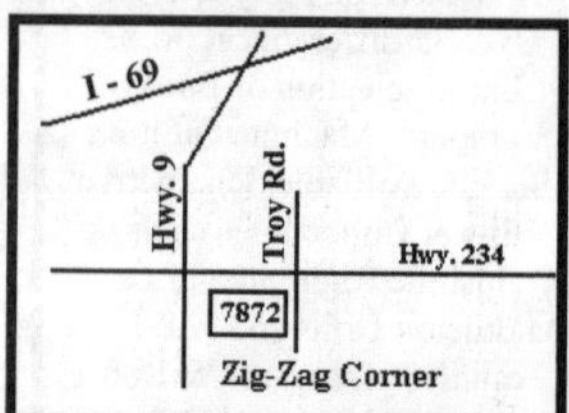

Liberty, IN #33

Mon - Fri 9 - 5
Sat 9 - 3

Stitching Nook

41 W. Union St. 47353
(765) 458-6443
thenook@myvine.com
www.stitchingnook.com
Owner: Diana Bruns Est: 1982

100% Cotton Fabrics, Quilting Notions, X-Stitch, Classes, Machine Sales, and Friendly Personal Attention.

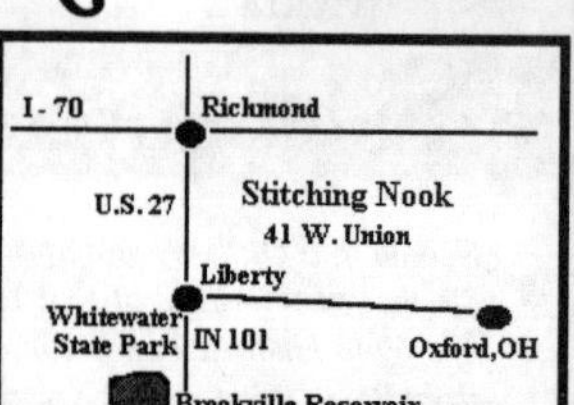

Liberty, IN #34

Pohlar Fabrics

Mon - Sat 9 - 5
Sun by Appt.

Over 3000 bolts of Fabrics.
- Moda - RJR - Hoffman - Benartex -
- Northcott - Thimbleberries -

Sewing & quilting notions, books, patterns and ready made gifts.
Machine Quilting.
Mail Order Welcome.
Exciting quilt classes!

6439 S. State Rd. 101 47353
(800) 357-3152

Or (765) 458-5466 fax also
E-mail: pfabrics@gte.net
Owners:
Kenny & Rose Pohlar
Est: 1984
1150 sq.ft.

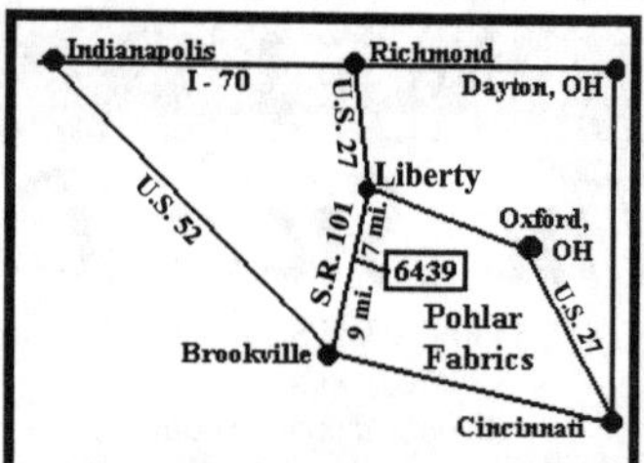

www.pohlarfabrics.com

Rushville, IN #35

Country Quilt Barn

Tues - Fri 9 - 5
Sat 10 - 5

5026 W U.S. 52 46173
(765) 663-5882
Owners: Judy & Harold Bowling

Good selection of Moda, Thimbleberries, Benartex, Springs, Mettler, Gutermann threads. Quilt classes, Patterns, Books, Stencils and Notions. Custom Machine Quilting Available.

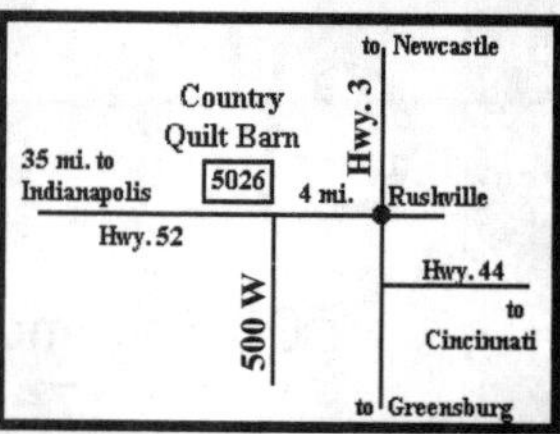

Rushville, IN #36

In Stitches

Mon - Fri 10 - 5
Sat 10 - 2

837 W. Third St. 46173
(765) 938-1818 Fax: (765) 938-1819
institches@mach1pc.com
Owner: Cathy Burkett Est: 2003
Over 500 bolts of 100% cotton fabrics including Benartex & Moda. Lots of samples to inspire. Classes, patterns & books.
"A fun place to shop!"

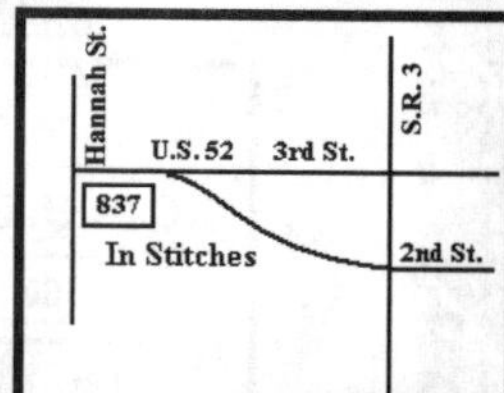

Morgantown, IN #37

Mon - Sat 10 - 5

Ady's Fabric & Notions

75 W. Washington St, P.O. Box 492 46160
(812) 597-0578 Fax: (812) 597-0593
lydiastout1@earthlink.net
www.adysfabrics.com
Est: 2001 2000 Bolts

Large selection of 100% cotton fabrics. Complete line of notions, patterns & classes. Gifts for the Quilter.

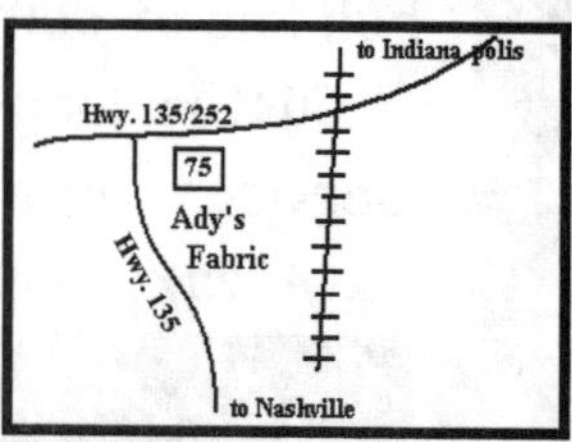

1748 E. 86th Street Northview Mall 46240
(317) 844-2446 or (800) 840-2241
E-Mail: shop@quiltsplus.com
Web Site: www.quiltsplus.com
Owner: Jeanne Moosey
Est: 1977 3800 sq. ft. 4000 Bolts

Indianapolis, IN #38

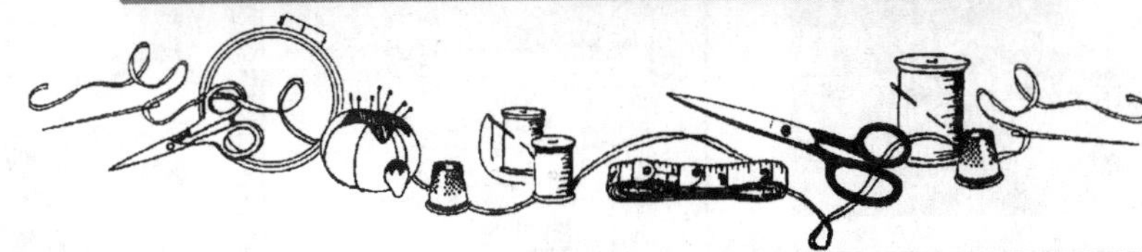

Mon - Sat
10 - 5
Thurs til
8:30
Sun 12 - 4

- We cater to all of your quilting needs
- Extensive Class Schedule
- Block of the Month Programs
- We ship anywhere!

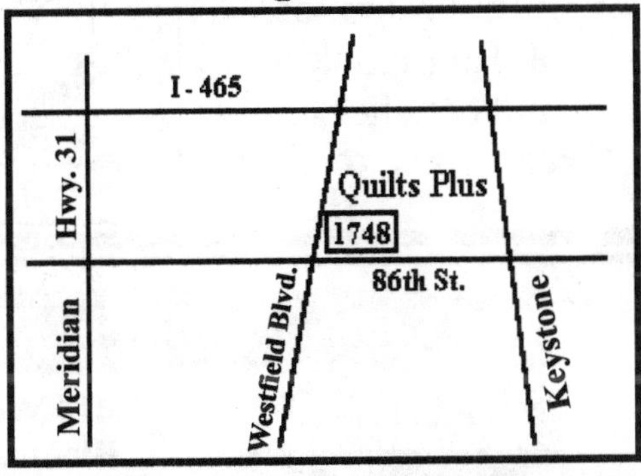

Quilt Quarters

Home of Kaye England Publications

Carmel, IN #40

1) 12405 North Meridian Street (Hamilton Crossing Centre)
Carmel, IN 46032
317-844-3636
317-844-7588 (fax)
email: north@quiltquarters.com
5000 sq. ft. - 7000+ bolts

Indianapolis, IN #39

2) 3137 East Thompson Road (Carson Square)
Indianapolis, IN 46227
317-791-1336
317-791-8289 (fax)
email: south@quiltquarters.com
5000 sq. ft. - 5000+ bolts

Avon, IN #41

3) 5201 E. US 36 (Prestwick Center)
Avon, IN 46123
317-745-2626
317-745-2774(fax)
email: west@quiltquarters.com
5000 sq. ft. - 3000+ bolts

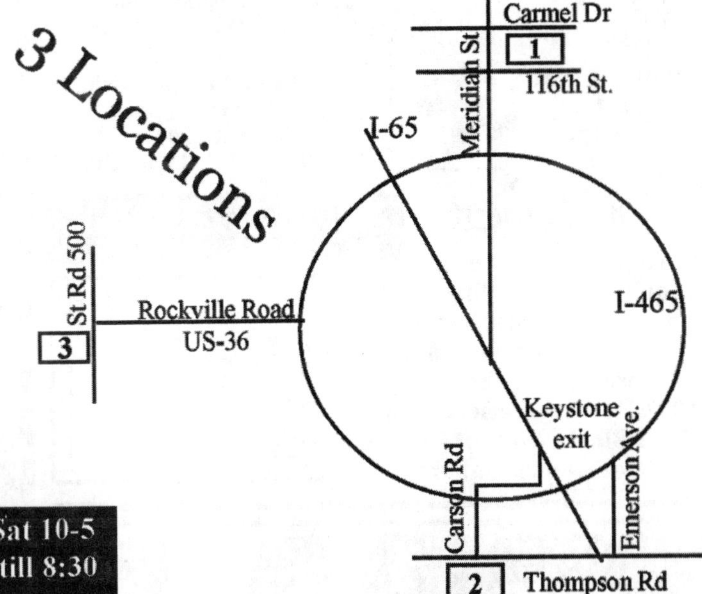

Mon- Sat 10-5
Thurs till 8:30

Indiana's largest selection of traditional and non-traditional fabrics. Authorized Bernina sales and service, patterns, books, notions, stencils, classes for all levels.

Nothing Sews Like A Bernina. Nothing.
BERNINA®

www.QuiltQuarters.com

Est: 1973

Greenwood, IN #42

5600 sq.ft.

The Back Door, Inc.

2503 Fairview Place #W 46142
(317) 882-2120 dttes@indy.net
www.backdoorquilts.com
Owners: Linda Hale & Teri Dougherty

Mon - Thur 9:30 - 9
Fri 9:30-6 Sat 9:30 - 5
1st & 3rd Sundays
Jan - Labor Day
All Sundays Labor Day to Christmas

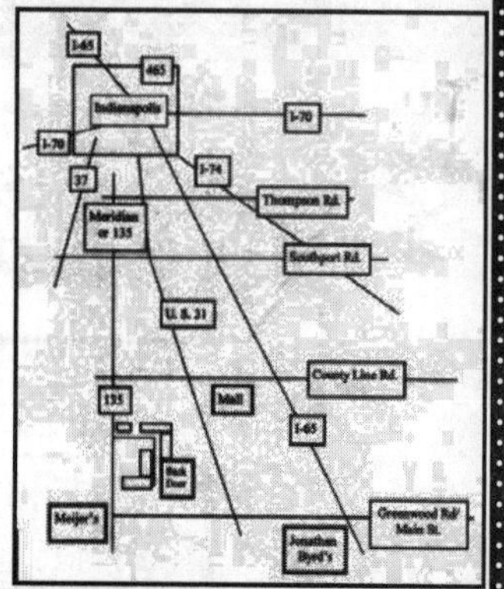

Quilting Supplies, Wool, Rug Hooking, and Stitchery
A Great place to shop!

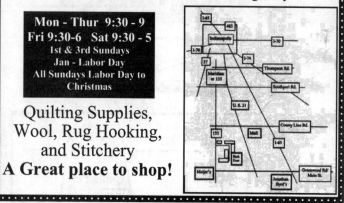

Columbus, IN #43

Mon - Thur 10 - 5
Fri 10 - 6
Sat 10 - 2

Columbus Sewing Center

2645 Eastwood Dr. 47203
(812) 372-4496
christine@columbussewing.com
Owner: Christine & Chris Lorimor
Est: 1974 1800 sq.ft. 900 Bolts

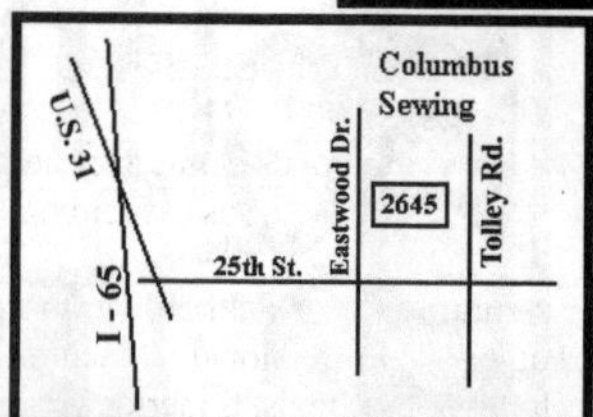

New Owner! New Location!
100% cotton fabrics, books, patterns & more.
Classes. Viking and White sales and service.

Bloomington, IN #44

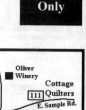

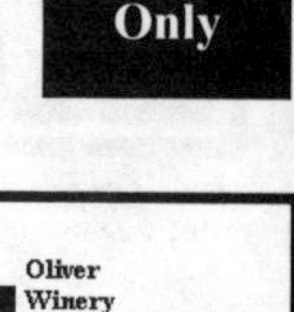

Cottage Quilters

111 E. Sample Rd. 47408
(812) 876-0700
CatQltr@aol.com
Owners:
Karen Blocher & Cathy Jackson
Custom Quilting by Machine. We Ship Throughout the U.S.
Commission Quilts from Start to Finish Available.

to Indianapolis 50 mi.
Oliver Winery
St. Rt. 37
Cottage Quilters
111
E. Sample Rd.
to Bloomington
Wylie's Floor Cov.
College Ave. Exit 2 mi.
Business 37

Bloomington, IN #45

Just Around The Block

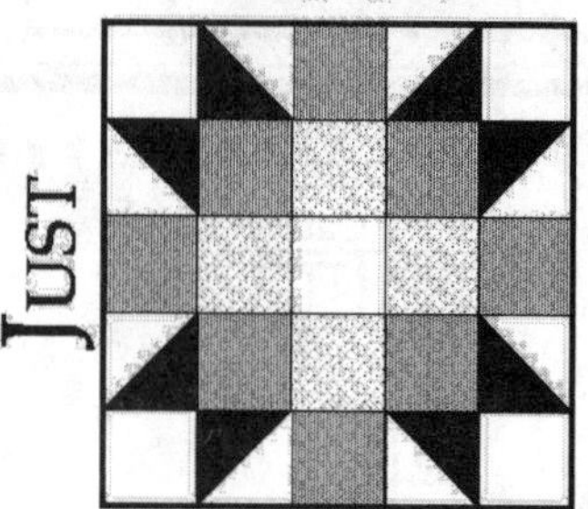

414 West 6th St.
Bloomington, IN
47404
(812) 333-1385
Owner: Nancy Hodson
Fax: (812) 339-2923
E-Mail:
Justaroundtheblock
@earthlink.net
Est: 2001
1900 sq.ft. 1800+ Bolts

Mon - Sat 10 - 5 Thur til 8

A complete, full service quilt shop carrying your favorite fabrics, books & notions. Classes too! Located in a charming 1902 House (Green & white), 2 1/2 Blocks West of County Courthouse Square.

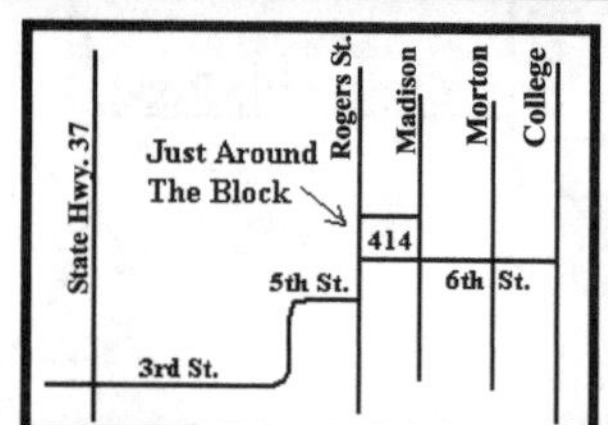

Seymour, IN #46

Mon - Fri 9 - 6
Sat 9 - 4

205 S. Maple St. 47274
(812) 524-2013 Fax: 523-0096
awest@hsonline.net Est: 2002
Owner:
Alice West
3500 sq.ft.
4000 Bolts
www.loosethreadsonline.com

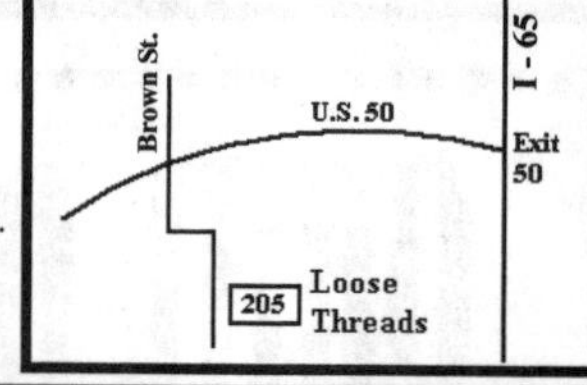

Loose Threads is truly the unique quilt shoppe. Offering 4000+ bolts of fabric, Hundreds of Books and Patterns. We are the authorized Bernina Dealer in Southern Indiana.

Aurora, IN #47

M, Tu, Th, F 10 - 5
Wd & Sa 10 - 3

Quilt Bug

214 Judiciary St. 47001
(812) 926-4939
Fax: (812) 926-1620
quiltbug@seidata.com
Owner: Bev DeSalvo Est: 2002

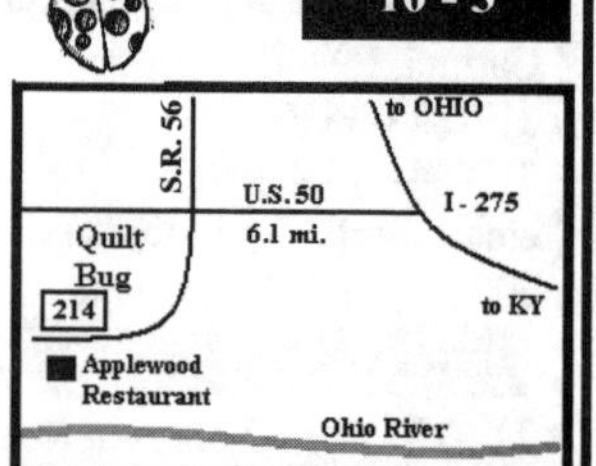

1500+ bolts of quality 100% cotton fabric at fantastic price. Complete line of notions, books, & patterns. We love to help you choose fabric!

Madison, IN #48

Mon - Sat 9 - 5

L & L Yard Goods

1814 Taylor St. 47250
(812) 273-1041
Owner: Lenora C. Green
Est: 1986

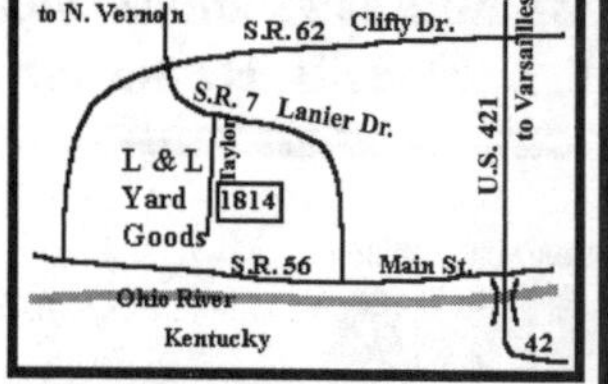

Selection of Fabrics from Moda, Thimbleberries, Batiks from Hoffman, & other quality Homespuns & prints. Lots of wonderful Samples! Classes.

Madison, IN #49

Mon - Sat 10 - 5
Sun 1 - 5

Margie's Country Store

721 W. Main St. 47250
(812) 265-4429
Owner: Marjorie Webb
Est. 1970 900 Bolts

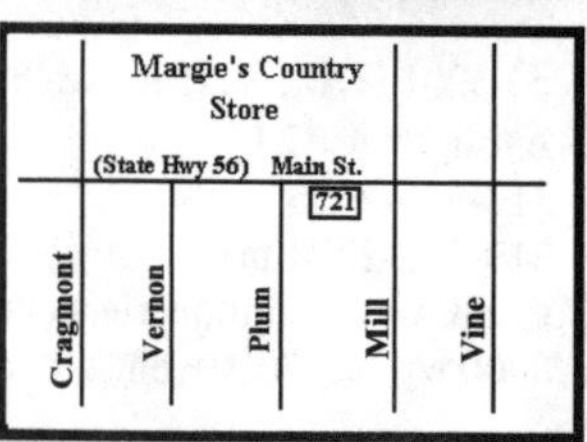

Quality fabrics, books, patterns. Many samples to inspire you. Gracious service. Large line of gifts and home decorations.

Salem, IN #50

Mon - Fri 9 - 5
Sat 9 - 3

The Quilted Cottage

203 E. Jackson St., Hwy. 60 47167
(812) 883-7577 Est: 2001
drygoods@blueriver.net
Owner: Susan Fleming

Premium Cotton Fabrics, Notions, Books & Patterns, Professional Machine Quilting, Home & gift Items, Superior Service.

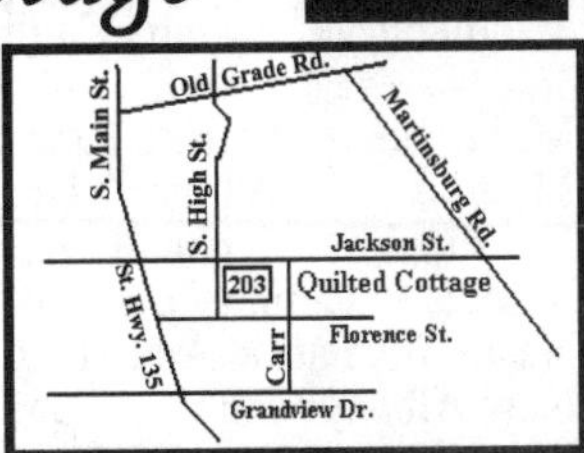

Montgomery, IN #51

Mon - Sat Daylight Hours

David V. Wagler's Quilts

R.R. 1 Box 73 450 E. 200 N.
(812) 486-3836 47558
Owners: David & Anna Wagler
Est: 1980 1900 sq.ft. 1500+ Bolts

Hand Made Quilts on display. Quilts made to order, applique, pieced, & wholecloth tops. 100% Cotton Fabrics, Stencils, Books, Patterns, Kits

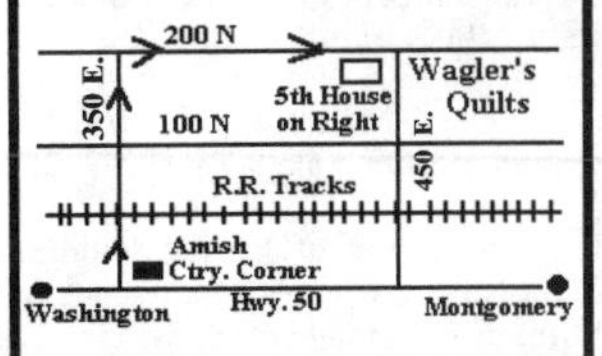

Washington, IN #52

Mon - Sat 10 - 5

The Stitching Post

401 E. Main St. 47501
(812) 254-6063
www.stitchingpostquilts.com
Owner: Mary Dell Memering
Est: 1986 4000 sq.ft.

Southwest Indiana's largest selection of quality quilting fabrics--6000 bolts 100% cottons including Plaids & Hoffmans. Quilting supplies, notions, books, & patterns.

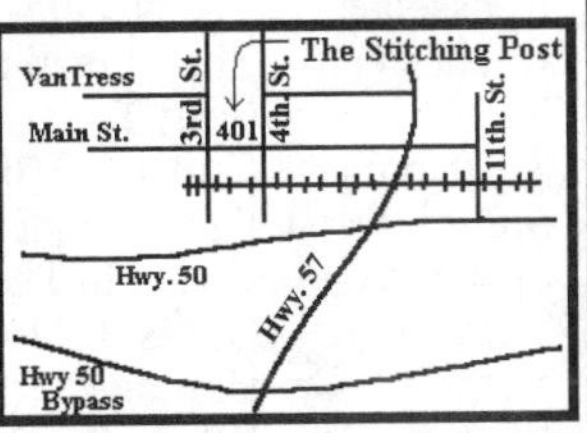

Haubstadt, IN #53

Tues 2 - 8
Fri & Sat 10 - 4

Quilts n' Bloom

R.R. #1, Box 53 47639
(812) 768-6009
Owners: Kathy & Rick Will

Quilting supplies, Books, Patterns, quality cotton Fabrics, Classes, Featherweight Parts & Service, Country Setting & Flower Garden.

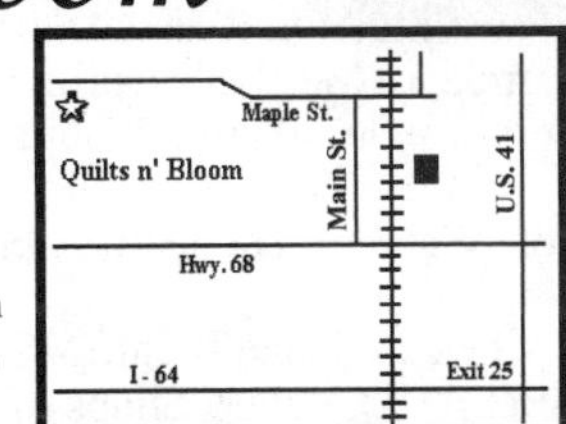

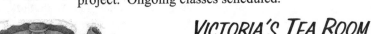

THE VILLAGE MERCANTILE

Boonville, IN #54

123 S. 2nd. St. 47601 (812) 897-5687
E-Mail: villagmerc@aol.com
Owners: Betty & Steve Cummings
Est: 1992 3000 sq.ft. 6000+ bolts

Tues - Fri 10 - 5 Sat 10 - 4

Turn of the century charm boasting a fantastic collection of 100% quilting cottons & homespuns. Hundreds of quilting books; patterns for quilts, critters & clothes; kits. Large selection of notions, stencils plus unique gifts for the quilt enthusiast. Be inspired by our many samples of wall hangings, clothing & critters. Kits available or to order on any project. Ongoing classes scheduled.

20 min. east of Evansville;
10 min. south of I - 64, exit 39
West side of the Historic Town Square

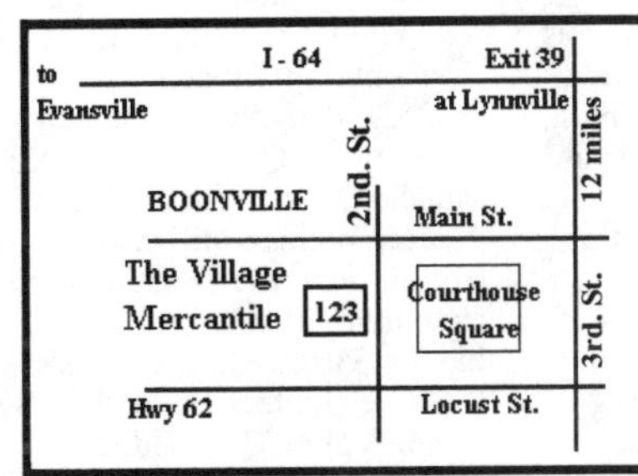

VICTORIA'S TEA ROOM

2nd Floor, Village Mercantile
Tues - Sat 11 - 2
Plan to join us for a delightful lunch in an airy atmosphere overlooking the Historic Town Square.
Scrumptious homemade everything, specializing in soups, desserts, hot grilled sandwiches, pasta salads, breads, flavored coffees & teas. Our chicken and tuna salads are the best.

Plan to spend the day with us - You won't be disappointed!

Pekin, IN #55

Quilt Corner

Mon - Fri 9 - 5
Sat 9 - 4

98 S. Shorts Corner Rd. 47165
(812) 967-4666
E-Mail: lorajn@wertc.net
Owner: Lora Nale Est: 1998 2000 Bolts

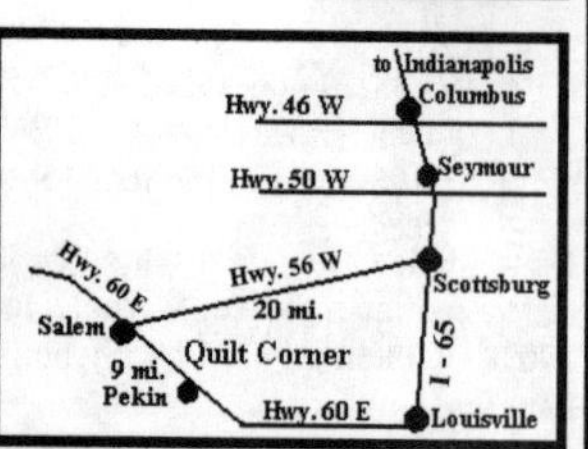

Large selection of Books, Patterns, Notions, Templates & Classes. Fabric includes Debbie Mumm, Thimbleberries, Moda, Fossil Fern, Hoffman, Flannels & More.

Other Shops in Indiana: *We suggest calling first*

Berne Hilty's Dry Goods Store, Hwy. 27 N
Brazil Dorothy's Quilts & Crafts, 5280 N. Murphy Rd. 812-446-5502
Brownstone Quilt N Baskets, 209 S. Sugar St. 812-358-2338
Elkhart My Sister's Choice, 2400 Broadmoor 219-262-5198
Evansville Aunt Rosies Quilt, 2803 N St Joseph 812-401-2850
Farmland Marilyn's Quilting Parlor, 201 N Main 765-468-9445
Fort Wayne Those 2 Quilt Ladies, 3675 N. Wells St. 260-484-6005
Fort Wayne The Quilt Fabric Shop, 481 E. Dupont Rd. 260-338-1050
Goshen Calico Point, 24810 County Rd. 40 219-862-4065
Grabill Country Shops of Grabill, 13756 State 260-627-6315
Indianapolis Carmel Quilting, 4340 W 96th St 317-802-6130
Kendallville Nancy's Stitches, 704 S Main St 260-343-2627
La Paz Homestead Shoppe 324 Vandallia St 219-784-2307
Linton Creative Uniques Inc., SR Rd 54th W 812-847-7780
Madison Joan's Quilts & Crafts, 115 E. Main St. 812-265-2349
Markleville Needle in the Haystack, 123 E. Main St.
Middlebury Country Quilt Shoppe, 200 W. Warren 219-825-9309
Middlebury Laura's Fabrics, 55140 G.R. 43
Monroe Wilmen's Country Store, 421 E 100 S
Morrisville Colonial Outlet, 490 E. St. Clair 317-831-0026
Muncie Country Designs, 705 Nebo Rd. 765-286-0505
Nashville Fabric Addict, 158 Old School Way 812-988-4993
New Albany Jan's Sewing, 2223 E. Spring St. 812-945-8113
New Albany Sew Delightful Quilting, 1613 E Market St 812-542-0079
Noblesville Arbuckle's Railroad Place, 1151 Vine 317-773-3915
Odon Hopes and Seams, 105 W. Main St. 812-636-4393
Paoli Stitch with a Twist, 1040 N Gospel St 812-723-0285
Pershing Quilting & Variety Shop, 119 N. Market St. 765-478-1224
Rensselaer The Needles Point, 125 N. Front 219-866-5353
Rochester The Thread Shed, 610 Main St. 574-223-4959
Salem Craft Town, 21 Public Square 812-883-6860
Scottsburg Quilts & More, 204 N Main St 812-752-6071
Shipshewana Fabric Outlet, 440 S. Van Buren 219-768-4501
Spencerville Cotton In The Cabin, 17727 St Rd #1 219-238-4620
Terre Haute Quilts & More, 1907 S. 3rd. St. 812-232-0610
Vernon Heritage Crafts, 23 E. Brown St. 812-346-7933
Wanatah Prairie Point Quilts, 213 N. Main 219-733-2821
Wheatfield Fabric Cottage, 30 E. Grove St. 219-956-4171
Zionsville Liberty Farmhouse, 25 Cedar St. 317-873-1776

Indiana Guilds:

Anderson Anderson Evening Guild, 1112 North Dr, 46011
Anderson Redbud Quilter's Guild, 111 E. 12th St, 46016
Battleground Americus Quilting Club, P.O. Box 312, 47920
Bedford Quarry Quilters, 47421
Bloomington Bloomington Quilter's Guild, P.O. Box 812, 47404
Clay City Clay City Calico Quilters, Box 107, 47841
Connersville Conner Quilters Guild, 704 W. Third St, 47331
Crown Point Heritage Quilters, P.O. Box 8, 46307
Danville Hendricks County Quilters Guild, 46122
Elkhart Heartland Quilters, 55922 Channelview Dr., 46516
Decatur Creative Quilters, 5342 N 400W, 46733
Fort Wayne Calico Cut-ups Quilt Club, 10013 Teton Court, 46804
Fort Wayne Crossroads Quilt Club, 3625 Amulet Drive, 46815
Fort Wayne Qu-Bees Quilt Club, 1512 Irene Avenue, 46808
Fortville Spring Valley Quilt Guild, 7164 W. Reformatory Rd, 46040
Greenfield Greenfield Guild, 3842 E. 200 S., 46140
Greenwood Quilt Connection Guild, 2321 Willow Circle, 46143
Indianapolis Quilter's Guild of Indianapolis, P.O. Box 68853, 46268
Indianapolis IQ's, 46222
Michigan City Dune Country Quilters, PO Box 8526, 46360
Indianapolis Quilt Connection Guild, 6630 Yellowstone Pkwy., 46217
Lafayette Common Threads
Millersburg New Paris Puzzle Quilters, 10729 CR 46, 46543
Mooresville Carolina Quilters, 413 Conduit Road, 46158
Muncie Muncie Quilters Guild, 812 W. Cromer, 47303
Nashville Pioneer Women of Brown County, P.O. Box 668, 47448
New Haven Hoosier Favorite Quilters, 1715 Duart Court, 46774
New Palestine Common Threads Quilt Guild, 5811 S. 500 W., 46163
New Paris Indiana Puzzle Quilt Club, 68535 CR 23, 46553
Newberg Raintree Quilters Guild, P.O. Box 118, 47630
Pendleton Spring Valley Quilt Guild
Salem Piecemaker's Quilt Guild, 211 N. Main Street, 47167
Terre Haute Vigo County Quilters Guild, 1907 S. 3rd St., 47802
Union City Randolph County Art Assoc., P.O. Box 284, 47390
Valparaiso String-along Quilt Guild, P.O. Box 2363, 46384
W. Lafayette Indiana State Quilt Guild, 3059 Sullivan, 47906
W. Lafayette The Old Tippecanoe Quilt Guild, P.O. Box 707, 47902
Meets: 1st & 3rd Tuesday 7:15 p.m. at Morton Comm. Ctr, 222N. Chauncey, North Lafayette
Waterloo Spinning Spools Quilt Guild, 4111 CR 16, 46793

Meets: 7pm at North Central Church of Christ
Columbus Columbus Star Quilter's Guild, P.O. Box 121, 47202
Corydon Quilt Patch Quilt Club, 47112
Cumberland Love 'N Stitches, 116 S. Muessing, 46229

Meets: 1st Tueaday @ 6:30pm at Country Creations Classroom

Indianapolis Hill Valley Quilting, 607 W. Ralston, 46217

Meets: 1st Thursday 7 p.m. at Community Church of Greenwood
Meets: 3rd Wednesday at Hanna Community Center, 1201 N. 18th
Millersburg Hands All Around Quilt Club, 10729 CR 46, 46453
Muncie Evening Quilter's Guild, 4001 W. St Rd 28, 47303

Portland Stitch & Chatter Quilt Guild, 221 W. 7th St, 47371
Meets: 1st Wednesday at 6:30 p.m. at St. Theresa Church
Meets: 1st Monday 6:30 p.m. at Pendleton Public Library
South Bend Sew-n-Sew Quilt Club, 19887 Alou Lane, 46637

Meets: 2nd Wednesday @ 7pm at Immanuel Lutheran Church

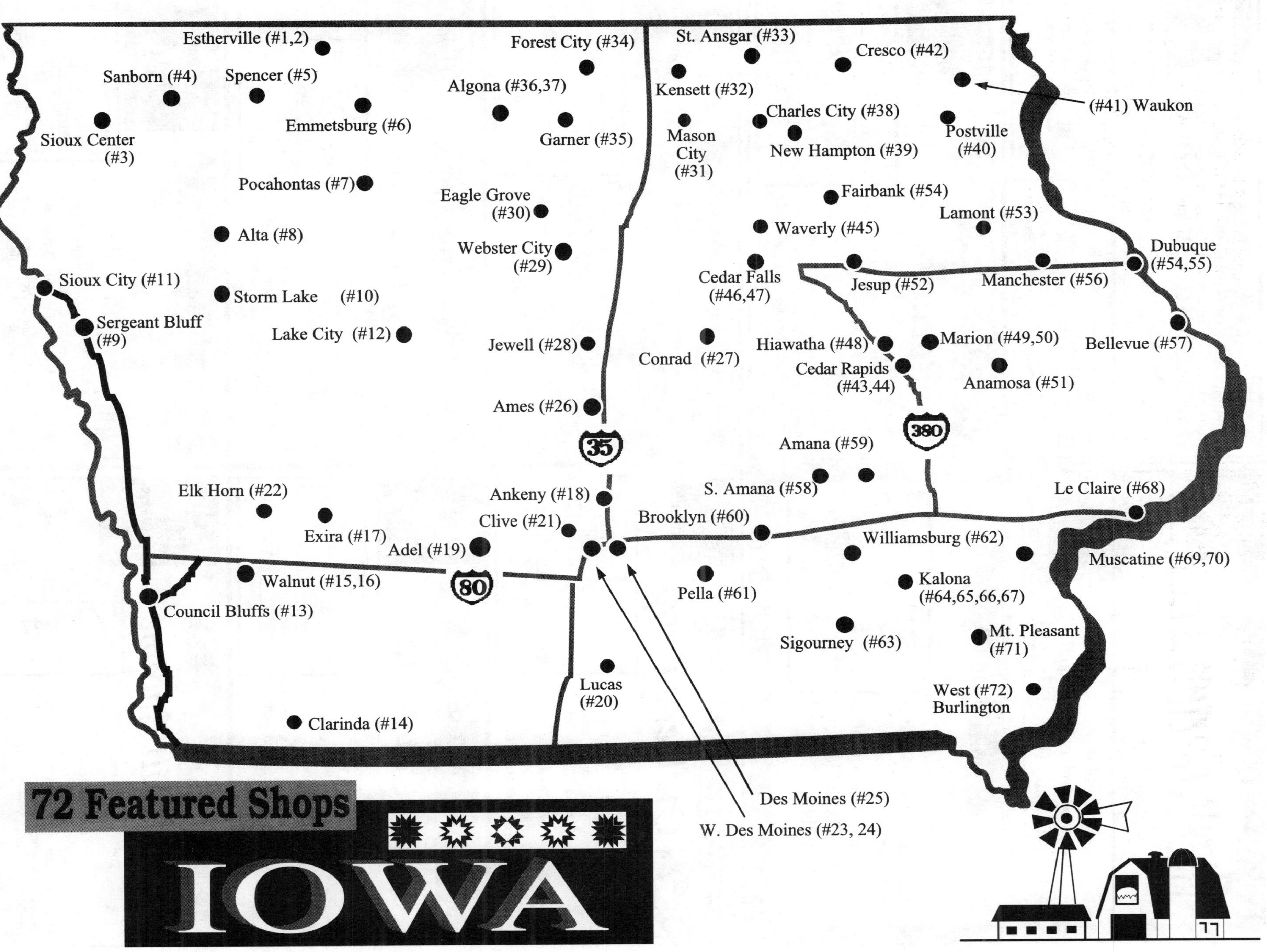
Estherville (#1,2)
Sanborn (#4)
Spencer (#5)
Sioux Center (#3)
Emmetsburg (#6)
Forest City (#34)
Algona (#36,37)
Garner (#35)
St. Ansgar (#33)
Kensett (#32)
Cresco (#42)
(#41) Waukon
Charles City (#38)
Mason City (#31)
New Hampton (#39)
Postville (#40)
Pocahontas (#7)
Eagle Grove (#30)
Fairbank (#54)
Lamont (#53)
Alta (#8)
Waverly (#45)
Webster City (#29)
Dubuque (#54,55)
Sioux City (#11)
Storm Lake (#10)
Cedar Falls (#46,47)
Jesup (#52)
Manchester (#56)
Sergeant Bluff (#9)
Lake City (#12)
Jewell (#28)
Conrad (#27)
Hiawatha (#48)
Marion (#49,50)
Bellevue (#57)
Cedar Rapids (#43,44)
Anamosa (#51)
Ames (#26)
380
35
Amana (#59)
Elk Horn (#22)
Ankeny (#18)
S. Amana (#58)
Le Claire (#68)
Clive (#21)
Brooklyn (#60)
Exira (#17)
Williamsburg (#62)
Adel (#19)
Muscatine (#69,70)
Walnut (#15,16)
Kalona (#64,65,66,67)
80
Pella (#61)
Council Bluffs (#13)
Sigourney (#63)
Mt. Pleasant (#71)
Lucas (#20)
West (#72) Burlington
Clarinda (#14)
Des Moines (#25)
W. Des Moines (#23, 24)
72 Featured Shops
IOWA

The Wooden Thimble

4 N. 16th St. 51334
(712) 362-2561
woodenthimble@netscape.net
www.woodenthimble.com
Owner: Mary Hart Est: 1983

Mon - Fri
9 - 5:30
Sat 9 - 4

Estherville, IA #1

Large selection of fabric, quilting, cross-stitch and craft supplies, books and patterns. Many hand made gifts and lots of friendly service.

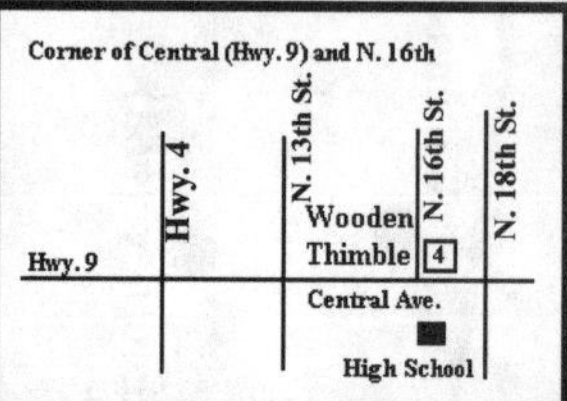

Estherville, IA #2

Mon - Fri
9 - 5
Sat 9 - 4

Homespun Quilt Shop

202 Central Ave. 51334
(712) 362-5100 Fax: Same
homespun@myexcel.com
www.homespunquiltshop.com
Owner: Candy Fredericksen

Quilting fabrics & supplies, Classes, Bernina Sales & Service. $5.00 quilt block. Gifts including pottery, McCalls candles & and much more. "The quaint house on the corner" one block east of the bridge on the West edge of town.

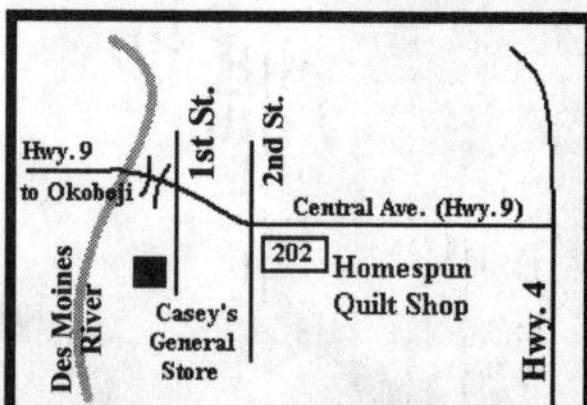

Sioux Center, IA #3

Mon - Sat
9 - 5:30
Thur til 9

Roelofs

24 3rd St. NW 51250
(712) 722-2611
Owner: Dixie Roelofs
Est: 1976 2000 sq.ft.

Quilting Fabrics & supplies; Fabric craft patterns and supplies; kits; hemstitched flannel receiving blankets ready for crochet edge; Bernina Sewing Machines.

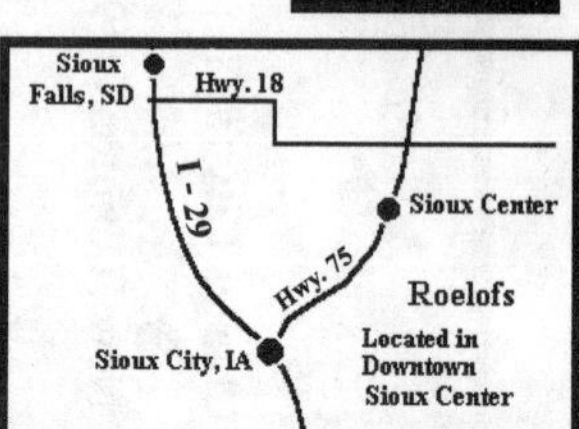

Sanborn, IA #4

Tues - Sat
10 - 5:30

Quilter's Coop

6063 - 280th St. 51248
(712) 736-2204
Owner: Judy Flanagan
Est: 1992 1280 sq.ft. 800 Bolts

Cotton Fabrics, Notions,
Patterns & Books, Original Patterns,
Country feel in an old Chicken Coop.

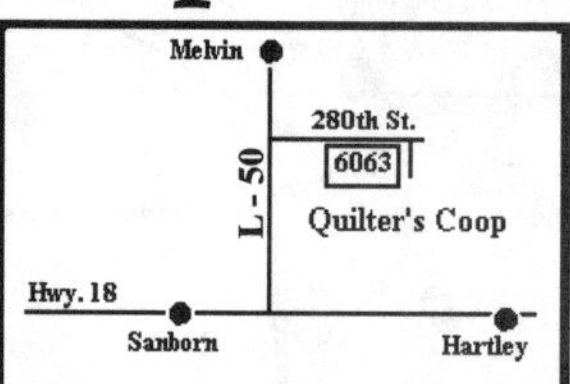

Spencer, IA #5

Mon - Fri
9:30 - 5:30
Thur til 8
Sat 9:30 - 4

211 Grand Ave. 51301
(712) 262-2738
quiltsog@ncn.net
Website: Coming Soon
Owners: Neila Rohan
& Sue Stevenson
Est: 2002 3000 sq.ft.
2500+ Bolts

Customer friendly.
Quality 100% cotton fabrics, flannels, books, notions, gifts, pottery, classes, finished quilts. Something for everyone. Buses welcome

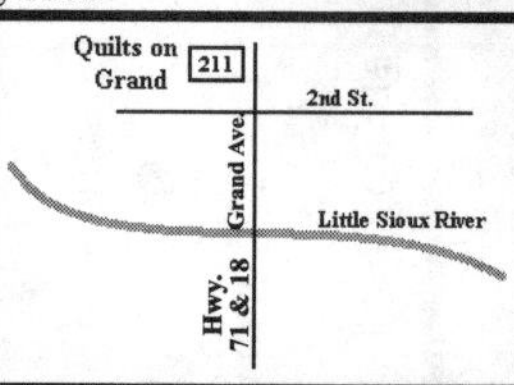

Emmetsburg, IA #6

Mon - Fri
9 - 5
Thur til 7
Sat til 4

Calico Cupboard

2201 Main St. 50536
(712) 852-2098
Owner: Deborah Hite
Est: 1981 2500 sq.ft. 700 Bolts

Large selection of quilting fabrics, notions, books, quilt & craft patterns and stencils. Great classes and friendly service !

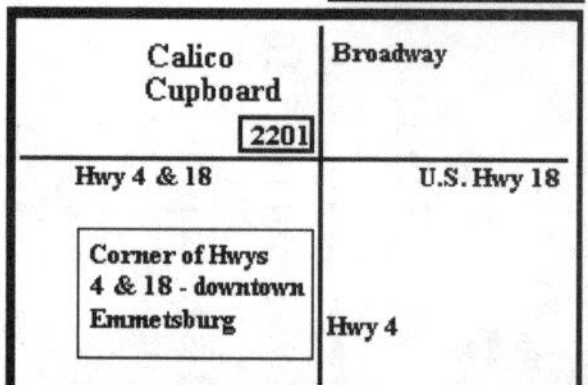

Pocahontas, IA #7

Mon - Fri
9 - 5
Wed til 7
Sat 9 - 1

Quilting on Main

229 N. Main 50574
(712) 335-3969 Fax: (712) 335-3972
patches@evertek.net
www.quiltingonmain.com
Owner: Bonnie Wood 2000 sq.ft.

Full line of fabrics, books, patterns & notions.
Great selection of kits & fat quarters.
Millennium Quilting Machine available for custom quilting.

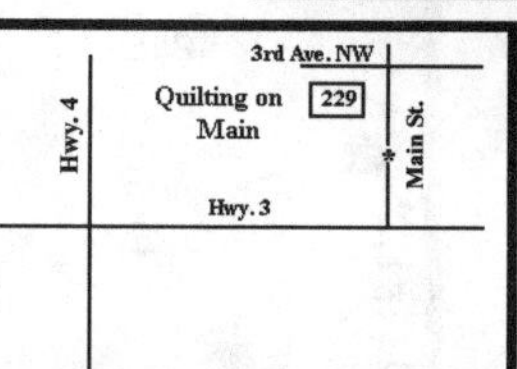

Alta, IA #8

Mon, Tue,
Thur, Fri
9:30 - 5:30
Thur til 8
Sat 9:30 - 3

The Quilt Shoppe

206 S. Main 51002
(712) 284-2724
Owner: Pat Patten
Est: 1987 1200 sq.ft.

All-cotton fabrics, books, patterns, notions, classes. Bus groups welcome. Personalized helpful service for all your quilting needs. STRETCH dealer - the affordable long-arm quilting system.

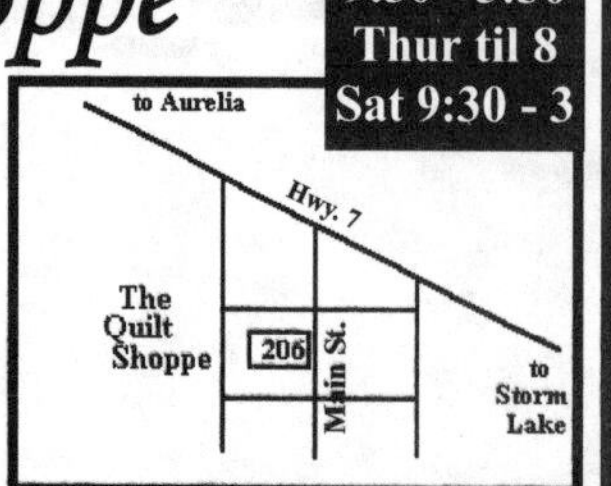

Sergeant Bluff, IA #9

Mon - Fri 10 - 5
Sat 10 - 4
Sun 12 - 4
Closed Sun July & Aug

206 1st St.
P.O. Box 314 51054
(712) 943-9486
Fax: (712) 943-9487
diamond3@longlines.net
www.kimsquilts.com
Owner: Kim Gray Est: 2001 1000 Bolts

Nestled inside the Pioneer Professional Plaza, we specialize in the novice quilter. Our shop is light & airy, our staff is patient and helpful, our fabrics are bright and beautiful!

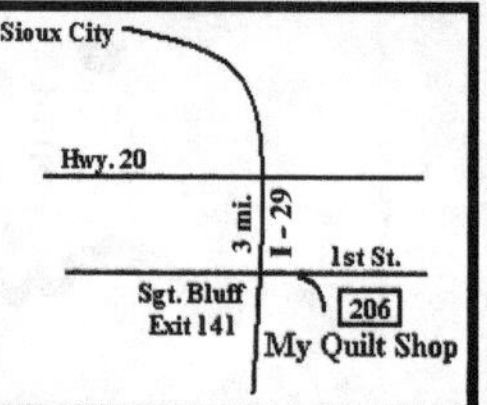

Storm Lake, IA #10

One of a Kind Quilts

617 Lake Ave. Storm Lake, IA 50588
(712) 213-1050 Owner: Bettie Sproul
Est: Feb. 2002 3700 sq.ft. 4000+ Bolts

Not your ordinary quilt shoppe.
100% cotton fabrics, kits
Complete line of notions, Books,
Patterns & Classes
Many Great Gift Ideas
Batiks, Flannels, Moda, Plaids,
30's prints, Award Winning Teachers
Custom Machine Quilting

Mon - Fri 9 - 5:30
Thurs til 8
Sat 9 - 4

6th St. W
6th St. E
Lake Ave.
617
One of a Kind Quilts
5th St. W
5th St. E

Heart & Hand Dry Goods Co.

1551 Indian Hills Dr. #6 51104
(712) 258-3161
Threadhead1@aol.com Est: 1996
www.heartandhand.com
Owner: Ann Brouillette
2000 sq.ft. 2500 Bolts

Mon - Fri 10 - 5:30
Thurs til 6 Sat 10 - 5

We feature an antique-filled atmosphere that compliments the quilting fabrics, patterns & books, sewing notions, gift items and greeting cards. A helpful staff and lots of samples on display.

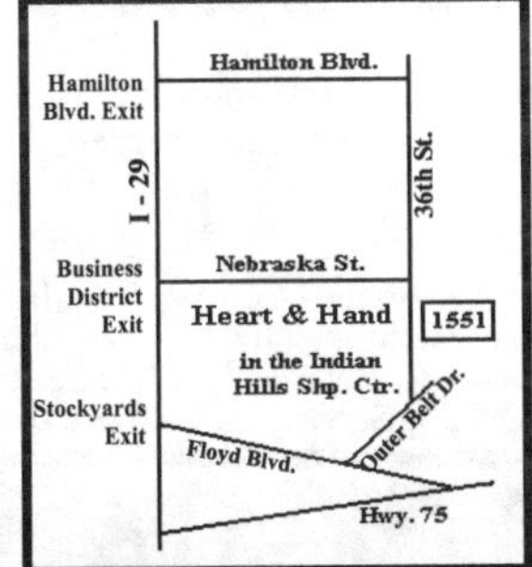

Featured in 1999 Quilt Sampler Magazine

Sioux City, IA #11

Towne Square
Quilt Shoppe

Mon - Fri 10 - 6 Sat 9 - 4

103 E. Main St.
Lake City, IA 51449
712-464-7477
tsqs@iowatelecom.net
Owner: Christi Savage
Est: 2001 1500 sq.ft.

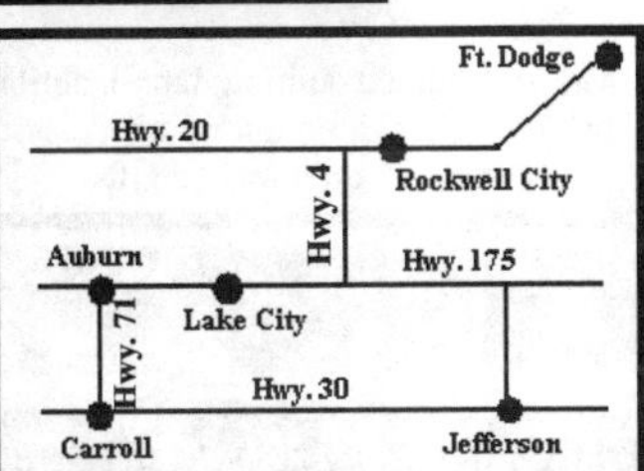

Located 25 miles NE of Carroll in Charming Lake City. Features fabric, patterns and quilting supplies. Come see the quilt block on the classroom floor. Authorized Thimblelady dealer.

Lake City, IA #12

Council Bluffs, IA #13

Kanesville Quilting Gingham Goose

19851 Virginia Hills Rd. 51503
(877) 294-1009 or (712) 366-6003
quilt@kanesvillequilting.com
www.kanesvillequilting.com
Owners: Mavis Hauser & Karen Krause
Est: 1990 3000 sq.ft.

Spacious, well lit shop, filled with 100% cotton fabrics, books, patterns, notions, and the latest magazines. We do machine quilting on your tops. Our friendly staff is always ready to assist you with your quilting needs.

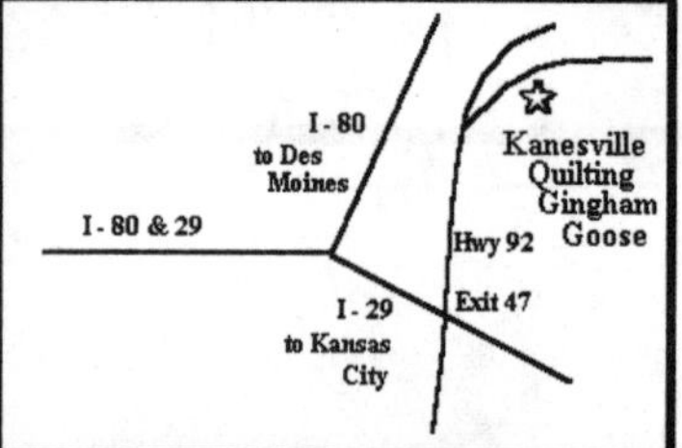

Mon - Fri 10 - 5:30
Sat 10 - 4

East on Hwy. 92

Clarinda, IA #14

Mon - Fri 9 - 5
Thur til 6
Sat 9 - 12

The Quilt Nest, Inc.

218 E. Main 51632
(712) 542-9578
qnest@iowatelecom.net
1500+ Bolts

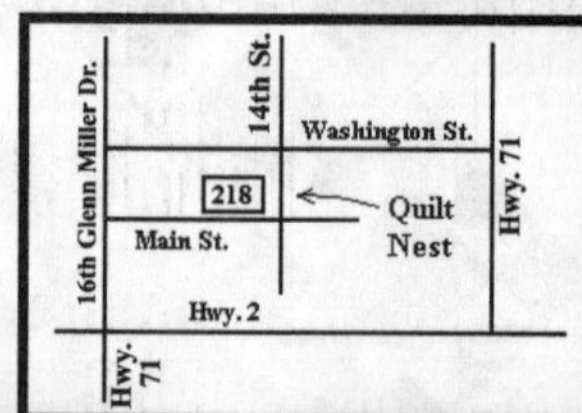

Quality quilting fabrics, plus fleece and felted wool. Notions, books, patterns and classes. Helpful, friendly staff with tons of samples!

Walnut, IA #15

Mon - Sat 9 - 5
Sun 1 - 5

DR's Kalico Krafts

206 Antique City Dr., P.O. Box 332 51577
(712) 784-3865
kalicokrafts@walnutel.net
Owner: Dorine K. Rasmussen
Est: 1995 1800 sq.ft.

Fabric, Books and Supplies for Quiltmaking. Finished Wallhangings to Quilts. Custom orders. Needlework finishing. Machine applique and preprinted shirts, gifts and fleece.

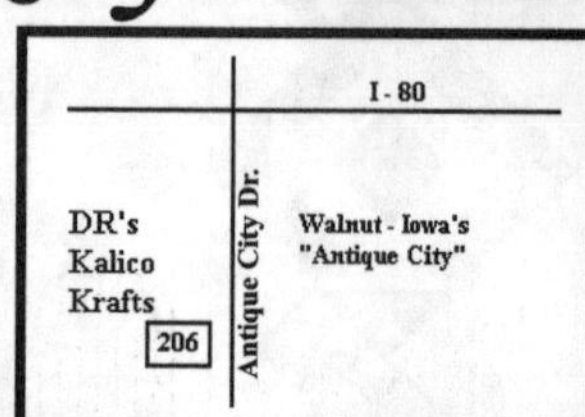

Walnut, IA #16

Mon - Sat 10 - 5

Olde Tyme Quilting

610 Country St.,
P.O. Box 705 51577
(712) 784-3653 or (888) 784-3661

Fabrics which include 108" cotton backing in many colors.
Quilting Notions.
Batting by the yard!

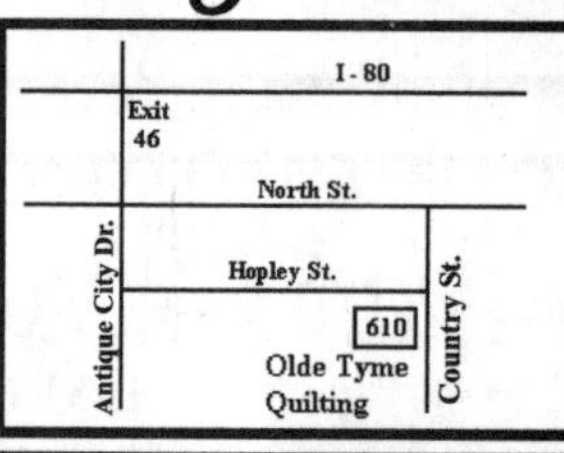

Exira, IA #17

Tues - Sat 10 - 5
Thur til 8

Log Cabin Quilting

111 W. Washington
P.O. Box 594 50076
(712) 268-2487
Owner: Margy Hansen

Machine guided quilting, fabric, notions, books / patterns, samplers / kits, classes, cabin & quilt related gifts.

W. Washington St.
111
Log Cabin
Quilting
Hwy. 71
6 miles
I-80

Ankeny, IA #18

Mon - Fri 10 - 5:30
Thur til 7
Sat 10 - 4

QUILTER'S HAVEN

520 SW 3rd St. 50021
(515) 964-2747
bailey5@netins.net
Owner: Judy Larsen Est: 1985
Group Appts. Available

Clean & Bright Quilt Shop featuring 1800+ bolts of fabric & quilt books. We offer classes and a Thimbleberries' Club. Long Arm Quilting Service. **A Quilter's Dream!**

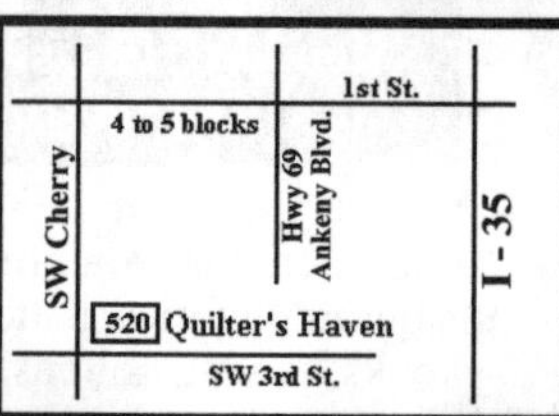

Adel, IA #19

Mon - Sat 9 - 5
Thur til 7

909 Prairie St. 50003
(515) 993-1170
JacmcLau@aol.com Est: 2002
Owners: Jacque & Frank Johnson

Come to the "Little Quilt Shop on the Prairie" for fabric, patterns, books, kits, notions, classes & friendly service.

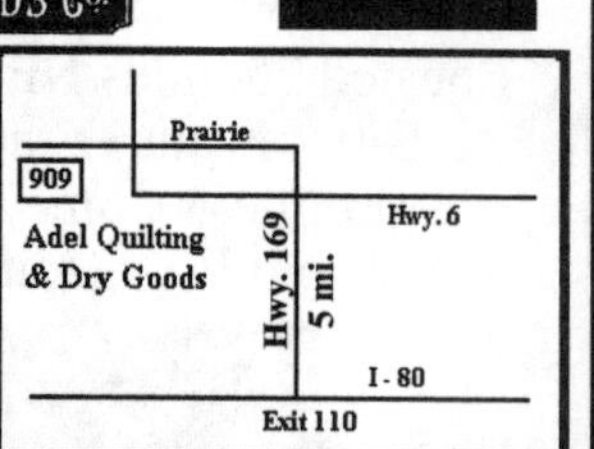

Lucas, IA #20

Mon - Fri 9 - 5
Sat 9 - 4

Quilt With Us

100 E. Front St., P.O. Box 89 50151
(641) 766-6486
quiltwithus@yahoo.com
Owners: Mary Kinsey & Jerri Holmes
Est: 2002

Small town friendly quilt shop located in 1915 hardware store featuring fabrics, notions, books, classes, Chenille by the inch, antiques & gifts.

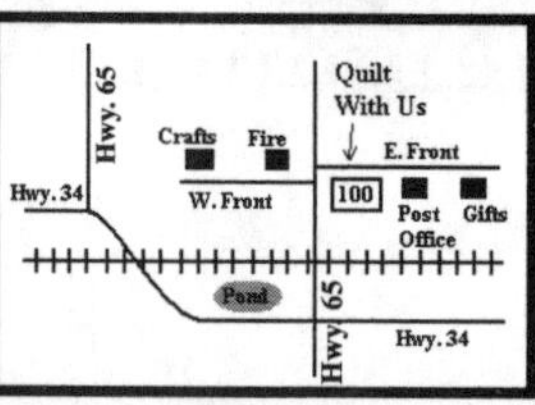

9926 Swanson Blvd. 50325
(515) 276-1977
Fax: (515) 276-2185
Owner: Connie Doern
Est: 2003 2700 sq.ft. C.doern@att.net
www.creekside-quilting.com

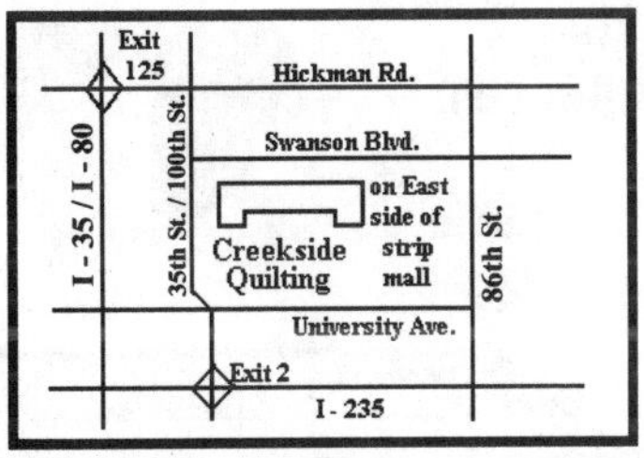

Exit 125
Hickman Rd.
Swanson Blvd.
I - 35 / I - 80
35th St. / 100th St.
Creekside Quilting
on East side of strip mall
86th St.
University Ave.
Exit 2
I - 235

Hours:
Mon - Wed 10 - 5:30
Thur 10 - 7
Fri & Sat 10 - 5
Sun 1 - 4

- 3600 Bolts of fabric from Moda, P&B, South Seas, Kaufman, Hoffman, Benartex, Maywood & Others
- Extensive selection of Marbles, Batiks, Reproduction fabrics, and new collections
- Over 200 Book titles, Patterns, & Magazines. Original Patterns.
- Wide assortment of notions, threads and stencils
- Dozens of samples and kits
- On-line Newsletter
- Friendly staff of experienced quilters dedicated to helping you
- Classes

Come and See us.
The coffee's always on !
Buses welcome; please call ahead

Clive, IA #21

Prairie Star Quilts

Elk Horn, IA #22

4132 Main St.
Elk Horn IA 51531
712.764.7012
psquilts@metc.net
on the Web at www.prairiestarquilts.com

The Friendliest Quilt Shop You'll Ever Visit!

Busses Welcome

Prairie Star Quilts
4132
Danish Windmill
Main St.
7 miles
Elk Horn Exit 54
I - 80

Mon - Sat 10 - 5

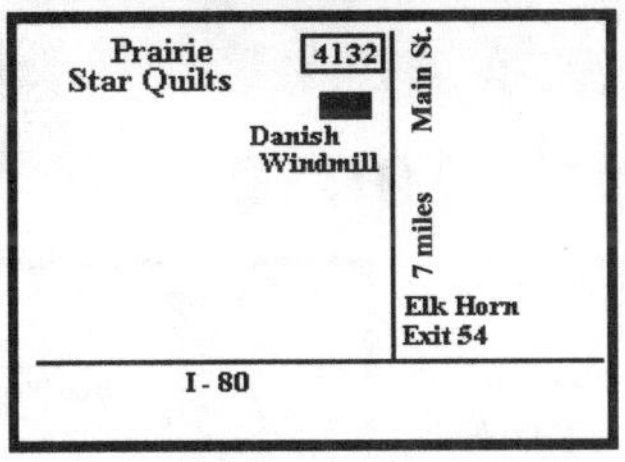

Selected by American Patchwork & Quilting Magazine as one of North America's 10 top Quilt Shops in 2002

Everything for the Quilter
Over 2000 bolts,
Including 400 flannels
Kits, Kits, Kits
Reproductions
Wool Felt
Embroidery
Fast Mail Order
Custom Machine Quilting
Original patterns & books by 5 on staff designers
Quilt Retreats

West Des Moines, IA #23

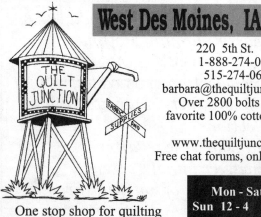

220 5th St. 50265
1-888-274-0660
515-274-0660
barbara@thequiltjunction.com
Over 2800 bolts of your favorite 100% cotton fabrics.

www.thequiltjunction.com
Free chat forums, online ordering

Mon - Sat 10 - 5
Sun 12 - 4 Thurs til 7

One stop shop for quilting supplies, notions, books, patterns, with a large selection of buttons and quilting threads. We also carry quilt bars and hangers to display your treasures. Mail and phone orders welcome. Dozens of samples on display, kits available for many items.

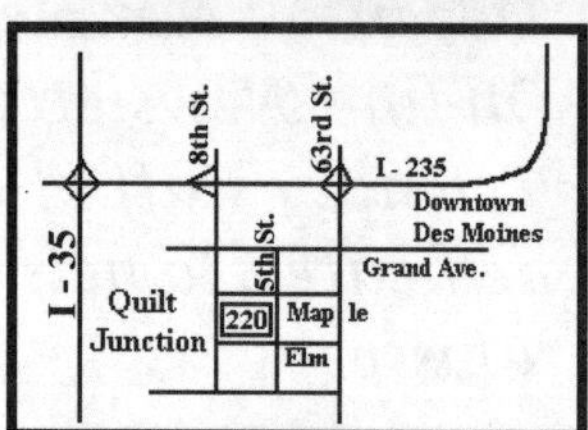

Located in historic Valley Junction

West Des Moines, IA #24

M -S 10 - 5
Thur 10 - 7
Sun 1 - 4

The Quilt Block

325 5th Street 50265
(515) 255-1010
Owner: Mary Miller
Est: 1987 3000 sq.ft. 2000 Bolts

Full line quilt supply store--fabrics, notions, books, patterns. Authorized Bernina dealer.

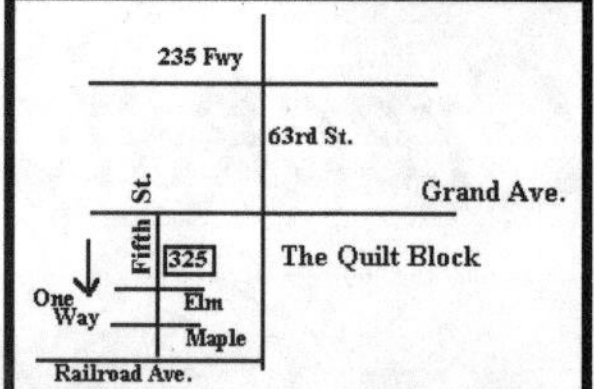

Des Moines, IA #25

M-F: 10-5
Sa: 10-4

Creative Sewing Center

Come and visit Lynda & Don at
3708 Ingersoll Avenue 50312
Phone: 515.279.0019
www.creativesewingcenter.com
Email: csew@earthlink.net
Est: 1992 2500 sq.ft. 1200 Bolts

"Come in as a customer... leave as a friend!"

HUGE Selection of
- Fabrics
- Notions
- Quilting Supplies
- Patterns
- Books
- Heirloom
- Kits
- Horn Cabinets
- Classes-all levels
- Service Department
- Viking & White Sewing Machines/Sergers
- Certified Martha Pullen Instructor

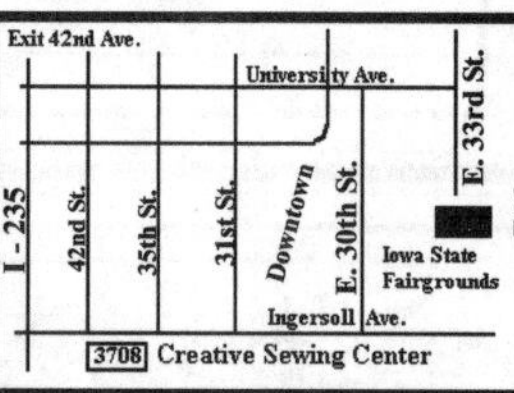

Husqvarna VIKING

Ames, IA #26

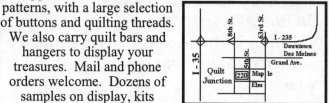

Quilting Connection

Mon & Thur 10 - 8
Tues, Wed, Fri 10 - 5:30
Sat 10 - 5
Check First on Sun.

238 Main St. 50010
(515) 233-3048 Owner: Jeanne Allen
iaquilts@netins.net www.iaquilts.com
Est: 1998 5000 sq.ft 4000+ Bolts

Husqvarna VIKING

Great selection of 100% cotton fabrics including Hoffman, Bali, RJR, Moda. Hundreds of books, patterns, & notions. Complete Line of Viking Sewing Machines.

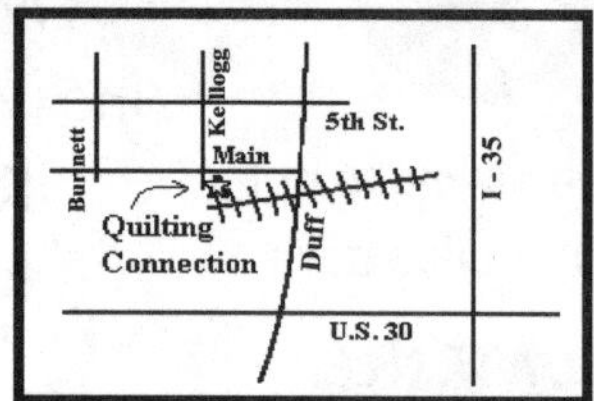

New Larger Location!

Conrad, IA #27

Mon - Sat 9:05 - 5:00
Mem. to Labor Day Sat 9:05 - 1

Conrad General Store

101 N. Main, P.O. Box 726
50621
(641) 366-2043 Fax: Same
conradgs@adiis.net
Est: 1983 2500 sq.ft.

This century old general store has over 2500 bolts of fabric plus notions, patterns, and gifts. Machine quilting and classes offered.

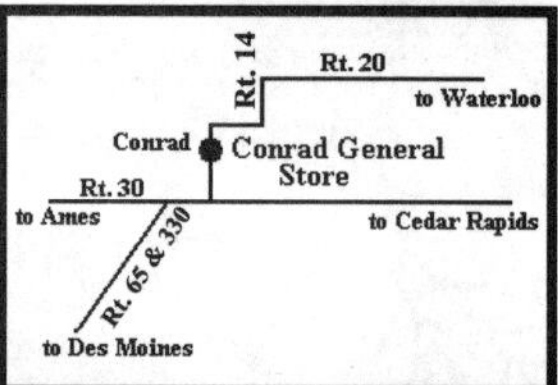

Jewell, IA #28

Tues - Sat 10 - 5
Thur til 8
June - Aug Sat 10 - 3

Prairie Rose Quilts & Gifts

629 Main St., P.O. Box 160 50130
(515) 827-6151 Fax: (515) 827-5670
www.prairierosequilts.com
Owners: Paula Ray & Sara Harless
Est: 2002

Over 2300 bolts in a restored 1900 storefront with original tin ceiling & wooden floors. Warm & welcoming environment.

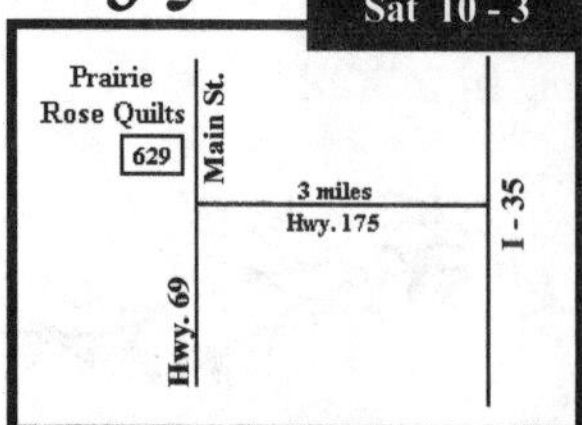

Webster City, IA #29

Mon - Sat 9:30 - 5:30

Gingerbread House

309 Bank St. 50595
(515) 832-1492
Fax: Same
Est: 1974 2000 Bolts

"as unique as you are"
CHECK US OUT
We are one of the most diversified stores around.

Eagle Grove, IA #30

Est: 1987

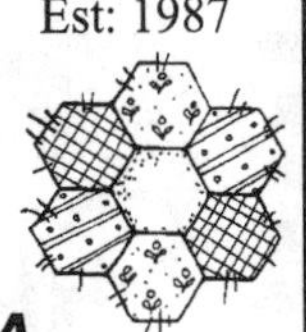

Grandma's Quilts

Formerly of Fort Dodge, IA

(866) 723-9442

1551 Xavier Ave. 50533 Owner: Mary Consier

I am retiring & would like to thank the many travelers who have stopped by. I will still have fabric, kits, teach classes and do quilt appraisals in a chicken coop on the farm. Just give me a call.

Mason City, IA #31

Mon - Fri 10 - 8
Sat 10 - 5

Beehive Quilt Shoppe

Willowbrook Mall
1631-4th St. SW
#120 50401
(641) 422-1027

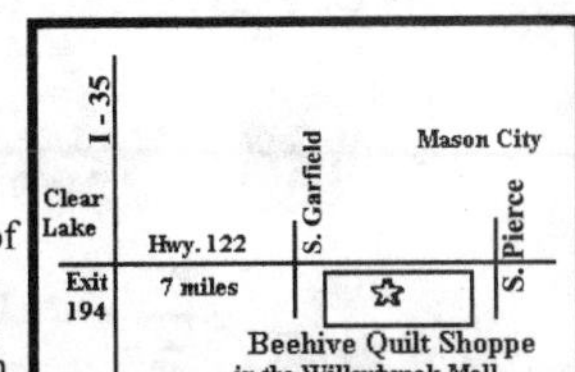

Enjoy our friendly service and large selection of quality quilting fabrics, supplies, notions, books, patterns, and classes for beginners and beyond. Thimbleberries Club and Buzz Bunch meet monthly. Valdani thread distributor.

Kensett, IA #32

Wed - Fri 10 - 5
Sat 10 - 3

Heart & Sew Quilts

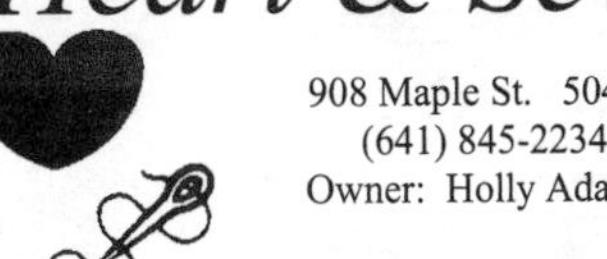

908 Maple St. 50448
(641) 845-2234
Owner: Holly Adams

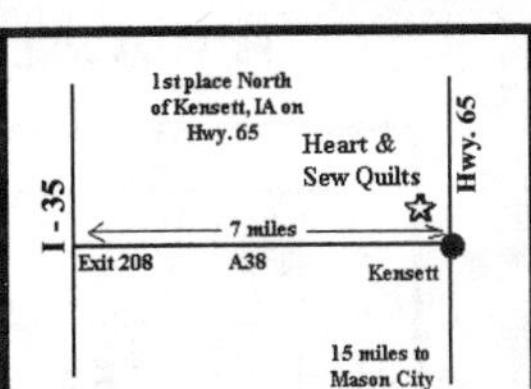

1895 Cottage in the country full of original, hand stitched Quilts of every size, (to warm your heart & home). Full size quilts, wall quilts, vests, santas and more.

St. Ansgar, IA #33

Mon - Fri 9 - 5
Sat 9 - 4

The Fabric Shoppe

230 W. 4th St., P.O. Box 17 50472
(641) 713-3669
Fabshop@omnitelcom.com
Owner: Pam Schaefer - Smith
Est: 1988 1900 sq.ft.

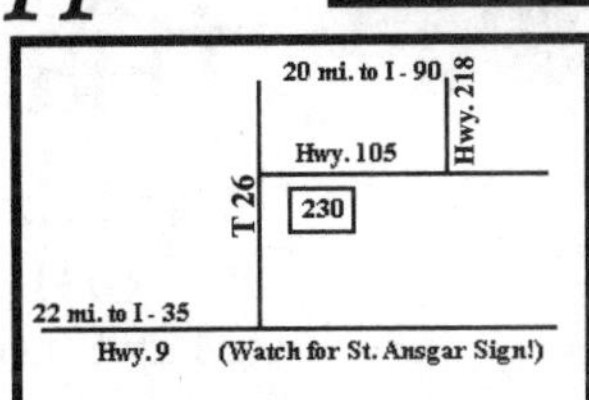

Over 3000 bolts quality 100% cotton fabrics. Large selection of books, patterns, & notions. Classes. Well worth the trip!

the Quilted Forest

Serving You:
9 am-5 pm
Mon.--Sat.
Thursday nights
Until 8 pm

Forest City, IA #34

Offering friendly service and an incredible selection of fabrics, The Quilted Forest has been inspiring America's quilters since 1998. We have hundreds of quilted models on display and plenty of space and light to see them all! The Quilted Forest has a great selection of kits, patterns, notions, books, and original patterns from Pieced Tree Patterns. Funky and Fine yarns for knitting or crocheting, Bernina Sewing Machine, Sewing cabinets, Quality Machine quilting and gifts for the quilter round out our diverse and growing inventory.

A tearoom (Open Tues - Sat) is located right next door and other unique specialty shops are located close by. Your visit to The Quilted Forest is well worth the drive.

The Quilted Forest, 109 North Clark, Forest City, IA 50436

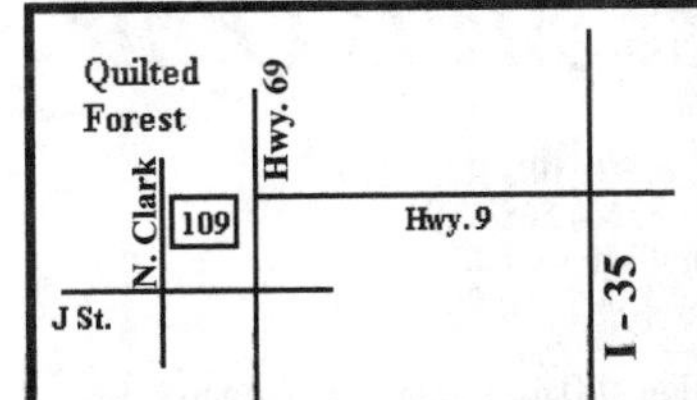

1-641-585-2438 Or 1-877-985-2438

Owner: *Shelley Robson*
Established: 1998
Email: tqf@wctatel.net

Bus Groups Welcome!

Welcome to Country Threads!
A World Class Quilt Shop on a working farm in North Iowa

Garner, IA #35

2345 Palm Ave. 50438
(641) 923-3893
Owners: Mary Etherington & Connie Tesene

Est: 1983 3500 Bolts

Hours:
April thru October
Mon - Sat 9 - 5
November thru March
Tues - Sat 9 - 5

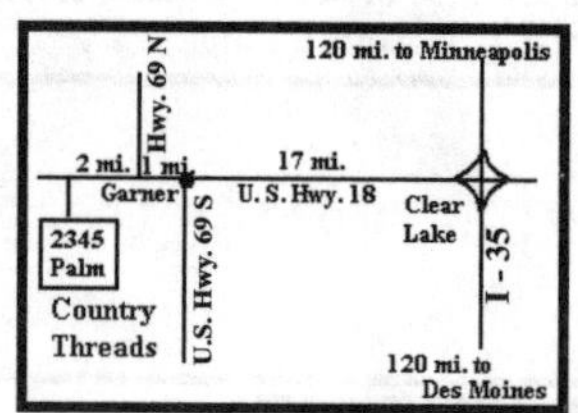

Take Exit 294 of I-35 at Clear Lake. West 17 miles.

Check our website: **www.countrythreads.com** for classes in the barn, what's new in the quilt shop and animal updates.

Algona, IA #36

Seams To Me

17 E. State St.
Algona, IA 50511
515-295-5841
kboyken@ncn.net
Owner: Karen Boyken
Est: 1987

www.seamstome.com

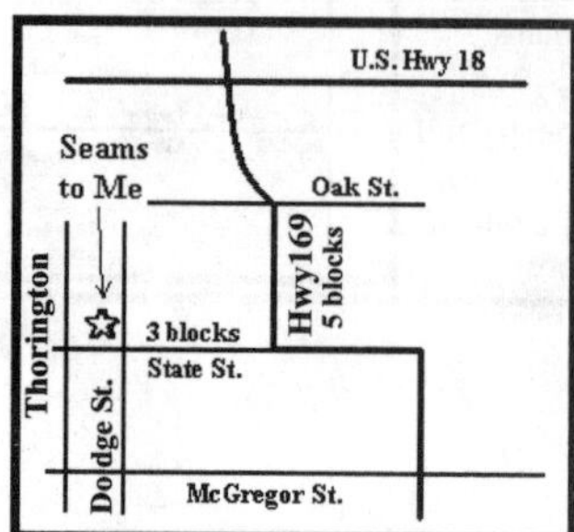

Mon - Fri 9 - 5
Sat 9 - 3

Quality 100% cotton fabrics.
Full line of notions & crafts.
Walls filled with models & displays.
Home of "Stitchin' Friends" patterns.
Mail Order.

Algona, IA #37

Mon - Fri 10 - 5
Sat 9 - 3

Heartland Quilt Shop

107 S. Harlan 50511
(866) 469-1428 or (515) 295-3036
Fax: (515) 295-3049
myquilts@netamumail.com
Website coming soon Est: 2001
Owner: Pat Lucas 2200 sq.ft. 1400 Bolts
Warm country style featuring large selections of Moda, Thimbleberries, Aunt Gracie's and much more! Classes, samples & friendly service.

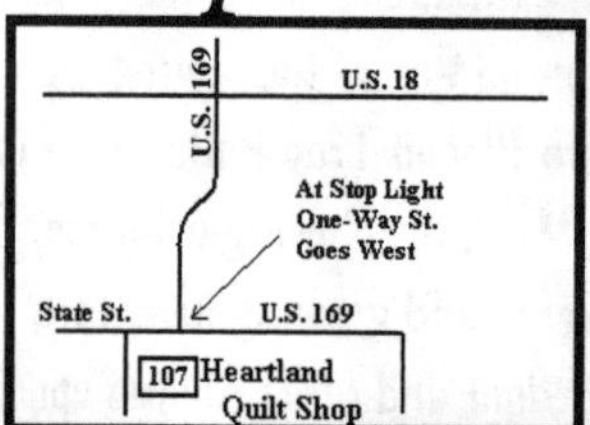

Charles City, IA #38

Mon - Fri 9 - 5:15
Sat 9 - 4

The Trading Store

209 N. Main St. 50616
(641) 330-6880
Owner: Edwin Benedict
Mgr: Marlene Kokal

125 year old building houses unique quilt shop. Visit us for the latest fabrics and quilting needs. Scheduled classes plus in-store machine quilter.

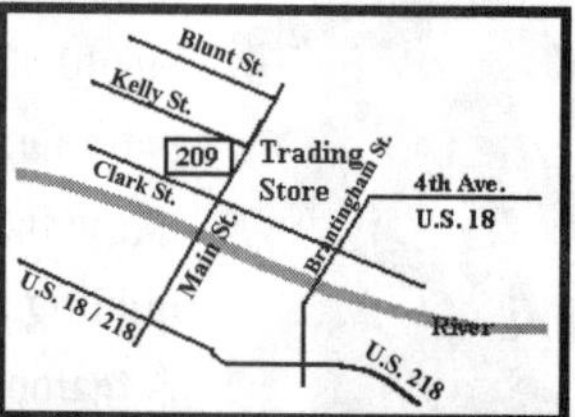

New Hampton, IA #39

Mon - Sat 9 - 5

Material Magic

22 E. Main 50659
(641) 394-2461

Large selection of 100% cotton fabrics, books, patterns & quilting supplies. Custom machine quilting. Hand-made crafts. Classes offered.

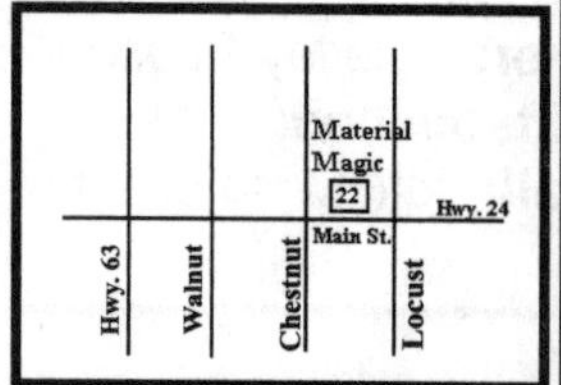

Postville, IA #40

Mon - Sat 10 - 6

Forest Mills Quilt Shop

650 Forest Mills Rd. 52162
(563) 568-3807
forestmillsquilts@direcway.com
Est: 2003 1000+ bolts

Large selection of Batiks, Moda. Gift items for the country enthusiast. Books and patterns always on sale. Fall Shop Hop.

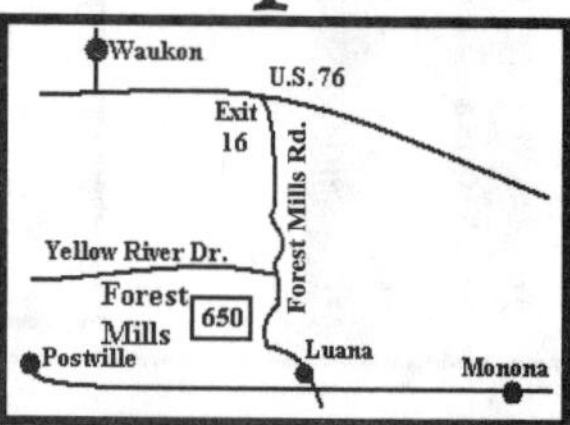

Waukon, IA #41

Country Stitchin'

915 Hwy. 76 South, Waukon, IA 52172
(563) 535-7376 Fax: (563) 535-4325
jsnitker@acegroup.cc
Owners: Jane Snitker & Peg Mathis
Est: 1997

"A Charming Country Atmosphere"

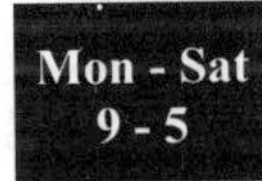

Unique Quilt shop, located on a 4½ acre farm. Specializing in Custom HAND Quilting.
Many samples on display.
All samples are for sale.
Quilt Tops--several to choose from
Quilt Classes Year Round
Large selection of fabrics, books, patterns & notions.

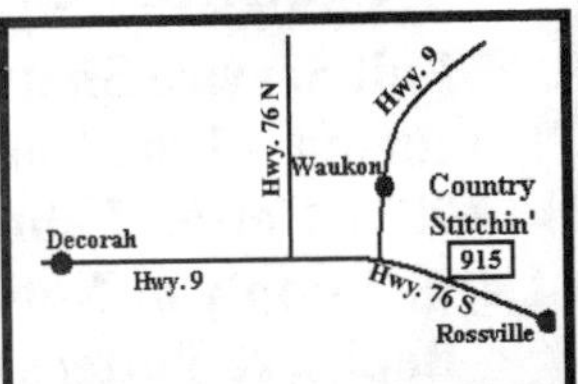

Cedar Rapids, IA #44

Mon - Sat 10 - 5
Sun 12 - 4

The Keeping Room

2345A Blairs Ferry Rd. NE 52402
(319) 743-9929
Owner: Nancy Wagner

Charming shop featuring quality quilting fabrics and supplies. Fabric line includes: Moda, Maywood, RJR, Batiks, P&B, Benartex, plus hand-dyed wool.
A complete selection of Cross Stitch Supplies.

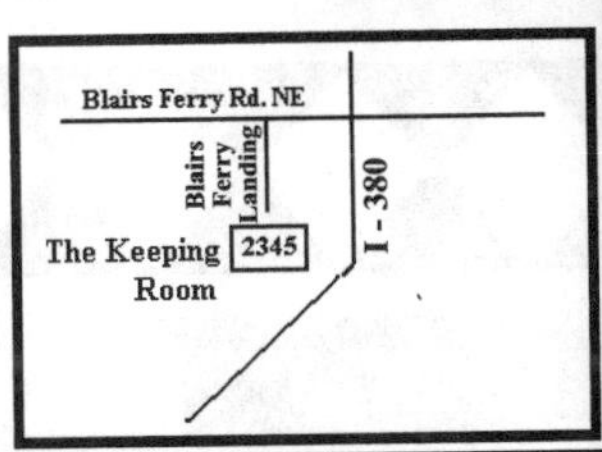

"A quilter's dream come true!"

The Moose Patch Quilt Shop
Waverly • Iowa

All the latest books, patterns & fabrics with lots of displays and samples to inspire you.

Mon - Sat 10 - 5
Thur til 8

205 E. Bremer
Waverly, IA 50677
(319) 352-5040
2000 sq. ft.

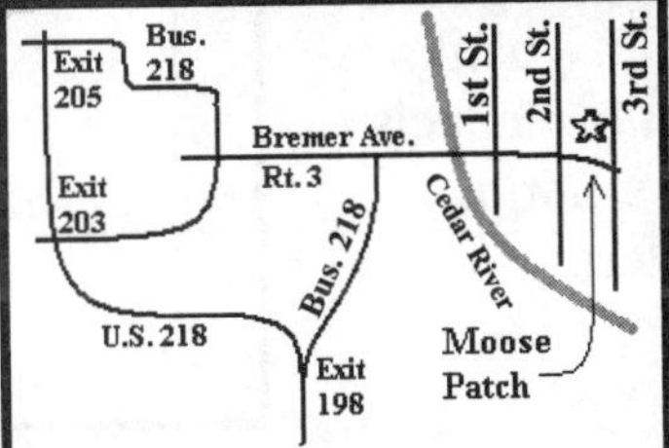

www.sewdear.com

Waverly, IA #45

Pine Needles

Quilt Shop - Sewing Center

People who sew dream in fabric and color. Let us inspire you to bring your dreams to cloth.

Pine Needles Quilt Shop - Cresco, Iowa
A featured store in
Better Homes & Gardens Quilt Sampler® 2004

Pine Needles Quilt Shop #42

105 2nd Avenue SW • Cresco, IA 52136
563 547-1212 • quilt@pineneedles.net
www.pineneedles.net

Store hours:
M-T-W-F 10-5 • Thur 10-8 • Sat 10-4

Est: 1999 - 7,000 square feet.
Spacious, well-lit atmosphere in a

Pine Needles Sewing Center #43

290 Blairs Ferry Rd. NE • Cedar Rapids, IA 52402
319 373-0334 • quilt@pineneedles.net
www.pineneedles.net

Store hours:
M-T-W-F 10-5 • Thur 10-8 • Sat 10-4

Est: 2003 - 4,000 square feet.
Bright and inspiring, located on Blairs Ferry Road in Cedar Rapids.

We service all machine brands.

Nothing Sews Like A Bernina. Nothing.
BERNINA®
We specialize in Bernina education, products and service.

www.pineneedles.net

Cedar Falls, IA #46

Mon - Fri 10 - 5:30
Thur til 8
Sat 10 - 4

Crazy to Quilt

602 State St. Suite C2, 50613
(319) 277-1360
lizctg@forbin.net
jeanette@cedarnet.org
Owners: Jeni Moravec & Liz Wehrmacher

Quality quilting supplies and fabrics; large selection of flannels and homespuns; friendly, helpful staff; a variety of classes; special order welcome. Authorized PFAFF Dealer Sales & Service.

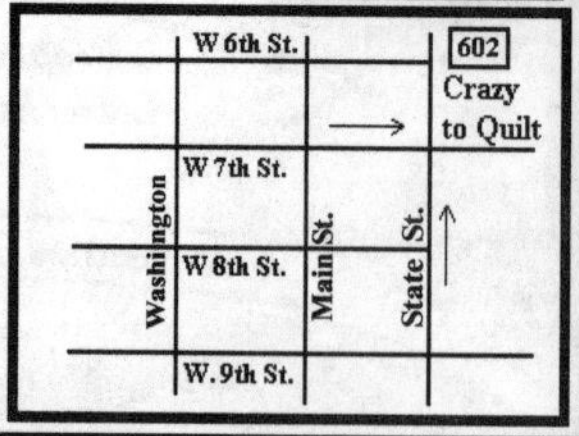

W 6th St. | 602 Crazy to Quilt | W 7th St. | W 8th St. | W.9th St. | Washington | Main St. | State St.

Cedar Falls, IA #47

Tues - Fri 10 - 5
Sat 10 - 4

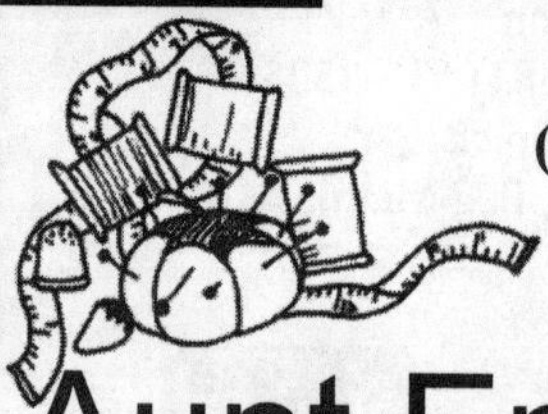

212 Main St. 50613
(319) 277-8303 Est: 1993
Owners: Sara Bockenstedt & Marsha Schoeder

Aunt Emma's Attic
A Quilter's Treasure Chest

Full Service Shop.
Featuring—1000 Bolts of 100% Cotton Fabric
Large Supply of Notions, Books, & Patterns
Mail Order Available.

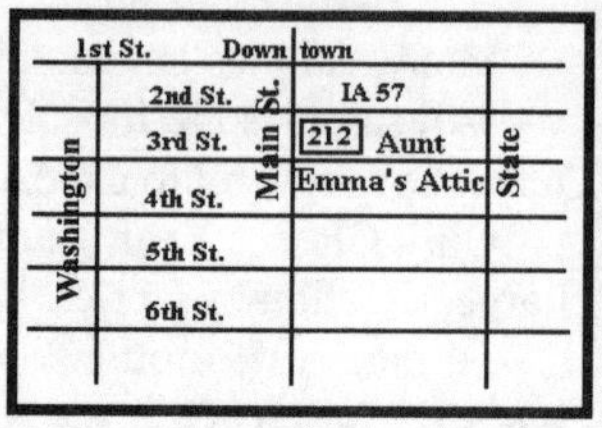

1st St. | Down town | 2nd St. | IA 57 | 3rd St. | 212 Aunt Emma's Attic | 4th St. | 5th St. | 6th St. | Washington | Main St. | State

A GREAT QUILTING EXPERIENCE!

Hiawatha, IA #48

Mon - Fri 8 - 4

Nolting Mfg., Inc.

1265 Hawkeye Dr. 52233
(319) 378-0999 Fax: (319) 378-1026
nolting@nolting.com
www.nolting.com
Est: 1987 12,000 sq.ft. Free Catalog

The original Longarm Quilting Machine Manufacturer. See machines being made. Try new and refurbished Longarms. Machine Quilting Shop, Patterns, Accessories.

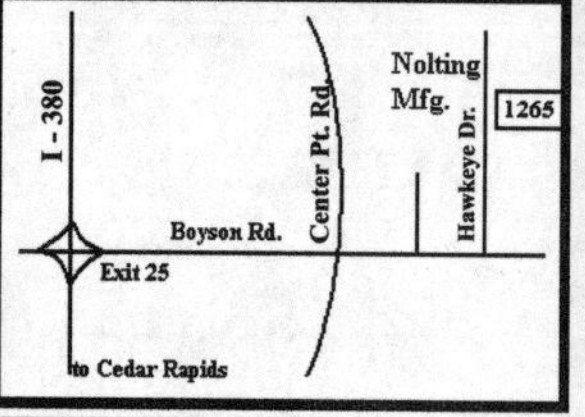

Marion, IA #49

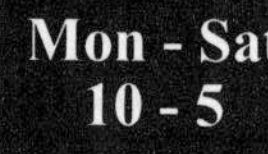

Connie's Quilt Shop

Owner:
Connie Moyer
Est: 1992

785 8th Ave. 52302
(319) 373-9455
Conniesquiltshop@wmconnect.com

We've expanded!! We now have four rooms full of your favorite fabric lines, including reproduction prints, batiks, brights, novelties, homespuns and one room full of flannels. We carry a large selection of books, patterns & notions; including English Paper Piecing and patterns.

Stop in and See Us!!

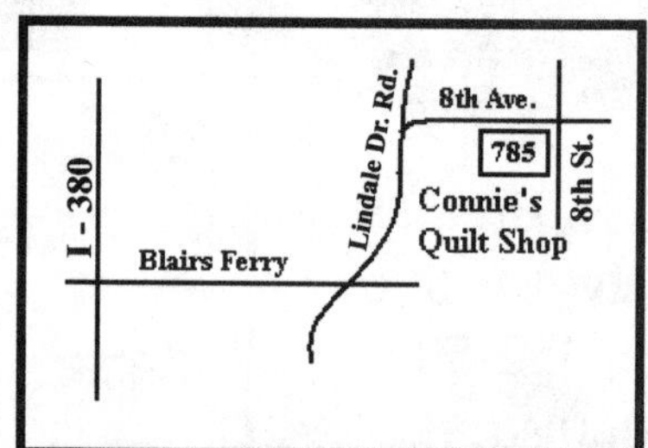

Marion, IA #50

Mon - Fri 10 - 6
Thur til 8
Sat 10 - 5
Sun 12 - 4

"the cottage rose"
a quilt shop

1048 7th Ave. 52302
(319) 377-1482
thecottagerose@aol.com
Est: 2001 1500 sq.ft. 1200 Bolts
100% Cotton Fabrics - Machine Quilting
Books - Patterns - Notions - Classes
Knowledgeable Personel and Always a
Friendly Smile, Seven Days a Week.

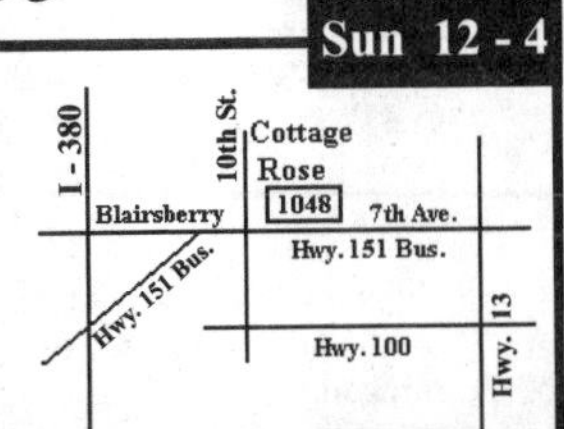

Jesup, IA #52

Tues - Fri 2 - 8
Sat 10 - 4
or by Appt.

Merry's Stitchins

1923 Baker Rd. 50648
(319) 827-6703
merrys@jtt.net
Owner: Merry Backes 3000+ Bolts

Custom machine quilting—Full line of thimbleberries & more. Quilting supplies. Oak quilt racks & Hangers.

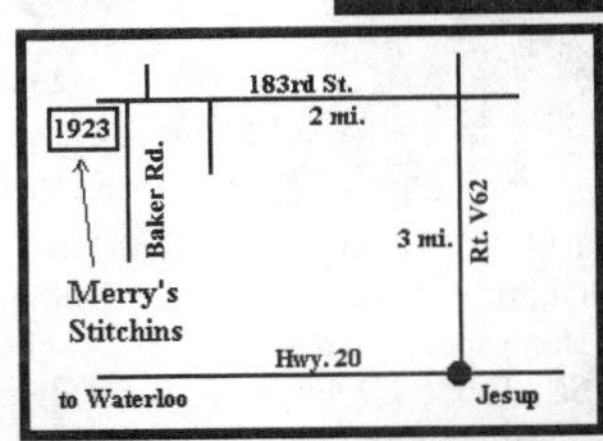

Quilt Basket

12435 229th Ave.
52205
(319) 462-2222
Est: 2000
1500 Bolts

www.thequiltbasket.net

Your Complete Quilt Store
A little off the beaten path,
but well worth the trip.

Tues - Sat 10 - 5
Closed May 15 - June 1
& Dec 21 - Jan 5

to Dubuque
Anamosa
Hwy. 151
Hwy. 1
Exit 49
to Cedar Rapids
to Iowa City

Anamosa, IA #51

Lamont, IA #53

Mon - Fri 1 - 7
Sat 9 - 5

Quilter's Quarters

3290 150th St. 50650
(563) 924-2216 5000+ bolts
info@quiltersquartersonline.com
www.quiltersquartersonline.com
Owners: Mark & Melinda Engelbrecht

Quality Quilting fabrics and flannels, Books, Patterns, Supplies, Notions. Authorized Dealer for PFAFF sewing machines.

Hwy. 3
Hwy. 187
Lamont
150th St.
3290
7 mi.
Quilter's Quarters
I - 20

Dubuque, IA #54

Mon - Fri 9 - 5
Sat 9 - 4

Oreck Plus

5020 Wolff Rd. 52002
(563) 556-2150
oreckplus@yousq.net
Owners: Dave Smith & Mary LeGrand
Est: 1992 3000 sq.ft. 1500 bolts
We carry Oreck vacuum cleaners, Viking & White sewing machines and sergers, notions & accessories, service all makes, quilt fabric, books, patterns & notions.

Wolff Rd.
Oreck Plus
5020
Radford Rd.
Pennsylvania Ave.
North West Arterial
Hwy. 20

Dubuque, IA #55

Est: 2000

The Cotton Cabin
Quilt Shop

374 Bluff St. 52001
563-582-0800
Fax: 563-582-5940
Daynabskts@aol.com
Joe & Dayna Haverland

Mon - Fri 10 - 5 Sat 10 - 4

A quaint & Cozy shop with a friendly staff and lots of primitive country charm. Large inventory of fat quarters, kits, 100% wool, flannel and homespun fabrics along with the latest 100% cotton collections. Classes are also avail.

The Quiltmaker's Shoppe

110 East Main St. Manchester, IA 52057
(563) 927-8017
Owner: Kathy Wilgenbusch

Tues - Fri 9 - 5
Thur til 8
Sat 9 - 4

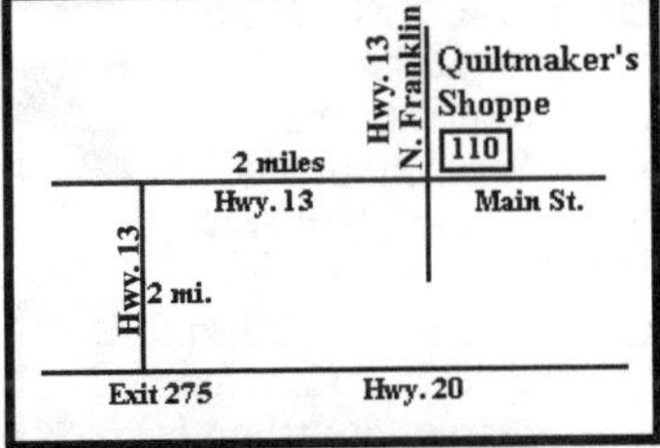

Manchester, IA #56

We offer 100% cotton fabric from the top lines, the latest in books & patterns and a full line of notions. We also have kits, antique buttons and hand-crafted quilt racks & hangers. Come in and see what we have in store for you!

Bellevue, IA #57

Thur - Mon 11 - 5

JoQuilter Fabrics

128 S. Riverview Dr.
52031
(563) 872-3473
joquilter@webtv.net
Owner: Jo Fifield
Est: 2002

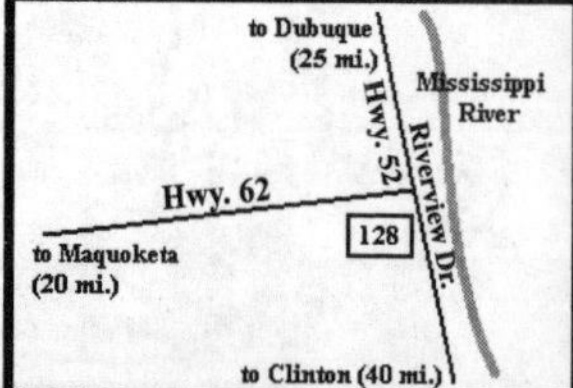

A cozy quilt shop on Bellevue's main street with a spectacular Mississippi River view.

South Amana, IA #58

Mon - Sat 9:30 - 5 Sun 11 - 4

Fern Hill Gifts & Quilts

103 - 220th Trail 52334
(319) 622-3627 Fax: (319) 622-6120
pasteph13@aol.com
Est: 1987 3400 sq.ft. 3000 Bolts

Relax & linger in our fabric loft with 3000 bolts of the latest fabrics. Antiques, architectural antiques, antique quilts, new quilts and wallhangings await your arrival.

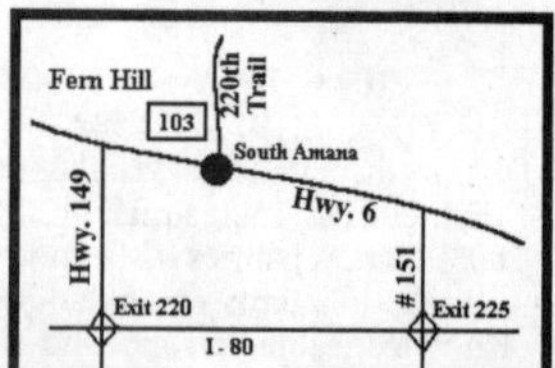

Amana, IA #59

Heritage Designs

Needlework & Quilting Supplies

4517- 220th Trail 52203 (319) 622-3887

Est. 1976 ~ 2000+ Bolts ~ 1200 sq. ft.

****OPEN DAILY**** **Mon, thru Sat. 9-5 & Sundays 11-4**

Ten miles off I 80 on the main street in the historic village of Amana. An exclusive shop featuring supplies, and unique accessories and gifts for quilting & needlework. Find beautiful fabrics, books, craft patterns, notions, buttons, cross-stitch, tatting, & hardanger supplies.

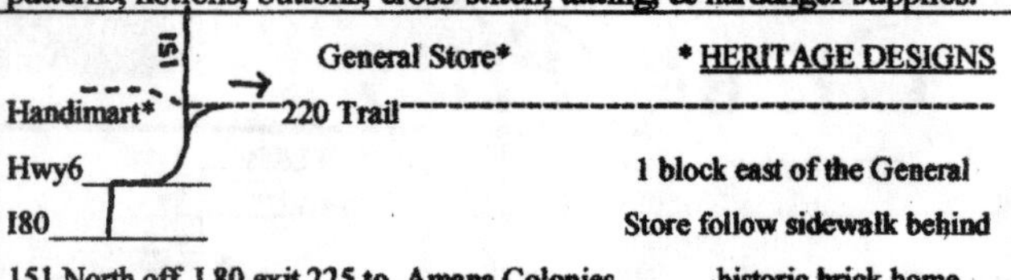

Hoffman - RJR - Moda - Benartex – Homespuns - Designer favorites.
Renowned for our fat quarter table & coordinated bundles!

Brooklyn, IA #60

Mon - Sat 8 - 6

True Value

118 W. Front St.
52211
(888) 522-7712
Free Newsletter

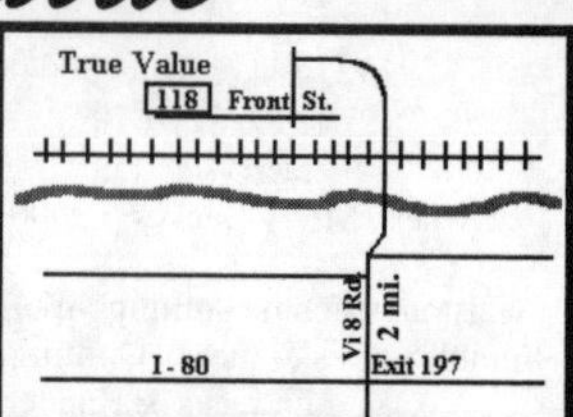

12,000 yards of Quality Cotton Quilting Fabric (Debbie Mumm, Moda, Homespuns), Craft Patterns, Rubber Stamps, Silk Ribbon. Quilting & Craft Supplies. Lots of Models. Memory items & ideas.

Rainbows & Calico Things

Wed - Sat 9 - 4 Other Times by Chance or Appt.

2811 240th St. 52361
(319) 668-1977
Owner: Barbara Wardenburg
E-Mail: barbaraw@avalon.net
Est: 1994 1100 sq.ft.
Web Site: www.avalon.net/~barbaraw/quiltshop.htm

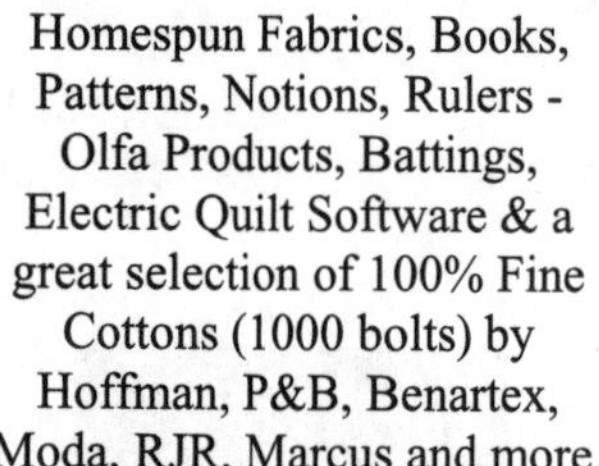

Homespun Fabrics, Books, Patterns, Notions, Rulers - Olfa Products, Battings, Electric Quilt Software & a great selection of 100% Fine Cottons (1000 bolts) by Hoffman, P&B, Benartex, Moda, RJR, Marcus and more.

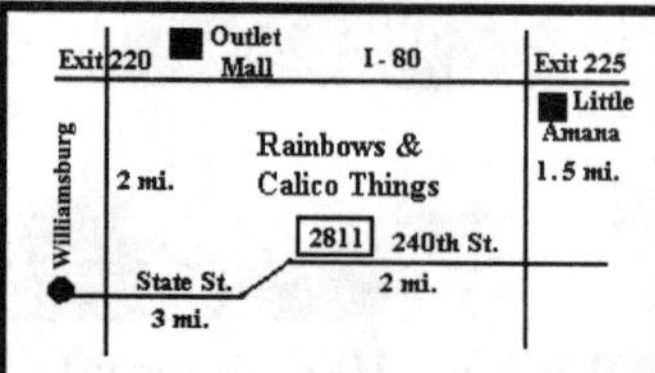

A unique shop located on a three generation farm just outside of historic Williamsburg, Iowa.

If coming from the **East** use I-80 Exit 225 follow map & signs. If coming from the **West** use I-80 Exit 220 go into Williamsburg. Turn east on **State St., (F-46)**, **240th St.** go 3½ miles.

Williamsburg, IA #62

Pella, IA #61

Vande Lune Fabrics

and Quilt Shop

701 Franklin St. 50219
(641) 628-3350
Fax: (641) 628-8968
Located on the Southeast corner of Town Square
Est: 1972

Mon - Fri 9 - 5:30 Thur til 8 Sat 9 - 5

Large selection of the latest Books, Notions & Fabrics (over 3,000 bolts). Come visit our Vibrant Store. We are known for our unusual samples with available kits.
* Authorized Bernina Dealer. *

Pella Tulip Festival
First Weekend in May - Thur, Fri, Sat

A touch of Holland

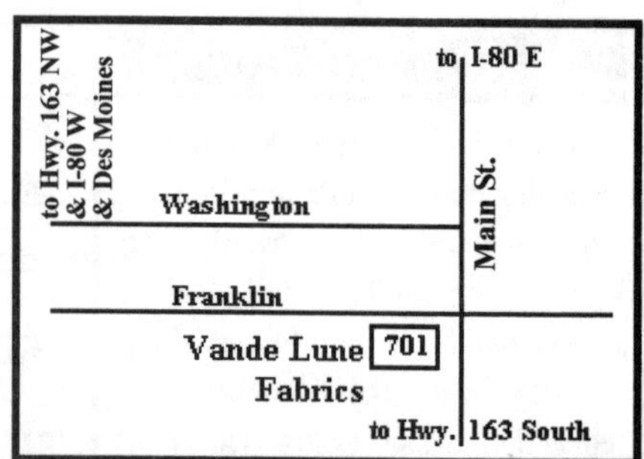

Sigourney, IA #63

Mon - Fri 9 - 4:30
Sat 9 - 12

In My Sewing Room

104 E Washington 52591
(641) 622-2212
Fax: (641) 622-2212
inmysewingroom@yahoo.com
www.inmysewingroom.com
Owner: Adrian Gentry Est: 1990

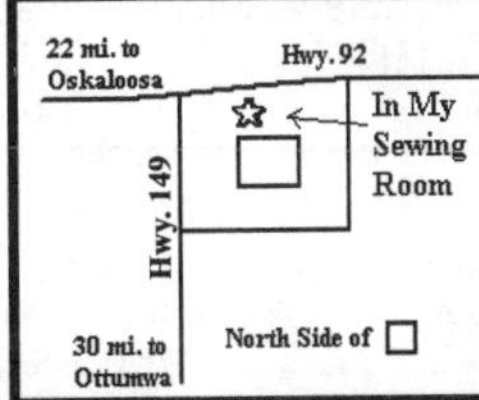

Full service quilt shop; notions, books, homespuns, brights, batiks, reproduction prints, Husqvarna Viking dealer. Southeast Iowa's best kept secret.

Kalona, IA #64

Mon - Sat 9 - 5

515 "B" Ave., P.O. Box 627 52247
(319) 656-2240

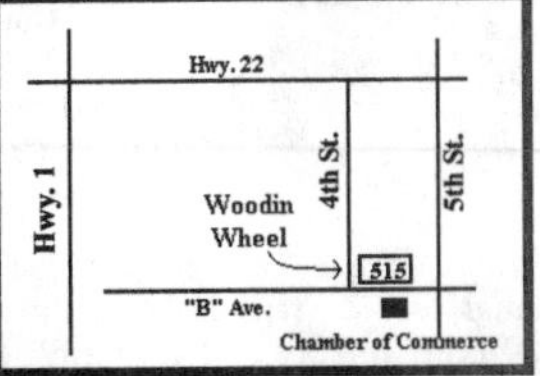

Over 300 New & Antique Quilts for Sale.
Sponsor of Annual Kalona Quilt Show & Sale.
Last Friday & Saturday of April

Kalona, IA #65

Mon - Sat 9 - 5

Stitch N Sew Cottage

207 4th St.
P.O. Box 351 52247
(319) 656-2923 Est: 1981

Custom made quilts, Fabrics, Notions, Quilting supplies, 1000+ Bolts.

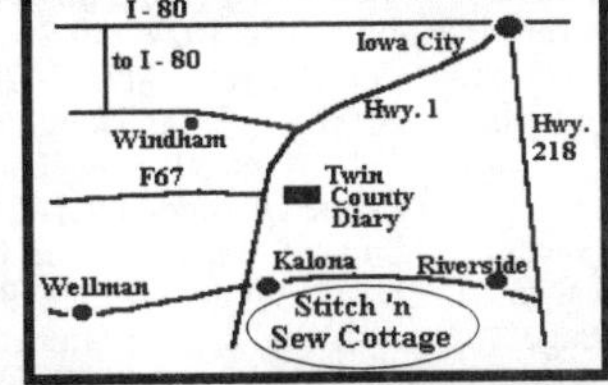

Kalona, IA #66

Summer 9:30 - 4
Winter 11 - 3

Kalona Quilt & Textile Museum

In the Kalona Historic Village on D Ave.
715 D Ave. 52247

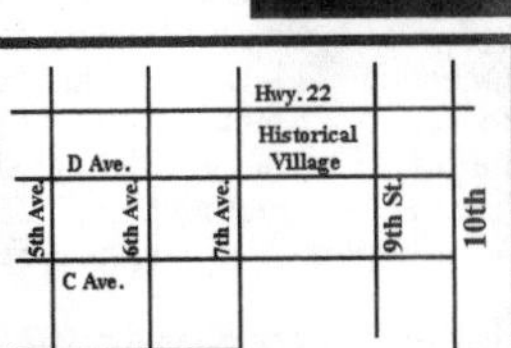

Museum with quilts dating 1830 - 1940
Shows change every 3 - 4 months
Admission $3

Kalona, IA #67

Mon - Sat 10 - 5

Willow Creek Quilting & Gifts

418 B Ave., P.O. Box 862 52247
(319) 656-3939
Owner: Juanita Troyer

NEW FLANNEL ROOM. 100% cotton flannels--specializing in homespuns. 100's of bolts of regular cotton fabrics. Huge selection of books & patterns for dolls, quilts, & stitchery with many models and quilts made up. Many quilt kits. Classes available.

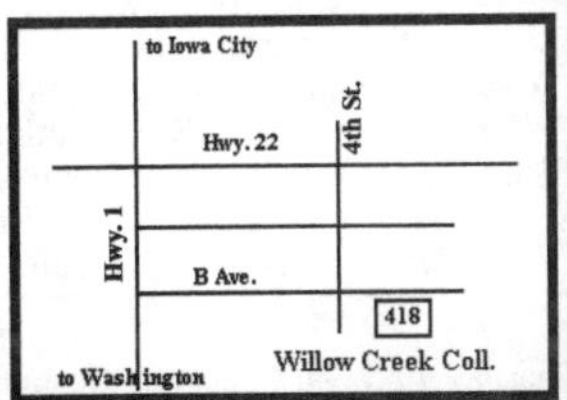

Le Claire, IA #68

Mon - Fri 10 - 5
Sat 10 - 4

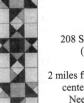

208 S. Cody Rd. 52753
(563) 287-6701
2800 sq. ft.
2 miles from the Iowa welcome center. Fine Fabrics and Needlework Supplies

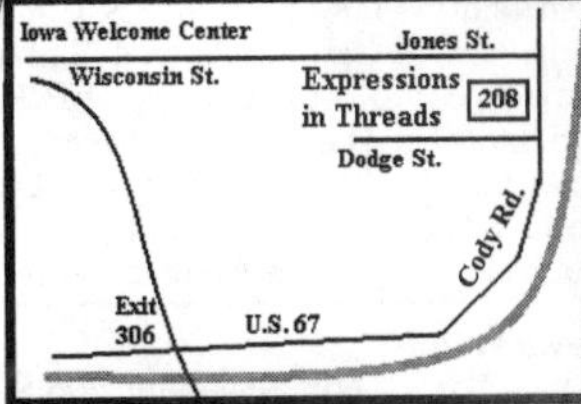

Muscatine, IA #69

Mon - Thur 9 - 5:30
Fri 9 - 8
Sat 9 - 5

Neal's Vacuum & Sewing Center

309 E. 2nd St. 52761
(563) 263-4543 or (800) 362-4543
Fax: (563) 263-7179 Est: 1951
nealssew@machlink.com
www.nealssew.com

Over 3000 bolts of fabric, books, patterns, and notions. Viking & White sewing machines and sergers. Lots of Personal Help!

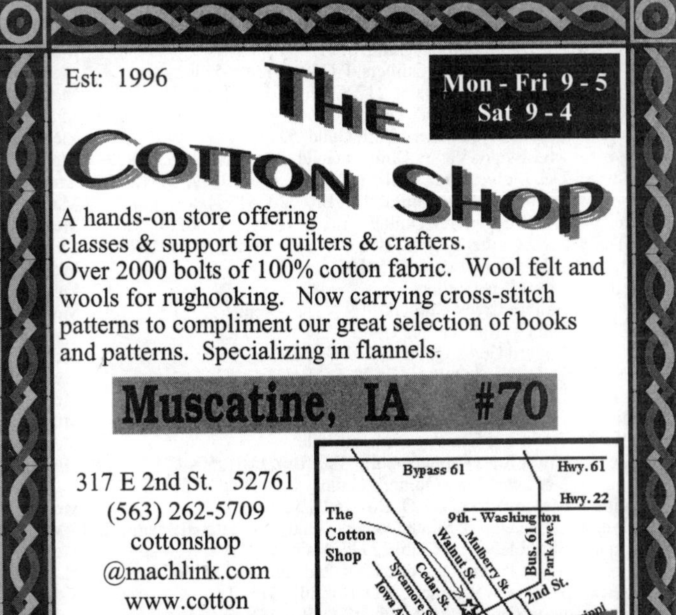

Other Shops in Iowa: *We suggest calling first*

Albia	Prairie Point Shoppe, 508 N. 10th St.	641-932-3866
Altoona	Back Door Fabrics, 106 2nd St. S.E.	515-967-2321
Amana	Fern Hills Back Porch, 708 47th Ave	319-622-3962
Arcadia	The Quilt Connection, 205 Gault St.	712-689-2446
Audubon	Country Quilting, 1752 210th St	712-563-3257
Audubon	Sweet Williams, 409 S. Park Pl.	712-563-3443
Bonaparte	La Donna's Quilting Shop, 411 Maple St.	319-592-3666
Boone	Memory Lane, 715 Carroll St.	515-432-3222
Burlington	The Sew 'N Sew Shop, 3206 Division	319-752-5733
Cedar Falls	Quilting Bug, 7125 N Union Rd	319-266-1098
Cedar Rapids	Treasures From The Attic, 212 Edgewood Rd NW	319-390-1929
Chariton	The Sampler, 102 S. Grand	515-774-2116
Clive	Creekside Quilting, 9926 Swanson Blvd.	515-276-1977
Colfax	Sugar Creek Sampler., 11627 N. 19th Ave. W	
Corydon	J's Nook, 105 S. Franklin	515-872-2709
Denison	Memory Lane Fabrics, 28 N. Main St.	712-263-8383
Des Moines	Bartlett's Quilts, 820 35th St.	515-255-1362
Des Moines	Miller's Perfect Place, 5255 NE 3rd	515-282-8605
Eldorado	Eldorado Store, 29014 State St.	319-422-3097
Elkader	The Backstitch, 20442 S Main	319-245-2967
Exira	Twigs Country Classics, 112 W. Washington	712-268-2622
Fairfield	CR Quilts, 621 S. Court	641-469-4534
Griswold	Quilting Party, 442 Main St.	712-778-2332
Hawkeye	Karol's Quilting, 103 E. Main St.	563-427-3736
Indianola	The Stitching Place, 127 N Buxtun	515-961-5162
Iowa City	Textiles Inc., 109 S. Dubuque St.	319-339-0410
Iowa City	Lasting Piece, 1029 E Court St	319-351-6531
Kalona	Yoders Antiques, Gifts & Quilts, 432 B Ave.	319-656-3880
Kelley	Fairlight Quilts, P.O. Box 177	515-233-4959
Lamont	Tailored Threads, 120 E Main St	515-784-8518
Ledyard	Quilted Plum, 211 Edmunds St	515-646-2034
Lineville	Quilt Loft, 304 W. 3rd St.	641-876-2265
Mapleton	DJ's Quilt Quarters, 322 Main St	712-881-2082
Marshalltown	Firehouse Country Gifts, 13 W Main St	641-752-3360
Monona	Suhdrons's The Mall, 120 W. Center	319-539-2135
Nevada	Julieann's, 1024 6th St.	515-382-5819
New London	Top Drawer, 19472 162nd St.	319-392-8142
New Market	Helen's Quilting Boutique, 2053 Garden Ave., R.R. #1, Box 228	712-585-3678
Newton	Fabric Quarters, Inc., 426 First Ave. E	641-792-6274
Oelwein	Louann's Fabrics, 21 E. Charles	319-283-5165
Onawa	Susie's Quilts-N-More, 904 Iowa Ave.	712-423-9625
Osage	Nolt Quilts, 3416 Orchard Ln.	641-732-1463
Panoca	Quilting Market, 4926 Lynn Dr	641-755-4151
Parkersburg	The Stitchery, 903 Muller	319-346-1691
Ponoca	Quilting Market, 317 W Market St	641-755-2118
Postville	Sudron's Fabrics, 138 W. Greene, Box 225	319-864-3919
Quemly	Quilting Adventures, 108 N Main St	712-445-2224
Red Oak	Quilting on the Square, R.R. #3, Box 39	712-623-3884
Remsen	Dog Gone Stitches, 407 Jackson St	712-786-5279
Rudd	Laughing Lady Quilt Shop, 416 Chickasaw St.	515-395-2638
St. Olaf	Country Calico, R.R. #1, Gunder Rd.	319-783-2445
Storm Lake	Country Stitches, 1122 N. Lake Ave.	712-732-5419
Strawberry Point	Keppler Krafts, 35536 Hwy. 13 N	319-933-6069
West Branch	B.R. Le'Quilt Shop, 106 W. Main	319-643-2344
West Des Moines	Donna's Dolls & Country Collections 234 5th St.	515-274-2522
Winterset	Fons & Porter Quilt Supply, 54 Court Ave.	515-462-1020

Iowa Guilds:

Alta	Quilt Sew-ciety, 206 S. Main, 51002	Meets: 1st Tuesday 7 p.m. at Lakeside Presbyterian Church, Storm Lake
Altoona	Eastern Polk Quilt Guild, P.O. Box 491, 50009	Meets: 3rd Monday 7 p.m. at Altoona Christian Church
Ames	Just Friends, 5712 Valley Rd., 50014	Meets: 2nd Tuesday 7 p.m. at various locations
Anamosa	Calico Cut Ups	Meets: at Lwarence Community Center, 600 E. Main St.
Ankeny	Ankeny Area Quilters Guild, P.O. Box 961, 50021	Meets: 2nd Tuesday 7 p.m. at Neveln Community Center, 320 SW Schat St.
Cedar Falls	Keepsake Quilters Guild, 50613	Meets: 3rd Monday @ 7pm at Bethlehen Lutheran Church
Cedar Rapids	East Iowa Quilters, P.O. Box 1382, 52302	Meets: 4th Monday 9 a.m. & 7 p.m. (except Dec) at American Legion Hall, Marion, IA
Cherokee	Cherokee Quilt Batts, 217 S. 9th St, 51012	Meets: 3rd Tuesday @ 7pm at United Methodist Church
Clear Lake	Lake Area Quilter's Guild	Meets: 1st Thursday 7 p.m. at City Hall Community Room
Cresco	Cresco Piecemakers Quilt Guild, 52136	Meets: 2nd Thursday 7 p.m. at Pine Needle Quilt Shop
Davenport	Mississippi Valley Quilters Guild, P.O. Box 2636, 52809	Meets: 1st Tues. 1 p.m. & 7 p.m. at First Congregational, 2201 7th Ave., Moline
Des Moines	Des Moines Area Quilt Guild, P.O. Box 12219, 50312	Meets: 4th Tuesday at WDM Methodist Church, 720 Grand Ave. Annual Show 3rd Weekend in Sept.
Estherville	North Star Quilt Guild, P.O. Box 330, 51334	Meets: 2nd Monday 7 p.m. at Public Library
Fort Dodge	Fort Dodge Area Quilters, 1422 1st Ave. N, 50501	Meets: 2nd Tuesday 7 p.m. at First Congregational United Church of Christ
Garden City	Iowa Quilter's Guild, Box 65, 31446 Prairie St., 50102	
Iowa City	Quilting for Fun, 52240	
Gilbert	Fabricators, Box 267, 50105	Meets at: 3rd Monday 7 p.m. at Gilbert Luthern Church, 135 School St.
Grinnell	Jewel Box Quilters	Meets: 2nd Thursday 7 p.m. at St. Mary's Parish Ed. Center
Huxley	Ballard Creek Quilters, 209 N 2nd Avenue	Meets: 2nd Tuesday @ 7pm at Fjeldberg Lutheran Church
Iowa City	Old Capitol Quilters Guild	
Juxley	Ballard Creek Quilters, 209 N 2nd Ave	Meets: 2nd Tuesday 7PM at Fjeldberg Lutheran Church
Kalona	Old Capital Quilters Guild, PO Box 252, 52247	Meets: 2nd Monday at Our Redeemer Lutheran Church, Iowa City
Laurens	Lauren Quilt Guild, 50554	Meets: 1st Monday at Methodist Church, 201 W. Main
Manchester	Heartland Quilters Guild, P.O. Box 134, 52057	Meets: 3rd Thursday at Good Neighbor Home
Maquoketa	Town and Country Quilters Guild	Meets: 1st Monday 6:30pm Senior Center
Mason City	North Iowa Quilters Guild, P.O. Box 1163, 50402	Meets: 2nd Wednesday
Orange City	Sioux Prairie Quilters, 116 Colorado NW, 51041	
Monona	Northeast Iowa Quilter's Guild P.O. Box 43 52159	
Muscatine	Melon Patchers, P.O. Box 1621, 52761	Meets: 4th Thursday 7 p.m. at Mulford Church, 2400 Hershey
New Hampton	Clip & Stitch Quilters Guild, c/o Material Magic, 22 E. Main, 50659	Meets: 3rd Monday 7 p.m. (Sept. - May) at New Hamton Community Center
Pocahontas	Thimbleberries Club, 229 N. Main, 50574	Meets: 3rd Tuesday 1:30 or 7 p.m. at Quilting on Main
Sioux Center	Sioux Prairie Quilters, 1689 2nd Ave. SE, 51250	Meets: 1st & 3rd Monday (Sept - May) and once a-month (June - Aug.)
Sioux City	Siouxland Samplers, P.O. Box 162, 51102	Meets: 2nd Monday at 7 p.m. at Council Oaks Community Center
Toledo	Stitch n Go Quilters	Meets: 3rd Monday 7 p.m. at Sewtique Fabrics
Sloan	Four Seasons Quilt Guild, P.O. Box 178, 51055	
Story City	Story City Quilt Guild, 626 Broad St., 50248	Meets: 3rd Tuesday 8:30 a.m. or 7 p.m. at Quilters Corner
Waverly	Friendship Quilters Guild, 50677	Meets: 2nd Thursday @ 7pm at Reedemer Lutheran Church
Wellman	Kountry Quilter's Guild, 52356	Meets: 3rd Monday 7 p.m. at Wellman Senior Center
West Des Moines	Des Moines Area Quilt Guild, 50265	Meets: 4th Tuesday at 1 or 7 p.m. at WDM Methodist Church
Williamsburg	Iowa Country Heartland Quilters	Meets: 3rd Monday at 7 p.m. at Presbyterian Church on Hwy 149

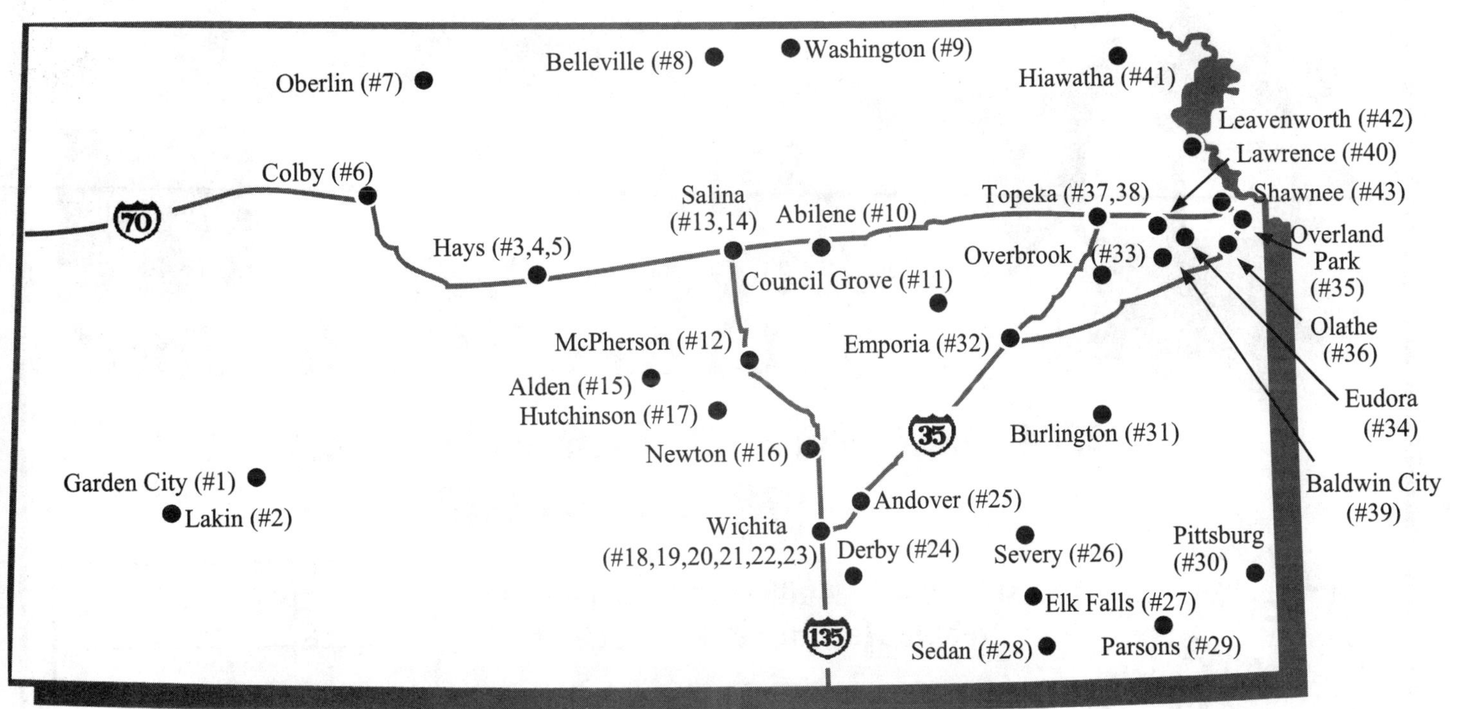
Oberlin (#7)
Belleville (#8)
Washington (#9)
Hiawatha (#41)
Leavenworth (#42)
Lawrence (#40)
Shawnee (#43)
Overland Park (#35)
Olathe (#36)
Eudora (#34)
Baldwin City (#39)
Colby (#6)
70
Salina (#13,14)
Abilene (#10)
Topeka (#37,38)
Overbrook (#33)
Hays (#3,4,5)
Council Grove (#11)
Emporia (#32)
McPherson (#12)
Alden (#15)
Hutchinson (#17)
35
Burlington (#31)
Newton (#16)
Garden City (#1)
Lakin (#2)
Andover (#25)
Wichita (#18,19,20,21,22,23)
Derby (#24)
Severy (#26)
Pittsburg (#30)
Elk Falls (#27)
135
Sedan (#28)
Parsons (#29)

KANSAS
43 Featured Shops

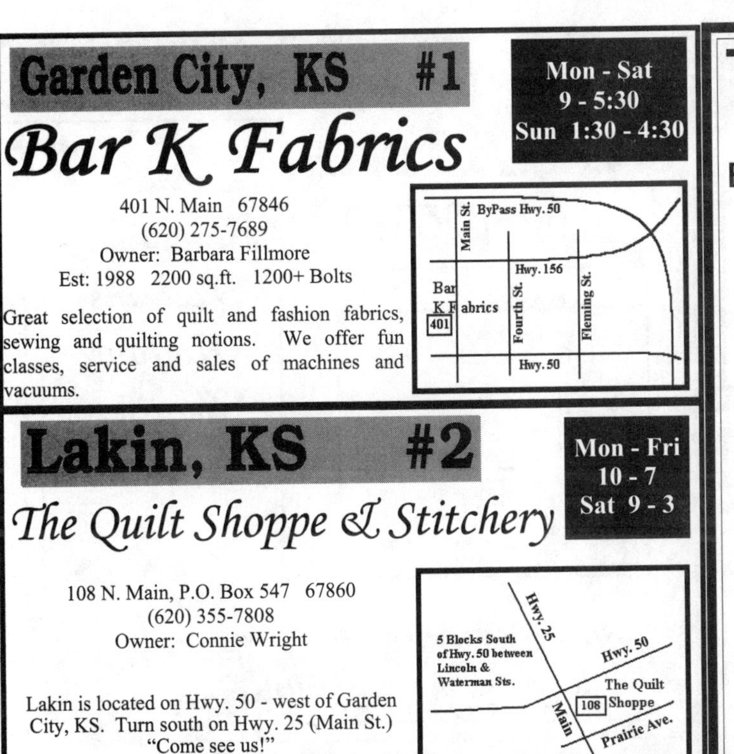
Garden City, KS #1
Mon - Sat
9 - 5:30
Sun 1:30 - 4:30
Bar K Fabrics
401 N. Main 67846
(620) 275-7689
Owner: Barbara Fillmore
Est: 1988 2200 sq.ft. 1200+ Bolts
Great selection of quilt and fashion fabrics, sewing and quilting notions. We offer fun classes, service and sales of machines and vacuums.
Main St.
ByPass Hwy. 50
Hwy. 156
Bar K Fabrics
401
Fourth St.
Fleming St.
Hwy. 50
Lakin, KS #2
Mon - Fri
10 - 7
Sat 9 - 3
The Quilt Shoppe & Stitchery
108 N. Main, P.O. Box 547 67860
(620) 355-7808
Owner: Connie Wright
Lakin is located on Hwy. 50 - west of Garden City, KS. Turn south on Hwy. 25 (Main St.)
"Come see us!"
Hwy. 25
5 Blocks South of Hwy. 50 between Lincoln & Waterman Sts.
Hwy. 50
The Quilt Shoppe
108
Main
Prairie Ave.

Tumbleweed Crossing
Quilt & Bridal Fabrics
1010 Main, 67601
(Historic Downtown Hays)
(785) 625-8122
Owners: Diane Werth & Frances Shearer
Est: 1995 2500 sq.ft. 2000 Bolts
Mon - Fri
9:30 - 5:30
Sat 9:30 - 4
I - 70
Exit 159
27th St.
Hwy. 183
Main St.
13th St.
1010
Tumbleweed Crossing
Hays, KS #3
www.tumbleweedcrossing.com

Hays, KS #4

Quilt Cottage Co. & Cross Stitch, Too!

Mon - Fri 10 - 5:30
Sat 10 - 3

2504 Vine (corner of Centennial and Vine) 67601
(785) 625-0080

NEW!!! We now carry yarn and knitting supplies

Est: 1994 4000 sq.ft. 2500 Bolts
Debbie Huebner & Kari Schultz

Top quality quilting fabrics.
The area's finest selection of books, patterns and notions.
Cross-stitch fabrics, patterns & DMC floss.

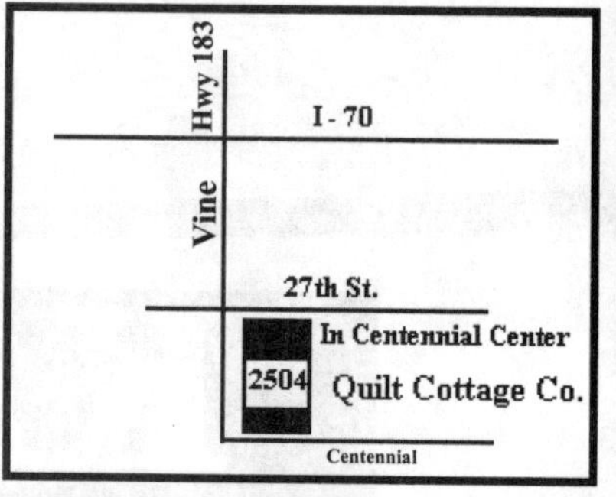

Hays, KS #5

Mon - Fri 10 - 4

Quilt & Sew

1111 E. 30th - White Dome 67601
(785) 625-5712 or (888) 625-5712
QuiltandSew@spidome.net
Est: 2003

Elna & Singer, Machine Quilting, Classes
Sewing Machines Sales & Service.
KenQuilt Quilting Machines - Sales & Service & Rental

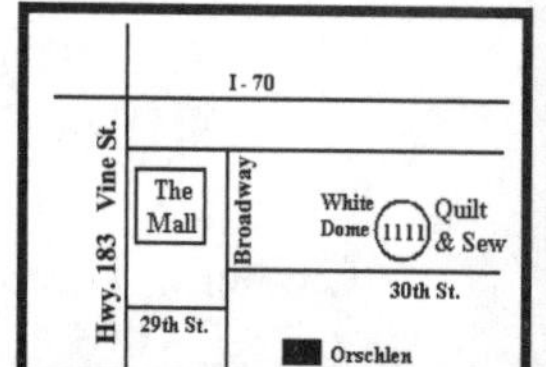

Colby, KS #6

Mon - Sat 9 - 5

Quilt Cabin

1525 S. Range Ave. 67701
(785) 462-3375
Est: 1988

Good Selection of quality 100% cotton fabrics.
Books, patterns, notions and classes.
Decorator fabrics. Custom window treatments.
Janome Sewing Machine Sales & Service.

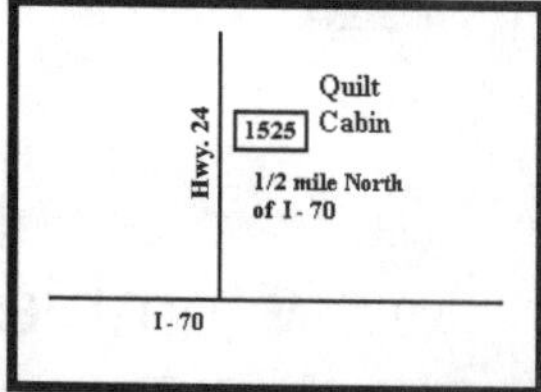

Country Quilting & Keepsakes

Mon - Sat 10 am - 5 pm

#7

Fabrics
Books
Patterns
Notions
Batting
Classes

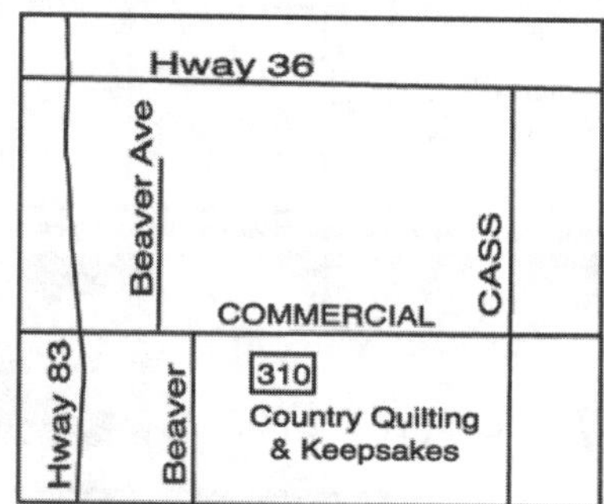

owner: Norma Carman

310 WEST COMMERCIAL; OBERLIN, KS. 67749
Ph: 785-475-2411 • Fax 785-475-2477

"Helping you create your quilt from start to finish."

Belleville, KS #8

Sew Country

Fabric ♥ Notions ♥ Gifts

Mon - Fri
9 - 5:30
Sat 9 - 5

1834 M St. 66935
Phone & FAX 785-527-2332
Sheila Cornett, Owner
Established 1992

We've Burst Our Seams!
Now Double the Space!

- 2,000 Bolts of Fabric!
- 100s of Patterns & Books!
- Shirts, Towels & Candles Handmade in Belleville
- Reasonably Price Gifts, Christian Books & Jewelry

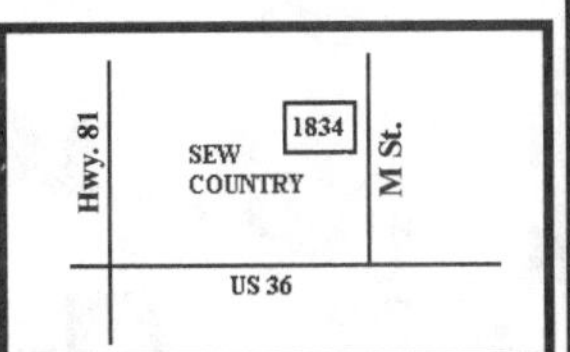

Look for us on the Web
In mid-2004!

Washington, KS #9

Tues - Sat
10 - 5:30

Honeysuckle Fabrics

311 "C" Street 66968
(785) 325-3432
honeyfabrics@hotmail.com
Owner: Terry & Ruth Bailey
Est: 2002 2500 sq. ft.

3rd St.
Honeysuckle 311
4th St.
5th St.
6th St.
C St.
Hwy. 15
Hwy. 36

Wonderful selection of 100% cotton fabrics, books, patterns and notions. Classes and the friendliest staff around.

Abilene, KS #10

Tues - Fri
9:30 - 5:30
Sat 9:30 - 3

Quilted Comfort
Quilt Shop & More

203 N. Broadway 67410
(785) 263-3915
acheathman@access-one.com

Books, Patterns, Notions, Fabrics, Workshops, Gifts, Sweat Shirts, Denim Shirts, Greeting Cards, Wind & Willow products & much, much more.
"Where Friendships are Sewn One Stitch at a Time"

I-70
Exit 275
14th St.
Cedar
Broadway
Spruce
3rd St.
Quilted Comfort

Council Grove, KS #11

Tues - Fri
10 - 5
Sat 10 - 4

Prairie Pieces

131 W. Main St. 66846
(620) 767-6628
twoquilt@cgtelco.net
www.prairie pieces.com
Owner: Toni Steere
Est: 1990 3000+ Bolts
Full line quilt shop. Hoffman, Moda and other fabric lines. Renown for our Fat Quarters. Small town service with a smile.

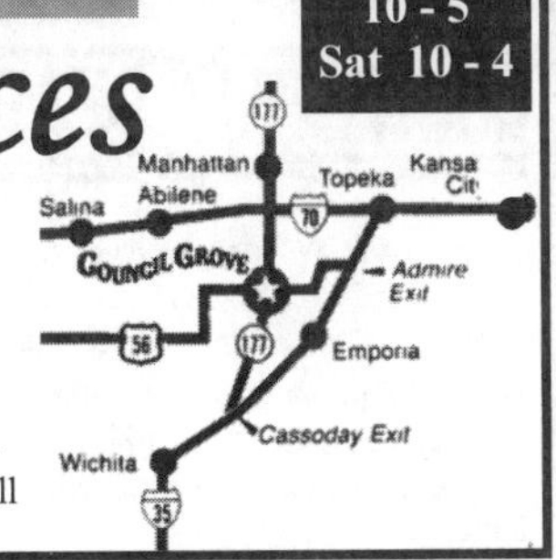

The Button Hole LC

FABRICS • NOTIONS • GIFTS

OVER 15,000 BOLTS

A Quilter's Heaven

Located in beautiful downtown McPherson, Kansas, The Button Hole is the fourth largest independently owned fabric store and quilt shop in the United States. Our elegantly decorated store has over 15,000 bolts of quilting, fashion, decorator, and novelty fabrics from all major manufacturers, including RJR (Thimbleberries), South Seas, Moda, and Hoffman. We also sell a full line of quilting supplies, patterns, and sewing notions plus Vera Bradley bags, Brighton Jewelry, Crabtree and Evelyn products, and a great selection of gift items. For your shopping break, stop in the Hearth Room and enjoy a variety of coffees, teas, pies, and pastries, located in The Button Hole. Quilting...wish you were here...and yes, we have a gazebo right in the middle of the store!

SEWING DIVISION

Home and commercial machines, machine sales, repair of all makes and models, embroidery software & supplies, scissors sharpening, sewing cabinets.

Dealers of Gammill, Singer, Pfaff, White Sewing Machines

101 N. Main Street, McPherson, KS 67460
620-241-5257 • 1-866-QUILTER
FAX: 620-241-5234
sales@thebuttonhole.net
www.thebuttonhole.net

Established 1996
10,000 sq ft. with over 15,000 bolts of fabric
Owner: Evelyn Birkhead

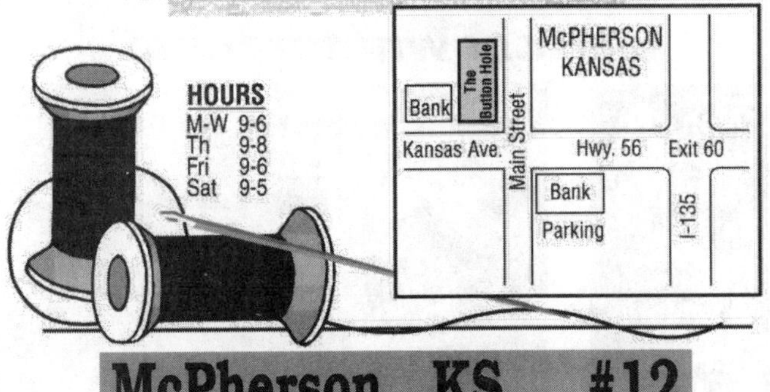

McPherson, KS #12

Salina, KS #13

Mon - Fri
9:30 - 5:30
Sat 9:30 - 5

Come visit our full line quilt shop! Where Quilters want to "Bee"!

We feature Kansas Troubles quilters fabrics, books & patterns plus a large selection of other fabrics including Moda, Thimbleberries, flannels, homespuns & felted wool. Lots of kits.

120 S. Santa Fe 67401
(785) 823-9376
Fax: (785) 823-7628
Owner: Sherril Bieberly
Est: 1979 4000 sq.ft.

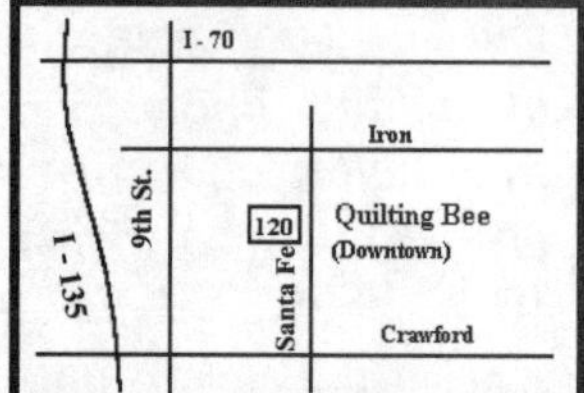

Visit us at: www.quiltingbee.net

Salina, KS #14

Quilting Station

Tues - Sat
12 - 6

212 E. Iron 67401
(785) 493-5625
kdperney@yahoo.com
Owner: Kathryne Perney Est: 2002

Located in cute antique gas station. Featuring giftware for the quilt lover; quilts by Kansas quiltmakers and provide long-arm quilting service.

Exit 252 | I-70 | Exit 253 | 9th St. | Iron | 212 | Quilting Station | Fourth St. | Ohio | I-135 | Exit 92 | Crawford

Alden, KS #15

Prairie Flower Crafts

205 Pioneer St. 67512-0158
(800) 527-3997
PrFlrCraft@aol.com
Owner: Sara Fair Sleeper
Est: 1970 6900 sq.ft.

A Specialty Fabric Shop for Quilters

RJR, Hoffman, Michael Miller, Alexander Henry, Liberty of London, Daiwabo of Japan, Clothworks, Kona Bay, SSI, Marcus Brothers, P&B, Robert Kaufmann, Benartex, Northcott, Timeless Treasures, In the Beginning, Free Spirit, UK, African and Oriental Fabrics.

Mon - Sat
10 - 4:30

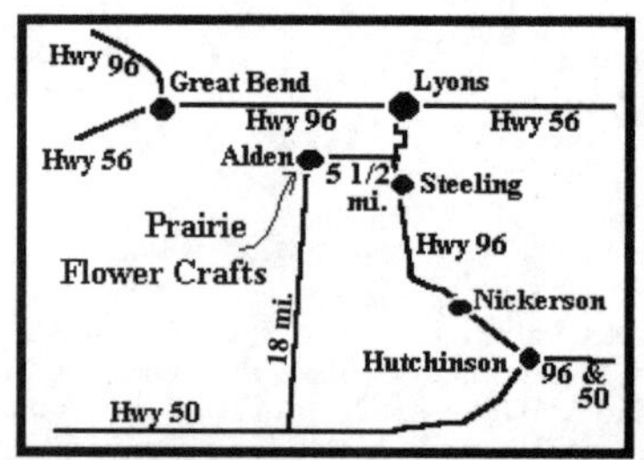

Newton, KS #16

Charlotte's Sew Natural

20th YEAR

UNIQUE FABRICS FOR QUILTING & FASHION

The BEST source for

Fabrics • Patterns • Buttons
Trims • Notions • Classes

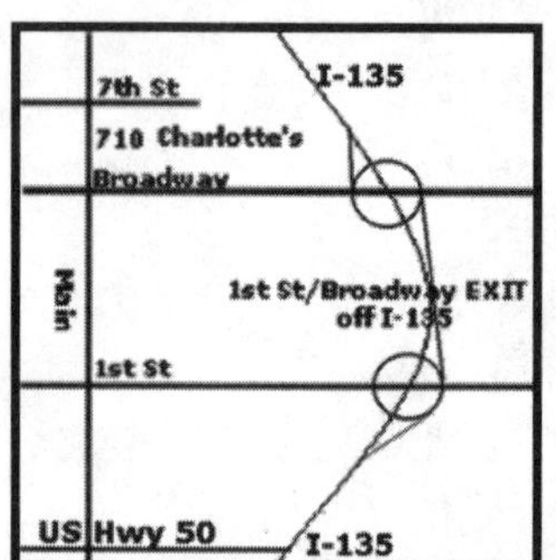

710 N. Main 67114
(316) 284-2547

Home of the "Fuzzy Wuzzy Couch Quilt"
Collect all of Charlotte's original patterns!

Owner:
Charlotte Wolfe

www.sewnatural.net

Mon - Fri
9:30 - 5:30
Thur til 8
Sat 9:30 - 5

Historic Downtown

Newton, Kansas

Hutchinson, KS #17

Mon - Sat
9 - 5:30

COUNTRY FABRICS

6411 W. Morgan Ave. 67501
(620) 662-3681 Est: 1977
Owners: Janet, Randy, & Leland Headings

100% Cotton Solids and calicos. Quilting Notions, Wood Quilt Frames, Books, & Batting. Fashion Fabrics, Sewing Notions & Patterns.

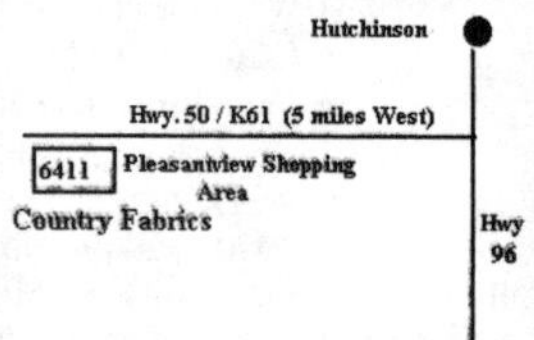

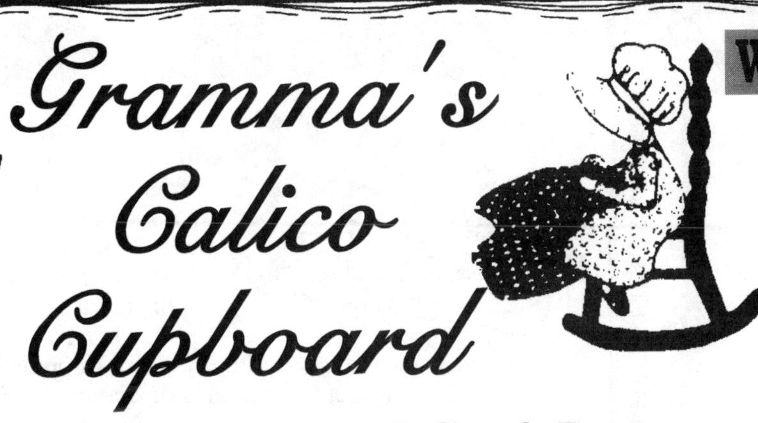

Wichita, KS #18

1945 S. Hydraulic 67211
(316) 264-0274
Owner: Betty Webb
Est: 1982 3500 sq.ft.
6000 Bolts

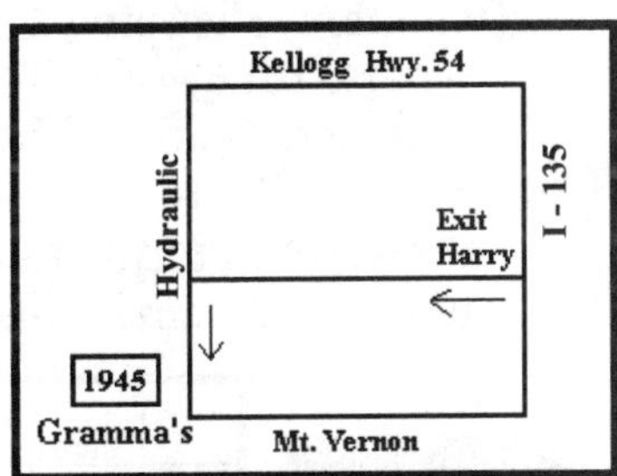

Quilting and Craft Patterns

Fantastic collections of fabric, includes 1930's reproductions, Hoffman florals, flannels, juvenile prints, wool felt, & homespuns Holiday fabrics always available. Christmas room open all year, full of fabrics, patterns and gifts. Handmade rag dolls, quilts, quilted animals and antiques

Mon - Sat 9:30 - 5

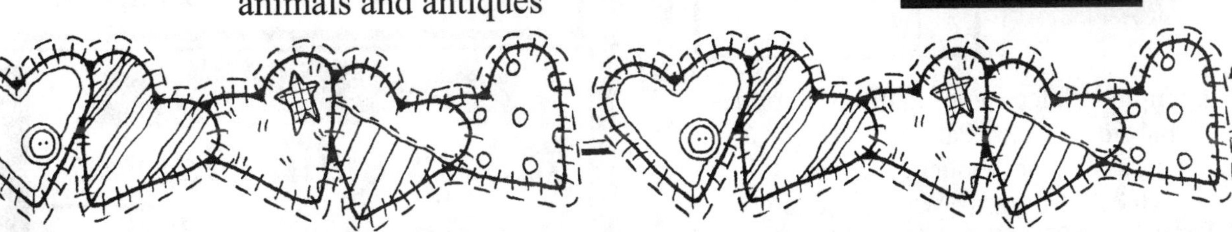

Attic Heirlooms

Needleart Shop #19

Heirloom Silk Ribbon
& Other Needle Art Supplies

Books • Classes • Lace
Accessories • Antique & Repro Linens
Embellishments & Related Items
Wired Ribbon / Fancy Fabrics
Buttons / Needle Tatting
Charms / Beaded Fringes
Ribbon Trims

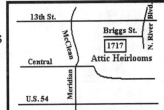

13th St.
McClean
Briggs St.
N. River Blvd.
1717
Attic Heirlooms
Central
Meridian
U.S. 54

MC / Visa Accepted
Julie Craig, Owner
1717 Briggs
Wichita, KS 67203
(316) 265-4646
Located in Historic Riverside
Tuesday - Saturday
11am - 5pm

Call for Class Schedule

Gift Certificates Available

Wichita, KS #20

Prairie Quilts

1010 S. Oliver 67218
(Parklane Shopping Center)
(316) 684-5855
Owner: Shirley Binder
Est: 1996 1300 sq.ft. 3000+ Bolts
www.prairiequilts.com
quiltsrfun@prairiequilts.com

Mon - Fri 9 - 6
Sat 9 - 5:30

Kellogg
Hwy. 54
Oliver
Lincoln
I - 135
1010 Prairie Quilts
Harry

Complete Selection of Quilting Supplies. Fabrics, Books, Patterns, Notions & Classes. Ask About our Block of the Month Program. We carry a large Selection of Batik Fabrics. Now carrying wool felt & 100% Wool fabrics for Wool Applique & Rug Hooking.

Wichita, KS #21

At Hen Feathers you will find great fabric and a friendly atmosphere. Our selection includes florals, batiks, westerns & reproduction prints, plus fabrics for pet lovers.
We are easy to find and definitely worth stopping by. Don't forget to visit our sale corner.

Mon, Wed, Fri 10 - 5:30
Tues & Thur 10 - 7 Sat 10 - 5

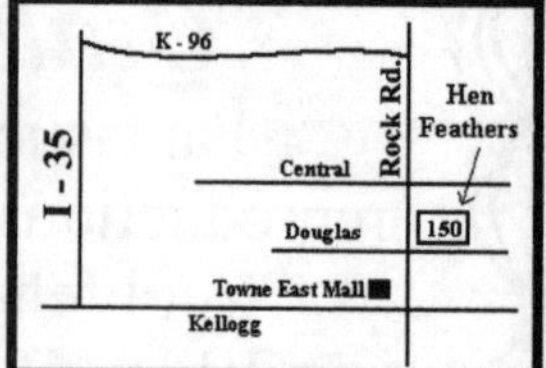

150 N. Rock Rd. 67206
316-652-9599
henfeathers@cox.net
www.henfeathersquilts.com

Wichita, KS #22

Mon - Wed 10 - 5:30
Thur til 8
Fri & Sat 10 - 5

Janet's Quilt Basket

7348 W 21st N #106 67205
(316) 773-0338 or (877) 744-8500
Owner: Janet Robinson
Est: 1996 2400 sq.ft.

Cottons, stencils, books, patterns, notions, classes, special events, Blocks-of-the-Month.

Wichita, KS #23

Mon - Sat 10 - 5

Crazy Quilters' Studio

1065 W. 53rd St. North 67204
(316) 838-1756 Fax: (316) 945-4007
vschneider@cqstudio.com
www.cqstudio.com
We cater to the Victorian Crazy Quilter with specialty threads, fabric, buttons, lace, charms, beads, books, patterns, needle supplies and silk prints. Gift Certificates Available.

Seneca
Broadway
53rd St.
1065
in the Riverview Village Mall
Crazy Quilters' Studio
I - 135

Andover, KS #25

Mon - Fri 10 - 5:30
Sat 9 - 5:30

Karen's Sew N Sew

211 W. Central Ave., P.O. Box 310 67002
(316) 733-2899
sewnsew@powwwer.net
www.karenssewnsew.com
Owner: Karen Hayes Est: 1992
Featuring Hoffman, P&B, Moda, and other fine fabrics. Books, notions, classes and an abundance of fun! We will gladly ship products. Come see us!

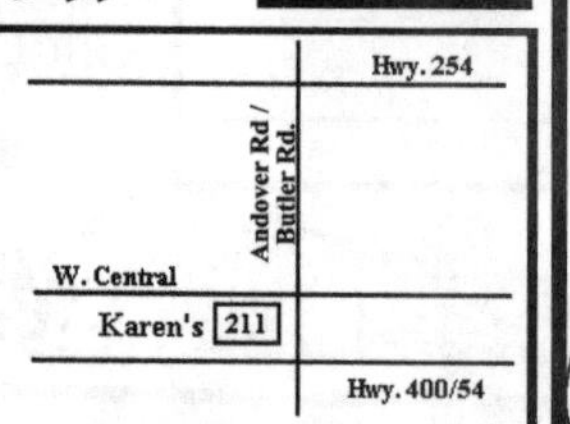

Derby, KS #24

Sunflower Quilts

Hwy. 54
Sunflower Quilts
K15
35
Madison
Rock Rd.
E 79th St. S
405

405 Osage Rd., Derby, KS 67037 (316) 788-5120
Website: www.sunflowerquilts.com
Email: sunflowerquilts@sbcglobal.net
Fabric - Notions - Patterns - Books
Classes - Wearables - Machine Quilting
Owner: Janeen Miller
Est: 2002 with 2800+ sq.ft., 2000+ bolts

Mon - Thur 9:30 - 6
Fri & Sat 9:30 - 5
Sun 1 - 5

Behind Dillons at Rock Rd. & Madison
A Thimbleberries Club Shop
Offering BOMs,
Quilters Dream Batting,
Fine fabrics from: Benartex, Clothworks, Hoffman, Kona Bay, Moda, RJR and more.

Needle In A Haystack

Severy, KS #26

207 Q Road 67137
(620) 736-2942
Fax: (620) 736-2222
Owner: Lois Klepper
Est: 1991 3000 Bolts

Mon - Fri 9 - 5
Sat 9 - 4
Sun 1 - 5

Fabric - Books - Notions
Machine Quilting
Handcrafted items for sale.

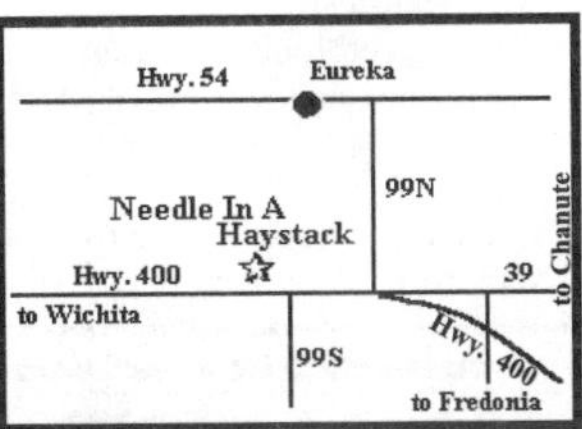

Elk Falls, KS #27

Tues - Fri 10 - 5:30
Sat 10 - 4

Quilts & More

Located in a "Living Ghost Town"
in the Heart of the Kansas Ozarks
105 N. 10th, P.O. Box 23 67345
(620) 329-4440 Owner: Edie Baker
quiltsandmore@sktc.net

Custom machine quilting, cotton fabrics, patterns, notions, & more. We specialize in novelty long arm quilting.

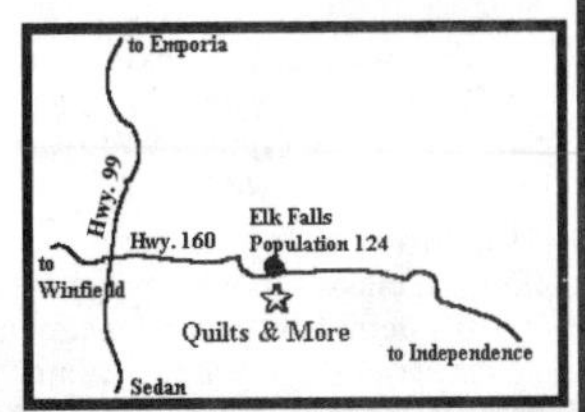

Sedan, KS #28

Tues - Sat 10 - 5

145 E. Main 67361
(620) 725-5499
Fax: (620) 725-5690
www.lilliesclassicquilts.com
Catalog $15.95
Est: 2001
We are a quilter's boutique, featuring complete lines of new & vintage fabrics. Moda Home and Robin Pundolph's Home Décor.

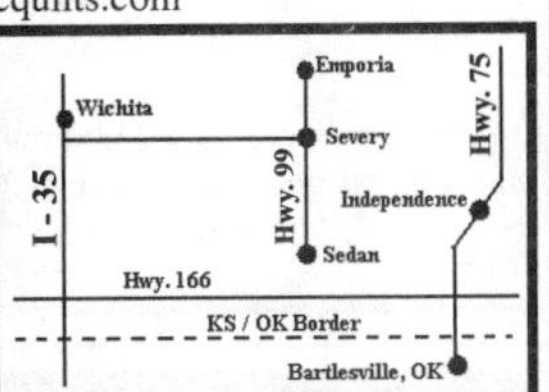

Parsons, KS #29

1777 E. Hwy. 400, Parson, KS 67357
(620) 421-5006
dieker@terraworld.net
Owner: Rhonda Dieker

Mon - Fri 10 - 5 Sat 9 - 4

Need'L Network

Largest Quilt Store in SE Kansas

- Over 3,000 bolts of 100% Cotton Fabric
- Wool & chenille by the yard
- 100's of books and patterns
- Custom Machine Quilting
- Mail Order Welcome

www.needlnetwork.com

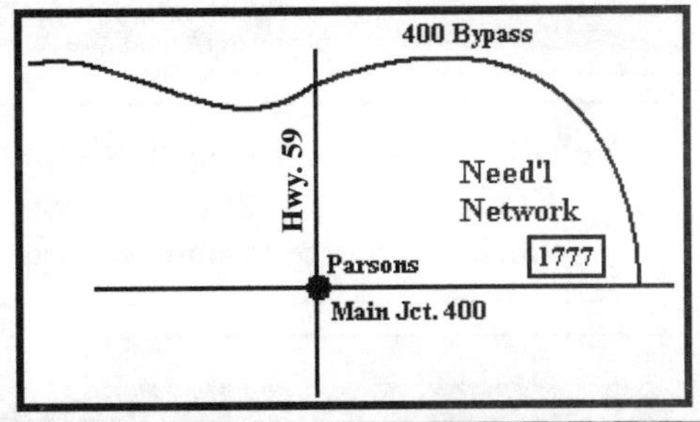

Pittsburg, KS #30

Mon - Fri 10 - 6 Sat 10 - 3

Three Women & A Blanket, Inc.

913 N. Broadway 66762
(620) 231-6083
threewomen&ablanket@wequilt.com
Owners: Debi Rankin, Debbie Walker, & Ginger McElwee
Est: 2001 3600 sq.ft. 1500+ Bolts

Bright, airy shop with great variety of fabrics, notions, classes, books, patterns and consigned gift items. Stop in for a unique quilting experience. Group programs available.

Three Women & A Blanket 913
5 1/2 blocks North of Hwy. 69 & 126 Junction
Hwy. 69
4th St.
Hwy. 126
Broadway

Burlington, KS #31

Mon - Fri 10 - 5:30 Sat 10 - 3 Sun by Appt.

Silver Threads & Golden Needles

321 Neosho 66839
Owner: Jerry Anne Hoyt
(620) 364-8233
Est: 1985 2000 sq.ft.

Quilters Discount Fabrics, Patterns, Notions, Crafts, Gift Items, Quilting Supplies & Craft Patterns.

Emporia, KS #32

Mon - Fri 9:30 - 5:30 Sat 9 - 5

FABRIC CORNER

627 Commercial
(620) 342-3040
Owner: Colleen Janssen
Est: 1992

We carry more than 2,000 bolts of quality quilting fabrics and more than 200 book titles for every quilter.

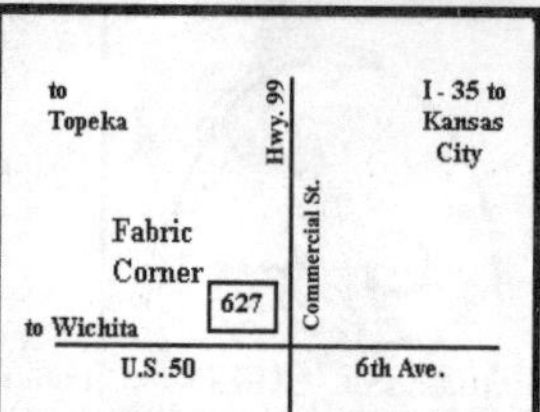

Overbrook, KS #33

Tue - Sat 10 - 5

Overbrook Quilt Connection

500 Maple P.O. Box 50 66524
(785) 665-7841 or (888) 665-7841
oqc@sftnet.org
www.overbrookquilts.com
Owners: Roxane Fawl & Carolyn Meerian
Est: 1994 4300 sq.ft.

2000 bolt inventory, books, patterns, notions, classes. Mailorder. Free flier.

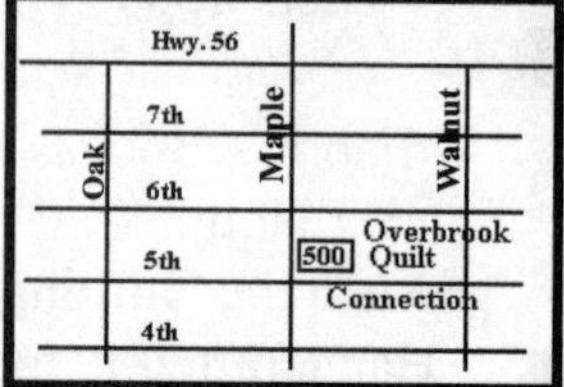

Quilts on Display

Quilting Bits & Pieces

2500+ bolts of quality fabrics with corresponding fat quarters, BOM's, classes, redwork, notions, books & patterns, kits and machine quilting.

Eudora, KS #34

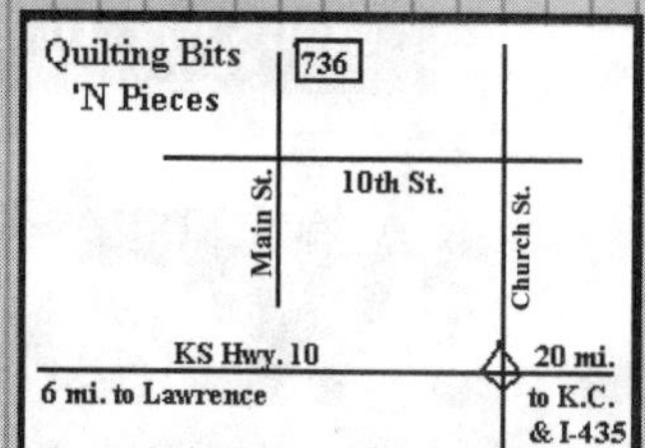

M, W, F, S 9:30 - 5 T & Th 9:30 - 7

Website: www.eudoraquiltshop.com
Est: 1997 (785) 542-2080
e-mail: bitsnpieces@sunflower.com

736 Main St. 66025 877-639-2080

Overland Park, KS #35

7917 Santa Fe Drive
Overland Park, KS
66204
(913)-648-2SEW
Toll-Free
(877)-780-2SEW

Owner: Elaine Johnson
Est: 1969

Mon-Fri 10-6 Sat 10-5 Sun 1-4

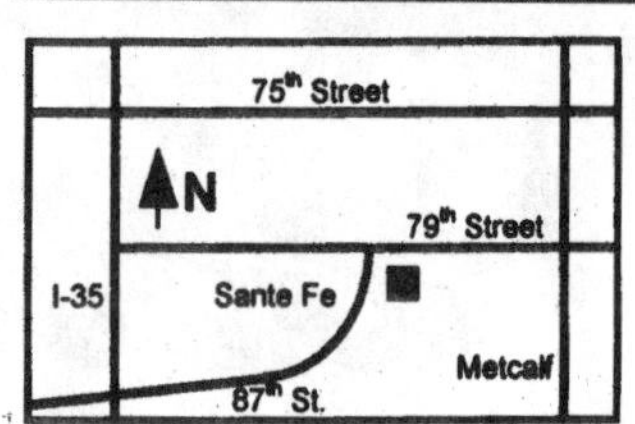

Large selection of Brand Name, 100% Cottons, Flannels, Kids Prints, Reproduction & Novelties, Books, Quilting Supplies & Notions, Classes, Seminars & Workshops.
Premier Husqvarna Viking Sewing Machines & Sergers

www.harpersfabricandquilt.com

Husqvarna VIKING

Sewing Machine Co. Located inside Jo-Ann stores at

11401 Metcalf Ave, Overland Park, KS 66212 (913) 491-4499

3810 CrackerneckRd, N 291 & 39th St Independence, MO 64055 (816) 350-3900

603 N Belt Hwy, St. Joseph, MO 64506 (816) 390-9800

Quilters' Haven

120-B So. Clairborne Rd. Olathe, KS 66062

3,000+ Bolts of Fabric

Large Selection of Batiks, Flannels & Orientals

Books 20% OFF Everyday

www.quiltershaven.com

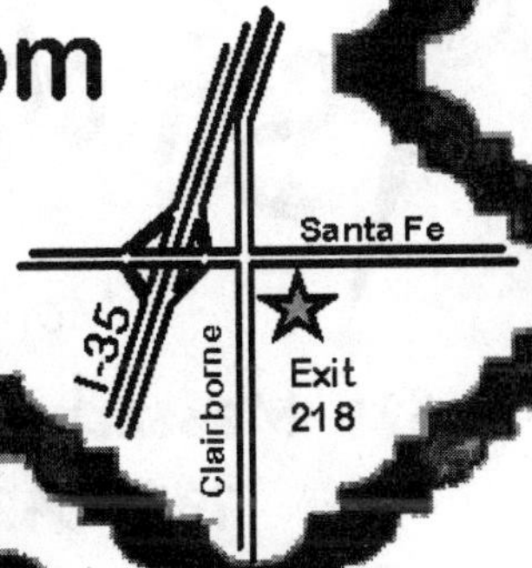

Mon. - Sat.
9:30 - 5:30
Thurs.
9:30 - 8:00

Olathe, KS #36

913.764.8600

866.464.8600
Toll Free

Santa Fe
I-35
Clairborne
Exit
218

FABRIC CORNER

5321 B SW 22nd Place
Topeka, Kansas 66614-1500
(785) 271-7667

Est: 1992
Owner: Colleen Janssen

Monday and Thursday 10-8
Tues, Wed & Fri 10-6
Saturday 10-5

Topeka, KS #37

Located in Fairlawn Plaza Shopping Center
At the Corner of 21st and Fairlawn

One can't imagine the awesome feeling of entering our more than 9,000 sq. ft. Space with more than 4,000 bolts of quality quilting and fashion fabrics.

We carry over 400 titles of books for quilting, sewing and home décor.

Authorized BERNINA dealer and comprehensive sewing center.

If you are traveling through our area, be sure to mention this ad and receive 10% off your purchase except our already discounted Berninas.

Nearly everything under one roof for the quilter or seamstress.

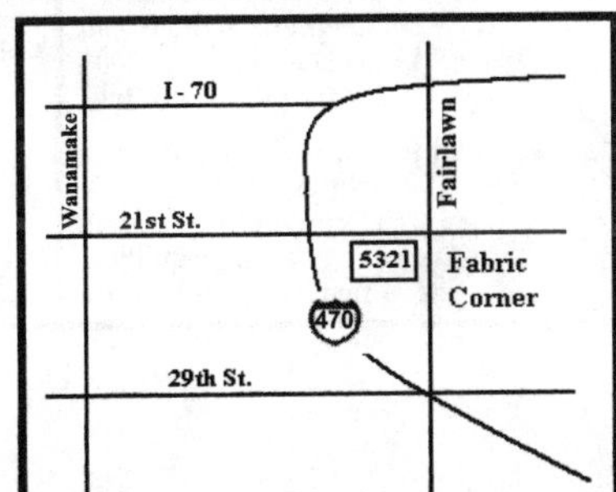

Topeka, KS #38

Mon - Fri 10 - 5
Thur til 7
Sat 10 - 3

3005 SW Topeka Blvd.
66611
(785) 266-4130

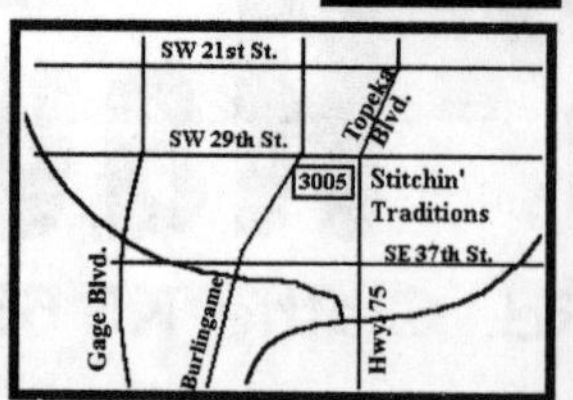

stitchintraditions@kscable.com
Est: 1997 1600 sq.ft. 750+ Bolts
Full service quilt shop serving Topeka and the surrounding area. We offer a large selection of fabric, books, patterns, notions and classes.

Baldwin City, KS #39

Mon - Sat 9:30 - 5
Tues til 6

Quilters' Paradise

713 8th St., P.O. Box 646 66006
(785) 594-3477 Est: 1986
quiltfabsupply@earthlink.net
www.quiltingfabricsupply.com
Owner: Sharon A. Vesecky

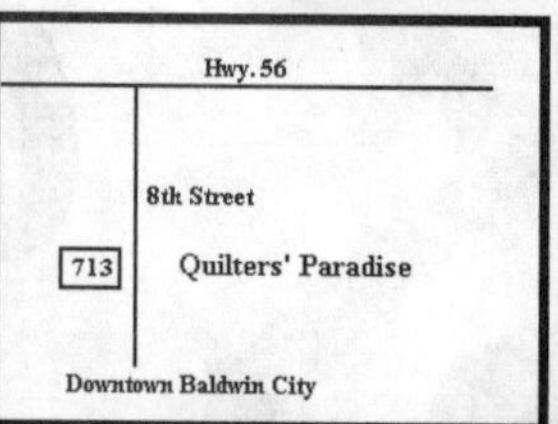

Quilting supplies, books, patterns, fabric—Hoffman, Jinny Beyer, Springs, Maywood Studio, Moda, Batiks & Flannels.
Machine Quilting.

Stitch On Needlework Shop

Mon - Sat 10 - 5:30 Thur until 8 pm Sunday 1 - 4

926 Massachusetts St., Lawrence, KS 66044
785-842-1101 stchon@aol.com
Est. 1976 3,000 sq.ft. 2500+ bolts of 100% Cotton

Batiks, Flannels, Homespuns, 1930's. Large selection of books, patterns and Models. Counted Cross Stitch and fun buttons. Large gift selection of Department 56, Radko, Old World Christmas, Yankee, Aromatique, Smokers, Nutcrackers and Much, Much more.

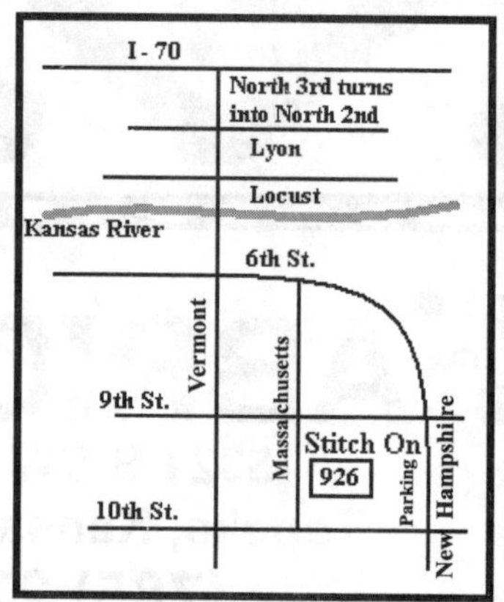

Lawrence, KS #40

Hiawatha, KS #41

Tues - Fri 10 - 6
Sat 10 - 4

Sunflower Quilt Shop

716 Oregon St. 66434 (785) 742-4343
sunqlt@carsoncomm.com
Owner: Linda Duesing Est: 2001
1550 sq.ft. 1000 Bolts

Full service quilt shop offering fabrics, notions, books, patterns, classes, custom machine quilting.
Friendly helpful service

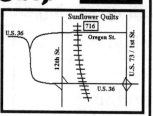

Sunflower Quilts
716
U.S. 36
Oregon St.
12th St.
U.S. 73 / 1st St.
U.S. 36

Leavenworth, KS #42

The Quilter's Quarters

219 Delaware, Leavenworth, KS 66048
(913) 651-6510
www.quiltersqtrs.com
Owner: Jerry Ann Stube

Mon, Tues, Thurs, Fri, Sat 9:30 - 5:30 Wed 12 - 8

Minutes from Kansas City, The Quilter's Quarters is dedicated to providing the best possible customer service in the friendliest atmosphere. Quilters will truly find a home in our civil war vintage building where the surroundings may be antique, but the fabric and ideas are cutting edge. Unlike a fabric museum, our merchandise is constantly being updated. You will find our large selection of fabrics, notions, books, kits, plus new and antique quilts just outside the front gate of historic Fort Leavenworth.

Featured in 2 books--"Kansas City Quilt Maker Portraits & Patterns" and "Kansas City Scrap Book" by Terri Atkinson.
Authorized PFAFF Dealer

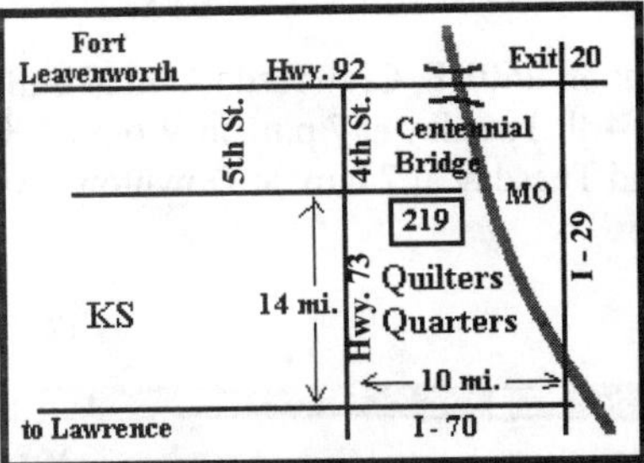

Shawnee, KS #43

Prairie Point

Fabrics, Quilting Supplies & Classes

- Great selection of the best new fabrics including flannels, novelty prints, ethnic designs, country homespuns and prints, contemporary jewel tones, 1930's and Civil War era reproduction prints, Bali Batiks, Japanese and more!
- Wide assortment of notions
- >1,000 books and patterns
- Many cotton, polyester and wool battings from which to choose
- Classes at all levels

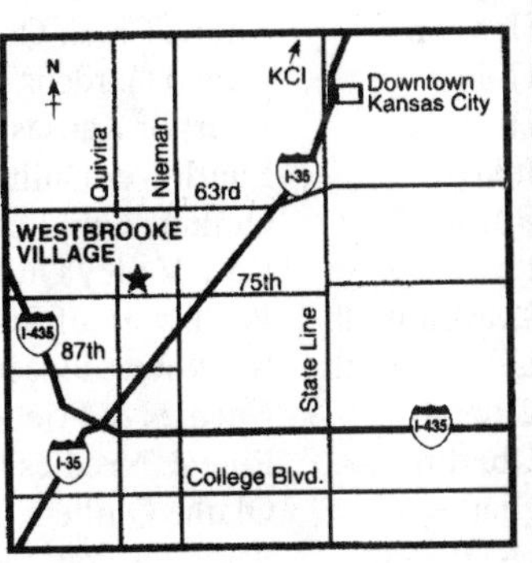

Store Hours:
Mon - Thurs 10:00 - 8:30
Fri & Sat 10:00 - 5:00
Sunday 1:00 - 5:00

Stop in for a visit. With so many inspirational samples, you're bound to find a project you just can't resist!

Located in Suburban Kansas City
7341 Quivira Rd.
Shawnee, KS 66216
(913) 268-3333
Toll Free (888) 268-5606

Web Site:
www.prairiepoint.com
email:
PrairiePTQuilts@aol.com

Other Shops in Kansas: *We suggest calling first*

Anthony	Pride of the Prairie, 131 W. Main St.	316-842-5945
Argonia	Quilters Nook, 106 N Main St	620-435-6961
Barnes	Downhome Quilting, 10 North Center St.	785-763-4400
Concordia	Country Cousins, 116 W 6th	785-243-4044
Emporia	Carol's Quilting, 511 S. Exchange St.	620-343-9197
Enterprise	Treehouse Quilting, 1225 Factory	785-263-8465
Ft. Scott	Country Cupboard, 12 N Main	620-223-5980
Galva	The Quilt Barn, 221 E. Hwy. 56	316-654-3400
Holton	Sunflower Quilting, 624 Colorado Ave.	785-364-5177
Hutchinson	Cottonwood Quilts, 126 N. Main	620-662-2245
Hutchinson	Advertising Specialities, 608 N. Main	620-662-6460
La Crosse	Patchwork Parlor, 812 Main St.	913-222-3536
Lakin	Patchwork Garden, 404 W. Hwy. 50	620-355-1441
Lawrence	Sarah's Fabrics, 925 Massachusetts St.	913-842-6198
Manhattan	Ideas Unlimited Quilt Shop, 523 S 17th	785-539-6759
Minneola	Quilts-N-More, 101 Olive St.	620-885-4500
Norton	The Sewing Box, 128 S. State	913-877-3821
Oakley	Quilt Shop, 423 Hudson Ave.	785-672-3870
Oberlin	Carrousel Quilt & Gift Shop, 141 S. Penn	785-475-3666
Osage City	Calico Cupboard, 513 Market	785-528-4861
Ottawa	Chris' Corner, 229 S. Main St.	913-242-1922
Overland Park	Addadi's Fabrics, 9629 West 87th Street	913-381-9705
Oxford	Variety Shoppe, 106 S. Summer St.	316-455-3698
Pomona	Quilted Blessings, 809 Hwy K 68	785-566-3510
Rose Hill	Patchwork Moon, 14855 SW 156th Ter	316-776-1600
Salina	The Emporium, 332 E Shilling Rd	785-823-1515
Seneca	Picture This, 420 Main St.	913-336-3296
Shawnee Mission	Back Porch Designs, 6416 W 83rd St	913-385-9082
Shawnee Mission	Bernina-Pfaff Sewing Center, 7251 W. 97th St.	913-371-6400
Topeka	Bennett's Sewing Center, 2125 N. Kansas	785-232-9117
Washington	Nutsch's Trading Post, 321 C St	785-265-3080
Wichita	The Picket Fence, 141 N. Rock Island St.	316-262-7774
Wichita	The Sewing Center, 2101 W. 21st St.	316-832-0819
Yates Center	Square Threads, 117 N State St	620-625-2300

Kansas Guilds:

North East Kansas Quilters Meets: 1st Tuesday, Cummings, KS
Assaria Silver Needles Quilt Guild, 5500 S. Ohio Rd., 67416
Baldwin City Maple Leaf Quilters Guild, P.O. Box 563, 66006
Meets: 4th Thursday 7 p.m. (except Nov & Dec, 1st Thur in Dec) at Baldwin Senior Center
Basehor Tonganoxie Sunflower Quilt Guild, P.O. Box 33, 66007 Meets: 2nd Monday 1 p.m. at Jenell's Quilt Patch
Colby Kansas Prairie Quilt Guild, 1525 S Range, 67701 Meets: 3rd Monday at 7pm, Community Building
El Dorado El Dorado Crazy Quilters Guild, 210 E. 2nd Ave., 67042 Meets: 2nd Thursday 7 p.m. at El Dorado Senior Center
Emporia Emporia Regional Quilt Guild, P.O. Box 1403, 66801 Meets: 2nd Monday 6:30pm at Emporia Senior Center
Eudora Eudora Quilting Bees, P.O. Box 9, 66025 Meets: 2nd Tuesday 7 p.m. at St. Paul Church, 8th & Church
Great Bend Central Kansas Thread-Benders, 67530
Hays Big Creek Quilt Guild, 67601 Meets: 3rd Thursday @ 7:30pm at Church of Christ, 1100 Centennial Blvd.
Hesston Emma Creek Quilt Guild, 67062 Meets: 4th Tuesday 7 p.m. at Hesston Senior Center, 108 E. Randall
Holton Calico Gardens Quilt Guild Meets: 3rd Wednesday 7pm at Colorado School
Hutchinson Heart of Kansas Quilt Guild, P.O. Box 27, 67504
Iola Sunflower Quilter's Guild, P.O. Box 69, 66749
Kansas City Quilters Guild of Greater K.C., 1617 W. 42nd Street
Lawrence Kaw Valley Quilters Guild, 924 Vermont, 66044
Leavenworth Patchwork of Sisters c/o Quilters Quarters
Leavenworth Sunflower Piecemakers, c/o Quilter's Quarters, 66048 Meets: 2nd & 4th Thursday 7 p.m. at Lansing City Hall, Lansing
Liberal Needles & Friends Quilt Guild, P.O. Box 72, 67901
Oberlin Pine & Needles Quilt Guild Meets: Last Monday 10 a.m. at Carrousel Quilt Shop
Olathe Olathe Quilters Guild, 66061
Overbrook Santa Fe Trail Quilt Guild, 500 Maple, P.O. Box 50, 66524 Meets: 1st Tuesday 7 p.m. at Overbrook Quilt Connection
Paola Miama County Quilters Guild, P.O. Box 453, 66071
Pittsburg Little Balken Quilt Guild, Inc., P.O. Box 1608, 66762 Meets: 3rd Monday 7 p.m. Presbyterian Church 6th & Pine
Rose Hill Country Rose Quilt Guild, P.O. Box 412, 67133 Meets: 3rd Tuesday @ 7pm at Rose Hill Senior Center
Salina Silver Needles Quilt Guild, P.O. Box 1132, 67402
Meets: 3rd Monday 7 p.m. at Presbyterian Manor, 2601 E. Crawford (Annual quilt show in late October)
Topeka Kansas Capital Quilters Guild, 66606 Meets: 2nd & 4rth Tuesday at 7 p.m. at Women's Club, 5221 SW West Dr.
Wichita Prairie Quilt Guild, P.O. Box 48813, 67201 Meets: 2nd Tuesday at 7 p.m. at Downtown Senior Center, 200 S. Walnut
Winfield Walnut Valley Quilters Guild, 1615 East 20th Ave., 67156
Winfield Kansas Quilters Organization, 1721 Weile, 67156

KENTUCKY

26 Featured Shops

Murray, KY #1

Pincushion Quilt Shop

Mon, Tues Fri 9:30 - 5
Wed & Sat 9:30 - 1
Thur 9:30 - 8

605 S. 12th St., Suite B 42071
(270) 753-8068 Fax: Same
Owner: Janeen Sutton
Est: 2001 1600 sq.ft.

Main St. (Rt. 94E)
Sycamore St.
S. 12th St. (Rt. 641)
Pincushion Quilt Shop

First quality 100% Cotton Fabrics from major manufacturers. Hundreds of Notions, Books, Patterns. Dealer for "Handi-Quilter" products. Full service store with classes year round.

Benton, KY #2

Odds & Ends

Mon - Fri 10 -5
Tues til 8 Sat 9 - 2
Closed Mon May - Aug.

"Home of Strippers & Hookers"

95 N. Main 42025
(270) 527-2487 Fax: (270) 527-2487
zar@wk.net
Est: 1995 1200 sq.ft.

If my hours do not meet your schedule, please call and we will work out something.

Fabrics by the yard & pound. Lace, books, & patterns. Sewing & quilting supplies, local crafts. Always friendly advice.

Paducah, KY #3

King's Quilting Studio

Open 10 - 5
Sundays by Appt.

119 N. 4th St. 42001
(270) 444-7577 Fax: Same
(888) 215-9282
sara@paducahquilts.com
www.paducahquilts.com
Owner: Sara Newberg King

Ohio River
MAQS
Convention Center
3rd St.
4th St.
119 King's
Harrison
Madison
Monroe
Jefferson
Broadway

Quilts, wallhangings, wearables, patterns. Silk ribbon embroidery, dyes, silks, books, classes, hand-dyed fabrics & ribbons, mail order.

Visit the World's Largest Quilt Museum

Museum of the American Quilter's Society

Open Year round
Mon - Sat 10 - 5
April - Oct
Also Sun 1 - 5

Ohio River
Take either Exit 4 or 11 from I-24
MAQS
Convention Center
3rd St.
4th St.
Harrison
Madison
Monroe
Jefferson
Broadway

See over 150 antique and contemporary quilts on display in three exhibit galleries

Don't miss our Museum Shop, where you will find fine crafts made by artists from around the country and over 400 books on quilting and textiles.

215 Jefferson St., P.O. Box 1540
42002-1540 Est: 1991
(270) 442-8856 Fax #: (270) 442-5448
info@quiltmuseum.org
www.quiltmuseum.org.

Paducah, KY #4

Paducah: Quilt City U.S.A.

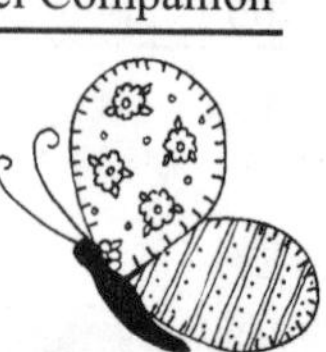

"The Little House with the Big Quilt Shop Inside"

Paducah, KY #5

(270) 443-5673
420 North 4th St. 42001
Owner: Pat English
Est: 1989

Designer Fabrics - Patterns - Classes - Books
Newest Notions - Brazilian Embroidery Supplies
Lace Making - Fabric Painting
Quilter's Jewelry - Tools or Gadgets
We do mail order on all those Hard-To-Finds
Janome/New Home &
Babylock Sewing Machines.

Quilters Alley

Ohio River
MAQS
Convention Center
3rd St.
Quilter's Alley
420
4th St.
Harrison
Madison
Monroe
Jefferson
Broadway

www.quiltersalleypaducah.com

Mon - Sat 10 - 5

Entrance on 3rd St. at 419
New Parking Area—Right across from Convention Center

Madisonville, KY #6

the QUILT DEPOT

19 N. Main St., Madisonville, KY 42431
270-824-8355 Owner: Kari Morton

Quilt Design, Professional Machine Quilting, Fabric (100% Cotton), Notions, Books, Consignment Selling, Classes & much more.

quiltdepot@madisonville.com
fax: 270-821-3814
Est: 2001
5500 sq.ft. 2500+ bolts

Mon - Fri 9:30 am - 5:30 pm
Sat 10 am - 4 pm

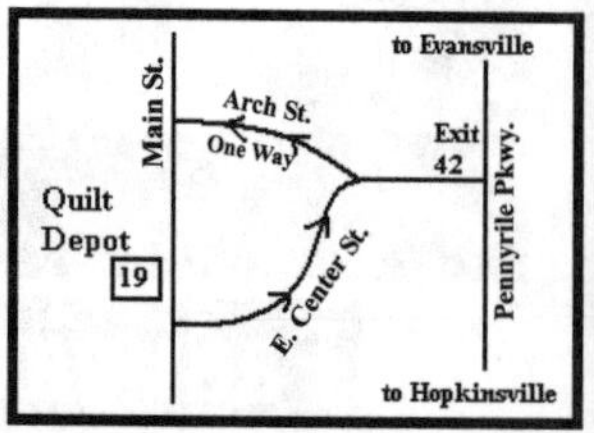

Henderson, KY #7

Tues - Fri 10 - 4
Sat 10 - 5

Bluegrass Quilts

8375 Pruitt-Agnew Rd.
(Hwy. 1217) 42420
(270) 826-5739
Owner: Pam Miller
Est: 2002 1200 sq.ft.

Large selection and friendly service! 100% cotton fabrics, quilting supplies, notions, books, and patterns. Classes too! Beautiful country setting.

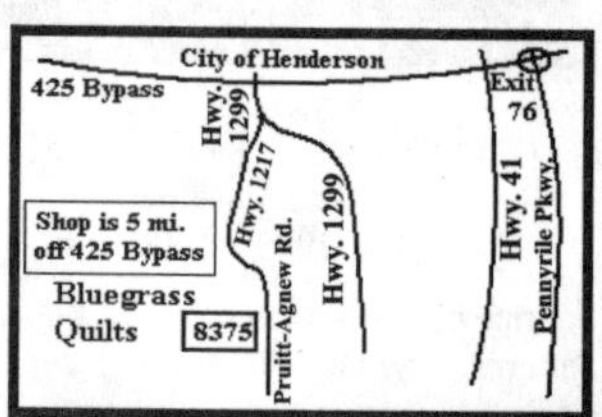

Owensboro, KY #8

Tues - Fri 10 - 5
Sat 10 - 4

Tab's Patchwork Place

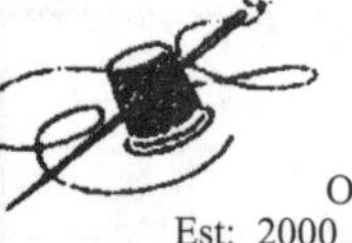

219 Williamsburg
Square 42303
(270) 683-9233
quiltbar@bellsouth.net
Owner: Theresa Barnett
Est: 2000 1600 sq.ft.

Fabrics, patterns, books, notions, needleart supplies. Large selection of hand-quilted quilts and friendly customer service.

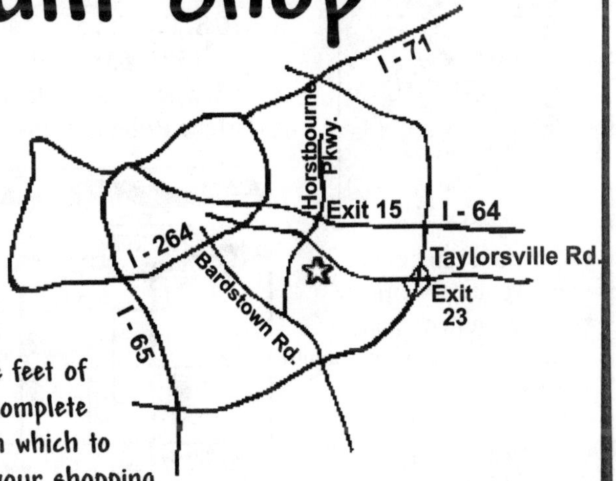

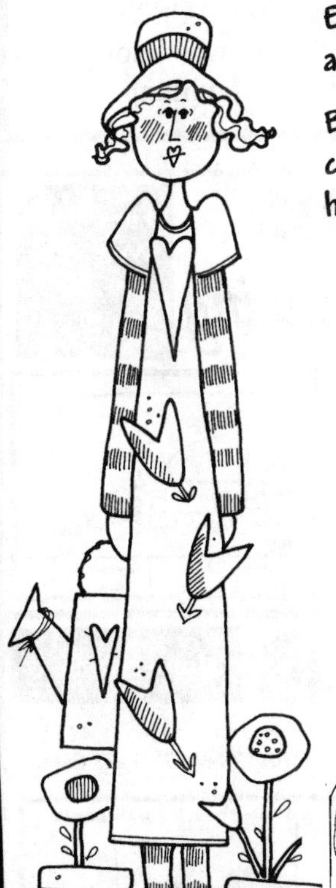

Louisville, KY #10

Est: 2001

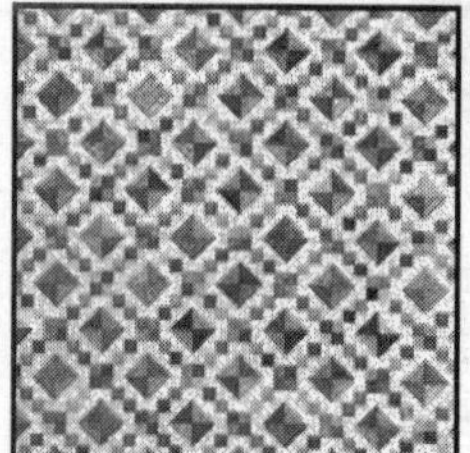

2116 S. Preston St. 40217
(502) 638-0630
Owners: Sue Clark, Darlene Roby & Carol Heil

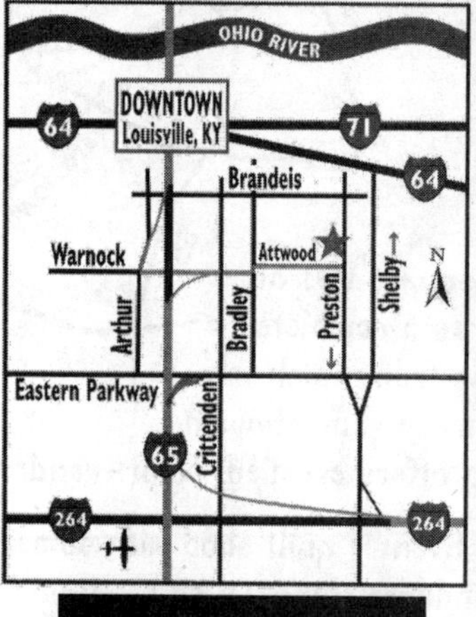

* Central location
* 3000 bolts of fabric
* Books, notions, patterns classes, block-of-the-month
* Friendly help
* National teachers
* Evening hours by appointment
* Ladies bring your spouse with you and enjoy bakery goods from Nord's Bakery next door, winner of the BEST IN LOUISVILLE DONUT AWARD

Mon - Fri 9:30 - 5
Sat 9:30 - 4

Louisville, KY #11

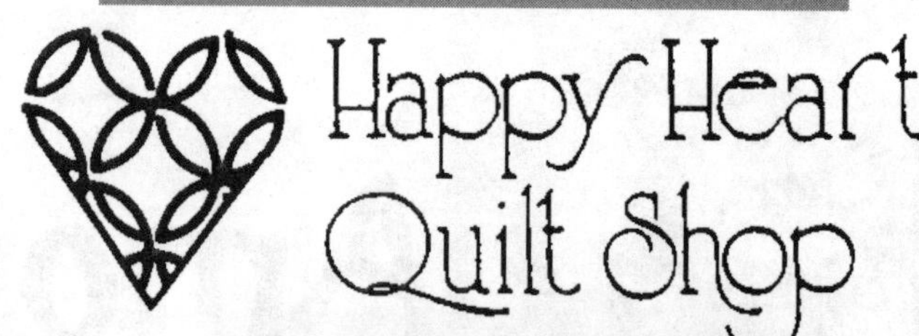

Mon - Fri 10 - 5 Sat 10 - 4

7913 3rd. St. Rd. 40214
(502) 363-1171
Owner: Yvonne Fritze
Est: 1985
3500 sq. ft.

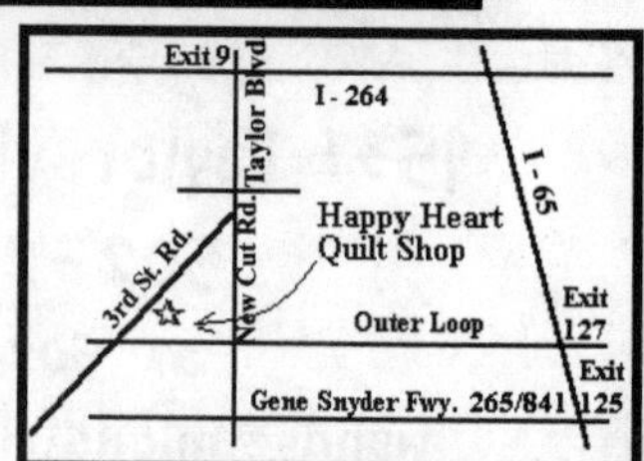

Happy Heart Quilt Shop is located ten minutes from I - 264, exit 9; or I - 65 exit 127, Kentucky Fair & Exposition Center and Louisville International Airport. There is a vast array of fabrics, 4000 bolts, in most major fabric lines, hundreds of books, patterns, stencils and notions in 3500 square feet of shopping space. Quilt kits are available—applique, cross-stitch, whole cloth, and pieced blocks. Merchandise is displayed on spacious shelving and antique pieces. Special features for customers include newsletters, classes, retreats, sales, demonstrations and problem solving. We also have two day-long bus trips to the AQS Shows in Paducah and Nashville each year. We are well known for our friendly service and our love of quilting.

Big Clifty, KY #12

Mon, Tues, Wed, Fri, & Sat 10 - 5

Quaint Quilts

16117 Leitchfield Rd. 42712
(270) 862-9708
quilts@quaintquilts.summit.ky.us
www.quaintquiltsummit.ky.us
Owner: Kathryn Richardson
Est: 1985 672 sq.ft.

Quilts, Curtains, Machine & Hand Quilting, Oil Paintings, Prints, Basketry, Rugs & Rug Weaving. Approx. 100 printed quilt top fabrics.

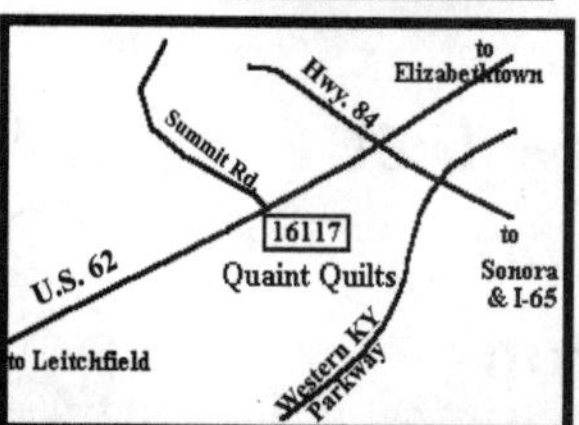

Bowling Green, KY #13

Tues 9 - 9
Wed - Fri 9 - 4
Sat 9 - 2

Sidekicks Quilting

1051 Searcy Way 42103
(270) 842-0045
Owner: Linda Rone
Est: 1999 3000+ Bolts

Look for the 2 story Blue Metal Building with chain link fence. Fabrics, notions, books, patterns, Thimbleberries club & more . . .

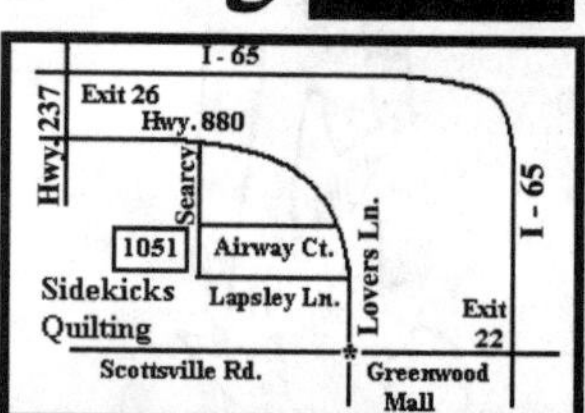

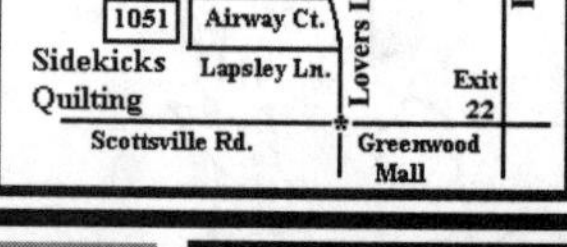

Glasgow, KY #14

Wed - Fri 10 - 4
Sat 10 - 3

The Barn Cat Quilting Shoppe

2897 Matthews Mill Rd.
42141
(270) 646-5468
barncat55@earthlink.net
Owners: Dorothy Bunch

Top name Fabrics, Notions, Books, Patterns and Classes. Email if you want to stop by on Monday or Tuesday.

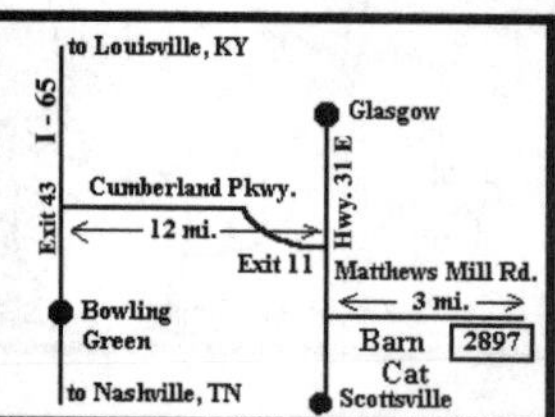

Magnolia, KY #15

Mon - Sat 9 - 5

10075 N. Jackson Hwy. 42757
(270) 528-3087 Fax: Same

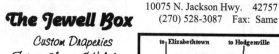

The Jewell Box
Custom Draperies
Fabric Shoppe & Upholstery

Owner: Doris Jewell Est: 1995
Quilting fabric & supplies. Machine quilting. Quilted purses & quilted material. Handmade quilts & machine quilts.
"Grab a Friend and Come On In"

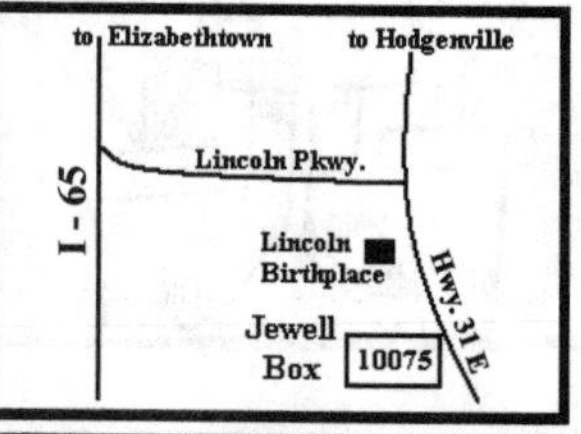

Elizabethtown, KY #16

Mon by Chance
Tues 3 - 9, Wed 9 - 6,
Thur 9 - 9, Fri 9 - 6
Sat 9 - 3
Sun Closed

Uniquely Yours Quilt Shop

2973 Rineyville Rd. 42701
(270) 766-1456
Mary@UniquelyYoursQuiltShop.com
Owner: Mary Sennott

Over 3000 bolts of 100% Cotton Fabrics. Books, patterns, notions and classes. Friendly, professional advice. Quilts for sale.

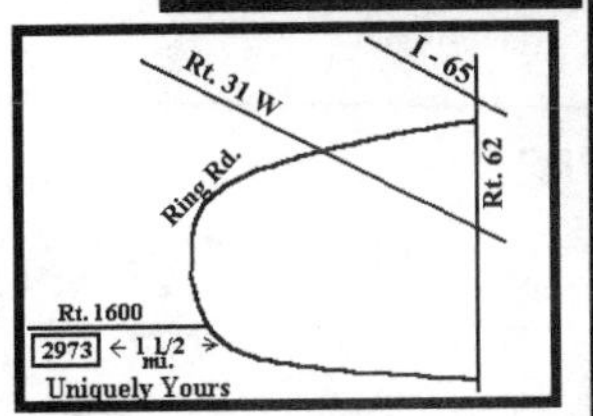

Lexington, KY #17

Mon - Sat
10 - 5:30
Thur til 7

Corner Quilt Shop

153 Patchen Dr. #67 40517
(859) 268-7467
Owner: Teresa Fritz

Large selection 100% cotton fabrics, books, notions, classes. Friendly staff always available to help if needed.

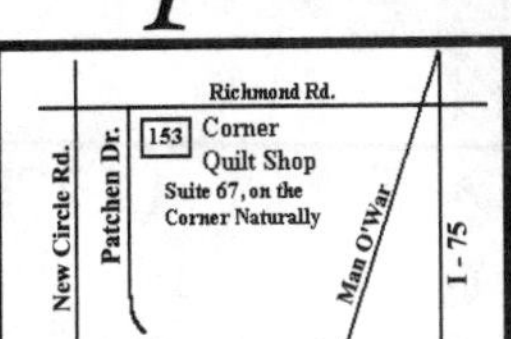

QUILTER'S SQUARE

2 Great Shops !

Friendly Service, Exceptional Selection of FABRIC, BOOKS, PATTERNS, NOTIONS & GIFT ITEMS.

Lexington, KY #18

140 Moore Dr.
Lexington, KY 40503
(859) 278-5010 Fax: (859) 278-0274

Monday - Friday 10 - 6
Thursday 10 - 9
Saturday 10 - 5:30

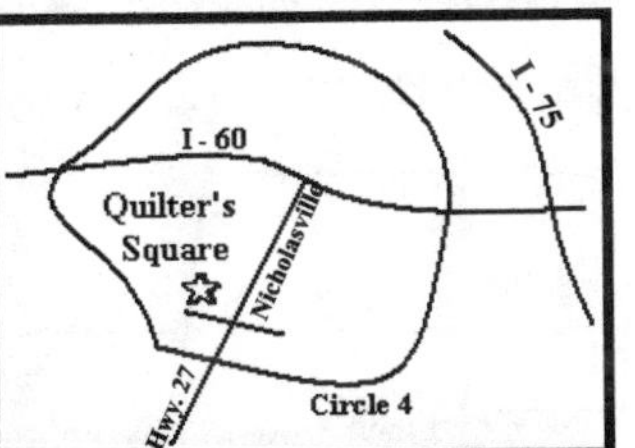

New Circle Rd. (Circle 4) to Nicholasville to Moore Dr. (behind Wendy's)

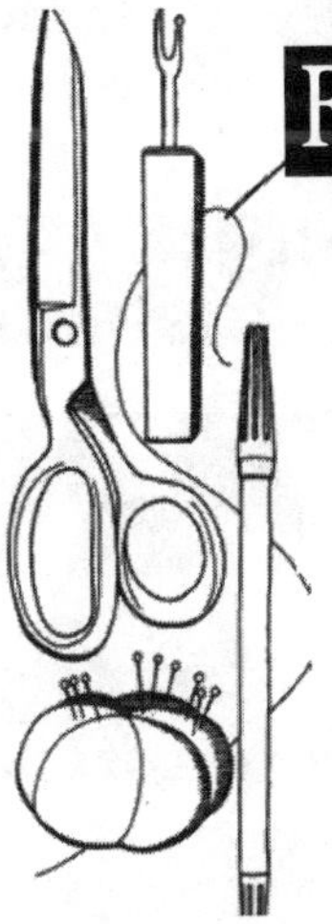

Florence, KY #19

8146 Mall Rd.
Florence, KY 41022
(859) 371-2160

Monday - Friday 10 - 6
Saturday 10 - 5:30

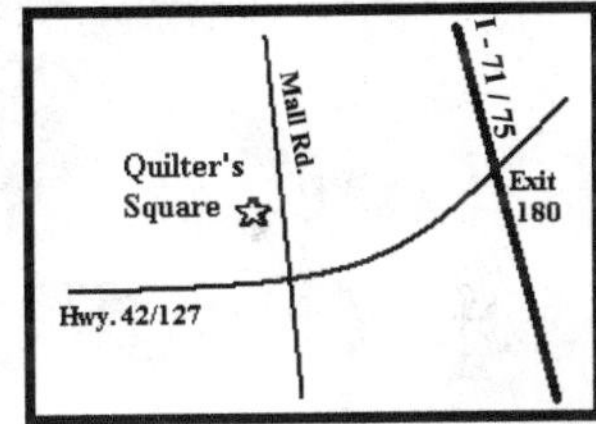

Exit I - 75 at Rt. 42
At the third light, turn right

Authorized BERNINA Dealer & Service

www.quilterssquare.biz

Burlington, KY #20

Mon - Fri
10 - 6
Sat 10 - 4

Cabin Arts

5878 N. Jefferson St. 41005
(859) 586-8021
cabinarts@nkol.net
www.nkol.net/cabinarts/
Owner: Linda Whittenburg
Est: 1992 1300 sq.ft. 5000 Bolts

Quality Quilt Fabrics plus notions, books & more. Local Handcrafted Treasures. Classes Available. Located in historic district in 1850's Log Cabin.

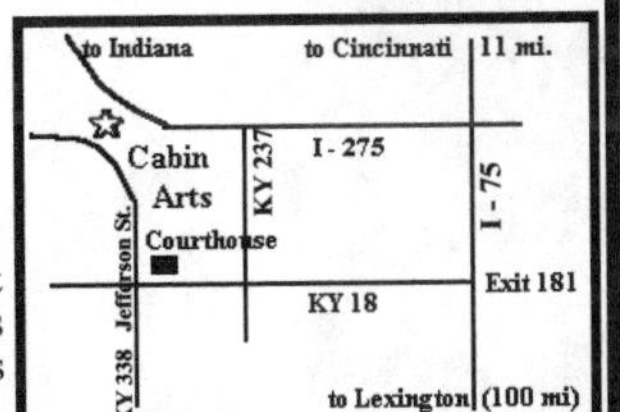

Winchester, KY #21

Tues - Sat
10 - 6

PieceWorks Quilt Shop

67 S. Main St. 40391
(859) 744-7404
pieceworksquilts@aol.com
Owners: Cleo Savala
& Jessica Allgire
Est: 2003 1200 sq.ft. 1000+ bolts

Located in Historic Downtown Winchester 20 minutes southeast of Lexington.
A wide selection of 100% cotton fabrics, books and notions.

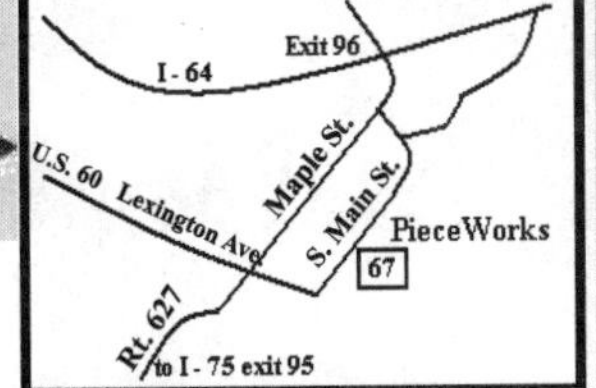

WILDERNESS ROAD QUILT CO.

(formerly World Wide Fabrics)
104 Man 'O War Dr
Danville, KY 40422

#22

We're your full line Quilt Shop and Bernina Sewing Center
Great selection of fine quilting cottons,
Books, Patterns, Quilting Necessities,
Custom Machine Quilting
Lots of Fun Classes

Store Hours
Mon - Fri 10AM to 6PM
Thursday 10AM to 9PM
Saturday 10AM to 4PM

Location:
On the Hwy 127 By-Pass across from the Boyle Co Fair Grounds. Danville, KY

Owner: Leslie Featherly **866-721-1175**
e-mail: fabrics@adelphia.net **859-236-1175**
Visit our website: www.wildernessroadquilt.com

Calico Patch Quilt Shop

155 Bluebank Road
Morehead, KY 40351
(606) 784-7235

TUE-FRI 10 - 5
SAT 9 - 2

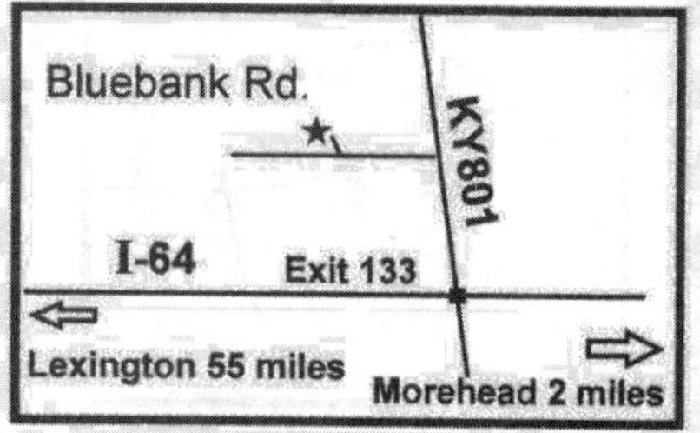

Nothing Sews Like A Bernina. Nothing.
BERNINA®

Morehead, KY #23

A Quilter's Garden of
Designer Fabrics, Notions, & Gifts

1.5 Miles From I-64

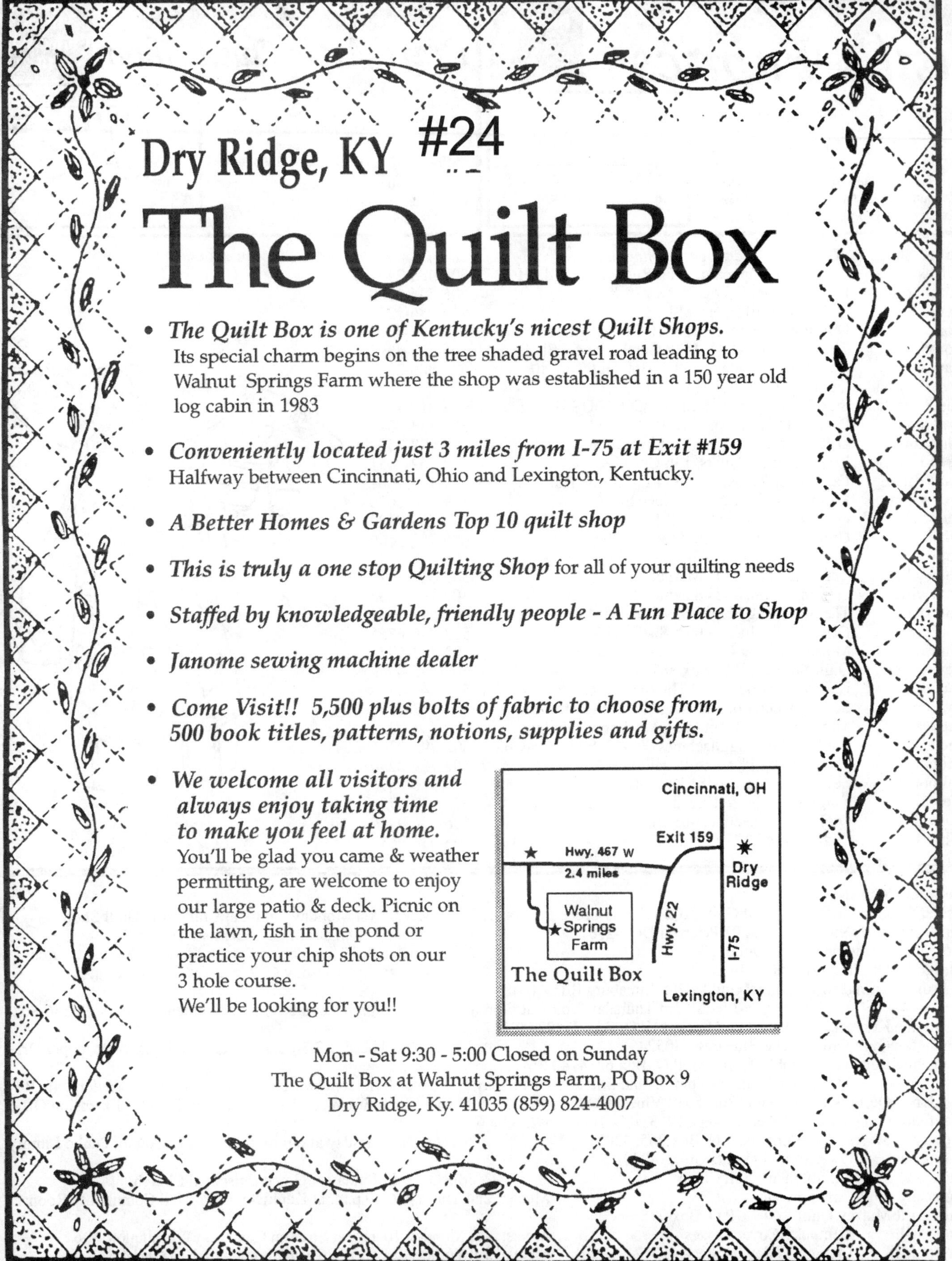
Dry Ridge, KY #24
The Quilt Box
• The Quilt Box is one of Kentucky's nicest Quilt Shops.
Its special charm begins on the tree shaded gravel road leading to Walnut Springs Farm where the shop was established in a 150 year old log cabin in 1983
• Conveniently located just 3 miles from I-75 at Exit #159
Halfway between Cincinnati, Ohio and Lexington, Kentucky.
• A Better Homes & Gardens Top 10 quilt shop
• This is truly a one stop Quilting Shop for all of your quilting needs
• Staffed by knowledgeable, friendly people - A Fun Place to Shop
• Janome sewing machine dealer
• Come Visit!! 5,500 plus bolts of fabric to choose from, 500 book titles, patterns, notions, supplies and gifts.
• We welcome all visitors and always enjoy taking time to make you feel at home.
You'll be glad you came & weather permitting, are welcome to enjoy our large patio & deck. Picnic on the lawn, fish in the pond or practice your chip shots on our 3 hole course.
We'll be looking for you!!
Cincinnati, OH
Exit 159
Hwy. 467 W
2.4 miles
Dry Ridge
Walnut Springs Farm
Hwy. 22
I-75
The Quilt Box
Lexington, KY
Mon - Sat 9:30 - 5:00 Closed on Sunday
The Quilt Box at Walnut Springs Farm, PO Box 9
Dry Ridge, Ky. 41035 (859) 824-4007

Other Shops in Kentucky: *We suggest calling first*

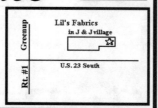

Allensville	Grandma's Cupboard, 5760 Russellville Rd., Hwy 79	502-483-2461
Barbourville	Kno Discount Fabric, Hwy. 229 & 25 E	606-546-9362
Berea	Quilt Shop, 102 Center St.	859-986-1239
Boaz	Quilting Kaleidoscope, 8510 Old Mayfield Rd.	270-534-4808
Corbin	The Kentucky Quilt, 1878 Cumberland Falls Hwy.	606-523-4393
David	David Appalachian Crafts, 6369 Highway 404	606-886-2377
East Bernstadt	Quilting B, 1870 E. Hwy. 30	606-843-2803
East Bernstadt	Star Tanning & Quilt Shop, 5506 N US Hwy 25	606-843-7336
Flatwoods	Penny's Quilt Shop, 1110 Powell Ln	606-833-8940
Glasgow	D & M Quilting Shop, 20 Flint Knob Rd.	270-678-2568
Grand Rivers	Rocky Hollow Quilts, 136 Chandler Ct.	270-362-2651
Harrodsburg	Farmhouse Treasures, 2784 Louisville Rd.	859-734-7001
Harrodsburg	Karen's Crafts, 723 N College St	859-734-0010
Hueysville	Quilt Shop, 738 Saltlick Rd.	606-358-9490
Liberty	Granny's Quilting, 12270 W Ky 70	606-787-4660
Louisa	Quilted Memories Quilt Shop, 201 E Madison St	606-638-0232
Louisville	Baer Fabrics, 515 E. Market St.	502-569-7016
Louisville	Quilting Shop, 3829 Staebler Ave	502-962-8232
Louisville	The Smocking Shop, 3829 Staebler Ave.	502-893-3503
Louisville	Dee's Crafts, Inc., 5005A Shelbyville Rd	502-896-6755
Murray	Murray Sewing Center, 942A S. 12th St.	502-753-5323
New Castle	Quilt Stitchin, P.O. Box 387	502-845-4987
Paducah	Hancock Fabrics, 3841 Hinkleville Rd.	502-443-4410
Paducah	Sewing Center of Paducah, 842 Joe Clifton Dr.	502-442-1661
Paducah	Michael Stewart Antiques, 136 Lone Oak Rd.	502-441-7222
Paducah	English's Sewing Machines, 7001 US Highway 68	502-898-7301
Philpot	The Quilting Place, 6845 Milton Rd.	502-729-2290
Philpot	Sew Much More, 6481 Ditto Rd.	270-926-8886
Pineville	Kathy's Needle & Thread, P.O. Box 118 Route #2	606-337-6753
Russell	Quilting Connection, 401 Belfonte	606-836-9920
Whitesburg	Cozy Corner, 127 E. Main St.	606-633-9637

Kentucky Guilds:

Ashland	Gone to Pieces Quilt Guild, 2027 Hoods Creek Pike, 41102	Meets: 1st Monday 7 p.m. at Craft Attic Quilt Shop
Elizabethtown	Ninepatchers, 201 Peterson Dr., 42701	Meets: 9:30, Hardin Cty. Extension Office
Florence	Stringtown Quilt Guild	Meets: 3rd Thursday @ 7pm at Florence Baptist Church
Glasgow	Quilting Friends, 42141	Meets: 2nd Tuesday @ 9:30am at Cultural Center
Hebron	Stringtown Quilters' Guild, 4706 Limaburg Rd., 41048	Meets: 3rd Thursday 7 p.m. at Florence Baptist Church Contact: Linda Whittenburg at (859) 586-8021
Lexington	Kentucky Heritage Quilt Society, P.O. Box 23392, 40517	
Lexington	Quilt Guild of the Bluegrass, 40524	Meets: 2nd Tuesday 7:30 p.m. at KET building, 600 Cooper Dr.
Louisville	Louisville Nimble Thimbles, P.O. Box 6234, 40207	Meets: 1st Thursday 7pm Sit and Stitch 3rd Thursday 6:30pm at Jeffersontown Community Ctr 10619 Taylorsville Rd
Lyndon	Quilters Choice Fan Club, 8012 Vinecrest Ave., 40222	Meets: 1st & 3rd Wed. 9 a.m. Jefferson Country Extension Office
Mayfield	Graves County Piecemakers, Rt. 3, P.O. Box 236-2, 42066	
Murray	Murray Quilt Lovers, P.O. Box 265, 42071	Meets: 3rd Tuesday at 6 p.m. at Calloway County Public Library
Owensboro	Owensboro Quilters Guild, 42301	
Paducah	Paducah Stitch 'n' Quilt Circle	Meets: 3rd Monday at Grace Episcopal Church
Paducah	Quilt And Sew On	Meets: 2nd Tuesday 6:30 p.m. at Kentucky Oaks Mall Community Room
Paintsville	Murray Quilt Lovers, P.O. Box 975	
Shelbyville	Kentucky Cover Lovers	Meets: 4th Monday 10 a.m. at Stratton Center on Whasington Ave.
Taylor Mill	Licking Valley Quilters, 41017	Meets: 3rd Wednesday @ 10am at Hilltop Church of Christ
Walton	Walton Christian Church Quilt Group	Meets: Every Wednesday @ 6:30pm at Walton Christian Church

18 Featured Shops

LOUISIANA

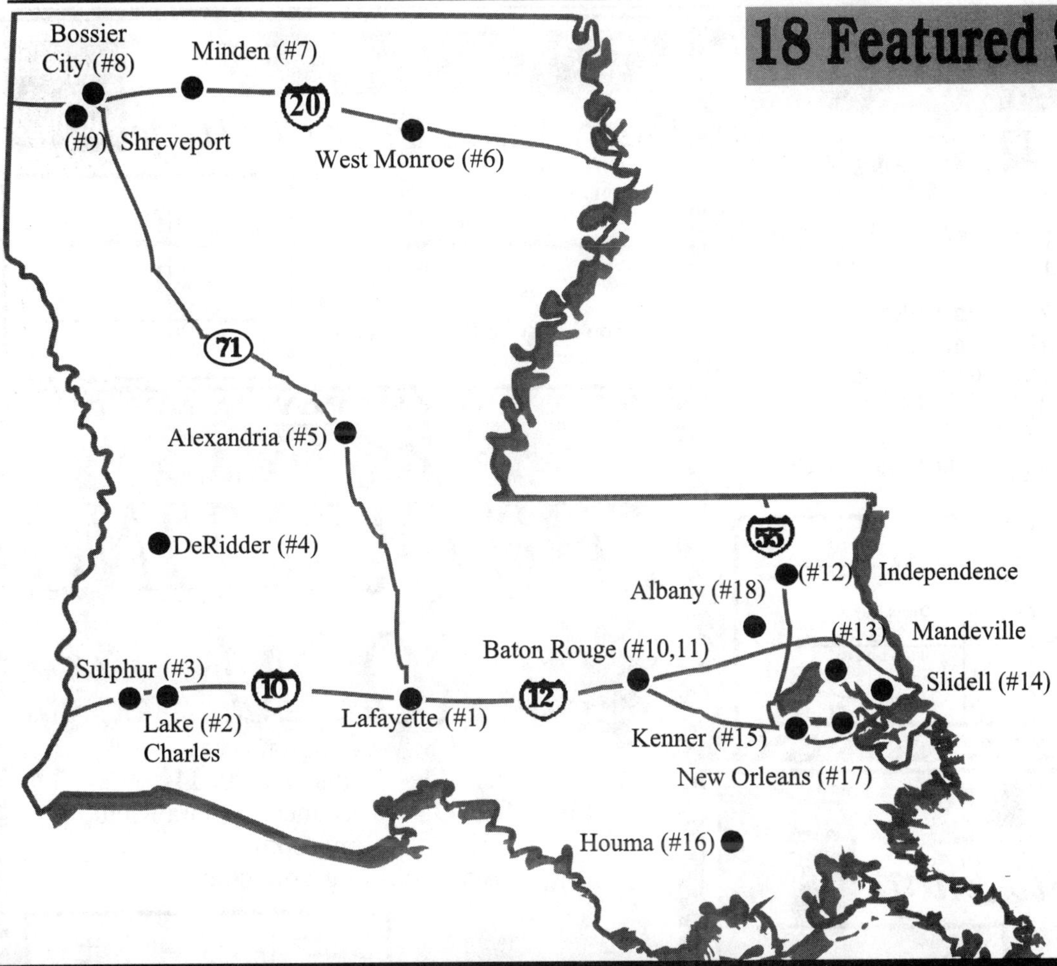

Bossier City (#8)
Minden (#7)
20
(#9) Shreveport
West Monroe (#6)
71
Alexandria (#5)
DeRidder (#4)
55
(#12) Independence
Albany (#18)
(#13) Mandeville
Baton Rouge (#10,11)
Sulphur (#3)
10
12
Slidell (#14)
Lake (#2) Charles
Lafayette (#1)
Kenner (#15)
New Orleans (#17)
Houma (#16)

Lafayette, LA #1

Ginger's Needleworks

Mon - Fri 10 - 5 and Sat 10 - 3

1001 East Gloria Switch Road 70507 (337) 232-7847

Owner: Ginger Moore Est:1984 1600 sq.ft. Quilting 200 sq.ft. Yarns

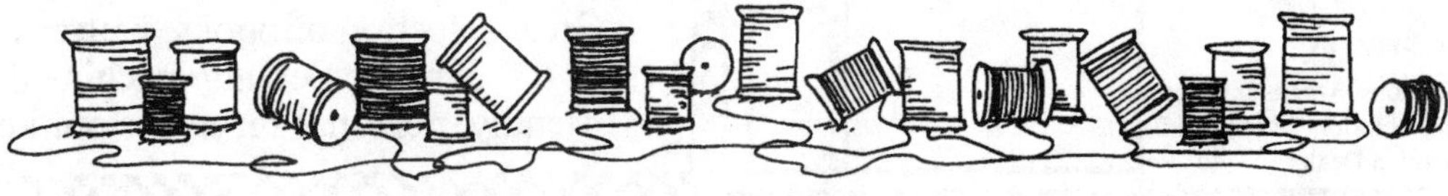

3500 Bolts of Fabrics
Specializing in Civil War and 1930's Reproductions and Oriental Fabrics. We also have a large selection of Novelty Prints.
Lots of Notions, Patterns & Books

Make www.quiltknit.com your one-stop online quilt store for all your quilting fabrics, notions, books and patterns.
Secure online ordering and fast service.

Ginger's Needleworks
Exit 2
1 1/2 mile
1001
Gloria Switch Road
I - 49
I - 10

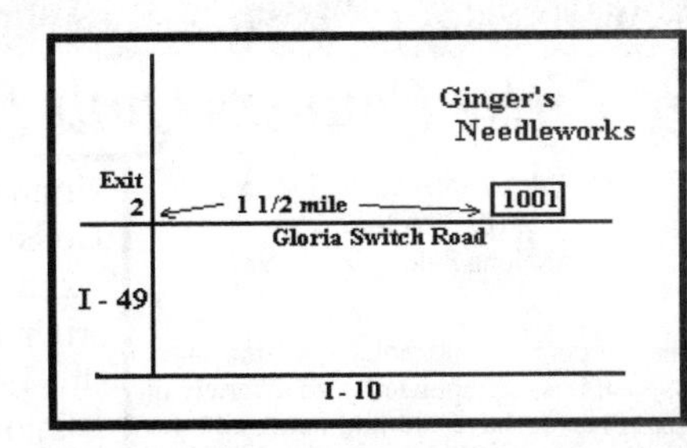

Lake Charles, LA #2

Quilts Bayou

South West Louisiana's premier quilt shop where stitching and laughter go hand in hand

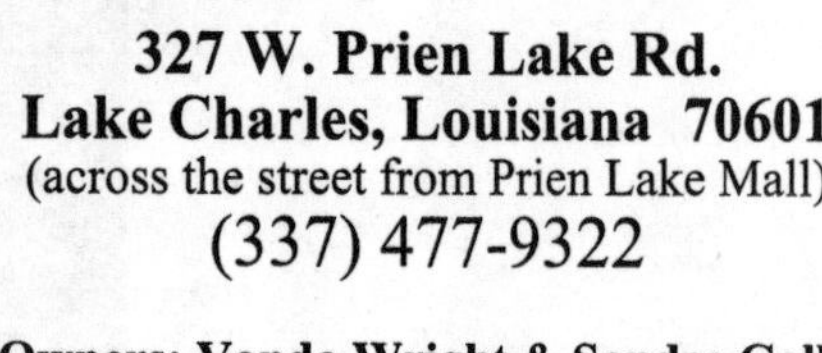

327 W. Prien Lake Rd.
Lake Charles, Louisiana 70601
(across the street from Prien Lake Mall)
(337) 477-9322

Owners: Vonda Wright & Sandee Golla

Mon - Fri
9:30 - 5
Thur til 8
Sat 9:30 - 3

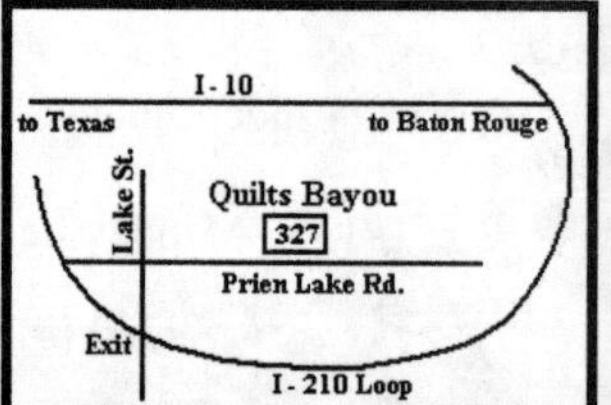

Sulphur, LA #3

Mon - Fri
9:30 - 5
Sat 10 - 3

Mary Ann's Fabric Cottage

1017 S. Beglis Pkwy. 70663
(337) 528-9190 Fax: (337) 528-9195
E-Mail: maryann@fabriccottage.com
Web Site: www.fabriccottage.com
Est: 1994

"Your one-stop quilter's paradise."
Quilt Fabrics, Quilt Kits, Patterns, Books

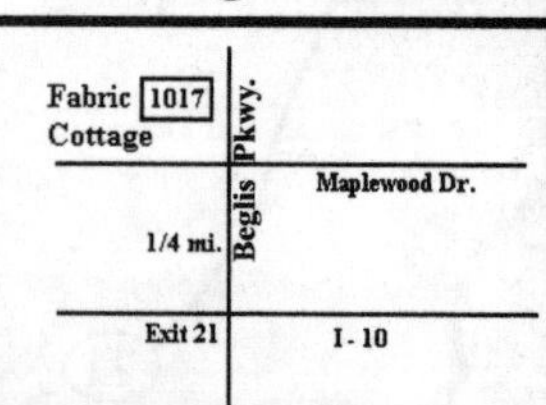

DeRidder, LA #4

THE QUILTING ROOM

113 S. Washington Ave.
DeRidder, Louisiana 70634
(337) 462-4944 Owner: Sandra Rich
srich@quiltingroom.com
www.quiltingroom.com

Tues - Fri
9:30 - 5:30
Sat 10 - 5

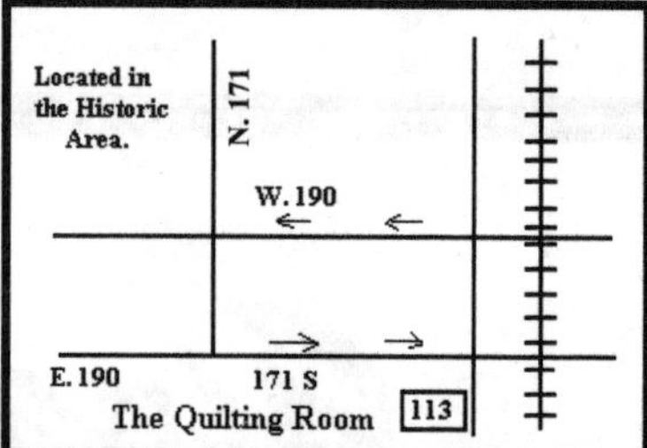

DeRidder is located 45 miles north of Interstate 10 on US Highway 171.

Over 2500 bolts of top quality 100% cottons
Complete selection of 30's reproduction Aunt Grace, Granny's Nine (Chanteclaire).
Large line of Civil War reproduction prints
Great selection of books, patterns, and notions
Janome Sewing machine dealer.
Friendly, personal service is our key to success.

Alexandria, LA #5

Mon - Fri
9 - 5
Sat 9-2

Red Roof Quilt Shop

5412 Masonic Drive 71301
(318) 443-1589
Quilts110@cox-internet.com
Owners: Faye Dantzler

We cater to quilters. 100% Cotton fabrics, from top companies with a wide selection of books & notions. Custom made quilts too.

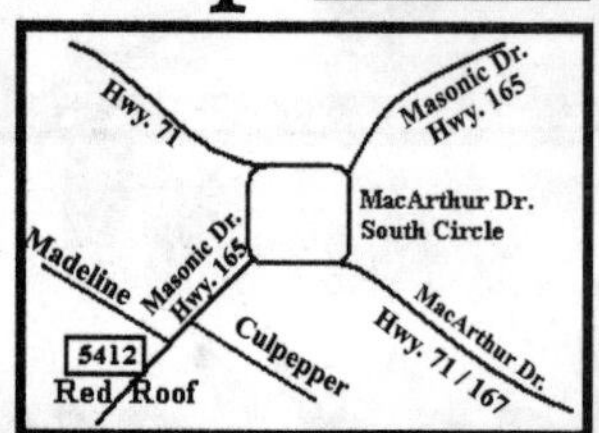

West Monroe, LA #6

Mon - Fri
9 - 5
Sat 10 - 4

Quilt 'N Stitch

6049 Cypress St. 71291
(318) 396-6020
E-Mail: qultstch@bayou.com
Web Site: www.quiltnstitch.com
2000+ Bolts

The store is located in a house where antiques nestle among the many fabrics, books, and notions. Authorized Bernina Dealer

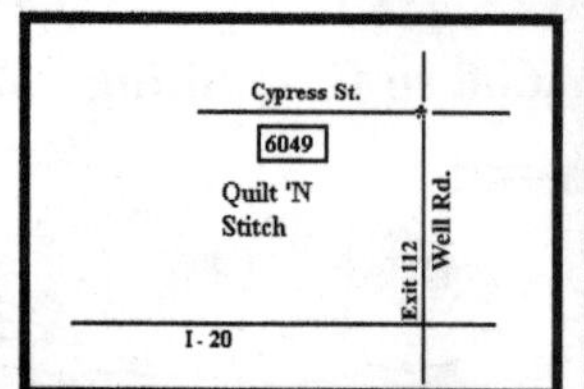

Minden, LA #7

Tues - Fri
10 - 5

The Little Country Quilt Shop

534 Old Arcadia Rd. 71055
(318) 377-2462
Owner: Nona Sale Est: 1983

From I - 20 take Exit 49. Go North 3½ miles to the 2nd traffic light. Turn right & stay in exit lane for 1/4 mile. Lane turns into Old Arcadia Rd. Shop is 1 mile on left.

We have approx. 1500 bolts. All the latest books, patterns, & supplies. Also a variety of classes. Plus we have old and new quilts for sale. Please drop by for our group meeting every Thursday.

Bossier City, LA #8

Mon - Sat
10 - 6

Fabric Boutique

Heart of Bossier Shopping Ctr.
1701 Old Minden Rd. 71111
Toll Free (877) SEW-ASAP (739-2727)
(318) 742-0047 Fax: (318) 742-5934
Owner: Shirley C. Warren
Est: 1972

Unique combination of classes, quilting supplies & fabrics. Authorized Bernina, Sewing Machine dealer.

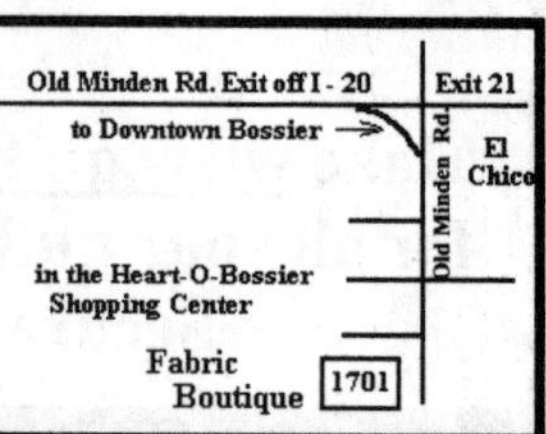

Introducing Northwest Louisiana's Only full Service Quilt Shop

2500+ bolts, classes, books, notions
Everything you need for quilting!
Long-arm Quilting Services -
"You piece it -- we'll quilt it!"

Mon - Sat 10 - 5

750 Drexel Drive
Shreveport, LA 71106
318-865-2662

From I-20, exit onto I-49 South
From I-49, take 2nd exit - 203, go East on Pierremont Rd. & take Line Ave. South

I-20 Exits 18A & 18D
I-49
Line Ave.
2nd Exit 203
Pierremont Rd.
750
Drexel
Superior Grill

Shreveport, LA #9

Tour Groups Welcome!!

Premier Dealer of
Husqvarna VIKING
Featuring
DAKOTA EMBROIDERY COLLECTIONS

www.materialgirlquiltsonline.com

Baton Rouge, LA #10

A Quilter's Workshop

8700 Airline Hwy. Suite A 70815
(225) 929-9902
aquiltersworkshop@cox.net
Owner: Pamela Grigsby

A full service quilt shop offering 100% cotton fabrics, notions, books, patterns & classes. Wonderful selection of blender fabrics & many batiks. We carry many quilt related gift items. Come by & pet our fabrics.

Please Call For Hours

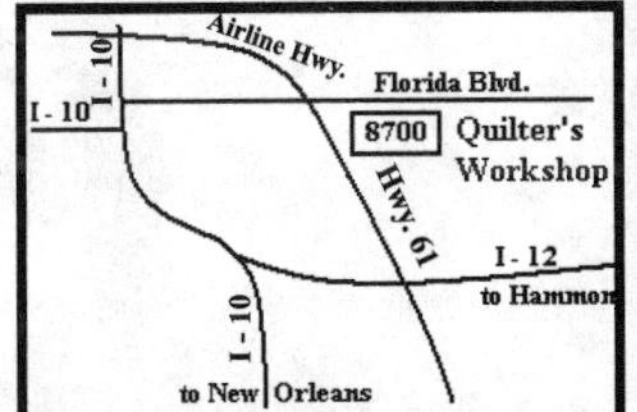

Conveniently located off Interstate 12. Take the Airline/Highway 61 N exit, go north 1.9 miles (6 lights). Turn right onto Vine St, then take an immediate left onto the service road. Go down the service road and we are located just past the curve on the right. Look for the large green signs.

Baton Rouge, LA #11

Piecing Memories Quilt Shop, LLC.

13847 Coursey Blvd., Suite 1
Baton Rouge, LA 70816
(225) 756-0542
Fax: (225) 756-0543
PMQuiltshop@yahoo.com
Owners: Paula St. Romain & Linda Burns
Established 2003

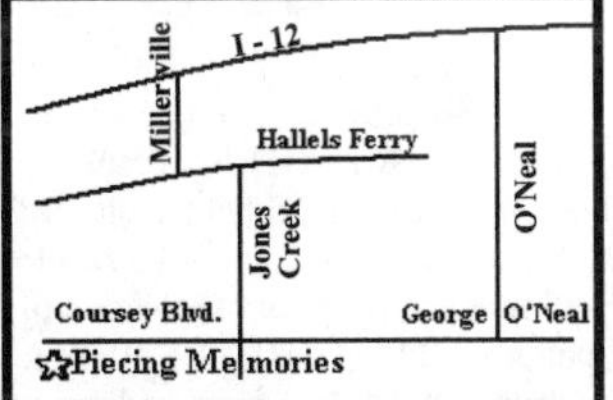

1000 Bolts of 100% cottons, Patterns, Books, Notions, Felted Wools, Classes, Friendly Service!!!

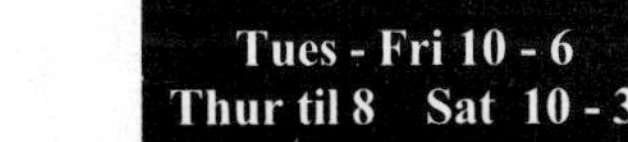

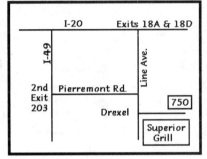

Independence, LA #12

15111 Catfish Farm Road 70443

985-878-6396

mamasquiltshop@yahoo.com
www.mamasquiltshop.com

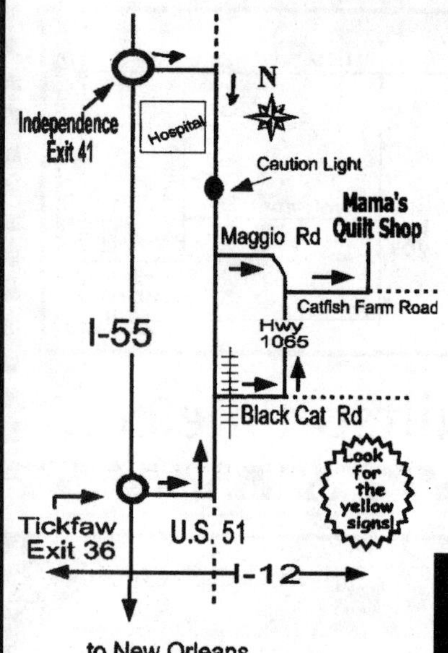

We carry over 2000 Bolts of fabric including RJR, Benatex, Marcus Brothers, Timeless Treasures, Hoffman, P&B and many, many more.
Best prices around!

Fabrics, notions, books, classes and lots of inspiration at the "quilt shop in the country."

Hours: 9 am - 5 pm
Mon-Sat

Mandeville, LA #13

Mon - Fri 9:30 - 5
Sat 9:30 - 3

Bright Hopes Quilting

5150 Hwy. 22, Suite C1 70471
(985) 845-9554 Fax: (985) 845-9599
brighthopes@bellsouth.net
www.brighthopesquilting.com
Owner: Pearl Squires
Est: 2003 2200 sq.ft. 1000 Bolts
Where quilters gather! We carry a wide variety of fabrics - brights, orientals, batiks, florals, plus classes, books & notions.

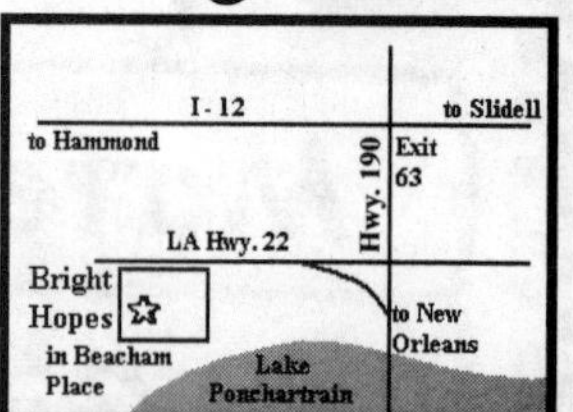

Slidell, LA #14

Mon - Fri 9 - 5
Sat 9 - 4

Nanny's Quilting Niche'

1922 First St. 70458
(985) 649-4411 Fax: Same
nickstep@prodigy.net
Owner: Blanche Nichols
Est: 2002 1600 sq.ft.

Longarm Machine Quilting & Fabrics, Notions, Books and Classes.

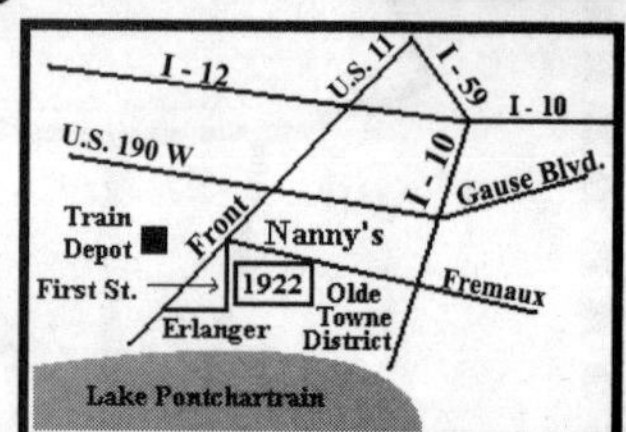

Kenner, LA #15

Mon - Sat 10 - 5

Scrap-Happy Quilter

2546 Williams Blvd. 70062
(504) 463-0094 Fax: Same
Owner Janice Andrews
Est: 1997 1400 sq.ft. 2000+ Bolts

Bright, Cheery Full Service Shop 5 minutes from New Orleans International Airport.

Houma, LA #16

Mon - Fri 10 - 5
Sat 10 - 3

The Quilting Niche, LLC

1220 St. Charles St. 70360
(985) 876-9077 Fax: (985) 876-9078
applenspice@peoplepc.com
Owner: Debra Frank
Est: 2004 2000 sq.ft. 600 Bolts & Growing
A complete collection of fabrics for your quilting needs. A large selection of books, patterns and notions. Also offering classes from basic to advanced and wearables.

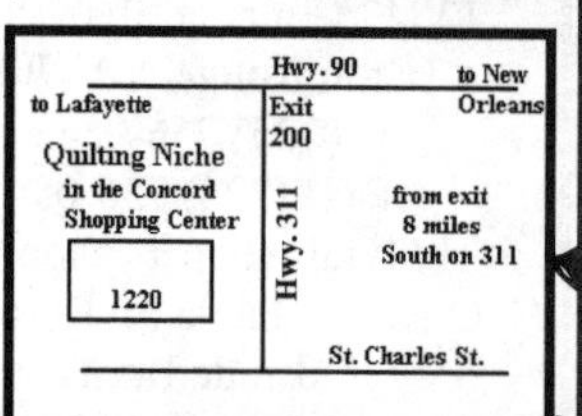

New Orleans, LA #17

(800) 453-6998

Quilt Cottage

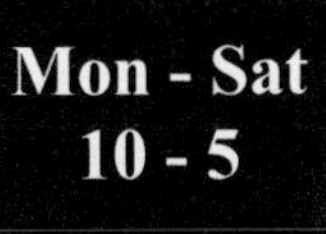

801 Nashville Avenue 70115 (504) 895-3791
Owners:
Carol Schiaffino
& Jeanne Lincks
Est: 1981 2000 sq.ft.

Your Complete Quilt Shop !

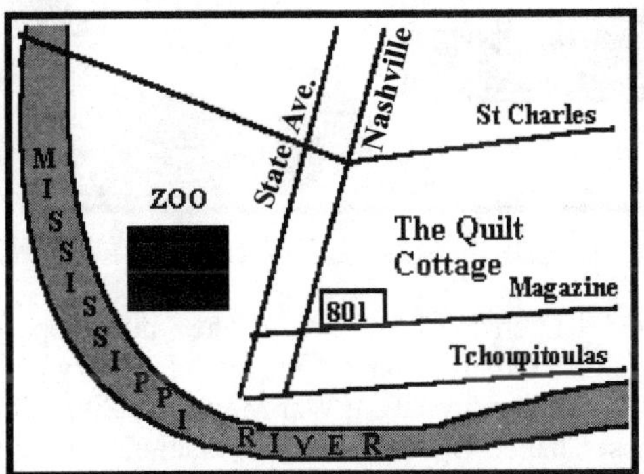

Room full of 100% cotton fabric. Over 2000 Bolts. The latest books, notions, & Patterns. New, Antique, Custom made quilts. Repair. Our own Mardi Gras Fat Quarter Packets, Patterns and Bolts of Mardi Gras fabrics are stocked year 'round.

Send us your name and address and we'll send you our free newsletter three times per year.

Albany, LA #18

**Mon - Fri
10 - 5
Sat 10 - 3**

The Quilt Shop

29937 S. Montpelier Ave., P.O. Box 1716, Albany, LA 70711
225/209-2097 225/209-2096 FAX thequiltshop@bellsouth.net
Owners: Judy Jensen & Rhoda Jordan
Est: 2001 3000 sq.ft. Over 2500 Bolts of 100% Cotton

"pursuing the heavenly art of quiltmaking"

Specializing in reproduction fabrics, as well as Aunt Grace, Thimbleberries, Batiks, flannels, orientals, juveniles, florals and redwork. Huge selection of books and patterns with over 100 samples hanging from our walls. Long-arm Gammill quilting services available. Send us your e-mail address and we'll send you our newsletter!

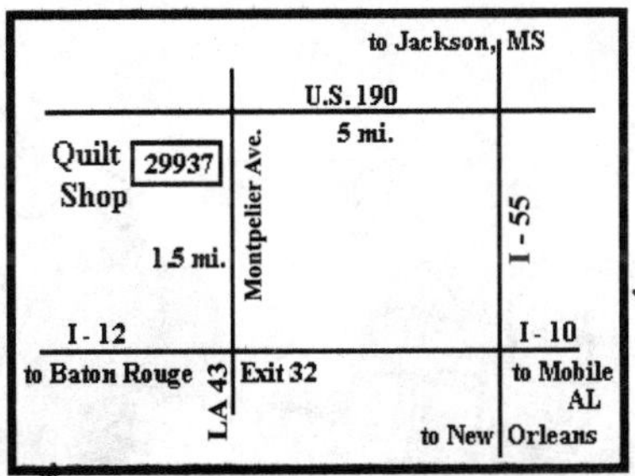

to Jackson, MS
U.S.190
5 mi.
Quilt Shop 29937
Montpelier Ave.
I - 55
1.5 mi.
I - 12
I - 10
to Baton Rouge
LA 43
Exit 32
to Mobile AL
to New Orleans

www.albanyquiltshop.com

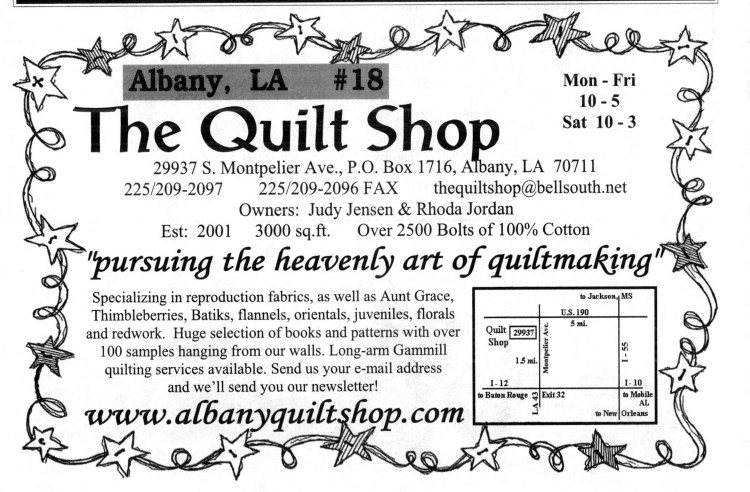

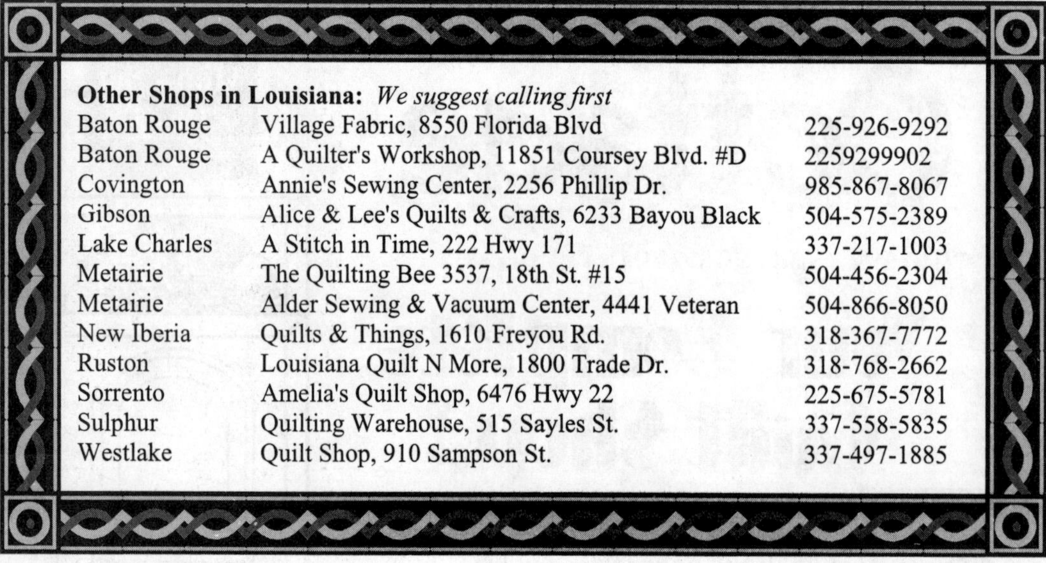

Other Shops in Louisiana: *We suggest calling first*

Baton Rouge	Village Fabric, 8550 Florida Blvd	225-926-9292
Baton Rouge	A Quilter's Workshop, 11851 Coursey Blvd. #D	2259299902
Covington	Annie's Sewing Center, 2256 Phillip Dr.	985-867-8067
Gibson	Alice & Lee's Quilts & Crafts, 6233 Bayou Black	504-575-2389
Lake Charles	A Stitch in Time, 222 Hwy 171	337-217-1003
Metairie	The Quilting Bee 3537, 18th St. #15	504-456-2304
Metairie	Alder Sewing & Vacuum Center, 4441 Veteran	504-866-8050
New Iberia	Quilts & Things, 1610 Freyou Rd.	318-367-7772
Ruston	Louisiana Quilt N More, 1800 Trade Dr.	318-768-2662
Sorrento	Amelia's Quilt Shop, 6476 Hwy 22	225-675-5781
Sulphur	Quilting Warehouse, 515 Sayles St.	337-558-5835
Westlake	Quilt Shop, 910 Sampson St.	337-497-1885

Louisiana Guilds:

Albany — Strawberry Patch Quilters

Albany — Pieces of Time, 29937 S. Montpelier, P.O. Box 1716 — Meets: 1st Thursday 10:30 a.m. at The Quilt Shop

Baton Rouge — River City Quilting Guild — Meets: 1st Thursday 7pm at Goodwood Library

DeRidder — Common Thread Guild, 1402 Meadowbrook Dr., 70634 — Meets: 3rd Tuesday 10 am War Memorial Civic Center

DeRidder — Piecemakers, 1334 Shadybrook St., 70634 Meets: Ft. Polk Main Post Chapel, Open to military personnel and wives

Jonesboro — Heritage Quilt Guild, 71251 — Meets: 1st Wednesday 9:30 a.m. at Jackson Parish Library

Leesville — Sew Crazy Quilters, 3699 Tank Tr., 71446 — Meets: 4th Tuesday 6:30 p.m. at Vernon Parish Library

Metairie — Gulf State Quilting Assoc., P.O. Box 8391, 70011

Metairie — Jefferson Parish Quilting Guild, 711 Ridgelake Dr.

Monroe — North Louisiana Quilters
Meets: Morning Stars Chapter--1st Tuesday 9:30 a.m., Sunshine Chapter--1st Thursday 1 p.m., Moonlight Chapter--1st Thursday 6 p.m. Call (318) 396-6020 for locations

Monroe — North LA Quilters Guild, 71201 — Meets: 1st Thursday 1 p.m. & 6:30 p.m. at Auacheta Extension Office.

Ponchatoula — Southern Samplers, 165 E. Pine St., 70454

Shreveport — Red River Quilters, P.O. Box 4811, 71134 Meets: 1st Monday 1 p.m. & 6:30 p.m. Broadmore Prebyterian Church.
Holds annual quilt show. Also classes and workshops offered. Seven community projects.

Slidell — Camellia Quilters, 70458 Meets: 3rd Thursday 9:30 a.m. & 7 p.m. Aldersgate Methodist Church, 360 Robert Blvd.

Westlake — Slightly Off Grain, 1034 Ann Street, 70669 — Meets: 3rd Tuesday at Heartstrings--Quilts & More

Westlake — Calcasicu Cut-Ups Guild, P.O. Box 1111, 70663 — Meets: 1st Thursday 10 a.m. or 6:30 p.m. at Managan Center, 1000 McKinley

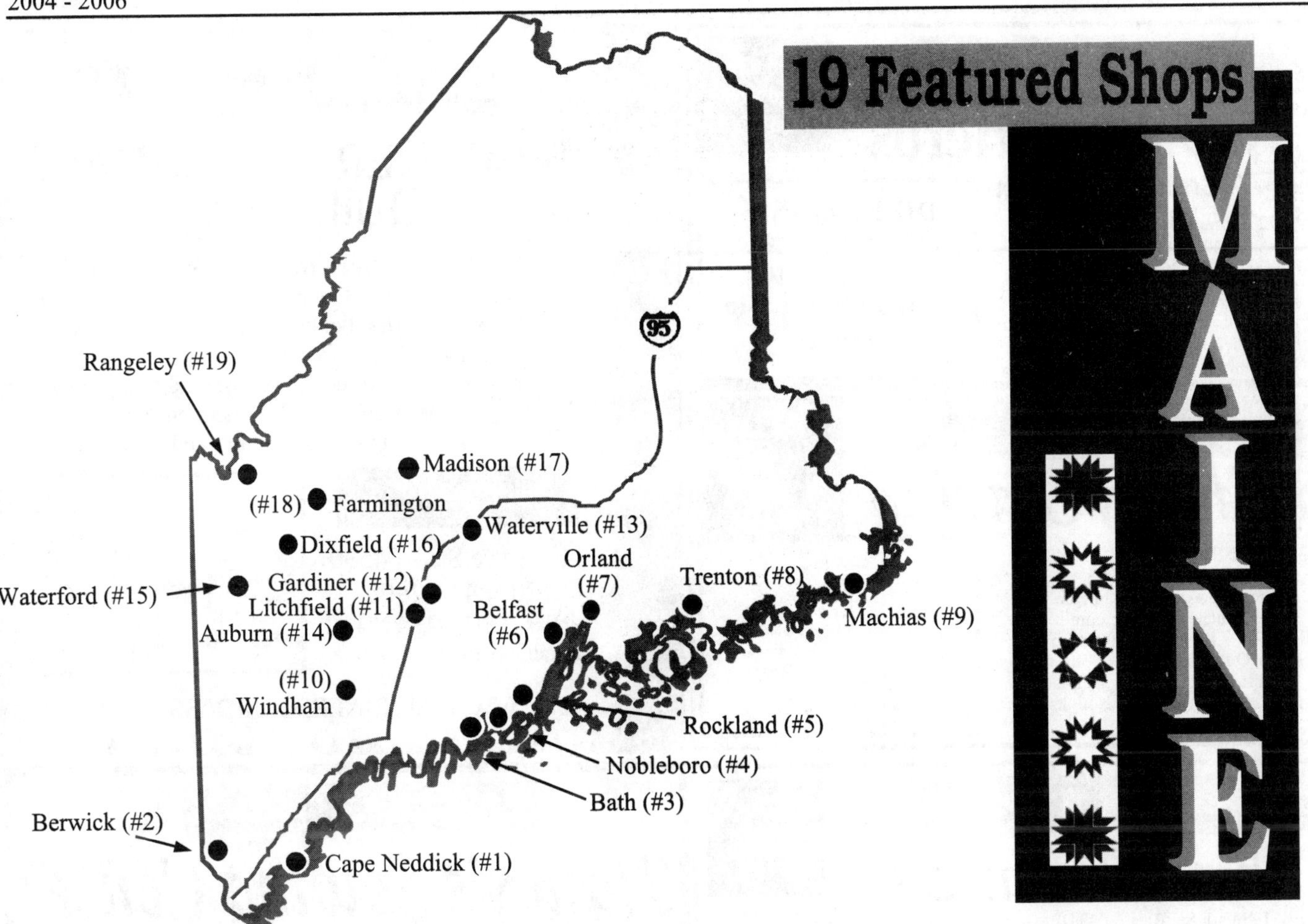
19 Featured Shops
MAINE
Rangeley (#19)
Madison (#17)
(#18) Farmington
Waterville (#13)
Dixfield (#16)
Orland (#7)
Waterford (#15)
Gardiner (#12)
Trenton (#8)
Litchfield (#11)
Belfast (#6)
Machias (#9)
Auburn (#14)
(#10) Windham
Rockland (#5)
Nobleboro (#4)
Bath (#3)
Berwick (#2)
Cape Neddick (#1)
95

Berwick, ME #2

Wed - Sat 10 - 5
Sun 1 - 5

Cottage Herbs
A Craft & Quilt Shop

372 Diamond Hill Rd. 03901
(207) 698-5507
Owner: Nancy Riley Est: 1980

We specialize in country fabrics--cottons, homespuns, wool, wool felt & great background fabrics for stitcheries. Many books, patterns, on doll making, penny rugs, quilts & stitcheries.

DIRECTIONS:
(We're easy to find)
Just Follow the signs on Route 9 in Berwick

Bath, ME #3

Mariner's Compass Quilt Shop

"Guiding Quilters to the City of Ships"

Join us in historic downtown Bath and shop amidst our 100% cotton fabrics, books, notions, patterns, wool, penny rug/rug hooking projects, and our own exclusive Fingerguard Safety Rulers, "The essential rotary rulers for safety minded quilters". Our selections range from batik and contemporary to country and primitive.

Tues - Sat 10 - 5

11 Centre St. 04530
(207) 443-2900
Fax: (207) 443-2904
Owner: Amanda B. Ulmer

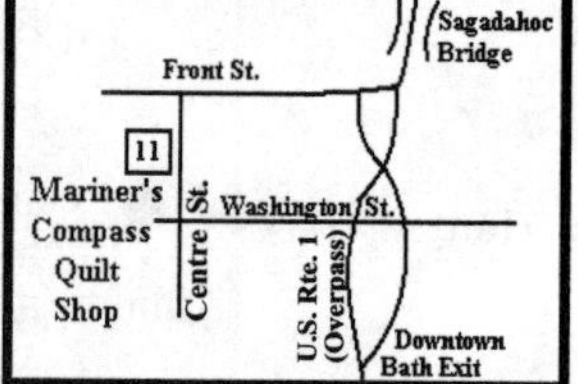

WWW.MARINERSCOMPASS.COM

Nobleboro, ME #4

Mon - Fri 9:30 - 5:30
Sat 10 - 4:30
Sun 12 - 4

Maine-ly Sewing

48 Atlantic Hwy., U.S. Rt. 1 04348
(207) 563-8445
mainelysewing@hotmail.com
www.mainelysewing.com
Est: 2001 100 sq.ft. 3000+ bolts

Catering to Quilters. 3000+ Bolts of high quality fabrics from top manufacturers. Hand-dyed fabrics, Batiks, Notions, Kits, Books & Patterns.

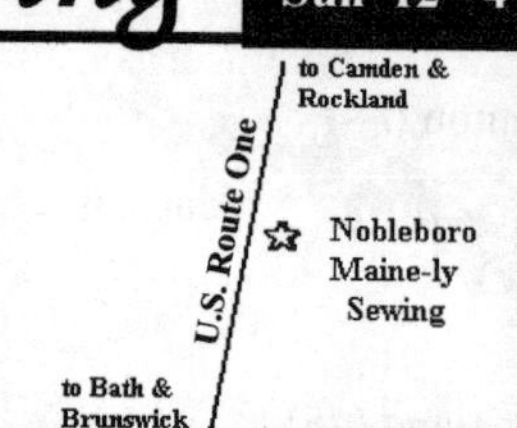

Rockland, ME #5

Mon - Sat 9 - 6
Sun 12 - 5

Fabric Bonanza

195 Park St., Rt. 1 04841
(207) 594-2555
info@fabfabrics.com
www.fabfabrics.com
Owners: Joel & Barbara Fishman
Est: 1976 8000 sq.ft. 2500 Bolts

Over 2500 bolts of 100% cotton top quality quilting fabric, supplies, books and patterns. Located on Route 1 in Mid-Coast Maine.

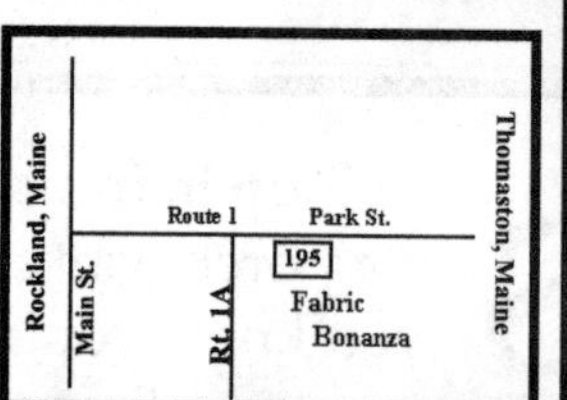

Belfast, ME #6

Nancy's Sewing Center

The "BIG" Little Quilt Shop in Belfast

216 Belmont Ave. 04915
(207) 338-1205
Owner: Nancy E. Black
Est: 1984 1200 sq.ft.
quiltfab@gwi.net

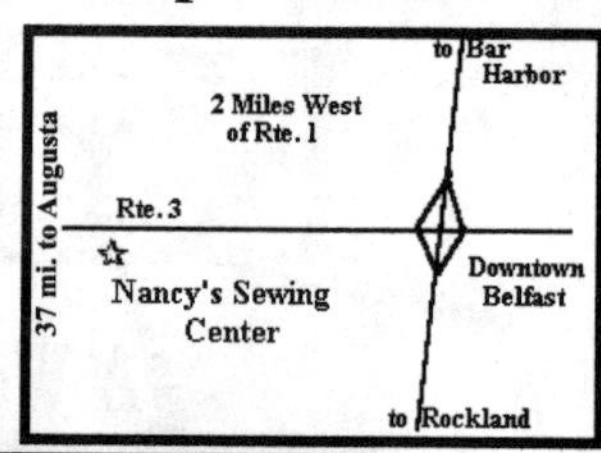

Mon - Fri 9 - 5 Weekends 10 - 4

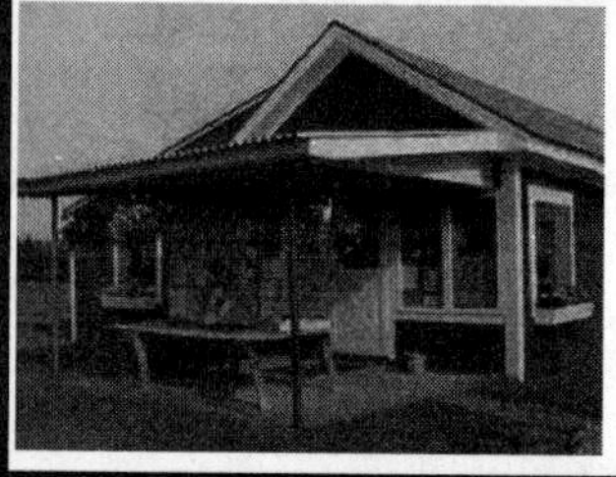

1500 Bolts of 100% cotton top quality quilting fabrics, quilting supplies, books, patterns, threads, Machine Quilting, Quilt Show every October
www.nancyssewingcenter.com

Orland, ME #7

Summer
Mon - Sat 9 - 5
Winter
Tues - Sat 10 - 5

The Quilted Cabin

4 Oak Hill Rd. 04472
(207) 469-7744
TheQuiltedCabin@aol.com
www.QuiltedCabin.com
Owners: Holly & Michael Simpson
Est: 2003 1200 sq.ft. 1500 Bolts

A log cabin full of 100% cottons, flannels & wool felt patterns, books, and qulting notions. "Come home to the cabin!"

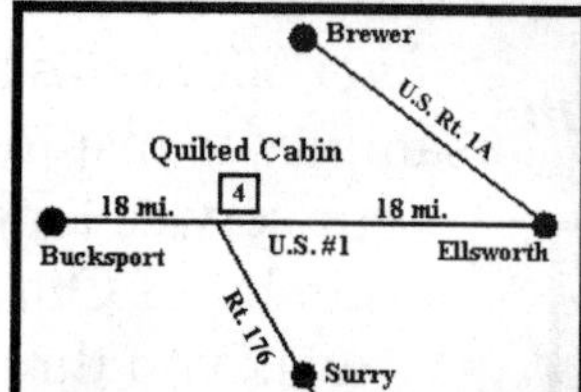

Trenton, ME #8

Mon - Fri 9:30 - 5:30
Sat 9:30 - 5

Sewing by the Sea, Inc.

11 Periwinkle Lane 04605
(207) 664-2558 Fax: (207) 664-2560
sewing2@midmaine.com
2000 sq.ft.

Downeast Maine's Sewing Resource
Quilt Cottons, Polartec™, Kwik Sew Patterns, Maine themed kits. Pfaff Dealer.

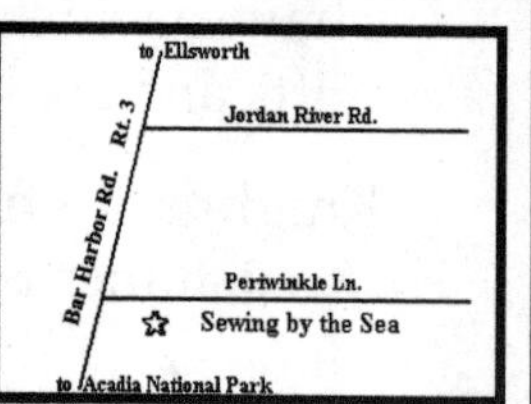

Machias, ME #9

Tues - Sat 10 - 4

Gingham Fabrics

Route 1 East
Mail: Box 286, Cutler, ME 04626
(207) 255-8238
Owner: Linda M. Throckmorton
Est: 1977 1700 sq.ft.

Eastern most quilt shop in the USA. Look for the geodesic dome midway between Ellsworth and Calais.

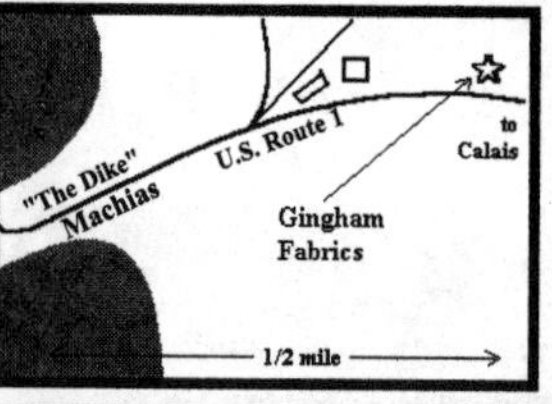

Windham, ME #10

Mon - Fri 9:30-4:30
Tues til 8
Sat 9:30-4
Sun 11 - 3

Calico Basket Quilt Shop

31 Page Road 04062
(207) 892-5606
CalicoBasketQlt@aol.com
Owner: JoAnne Hill
Est: 1982 1300 sq.ft.

Over 5000 Top Quality Fabrics.
The Latest Books, Notions, Craft Patterns, and Quilting Supplies.

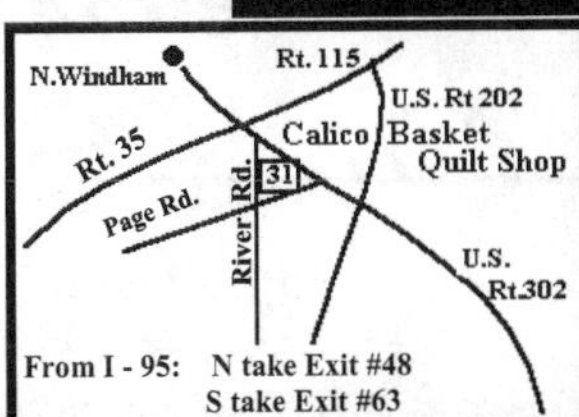

Litchfield, ME #11

Mon - Sat 10 - 4
Sun by chance

The Busy Thimble

2040 Hallowell Rd. 04350
(207) 268-4581 Est: 1990
bsythmbl@ctel.net
Owner: Cynthia Black 1000 sq.ft.
Only 6 1/2 mi. west of I - 95, Exit 51

More than 2000 bolts of antique reproduction fabric and homespuns.
Complete Library & Notions galore!

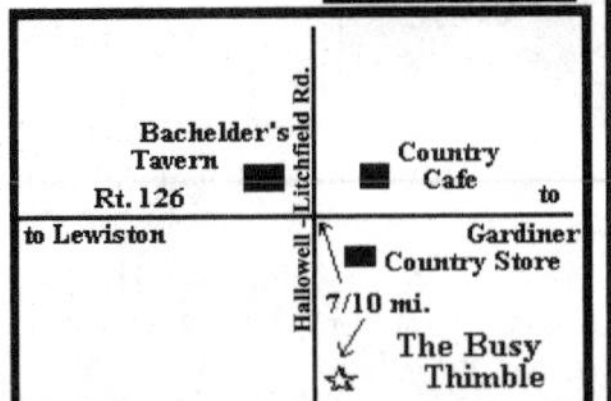

Gardiner, ME #12

Mon - Fri 9 - 6
Sat 10 - 5
Sun 11 - 4

Mystic Maine Quilts

287 Water St. 04345
(207) 582-0312 Fax: (207) 582-0314
mysticmequilts@aol.com
www.mysticmequilts.com
Owner: Roxy Getchell
Est: 2003 1800 sq.ft. 1500+ Bolts
100% cotton fabrics, notions, books, & patterns. Authorized Janome dealer.
Plus custom machine quilting & classes.

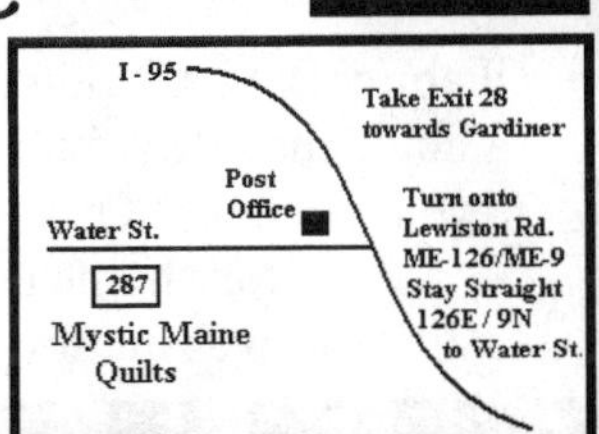

Waterville, ME #13

• FOUR FLOORS TO EXPLORE •

Friendly service and unique offerings since 1949

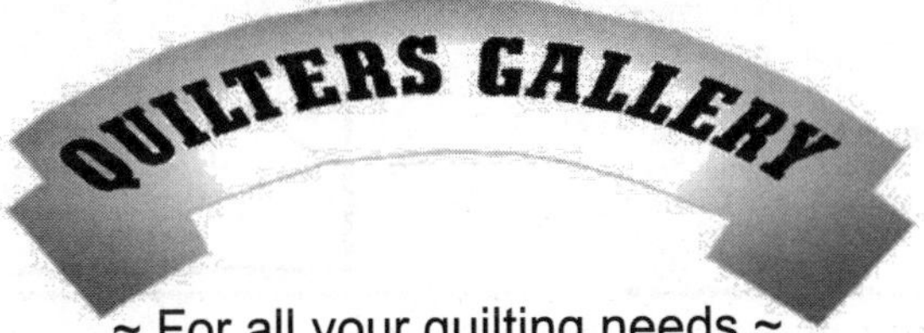

~ For all your quilting needs ~

* Thousands of newest fabrics
* Hundreds of books
* Quilters potpourri section
* Quilt in a Day Shop
* Long-arm Quilting systems

207-872-5403
Est: 1949
10,400 sq.ft.

E-mail:
vlodek@yardgoods.com
Website:
Coming Soon
Fax: 207-872-2118

Mon - Sat 9:30 - 5

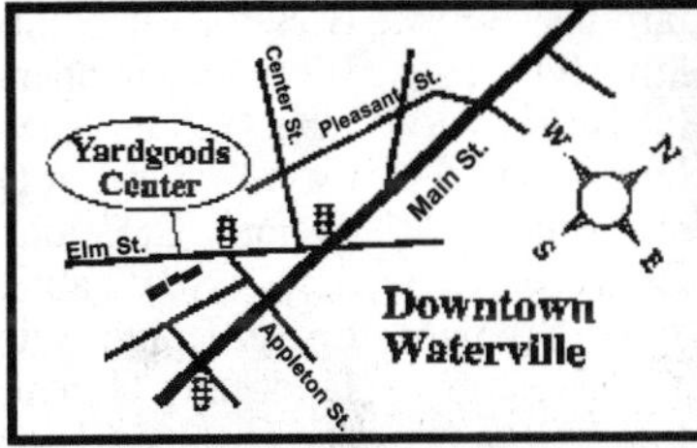

Just 4 Minutes from I-95

Yardgoods Center
Since 1949

MAINE'S CREATIVITY SUPER STORE
10 STORES IN ONE

- Designer / Fashion Fabrics
- Quilting
- Decorator Fabrics
- Home Designs
- Rubber Stamps
- Craft Supplies
- Needlework
- Fashion Yarns
- Sewing Machines

DOWNTOWN SHOPPING CENTER • WATERVILLE, MAINE 04901

Auburn, ME #14

Quiltessentials

Great selection of contemporary fabrics, batiks, brights, and much more. Lots of notions, books and patterns along with an interesting selection of handmade baskets. We carry a wide array of hand knitting yarns, novelty yarns and sock yarns. Books, patterns and knitting notions round out an enticing array of color and texture.

909 Minot Ave. 04210
(207)784-4486
www.quilt-essentials.com
info@quilt-essentials.com

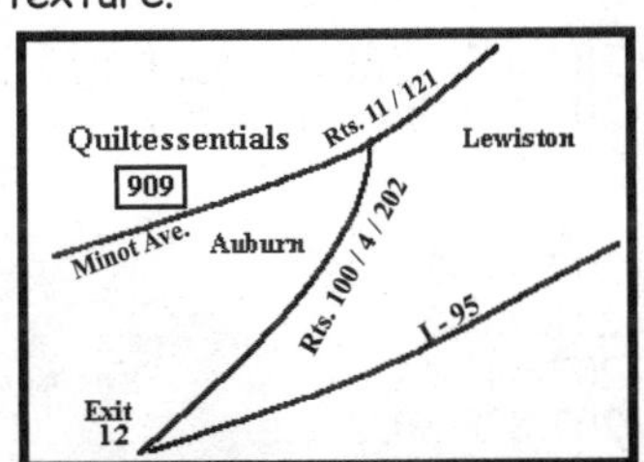

Store Hours: M-F 10-5, Tue 10-8, Sat 10-4

Waterford, ME #15

Mon - Sat 9:30 - 6
Sun 10 - 5

Kedar Quilts

Rt. 35, Box 61 04088
(207) 583-6182
Fax: (207) 583-6424
kedar@kedarquilts.com
www.kedarquilts.com Est: 1989
Owner: Margaret Gibson 4000 Bolts
Fine 100% Cotton Fabrics, Notions, Classes, Books. FOR SALE: New Quilts, Wallhangings and much more. Quilt Weekends and Retreats.
Located at Kedarburn Inn.

Dixfield, ME #16

Tues 9:30-8
Wed - Fri 9:30 - 5
Sat 9:30 - 1

Log Cabin Craftworks

31 Main St. on U.S. Route 2 04224
Phone/fax: (207) 562-8816
Owner: Norine Clarke
Est: 1981 550 bolts 2500 sq. ft.

Located in the foothills of Western Maine for over 20 years, we offer supplies for quilting, counted cross stitch, rubber stamping, scrapbooking, painting crafts and more.

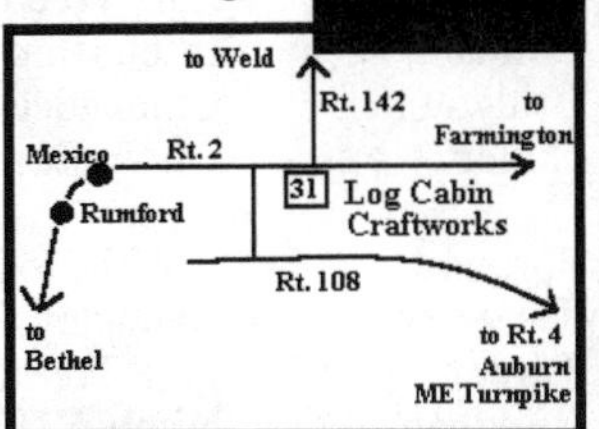

Madison, ME #17

The Fabric Garden

Mon - Fri 9 - 6
Sat 9 - 5
Sun 12 - 5

167 Lakewood Rd. 04950
(207) 474-9628
www.fabricgarden.com
Owner: Michaela Murphy
Est: 1978 2400 sq.ft.

The store for all your sewing and quilting needs. Name brand fabrics, books, patterns & notions. Janome sewing machines sales and service. "A Quilters must stop shop!"

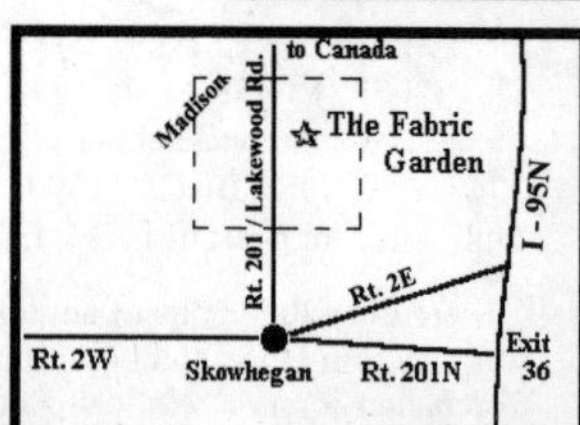

Farmington, ME #18

Fabric Inn

Open 7 Days a Week

413 Wilton Rd. 04938
(207) 778-4288
Est: 1976 2000 sq.ft.

The store for all your sewing, quilting and knitting needs. Name brand fabrics, books, patterns & notions. Janome sewing machines sales and service. Easy to find.

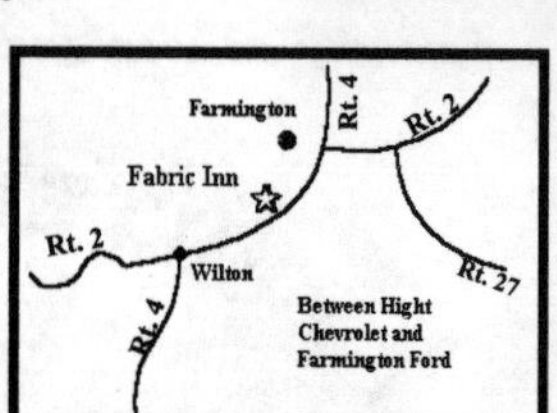

Rangeley, ME #19

Threads Galore Quilt Shop

Tues - Sat 10 - 5

27 Pleasant St.
P.O. Box 219 04970
(207) 864-5752
Est: 1996
carol@threadsgalore.com
www.threadsgalore.com
Owners: Carol & Dan Perkins

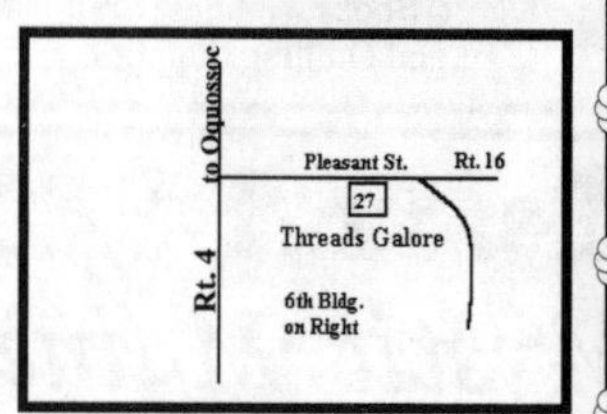

Fabric, Books, Notions, Classes. Quilted items for sale. Schedule a fun and relaxing quilt retreat with your friends at Quilt Inn Rangeley, a circa 1891, two-story home designed just for quilters! Visit our website for more info or to take a tour!!

Other Shops in Maine: *We suggest calling first*

Alton	Cotton Petals Fabric Shop, 2836 Bennoch Rd	207-394-3472
Boothbay Harbor	McKown Square Quilts, 14 Boothbay House Hill Rd.	207-633-2007
Caribou	Country Farm Fabrics, 204 Bailey Rd	207-498-8682
Dover	Foxcroft Quilting Mania, 27 North St	207-564-3533
East Waterboro	Bumble Bee Quiltworks, Rt 202	207-247-2008
Farmington	Pins & Needles, 133 Davis Rd	207-779-9060
Freeport	Quilt & Needlecrafts, 22 Main St. R.R. #1	207-865-3224
Gardiner	Honey Bear Quiltshop, 445 Water St	207-588-0012
Hallowell	Whipper Snappers, 100 Second St	207-622-3458
Harrison	Jan's Golden Needle, 24 Zakelo Rd.	207-583-2654
Hermon	David's Wife, A Quilt Shop, 603 Coldbrook Rd.	207-848-7222
Jefferson	Country Creations, Route 32, P.O. Box 949	207-549-7424
Liberty	Sew N Sew Fabrics, 343 Belfast Augusta Rd	207-589-3227
Lovell Village	Rocky Ridge Quilters, Route 5, 222 Main St.	207-925-3088
Millinocket	Jandseau's Greenhouse, 220 Iron Bridge Rd.	207-723-6332
New Harbor	Duck's, 2634 Bristol Rd.	207-677-3741
Newcastle	Alewives Fabrics 10 Main St., Box 480	207-563-5002
North Edgecomb	On Board, Route 27 Booth Bay Rd., PO Box 14	207-882-7536
Old Town	Sandi's Hideaway, 525 Kirkland Rd	207-827-3876
Pittsfield	Quilter's Dream, 9 Easy St.	207-938-3524
Saco	Patchwork Boutique Quilt Shop, 304 Beach St.	207-284-7287
Sidney	Mystic Maine Quilts, Middle Rd.	207-547-4331
So. Portland	Craft-Mania, Inc., 333 Clarks Pond Pkwy	207-828-8033
Topsham	Fabric Den, 125 Main St.	207-373-1468
Troy	Sew Many Things, 571 Detroit Rd	207-948-3084
Wales	Quiltworks Unlimited, 99 Avenue Rd	207-375-8221
West Forks	Cabin Fever Treasurers, RR 201	207-663-2268
West Paris	Maine Balsam & Fir Co, 16 Morse Hill Rd	207-674-5073
Wiscasset	The Marston House, PO Box 517	207-882-6010
Yarmouth	Yarmouth Quilt Company, 267 U.S. Rt #1	207-846-1550

Maine Guilds:

Augusta	Pine Tree Quilters Guild, Inc., P.O. Box 5405, 04332-5405 Meets: Jan, May, Sept. Veterans Adm. Bldg. @ Togas
Belfast	Friendship Sampler Quilters, 04915 Meets: 2nd & 4th Thursday 10 a.m. St. Margaret Church, 49 Court St.
Bridgeton	Chickadee Quilters Meets: 1st & 3rd Thursday @ 7pm at the Annex
Cutler	Down East Chapter, Pine Tree Quilters Guild, PO Box 286, 04626 Meets: 4th Thursday at 1 p.m. at Porter Memorial Library in Machias
Portland	Cobblestone Quilters
Rangeley	Rangeley Quilters Guild Meets: 1st & 3rd Thursday (Sept - June) 7 p.m. at Rangeley Congregational Church
Turner	Pine Tree Quilter's Guild, RD Box 252, 04282
Windham	Nimble Thimbles , 04062 Meets: 2nd & 4th Thursday 7 p.m. at Windham Library, Windham Ctr. Rd.

Catonsville (#19)
Grantsville (#20)
Jacksonville (#14)
Hagerstown (#15,16)
Towson (#10)
Frederick (#12,13)
Crofton (#9)
Dayton (#17)
Annapolis (#7)
Gaithersburg (#18)
Ellicott City (#11)
Centreville (#6)
Easton (#8)
Waldorf (#3)
Prince Frederick (#2)
La Plata (#1)
Salisbury (#4)
Snow Hill (#5)

20 Featured Shops

MARYLAND

LaPlata, MD #1

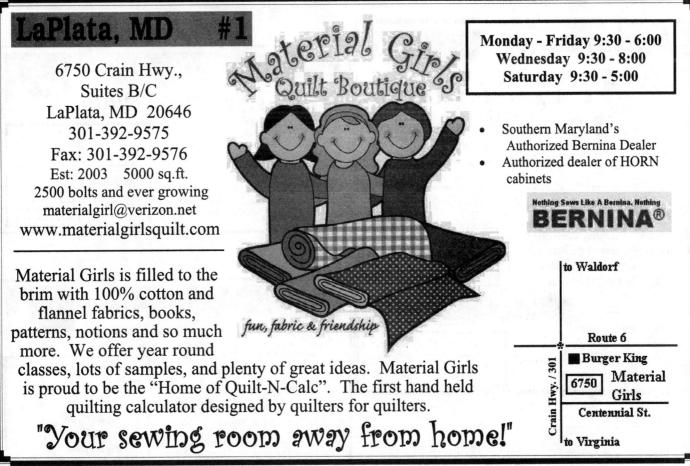

6750 Crain Hwy.,
Suites B/C
LaPlata, MD 20646
301-392-9575
Fax: 301-392-9576
Est: 2003 5000 sq.ft.
2500 bolts and ever growing
materialgirl@verizon.net
www.materialgirlsquilt.com

Material Girls Quilt Boutique

Monday - Friday 9:30 - 6:00
Wednesday 9:30 - 8:00
Saturday 9:30 - 5:00

- Southern Maryland's Authorized Bernina Dealer
- Authorized dealer of HORN cabinets

Nothing Sews Like A Bernina. Nothing
BERNINA®

Material Girls is filled to the brim with 100% cotton and flannel fabrics, books, patterns, notions and so much more. We offer year round classes, lots of samples, and plenty of great ideas. Material Girls is proud to be the "Home of Quilt-N-Calc". The first hand held quilting calculator designed by quilters for quilters.

fun, fabric & friendship

"Your sewing room away from home!"

to Waldorf
Route 6
Burger King
6750 Material Girls
Crain Hwy. / 301
Centennial St.
to Virginia

Calvert Quilt Shoppe

Prince Frederick, MD #2

Mon - Thur 9 - 6
Fri to 7
Sat 9 - 4

MD Rt. 4 at 20 Industry Lane 20678
(410) 535-0576 Fax: (410) 535-1197
marti@softhome.net
www.calvertquiltshop.com
Est: 1966 6000+ Bolts

We carry major manufacturers of Quilting Products.
100% Cotton, Name Brand Fabrics, Notions, Quilting Classes.
Janome Sewing Machine Sales and Service.

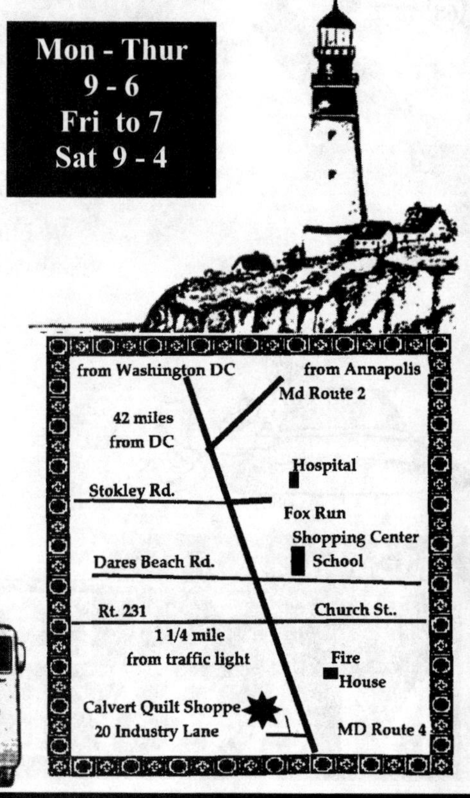

Cheasapeake Bay Q·U·I·L·T·I·N·G

Mon - Sat 10 - 5

12096 Ell Ln., Bus. Rt. 5 20602
(301) 638-5300 or (877) 227-1354
cbquilting@cs.com
www.chesapeakebayquilting.com
Owner: Nancy Gorski

Located in historic southern Maryland - a friendly shop offering a full complement of quilting fabric, notions, books, & patterns.

- Vintage Sewing Machines
- Gift Items/Cards
- Machine & Hand Embroidery Supplies
- Magazines - CD's - Videos
- Custom-made wood quilt hangers
- Quilt Classes for all Levels

Waldorf, MD #3

Bring in your QTC & receive a 10% discount on your fabric purchase. One time use only.
Not Valid with other offers. Expires Dec 31, 2006

Salisbury, MD #4

Mon - Sat 10 - 6

Jenny's Sewing Studio

311 Civic Ave. 21804
(410) 543-1212
jenny@jennys-sewing-studio.com
www.jennys-sewing-studio.com
Owner: Jennifer Friedel
Est: 1982 3200 sq.ft.

Full service quilt shop & sewing machine dealer. (New Home, Singer, Babylock, Janome) Over 2000 bolts of fabric and approx. 20 classes offered.

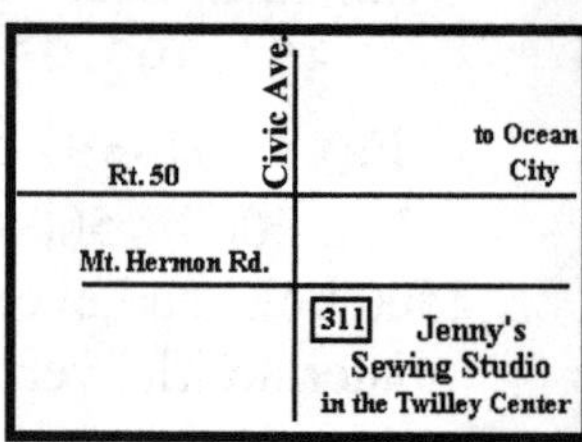

Snow Hill, MD #5

Tues - Sat 10 - 5

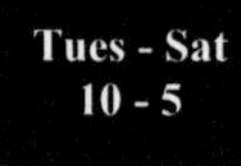

The Fine Needle

121 South Dr. 21863
(410) 632-0772

quilts@fineneedle.com
www.fineneedle.com
Owner: Stacy Mitchell
Fine fabric, fine yarns, and friendly service!

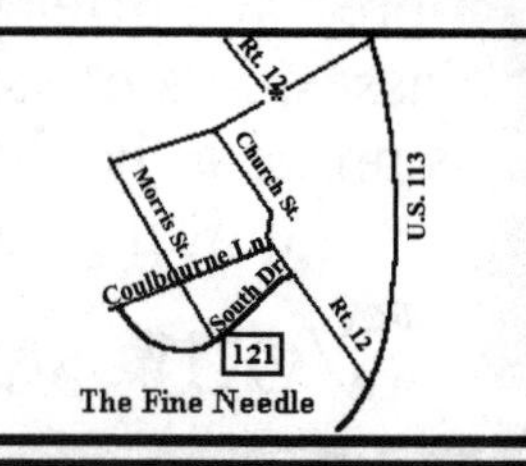

PEGGY'S SEWING CENTER AND QUILTING STUDIO

On The Beautiful Eastern Shore of Maryland

LARGE SELECTION OF 100% COTTON FABRICS. COMPLETE LINE OF NOTIONS, QUILT SUPPLIES, THREADS AND MORE THREADS.

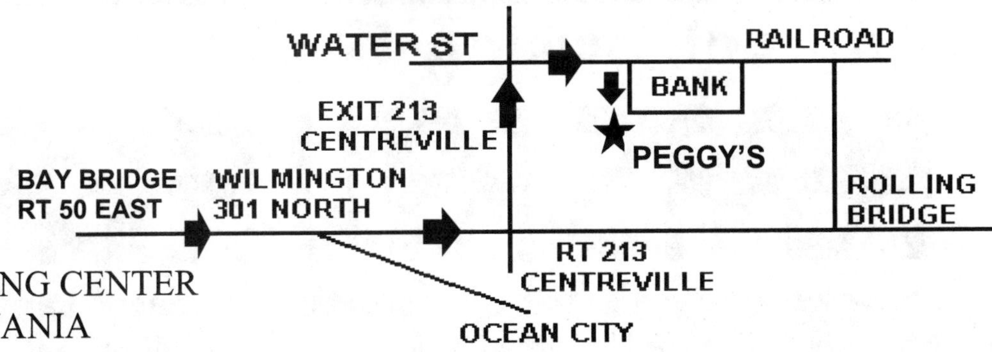

★PEGGY'S SEWING CENTER
210 PENNSYLVANIA
CENTREVILLE, MD 21617

VIKING, JANOME
SEWING MACHINES

Centreville, MD #6

WWW.PEGGYSEWING.COM
MACHINE QUILTING AVAILABLE
410-643-7202
800-643-7775 (Maryland Only)

Cottonseed Glory

Est: 1978

Annapolis, MD #7

4 Annapolis St. 21401
(410) 263-3897
Owner: Pat Steiner
www.cottonseedglory.com

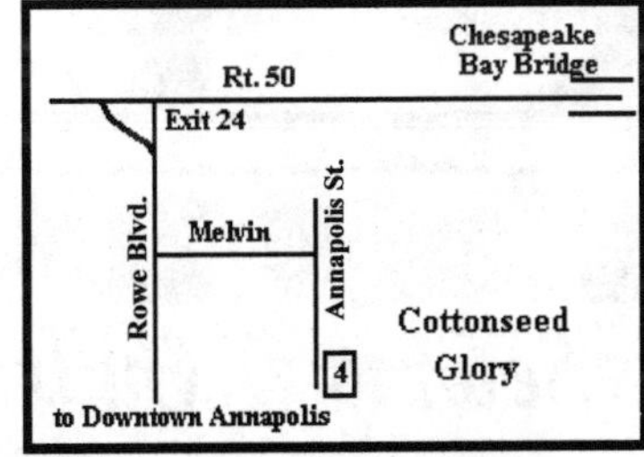

1/2 miles from U.S. Naval Academy & Historic area of Annapolis
1 mile and 2 traffic lights from Rt. 50
Free parking on our lot

Mon - Sat 10 - 5
Sundays 1 - 4
(No Sun hours June - Aug)

6000 bolts from over 50 manufacturers.

Books, Gourmet Notions, Classes year round
Friendly, knowledgeable help, free parking.
PATTERNS, PATTERNS, PATTERNS!

Easton, MD #8

Mon - Sat 10 - 5

Lilies of the Field
101 Marlboro Ave.
Easton Plaza
Easton, MD 21601
410-822-9117

Web Site: www.sew 2000.com\liliesoffield
Owner: Regina Chapman

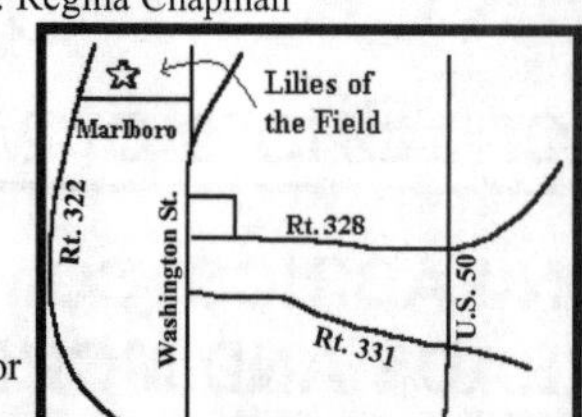

Fine Fabrics, notions, equipment and classes for the discriminating woman who sews.

Crofton, MD #9

Mon - Sat 9:30 - 5 Tues & Thur til 7

Tomorrow's Treasures

2110 Priest Bridge Dr., Suite 12 21114
(410) 451-0400 Fax: (410) 451-4858
vbozick@erols.com
Owner: Vickie Bozick
Est: 1998 5800+ Bolts

Friendly quilting and heirloom store. Authorized Husqvarna Viking dealer. Wide range of classes, fabric, laces, patterns, books, notions, embroidery supplies.

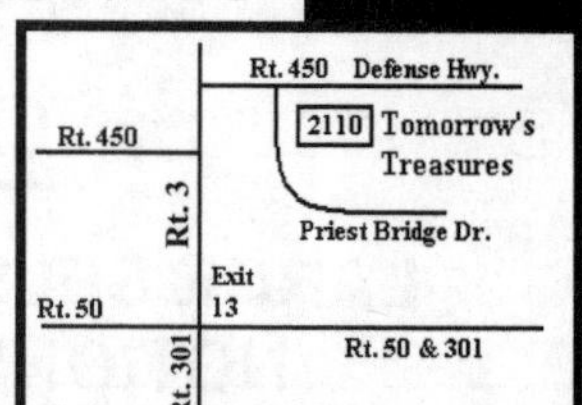

A Different Sewing Experience

BEAR'S PAW FABRICS

We welcome you to the world of Bear's Paw Fabrics and Bernina.
We hope you can take the time to visit our of our conveniently located shops.

- Over 2000 beautiful cotton fabrics for the quilter or home sewer
- Books, notions, patterns, embroidery stabilizers, threads
- Authorized Bernina Dealer

Owners: Doug and Judy Monro
info@bearspawfabrics.com

Towson, MD #10

8812 Orchard Tree Lane 21286
410-321-6730 ~ 800-761-2202
695 to Exit 29B (Loch Raven Blvd.)
right on Joppa Rd.
right on Orchard Tree Lane
5th store on left

Ellicott City, MD #11

8659 Baltimore National Pike
410-480-2875 ~ 888-877-4898
695 to Exit 15B (Route 40 W)
Rt. 40 West to Ridge Rd
U-turn at Ridge
Store immediately on right

Frederick, MD #12

Mon - Sat 10 - 6 Mon & Thur 10 - 8

Sisto's Sewing & Quilting

1911 N. Market 21701
(301) 695-0643 Fax: (301) 695-1653
sistosquilting@erols.com
Owner: Linda M. Sisto
5,200 sq.ft. 5,000+ Bolts

Fabrics, Patterns, Books, Notions. Brand names: RJR, Hoffman, Moda, Kauffman. Authorized dealer for Bernina, Brother, Janome and Singer Sewing Machines.

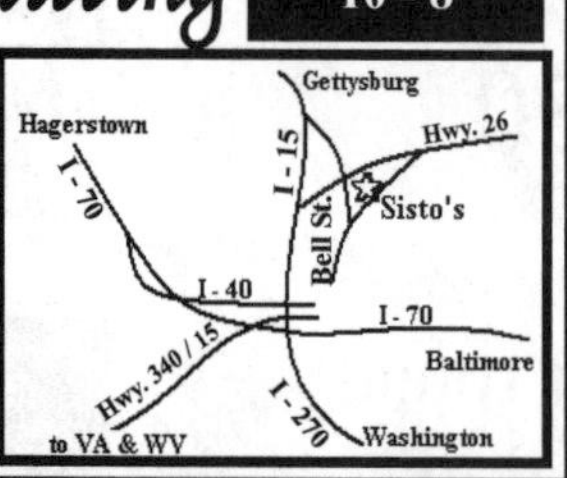

Needles & Pins

FREDERICK MARYLAND'S PREMIER QUILTING, STITCHERY AND DOLLMAKING SHOP

Frederick, MD #13

Just a pretty country drive north of Baltimore!

Stitches Etc, Inc.

Jacksonville, MD #14

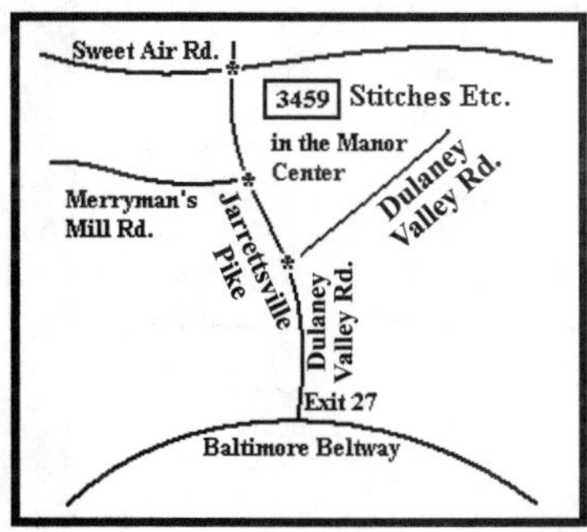

Manor Shopping Center
3459 Sweet Air Rd.
(Mail: P.O. Box 266,
Phoenix, MD 21131)
410-667-9522

Store hours:
Tuesday - Friday
11:00 am--5:30 pm
Saturday
11 am--4 pm
Evening hours by appointment for your convenience!

3,000 bolts of quality quilting fabrics, specializing in novelties, 1930's and civil war reproductions.
A THANGLES shop--
stocking all sizes and patterns.
Authorized Janome Sales and Service.

Hagerstown, MD #15

Traditions at the White Swan

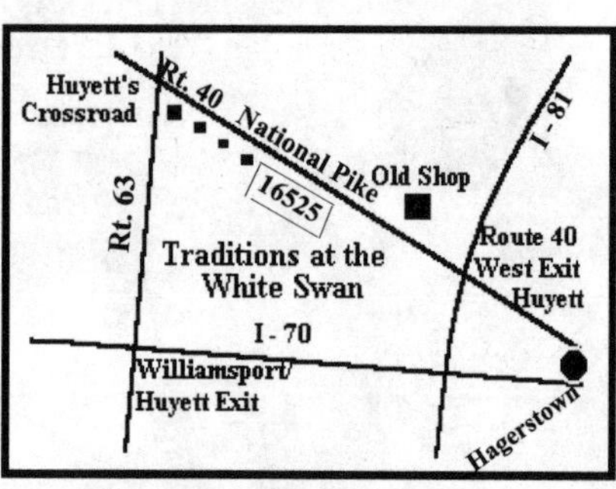

3½ miles West of town

Largest Quilt Shop in the area with everything for the quilter—beginner thru advanced. 2500 bolts of fabric including—Hoffman, RJR, P&B, Benartex, Marcus Brothers & Mums the Word. Notions, Books, Patterns, Stencils, & Classes

16525 National Pike 21740
(301) 733-9130 Est: 1985
Owners: Dick & Wendy Shank 1700 sq.ft.

Monday - Saturday 10 - 5
Sunday 1 - 5

The Prettiest Quilt Shop in Western Maryland!

Wilson's, *Your Favorite Quilt Shop*, offers:

- Over 2,000 bolts of "only the prettiest" fine, Quality fabrics by supplies including Moda, Hoffman and many more
- Check out our Book Nook comtaining a Large selection of books and patterns
- Get great inspiration from our finished Samples and grab a kit to take home!

Country Setting • Buses Welcome
Close to the Interstate • Easy-Off/Easy-On

#16

13516 Marsh Pike, Hagerstown, MD 21742
(301) 790-3526

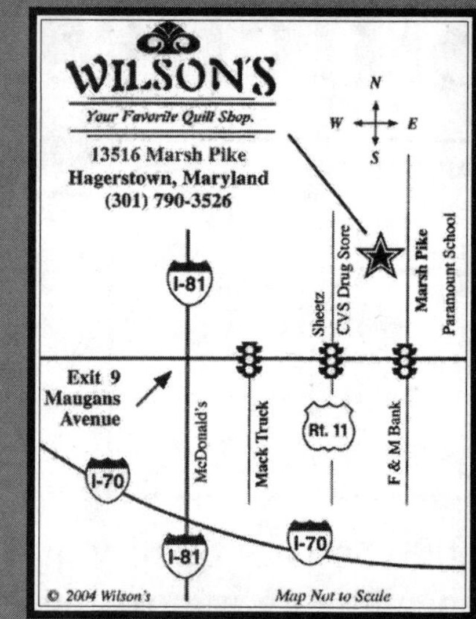

Store Hours;
Mon., Tues., Thurs., & Fri. 9 a.m. - 5 p.m.
Sat. 9 a.m. - 2 p.m. • Wed. CLOSED

Don't go home without being able to say you were at Wilson's in Hagerstown!

Ladybug Quilts

4714 Linthicum Road
Dayton, MD 21036
www.ladybugquilts.net
(410) 531-5723
Toll Free: (877) Go-Quilt
(1-877-467-8458)

Open Monday thru Saturday 10 - 5
Open Late 'til 8 on Thursdays

Friendly, knowledgeable staff

More than 1,500 bolts of fabric

Notions Kits Classes

Dayton, MD #17

Located just off of
Route 32 north of Clarksville

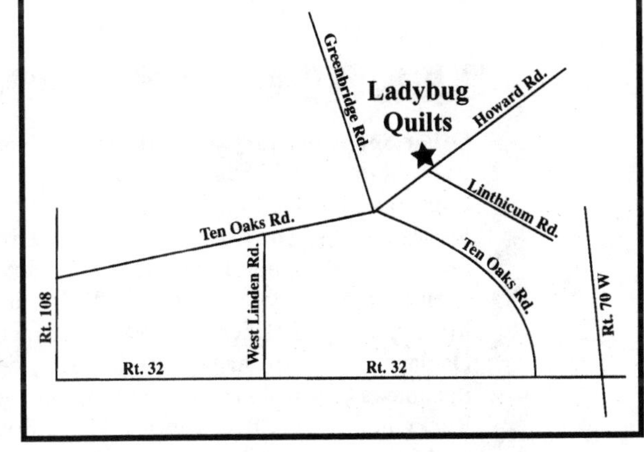

Gaithersburg, MD #18

15926 Luanne Dr. 20877
(301) 527-0598 Est: 1995 3000 sq.ft.
Owners: Susan & Gary McLaughlin

Mon - Sat 10 - 6
Sun 12 - 5
Class Eve.

CAPITAL QUILTS

Great selection of high quality fabric and a full range of necessities and niceties for the quilter. The largest selection of books in the area, we feature patterns by local artists. We're proud of our many classes. Service is friendly & helpful. Bring in your 'Problem Pieces'. Authorized Pfaff dealer. Easy Access by Public Trans.

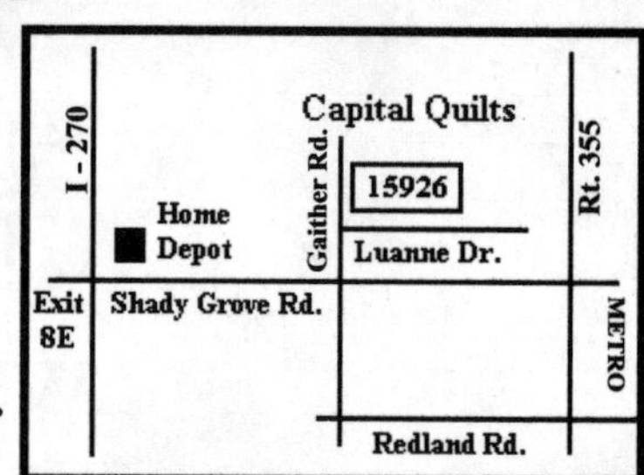

We Are Very Easy to Find!

QUILTING EACH DAY...
KEEPS THE DOCTOR AWAY!

Other Shops in Maryland: *We suggest calling first*

Boonsboro	Old School Fabrics, 230 Potomac	301-432-6195
Flintstone	Cathy's Country Quilts, 12712 Murleys Branch Rd. NE	301-478-2589
Fruitland	The Dusty Attic, 301 S. Division St., P.O. Box 556	410-546-1656
Fulton	Quilt Studio, Inc., P.O. Box 243	301-490-3544
Glen Burnie	Fabric Chest, 337-F Hospital Dr	410-768-5233
Mt Airy	Patches Quilting & Sewing, 308 S Main St	301-831-0366
Oakland	Not Just Quilts, 210 E. Alder St.	
Pocomoke City	Robinanne's Quilting Service, 145C Market St.	410-957-4766
Rockville	G Street Fabrics, 11854 Rockville Pike	301-231-8998
St. Michaels	Sewing Factory, 609 S. Talbot St.	410-745-3178
Upper Marlboro	Stitches & Sew On, 9020 Trumps Hill Rd.	301-627-2990

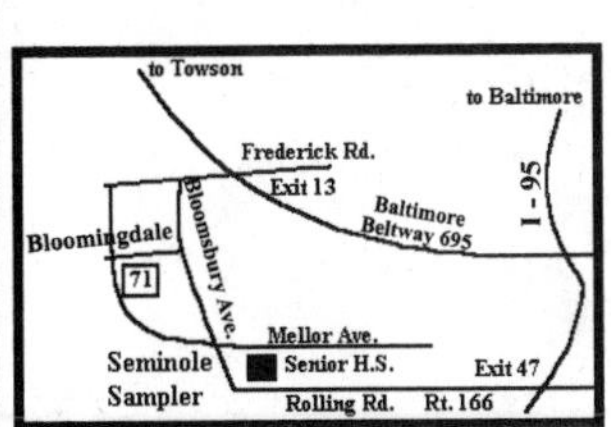

- Fine Cotton Fabrics
- Quilting Books and Patterns
- Quilting and Sewing Notions
- Batting and Supplies
- Unique Block of the Month Patterns
- Wearable Art Patterns
- Classes for Every Level

SEMINOLE SAMPLER

71 Mellor Ave. 21228
(410) 788-1720
seminolesampler@erols.com
www.seminolesampler.com

Mon & Thur: 10 - 8
Tue, Wed, Fri, Sat: 10 - 5
Sun: 1 - 5

3600+ sq.ft. of quilt store featuring more than 4000 bolts of fine cotton fabrics; especially known for extensive collections of solid color, batik, contemporary and oriental fabrics. Excellent offering of books and patterns, notions and supplies. Regularly scheduled classes in every aspect of quilting, for all levels of experience. Service oriented staff cheerfully willing to assist with all quilt project needs. Guild discount on Mondays.

Catonsville, MD #19

Grantsville, MD #20

FOUR SEASONS STITCHERY

The place to go for calico and "sew" much more

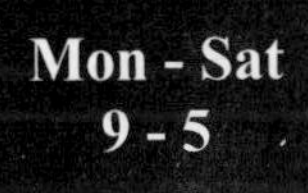

A VERY SPECIAL FABRIC SHOP with 1500 bolts of cotton quilting fabrics as well as WAVERLY decorator fabrics and apparel fabrics. Special threads, ribbons and fabrics for counted cross stitch, silk ribbon and Brazilian embroidery and other needlework.

Instruction books and patterns

We have a friendly and knowledgeable staff ready to help you with your project.

Just minutes from I - 68, Exit 19
116 Main Street
Grantsville, MD 21536
www.4seasonsstitchery.com
301-895-5958

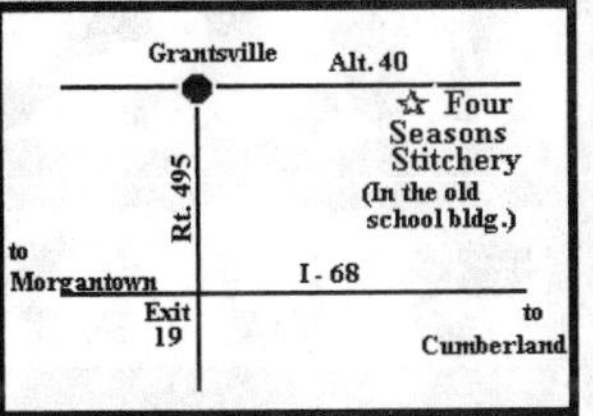

QUILTERS DON'T DO BUTTONS!

Maryland Guilds:

Annapolis	Annapolis Quilt Guild, P.O. Box 4278, 21403 Meets: 7 pm first Monday at St. Martin's Lutheran Church corner of Spa Rd. and Hilltop Ln.
Baltimore	Baltimore Heritage Quilters' Guild, 21239
Bel Air	Flying Geese Quilt Guild, P.O. Box 1894, 21014
Centreville	Queen Anne County Quilt Guild Meets: Last Wednesday @ 7:30pm at Kramer Senior Center
Columbia	Faithful Circle Quilters, 5012 Lake Circle W, 21044
Gaithersburg	Friendship Star Quilters, P.O. Box 8051, 20898 Meets: 1st Monday @ 7:30 pm at Gaithersburg Church of the Nazarene
Hagerstown	Friendship Quilters Guild, 21740 Meets: 2nd Tuesday @ 7pm at Seventh Day Adventist Church
Hebron	Lydia Guild, 21830 Meets: 2nd Monday 7 p.m. at Rockawalkin UMC, newly formed--mostly beginners
LaVale	Creative Needle Quilters, 21502
LaVale	Schoolhouse Quilters' Guild, 888 Weires Ave., 21502
Millersville	Eternal Quilter, 346 Chalet Dr., 21108
Salisbury	School House Quilts, c/o Joan Norman, 4705 Fleming Mill Rd., Pocomoke, MD 21851 Meets: 3rd Wednesday 7 p.m. at Holly Center, Snow Hill Rd., Salisbury

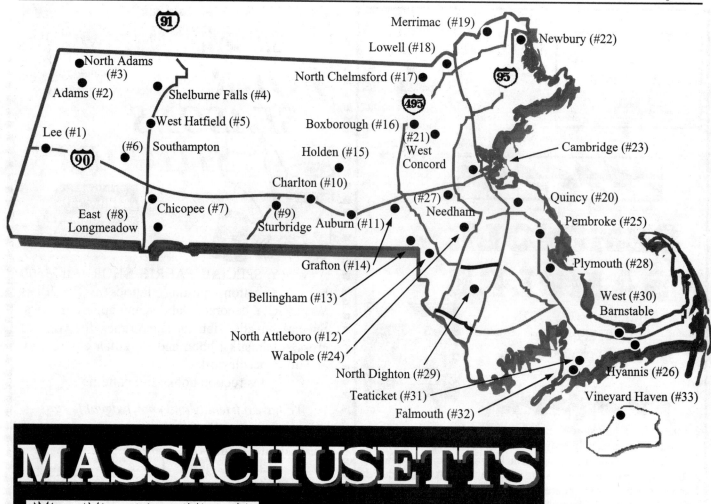

Merrimac (#19)
Newbury (#22)
Lowell (#18)
North Adams (#3)
North Chelmsford (#17)
Adams (#2)
Shelburne Falls (#4)
West Hatfield (#5)
Boxborough (#16)
Lee (#1)
(#21) West Concord
(#6) Southampton
Holden (#15)
Cambridge (#23)
Charlton (#10)
(#27) Needham
Quincy (#20)
Chicopee (#7)
East (#8) Longmeadow
(#9) Sturbridge
Auburn (#11)
Pembroke (#25)
Grafton (#14)
Plymouth (#28)
Bellingham (#13)
West (#30) Barnstable
North Attleboro (#12)
Walpole (#24)
North Dighton (#29)
Hyannis (#26)
Teaticket (#31)
Vineyard Haven (#33)
Falmouth (#32)

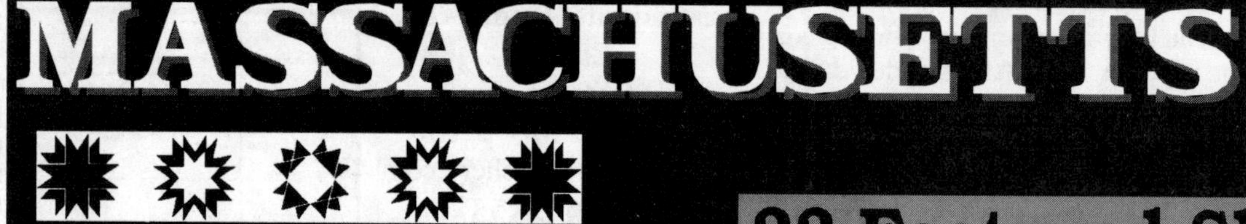

33 Featured Shops

Lee, MA #1

Mon - Sat 10 - 6 Sun 12 - 6

Pumpkin Patch

58 W. Center St. (Rt. 20)
(413) 243-1635 01238
Owners: Susan & Dan Sullivan
Est: 1985 800 sq.ft.

Located in the beautiful Berkshires!
Cotton fabrics, books, patterns, etc. . . .
Classes, machine quilting . . . .
Bernina Sewing Machines

Adams, MA #2

Mon - Sat 10 - 5 Thur til 9

A Stitch in Time

45 Commercial St. 01220
(413) 743-7174
a_stitchintime@yahoo.com
Est: 1996

Great selection of 100% Cotton Fabrics "To Die For". Quilting Supplies, Books, Gifts and Quilts. Variety of Yarns, Patterns and Needles.

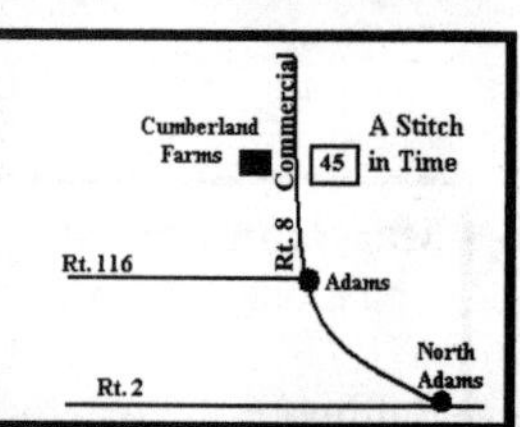

North Adams, MA #3

Mon - Sat 10 - 5 Sun 12 - 4

Tala's Quilt Shop

Heritage State Park-Furnace St. 01247
(413) 664-8200
tquilting@hotmail.com
www.talasquiltshop.tripod.com/
Owner: Tala Neathawk Est: 2001
Over 3900 Bolts - 800 Flannels. Featured in "Quilt Samplers" 2004 magazine as one of the top ten shop in the U.S. & Canada.

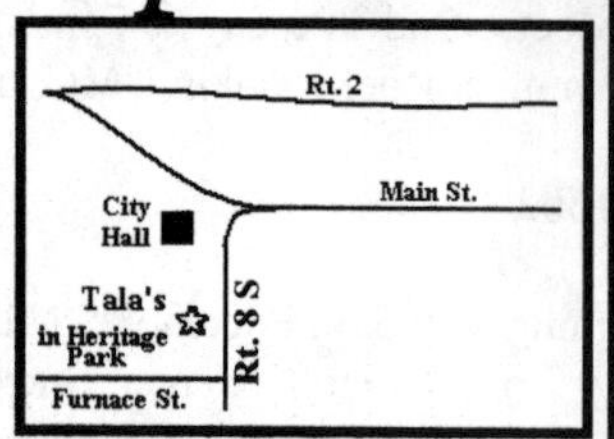

Shelburne Falls, MA #4

Call for Hours

Notion to Quilt, LLC

1 Deerfield Ave. 01370
(413) 625-9644
ellendegrave@hotmail.com
Owner: Ellen DeGrave Est: 2003
"On the road to the Glacial Potholes"
Notion to Quilt offers Fabric, Supplies, Notions, Quilted Products and Classes.

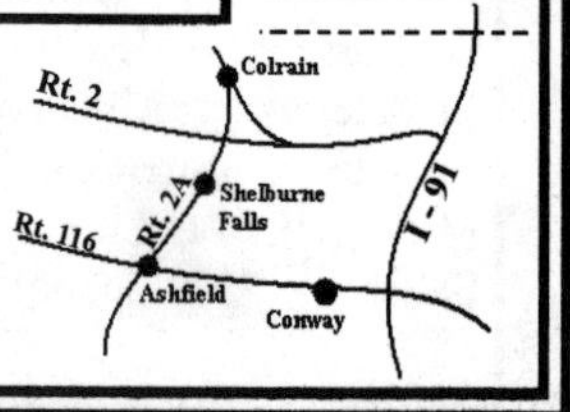

West Hatfield, MA #5

Calico Fabric Quilt Shop

10 West St. 01088
(413) 247-9989
www.calicofabric.com

Owner: Joan Trecartin
Est: 1980 2500 sq.ft.

Mon - Fri 10 - 5
Sat 10 - 3

Choose from 4000+ bolts of top name Fabrics. Hoffman, RJR, P&B, Kaufman, Moda, Kona Bay. Books, Quilt Supplies and Classes. Handicapped Accessible Bus Tours Welcome

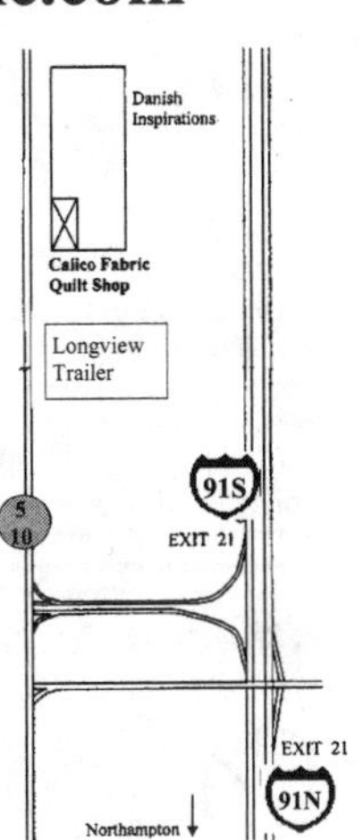

Largest Quilt Shop in the Area!

Southampton, MA #6

Tues - Thur 10 - 8
Fri & Sat 10 - 4
Sun noon - 5

Southampton Quilts

162 College Hwy. 01073
(413) 529-9641
Owners:
Maureen Mason & Nancy Aurnhammer

info@southamptonquilts.com
www.southamptonquilts.com

We are a cozy shop dedicated to all quilters. Featuring 3000+ bolts of the latest quality cottons. Easy to get to, friendly atmosphere.

162
Southampton Quilts
Rt. 10N
7 miles
Exit 3
Mass Turnpike

Chicopee, MA #7

Bayberry Quilt & Gift Shoppe

- Full line of quilting fabrics, supplies, books & patterns displayed in a 10 room Victorian farm house.
- We offer quilting classes ….
- We also offer a CUSTOM MACHINE QUILTING SERVICE Visit us online for available patterns and price list...4 years experience….currently a 2 to 3 week turnaround time.
- COME IN AND SEE OUR NEW ADDITION...increased space, more fabric and supplies...handcrafted gifts and quilt for sale and so much more.
- UNIQUE SHOPPE

Hours: Tues 10-4…Wed & Thurs 10-4 and 5:30-8…Sat 10-3

137 Sheridan St.
Chicopee, MA 01020
(413) 592-9653
www.bayberryquilts.com
Laura J. Knapp/Owner
Est: 1999

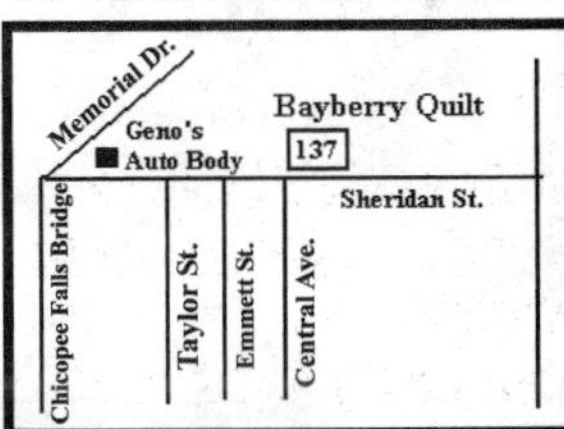

East Longmeadow, MA #8

Thimbleworks

56 Shaker Rd. 01028
(413) 525-4789
www.thimbleworks.org

Mon - Thur 10 - 9
Fri & Sat 10 - 5
Closed Mondays in July & Aug.

Sewing Machine Center

Great selection of 100% cotton Fabrics, Books, Patterns & Quilting Supplies. Authorized Pfaff dealer.

to Springfield
Rt. 83 N. Main St.
Rt. 21 Elm St.
Rotary
Maple St.
Pleasant St.
Rt. 220 Shaker Rd.
Rt. 83 Somers Rd.
56
to Enfield, CT
Thimbleworks

THE Quilt AND Cabbage

Enter a relaxing & warm atmosphere of 2000 bolts - select cottons, homespun, batiks, flannels, wool, fleece & wool yarn. Best array of books, patterns, stencils. Custom quilts & gifts. Leave with inspiration, treasures & a smile!

P.O. Box 534 01566
538 Main St. (Rt. 20)
(508) 347-3023

Sturbridge, MA #9

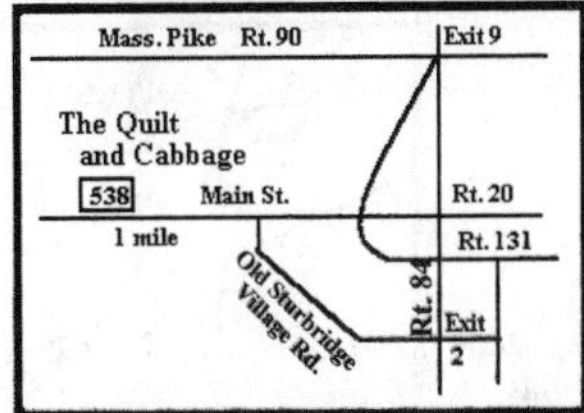

Mon & Wed - Sat 9:30 - 4:30
Sun 11 - 4
Closed Tues

Est: 1991

Charlton, MA #10

The Fabric Stash, Inc.

Large enough for a good selection,
Small enough for good service.

Tues - Thur 9:30 - 6:30
Fri 9:30 - 8
Sat 9:30 - 5
Sun 12:30 - 4

FABRICS for: quilting, clothing, home decorating
YARN, NOTIONS and BUTTONS
QUILTS for Sale
CLASSES in: quilting, knitting and sewing.
LONG ARM QUILTING $16. PER SQ. YD.
Edge to edge, stippling or swirls and loops

16 Sturbridge Rd.
(Rt. 20)
P.O. Box 705
Charlton, MA 01507
(508) 248-0600
Owner: Laurel Wilber

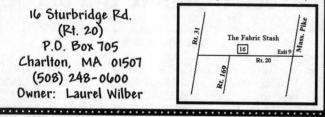

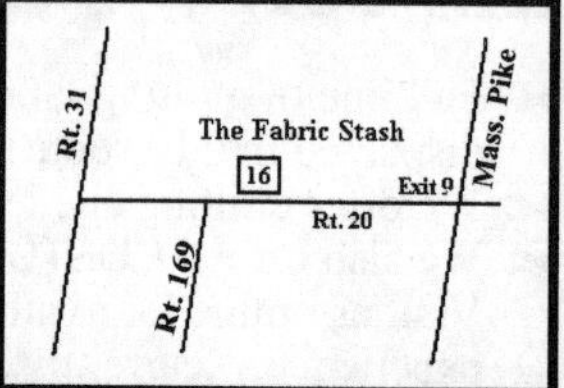

Auburn, MA #11

Mon - Wed 10 - 8
Thur - Sat 10 - 5
Sun 12 - 3
(Oct-May)

Appletree Fabrics

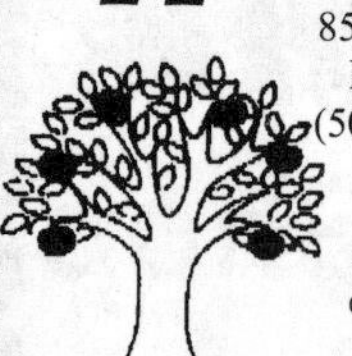

850 Southbridge St. 01501
Rts 12/20, Westside Plaza
(508) 832-5562 Est: 1991
Owner: Lois Therrien

Over 2500 bolts of fine quality quilting cottons. Hundreds of books & patterns.

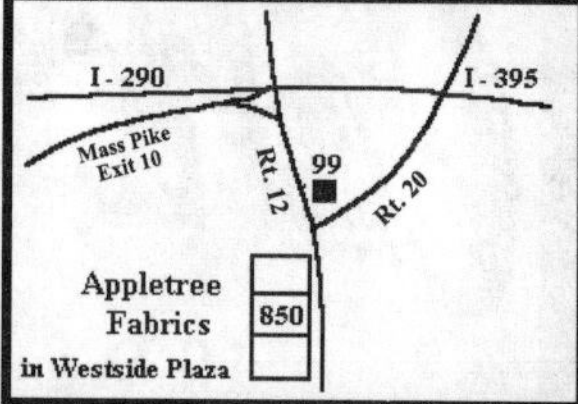

North Attleboro, MA #12

Mon - Sat 10 - 6
Thur til 8

Quilter's Stash

560 Kelley Blvd., (Rte. 152), 02760
(508) 699-3010 Owner: Sue Kassler
qstash@msn.com www.quilters-stash.com

A fun and friendly shop filled with fabulous fabric! 1500+ bolts of quilting cottons, flannels and Woolfelt, plus batiks and Kaffe Fassett/Westminster fabrics, too. We stock notions, books, patterns and gifts for the quilter and quilt lover and an ever-changing selection of antique quilts and textiles. Visit our website for an extensive schedule of classes for all skill levels and complete direction to the shop. Convenient to all major routes: Interstates 95, 495, and 295 and US Route 1.

Bellingham, MA #13

Tues - Sat 10 - 5

Quilt Center

373 Center St. 02019
(508) 876-9955
quiltcenter@cs.com
www.quiltcenter.net
Owner: Terri Vadenais
Est: 2000 1300+ Bolts
Fabrics, Notions, Books and Various Quilting Items.

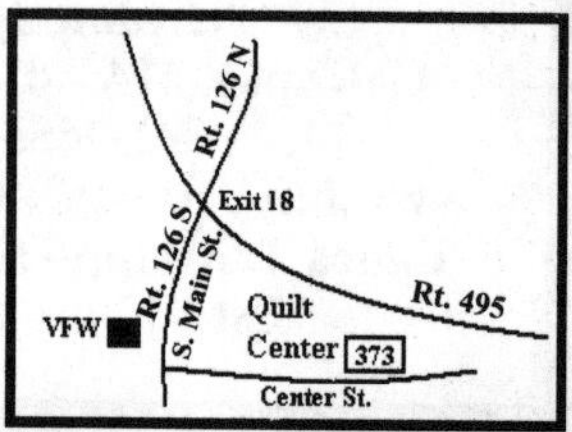

Grafton, MA #14

Tues - Sat 10 - 5
Sun 12 - 5

Calico & Co.

2 Grafton Common (Rear) 01519
(508) 839-5990
Owner: Joanne & Richard Erenius
Est: 1984 1000 sq.ft. 800 Bolts

Helpful & Friendly Service & Supplies for your every Quilting need. Classes to inspire your creativity.

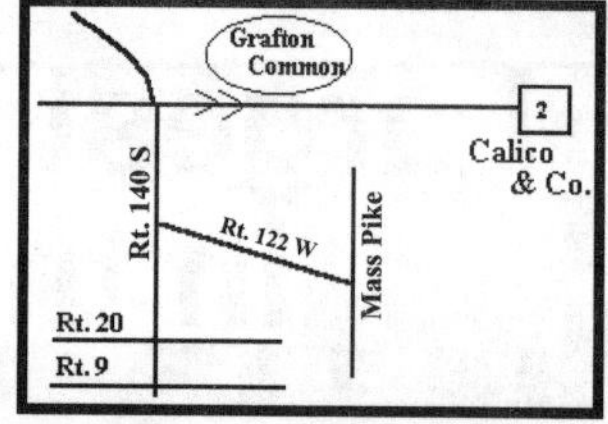

Holden, MA #15

Wed - Sat 10 - 4:30
Thur til 8
June thru Aug Closed Sat

Betsey's Sewing Connection & Quilt Shop

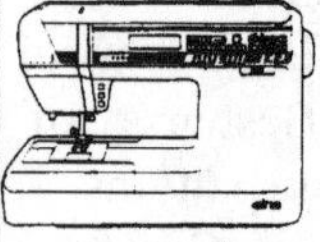

1085A Main St. 01520
(508) 829-6411
betseysquiltshop@yahoo.com
Owner: Betsey Berry
Est: 1973

30 years sharing sewing & quilting knowledge. Excellent cotton fabrics, quilting notions, books. Elna sales & service.

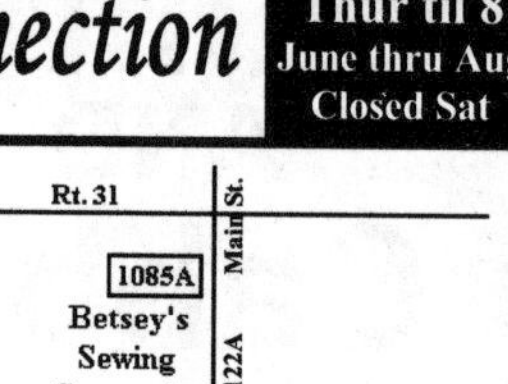

Boxborough, MA #16

Mon - Sat 10 - 4
Sun 12 - 4

The Quilted Crow

61 Stow Rd. 01719
(978) 266-9102
info@thequiltedcrow.com
www.thequiltedcrow.com

2004 Quilt Sampler Shop specializing in folkart, and reproduction fabrics and gifts. Located in 18th century farmhouse with adjacent tearoom.

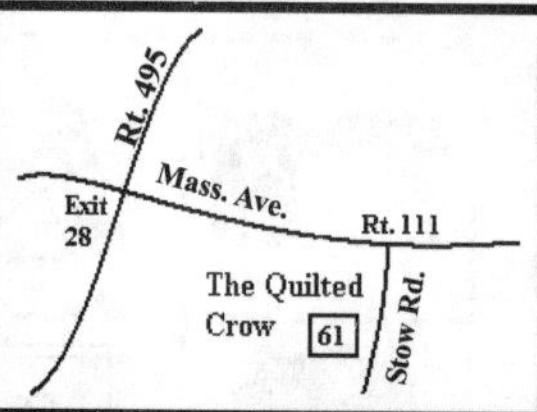

N. Chelmsford, MA #17

Mon - Sat 9:30 - 5
Thurs til 8:30

Mill Girl Quilts

2 Kennedy Dr. 01863
(978) 251-8118 Fax: (978) 251-9807
millgirl@ix.netcom.com
millgirl.home.netcom.com
Owner: Susan Dillinger
Est: 2000 3200 sq. ft.

Friendly, service-oriented staff. Close by New England Quilt Museum. Over 2400 bolts, books, patterns, notions, classes, machine quilting service. Bernina Dealer.

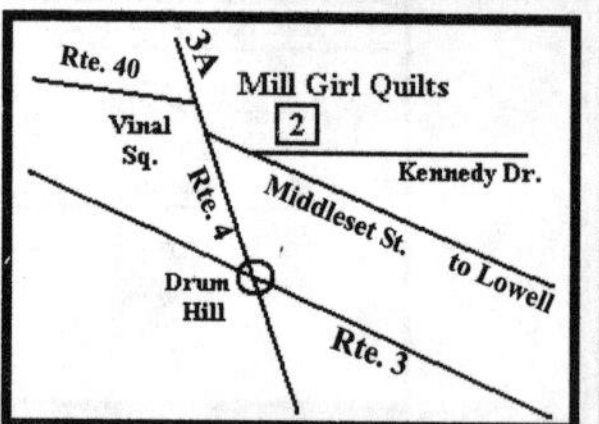

Lowell, MA #18

Tues - Sat 10 - 4
Sun May - Nov 12 - 4

The New England Quilt Museum

18 Shattuck St. 01852
(978) 452-4207 Free to Members
www.nequiltmuseum.org
Adm: $5, $4 Seniors & Students

We are the only museum in New England dedicated solely to the preservation, education and interpretation of American quiltmaking past and present. Exhibitions, workshops, programs and our library are a wonderful resource for quilters and collectors.

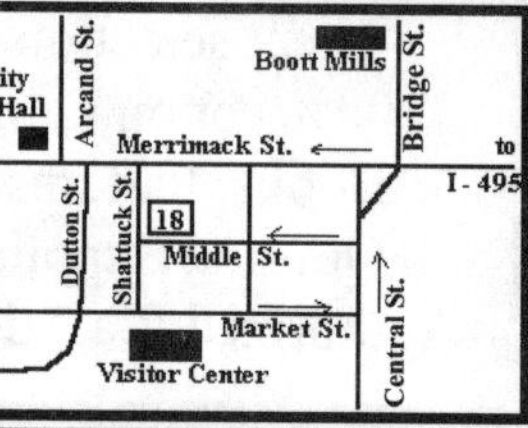

116 W. Main St. Rte. 110 01860 (978) 346-9292
redbarn@greennet.net
Owners: Helen Gosselin & Linda Ouellette
Est: 1978 2000 sq.ft.

Mon - Fri
9 - 5
Sat 9 - 4

Merrimac, MA #19

Over 3000 bolts of quality 100% cotton fabrics,
Books - Patterns - Notions - Yarns
Quilting Classes
Authorized Janome/New Home
Sewing Machine Dealer
Celebrating 26 years

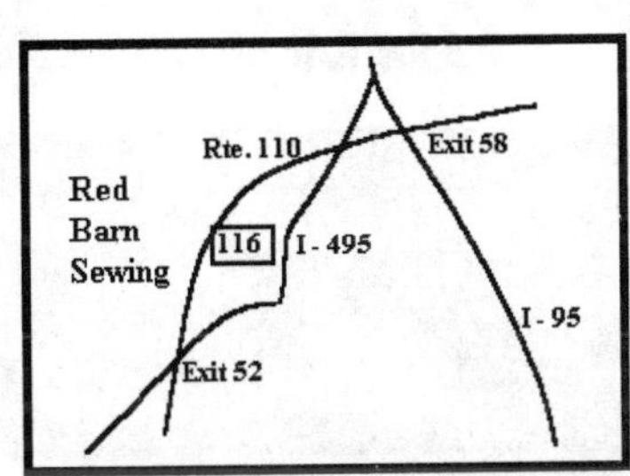

Quilters' Compass

27B Cottage Avenue, Quincy, MA 02186
(866)-4QUILT1 (Toll Free), (617)-479-2206
www.quilterscompass.com
Proprietor: Pat Fay
E-mail: Pat@quilterscompass.com

Store Hours
Tues, Fri, Sat. 9-5
Weds, Thurs 9-9
Sun 12 Noon –5
Sept. - June

Located in historic Quincy, Massachusetts, Quilters' Compass **is a bright, open, friendly quilt shop. We stock over 1000 bolts of top quality quilting fabric, hundreds of notions, books and other quilting supplies. Classes offered for all levels.**

Located next to tons of free parking
Easily accessible by MBTA Red Line or Commuter Rail

Quincy, MA #20

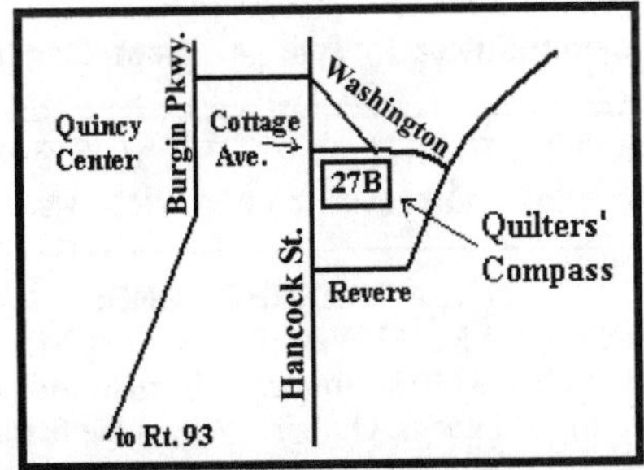

A Quilt Shop For Today's Quilter!

STORE HOURS:
Tuesday, Thursday 10am - 9pm
Wed, Fri, Sat 10am - 6pm
Sunday noon - 5pm
Closed Mondays

Quilter's Way is a great travel destination! Our sunny shop is located in the artisan village of West Concord. We are widely known for our friendly, helpful staff and for our large, eye-catching selection of the latest in contemporary and reproduction quilting fabric, books, magazines and notions. You'll also find a unique collection of embellishment supplies.

After shopping with us, you can enjoy great food and other boutique shops in the village, including a Five & Ten Cent Store that hasn't changed in over 30 years.

Come visit - we'd love to welcome you!

West Concord, MA #21

75 Commonwealth Ave • West Concord, MA 01742

Phone: 978-371-1177 Fax: 978-371-1192
Email: Info@quiltersway.com Web: www.quiltersway.com

DIRECTIONS:
Take Rte 2 to Rte 62 West. Follow Rte 62 for 2 miles then take right fork at 99 Restaurant and the right fork again to cross the railroad tracks. Quilter's Way is the first shop on left.

Newbury, MA #22

Tues - Sat 9:30 - 4:30

The Crazy Ladies at The Quilted Acorn Shoppe

72 Newburyport Tpk. (Rt. 1) 01951
(978) 462-0974 Est: 1983
Schedule of Classes & Sales
www.QuiltedAcorn.com
Owners: Cynthia Erekson & Sandra Schauer
Unique combination of Quilting, Folk Art Painting and Stenciling: supplies and classes. We specialize in Homespuns & Antique Reproduction Fabrics. Doll Patterns & Gail Wilson Kits.

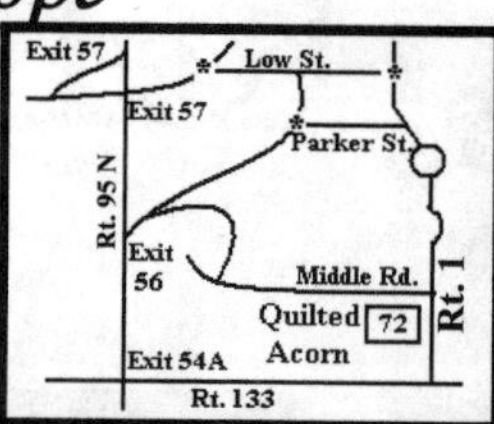

Cambridge, MA #23

Mon - Sat 10 - 6
Thurs 10-8:30
Sun 12 - 5

Cambridge Quilt Shop

95 Blanchard Rd. 02138
(617) 492-3279
Owners: Lynn Gorst, & Shannon Krasnov
Est: 1996 1100 sq.ft.

Our shop maintains 1500 bolts of fabric and over 400 current quilt books, plus the latest in quilting supplies and classes!

quilters@cambridgequilts.com www.cambridgequilts.com

Walpole, MA #24

Please Call for Hours

All About Quilts

958 Main St. 02081
(508) 668-0145
www.allaboutquilts.com
Owner: Linda & Mike Publicover

Quilting fabric, supplies, classes for all levels. Day, Night and Weekend Marathons.

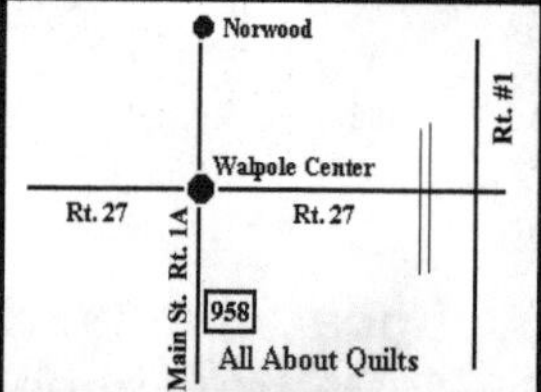

Pembroke, MA #25

Mon - Sat 10 - 5:15
Sun 12 - 5
Thur Eves.

Tumbleweed

158 Center St. 02359
(781) 293-6400
Est: 1973 1000 sq.ft.

Large selection of fabrics, hundreds of books, notions, batting & more. In a pre-civil war house. Classroom in barn.

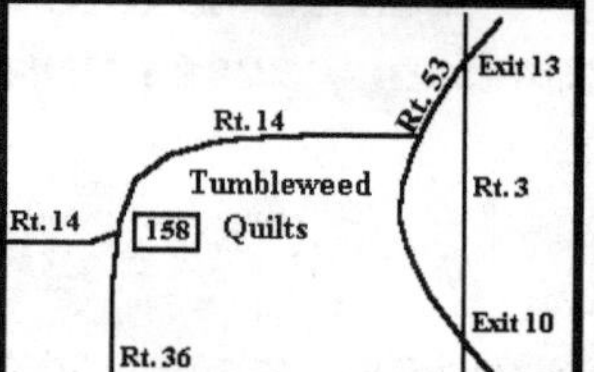

The Button Box Quilt Shop

Needham, MA #27

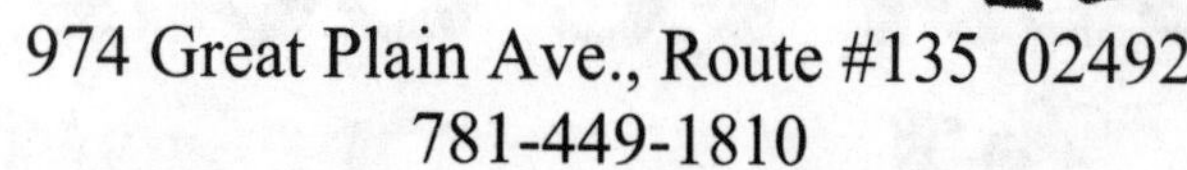

974 Great Plain Ave., Route #135 02492
781-449-1810
Toll Free 866-IQUILT2 (866-478-4582)
E-Mail: buttonbox@gis.net Est: 1995
Owner: Catherine Gentile 2800 sq.ft. 4000 Bolts
www.buttonboxquiltshop.com

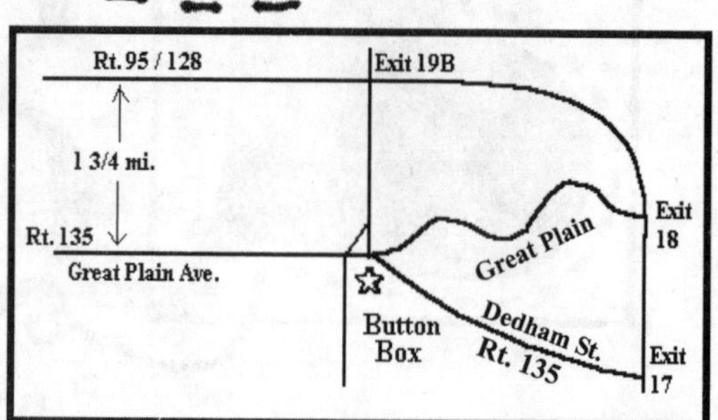

Mon - Sat 9:30 - 5:30
Wed & Thur til 8
Sundays 12 - 5
Sept. thru June

Documentary/Vintage Reproduction and Contemporary Fabrics our Specialty.
Boston's Largest Selection of Japanese Fabrics.
The Best Button Shop in Massachusetts.

Authorized Dealer for Pfaff Sewing Machines

Plymouth, MA #28

Mon - Sat 9 - 4:30

Sew Crazy

5 Main St. Extension Rt. 3A
(508) 747-3019 02360
Owner: Dottie Krueger
Est: 1977

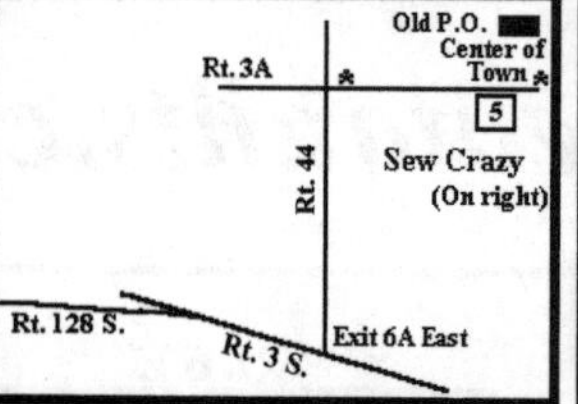

Over 1000 bolts of fabric and more coming.
Notions & Lots of Patterns.

West Barnstable, MA #30

Mon - Sat 10 - 5:30
Sun 12 - 5
Thur Eves.

Tumbleweed™

Corner of Rt. 6A & Rt. 132
(781) 362-8700 02668
Est: 1985 3200 sq.ft.

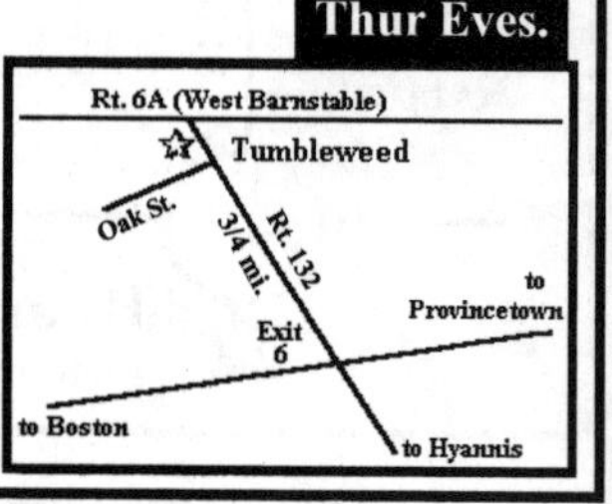

Wonderful fabric gathered from the best mills for quilts, clothing and home decoration where the contemporary mixes with the traditional.

Olde Carriage House Quilt Shoppe

Homespun - Reproduction Fabric
Notions - Books - Patterns

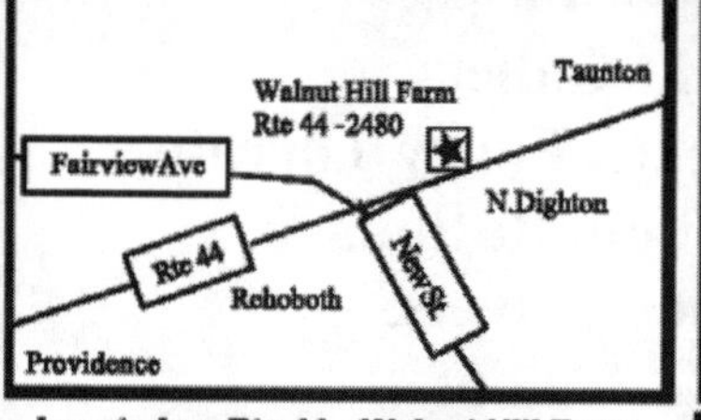

"Visit our 1860's Carriage House and take a step back in time. Relax by the pot belly stove with a hot apple cider while searching through books and patterns to find your next quilt project."

Located on Rte 44 - Walnut Hill Farm
Dighton - Rehoboth Line
2480 Winthrop St.,
N. Dighton, MA 02764

#29

Tues - Fri 10 - 6
Sat 10 - 5 Sun 12 - 5
Closed Mon.

508-252-5600

www.OldeCarriageHouseQuiltShoppe.com
email:OldeQuiltShoppe.com

Teaticket, MA #31

Mon - Fri 10 - 5
Sat 10 - 4

Sit n Stitch
Bernina Corner

192 Teaticket Hwy. 02536
(508) 540-9188 Fax: Same
Imaquilt8@aol.com
Owner: Lois Atkinson Est: 1997

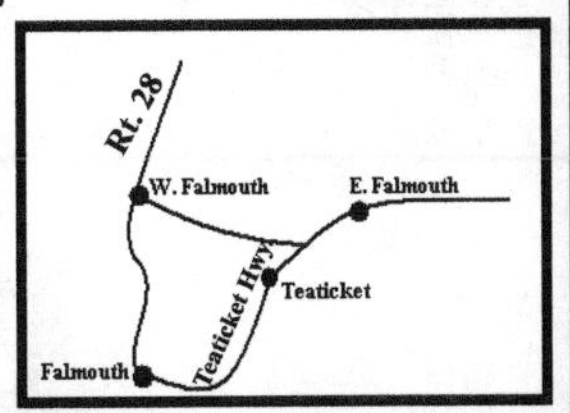

100% cotton quilting fabric. Patterns, books & notions. Full line of Bernina Sewing & Embroidery Machines. Classes.

Falmouth, MA #32

Offering Fabric • Quilt Supplies • Classes

97 Davis Straits Rd. (Rt. 28)
Falmouth, MA 02540
(508) 495-4400 Fax: (508) 495-4401
ComThreadQuilts@aol.com
www.CommonThreadQuilts.com
Owner: Linda McCarthy
Est: 1998

Open Year Round

Featuring a Barn full of inspiration! Offering both Quilts for Sale and Kits to make your own Cape Cod Memories.

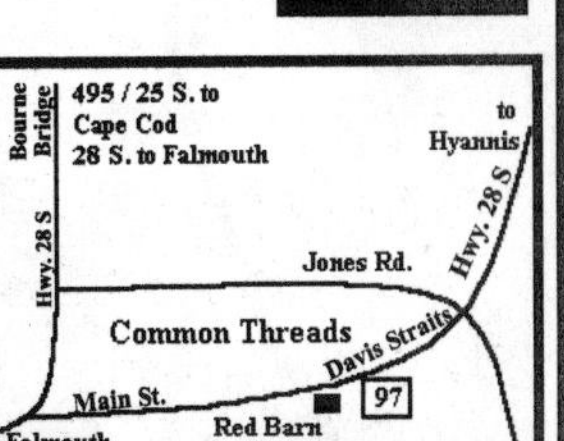

Vineyard Haven, MA #33

Mon - Sat 10 - 5
Wed til 6

Heath Hen Quilt Shop

79 Beach Rd. Tisbury Market Pl. 02568
(508) 693-6730
lbenson@geoserve.net
www.heathhen.com
Owner: Lynne A. Benson
Est: 1985 1000 sq. ft.

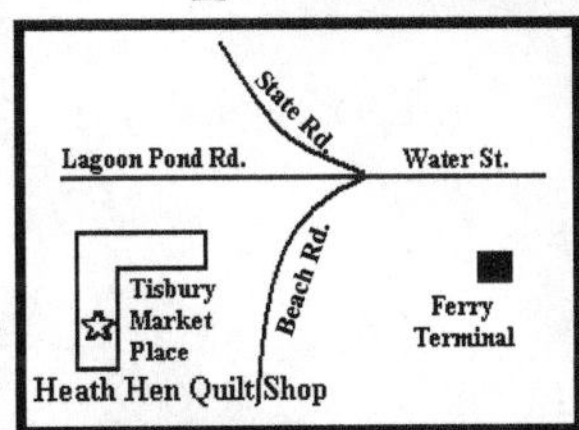

Located .4 mile from steamship dock. Full line of quilting fabrics, exquisite yarns, notions, books, Bernina sewing machines and classes.

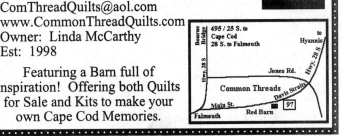

Other Shops in Massachusetts: *We suggest calling first*

Acushnet	Perry Farm Patchworks, 196 Perryhill	508-995-1555
Arlington	Fabric Corner, 783 Massachusetts Ave.	781-643-4040
Bellingham	Stitch by Stitch, 234 Pulaski Blvd.	508-876-9005
Belmont	Comfortables, 1 Stewart Terrance	617-484-0692
Brewster	The Yankee Craftsman, 230 Route 6A W	508-385-4758
Chelmsford	The Quilted Garden, 9 Rolling Green	978-250-3300
Dracut	Snip N Stitch Quilt Shop, 395 Textile	978-674-0137
East Brookfield	Calico Crib Quilt & Fabric Shoppe, 108 Howe St.	508-867-7389
Easthampton	Christina's Cottage, 116 Cottage St.	413-529-1060
Easthampton	Quilts & Needlework Go, 56 Cottage	413-527-4456
Falmouth	Fabric Corner, 12 Spring Bars Rd.	508-548-6482
Fiskdale	Colonial Crafts, 479 Main St.	508-347-3061
Florence	Glorious Fabrics, 60 Pioneer Knolls	413-586-0092
Framingham	Fabric Place, 136 Howard St.	508-872-4888
Franklin	Mayflower Textiles, 305 Union St	508-528-3300
Greenfield	Bear's Paw Quilts, 1182 Bernardston	413-773-9876
Greenfield	The Textile Co., Inc., Power Square	413-773-7516
Hingham	Purrfect Quilts, 13 Amber Rd.	781-749-2423
Ipswich	Loom N' Shuttle, 190 High St.	508-356-5551
Lawrence	Malden Mills, 46 Stafford St.	978-685-6341
Lowell	Quilters Corner, 308 Trotting Park Rd.	978-441-9225
Marlboro	A Quilter's Garden, 33 Main St.	508-485-5481
Medway	House on the Hill Quilt Shop, 121 Main	508-533-1203
No. Eastham	Fabric Basket, Rt 6 Nmain St Mercantile	508-255-8909
Reading	Mary Rose's Quilts, 159 Ash St.	781-942-9497
Rehoboth	The Store on 44, 224 Winthrop St.	508-252-5640
Salem	Marketplace Quilts, 6 Front St	978-740-3890
South Hadley	The Calico Shop, 40 Searle Rd.	413-536-3245
South Hamilton	Cranberry Quilters, 161 Bay Rd.	508-468-3871
Springfield	Osgood Textile Co., 30 Magaziner Pl.	413-737-6488
Sturbridge	Wrights Factory Outlet, 559 Main St	508-347-2731
Vineyard Haven	Beas Fabrics, State Rd., P.O. Box 1296	
Wales	Ilona's Whim, 10 Stafford Rd.	413-245-3827
Woburn	Fabric Place, 300 Mishawun Rd.	781-938-8787
Worcester	Shirley's Sewing Center Inc., 452 W. Boylston	508-853-8757

Massachusetts Guilds:

Amherst	Hands Across the Valley, P.O. Box 831, 01002	
Aqawam	Pioneer Valley Quilters, P.O. Box 202, 01001	
Arlington	Quilter's Connection, 02174	
Burlington	Burlington Quilters Guild, 61 Center St, 01803	Meets: 2nd Thursday 7:30pm at Burlington Senior Center
Carver	Plymouth Country Cranberry Quilters, P.O. Box 149, 02330	
Chelmsford	Chelmsford Quilters Guild, P.O. Box 422, 01824	
Concord	Concord Piecemakers	
Dalton	Friendship Knot Quilters	Meets: 3rd Thursday @ 6:30pm at Gus County Community Bldg
Falmouth	Crazy Quilters Of Cape Cod, P.O. Box 2058, 02536	
Falmouth	Hollyberry Quilters	
Great Barrington	Berkshire Quilt Guild, 47 W. Sheffield Rd., 01230	Meets: 2nd Tuesday eve. at Searles Middle School
Haverhill	Merrimack Valley Quilters, P.O. Box 1435, 01831	Meets: at Holy Angels Church, Plaistow, NH
Hollister	Gavilan Quilt Guild, 191 San Felipe Rd. #M-1, 95023	Meets: 1st Monday at Methodist Church
Leominster	Material Girls, 23 Battles St., 01453	
Lowell	New England Quilters Guild, P.O. Box 7136, 01852	
Mendon	Thimble Pleasures Quilt Guild, P.O. Box 387	Meets: 3rd Thursday
Orleans	Bayberry Quilters of Cape Cod, P.O. Box 1253, 02653	
Pittsfield	Yankee Pride Quilt Guild, P.O. Box 833, 01201	
Southboro	County Line Quilt Guild	Meets: 2nd & 4th Tuesday 7 p.m.
Sudbury	Wayside Quilters	
Tewksbury	Tewksbury Piecemakers	
Topsfield	Common Threads, 01983	Meets: Last Tuesday @ 7pm at 4-H Building - Topsfield Fair Grounds
Townsend	Squanicook Quilt Guild	
Walpole	Rhododendron Needlers Quilt Guild	Meets: 3rd Wednesday (except July & Aug.)
Westford	East Coast Quilters Alliance, P.O. Box 711, 01886	
Yarmouth	Bayberry Quilters	

For the Upper Peninsula Shops #86-96 See Page 238
75
(#2) Petoskey
East Jordan (#3)
Bellaire (#4)
Gaylord (#6)
Cedar (#7)
Grayling (#10)
Lewiston (#5)
Harrisville (#11)
Traverse City (#12,13)
Williamsburg (#8,9)
Beulah (#1)
East Tawas(#19)
West Branch (#16,17,18)
Custer (#14)
Gladwin (#20)
75
Farwell (#15)
Midland (#21)
Bay City (#23,24)
Caro (#22)
Whitehall (#76)
Alma (#75)
Ortonville (#28)
Greenville (#74)
69
Port Huron (#32,33)
Lake Orion (#27)
Davison (#30,31)
Norton Shores (#77)
Comstock Park (#72)
Imlay City (#26)
Lapeer (#25)
Grand Rapids (#70,71,73)
Flushing (#29)
Richmond (#34)
Portland (#69)
Zeeland (#78)
Clinton Twp. (#35)
Troy (#40)
Fenton (#59)
Holland (#80)
Hastings (#68)
Charlotte (#61)
St. Clair Shore (#36)
Kalamazoo (#65,66,67)
South Lyon (#43)
Sterling Heights (#37)
Battle Creek (#64)
Berkley (#38,39)
Mason (#52)
South Haven (#79)
Walled Lake (#58)
Jackson (#57)
Livonia (#41)
East Leroy (#63)
Marshall (#62)
Holt (#53)
Wayne (#42)
94
Lansing (#60)
Wyandotte (#44)
Tecumseh (#54)
(#81,82) St. Joseph
Benton Harbor (#83)
East Lansing (#56)
Southgate (#45)
(#84,85) Stevensville
Belleville (#48)
Montgomery (#51)
Ypsilanti (#47)
Monroe (#49,50)
Ann Arbor (#46)
Howell (#55)
MICHIGAN
96 Featured Shops

Petoskey, MI #2

Mon - Fri 9 - 9
Sat 9 - 6
Sun 11 - 5

Calico Crafts

1691 U.S. 131 South 49770
(231) 347-1511 Fax: (231) 347-5914
Owner: Judith A. Hills
Est: 1979 3700 sq.ft. 3000 Bolts

3000 of the Finest Quality Quilt Fabrics from all the main companies. Friendly & knowledgeable staff to serve you!

East Jordan, MI #3

Mon - Sat 10 - 5
Tues 8 - 5
Wed 10 - 8

The Quilt Cottage

301 Water St. 49727
(231) 536-3363
www.thequiltcottage.net
A full line of quilting fabrics, notions & books. Newly remodeled shop located ½ miles east of M-66, on M-32 (Water St.)

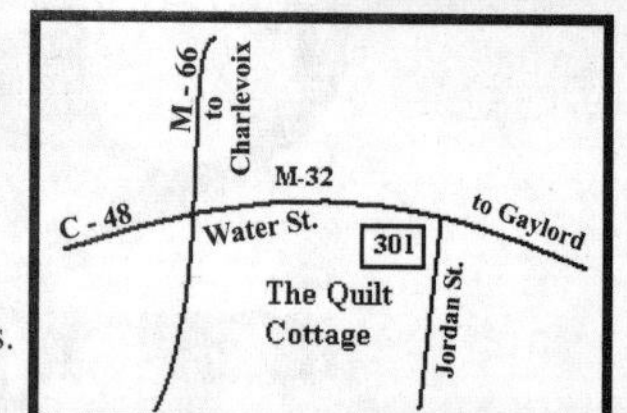

Bellaire, MI #4

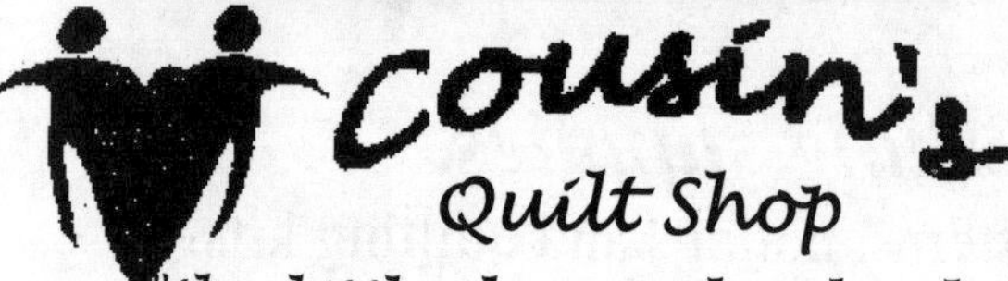

"the little shop with a big heart"

732 E. Cayuga St.
Bellaire, MI 49615
(231) 533-4661 Est: 2001
hartwig@torchlake.com
Owner: Carmen Hartwig

Bernina *of Bellaire*
Located within Cousins' Authorized Bernina Sales & Service
Software
OESD & Mettler Threads.

* Threads
* Fabrics
* Books
* Patterns
* Classes!!
* Mail Order
* BOM's
* Quilt Kits

Mon - Sat 10 - 5

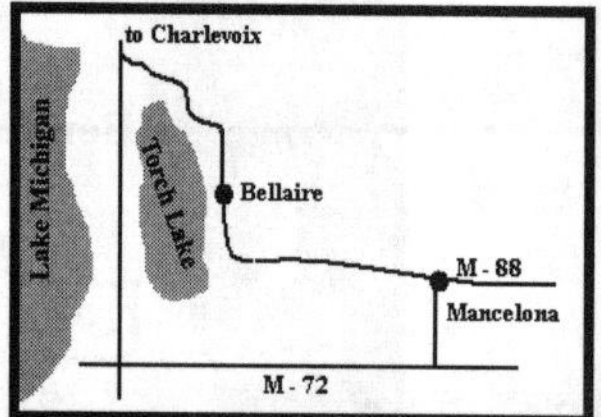

Lewiston, MI #5

Mon - Fri 10:30 - 4:30
Closed Wed
Sat 11 - 2
July Sun 11 - 2

Pine Tree Quilt Shoppe LLC

3060 Kneeland St. 49756
(989) 786-2804 Fax: (989) 786-9946
www.pinetreequiltshoppe.com
gortonhouse@i2k.com
Est: 2001 1500 sq.ft.
A quaint shop located in a 110 year old victorian farmhouse. Featuring Brights, Batiks, Cathy Parker redwork, local & Michigan artisans, pottery and American Spoon products. Guild Retreats. Bed & Breakfast.
"A Legacy Through Quilting"

Gaylord | Michaelson | Alpena | Pine Tree Quilts 3060 | Ct. Rd. 612 / Salling | Grayling | Kneeland | Ct. Rd. 489 / 491 | East Twin Lake

Gaylord, MI #6

Mon - Fri 9 - 6
Sat 9 - 5

Quilters General Store

132 W. Main St. 49735
(989) 732-1252
miker@dunnsonline.com
www.gaylordchamber.com
Owner: Lynda Ryan 600 bolts

A small town Quilt Shop with a large variety of fabrics and notions. Next to Sue's Stamps & Things -- just off I - 75.

to Mackinac Bridge | I - 75 | Quilters General Store | M - 32 (Main St.) | 132 | to Petoskey | Exit 183 | to Alpena | Coret House | 1/2 mile east of I-75 | to Grayling

Cedar, MI #7

Williamsburg, MI #8

Mon - Sat 10 - 5:30
Sun 12 - 5:30

Cranberry Christmas & Country Store

3997 M 72 East 49690
(231) 938-5944 Est: 1994 600+ Bolts
E-Mail: cranberrychristmas@yahoo.com
Web Site: www.cranberrychristmas.com

Growing inventory of 100% cotton fabrics & homespuns, patterns & stitcheries set amongst primitive antiques, gift & food items.

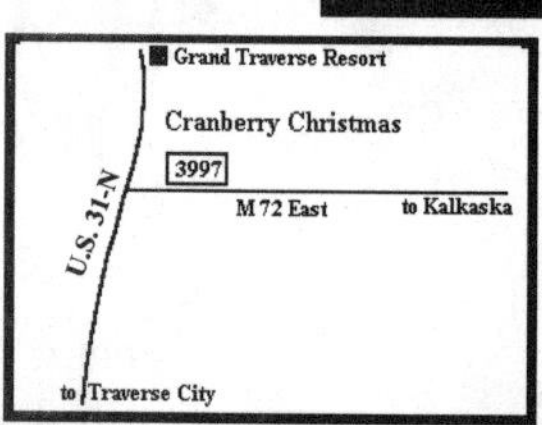

Williamsburg, MI #9

Mon - Fri 9:30 - 7
Sat 9:30 - 5:30

8995 M 72 East 49690
(231) 267-5895
Reneeshouseofquilting@yahoo.com
Owner: Renee Savage
Est: 2004

We have a vast selection of Children Brights, Flannels, Kona Bay, Hand-dyed batiks, etc. Over 2000 bolts to choose from. Tons of notions and books also. Come in for a visit and make yourself at home in our quilting house. Customer service our top priority.

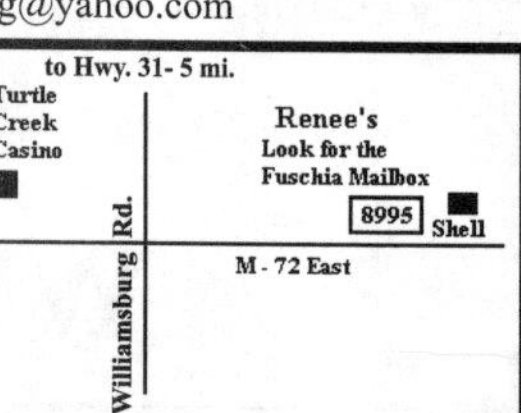

Mon - Fri 9:30 - 6:00
Sat 9:30 - 5:00

"Stop In And See What The Buzz Is All About"

- Over 1,000 bolts of high quality quilting fabric
- Collections by Moda, Benartex & Hoffman
- Smocking & Silk Ribbon Embroidery Books, Patterns & Supplies
- Heirloom Fabrics from Spechler-Vogel
- Inspirational Samples
- Hundreds of the Latest Books, Patterns & Notions
- Unique Gift Items & Kits Galore

Experienced and friendly staff ready to serve you!

1425-C S. Airport Rd. West
(231) 922-6766
Fax: (231) 946-1182
www.quiltnbee.com
Established: 2003 2,000 sq. ft.
Owners: Sharon Kaiser & Laura Hazen

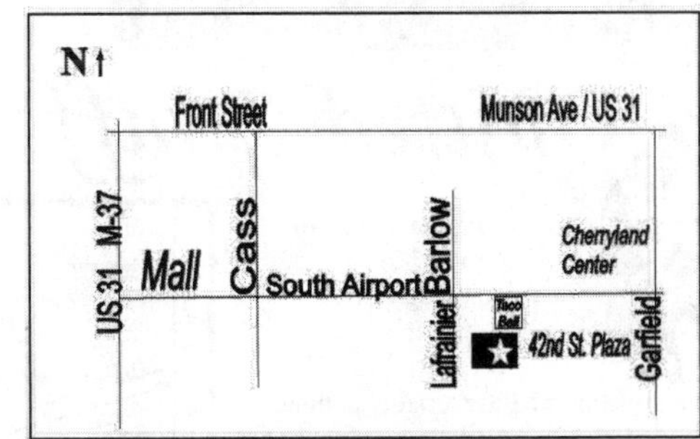

Traverse City, MI #13

Custer, MI #14

1200+ bolts of 100% cotton fabric plus patterns, books and notions all located in a 100 year old brick farm house

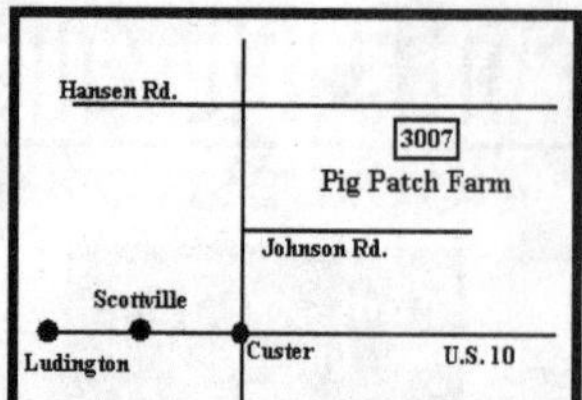

Mon - Sat 10 - 5

3007 E. Hansen Rd. 49405
(231) 757-2812
E-Mail: pigpatch@t-one.net
Web Site: www.pigpatchfarm.com
Owner: Sue Riffle Est: 1998

Farwell, MI #15

Elm Creek Ltd.

Mon - Sat 8 - 7
Sun 9 - 5

2609 W. Surrey Rd. 48622
(989) 588-6061 Fax: 588-3562
jjcrafty1@hotmail.com
www.elmcreekltd.com
Est: 1988 10000sq.ft.

Mid Michigan's Largest Fabric, Craft, Gifts & Garden Store! 5000 Bolts of Fabrics. Moda, South Seas, Homespuns & More. Specializing in Northwoods Fabrics & Gifts!

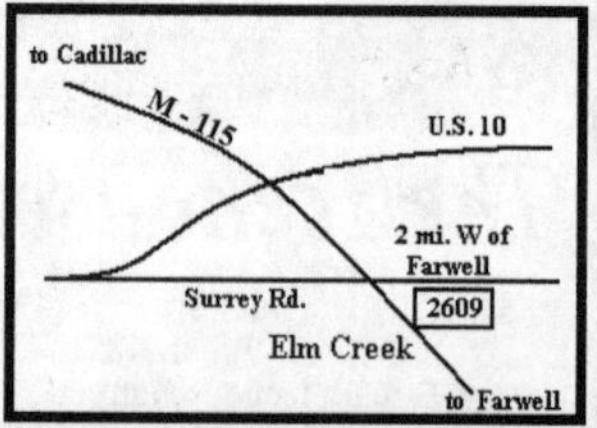

West Branch, MI #16

Crocker's Attic

Winter Hrs. Vary
May thru Dec.
Mon - Thur 11 - 4
Fri & Sat 10 - 5

3156 W. M-55 48661
(989) 345-1780 Est: 1993
E-Mail: crocker@voyager.net
Owner: Jolee Crocker 600+ Bolts

Primitive home furnishing and gift shop featuring Moda, Indo, Aunt Gracies and Homespuns. Specializing in Reproduction Fabrics, Thimbleberry prints and more.

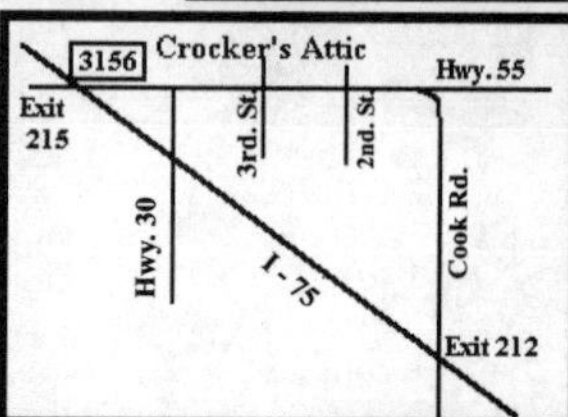

West Branch, MI #17

Caroline's Sewing Room

Mon - Fri 9 - 6
Sat 10 - 5

3197 W. M-55, P.O. Box 233 48661
(989) 345-9180 Fax: (989) 345-3578
Est: 1994 3000 bolts

Unique friendly - Large Selection of Books
100% Cotton Fabrics - Lots of Flannels
Patterns - Classes - Notions - Homespuns
Plaids - Color of the month sale.

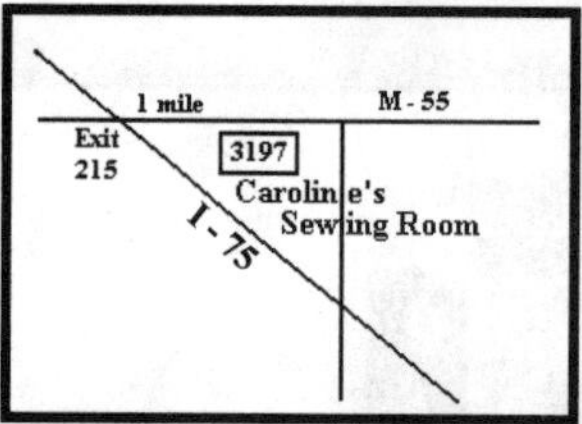

West Branch, MI #18

Button Hole

Mon - Fri 9 - 6
Sat 9 - 5

218 West Houghton 48661
(989) 345-0431
Web Site: www.buttonholeshop.com
Owner: Darlene Jones
Est: 1981 3300 sq.ft.

We have Everything for the Quilter !!
Located in a Victorian, downtown West Branch on Business Loop I - 75

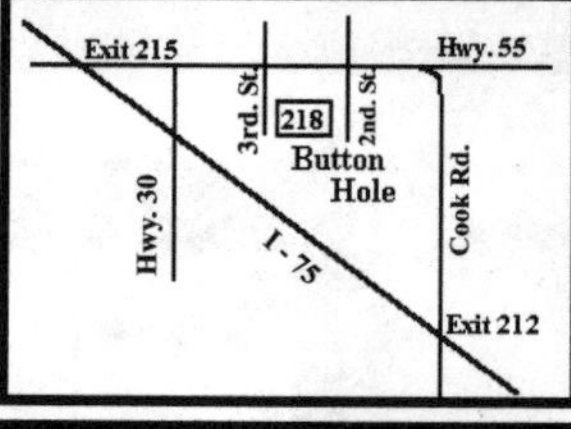

East Tawas, MI #19

Cotton Patch Quilt Shop

Mon - Sat 10 - 5
Summer Sun 12 - 4

306 Newman St. 48730
(877) 362-6779 or (989) 362-6779
ctnpatch@alpena.cc.mi.us
www.cottonpatchfabrics.com
Owner: Doni Butzin
Est: 1996 3000 sq.ft. 3000+ Bolts

Full Service Quilt Shop.
Block of the Month Clubs.
Machine Quilting Services.

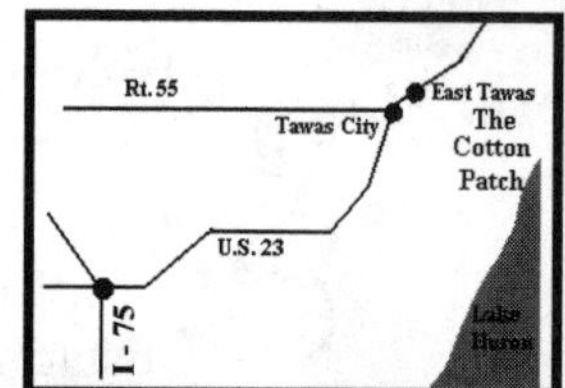

Gladwin, MI #20

The Log Cabin Fabric Shoppe

Tues - Sat 10 - 4

1902 Lakeshore 48624
(989) 426-1422
Owner: Cherie Thornton

We are now located in a beautiful shop in the country. Come visit our brand new barn full of quilting delights.

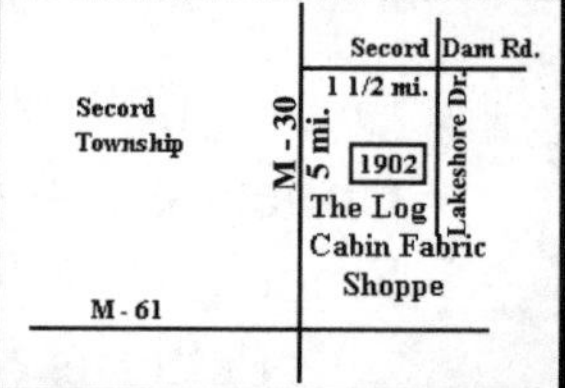

Midland, MI #21

Quilted Giraffe

Mon - Thur 9:30 - 6
Fri & Sat 9:30 - 5

1016 Haley St. 48640
(989) 837-2666
www.quiltedgiraffe.net

Large selection of 100% quality cottons, supplies, and classes. A year-round mini quilt show. Fun, Friendly and Knowledgeable Staff.

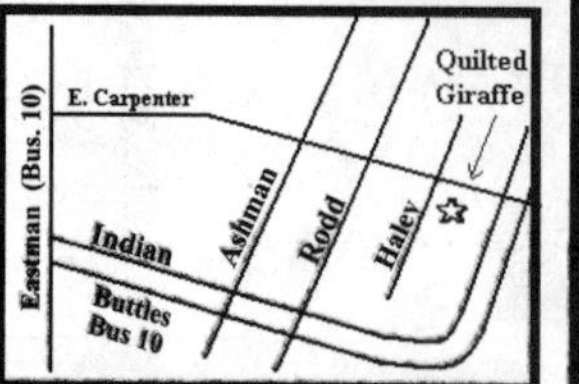

Caro, MI #22

Ruby's Yarn & Fabric

Tues - Fri 9 - 5
Thur til 6
Sat 9 - 4

326 S. State St. 48723
(989) 673-3062
beth@rubysyarnandfabric.com
www.rubysyarnandfabric.com
Owner: Beth A. Phillips

The ONLY shop of it's kind in the Thumb of Michigan. Designer yarns and quilting fabric. A definite "must see".

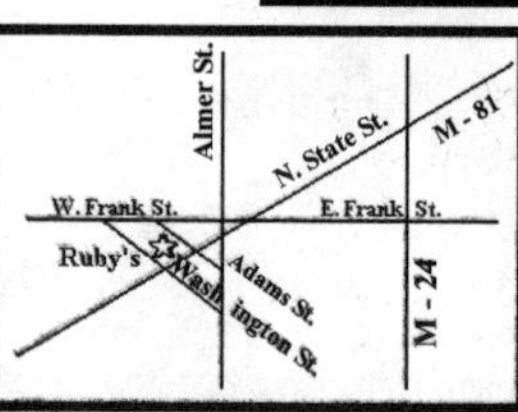

The Fabric Fair

206 Fifth Street
Bay City, MI 48708
989-893-8971
www.thefabricfair.com
Monday-Friday 9:30-7:00,
Saturday 9:30-5:00

BERNINA
The Art and Science of Sewing

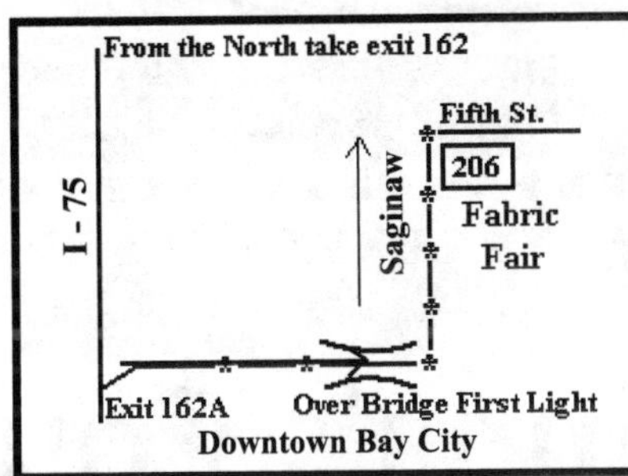

Bay City, MI #23

We are located in Bay City's Historic Downtown District
A Fabric Store since 1955
50,000 Bolts of fabric
Proprietor: Cecelia Wieland

- Quilters Cotton, notions and frames
- Bridal, Formal and Special Occasion
- Quality Woolens, Knits & Ribbing
- Linen, Tencel, Silk & Ultra Suede
- Heirloom Fabric and Laces
- Polar Fleece, Berber & Flannel
- Homespuns and Tapestries
- Tricot, Swim and Dancewear Fabric
- Dill Buttons * Just Another Button
- Stretch & Sew and Burda Patterns
- Silver Cloth, Linen Toweling, Ticking

YOUR ONE STOP FABRIC SHOP

Bay City, MI #24

Mon 12 - 9
Tues - Fri 10 - 5
Sat 10 - 2

Snail's Trail Quilt Shop

214 S. Henry 48706
(989) 895-9003
trail214@famvid.com
Owners: Pat LaRoche & Kathy Baker

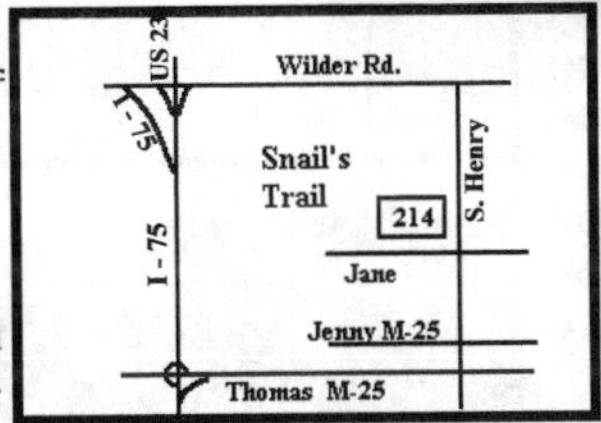

Fabrics including Hoffman & South Seas. Crafters, you'll love our Button Crock! Large Selection of Patterns. Classes. Featuring wearable art.

Lapeer, MI #25

Sandra's Sewing Center

458 W. Nepessing St. 48446
810-667-5400

Quilt shop in lovely downtown Lapeer. Many creative and traditional samples, kits and magic thread dolls. Featuring Jinny Beyer and Laurel Burch collections.

Mon - Fri 9:30 - 5:30
Sat 10 - 4

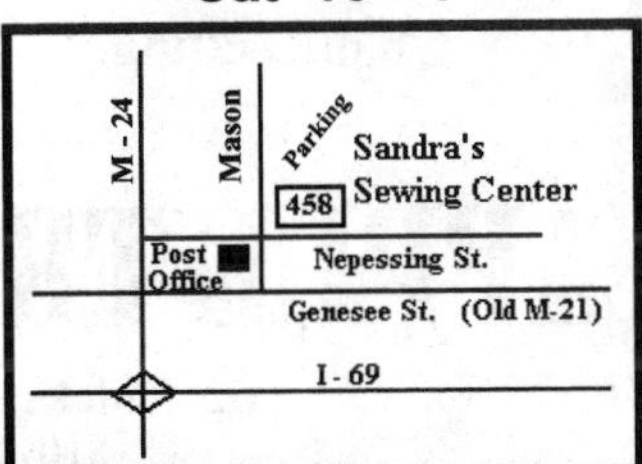

Come see Sara's beautiful portrait quilts. Watch for the mural on the side of our building!

Imlay City, MI #26

Mon - Fri 9:30 - 5:15
Sat 9:30 - 5

The Pincushion

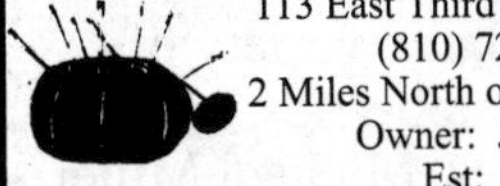

113 East Third Street 48444
(810) 724-7065
2 Miles North of I - 69 & M-53
Owner: Joyce Schihl
Est: 1971

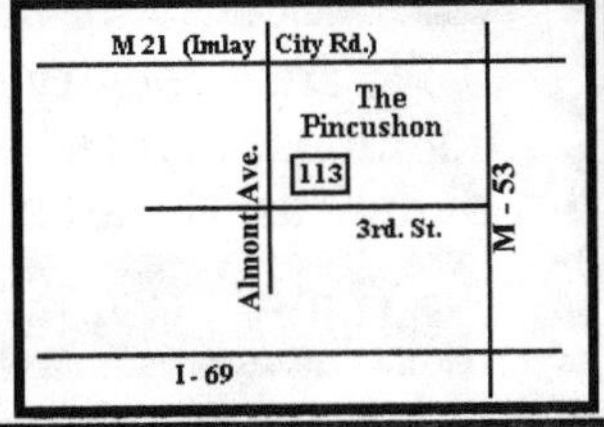

Everything For The Quilter.
Quality Quilting Fabric & Supplies.
An Extensive Book Inventory. Small town Friendly service. Our customers are our friends.

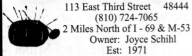

Lake Orion, MI #27

2369 Joslyn Ct. Lake Orion, MI 48360
(248) 391-5727
Est: 2004 3000 sq.ft.

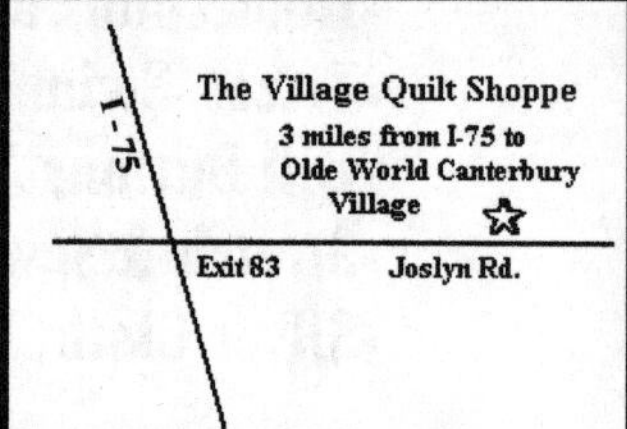

Mon - Sat 10 - 5:30
Sun 11 - 5:30

- Located at Olde World Canterbury Village.
- Large Selection of 100% Cotton - RJR, Moda, Benartex, Hoffman, Michael Miller & More
- Come Join our thimbleberries Club
- Lots & lots of Books and Patterns
- Classes - Notions - Gifts

mabelena

quilting supplies and comforts

470 Mill St., P.O. Box 804
Ortonville, MI 48462
248-627-9100 Fax: 248-627-9101
mabelenas@aol.com
Owner: Brenda Heffernan
Est: 2002 2000 sq.ft. 2000 bolts

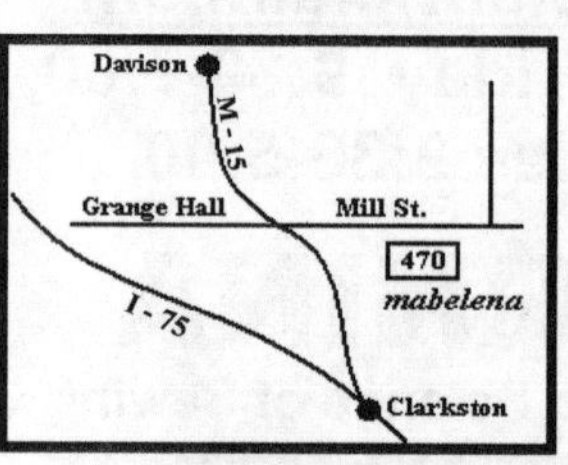

Brenda's shop is named after her grandmothers, Mabel and Lena. The shop's dedicated, friendly staff will be happy to assist you in selecting fabric for your next quilting project.

Ortonville, MI #28

Flushing, MI #29

100% Cotton fabrics.
Quilting books & patterns.
Notions.
Lots of classes.
Warm and personal service.
Quaint setting.

Mon - Sat 10 - 5
Sun 1 - 4

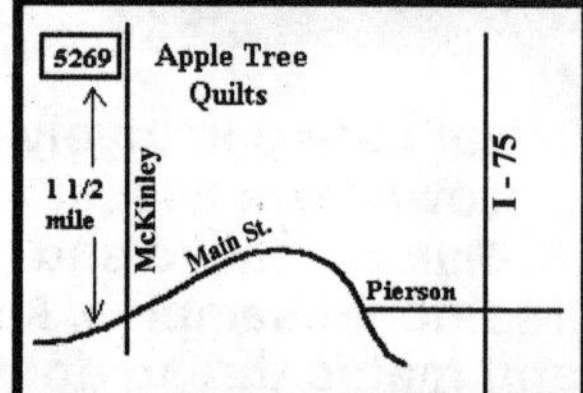

APPLE TREE QUILTS

5269 McKinley Rd. 48433
(810) 659- 4190
Owner: Judie Martin
Est: 1996
2000 sq.ft. 1000+ Bolts

Davison, MI #30

Linda's Country Quilt Shop

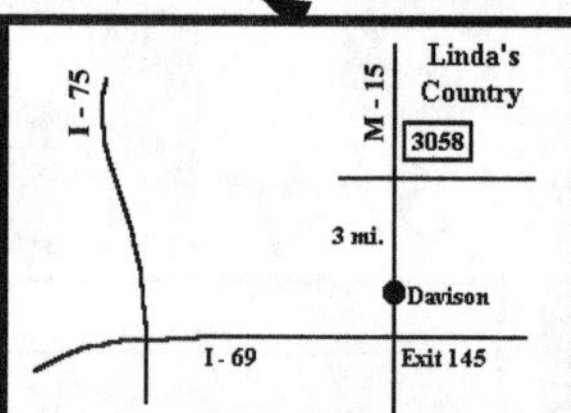

3058 N. State Rd. Unit F
M - 15 48423
(810) 658-9051
Owner: Linda Jacobsen
Est: 1998
2500 sq.ft. 2500 Bolts

We are a country store with a large variety of traditional fabrics by RJR, Thimbleberries, Moda, South Seas, Benartex, P&B Fabrics, Michael Miller Marcus Brothers and more.

Mon - Sat 9 - 5

Davison Fabrics

Thousands of Fabric Bolts Including:
Benartex ◆ Thimbleberries ◆ Kaufman
RJR ◆ Hoffman ◆ Moda ◆ Roberta Horton
P&B ◆ South Seas ◆ Debbie Mumm
Timeless Treasures ◆ In the Beginning
Monarch ◆ Pinwheels Japanese Fabrics
Theresa Kogut ◆ Fasco ◆ Hi Fashion
Bali ◆ Spechler-Vogel ◆ And Many More!

Lots of Batiks and Novelty Prints

Est. 1944
Owners: Greg & Ramona Nolan
Over 6000 square feet

Hours:
Mondays - Saturdays
9 a.m. - 5:30 p.m.

Davison, MI #31

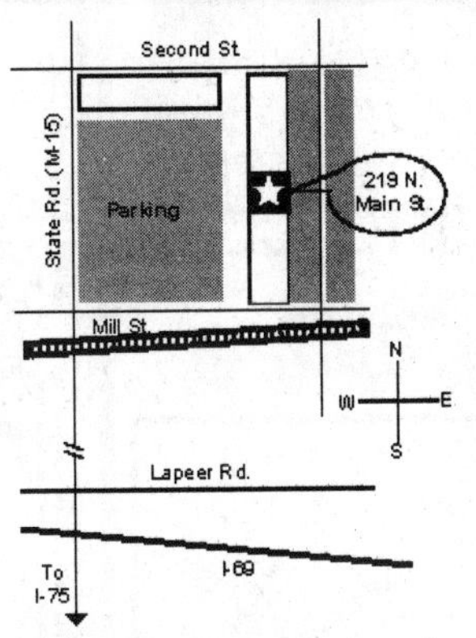

219 N. Main Street
Downtown Davison
(810) 653-2641
www.davisonfabrics.com

Less than 5 minutes from the expressway!

Over 400 classes annually
100's of Book Titles
Quilting & Sewing Gifts
Wonderful Selection of Buttons
Heirloom & Smocking Supplies
Many of those Hard to Find Notions

Largest Selection of Craft Patterns in the State

Nothing Sews Like A Bernina. Nothing.
BERNINA®
Authorized Sales & Service

Commercial & Residential
We Service All Brands

Port Huron, MI #32

Sew Elegant

Quilt Shoppe

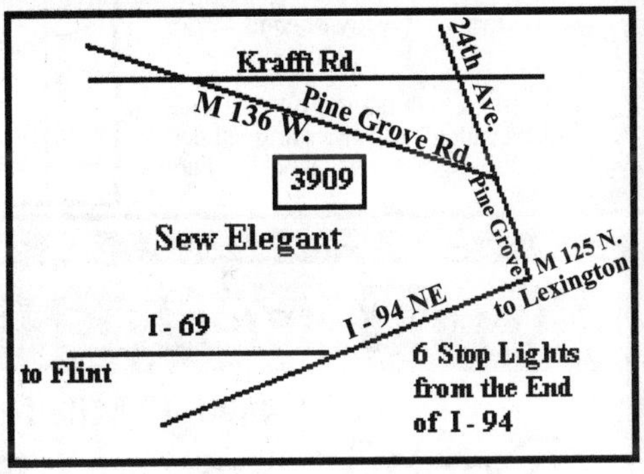

VAST SELECTION OF
BOOKS, PATTERNS AND SEWING
NOTIONS FOR QUILTERS.

PFAFF MACHINES
SALES & SERVICE

Mon - Sat
10 - 5
Sun 12 - 4:30

Krafft Rd.
24th Ave.
M 136 W.
Pine Grove Rd.
3909
Pine Grove
Sew Elegant
M 125 N. to Lexington
I - 69
I - 94 NE
to Flint
6 Stop Lights from the End of I - 94

3909 Pine Grove Rd. 48059
(810) 982-6556
Fax: (810) 982-6996
E-Mail: elsew@aol.com
Web-Site: www.sewelegant.com
Owner: Linda Anderson
Est:1986 4880 sq.ft.

Eastern Michigan's Largest Quilt Shop!
Our Shop is full of 100% cotton Fabrics--
over 8,000 bolts

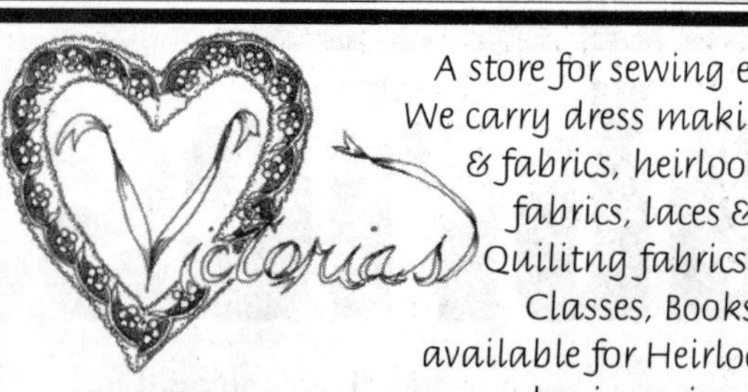

A store for sewing enthusiasts. We carry dress making supplies & fabrics, heirloom supplies, fabrics, laces & insertions. Quilitng fabrics & supplies, Classes, Books & Patterns available for Heirloom sewing, basic sewing & quilting. Authorized Husqvarna Viking, White and Brother Sales & Service.

Mon 10 - 5
Tues & Thur 10 - 9
Wed, Fri Sat 10 - 6:30

www.victoriassewing.com

Port Huron, MI #33

2708 14th Ave. 48060
(810) 966-9600
Fax: (810) 966-9027
Victoriassewing@sbcglobal.net
Owners: Victoria A. Essery & Sally Kiewicz
Est: 1996

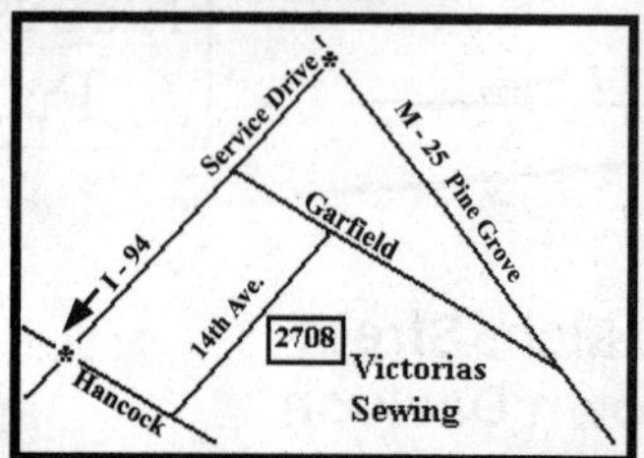

Richmond, MI #34

Sew Together

Tues - Thur 10 - 5
Fri 10 - 7
Sat 10 - 4

69295 Main St. 48062
(586) 727-1555
quilting@massnet1.net
www.geocities.com/sewtogetherquiltshop
Owners: Gina Kaszynski & Susan Weinert

A large variety of cotton fabrics, many different threads and embellishments. Huge assortment of books and patterns. We now carry knitting supplies and have some gorgeous yarns. Inquire about our doll club and bear classes.

St. Clair Shore, MI #36

The Quilters Patch

Mon,Tues, Fri 10 - 6
Thur 10 - 9
Sat 10 - 4

31384 Harper 48082
(586) 293-1999
Owner: Beverly Maxvill
Est: 1981 1200 sq.ft.

Victorian Block of the Month as seen in "Keepsake Catalog" and many original designs available for Quilts & Blocks. Fabrics-Notions-Books.

Masonic
I - 94
I - 94
31384 The Quilters Patch In Landmark Plaza
Little Mack
Harper
13 - Mile

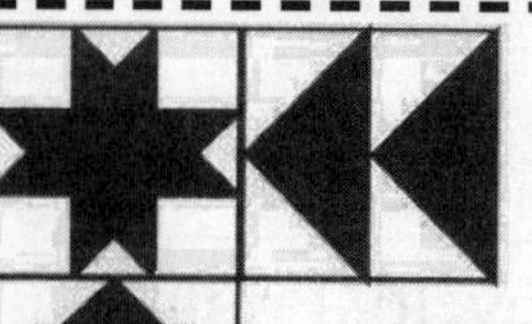

QUILTER'S CORNER

36743 Garfield Rd.
Clinton Twp., MI 48035
(586) 790-8292; Fax (586) 790-8293

M & F 9 TO 5; T-W-Th 9 to 8; Sat 10 to 4;
Sun Closed (Open Super Bowl Sun. 12 - 4)

Friendly, fun staff!!
Great selection of 100% cotton fabrics,
Books, patterns, notions,
Classes to suit everyone.
Host shop for Thimbleberries Quilt Club.

GIFT CERTIFICATES
VISA - MASTERCARD - DISCOVER

Take I - 94 to Exit 236. West on Metro Pkwy. 4 miles to Garfield Rd.

On SW corner (near bank) in Hitching Post Shopping Ctr.

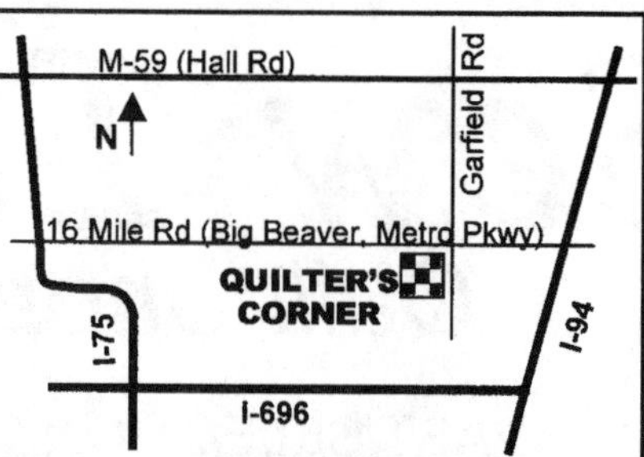

Clinton Twp, MI #35

Sterling Heights, MI #37

4090 17 Mile Road 48310
(586) 979-7422
Gretchen L. Tatge
Est: 1983

Quilt-n Friends

2500 bolts of 100% Cotton Fabrics
Notions ... Books ... Patterns
Gifts ... Machine Quilting
Newsletter every 2 months ... Friendly Staff
Classes Year Round ... Michigan's Finest Teachers

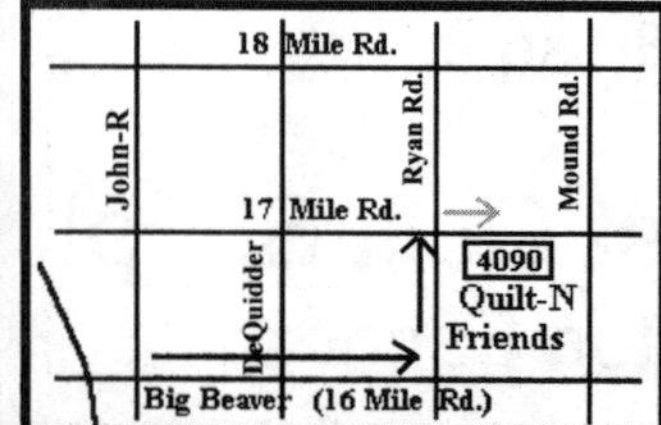

"The Complete Quilt Shop"

Mon - Fri 9 - 5 Sat 9 - 3
Thurs Eve til 8:30

Berkley, MI #38

By Appt.

Cheryl's Heirloom Quilting

(248) 544-1113
Owner: Cheryl Mathe—designer

Please Call for Directions

Experienced long-arm machine quilting.
100's of designs or custom design available.
Excellent service. Call for information.

Berkley, MI #39

Once Upon a Time

In A Land Not Far Away...

Guildcrafters
QUILT SHOP

OPEN 7 DAYS:
M, Tu, Th, F, 10-6 - W, 10-9
Sat, 10-5 - Sun, 12-3

Est 1982

2790 W. 12 Mile Berkley, MI 48072 • 248-541-8545

12 Mile
I-275
Coolidge
Woodward
I-75
I-696
200
10 Mile

5000 Bolts / Kits

Guildcrafters.com

2 mi North of 696 - 5 mi west of 175

Where the quilt of your dreams can come true

The Quilted Goose offers custom machine quilting services. Award winning quilter with design imagination can make the most of your creation. We offer four levels of quilting, from simple all-over designs to heirloom quality quilting. Your quilts will be treated with loving care in our smoke-free studio.

Be sure to ask for a copy of our brochure **"What Our Customers Have to Say About The Quilted Goose"** and find out what our customers already know!

Let us help you get your quilt tops out of the storage closet and onto a bed or a wall! **Call or email today for current turn-around time or to request a copy of our free brochure.**

Custom Machine Quilting Services

For your convenience we stock several types of batting and backing fabrics to make completing your quilt even easier!

Troy, MI #40

The Quilted Goose

646 East Long Lake Road, Troy, MI 48085

248-740-8867

248-740-8869 FAX

www.thequiltedgoose.com

Email: info@thequiltedgoose.com

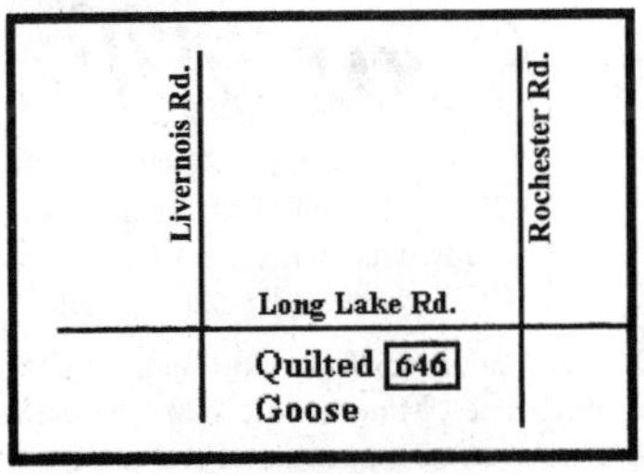

Livernois Rd.
Rochester Rd.
Long Lake Rd.
Quilted Goose 646

Linda M. Thielfoldt, Designer
Hours By Appointment - please call.
Member of IMQA

Livonia, MI #41

Please Call for an Appt.

Creative Quilting

36749 Angeline Cir. 48150
(734) 425-6385
Owner: Jean Coleman Est: 1990

The Finishing Touch

A MACHINE QUILTING SERVICE

Custom machine quilting. Quilts accepted from UPS and U.S.P.S. Design choices by mutual agreement per letter or phone. Call for a flyer.

Bits 'n Pieces

34629 W. Michigan Ave.
Wayne, MI 48184
Est. 1981
(734) 641-4970 **#42**

www.bitsnpieces.net

Cotton Fabrics
Quilting Supplies
Books • Patterns • Kits • Block-of-the-Month
BERNINA Sewing Machines
Sales • Service • Repair

Mon - Sat 10 - 5 Tues & Thurs 'til 7
(closed Mondays during July and August)

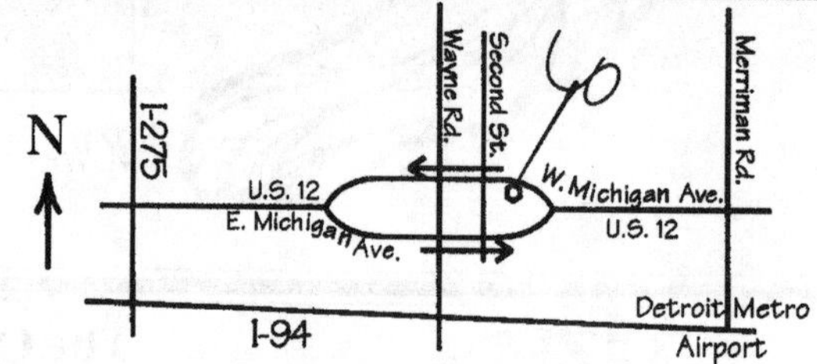

On the south side of Westbound Michigan Ave.
Approximately 3½ miles east of I-275, 1½ miles west of Merriman Rd. and 4 miles north of I-94.

Lake St. Mercantile

Located in a beautifully restored 100 year old Bank Building in Downtown South Lyon

Quilting • Lessons • Supplies
Wool Penny Rugs & Projects
Girl Gang Club Member

We carry a large selection of 100% cottons from Moda, RJR, Benartex, Free Spirit, In the Beginning & more, along with Wool from York & a new assortment of Hand Dyed from WICKED WOOL! Of course, let's not forget our books, patterns and kits made to order.

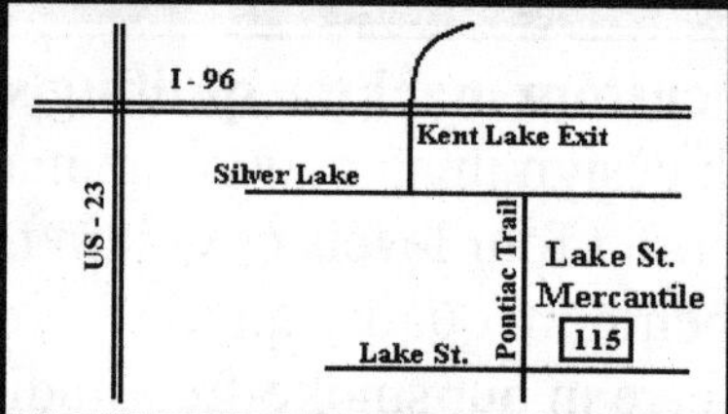

Gifts Cards Available • Credit Cards Accepted
115 E. Lake St.
South Lyon, MI 48178
248-486-4410
mercantile@cablespeed.com

HOURS: Mon, Tues, Wed, Fri 10-6
Thurs 10-8 • Sat 10-4 • Sun 12-3

South Lyon, MI #43

Sew Fun Fabrics Inc.

This quilt shop is in an old house at the corner of Oak and 7th Street. Many services are brought to our customers in one relaxed and comfortable setting. Freehand long-arm quilting is available in the shop. Our knowledgeable and creative staff has more than 30 years of experience.

Tues - Sat 10 - 5
Sun 11 - 4

664 Oak St., P.O. Box 42
Wyandotte, MI 48192
(734) 284-1405
dmoffitt@wideopenwest.com
Owner: Deb Moffit
Est: 2003 1200 sq.ft. 800 bolts

www.sewfunfabrics.com

Wyandotte, MI #44

Southgate, MI #45

Mon - Sat 10 - 5
Winter Sun 12 - 4

Sew What

13736 Fort St. 48195
(734) 281-1344 Fax: Same
sewwhat59@aol.com
Est: 1997 1400 sq.ft. 2000+ bolts

100% cotton fabrics from Hoffman, Benartex, Thimbleberries, Mumm's the Word, Moda and more. Quilting supplies, books & patterns. Special orders welcome.

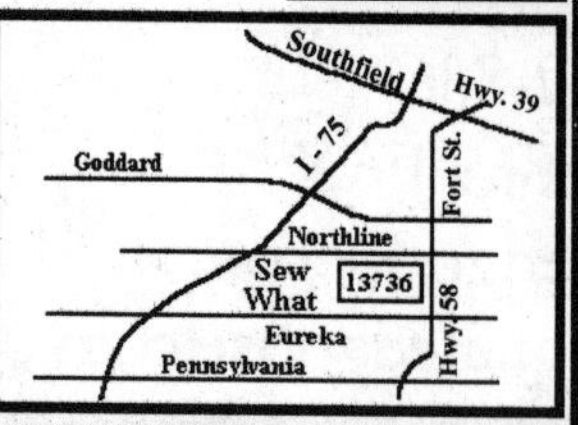

The Quilting Season

5150 W. Michigan Ave.
Ypsilanti, MI 48197
(734) 528-1740 Fax: (734) 528-1749
www.quiltingseason.com
Est: 2001 1800 sq.ft.

Ypsilanti, MI #47

1500 Quilting Fabrics that Enchant and Inspire

RJR Fabrics, Moda Fabrics, Hoffman California, Benartex, Bali Fabrics & more.

Quilting Books, Patterns, Supplies and Classes

Located 3/4 mile East of US-23 on US12 in the big red barn at Schmidt's Antiques.

Mon - Sat 9:30 - 5
Sun 12 - 5

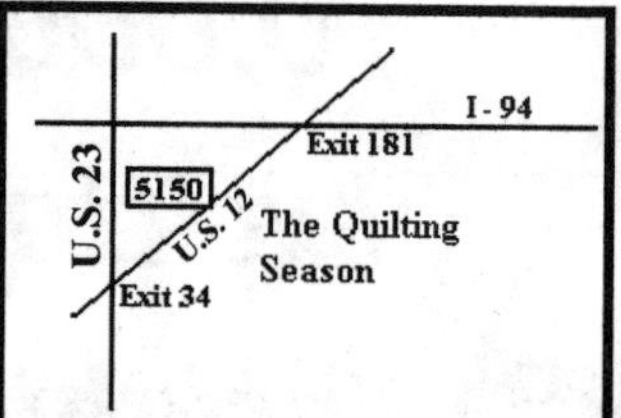

Belleville, MI #48

Mon - Sat 10 - 6
Sun 12 - 5

Threads 'n Treasures Quilt Shop

129 South St. 48111
(734) 697-9376 Fax: Same
katkins@provide.net
Owner: Kay Atkins Est: 1996

"We've added 800 square feet & lots of fabric" Save 25% when you buy 1/2 yard or more per cut, excluding panels. Notions, books, patterns.

Monroe, MI #49

Mon 10 - 9
Tues, Wed, Thur 10 - 6
Fri & Sat 10 - 5
Sun 12 - 5

Kinder's Corner

4531 E. Dunbar 48161
Phone/Fax (734) 457-9111
info@cattalesquilts.com
www.cattalesquilts.com
Est: 1999 2000sq.ft.

Full service Quilt Shop.

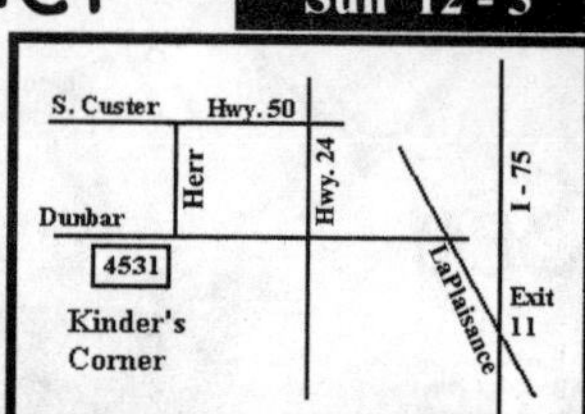

Monroe, MI #50

Sadie Sewing Shoppe

Mon - Fri 10 - 5
Thur til 8
Sat 10 - 4

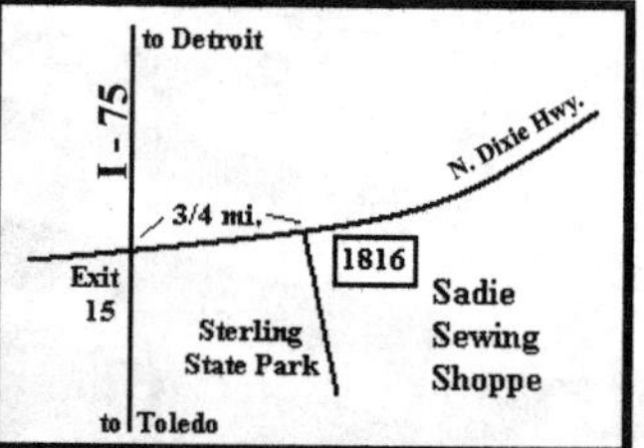

Quality Quilting Materials,
Lots of Notions,
Classes of all Types,
We are the Friendliest Quilt Shoppe on the Lake (Erie).

Conveniently Located 3/4 of a mile off I-75.
Right next to Sterling State Park

1816 N. Dixie Hwy. 48162
sadiesewing2003@yahoo.com
Owner: Barbara Peterson
(734) 289-1213

Montgomery, MI #51

Mon - Sat 10 - 5
Closed Thur

Quilting Nest

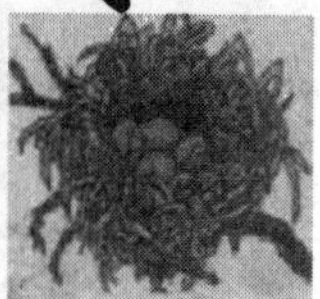

801 S. Fremont Rd. 49255
(517) 238-4041
Owner: Rae B. Easterday
Est: 2000 850 sq.ft.

Over 200 Bolts of Flannels, 400 Bolts of 100% Cottons. Machine Quilting

U.S. 12
St. Rd. 27
I - 69
Fremont Rd.
Copeland Rd.
3 mi.
801
Quilting Nest
to Indiana 3.5 mi.

Mason, MI #52

Mon - Fri 9 - 8
Sat 9 - 5:30
Sun 12 - 5

Kean's Store Co.

406 S. Jefferson St. 48854
(517) 676-5144

Large selection of quality quilting fabrics, bear supplies, mohair, quilt books, patterns, books, & notions.
Bring a friend, spend the day, lots to see!

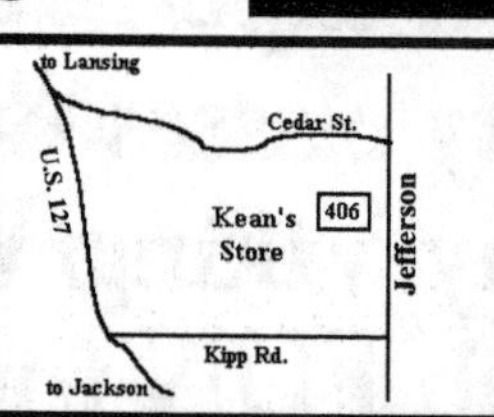

Holt, MI #53

Mon - Fri 9:30 - 6
Thur til 8
Sat 9:30 - 4
Sun 11 - 3

Everlasting Stitches, Inc.

2040 N. Aurelius Rd. 48842
(517) 699-1120 Fax: (517) 699-1122
Owner: Pam Henrys
Est: 2002 1500 sq.ft. 1600+ Bolts
High Quality Cottons from Top Companies.
Rughooking and Supplies.
Long-arm machine rental
Handcrafted Sewing Collectables.
Friendly, helpful customer service. Coffee's On.

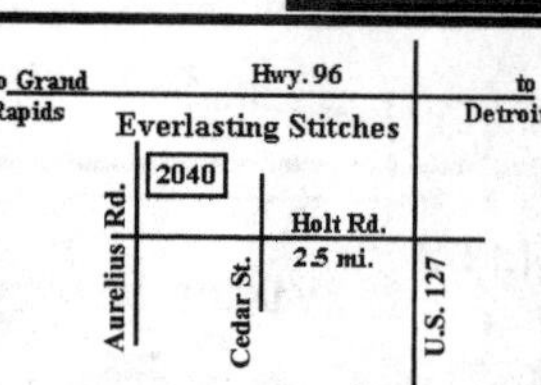

We will be
MOVING
from 123 W. Chicago Blvd.
across the street to our
NEW PLACE

112 N. EVANS STREET
Tecumseh, MI 49296

SUMMER 2004

517-423-0053
WEBSITE: www.thequiltpatch.com

Tecumseh, MI #54

- Enjoy 9000 Sq. Ft. of Quilter's Paradise
- Thousands of Bolts, Books & Patterns
- Classes for Every Skill Level
- Full Sewing Machine Repair & Service
- Scissor & Knife Sharpening

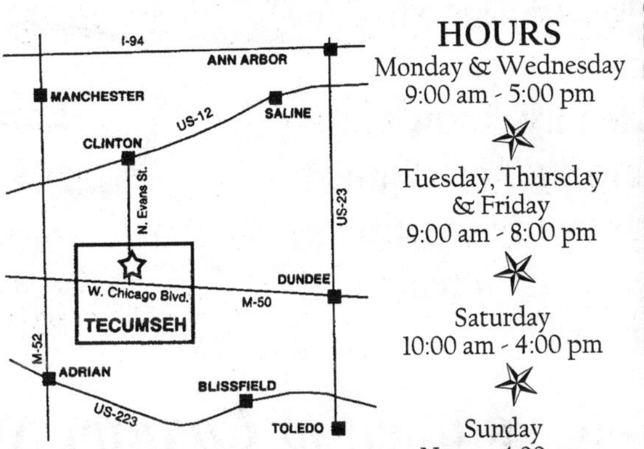

HOURS
Monday & Wednesday
9:00 am - 5:00 pm

Tuesday, Thursday & Friday
9:00 am - 8:00 pm

Saturday
10:00 am - 4:00 pm

Sunday
Noon - 4:00 pm

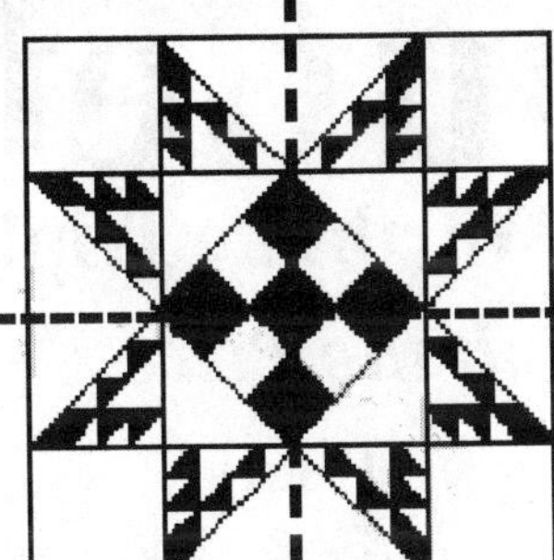

The Stitchery

1129 E. Grand River Ave - Howell, MI 48843 - (517)548-1731
E-Mail:st1tchery@sbcglobal.net - www.thestitcheryonline.com
Owner: Susan Reid

Howell, MI #55

Friendly, knowledgable staff ready to give you personalized service. Over 4000 bolts of fabric from major manufactures including quality cotton, flannels, wools and batiste. Quilting Supplies, Heirloom Sewing Supplies, Books, Patterns, Notions and Classes for all skill levels. Servicing all makes and models of sewing machines and sergers.

Authorized **JANOME** Sewing Machine Dealer

Mon-Fri 9 A.M.-6 P.M. Sat 9 A.M.-4 P.M.

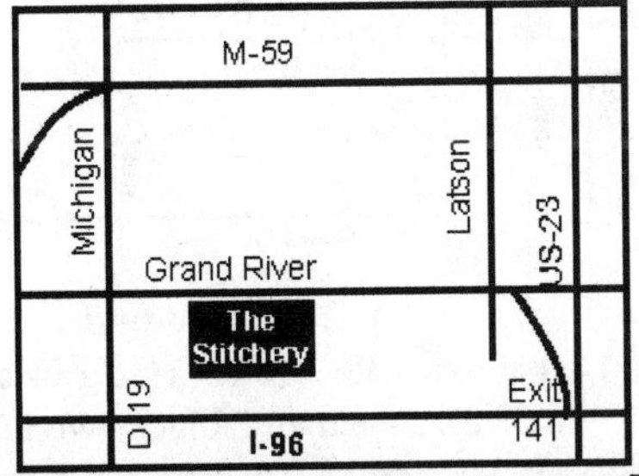

Country Stitches

Our Destination Store

America's Largest Quilt Shop is a Quilter's Heaven!

- Over 6000 bolts of 100% cotton fabric line the shelves.
- A continuous quilt show and year-round Christmas displays offer ideas and inspiration.
- Friendly, knowledgeable staff are trained and ready to help with your creative project.

Hours:
Monday - Thursday
9:30 am - 8:00 pm
Friday
9:30 am - 6:00 pm
Saturday
9:30 am - 5:30 pm
Sunday - Closed

Call **517-351-2416**
or **1-800-572-2031**
for more information

We're easy to find:
One block east of US 127
on Lake Lansing Rd.
across from Meijer

East Lansing, MI #56

Web Site: countrystitches.com

Treat yourself to Country Stitches, truly a unique quilt shop.

Country Stitches Outlet

It's Worth the Trip!

Over 3000 Bolts

of 100% Cotton Fabric

$4.99/yd or less!

Great Quality Fabric - At Half the Price

PLUS...

Hundreds of Patterns $1.00
Threads 50% Off
Gift Items 50% Off

Visit Our Outlet Store for Fabric & Notions along with Discount Sewing Machines
(Repacks, Blems, One-of-a-Kind)
Husqvarna Viking, Pfaff & White

Hours:
Mon & Wed
10 am - 8 pm
Tue, Thur, Fri
10 am - 6 pm
Sat 10 am - 5 pm
Sun 12 pm - 4 pm

Call **517-782-7100**
or **1-800-782-3830**
for more information

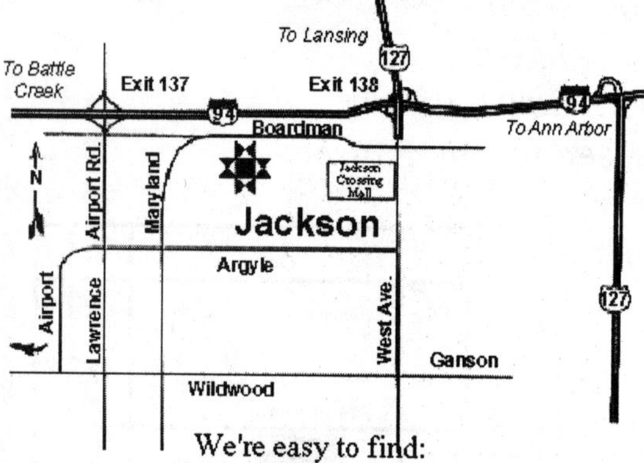

We're easy to find:
I-94 at exit 138 (US-127) Go 1 block south
on West Ave then 2 blocks west (right)
on Boradman Rd. (just past Lowe's)

Jackson, MI #57

Web Site: countrystitches.com

Walled Lake, MI #58

Mon 12 - 9
Tues - Fri 10 - 6
Sat 10 - 4

Cross-vine Quilting, Inc.

500 Pontiac Tr. 48390
(248) 668-2700
Crossvinequilts@cs.com
Owners: Cheri & Joe Stephan
Est: 2002 1500 sq.ft. 1500+ bolts

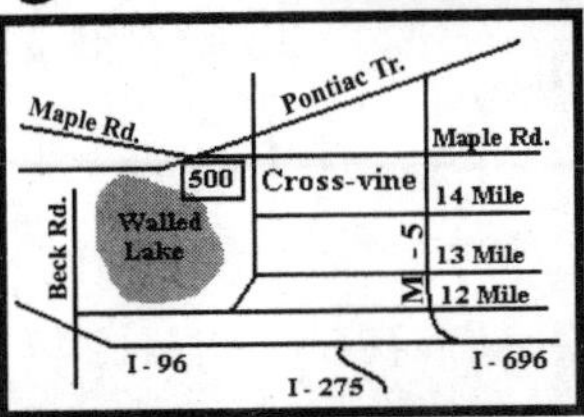

Fine 100% cotton fabrics, excellent classes, inspiring books and patterns, long-arm finishing services.

Fenton, MI #59

The Quilters Garden

Mon, Tues, Wed, Fri 9:30 - 6
Thursday 9:30 - 8:30
Sat 9:30 - 4

Providing a variety of high quality 100% cotton quilting fabric, books, patterns, quilting supplies and classes.

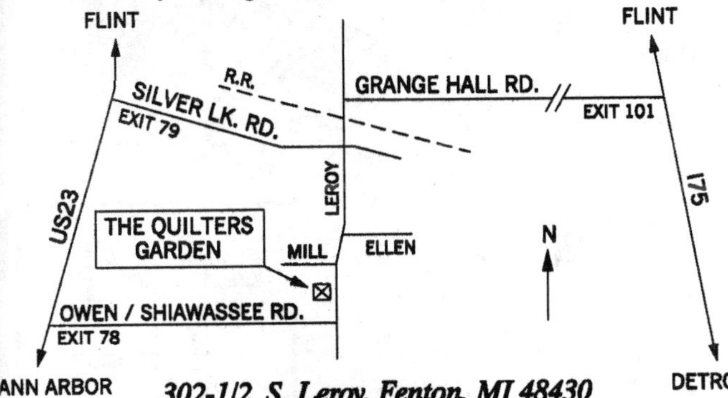

302-1/2 S. Leroy, Fenton, MI 48430
810-629-0331
quilt@thequiltersgarden.com
www.thequiltersgarden.com

Lansing, MI #60

Mon - Thurs 10 - 9
Fri & Sat 10 - 6

The Quilt Depot

323-B S. Waverly Rd. 48917
(517) 323-3090 (888) 809-9323
Fax: (517) 323-3313
tqdepot@thequiltdepot.com
www.thequiltdepot.com
Owner: Patti Parmenter
Est: 1998 4500 sq.ft. 1500 Bolts.

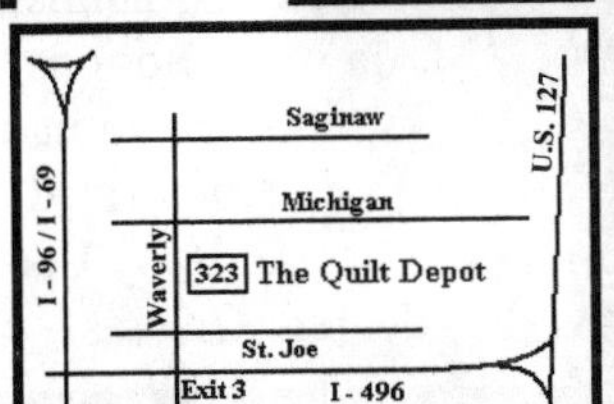

The friendly shop with great fabrics and fun!

Charlotte, MI #61

Mon - Sat 10 - 5:30

Hen House of Charlotte

211 S. Cochran 48813
(517) 543-6454
Owner: Nancy Conn Est: 1974

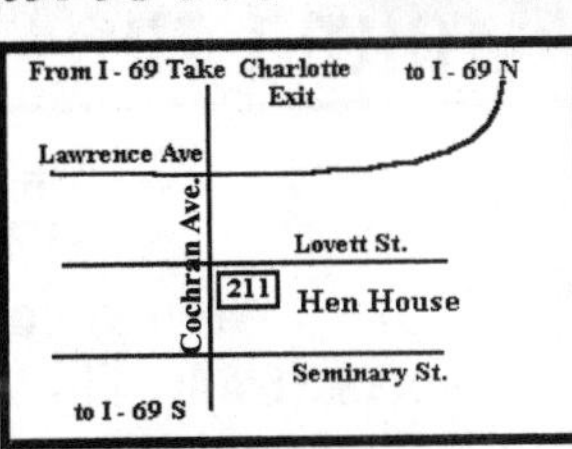

A primitive quilt and craft shop specializing in quality materials including 100% cotton and homespun fabrics, wool and rug hooking supplies, stenciling, floor canvas painting, cross stitch materials, and basket making supplies.

Shops at the MARSHALL HOUSE

Marshall, MI #62

100 Exchange St. 49068 269-781-9450
Est. Dec. 2003 1500 sq.ft. 1000+ bolts

Tues - Sat 10 - 5 Thur til 7 Sun 12 - 4 Mon by Chance

Quilting supplies, antiques and knitting in one of the oldest building in historic Marshall, MI. Concentrating in Asian, Batik, and 19th Century reproduction fabric.

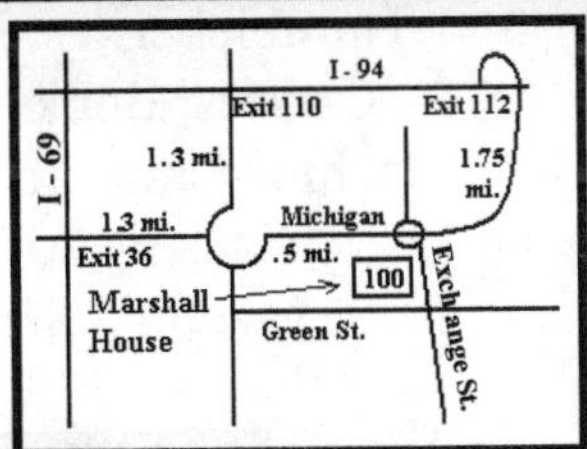

Parking in front of the building on Green St. and in the city lot directly to the west.

East Leroy, MI #63

Quilt N Go

"Your quilt shop in the country"
7212 6-1/2 Mile Rd * East Leroy, MI 49051
(south of Battle Creek)
269-979-2347 ruth@quiltngo.com
Owner: Ruth Dean

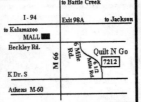

to Battle Creek
I - 94
Exit 98A
to Jackson
to Kalamazoo
MALL
Beckley Rd.
6 Mile Rd.
Quilt N Go
7212
6 1/2 Mile Rd.
M 66
K Dr. S
Athens M-60

Mon - Fri 9 - 6
Thur til 8
Sat 9 - 1

Receive 10% off your purchase when you show us your QTC!

www.quiltngo.com

We offer classes from beginning to advanced with all the notions, books, and patterns that you need.

Over 2,000 bolts of fabric from Thimbleberries, Moda, 1930's reproductions, wool, wool felt, South Seas, Benartex, homespuns and more.

Battle Creek, MI #64

Tues - Fri 10 - 5
Sat 10 - 1

The Quiltery

1540 East Columbia Ave. 49104
(269) 965-2116
Est: 1981 2500 sq.ft.
Owner: Lynne Evans

HUGE selection of quality 100% cottons by Hoffman, RJR, Benartex, and others; notions, books, and patterns. Hand knitting yarns, knitting tools, patterns and books. Call for a free newsletter listing classes & sales.

Kalamazoo, MI #65

Bernina Sewing Center

Mon - Fri 9:30 - 5:30
Wed til 8
Sat 9:30 - 4

4205 Portage Rd. 49001
(269) 383-1244 Fax: (269) 383-5913
berninakzoo@ameritech.net
www.berninakzoo.com
Est: 1992 5600 sq.ft. 2000+ Bolts

2000+ bolts of 100% cotton, batiks, flannel, Moda wool, notions, books, patterns, threads galore. Authorized Bernina and Baby Lock dealer. Classes.

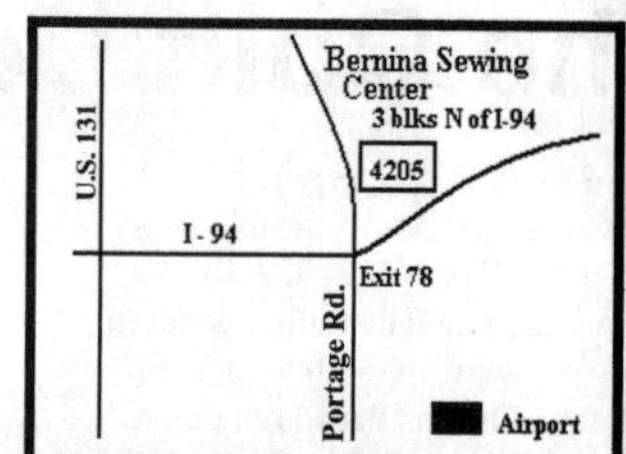

Kalamazoo, MI #66

Quilts Plus

Mon - Fri 10 - 6
Thur til 8:30
Sat 10 - 4

- Fabrics
- Classes
- Quilting Supplies
- Books & Patterns
- Hoops
- Blocks of the Month
- Quilt Kits & Fabric Packs
- Hinterberg & Ulmer Quilt Frames
- Gifts
- Samples Galore

4644 W. Main
Kalamazoo, MI 49006
Tel: (269) 383-1790
Fax: (269) 383-2182
quiltspluskazoo@hotmail.com
Owner: Kathleen Edwards Est: 1996

20% off--Empty a Bolt--Last Business Day of the Month

Portland, MI #69

Around the Block Quilt Shop

120 Maple St. 48875
(517) 647-5430
Aroundblockquilt@aol.com
Owners: Cathy Norton, Steve & Cathy McCann
Est: 1999 2500 sq.ft.

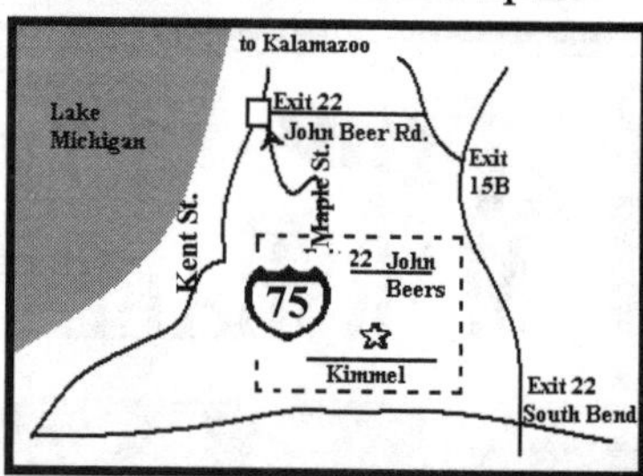

Web: sew2000.com/aroundtheblock

100% Cotton Fabrics by Hoffman, Benartex, Thimbleberries, Debbie Mumm & RJR.
Classes, Books, Patterns, & Notions.
Machine Embroidery Supplies from OESD
Lansing Area Bernina Dealer.
Machine Service—All Brands.

Mon, Wed, Fri, Sat 10 - 5
Tues & Thurs 10 - 8

Kalamazoo, MI #67

Mon - Fri 9 - 5:30
Wed til 7
Sat 9 - 4

Viking Sewing Center

5401 Portage Rd. 49002
(269) 342-5808
Owners: Phil & Julie Rotzien
2500 sq.ft.

1000+ bolts of 100% cotton fabric. Quilting, heirloom, garment and specialty sewing classes. Viking & White sewing machine sales & service.

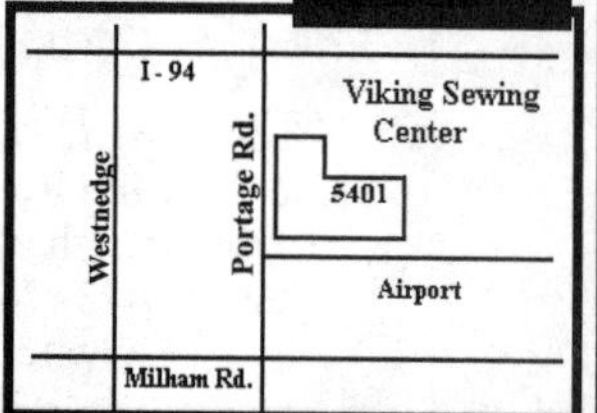

Hastings, MI #68

Mon - Thur 8 - 5:30
Fri 8 - 7
Sat 9 - 5:30

Sisters Fabrics

218 E. State St. 49058
(269) 945-9673

Large selection of calico, books, patterns, quilting supplies, fleece, dress fabrics, JHB and Streamline buttons, etc.

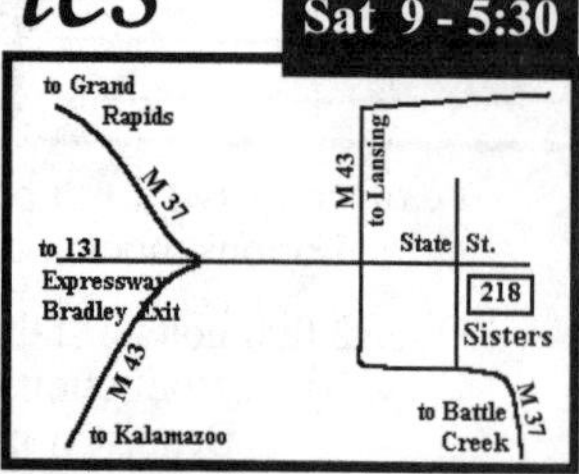

Western Michigan's largest Quilt Shop

Check on the latest in books, notions, and patterns. Many Quilts and wall hangings on display in our showroom.

4051 Plainfield NE
Grand Rapids, MI 49525
(616) 361-5484
www.smithowensew.com

Get off I-96 at Plainfield exit #33. Go north 2 miles. Smith-Owen is on the left across from Kentucky Fried Chicken.

Hours
Mon & Thur 9 - 8
Tues, Wed, Fri 9 - 5
Sat 10 - 3

Check out our different quilting models of sewing machines.

- **Viking Quilt Designer**
- **Pfaff QuiltStyle**
- **Juki Quilter**

Grand Rapids, MI #70

Grand Rapids, MI #71

West Michigan's "one-stop" quilt shop!

Grand Quilt Co.

5290 Alpine Ave. N.W. (M-37)
Comstock Park, MI 49321
(Just three miles north of Grand Rapids)

(616) 647-1120 grandquiltco@aol.com
Owner: Gay Bomers
Est: 1997 4500 sq. ft.
4,000+ bolts of 100% cotton fabric!

Ask how to join The Material Girls, our bi-monthly fat quarter club!

Every quilting goodie a quilter's heart desires in a friendly atmosphere. Ask to receive our quarterly 16-page newsletter, filled with fun classes, new product info and special store events!

Weekdays 10 - 9
Saturdays 10 - 5
Closed Sundays

Take I-96 to Alpine Ave. exit (Exit 30). Go North 3 miles. Grand Quilt Co. is just beyond the traffic signal at 6 Mile and Alpine.

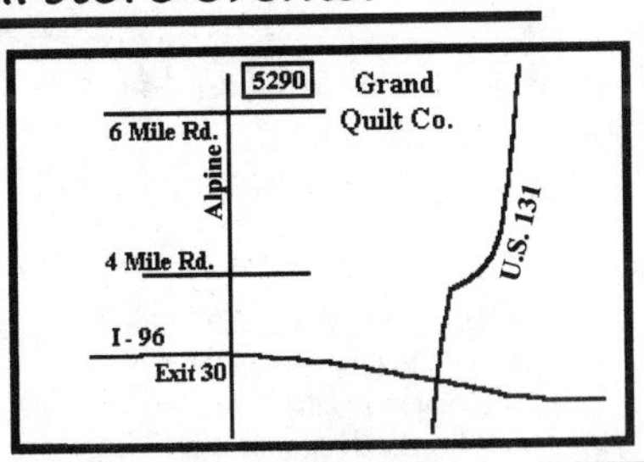

Comstock Park, MI #72

Attic Window Quilt Shop

Est: 1997
1200 sq.ft.

**Mon 10 - 8
Tues - Fri
10 - 5:30
Sat 10 - 3**

5307 Alpine NW 49321
(616) 785-3357 Fax: (616) 785-3358
atticwindowquiltshop@altbi.com
Owner: Sally Johnson

Nice selection of fabric, books, patterns, and notions. Specializing in reproduction fabrics 1800's - 1940's Special order and hard-to-find items. Classes, mail order and more.

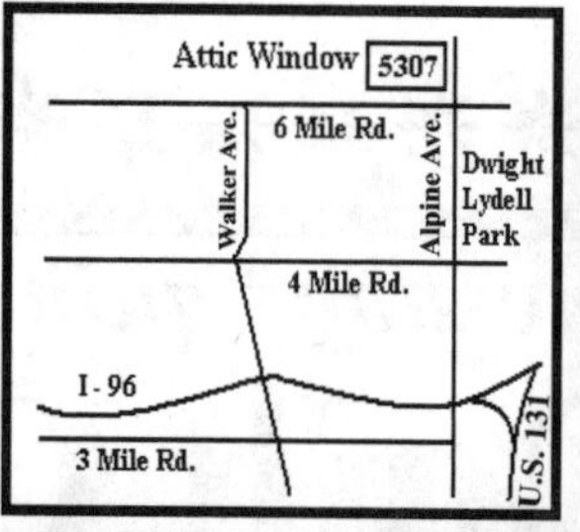

Grand Rapids, MI #73

**Mon - Fri
10 - 8
Sat 10 - 5**

Wooden Spool Quilts & Gifts

1760 44th St. SW, Suite 2B 49509
(616) 249-3744
woodenspool@msn.com
Est: 2002 2400 sq.ft

Friendly and fun shop with over 1200 bolts of quality fabric, over 500 book titles, plus patterns, notions and batting.

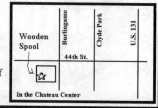

Wooden Spool
Burlingame
Clyde Park
U.S. 131
44th St.
in the Chateau Center

Greenville, MI #74

**Mon - Fri
10 - 6
Sat 10 - 2**

Forever Fabrics

214 S. Franklin St. 48838
(616) 225-8486
o1sewandsew@chartermi.net
Owners: Sheila Crawford & Judy Jensen
Est: 2002

Relax as you enjoy our great selection of quilting fabrics, notions & books. Customer Service is our #1 goal.

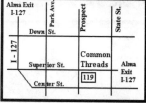

Forever Fabrics
214
Cass St.
Washington St.
M-57
Franklin St.
M-91
Lafayette St.

Alma, MI #75

**Mon - Fri
10 - 5
Sat 10 - 3**

Common Threads

119 W. Superior 48801
(989) 466-6966
Est: 2000 1200 sq.ft. 1500 Bolts

100% Cotton fabrics, wools, kits, books, patterns and supplies.
Thimbleberries - 30's Reproduction - Moda & More! Located in downtown Alma

Alma Exit I-127
Park Ave.
Prospect
State St.
Down St.
I-127
Superior St.
Common Threads
119
Alma Exit I-127
Center St.

Whitehall, MI #76

**Mon - Sat
10 - 5**

103 E. Colby St. 49461
(231) 894-2164

Two floors of unique merchandise. The finest quality quilting fabrics and notions.

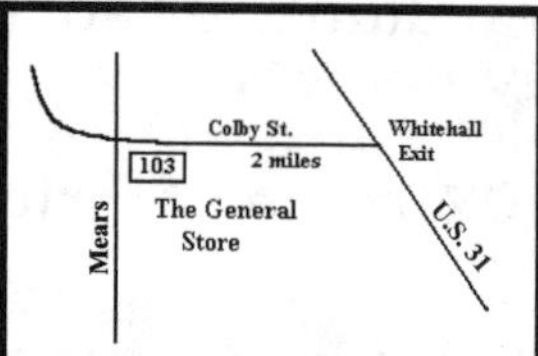

Norton Shores, MI #77

**Mon - Sat
11 - 6
Sun 12 - 6**

Stitched Heart

in the Airport Antique Mall
4206 Grand Haven Rd.
(231) 798-3318
Owners: Sue Steinhauer & Mike Chaban

New & Used Quilting Supplies - Quilts - Wall Hangings - Wearable Art - Vests - Fine Antiques Collectables - Fat Quarters - No Bolts of Fabric

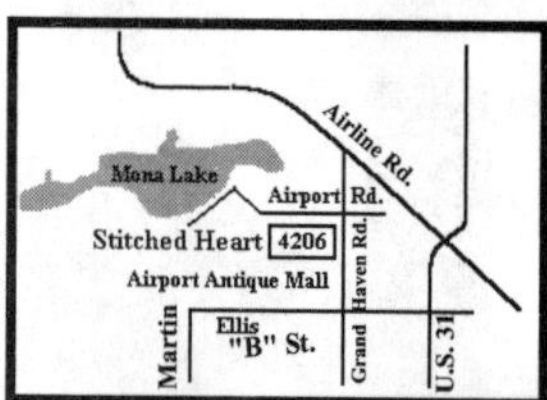

Zeeland, MI #78

**Mon - Fri
9 - 5:30
Fri til 8
Sat 9 - 2**

It's Stitching Time

150 E. Main 49464
(616) 772-5525

Complete Needlework and Quilt Shop.
Over 350 Quilt Books.
Lots of patterns, fabric, rulers.
A Quilter's Dream Shop.

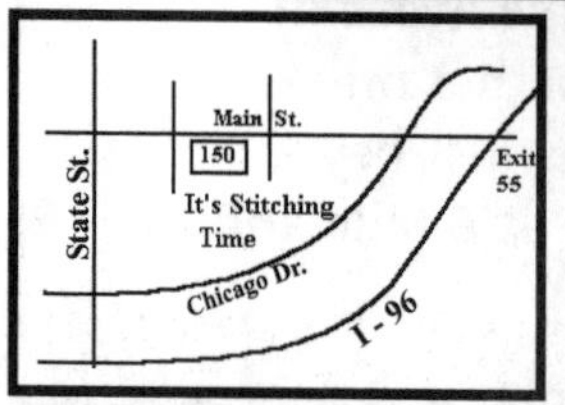

South Haven, MI #79

**Sept - May
Weekdays 4:30 - 8
(please call first)
June-Aug Mon-Fri 10-5
Always
Sat 8 - 5 Sun 1 - 4**

Calico Creations

70325 16th Ave. 49090
(616) 637-5558
Owner: Cornelia Miller

Quilt supply shop; SW Michigan Largest Supply of Quilt Books. Offers Classes: basic, traditional hand piecing & quilting to advanced machine piecing & quilting. Large supply of quilting fabrics & notions along with gifts for quilters.

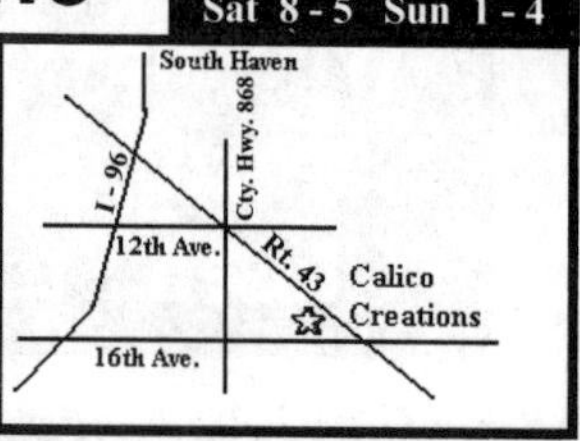

Holland, MI #80

Packed with Fabrics! 10,000+ Bolts, Many Unique Prints.

www.fieldsfabrics.com

281 East 8th Street
(616) 392-4806

Quality Fabrics for Creative People

Owned by:
Jack Veldman
Est. 1953
12,000 sq. ft.

Celebrating 50 years of service

Open Mon.-Sat. 9-9 Closed Sunday

St. Joseph, MI #81

Call for Appt.

Eileen's Design Studio

4503 Bacon School Rd. 49085
(888) 240-6002 Fax: (616) 429-1876
Eileen@parrett.net
www.eileensdesignstudio.com
www.quiltbooksusa.com
www.craftstoreusa.com Free Catalog
Owner: Eileen Chapman Est: 1993

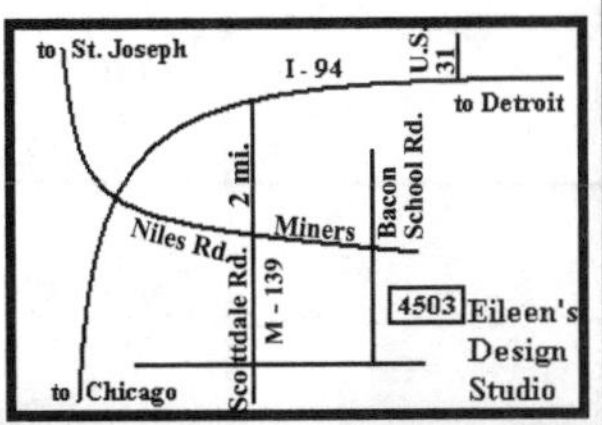

Tour a "working studio", located in the barn behind Eileen's 130-year-old home. Eileen's patterns, books and fabric kits are available.

St. Joseph, MI #82

Mon - Sat 10 - 5:30

The Silver Needle

415 State St. 49085
(269) 982-8521
Owners: Sherry Krause & Joyce Patrick
Est: 1998

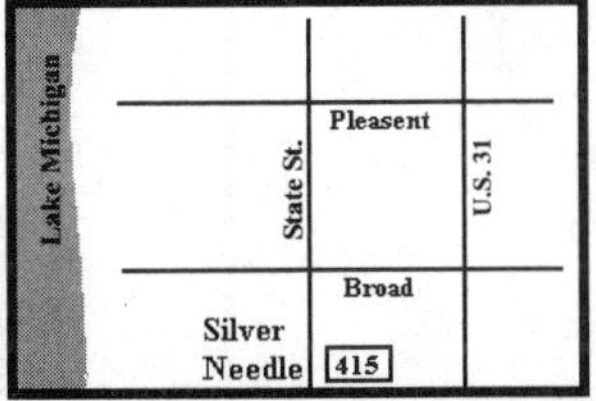

Located in the lovely lakefront town of St. Joseph, we carry bright, bold fabrics, patterns, books, notions & Quilt Magics. We also have some prepackaged kits.

Benton Harbor, MI #83

Tues - Sat 10 - 4

Carol's Quilt Cottage

1985 Zoschke Rd. 49022
(269) 849-4065
Owner: Carol Frosolone
Est: 1997

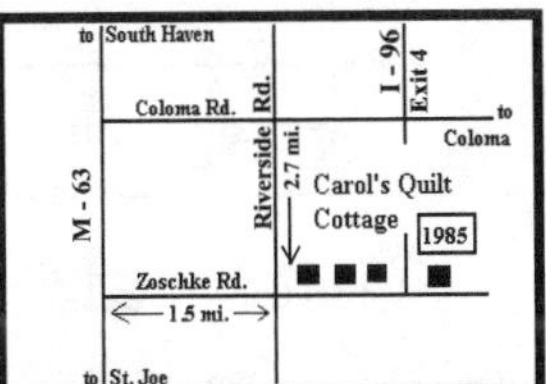

Available will be a wide variety of notions, patterns, books, quality 100% cotton fabric, and many gift ideas. Full service quilt shop. Lectures & workshops on Hawaiian quilting.

Stevensville, MI #84

Accomplish Quilting.com

Your sewing and maching quilting headquarters! Authorized Gammill Quilting Machines, Statler Stitcher & PFAFF dealer. Long-arm and Sewing Supplies. Classes.

Mon - Sat 9 - 5

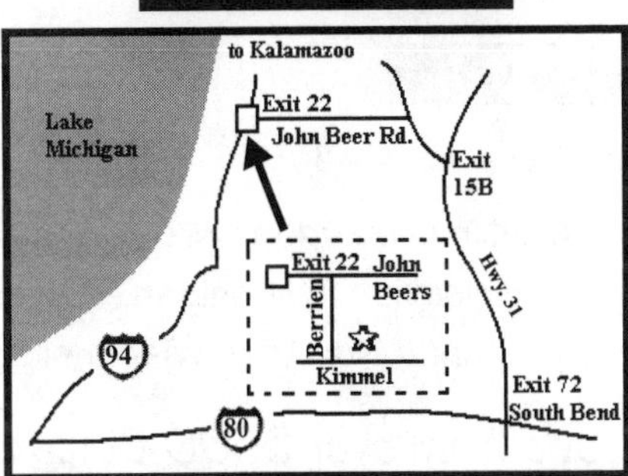

2797 Kimmel St. 49127-1220
(269) 556-2552
Fax: (269) 556-0406
Est: 2001 2400 sq.ft.
www.accomplishquilting.com

Stevensville, MI #85

Loving Stitches QUILT SHOP LLC

Est: 1996

Owner: Holly Martin

WWW.LSQUILTSHOP.COM

Over 3000 100% cotton fabrics to choose from!!
Patterns, Books, Supplies
See our perennial garden in season.

Exit 23 Stevensville, MI
I-94
Red Arrow Highway
Loving Stitches
Linco Road
Exit 16 Bridgman, MI

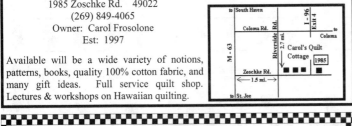

Located 1/2 mile North of Cook Information Center Easy on/Easy off between Exits 16 and 23 of I-94

7291 Red Arrow Hwy.
49127
(269) 465-3795
WWW.LSQUILTSHOP.COM

e-mail:
HOLLY@LSQUILTSHOP.COM
HEATHER@LSQUILTSHOP.COM

Mon. Thru Fri. 10-5
Sat. 10-3

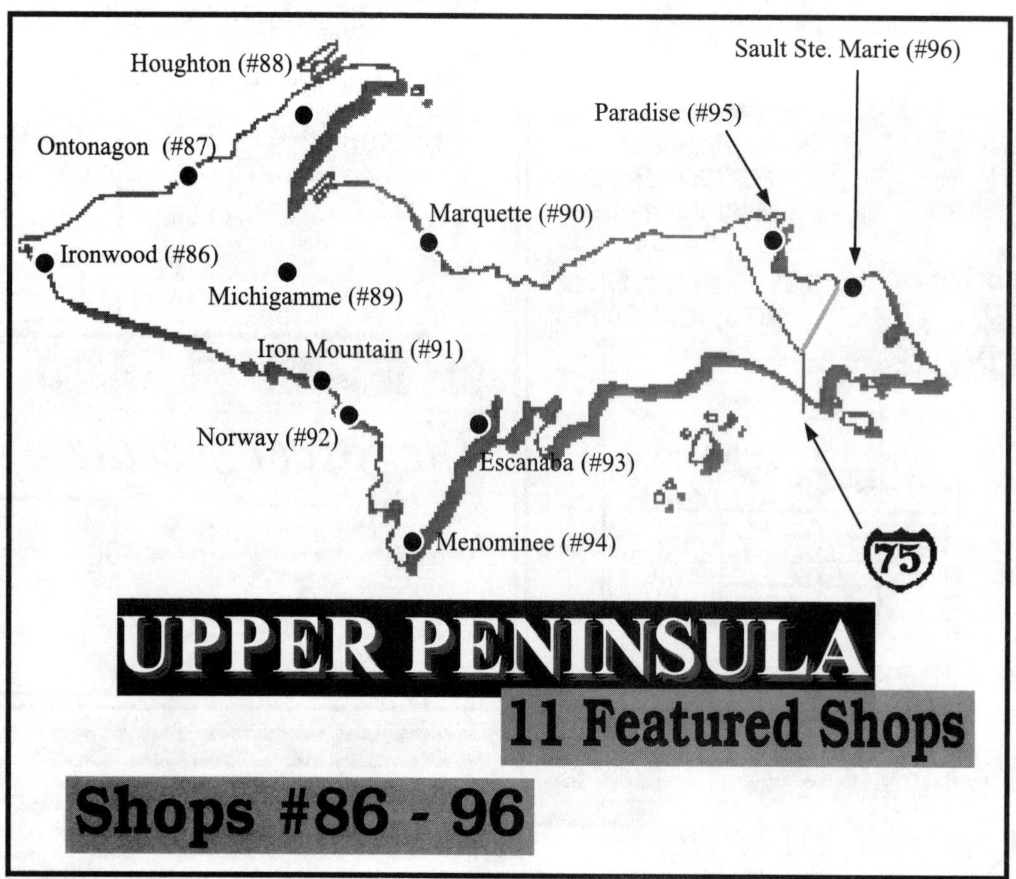

Ironwood, MI #86

Visit us at: www.fabricpatch.com

The Fabric Patch

121 N. Lowell St. 49938
(906) 932-5260 Fax: (906) 932-5004
E-Mail: fabric@myvine.com Est: 1981

Mail Order Available.

Quilting Headquarters of the North.
Largest Selection in Michigan's Upper Peninsula and Northern Wisconsin.

Authorized Dealer for Husqvarna Viking Sewing Machines & Sergers.

Choose from over 3500 Bolts of Quilting Fabrics Huge Selection of Quilting Books and Craft Patterns.
Ongoing Block of the Month Kits
Call or Stop In for Details

Mon - Fri 9:30 - 5
Sat 9:30 - 4

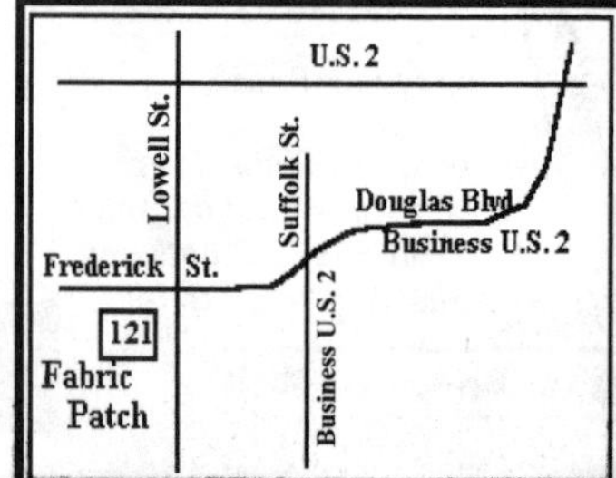

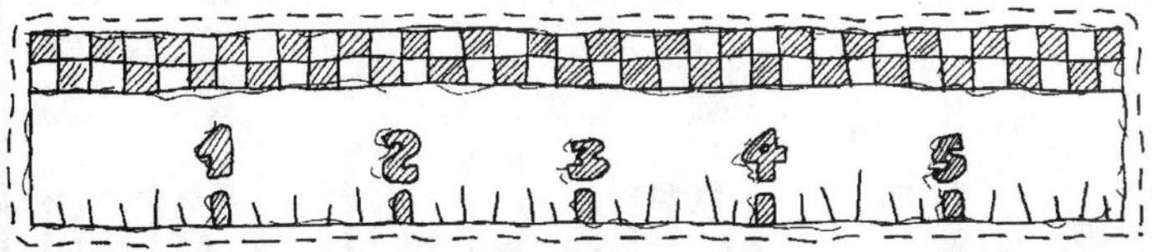

Ontonagon, MI #87

Mon - Fri
11 - 5:30

Quilter's Closet

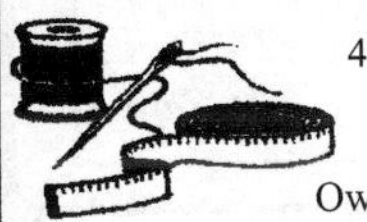

409 Lake St. 49953
(906) 884-2225
Est: 2001
Owner: Laura D. LaHaie

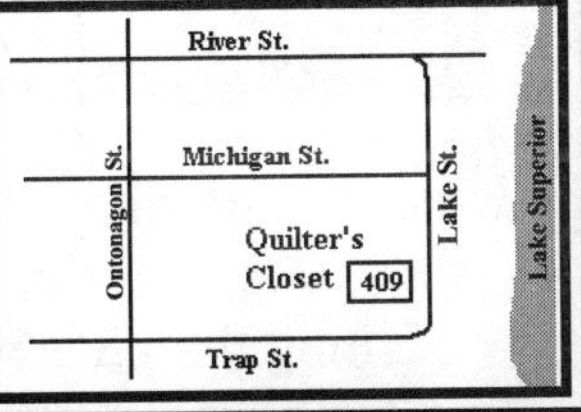

Fabrics, Sewing Notions, Yarns & Notions, Craft Kits & Supplies, Craft Books, Teas & Spices.

Michigamme, MI #89

Nov - April
Thur - Sat 11 - 5
May - Oct
Mon - Sat 10 - 5
Sun 1 - 5

Country Garden Quilts & More

103 W. Main, HCR 1, Box 3375 49861
(906) 323-6203
cgquilts103@aol.com
Owner: Roy (Bud) & Mary Poirier
Est: 2003 800 Bolts
Fabrics, patterns, books, notions & classes. Friendly, helpful customer service. Located in quaint village - a shopping destination.

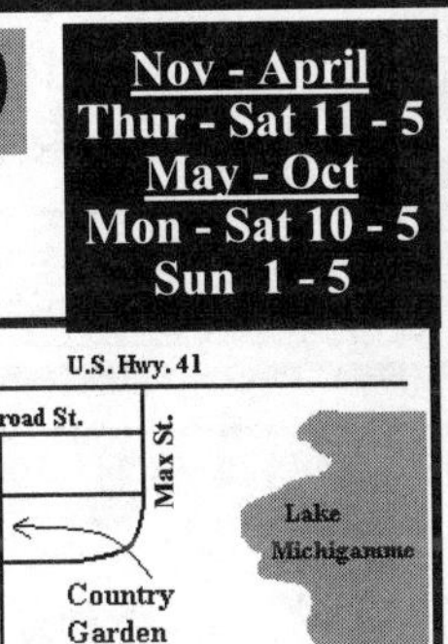

Houghton, MI #88

Mon - Sat
10:30 - 5:30

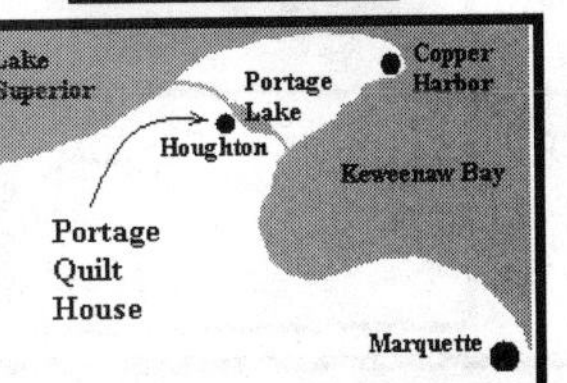

The "Copper Country's" only Full-Service Quilt Shop. Located between Chassell and Michigan Tech University in the big yellow house.

46509 U.S. Hwy. 41
Houghton, MI 49931
906-487-5500
Fax: 906-486-5600
Est: 2002 1500 sq. ft.

Portage Quilt House
Fabrics & Gifts

Marquette, MI #90

Quilting by Lake Superior

Marquette Lighthouse

Merricks
dba Ben Franklin

40% off One Cut Of Fabric

3,000 Bolts of Fabric Including 100% cottons and flannels from top designers

Fleece, Upholstery, Yarn

Also gift items, notions, kits and books

Long Arm Gammil Quilting Machine

Drop in for a cup of coffee and meet with new friends.

Custom picture framing and matting is offered.

100 Coles Dr., Marquette, MI 49855
(906) 226-9613 Fax: (906) 226-8004
Jwm2180@yahoo.com
Owners: Jim & Sarah Martin
Est: 1963 6,000 sq.ft. 3,000 Bolts

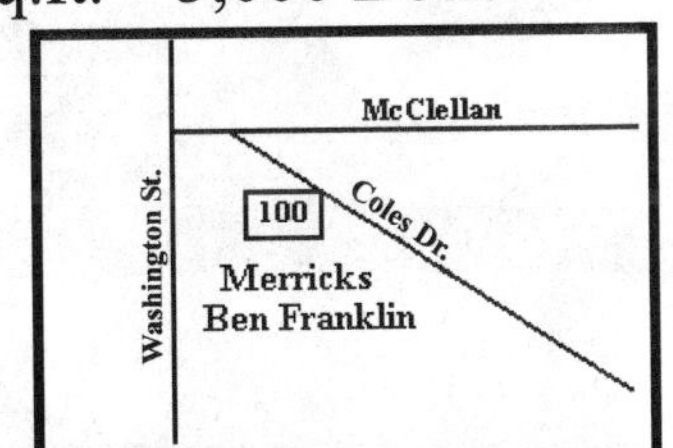

Mon - Thur 9 - 6
Fri 9 - 7 Sat 9 - 5
Sun 12 - 4

BERNINA

Iron Mountain, MI #91

M,T,W,F 10 - 5
Thur 11 - 6
Sat 10 - 3

From the Heart

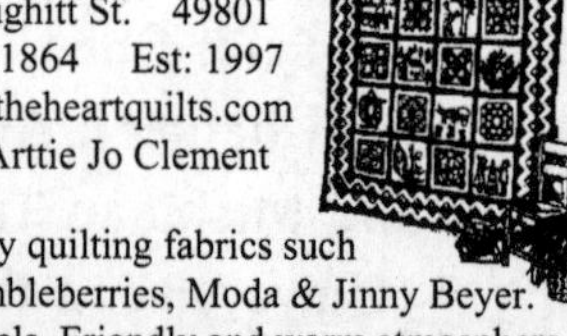

211 E. Hughitt St. 49801
(906) 779-1864 Est: 1997
www.fromtheheartquilts.com
Owner: Arttie Jo Clement

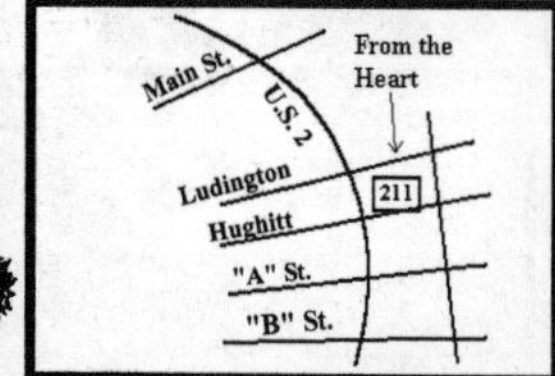

We carry only quilting fabrics such as RJR, Thimbleberries, Moda & Jinny Beyer. Lots of flannels. Friendly and warm atmosphere.

Norway, MI #92

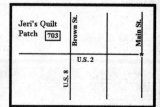

Jeri's Quilt Patch

703 Brown St. U.S. 2 49870 (906) 563-9620
www.jerisquiltpatch.com

Mon - Sat
10 - 5

Yearly Quilt Show & Fabric Sale
2004 JQP Quilt Show Aug 28 - Sept 6
2005 JQP Quilt Show Aug 27 - Sept 5
2006 JQP Quilt Show Aug 26 - Sept 4

Unique Quilt Shop, 100% Cotton Fabric, Quilting Supplies plus Antiques & Gifts. Featuring Antique Linens, Fabric, Quilts & Quilt Tops.

Jeri's Quilt Patch 703
Brown St.
Main St.
U.S. 2
U.S. 8

Bring in this ad & receive **one** of your choice
1 Free Fat Quarter - 50% off one pattern - 50% off 1 yard of fabric

Escanaba, MI #93

Mon - Fri 10 - 5
Sat & Sun by Appt.

Quilts 'n Stuff by Glenna

608 S. 14th St. 49829
(906) 786-3436 Fax: (906) 789-1483
garkens@quiltsnstuff.net
www.quiltsnstuff.net
Owner: Glenna Arkens Est: 1992

U.S. 2 & 41
Ludington St.
M 35
14th St.
High School
5th Ave. South
Quilts 'n Stuff 608

Featuring: quilting fabric (lots of batiks), silk ribbon, applique patterns, Upper Peninsula & floral art quilts.

Menominee, MI #94

Mon - Fri 9:30 - 5:30
Thur til 8
Sat 10 - 4
Sun 1 - 4

Quilter's Haven, Ltd.

707 1st St. 49858
(906) 864-3078
c_caselton@hotmail.com
Owner: Chris Caselton
Est: 1996 2000 sq.ft. 3000 Bolts

A friendly quaint quilt shop along the beautiful shore of Lake Michigan. Notions, books, patterns galore!! Bernina Sewing Machine Dealer

Paradise, MI #95

Open 7 Days
Summer 10-7
Winter 10 - 5

Village Fabrics & Crafts

32702 W. Hwy. M-123 P.O. Box 254
(906) 492-3803 49768
villagefab@sault.com
www.VillageFabricsAndCrafts.com
Owner: Vicki Hallaxs Est: 1986

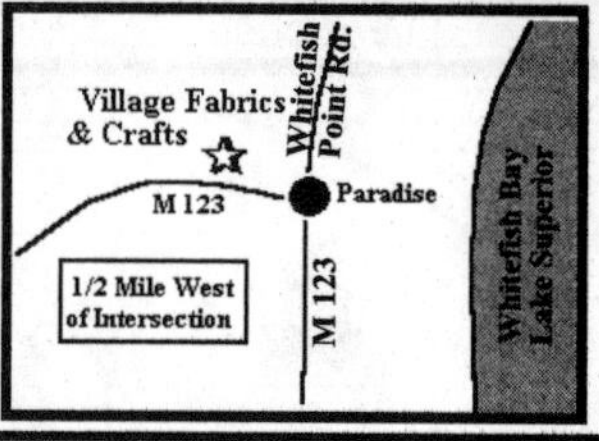

New 2400 square foot addition.
Quilting, yarns, counted cross stitch, embroidery, & gifts. Year round classes and retreats. Tour buses welcome.

Sault Ste. Marie, MI #96

May 1 - Oct 15
Mon - Fri 9 - 5
Sat 9 - 3
Oct 16 - Apr 30
Tues - Sat 9 - 5

Gloria's Happy Hooker

Quilting & Needlecraft Supplies

M - 129 (2733 Ashmun St.) 49783
(906) 635-9937
Owner: Gloria Larke

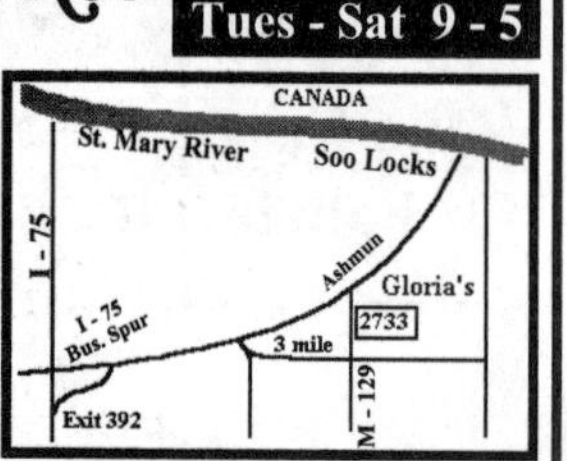

Quilting Fabric including RJR, Hoffman, Moda. Yarn, counted cross-stitched, needlepoint books & supplies. Home of the Famous Soo Locks.

Other Shops in Michigan: *We suggest calling first*

Ann Arbor	Cloth Encounters, 1731 Plymouth Rd	734-332-0070
Au Gres	Bayview Calicoes and Ceramics, 3631 E. Huron Rd. #2	989-876-6933
Bath	Quilting Memories, 13630B Main St., P.O. Box 367	517-641-6522
Beaverton	Lelia's Place, 1333 McKimmy Dr.	517-435-3275
Belleville	Sue's Quilt Shop, 48120 Harris Rd.	313-461-6540
Beulah	Margie Ann's, 194 S Benzie Blvd	231-882-4024
Bloomfield Hills	For Pause Quilting, 3985 Lincoln Rd	248-258-0964
Bloomingdale	Xzanthus, 46560 County Rd 380	616-521-7782
Brethren	Studio North, 5630 Farnsworth Rd.	616-477-5679
Brown City	Ann's Fabric Shop, 5044 Bailey Rd.	810-346-3237
Cadillac	Julie Ann Fabrics, 109 S. Mitchell	231-775-8301
Caledonia	Rainbow's End, 9343 Cherry Valley Ave.	616-891-1106
Calumet	Traditions, 51950 US 41, PO Box 86	906-482-8674
Caro	Primrose Lane, 1545 Pine Crest Dr	514-673-7180
Carp Lake	Quilting & Crafts by Mercer, 8815 Paradise Trl	231-537-2180
Croswell	Wanda's Fabric Shop, 61 N. Howard Ave.	810-679-3482
Dearborn	Lace, Quilts N' Roses, 22037 Michigan Ave	313-792-8804
Dearborn	Cheryl's Inspired Designs, 5472 Argyle St	313-945-5364
Dryden	Quilt House, 5510 Main St	810-796-4272
Frankenmuth	Abbey Rose Quilts, 925 S Main St	989-982-2433
Frankenmuth	Frankenmuth Woolen Mills, 570 S. Main St.	517-652-8121
Grand Haven	The Wooden Spool Quilts & Antiques, 210 Washington	616-844-0885
Highland	More Than Quilting, P.O. Box 541	248-698-3020
Hillsdale	Laurie's Farmhouse Quilting, 6551 Cambria Rd.	517-357-4478
Houghton	Lake Suzie's Stitch'n, 1970 W Houghton Lake Dr	989-366-5252
Ida	Quilt Corner, 2005 Geiger Rd	734-269-2972
Jenison	Country Needleworks, Inc., 584 Chicago Ave.	616-457-9410
Kingsley	Whispering Needles, 107 Blair St	231-263-5902
Lambertville	Village Fabrics & Crafts, 8019 Summerfield Rd.	313-856-5350
Lapeer	The Quilt Block, 2268 N. Lapeer Rd.	810-715-1324
Lapeer	Lapeer Fabrics, 110 W. Park	810-667-9098
Lapeer	Piece Full Quilting, 611 Vista Del Sol	810-664-9452
Macomb	Hearthstone Quilts, 23404 Harrellson St.	810-598-5936
Marquette	Needleworks, 219 W. Washington St.	906-228-6051
Mason	Yards of Fabric, 116 E. Ash	517-676-2973
Midland	Material Mart, 86 Ashman Circle	517-835-8761
Milford	Quilter's Shoppe, 4458 Country View Ln.	
Mohawk	Phyl's Fabrics, 1020 N. Ahameek St., P.O. Box 229	906-337-0567
Montague	Quilted Memories, 9919 US Hwy 31	231-893-0096
Muskegon	Harbor Star Quilts, 1347 Peck St	231-722-8356
New Era	Needle Nook, 4708 1st St.	231-861-4077
Omer	Quilt Patch Antiques, 429 E. Center St.	517-653-2332
Perrinton	Calico Cupboard, 4625 MacArthur	517-236-7728
Port Huron	Mary Maxim, Inc., 2001 Holland Ave.	810-987-2000
Portland	Quilters Gallery, 1419 E. Grand River	517-647-7716
Prudenville	Chris' Frabrics, 960 W. Houghton Lake Dr.	517-366-4790
Reading	Kathryn's Country Fabrics, 7911 S. Edon Rd. M-49	517-268-5815
Riley	Pins & Needles, 1280 Kinney Rd	810-392-2353
Riverdale	Sheila's Fabrics, 11995 W. Monroe Rd.	517-833-7835
Rockford	Material Girls, 8321 Atlanta Dr. NE	616-866-3721
Saginaw	Saginaw Quiltworks, 7408 Grabot Rd	989-781-1057
Saranac	Candy Corner Emporium, 7129 Bliss Rd.	616-527-1170
Schoolcraft	Timeless Quilting, 11598 S 8th St	269-679-5717
South Lyon	The Artcraft Shop, P.O. Box 276	810-437-3830
Sterling Heights	Sewing Products Co. Inc, 43638 Schoenherr	810-566-4500
Sturgis	Peacock's Pieces, 1515 E Chicago Rd	269-659-6001
Suttons Bay	Sew Central, PO Box 248	231-271-6331
Swartz Creek	Mary's Quilts & Things, 5353 Chin Maya Dr.	810-635-3803
Traverse City	Boyd's and Sew Much More, 966 S. Airport Rd. W	616-946-4011
Walled Lake	Grandma Honey's Quilts, 1925 Shankin Dr.	248-624-4677
Washington	Creative Corner, 66800 Van Dyke Rd.	810-752-7444
Williamston	Fabric Gallery 146 W Grand River	517-655-4573
Yale	Sew 'N Sew, 1 N. Main St.	

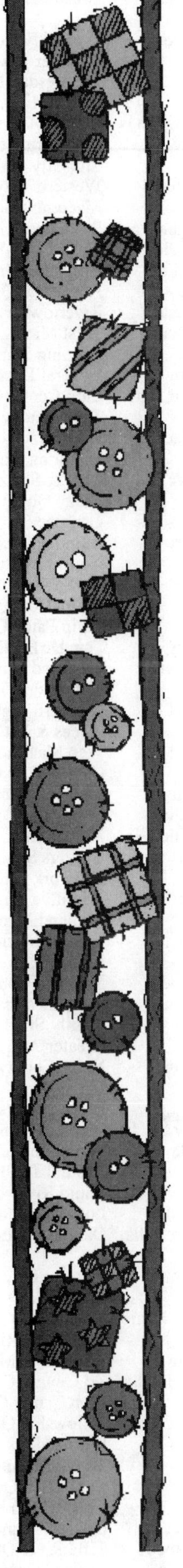

Michigan Guilds:

Allen Park — Trinity Piecemakers, 9077 Allen Road, 48101
Ann Arbor — Greater Ann Arbor Quilt Guild, P.O. Box 2737, 48106-2737 Meets: 3rd Saturday (odd # months, except May) at Washtenaw Community College, Morris Laurence Bldg., Nationally known Speakers and classes offered
Ann Arbor — U of M Faculty Women's Quilters, 2481 Trenton Court, 48105
Atlanta — Thunder Bay Quilters, P.O. Box 960, 49709
Atlanta — Michigan Quilt Network, P.O. Box 339, 49709
Au Gres — Wednesday Night Strippers Quilt Guild, 3631 E. Huron, 48703 Meets: 4th Wednesday at Bayview Calicos
Augusta — McKay Library Quilters, 105 S. Webster Street, 49012
Barrien Springs — Berrien Towne & Country Quilters, 4218 E. Tudor Road, 49103
Battle Creek — Cal-Co Quilters' Guild, P.O. Box 867, 49016
Bay City — Bay Heritage Quilters Guild, 321 Washington Ave., 48708
Belding — Silk City Quilters' Guild, 108 Hanover, 48809 Meets: 1st Wednesday 6:30 at the Community Center
Belleville — Western Wayne County Quilting Guild, 129 South St., 48111
Berkley — Macomb County Quilt Guild Meets: 2nd Monday 7pm at Trinity Lutheren Church
Birmingham — Pieceable Friends, 1991 E. Lincoln, 48009
Bloomfield Hills — Needlework & Textile Guild, 3219 Woodside Court, 48013
Bloomfield Hills — Great Lakes Heritage Quilters Meets: 2nd Thursday @ 7pm Sept. thru June at Birmingham Unitarian Church
Brighton — Brighton Heritage Quilters, 10281 Carriage Drive, 48116
Brighton — Casual Quilter's, 5418 Ethel, 48116
Cadillac — North Star Quilters, 8436 E. 48th Road, 49601
Calumet — Keweenaw Heritage Quilters, 49913
Cheboygan — Rivertown Patchworkers, 1849 Richmond, 49721
Clifford — Thumb Thimbles Quilt Guild, 5140 English Road, 48727
Coopersville — West Michigan Quilters Guild, 13646 48th Ave., 49404
Davison — Evening Star Quilters, 1034 Carla Blvd., 48423 Meets: Last Wednesday at 6:30 p.m. at Davison Senior Center, 334 N. Main
Dearborn — General Dearborn Quilting Society, 915 Brady Road S., 48124
Dearborn Hgts. — Eton Center Quilters, 4900 Pardee, 48125 Meets: Tuesdays 8:30 pm, Eton Center 4900 Pardee
Decatur — The Monday Night Quilters, 79939 40th Street, 49045
Detroit — St. Raymond's Quilters, 20212 Fairport, 48205
Dowagiac — The Crazy Quilters, 51106 Glenwood Rd., 49047
Eaton Rapids — Island City Piecemakers, P.O. Box 14, 48827
Empire — Victorian Quilters Guild, P.O. 149, 49630
Escanaba — Bay deNoc Quilt Guild, 49829
Fairgrove — Care & Share Quilters, 4052 Fairgrove Rd., 48733
Farmington — Greater Ann Arbor Quilt Guild, 36437 Saxony, 48335
Farwell — Crazy Quilters, 7870 Peninsula, 48622
Flint — Evening Star Quilters, 5327 Hopkins, 48506
Flint — Genesee Star Quilters, G-4324 W. Pasadena, 48504 Meets: 3rd Friday at 9:30 a.m. at Nazarene Church, 2254 Dye Rd.
Frankfort — Rumpled Quilts Kin, P.O. Box 587, 49635
Fremont — Tall Pine Quilters, 2073 Baldwin, 49412
Glennie — North Country Piecemakers, P.O. Box 10, 48737
Grayling — Au Sable Quilt Guild, c/o Icehouse, 509 Norway, 49738 Meets: 1st Wednesday 1 p.m. at St. John's Lutheran Church
Harrison — Claire County Crazy Quilters, 5189 Hamilton, 48625
Hartford — Tuesday Night Crazy Quilters, 18 N. Center St.
Holland — Tulip Patch Quilting Organization, 600 Woodland Drive, 49424
Imlay City — Thimble Buddies Quilt Guild, 2937 Henesy, 48444 Meets: 6:30 p.m. 2nd & 4th Mondays at Trinity United Methodist, 1310 N. Main St., Lapeer
Interlochen — Rumpled Quilts Kin Meets: 1st Monday 7 p.m. at Interlochen Fellowship Hall
Iron River — Composing Threaders, P.O. Box 227, 49935
Iron River — Carrie Jacobs-Bond Composing Threaders
Ironwood — Northern Lights Quilting Guild, P.O. Box 125, 49938 Meets: 7 p.m. at Salem Lutheran Church, Sept. 23, Quilt Show
Jackson — Pieces & Patches Quilt Guild, Box 6294, 49202
Kalamazoo — Log Cabin Quilters, 6632 Woodlea, 49004
Kentwood — West Michigan Quilter's Guild, P.O. Box 8001, 49518 Meets: 4th Tues. 7 p.m. Jan, Mar, May, July, Sept, Nov at Calvary Christian Reformed
Lansing — Capitol City Quilt Guild, 7131 Willow Woods Cr., 48917
Lansing — Lansing Area Patchers, 3305 Sunnylane, 48906
Lewiston — Lewiston Lakes Quilt Guild, P.O. Box 512, 49756
Marine City — Anchor Bay Quilters, 48039
Marquette — Marquette County Quilters Assoc., PO Box 411, 49855 Meets: 1st Wednesday 6:30 p.m. at Peter White Public Library
Menominee — Northwoods Quilters, 707 1st St., 49858 Meets: 9:30am & 6:30pm alternating months at Pioneer Predbyterian Church
Midland — Quilters Squared Quilt Guild Meets: 2nd Tuesday at Quilted Giraffe
Midland — Redwork Club, 86 Ashman Cir., 48640 Meets: 4th Tuesday 6:30 p.m. at Material Mart
Midland — Primitive Club--Girl Gang, 86 Ashman Cir., 48640 Meets: 3rd Tuesday 7 p.m. at Material Mart
Midland — Midland Mennonites, 364 E. Gordonville, 48640
Niles — Niles Piecemakers, 1347 Louis Street, 49120
Midland — Thimbleberries Club, 86 Ashman Circle, 48640 Meets: 2nd Tuesday 1 p.m. at Material Mart
Monroe — Monroe Cty. Quilt Guild Meets: 2nd Thursday 7 p.m. at Trinity Lutheran Church, 323 Scott
Mt. Clemens — Macomb County Quilt Guild, 124 Parnacott, 48043 Meets: 2nd Monday @ 7pm at Trinity Lutheran Church
Muskegon — Patchers at the Lake Shore, 926 Wellington Court, 49441 Meets: 1st Monday 6:30 p.m. at Central Methodist Church, 1011-2nd St.
Norway — Saintly Stitchers, 407 Mine St., 49870 Meets: 6:30 at St. Mary's Catholic Church
Novi — Greater Ann Arbor Quilt Guild, 22452 Meado Brook, 48375
Oxford — Calico Patch Quilters, 1550 W. Drahner Rd., 48371
Ontonagon — North County Quilters, 19545 Firesteel Rd, 49953 Meets: 1st Thursday @ 12:30pm & 3rd Thursday @ 6pm at St. Paul's Lutheran

Petosky — Little Traverse Bay Quilters Guild, 49770 Meets: 2nd Wednesday 7:30 p.m. at NCMC College
Pinckney — Pinckney Quilting Sisters, 11383 Cedar Bend Dr., 48169
Plainwell — Island City Quilters, 180 S. Sherwood, 49080
Plymouth — Plymouth Piecemakers, 48170
Portage — Portage Quilt Guild, 49002
Portland — Around The Block Quilters, 120 Maple St., 48875 Meets: 4th Wednesday @ 6:30 at Around the Block Quilt Shop
Rapid River — Rapid River Quilt Guild, 7653 26th Rd, 49878 Meets: 2nd Monday @ 6:30pm at St. Charles parish hall
Richmond — Loose Threads, 37550 Hebel Road, 48062
Rochester Hills — Oakland County Quilt Guild, P.O. Box 81096, 48308 Meets: 1st Thursday @ 7pm Sept. thru June at Rochester Community House, 816 Lidlow St
Rosebush — Piece to Peace Quilting Club, 3914 Mission, 48878
Saginaw — Piecemaker's Quilt Guild Meets: 3rd Wednesday 7 p.m. at Presbyterian Church, 2665 Midland Rd.
Sault Ste. Marie — Keeping the Piece Quilt Guild, 5370 S. Riverside, 49783
Shelby — Friendship Ring Quilt Guild, 305 E. Harrison St., 49455
Southgate — Wyandotte Museum Quilters, 13407 Pullman, 48195
St. Charles — Piecemakers Quilt Guild, 202 Jay Street, 48655
Sterling Heights — Tri County Quilt Guild, 4619 Hatherly Place, 48310
Tawas City — Sunrise Quilters, 318 N. McArdle Road, 48763
Taylor — Eton Center Quilters, 7946 McKinley, 48180
Traverse City — Fellowship Quilters Meets: At Presbyterian Church
Traverse City — Pineneedlers Meets: 2nd Wednesday 7 p.m. at Senior Center
Trenton — Trenton Quilters, 3398 Norwood Dr., 48183
Vassar — Cass River Quilters' Guild, 6977 Sohn Road, 48768
Wakefield — Northern Lights Quilt Guild, 1315 Dewey, 49968
Warrren — Greater Ann Arbor Quilt Guild, 29807 Autumn Lane, 48093
Washington — Metro Detroit Quilt Guild, 6148 28 Mile, 48094
Watervliet — Barrien County Coverlet Guild, PO Box 529, 49098
West Bloomfield — Quilt-N-Friends, 6332 Aspen Ridge Blvd., 48332
West Branch — Rifle River Quilt Guild, 2831 Highland Dr., 48661 Meets: 4th Tuesday 7 p.m. at Ogemaw Hills Free Methodist Church
Zeeland — Zeeland Crazy Quilters, 150 E Main, 49464 Meets: 1st Monday 6 p.m. at It's Stitching Time

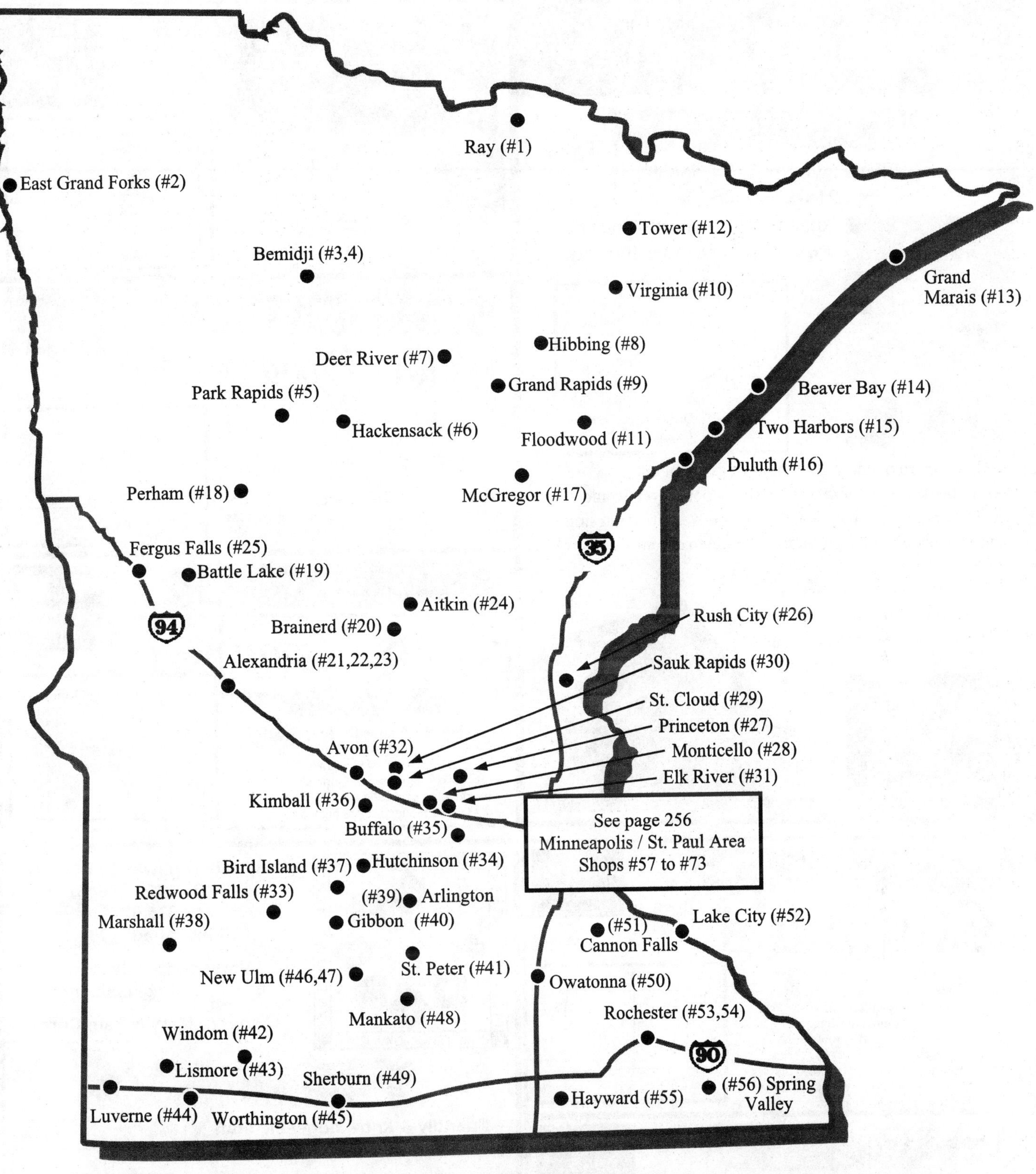
Ray (#1)
East Grand Forks (#2)
Tower (#12)
Bemidji (#3,4)
Virginia (#10)
Grand Marais (#13)
Hibbing (#8)
Deer River (#7)
Grand Rapids (#9)
Park Rapids (#5)
Beaver Bay (#14)
Hackensack (#6)
Two Harbors (#15)
Floodwood (#11)
Duluth (#16)
Perham (#18)
McGregor (#17)
35
Fergus Falls (#25)
Battle Lake (#19)
Aitkin (#24)
94
Rush City (#26)
Brainerd (#20)
Alexandria (#21,22,23)
Sauk Rapids (#30)
St. Cloud (#29)
Princeton (#27)
Avon (#32)
Monticello (#28)
Elk River (#31)
Kimball (#36)
See page 256
Minneapolis / St. Paul Area
Shops #57 to #73
Buffalo (#35)
Bird Island (#37)
Hutchinson (#34)
Redwood Falls (#33)
(#39) Arlington
Marshall (#38)
Gibbon (#40)
(#51) Cannon Falls
Lake City (#52)
St. Peter (#41)
New Ulm (#46,47)
Owatonna (#50)
Mankato (#48)
Rochester (#53,54)
Windom (#42)
90
Lismore (#43)
Sherburn (#49)
(#56) Spring Valley
Hayward (#55)
Luverne (#44)
Worthington (#45)

MINNESOTA

73 Featured Shops

Quilter's Corner

Ray, MN #1

4794 Town Rd. 180 56669
218-875-3805
diannekrenik@northwinds.net
www.quilterscorner-mn.com

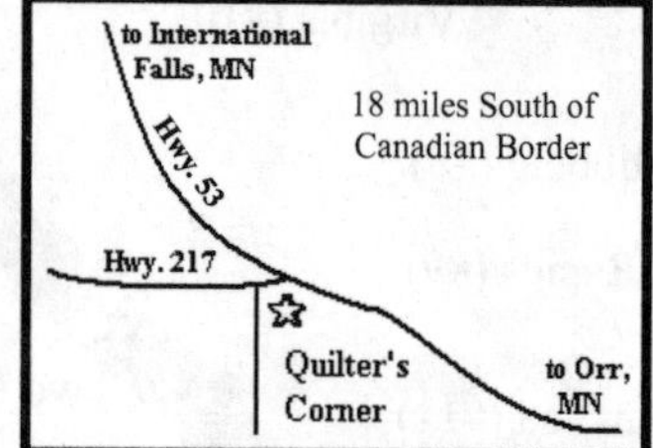

We have approximately 2000 bolts of fabric in the shop and tons of books and patterns. Almost any notion you would want or need. We have visitors from all over the world stop in to see the shop or look for fabrics unique to our area. Living in the Voyageur National Park and Boundary Waters brings a lot of people from all walks of life to our shop.

Mon - Sat 10 - 5
Tues 10 - 8
Summer Sundays
June 30 - Oct. 1 1-4

East Grand Forks, MN #2

Mon - Fri 10 - 8
Sat 9 - 6
Sun 11 - 5

223 DeMers Ave. 56721
(218) 773-0773
Fax: (218) 773-0772
www.quilterseden.com

Quilter's Eden offers premium quilt fabrics, books, patterns, notions. Long-arm quilting service. Janome Sewing Machines.

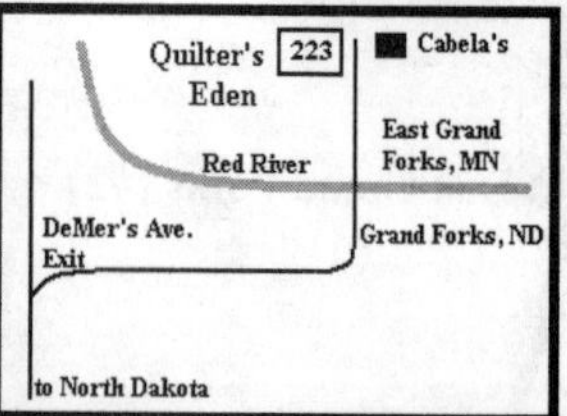

Bemidji, MN #3

By Chance Or Appt.

Willow Wood Market

23621 Cty. Rd. 9 56601
(218) 759-2310
lundorff@paulbunyan.net
Est: 1997

Tucked in the woods, our shop / studio offers unique woolfelt and primitive stitchery patterns, supplies and inspiration. Mail Order Available.

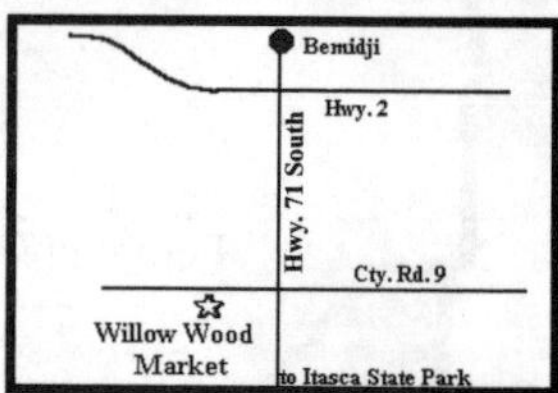

Bemidji, MN #4

Mon - Fri 10 - 6
Sat 10 - 4:30

The Quilted Loon

1285 Paul Bunyan Dr. NW 56601
(218) 444-2290
Owner: Mary Strand
Cozy Northwood Quilt Shop.
Conveniently Located Next to Paul Bunyan Mall & Ganden Mountain Sporting Goods Store.

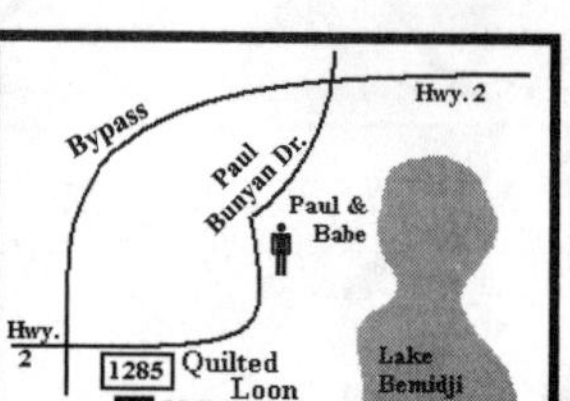

Park Rapids, MN #5

Mon - Sat 9 - 5

Monika's

210 S. Main 56470
(218) 732-3896 Fax: (218) 732-3821
monikas@unitelc.com
Owner: Monika Wilkins
Est: 1984 5000 sq.ft. 4000 Bolts
Large Selection of name brand fabrics, quilting, needlework, patterns, books, classes, and yarn for knitting and crochet available.
Heritage lace showcase store.

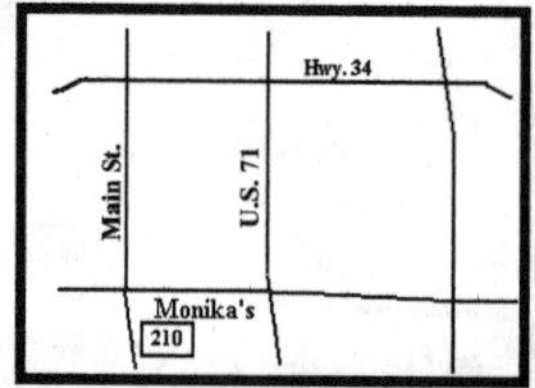

Deer River, MN #7

Mon - Sat 9 - 5
Sun 12 - 4

Heart to Hands Quilt Shop

509 Division St. 56636
(218) 246-2555 Fax: (218) 246-2066
holloway@paulbunyan.net
www.hearttohands.com
Owner: Karen Holloway Est: 2003

3000+ bolts of 100% cotton fabrics from top manufacturers. Large selection of books, patterns and notions. Machine quilting available. Finished quilts for sale.

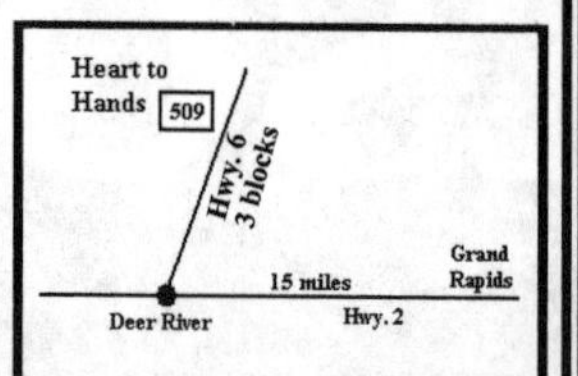

PIECEMAKERS QUILT SHOP

313 State Highway 371 South
P.O. Box 129 56452
218.675.6271
Established: 1984

www.cottontales.net
Email: quiltr@uslink.net

Owners: Mary & Pam Curo

Hackensack, MN #6

Friendly & knowledgeable staff
Inspiration is our specialty!

Custom made Quilt Hangers

Quality Cottons & Supplies
Quilt Kits, Wool & Wool Felt
Wonderful Samples, Girl Gang Club
Quarterly Newsletter, Classes
100's of Books & Patterns
Home of Cotton Tales Patterns

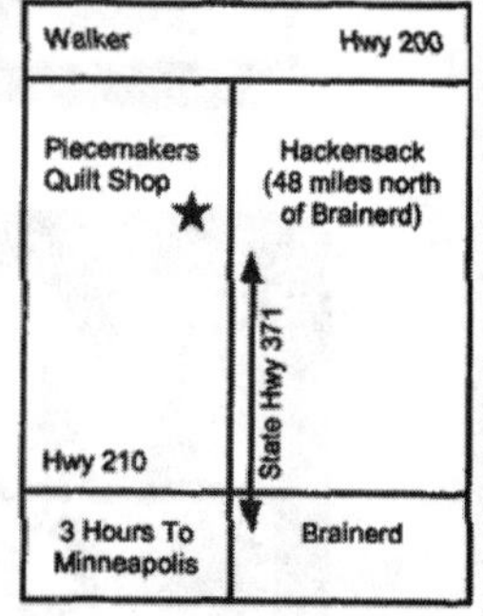

Mon - Sat 10-5 Sun 12-4 Closed Sun Dec & Jan

Hibbing, MN #8

Mon - Fri 9 - 5
Sat 9 - 2

PINS-N-NEEDLES

314 E. Howard St. 55746
(218) 262-5531
pins@rangebroadband.com
Owner: Jean Stimac
Est: 1993

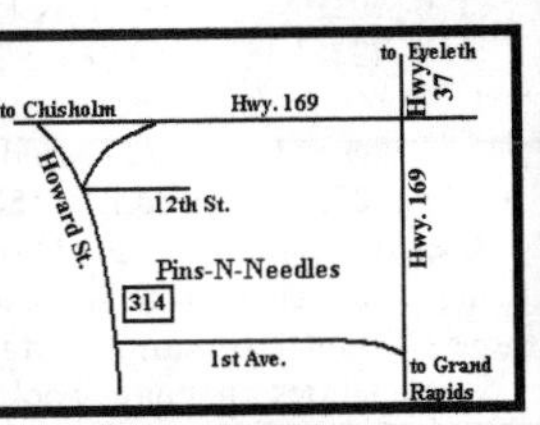

Over 2000 bolts of fabric, supplies, books, patterns, needlework & yarn for all your quilting & hand work needs.

ABC's of Quilting

Mon - Sat 9:30 - 5
Thur 10 - 7
Labor Day to Mem. Sun 10 - 3

10 NW 5th St. 55744
Junction of Hwy. 2 & 169
Downtown - Old Central School
(218) 326-9661
abcofq@2z.net
Est: 2000 2000+ Bolts

Grand Rapids, MN #9

Located downtown in the Old Central School, built in 1898.

Fabrics from quality companies.
Large selection of flannels.
Books, Patterns, Notions & Kits Available.

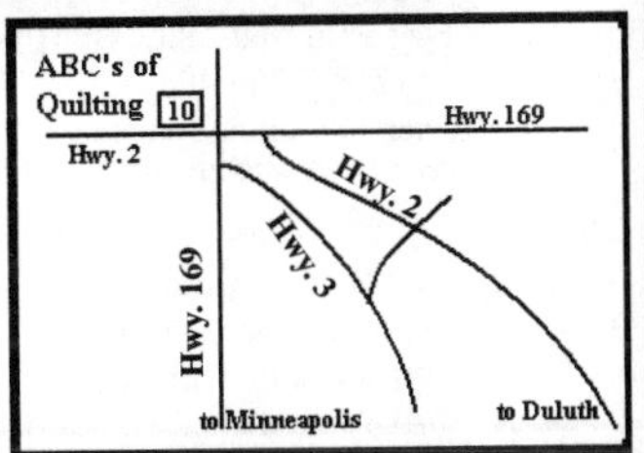

Virginia, MN #10

Mon - Sat 9 - 5
Thur til 8
Summer:
Sat 9 - 2

Pinberries

406 Chestnut St. 55792
(218) 741-8446
www.pinberries.com
Owners: Betsy Nelson & Sheril Prebeg

Take a beautiful drive "Up North" to Virginia and Pinberries. We have a friendly Northwoods atmosphere and a wonderful assortment of cozy flannels, homespuns and 100% cotton fabrics. While you're here, take a minute to enjoy our unique gift shop!

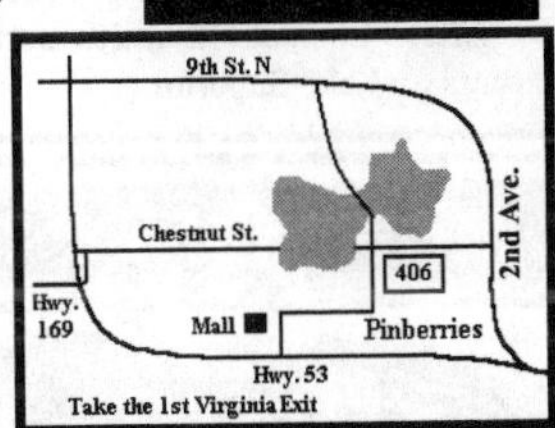

Floodwood, MN #11

Mon - Fri 10 - 5
Sat 9 - 4
Sun 11 - 4
May - Nov.

We have a 10,000 Bolt Attitude!

11284 Hwy. 2 Floodwood, MN 55736
218-476-3139
Opened December 2000 2600 Bolts & growing
HingeleyRoadQuilting@msn.com

Top Quality Quilt Fabric

Moda	Benartex	Maywood Studios
RJR	Clothworks	Timeless Treasures
P&B	Free Spirit	Michael Miller
Hoffman	Northcott	In the Beginning
SSI	Kaufman	Alexander Henry

Block of the month kits & patterns

We carry the entire line of:
Hoffman Bali Handpaints - 100 plus colors
Moda Marble Mates
Benartex Fossil Ferns woven and flannel

Events: Large meeting/classroom facilties
Spring and Fall Shop Hops

Guilds/groups and buses welcome anytime
Discounts available

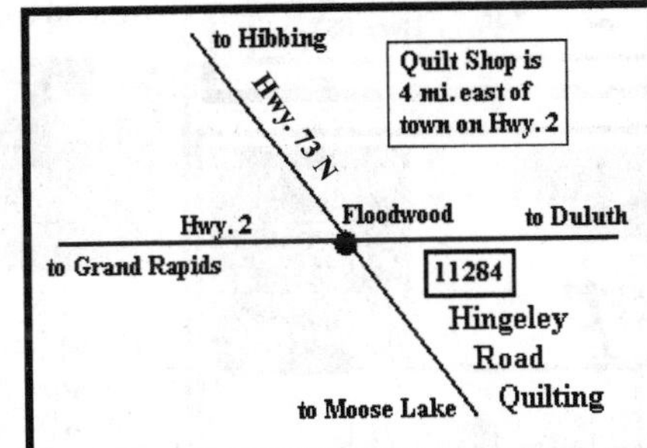

Quilt Supplies:
Notions/thread
Books & Patterns
Batting--wool & cotton

Large Suppply of Original Kits

Australian Patchwork - Quilting Magazine

www.quickquiltkits.com

Tower, MN #12

Tues 10 - 6
Wed - Sat 10 - 5
June - Sept
Mon 10 - 5

North Country Quilts

504 Main St. 55790
(218) 753-4600
northcountryquilts@yahoo.com
Owners: Dan & Corrine Hill

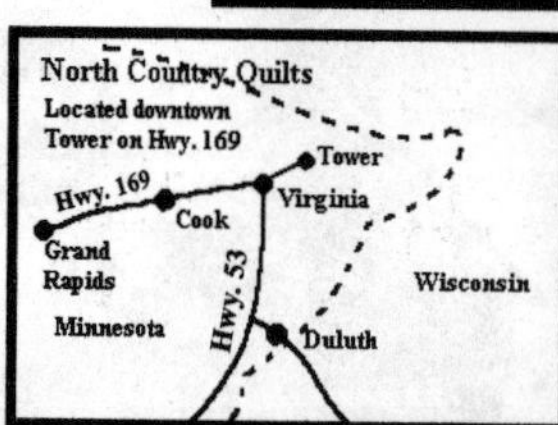

Full service shop. Fabric, books, patterns, notions, classes and machine quilting. Personal attention with a smile is our specialty.

Grand Marais, MN #13

Mon - Sat
9 - 4
Sometimes
More

Crystal's Log Cabin Quilts

1100 W. Hwy. 61, P.O. Box 155 55604
(218) 387-1550 Fax: Same
trailside@boreal.org
Owners: Crystal & Harold Nelson
Est: 2001 1500 sq.ft. 1500+ bolts

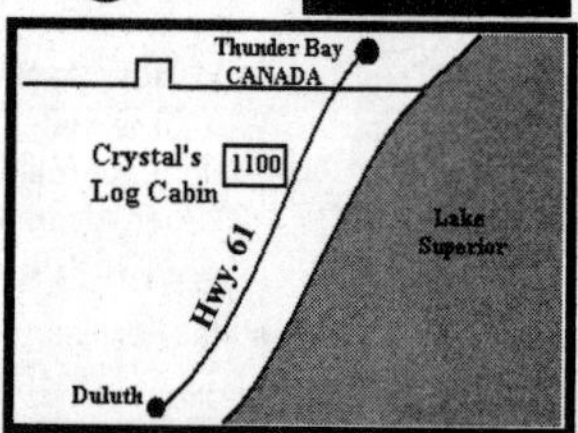

Creative learning studio. On-going mini demonstrations. Seasonal retreats at Trailside Cabins & Motel. Beautiful Northwoods Quilts. Nature fabrics - notions - books - supplies.

Beaver Bay, MN #14

Mon - Sat
10 - 4
Sun 12 - 4

Quilt Corner

Beaver Bay Mini Mall, P.O. Box 304
(218) 226-6406
Owner: Roxanne Johnson
Est: 1990 800 sq.ft.

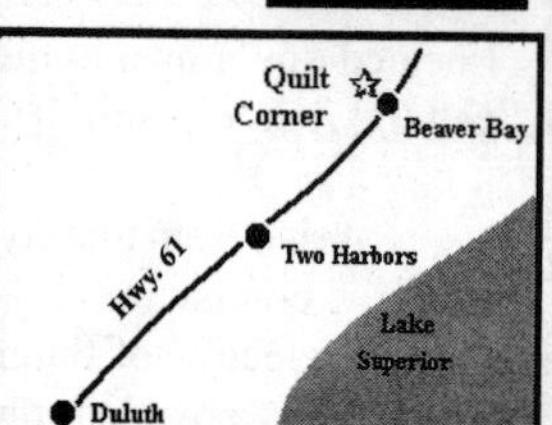

Over 2000 Bolts of Cotton Fabric. Books, Notions, Patterns, & Stencils. Many Quilts for sale. Gifts too.

Two Harbors, MN #15

Mon 12 - 6
Tues - Sat 10 - 5
Sun 11 - 4
Closed Mon Nov - April

Quilter's Cabin

3067 E. Castle Danger Rd. 55611
(218) 834-4303
Owner: Debbie Lind Est: 2002

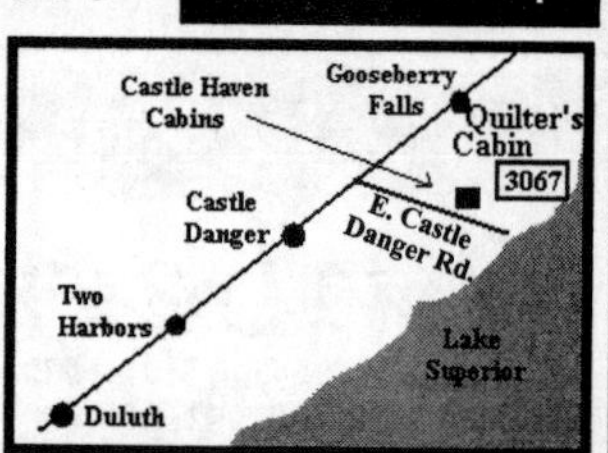

Over 2000 bolts of fabric, supplies, patterns, and gifts. Located 12 miles north of Two Harbors on Lake Superior.

Kelly J's SEWING CENTER & QUILT SHOP

4313 Haines Road, Duluth, MN 55803 **#16**
218-724-8781 • Toll Free: 1-800-638-1911
Website: www.kellyjs.com - Email: kellyjsews@msn.com

Approximately 5000 sq. feet, 2800+ bolts of 100% cotton quilting fabrics, 100+ bolts of genuine Malden Fleece, books, notions, patterns & more? Authorized dealer for the SuperQuilter quilting frame and Bernina, Janome New Home and Juki machines. Established in 1987, we've been awarded nationally for outstanding customer service 14 years in a row.

Mon.-Sat.
9am-6pm
Tues. 'til 8pm
Closed Sunday

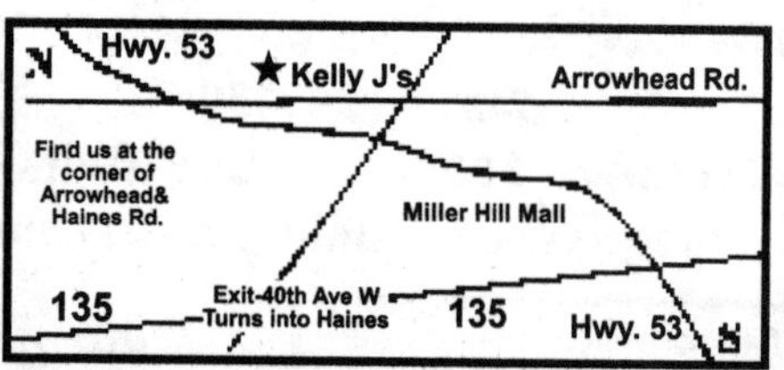

McGregor, MN #17

Tues - Fri 10 - 5
Sat 10 - 4
Summer Mon
10 - 5

Timeless Treasures

of McGregor
Quilt & Scrapbooking Supplies
DOWNTOWN McGREGOR, MN

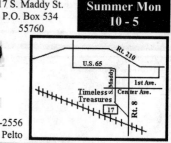

17 S. Maddy St.
P.O. Box 534
55760

(218) 768-2556
Owner: Diane Pelto

Bay Window Quilt Shop

Visit one of Minnesota's premier quilt shops! Enjoy two levels of shopping enjoyment featuring a huge selection of quality fabrics from over 30 companies, great books, patterns, notions, and our own in-house quilt pattern designer. Don't miss our new gift shop featuring quilts for sale & antiques! Classes. Custom Quilting. Terrific Service! Thimbleberries Quilt Club, Embroidery Club, Book Club, and Thimbleberries Quilt Club by Mail.

Mon - Fri
9 - 5:30
Sat 9 - 4

116 2nd Ave. SW 56573
(888) 346-7275 or (218) 346-7272
katie@baywindowquiltshop.com
www.baywindowquiltshop.com
Owner: Sarah Hayden Est: 1989
3500+ Bolts, 800+ Flannels Bolts

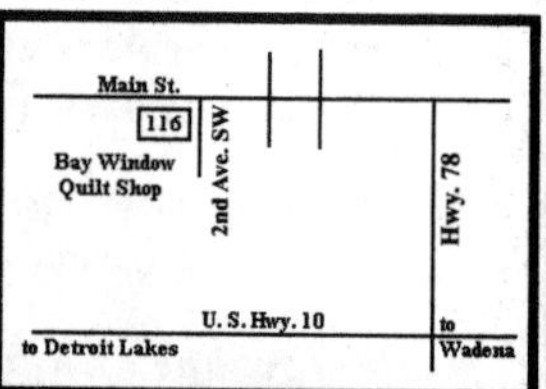

Perham, MN #18

Battle Lake, MN #19

Mon - Sat
9 - 5
Sun 12 - 3
Mem. Day to
Labor Day

B's Quilt Shop

122 Lake Ave. S, P.O. Box 516 56515
(218) 862-2230
Owners: Carol Boyum, Pam Boyum & MarJean Martelle

Machine & custom quilting, fabrics, notions, patterns, classes. Helping you create your quilt from start to finish.

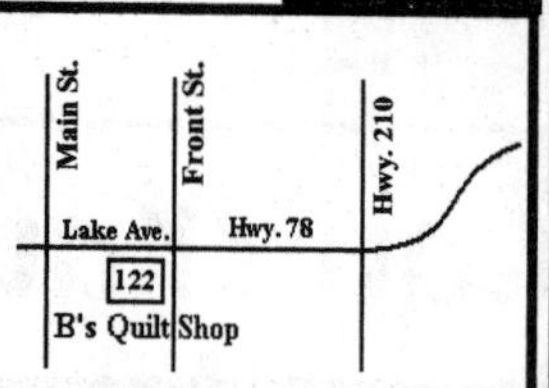

Est: 1971

Brainerd, MN #20

909 S. 6th St. 56401
(218) 829-7273 or (888) 441-7273

Country Fabrics, Quilts, & Collectibles

210 W Washington St. 210 E
Water Tower
6th St.
909 S. 6th St.
Country Fabrics, Quilts, & Collectibles
371N

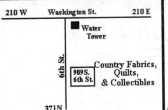

Show us this coupon and receive 10% off your purchase. 1 time only.

Mon - Fri 9:30 - 5:30
Sat 9:30 - 5

Our 1800 Mercantile is filled with over 5000 calicoes by the leading designers: Moda, Thimbleberries, Reproduction Prints, Batiks by Hoffman and much more. Check out our large selection of 100% wool for rug hookers and primitive appliqué. Our store is filled with 100's of samples. There is something to inspire everyone. We are your authorized Elna & Baby Lock dealer. We service all brands of machines and sergers. If you're not into quilting--visit our quaint 2nd floor. It's filled with unique gifts and antiques.

Heartland Sewing Co.

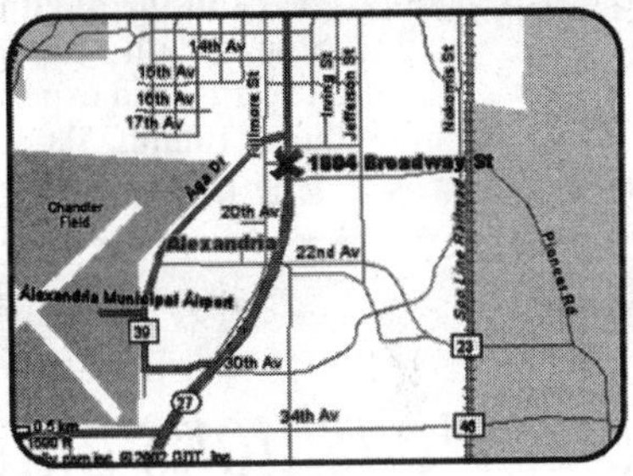

CARDINAL PLAZA
(store entrance facing Juettner Motors)
1804 S. Broadway ♥ ALEXANDRIA, MN
320-763-6739 ♥ www.qheartland.com

Manitoba
Ontario
North Dakota
STATE OF MINNESOTA
Fargo/Moorhead
Duluth
Alexandria
Wisconsin
St. Cloud
St. Paul
Minneapolis
Mankato
Rochester
Iowa

1804 Broadway St

STORE HOURS
Mon-Fri 9am-5pm
Sat 10am-4pm

QUILTING SUPPLIES ♥ FABRIC ♥ GIFTS ♥ CLASSES ♥ MACHINE QUILTING ♥ HUSQVARNA VIKING SEWING MACHINES

#21

Alexandria, MN #22

The Common Threads Quilt Shop, Inc.

109 15th Ave. E 56308
(320) 763-6771
common@rea-alp.com
www.commonthreadsquilt.com

Mon - Fri 10 - 5
Thur til 6
Sat 10 - 3

"BLESSED ARE THE QUILTERS FOR THEY SHALL BE CALLED PIECEMAKERS"

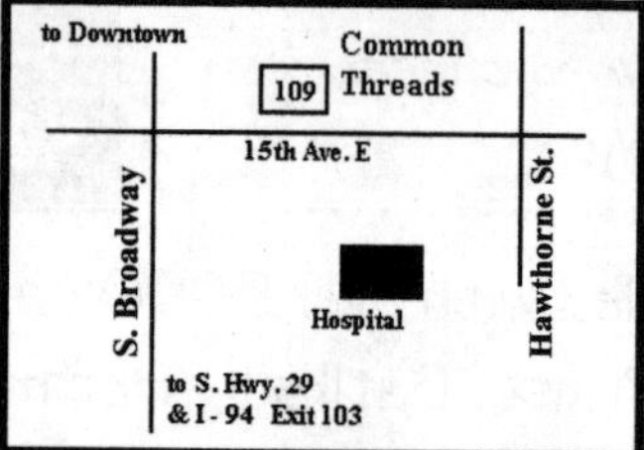

We specialize in 100% quality cotton fabrics made by leading designers, the newest quilting books, unique patterns, specialty quilting notions, primitive wool rug hooking, gifts and classes starting at the "beginner" level. Browse through our "garden" of inspiring samples and displays, reproduction prints, homespuns and flannels and meet with our friendly and knowledgeable staff. Free inspiration and advice is always available. We would be happy to help you coordinate fabrics for your projects and make up kits on request. Ongoing "Block of the Month" kits and patterns are also available. Stop in with a friend, spend time with kindred spirits, and experience the common thread running through our lives.

Alexandria, MN #23

Mon - Fri 9:30 - 5
Sat 10 - 5

612 Broadway 56308
(320) 763-3400
www.stitchinpostmn.com

Stitchin' Post 612
Travel about 3 miles to downtown then look for us on the left.
Fargo
Alexandria Exit 103
I - 94
Minneapolis

Owner: Terilyn Kennedy Est: 1996 2000 sq.ft.
A "Must See" shop in downtown Alexandria! Color is our specialty and lots of it. Our shop is known for it's huge selection of batiks, brights and flannels. Over 1500 bolts of highest quality fabrics for you to choose from.

Aitkin, MN #24

Mon - Fri 9:30 - 5
Sat 9:30 - 4

Hooked on Quilting

117 Second St. NW 56431
(218) 927-4699
hookedonquilting@internetdrive.com
Est: 2003

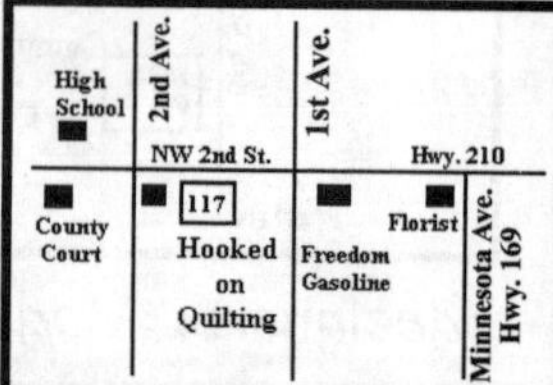

Great selection of books, patterns, fabrics & notions. Located 1 block east of the Courthouse next to Jacques Art Center.

Fergus Falls, MN #25

Mon - Fri 10 - 5
Sat 10 - 3

316 N. Tower Rd. 56537
(218) 739-9652
Fax: (218) 739-0722
quilters@prtel.com
Est: 1988 2000 Bolts
www.quilters-cottage.com

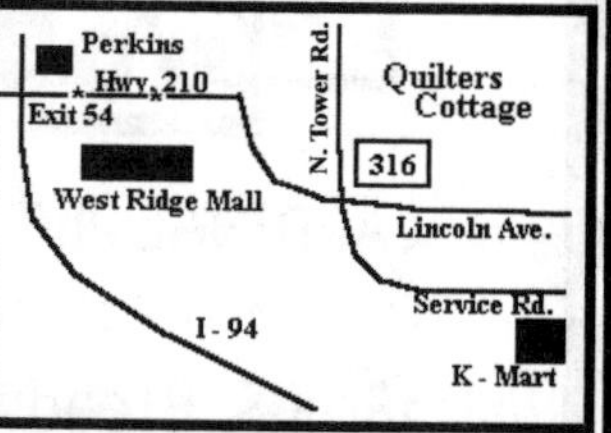

**Your one stop quilt shop.
We supply everything but the time.**

Rush City, MN #26

Fabrics Fashions and More

Mon - Fri 9 - 5
Sat 9 - 4

485 S. Dana, Box 21 55069
(320) 358-3693 Est: 1994
vthorn@fabricfashions-more.com
www.communityshowcase.net
Owner: Virginia Thorn 1900 sq.ft.

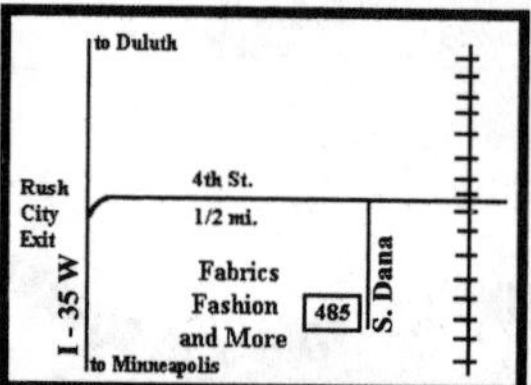
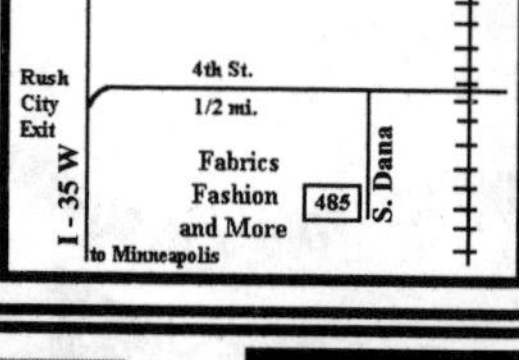

Well worth the stop! Fabrics, Books, Notions & more. Home of PFAFF Integrated Dual Feed. Authorized PFAFF Sales & Service.

Princeton, MN #27

Cole's Country Treasures Quilt Shop

Mon - Fri 9:30 - 5:30
Thur til 7
Sat 9:30 - 4

105 N. Rum River Dr. 55371
(763) 389-0680
Fax: (763) 631-0080

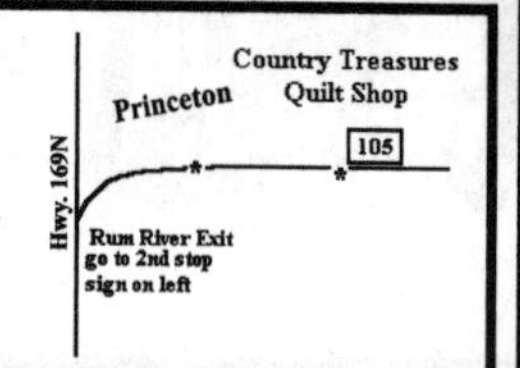

Hundreds of Books, 1,000's of Fat Quarters 3500 Bolts of Fabric. Frequent buyers cards / no expiration, Free Newsletter, Lots of Samples for Sale, We specialize in 1930's Reproduction Fabrics with over 300 in Stock.

Monticello, MN #28

Little Mountain Quilt Shop

Mon - Fri 10 - 6
Thur til 8
Sat 10 - 5
Sun 12 - 4

219 W. Broadway, P.O. Box 1153 55362
(763) 295-3777 Fax: (763) 295-3742
Lmqs219@yahoo.com
www.littlemountainquilts.com
Est: 2002 1800 sq.ft. 1100+ Bolts

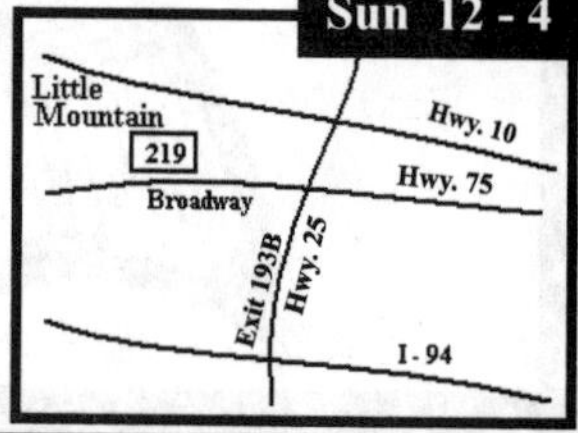

In downtown Monticello. Exit 193B from I-94. North on Hwy 25. Left on Hwy. 75. Fabric, Patterns, Notions, Friendly Staff.

The Must See Quilt Shop

St. Cloud, MN #29

in "Waite Park"—310 4th Ave. NE
320-259-4360 / 1-877-778-7793
www.grubersquiltshop.com
Owner: Sue Poser

Selected one of the top 10 Quilt Shops in North America 2001 by American Patchwork & Quilting Magazine

Mon-Fri, 9 - 7
Sat, 9 - 6
Sun, 12 - 5

Shop over 9,000 bolts in our spacious store and a complete collection of patterns, books and notions. Even book a stay with your friends at our Retreat Center! Hundreds of samples and displays to inspire you.
Located at DanTree Court in Waite Park.

DanTree Court
Cnty Rd 138
Hwy 15
33rd Ave.N.
25th Ave.N.
3rd St. N.
Crossroads Center
Hwy 23
Division St.
2nd St. S.
West St.Germain
Hwy 75

Sauk Rapids, MN #30

Bound in Stitches Quilt Village

2078 - 45th Street N.E.
Sauk Rapids, MN 56379
Phone: (320) 255-9021
Owners: Michelle & Wayne Johnson

Show us this ad & receive a special discount on your purchase. Certain exclusions apply. One time purchase only.

Store Hours:
Monday - Friday
10 a. m. - 5 p. m.
Saturday
9 a. m. - 3 p. m.

Closed Mondays:
Memorial Day - Labor Day

Quality Quilting Supplies

- 100% Cotton Print Fabrics ~ Moda, Hoffman, Bali, Benartex, Thimbleberries, South Seas, RJR, Nancy Crow & more
- **Peaceable Hand Dyed Fabrics**
- **Bound-in-Stitches Patterns**
- Books & Patterns
- Quilting Notions
- Kits
- Block of the Months
- Quilting Giftware
- Classes year round
- Friendly, Knowledgeable Staff
- Specializing in Color Expertise
- Many Samples on Display
- Unique & Relaxed Country Setting
- Ample Parking for RV's and Buses!

Directions: From St. Cloud, take Hwy. 15 North. Exit right on County Road 29 East. At stop sign, turn left on County Road. 1. Go one mile. Turn right on County Road 15. Continue east for 1/2 mile. Quilt Shop is located on the right.

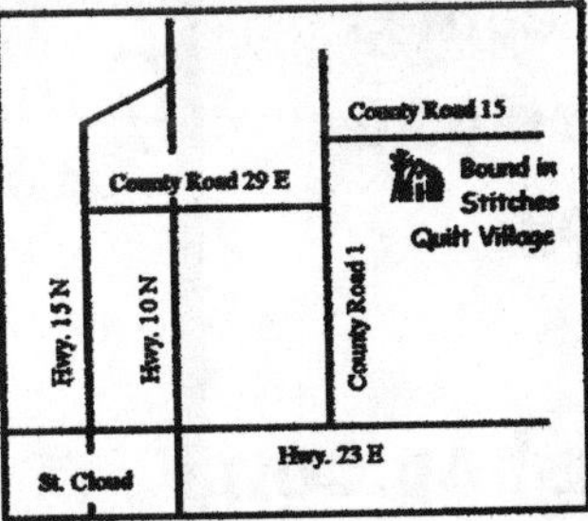

MasterCard & Visa Accepted

www.bound-in-stitches.com

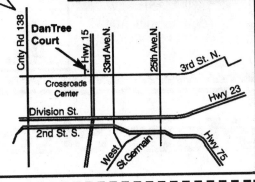

Elk River, MN #31

Cottage Quilts & Fabrics

Come visit us in our new location across the highway!

Mon - Fri 10 - 6
Thur til 7:30
Sat 10 - 4
Sun 12 - 4

Large selection of 100% cottons, quilting supplies, notions, patterns, books and classes. "Come Quilt With Us!"

16860 Hwy. 10 NE 55330
(763) 241-1490
Owner: Lynn Grant
Est: 1994 3500 Bolts

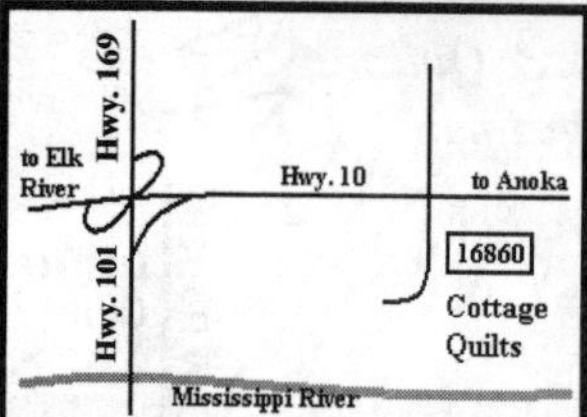

Avon, MN #32

Aunt Annie's Quilts & Silks

Visit our newly expanded shop.
Over 2400 sq.ft. of well lit shopping & classroom area.
3500+ bolts of fabrics including African, Bali, Japanese, Australian, Alexander Henry, Hoffman, Kaufman, RJR, Moda, Kona Bay, Monarch, Nancy Crow, hand-dyed & painted and many others.
Fine woolens, silks, rayons & flannels.
Inspiring samples & displays.
Local & international books and magazines.

Known for color assistance, enticing & unique fabrics, knowledgeable & helpful staff. Fabrics chosen by working artists for creative quilters and sewers.

Tour groups welcome, please call ahead.

Mon - Fri 9 - 6
Sat 9 - 4

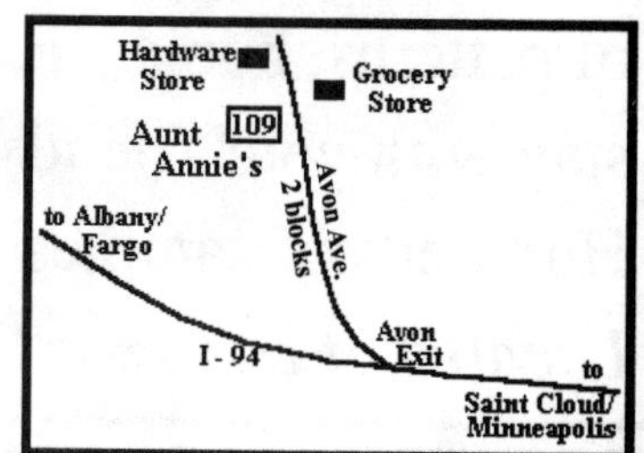

109 Avon Ave. S, P.O. Box 359 56310
(320) 356-1061
Auntanniesquilts@aol.com
Owners: Lucy Senstad

Main Street Cotton Shop

2 Great Locations

Redwood Falls, Mn #33
Selected Top Shop in Premier issue of APQ Sampler

#34 Hutchinson, Mn.
Located in the Thimblebrries design studio building

Free Full Color Catalog
800.624.4001
24 Hour Mail Order Service

Order On-line
www.mainstreetcottonshop.com

Buffalo, MN #35

Lady of the Lake Quilts & Fabrics

Mon - Sat 10 - 5
Thur til 7

One West Division St. 55313
(763) 682-1990
Owner: Karen Sargent
Est: 1997 1400 sq.ft.

Hundreds of Yards of Cottons, also Books, Notions, and Gifts.

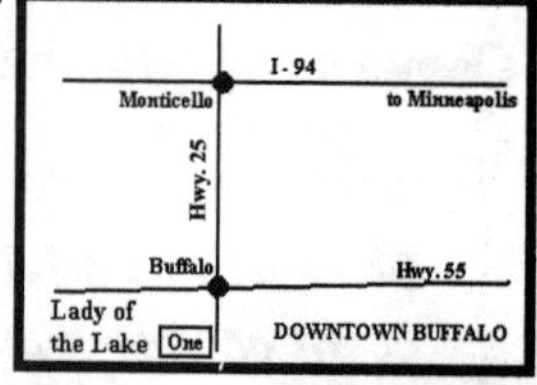

Kimball, MN #36

Gone to Pieces Quilt Shop

Mon - Fri 9 - 5
Sat 9 - 3

1 East Hazel Ave., P.O. Box 186 55353
(320) 398-5300
gonetopieces@meltel.net
Owner: Penny Callander Est: 2002

Located two blocks south of Hwy. 55 and Hwy 15 intersection. Carefully selected 100% cotton quilting fabric along with the latest books, patterns, notions and classes.

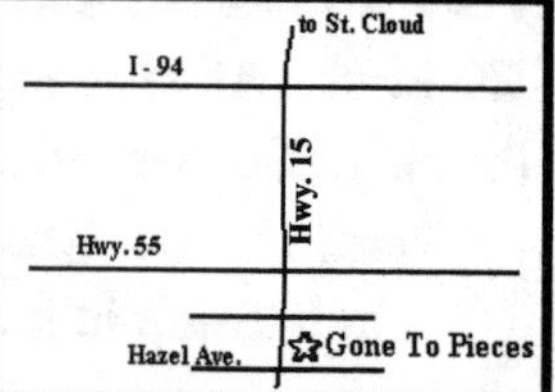

Bird Island, MN #37

Mon - Fri 9 - 5
Sat 9 - 3

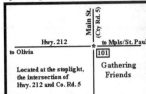

GATHERING FRIENDS
Quilt Shop

101 S. Main, P.O. Box 189 55310
gfriends@willmar.com
www.gatheringfriendsquiltshop.com
(320) 365-4670
Owners:
Deb Jacobs &
Kathy Squibb
Est: 1998
2500 bolts

Hwy. 212
Main St. (Cty Rd. 5)
to Olivia
to Mpls/St. Paul
101
Gathering Friends
Located at the stoplight, the intersection of Hwy. 212 and Co. Rd. 5

Large selection of 100% cotton fabrics & flannels, gift items and quilting kits.

Marshall, MN #38

Fabrics Plus

307 W. Main 56258 (800) 215-6246
elaine@fabricsplus.com www.fabricsplus.com
(507) 537-0835
Fax: (507) 537-1320
Owner: M. Elaine Nyquist
Est: 1985 2500 sq.ft.

Mon - Fri 9:30 - 6 Thur til 8 Sat 9:30 - 5

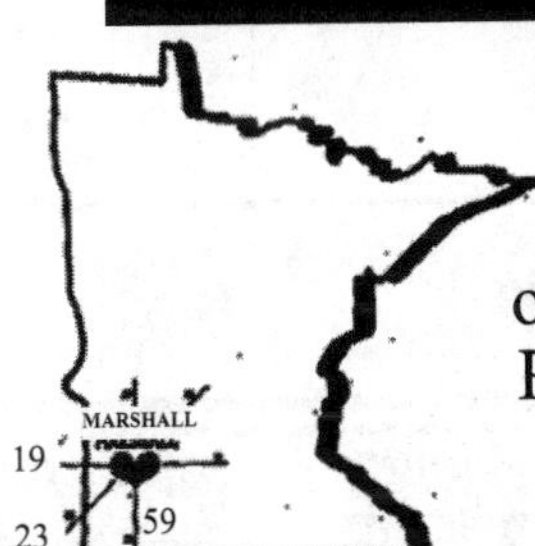

Southwest Minnesota's Largest Quilt Shop.
Over 3500 bolts of Fine Quilting Cottons.
Plus Books, Notions and Sewing Machines.

Arlington, MN #39

Ada Kate's Quilted Heart

Tues - Fri 9 - 5:30
Thur til 9
Sat 9 - 4

109 3rd Ave. SW, Box 159 55307
(507) 964-2667 Fax: (507) 964-2994
Adakatesquiltedheart@frontiernet.net
Owner: Kathryn Gail Hildebrandt
Est: 2003 1800 sq.ft. 1000 Bolts

We are a quilt shop in a wonderful small town. Our focus is beginner quilters. We have a 6 week basic "Quilting 101" for beginners. Beginners and experienced quilters will find beautiful fabrics and samples in our store.

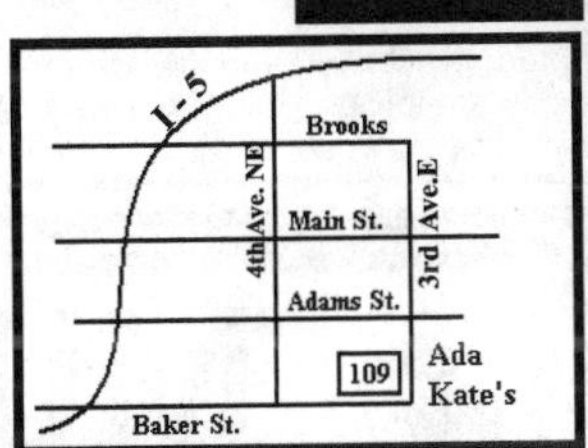

Gibbon, MN #40

Gallagher's Cafe Quilt Shop

A different menu each day. We specialize in panini sandwiches and extravagant desserts.

Cafe Hours:
Daily 10 - 4

1059 1st Ave. 55335
(507) 834-6886 or (888) 610-6886
ggallaghers@mchsl.com 1700 sq.ft.
Owner: Rita Gallagher

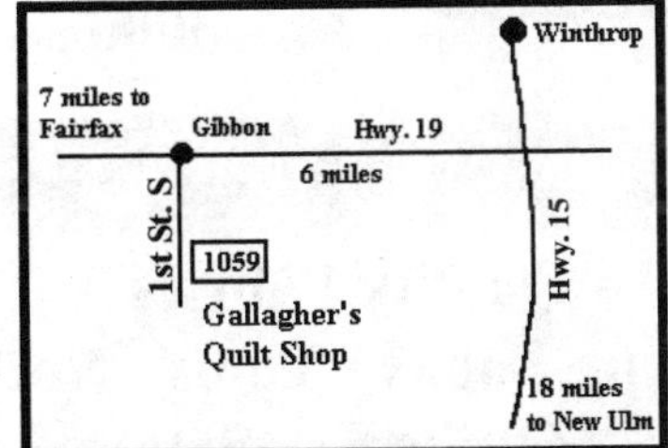

Mon - Fri 10 - 5
Sat 10 - 4

A Quilt Shop and Restaurant housed in a 1903 reclaimed building.

Wonderful colors and great food. Moda, Benartex, Chanteclair, Hi Fashion, P&B, Alexander Henry, Kona Bay, Marcus Bros

Mary Lue's Yarn & Quilt Shop

at the Historic St. Peter Woolen Mill

Fabrics, Patterns, Books, Gifts, Yarns
Wool Processing & Batting
Machine Quilting

Web: www.woolenmill.com
Email: spwoolen@prairie.lakes.com

Mon - Sat 9 - 5
Sept - May Sun 12 - 4

101 W. Broadway
St. Peter, MN 56082
(507) 934-3734

75 mi. to Minneapolis
St. Peter Woolen Mill 101
Broadway
Hwy. 169
Front St.
10 mi. to Mankato

St. Peter, MN #41

Windom, MN #42

Prairie Quilting

Mon 9 - 6:30
Tues - Fri 9 - 5
Sat 9 - 3

1293 Hale Place 56101
(507) 831-2740
jrkp@rconnect.com
Owner: Kay Peterson

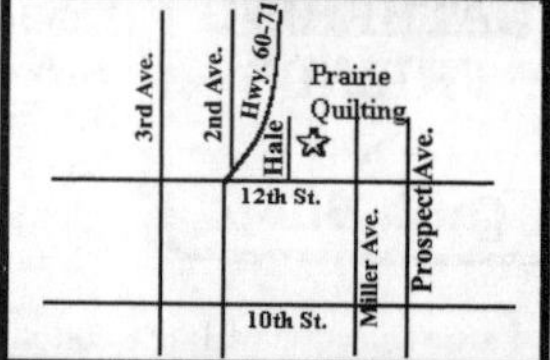

Unique Quilt Shop location next to feed store. Great selection of 100% cotton fabrics, books, patterns, and notions. Quilts for sale.

Lismore, MN #43

Country Hearts

Jan - April
Tues - Sat 9 - 5
May - Dec
Tues - Sat 9 - 5
Sun 12 - 5

12405 State Hwy. 91 56155
(507) 472-8707 Est: 1998
Chearts@frontiernet.net
Owner: Karon Nagel 2600 sq.ft.

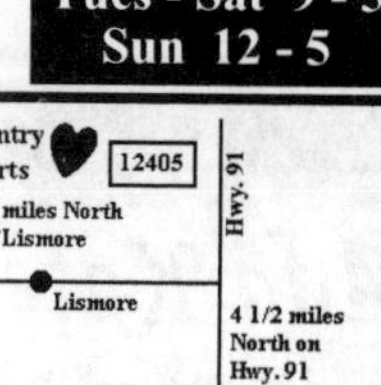

Quilting Fabrics, Notions, Patterns, Books and many samples. Quaint Country Shop. Many handcrafted wood items.

Luverne, MN #44

The Sewing Basket

Tues - Fri 9 - 5
Thurs til 8
Sat 9 - 12

204 E. Main 56156
(507) 283-9769
sewing@ideasign.com
Owner: Barbara Bork

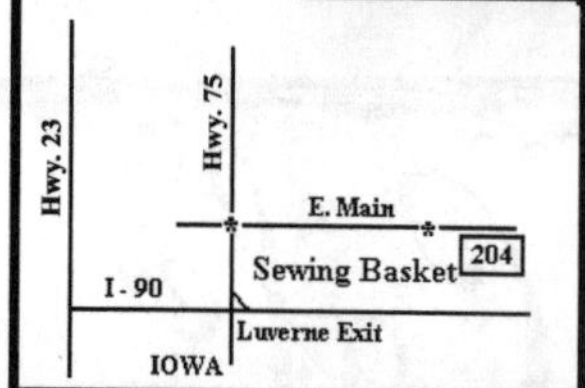

Your full service Quilt Shop!

Worthington, MN #45

Mon - Thur 9 - 5:30
Fri 9 - 9
Sat 9 - 4

1820 Oxford St. 56187
(800) SEW-MORE or (507) 372-2707
Owner: Zuby Jansen
Est. 1982 3600 sq.ft.

CRAFTY CORNER
Quilt & Sewing Shoppe

We sell 100% cotton fabrics.
6221 bolts in stock.
Many Patterns Bernina Sewing Machine sales & Service. Quilting Supplies!
Singer Featherweights in stock

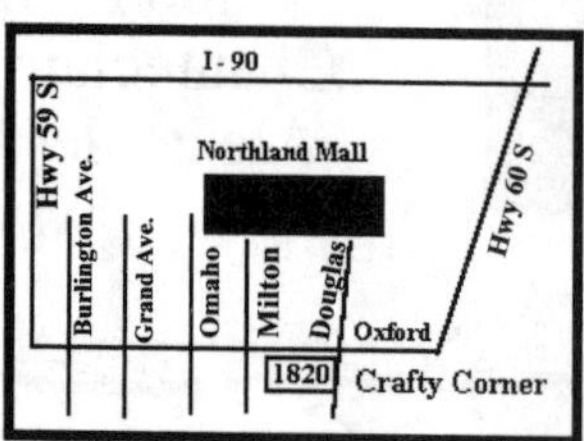

MUGGS Fabric

Owner: Margaret (Muggs) Meyer

Mon & Thur 9:30 - 8
Tues, Wed, & Fri 9:30 - 5:30
Sat 9:30 - 5 Sun 12 - 4
Closed Sun May 1st to Labor Day

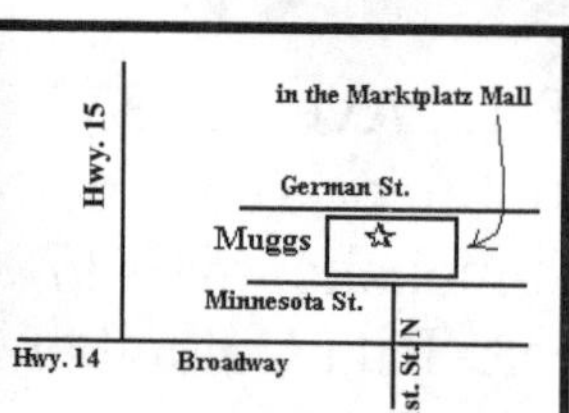

101 N. German
Marktplatz Mall
56073
(507) 359-1515
Fax: (507) 359-1405
3000 sq.ft.

New Ulm, MN #46

- **Quality Fabrics**
- **Quilting Books • Tools • Notions**
- **Quilts For Sale**

Expert Advice always gladly given

The Thimble Box

New Ulm, MN #47

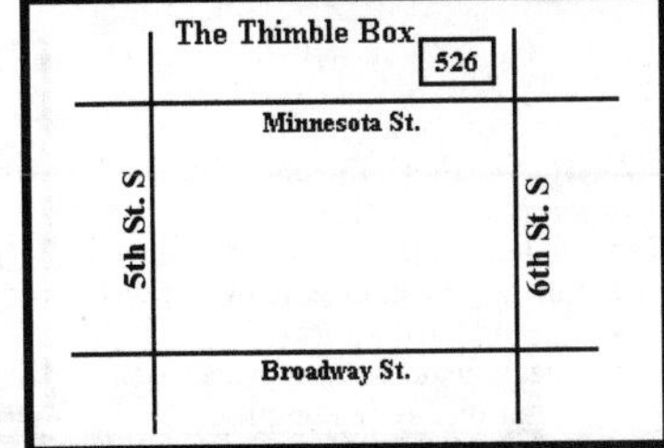

526 S. Minnesota St. 56073
(507) 354-6721
www.thimblebox.com

Owners: Toni and Duane Laffrenzen

thimble@newulmtel.net

Enter the nostalgic atmosphere of a turn-of-the-century corner store, complete with old wooden floors and tin ceiling.

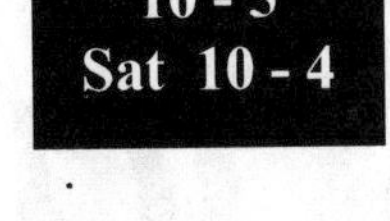

Find an inviting warm quilt shop that combines the joy of quilting and an intriguing array of time-gone by gifts.

A large supply of flannels, homespuns, Batiks, 30's, Thimbleberries and 100% cotton fabrics are available.

Machine quilting is also available.

Prints, custom picture framing and matting are offered.

The Quilter's Mercantile

Mankato, MN #48

Est: 2001

1400 Madison Ave. Suite #404, Mankato, MN 56001
(507) 385-7777 Fax: (507) 385-0187
www.quiltersmerc.com quiltersmerc@aol.com
Owners: Susan & Mike Brown

Mon - Sat 9 - 5
Tues & Thur til 8
Sun 1 - 4

Lots of Books, Patterns and Notions.
Come and visit our antique filled shop where inspiration abounds. We carry 3500+ Bolts of 100% cotton dry goods for the traditional and contemporary quilters; from batiks to homespuns, there's something for everyone.
"Friendly Service & Free Advice"

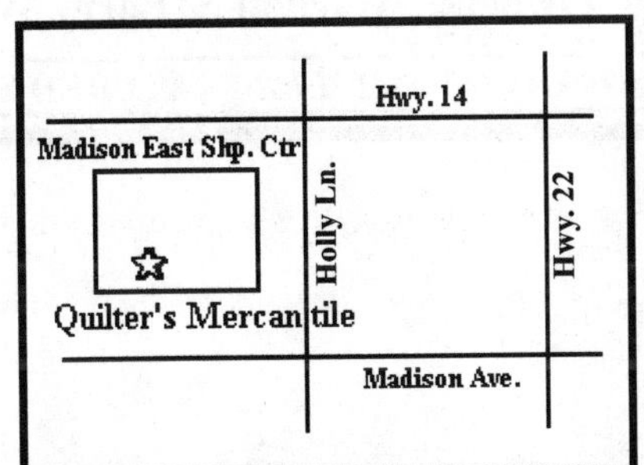

Take Hwy. 14 to Hwy. 22 South. Go to Madison Ave. - Turn Right - Go about 1 Mile West to the Madison East Shopping Center. We are located in the mall.

Sherburn, MN #49

Old Alley Quilt Shop

Opening Fall of 2004 !

115 N. Main St. (Hwy. 4)
P.O. Box 143 56171
(507) 728-8851
detert@oldalleyquiltshop.com
www.oldalleyquiltshop.com

We are remodeling the old bowling alley in Sherburn into a quilt shop. Check our web site for updated information!

quilting machine, classes, fabrics, books, patterns, notions, & reading room

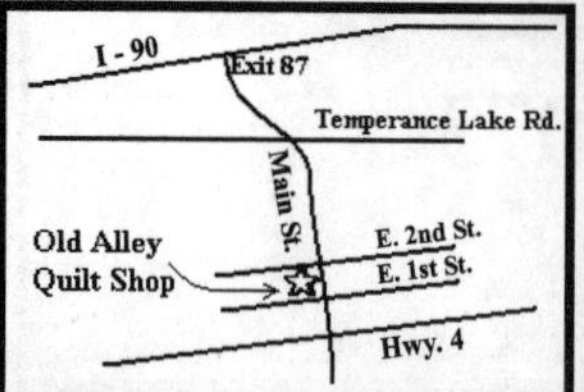

Owatonna, MN #50

The Cotton Patch

Mon - Fri 9 - 5:30 Sat 9 - 4:30

110 W. Broadway 55060
(507) 451-5979 Est: 1993 2000 Bolts
www.thecottonpatchquilts.com
Owners: Cathy Torrey & Laura Wertwijn

Spacious, well-lit shop staffed by helpful, experience quilters. An abundance of quality 100% cotton fabric & supplies for all your quilting needs. Located on downtown's charming Central Park, just 1 mile off I - 35 and 5 minutes from Cabela's.

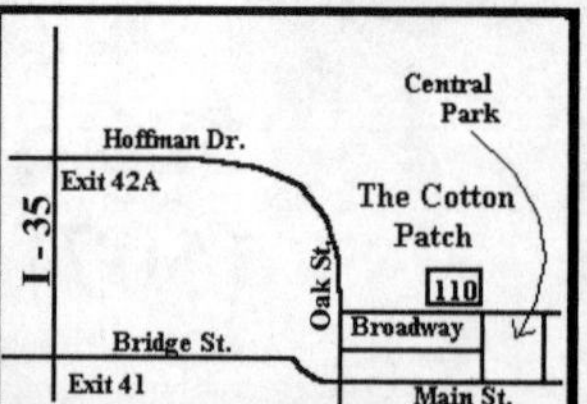

Create a treasured heirloom for someone you love or for your own home.

Cannon Falls, MN #51

Quilts by the Falls

Mon - Fri 9 - 5 Thur 9 - 8 Sat 9 - 4

* **3500+ bolts of quality quilting**
* **fabrics & homespuns**
* **100's of books & patterns**
* **16 feet of notions, Gifts - classes**
* **100's of models for inspiration**

Map: To Mpls./St. Paul; Hwy. 52; 402 W. Mill St.; Quilts by the Falls; Mill Street; 4th Street; To Northfield; Cannon Falls; To Red Wing; State Hwy. 19; To Rochester

Offering You Small Town Friendly Service!

Free Inspiration & Advice Always Available

402 W. Mill St. 55009
(507) 263-2528 or (888) 899-2528
www.cannon.net/~quilts
e-mail - quilts@cannon.net
Owners: Marilou & Larry Welt

1999 *QUILT SAMPLER* FEATURED SHOP

"Where all the pieces come together!"

Lake City, MN #52

116 S. Washington
55041
(651) 345-3958
Owners: Janet Bruce & Judy Rutz
Est: 1998

Mon - Sat 9 - 5 Closed Sundays

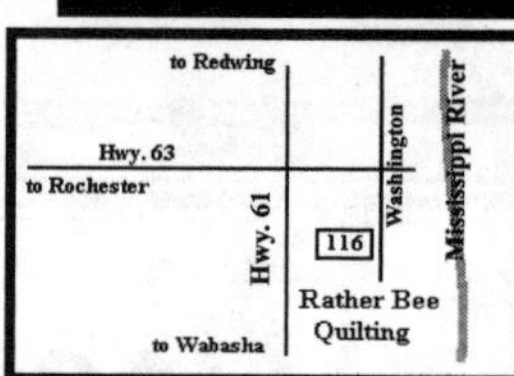

Known for beautiful fabrics, innovative classes and friendly, knowledgeable help.

www.ratherbeequilting.com

Just A Little Something

304 Sixth Street SW
Rochester, MN 55902
507-288-7172

Quilting Fabrics, Patterns, Books, Notions and Classes

Friendly Help and Advice In a Unique Historical Setting

Hand Knitting Yarn, Patterns, Books, Needles and Classes

Store Hours
Monday through Friday
10 am to 6 pm
Saturday 10 am to 5 pm

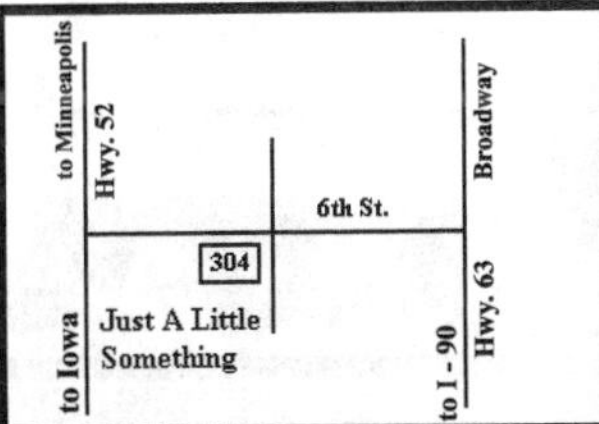

Rochester, MN #53

Rochester, MN #54

Mon - Fri 9 - 5
Sat 9 - 1

The Quilting Cupboard

115 N. Broadway 55906
(507) 281-9988
thequiltingcupboard@hotmail.com
www.thequiltingcupboard.com
Owners: Susan & Jim Kisro
Est: 2003
Convenient downtown location 3 blocks from Mayo Clinic campus. Original pattern designs. Custom quilt racks and stands. 100% soy candles.

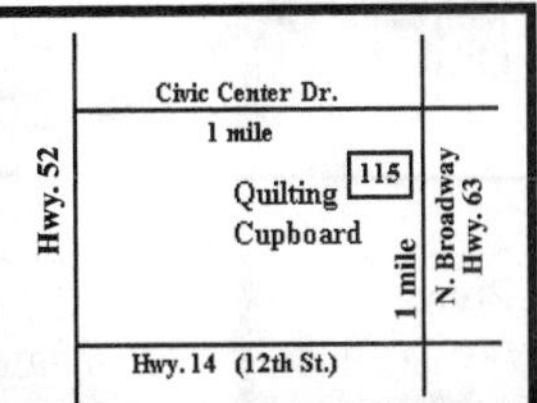

Hayward, MN #55

Mon - Fri 10 - 5
Sat 10 - 3

Calico Hutch

100 W. Front St., P.O. Box 482 56043
(507) 377-1163
ckmatson@smig.net Est: 1982
Spacious quilt shop with over 2,000 bolts of 100% cotton fabrics by RJR, Moda, South Seas, Maywood, Hoffman and more. Hundreds of samples and kits. Small-town, friendly shop with large-town service and products.

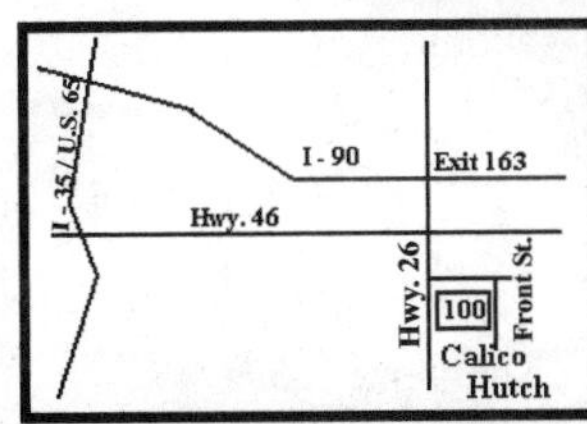

Spring Valley, MN #56

Quilter's Quarters

616 N. Broadway
Spring Valley 55975
(507) 346-2555
Fax: (507) 346-2528
cmarzolf@deskmedia.com
Est: 2004 2000 sq.ft.
1200+ Bolts

Brand new shop!
Fabric, patterns, books, and notions; all to inspire beautiful new projects for you. Fun and friendly atmosphere. Great customer service.

Mon - Sat 9:00 - 5:30

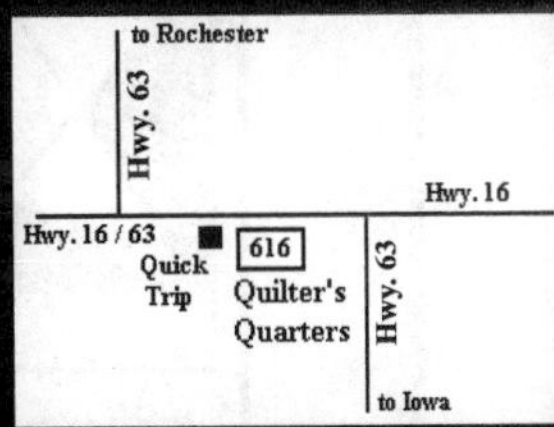

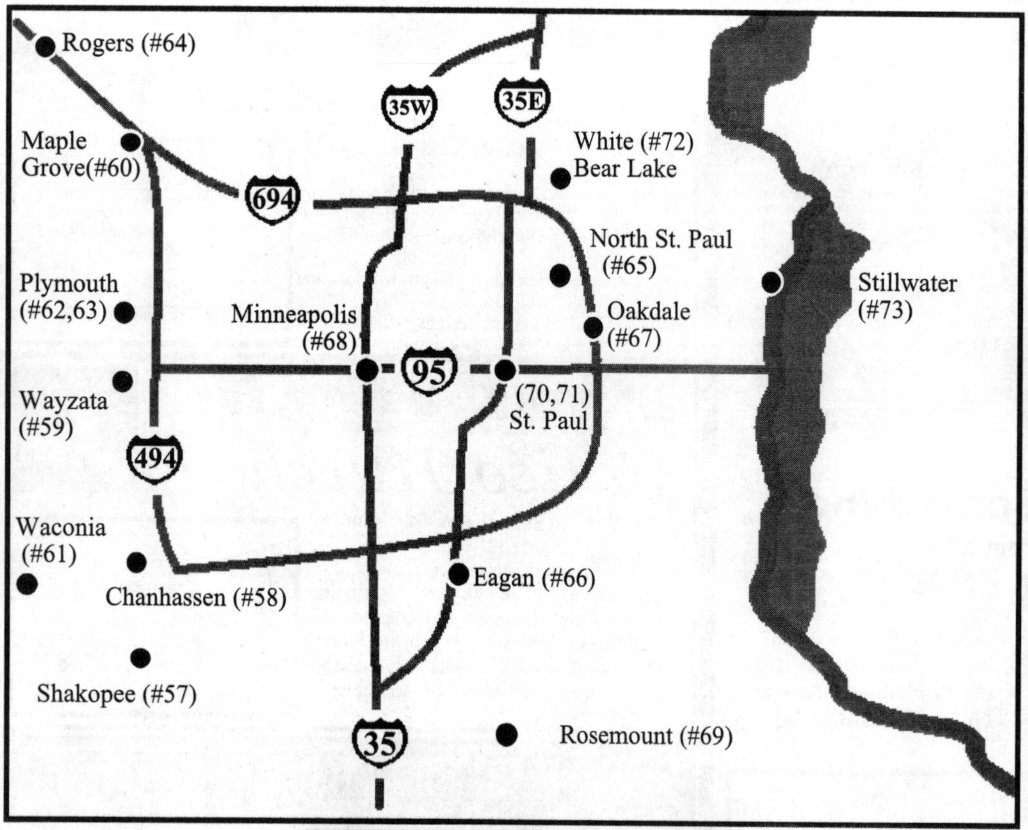

Rogers (#64)
Maple Grove(#60)
694
35W
35E
White (#72) Bear Lake
North St. Paul (#65)
Plymouth (#62,63)
Minneapolis (#68)
Oakdale (#67)
Stillwater (#73)
95
(70,71) St. Paul
Wayzata (#59)
494
Waconia (#61)
Chanhassen (#58)
Eagan (#66)
Shakopee (#57)
35
Rosemount (#69)

MINNEAPOLIS ST PAUL AREA

Shops #57 - 73

17 Featured Shops

Shakopee, MN #57

EAGLE CREEK QUILT SHOP

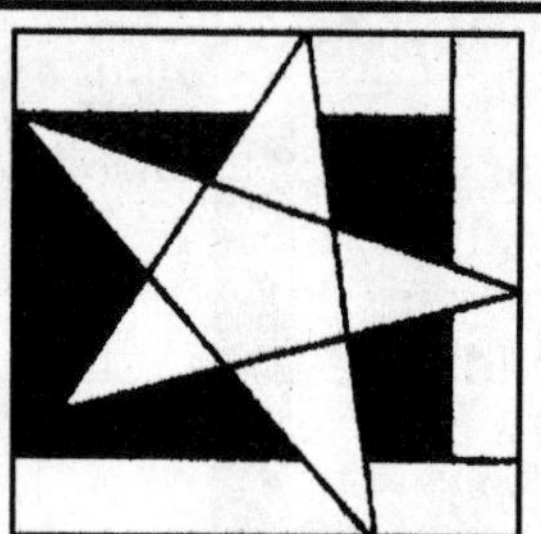

333 2nd Ave. W, Shakopee, MN 55379
(952) 233-3774
Owners: Lori Gillick & Becky Kelso
2300 sq.ft. 3000 Bolts
A Top Ten Shop - Quilt Sampler 2003

Located in an enchanting turn of the century railroad depot, our shop features hundreds of plaids, homespuns and flannels as well as complete lines of 1800's - 1930's reproduction fabrics.
You'll find wonderful samples to inspire you and many kits to entice you.
Conveniently located two miles west of Valley Fair on Hwy. 101, just 20 min. from the Mall of America.

Eagle Creek Quilt Shop
Scott St.
Hwy. 101
Hwy. 13
333
2nd Ave. W
I - 35
Marschall

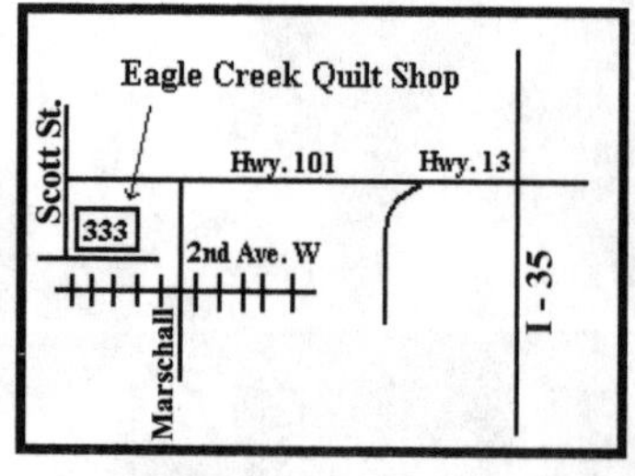

www.eaglecreekquiltshop.com

Mon 10 - 5 Tues 10 - 8 Wed - Sat 10 - 5

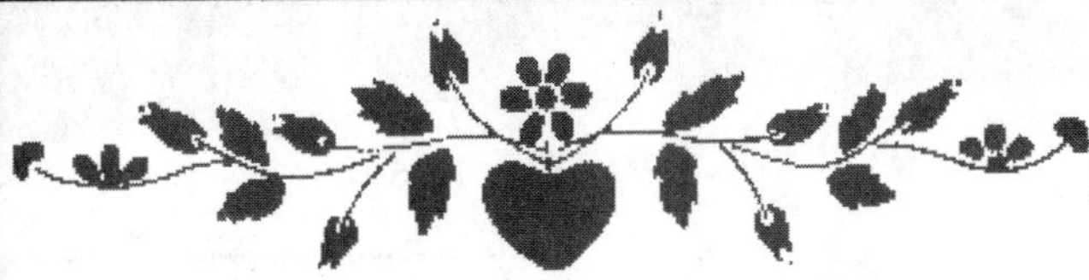

The Sampler

a quilt shop and more.....

A New and Larger Store creates an even more "exciting" shop to visit if you are Minnesota Bound! Located in the SW suburbs and easy to find, we're only 20 minutes from the Mall of America. Our diverse Fabric Selection helps you create Fabulous Quilts. The Sampler is known for carrying the Entire Kaffe Fassett Collection, a Hugh Selection of Bali Batiks, Japanese, African, Brights and so much more! Lots of Kits, Fat Quarter Bundles, Unique Gifts, Innovative Classes plus a creative and talented Staff! We also do mail order.

551 W. 78th St.
Chanhassen, MN 55317
(952) 934-5307
sampler@pconline.com
www.the-sampler.com
Owner: Karol Thompson
Estab: 1977 3400 Sq.ft.

Mon & Wed 9:30 - 6:30
Tues & Thur 9:30 - 8:30
Fri & Sat 9:30 - 5
Sun 12 - 4:30

Directions:

Take Highway 494 to Highway 5 West - go to Great Plains Blvd (Chanhassen exit) — turn Rt. — Follow street around Chanhassen Dinner Theater to first left.

Chanhassen, MN #58

Wayzata, MN #59

WAYZATA Quilting Emporium

... Eclectic collection of fabrics — from traditional to contemporary
... 2000+ bolts of cotton fabric
... 300+ book titles, large selection of patterns
... Quilting tools and supplies
... Kits, bundles and fat quarters
... Classes year round
... Friendly, knowledgeable staff

Mon - Thurs 9 - 8:30
Fri & Sat 9 - 5

927 East Lake Street 55391
Located in Wayzata Bay Center Mall.
(952) 475-2138
Owners: Deb Buchholz & Wendy Fedie
Est: 1980 1650 sq.ft.

www.wayzataquilting.com

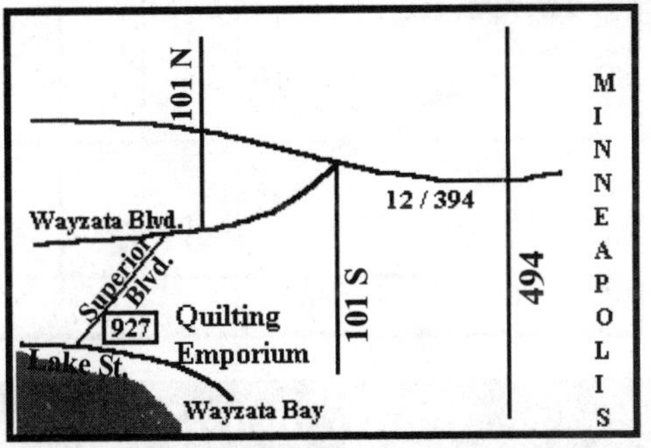

Twenty minutes west of Minneapolis — over 2000 bolts of cotton —

A complete quilt shop !

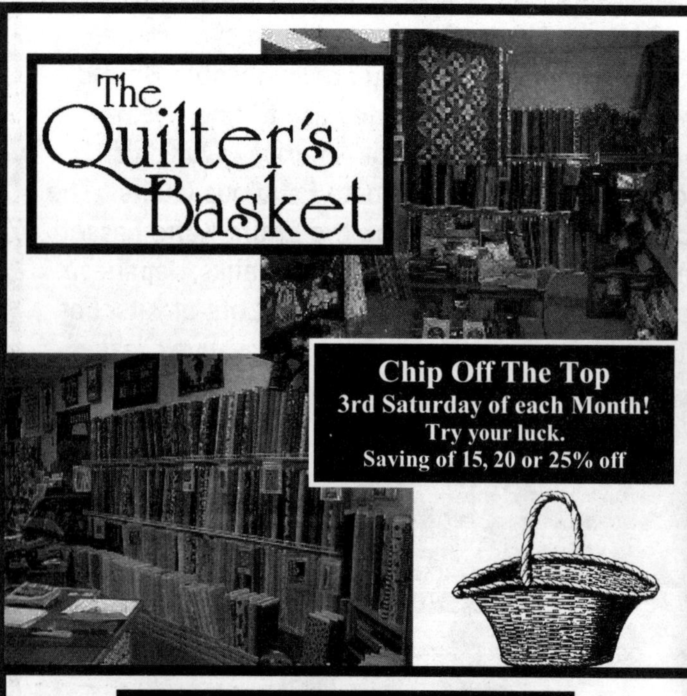

Maple Grove, MN #60

Zachary Square Shopping Center
11375 96th Ave. N 55369
(763) 493-5577
tqb97@aol.com
Est: 1997 1700 sq.ft. 3000 Bolts

- 100% Cotton Quilting Fabrics
- Quilting Books & Patterns
- Reed
- Gift Items
- Quilting & Basket Notions

Classes for all Ages & Abilities

www.TheQuiltersBasket.com

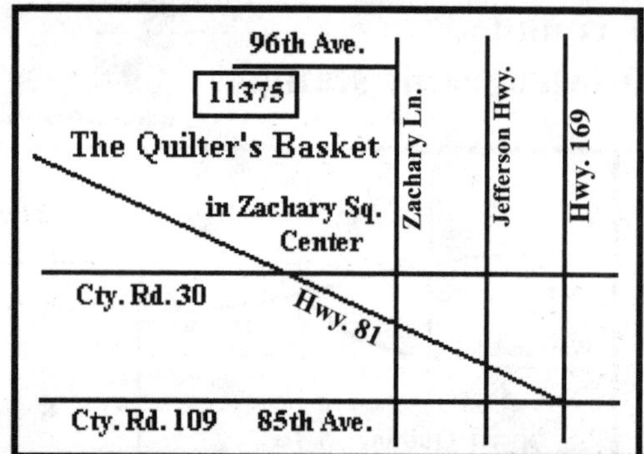

Store Hours:
Mon-Th 9:30 am - 8:30 pm
Fri-Sat 9:30 am - 5:30 pm
Sun 12:30 pm - 5:00 pm

Waconia, MN #61

Mon - Fri 9 - 6
Sat 9 - 4

Heavenly Patchwork Quilt Shop

115 S. Olive St. 55387
(952) 442-8677

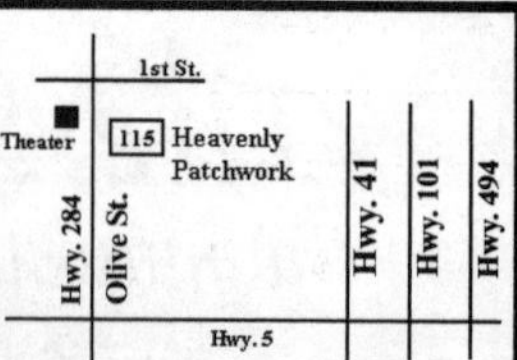

heavenlypatchworkqs@gbronline.com
Owner: Kay R. Derner Est: 2003
Located in 1900 year old House - Downtown Waconia - across the street from Theatre on the second floor of Green Door Frame/Floral Shop.

Plymouth, MN #62

FOUR SEASONS QUILTS

4172 Lancaster Ln. 55441
(763) 557-5899 Fax: (763) 557-5894
Fourseasonsquilts@popp.net
Owner: JoAnn Atkins
Est: 2003 2600 sq.ft. 2000+ Bolts

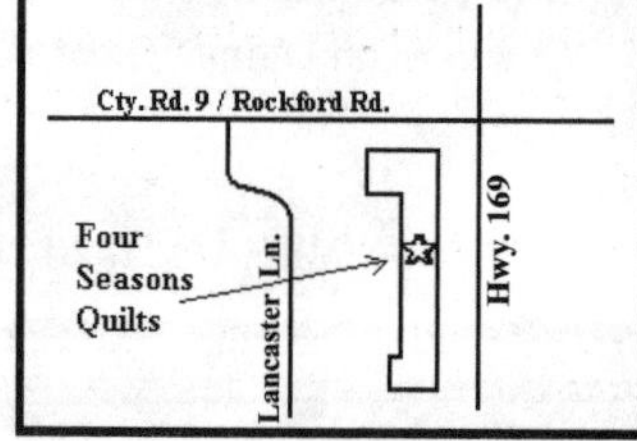

Mon - Thur 10 - 9
Fri 10 - 7
Sat 9 - 5
Sun 12 - 4

A warm & friendly quilt shop providing a wide variety of 100% cottons including reproductions and the complete Jinny Beyer palette, a large selection of books, patterns, kits & notions.

Plymouth, MN #63

SnuggleBug, A Quilt Shop

You will be pleasantly surprised as you enter SnuggleBug's world of bright, *bold, vivid colors.*

- Great Selection of ***Beautiful Batiks***
- Bright Children's ***Novelty Prints***
- ***Moda Marbles*** & More
- 100's of ***Books & Patterns***.

3900 Vinewood Ln. N, Suite 9
Plymouth, MN 55441
in Cottonwood Plaza
(763) 557-8656
Owner: Alexis Lair
Est: 2001 1500 sq. ft.

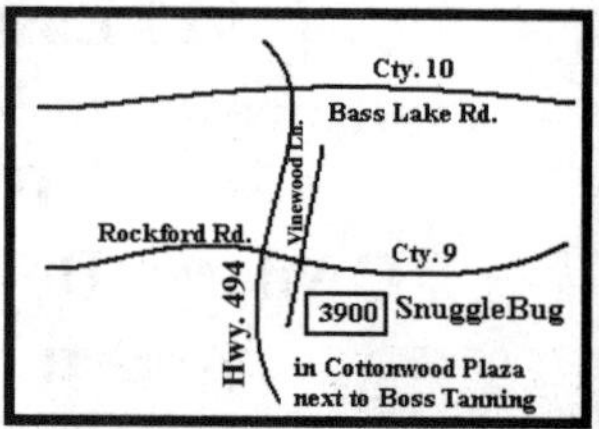

Mon - Wed 9:30 - 6:30
Thur 9:30 - 8
Fri & Sat 9:30 - 5

Southeast corner of Hwy 494 & Rockford Rd. (Cty Rd 9) South on Vinewood Ln. in Cottonwood Plaza.

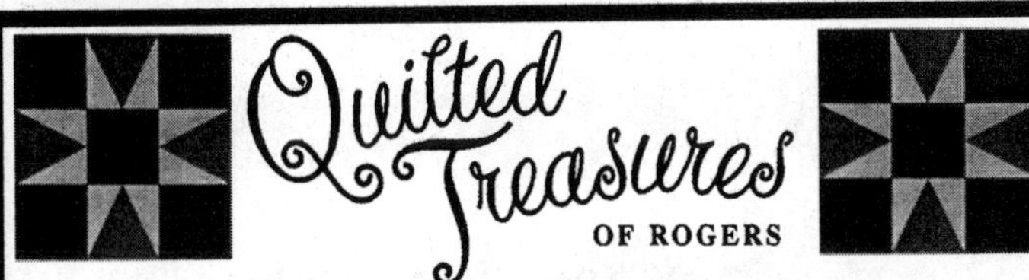

QUILTING SUPPLIES • COTTON FABRICS • CLASSES • KITS

1 Mile North of 94 on Hwy. 101
14178 Northdale Blvd.
(763) 428-1952
www.quiltedtreasures.net

Rogers, MN #64

OUR SHOP FEATURES

- **Over 150 quilts in full view to inspire your next project**
- **True color lighting.**
- **Spacious classroom and year round classes.**
- **4500 bolts of fabric including Batiks, North Woods and Reproductions. Line from Moda, Hoffman, Alexander Henry, Michael Miller, Timeless Treasures, Thimbleberries, RJR and Benartex.**
- **Thimbleberrie Clubs.**
- **Friendly, knowledgeable staff.**
- **Seasonal Retreats & Special Events.**
- **Regional Designers featured.**
- **Buses Welcomed**

Shop Hours

Monday, Wednesday, Friday 10 - 5
Tuesday & Thursday 10 - 8
Saturdays 10 - 4
Sundays 12:30 - 4

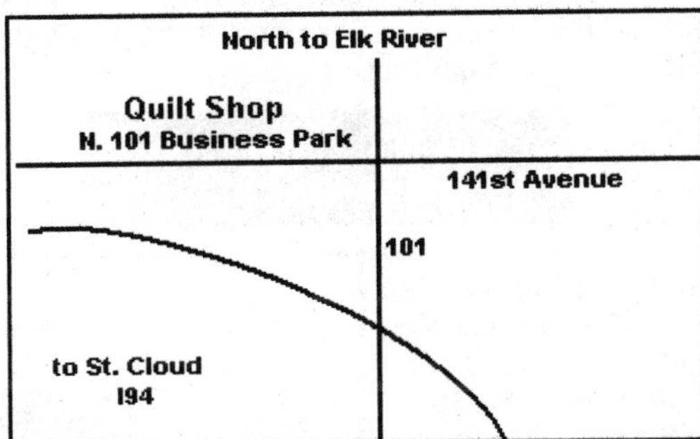

FROM 94: Go North on 101 two stoplights. Turn West on 141st Avenue. and an immediate right into North 101 Business Park.

North St. Paul, MN #65

2580 SEVENTH AVE - NORTH ST PAUL MN 55109
(651) 426-1885 WWW.ROSEBUDS-COTTAGE.COM
Owner: Roseann Meehan Kermes Est: 1997

Mon - Fri 10 - 5
Sat 10 - 3

A HAVEN FOR THE PRIMITIVE FOLK ART LOVER! You'll find quilting fabric, homespun, brushed cottons and hand dyed wool perfect for projects from your favorite primitive designers. Unique designs from Rosebud's Cottage and Plain Jane Creations - penny rugs and wool applique are our specialty. Don't miss our Vintage Postcard Block of the Month and other vintage projects.

"A 2004 Quilt Sampler Shop"

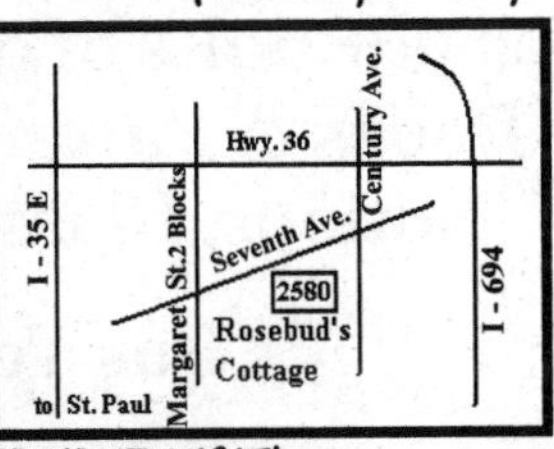

WE'RE LOOKING FORWARD TO YOUR VISIT!

Eagan, MN #66

QUILT COVE

1960 Cliff Lake Road, Suite 134
Eagan, MN 55122
651-452-8891 • www.quiltcove.com

Owner: Susan Herzberg
Est: 1989 • 3800 sq.ft. • 4000 bolts

A Quilt Shop offering the finest in cotton fabrics, books, patterns and quilting supplies.
Classes & Gift Certificates Available.

Hours:
Mon-Fri
10:00 - 8:30
Saturday
10:00 - 5:00
Sunday
1:00 - 5:00

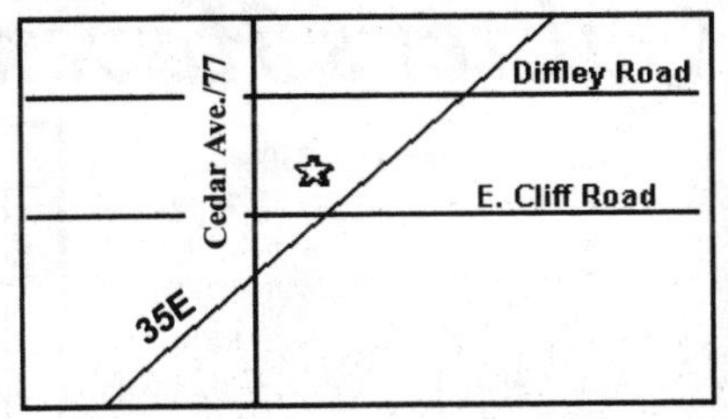

Located just 5 miles south of the Mall of America (off 35E and Cliff Road between Target and Cub)

Oakdale, MN #67

Owners: Carolyn & Charles Peters

7166 10th St. N 55128
(651) 731-4700 - Fax (651) 731-5420
www.thequiltedshingle.com
e-mail: info@thequiltedshingle.com

Quilting Supplies, Classes, Friendly Folks - All Under one Roof!

2500+ Bolts of quality quilting fabrics.
Books & Patterns, Quilt-Related Gifts
Notions, Classes, Buttons & Batting

Bus Tours Welcome!

Online Shopping

Mon - Thurs: 10 to 6, Fri - Sat: 10 - 5
Sun: 12 to 4

Roxanne Thimble Certified Fitters
BlockWatchers, Samplers
Stitchin' Red Hats - Red Hat Society

Located just west of the intersection of Interstate 694 and 10th St. N in the Oakdale Center

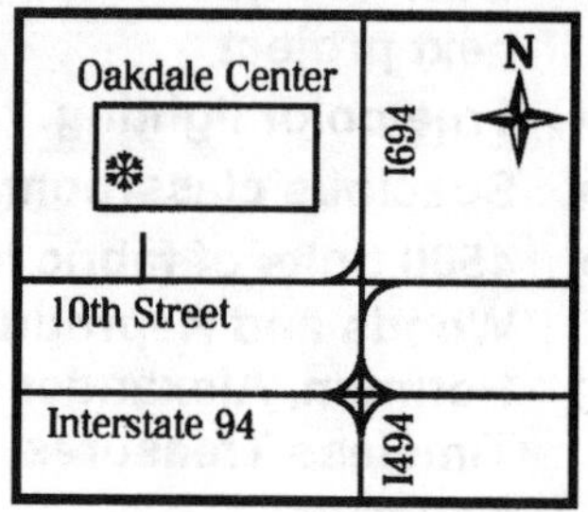

Minneapolis, MN #68

Mon - Sat
9:30 - 5

Glad Creations, Inc.

3400 Bloomington Ave. S 55407
(612) 724-1079 Fax: (612) 276-0275
E-Mail: nancy@gladcreationsquilts.com
Web Site: www.gladcreationsquilts.com
Est: 1976 1500 sq.ft. 3000 Bolts

Great selection of fabrics, books and quilting supplies. Original line of patterns for rotary cut machine pieced quilts.

downtown Minneapolis
Glad Creations 3400
34th St.
35th St.
36th St.
1 mile
I - 35W
Bloomington Ave.
Cedar Ave.
Mall of America

Rosemount, MN #69

Tues - Fri
10 - 9
Sat 10 - 6
Sun 12 - 5

Quilter's Haven

14680 S. Robert Tr. 55068
(651) 322-7071 Fax: (651) 322-4994
E-Mail: Quilthav@frontiernet.net
Owners: Kathy Watson & Jean Graham
Est: 2002 1500 sq.ft. 750+ Bolts

Visit our quaint 100+ year house, 5 rooms full of new fabrics, patterns & notions. European country florals, brights, & children's prints.

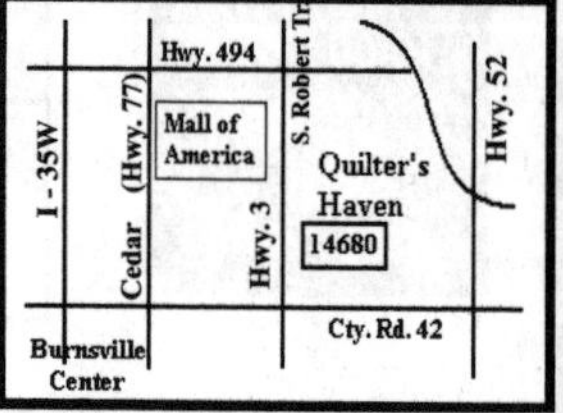

St. Paul, MN #70

Colorful Quilts & Textiles

Contemporary and Asian-style prints, a huge inventory of Bali fabrics, artist-dyed fabrics from nine dyers, lots of imported batiks and molas, and unusual garment fabrics. Also contemporary books and patterns, plus classes in surface design, artwear, dollmaking, beading on fabric, embellishment, and quilting.

Mon - Sat 10:30 - 5:30
Tues & Thur til 8

NEW LOCATION
On Hwy. 280 between St. Paul & Minneapolis
2233 Energy Park Dr. 55108
(651) 628-9664
www.colorfulquilts.com

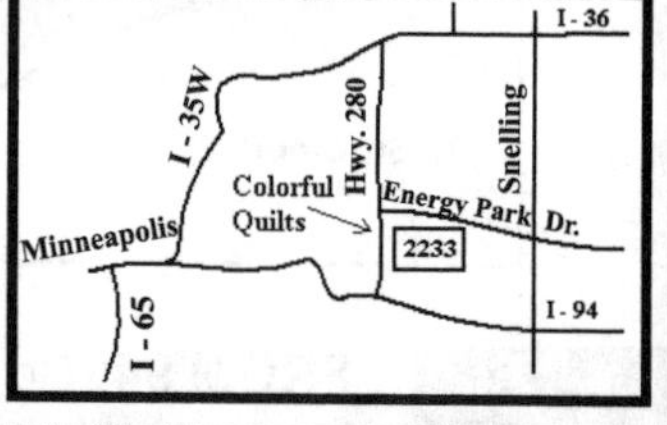

Quilter's Courtyard

A haven for quilters, quilt lovers, and friends.

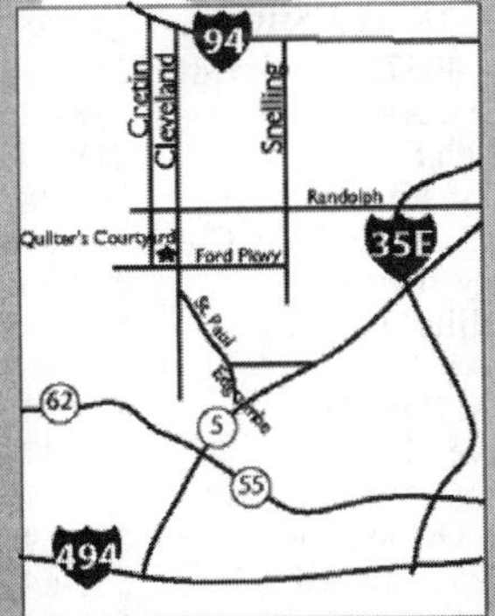

shop hours

monday - friday 10am–9pm
saturday 9am–9pm
sunday noon–5pm

news & classes online

www.quilterscourtyard.com

Mary Harreld
Owner

2112B Ford Parkway
St. Paul, MN 55116
651.698.1816

also located in South Burlington, Vermont!

Visit our beautiful courtyard, just brimming with delightful treasures!

- A spectacular selection of contemporary and traditional fabrics.
- Exquisite fabrics and trim imported from Japan, Australia, England, and Switzerland.
- Extensive collection of the latest books, notions, and patterns.
- Specialty thread and floss collections for hand and machine embroidery.
- Many uniquely wonderful gifts.
- Personalized weekend getaways for your group or guild.
- Tour groups welcome.
- Visit us in South Burlington, Vermont as well!

St. Paul, MN #71

White Bear Lake, MN #72

Bear Patch Quilting Co.

2001 TOP TEN QUILT SHOP

A Quilter's Heaven filled with 100% cotton fabrics, patterns, books, notions, and lots of samples and great ideas to inspire your creativity. Meeting all your quilting needs with year-round classes, stitchery clubs and friendly, knowledgeable staff.

651-429-1039
2199 Fourth St. 55110
e-mail: bearpqc@aol.com
Est: May 1997
4600 sq.ft. 4000+ Bolts

Mon - Fri 9 - 9
Sat 9 - 5
Sun 12 - 4

www.bearpatchquilting.com

St. Paul's Authorized Bernina Dealer serving the Twin Cities.

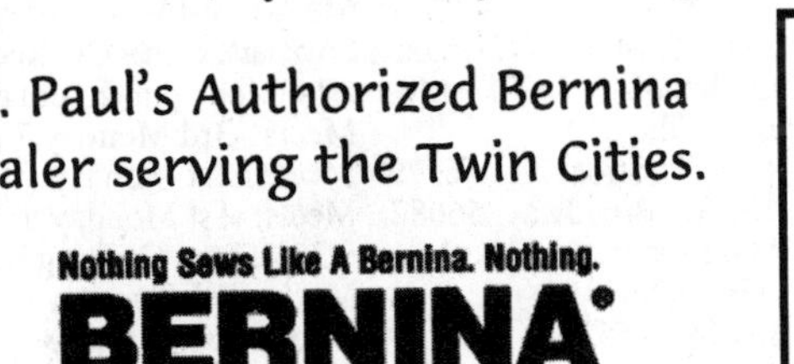

Join us for Patchwork Thursdays

Other Shops in Minnesota: *We suggest calling first*

Afton	Afton Quiltworks, 3192 Saint Croix Trail S	651-436-4065
Alexandria	The Quilt Shop, 1903 Cty. Rd. 22 W	320-763-7177
Anoka	Always Reach for the Stars, 7731 172nd NW	763-753-5074
Apple Valley	Fabric Town, 7655 W. 148th St.	952-432-1827
Bagley	Gram's House Of Quilts, RT 2 Box 55A	218-694-3000
Baxter	Tangled Threads, 149 Norway Dr. N	218-828-3087
Bemidji	Quilting Keepsakes, 8732 Country Club NE	218-751-5954
Bloomington	Stretch & Sew, 521 W 98th St	612-884-7321
Brainerd	Colorz for Quilts, 317 W Washington St	218-825-9101
Burnsville	Heavenly Jugs, 13211 Upton Ave S	952-220-2946
Chanhassen	QuiltSMART, 775 West 96th St.	612-445-5737
Cokato	Moose Tree Village, 290 Millard Ave. SW	320-286-5900
Crookston	Veronica's Quilt Haven, 303 S. Main St.	218-281-5374
Crosslake	Stone Creek Craft Supplies, 34257 Cty Rd 3	218-692-1755
Dassel	The Quilted Barn, 72985 - 215th St.	320-275-0155
Deer River	Needle Nook, 37584 County Road 129	218-246-2794
Duluth	Cindy's Creative Quilting, 2904 W 3rd St	218-924-8337
Duluth	Quilters Coop, 319 N. Central Ave.	218-628-2900
Duluth	Pine Needle Quilting, 3566 W. Tischer Rd.	218-728-6950
Farmington	Homemade Stitches, 3731 Upper 204th St. W	612-460-6213
Fosston	Best Friends Quilting, 808 Mark Ave N	218-435-2087
Hoffman	Nuts & Bolts Quilt Shop, 213 1st St. N	320-986-2447
Hollandale	The Seed Room, 103 Central Ave. S	507-889-6351
Howard Lake	Piece Makers Quilt Shoppe, 809 6th	320-543-3107
Janesville	Treasures of the Heart, 235 390th Ave	507-234-6804
Lake Crystal	Mustard Seed Quilting, 753 Fox Ct	507-726-6644
Le Sueur	River Bobbin, 119 S. 5th St.	507-665-4057
Mabel	Quilter's Heaven & Gifts, 121 N. Main St.	507-493-5666
Mahnomen	Back Porch Quilts, 117 N Main St	218-936-5607
Menahga	Lorraine's Sewing & Quilting, 214 1st St. NE	218-564-4047
Merrifield	K Dee Quilt Shop, 21755 Cty. Rd. 3	218-833-0176
Minneapolis	Bernina Sewing, 10550 France Ave. S	952-888-5100
Mora	Miss Fannie Turgeon's, 206 W. Forest Ave.	320-679-4842
Mountain Lake	Quilts & More, 1104 6th Ave.	507-427-2728
New London	Flying Goose Quilt Shop, 13 N. Main St.	320-354-3535
Oklee	The Oklee Quilt Shop, 128 S. Main St.	218-796-5151
Owatonna	The Doll House, 720 S. Oak Ave.	507-451-6642
Park Rapids	Miss Molly's Mercantile,105 Lake Ave.	218-732-6537
Pelican Rapids	Calico Cupboard 25 1st Ave. NW	218-863-4681
Pelican Rapids	Skunk Hill Quilting, 40575 Skunk Hill	218-863-4748
Perham	Quilt It by the Bay, 116 2nd Ave. SW	218-346-7399
Perham	Quilter's Cabin, 49684 440th St	218-346-6261
Princeton	Cindy's Stitches, 13920 Cty. Rd. 42	763-389-8788
Redwood Falls	Crow Creek Quilting, 36248 Crow Creek	507-644-3261
Rochert	Cotton Hive, 20413 County Hwy 32	218-847-7080
Rochester	Quilts Galore, 357 Elton Hills Dr. NW	507-288-2220
Roseau	Quilt S'more, 32105 St. Hwy. 310	218-463-3867
St. Charles	Amish Market Sq., I - 90 & Hwy 74	507-932-5907
St. James	Stitch-A-Quilt, 806 1st Ave. S	507-375-7757
St. James	Sue's Quilt Stitchery, 504 1st Ave S	507-375-5588
St. Paul	Treadle Yard Goods, 1338 Grand Ave.	651-698-9690
St. Paul	Moose Country Quilting, 957 Cty. Rd. BW	651-646-5218
St. Paul	Roses' Vintage, 1330 Grand Ave	651-696-5242
Thief River Falls	Quiltingly Yours, 212 Parkview St.	218-681-6780
Thief River Falls	Annette's Fabrics, 212 E. 3rd St.	218-681-3501
Truman	Quilting Thimble, 105 E 6th St	
Walnut Grove	Plum Creek Patchwork, Rt. 2, Box 95	
Wells	The Creative Needle, 135 S. Broadway	507-553-3195
West Concord	Pieces Be With You, 54336 237th Ave.	507-356-4255
Willman	Material World Quilt Shoppe, 101 1st St S	320-235-8080
Zimmerman	Blue Hill Quilting, 29844 152nd St NW	763-633-8322

Minneapolis Guilds:

Alexandria	Lakes Area Quilting Guild, 1219 S. Nokomis, 56308	Meets: 3rd Monday (Sept - Nov & Jan - May) 7:30 p.m. at County Historical Society
Anoka	Peace-By-Piece Quilt Guild	Meets: Last Tuesday 10 a.m.
Austin	Keepsake Quilters, 810 2nd Ave. NW, 55912	Meets: 1st Thursday 7 p.m. at St. Johns Lutheran Church, 704 7th Ave. SW
Bemidji	Headwaters Quilters, 1285 Paul Bunian Dr NE, 56601	Meets: 1st Tuesday @ 6:30 at Bethel Lutheran Church
Braham	Hands all around Quilters, P.O. Box 329, 55006	
Brainerd	Pine Tree Patchworkers, P.O. Box 935, 56401	Meets: 2nd Monday at various locations
Buffalo Lake	Quilters along the Yellowstone Trail, P.O. Box 261, 55314	
Cannon Falls	Common Threads, 500 E. Minnesota St., 55009	
Grand Rapids	Loon Country Quilters, 4646 Hwy. 2 E., 55744	
Cannon Falls	Piece Makers Quilting Group, 402 W. Mill St.	Meets: 2nd Tues. & Thur. 9:30, also 2nd Thursday 1:30 and 7 p.m. Quilts by the Falls
Chaska	Chaska Area Quilt Guild, P.O. Box 44, 55318	
Hackensack	Heartland Quilters	
Coon Rapids	WOW - (Women of the West), 251 - 110th Ave N, 55448	Meets: 4th Monday @ 7pm at Medina Entertainment Center, Medina MN
Eden Prairie	Minnesota Quilter Inc., 55344	
Gibbon	Piecemakers Quilt Guild, R.R. #1, Box 150	
Elk River	Pieceful Hearts Quilt Club	Meets: 3rd Monday 7 p.m.
Fergus Falls	Country Quilters	Meets: 3rd Tuesday 9 a.m. at First Baptist Church, 629 Channing Ave. E
Fergus Falls	Evening Guild	Meets: 1st Monday 7 p.m. at Pioneer Nursing Home Comm. Room, 1006 Sheridan Ave. S
Hoffman	Thimbleberries Quilt Club, 213 1st St. N 56339	Meets: 4th Tuesday 7 p.m. at Nuts & Bolts
International Falls	Northern Lights	Meets: Monday's 11:30 a.m. at First Lutheran Church
Lake City	Flying Bobbins	Meets: 3rd Thursday 7 p.m. at First Lutheran Church
Luverne	Blue Mound Quilters, 56156	Meets: 1st Monday 7:30 p.m. in the Library Basement
Mankato	Deep Valley Quilters, 207 McConnel St	Meets: 2nd Thursday 1:30 PM & 7 PM at Christ The King Lutheran Church
Marshall	Threadbenders	Meets: 1st Monday
New Ulm	Prairie Piecemakers, 101 N. German, 56073	Meets: 2nd Thursday 7 p.m. at Marktplatz Mall
North St. Paul	Northern Material Girls, 2580 7th Ave 55109	Meets: 3rd Monday @ 7pm at Silver Lake United Methodist Church
Owatonna	Heritage Quilt Guild of Southern Minnesota, 110 W Broadway, 55060	Meets: 2nd Thursday 7 p.m. at United Prairie Bank
Perham	Thimbleberries Quilt Club	Meets: 3rd Wednesday 9:30 a.m., 1 p.m., and 6 p.m. at Bay Window Crafts
Plymouth	W.O.W.--Women of the West	Meets: 7 pm 4th Mon Plymouth Covenant, corner Old Rockford Rd. & Vicksburg Ln. www.winternet.com/~milo/wow
Rochester	Rochester Quilters' Sew-Ciety, P.O. Box 6245, 55903	Meets: 1st Mon 1pm & 7pm at Calvary Evangelical Free Church 5500 25th Guenive NE
Rush City	Rush City Piecemakers Quilt Guild, 55069	Meets: 3rd Monday 7 p.m. at Community Center
Sauk Rapids	Rapid Quilter's Quild, 2078 - 45th Street NE, 56379	Meets: 1st Monday @ 7pm at Bound in Stitches Quilt Village
St. Peter	Ewenique Quilters Guild, 101 W. Broadway, 56082	Meets: 1st Monday at Mary Lue's Yarn & Quilt
Staples	Piecemaker's Quilt Club, P.O. Box 26, 56479	Meets: 3rd Thurs Quilting Memories, Holds a quilt show every other year (05 next)
Thief River Falls	Thief River Falls Quilter's Guild, 56701	Meets: 4th Tuesday at Northland Community College
Tower	Vermilion Dream Quilters, PO Box 597 55790	Meets: 1st Thursday @ 6:30 p.m. at North Country Quilts
Virginia	Going to Pieces Quilters	Meets: 3rd Tuesday 7 p.m. at First Covenant Church
Wabasha	River City Quilters	Meets: 1st Tuesday 7 p.m. at St. Elizabeths Hospital Community Room
Waseca	Stitchers In Time Quilt Club, 107 2nd St. NW, 56093	Meets: 2nd Tuesday 10 a.m. at Happy Hands Shoppe
Willmar	Country Quilters, 56201	Meets: 2nd Tuesday at 7 p.m.

The Quilting Bee

Large selection of brand name fabrics, books, patterns, kits and notions.
Located in historic downtown Ocean Springs. A quilter's destination on the Gulf Coast!

Mon - Fri 9 - 5:30
Thur til 8 Sun 12 - 4 Closed Sat

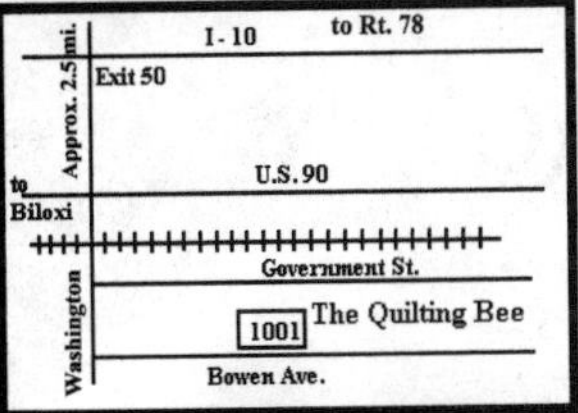

1001 Bowen Ave 39564
(228) 818-9560
thequiltingbee@bellsouth.net
Owner: Cheri Leffler
Est: 2003 3000 sq.ft.

Ocean Springs, MS #1

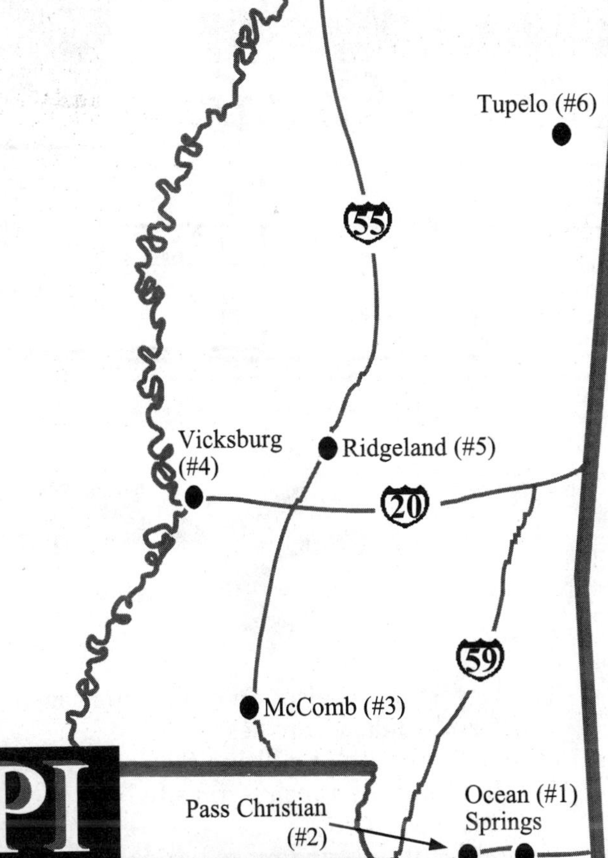

MISSISSIPPI

6 Featured Shops

Looking for a great place to visit?

The Mississippi Gulf Coast is *THE* Place!

Pass Christian, MS #2

Fabrics, Patterns, Books, Classes and Notions of the finest quality from top manufacturers and designers.

Our gift department will delight and appeal to your sense of fun.

Oakes & Acorns, Inc.

106 W. Second Street
Pass Christian, MS 39571
228-452-1221
www.oakesandacorns.com

Tues - Fri 10 - 5
Sat 10 - 4

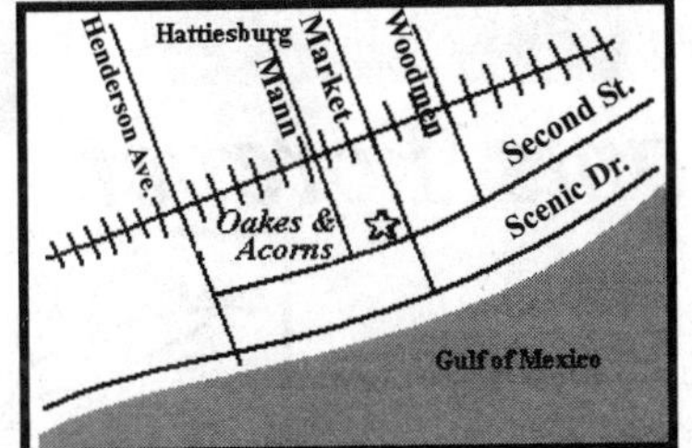

Just 10 Miles from I-10 !
Take I-10 to Exit 24 (Menge Ave), go south to E. Second Street, turn right. We are just past Market Street.

McComb, MS #3

Mon - Fri 9 - 5
Sat 9 - 1

Fast Threads

111 Burke St. 39648
(601) 249-0787
Est: 2000

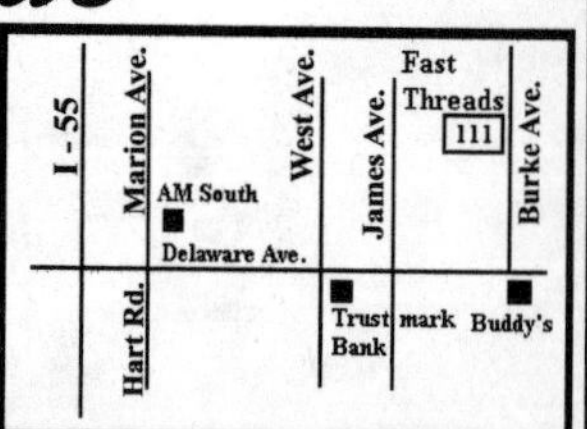

Over 1500 bolts of 100% cotton fabrics! Books, patterns & notions for all your quilting needs. Best (only) quilt shop in Southwestern Mississippi.

Vicksburg, MS #4

Mon - Sat 9 - 5:30

Stitch-N-Frame

2222 S. Frontage Rd., Suite D 39180
(601) 634-0243 Fax: (601) 634-0287
kmccoy@vicksburg.com
www.stitch-n-frame.net

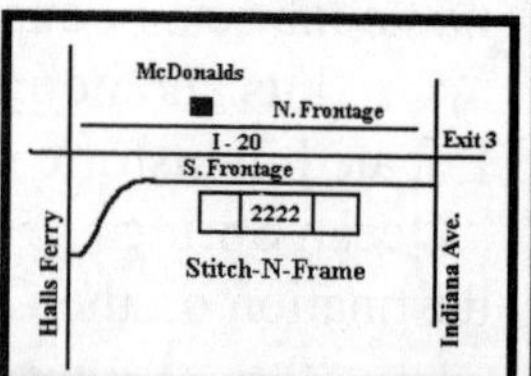

Owner: Kay Elliott Est: 1983 2800 sq.ft. Home of Ulmer Quilt frames. Anywear Shoes. Over 5000 bolts plus all the supplies you'll need. Join our on-line newsletter to get our "Thursday Specials". Numerous Blocks of the Month. Toll free # (877) 634-1462

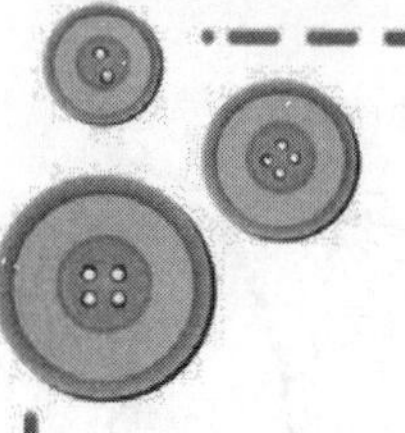

- The largest local selection of Bernina sewing machines
- Great embroidery supplies
- Over 2,500 bolts of quilting fabric
- Bernina machine repairs—on site by our technician
- Notions, notions, and more notions....
- State of the art classroom with the most comfortable seating in Mississippi

Mon-Sat 9-4
Thursday til 7

#5 665 S. Pear Orchard Rd. , Ste 104
Ridgeland, MS 39157
(601)991-2120 (601)991-2123—fax
E-mail: ann@berninasewingetc.com
Owners: Ann & Nolen Hudson

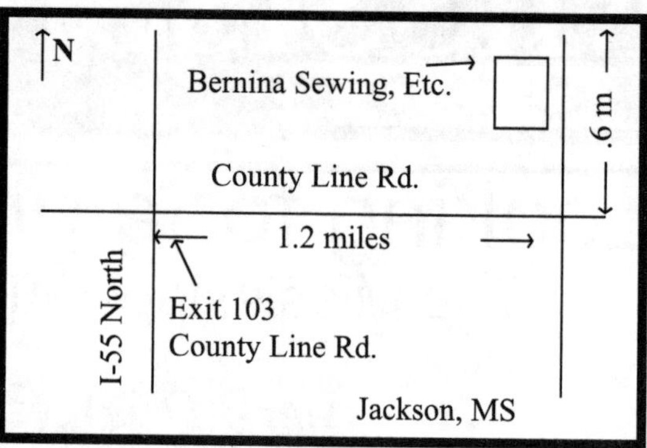

Visit our website at www.berninasewingetc.com!!!!

Tupelo, MS #6

Mon - Sat 10 - 5:30

Heirlooms Forever

3112 Cliff Gookin Blvd. 38801
(662) 842-4275 or (800) 840-4275
Fax: (662) 842-2284 Est: 1983
kathy@sews.com 7000 sq.ft.
www.sews.com

Over 1500 bolts of fabrics, quilting supplies, books, notions, threads, Bernina, Brother, Pfaff & Viking Machines Sales & Service. Helpful & Friendly.

Other Shops in Mississippi: *We suggest calling first*

Bay St. Louis	Bungalow, 136 Main St	228-466-2651
Booneville	Quilt Gallery, 1114 Hwy. 30	601-728-3302
Brookhaven	Melanie's Fabric, 128 W. Monticello St.	601-833-4608
Jackson	Continental Sewing Center, 1491 Canton Mart Rd	601-956-6376
Meridian	The Corner Stitch, 1820 23rd Ave	601-693-2739
Meridian	The Craft Cottage, 2034 40th St	601-482-2821

Mississippi Guilds:

Carriere	Piecemakers Quilt Guild, 39426	Meets: 1st Saturday 9:30 a.m. at Baptish Church, 7264 Hwy. 11 N
Hattiesburg	Pine Belt Quilters	
Hattiesburg	Mississippi Quilt Association 909 N. 31st Ave. 39401	
Purvis	Pine Belt Quilters50 Timberland Dr., 39475	Meets: 3rd Wednesday at 9:30 a.m. at University Baptist Church
Tupelo	Sew Pieceful Quilting Guild, 3112 Cliff Gookin Blvd, 38801	Meets: 1st Tuesday @ 7pm at Heirlooms Forever
Vicksburg	Vicksburg Quilters	Meets: 2nd Saturday 9:30 a.m. at Stitch-n-Frame

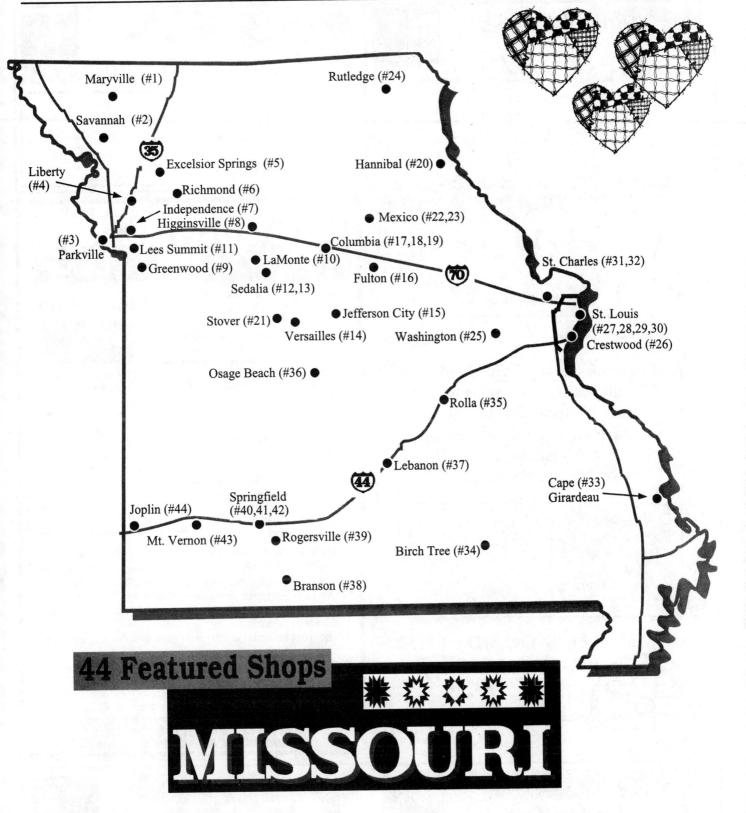

Maryville (#1)
Savannah (#2)
(#3) Parkville
Liberty (#4)
Excelsior Springs (#5)
Richmond (#6)
Independence (#7)
Higginsville (#8)
Greenwood (#9)
LaMonte (#10)
Lees Summit (#11)
Sedalia (#12,13)
Versailles (#14)
Jefferson City (#15)
Fulton (#16)
Columbia (#17,18,19)
Hannibal (#20)
Stover (#21)
Mexico (#22,23)
Rutledge (#24)
Washington (#25)
Crestwood (#26)
St. Louis (#27,28,29,30)
St. Charles (#31,32)
Cape (#33) Girardeau
Birch Tree (#34)
Rolla (#35)
Osage Beach (#36)
Lebanon (#37)
Branson (#38)
Rogersville (#39)
Springfield (#40,41,42)
Mt. Vernon (#43)
Joplin (#44)
35
70
44

44 Featured Shops

MISSOURI

Maryville, MO #1

Tues - Fri 10 - 5:30
Sat 10 - 4:30

Thimble 'n Thread

1312 S. Main St. 64468
(660) 562-4955
Owner: Patty Bagby
Est: 1994 1400 sq.ft. 1500 Bolts

Area's largest selection of quilting books, patterns, fabric. Enjoy charming displays, friendly helpful service. Classes. Bernina Machines. Custom quilting service.

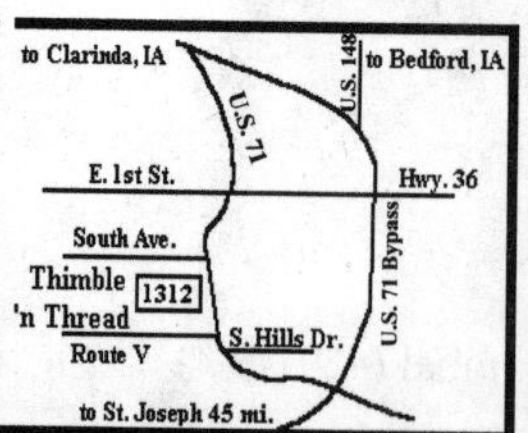

Savannah, MO #2

Mon - Fri 9 - 5
Tues til 9
Sat 9 - 4

Wild Hare Quilt Shop

420 Court St. 64485
(816) 324-4053
wildhare@ponyexpress.net
Owner: Melanie Rouse 3000+ bolts

Fabrics, Books, Patterns, Notions, Classes

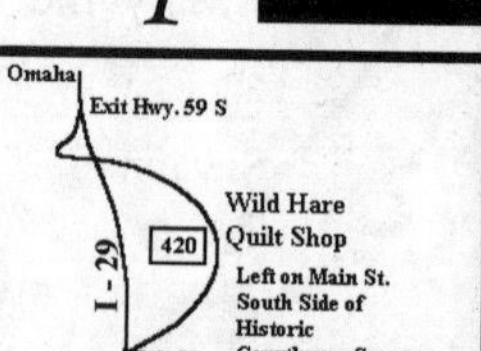

Parkville, MO #3

Peddler's Wagon

Everything a quilter needs plus friendly smiles and expert help.
Huge Collection of Models
***Featured in 1996 Quilt Sampler Magazine ***
Est: 1982 3400 sq.ft.

Hours:
10 - 5
Tues. - Sat.
Extended Holiday hours

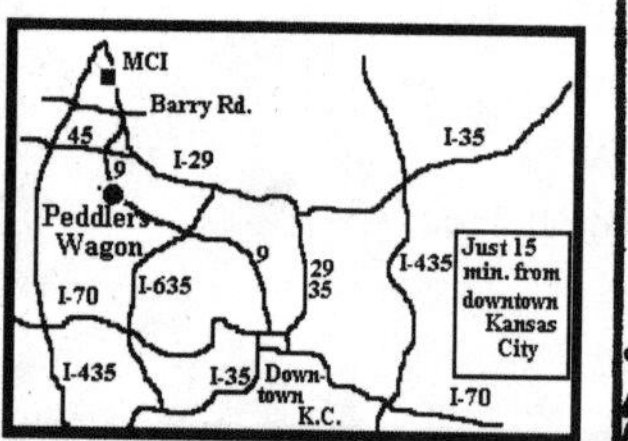

115 Main Parkville, MO 64152
816-741-0225

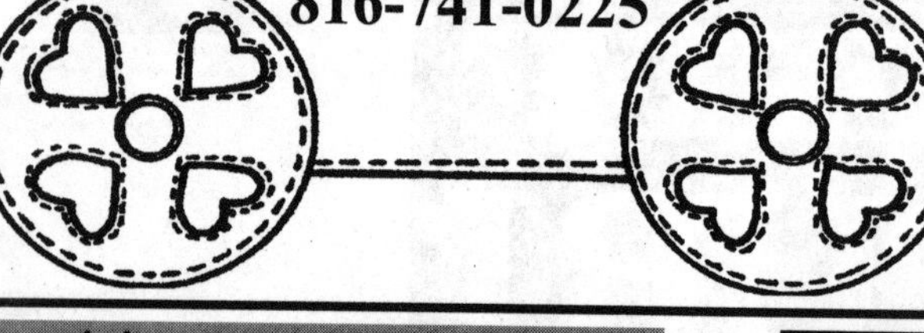

Winding River Quilt Shop

Owner: Lisa Winkler

249 W. Mill St., Suite 101 64068
816-415-2686
wrquilting@sbcglobal.net
www.windingriverquiltshop.com
Est: 2002 2400 sq.ft.

Mon - Fri 10 - 6
Sat 10 - 4

Winding River Quilt Shop is where quilters go to shop. With a wide selection of beautiful fabrics and hundreds of books and patterns, it is no wonder that thousands of quilters from all over the world rely on Winding River for their quilting needs. Come experience the fun of beautiful fabrics including; period, reproductions, contemporary, and traditional designs from the top fabrics makers - Moda, RJR/ Thimbleberries, P&B, Hoffman, Benartex and more.

I - 35
Hwy. 291
Ridge
Kansas St.
Hwy. 152
Exit 16
Mill St.
Sunset
249
Liberty Dr.
Winding River

While visiting Winding River be sure you experience:

* The Notions Nook for a great selection of the latest notions.
* The Wool Corner has a wide selection of hand-dyed wools.
* Our fully equipped classroom - classes for all levels.
* The Thimbleberries Collection for the latest in Lynette's fabrics & patterns.
* The most beautiful selection of quilt samples and kits using the latest designs and fabrics.

Winding River offers long-arm quilting services using the latest in Gammill stitch-regulating technology and you get your quilt back in weeks - not months. Come see why Winding River has quilting customers in 48 states!

Liberty, MO #4

Excelsior Springs, MO #5

Tues - Sat 10 - 5

The Wooden Spool

233 E. Broadway 64024
(816) 630-5063
Owner: Jamie Fondren

Great quilt shop opened in May 2002 in our newly renovated turn of the century building. For all of your quilting needs: Fabric, Notions, Books, Patterns, Kits and Classes.

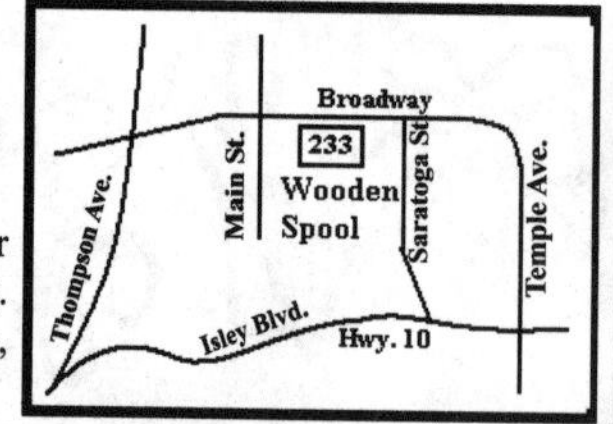

Richmond, MO #6

Mon - Fri 10 - 5
Sat 9 - 5

I'D RATHER BE QUILTING

108 Wollard Blvd. 64084
(816) 776-7622
Owner: Laurel Kindley
Est: 2003

kindley@idratherbequilting.com
www.idratherbequilting.com

Full service quilt shop with all your quilting supplies. Professional long-arm quilting, classes, and quilt finishing services available.

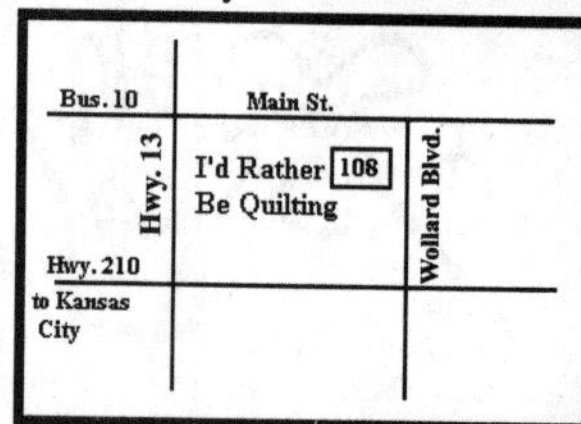

Independence, MO #7

RUSTIC YEARNINGS

17601 A East 40 Hwy. Colonnade Shopping Center 64055
(816) 373-2423 rusticy@aol.com
Est: 1993 8500 sq.ft. 6000+ Bolts
www.rusticyearnings.com

Large Selection of Books, Notions, Patterns & Fabrics for Quilting and Crafting. Also unique Home Accessories & Gifts plus P. Buckley Moss Gallery.

Open 7 Days

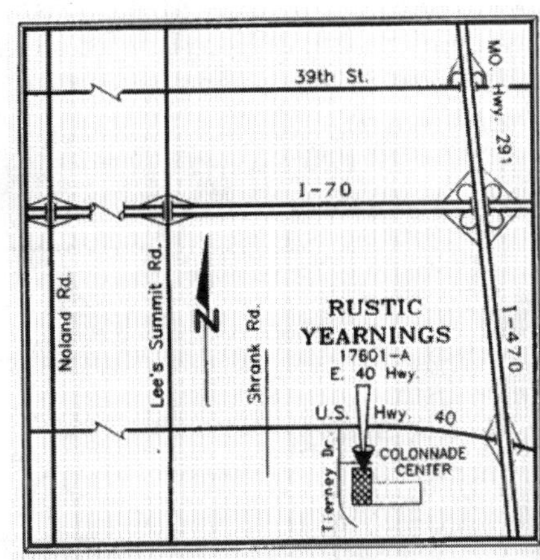

Higginsville, MO #8

Mon - Fri 9:30 - 6
Thur til 8
Sat 10 - 4

Quilter's Harvest

1913 Main St. 64037
(660) 584-3399
quilter@ctcis.net
www.quiltersharvest.com
Owners: Pam Fisher & Donna Campbell
Est: 2000 1300 sq.ft. 1600+ Bolts

Everything a quilter needs! Quality fabrics, notions, books, patterns and kits. We now carry Koala sewing machine cabinets and chairs. Always ready to help with friendly service.

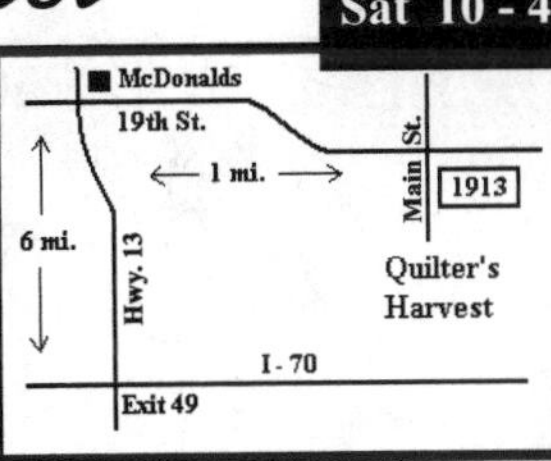

Greenwood, MO #9

Tues - Sat 10 - 5

Calico Cat Quilt Shop

106 5th Ave. S 64034
(816) 537-8855 Est: 2003
calicocatquiltshop@earthlink.net
Owners: Betty Mathis & Sherrie Montgomery

Located in the heart of Greenwood's Antique Shopping area. Broad selection of fabrics, especially 1930's and 1800's Reproductions.

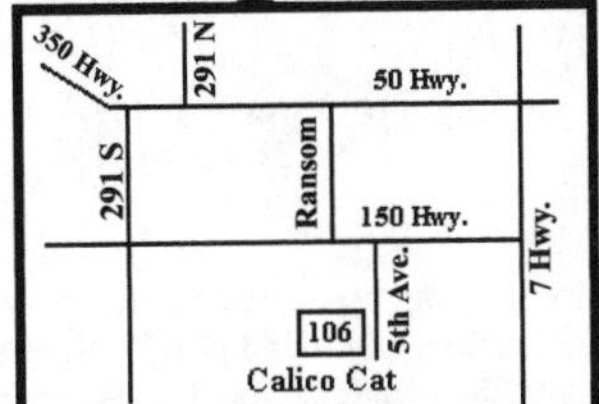

LaMonte, MO #10

Mon - Thur 9 - 6
Fri 9 - 7
Sat 9 - 4

Patches Place

Hwy. 50 & Pleasant Green Rd.
P.O. Box 98 65337
(660) 347-5150 Fax: Same
Owner: Valerie Studer

Large selection of quilting & Fashion Fabrics. Notions, books, patterns, Embroidery CD's Quilt Squares. Everyday Low prices!

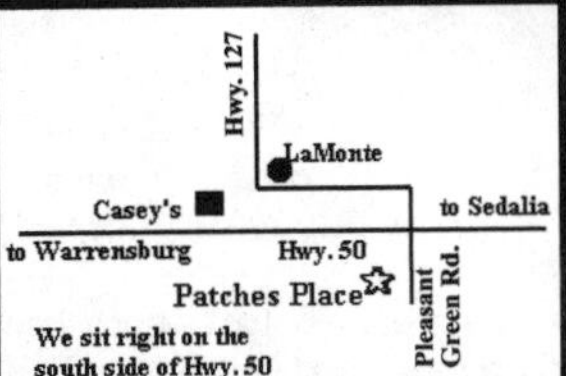

824 SW Blue Parkway
Lee's Summit, MO 64063

(816) 525-8955
quiltersstation@prodigy.net
www.quiltsstation.com

Toll Free 1-866-649-8024

Over 5000 bolts of the latest in fabrics including, Benartex, Moda, Hoffman, RJR, Kona Bay and others. As well as a large selection of books, patterns, and notions. Classes available.

Lees Summit, MO #11

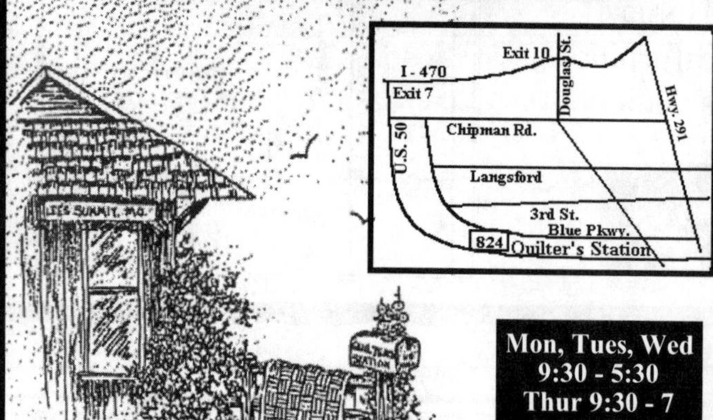

Mon, Tues, Wed 9:30 - 5:30
Thur 9:30 - 7
Fri 9:30 - 5
Sat 9:30 - 4

Sedalia, MO #12

Mon - Fri 9 - 5
Sat 9 - 4

D & T Quilt Shop

3620 S. Marshall 65301
(660) 826-4788 Fax: (660) 826-4788
dandt@murlin.com
Owner: Theresa Gerber
Est: 1991 1200 sq.ft.

Fabrics, Notions, Embroidery Blocks, Classes. 4500+ Bolts. Buttons by the Lb. $4.99. Happy to ship orders. Hand & Machine Quilting. We'll also sew your tops together. Friendly Country Atmosphere

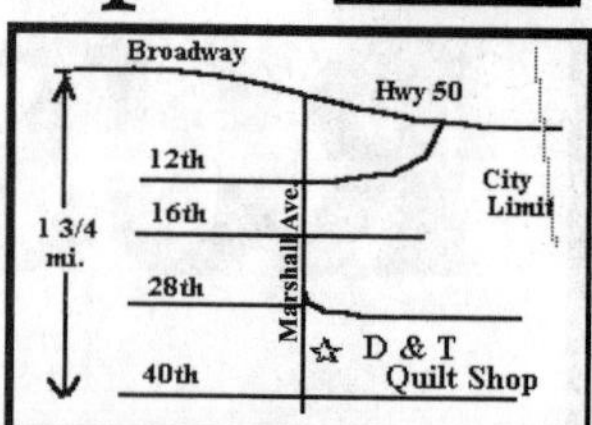

Sedalia, MO #13

The Nimble Thimble

Located in historic downtown Sedalia, we offer the most exciting cotton fabrics in town along with books, notions, unique patterns, wool and hand crafted gifts and jewelry. Authorized Viking Sales and service. Machine embroidery supplies, Sulky & Mettler threads, Moda, Thimbleberries, Debbie Mumm and friendly, helpful service.

Mon - Fri 9 - 5 Sat 9 - 2

214 S. Ohio 65301
(660) 827-7400
Fax: (660) 827-7469
Nimble_Thimble@sbcglobal.net
Owners: Julia Vandiver
And Lois Boggs
Est: 2002 2000 sq.ft.

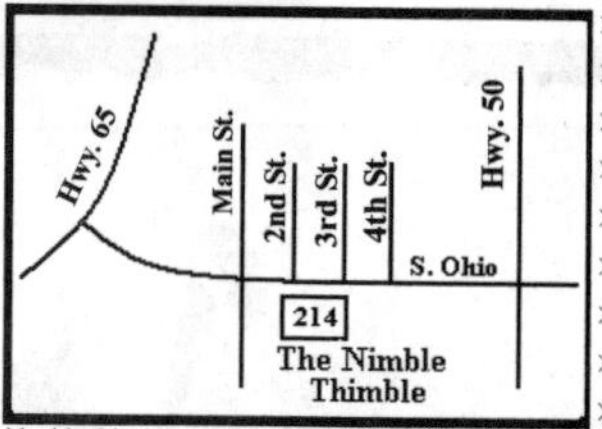

Versailles, MO #14

Mon - Sat 9 - 5

Clark's Fabrics

813 W. Newton 65084
West Vue Shopping Center
Hwy 5 & 52 W. Est: 1964
(573) 378-5696 1800 sq.ft. 1700 Bolts
Owner: Kirk Chapman

Great selection of all types of fabric, including quilting, clothing and home decorating.

Buttons, Buttons, Buttons !

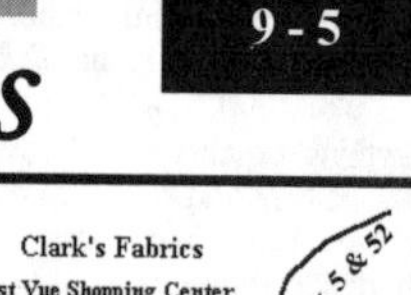

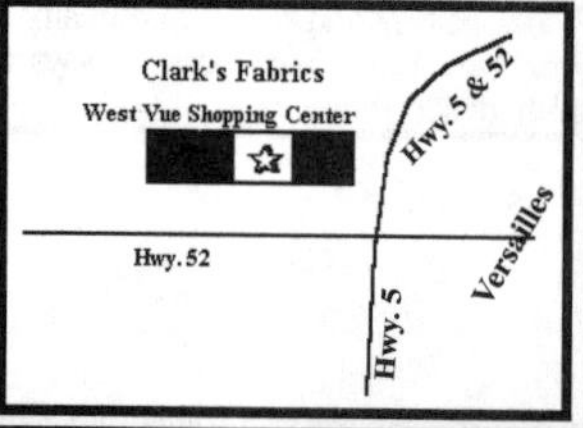

Jefferson City, MO #15

Mon & Sat 10 - 3
Tu, Th, Fri 10 - 6
Wed 10 - 8

The Quilter's Haven

2503 Industrial Dr. 65109
(573) 556-8900 Fax: (573) 556-8909
lori@thequiltershaven.com
www.thequiltershaven.com
Est: 2000 3000 sq.ft. 1000+ bolts
"Where quilters go to pieces!"
High quality fabrics, notions, books, patterns, embroidery blocks, handmade oak wood products, classes and clubs.

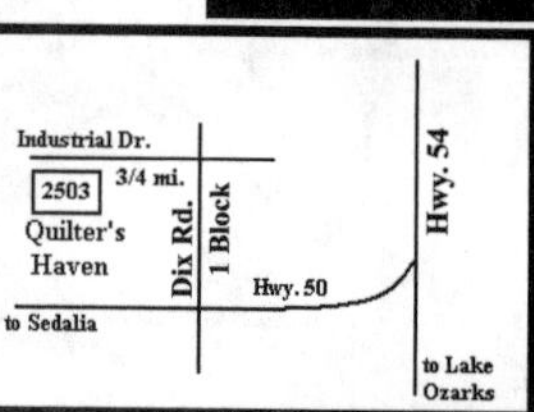

Fulton, MO #16

Tues - Fri 10 - 5
Thur til 6:30
Sat 10 - 4

Quilting Bee

517 C Court St. 65251
(573) 642-4100
jmehmert@coin.org
Est: 2003 2000+ bolts

2,000 Fabric Bolts, Notions, books, patterns, classes too. Just 7 miles from Exit 148 on I - 70.

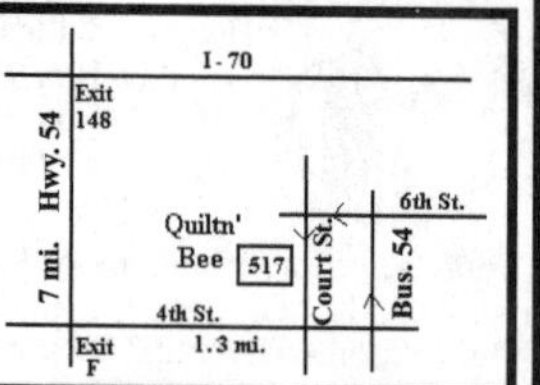

Columbia, MO #17

Tues - Thur 10 - 6
Fri & Sat 10 - 5
Sun 12 - 4

Miss Millie's Quilt Shop

3601 Buttonwood, Suite G 65201
(573) 449-8844
2400 sq. ft.

Specializing in Thimbleberries & Jinny Beyer fabrics. Our own line of Gingham Lace (Chicken Scratch) patterns and books.

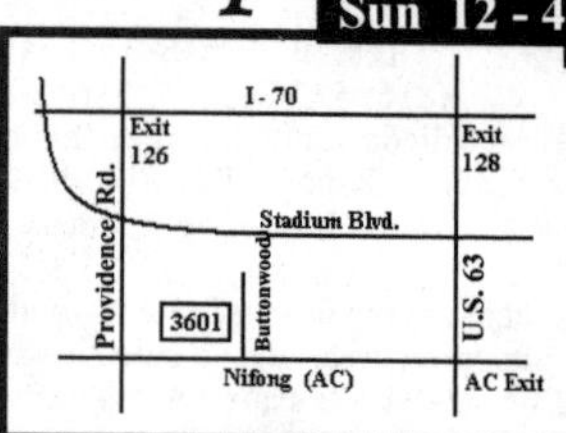

#18

Husqvarna VIKING

Come Quilt with Us .... Visit Silks & More on your next trip to the Midwest.

We're sew much more than just a fabric store.

KEEPING THE WORLD SEWING

- 5,000 sq. ft. of Quilting Paradise
- Extensive Quilting Department
- Heirloom Sewing & Smocking Supplies
- Great Selection of Quilting Books
- Wide Assortment of Patterns & Notions
- Husqvarna Viking Sewing Machines
- Lots of Fun Sewing Classes including Quilting, Fashion, Wearable Art, Heirloom Sewing, & Sew Much More!

Directions:

Silks & More Fine Fabrics is located in the heart of Missouri quilting country half way between St. Louis and Kansas City on Interstate 70. Take exit #124 - Stadium Blvd. Turn south on Stadium, then turn right on to Bernadette Dr. (second stop light at Wendy's Restaurant). We are located in Bernadette Square, a shopping center on your right, across from the Columbia Mall.

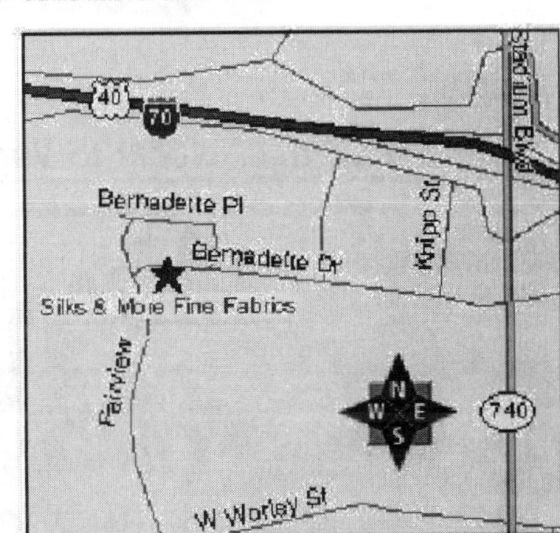

We also now have four additional Viking Centers located inside these JoAnns Fabrics Centers:

Affton, MO	St. Charles, MO
Ferguson, MO	and in Columbia, MO

www.silksnmore.com
Email: sewing@silksnmore.com
Established 1985

Hours:

10 - 7	Mon - Thr
10 - 5	Fri & Sat
12 - 4	Sundays

SILKS & MORE FINE FABRICS & VIKING CENTERS

2541 Bernadette Dr.
Columbia, MO 65203

573-446-2655
1-800-269-2655

Satin Stitches
SEWING & EMBROIDERY

FABRICS $2.00 OFF EVERYDAY!

* FABRICS *
* HANDI QUILTER - HQ16 *
* CLASSES *
* GENERATIONS *
* ORIGINS * SOFTWARE *
* NOTIONS * BOOKS *

MACHINES AS LOW AS $159.00

Financing Available!

PFAFF
Authorized Dealer

brother
Authorized Dealer

Columbia, MO #19

705 D VANDIVER DR. COLUMBIA, MO 65202
573-817-0006 800-463-2483
Mon. - Thurs. 10:00-5:30 Fri. & Sat. 9:30-3:30
www.marcysewing.com

Where Sewing FUN begins!

Directions:
Interstate 70 to EXIT 127 (east or west)
Go North (1 block) to Vandiver Drive, Inside Vandiver Village

---

Hickory Stick

Hannibal, MO #20

Quilt & Gift Shop

326 N. Main
Hannibal, MO 63401
(573)221-4538
Fax: (573)248-0396

Extensive Collection Of Redwork

email: jframe@socket.net
Located across from Mark Twain's Home

- Fabrics *including* Cotton, Wools, Flannel, and 54" Decorator
- Quilting Supplies
- Books & Patterns
- Primitive Stitchery
- Stamped Embroidery Kits & Floss
- Unique Buttons
- Wholecloth Quilt Tops
- Handbags & Tote Accessories

- Open Daily-

4 Beautiful Rooms of Home Decor Accesories

- Table Settings
- Retro Decor
- Florals & Wall Decor
- Lamps
- Fine Linens & Quilts

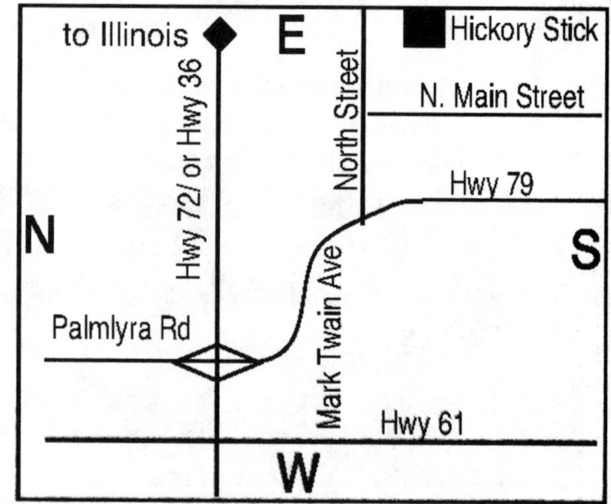

Est: 1998

Mexico, MO #22

Sticky Wicket

"Shopping at Sticky Wicket is like coming home."

110 N. Jefferson St., Mexico, MO 65265
(573) 581-6262
www.stickywicketquilt.com
Owner: Mona Leonard
2000+ sq.ft. 2000+ Bolts 2000+ Fat Quarters

Mexico exit off I-70, Highway 54 North (East) to first Mexico exit. Straight on S. Clark to Jackson. Right on Jackson to N. Jefferson, turn left, ½ block on right.

Mon - Sat 9 - 5
Thur til 7

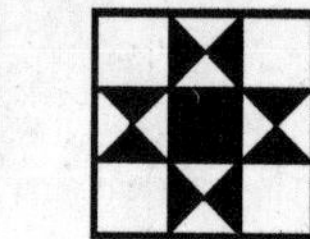

Quality Cotton Fabric, Thimbleberries, Moda, 30's, Benartex, Homespuns and more. Quilt Supplies, Redwork, Stamped Embroidery Blocks, Books & Patterns, Cards, Craft Gift Items, Gifts, Teas, Cocoas, Oak Furniture, Candles, Baskets & much more.

Mexico, MO #23

105 N. Coal 65265
(573) 581-1966
www.homesteadhearth.com
info@homesteadhearth.com
Est: 2002 5500 sq.ft

HOMESTEAD HEARTH

Homestead Hearth is your one-stop resource for:

- Over 3500 bolts of fabric
- Over 7,000 fat quarters -- the largest selection in mid-Missouri
- Books, patterns & notions
- Unique classes on quilting, garments, rug hooking and more
- Gourmet foods, coffees and teas
- Candles, pottery & gift items
- Authorized Janome Dealer

Don't miss the café in the building serving breakfast, sandwiches, salads & desserts

Monday 10 - 5
Tues, Wed 10 - 6
Thursday 10 - 8
Fri & Sat 10 - 5

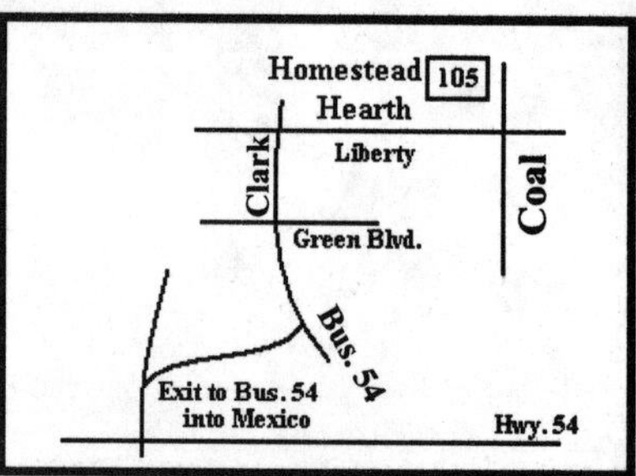

Rutledge, MO #24

Mon - Sat 8 - 5

Zimmerman's Store

Main St., Box 1 63563
(660) 883-5766 Est: 1974
Owners: Paul & Lydia Zimmerman
Mgr: Ellanor Zimmerman

2000 bolts of 100% cotton fabrics at reasonable prices. Batting, quilt patterns & books, sewing notions, hand quilted quilts, pillows, aprons etc.

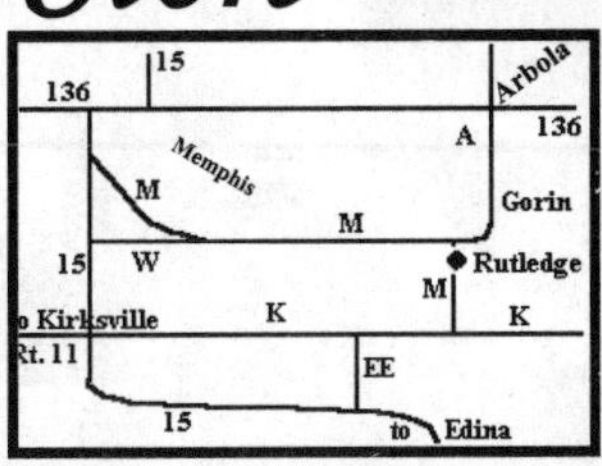

Washington, MO #25

Mon - Fri 10 - 5:30 Sat 10 - 3

Quilt-A-Lot Fabrics

422 E. 5th St., Ste A
(636) 239-1700
quiltalotmo@yahoo.com
www.quiltalot.com Est: 1998

Come visit our new shop located in an historic 1924 Arts & Craft home. Cotton Fabrics, Stencils, Books (pattern, quilt mystery & children's quilt stories). Quilt block by Fairway Needlecrafts, Gifts & more.

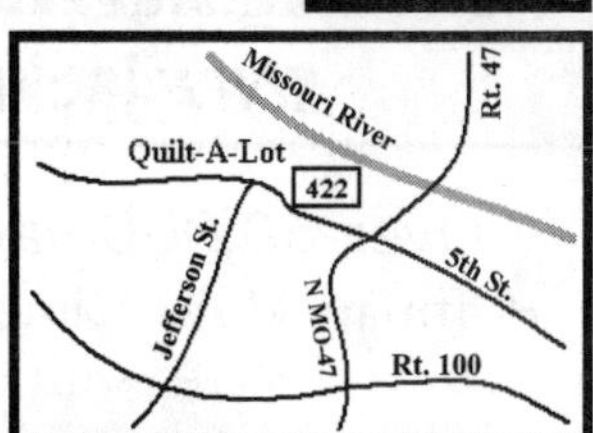

Crestwood, MO #26

Mon - Fri 9:30 - 5 Wed til 8 Sat 9:30 - 4:30

Quilt 'N' Stitch

9109 Watson Rd. 63126
(314) 961-0909 or (888) 681-0909
qltnstitch@aol.com
www.quiltnstitch.net
Owner: Connie Ewbank
Est: 1992 2400 sq.ft. 2000 Bolts

Large selection of fabrics - Christmas, homespuns, contemporary. Books, patterns, notions, classes. Also counted cross stitch.

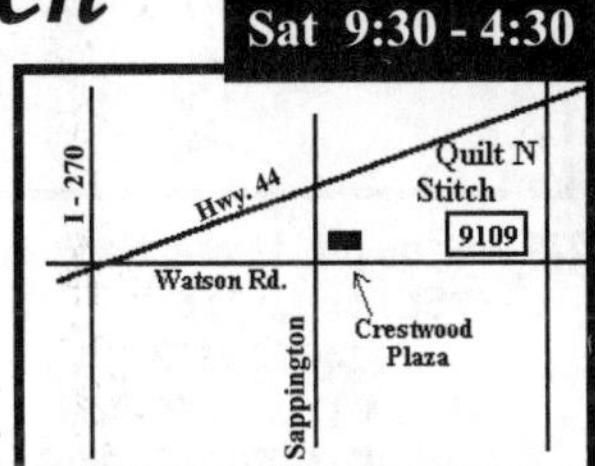

St. Louis, MO #27

Tues - Sat By Appt.

Treasured Keepsakes

1771 Parker Rd. 63138
(314) 741-4018
(800) 300-6316
Est: 1998 Catalog $2

We have a large selection of stamped embroidery. Pearl Cotton. Hand & Machine quilting also special order quilts.

Moving Fall of 2004
For New Location
Call 636-343-0508
or Directory
Information

St. Louis, MO #28

M, W 9:30 - 5
T, Th 9:30 - 6:30
Fri & Sat 9:30 - 4:30

THE QUILTED FOX

SELECTED AS ONE OF THE TOP TEN FEATURED SHOPS
2001 QUILT SAMPLER MAGAZINE
BY BETTER HOMES AND GARDENS

4000 bolts of unique quilting fabrics
International, Asian, Australian, African and more
Fox Fabric club for the out-of towner

Easy Access off & on the highway
Mail Orders always welcome
Handicap Accessible

10403 Clayton Rd., St. Louis, MO 63131
(314) 993-1181
info@quiltedfox.com www.quiltedfox.com
Established 1994; 2500 sq. ft.
Owner: Louise L. Georgia

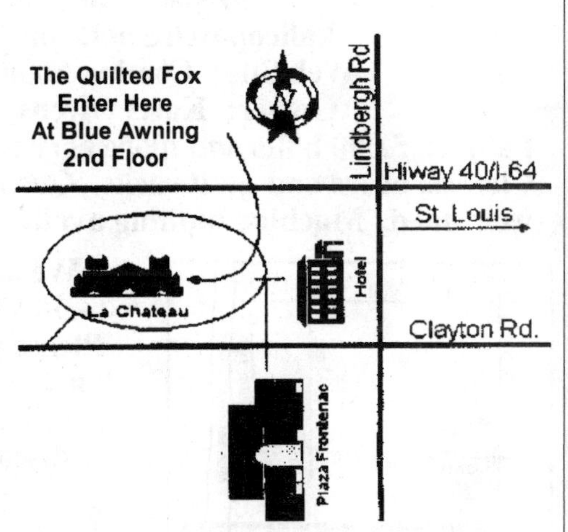

Jackman's Fabrics

Since 1903

www.jackmansfabrics.com

Over 50,000 yards of quilting cottons!
Hoffman, Moda, Timeless Treasures, Benartex, RJR, P&B, South Seas and more . . .

Fabrics designed by Mary Engelbreit, Laurel Burch, Nancy Halvorson, Robin Pandolph, etc.

Huge collection of batiks, marbles, Novelties, patterns, books, etc.

Tremendous displays! Great new ideas!

Baby lock & elna
Sergers, Embroidery & Sewing Machines

Show us this ad and you will receive a 1 time 20% discount on your entire non-sale purchase.

St. Louis, MO #29 & 30

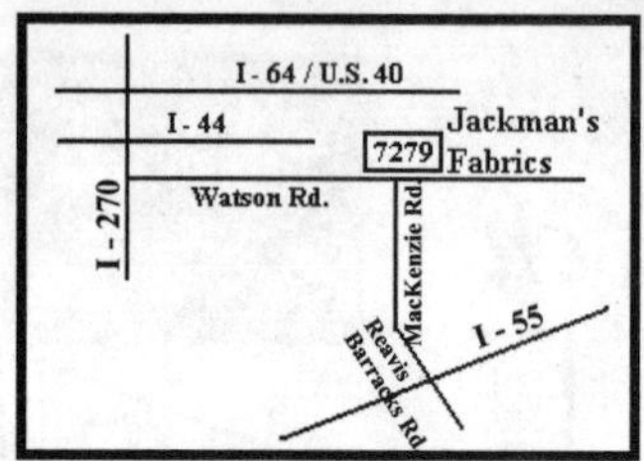

7279 Watson Rd., Mackenzie Pt. Plaza
St. Louis, MO 63119
314-352-7979
Mon. & Thur. 10:00-9:00
Tues., Wed., Fri 10:00-6:00
Sat. 10:00-5:30 • Sun. noon-5:00

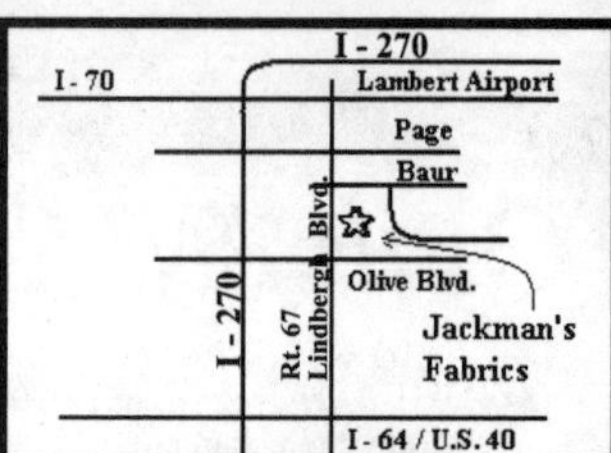

1234 North Lindbergh
St. Louis, MO 63132
314-994-1060
Mon. & Thur. 9:30-9:00
Tues., Wed., Fri 9:30-6:00
Sat. 9:30-5:30 • Sun. noon-5:00

St. Charles, MO #31

"Out of the scraps of my life God has made a beautiful quilt."

Kalico Patch

412 Boone's Lick Rd. 63301
636-946-9520
kalicopatch@aol.com
Web Site: Coming Soon
Owner: Karel Owens

Fabric: 5,000 bolts and more arriving weekly. Classes, bears and quilt racks. Custom orders welcomed. Machine quilting available.

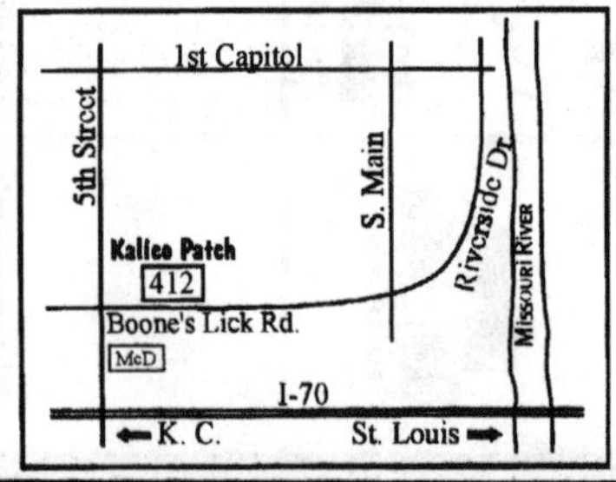

We are a convenient stop for traveling quilters. Our shop is just off I - 70. To accommodate our travelers we offer half-day quilting classes. Please send a SASE for a schedule of our classes. If you are planning a bus tour to the St. Charles area, we will schedule special classes for your quilt group. On your first visit to our store, bring this ad for a 15% discount on fabric and books. In addition, if it happens to be your birthday, bring proof and this ad for a 20% discount.

HOURS: Mon - Sat 9 - 5 Sun 12:30 - 5

Patches Etc. Quilt Shop

First | Capitol Dr. | Fifth St. | Patches Etc. | 337 | South Main | Frontier Park | Missouri River | Boonslick Rd. | I-70

Visit us at: www.patches3.com

Quilts, Fabric and Patterns -- Home of 'Redwork'.

Mon - Sat 9:30 - 5
Sun 11 - 5

Patches etc.

337 South Main 63301
(636) 946-6004
Owner: Ann Watkins-Hazelwood
Est: 1979 1500 Bolts
E-mail: 3patches@prodigy.net

Voted one of the 10 Best Quilt Shops in the 1st edition of Better Homes and Gardens Quilt Magazine.

Historic St. Charles, MO #32

Certified appraisals by Ann Watkins-Hazelwood.

2504 William St.
Cape Girardeau, MO 63703-5763
Toll Free: 1-877-339-7667
I - 55 Exit 96 • East 1 Mile

HOURS:
Mon. - Fri. 9:30 a.m. - 5:30 p.m.
Sat. 9:30 a.m. - 4:00 p.m.

Moda • Hoffman • RJR
Over 1200 bolts

Cape Girardeau, MO #33

Birch Tree, MO #34

Tues - Sat 9 - 5

The Hideaway Quilt Shop

3217 W. 1st St.
P.O. Box 57 65438
(573) 292-1008

Name brand fabrics.
Ready made quilts, too.
Love to share quilting stories.
Come spend an hour or two.

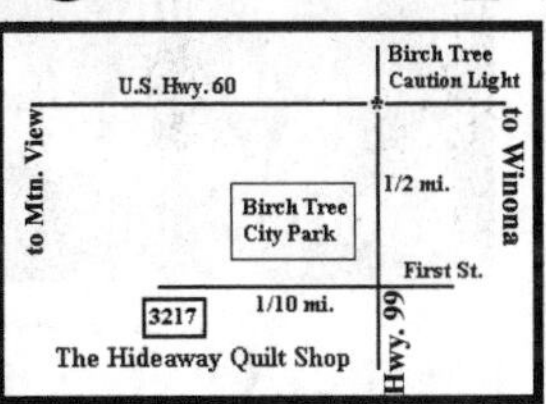

Rolla, MO #35

Mon - Fri 9 - 6
Sat 9 - 4

Fabrics Unlimited

13795 U.S. 63 S 65401
(573) 364-5245
Owner: Betty I. Lewis 1600 sq.ft.
2500 total bolts, 1100+ quilt fabric

Quilting Fabrics, Notions, Batting, Quilt Books. Machine Quilting. Machine Binding. Our main business is quilt supplies.

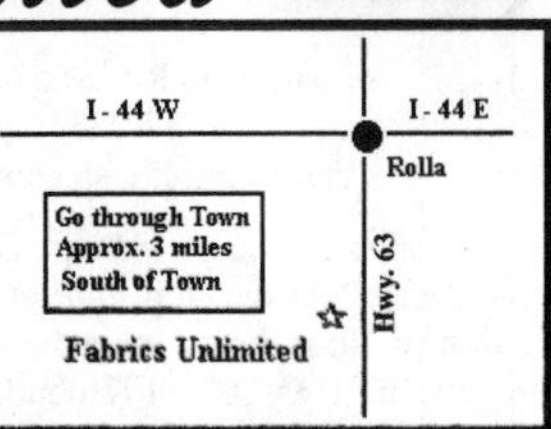

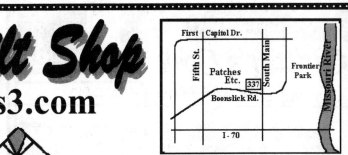

Osage Beach, MO #36

Mon - Fri 10 - 5
Sat 10 - 4

Quilter's Cove

Sewing & Embroidery

3877 Hwy. 54 65065
(573) 302-9923 Est: 2002
E-Mail: Quilterscove1@aol.com
Fabrics - Notions - Books - Patterns. Machine Embroidery Supplies. Sewing & Embroidery Machines. Offering a variety of classes. Authorized Husqvarna Viking Dealer

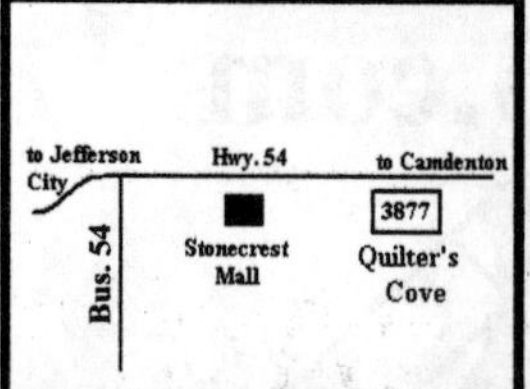

Lebanon, MO #37

Mon - Fri 10 - 6
Sat 10 - 5

Up-In Stitches
QUILT SHOP

1516 N. Jefferson 65536
(417) 588-3808
Est: 2002

I-44
Exit 129
High School
Up-In Stitches
1516
Jefferson

upinstitches@earthlink.net
Beautiful 100% cotton fabrics. From the deep hues of Kansas Troubles to the vibrant tones of Jinny Beyer's palette.

Of all the 'shows' in Branson our shop is the best one!!

Quilts & Quilts

1137 West Hwy. 76 65616
in Branson Heights Shopping Ctr.
(417) 334-3243
Owner: Marlys Michaelson Est: 1981 8,000 sq.ft.

Branson, MO #38

Summer
8 - 7 Mon - Sat
9 - 6 Sun
Winter
9 - 5 Mon - Sat
10 - 4 Sun

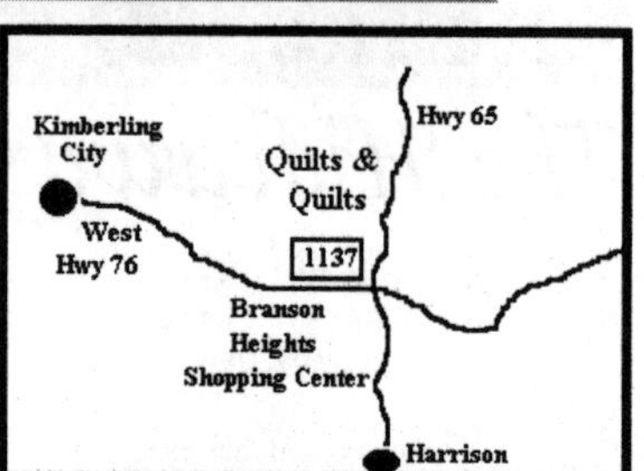

PATTERNS FOR CRAFTS AND QUILTS. Extensive collection of patterns for quilts, applique, and clothing (including the entire Eleanor Burns line) and much more. GREAT line of FAST and EASY "iron-on" projects.

COLOR AND FABRIC MAKE THE QUILT and we love to offer our years of experience in selecting the "perfect" combination so you end up with the "perfect" quilt.

OVER 500 BOOK TITLES - if we don't have it - we can order it and ship it to you.

FABRICS TO DIE FOR - Huge collection of Aunt Gracies, Modas, Hoffmans, Flannels, & State Flower Fabrics.

GREAT SELECTION OF GIFT ITEMS

Lots & Lots of Models--It's a Quilt Show Everyday

Rogersville, MO #39

Mon - Fri 10 - 5
Sat 10 - 4

Quilt'in Time Quilt Shoppe

424 Redbud Rd. 65742
(417) 753-7373
quiltintime@msn.com

Fabric, notions, patterns, classes, Grace Quilting frame dealer. At the stop light at Hwy. 60 and VV turn south, make an immediate left between Hardee's and Hwy. 60 on Redbud, go 1/8 mile, on left side of street.

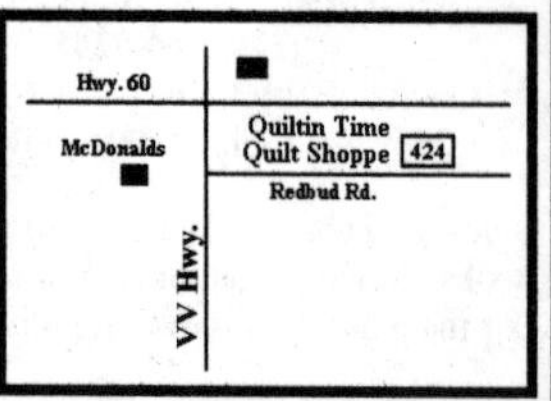

Springfield, MO #40

Tues - Fri 9:30 - 5:30
Sat 10 - 4

The Quilt Shoppe

2762 South Campbell 65807
(417) 883-1355
Owners: Rosalie Carey & Gilda Young
Est: 1978 2100 sq.ft.

100% cotton fabrics(1500 prints, 300 solids), 200 stencils, books, patterns, notions, Q-Snap frames, Hinterberg frames.
"Down the street from Bass Pro"

Sunshine
Bass Pro
Campbell
National
Glenstone
The Quilt Shoppe
2762
Battlefield Mall
Battlefield

THE QUILT SAMPLER, INC.

www.quiltsampler.com
1802A South Glenstone
"On The Plaza" • Springfield, MO 65804
Mon - Fri: 10 - 5 • Thurs: 10 - 7 • Sat: 10 - 4 • Sun: 12:30 - 4
417-886-5750 • Toll Free 1-877-452-3773
Qltsampler@aol.com
Est. 1994 • 5500 sq.ft. • Cristen Powell, owner

 Pfaff & Bernina dealership

5000 Bolts of Cotton Fabrics, 1000 Bolts of Flannels

 Books, Patterns, Notions, Software & More

 Friendly, Knowledgeable Staff

Springfield, MO #41

A full service quilt shop offering two complete lines of sewing machines & sergers, many kits, block of the months & a wide variety of machine accessories. Easy to find location.

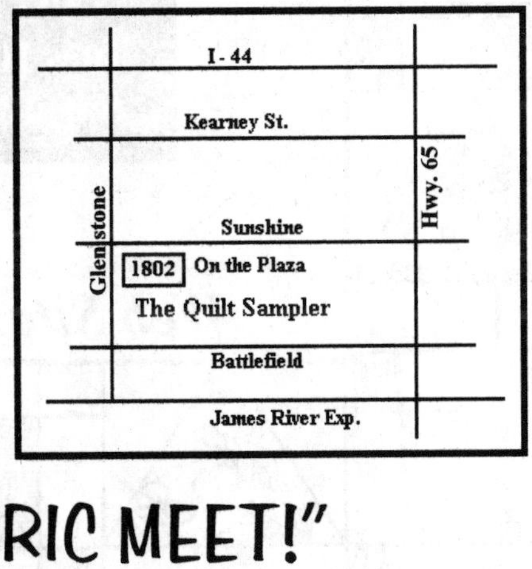

I-44
Kearney St.
Hwy. 65
Glenstone
Sunshine
1802 On the Plaza
The Quilt Sampler
Battlefield
James River Exp.

"WHERE FRIENDS AND FABRIC MEET!"

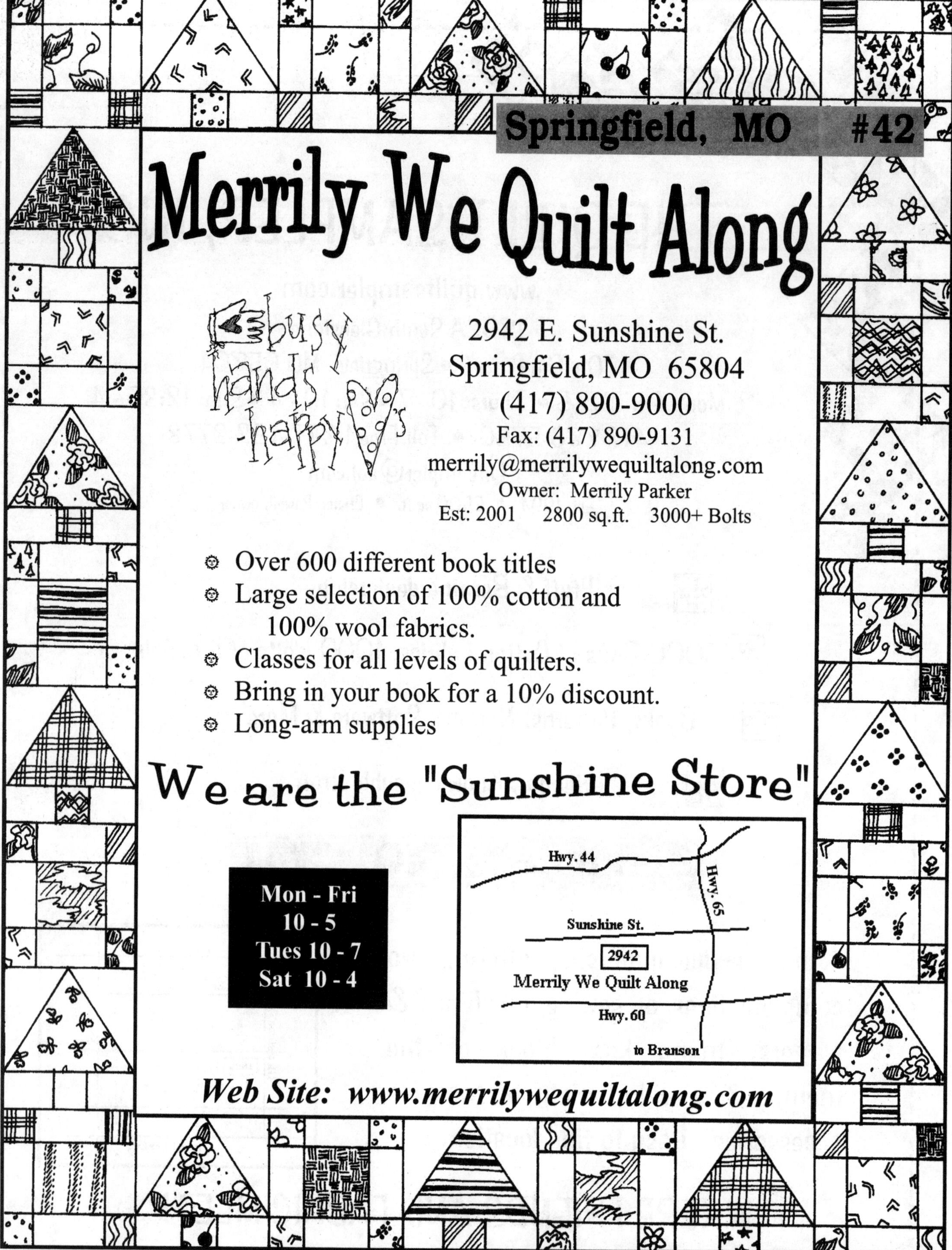
Springfield, MO #42
Merrily We Quilt Along
busy hands happy hearts
2942 E. Sunshine St.
Springfield, MO 65804
(417) 890-9000
Fax: (417) 890-9131
merrily@merrilywequiltalong.com
Owner: Merrily Parker
Est: 2001 2800 sq.ft. 3000+ Bolts
Over 600 different book titles
Large selection of 100% cotton and 100% wool fabrics.
Classes for all levels of quilters.
Bring in your book for a 10% discount.
Long-arm supplies
We are the "Sunshine Store"
Mon - Fri 10 - 5
Tues 10 - 7
Sat 10 - 4
Hwy. 44
Hwy. 65
Sunshine St.
2942
Merrily We Quilt Along
Hwy. 60
to Branson
Web Site: www.merrilywequiltalong.com

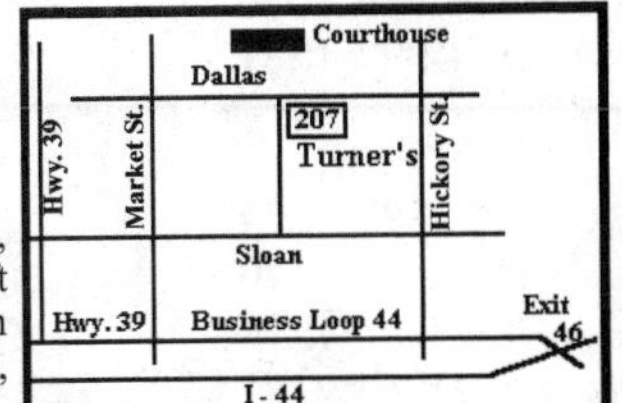

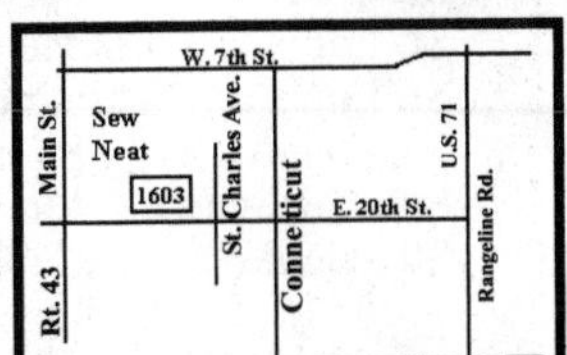

City	Store Name Store Address	Phone
Ballwin	In Stitches, 14664 Manchester Rd.	314-394-4471
Beaufort	Quilt N Time Quilt Station, 4149 Hwy. 50, R.R. #1,	573-484-3120
Bismarck	Dogwood Mountain Quilt Shop, 1567 Loughboro Rd.	573-734-2336
Bolivar	Buttons & Thread, 115 N. Main	417-777-6510
Branson	Carolina Mills Factory Outlet, 3617 W. Hwy. 76	417-334-2291
Branson	Amish Country Store, 3100 N. Gretna Rd.	417-334-6523
Branson	Quilt Cottage, 122 Skyview Dr.	417-339-3445
Branson	Log Cabin Quilts, 3612 Shepard of the Hills Expy	417-335-4236
Branson	Ozark Mountain Quilt Co., 3562 Shepherd Hill Expy.	417-336-6294
Branson	Country Sampler Quilt Shop, 3044 Shepherd of the Hills Exp.	417-336-5090
Branson	Ivy Rose Quilts & Gifts, 118 W. Main St.	417-337-7585
Branson	Brier Rose Quilts, 117 E Main St	417-336-3436
Branson	Ozark Mountain Quilts, 1000 Pat Nash Dr	
Brookfield	Grandma's Hope Chest, 616 W. Lockling St.	660-258-7665
Cape Girardeau	Quilting Shop, 134 Dena Ln.	573-335-0761
Centerview	Country Cottage Fabrics, 537 SW BB Hwy.	660-747-5368
Centerview	A Stitch in Time, 229 NW 601st Rd	660-656-3577
Craig	Fabrics Unique, Rt. 1	816-683-5757
Deepwater	Mary Jane's Fabrics, 947 SE 901st Rd.	
Ellington	Pin Cushion, 104 Hwy. 106, PO Box 9	573-663-2921
Florissant	Helen's Hen House, 180 W. Dunn Rd.	314-837-7661
Fredericktown	Carolina Fabric Center, 323 N Chamber Dr	573-783-2222
Hannibal	Yore Quilts, 403 Broadway	573-221-2480
Higginsville	Final Stitch, 711 W 34th St	660-584-7563
Hopkins	Young's Craft & Sewing, 415 E. Barnard St.	660-778-3272
Jamesport	Sherwood Quilt & Crafts, 1091 Hwy. U	no phone
Jamesport	Ropp's Country Variety, Rt. 2, Box 173	no phone
Jamesport	Leona's Amish Shop, Rt. 2	816-684-6628
Jamesport	Fabric Barn, 21914 St. Hwy. 190	no phone
Jamesport	The Garden Cottage Quilt Shop, 21870 Hwy. 190	no phone
Jefferson City	Meadow Ridge Train Depot, 5824 Meadow Ridge	573-395-4910
Jefferson City	Bertha's Sewing Center, 633 E High St	573-635-3571
Jefferson City	Quilter's Cove Sewing, 3600 Country Club Dr	573-636-5278
Kansas City	Kaplan Fabrics, 438 Ward Parkway	816-531-4818
Kirksville	Kaye's Fabrics, RR 3 Box 102	816-665-0123
Lebanon	H & H Fabric and Quilt Center, 326 W. Commercial	417-532-2378
Lebanon	Quilt Basket, 22993 Professional Ln	417-532-0883
Linn	Quilts & More, 205 E. Main St.	573-897-0355
Macon	J.M. Variety, 103 N Rollins	660-385-5751
Mercer	Quilter's Place, 1 State St	660-382-5890
Mountain View	Calico Cupboard Quilt Shop, 116 N. Oak St.	417-934-6330
Nevada	Mary's, 111 W. Walnut	417-667-3151
Oak Grove	Phanora's Variety, 1560 S. Broadway St.	816-625-8531
Osceola	Quilts and Crafts, 312 2nd St.	417-646-7746
Potosi	Quilter's Corner, 201 E. High St.	573-438-6718
Potosi	Busy Bee Quilt Shop & Florist, 103 Fissell St.	573-438-8660
Richmond	I'd Rather Be Quilting, 108 Wollard Blvd.	866-306-7622
Rocheport	Micki's Fabric & Yarn Shop, 10300 W. Sontag Dr.	573-446-8085
Rolla	Uniquely Yours, 404 E. St. Rt. 72	573-364-2070
Sedalia	Kaye's Kreations, 218 S Ohio	660-827-5297
Shelbina	Pieced Together, 6608 Shelby 468	573-588-4281
Shell Knob	Stitches, TimbeRoc Village, P.O. Box 117	417-858-2990

Springfield	Patchwork Corner, 702 E. Commercial St.	417-866-6160
Springfield	Crafters Delight, 2717 W. Kearney St.	417-866-4184
Springfield	Country Sampler Quilt Shop, 2904 S. Cambell St.	417-889-4646
St Louis	Aunt Toni's Quilting, 6815 Gravois Ave	314-752-1001
St. Charles	Lococo House, 1309 N. 5th St.	636-946-0619
St. Charles	Stitches Etc., 341 S Main St	636-946-8016
St. Louis	Eunice Farmer Fabrics, 9814 Clayton Rd.	314-997-1531
St. Louis	Thimble & Thread, 2629 Yeager Rd.	
Ste Genevieve	Becky's Quilts & Supplies, 185 Market	
Ste. Genevieve	Monia's Unlimited, 316 Market	573-883-7874
Ste. Genevieve	Cabin Fever Quilt Shop, 19803 State Rte P	573-883-7340
Troy	Quilter's Caboodle, 250 S. Lincoln Dr	636-528-2416
Versailles	Linda's Cottonpatch, 13501 Hwy. 52 E	573-378-6191
Versailles	Excelsior Fabrics, 19346 Excelsior Rd.	
Viburnum	Seams Sew Sweet, 60 Walnut St	573-244-3576
Vienna	GS Fabric and Gifts, Hwy. 42 W.	314-422-3500
Warsaw	Wooden Wagon, 242 W. Main	660-438-6400
Weston	Missourie River Quilt Co., 519 Main St. #A	816-640-5308

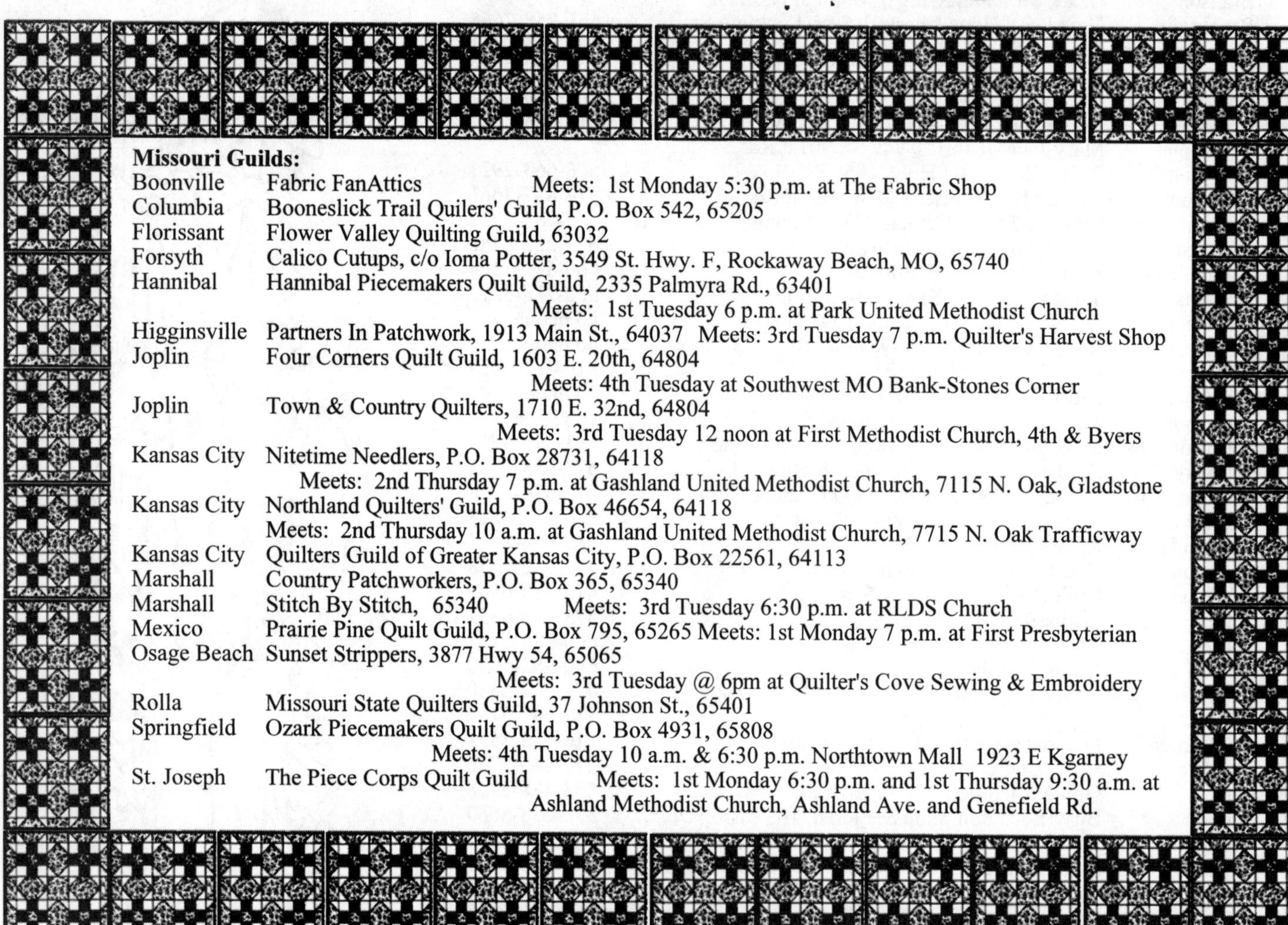

Missouri Guilds:

Boonville Fabric FanAttics Meets: 1st Monday 5:30 p.m. at The Fabric Shop
Columbia Booneslick Trail Quilers' Guild, P.O. Box 542, 65205
Florissant Flower Valley Quilting Guild, 63032
Forsyth Calico Cutups, c/o Ioma Potter, 3549 St. Hwy. F, Rockaway Beach, MO, 65740
Hannibal Hannibal Piecemakers Quilt Guild, 2335 Palmyra Rd., 63401
Meets: 1st Tuesday 6 p.m. at Park United Methodist Church
Higginsville Partners In Patchwork, 1913 Main St., 64037 Meets: 3rd Tuesday 7 p.m. Quilter's Harvest Shop
Joplin Four Corners Quilt Guild, 1603 E. 20th, 64804
Meets: 4th Tuesday at Southwest MO Bank-Stones Corner
Joplin Town & Country Quilters, 1710 E. 32nd, 64804
Meets: 3rd Tuesday 12 noon at First Methodist Church, 4th & Byers
Kansas City Nitetime Needlers, P.O. Box 28731, 64118
Meets: 2nd Thursday 7 p.m. at Gashland United Methodist Church, 7115 N. Oak, Gladstone
Kansas City Northland Quilters' Guild, P.O. Box 46654, 64118
Meets: 2nd Thursday 10 a.m. at Gashland United Methodist Church, 7715 N. Oak Trafficway
Kansas City Quilters Guild of Greater Kansas City, P.O. Box 22561, 64113
Marshall Country Patchworkers, P.O. Box 365, 65340
Marshall Stitch By Stitch, 65340 Meets: 3rd Tuesday 6:30 p.m. at RLDS Church
Mexico Prairie Pine Quilt Guild, P.O. Box 795, 65265 Meets: 1st Monday 7 p.m. at First Presbyterian
Osage Beach Sunset Strippers, 3877 Hwy 54, 65065
Meets: 3rd Tuesday @ 6pm at Quilter's Cove Sewing & Embroidery
Rolla Missouri State Quilters Guild, 37 Johnson St., 65401
Springfield Ozark Piecemakers Quilt Guild, P.O. Box 4931, 65808
Meets: 4th Tuesday 10 a.m. & 6:30 p.m. Northtown Mall 1923 E Kgarney
St. Joseph The Piece Corps Quilt Guild Meets: 1st Monday 6:30 p.m. and 1st Thursday 9:30 a.m. at
Ashland Methodist Church, Ashland Ave. and Genefield Rd.

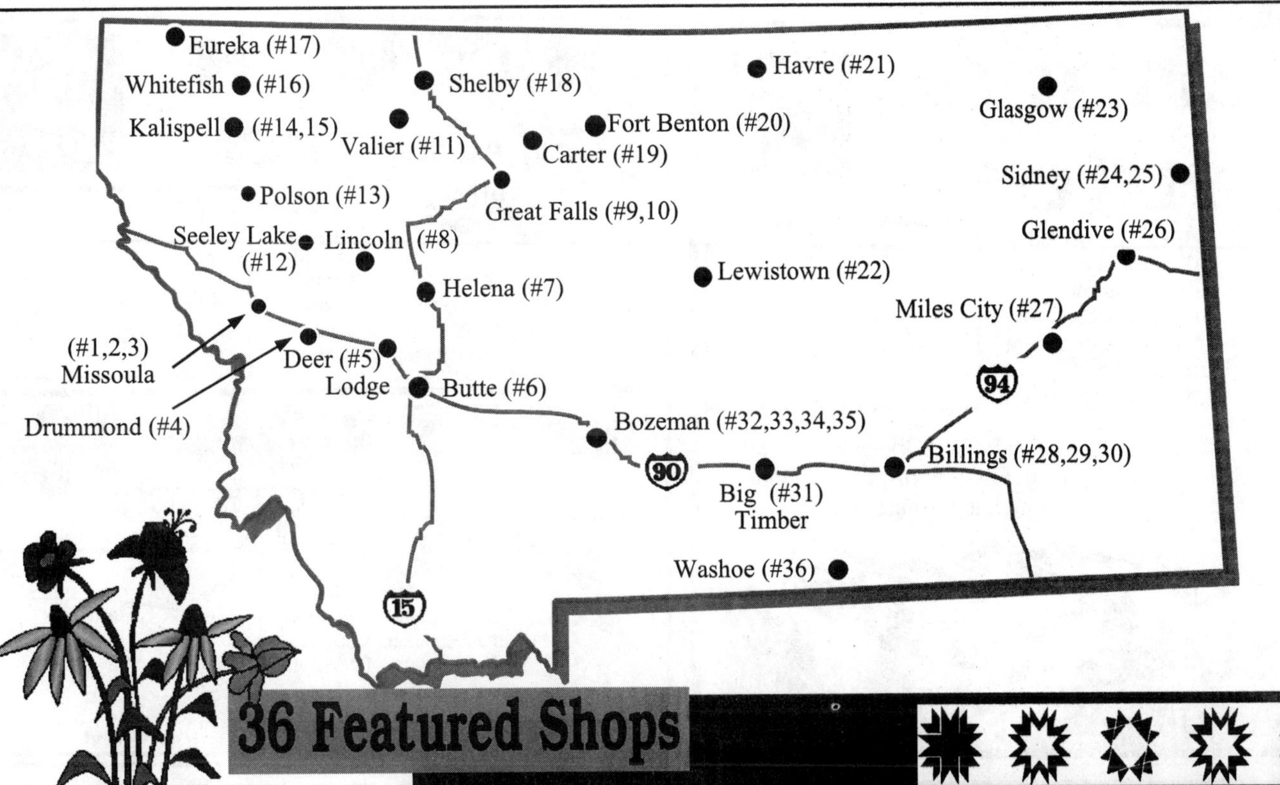

36 Featured Shops

MONTANA

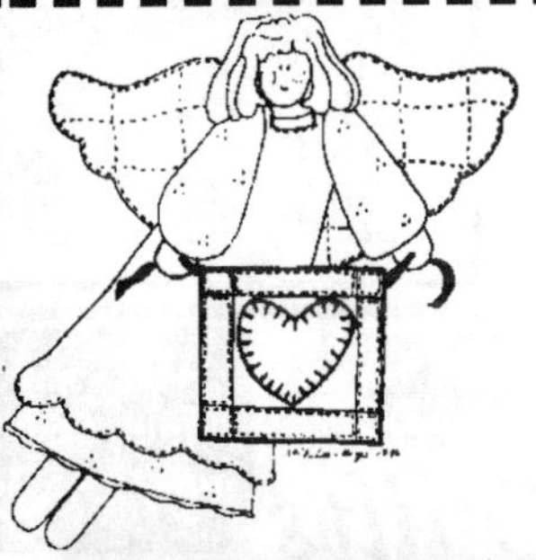

Missoula, MT #1

Timeless Quilts & Friends Quilt Shop

Located in the Towne Court at Reserve St.

2412 River Rd. 59804
(406) 542-6566 Fax: (406) 327-0742

www.tqandf.com

info@tqandf.com

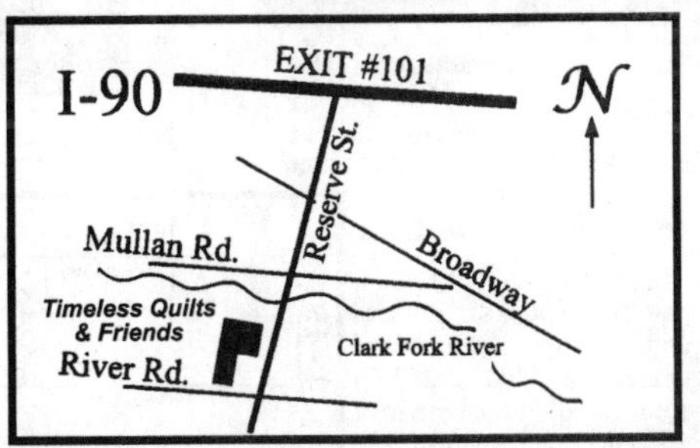

*** Featuring Fine Cotton Fabrics ***
*** Books, Patterns, Notions & Classes ***
*** Quilts for Sale ***

Custom Hand-Guided Machine Quilting
Bring your finished quilt tops along - we'll quilt them and then ship them back to you!

Mon - Fri 10 - 5
Sat 10 - 4

PROFESSIONAL MEMBERSHIPS:
International Machine Quilter's Association
American Quilter's Society
Missoula Quilter's Guild
Bitterroot Quilter's Guild

Bernina Center

Mon - Fri 10 - 5:30
Sat 10 - 4

1900 W. Broadway 59808
(406) 728-2119
Fax: (406) 728-3394
sharonmm@marsweb.com
ww.sewingmachinedealers.com / berninacenter
Est: 1986 4250 sq.ft. 1500+ Bolts

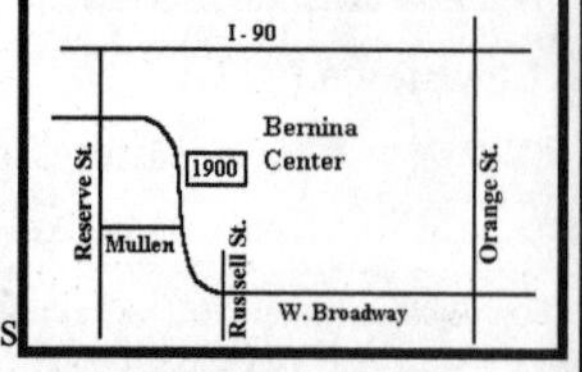

Quilting Fabrics specializing in Batiks, Orientals, Flowers, & Childrens. Complete line of Fossil Ferns, Fleece, Books, Patterns & Notions. Full line Bernina Dealer.

Missoula, MT #2

Missoula, MT #3

Mon - Fri 10 - 5
Thur til 7
Sat 10 - 4

3800 Russell St. #130 59801
at Russell Square
(406) 542-6644
Fax:
(406) 542-6650
Est: 2002
1350 sq.ft.
E-Mail: berrypatchquilts@msn.com
Owners: Sheila McIntosh & Louise Yamasaki

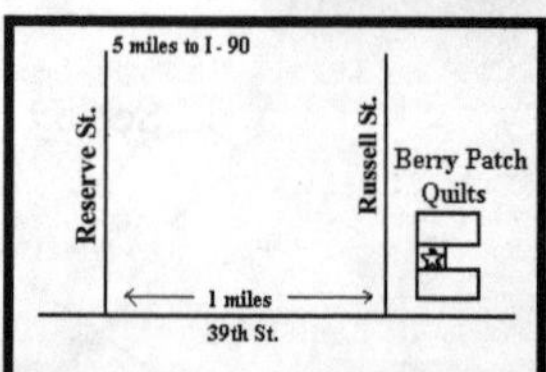

Our cozy shop offers friendly hometown service. Call ahead and we'll accommodate your travel plans. Looking forward to meeting you.

Drummond, MT #4

Mon - Sat 10 - 5

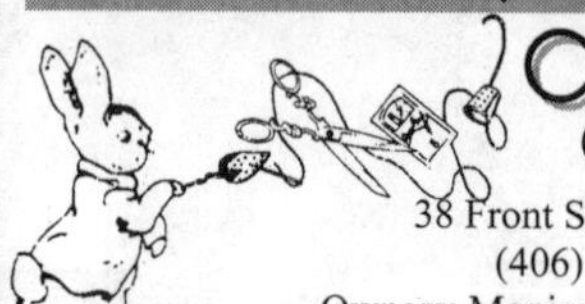

38 Front St. 59832
(406) 288-3297
Owners: Monica Prince & Mary Ellen & Maretta McGowan
Est: 1999 1800 sq.ft.

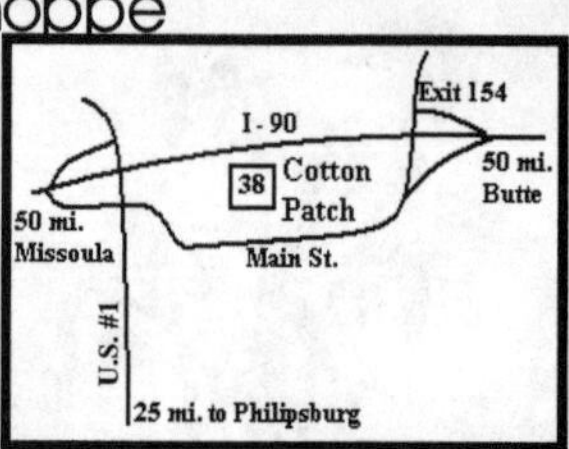

1500 Bolts of 100% cotton fabric. Specializing in Western, Wildlife and Floral Fabric. Books, Notions, & Patterns. Friendly, personal service.

Deer Lodge, MT #5

Mon - Sat 10 - 5:30
Sun 1 - 5

Quilters Corner, Etc.

401 Main St. 59722
(406) 846-3096
Fax: (406) 846-2298
donnamaccpt@aol.com
www.quiltsinmontana.com
Owner: Donna McCarthy

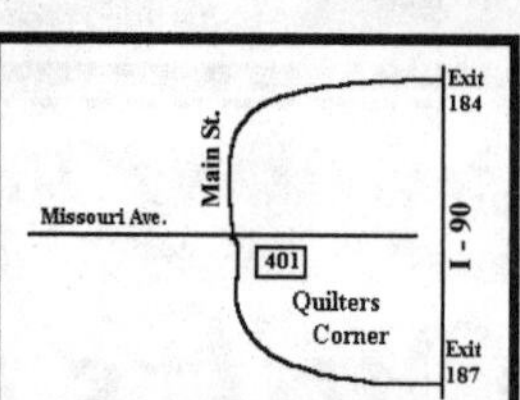

A bank built in 1912 is the home of 3000 Bolts of fabric, patterns, books and quilting ideas.

Butte, MT #6

Mon - Sat 10 - 5:30
Sat 10 - 4

the Silver Thimble Inc.

3104 Busch St. 59701
(406) 494-1633
E-Mail: Lstanhope@prodigy.net

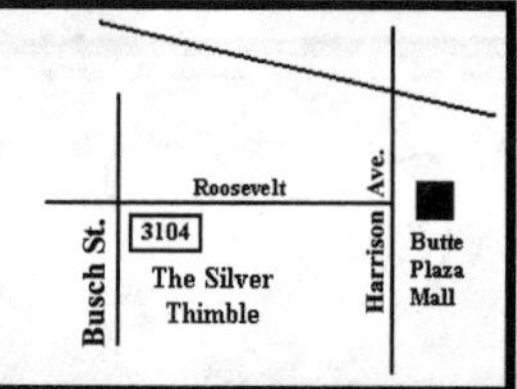

Quilting cottons, specialty fabrics, tools, notions, patterns & more. Authorized Husqvarna Viking Dealer.

Helena, MT #7

Mon - Fri 10 - 6
Sat 10 - 5
Sun 12 - 4
Summer Hrs. Vary

Sue's Sewing Palace Bernina

1103 Helena Ave. 59601
(406) 443-5724
Fax: (406) 443-3924
www.suessewingpalace.com

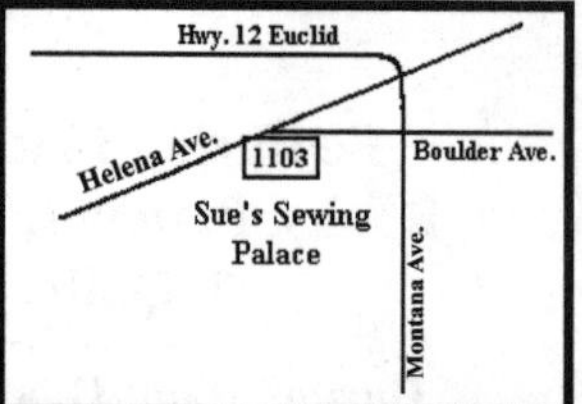

Largest in-town selection of quality 100% cottons, specializing in batiks, flannels and brights. Large selection of specialty threads, books, patterns, and classes. Award winning Bernina dealer.

Lincoln, MT #8

Wed - Sat 9:30 - 5:30
Sun 12 - 5:30

BackCountry Quilts

223 Main St., P.O. Box 476 59639
(406) 362-4373
tammy@bcquilts.com
www.bcquilts.com Est: 2003
Owners: Tammy & Dick Lewis 1000+ bolts

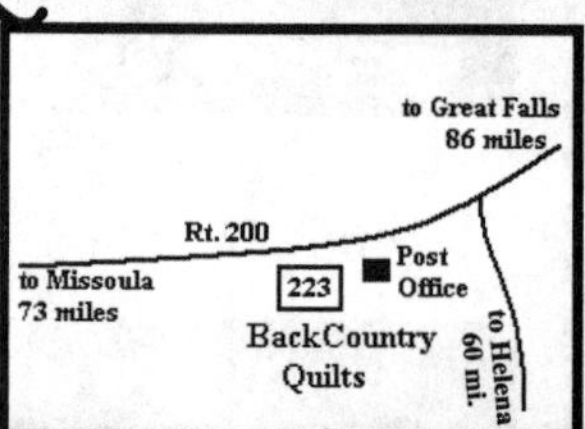

We feature Thimbleberries and a large selection of wildlife and outdoor prints and patterns. Over 1000 fat quarters to choose from!

Great Falls, MT #9

Mon - Fri 10 - 6
Sat 10 - 5
Sun 11 - 4

The Quilt-A-Way

222 13th St. S 59401
(406) 453-2788
quiltawy@mt.net
Owner: Toni Echart

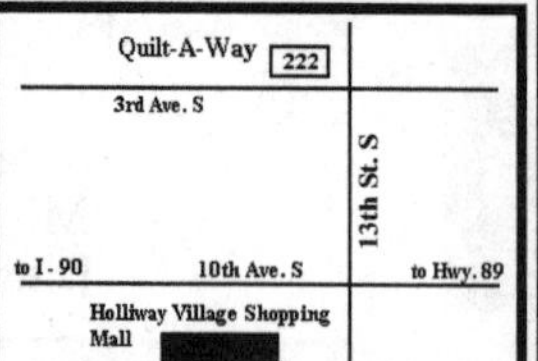

We are a Full-Service Quilt Shop. Over 2500 bolts of 100% designer Cottons. Friendly, expert staff.

Great Falls, MT #10

Mon - Sat 10 - 5

Big Sky Quilts

101A Central Ave. 59401
(406) 727-1757 Fax: (406) 965-3671
jw@bigskyquilts.com
www.bigskyquilts.com
Est: 1999
3000 sq.ft. 3500+ Bolts

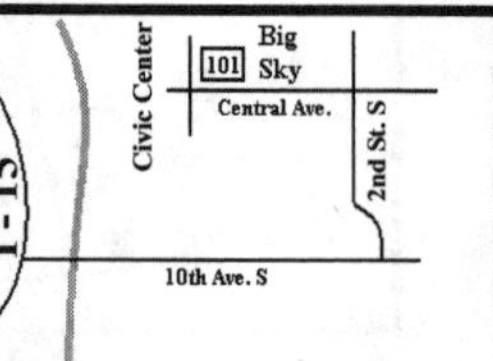

Top quality fabrics, patterns, books, notions and supplies. Authorized dealer for Elna and Juki sewing machines. We are located on the corner of Central Avenue and Park Drive across from the Civic Center.

#11

Reasonable Rates
Fast Turn Around Time
Friendly, Helpfull, Artistic Quilters

Fabrics
Notions
Classes
Quilts
Patterns
Books

Open Tues thru Sat

P.O. Box 154
Valier, MT 59486

www.rockcityquilts.com

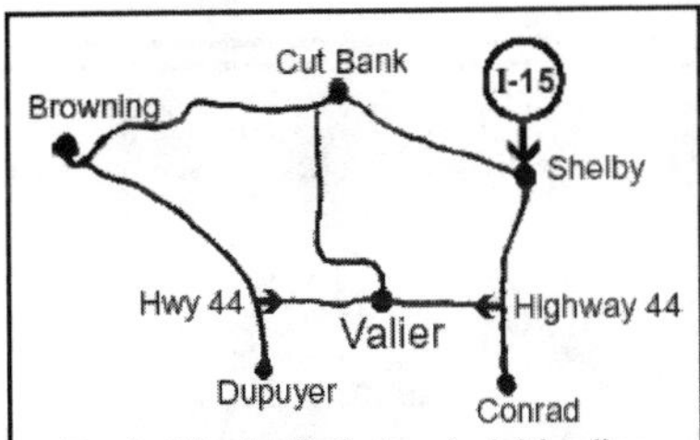

Rock City Quilts is located 14 miles east of Interstate15 on Highway 44 (518 Teton Ave) in Valier, MT. The shop is in the One Stop Conoco building. Valier has 3 very nice restaurants and a wonderful bed & breakfast.

Seeley Lake, MT #12

Mon - Sat 10 - 5:30
Sun 12 - 4

Deer Country Quilts

Hwy. 83, P.O. Box 808 59868
(The log store in the center of town)
(406) 677-2730 Fax: (406) 677-2885
www.deercountryquilts.com
Owner: Penny Copps & Pam Rose
Est: 1996 4200 sq.ft. 4000 Bolts
Selected by American Patchwork and Quilting as an outstanding store in North America in 2004
Everything you need including inspiration

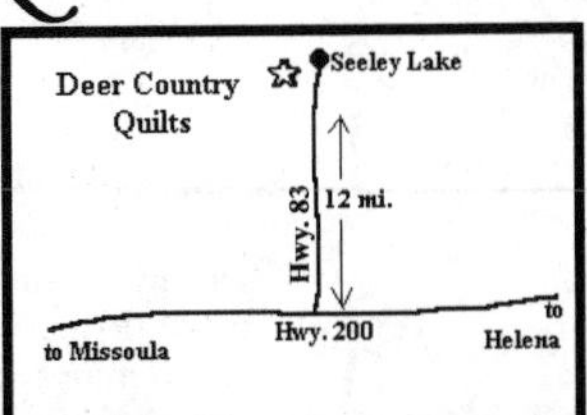

Polson, MT #13

Mon - Sat 9:30 - 5:30

All In Stitches

210 Main St. 59860
(406) 883-3643
aistitch@digisys.net
Est: 2000 2000 sq. ft. 2000 Bolts

All In Stitches carries a wide selection of batiks, orientals, brights, books, patterns & kits. We offer a variety of classes year round.

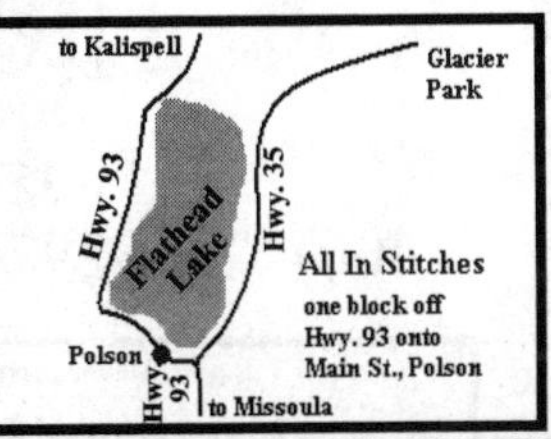

Kalispell, MT #14

Quilts • Fabrics • Supplies
Unique Patterns • Gifts •
Lessons

Large selection of antique, handquilted, novelty and machine Quilts.
Mail Orders Welcome
Owner: Joan P. Hodgeboom
Est: 1983 4700 sq.ft.

1710 Hwy. 93 S. 59901
(406) 257-5799
Next to Diamond Lil Inn

Mon - Fri 9:30 - 5:30
Sat 9:30 - 5

Selected by American Patchwork & Quilting magazine readers as one of the Top 10 quilt shops in the nation.

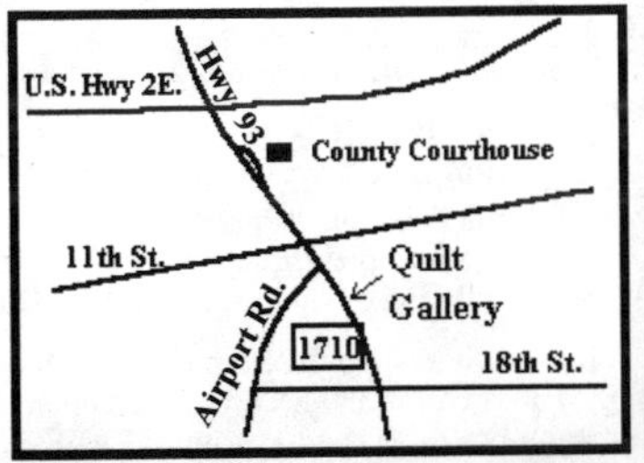

Kalispell, MT #15

Glacier Quilts

2960 Hwy. 2 East
P.O. Box 7274 59901
(406) 257-6966
Mgr: Coni Bjelland
Owner: Susan Gilman
info@glacierquilts.com

Mon - Fri 10 - 5:30
Sat 10 - 4

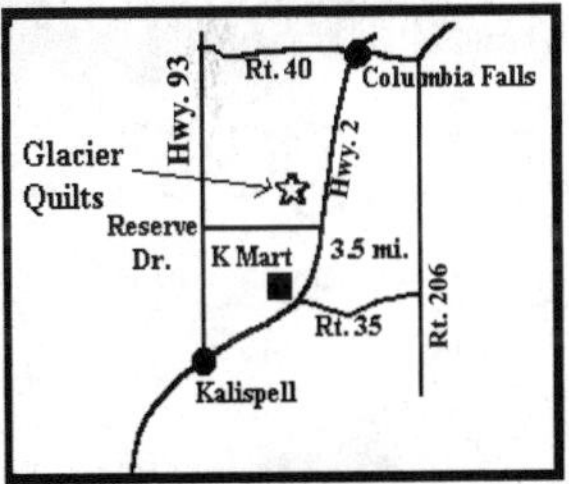

Authorized Elna Dealer

www.glacierquilts.com

Quality 100% Cotton Fabrics - Flannels - Books - Patterns - Notions - Quilts - Classes
Mail Orders Welcome / Online Ordering Available
Class Schedule/Newsletter available on request.

Come in and check out the quilts on the ceiling!

Whitefish, MT #16

Mon - Sat 9:30 - 5:30
Sun 11 - 4
Extended Hours May - Sept.

Moosetrack Quilts

633 Denver Ave. 59937
(406) 862-5429 Fax: (406) 862-5439
moosetracks@centurytel.net
Owner: Karla Reinhart
Est: 2003 1200 sq.ft. 1600 Bolts

All your quilting needs and friendly, helpful customer service in one stop. Classes and clubs offered, adults and kids welcome.

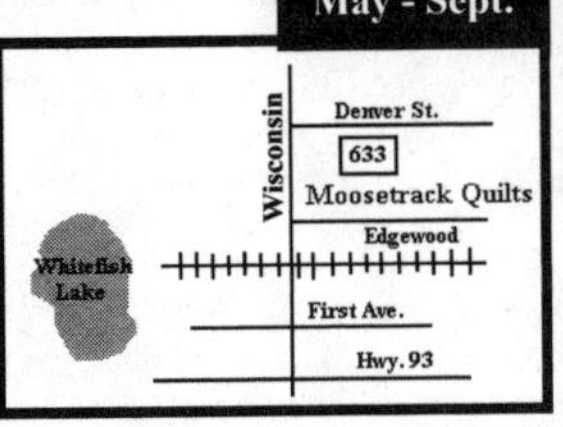

Eureka, MT #17

Bobbins, Buttons & Bears

993 Hwy. 93 N 59917
(406) 297-3233
Fax: (406) 297-7245
Email: bobbins@interbel.net
Owner: Mickey Richard
Quality quilting cottons, batiks, large selection of notions, crafts and yarn. We specialize in flannels!

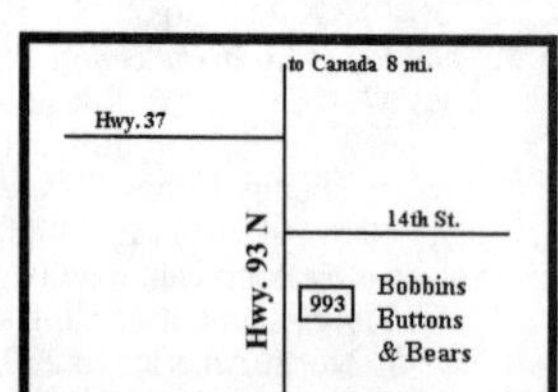

Shelby, MT #18

Mon - Fri
9:30 - 5
Sat 10 - 4

Quilt With Class

860 Oilfield Ave. 59474
(406) 434-5801
(800) 474-5801 (MT only)

Large variety of classes. Friendly, personalized service. Excellent selection of finest fabrics, notions, books. Phone orders welcome. Will mail anywhere.

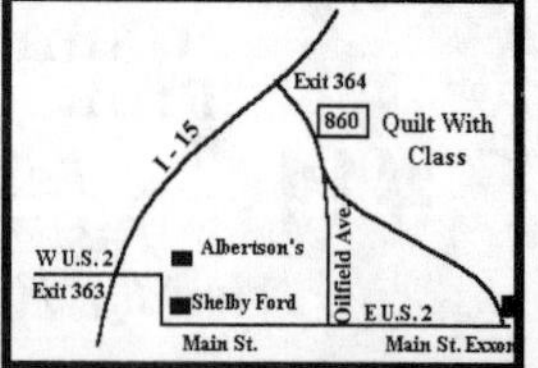

Carter, MT #19

The Quilting Hen

1156 Buck Bridge Rd. 59420
(406) 734-5297 www.quiltinghen.com

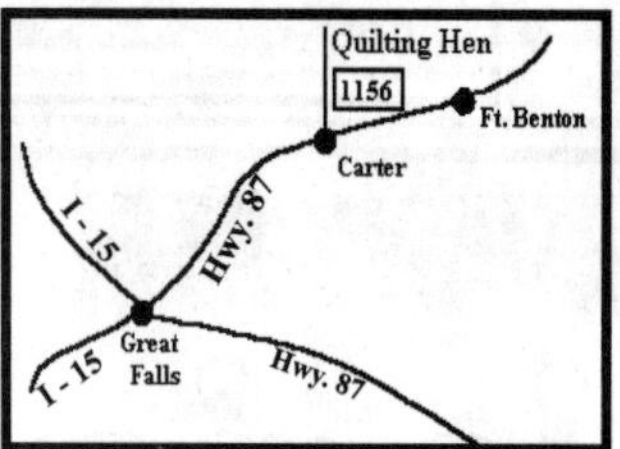

Tues - Sat 9 - 5

Best Prices on the Prairie!

Only 25 miles north of Great Falls, MT
Annual Outdoor Quilt Show 2nd Saturday in June
Free entry of quilts, open to all, big prizes
Show and event info on our website
PFAFF Authorized sales and service

Fort Benton, MT #20

Wed, Thur, Fri 12 - 7
Sat 10 - 5
Sun 11 - 4

Owners: Paulette Albers, Maggie Onstad & Gini Onstad

1514 Front St. Box 1420 59442
(406) 622-5150
blessmybuttons@mtintouch.net
www.blessmybuttons.biz

Featured in "Quilt Sampler 2004" as one of Top 10 Quilt shops in North America

Havre, MT #21

Mon - Fri
10 - 5:30
Sat 10 - 5

126 Third Ave.
59501
(406) 265-7212

2000 bolts of fabric - batiks, Thimbleberries, Kaffe Fasselte wools and wool felts and much more. Books, patterns & notions too.

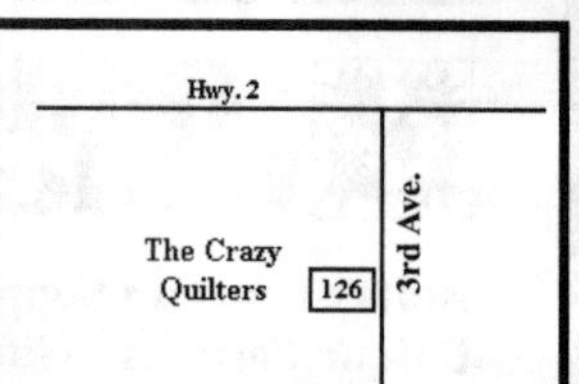

Lewistown, MT #22

Mon - Sat
9:30 - 5

Gingerbear Quilt-n-Gift Shop

305 W. Virginia St.
59457
(406) 538-2847
Owner: LaVerna Conard

Quilting Supplies, Classes & Patterns.

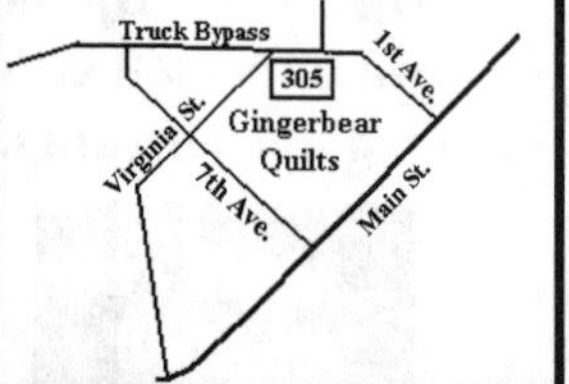

Glasgow, MT #23

Mon - Fri
9:30 - 5:30
Sat 10 - 3
Winter Sat
9:30 - 5:30

The Plaid Square

513 1st Ave. S 59230
(406) 228-9665 Est: 1999
dellab@plaidsquare.com
www.plaidsquare.com
Owner: Della Berg 1500 sq.ft. 1400+ Bolts

Full line quilting shop in North Eastern Montana. Many 100% cotton flannels, batiks, conversation prints and basics to choose from. PFAFF dealer. Custom machine quilting available.

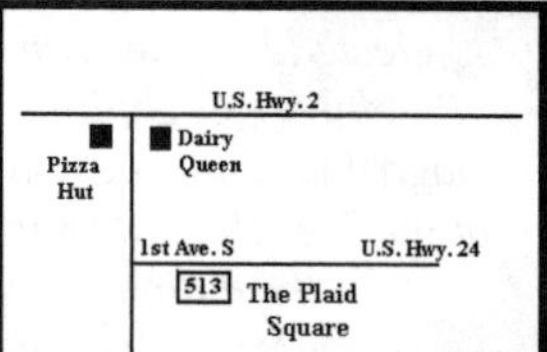

Sidney, MT #24

Mon - Fri
9 - 5

Quilted Treasures

609 S. Central Ave., Suite 2 59270
(406) 433-5586 Est: 2003
Custom long-arm quilting service.
2 - 3 week turn around.
Batting & wide backing fabric available.
Contact Jodi at jodirayk@midrivers.com or Trish at neiss@midrivers.com

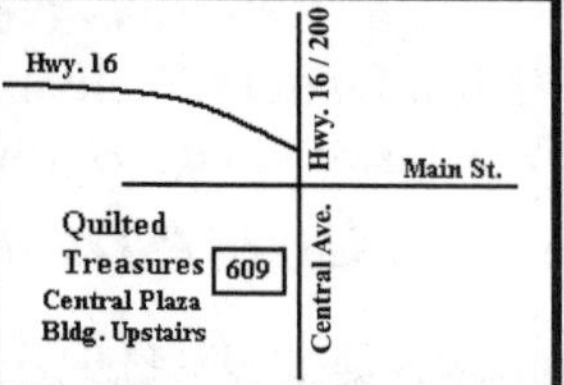

Sidney, MT #25

Mon - Fri
10 - 5:30
Sat 10 - 3

Quilts & More

Route 2, Box 2150 59270
(406) 482-3366 Fax: (406) 482-6772
vanhook@midrivers.com
Est: 1999 1440 sq.ft. 2100 bolts

Specializing in 30's, western, flannels, batiks and jewel tones. Machine quilting available. Annual outdoor quilt show, weekend after Labor Day

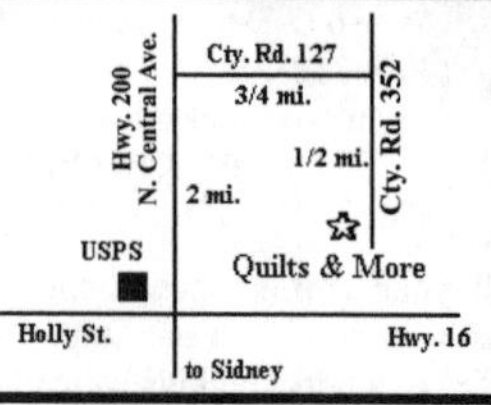

Glendive, MT #26

Mon - Sat 10 - 5

The Enchanted Room

222 W. Towne St. 59330
(406) 365-4745
Owners: Myrna Quale & Laura Gluecker

Quilt Shop located in Restored Historic Home. Excellent Selection of Quilting Fabric, books, & notions. Unique gifts, Custom Floral, Home Decorating accessories.

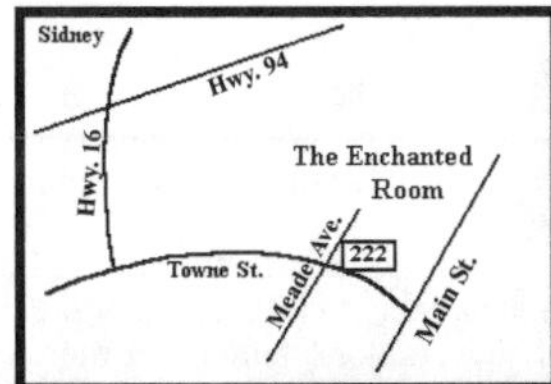

Miles City, MT #27

Mon - Sat 9 - 5:30

Copper Thimble
FABRICS & QUILTS

709 Main St. 59301
(406) 234-7226
Fax: (406) 234-7226
Est: 1980
7000 sq.ft.

cprthmbl@midrivers.com 1000+ Bolts
Owners: Gayle Muggli & Vicki Hamilton

Quality fabrics — Hoffman, Henry, Benartex & more. Books, patterns, notions, gifts. Viking dealer. Commercial quilting.
Eastern Montana's largest quilt store.

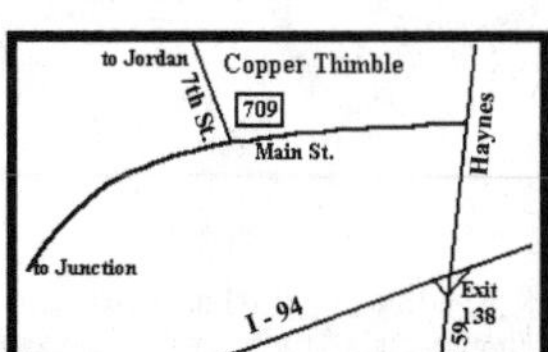

Billings, MT #28

Mon - Sat 9:30 - 5:30

Bernina Sewing Center

1505 Rehberg Ln. 59102
(406) 656-4999
Owner: Doris Holzer

Authorized Bernina Dealer.
Quilting books, patterns, supplies.
Large selection of 100% cotton calicos & solids. Classes. Friendly & helpful

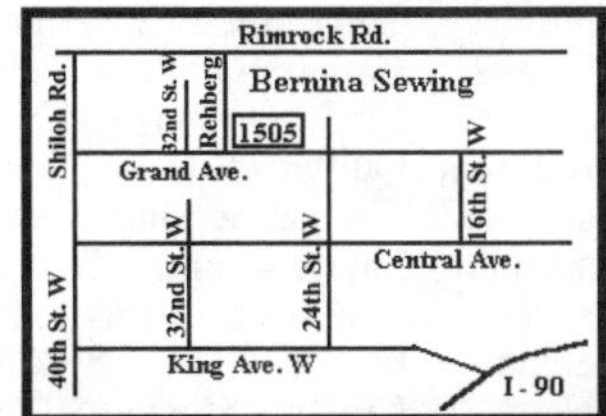

Billings, MT #29

Mon, Tues Wed 10 - 6
Thur 10 - 8
Fri & Sat 10 - 5
Sun 12 - 5

Fiberworks

3213 Henesta Dr. 59102
(406) 656-6663 Fax: (406) 656-3363
www.fiberworks-heine.com Est: 1994
Owner Laura Heine invites you to her 6100 sq.ft. building to see the largest selection of fabrics, books, notions and quilt patterns around. Also see Laura's newest line of fabrics, have her sign one of her many book selections or take a long-arm quilting class. Fiberworks is touted as the "quilters haven".

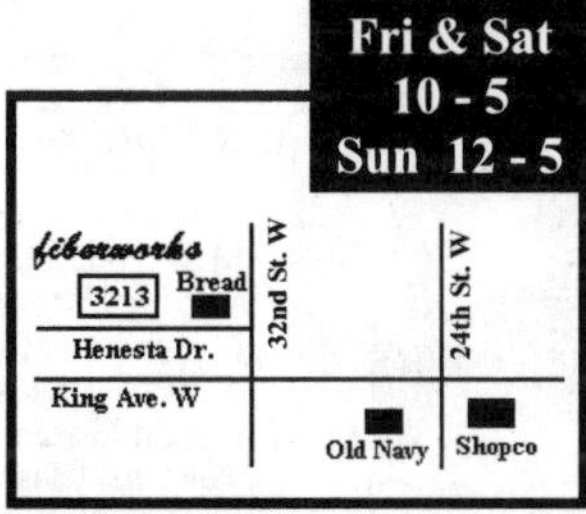

Billings, MT #30

Mon - Fri 9 - 7
Sat 9 - 6
Sun 12 - 5

Backdoor Quilt Shoppe

712 Carbon St. #A, P.O. Box 80833 59102
(406) 655-1001 (Fax: (406) 655-0009
Est: 2002 5000 sq.ft. 4000+ Bolts

Authorized Brother Pacesetter dealer.
Full Service Quilt Shop. Classes.
Antique Machines.

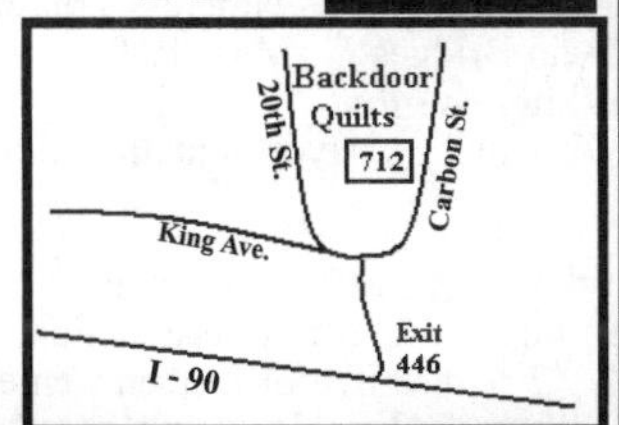

Big Timber, MT #31

Mon - Sat 10 - 6

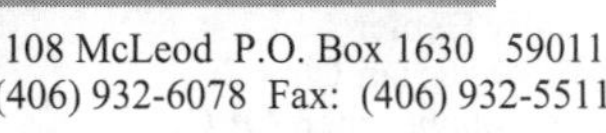

108 McLeod P.O. Box 1630 59011
(406) 932-6078 Fax: (406) 932-5511

Owner: Susie Mosness
Est: 2001 3500 sq.ft.
Friendly small town store with big ideas, great flannels, batiks and cottons.
Home of Janome Memory Craft machines.

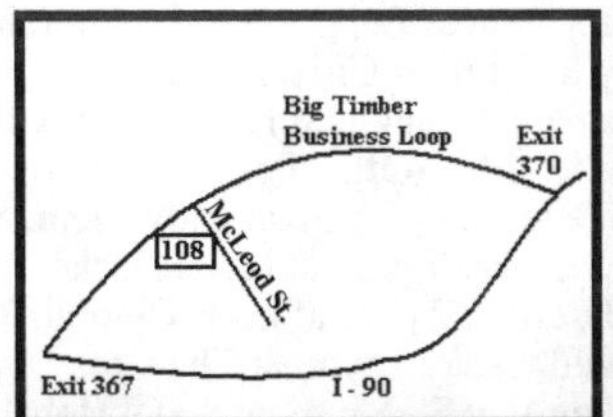

Bozeman, MT #33

Mon - Sat 9:30 - 5:30

Bear Comforts
Quilters Headquarters

126 E. Main St. 59715
(800) 757-6097 Fax: (406) 586-5239
www.bearcomforts.com
(406) 586-6097

Owner: Sandy Taylor bearcomf@avicom.net
Est: 1977 2500 sq.ft. 2000 Bolts
Bozeman's only complete quilting store offering hundreds of bolts of 100% cotton, the latest notions, patterns & books for your selection. Custom machine quilting services.

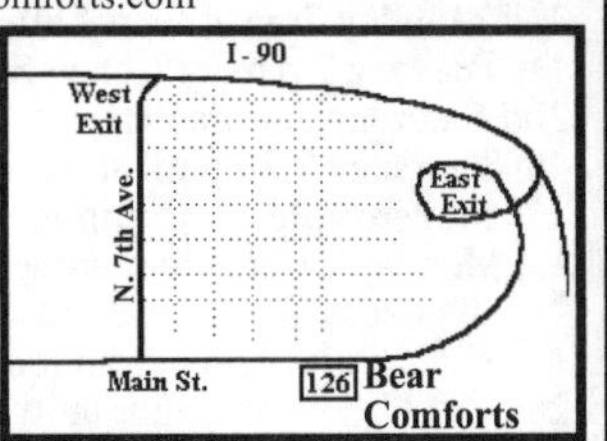

ReproductionFabrics.com

Welcome to Bozeman
Featuring authentic reproductions 1775 – 1970 and Natural Indigo dyed prints

Visit our Website.
You'll want to Visit us!
***Free* Electronic Newsletter**

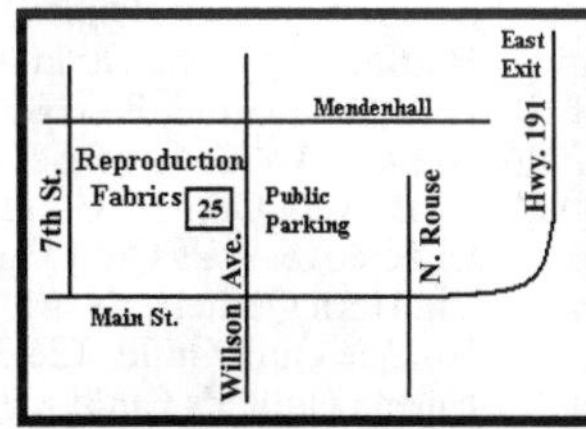

www.reproductionfabrics.com

Bozeman, MT #32

Mon-Fri 9-5 / Saturdays 9-Noon

25 N. Willson Ave. Bozeman, MT
406-586-1775 --- toll free: 888-728-2495

Bozeman, MT #34

Mon - Sat 11 - 4 Wed til 9 Thurs til 6

Quilting In The Country

5100 S. 19th Rd. 59718
(406) 587-8216
Owner: Jane Quinn

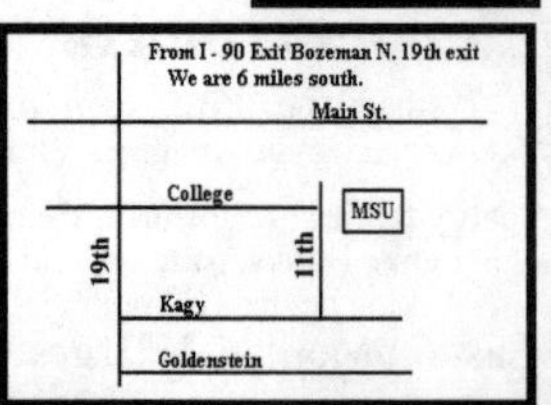

jquinn @quiltinginthecountry.com
www.quiltinginthecountry.com

Charming shop in bunkhouse on 130 year old homestead. 3 miles south of Bozeman. Classes. End of summer outdoor quilt show. Featured in "Quilt Sampler" & "Simply Quilts".

Bozeman, MT #35

Mon - Sat 10 - 5:30 Sat 10 - 4

the Silver Thimble Inc.

11 E. Main 59715
In the heart of downtown Bozeman
(406) 587-0531
Lstanhope@prodigy.net

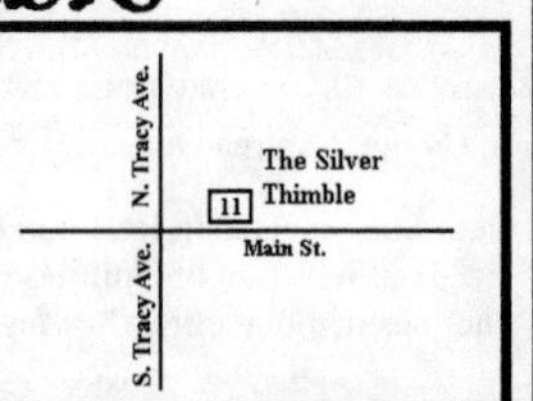

Bozeman's unique sewing boutique! Specializing in high end quilting cottons, polar fleece, notions, patterns & more. Authorized Husqvarna Viking Dealer.

Washoe, MT #36

Sun - Wed 10 - 6

Washoe Quilt Shoppe

406 Hwy. 308,
HC 41, Box 15 59007
(406) 446-4094

Owner: LuDon DeVille
Est: 2002 1200 sq.ft.
750 Bolts
Located in a former mine office. Check out our local history. Fabric, Patterns, Classes, Quilts, Notions.

Population 21
When we're all home

to Billings
Rt. 212
Rt. 72
Washoe Quilt Shop
406
Hwy. 308
Red Lodge
Washoe
Bearcreek
to Yellowstone
to Cody, WY

Other Shops in Montana: *We suggest calling first*

Baker	Gathering Place, 238 S 1st St W	406-778-2114
Basin	Quilting Corral, 60 Frontage Rd	406-225-4306
Big Fork	Merry Gems, 469 Electric Ave	406-837-1247
Bigfork	Lynn's hip hop Shop, 1847 Hwy. 209	406-837-6634
Billings	Thread Mill, 712 Carbon St. #A	406-652-3098
Billings	Pin Cushion, 2646 Grand Ave. #9	406-652-6328
Billings	Grand Quilts, 1827 Grand Ave. #1	406-256-8338
Billings	Mom's Quiltin Closet, 2130 Whitewater Cir	406-651-4285
Billings	Billings Sewing & Vac, 1212 Grand Ave.	406-252-6989
Billings	Butterfly Fabrics, 501 Hansen Ln #B	406-256-3985
Bozeman	Quilting in the Rockies, 19 Cloninger Ln	406-587-2045
Bozeman	The Quilting Hen, 1716 W. Main St. #8C	406-556-8100
Broadus	Fabric to Fashion, 106 Crane Ave.	406-436-2963
Butte	Top of the Hill Bernina, 1440 Holmes Ave	406-494-6508
Chinook	Country Quilts & Fabrics, 16 Clear Creek Hght	406-357-2891
Dillon	Crafty Quilter, 104 N. Montana St.	406-683-5884
Drummond	Quilter's Rose, 282 Airport Rd.	
Hamilton	The Fabric Shop & Quilts, 410 N. 1st St.	406-363-3471
Hamilton	Fabric Country, 1659 N 1st St #3	406-363-3341
Havre	The Silver Thimble, 104 3rd Ave.	406-265-4531
Helena	Scraps of Heaven, 828 N. Rodney St.	406-449-7467
Helena	Creative Stitches, 1060 Helena Ave	406-443-7540
Laurel	LeDuc's, 13 1/2 Colorado	406-628-4817
Lewistown	Megahertz, 223 W. Main St.	406-538-8531
Libby	Quilters' Cottage, 910 Main St.	406-293-6306
Libby	Sue Bee's Quilting, 305 California Ave	406-293-7832
Red Lodge	Cottage Quilts, 316 S Broadway Ave	406-446-2581
Scobey	Bev's Sewing Center, 123 Main St.	406-487-2841
Shelby	The Creative Needle, 225 Main St.	406-434-7106
Twin Bridges	Timeless Treasures Quilt, 150 Melrose	406-684-5719
Twin Bridges	Mary R. Originals, 204 South Main	406-684-5878
Whitefish	Pine Mountain, 124 Obrien Ave.	406-862-5519
Whitehall	Cozy Mountain Quilts, 1 E Legion	406-287-9984

Montana Guilds:

BakerLife's Patchwork Quilting Guild, 59313 Meets: 4th Wednesday 1 p.m. at Thee Garage
Big Fork Piecemakers Quilt Guild, P.O. Box 176, 59911 **Billings** Quilt by Association, P.O. Box 22233, 59104
Bigfork Bigfork Piecemakers Guild Meets: 3rd Thursday 7 p.m. at Senior Citizen Center
Billings Yellowstone Valley Quilt Guild, 3114 Country Club Cir, 59102 **Billings** Nimble Thimble Quilters, 1917 Ave. C, 59101
Bozeman Quilters Art Guild, P.O. Box 4117, 59772 **Bozeman** Quilter's Art Guild of Northern Rockies, 59772
Broadus Stitch & Chatter Quilt Club, Box 318, 59317 Meets: 2nd & 4th Tuesday at County Courthouse Election Room
Butte Chateau Quilters, 3104 Busch, 59701 Meets: 2nd & 4th Thursday eves and Every Friday morn. at Quilt Essentials
Columbia Falls Teakettle Quilters' Guild Meets: 3rd Daturday 10am at Community Center
Dayton West Shore Quilters Guild Meets: 3st Monday 10am at Dayton Presbyterian Church
Dillon Piecemakers, Box 212, 59725 **Lewiston** Central Montana Fiber Art Guild
Eureka Scraps & Threads Quilt Guild Meets: 2nd Thursday 9am at Eureka Baptist Church
Glasgow Heirloom Quilters Guild, 68 Kampfer Dr Meets: 1st Monday at 7pm, Sr Citizenz Center
Great Falls Falls Quilt Guild, P.O. Box 6592,, 59406 Meets: 2nd Tuesday 7 p.m. at Great Falls Senior Citizens Center, 1004 Central Ave.
Great Falls Quilters Art Guild of the Northern Rockies, P.O. Box 242, 59403 **Missoula** Peace Quilt Guild, 2136 Collins Ln., 59802
Hamilton Bitter Root Quilters Guild, P.O. Box 943, 59840 Meets: 4th Wednesday 7 p.m. at Daly Elem. School
Hardin Undercover Gals Quilt Guild, P.O. Box 508, 59034 Meets: 4th Thursday 7 p.m. at Hotel Becker
Hardin Big Horn Quilters, Rt. #1, Box 1238, 59034 Meets: 2nd Tuesday 7 p.m. at E&R Church, 703 N. Cheyenne
Havre Hi-Line Quilt Guild, 126 3rd Ave, 59501 Meets: 1st Wednesday 7 p.m. at The Crazy Quilters
Helena Helena Quilter's Guild, P.O. Box 429, 59624 Meets: 2nd Tuesday 7:15 p.m. at 800N Hoback
Kalispell Flathead Quilters Guild, P.O. Box 9845, 59904 Meets: 1st Thursday 7 p.m. at the Epworth United Methodist Church
Libby Kootenai Valley Quilters, P.O. Box 490, 59923 Meets: 2nd Monday 7:30 p.m. at Christ Lutheran Church
Malta Hands All Around Quilters, P.O. Box 697, 59538 Meets: 2nd Tuesday except Aug.
Marion Marion Sew'n Sews Quilt Guild Meets: Every Monday 9am at 440 Sickler Creek Rd
Miles City Miles City Centennial Quilters, 709 Main, 59301 Meets: 1st Tuesday 7 p.m. at Copper Thimble
Missoula Missoula Quilter's Guild, 2401 Brooks, Box 325, 59801 Meets: 2nd Wednesday @ 7pm at Best Inn Conference Center, 3803 Brooks St.
Plains Plains Piccers Quilt Guild, 1010 River Rd., 59859 Meets: 2nd Monday 7pm at First Lutheran Church
Ronan Mission Mountain Quilters, 4185 Cheff Ln., 59864 Meets: 1st Tuesday 7 p.m. at Ronan Senior Center
Roundup Cross Country Piecemakers, 137 Main St., 59072 Meets: 2nd Saturday at Scrap Happy
Seeley Lake Seeley Lake Quilt Guild, P.O. Box 205, 59868 Meets: 4th Thursday 7:30 p.m. at Deer Country Quilts
Shelby Triangle Squares Quild Guild, 124 6th Ave. S, 59474 **Stevensville** Sapphire Quilters, 317 Main St., 59870
Thompson Falls Flat Iron Quilt Guild Meets: 1st Monday 7 p.m. alternating between Thompson Falls & Trout Creek
Townsend Quack-N-Quilters, 63 Manor Dr., 59644 Meets: 2nd Thursday 7 p.m. at Elementary School
Troy Tender Loving Quilters, 59935 Meets: 1st Monday 7:30pm at Methodist Fellowship Hall
Whitefish Stumptown Quilter's Society Meets: 2nd Sat 11 a.m. at Community room North Valley Hospital

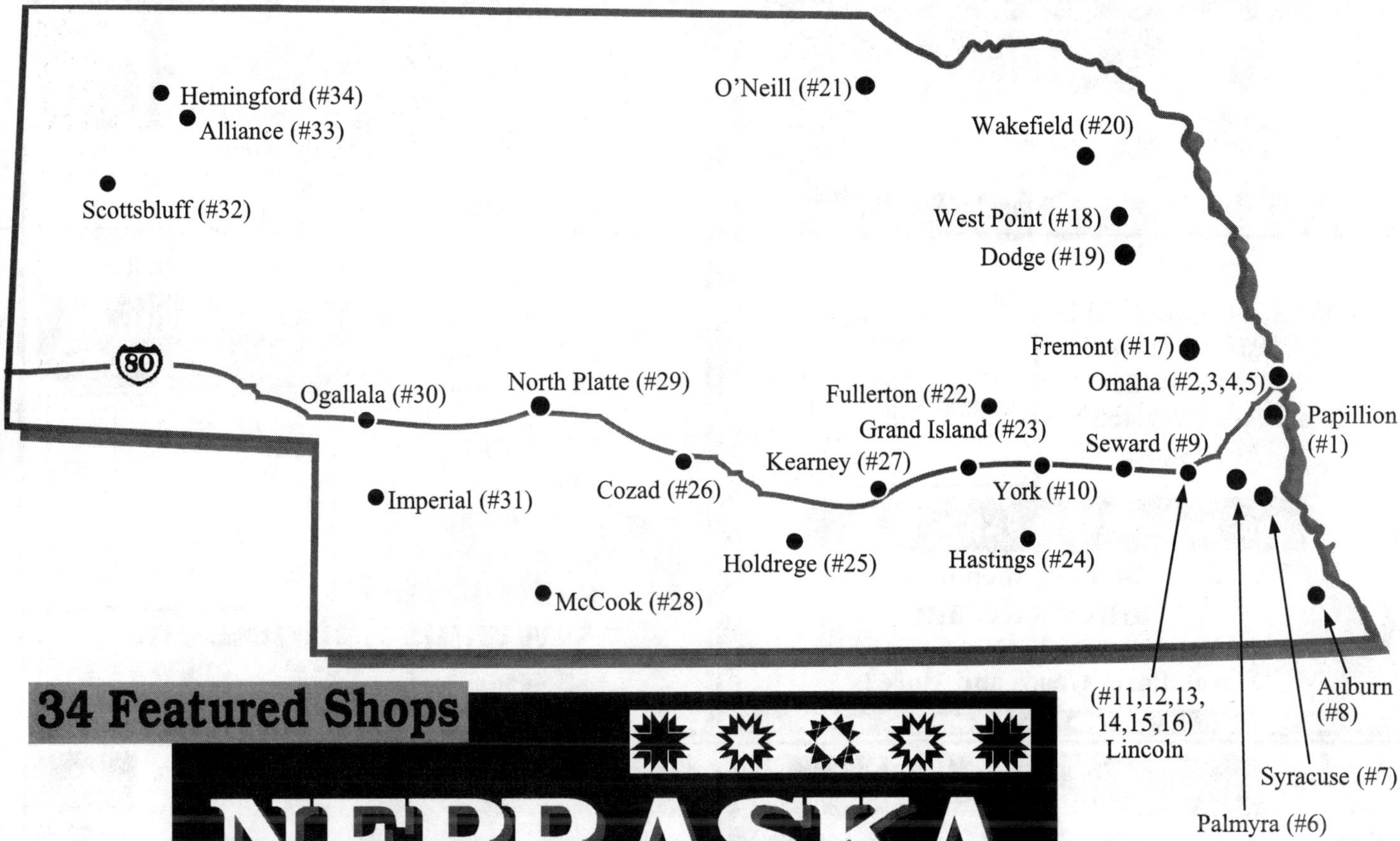
Hemingford (#34)
Alliance (#33)
Scottsbluff (#32)
O'Neill (#21)
Wakefield (#20)
West Point (#18)
Dodge (#19)
Fremont (#17)
Omaha (#2,3,4,5)
Papillion (#1)
80
Ogallala (#30)
North Platte (#29)
Fullerton (#22)
Grand Island (#23)
Seward (#9)
Kearney (#27)
York (#10)
Imperial (#31)
Cozad (#26)
Holdrege (#25)
Hastings (#24)
McCook (#28)
(#11,12,13, 14,15,16) Lincoln
Auburn (#8)
Syracuse (#7)
Palmyra (#6)

34 Featured Shops

NEBRASKA

Two Locations in the Omaha Area

Country Sampler

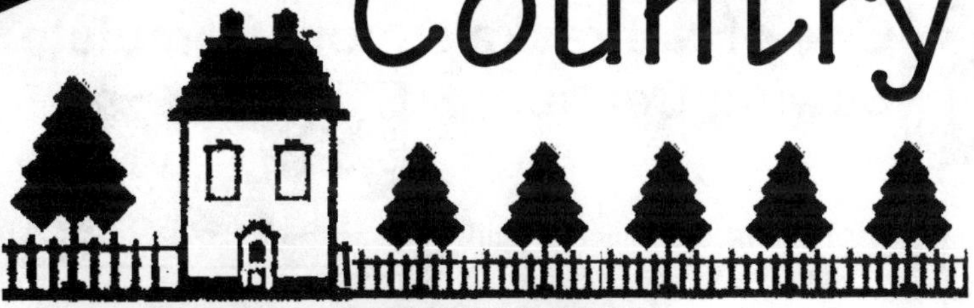

Mon - Sat 10:00 - 5:30
Thurs til 8:00 Sun 12:00 - 5:00

Omaha, NE #2

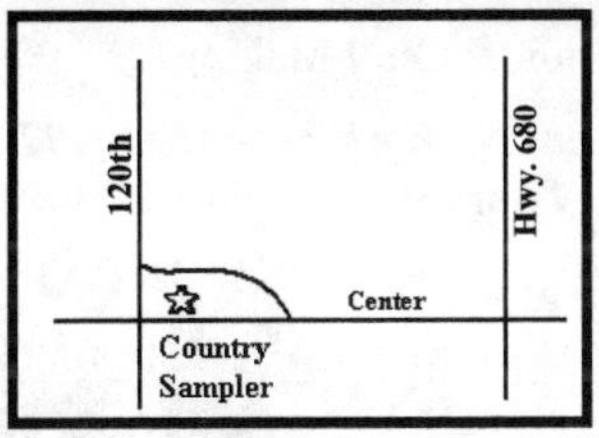
120th
Hwy. 680
Center
Country Sampler

11928 W. Center Rd.
Omaha, NE 68144
(402) 333-6131
Est: 1990 3400 sq.ft.

Papillion, NE #1

841 Tara Plaza
Papillion, NE 68046
(402) 537-9515
Est: 1998 3100 sq.ft.

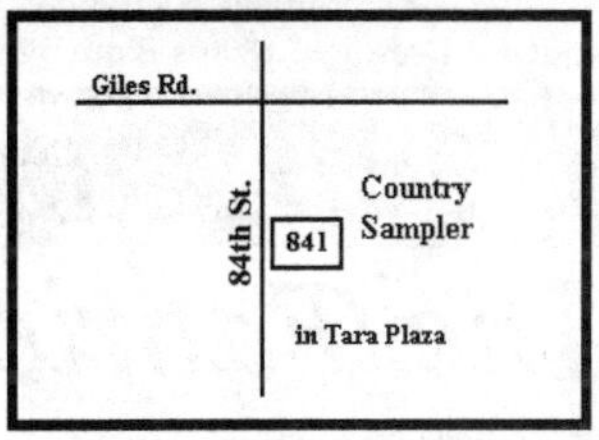
Giles Rd.
84th St.
841
Country Sampler
in Tara Plaza

Owner: Deb Cizek

Come and see why Country Sampler was selected as a featured shop in the Better Homes & Gardens Quilt Sampler Magazine for 2002! Over 3,000 bolts of 100% cottons, flannels and homespuns! Tons of kits, patterns and books, block of the months, stitcheries, and rug hooking supplies.

Omaha, NE #3

Family Owned Since 1961

David M. Mangelsen's®

3457 S. 84th St. 68124
Westgate Plaza
(402) 391-6225
Fax: (402) 391-4659
37,000 sq.ft.

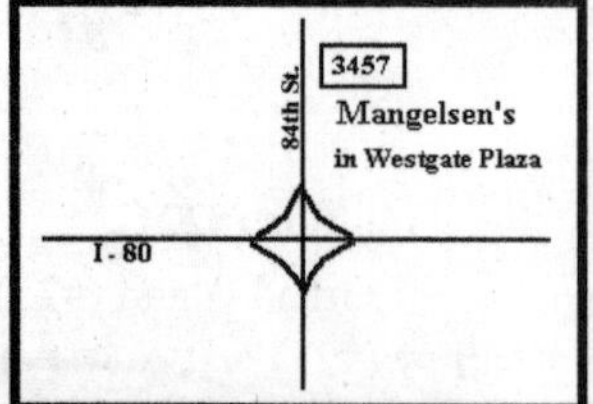

Mon - Fri 9 - 9 Sat 9 - 8 Sun 10 - 5

The store where you shop for FUN !
A Quilter's dream.
Fabric, Patterns, Books, Notions, Crafts, Floral, Party Goods and More !

JUST FaBRIC

We have "pressed" a lot of fabric into our user friendly store. Plenty of inspiration for quilters; including wide cotton for quilt backs. We have a variety of cottons, imported prints, knits, fleece, wool, corduroy, fashion, bridal, fleece, upholstery, & more. Come visit us!

402-393-2422
Fax: 402-393-2522
justfabric@earthlink.net
Mike & Cheryl Zach
Est: 2003 2000 sq.ft.
3000 bolts

2329 N. 90th St.
Just S. of Hobby Lobby

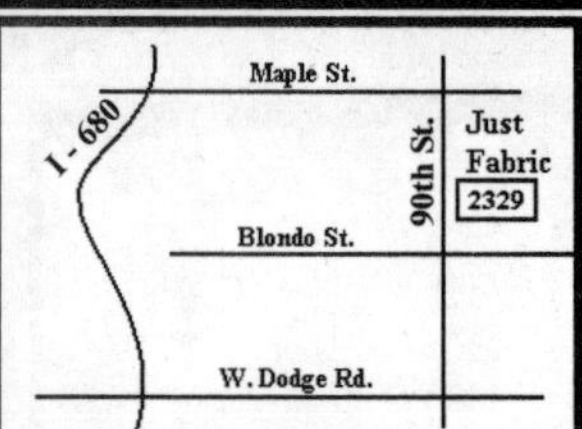

Mon - Wed - Fri - Sat 9 - 5
Tue & Thu 11 - 7

www.justfabric.com

Omaha, NE #4

Omaha, NE #5

Log Cabin Quilt Shop

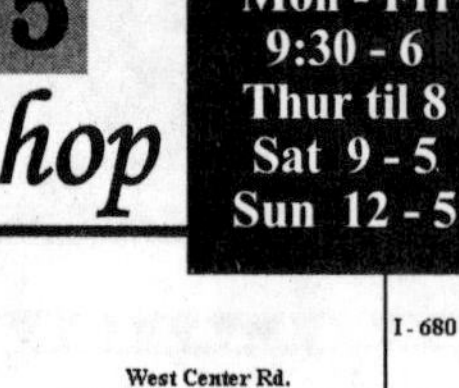

2809 South 125 Avenue #283 68144
In Westwood Plaza
sue@logcabinquilts.com
www.logcabinquilts.com
(402) 333-5212
Est: 1980 1700 sq.ft.
Complete line of books, patterns, fabrics, and notions for quilters.
Service with a smile !

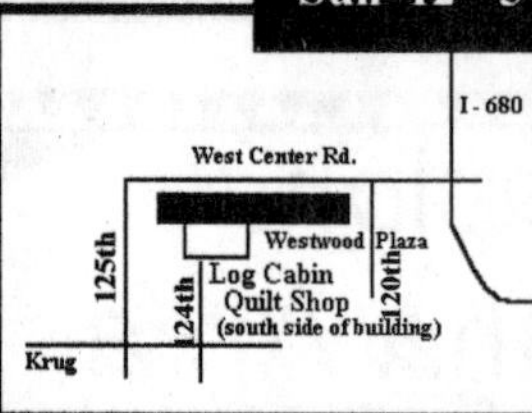

Palmyra, NE #6

Owner: Gloria Hall
Est: 1989
600 sq.ft.
Price List Avail.
(800) 284-8574

By Appt.

296 N. 10th Rd.
68418
(402) 780-5773

We have over 100 quilts dating from 1870's to 1960's
Vintage Fabric, Tops, Blocks, Feed Sacks & Old Linens.

grandma@grandmasquilts.com
www.grandmasquilts.com

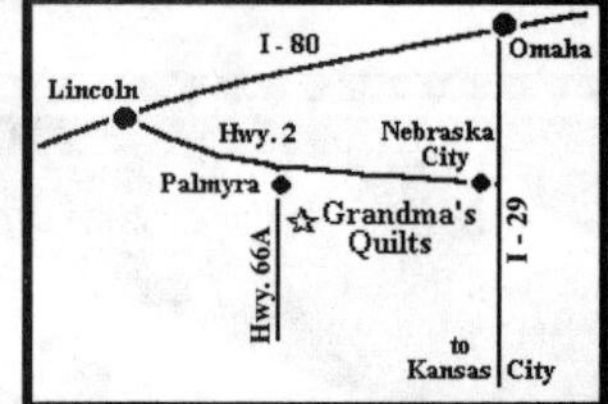

Syracuse, NE #7

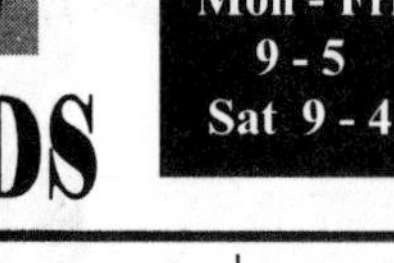

COMMON THREADS

325 5th St. 68446
(402) 269-2235
Owners: Julie & David Zahn
commonthreads@alltel.net
Est: 1997 1800 sq.ft. 800 Bolts

Nice selection of 100% Cotton fabrics, books, patterns & gifts.
Located in a restored 1890's Bank Building!

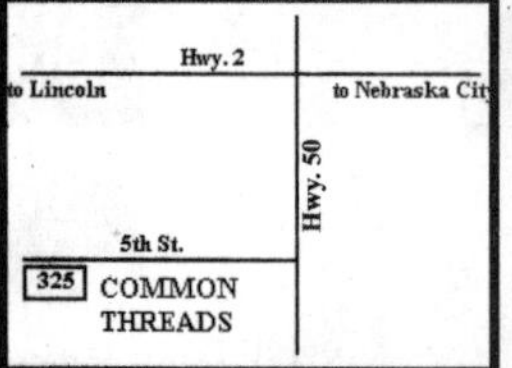

Auburn, NE #8

The Fabric Fairie

Tues, Thur, Fri 11 - 7
Wed 11 - 6
Sat 9 - 3

900 Central Ave. 68305
(402) 274-4454
pamelasfirst@alltel.net
Owner: Pamela Estrada
Est: 2002 1000 sq.ft. 700 Bolts

Small town shop, big on service. Shop in a relaxed, cozy atmosphere. Let our top quality fabrics stimulate your creativity.

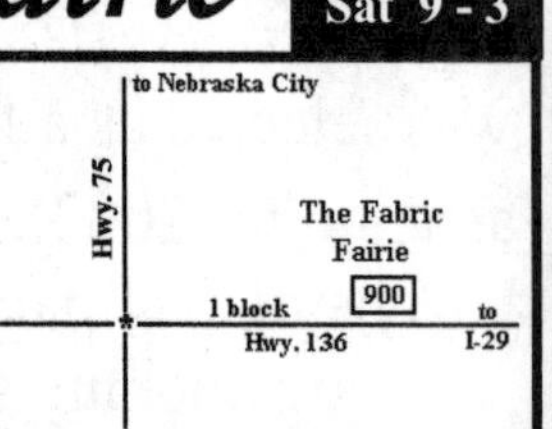

One of Nebraska's most Complete Sewing Centers!

- Full line of Fashion & Quilt Patterns
- Janome Sewing Machines & Sergers
- Large Selection of Quilt Fabrics & Books
- Supplies: Templates, Frames, Needles, Etc.
- Bridal Specialties
- Classes in Clothing Construction & Quilt Making

636 Seward St. 68434 Owner: Nancy Fleecs Est: 1970
Hrs: Mon -Sat 9 - 5:30 Thurs til 9 Sun 1 - 4

Seward, NE #9

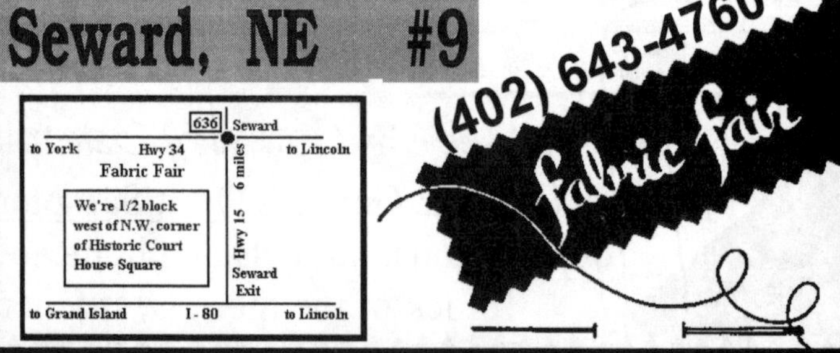

York, NE #10

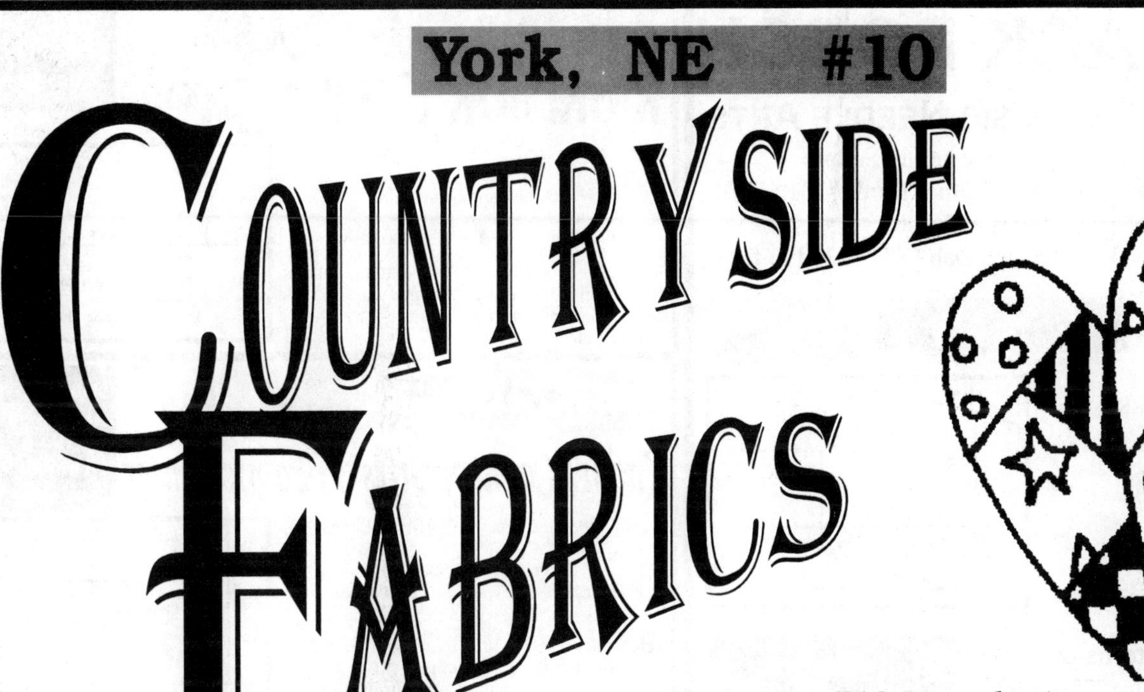

718 Lincoln Ave. 68467
Phone & Fax (402) 362-5737
countrysidefabrics@alltel.net
Owners: Ed & Lola Schall
Est: 1970 4000 sq.ft.

Mon - Fri 9:30 - 5:30
Thursdays til 8:00 pm
Sat 9am - 5pm

- Over 3000 bolts of 100% cotton, major brand fabrics
- A large selection of books, patterns, notions, and specialty threads
- National, State and Local Trunk Shows, Retreats, Seminars and Special Programs, Classes, Bernina & Thimbleberries clubs.
- Local Quilt and Thread Artists are featured
- Fashion, Bridal & Special Occasion Fabrics
- Free Newsletter on request
- Authorized Bernina Sewing Machine, Sergers, and Embroidery Systems dealer
- Friendly, Knowledgeable staff
- Free Parking
- Mail Order Welcome
- Over 4000 square feet of shopping pleasure
- Experience York

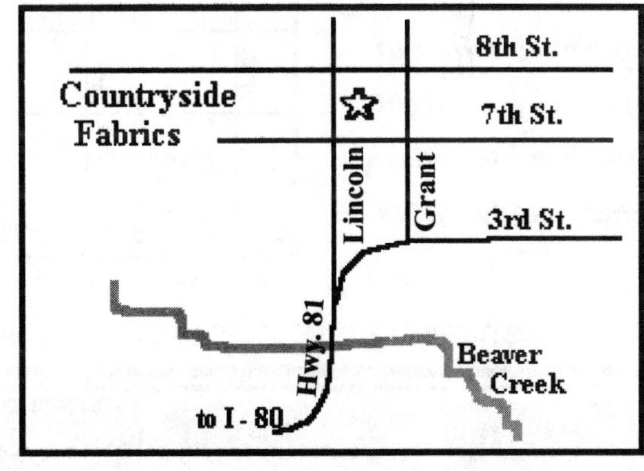

York's One-Stop Fabric Center

BERNINA

ONLY FIVE MINUTES OFF HWY 80/81
JCT. IN DOWNTOWN YORK

Use your... VISA ... MasterCard ... DISCOVER ...BERNINA CREDIT Cards

THE BACK PORCH

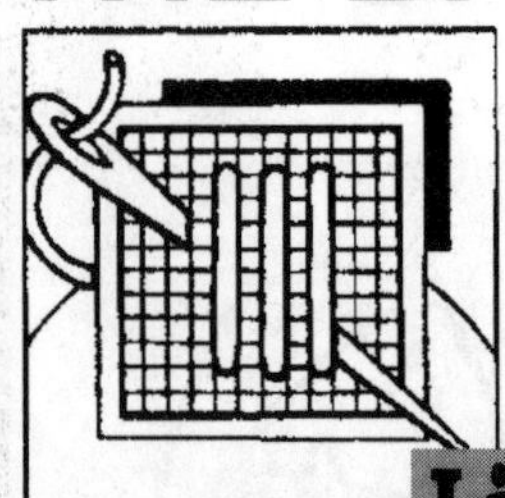

CLASSIC NEEDLE ARTS

Piccadilly Square
1415 N. Cotner Blvd. #101 68505
(402) 465-0000 Est: 2001
Owner: Deb Fick 2200 sq.ft.

Lincoln, NE #11

- Fabric
- Patterns & Books
- Smiles
- Notions
- Perle cotton
- For the crazy quilter--specialty threads, ribbons, & lace.
- Cross stitch patterns & books.
- Weeks & Sampler Threads.

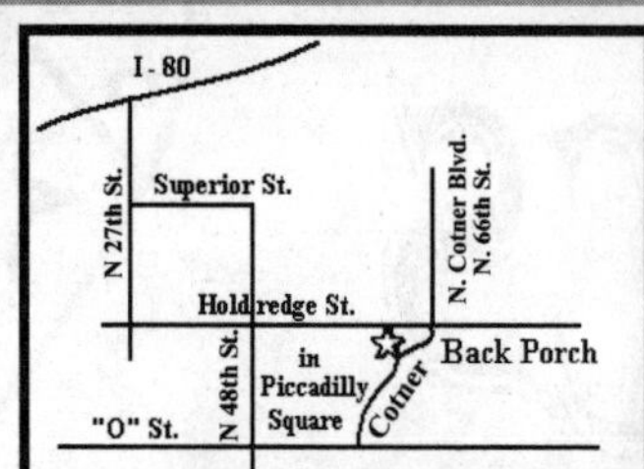

Mon - Sat 10 - 5

Lincoln, NE #12

Mon - Sat 10 - 5:30 Tues til 8

Rickrack Fabric Shop

1501 Pine Lake Rd. #13 68512
(402) 423-7227 Fax: Same
Rickrackfabric@aol.com
Owner: Linda Thompson
Est: 2003 750 sq.ft. 700 Bolts

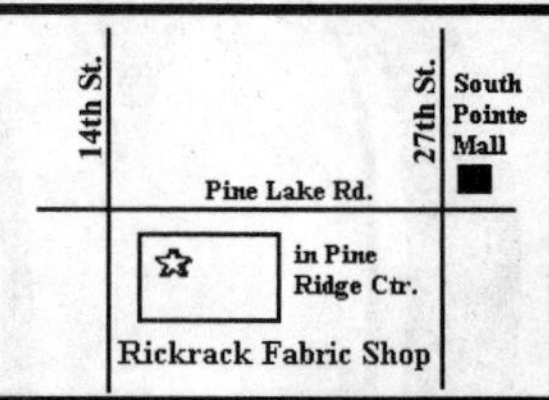

Fun collection of 100% cotton fabrics. Reproduction, novelties, brights and batiks. Books, patterns, notions, classes--All with a vintage flair.

Lincoln, NE #13

Mon 10 - 6 Tues - Sat 10 - 6 Thur til 9 Sun 12 - 5

Karen's Country Gifts & Fabric Center

5500 Old Cheney Rd. #14 68516
(402) 421-6151 Fax: Same
Karenhunt001@msn.com
Est: 1989 5500 sq.ft. 2500 Bolts

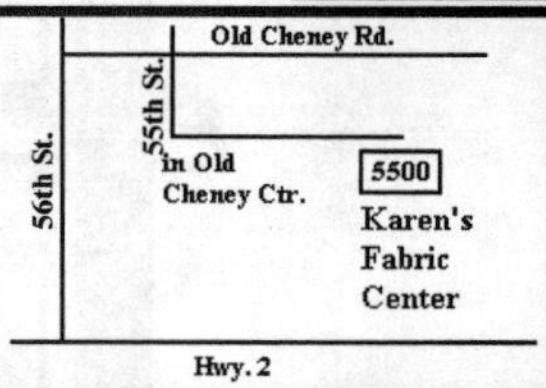

Nebraska's largest Quilt Store with over 2500 bolts of fabric & patterns. Big upstairs classroom you can rent. Come for lunch in our tearoom.

Lincoln, NE #14

Mon - Sat 10 - 5 Sun 1 - 4

5221 S. 48th St., Suite 4
Sutter Place Mall
Lincoln, NE 68516
(402) 489-1067
calicohouse@ned.rr.com

the CALICO HOUSE

Great selection of fabrics from light and brights to dark and muddy colors.

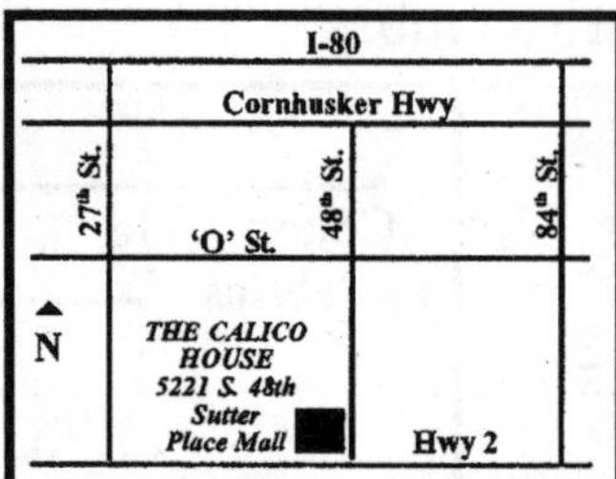

· Distances on map are not shown in accurate proportion

HOFFMAN BATIKS · MODA · FREE SPIRIT · FLANNELS

Lincoln, NE #15

Mon - Sat 10 - 5 Sun 1 - 4

Creative Hands

5220 S. 48th St. 68516
(402) 483-1538

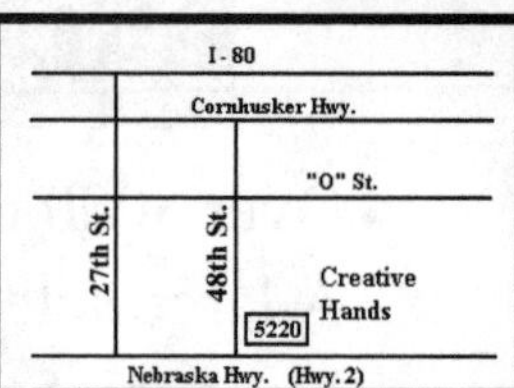

Specializing in quality cotton fabrics and friendly service.
Books, patterns, quilting supplies available.

Lincoln, NE #16

Mon - Sat 10 - 5:30

Hooper Creek Sewing & Quilting

110 S. 56th St. 68510
(402) 488-2766 Est: 1999
www.hoopercreek.com

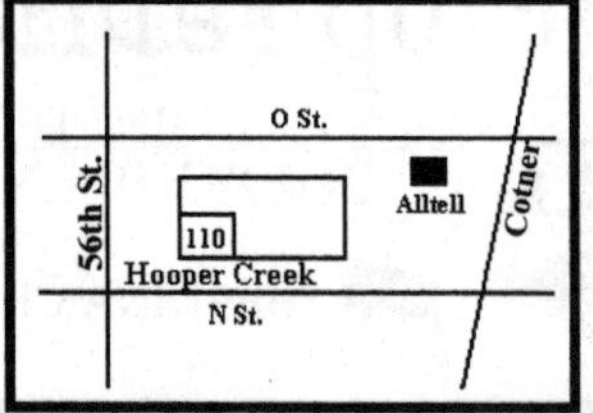

Quilting fabrics, notions, and patterns. Dealership for Pfaff and Elna Sewing Machines. Machine Quilting Service.

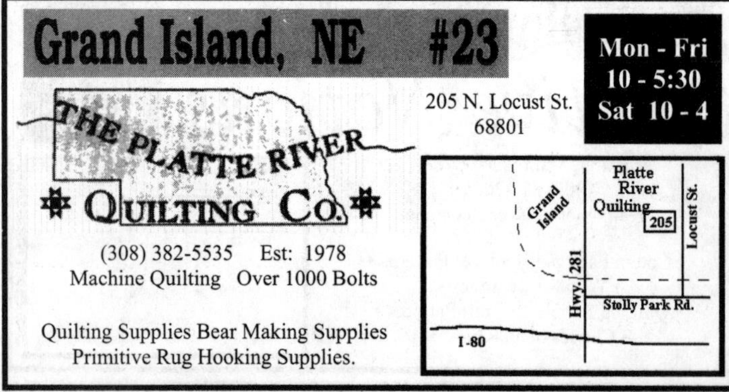

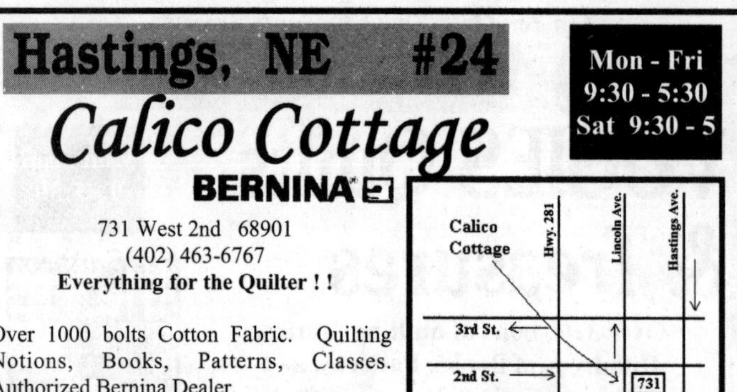

Prairie Point Junction

124 East 8th PO Box 184
Cozad, NE 69130
308-784-2010
prairiepointjunction@yahoo.com

Mon - Fri
10 - 5
Sat 10 - 4

Cozad, NE #26

Our shop is bursting with tons of displays.
You're sure to find inspiration with:

- 2000+ bolts of cotton fabrics
- 100's of patterns and books
- Lots of kits
- 50+ colors of wool felt too!

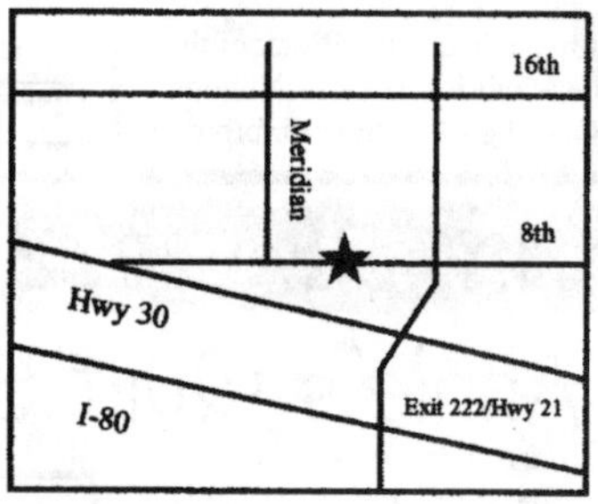

16th
Meridian
8th
Hwy 30
I-80
Exit 222/Hwy 21

Visit us on the web at www.prairiepointjunction.com

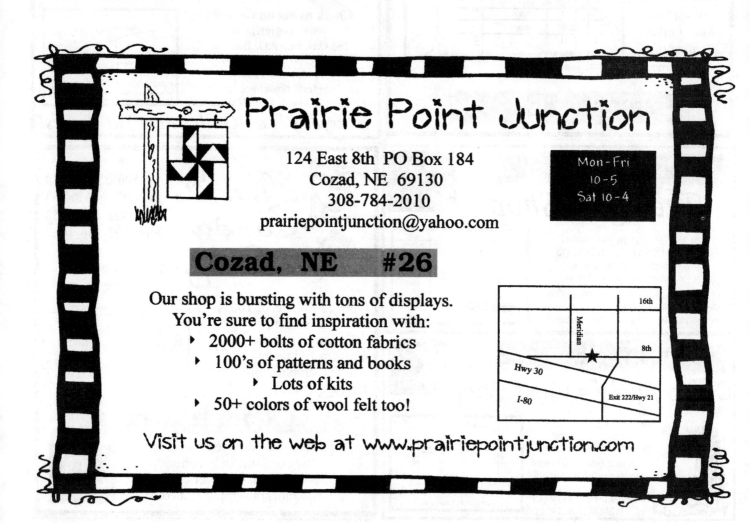

Kearney, NE #27

Mon - Fri 9:30 - 5:30
Sat 10 - 4

Quilter's Trunk

2114 Central Ave. 68847
(308) 236-6286
Fax: (308) 236-6156

100% Cotton Fabrics, notions, hundreds of books, PFAFF and Bernina Sewing Machines.

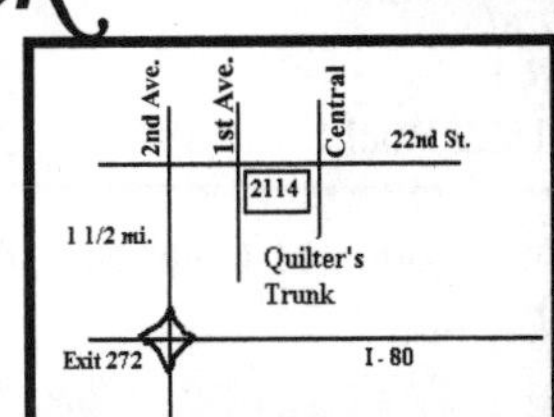

McCook, NE #28

Mon, Tues Thur, Fri 9:30 - 5
Sat 10 - 4

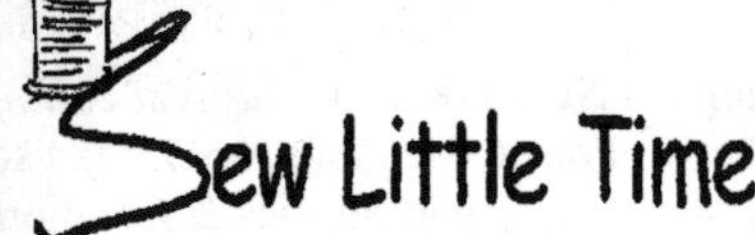

213 Norris Ave. 69001
(308) 345-4572

Quilting books, notions, patterns, 100% cotton fabrics. Great Displays. Smocking plates and supplies.

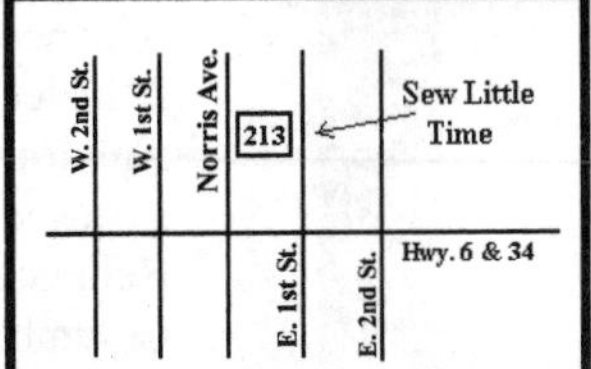

North Platte, NE #29

Mon - Fri 9:30 - 6
Wed til 7
Sat 10 - 4
Sun 1 - 4

The Quilt Rack

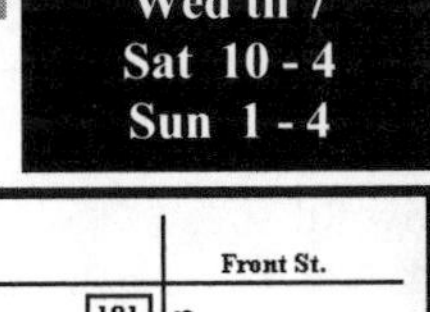

101 W. Front St. 69101
(308) 532-2606
lisa@the-quilt-rack.com Est: 2002
www.the-quilt-rack.com 3100 sq.ft.
Owner: Lisa DeBord

North Platte's only full-service quilt shop. Over 1500 bolts of quality fabrics. The best selection of books, patterns, and notions. A dedicated, knowledgeable staff to assist you with your projects.

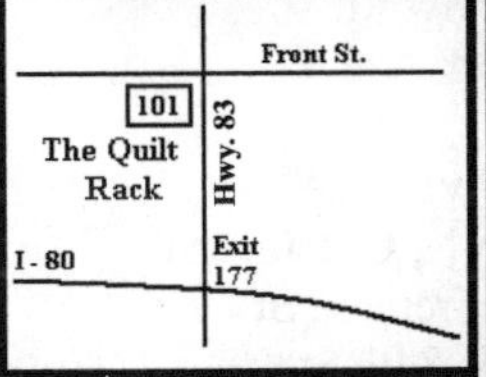

Silver Thimble Sewing Center

108 N. Spruce 69153
(308) 284-6838
Fax: (308) 284-8945
Owner: Julie Peterson
Est: 1988 2500 sq.ft.

Show us this ad and Receive a Free Gift.

Mon - Sat 9 - 5:30
Thur til 8

Ogallala, NE #30

6000+ Bolts of Cottons, Quilt Fabrics and Supplies. Books, Notions, Batting, Classes.
Pfaff Sewing Machine Sales and Service.
Full line fabric store.

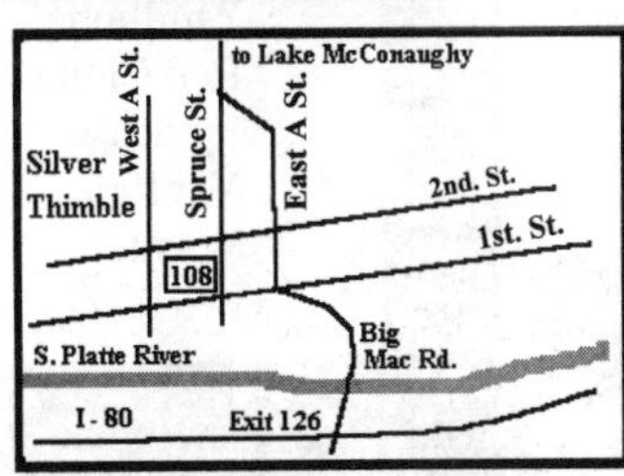

Less than 5 min. off I - 80

Imperial, NE #31

Mon - Fri 9 - 5:30
Sat 9 - 5

PRIOR'S AND SEW FORTH

525 Broadway,
P.O. Box 668 69033
(308) 882-4354
Owner: Lila V. Prior

Fabrics — quilting (4000+ Bolts) and fashion; all top quality. All your quilting supplies and other sewing notions.

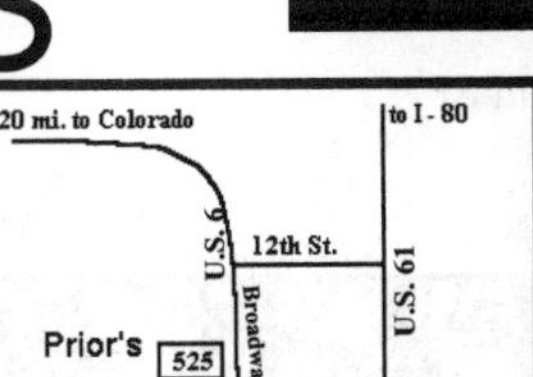

Scottsbluff, NE #32

Tues - Fri 10 - 5
Sat 10 - 4

Prairie Pines Quilt Shop

70756 County Rd. 20 69361
(308) 632-8668

Supplies and classes for Quilting and Cross-Stitch. Including 2000 bolts of 100% cotton fabrics. Authorized Bernina & New Home Sales & service.

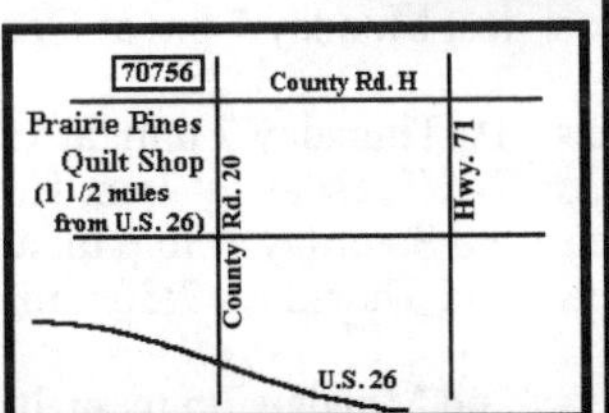

Alliance, NE #33

Mon - Sat 9 - 5:30

Special Stitches

316 Box Butte Ave. 69301
(308) 762-3784
rthiems@aol.com
www.specialstitches.com
Owner: Deb Thiems Est: 1987

Quilting Supplies, Counted Cross Stitch, Machine Quilting, Viking Sewing Machines & Sergers.

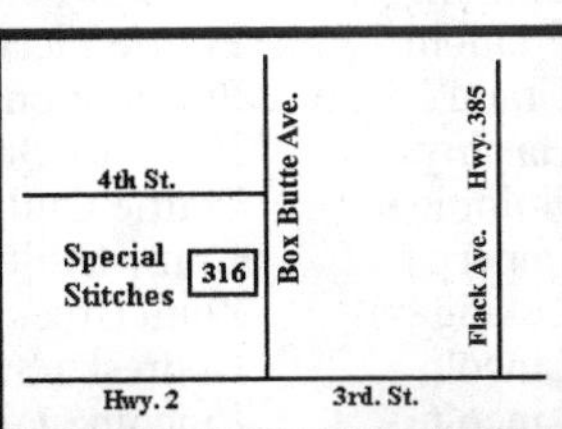

Check out our website
for the latest shops
www.chaletpublishing.com

Hemingford, NE #34

Mon - Fri 10 - 5
Sat 10 - 4

PAT'S CREATIVE

7355 Gage Rd. 69348
(308) 487-3999
Fabricfun@bbc.net
Owners: Sonya - Toni - Shelley
Est: 1975 2700 sq.ft. 2500 Bolts

Over 3000 quilting cottons - 500 flannels
Books, Patterns, Threads & Notions.
We sell Bernina & Janome Sewing Machines.
YOUR 1 STOP SEWING SHOP

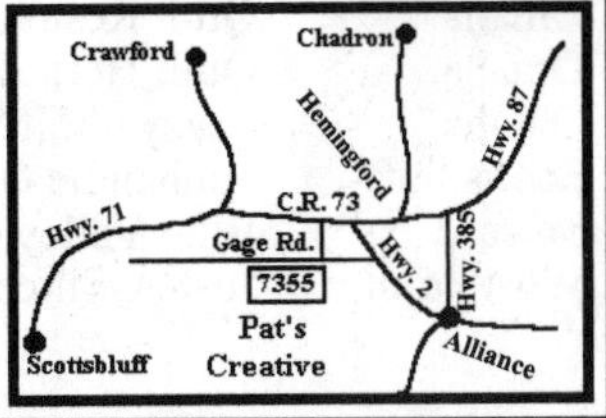

Other Shops in Nebraska: *We suggest calling first*

Alliance	Prairie Creations, 5611 Madison Rd	308-762-8365
Alliance	Quilting Memories & Creations, 1629 Buchfinck Ave.	308-762-2893
Auburn	Needles I, Rt 1 Box 11	
Beatrice	Loper's Sewing & Embroidery Workroom, 311 Court St.	402-223-3108
Bellevue	Country Corner, 1323 Harrison St	402-731-8707
Columbus	Sew - What, 3411 21st St.	402-563-3900
Crawford	K & J's Korner Quilt Shop, 120 McPherson St	308-665-1288
Curtis	Quilter's Cottage, 108 Pope Ave	308-367-8728
Fremont	Sunshine Stitches, 2625 N. Broad St.	402-727-9233
Grand Island	Y Knot Quilt, 4604 Deva Dr	308-382-1716
Gretna	Quilted Moose, 109 Enterprise Dr	402-332-4178
Homer	Wish & A Prayer, 102 S. 1st St., P.O. Box 453	402-698-2221
Kearney	Quilt Blocks Etc., P.O. Box 63	308-236-8973
Lincoln	The Quilted Kitty, 5000 Fir Hollow Rd	402-420-9292
Lincoln	Circle H Sstudios, 6220 Havelock Ave	402-467-3484
Lincoln	Sew Creative, 5221 S. 48th St.	402-489-6262
Norfolk	Pieceful Pastime, 322 Norfolk Ave	402-371-0045
North Platte	Jo's Stitchery & Quilt Shop, 408 N. Chestnut St.	308-532-3225
O Neill	Shanette's Quilt Corner, 404 W Fremont St	402-336-1632
Omaha	Bernina Sewing Centers, 3407 S. 84th St.	402-392-0430
Omaha	SunShine Stitches, 595 N. 155th Plaza	402-504-1345
Oxford	Alaska Dyeworks, 322 Ogden St	308-824-3540
Papillion	Quilt Boutique, 546 N. Washington St.	402-339-6984
Red Cloud	Sewing Box, 422 N. Webster St.	402-746-3592
Syracuse	Hobnobbers, 331 5th St	402-269-2233
Verdigie	Verdigie Creek Quilts, 304 S Main St	402-668-7497
Wayne	Jest Sew, 512 E. 7th	402-375-4697

Nebraska Guilds:

Beatrice	Beatrice Quilters' Guild	Meets: 2nd Tuesday 10:30 a.m.
Cozad	Hands All Around	Meets: 3rd Tuesday 7 p.m. at Wilson Center
Elkhorn	Cottonwood Quilters, P.O. Box 27, 68022	Meets: 3rd Monday at St. John's Lutheran Church, Bennington
Fremont	Prairie Piecemakers, P.O. Box 1202, 68025	Meets: last Monday 7 pm at Good Shepherd Church, 1544 E. Military
Grand Island	Prairie Pioneer Quilters, P.O. Box 675, 68802	
Hastings	Hastings Quilters Guild, P.O. Box 442, 68901	Meets: 1st Thursday 7 p.m. at 1st St. Paul's Lutheran Church Basement
Holdrege	Prairie Quilt Guild, 323 West Avenue, 68949	Meets: 2nd Tuesday @ 7pm, Holdrege Library
Imperial	Crazy Quilt Guild, P.O. Box 100, 69033	Meets: 2nd Saturday 1:30 p.m. at Senior Center
Lexington	Plum Creek Quilters	Meets: 2nd Thursdays 7:30 p.m. at Grand Centeration Center
Lincoln	Nebraska State Quilt Guild, 68516	
Lincoln	Lincoln Quilters Guild, P.O. Box 6861, 68506	Meets: 2nd Monday 7 p.m. at 7th Day Adventist Church
Nebraska City	Heritage Quilt & Needlework Guild, 315 S. 16th, 68410	Meets: 4rth Tuesday at 7 p.m.
Norfolk	Country Piecemakers Quilt Guild, 509 Norfolk Ave.	Meets: 3rd Monday (except Dec.) 7:30 p.m. at Norfolk Senior Center, 307 Prospect St.
North Platte	Heartland Quilters' Guild, PO Box 1896, 69101	Meets: 1st Thursday at 7:30pm, McKinley Education Ct, 301 W F St.
Ogallala	Ogallala Boot Hill Stitchers, 108 N. Spruce, 69153	Meets: 3rd Saturday, 1 p.m. at Silver Thimble Sewing Center
Omaha	Omaha Quilters Guild, 108th and Grover	Meets: 2nd Tuesday (Sept - May) at Westside Community Center
Omaha	Quilt Restoration Society & Conference, P.O. Box 19452, 68119, Fax: 800-811-1610	
Omaha	Quilt Heritage Foundation--Quilt Rescue Squad, P.O. Box 19452, 68119, Fax: 800-811-1610	
Omaha	Crazy Quilt Society & Conference, P.O. Box 19452, 68119, Fax: 800-811-1610	
Scottsbluff	Panhandle Quilt Guild, 180009 Thomas Dr., 69361	Meets: 3rd Saturday at various locations
Seward	Blue Valley Quilters, 636 Seward St., 68434	Meets: 3rd Monday 7pm at Civic Center
West Point	Just-A-Stitch Quilt Guild, 107 N. Main St., 68788	Meets: 7pm at Creative Notions

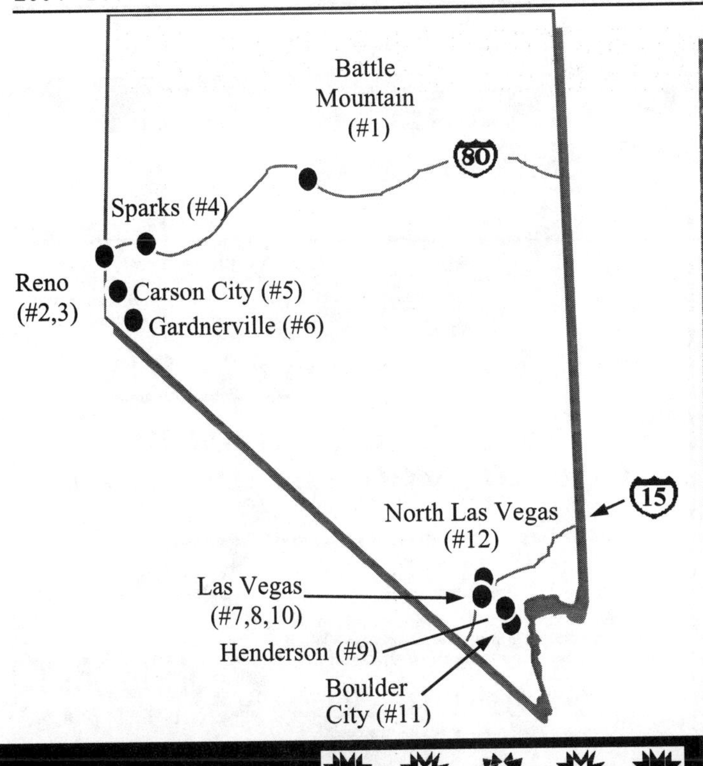

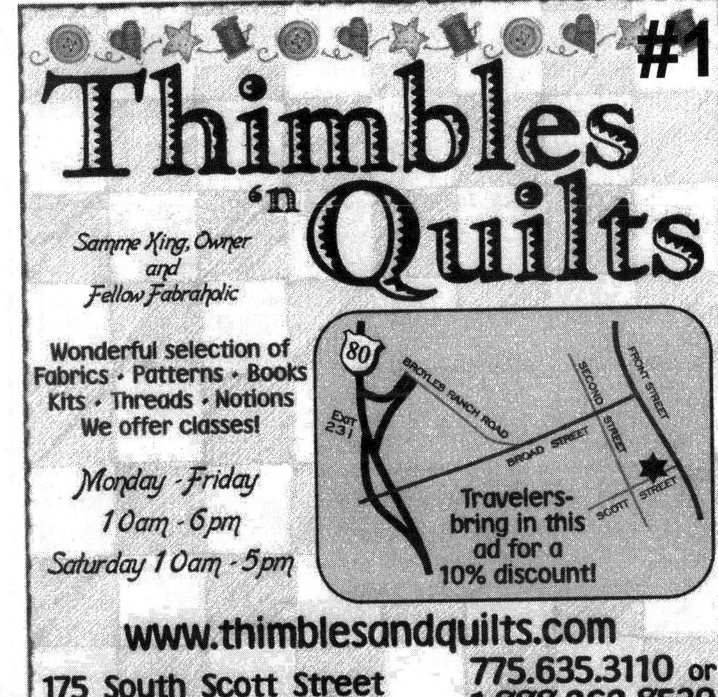

NEVADA

12 Featured Shops

Reno, NV #2

440 Spokane Street 89512

6,000 sq. ft. of fabric, books, notions, patterns, classes, gifts, and quilting help.

All the Quilter's Needs

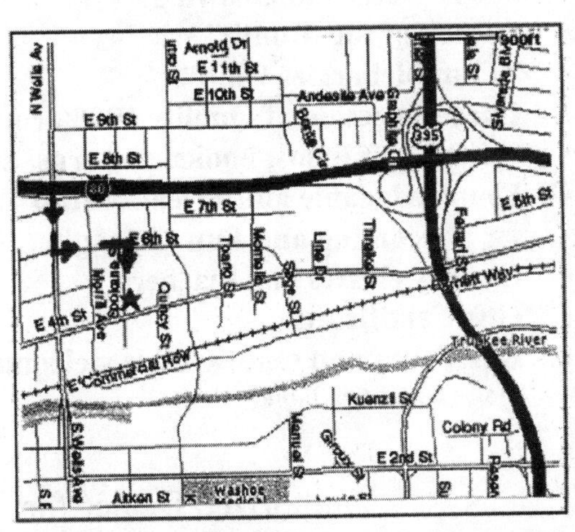

"Biggest little Quilt Shop in the West"

Visit, Call or Fax
Monday - Saturday 10 - 6
Sunday 11 - 5
(775) 323-4777 or (800) 622-8082
FAX (775) 323-4790

Shop on Line → www.windymoonquilts.com

Reno, NV #3

Mon - Sat 9:30 - 5:30

Sierra Sewing

4145 S. Virginia St. 89502
(775) 823-9700
Owner: Lee Levin

Great Quilt Fabrics and all the latest notions and Viking, Pfaff & White Machines.

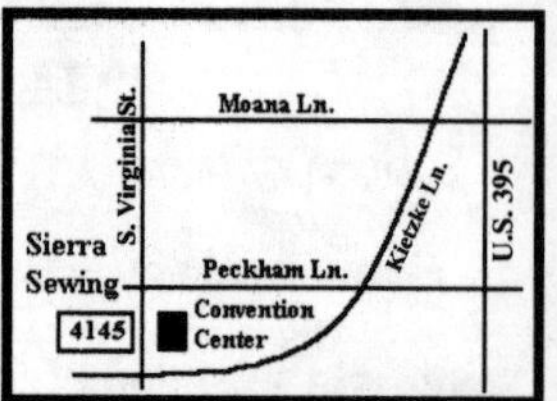

Sparks, NV #4

Mon - Sat 10 - 4

Quilt Stop

101 15th St. 89431
(775) 355-3233
Owner: Joan Carroll 6000 Bolts

100% Cotton Fabric, Classes, Books, Patterns, Notions, Quilts on Display. Also mail order. Call for info.

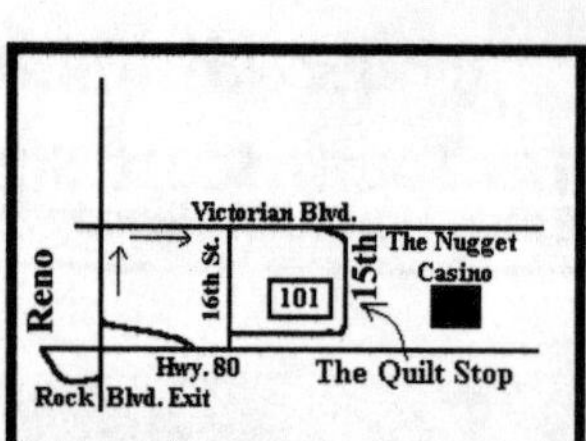

Carson City, NV #5

Cloth Cottage
Northern Nevada's Premium Quilt Store

We've expanded our floor space and inventory to better serve all your sewing and quilting needs. With over 3,000 sq. ft. we are known as the purveyor of the finest fabrics for quilting and home decorating. You will be inspired!

(775) 841-9191
www.clothcottage.com

Two great stores in one convenient location
Monday-Saturday 9:30 a.m until 5:30 p.m. Closed Sunday

We feature only the best in sewing machines!
PFAFF
authorized dealer

Experienced staff with show you how to get the most out of your new machine. We'll be with you every stitch of the way.

(775) 884-9500
e-mail: sewbizi@sierrasewing.com

Sierra Sewing CENTER INC

511 Fairview Drive, Carson City, Nevada 89701
Follow Highway 395 to Carson City. Turn on Fairview Drive.
We are across the street from Lowe's Hardware and 30 minutes from Reno and Lake Tahoe.

"Experience the FUN with us !!!" Gardnerville, NV #6

The Quilt House Inc.

Est: 1999

VISA MasterCard

1328 N. Hwy. 395 #105 , 89410
(775) 782-8845 Fax: (775) 782-5004
theqlthouse@aol.com
www.TheQuiltHouse.net
Owners: Janet Pierce & Gary Pierce

Monday - Saturday 10am - 5pm
Closed Sundays

- 3000+ Bolts and Growing
- "Block of the Month"
- "Thimbleberries Club"
- Large selection of Quality 100% cotton fabrics
- "Kits", gift items, books, patterns, and notions
- Knowledgeable and Friendly staff and welcoming and Fun atmosphere.
- Quality classes and teachers
- Gift Certificates
- Bus Tours and Quilt Guilds welcome (please call ahead)
- Mail Order Available

Chosen one of ten *"Award Winning" Quilt Shops* featured in the September 2004 issue of **"Quilt Sampler"**

In the "Park Place" Center

395
To Carson City And Reno
N
MINDEN
GARDNERVILLE
88
TOLER AVE.
WATERLOO LANE
The Quilt House
207
756
395
756
To Markleeville
To Bridgeport

Authorized Dealer for: Nothing Sews Like A Bernina. Nothing. BERNINA® HORN of America The Perfect Sewing Chair™

Fabric Boutique
Quilt Shop
4465 W. Charleston,
Las Vegas, NV 89102
www.fabricboutique.com
(702) 878-0068
Owners: Helen Clapp, Ev Dahl
Las Vegas, NV #7
Be sure to visit us
on your next trip
to Las Vegas!
You'll find:
11,000 Sq. Ft. of Pure
Quilting Heaven
Over 5,000 Bolts of
Quilting Cottons
Huge Selection of
Books and Patterns
Classes
Pfaff Sewing Machines
Space and Machine
Available for Visitors
to Sew!
Open 7
Days A Week
W. Charleston
Taco Bell
Decatur
Fabric
Boutique
4465
Walmart Super Center
2 1/2 mi. to Strip

Est: 1993

The Christmas Goose

5,000 sq.ft.

Las Vegas, NV #8

4750 W. Sahara #6
Las Vegas, NV 89102
(702) 877-1158
E-Mail: Cmasgoose@aol.com
Owner: Jeanette Sherrick

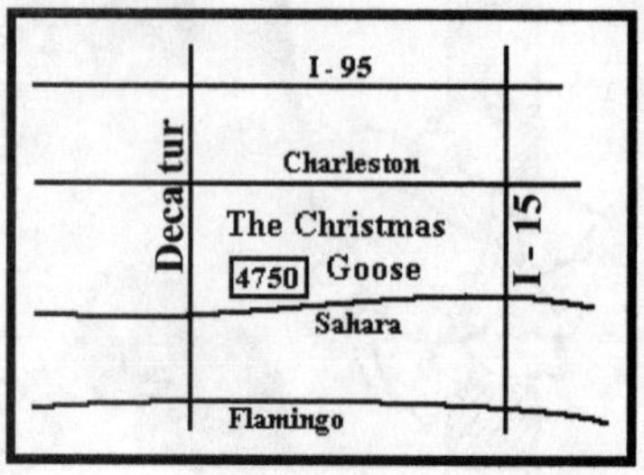

I-95
Charleston
Decatur
The Christmas Goose
4750
I-15
Sahara
Flamingo

www.Christmasgoose.com

We carry a large selection of cotton fabrics, Patterns, Books, Notions and Quilting Supplies. Plus Country Gifts like Boyds Bears, Warm Glow Candles, Williraye collection and home décor items.

Mon - Sat
10 - 6
Sun 12 - 4

QUILTIQUE

Las Vegas' Newest Quilt Shop

- 4000+ Bolts of 100% Cotton Fabrics
- Full Line of Quilting Supplies
- Antiques & Gift Items Too!!

#9

Open Monday thru Saturday
10 am - 6 pm

213 N. Stephanie, #E
Henderson, NV
89074

(702) 563-8600

www.quiltique.com

DRIVING DIRECTIONS from the LV Strip

South on I-15 to Henderson/Las Vegas;

Exit onto East I-215 (Henderson/McCarran Airport Exit);

Exit onto Stephanie St., turn left to travel north;

Approx. 1 mile turn left at American Pacific into the Stephanie Promenade Center & you're there!

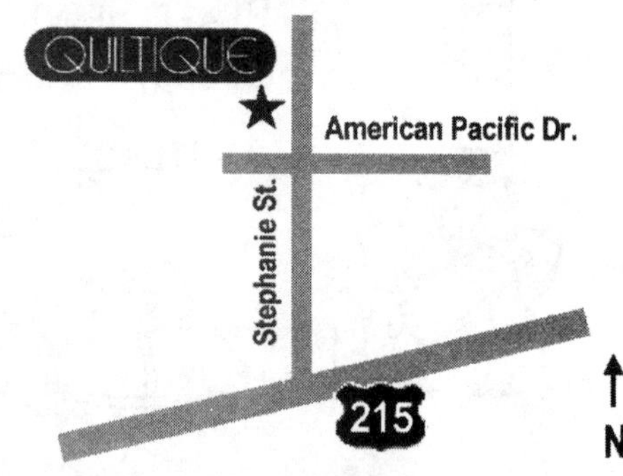

Nancy's Quilt Shop

3290 N. Buffalo Dr.
Las Vegas, NV 89129
702-839-2779
Hours: Mon-Sat 9am-6pm
www.nancysquiltshop.com

Est: 2002 5500 sq. ft. Over 6000 bolts

We are located on the northwest side of town near Summerlin: take Interstate 15 north to Interstate 95 north, exit at Cheyenne, turn left (heading west). Go 1/2 mile to Buffalo and take a right. We are 1 1/2 blocks on your right in a free standing building.

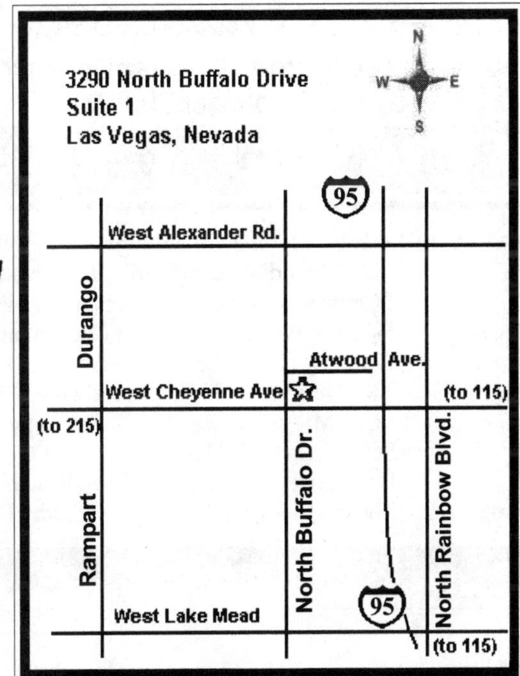

Nancy's offers you a wonderful variety of quality cotton quilting fabric including the full lines of Benartex Fossil Ferns and Moda Marbles. We carry a large selection of flannels, Asian fabrics and batiks as well as the popular reproduction fabrics. Books, patterns, notions, kits, stitchery and locker rug hooking supplies are available.

Our sale room is always full of great value; use our convenient carts to "load up".

Visit our website for online shopping, newsletter, class schedule, calendar and coupon to print out.

We are known for our great customer service.

Owners: Nancy & Mark Laussade

Las Vegas, NV #10

fiddlesticks

quilts and other works of heart

Mon - Fri 10 - 5:30
Sat 10 - 4:30

(702) 293-2979

Owner: Nanci Bowen

www.fiddlesticksquilts.com

Located in Historic Old Town... come visit a gentler time and treat your senses. We have a unique selection of quilt fabrics, books and notions, all carefully chosen with our customers in mind. Among our favorites are warm Moda plaids and beautiful vintage prints, bark cloth, linens and velvets. You'll find antiques, gifts and one-of-a-kind treasures made by local craftspeople as well as many classes taught by these artists. More than just a fabric store, we specialize in new ideas and personal customer service. Come stretch your creativity and let us spoil you... the tea kettle is always on!

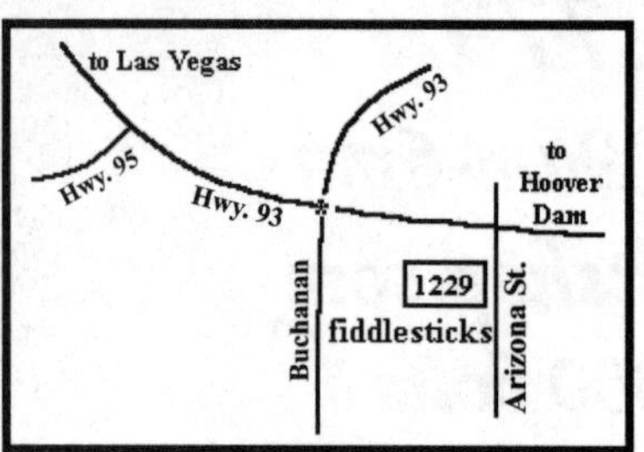

1229 Arizona St. 89005

Between the Historic Boulder Dam Hotel and the Boulder Theater

Boulder City, NV #11

N. Las Vegas, NV #12

Mon - Fri 10 - 5
Sat 10 - 4

Uncommon Threads

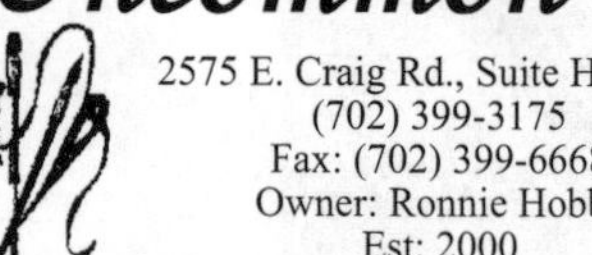

2575 E. Craig Rd., Suite H 89030
(702) 399-3175
Fax: (702) 399-6668
Owner: Ronnie Hobbs
Est: 2000

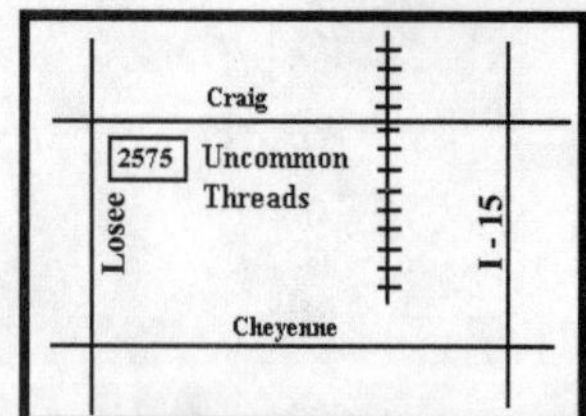

2000 square feet of over 2000 bolts of 100% Cotton Fabrics, Notions, Books & Patterns. Classes available. 1/2 mile west of I-15 on Craig Road.

Other Shops in Nevada: *We suggest calling first*

Elko	Elko Floral Fabric and Gifts, 180 Idaho St.	775-738-4728
Fallon	Workman's Farms Crafts & Nursery, 4990 Reno	702-867-3716
Las Vegas	Quilts in the Attic, 4465 W. Charleston Blvd.	702-880-4558
Las Vegas	Julia's Quilting, 1271 Finale Ln	702-274-1869
Minden	TRS Designs, 1731 Westwood Dr.	775-782-6179
Pahrump	I Can Make That …., 111 S. Frontage Rd.	775-727-0994
Reno	Sew-N-Such, 3702 S Virginia St #G8	775-825-6677
Sparks	Ben Franklin Crafts, 530 Green Brae Dr.	775-331-5755
Winnemucca	Those Moody Girls, 4695 Weatherby Dr.	775-625-2711

Nevada Guilds:

Battle Mountain	Battle Mountain Quilt Guild, P.O. Box 7, 89820	Meets: 3rd Thursday 7 p.m. at Thimbles 'n Quilts
Elko	Silver Sage Quilt Guild, P.O. Box 6262, 89802	Meets: 4th Monday at the Girl Scout House
Gardnerville	Carson Valley Quilt Guild, 89410	
Las Vegas	Desert Quilters of Nevada, P.O. Box 28586, 89126	Meets: Quarterly (July, Oct, Jan, April) various locations
Minden	Carson Valley Quilt Guild, P.O. Box 2541, 89423	Meets: 4th Monday 6:30 p.m. at Carson Valley United Methodist
Reno	Creative Quilters of Nevada, P.O. Box 3725, 89505	
Reno	Truckee Meadows Quilters, P.O. Box 5502, 89513	Meets: 1st & 3rd Friday 7 p.m. and 2nd & 4th Friday 10 a.m. at Silver Connection, 601 W. 1st St.
Wells	Hummin'bolt Quilters Guild	Meets: 3rd Monday at Senior Center
Winnemucca	Winnemucca Crazy Quilters	Meets: Every Monday at meeting room at the fair grounds

Rumney, NH #1

Main Street 03266
(800) 348-9567 or (603) 786-9567
E-Mail: info@calicocupboard.com
Web Site: www.calicocupboard.com
Est: 1978 2000 sq.ft.
Owners: Joe & Nancy Kolb

A Delightful Experience

In A Quaint New England Village

* Super collection of the newest quilting fabrics.
* Terrific selection of cozy flannels and bright, whimsical kids' prints.
* Outstanding variety of quilting books.
* Warm atmosphere and friendly service.

Mon - Sat 9:30 - 5:30
Sun 9:30 - 5
Closed April

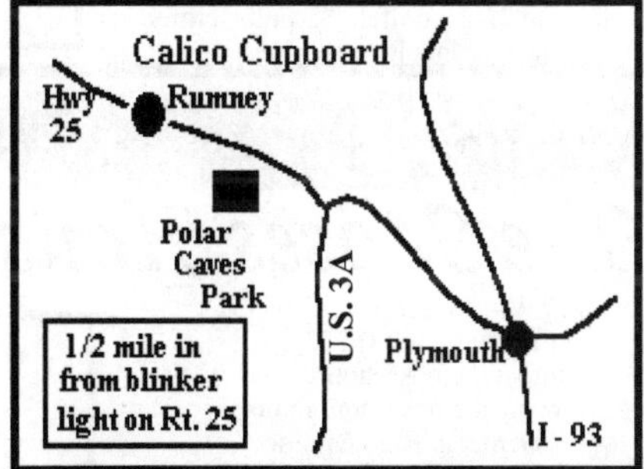

We're Worth the Trip!

Woodsville, NH #2

Tues - Sat 9:30 - 5 Fri til 6

Seams Sew Easy Fabric Shoppe

65 Central St. 03785
(603) 747-3054
Owners: Chris & Lloyd Steeves

A complete fabric store featuring a large selection of quilting fabrics and supplies. Quality Paton's & Plymouth yarns.

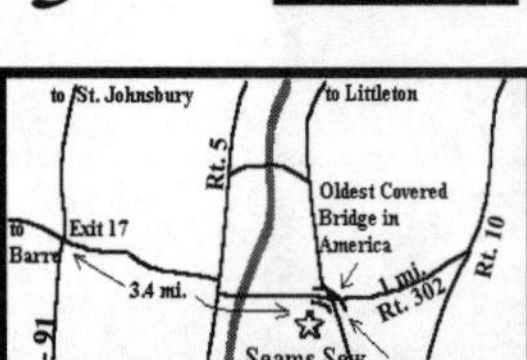
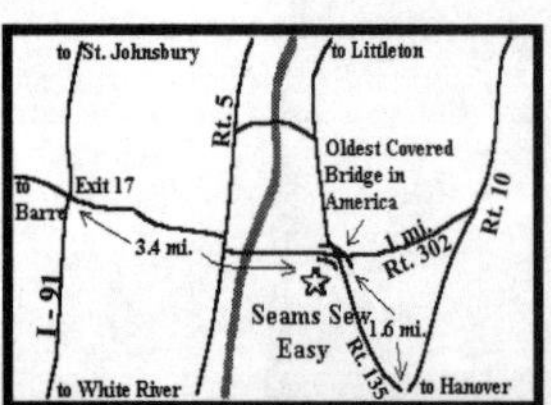

Littleton, NH #3

Mon- Sat 9:30 - 6 Sun 11 - 5

Cut 'n Sew Fabrics

562 Meadow St. 03561
(603) 444-7760
Owner: Jane Ladd
Est: 1970 3200 sq.ft.

Large store filled with quilting fabrics and supplies, drapery - slipcover and garment fabrics, yarns, needlework kits; NASCAR clothing & cars.

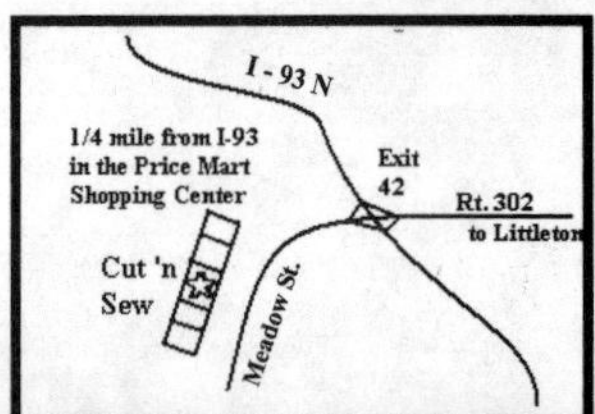

Lincoln, NH #4

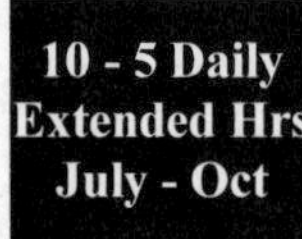

Pinestead Quilts

Main St. 03251
(603) 745-8640
Owner: Kathleen Achorn Sherburn
Est: 1980

A personal quilt shop where your projects interest us. Quilting, knitting, cross-stitch & craft supplies. Fabrics, books, patterns, kits. Ready-made quilts, wallhangings & crafts.

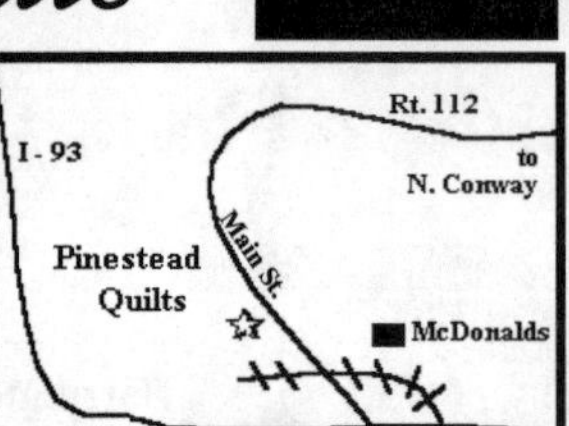

Conway, NH #5

Mon - Sat 9 - 5:00 Sun 10-4

THE QUILT SHOP AT VAC N SEW

Over 2000 Bolts of Cottons
All at Discounted Prices
Books, Patterns, Bernina, Elna, PFAFF

Rt. 16 Next to Family Dollar
Toll Free 888-447-3470
www.quiltshopnh.com

Center Harbor, NH #6

Mon - Sat 9 - 6 Sun 9 - 5 Extended Summer hrs.

Keepsake Quilting

In Senters Marketplace
Route 25B P.O. Box 1618 03226
(603) 253-4026
Est: 1988 Free 128 pg. Catalog

America's largest quilt shop with over 10,000 bolts of cotton! Hundreds of finished Quilts.
Don't miss it. It's a Quilter's Paradise!

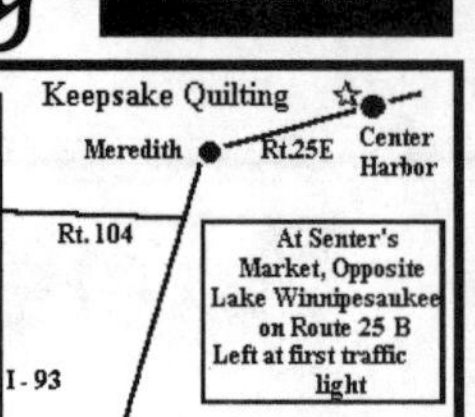

Grantham, NH #7

Mon - Fri 9:30 - 5 Sat 9:30 - 3

Sunshine Carousel Quilt Shop

Sawyer Brook Plaza, Route 10 03753
(603) 863-5754
scqs@srnet.com
www.scqs.com
Owner: Elaine Pillsbury
Est: 1990 5000 sq.ft.
4000+ Bolts

Full Service Quilt Shop
"Let us help you make a memory!"

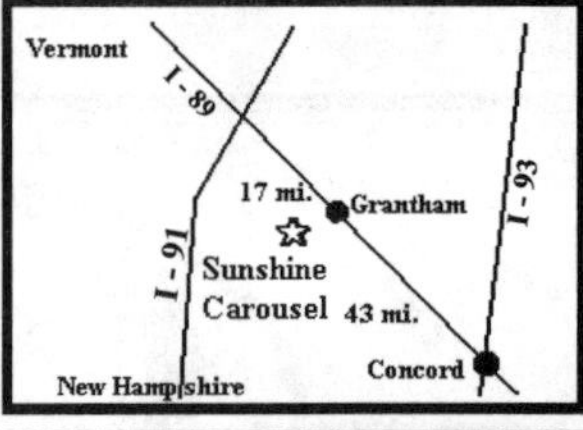

Hillsboro, NH #8

APPLE TREE FABRICS

282 Henniker St. 03244
(603) 464-5510 Est: 1980
whijer@tds.net 1300 sq.ft.
www.appletreefabrics.com 1100+ Bolts
Owner: Carole Whitney
"Friendly Country Town Fabric Shop"
Quilting supplies, notions, 100% cotton fabric, books, patterns, woolfelt™, quilts, crafts, classes, Janome machines.

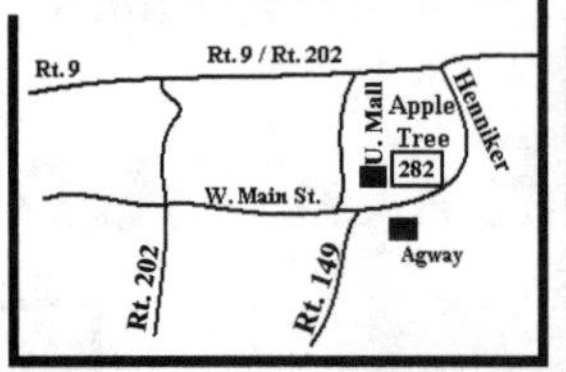

Keene, NH #10

Mon - Fri 10 - 5:30 Sat 10 - 4

The Moses House

423 Winchester St. 03431
Phone/Fax: (603) 352-2312
info@themoseshouse.com
www.themoseshouse.com
Owners: Russ Moline
Est: 1987 1800 sq.ft.

The best quilting fabrics, books, patterns, and supplies. Many reproduction fabrics. Redwork. Grace Quilting frames on display. NOLTING Longarm Quilting Machine dealer.

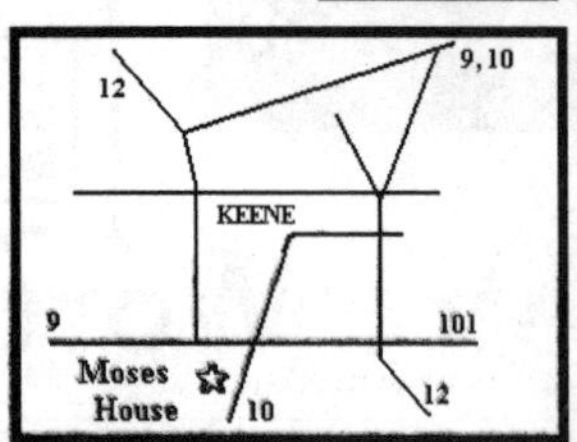

Keene, NH #9

Mon - Sat 9:30 - 5:30 Fri til 8

NEW ENGLAND FABRICS

– & Decorating Center –

Tremendous Selection of Beautiful Fabrics for:

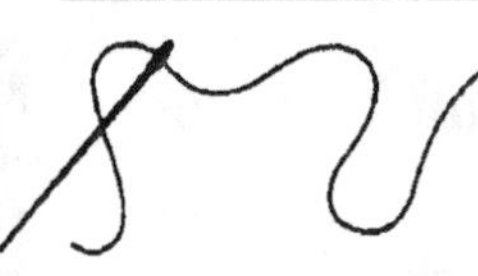

- Quilting • Apparel • Bridal
- Draperies • Slipcovers
- Upholstery & More!

Plus Yarn & Sewing Machines

Central New England's Largest Fabric & Home Decorating Center!

55 Ralston St., Keene, NH 03431
(603) 352-8683
www.nefabrics.com

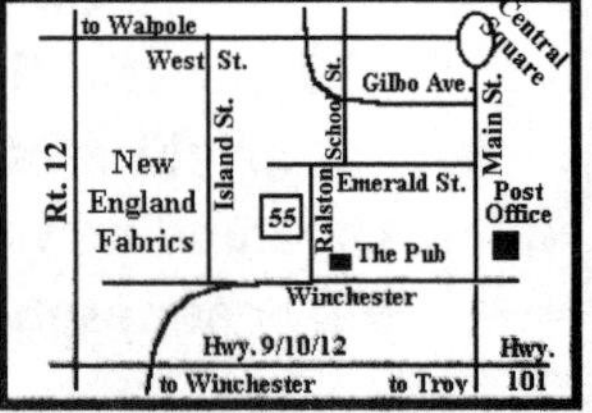

Amherst, NH #11

The Little Quilt Shop

We have a great selection of fine quality 100% cotton fabrics including: Thimbleberries, Moda, Thirties, Kids, Ethnic and much more. Classes, Notions, Machines and 100's of Books and Patterns.

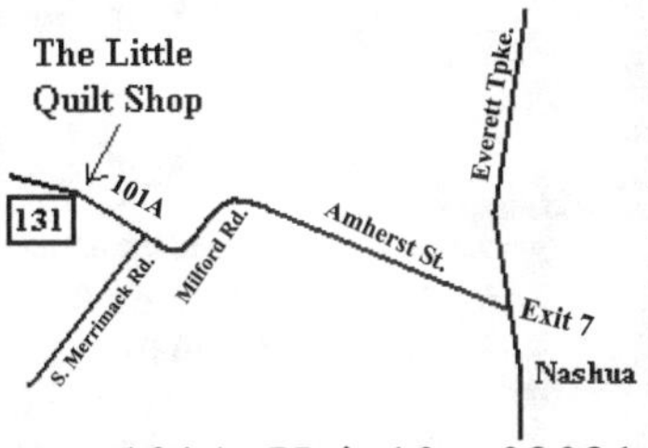

The Little Quilt Shop
101A
131
S. Merrimack Rd.
Milford Rd.
Amherst St.
Everett Tpke.
Exit 7
Nashua

Mon 9:30 - 5:30
Tues 9:30 - 9
Wed, Thur, Fri 9:30 - 7
Sat 9:30 - 4

131 Route 101A, Unit 10 03031
"Amherst Plaza" (603) 886-6084
Fax: (603) 886-6085
info@fatquarters.com
www.thelittlequiltshop.com

Owner:
Shirley Collins

Hollis, NH #12

Tues - Sat 10 - 5

Quiltopia

Hollis Village Marketplace 03049
(603) 465-9119
jdamon@quiltopia.com
www.quiltopia.com
Owner: Judy Damon
Est: 1999 1000 sq. ft. 1200 Bolts.

Colorful fabrics from top manufacturers, including Balis, brights, orientals. Oceans of notions, plus books, patterns, stencils. Friendly, helpful service & expert advice.

Concord, NH #13

Mon - Sat 10 - 5
June, July, Aug
Mon-Fri 10 - 5
Sat 10 - 1

Golden Gese Quilt Shop

22 Liberty St. 03301
(603) 228-5540
Owner: Nancy Gesen
Est: 1987 1200 sq.ft. 2000 Bolts

100% Cotton Fabric, Books, Patterns, Notions & Classes. Helpful Assistance.

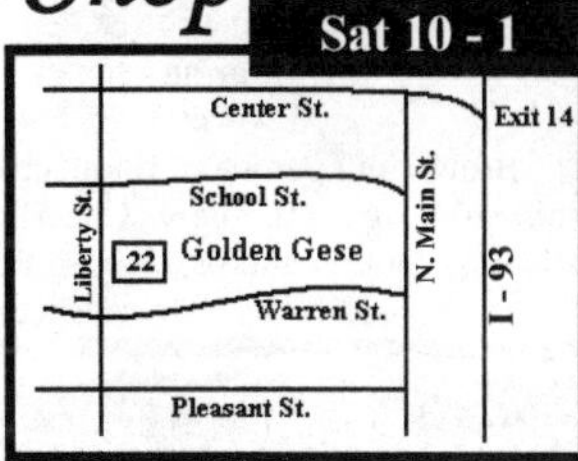

Est: 2003

PEGGY ANNE'S
Quilting & Sewing Co.

Peggy Anne's Quilting & Sewing Co.
Offers Liberty of London, Tana Lawn, Kaffe Fasset, fine British heirloom quilter's tools, as well as over 1,000 bolts of premium quilter's cottons!

BERNINA sewing machines are our specialty, we offer a full range of quilting, heirloom, dollmaking and designer classes!

www.peggyannes.com

Concord, NH #14

57 North Main St. • Concord, NH 03301
603-223-2344
Fax: 603-223-2303

Mon - Thurs 10 - 5 • Fri 10 - 9 • Sat 10 - 5

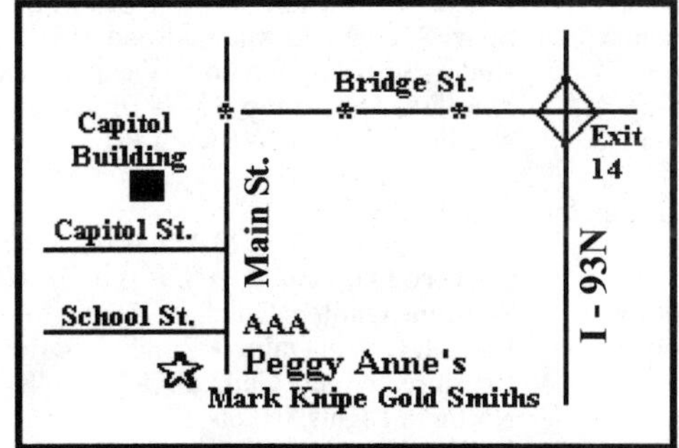

Hooksett, NH #15

Mon - Fri 8 - 6
Sat 9 - 3

Levesque's Sewing Machine, Vacuum & Quilt Shop

1261 Hooksett Rd. 03106
(603) 645-1661 Fax: Same
lele102@hotmail.com
www.levesquesewvac.com
Owner: Dennis P. Levesque
Est: 1994 2400 sq.ft.
Warm, full service sewing center, personalized attention, 100% quality cotton fabrics, books, notions, supplies plus special orders and classes.

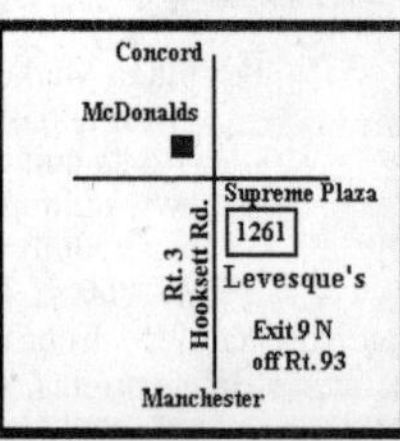

Manchester, NH #16

Mon - Fri 9:30 - 4
Thur til 6
Sat 9:30 - 2

The Chestnut Quilter

76 Lowell St. 03101
(603) 647-8458
E-Mail: chestnutquilter@hotmail.com

Fine Quilting Supplies, Quilting Classes

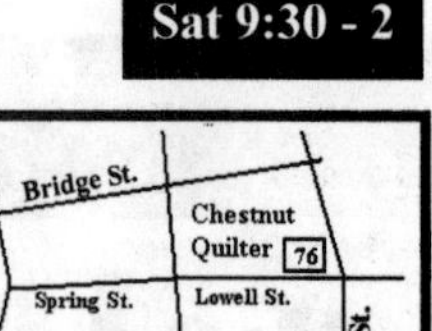

Barrington, NH #17

Tues & Thur 4 - 8
Sat 9 - 4
Extended Hrs During School Vacations

The Fabric Garden

4 Rte. 125 03825
(603) 868-2002
krhodes@metrocast.net
Owner: Katrina Rhodes
Est: 2003
Browse our garden of florals, batiks, children's, 30's, and fillers. Cheerful service, notions, books, patterns, classes, friendship opportunities in abundance!

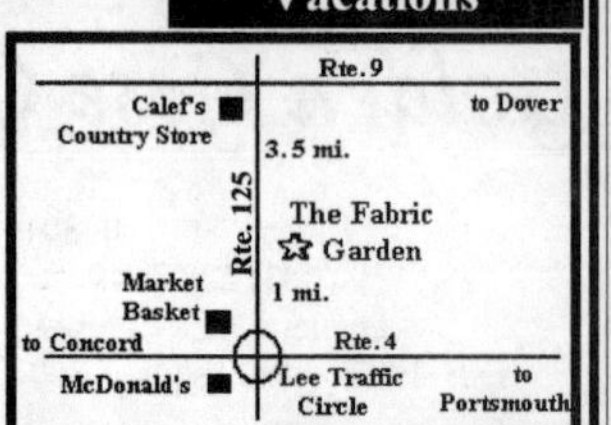

Portsmouth, NH #18

Mon - Sat 9:30 - 5:30
Sun 12 - 5

Portsmouth Fabric Co.

112 Penhallow Street 03801
(603) 436-6343 Fax: (603) 430-2943
E-Mail: pfc@portsmouthfabric.com
Web Site: www.portsmouth.com Est: 1979
1100 sq. ft. 6000 Bolts Online Catalog
An exceptional selection of natural fiber and designer fabrics, fine laces and silks. An expanded collection of contemporary quilting cottons, batiks and ikats, buttons, fiber art magazines and books. Swiss Bernina machines.

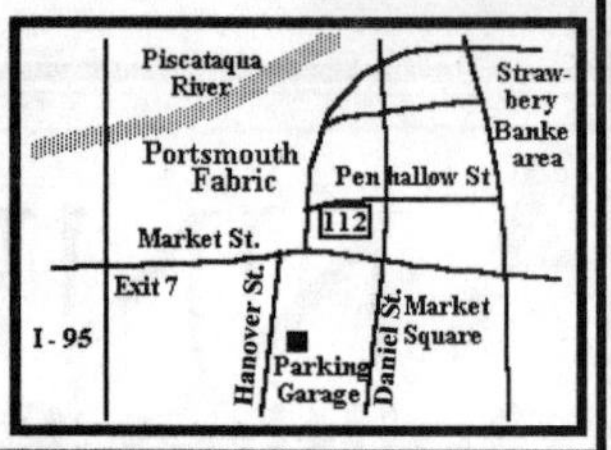

Silver Thimble Quilt Shop

53 Church St., Box 86, Kingston, NH 03848
(603) 642-4615 Fax: (603) 642-4386
silverthimble@ttlc.net
www.silverthimblequiltshop.com
Store Hours:
Mon - Fri 10 - 5 Sat 10 - 4

Silver Thimble Quilt Shop offers over 1800 bolts of fabric for you to choose from. We specialize in elegant florals and Bali's. A large selection of books and patterns are also available. Stop in today!!

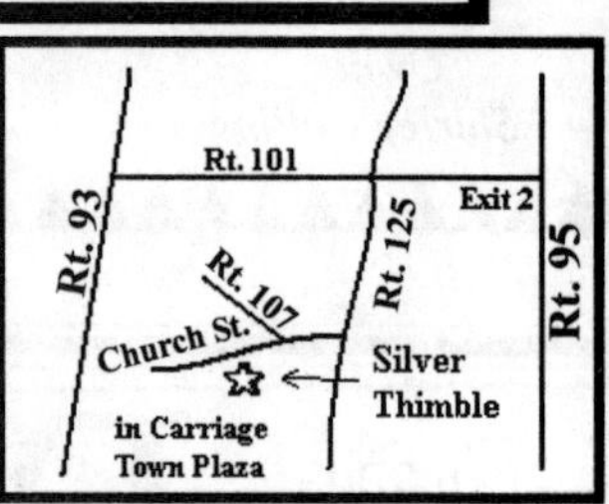

Kingston, NH #19

Other Shops in New Hampshire: *We suggest calling first*

Andover	Wilcox Farm Quilts, Rt. 11, 322 Main St.	603-735-5891
Ashland	Quilt Studio, P.O. Box 576	603-968-3492
Bedford	Saginaw Quilted Apple, 99 Powder Hill Rd.	
Bedford	The Patchworks, 133 Bedford Center Rd.	603-472-3002
Center Barnstead	Barn Door Quilting, 665 Barn Door Gap Rd	603-269-3480
Chocorua	Patchwork House, 1808 Chocorua Mtn. Hwy.	603-367-9269
Concord	Bittersweet Fabric Shop, 8 Cottage St.	603-753-4920
Effingham	Attic Cat, Town House Rd	603-539-4669
Guild	The Dorr Mill Store, P.O. Box 88	800-846-3677
Henniker	Quilted Threads, 16 Bradford Rd., P.O. Box 778	603-428-6622
Kingston	Pieced Pastimes Quilt Shop, 4 Stoney Brooke Lane	603-642-8251
Lancaster	Weaving Edge, 48 Prospect	603-788-4417
Manchester	Quilter's Courtyard, 700 Elm St	603-622-0939
Pellham	Bits & Pieces Quilt Shop, 71 Bridge St #1	603-635-9705
Portsmouth	Merri Stitches, 72 Mirona Road #15	603-431-9922
Salem	Audrey's Sewing Studio & Vacuum Center, 26 Ermer Rd.	603-898-0777
Salem	Pine Tree Quilt Shop, 224 N Broadway	603-870-8100
Sanbornville	Needleworks, 126 Witchtrot Rd	603-788-2965

New Hampshire Guilds:

Concord	Capital Quilter's Guild, P.O. Box 192, 03302	Meets: Havenwood Nursing Home
Dover	Cocheco Quilt Guild, P.O. Box 1153, 03821	Meets: 3rd Tuesday at First Parish Church
Grantham	Sunshine Quilters Guild, 03753	Meets: 3rd Tuesday 7 p.m. at Grantham Town Hall
Hudson	Hannah Dustin Quilters Guild, P.O. Box 121, 03051	
Keene	Cheshire Quilters Guild, P.O. Box 1481, 03431	
Lebanon	Northern Lights, 03766	Meets: 2nd Wednesday @ 7pm at Methodist Church
Littleton	Ltiileton Quilt Guild	Meets: 3rd Thursday @ 7pm at Littleton Community House Annex
New London	Sunshine Quilters Guild, P.O. Box 713, 03257	Meets: 3rd Tuesday 7 p.m. at Grantham Town Hall
W. Peterboro	Monadnock Quilters Guild, P.O. Box 140, 03468	Meets: 3rd Friday at 7 p.m.
Wolfeboro	Ladies of the Lakes Quilters', GuildP.O. Box 552, 03894	

15 Featured Shops
New Jersey

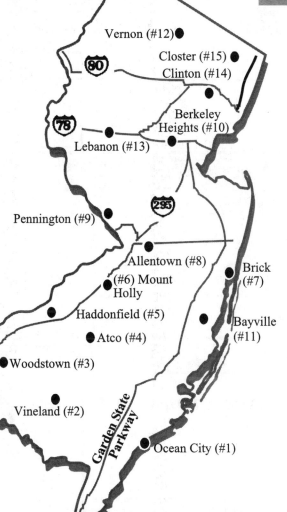

Vernon (#12)
Closter (#15)
Clinton (#14)
Berkeley Heights (#10)
Lebanon (#13)
Pennington (#9)
Allentown (#8)
Brick (#7)
(#6) Mount Holly
Haddonfield (#5)
Bayville (#11)
Atco (#4)
Woodstown (#3)
Vineland (#2)
Garden State Parkway
Ocean City (#1)
80
78
295

Ocean City, NJ #1

Calico N Cotton

715 Asbury Ave. 08226
(609) 399-7166
Owner: Holly Flanders
Est: 1990 1900 sq.ft.

Summer
Mon - Sat
10 - 5
Sun 12 - 4
Winter
Wed - Sat
10 - 5
Sun 12 - 4
Closed Mon & Tues Nov. 1 thru March 31

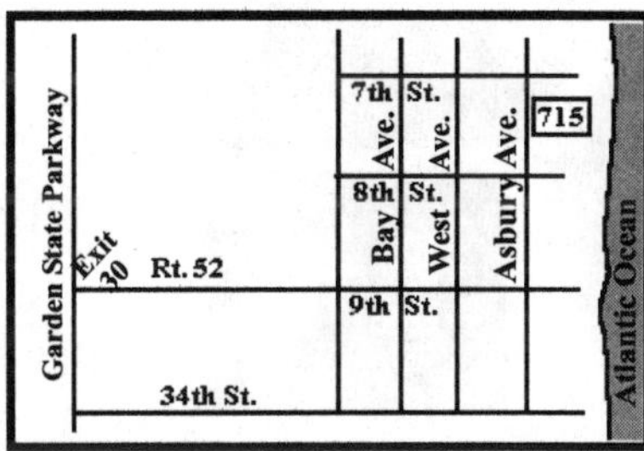

1500 Bolts of 100% Cotton
Classes ◆ Books ◆ Notions
Craft Patterns ◆ Gifts

Vineland, NJ #2

Mon - Fri
9:30 - 6
Thur til 8
Sat 9:30 - 5:30

The Pin Cushion

36 Landis Ave. 08360
(856) 692-5460
Est: 1972 4000 sq.ft.
2000 Bolts (Quilt Prints)

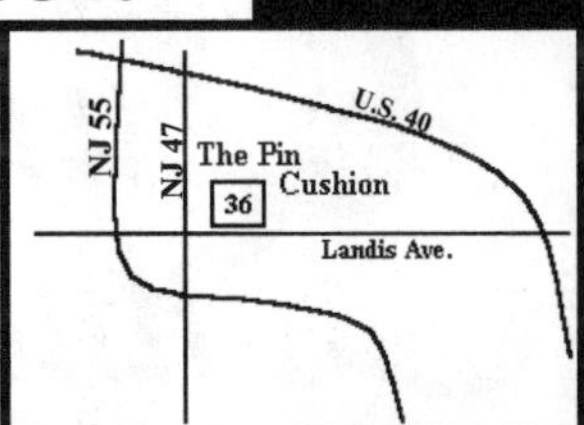

Dress, Bridal, Quilt Fabrics.
Notions, Patterns & Accessories.

Woodstown, NJ #3

Tues - Fri
10 - 4
Sat 10 - 3

Pieceful Stitches
A Quilt Shop

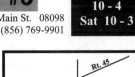

4 S. Main St. 08098
(856) 769-9901

Owner: Kristine DeJohn

This quilt shop is filled with classes, fabric, books, & patterns topped off with lots of laughter. A great day out. Woodstown is a wonderful small home town.

Atco, NJ #4

T, W, Th
10 - 5
Fri 12 - 7
Sat 10 - 3

2212 Atco Ave. 08004
(856) 768-2222
Owner: Lynn Hannigan

Small but growing Quilt Shop offering quilting Fabric, Lessons and Supplies. On site Long-Arm Quilting Service by Janet Eisnen.

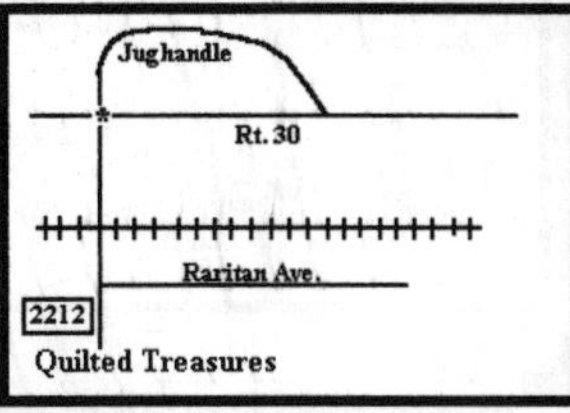

Haddonfield, NJ #5

The Little Shop

Mon - Sat
10 - 5
Sun 12:30 - 4
Class Nights
7 - 9

143 Kings Hwy. East 08033
(856) 429-7573 Est: 1960
Owner: Deborah Hagy Hansen 3000 bolts

10 minutes from Philadelphia.
Quality cotton fabric.
Instruction & Gifts. All the latest books & notions.

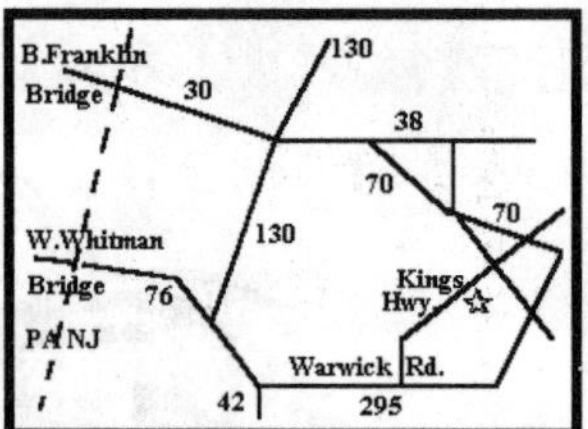

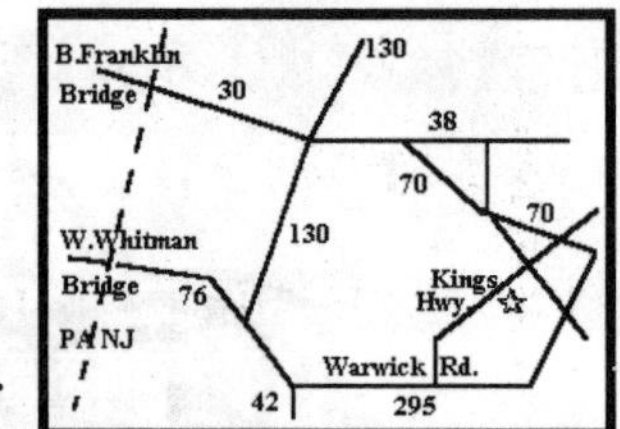

Visit our website at: "Littlequiltshop.com"
e-mail us at: LSQUILTS@aol.com

Mount Holly, NJ #6

The Village Quilter

Tues 11 - 4
Wed - Sat
11 - 6
Thur til 8
Sun 12 - 4

10 Charles St. 08060
(The Shoppes at Mill Race Village)
(609) 265-0011 Fax: (609) 265-9010
www.millraceshops.com
Owner: Susan Di Bartolo
Est: 2002 750 sq.ft. 1000 Bolts

This charming quilt shop offers quilters a colorful selection of current fabrics, patterns, and notions. Located at the SE corner of the main parking lot off of Charles Street.

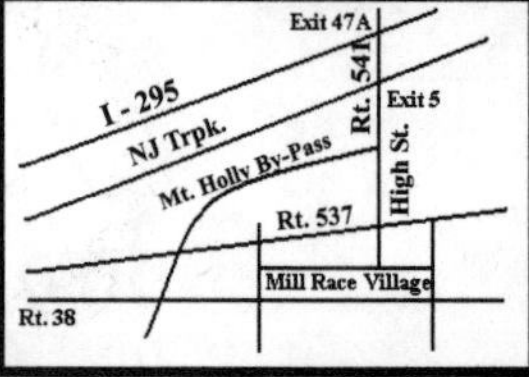

Brick, NJ #7

Crafty Fabrics

Tues - Fri
9:30 - 4:30
Sat 11 - 4

750 Mantoloking Rd. (Rt. 528) 08723
(732) 920-6220
Owner: Diane McColley 1200 sq.ft.
Est: 2002 Formerly in Toms River for 17 years

First Quality Cotton Fabrics at Discounted Prices. Books - Patterns - Notions - Gifts
Day & Evening Classes with 6 machines for your use.

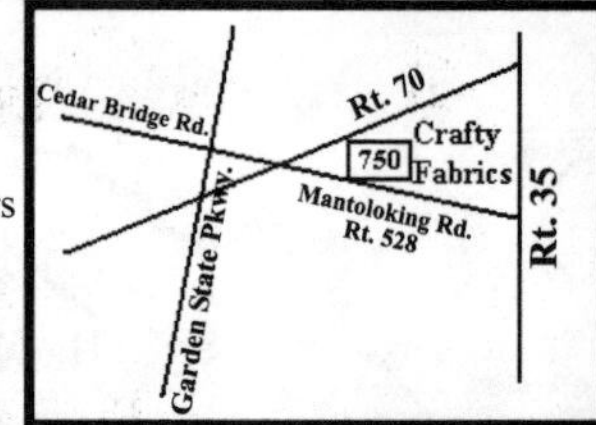

Allentown, NJ #8

Quilter's Barn

Tues - Sat
9:30 - 4
Thur til 7:30
Sun 12 - 5
Closed Sun July & Aug

34 South Main St.
P.O. Box 295 08501
(609) 259-2504 Est: 1975
qbpatti@aol.com
www.Quiltersbarn.com

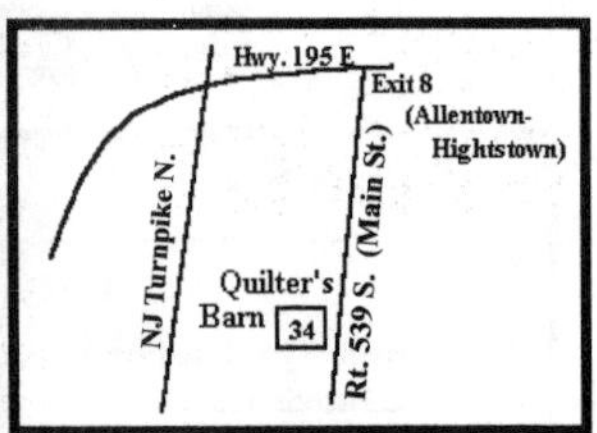

Over 1,500 bolts of fabric, Books
Patterns Notions
Batting Classes
Blocks of the Month
Friendly personal service

Pennington, NJ #9

Pennington Quilt Works

Mon - Thur
10 - 5
Fri 10 - 7
Sat 10 - 4
Sun 12 - 4

Pennytown Shopping Village
Route 31 North
(609) 466-5722
E-Mail: pqworks@aol.com
Owner: Jan Crane Est: 1996

Wonderful selection of fabrics, books and supplies. All the basics, but always something new. Fun Classes. Warm expert service.

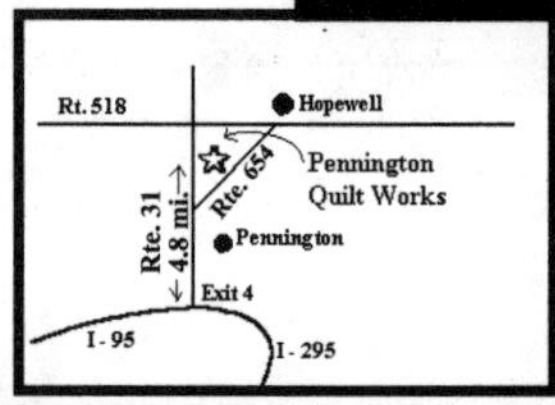

Berkeley Heights, NJ #10

Quilt Connection

Tues - Fri
10 - 5
Thur til 9
Sat 10 - 4
Sun 12 - 4

Fabulous selection of fine cottons including Alexander Henry, Hoffman Batiks, P&B, & Kaufman. Classes, notions, books & patterns. Gift Items especially for quilters.

432F Springfield Ave. 07922
(908) 286-0200
Fax: (908) 286-1100
Owner: Sally Davis
Est: 1998
1400 sq.ft. 3000+ bolts

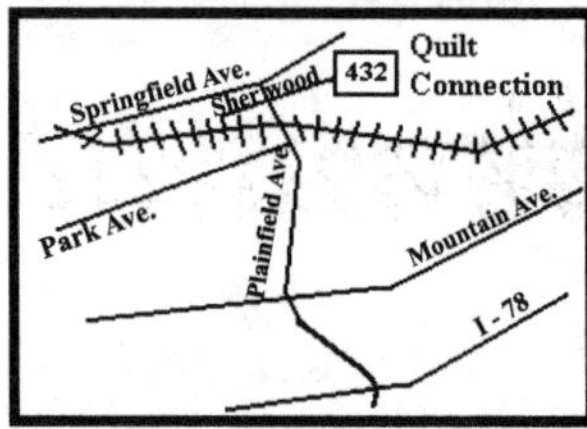

Web Site: www.njquiltconnection.com

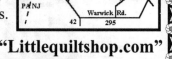

Bayville, NJ #11

Est: 1994

Quilting Possibilities

Rt. 9 08721
(732) 269-8383
Owners: Debbie & Jim Welch
qps@quiltingposs.com

www.quiltingposs.com

We are an authorized Bernina, Elna, and baby lock dealer, and carry a full line of sewing machines, sergers, and supplies. We repair and service all brands of sewing machines. Name Brand 100% cotton fabric (4000+ bolts), books, notions, patterns. Horn of America and Koala Sewing machine cabinets and cutting tables.

One of New Jersey's Largest Quilt Stores

elna

Nothing Sews Like A Bernina. Nothing.
BERNINA®

baby lock

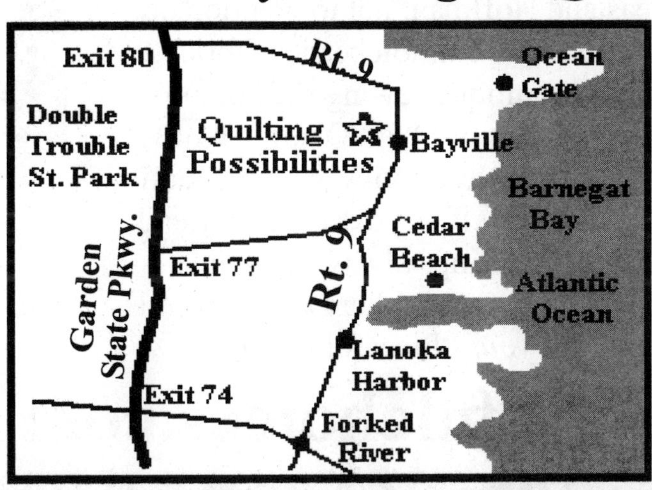

Tues - Sat
10 - 5
Sun 12 - 4

Pieceful Choices Quilt Shop

Est: 2001

Vernon, NJ #12

99 Route 94
Vernon, NJ 07462
(973) 823-9297
E-mail: moestuf@earthlink.net
Owners: Maureen & Jon Lasslett

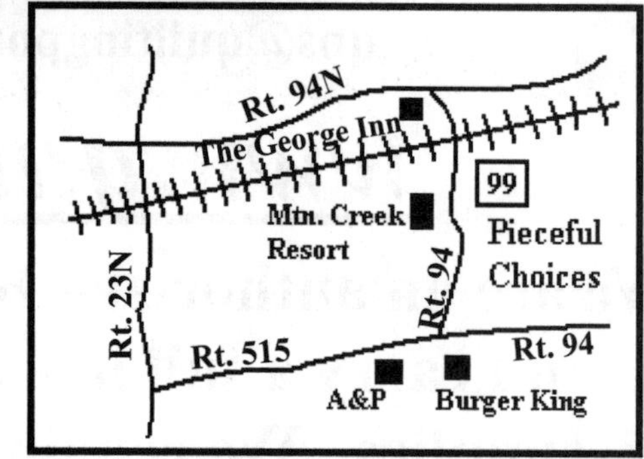

Tues, Wed, Fri
10 - 5
Thurs 10 - 8
Sat 10 - 4
Sun 11 - 2

Come and visit our lovely quilt shop in Northern NJ, just minutes away from NY and PA! We proudly offer you 1000+ bolts of quality cottons, flannels, batiks and extra wide backings from your favorites like Moda, Kona Bay, P&B, Maywood, South Seas and Hoffman, not to mention our *superior* selection of the newest Thimbleberries fabrics and books in the area! Enjoy the antique sewing memorabilia as you make your way to our famous "Fat Quarter Wall". We are fully stocked with the newest books, patterns, notions and quilt related gifts for yourself or your special friend. Classes and delightful gatherings always available. You'll appreciate the friendly atmosphere and cheerful experience as you make *your* "Pieceful Choices"!

www.piecefulchoices.com

Lebanon, NJ #13

Mon - Sat 10 - 5:30
Sun 1 - 4

Budding Star Quilts

Rt. 22 E, Lebanon Plaza 08833
(908) 236-7676
Web Site: www.buddingstarquilts.com
Owner: Kathy Verser Est: 1987 2000+ Bolts

We Specialize in Kits for all Levels!
Thimbleberries Club

Over 2000 Bolts 100% Cotton Fabric.
Large selection of flannels.
Classes. We carry all current Thimbleberries Fabrics and products.

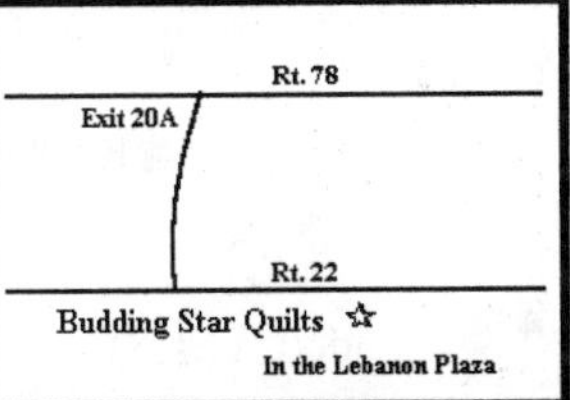

Clinton, NJ #14

Mon - Sat 10 - 5
Thur til 7:30
Sun 12 - 4

Kindred Quilts

21 E. Main St. 08809
(908) 730-8896
E-Mail: kindredquilts@att.net
Web Site: www.kindredquilts.com
Owner: Toby Preston
Est: 1999 1500 sq.ft.

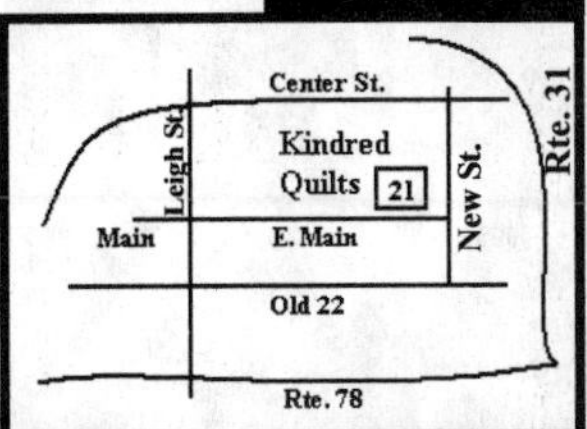

2,000 bolts of 100% cotton fabric, notions, primitive stitcheries, hand-dyed fabrics, as well as wool-felt for penny rugs.

Closter, NJ #15

Mon - Fri 10 - 6
Sat 10 - 5

Quilt Plus

223 Closter Dock Rd. 07624
(201) 767-0506
Fax: (201) 767-1781

E-Mail: QuiltPlus@mail.com
Owner: Connie Woo

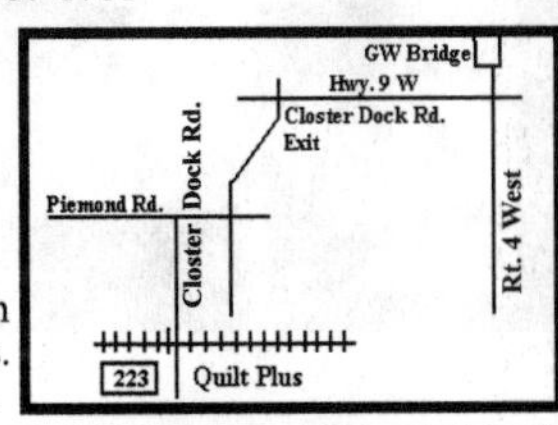

Only quilt Shop in Bergen County! Selected High Quality Fabrics. Unique Japanese Fabrics. Sashiko Books & Patterns. Special Bag Supplies.

Other Shops in New Jersey: *We suggest calling first*

Absecon Sew Distinctive, 144 E Mourning Dove 609-652-2260
Allenwood Jacob's Ladder Quilt Shop, 3203 Atlantic Ave #4 732-223-7774
Bay Head Quilt By The Number, 336 Main Ave 732-899-3151
Bedminster Lamington General Store, 285 Lamington Rd. 908-439-2034
Bridgeton Broad Meadows Country Fabrics, 100 Mary Elmer Dr. 856-451-2433
Browns Mills Pastimes, 13 Trenton Rd 609-893-3311
Collengswood Daisy Patchworks, 702 Haddon Ave 856-869-8869
Delran Simply Stitches, 263 Southview Dr.
Denville Bows, Bits & Stitches, 9 Broadway
Elmer The Fabric Place, 160 Dutch Row Rd. 609-358-7375
Flemington Fabric Factory, 17 Reaville Ave 908-788-5444
Forked River Country Sisters, 110 N. Main St. 609-693-7224
Hackensack Julia's Fabrics, 137 Main St. 201-487-4110
Hopatcong Needle Niche, P.O. Box 592 973-398-8412
Howell Beary Unique Quilt Shoppe, 4134 Rt. 9 S 732-905-5445
Lakewood Stitch N'Sew Center, 123 E County Line 732-363-2220
Mercerville Sew Diff'Rent, 528 Hwy 33 609-586-1440
Millstone Millstone Workshop, 1393 Main St 908-874-3649
North Plainfield Fabric Land, 855 Rte. 22 908-755-4700
Phillipsburg Prescription Quilts, 105 Cty Rd. 519 908-995-9650
Princeton Pines & Needle, 8 Chambers St 609-921-9075
Red Bank Funky Quilt, 30 Monmouth St 732-219-0972
Rio Grande Olsen Sew & Vac Center, 1121 Rt. 47 S. Robbins Nest Plaza 609-886-5510
Scotch Plains Cozy Corner Creations Quilt Shop, 1636 E. 2nd St. 908-322-8480
Sussex Ben Franklin, 455 Rt. 23 973-875-7444

New Jersey Guilds

Bridgewater Pieced Together Quilters, P.O. Box 8097, 08807
Chatham Garden State Quilters, P.O. Box 424, 07928
Meets: 2nd Monday @7pm Sept-June at Chatham United Methodist
Cherry Hill Love Apple Quilters, P.O. Box 3734, 08034
Cinnaminson Cinnaminson Quilters
Egg Harbor City Lafayette Quilters Guild
Meets: 2nd Saturday at the Senior Nutrition Ctr., Cincinnati and Buerger Sts.
Freehold Molly Pitcher Stitchers
Glendora Love Apples, 08029
Howell The State Quilt Guild of NJ, 46 Old Tavern Rd., 07731
Island Heights Beach Plum Quilters, P.O. Box 204, 08732
Jamesburg Turtle Creek Quilters, 27 W. Church St., 08831
Jersey City The Jersey City Quilters, 181 Pearsall Ave., 07305
Manahawkin Pieceful Shores Quilters Guild, P.O. Box 351, 08050
Marmora South Shores Stitchers, P.O. Box 1103, 08223
Meets: 2nd Mon @ 7pm Tuckahoe United Methodist, 112 Rt. 49, Tuckahoe
Middletown Rebecca's Reel Quilters, P.O. Box 36, 07748
Moorestown Moorestown Area Quilters, 08057
Point Pleasant Jersey Shore Quilters, 415 Foreman Avenue, 08742
Ringoes Courthouse Quilters Guild, 121 Back Brook Rd., 08551
Southampton Berry Basket Quilters, 509 Paige Dr., 08088
Tennent Molly Pitcher Stitchers, P.O. Box 467, 07763
Toms River Beach Plum Quilters, PO Box 743, 08753
Toms River Tri-State Quiltmaking Teachers, 20 Pine Tree Rd., 08753
Tuckahoe New Jersey State Quilt Guild, P.O. Box 305, 08250
Meets: 3x a year at various locations
Waldwick Brownstone Quilters Guild, P.O. Box 228, 07463
Woodbridge Woodbridge Heritage Quilters, P.O. Box 272, 07095

NEW MEXICO

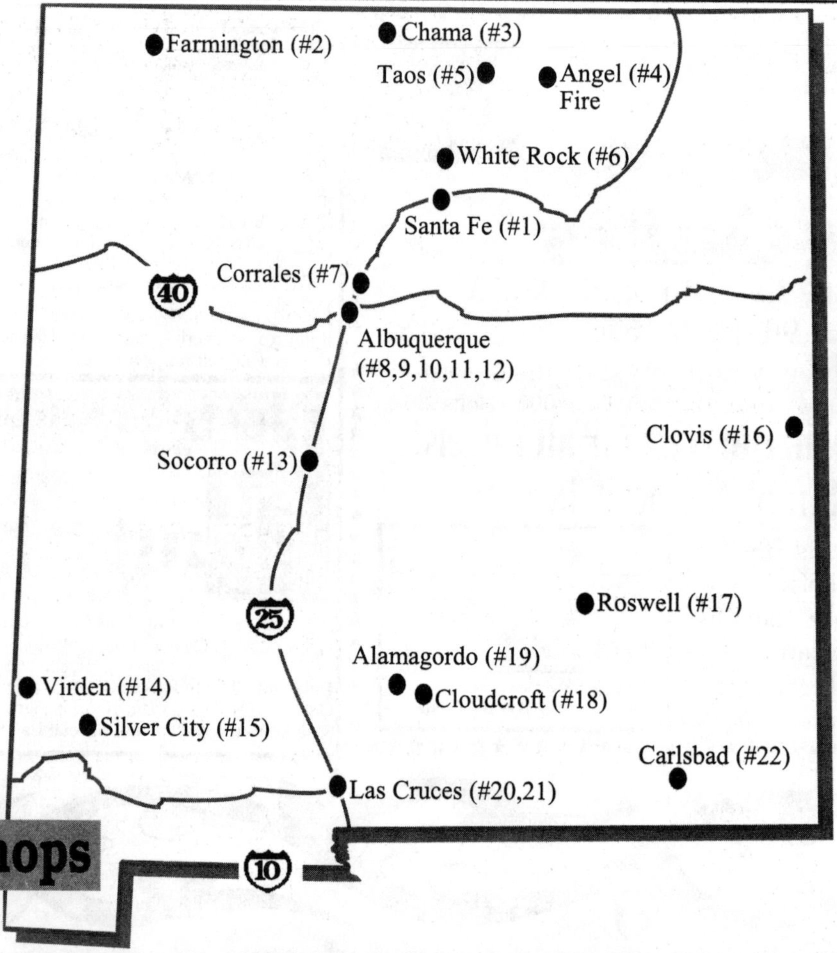

Farmington (#2)
Chama (#3)
Taos (#5)
Angel (#4) Fire
White Rock (#6)
Santa Fe (#1)
Corrales (#7)
40
Albuquerque (#8,9,10,11,12)
Clovis (#16)
Socorro (#13)
25
Roswell (#17)
Alamagordo (#19)
Cloudcroft (#18)
Virden (#14)
Silver City (#15)
Carlsbad (#22)
Las Cruces (#20,21)
10

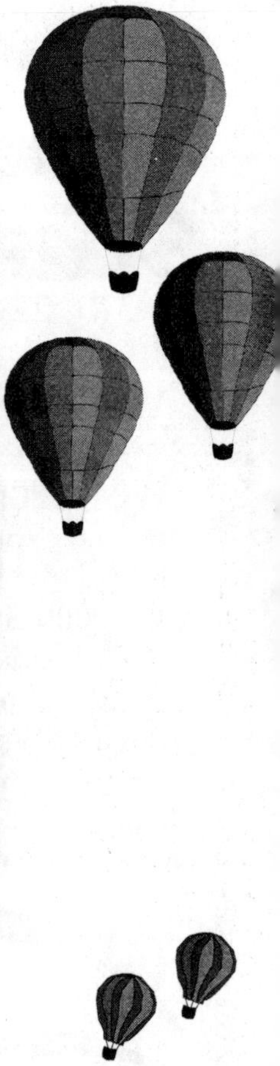

22 Featured Shops

Santa Fe Quilting, Inc.

3018-A Cielo Court, Santa Fe, NM 87507
(505) 473-3747
Fax: (505) 473-9510 info@santafequilting.com
Owners: Mary McCusker & Allen Winchester
Est: 2000 2400 sq.ft. 3500 Bolts
www.santafequilting.com

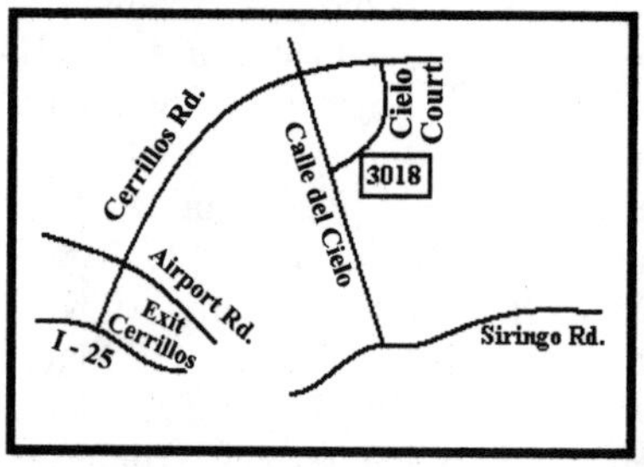

Cerrillos Rd.
Calle del Cielo
Cielo Court
3018
Airport Rd.
Exit Cerrillos
I - 25
Siringo Rd.

Mon - Sat 10 - 5:30 Thur til 8 Sun 1 - 5

Bright cottons, including a wide selection of Batiks. Cottons from Japan. Oriental and Southwest Fabrics and Patterns. Sashiko Supplies, Numerous Flannels. Books & Time Saving Notions. Block of the Month Kits & Classes. Sewing Machines available for classroom use by travelers. Fabrics from most major fabric companies are available in our store.

Santa Fe, NM #1

Farmington, NM #2

Mon - Fri 10 - 5
Thur til 7
Sat 10 - 3

Patchwork Pig

3030 E. Main, Ste E-3 87402
(505) 326-6465
Fax: (505) 326-6498
patchworkpig@cptnet.com
www.patchworkpig.biz
Owner: Deborah K. Williams
Est: 2003 2500 sq.ft.

3000+ Bolts of 100% cotton, Civil War, 30's, Flannel, Batiks, Thimbleberries and Wool. Long-arm quilter on site.

Little Foot Ltd.

Quilt Shop Est: 1999 Business Est: 1988

#3

Owner: Lynn Graves

798 Terrace Avenue • Chama, NM 87520
1-800-597-7075 • 505-756-1412

The Home of Little Foot®
Big Foot®
Jaws™ • That Purple Thang™
The Setting Triangle™
Notions for the Quilter
Top Piecing Foundation Sheets

SUPPORT YOUR LOCAL QUILT SHOP!

Authorized Brother Sewing Machine Dealer

Largest selection of Flannels in the Southwest!

Mon - Fri • 8:30 - 4p.m.
Closed Sat & Sun

Angel Fire, NM #4

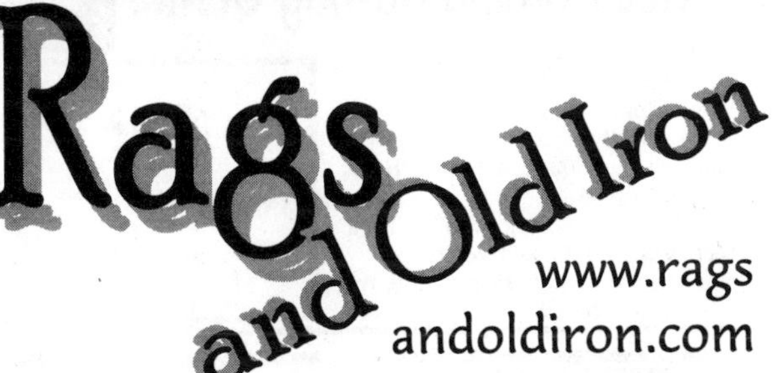

www.rags
andoldiron.com

- ❖Full service quilt shop
- ❖More than 1800 bolts
- ❖Friendly, knowledgeable staff
- ❖You'll always feel welcome
- ❖Janome sewing machines
- ❖Featherweight parts
- ❖Classes
- ❖Gifts for quilters
- ❖Large selection of flannels
- ❖Visa & Mastercard accepted
- ❖The very latest fabrics from your favorite manufacturers: Hoffman - Timeless Teasures

Mon - Sat
10 - 5

3453 Mountain View Blvd.
Suite 100
P.O. Box 145,
Angel Fire, NM 87710
505-377-3456
kathy@ragsandoldiron.com
Fax: (505) 377-3999

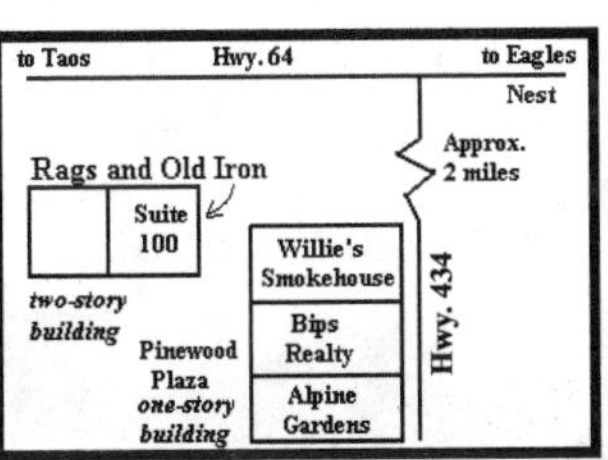

Taos, NM #5

Mon - Sat
10:30 - 5:30
Sun 12 - 4

Taos Adobe Quilting

102 Teresina Lane 87571
(505) 751-3219 Fax: Same
taostogs@taosnet.com
Owners: Peter & Jan O'Donohue

Features Quilts, southwestern and juvenile fabrics in 100% cotton and hard to find prints, notions, patterns & classes.

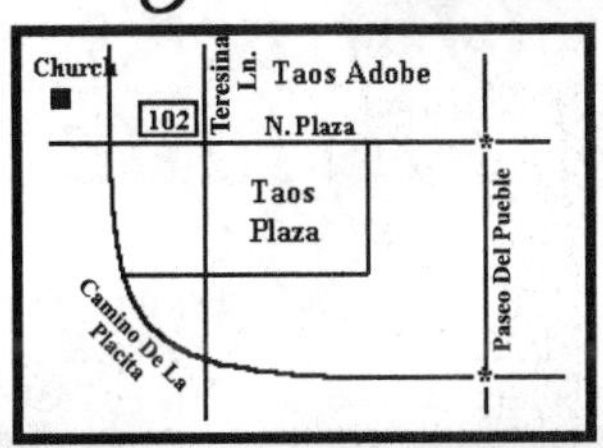

White Rock, NM #6

Tues - Fri
10 - 5:30
Sat 10 - 4:30

PANDY'S Quilt Store

13 Sherwood Blvd. 87544
(505) 672-2004 Est: 1999
pandy@pandysquiltstore.com
www.pandysquiltstore.com
Owner: Pandy Lolos 1600 sq.ft. 1200 Bolts

We carry brights, batiks, marbles and oriental fabrics plus PFAFF sewing machines.

Corrales, NM #7

Mon - Fri
10 - 5:30
Sat 10 - 5
Sun 12 - 4

4908 Corrales Rd. 87048
(505) 890-9416 Fax: (505) 890-9451
www.quiltsole.com
Owner: Cathy Gormley
Est: 2000 1500 sq.ft. 1400+ Bolts

Located in a quaint village, northwest of Albuquerque. Specializing in brights, batiks & unusual prints. Notions, books, classes too!

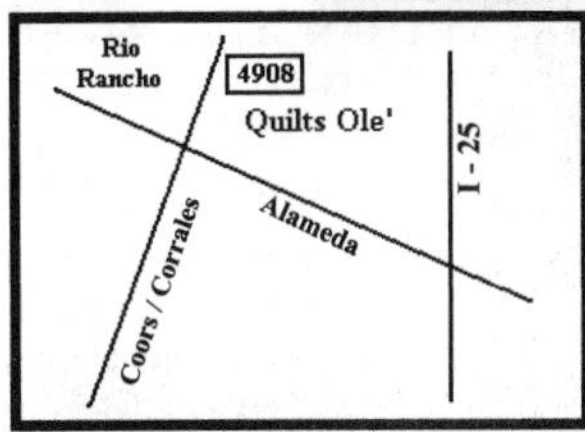

Albuquerque, NM #8

Mon - Fri 9 - 6
Sat 9 - 5
Sun 2 - 5

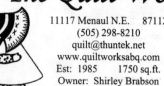

The Quilt Works

11117 Menaul N.E. 87112
(505) 298-8210
quilt@thuntek.net
www.quiltworksabq.com
Est: 1985 1750 sq.ft.
Owner: Shirley Brabson

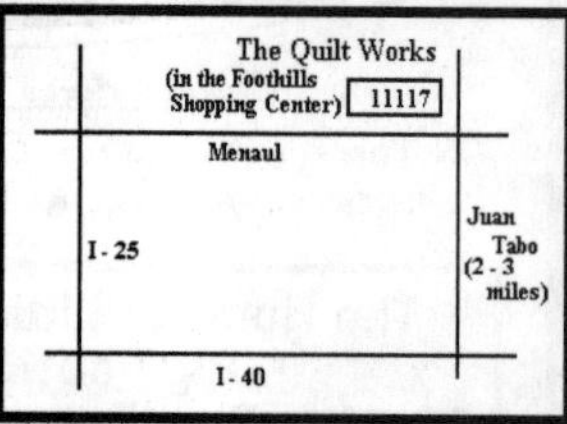

We have over 3000 bolts of cotton fabric. We're Friendly and Helpful !

Albuquerque, NM #9

Mon - Sat
9 - 5
Sun By Appt.

SOUTHWEST DECORATIVES

5711 Carmel Ave. NE, Ste. B 87113
(505) 821-7400 Fax: (505) 821-6556
swd@swdecoratives.com
www.swdecoratives.com
Owner: Mary-Jo McCarthy
Est: 1994 5000 sq.ft. 3000 Bolts

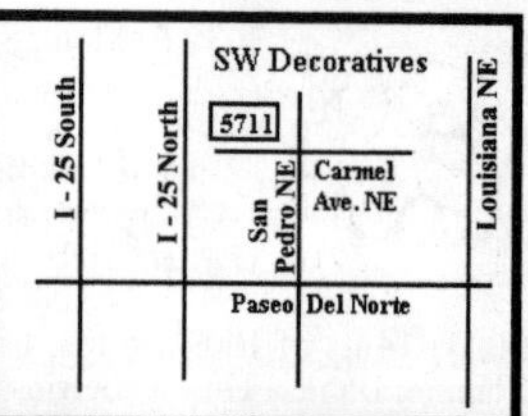

Beautiful Southwest theme fabrics, patterns and lots more! Long-arm quilting available.

Albuquerque, NM #10

Mon - Sat
10 - 5
Thurs til 9

Quilt from the ☐

417 Tramway NE #1 87123
(505) 292-8560
Owner: Leta Brazell

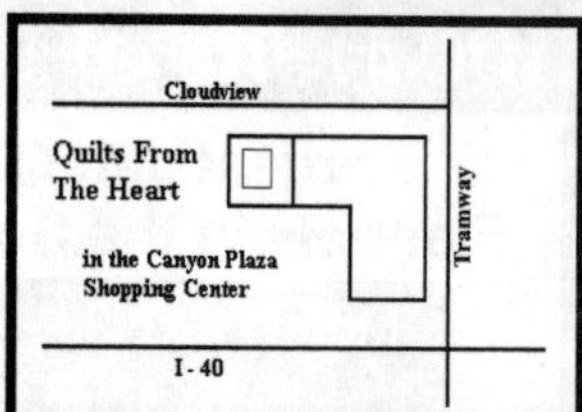

A Full Service Quilt Shop !
Quilts for Sale, Custom Quilts, Finishing, Classes, Fabric, Books, Notions & More.

Albuquerque, NM #11

Mon - Thur
9 - 8
Fri & Sat
9 - 5

Ann Silva's Bernina Sewing Center

3101 Menaul NE 87107
(505) 881-5253 Fax: (505) 881-3127
silvainc@nmia.com Est: 1980
www.annsilvasbernina.com
Owner: Ann Silva 6600 sq.ft. 1500+ Bolts

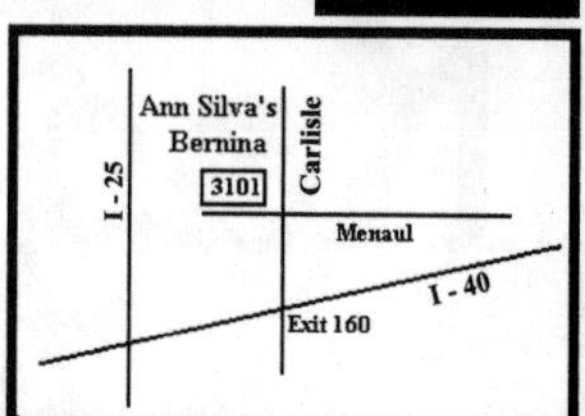

Top ranking Bernina dealership. We carry a complete line of Bernina accessories. Specializing in Southwestern fabrics, patterns, books, threads & more!

Albuquerque, NM #12

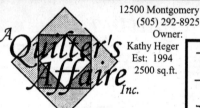

Mon - Fri
10 - 6
Sat 10 - 5
Sun 12 - 5

12500 Montgomery 87111
(505) 292-8925
Owner:
Kathy Heger
Est: 1994
2500 sq.ft.

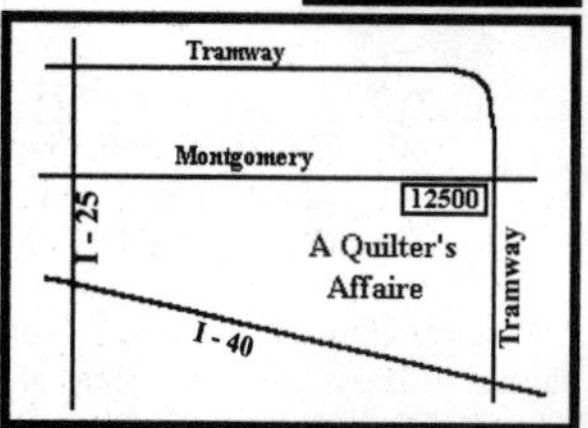

Featuring over 1500 bolts of fabric, notions, books, & patterns for quilting and crafting. Classes Too!

Bobbie's Bobbin

107 N. California St. 87801
(505) 838-0001 Fax: (505) 838-1094
bbobbin@zianet.com
Owners: Bobbie & Gary Stendel

Custom embroidery, Sensational Fabrics, Quilters Supplies, Notions, Books, Beads and Sewing Machine Service/Repair.
"Best Little Sewing Store in Socorro!"

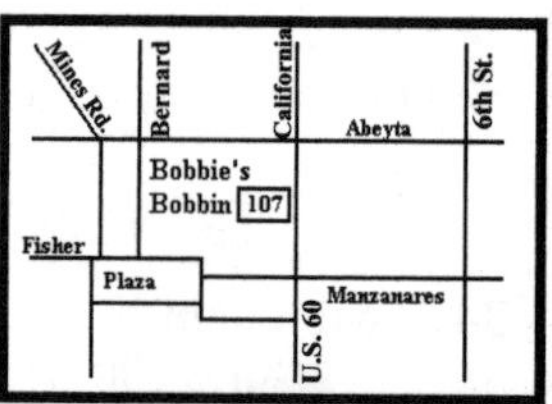

Mon - Sat 10 - 6

Socorro, NM #13

Virden, NM #14

Mon, Wed
Fri 1:30 - 6
Thur 9 - 7

Nelda's Quilt Shop

309 Richmond Ave.
Mailing: Rt. 1, Box 194, Duncan, AZ 85534
(505) 358-2184 Fax: (505) 358-1000
neldapotter@aznex.net
Owner: Nelda Potter
Est: 2002 1200 sq.ft. 1200+ Bolts

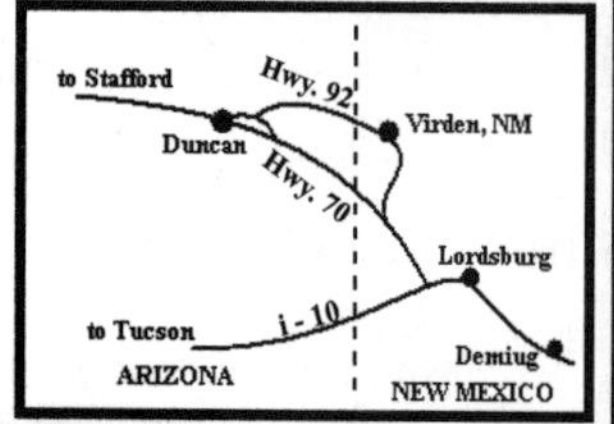

1200 Bolts of Fabric, Notions, College Classes, Hemstitching, Receiving Blankets, Long-arm Quilting and More.
Brother Sewing Machine Dealer.

Silver City, NM #15

Mon - Sat
9 - 5

Thunder Creek Quilt Company

1330 N. Hudson St. 88061
(505) 538-2284 or (800) 376-4201
Owners: Cindy Ugarte & Nancy Coryell
Est: 1995 700+ Bolts

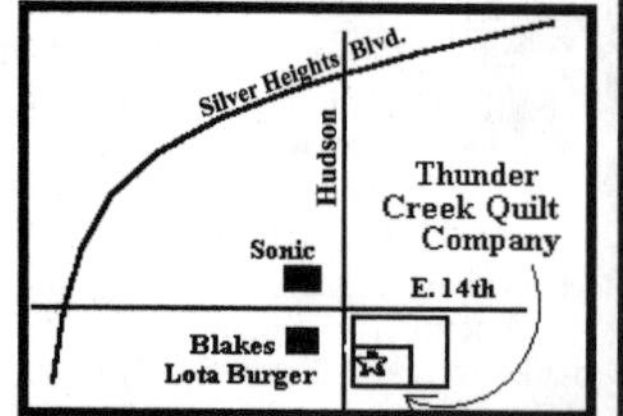

Specializing in Southwestern Fabrics & Patterns. Cotton Fabric. Notions, Sulky & Gutermann Threads. Gingher Scissors. Classes. Gifts.

Clovis, NM #16

Mon - Sat
10 -5

The Patchwork House

519 Main St. 88101
(505) 769-8072
quiltpatches4@hotmail.com
Owner: Judy Matthews

Best Selection of Quality Quilting Fabrics, Books, Patterns, Notions for 100 miles. Classes and custom Quilting Service Avail.

Roswell, NM #17

Mon - Fri 10 - 5
Sat 10 - 3

Calico Cow Quilt Shop

318 N. Main 88201
(505) 623-8647 Est: 2001
Carolynnoling@aol.com
Owner: Carolyn
Pollard Noling

Cotton Fabrics, Flannels,
Notions, Books & Patterns.

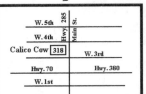

W. 5th
W. 4th
Hwy. 285
Main St.
Calico Cow 318
W. 3rd
Hwy. 70
Hwy. 380
W. 1st

Cloudcroft, NM #18

Daily 10 - 5

The Scrap Basket

Located in Pine Stump Mall
300 Burro, P.O. Box 478 88317
(505) 682-1468
pdrake@pvtnetworks.net
www.pvtnetworks.net/~pdrake
Small shop in a mountain village.
Retail Quilts, Fabric, Supplies, Related Gifts,
Books & Patterns & Classes

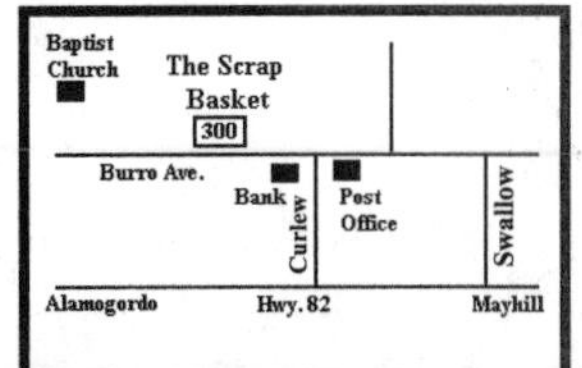

Alamogordo, NM #19

Mon - Sat 10 - 4

Forever Quilting Studio

700 E. First St. #754
Granada Center 88310
(505) 439-0346
foreverquilting2003@yahoo.com
Owners: Deborah Goldberg
Est: 2003 1000 sq.ft. 1400 bolts
A wonderful shop with everything you need
for your projects.

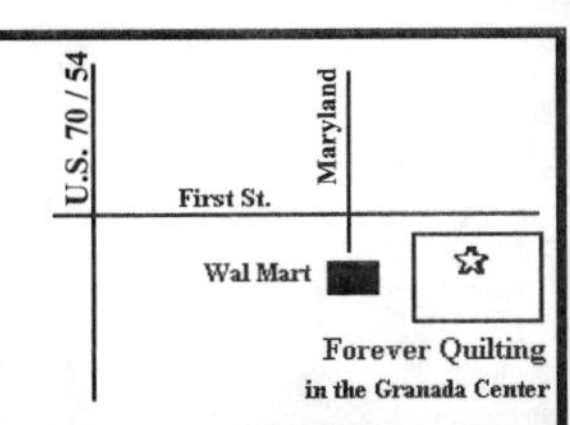

Las Cruces, NM #20

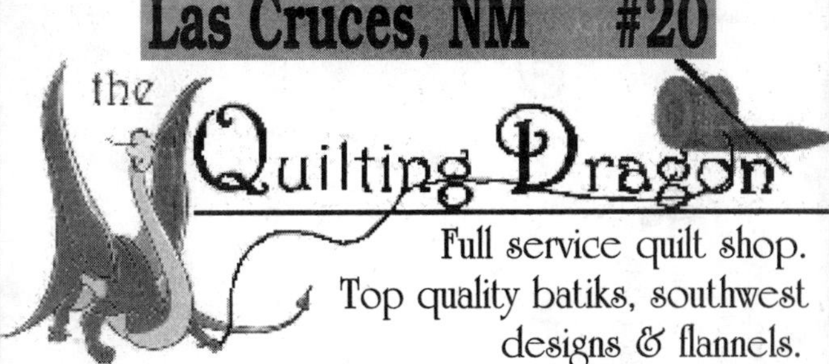

Full service quilt shop.
Top quality batiks, southwest designs & flannels.
Books, patterns, kits, threads, notions & gifts.
Authorized Brother, Elna & Janome dealer.

201 S. Solano, Suite A
Las Cruces, NM 88001
505-647-4022
Fax: 505-647-8008
qdragon@zianet.com
www.quiltingdragon.com
Est: 2003 1600 sq. ft.
Over 1600 bolts

Mon - Sat 10 - 5

to Albuquerque
Griggs Ave. E
May Ave. E
Amador Ave.
Lohman Ave.
201 Quilting Dragon
Walnut St.
I - 25
Lohman Exit
Solano Dr.
to El Paso

Las Cruces, NM #21

Sun - Fri 12 - 5
Sat 9 - 5

Soft Creations

207 Avenida de Mesilla 88005
(505) 525-8155
tinadal@zianet.com
Owner: Tina Dalcour
Est: 1996 2000+ sq.ft.

Come for inspiration, ideas and the greatest
place to buy supplies and fabric!

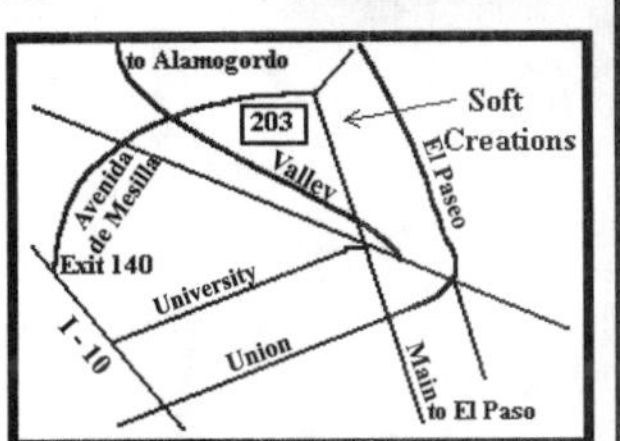

Carlsbad, NM #22

Mon - Fri 10 - 5:30
Sat 10 - 4

Jill's Fabric & Design

121 S. Canyon 88220
(505) 885-1184
Owners: Jill Balderrama &
Sherry Bowman
Est: 1994 4000 sq.ft.

Over 3000 bolts of fabrics - cotton, flannels,
wedding & dress. Also books, notions, patterns for all your sewing & quilting needs.

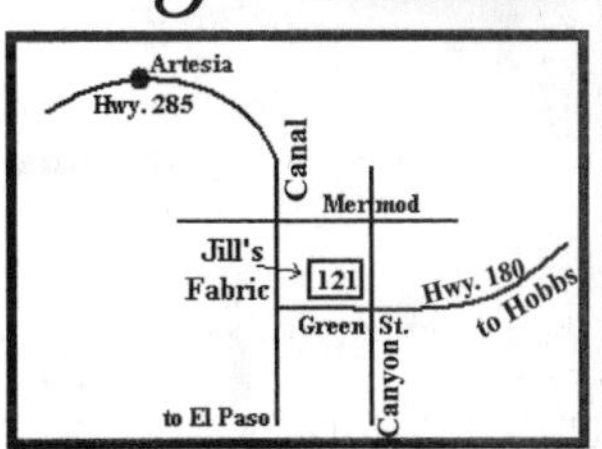

Other Shops in New Mexico: *We suggest calling first*

Alamogordo	Charmar's Cupboard, 7207 Hwy 5470	505-437-2266
Albuquerque	Quiltiques, 6040 Aspen Ave. NE	505-266-7276
Edgewood	A Quilter's Niche, 150 State Rd 344 #J	505-281-0940
Farmington	Quilted Threads, 5501 Evergreen Dr.	505-325-4490
Farmington	Apple Barn, 5991 Hwy. 64	505-632-9631
Lincoln	Lincolnworks, PO Box 32	505-653-4693
Raton	Quilter's Keepsakes, 104 Pecos Ave.	505-445-2092
Santa Fe	Moxie, 205 W. San Francisco St.	505-986-9265
Santa Fe	The Bedroom, 304 Catron St.	505-984-0207
Taos	Yukio's, 226 Pasio Del Puello Norte	505-758-2269

New Mexico Guilds:

Alamogordo	Enchanted Quilter's Guild, 900 Catalina, 88301	
Albuquerque	New Mexico Quilters' Association, P.O. Box 20562, 87154	
Cloudcroft	Sacramento Mountain Dears, P.O. Box 478, 88317	Meets: weekly at The Scrap Basket
Clovis	Clovis Quilters	Meets: 3rd Monday 1:30 p.m. at Cheyenne Meadows Community Room
Clovis	BlockBusters, 519 Main St., 88101	Meets: 2nd Thursday 7 p.m. at 519 Main St.
Farmington	San Juan Quilters' Guild, P.O. Box 5541, 87499	Meets: 2nd Tuesday 10am & 7pm at Farmington Civic Center
Los Alamos	Los Alamos Piecemakers Quilters, P.O. Box 261, 87544	
Portales	Piecemakers, 88130	Meets: 2nd Wednesday 9:30 a.m. at Eastern New Mexico Rural Electric
Roswell	Pecos Valley Quilters, 807 N. Missouri, 88201	
Santa Fe	Northern New Mexico Quilters, 87504	

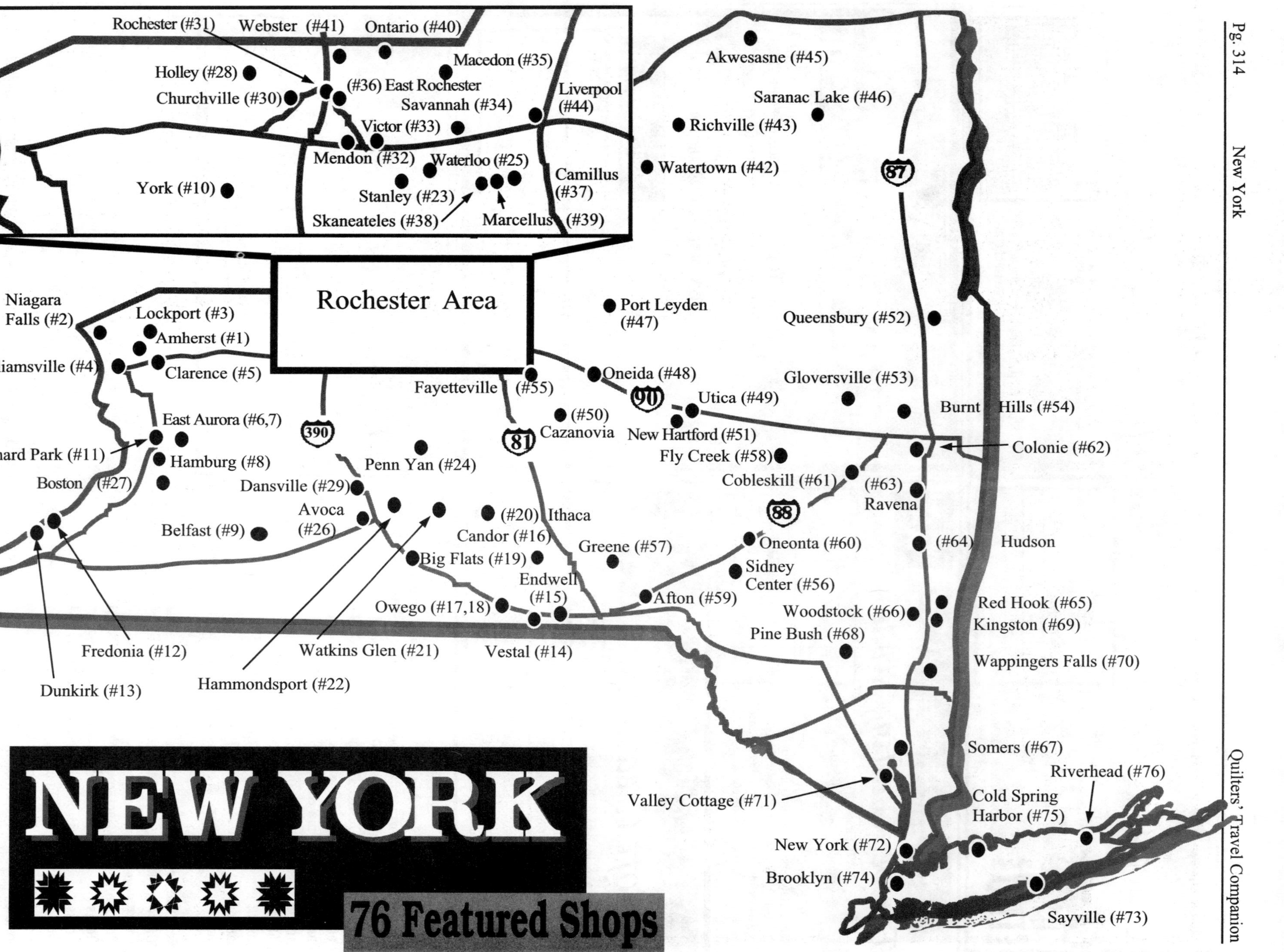

Rochester (#31)
Webster (#41)
Ontario (#40)
Macedon (#35)
Holley (#28)
(#36) East Rochester
Churchville (#30)
Savannah (#34)
Liverpool (#44)
Victor (#33)
Mendon (#32)
Waterloo (#25)
Camillus (#37)
York (#10)
Stanley (#23)
Skaneateles (#38)
Marcellus
(#39)
Akwesasne (#45)
Saranac Lake (#46)
Richville (#43)
Watertown (#42)
87
Rochester Area
Niagara Falls (#2)
Lockport (#3)
Amherst (#1)
Williamsville (#4)
Clarence (#5)
Port Leyden (#47)
Queensbury (#52)
Oneida (#48)
Gloversville (#53)
Fayetteville
(#55)
90
Utica (#49)
Burnt
Hills (#54)
East Aurora (#6,7)
390
(#50)
Cazanovia
81
New Hartford (#51)
Colonie (#62)
Orchard Park (#11)
Hamburg (#8)
Penn Yan (#24)
Fly Creek (#58)
Cobleskill (#61)
(#63)
Ravena
Boston
(#27)
Dansville (#29)
Avoca (#26)
88
Belfast (#9)
(#20)
Ithaca
Candor (#16)
Greene (#57)
Oneonta (#60)
(#64)
Hudson
Big Flats (#19)
Sidney Center (#56)
Endwell (#15)
Afton (#59)
Red Hook (#65)
Owego (#17,18)
Woodstock (#66)
Kingston (#69)
Pine Bush (#68)
Fredonia (#12)
Watkins Glen (#21)
Vestal (#14)
Wappingers Falls (#70)
Dunkirk (#13)
Hammondsport (#22)
Somers (#67)
Riverhead (#76)
Cold Spring Harbor (#75)
Valley Cottage (#71)
NEW YORK
New York (#72)
Brooklyn (#74)
76 Featured Shops
Sayville (#73)

Amherst, NY #1

Visit Us At: www. threadsoftimesewing.com

Threads of Time

Mon - Fri 10 - 9
Sat 10 - 5

Northtown Plaza,
3125 Sheridan Dr. 14226
(716) 837-1372
Email - tot@buffnet.net
Owners: Mari Wojcik & Jeanette Rogers

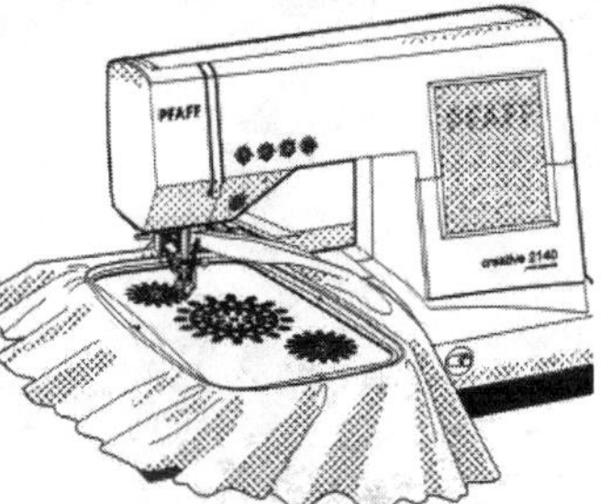

We carry over 3500 of bolts of fine cotton fabrics for all your quilt dreams.
Classes, books, patterns, a great variety of threads, notions & . . . lots of ideas.
PFAFF Authorized Sales & Service

"If You're a Quilter -- Then You're a Friend"

Niagara Falls, NY #2

Quiltmakers & Friends

Tues 10 - 2:30
Wed & Fri 10 - 8:30
Thur 10 - 4:30
Sat 10 - 3

4716 Military Rd. 14304
(716) 297-4067
Owner: Florence M. Rhodes

Hundreds of bolts — 100% cotton fabrics. Large selection of quilt books, notions, patterns & gifts. Classes offered.

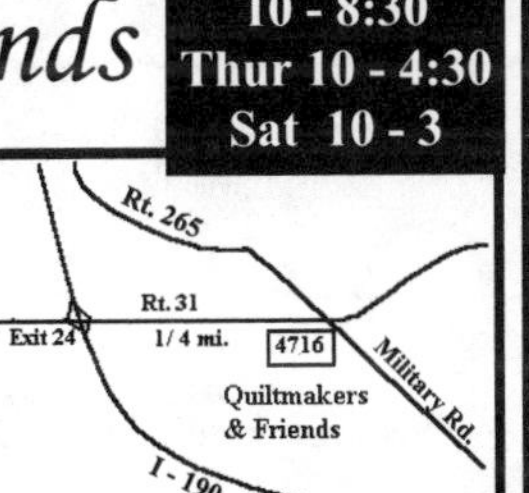

Lockport, NY #3

5410 Stone Rd. 14094
(716) 433-5377
Owner: Judith Farnham
Est: 1982

Pine Grove Workshop

Mon - Sat 10 - 4:30

2500 Bolts 100% Cotton
Antiques
Hundreds of Books, Patterns, & Notions
Spring Seminar

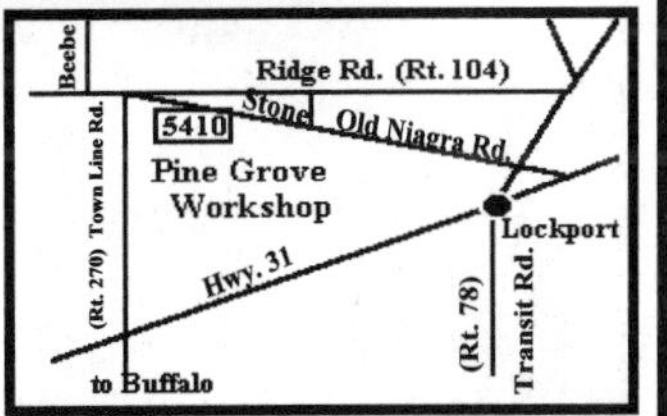

Williamsville, NY #4

Sew What?

Tues & Wed 10 - 7
Thur - Sat 10 - 5

6816 Main Street 14221
(716) 632-8801
Owner: Ann Shaw
Est: 1990 1500 Bolts 1900 sq.ft.

Large selection of unique and unusual quilting fabrics, the newest books and notions. Quilting classes and professional quilting service available.

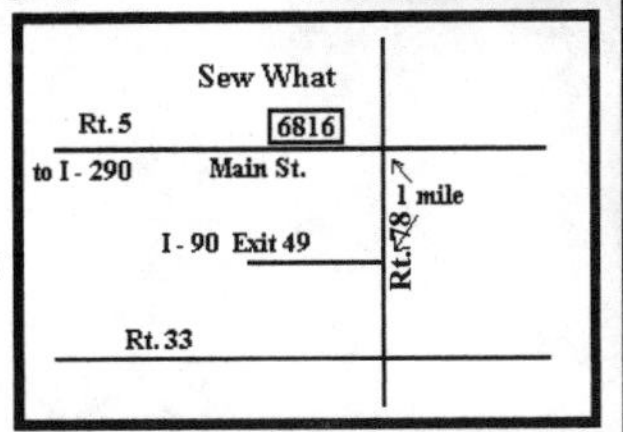

East Aurora, NY #6

659 Main St. 14052
(716) 652-2811
Fax: (716) 652-2863
Est: 1978 3500 sq.ft.

Clarence, NY #5

10750 Main St. 14031
(716) 759-8081
Fax: (716) 759-1715
Est: 1996
3000 sq.ft.

Aurora Sewing Center

Mon 10 - 8
Thur 10 - 9
Tues, Wed, Fri 10 - 5:30
Sat 10 - 4

Owners: Regis Boire & Barb Perry
www.Aurorasewingcenter.com
E-Mail Questions ASCBARB@aol.com

Stop in and visit our shops — You'll be pleasantly surprised!

- ♥ *We have over a 1000 Bolts of fabric to choose from.*
- ♥ *Thousands of book titles, quilting, sewing, applique & more.*
- ♥ *The latest in craft, quilting, & applique patterns — with lots of displayed samples!*
- ♥ *Look-in on our classroom activities — we have over 90 different classes offered each semester.*
- ♥ *Bernina sewing machines, sales and service.*
- ♥ *Service of all makes and models*
- ♥ *Large display of Horn cabinets.*

Rt. 5 (Main St.)
Rt. 33
I - 90
Ransom Rd.
Clarence Location
Aurora Sewing Center
East Aurora Location
Rt. 400
Girdle Rd.
U.S. 20A
(Main St.)
Maple

BERNINA®

2 Great Locations ! !

East Aurora, NY #7

THE CARRIAGE QUILT SHOPPE

593 Main St (By the Viaduct)
East Aurora, NY 14052
(716) 655-4561

- Amish Carriage in shoppe
- Amish quilts
- Amish Mustache Rugs
- Amish Gifts

MACHINE QUILTING SERVICE IN SHOPPE!

READYMADE QUILTS
CUSTOM ORDER QUILTS
100% COTTON FABRICS
BOOKS
PATTERNS
NOTIONS
CLASSES IN THE LOFT

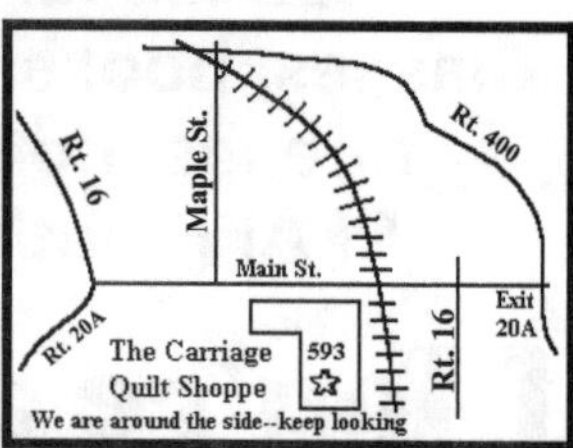

-call for summer hours!

Mon, Thur & Fri 10 - 6
Tues & Wed 10 - 5 Sat 10 - 4

Hamburg, NY #8

Tues - Fri 10 - 5
Thur til 9
Sat 10 - 4

Creative Needleworks

21 Main St. 14075
(716) 646-3013
Toll Free: (866) Stitch'n
E-Mail: cneedleinc@aol.com
Owner: Jane Macchioni Est: 1998

Inspiration abounds for both quilters and cross stitchers in this cozy shop. Friendly, knowledgeable staff welcome your visit!

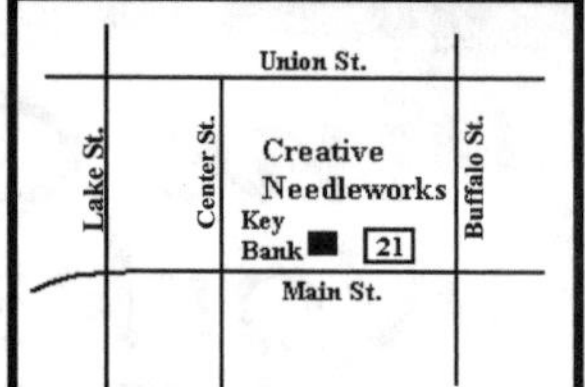

Belfast, NY #9

Tues - Fri 10 - 5
Sat 10 - 4

Quilts and Other Legacies

41 Main St. 14711
(585) 365-2493 Fax: (585) 365-2491
gwbouldin@wnyweb.net
www.quilts-legacies.com
Owner: Gail Wightman-Bouldin
Est: 1998 3200 sq.ft.

We are located in Amish country and we invite you to shop in the ambiance of our turn-of-the century store and beautiful antiques setting for cotton fabrics, books, pattern and other supplies. Local Amish goods and country hospitality.

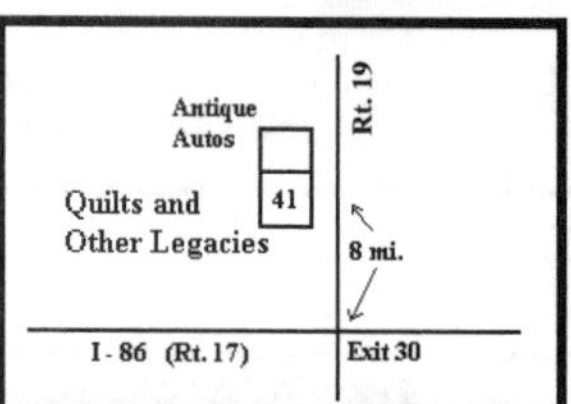

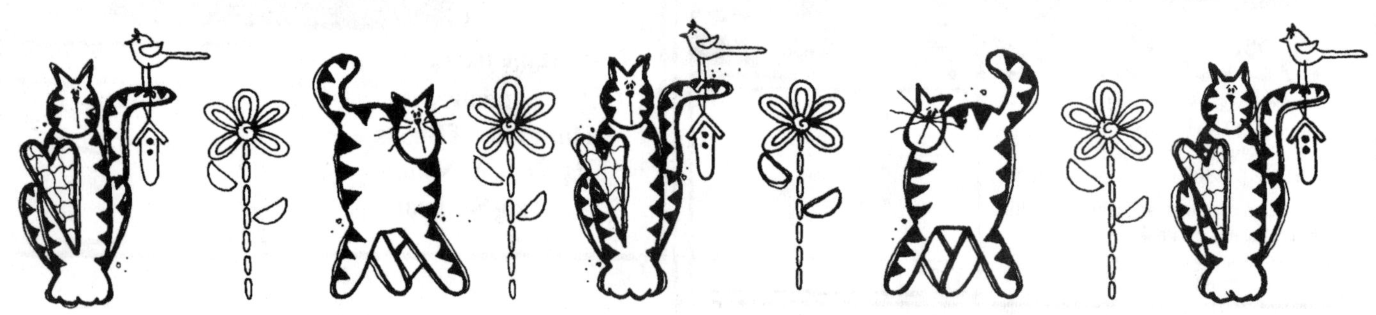

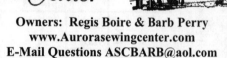

Mt. Pleasant

Quilting Company

Large selection of books, patterns, notions, supplies, kits & gift items.

Classes for all levels
~ from beginner through advanced ~

Longarm Machine Quilting Services

Store Hours:
Tuesday-Friday 10-5:00
Wednesday Evening 'til 8:00
Saturday 10-3:00
CLOSED Sunday & Monday

***30 min. SW of Rochester
75 min. SE of Buffalo
30 min. S of Batavia
60 min. NW of Corning***

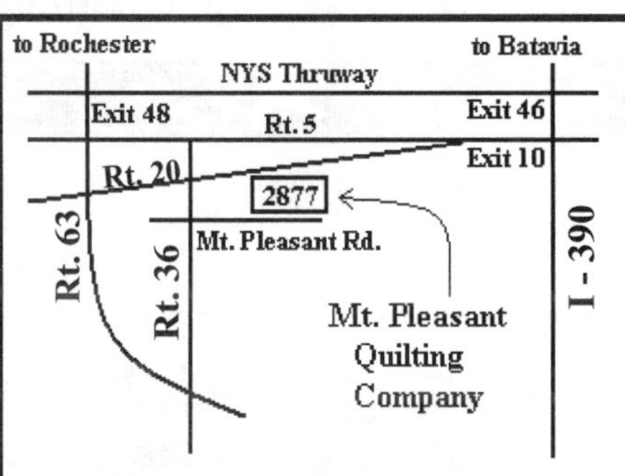

2877 Mt. Pleasant Rd., York, NY 14592
585-243-0767
Barbara J. Miller Est: 2002
mtpquilt@rochester.rr.com

Our friendly and knowledgeable staff invites you to visit soon! The coffee pot's always on!

York, NY #10

Over 2,500 bolts of 100% cotton fabrics from Andover, Benartex, David Textiles, Erlanger, Hoffman, Kona Bay, Marcus Brothers, Moda, Monarch, P&B Textiles, Indo, RJR, Thimbleberries, Seattle Bay, South Sea Imports, Timeless Treasures, & many more.

Visit us online!
www.mtpleasantquiltingcompany.com

Quaker Street West

"Home of the Mountain Fairies"

Tue. 10-7
Wed. 10-5
Thur. 10-7
Fri. 10-5
Sat 10-5

1000 + Bolts Est. 1999
2000 Sq.ft. Barn
Specialize in *Flannel & Batiks*

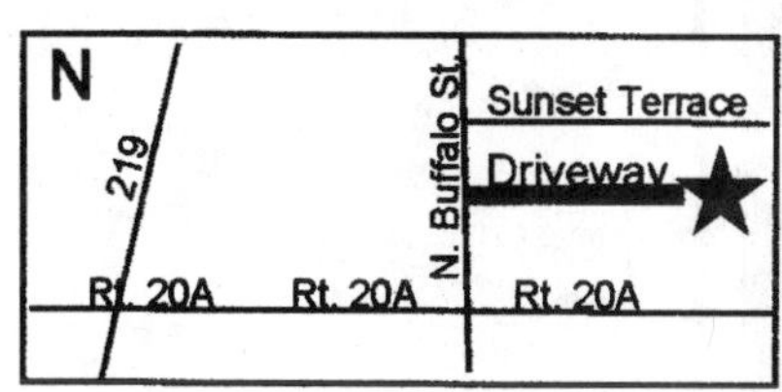

Quaker Street West Originals

The Quilters Blade
Full Line of Patterns
Block Party Programs

4109 N. Buffalo St., Orchard Park, NY 14127
716-662-3037

Orchard Park, NY #11

Fredonia, NY #12

Tues - Fri 9:30 - 6
Sat 9:30 - 4

Mauzy's SEWING CENTER

40 E. Main St. 14063
(716) 672-2242 mmauzy1@juno.com
Owner: Mary Mauzy Morales
Located in a White Victorian house.
We carry sewing machines, cabinets, fabrics, patterns, books & more. Classes all year.
Two Quilt retreats each year.

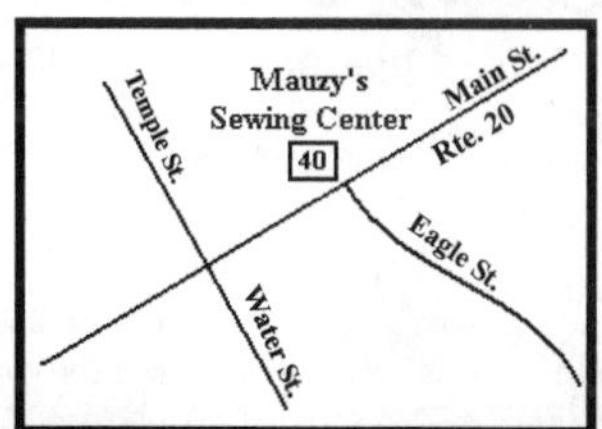

Dunkirk, NY #13

Tues - Fri 10 - 6
Thur til 7
Sat 10 - 4

Quilted Memories

3375 E. Main Rd. (Rt. 20) 14048
(716) 672-7472 Fax: (716) 672-7462
Owner: Mary Elfman
Est: 2003 1200 sq.ft. 1100 Bolts

Come In ... Enjoy the Friendly Atmosphere and Browse through the High-Quality Fabrics and Wide Selection of Books & Patterns.

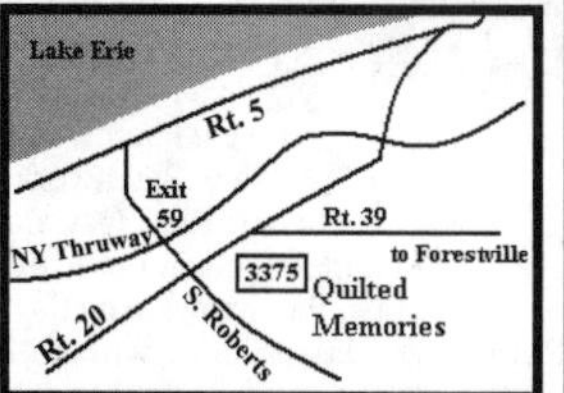

Vestal, NY #14

Grandmother's Thimble

Quilt Shop and Sewing Machines

Authorized **BERNINA**® Sales and Service

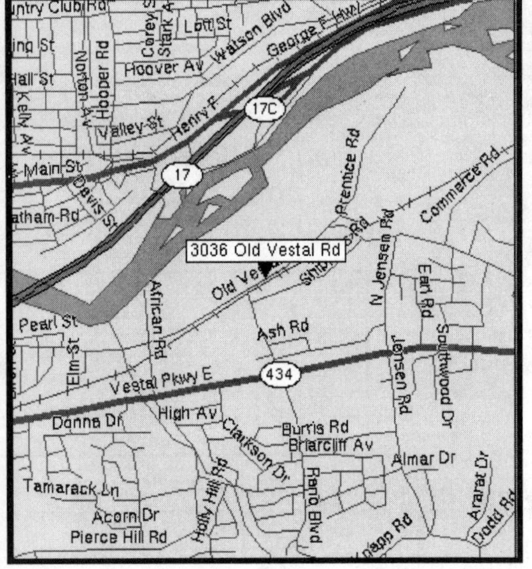

Store Hours: M,T,W,F 10-5:30
Thurs. 10-7, Sat. 10-4

www.grandmothersthimble.net

E-mail: gthimble@stny.rr.com

3036 Old Vestal Rd.
Vestal,NY 13850
607-797-7022

Owner: Justine Layman

Bernina Tech: Jim Layman

We have 2000 bolts of 100% cotton fabric, quilting notions, books, classes and a full line of Bernina sewing machines.

Endwell, NY #15

Mon - Fri 10 - 5:30
Thur til 8
Summer Sat 10 - 1
Winter Sat 10 - 4

Sew Much More

2010 East Main St. 13760
(607) 748-8340
Owner: Nancy Valenta
Est: 1990 8500 sq.ft.

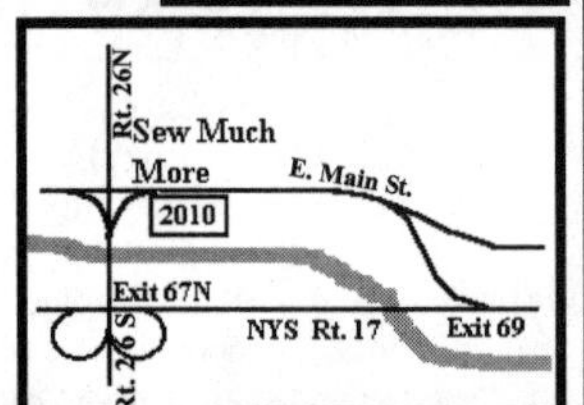

Over 6000 bolts of 100% cottons. Heirloom sewing, specialty threads, books and patterns galore. A delightful experience for your palette. HUSQVARNA VIKING Authorized Dealer.

Owego, NY #17

Mon 6 - 9
Tues & Thur 11 - 7
Fri 11 - 9
Sat 9:30 - 4

Patchwork Angels Quilt Shop

313 Front St. 13728
(607) 687-7999
Fax: (607) 687-3113
Rose@PatchworkAngels.com
www.PatchworkAngels.com
Owner: Rose Oswald Est: 2003

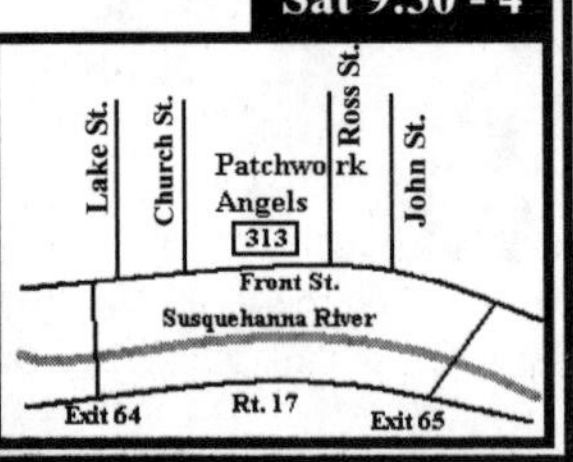

Located in Angels in the Attic Bed & Breakfast, Patchwork Angels provides Retreats & Classes along with notions, fabrics & Janome Sewing Machines.

Pucky Huddle Delight

Quilting Fabrics & Supplies
~Est. 2002~

~100% Cotton Fabrics
~Flannels
~Wool Felts
~Batting
~Fat Quarters
~Patterns
~Books
~Notions

Between Owego and Ithaca
12 miles from NYS Rt. 17 (86)

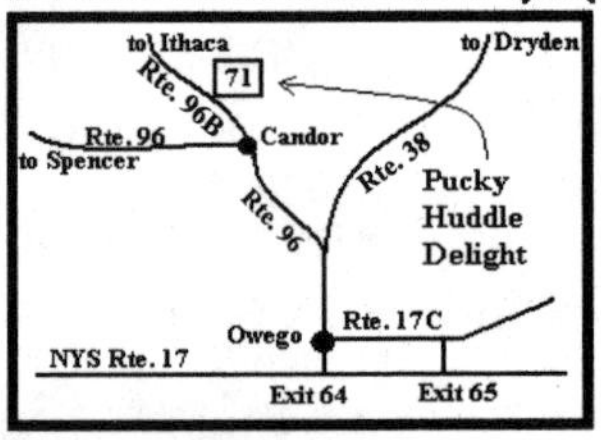

to Ithaca
to Dryden
71
Rte. 96B
Rte. 96
to Spencer
Candor
Rte. 38
Rte. 96
Pucky Huddle Delight
Owego
Rte. 17C
NYS Rte. 17
Exit 64
Exit 65

~Quilt Guild Members receive a 10% discount!
~Gift Certificates Available!

#16

Jennifer Kopcho ~ Proprietor

(607) 659 – 7PHD Fax: (607) 659-7744

www.puckyhuddledelight.com

Tues. – Fri. 11-8
Sat. & Sun. 11-6

71 Owego Rd. Rt. 96B
Candor, NY 13743

~ Open evenings for your convenience! ~

jen@puckyhuddledelight.com

Owego, NY #18

Mon - Fri 10 - 4:30
Thur til 6:30
Sat 10 - 3

The Churn Dash

6 McMaster St., Suite 4 13827
(607) 687-6811 Fax: (607) 687-6812
Churndashfabric@aol.com
Owners: Leonore & Gene Gill
Est: 2001 2500 sq.ft. 2000+ Bolts

Quality 100% cotton fabric, notions, books, patterns, classes, Pfaff dealer, machine quilting services available.

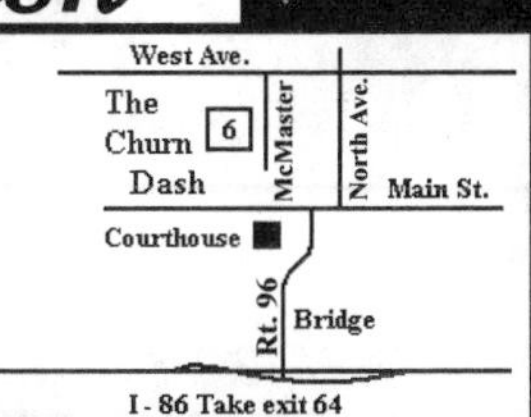

Ithaca, NY #20

200 Pleasant Grove Rd. 14850
(607) 266-0850
quilters@e-quilterscorner.com
www.e-quilterscorner.com
Owners: Katie Barnaby,
Cyndi Slothower,
Linda Van Nederynen & Merrie Wilent
Est: 1995 3500 Bolts

A diverse collection of exciting fabric selected by four wild women. Huge book selection, patterns, notions, and gifts. Authorized Pfaff dealer. Bus tours welcome, please call in advance so we may better serve you. Special promotions and projects available on our web site. Gallery of constantly changing quilts decorate our walls. New York's headquarters for Bali batiks. Block of the month quilts and kits with our original fabric packs.

Mon - Fri 10 - 6
Sat 10 - 5 Sun 1 - 4

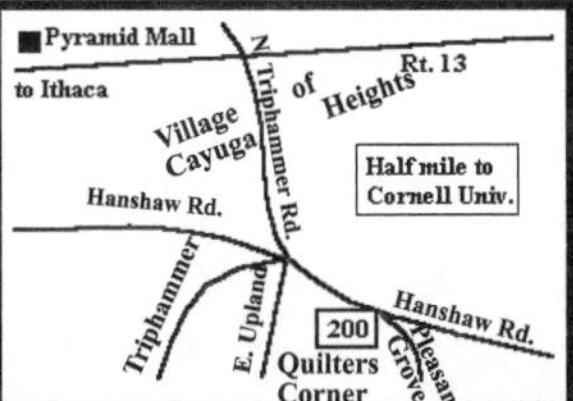

We're located on the north side of Ithaca at Community Corners.

Come . . . and enjoy a unique shopping experience in the ambiance of our renovated 19th century country church

18 Canal St.
14814
(607) 562-7596
Owner: Jody Kravec
Est: 1986
4500 sq.ft.

- The Finest 100% Cotton Fabrics Available, Quilting Books, Notions, Gadgets & Gifts
- Out-of-the-Ordinary Patterns for Dolls, Quilted Clothing & Home Decor
- Models & Samples to Inspire Creativity
- Quilts & Wallhangings for Sale
- Counted Cross Stitch Patterns, Threads & accessories
- Gifts—Candles, Boyds Bears, Cards
- Christmas Throughout the Year

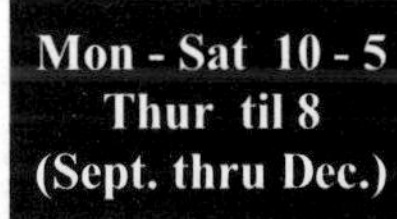

The Village Sampler is easily accessible from Exit 49, Route 17 / I-86

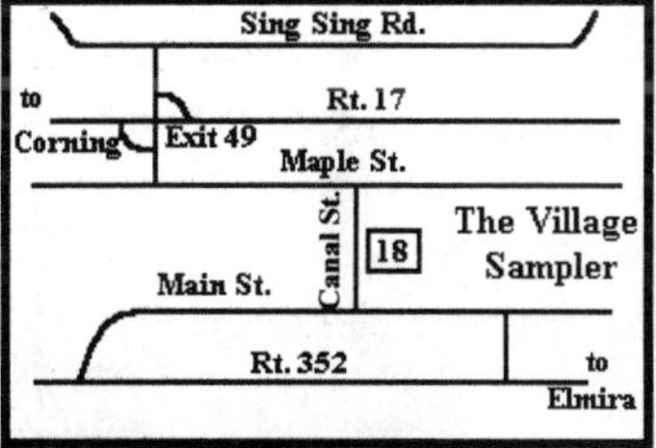

Big Flats, NY #19

Watkins Glen, NY #21

Mon - Sat 10 - 5:30
Closed Wed
Sun 11 - 3
June - Oct

O'Susannah's Quilts & Gifts

111 W. Fourth St. 14891
(607) 535-6550 Est: 2004
www.osusannahsquiltshop.com

Independent Quilt Shop with a wide selection of books to entice you and just the right fabrics to delight you!

Hammondsport, NY #22

Mon - Sat 10 - 5
Sun 11 - 4

Lake Country Patchwork

67 Shether St.
P.O. Box 332 14840
(607) 569-3530 Est: 1996
Owner: Candace Hosier

Let the natural beauty of the Finger Lakes inspire your next quilt. We have 100% cotton fabrics, quilting supplies and books. Quilts & gift items.

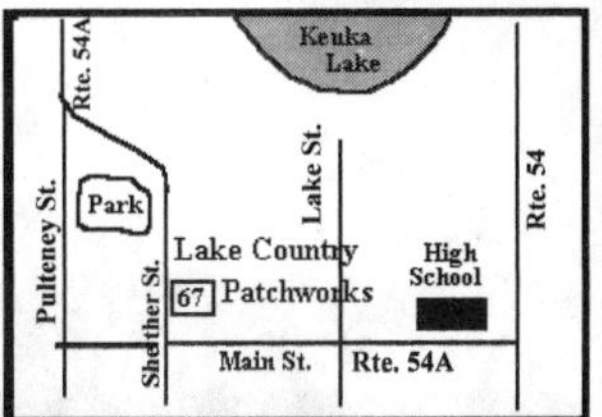

Stanley, NY #23

Wed - Fri 1 - 8
Sat 10 - 3

From The Heart

1725 Rte. 245 14561
(585) 526-4429 Fax: Same
fromtheheart@fontiernet.net
Owners: Michael & Jean Salone
Est: 2003 1500 sq.ft. 600+ Bolts

Fabrics - featuring Thimbleberries, Moda, Flannels and others. Notions, books, Classes, Clubs. Gifts - Candles, Soap, Quilt Racks and Shelves.

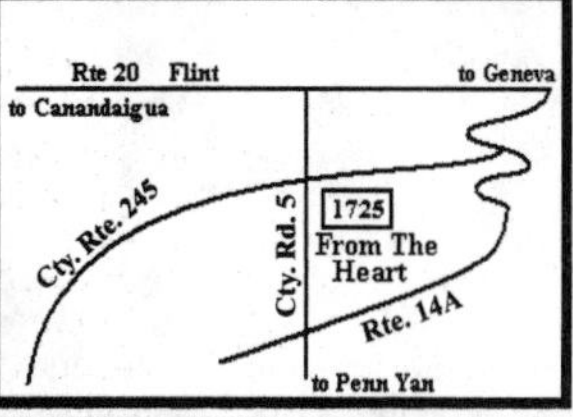

1190 Earls Hills Road · Penn Yan, NY 14527

Open Year 'Round -- Closed Sundays & Religious Holidays

1-315-781-2571

www.weaverviewfarms.com

150+ HANDSTITCHED QUILTS • HOMESPUNS
QUALITY COTTONS • FLANNELS • BOOKS
PATTERNS • FAT QUARTERS • HOMEMADE FOODS

Magical history abounds in the Finger Lakes region, never more so than on this 1800's working dairy farm.

Mention this ad and receive 20 fat quarters for $20!!! brand name fabrics

With over 4,500 sq. ft. there is something for everyone!

Our Amish quilts are made by friends and family. Coordinate your quilt with our selection of specialty fabrics. Homespun aprons, tablerunners & handquilted pillows, Gingham dresses & bonnets for little girls. Oak & iron quilt hangers.

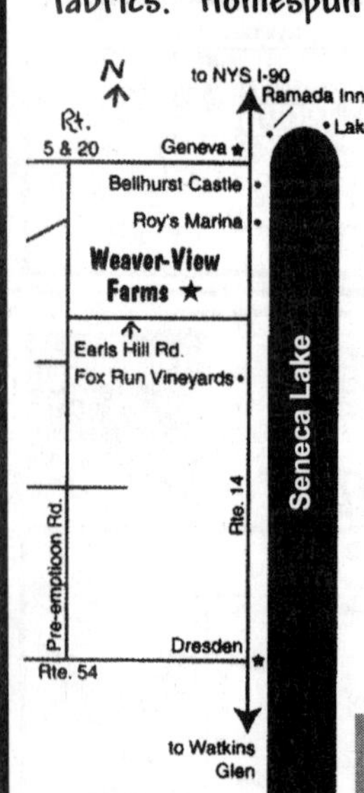

This map shows only major routes.

From Rochester & North:
Take 1 - 90 to the Geneva exit (exit 42) or follow Routes 5 & 20 into Geneva. Follow Route 14 South along Seneca Lake, approximately 7 miles. Watch for sign on right. Turn right onto Earls Hill Road, farm is on the right.

From Elmira & South:
Follow Route 14 North through Watkins Glen, along Seneca Lake, approximately 28 miles. Watch for signs on the left, turn left onto Earls Hill Road, farm is on the right.

Penn Yan, NY #24

Waterloo, NY #25

Ladybug Fabrics & Quilts

Main St Shop Center Suite 108
Waterloo NY 13165

www.ladybugfabrics.com/fabrics

Est: 2002 800 sq.ft. 800+ Bolts

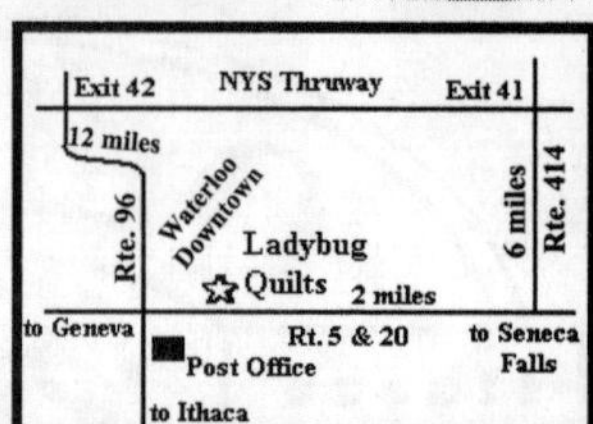

Mon - Fri 10 - 5 Thur til 8 Sat 9 - 4

Also dealer of Ulmer Quilter Frame. Handmade quilts, quilt racks and other fine gifts. Friendly, helpful customer service.

Exit 42 · NYS Thruway · Exit 41 · 12 miles · Rte. 96 · Waterloo Downtown · Ladybug Quilts · 2 miles · 6 miles · Rte. 414 · to Geneva · Rt. 5 & 20 · to Seneca Falls · Post Office · to Ithaca

100% cotton quilting fabrics, books, & notions.

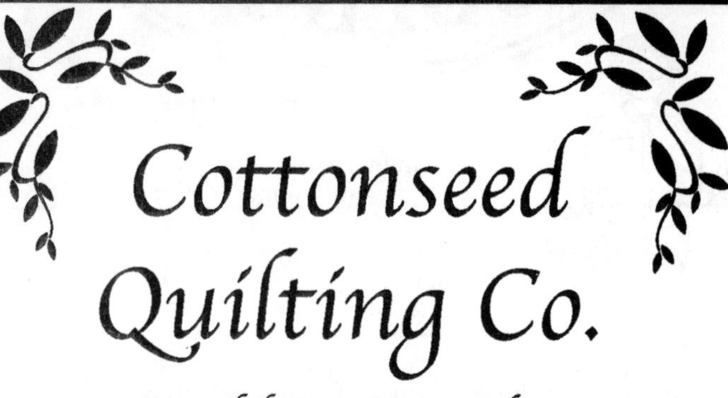

Beautiful 100% Cotton Fabrics
Handspun Wool Yarn -- Raised Locally
Haberdashery of Quilting Needs
Come & Enjoy Our Friendly Relaxed Atmosphere

Quality Custom Machine Quilting On Premises
Custom Embroidered Quilt Labels & Monograms

9 Charlesworth Ave. 14809
607-566-9264
qlt@infoblvd.net
www.cottonseedquilting.com
Owner: Susan Haneline

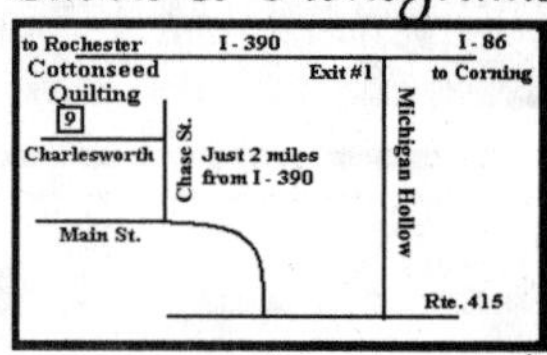

Avoca, NY #26

Tues - Fri 10 - 5
Sat 10 - 4 or By Appt.

Boston, NY #27

The Quilt FARM

est. 1989
3600 sq.ft.

Tues - Sat 11 - 5
Tues & Thurs evenings til 7
Closed Sun & Mon

"WORTH THE DRIVE"

The Answer to a Quilter's Prayers in God's Country

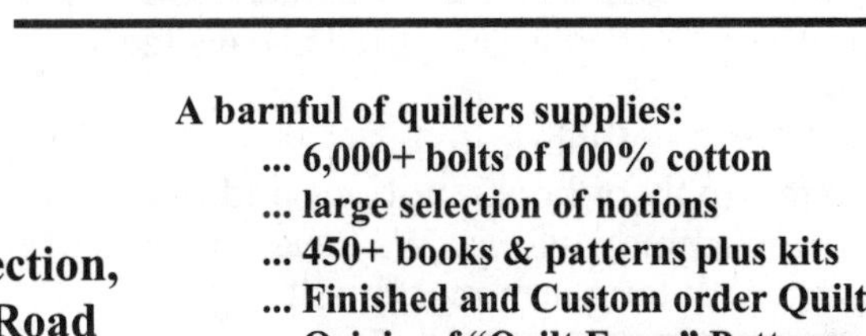

5623 South Feddick Road 14025
(716) 941-3140
Owner: Isabell Schmit
Staffed by Family and Friends

DIRECTIONS: (a scenic country drive 30 minutes South of Buffalo)
I - 90 to Route 219 South, Exit at Rice Road
Off exit ramp turn west & go (up hill) to first intersection, left on Zimmerman, then right on South Feddick Road
Call for specifics . . . It's a challenge.

A barnful of quilters supplies:
- **... 6,000+ bolts of 100% cotton**
- **... large selection of notions**
- **... 450+ books & patterns plus kits**
- **... Finished and Custom order Quilts**
- **... Origin of "Quilt Farm" Patterns**
- **... Classes**

"Shop 'til the Cows come home."

Apple Country Quilt Shop & Café

Authorized Gammill Quilting Systems Dealer

Remember us on your next road trip!
51 State St. (Route 31 on the curve)
Holley, NY 14470
1-585-638-5262
Toll free 1-866-340-6100
www.applecountryquilts.com

Tues - Sat 10 - 4

Holley, NY #28

Our Café is open during shop hours and for dinners Friday & Saturday 4:30 - 7:30 pm

After you have completely indulged yourselves in quilting goodies stop in at the Apple Country Café for a delectable lunch. Homemade soups, sandwiches and our Chef Vicki's specials of the week. Then how about one of our many totally Homemade desserts, all done right here in house by our own pastry chef Carol. Everything from Crème Brule to our always favorite bread puddings.

Apple Country Quilt Shop & Café has so much more to offer. Now boasting over 1500 bolts of the best quilters cottons, notions, books, quilting classes and long arm classes. You can also take a test drive on a new Gammill Quilting Machine. Only 20 minutes off the New York State Thruway exit 48 coming from the west or 35 minutes west of Rochester. Visit us on the web at www.applecountryquilts.com from there you can access a map, send us an email or see what we have in store in the up coming months including classes, sales, dinner specials and the like!

Dansville, NY #29

Material Rewards

10160 Sandy Hill Rd. 14437
(585) 335-2050
quilts@materialrewards.com
www.materialrewards.com

Tues - Fri 9:30 - 5:30
Sat 9:30 - 5

* Full service quilt shop where you'll always feel welcome!
* Over 5000 bolts of fabric
* Up to date supply of books, notions and patterns
* Long arm machine quilting. We have 15 years of experience with long arm machines!!

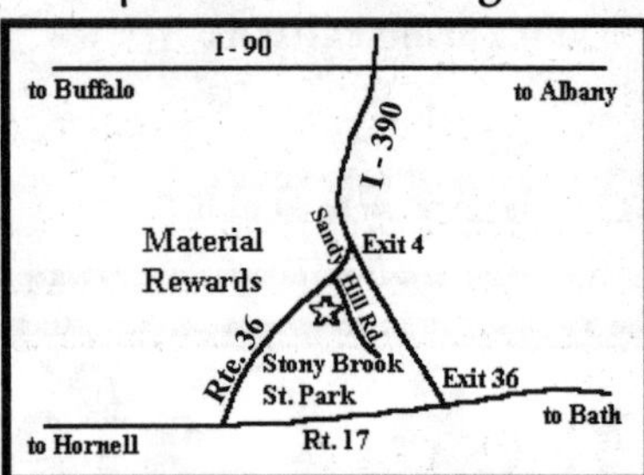

Enjoy one of the state's largest Quilt Shows - Labor Day Weekend (every other year - 2004). Contact us if you would like to submit an item or for more information

All the Creative Comforts for Quilters.

The Quilting Parlor

4001 Westside Dr. 14428
(585) 293-0762
thequiltingparlor@yahoo.com
www.quiltingparlor.com
Owner: Susan Zuber Est: 2002

Tues - Fri 10 - 4 Sat 10 - 2

100% High Quality Cottons, always 15% off to everyone. Notions, books, patterns, & classes available as well as long-arm services. Friendly & knowledgeable staff.

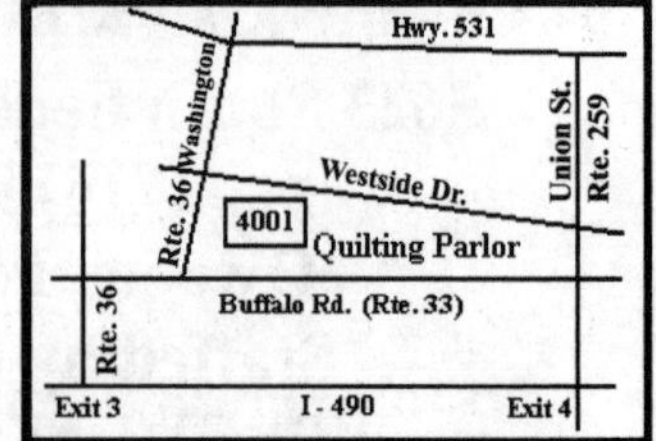

Churchville, NY #30

Rochester, NY #31

Mon - Sat 10 - 6
Tues & Thur Til 8

Discount Sewing & Jackie Lynn's Fabric Center

475 Ridge Rd. E 14621
(585) 544-4110 Fax: (585) 544-4252
www.discountsewingcenter.com
www.jackielynnsfabrics.com
Est: 1994 8000 sq.ft.

100% cotton quilting fabrics plus bridal, wools, knits and fashion fabrics. Authorized Brother, Janome, Singer and Nolting Longarm Dealer.

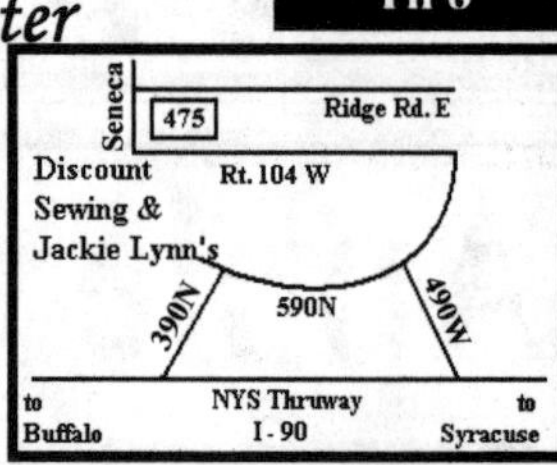

Mendon, NY #32

Mon - Fri 10 - 5
Sat 10 - 4

Mendon Village Quilt Shop

1350 Pittsford-Mendon Rd. 14506
(585) 624-3130
www.mendonvillagequiltshop.com
Owners: Linda Liljequist & Dorothy Lindblom

A hands-on shop with quality fabrics, quilting supplies, gifts, classes and knowledgeable staff offering friendly service and support.

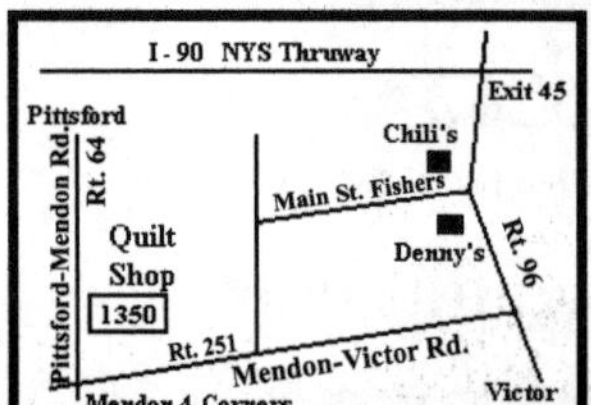

Victor, NY #33

Mon - Wed 9:30 - 5
Thur 9:30 - 7
Fri & Sat 9:30 - 4

Ivy Thimble Quilt & Gift Shop

27 E. Main St. 14564
(585) 742-2680 Fax: (585) 742-2696
www.ivythimble.com
Est: 2003 1400 sq.ft. 1000+ Bolts

We're not just a quilt shop!
Along with over 1000 bolts of high quality fabric, patterns, books & notions we have a great selection of gifts and greeting cards.

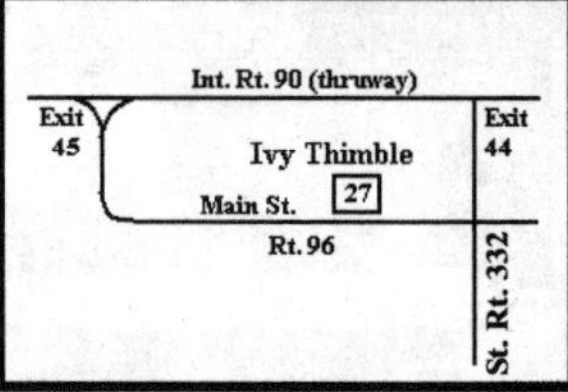

Savannah, NY #34

Mon - Sat 9 - 5
Thur & Fri til 8

4219 Yates Rd. 13146
(315) 594-8485
Owner: Arlene Zimmerman

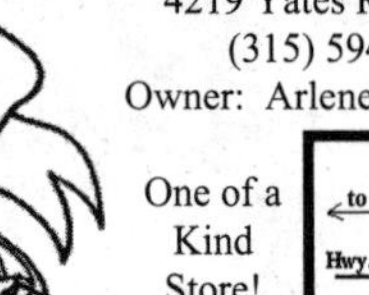

One of a Kind Store!

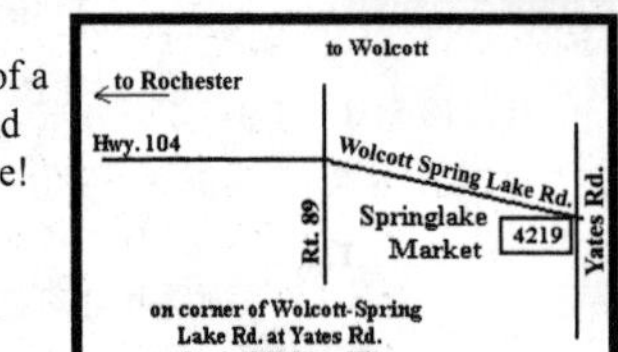

Great selection ... name brand fabrics unbeatable prices ... with a dutch country flair ... notions ... books ... crafts.

Macedon, NY #35

Sun 12 - 6
Mon - Thur 9 - 8
Closed Fri & Sat

QUILTWORKS

235 Pittsford-Palmyra Rd. (Route 31) 14502
(866) 506-5800 or (315) 986-5800
info@quiltworks.biz
www.quiltworks.biz
Owner: Judy Orsburn

Metropolitan Rochester's newest quilt shop located 1-1/2 miles east of Lollipop Farm on NY Route 31 across from the Old Barnworks.

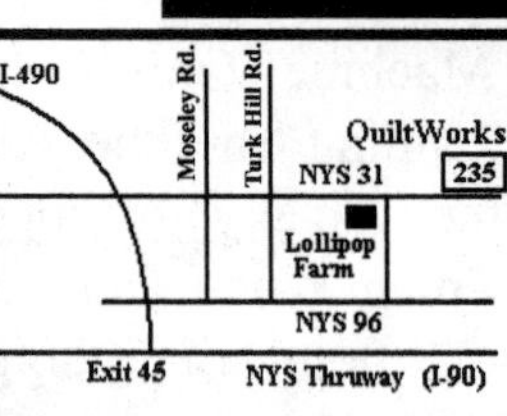

East Rochester #36

patricias' fabric house

333 W. Commercial St. 14445
585-248-2362
Monday-Thursday 10-9, Friday & Saturday 10-5

WE'VE GOT YOUR QUILTING NEEDS ALL SEWED UP!

5400 sq.ft. 3500+ Bolts Bus Tours Welcome

- Outstanding collection of fine quilting cottons: Kona Bay, Moda, Hoffman, RJR, etc.
- Also Batiks, Orientals, Novelty Prints, Homespuns & Florals
- Unique Threads, Unusual Buttons, Books, Notions, Classes
- Bridal & Special Occasion & Fine Dress Fabrics.
- Complete Line of **elna** Sewing Machines & Sergers.

Visit our Website
patriciasfabrichouse.com

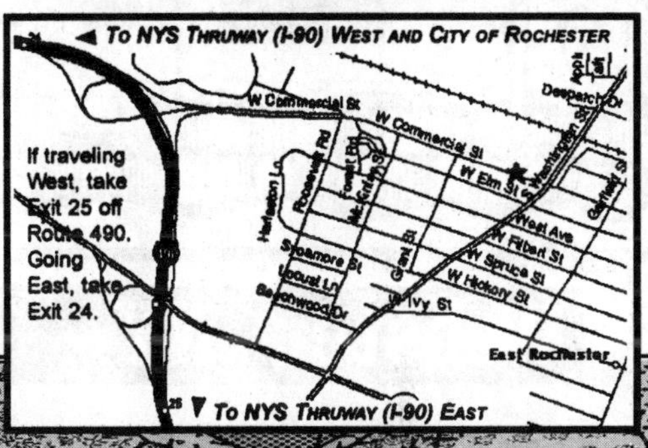

Little Ladies and Lace

CNY's Best Kept Secret

Located in the village. We feature quality quilting cottons, flannels, books, patterns, notions, classes, friendly service, and an on site long-arm quilting system.

Mon - Wed 10 am - 6 pm
Thurs - Fri 10 am - 7 pm
Sat 10 am - 5 pm

70 Genesee St., Camillus, NY 13031
315-672-9284 Fax: 315-672-3288
Kimberly@littleladiesandlace.com

Est: 1998 2800 sq.ft. 1200 Bolts & Growing

Camillus, NY #37

www.littleladiesandlace.com

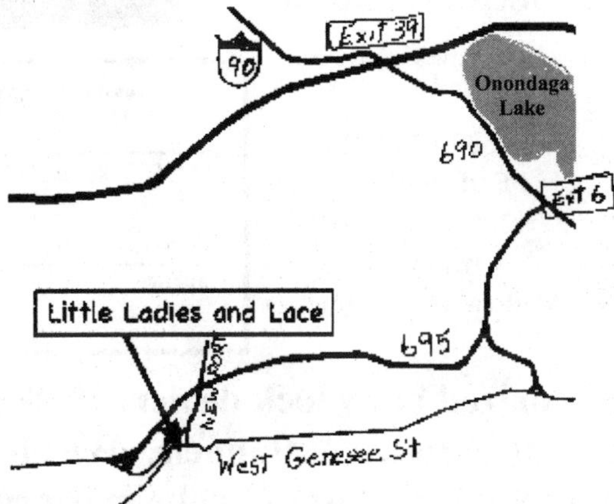

190 Exit 39 to 690. Merge onto 690 East. Exit 6 to the 695 bypass. Stay toward Auburn. Take Camillus Warners Exit. Left onto Newport. Take a right onto Genesee Street. We are located on right at #70

Skaneateles, NY #38

Patchwork Plus

36 Jordan Street 13152
(315) 685-6979
Owner: Judi West Est: 1987

4000 bolts of 100% cottons, books, notions, patterns;
Bernina Sewing Machines;
Plus friendly service in Skaneateles;
Gateway to the Finger Lakes

Mon - Sat 10 - 4

Webster, NY #41

Crosstowne Quilting LLC

182 North Avenue
Webster, NY 14580
585-872-2080

Mon - Thurs 10 - 5
Wed 10 - 8
Fri & Sat 10 - 4
Call for Evening Hours

Fax: 585-872-9728
Est: 2003
2000 sq.ft.
Owner:
Melissa Morgante

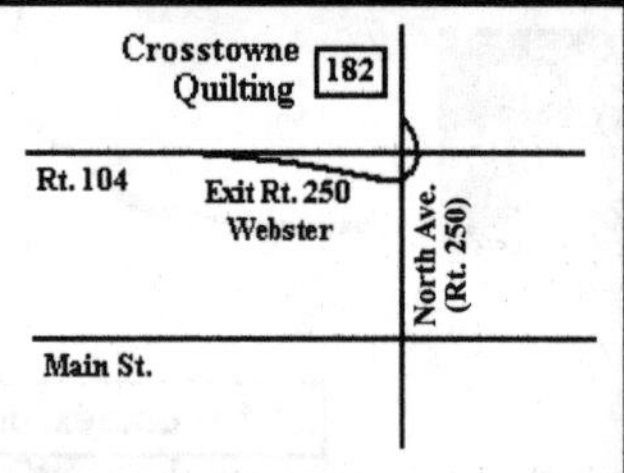

Authorized baby lock dealer. 2500+ bolts of quilting cottons, & flannels. We also have a large assortment of books, patterns, and notions for quilting. Free seminars for quilt guilds and tour groups. Call for details.
Numerous classes available for the hearing impaired

Marcellus, NY #39

By Appt. Or Chance

The Quilting Shoppe

2162 Lawrence Rd. 13108
(315) 673-1126
Owner: Elaine Lyon
Est: 1983 1800 sq.ft. 1800+ Bolts

MACHINE QUILTING SERVICE
Custom Made Quilts. Quilted Jackets
Quilts for Sale.

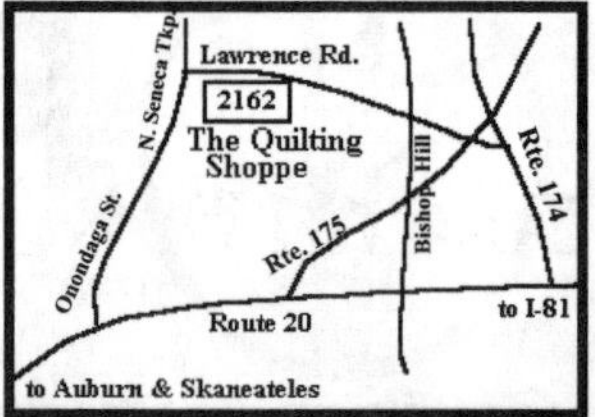

Heart in Hand
Fabrics & Quilts

A warm and friendly quilt shop with a full line of quality fabrics, books, patterns and notions.
Located at the L.W. Emporium, an antique and craft coop.
Authorized Janome Dealer.

Tues - Sat 10 - 5
Wed til 8
Sun 12 - 4

www.heartinhandfabrics.com

6365 Knickerbocker Rd. 14519
315-524-3363 1440 sq.ft. 1200 Bolts
Owner: Kathleen Wagner Est: 2002

Ontario, NY #40

Watertown, NY #42

Tues - Sat 10 - 5

KAP Quilting & Fabric

18486 Woodard Rd. 13601
(315) 658-4216
kapquilting@juno.com
Owner: Kenneth Alberry Est: 2000
2000 sq.ft. & growing 500+ bolts
Long-arm quilting -- pantographs and custom services. Fabric, batt and backing fabrics to 120". Books, Lasar Rulers and Notions.
Personalized service.

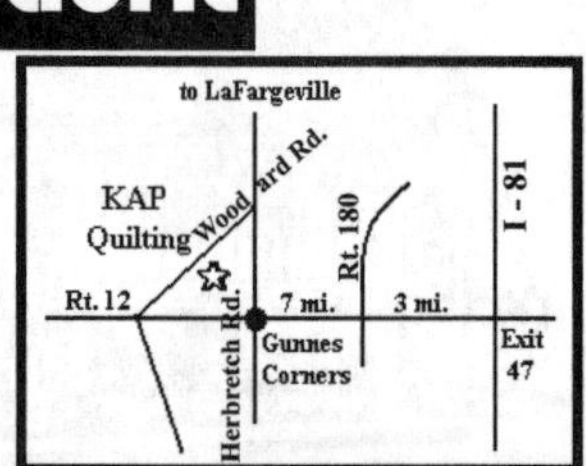

Richville, NY #43

Tues & Thur 4 - 8
Wed & Sat 10 - 4
and whenever we are home,
closed Sat June & July

Fabric Arts

20 Phelps Rd., P.O. Box 349 13681
(315) 287-2145
fabricrt@twcny.rr.com
www.sew2000.com/fabricarts
Owners: Norb & Dorothy Hall
Est: 1985 2500 sq.ft.
Machine Quilting Services, Fabrics, Books, Notions, Classes, Sewing Machines—
for all your quilting needs see us.

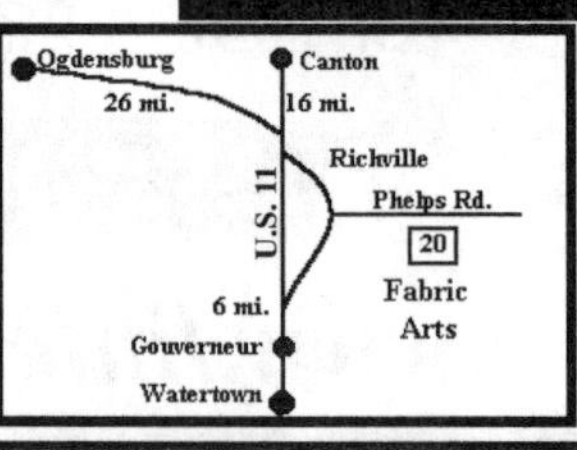

Liverpool, NY #44

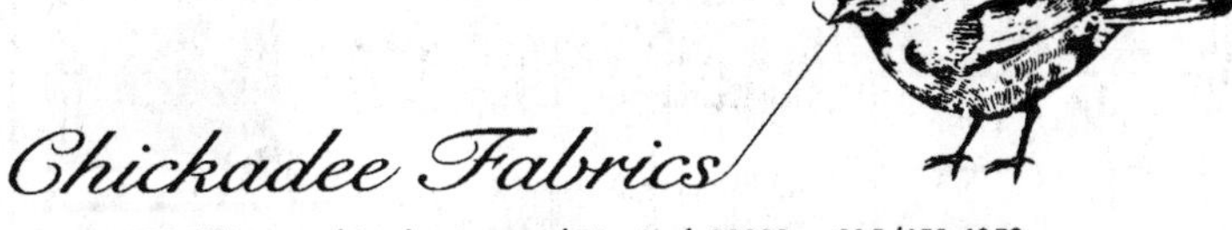

526 Old Liverpool Road • Liverpool, New York 13088 • 315/453-4059

Central New York's Premier Quilt Shop

Fabrics, Books, Notions, Classes, and Quilt restoration. Staffed by knowledgeable quilters

1865 square feet with over 2500 bolts of fabric and 2 dedicated classrooms

Featuring fabrics by Hoffman, P&B Textiles, Kona Bay, RJR, and many others.

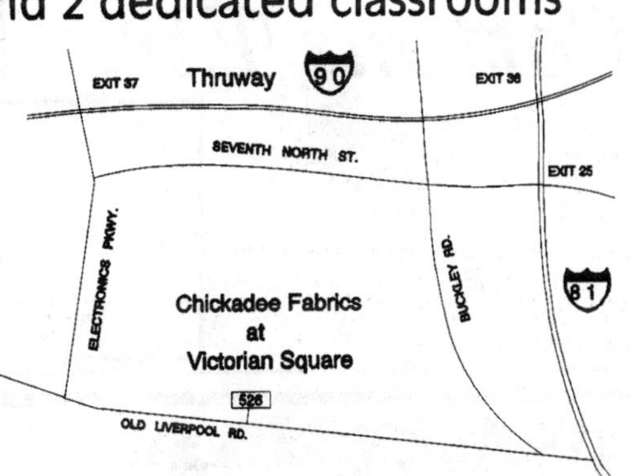

Books by That Patchwork Place, C&T Publishing, and Quilt Digest Press.

Over 100 classes offered per year with day, night, Saturday, custom, and private classes

Easily accessible from both interstate highways.

Store Hours: Mon - Sat 10:00 - 5:00

6 miles from Canadian Border

Dreamcrafter's Quilt Shop

Akwesasne, NY #45

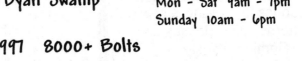

Located at the Wolf Pack Gift Shop on Rte. 37
1422 State Route 37, Hogansburg, NY 13655
(518) 358-4285 Owner: Dyan Swamp
E-Mail: dreamquilt@aol.com
Website: Coming Soon Est: 1997 8000+ Bolts

Store Hours
Mon - Sat 9am - 7pm
Sunday 10am - 6pm

LARGEST QUILT SHOP IN NORTHERN NY
SUPPLIES FOR ALL YOUR
"DREAM" CREATIONS

- 8000+ Bolts of 100% Cottons, Hoffman, Kaufman, Batiks
- Notions: Batting, Thread & Stencils
- Huge Selection of Books & Patterns.
- Quilts For Sale
- Fat Quarters Galore!!!
- Yard Cuts & 1/2 Yard Cuts
- Kits
- Quilter's Gifts
- All purchases are tax-free

Saranac Lake, NY #46

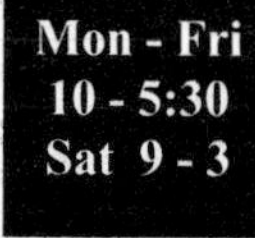

110 Church St. 12983
(518) 891-8899
quiltess@northnet.org
www.quiltessencequiltshop.com
Est: 2002 1200 Bolts

Supplies for the devoted quilter. Quality Fabrics. Notions - Patterns
Large selection of Books
Friendly and Competent Service - French Spoken

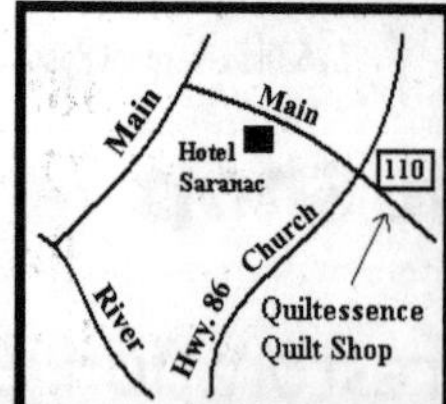

Oneida, NY #48

Mon - Sat
10 - 5
Thur til 8

Cottons Etc.

228 Genesee Street 13421
(315) 363-6834 Est: 1980
Owner: Paula Schultz 1700 sq.ft.
Swatch Set $2 and LSASE.
cottons@ny.tds.net

Our motto is "You Can Never Have Too Much Fabric!" A Pot-pourri of Quilting & Fashion Fabrics, Notions, Books & Patterns. Ask for free gift!

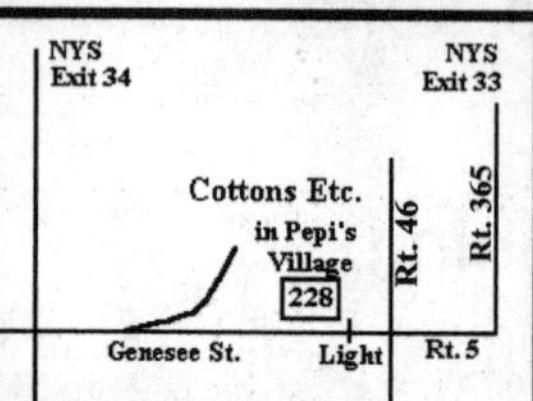

Port Leyden, NY #47

3331 Lincoln St. 13433
(315) 348-4544
Fax: (315) 348-6218
Lisa@aquiltedheart.com
Owner: Lisa Covey
Est: 2003 4500 sq.ft.
www.AQuiltedHeart.com

- Located in a church built in 1895
- Huge selection of Adirondack ("woodsy") prints in flannels and 100% cottons
- Many batiks and hand-dyed fabrics
- Books, patterns, notions and lessons
- Fresh coffee's always on!

Mon - Fri 10 - 5
Sat 10 - 4

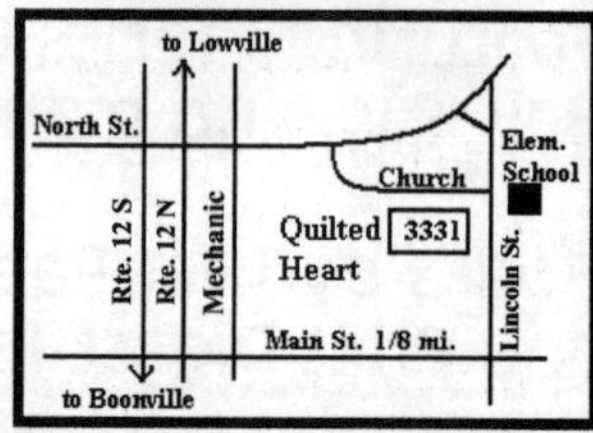

Utica, NY #49

2336 West Whitesboro St. 13502
(315) 735-5328 Est: 1991
Owners: Susan Kowalczyk & Sandra Jones

A shop with unusual fabrics for quilting & sewing. Books, notions, patterns, gifts, classes and newsletter. Bernina Affiliate.

Mon - Fri
9:30 - 5:30
Sat 10 - 4

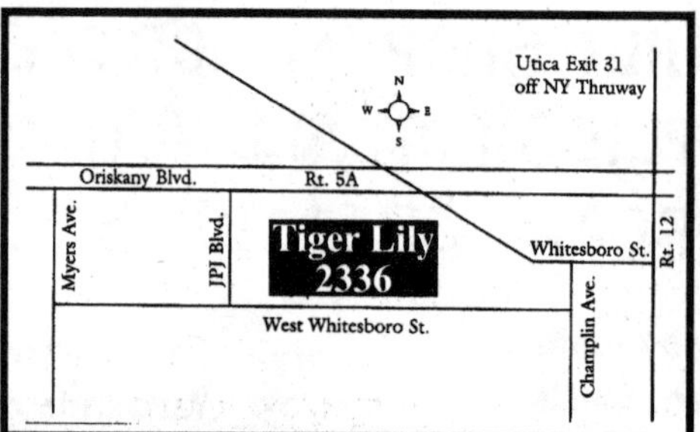

Directions to Tiger Lily: Thruway Exit #31, follow signs to Route 12, then to Route 12 South. Exit at 5A West (Oriskany Blvd.) and proceed through 3 lights. Turn left at JPJ Blvd. Immediately after 3rd light.

Cazenovia, NY #50

Mon - Sat
9:30 - 5

Cazenovia Fabrics

45 Albany St. 13035
(315) 655-8500 Fax: (315) 655-8555
cazfab@netzero.com
Est: 1969 1850 sq.ft.

Located on Rt. 20 in historic Cazenovia is this delightful shop of fabrics for quilting and fashion; giving special attention to the bridal party.

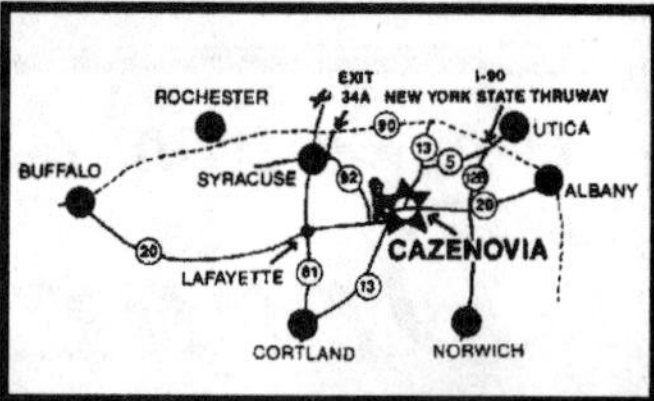

New Hartford, NY #51

Tues - Sat
9 - 5
Fri til 9
Sun 12 - 5

Quiltmaker's Paradise

50 Genesee St. 13413
(315) 797-9366 Fax: (315) 797-8983
Q@quiltmakersparadise.com
www.quiltmakersparadise.com
Est: 2003 5000 sq.ft.

Full service quilt shop. Authorized PFAFF dealer. Service & repair shop for ALL brands & models. Large selection of 100% cotton fabrics, from top manufacturers; notions, books, patterns, kits, classes, BOM's & clubs.

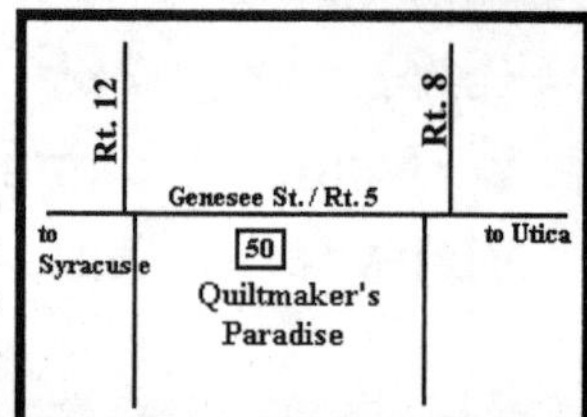

Queensbury, NY #52

Mon - Sat
10 - 5
Sun 12 - 4

The Quilting Bee

974 Rt. 9 12804
(518) 792-0845
Owner: Pat Strain
Est: 1987 1500 sq.ft. 3300+ Bolts

Cotton fabrics include designer's calicos & solids, books, patterns & notions.
Banner flag supplies, Gifts and Quilts.

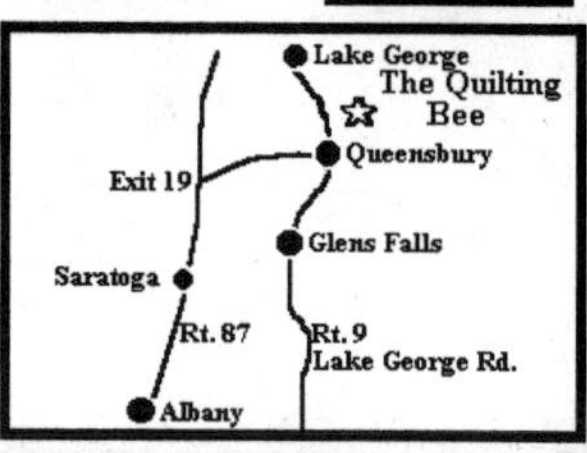

Gloversville, NY #53

385 S. Main St. 12078
(518) 725-4919 or (800) 336-9998
Fax: (518) 773-4166
www.gloversvillesewingcenter.com
Owners: Diana & John Marshall
Est: 1981 4600 sq.ft. 3000+ Bolts

Specializing in Sales & Service of
Bernina • Brother

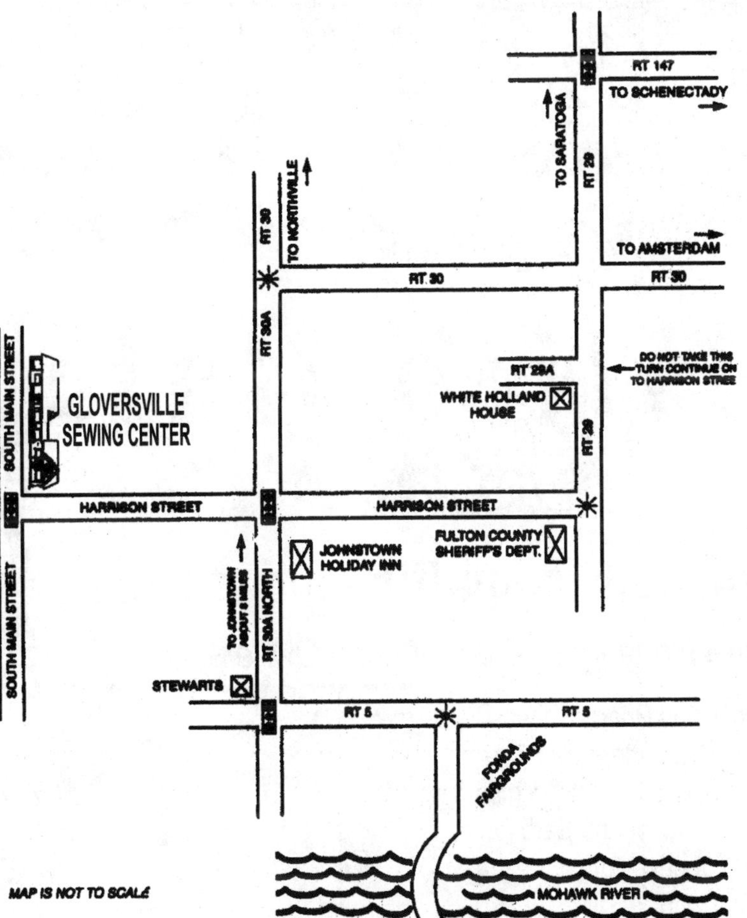

NYS THRUWAY
FONDA-FULTONVILLE EXIT 28
FOLLOW SIGNS FOR RT. 30A NORTH AND JOHNSTOWN AFTER YOU EXIT THRUWAY

Area's Largest Selection of
Quilting Books & Patterns

Over 3000 Broadcloths in Stock
Including Hoffman
Michael Miller
Robert Kaufman
P&B • RJR

Large Assortment of
Decorative Threads
Silk Ribbons
Specialty Needles
Sewing Machine Attachments

Classes in Everything
8 Instructors to Assist You

From A to Z -- It's all here!

Mon - Fri 9 - 5:30
Thur til 8 Sat 9 - 5

Burnt Hills, NY #54

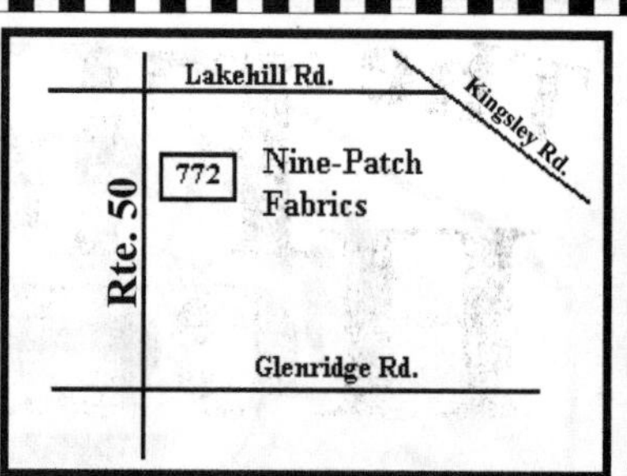

Nine-Patch Fabrics

Located on Route 50. 1/3 miles south of Lakehill Road in the Shopping Plaza on your left 5 miles North of Glenridge Road in Scotia.

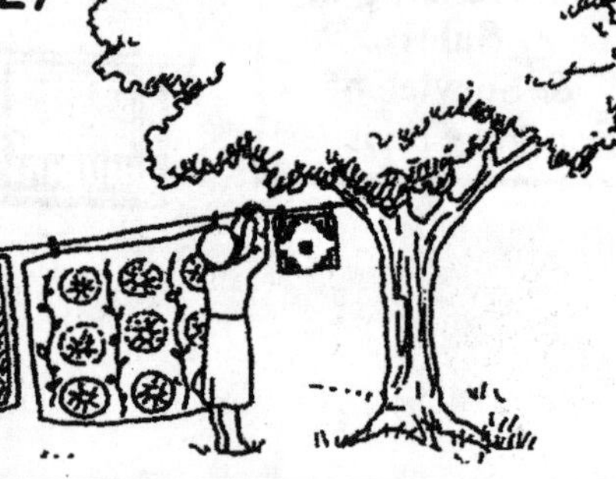

We specialize in Batiks and Flannels with a Large Selection of other Prints by Top Manufacturers.

Mon-Fri 10-6 Tues 10-8 Sat 10-4

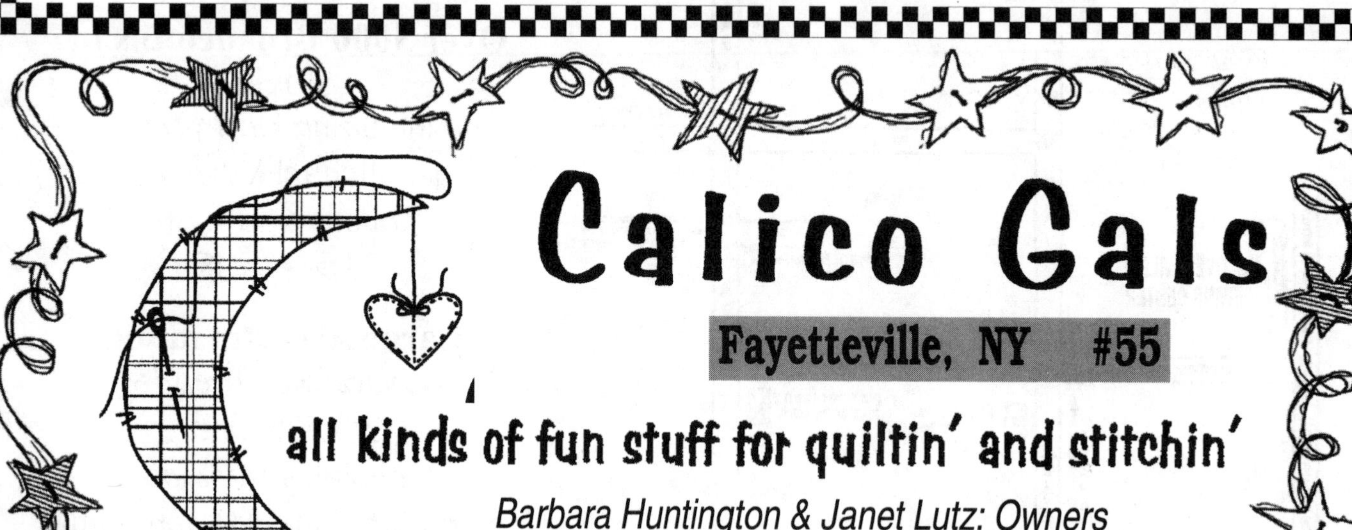

772 Route 50, Burnt Hills 12027
518-399-1999
www.ninepatchfabrics.com
Mary Hoover Est. 1999

Calico Gals

Fayetteville, NY #55

all kinds of fun stuff for quiltin' and stitchin'

Barbara Huntington & Janet Lutz: Owners

Located in the Canal Barn at 7070 Cedar Bay Road on the historic Erie Canal. Our barn is filled to the rafters with quality cottons, books, patterns, notions and wool felt, unique gifts and lots of inspiration. Authorized Elna dealer. Janet and Barb have recently doubled their space. There's loads of new stuff and even more fun quilters to hang out with.

The Barn Shops are Open: 10:00 - 5:00 Mon thru Sat
315-445-0617 www.calicogals.com

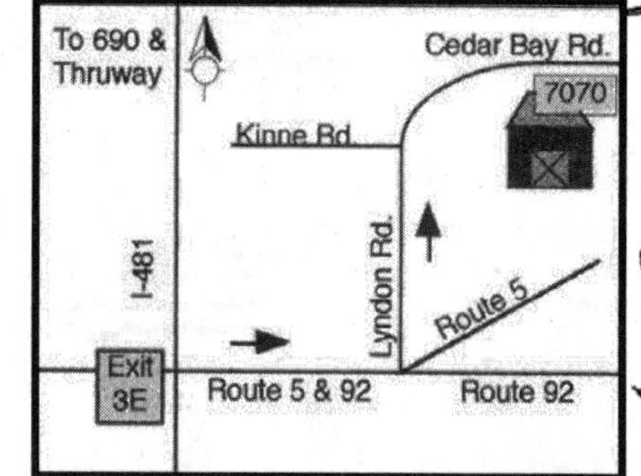

The Fieldstone House

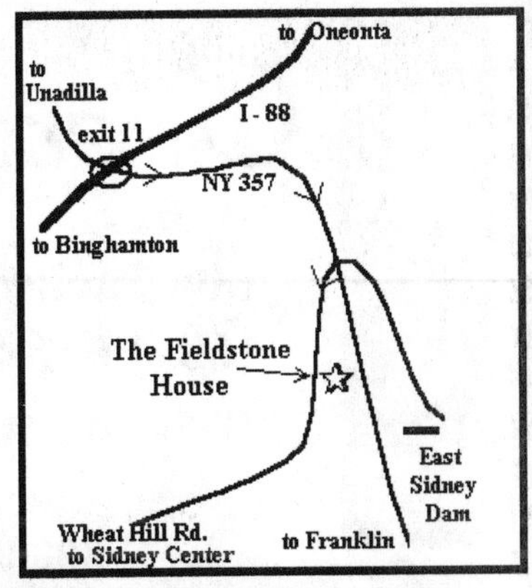

1884 Wheat Hill Rd. 13839
(607) 369-9177
Proprietors: Jane & Allan Kirby
fieldstonehouse@frontiernet.net
www.fieldstonehouse.com

Sidney Center, NY #56

Featuring a:
Fabric Shop
Country Tea Room
Gift Collection
Bed & Breakfast

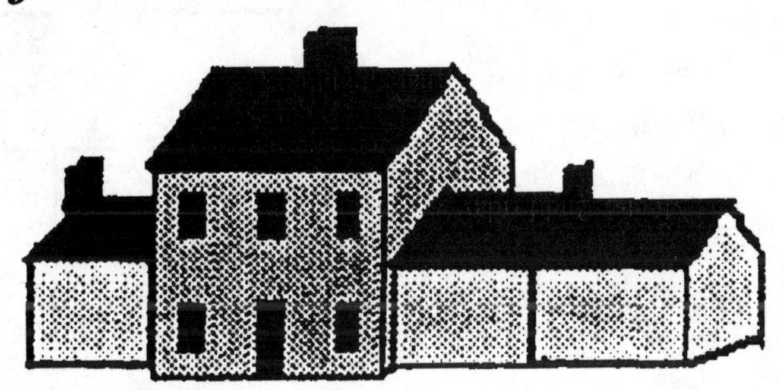

The Fabric Shop

Four rooms are filled to capacity with more than 14,000 bolts
This outstanding selection includes all of your favorite designs from . . .
Andover • Alexander Henry • Bali Fabrications • Clothworks • Debbie Mumm • Hoffman • Indo-Sales In the Beginning • Faffe Fassett • Kona Bay • Makower • Marcus Brothers • Michael Miller Moda • Northcott • P&B • Robert Kaufman • RJR • Timeless Treasures .... and more.
Books, Threads, Needles, Muslin, Battings, Templates, Buttons, Cutting Tools, Flannels, Clothing Patterns

"A quilter's dream come true"

The Gift Collection

Baskets ❖ Candles ❖ Pottery ❖ Stuffed Animals ❖ Wrought Iron ❖ Tinware

"Come Browse for that Special Gift"

Hours: 7 days a week 11 - 5
Closed Occasionally for Quilt Shows and Family Events
We recommend calling in advance.

The Country Tea Room

A delightful lunch is served daily; reservations recommended. Breakfast & dinner are also available by reservation only. Small group gatherings such as quilt guilds are a specialty.

The Bed and Breakfast

The Kirby Homestead, a fieldstone house in a quiet country hill side, is located on the same property approximately one-half mile from the shop. Three comfortable rooms are available, each with a double bed. A full breakfast is served to guests at the Country Tea Room. This is the perfect location for a quilting retreat!

"Relax & Enjoy with Friends & Family"

"Enjoy the Peace & Quiet of this Country Home"

Creative Threads

Mon - By Appt Only
Tues thru Fri - 10 AM to 5 PM
Sat - 10 AM to 4 PM
Sun - 1 PM to 4 PM

604 Jackson Hill Rd 13778
(607) 656-8883
web: www.creativethreads.net

brother At your side

3000+ bolts of fabric in this friendly, family run quilt shop.
We are an authorized dealer and service center for Brother and Elna.
A full service quilt shop with custom machine quilting available.

- Kits
- Notions
- Fabrics
- Machines
- Classes
- Battings
- Books
- Patterns

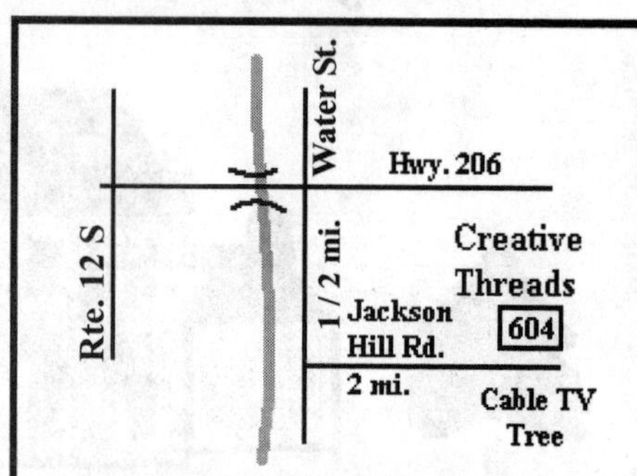

Greene, NY #57

Fly Creek, NY #58

3 miles North of Cooperstown, NY

Heartworks Quilts and Fabrics

Open Year Round
Mon - Sat
10 - 5

6237 St. Hwy. 28, P.O. Box 148 13337
Owners: Margaret & Jim Wolff
(607) 547-2501
hrtworks@telenet.net

Est: 1989

Original Design Block of the Month

A real country quilt shop with over **3000 bolts of Fine Cotton Fabrics** and Cotton Flannel Fabrics, Batting, Books, Stencils and a full line of notions. One-of-a-kind **full size quilts** (made here in NY,USA), quilt repair, custom design of quilts for interior decorators, and hand quilting of your quilt tops.

I - 90 | Mohawk | Exit 30
Rte. 20
Fly Creek
Rte. 28 | Cooperstown
I - 88
Oneonta

Albany 70 mi. E
Binghamton 85 mi. W
Utica 60 mi. NW
Oneonta 30 mi. S

Authorized dealer for
Elna Sewing Machines and
Baby Lock Sewing Machines

Between visits to our shop, please visit us on the world wide web at:
www.heartworksquilts.com
featuring our applique kits & is updated monthly

Afton, NY #59

Mon, Wed Thur, Fri 9 - 5
Tues 9 - 2
Sat 9 - 3

Sew Clever

195 Hwy. 41 S, P.O. Box 303 13730
(607) 639-2460 Fax: (607) 639-3436
c303@tds.net
Est: 1979 2000 sq.ft. 3000 Bolts

Husqvarna Viking Sewing Machines
Thousands of Bolts of Fine Cottons, Batiks, Homespuns; Books Galore, Many Notions.

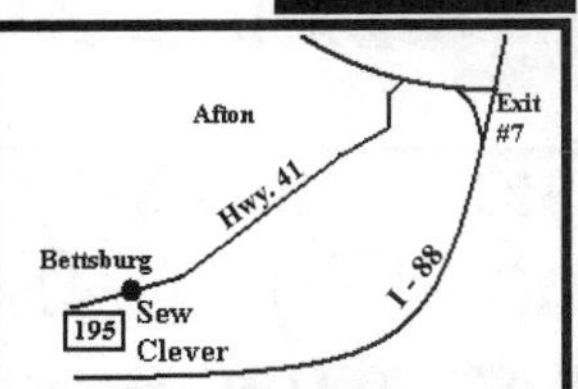

Oneonta, NY #60

Mon - Fri 8:30 - 5:30
Thur til 7
Sat 8:30 - 3:30

Country Fabrics

3200 Chestnut St., Suite 114 13820
(607) 432-9726
piecework@stny.rr.com
www.pieceworkcompany.com
Est: 1990 2000 sq. ft.
Over 2500 bolts of cotton fabrics plus notions, books, & patterns. Also fleece, knits, corduroy, rayon & denim.

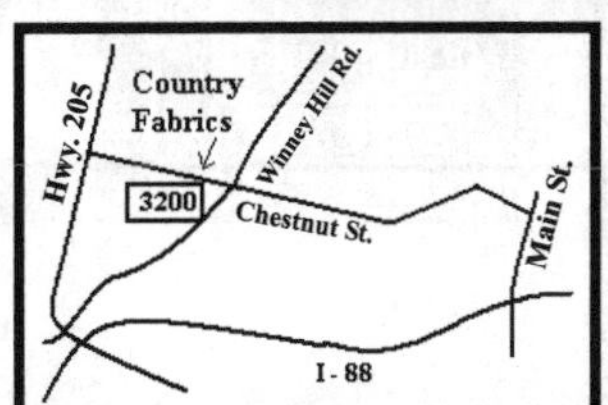

Cobleskill, NY #61

Mon - Sat 9 - 6
Thur til 8
Sun 11 - 5

The Yardstick

115 Plaza Ln., Suite 8 12043
(518) 234-2179 Est: 1975
yardstic@telenet.net
www.yardstickny.com
Owner: Merilyn Ludwig 2500 sq.ft.

Husqvarna Viking sewing machines sales & service. Over 2000 bolts of 100% cotton fabrics, books, notions, patterns, & classes. Friendly Knowledgeable Staff.

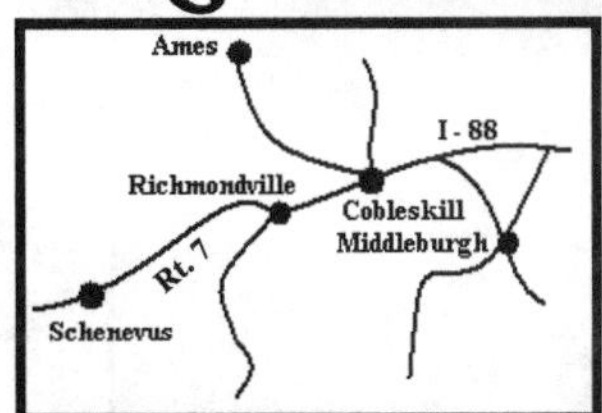

Flying Geese Fabrics

It's not just a Quilt shop . . .
It's an experience

Fine Quilting Fabrics
Designer Prints
The Newest Books, Patterns & Notions
Quilting Classes
Blocks of the Month

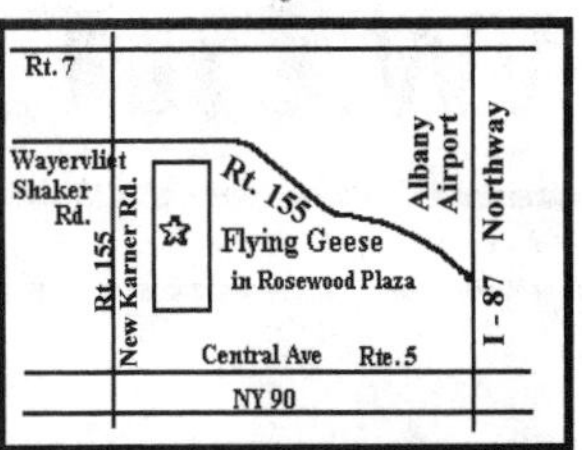

Just 3 miles West of I - 87—Exit 4, 155 West

Colonie, NY #62

Rosewood Plaza 501 New Karner Rd. 12205
(518) 456-8885 Est: 1996 2000 Bolts
flyinggeesequilts@yahoo.com
Owners: Donnie Brownsey, Tara Conlon & Joanne Skudder.

Mon - Sat 10 - 5 Wed & Thur 10 - 8
Sun 12 - 4 (Closed Sun July & Aug)

Ravena, NY #63

Log Cabin Fabrics

702 Starr Rd. 12143 (518) 767-9236
Owner: Londa VanDerzee Est: 1987

Visit a country quilt shop, 15 minutes south of Albany.
Over 2500 bolts, classes, books & patterns.

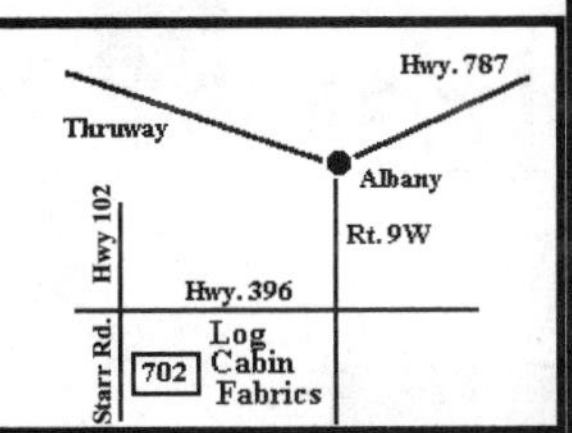

www.logcabinfabrics.net

Tue 10 - 9
Wed - Fri 10 - 5
Sat 10 - 4

Hudson, NY #64

Thur - Mon 10 - 5:30
Sun 12 - 5

FABRICations Quilt Shop

558 Warren St. 12534
(518) 822-0772

Over 3000 bolts of 100% cotton quilting fabric, featuring international & contemporary fabrics along with traditional. Books, notions, supplies & Classes.

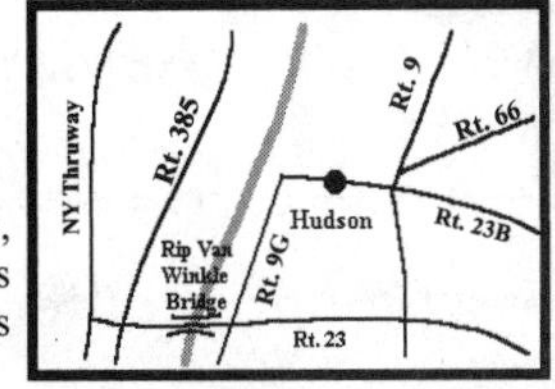

Red Hook, NY #65

Tues - Fri 10 - 5
Sat 10 - 4:30

The Village Fabric Shoppe

33 W. Market St. 12571
(845) 758-8541 Fax: (845) 758-4334
Web Site: www.villagefabricshoppe.com
Est: 1981

We specialize in fine, quilting fabrics - Hoffman, P&B, Thimbleberries & More - year round classes, supplies, books, patterns, gifts, kits - Friendly Service.

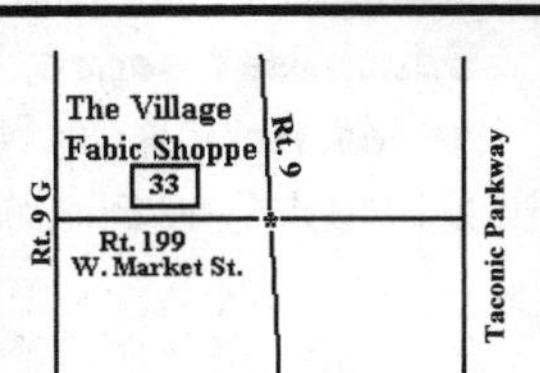

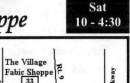

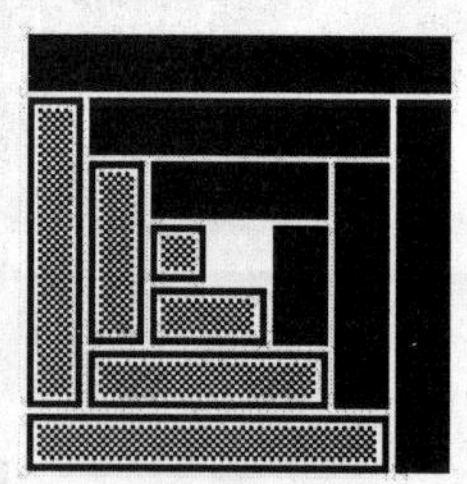

woodstock**quilt**supply

79 tinker street | woodstock, new york 12498
(845) 679-0733 | toll free (866) 679-0733
owners: bob silverman & jim helms

for all your quilting needs!

Woodstock, NY #66

store hours
mon-sat 10-6 | sun 11-5

web site 24/7
www.**quilt**stock.com

rock city road
NY 212 (tinker street)
NY 212 (mill hill road)
(8 miles)
exit 20 saugerties
woodstock quilt supply
NY 375
87 NY Thruway
NYS RT 28
to pine hill
(8 miles)
exit 19 kingston

The Country Quilter

Somers, NY #67

344 Route 100, Somers, NY 10589

Phone: (914) 277-4820
(888) 277-7780 toll free
Fax: (914) 277-8604
Email: qtc@countryquilter.com
Owner: Claire Oehler
Opened: 1990
1800 sq.ft.

Home of Country Quilter patterns and books -- Transportation series, Southwest series, Lighthouse series, Arts & Crafts, Kid's Quilts & Sew Simple Quilts

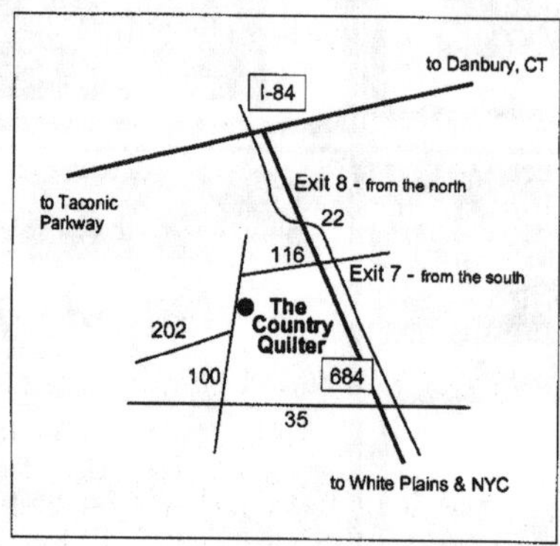

Quality Quilting Supplies

Over 2500 Bolts of 100% Cotton Fabrics
Over 900 Book Titles
Basic as well as Unusual Notions
100s of Patterns
Comprehensive Art Quilt Books & Supplies
100s of Quilt Stencils
Quilting Classes Year-Round
Gifts for Quilters and Quilt Lovers
Lots of Samples on Display
Fast Mail Order Service
Come in and meet our Friendly, Helpful Staff!

Visit us on the web at: www.countryquilter.com

Quilter's Attic

Est. 1994
Owners: Kathy and Wayne Joray

Route 302, Pine Bush, New York 12566
845-744-5888

Pine Bush, NY #68

New Customers: Bring in this ad for a FREE GIFT!!

Q.A is located in a wonderful old Victorian, packed full of samples to inspire you. Visit our shop for a delightful quilting experience.

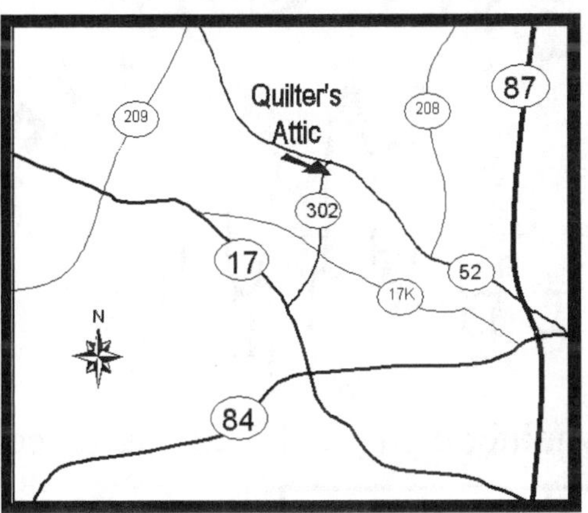

2000 Bolts of Fabric
PFAFF Sewing Machines
Koala Cabinet Dealer
Horn Cabinet Dealer
Large Selection of Books, Patterns, Notions
Dozens of Quilt Kits
Machine Embroidery Supplies
Huge Assortment of Threads
Wool & Stitchery Kits
Rug Hooking Kits
Year Round Classes
Retreats

Just minutes from Major Highways

From Route 17: Exit 119 (Route302N) to Pine Bush. 10 minutes on right.
From Route 84: Exit 8 (Route 52W) 15 miles to Pine Bush. Left on Rt. 302 - 1/10th mile on left.

Our friendly knowledgeable staff look forward to meeting you.
Bus tours welcome - please call ahead.

Shop Hours:
Tuesday - Saturday 10:00 - 4:00
Sunday 1:00 - 4:00
Closed holidays - call ahead

Visit us on-line at www.quiltersattic.com

Kingston, NY #69

Mon - Fri 10 - 7
Sat 10 - 6
Sun 12 - 5
Closed Sun
July & Aug.

Style Fabrics

Kingston Plaza, 222 Plaza Rd. 12401
(845) 338-1793 Fax: (845) 338-2659
Eileen.Style.Fab@juno.com
www.style-fabrics.com
Owner: Eileen Brophy
Est: 1995 3000 sq.ft. 2000 Bolts of Cottons
Quality quilting cottons - lots of novelty prints, batiks, Oriental prints and More! Plus: great dress fabrics! We're easy to get to!

Wappingers Falls, NY #70

Quilt Basket

Cambridge Commons #4
939 Route 376 12590
(845) 227-7606
Visit our Online Catalog:
www.quiltbasket.com
Owners: Cathy & Allan Anderson
Est: 1989 1800 sq.ft. 3000 Bolts

All Fabrics, & Books Discounted.

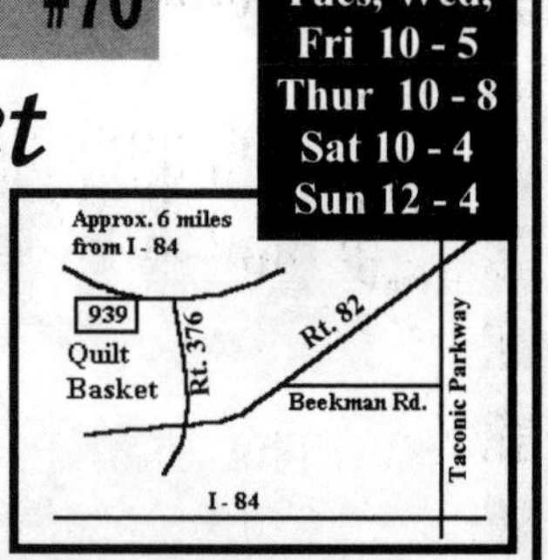

The Happy Quilter

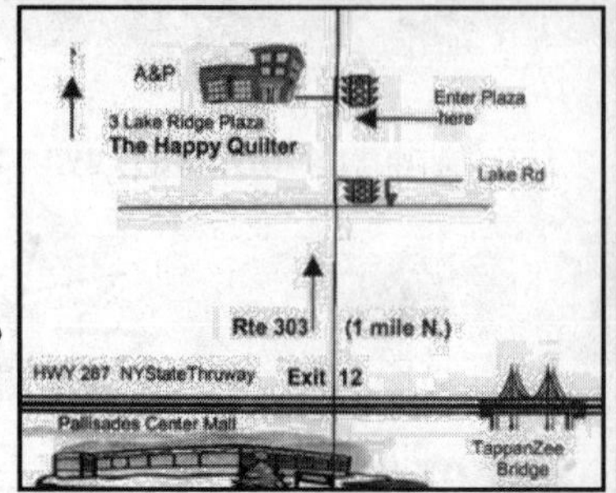

3 Lake Ridge Plaza - Route 303 10989
845-268-8744 Fax: 845-268-8753
www.Happyquilter.com
Est: 2003 1200 sq.ft. 1000+ Bolts

Tues - Sat
10 - 6
Thurs 10 - 8
Sun 11 - 4

Our quaint and cozy shop features the latest in premium quilting fabrics. We carry a large selection of books, notions, patterns, and gifts for the quilting connoisseur. Our class schedule is available 3-4 times a year. We are open six days a week and are only 35 minutes outside NYC. Come sit on our sofa, browse our selection and we will provide the cup of tea.

Valley Cottage, NY #71

New York, NY #72

Tues - Fri
11 - 7
Sat 10 - 6
Sun 11 - 5

133 West 25th St. 10001
(212) 807-0390
Fax: (212) 807-9451
Owner: Cathy Izzo

info@cityquilter.com www.cityquilter.com

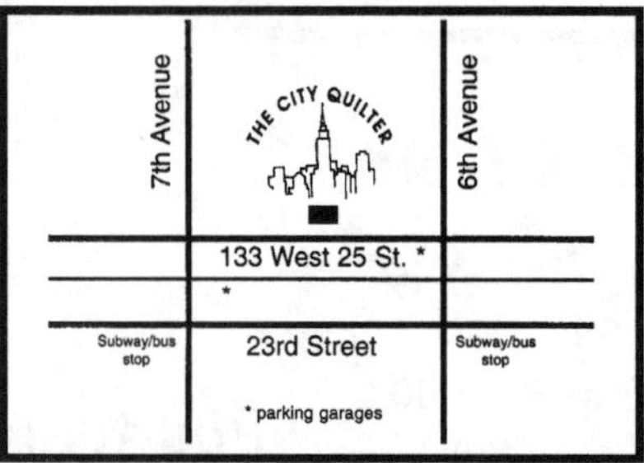

Outstanding selection of 100% Cotton Fabrics. Gifts, books, patterns, notions and classes.

Sayville, NY #73

PATCHWORKS Quilting GALLERY

Mon - Fri
10 - 6
Sat 10 - 5
Sun 12 - 4

A Complete Quilt Shop featuring Pfaff Sewing Machines, the latest 100% cotton fabrics, notions, books, patterns and classes.

www.patchworks.com

122 Main St. 11782
(800) 647-5596
Est: 1979 2000 sq.ft.
2000 Bolts
Owner: Carolyn Leyboldt

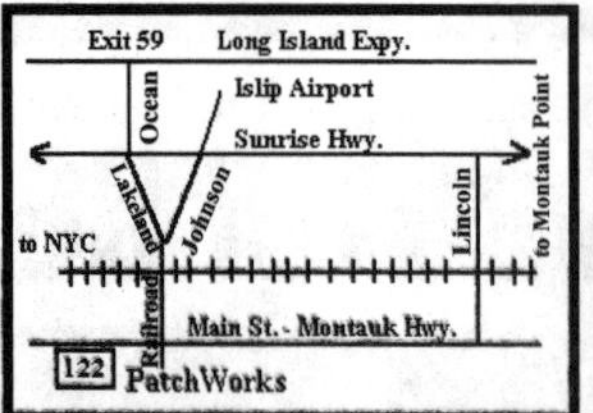

Brooklyn, NY #74

By Appt. Only

1025 E. 28th St. 11210
(718) 951-3973
Est: 1993
Owner:
Marcie Brenner

A Shoppe for Quilters! Large selection of 100% cotton Fabrics, Books, Patterns, Tools, Supplies, Battings, Gifts & Classes

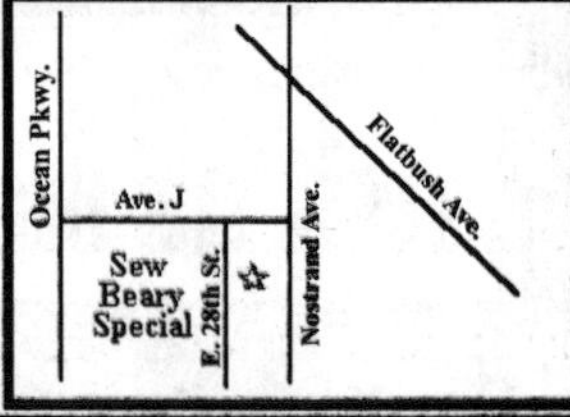

Sentimental Stitches

The latest in 100% Cotton Fabrics and Quilting Supplies.
Notions — Books
Classes
1800 sq.ft.

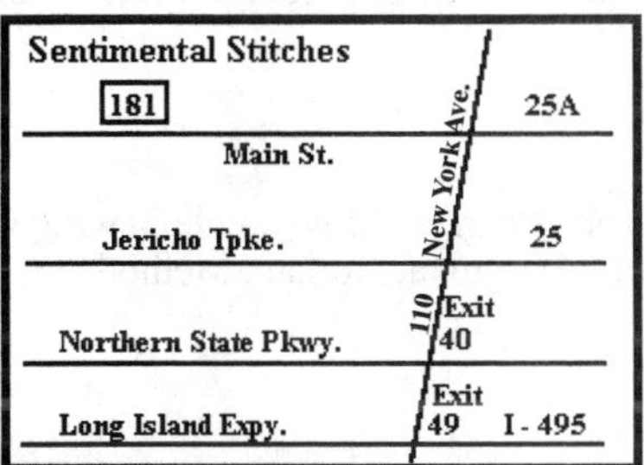

Mon - Sat 10 - 5
Sun 12 - 5

Cold Spring Harbor, NY #75

181 Main St. 11724 (631) 692-4145
Owner: Norma Gaeta Est: 1981

Riverhead, NY #76

Heirloom Country Collectibles

Mon - Sat 10 - 5
Sun 12 - 4
Closed Sun July & Aug

31 McDermott Ave. 11901
(631) 727-5909
hccrose@optonline.net
www.heirloomcountryquilting.com
Owners: Bobbie Lockman & Peggy Rose
Est: 1983 1600 Bolts

Fantastic assortment of 100% first quality cottons for quilting. Books, patterns, notions, quilt kits, color coordinated fabric packs, classes too.

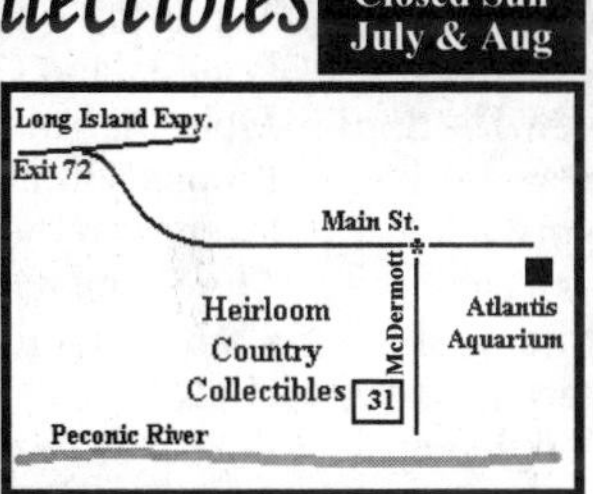

Other Shops in New York: *We suggest calling first*

Albany	The Sewing Store, 265 Osborne Rd.	518-482-9088
Altona	Maw & Paw's Fabrics, 4954 Military	518-236-5762
Baldwin	Sue's Fabric World, P.O. Box 383	914-855-0196
Brockport	Country Treasures, 27 Market St.	716-637-5148
Brooklyn	Sew Materialistic, 1310 Coney Island Ave.	718-338-6104
Cairo	Traditions, 185 Agnes Drive	518-622-3795
Clayton	Patchwork North, 425 James St.	
Croton-on-Hudson	Pinwheels, 416 Albany Post	914-271-1045
Dundee	The Fabric Shop, 8 Main St.	607-243-7052
East Aurora	Vidler's, 690 Main St.	716-652-0481
Elmira	Nancy's Bunny Hutch, 964B Pennsylvania	607-732-2480
Floral Park	Patchwork Patch, 32 Hemlock St.	516-326-0774
Ft. Edward	Cajon Creations, 147 Broadway	518-746-1647
Fulton	Herron's Fabric Center, 121 Cayuga	315-592-4031
Gilbertsville	Gilbert Block Shop, 9 Commerical	607-783-2872
Greenport	Calico Square, Inc., 1500 Brecknock	516-676-5577
Hamilton	The Pin Cushion, 37 Milford	315-824-5410
Hartsdale	Hartsdale Fabrics, 275 S. Central	914-428-7780
Hillsdale	K & K Quilted's, 2654 St. Rt. 23	518-325-4502
Huntington	Homespun Quilting, 18 Austin Ln.	631-757-3029
Hurleyville	Chris-Sans Nubian Quilt House, Meyerhoff Rd.	914-434-6667
Ilion	CD's Quilt Emp., 51 Central Plaza	315-894-6482
Ithaca	Homespun Boutique, 314 E. State St.	607-277-0954
Lake Placid	Dell's Gifts, 125 Main St	518-523-0155
Loudonville	Quilt Essentials, 2 Lacy Lane	518-489-2229
Manhasset	Watermelon Patch, 500 Plandome	516-365-6166
Maryland	Smitty's Stitchery, 208 Lake Shore N	607-433-5292
Monsey	Patchwork Sampler, 7 Fieldcrest St.	914-357-1011
Mt. Kisco	Pins and Needles, 161 Main St.	914-666-0824
New York	Quilts Plus, 86 Forsyth	212-334-0123
New York	B&J Fabrics, 263 W. 40th St.	212-354-8150
New York	Laura Fisher Antique Quilts, 1050 2nd. Ave.	212-838-2596
Norwood	Quiltin' Bee, 1140 River Rd.	315-353-4687
Penfield	Teddy's Threads, 11 Colonial Dr.	716-381-4987
Penn Yan	Edgewood Country Store, 1427 Voak	315-536-7562
Plainview	Melani's Moods Ltd., 14 Manetto Hill Mall	516-935-4644
Port Chester	Nimble Thimble, 509 N. Main St.	914-934-2934
Port Jefferson	Stitchin Time, Inc., 326 Main St.	516-928-4544
Roslyn	Arbor House, 22 Arbor Lane	516-538-0009
Sag Harbor	Do Your Own Thing, Main St	516-725-0858
Salt Point	Cotton Yard Quilt Shop, 2410 Rte 44 #A	845-677-3770
Seneca Falls	Country Quilting Shoppe, 3600 Rt. 89	
South Dayton	Block in the Square, 30 Maple St.	716-988-3013
Southold	Old Country Charm, Inc, Main Rd @ Beckwith Ave	516-765-3940
Sugar Loaf	Quilted Corner, 1 Romers Alley	845-469-7119
WatertownJudy	Quick Quilting, 27081 Cty Rt 160	315-788-7349
Watertown	Country Quilter28225 Bonney Rd	315-788-9457
Webster	Pam's Sewing Shop, 182 North Ave,	716-872-2080

New York Guilds:

Albany Q.U.I.L.T., 79 Edgecomb St., 12209
Amherst Amherst Museum Quilt Guild, 3755 Tonawanda Creek Rd.14228 Meets: 3rd Thursday 7 p.m. at Amherst Museum
Athens Athens Schoolhouse Quilters
Baldwinsville Candlelight Quilter's
Batavia Museum Quilt Guild, 131 W. Main St., 14020
Brewerton Tea Time Quilters
Brooklyn The Quilter's Guild of Brooklyn Meets: 3rd Saturday 11 a.m. at Holy Name Church, Windsor Ter.
Candor New Quilters on the Block Meets: 1st & 3rd Saturday 9:30am at Candor Emergency Building
Cazenovia Quilting By the Lake
Centerport Huntington Quilters, Little Neck Rd. Meets: 1st Tuesday at Centerport Methodish Church
Chazy Champlain Valley Quilter's Guild
Cicero Plank Road Quilters Guild, P.O. Box 1579, 13039
Clarence Clarence Log Cabin Quilters, 4895 Kraus Road, 14031
Clarence Creative Sewing Club, 14031
Clay Plankroad Quilt Guild
Clay Twilight Stitchers
Delmar Q.U.I.L.T., 12054 Meets: 2nd Friday 9:45 a.m. at United Methodist Church
Dresden Lake to Lake Quilt Guild
East Aurora Southtown Piecemakers Quilting , PO Box 340, 14052 Meets: 2nd Tuesday @ 7pm at St. Matthias Church
East Aurora Morningstar Quilt Guild, 14052 Meets: 2nd Wednesday @ 10am at St. Matthias Church
Eden Eden Quilt Guild, Church St., 14057 Meets: 3rd Monday (alternate months) 7 p.m. at United Methoidst Church of Eden
Fairport Perinton Quilt Guild
Fayetteville Towpath Quilt Guild, P.O. Box 188, 13066
Fulton Lake Country Quilt Guild
Glens Falls Wings Falls Quilter's Guild, Bay & Washington Sts.
Gloversville Sew Busy Quilt Guild, 385 S. Main St., 12078 Meets: 3rd Monday @ 7 p.m. at Gloversville Sewing Center
Gorham Lake to Lake Quilt Guild, Box 67, 14461 Meets: 1st Wednesday (Sept - June) 9:30 a.m. at Gorham Methodist Church
Grand Central Station Empire Quilters, P.O. Box 6175, 10163
Grand Island River Lea Quilters Guild
Hamilton Americana Village Quilters, P.O. Box 292, 13346
Holland Patent Mohawk Valley Quilt Guild
Holley Country Neighbors Quilt Guild, 51 State St., 14470 Meets: 2nd Wednesday @ 7pm at Apple Country Quilt Shop
Hudson Columbia County Quilt Guild, 558 Warren St., 12534 Meets: 2nd Tuesday 7 p.m. at Fabrications Quilt Shop
Ithaca Tompkins County QuiltersWomen's Community Bldg., Senecca St., 14850
Kingston Wiltwyck Quilter's Guild, P.O. Box 3731, 12401
Lisbon Borderline Quilters, 525 Murphy Rd., 13658 Meets: 1st Wednesday @ 1pm & 7pm at Canton Library
Lockport Kenan Quilters Guild, 433 Locust Street, 14094
Manlius Towpath Quilt Guild
Marcellus Tumbstall Quilt Guild
Mineola Long Island Quilters' Society Inc. P.O. Box 1660 11501
New Hartford Mohawk Valley Quilt Club, Inc, P.O. Box 595, 13413 Meets: 4th Mondays @ 7pm at New Hartford 1st United Methodist
New York Empire Guild, P.O. Box 20673, 10025 Meets: 2nd Saturday at Fashion Institute of Technology
Norwich Chenango Piecemakers Quilt Guild, P.O. Box 583, 13815
Oswega The Scriba Quilter's
Pine Bush Country Quilters Guild, 12566 Meets: 2nd Wednesday 7 p.m. at Pine Bush Schools
Porter Corners Hudson River Piecemakers
Poughkeepsie First Dutchess Quilters' Guild, P.O. Box 3182, 12603
Meets: 3rd Wednesday 7:30 p.m. at Arlington High School South Campus, Stringham Rd, LaGrangeville
Richville North Country Quilt Guild Meets: 4th Tuesday 7 p.m. at Black River Elementary School (Sept. - May)
Richville Borderline Quilter's Meets: 1st Wednesday 1 p.m. and 7 p.m. at Canton Public Library
Rochester Genesee Valley Quilt Club, 14618
Rochester Irondequoit Quilt Club
Rushville Lake to Lake Quilt Guild, 4594 Harvey Road, 14544
Saranac Lake Cabin Fever Quilters
Schenectady Q.U.I.L.T.S., 1068 Maryland Avenue, 12308
Sherrill Thread Bears Quilters' Guild, 13461 Meets: 1st Tuesday @ 7pm at St. Helena's Catholic Church
Skaneateles Thumbstall Quilt Guild, PO Box 320, 13152 Meets: 3rd Tuesday @ 7:30pm at United Methodist Church of Marcellus
Smithtown Smithtown Stitchers, P.O. Box 311, 11787
Somers Northern Star Quilters Guild, P.O. Box 232, 10589
Southampton East Long Island Quilters Guild
Union Springs Cayuga Lake Quilt Guild, 5 Park St., 13021 Meets: 2nd Wednesday at 7 p.m. at A. J. Smith Elementary School
Waverly Quilter's Consortium of New York State, P.O. Box 769, 14892
Waverly Endless Mountain Quilt Guild
Webster Webster Quilt Guild, 169 E Main Meets: 3rd Friday 10am at Methodist Church
Westfield Westfield Quilt Guild, S. Portage St., 14787
Meets: 4th Monday 7 p.m. at Westfield YMCA, biannual Quilt Show, Sept. 18-19th 1998
Whitesboro Mohawk Valley Quilt Club, 31 Capardo Drive, 13492

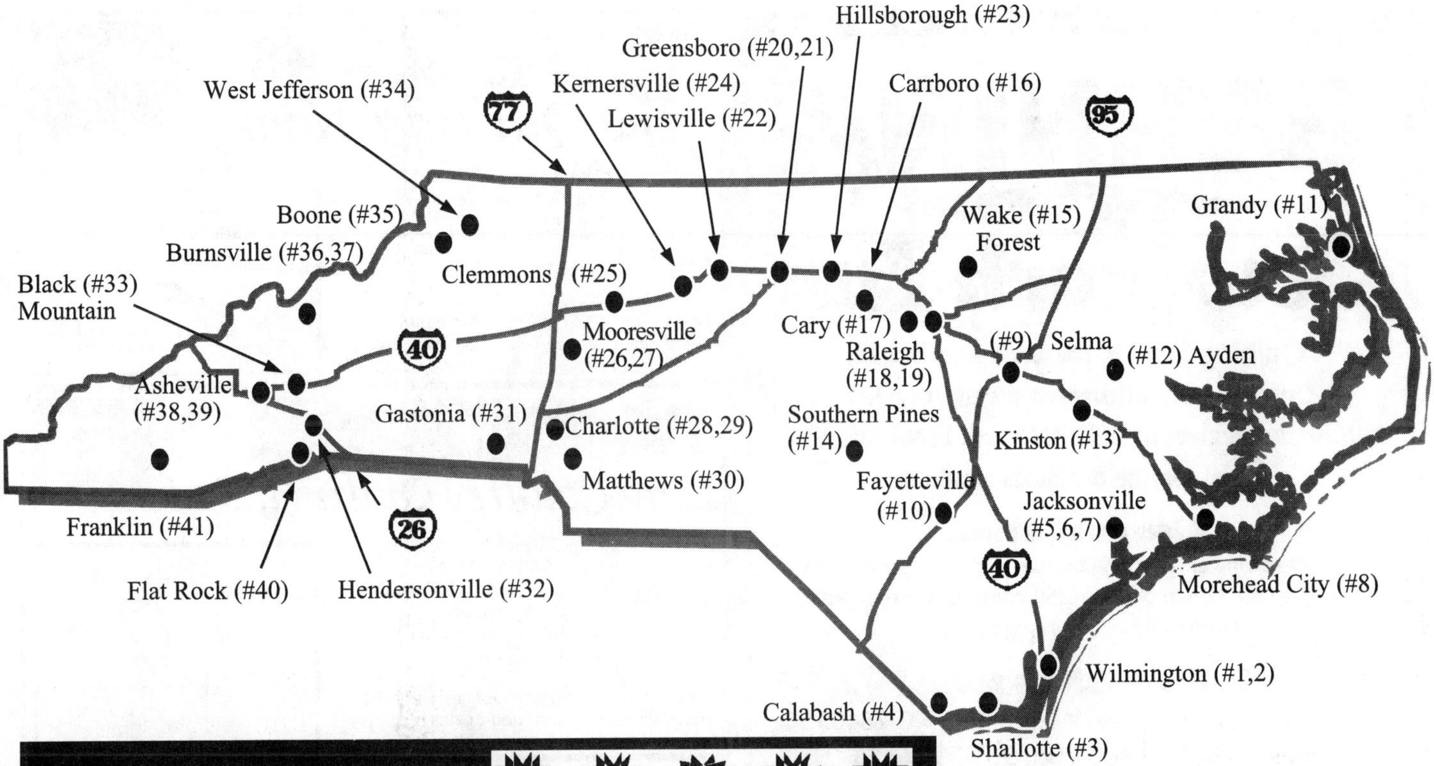

Hillsborough (#23)
Greensboro (#20,21)
West Jefferson (#34)
Kernersville (#24)
Carrboro (#16)
77
Lewisville (#22)
95
Boone (#35)
Grandy (#11)
Wake (#15) Forest
Burnsville (#36,37)
Clemmons (#25)
Black (#33) Mountain
Cary (#17)
40
Mooresville (#26,27)
Raleigh (#18,19)
(#9) Selma
(#12) Ayden
Asheville (#38,39)
Gastonia (#31)
Southern Pines (#14)
Charlotte (#28,29)
Kinston (#13)
Matthews (#30)
Fayetteville (#10)
Jacksonville (#5,6,7)
Franklin (#41)
26
40
Morehead City (#8)
Flat Rock (#40)
Hendersonville (#32)
Wilmington (#1,2)
Calabash (#4)
Shallotte (#3)

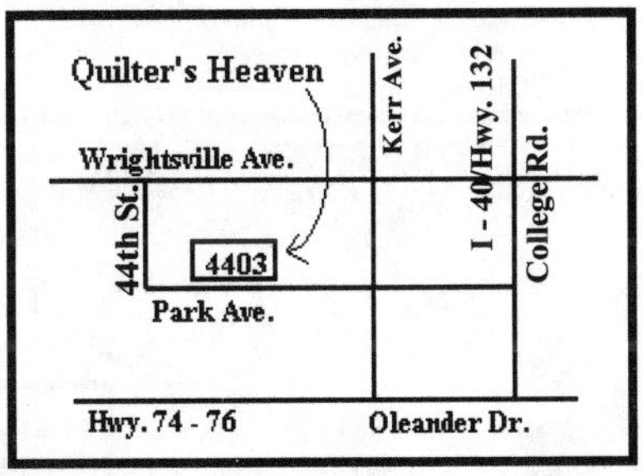

NORTH CAROLINA

41 Featured Shops

BERNINA®

is

Sew-Much-Fun

Quilting fabrics, patterns and books.
Current collections from quilt market.
Authorized dealers of BERNINA and ELNA machines.
Sales, service & classes available.

Also available...

Mettler sewing and quilting threads • Fat Quarter Friendly
OESD embroidery products • 350 colors of Isacord thread
Horn of America sewing cabinets

#2

Call or visit us today!

5221 Oleander Drive, Wilmington, NC 28403
phone: 910-791-6868 • fax: 910-791-6878
tollfree: 877-791-6868 • www.sew-much-fun.com

Hours:
Monday – Friday
10am till 6pm
Saturday
10am till 4pm

Owners:
Dana Stirling
Deborah Scheu

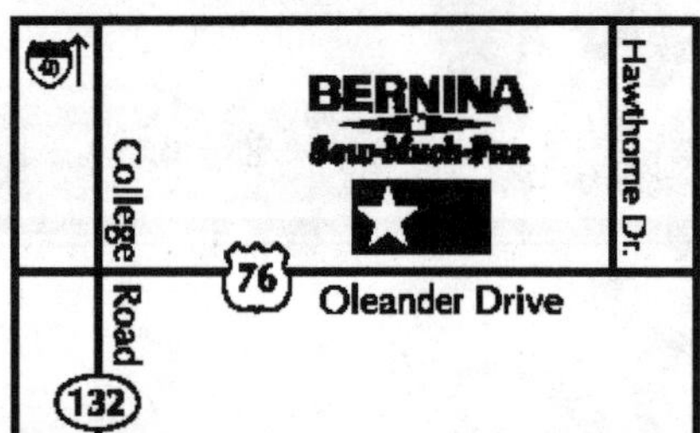

Shallotte, NC #3

Tues - Fri 10 -5
Sat 10 - 4

The Quilting Nook

150 Holden Beach Rd. Unit 3
Eastgate Plaza 28470
(910) 754-3845
thequiltingnook@msn.com
Est: 2003 1000 sq.ft.

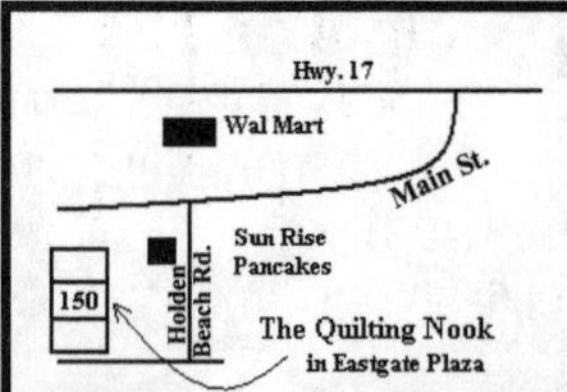

Large selection of books, patterns, notions, & top quality cotton fabrics to choose from Along with a friendly Southern atmosphere.

Calabash, NC #4

Mon - Sat 10 - 4

Low Country Quilting, Ltd

10138-2 Beach Dr. SW
P.O. Box 4036 28467
(910) 575-6632 Fax: (910) 575-6635
sewsquirly@aol.com
Cheryl Mills, owner, quilter
Est: 2001 500 bolts

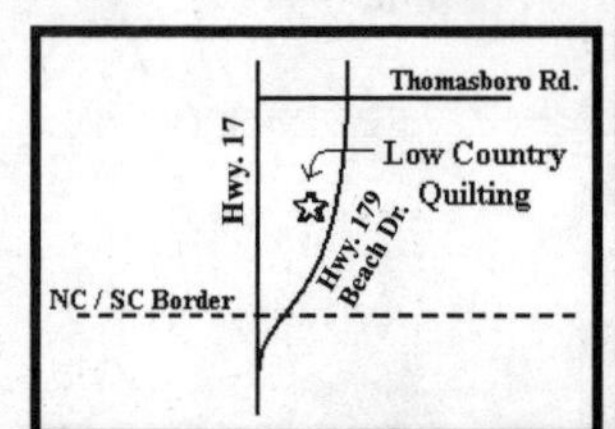

Charming quilt store with folkart flair offering fine fabrics, books, notions, patterns, classes and long-arm quilting.

Jacksonville, NC #5

Tues - Fri 10 - 4
Sat 10 - 2

The Country Collection

2864 Wilmington Hwy (Hwy 17 S) 28540
(910) 347-1960 Fax: Same
countrycollection@ec.rr.com
Owner: Frances Cauley
Est: 1994 1800+ sq. ft. 2000+ Bolts

100% cotton designer fabrics. Books, patterns, notions & classes. Jinny Beyer & Thimbleberries Quilt kits. Pfantastic Pfaff sewing machines. Friendly professional guidance. Mail order.

Jacksonville, NC #6

Tues - Fri 10 - 5
Sat 10 - 4

The Cotton Patch Quilt Shoppe

112 Phillips Rd. (Hwy. 17) 28540
(910) 938-1395
Fax: (910) 938-7543
Owner: Sharon C. Turner
Est: 1993
2750 sq.ft. 6000 Bolts

Large selection Fabrics, Books & Patterns, Kits, Notions, Classes.
"A Really Great Quilt Store."

Jacksonville, NC #7

Mon - Fri 10 - 5
Thur til 7
Sat 10 - 4

All About Quilting

118 Henderson Dr. 28540
(910) 577-9200 Fax: (910) 577-9300
Kirsta@wna-linknet.com
Owners: Jane Burger & Kirsta Meadows
Est: 2003

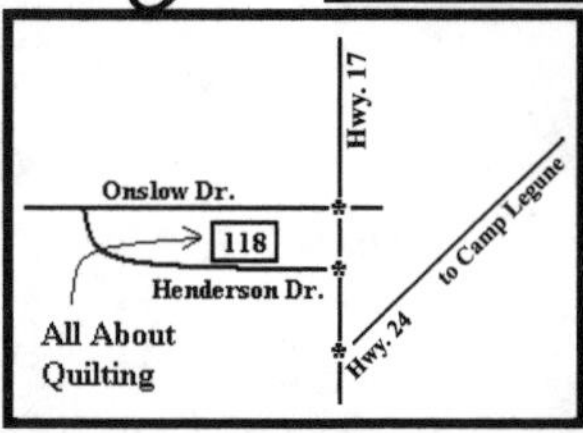

Fabric, Books, Classes with certified teachers, Gift Items and friendly service. Authorized Elna Sewing Machine Dealership. Sales & Service. Financing Available.

Morehead City, NC #8

Tues - Sat 9:30 - 5

Sew It Seams

905 Arendell St. 28557
(252) 247-2114

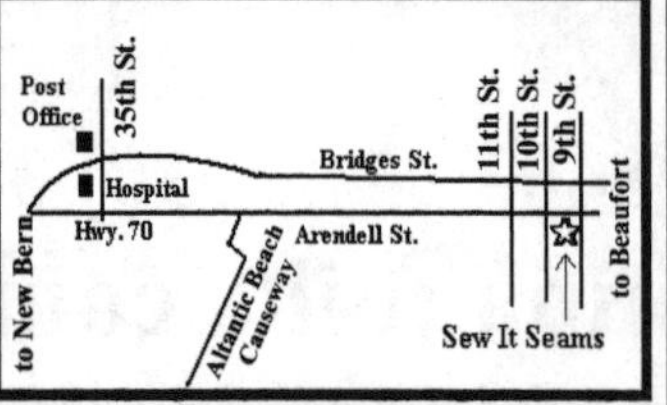

Personal Service and Southern Hospitality. Great Selection of 100% cotton fabrics, books, patterns, notions and classes.

WHISTLE STOP

Quilt Shop

Selma, NC #9

104 E. Anderson Street,
Selma, NC 27576
919/975-0404

Connie Walker, Owner Est: 2001
1100 sq.ft. 2400+ Bolts
www.whistlestopquiltshop.com

A destination for quilters & friends.

Bolts & Bolts of Fabric

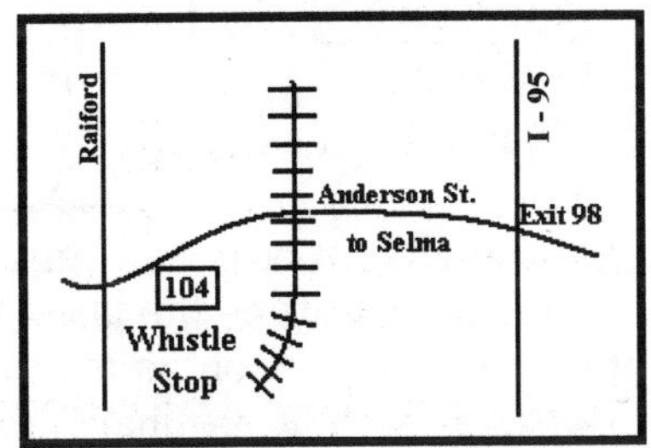

Mon - Sat 10:00 - 4:30 Closed Wed
1st Sunday of each Month 1 - 4

Conveniently located less than 1 mile off I - 95, exit 98.

Over 2400 bolts of 100% designer cottons, books, patterns, notions & more including batiks, homespuns, novelties, 30s & Civil War reproductions. Kits are our specialty!
Plan a trip to the Whistle Stop and discover Uptown Selma, home to over 20 shops and more than 100 antique dealers -- all within walking distance!

Est: 1996
9000 sq.ft.

Fayetteville, NC #10

Loving Stitches

New Location!!
7076 Ramsey St. 28311
North of Kelly Springfield tires
Very Convenient to I-95
(910) 630-3912
quilts4u@loving stitches.net

www.lovingstitches.net

From I-95 take exit 61 through the town of Wade.
Stay on River Rd. until you see sign for Ramsey St./Hwy. 401.
Turn onto new Freeway until it ends on Ramsey St. and turn right. We're 2 miles north on Ramsey on the right.

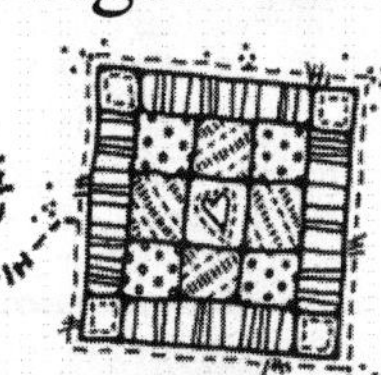

Mon - Sat
10 - 6

- Everything you could want for all your sewing & quilting needs
- Over 4000 bolts of current 100% cotton fabrics
- Repairs on all brands of sewing machines
- Authorized BERNINA dealer
- Specially made Quilt kits & Blocks of the Month
- Enjoyable sewing & quilting classes for all ages
- Quilting services available
- Busses Welcome! Call ahead and we'll wait for you.

Nothing Sews Like A Bernina. Nothing.
BERNINA®

Grandy, NC #11

Quilt Shoppe

Cindy Holland
Est: 2001

Mon - Sat
10 - 5

6599 Caratoke Hwy.
Grandy, NC 27939
252-453-8944
Fax:
252-232-3415
jandcholland
@yahoo.com

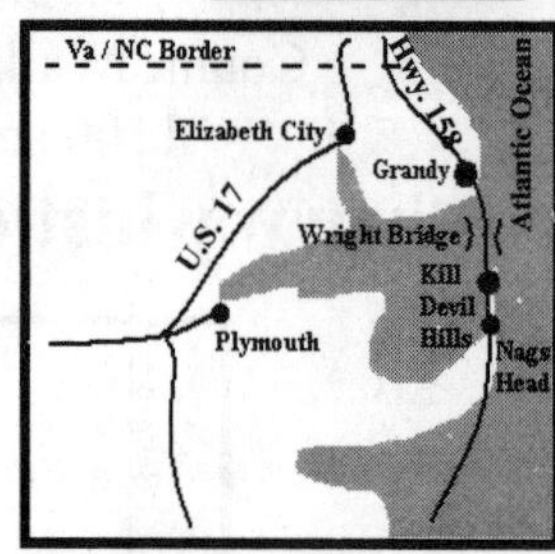

Specializing in brights, batiks, nautical and tropical. Featuring the latest in books and patterns. Stop by on your way to the Outer Banks of North Carolina, 12 miles north of the Wright Memorial Bridge.

Ayden, NC #12

Mon - Fri
11 - 6
Sat 10 - 3

4159 Emma Cannon Rd. 28513
(252) 746-7900
Owner: Wanda Conklin Est: 1997

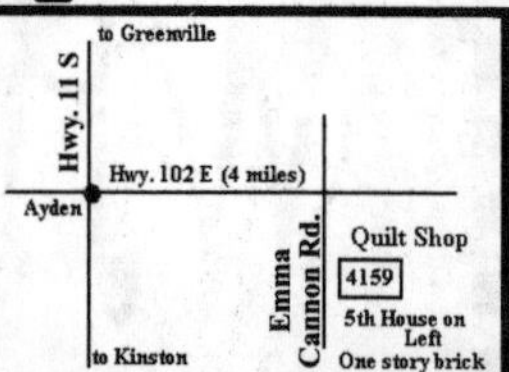

Machine Quilting, reasonable rate and fast service. Quilts old & new, 100% cotton fabric & notions, frames and hoops plus much more.

Kinston, NC #13

The Country Collection

Tues - Fri
10 - 4
Sat 10 - 2

1685 Highway 258 North 28504
(252) 522-3521 Fax: (252) 522-3521
countrycollection@ec.rr.com
Owner: Frances Cauley
Est: 1999 1500 sq. ft. 1500+ Bolts

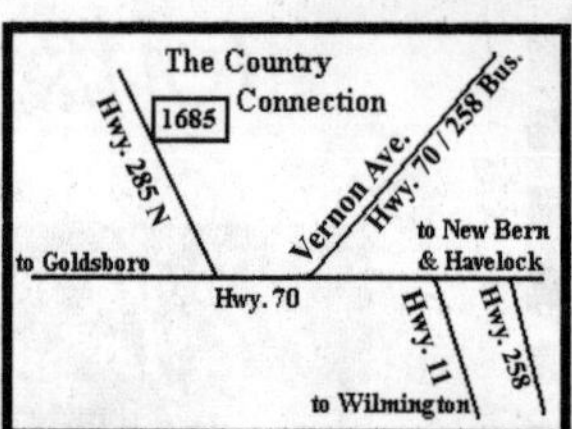

100% cotton designer fabrics. Books, patterns, notions & classes. Jinny Beyer & Thimbleberries Quilt kits. Pfantastic Pfaff sewing machines. Friendly professional guidance. Mail order.

Southern Pines, NC #14

Eastern Star Quilting Co.

Mon - Fri
10 - 5
Sat 10 - 3

129 E. Pennsylvania Ave. 28387
(910) 692-9709 Fax: (910) 692-9156
info@easternstarquilting.com
www.easternstarquilting.com
Owner: Mae H. Williamson
Est: 2004 1600 Sq.ft. 1000 Bolts

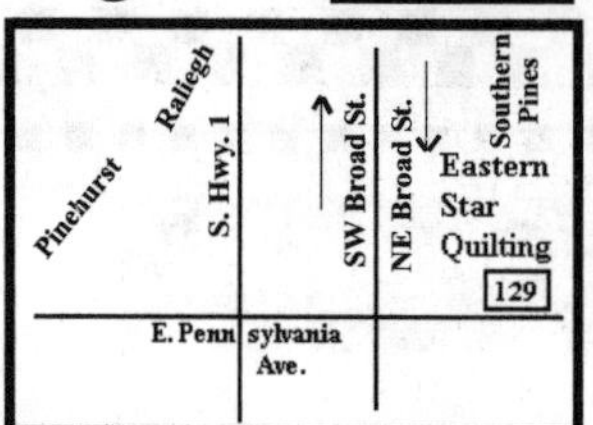

Best Selection of Fabrics, over 1000 bolts complete line of notions, books, classes specializing in Asian prints.

Wake Forest, NC #15

Quilts Like Crazy

Mon - Sat
10 - 5

1241 S. Main St. 27587
(919) 562-3425
nancy@quiltslikecrazy.com
www.quiltslikecrazy.com
Owner: Nancy Pease

We have a large selection of fabrics, books, patterns and notions. You'll be inspired by our many quilts and samples!

Carrboro, NC #16

Thimble Pleasures

Mon - Fri
10 - 6
Sat 10 - 5
Sun 1 - 4

205 W. Main St. 27510
(919) 968-6050
thimblepleasures@mindspring.com
www.thimblepleasures.com
Owner: Julie Holbrook
Est: 1993 2000 sq.ft.

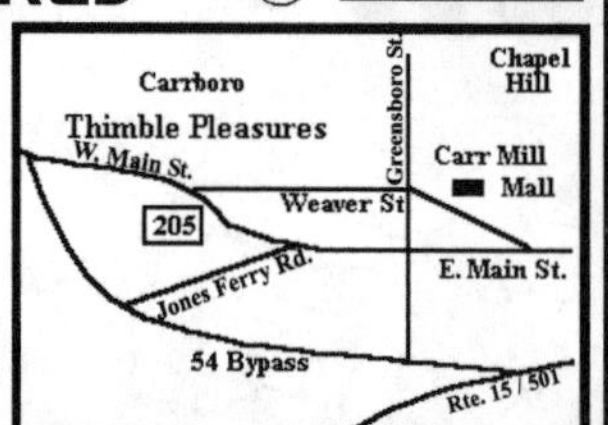

Over 5000 Bolts of 100% Cotton Designer Fabrics. Books, Patterns, Notions. Wide variety of classes. Quarterly Newsletter.

Cary, NC #17

Etc. Crafts

Mon - Fri
10 - 6
Sat 10 - 5

226 E. Chatham St. 27511
(919) 467-7636
Owner: Jean Petersen

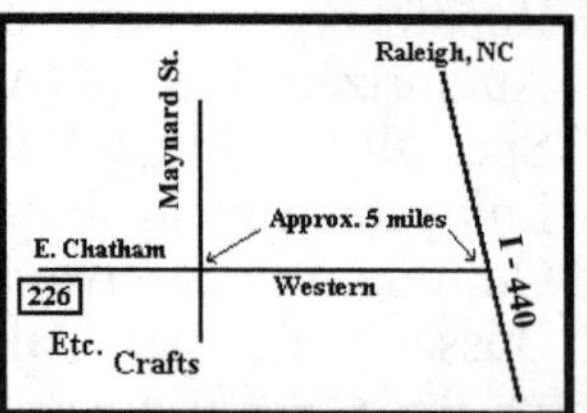

Large selection of 100% Cotton Quilting Fabrics. Books and Notions.

Raleigh, NC #18

Bernina World of Sewing

3500 bolts of 100% cotton fabric. Authorized Bernina Dealer. Wide variety of specialty patterns, threads, notions and sewing accessories. Large selection of sewing cabinets and work tables.

"Come Visit Us and be a part of the excitement"

Mon - Sat 10 - 5
Thur til 7

6013 Glenwood Ave. 27612
(919) 782-2945
Visit Us on the internet:
www.bernina
worldofsewing.com

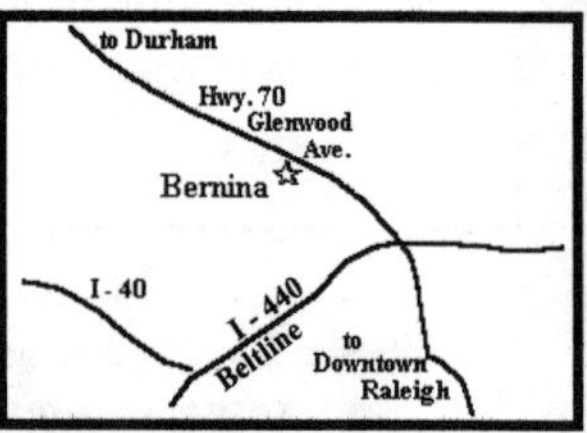

Located 1- 1/4 miles West of Crabtree Valley Mall on Hwy. 70 in Oak Park Shopping Center.

Archangel Fabrics

1612 N. Market Dr. 27609
(919) 790-7792
Fax: (919) 790-1834
E-Mail: archangelfabrics@mindspring.com
Owner: Sandy McKenzie
Est: 1995 2500 sq.ft.
Web Site: www.archangelfabrics.com

Tues - Sat 10 - 5 Thur til 10 - 7

Over 4000 bolts 100% designer cottons, classes, supplies, gifts, notions, books & patterns.
Machine quilting service available.

20 Randy's Quilt Shop

2417-C Lawndale Drive, Greensboro, N.C. 27408

Over 8500 bolts of fabric

Thousands of Batiks

Notions, Books & Patterns

Classes from Beginner To Advanced

Professional, Knowledgeable Staff Years of Experience in all aspects of Quiltmaking

Authorized Bernina, Elna, & Babylock Dealer

Store Hours
Mon—Sat
10-6
Sun– 1-6

Tel– 336-545-5558
Fax- 336-545-5805
randysquiltshop@triad.rr.com

www.randysquiltshop.com

Owner: Randy Silvers

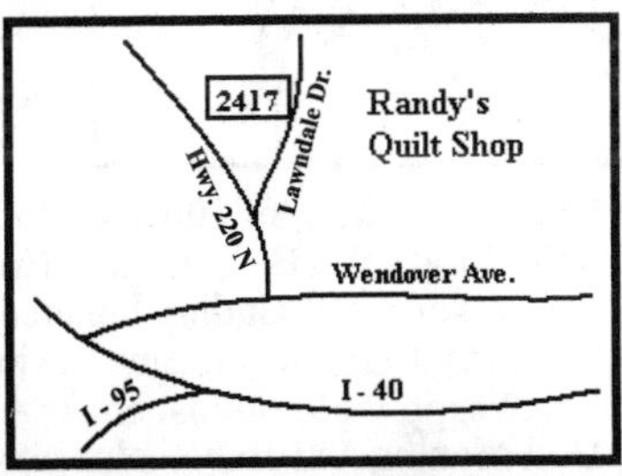

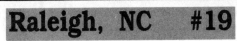

New Quilt Shop!

Sewingly Yours

- Quilt Threads
- Batting
- Quality Fabrics
- Great Prices

We specialize in quality quilt fabrics, notions, & classes. Expert repairs and tune ups are also available. We offer friendly service and share our love of sewing & quilting.

Mon-Thur 10-8
Fri-Sat 10-5

Quilting & Sewing notions
Embroidery threads and notions
Stabilizers & Design CDs
Books, Patterns
Needles

Greensboro, NC #21

4604 W. Market St. #122
336-834-0230

Located behind Bert's Seafood Restaurant on West Market St.

Lewisville, NC #22

1329 Lewisvile-Clemmons
336-766-8271

Located on the corner of Hwy. 421 and Lewisville-Clemmons Rd.

"Sharing the Joys of Sewing"

Hillsborough, NC #23

THE QUILT MILL

345 Ja-Max Drive 27278
(919) 644-2200
Email: thequiltmill@earthlink.net
Web Site: www.thequiltmill.net
Owner: Kathi Perry
Est. 2002 2000 sq. ft. 1200+ bolts
Located just one block off Historic Hillsborough's main street behind KFC ! (1/3 mile from I-85)

Mon - Sat
10 - 6
Last Sun
1 - 5

100% Cotton Fabrics
Notions * Books
Patterns * Classes
Authorized
Bernina Sewing Machines
Parts & Service

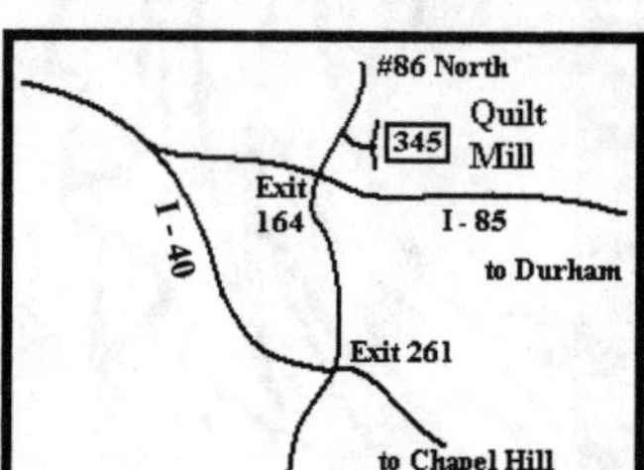

Kernersville, NC #24

Hi! Sew-Ciety
YOUR COMPLETE SEWING CENTER
&
QUILTING PEACE BY PIECE

Visit us at our 3000 sq.ft. shop, with loads of fabrics, patterns, books, templates, supplies and best of all a knowledgeable and friendly staff.

Plaza 66 South
Shopping Center
(Between the two I-40's)
806-R NC Hwy 66 South
Kernersville, NC 27284
336-993-1500
or 336-993-7770

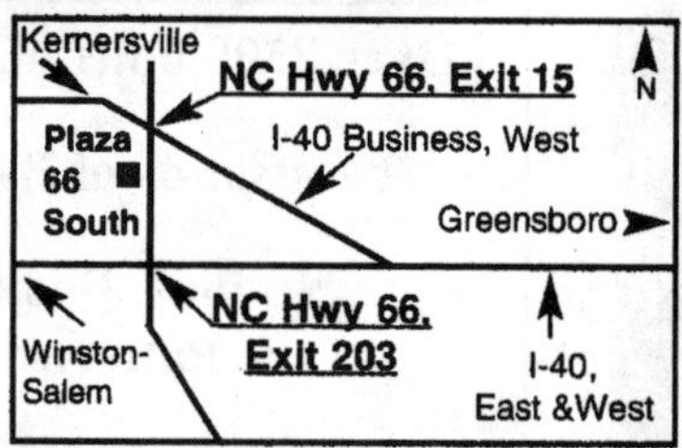

Clemmons, NC #25

The Quilting Corner

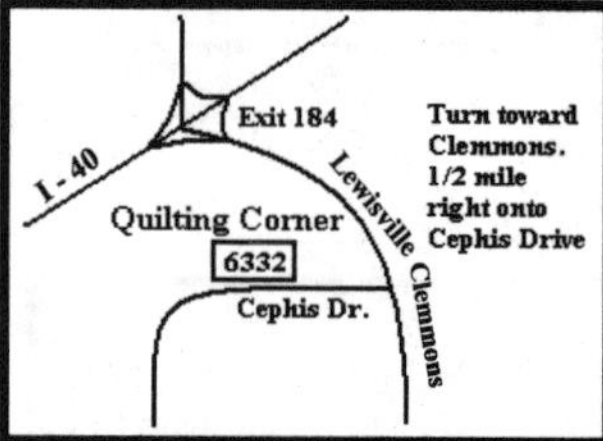

6332 Cephis Dr. 27012
(336) 766-6208
Quiltcorner@aol.com
Est: 1980
8000 sq.ft. 5000+ Bolts
Mon - Fri 10 - 5:30
Sat 10 - 3

- Over 5,000 Bolts of 100% Cotton Quilting Fabrics
- RJR, Moda, P&B, Benartex, Hoffman and many more of your favorites, including hundred's of beautiful Batiks
- We carry Bernina and Elna sewing machines and sergers
- Large supply of notions, books and patterns
- Doll Making and embellishment supplies
- Friendly, knowledgeable staff to assist you

Mooresville, NC #26

Rene's Quilt Shop

Mon - Fri
10 - 5:30
Sat 9:30 - 3:30

195 W. Statesville Ave. 28115
(704) 799-2829
Owner: René Crowder
Est: 2001 1600 sq.ft. 1000 Bolts

Fabrics, Books, Patterns, Notions, Classes.
Helpful, friendly staff.
Hand and machine quilting services.

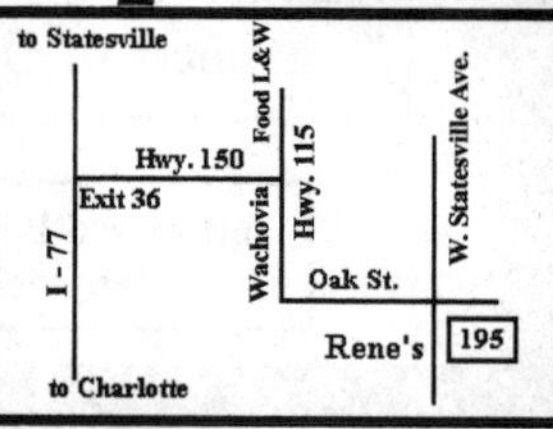

Mooresville, NC #27

Tues - Sat 10 - 5

Quilters Loft Company

188 N. Main St. Suite B 28117
(704) 662-8660
Owner: Erica Ransom

Fabrics, patterns, books, notions, classes. Corner of N Main & W Moore Sts. Entrance on Moore-upstairs.

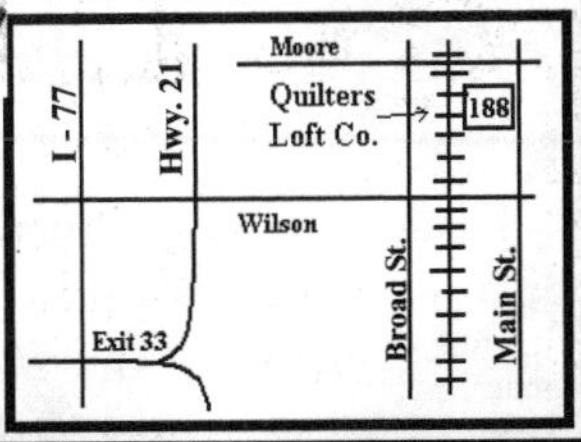

Moore
Quilters Loft Co.
188
I - 77
Hwy. 21
Wilson
Exit 33
Broad St.
Main St.

Charlotte, NC #28

Mon - Fri 10 - 5:30
Sat 10 - 4

The Sewing Bird

4247-B Park Rd 28209
(704) 676-0076 Fax: (704) 676-0179
sewinbird@aol.com
www.sewingbird.com
Owner: Anne Schout
Est: 1990 2500 sq. ft. 1200+ Bolts

Great selection of fabrics from around the world not your average quilting cottons. Notions, patterns, books, friendly service. We just added knitting yarns too!

JANOME

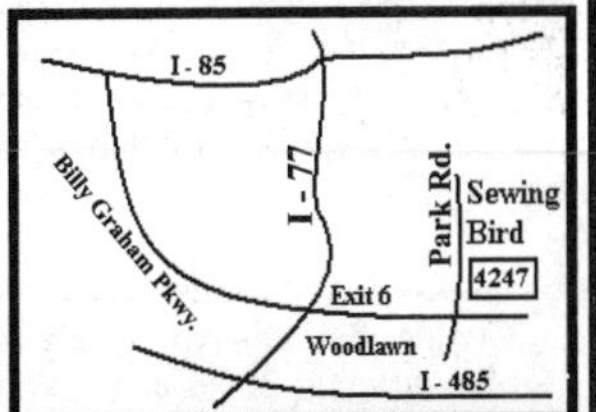

Charlotte, NC #29

Mon - Sat 10 - 4:30

Quilter's Gallery

310 Meacham St. 28203
(704) 376-2531
Owner: Patti Cline & Cindy Page
Est: 1981 2500 sq.ft. 2000+ Bolts

Cotton Fabrics--Traditional and unusual prints, Batiks, and homespuns. Wide range of books and patterns. German Mohair for Teddy Bears Lots of classes.

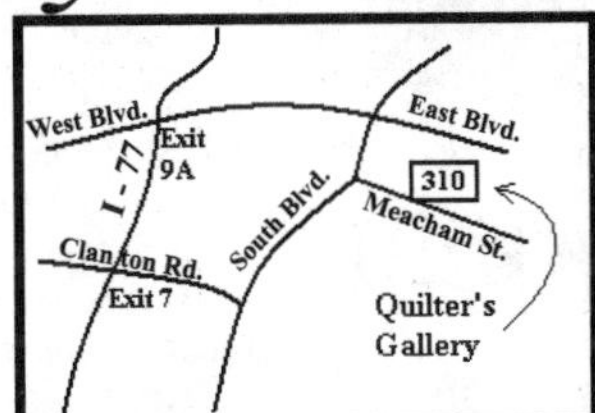

Matthews, NC #30

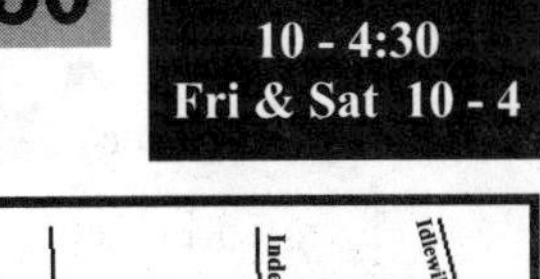

Mon - Thur 10 - 4:30
Fri & Sat 10 - 4

QUILT PATCH FABRICS

1017 Stallings Rd. 28104 (704) 821-7554
www.quiltpatchfabrics.com
Owners: Charlotte Harkey, Bryan Gregory, Janice Cooper Est: 1996
Full color range of 100% cotton fabrics (3000+ bolts), books & patterns, notions, hand & machine technique classes, machine quilting service available.

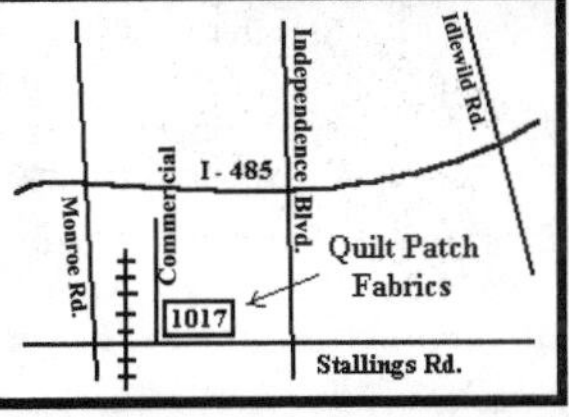

Gastonia, NC #31

(800) 627-9567

Mary Jo's Cloth Store

Mon - Sat 9 - 5:45
Mon & Thur til 8:45

"The Place" for investment sewers.
Where variety is the greatest. Prices are the lowest and large quantities can be found.

401 Cox Rd.
Gaston Mall
Gastonia, NC 28054
Owner: Mary Jo Cloninger

Est: 1951
32,000 sq.ft.

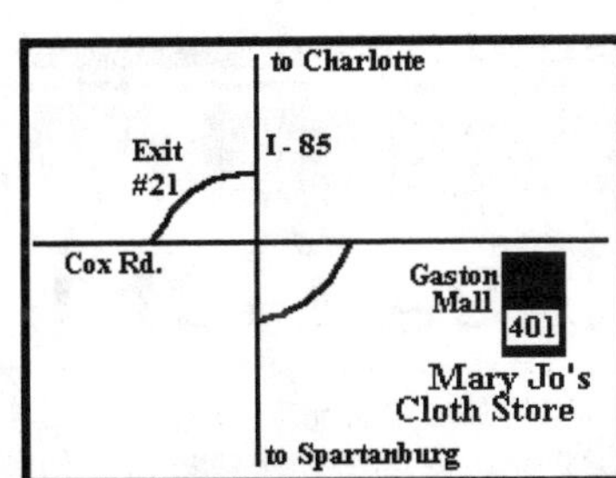

visit our website: www.maryjos.com

Hendersonville, NC #32

Mon - Sat 10 - 5 Tues & Thur Til 7

Material Things Quilt Shop

2021 Asheville Hwy. 28791
(828) 698-5556 Fax: (828) 698-5513
mthings@bellsouth.net
www.materialthingsquiltshop.com
Owners: Andi & Cindy Edwards
Est: 2001 2000 sq.ft.
Over 3,000 bolts of Fabric, featuring Civil War & 30's reproductions. 1,000 different Books and Patterns.

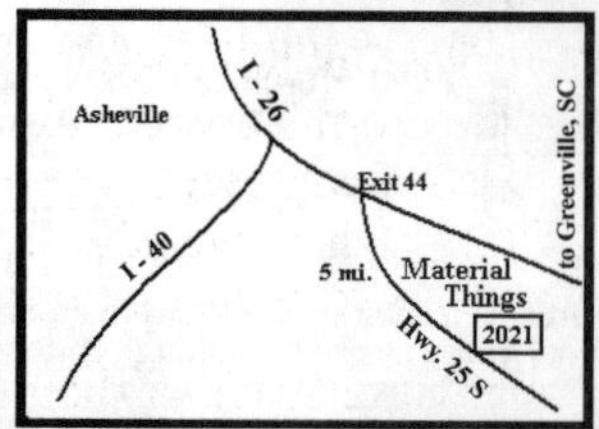

Black Mountain, NC #33

Mon - Fri 10 - 5 Sat 11 - 4

Marti's Patchwork Cottage

206 Sutton Ave. 28711
(828) 669-9005
www.martispatchworkcottage.com
Owner: Marti Cummins
Est: 1996 950 sq.ft. 1200 Bolts

Best little quilt shop anywhere dedicated to helping you make a wonderful, unique masterpiece.

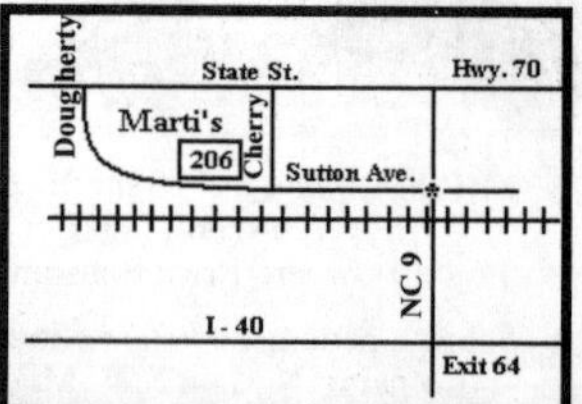

West Jefferson, NC #34

Mon - Sat 10 - 5

The Quilt Gathering

103 S. Jefferson Ave. 28694
(336) 246-5655 Est: 1999
quilt-gathering@fastransit.net
Owner: Gail Brandt 2000 sq.ft.

Designer Fabrics, Jinny Beyer, Thimbleberries, Princess Mirah: just a few of our fabulous fabrics. Notions, buttons, and patterns too!

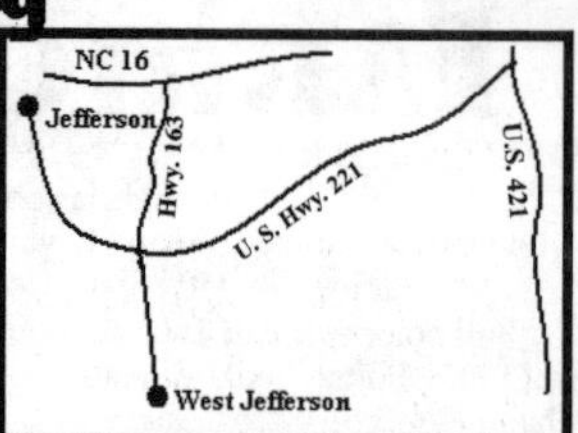

Boone, NC #35

Mon - Sat 10 - 5:30 Thur til 8

The Quilt Shop inc.

199 New Market Center 28607
(828) 263-8691 Fax: (828) 263-8718
thequiltshop@earthlink.net
Est: 2003 1400 sq.ft.

The friendliest quilt shop in the High Country. We carry a great selection of designer fabrics, notions, books, and patterns. Long arm quilting services available.

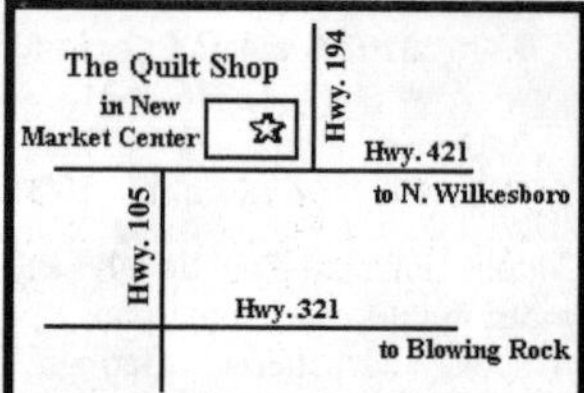

needle • me • this

2000 square feet of Fabrics with a Flair
Not your everyday Cottons • Notions • Books • Patterns Classes • Friendly Service.
Authorized Dealer for Janome Memory Craft 10,001, light weight Jem Gold and all models in between.

Mon - Fri 9:30 - 5:00 Sat 9:30 - 3:00

Look for the Blue Building with the Yellow Awnings.

Burnsville, NC #36

112 W. Main St. 28714
(828) 682-9462
Fax: (828) 682-9462
Owner: Carol McCroskey
Est: 1987
2000 sq.ft. 2000 Bolts

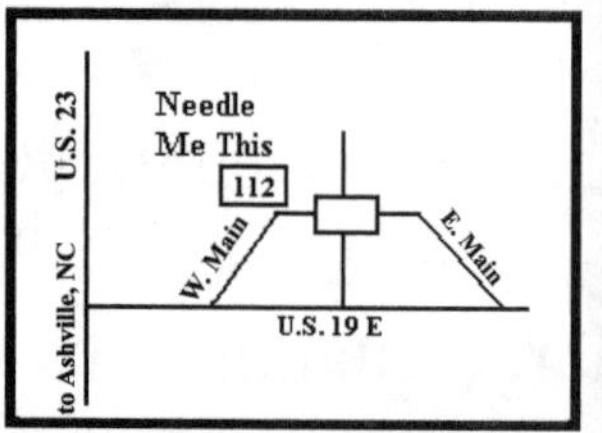

Burnsville, NC #37

Mon - Fri 9 - 5 Sat 9 - 3

The Country Peddler

3 Town Square 28714
(828) 682-7810
Owners: Barbara & Tommy Pittman
Est: 1980

Great selection of quilts, fabrics, & notions. Custom quilts made to order. Quilted and fabric gifts.

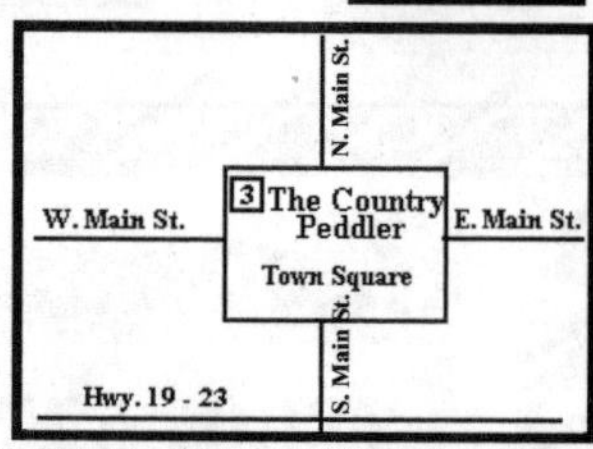

Asheville, NC #38

Mon - Sat 10 - 5

Piece Gardens

51 College St. 28801
(828) 254-3116 Fax: (828) 254-3088
piecegardens@hotmail.com
www.piecegardens.com
Owner: Amy Moore Est: 2003

Colorful quilt shop in a downtown walking district. Batiks, Asians, Cotton Lamē, elegant florals, sweet children's motifs, bold whimsical prints.

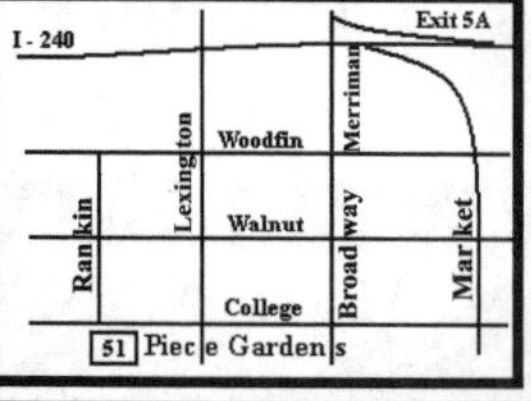

Asheville, NC #39

Mon - Sat 10 - 5:30

Asheville Cotton Co.

River Ridge Marketplace ~ 800 Fairview Rd. C-2 ~ 28805
828-299-8888 ~ ashevillecottonco.com ~ Exit 8 off I-240

Come see our large selection of beautiful quilting fabric, patterns, notions & books. We love machine embroidery, too!

We're conveniently located near I-40, I-240 and I-26. From I-40, take Exit 53B, then the first Exit (8) off I-240. At the end of the ramp, go straight across into our shopping center. We're to the right.

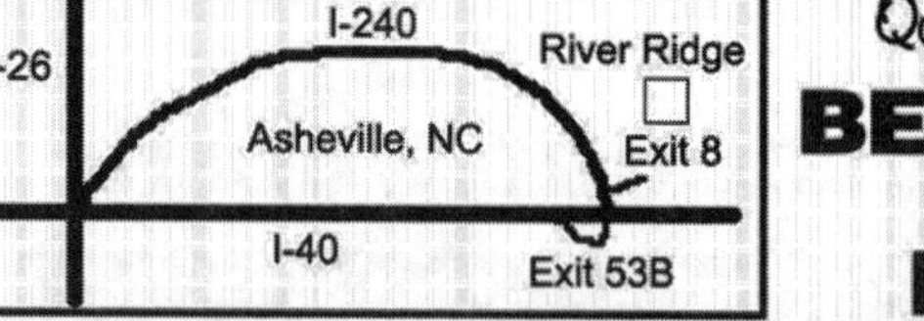

3200 sq. ft. with 4500+ bolts of Quilting Cotton!

BERNINA PFAFF baby lock

My Quilt Shoppe

One Stop Quilt Shoppe

Est: 2001
Bldg. #1 2000 sq.ft.
Bldg. #2 1200 sq.ft.

Flat Rock, NC #40

2689 Greenville Hwy.,
P.O. Box 1340 28731
(828) 692-8870 Fax: (828) 692-2821
Lanna@MyQuiltShoppe.com
www.MyQuiltShoppe.com

My Quilt Shoppe is the cutest little quilt shoppe in Western North Carolina. It is nestled in historic Flat Rock adjacent to the Flat Rock Playhouse. This is a shoppe where we have husband rockers and husband magazines to keep the quilter's spouses relaxed as they shoppe.

You will discover a shoppe full of fine fabrics such as Northcott, Moda, Kona Bay, Benartex and many other featured designer fabrics. You will be greeted by experienced quilters that will be happy to assist you with your quilting dreams.

And while you are here be sure to stop by Georgia Bonesteel's Quilt Corner where you can enjoy a lavish encounter with the tools and toys of the quilters' trade. Georgia Bonesteel is the host of the PBS series "Lap Quilting". All of her books are featured at the shoppe. Perhaps you'll visit on a day when Georgia is in and meet her in person.

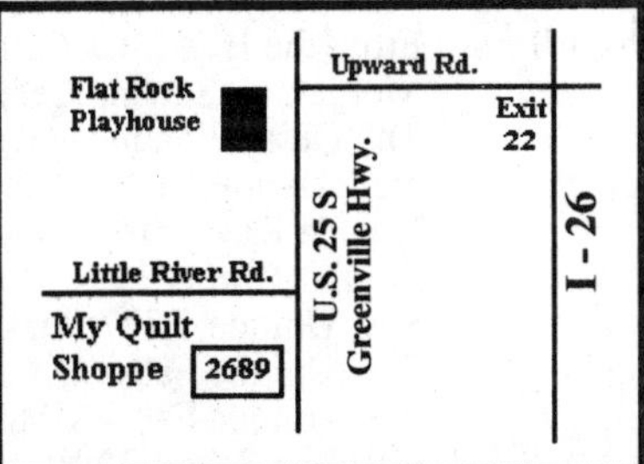

Mon - Sat
10 - 5

Directions: From !-26 take Exit 22 onto upward Road. If you're coming from the east turn left, from the west turn right. Stay on Upward Road until you dead end on 25 South. Turn left. Stay on 25S. We are on your right, adjacent to the Flat Rock Playhouse. We are in the same building as the Flat Rock Post Office.

On The Way to Ann's Needle & Hook Depot

"The Fun Place To Be"

- Quilting Fabrics -- Homespuns, Wool, Cottons, Batiks,
- Moda, P&B, Hoffman, Clothworks, Flannels

Husqvarna VIKING
Sewing Machine/Serger

- Notions
- Rug Hooking
- Patterns & Books
- Wearable Arts / Classes
- Lots of Sample Models

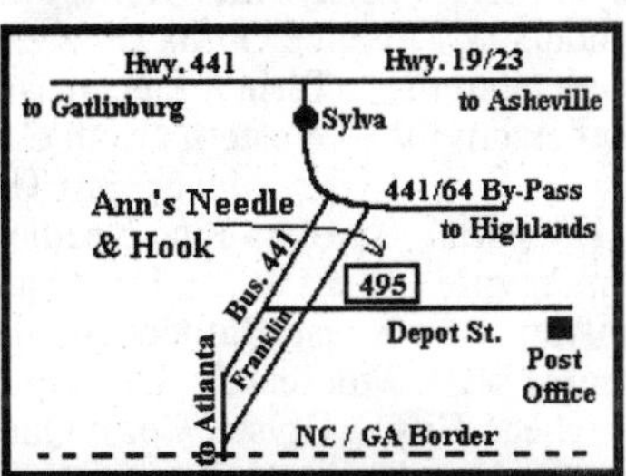

Mon - Fri 9 - 5
Sat 10 - 5

- **Unique Gifts**
  Lamps, Folk Art, Jewelry, Primitives, Candles

Owner: Ann Warren
Est: 1997

Franklin, NC #41

495 Depot St. • Franklin, NC • 28734 • (828) 524-9626

Other Shops in North Carolina: *We suggest calling first*

Asheville	Street Fair, 42 Battery Park Ave.	704-253-0836
Asheville	Waechter's Silk Shop, 94 Charlotte St.	828-252-2131
Burlington	Sewing & Oreck Center, 3127A Garden Rd.	336-584-7708
Burlington	Threaded Needle Quilt Shop, 554 Huffman Mill Rd	336-585-0170
Chapel Hill	Cotton Boll Creative Sewing Center, 91 S. Elliott Rd.	919-942-9661
Cornelius	Crafty Needle, 20722 N Main St	704-896-1688
Elizabeth City	Quilts & More, 1092 Commissary Rd.	252-338-9500
Fayetteville	Crafts, Frames & Things, Inc., 108 Owen Dr.	910-485-4833
Fayetteville	The Sewing Center, 1916 Skibo Rd. #315	910-864-3101
Fletcher	Carolina Fabric Outlet, 6024 Hendersonville Rd.	704-684-0801
Franklin	La Poma & La Poma, P.O. Box 777	828-524-5114
Franklin	Sew Creative, 91 Highlands Rd.	
Franklin	Maco Crafts, 2846 Georgia Rd.	828-524-7878
Goldston	Calico Quilt Antiques, Belview Ave.	919-898-4998
Greensboro	Log Cabin Craftshop, 5435 N. Church St.	336-282-7331
Greensboro	Quilts 'N Silks, 3000 Lawndale Dr.	336-286-1288
Greensboro	McKinney Sewing, 1710 Battleground Ave	336-274-6793
Greensboro	From the Heart, 1015 Bear Hollow Rd	336-547-9026
Morganton	Morganton Sewing Center, 128 N. Sterling St.	828-439-8050
New Bern	The Quilt & Stained Glass Company, 319 Middle St.	252-635-1054
New Bern	New Bern Fabric Center, 1218 S. Glenburnie Rd.	252-633-4780
Newland	Brenda Kay Crafts, Rt. 4, Box 489	
Newton	Phyllis' Crafts, 19 N. College Ave.	704-464-7770
Raleigh	Sew Unique, 1277 Buck Jones Rd	919-460-8159
Raleigh	Sew Unique Fabrics, 8800 Harvest Oak Dr #100	
Raleigh	Sew Unique Fabrics, 8801 Leadmine Rd	919-845-8802
Raleigh	Carolina Sew N Vac Center, 6320-111 Capital Blvd.	919-873-1981
Salisbury	Ruby's, 108 South Main St	704-636-8191
Shelby	Quiltique Shop, 1008 N Post Rd	704-482-4272
Spindale	The Mitchell Fabrics, 400 Spindale St.	800-870-5312
Stallings	A Stitch in Tyme, 2709 Old Monroe Rd.	704-684-0609
Washington	Cotton Fields Quilt Shop, 3751 Whaarton Station Rd	252-948-0372
Waynesville	W K Fabrics, 2348 Russ Ave.	828-456-3250
Wilmington	Sewing in the Carolinas, 25 Van Campen Blvd. #103	877-276-7393
Winston Salem	Sewing in the Triad, Newton Sq., 420 Jonestown Rd.	336-659-8212
Winston Salem	Knit One Smock Too, Inc., 3905-A Country Club	336-765-9099

North Carolina Guilds:

Albemarle Three Rivers Quilt Guild c/o HPC, 245 E. Main St., 28001

Asheville Asheville Quilt Guild, P.O. Box 412, 28793 Meets: 3rd Tuesday, alternates day and night, at Trinity United Methodist

Burnsville Mountain Piecemakers, P.O. Box 1347, 28714 Meets: 2nd Tuesday at First Prebyterian Church

Charlotte Charlotte Quilter's Guild, P.O. Box 221035, 28222

Durham Durham-Orange Quilters' Guild, P.O. Box 51492, 27717 Meets: 3rd Monday 7:30 p.m. at Church of Reconciliation, 110 N. Elliott Rd., Chapel Hill

Fayetteville Cape Fear Quilters Guild, 500 Southland Dr., 28311 Meets: 3rd Sunday at 1:30 p.m. at Loving Stitches

Fayetteville Tarheel Quilters Guild, P.O. Box 36253, 28303 Meets: 3rd Sunday at 2 p.m. at Westminister Presbyterian Church

Franklin Smoky Mtn. Quilt Guild, P.O. Box 1381, 28734 Meets: 2nd Monday 9 a.m. and 7 p.m. at Jaycee Bldg., West Main, Quilt Show Oct. 1998, and every other year.

Greensboro Piedmont Quilters Guild, P.O. Box 10673, 27404

Hayesville Misty Mtn Quilter's Guild, P.O. Box 913, 28904 Meets: 4th Monday 1 p.m. at Sharp Memorial, Young Harris, GA

Henderson Vance Quilts R Us, 27536

Hendersonville Tarhell Piecemakers Meets: 2nd Wednesday morning at Balfour Methodist Church

Hendersonville Western North Carolina Quilters Guild, 1735 5th Ave. W, 28793 Meets: 3rd Thursday, alternates day & night, at First Congregational Church, 5th & White Pine St.

Jacksonville Carolina Pine Needle Quilters Guild Meets: 2nd Tuesday 7 p.m. at Saint Anne's Episcopal Church

Kernersville Heart of the Triad Quilt Guild, 1018 Piney Grove Rd., 27284 Meets: 1st Monday 6:30 p.m. at Piney Grove Methodist

Kinston Neuse Quilters Guild P.O. Box 5226 28503 Meets: Wednesdays 10 a.m. at Arts Council of Kinston

Mooresville Mooresville Centerpiece Quilters Guild, Main St., 28117 Meets: 1st Monday 10am at Mooresville Citizen Center

Morehead City Crystal Coast Quilter's Guild, P.O. Box 1819, 28557 Meets: 3rd Thursday 7 p.m. at St. Paul's Episcopal, Beaufort

New Bern Twin Rivers Quilters Guild, P.O. Box 151, 28563 Meets: Every Thur. 10 a.m. the Tabernacle Baptist Church, 616 Broad

Raleigh North Carolina Quilt Symposium, 200 Transylvania Ave.

Raleigh Capital Quilters Guild, P.O. Box 20331, North Hills Station, 27619 Meets: 3rd Thur. at Wake County Office, off Poole

Sanford Sandhills Smocking Guild, 2816 Stonecliff Ln., 27330 Meets: Last Thursday at 7 p.m. at Loving Stitches

Southern Pines Sandhill Quilter's Guild, P.O. Box 1444 Meets: 3rd Tuesday at 9:30 a.m. at Brownson Memorial Presbyterian

Wilmington Quilters by the Sea, P.O. Box , 28401

Winston-Salem Forsyth Piecers & Quilters, P.O. Box 10666, 27108 Meets: 2nd Monday 7 p.m. at Parkway Presbyterian Church

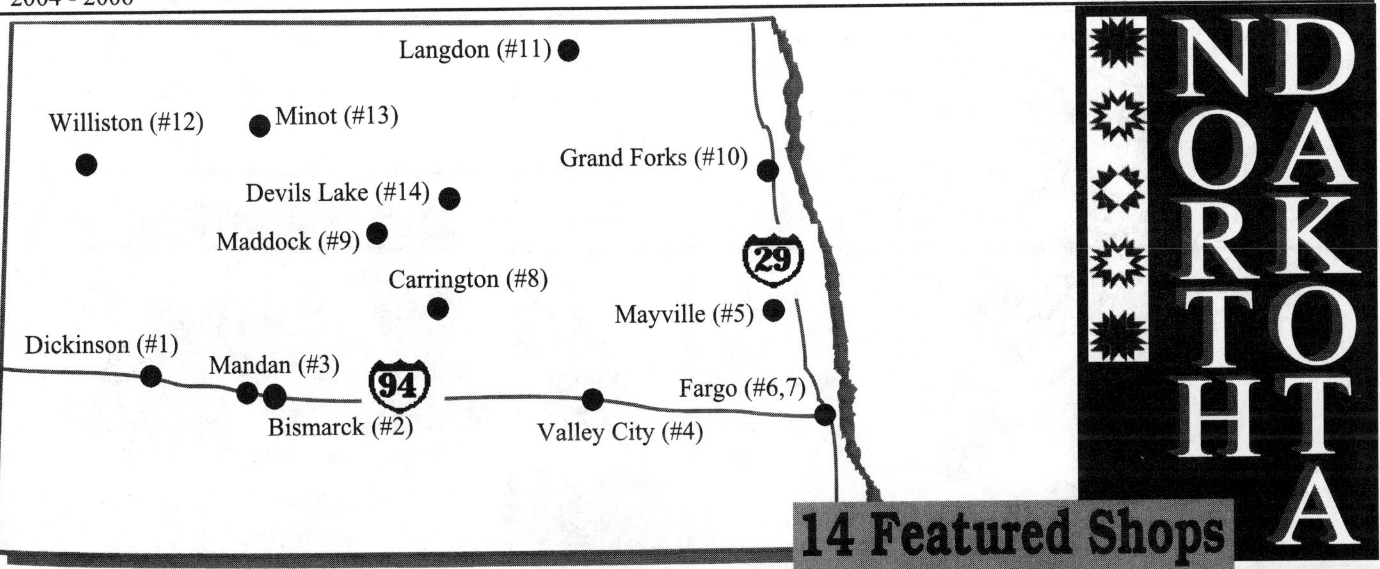

Dickinson, ND #1

Mon - Sat
9:30 - 5:30

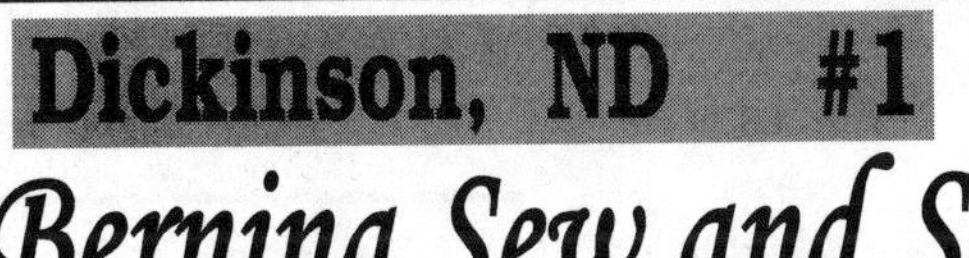

38 1st St. W 58601
(701) 225-1408 7200 sq.ft.
Owners: Holly Martinson

Dakota's Largest Fabric Store.
Mail order and newsletter available upon request. Quilt, Bridal, Fashion Fabrics. Bernina and Janome Dealer.

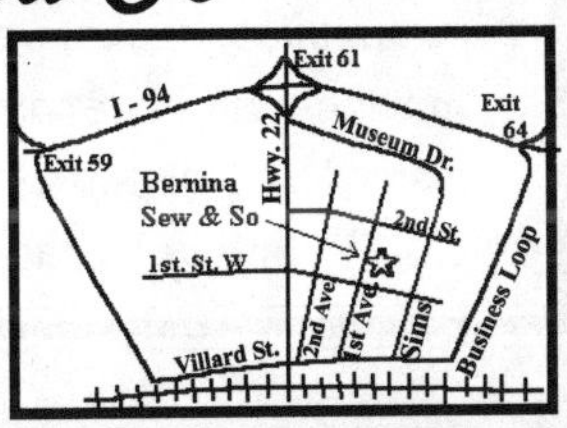

Bismarck, ND #2

Mon 10 - 8
Tues - Fri
10 - 5:30
Sat 9:30 - 5:30

Inside J & R Vacuum & Sewing
223 E. Main 58501
(701) 258-5619
(800) 371-5515
Owners: Jim & Rene Barnhardt

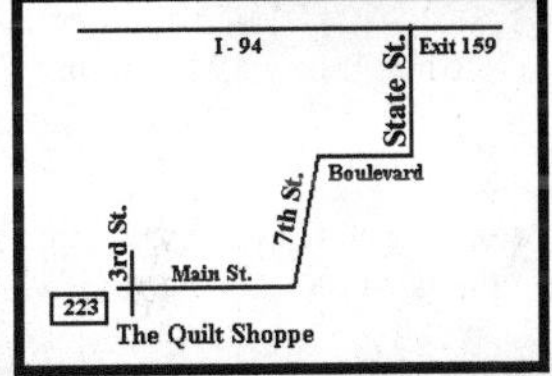

Quilt Supplies, classes, name brand 100% cotton quilting fabrics, books, patterns, notions, cabinets, PFAFF & Viking sewing machines.

Mandan, ND #3

Sewing Machines Plus!

Your Friendly Sewing & Quilting Place - Established 1998
322 West Main Street (Corner of 3rd Avenue NW & Main Street)
Mandan, North Dakota 58554 - (701) 663-9025
sewing_art@hotmail.com

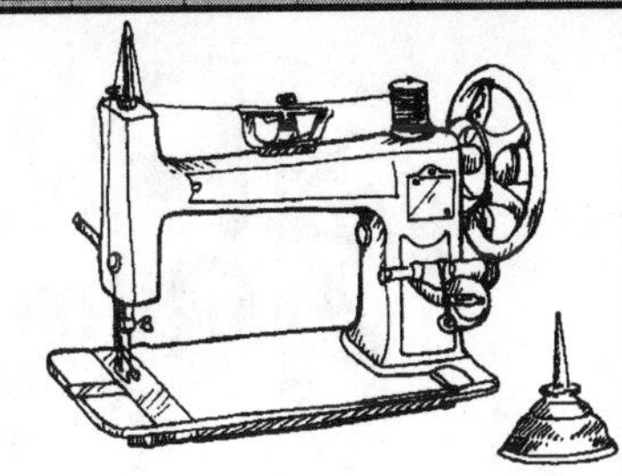

Monday 9-8
Tues-Fri
9-5:30
Saturday 9-4

- 100% Cotton Quilt Fabrics
- Threads; Notions
- Quilting Supplies
- Patterns & Books
- Machine Embroidery Designs
- Software & Supplies
- Classes
- Authorized Bernina Dealer
- Guaranteed Repair & Service on all Brands.

Mayville, ND #5

Mon - Sat
9 - 5:30
Tues til 9

37 Center Ave. North, Mayville, ND 58257
(701) 786-3790
Website: www.fayesquiltshop.com
Owner: Faye Grandalen
Est: 1996 3200 sq.ft. 5000+ Bolts

Fine cotton fabrics, quilting supplies, books, patterns, notions, and custom machine quilting, classes, gift items, and quilt racks.

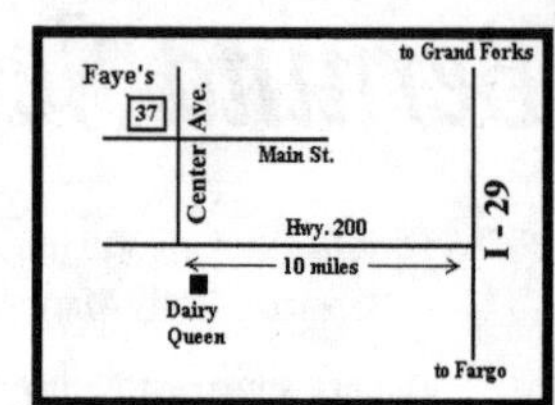

Valley City, ND #4

Mon - Sat
9:30 - 5:30

Cotton Patch Treasures

330 Central Ave. N 58072
(701) 845-4926
Owner: Georgia Manstrom
Est: 1993 2100 sq.ft.

Distinctive gifts such as Boyds Bears. Fabrics, classes, Books, Patterns, Quilting Supplies. Pfaff Sewing Machine Dealer.

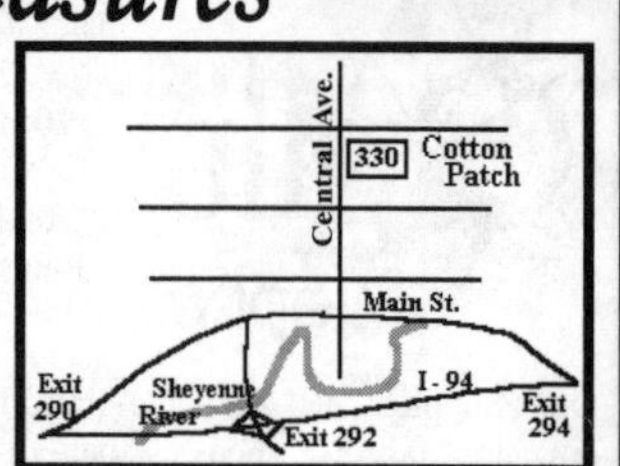

Rae-Bon
Quilt & Sewing Center

4325 13th Ave. SW #5
Fargo, ND 58103 (701) 433-7203

Mon 10 - 8
Tues - Fri 10 - 5:30
Sat 10 - 4 Closed Saturdays in the Summer

- Over 2000 bolts of 100% cottons, flannels, batiks, heirloom fabric and wools
- Books, patterns, kits
- Machine embroidery supplies
- Handy Notions and Unique Threads
- Inspiring Samples on Display

Fargo, ND #6

email: raesew@aol.com
Website: www.rae-bon.com
Fax: (701) 433-7204 Est: 1995

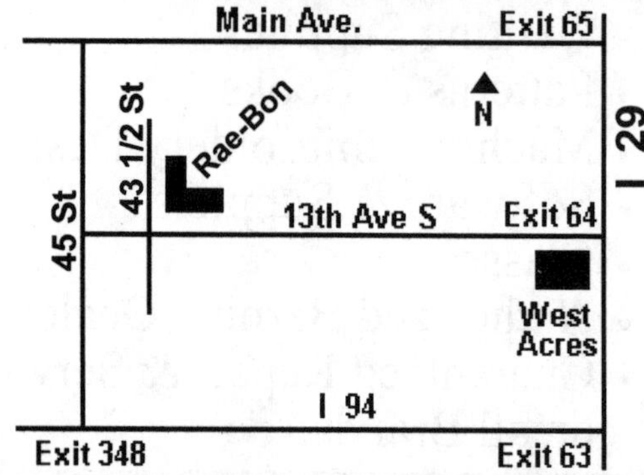

Owner: Tanya Zink
dfabqlt@daktel.com

2 Great Shops !!

Carrington, ND #8

929 Main St. 58421
(701) 652-3535
Est: 1992

Mon - Sat 10 - 5

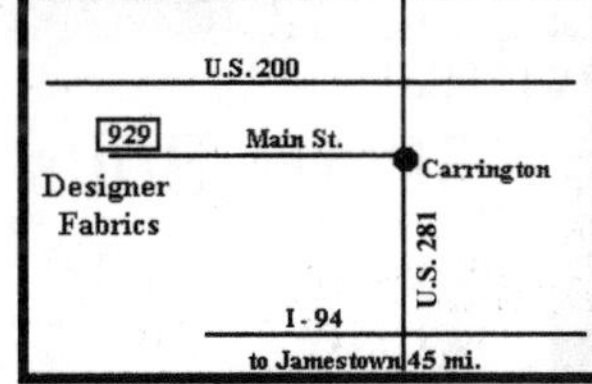

Complete quilt shop located in a historical building, specializing in traditional quilting. Many books, patterns, notions & classes. Friendly, helpful staff.

Fargo, ND #7

745D 45th St. SW 58103
(701) 277-1899

Mon - Fri 10 - 6:30
Sat 10 - 5

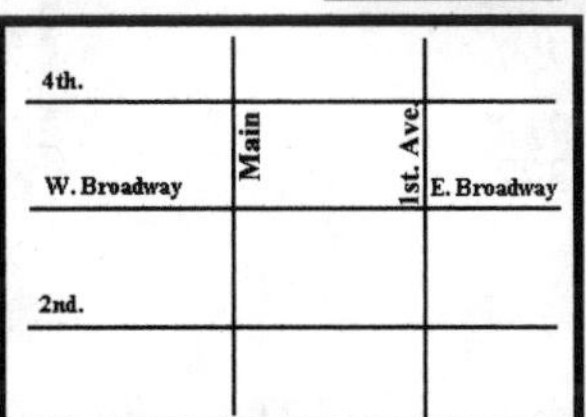

Come and visit our second location. Here you will find a warm friendly atmosphere filled with thousands of bolts of cotton fabrics, quilting supplies, Bernina sewing machines and Horn cabinets. Our knowledgeable, friendly staff will assist you with all your quilting, sewing and embroidery needs.

Maddock, ND #9

Tues - Sat 10 - 6

CABIN FEVER
Quilt Shop & Quilters' Cabin

407 2nd St., P.O. Box 328 58348
(701) 438-2151
kimkenner@hotmail.com

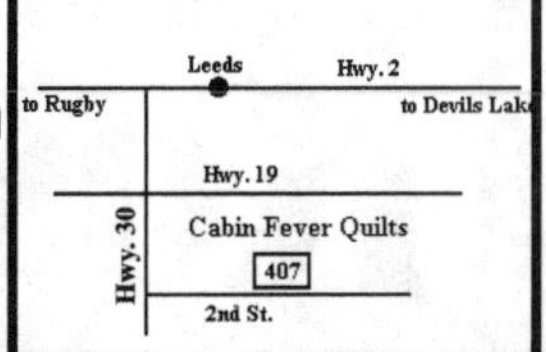

www.cabinfeverquiltshop.com
Quaint house filled with 100% cotton fabrics, notions, books, patterns and gift items. Machine quilting, classes and now a classroom/retreat center adjacent to the quilt shop in the house next door.

Grand Forks, ND #10

Mon - Fri 10 - 6
Sat 10 - 4

Quilted Rabbit

8 S. 3rd St. 58201
(701) 772-7173
Owner: Tes Weekesmurphy
Est: 1994

Country Gifts, Fabric, Machine Quilting & More
"A little out of the way, but a little out of the ordinary!"

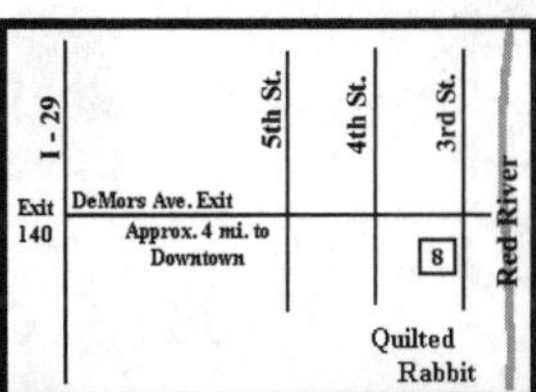

Langdon, ND #11

Mon - Sat 9:30 - 5:30

Homespun

802 3rd St. 58249
(701) 256-2609

barbkr@utma.com
Owner: Barbara Boesl

Quality Quilting fabrics, books, patterns, notions and quilting classes.
Friendly, Knowledgeable staff.

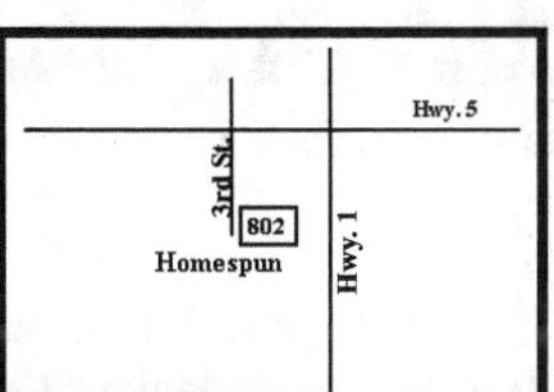

Williston, ND #12

Mon - Fri 10 - 5:30
Sat 10 - 4

Sylvia's Quilt & Sew

We will be moving soon, please call
(800) 246-0718 or (701) 572-0718
Fax: (701) 572-7018
sewquilt2@nemontel.net
www.sylviasquiltandsew.com
Est: 1988 4000+ Bolts 600+ Books
100% cottons including Hoffman, Moda, RJR, Debbie Mumm & many others. Large selection of books, patterns & notions.
Authorized Pfaff & Bernina Dealer.

4th.
W. Broadway
Main
1st. Ave
E. Broadway
2nd.

Call us with any new shop or guild information
You're our best source to keep everybody up-to-date!
Thanks
(800) 959-4587 or
info@chalet-publishing.com

Minot, ND #13

PRAIRIE ROSE
QUILT SHOP
(701) 852-2835
1500 53rd Ave. SW 58701
prairierosequilt@hotmail.com
www.prairierosequiltshop.com

Owner: Carmen R. Haugen
Est: 1998 1750 sq.ft.
2500 Bolts

Mon - Fri 10 - 5
Sat 10 - 2

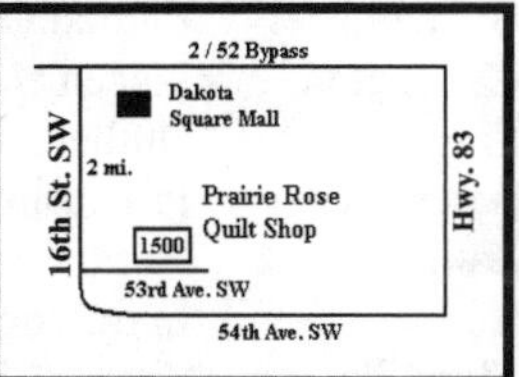

Full service quilt shop offering quality quilting fabric and machine quilting. Specializing in florals, plaids, batiks, flannels & wool.

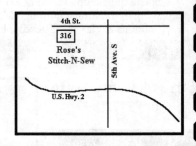

Other Shops in North Dakota: *We suggest calling first*

Burlington	Unique Creations, 9020 Project Rd S	701-839-6580
Devils Lake	Lone Star Quilting, 316 4th St.	701-662-3634
Hampden	H & H Quilting & Crafts, 215 Main St	701-868-3040
Minot	Carol's Etc., 112 S. Main St.	701-839-6183
Minot	Quilter's Cottage, 106 4th Ave NW	701-838-6376
New Town	J & J Quilt Shop, PO Box 219	701-627-2553
Northwood	From The Heart, 22 44th St.	701-587-6019
Wahpenton	Pin Cushion Quilt Shop, 500 Dakota Ave.	701-642-9757
Williston	Quiltmakins, 12542 Hwy. 1804	701-774-3315
Willow City	Ye Olde Sew & So, 365 Main St.	701-366-4372

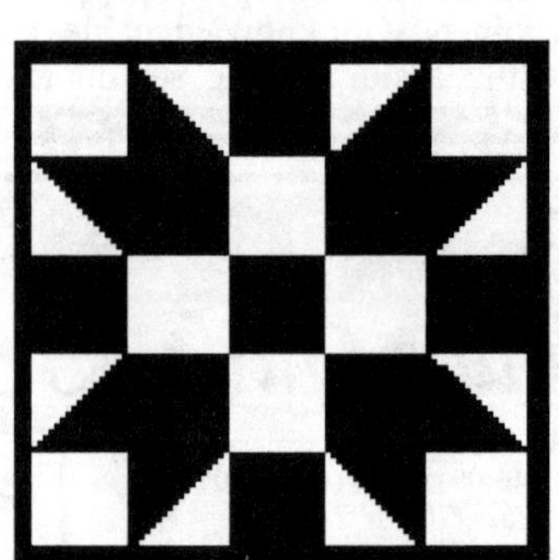

North Dakota Guilds:

Battineau	Northern Lights Quilters, 52 Main St., 58318	Meets: 1st & 3rd Thursday
Bismarck	Capital Quilters, 58501	
Carrington	Piecemakers Quilt Guild	Meets: 3rd Tuesday 7 p.m. at NDSU R/E Center North of Town
Fargo	Quilters' Guild of North Dakota, P.O. Box 2662, 58107	Meets: 3rd Saturday
Langdon	Friendship Star Quilt Guild, 802 3rd St, 58249	Meets: 1st Thursday @ 7pm at County Courthouse Meeting room
Langdon	North Star Quilt Guild	Meets: 1st Saturday 1 p.m. at University Lutheran Church
Lisbon	In Stitches Quilt Club	Meets: 2nd Thursday 7 p.m. at Ingeborg & Frannie's Quilt Shop
Mayville	Sisters Choice Quilt Club, 37 Center Ave N., 58257	Meets: 1st Thursday @ 6:30pm at Ebenezer Luthren Church
Rugby	Quilting from the Heart, 1102 Unique Dr., 58368	Meets: 2nd Tuesday
Williston	Dakota Prairie Quilt Guild, P.O. Box 1723, 58801	Meets: 2nd Saturday

Southington (#72)
Lordstown (#71)
Chesterland (#67)
Painesville (#63)
Warren (#70)
South Amherst (#34)
Toledo (#33)
Avon (#41)
North (#66) Kingsville
Sylvania (#32)
North Olmsted (#37)
80
90
Milan (#35)
Olmsted Falls (#38)
Wauseon (#31)
(#61,62) Middlefield
Cortland (#68,69)
Maumee (#29)
Pemberville (#28)
Aurora (#65)
Bettsville (#27)
Twinsburg (#64)
Oberlin (#36)
Findlay (#26)
Medina (#42)
Cuyahoga Falls (#60)
Van Wert (#30)
Bluffton (#25)
(#73) Youngstown
Wadsworth (#59)
Akron (#58)
Hartville (#57)
Ashland (#43)
Kidron (#54)
Mansfield (#39)
North Canton (#56)
Berlin (#47,48,49)
(#55) Mt. Eaton
Wilmot (#51)
Lexington (#40)
75
Charm (#46)
(#52,53) Sugarcreek
Greenville (#11)
Middleburg (#18)
Mt. Vernon (#44,45)
Stone Creek (#50)
Plain City (#23)
Hilliard (#24)
Englewood (#12)
Newark (#21)
Cambridge (#74)
(#13) Springfield
Pataskala (#19,20)
Fairborn (#10)
70
Columbus (#14,15,16,17)
Beavercreek (#9)
71
Cumberland (#75)
Lancaster (#22)
Woodsfield (#76)
Centerville (#8)
McConnelsville (#77)
77
Waynesville (#6)
Chillicothe (#5)
Fairfield (#7)
Marietta (#78)
Sharonville (#4)
Pomeroy (#79)
Cincinnati (#1,2,3)
OHIO
79 Featured Shops

OPEN SUNDAY!

- Roxanne Thimbles!
- Electric Quilt Software!
- The Famous Wall of Flannels!
- Thimbleberries Club!
- Machine Quilting & Binding!

The only place in town to "Try It Before You Buy It with EQ5!"

#1

Home of the original Friendly Quilt Challenge!

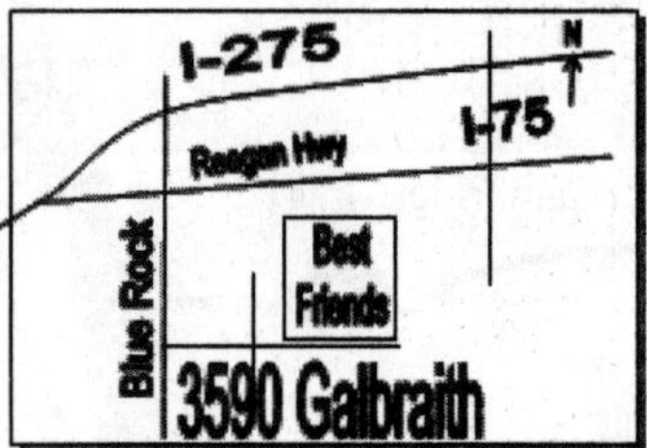

Easy access from I-275 on Cincy's West Side!

Mon-Fri 10-9, Sat 10-5, Sun 12-4
(513)385-2200
email:qshoppe@cinci.rr.com
www.bestfriendsquilts.com
3590 W. Galbraith Rd Cincinnati OH 45239

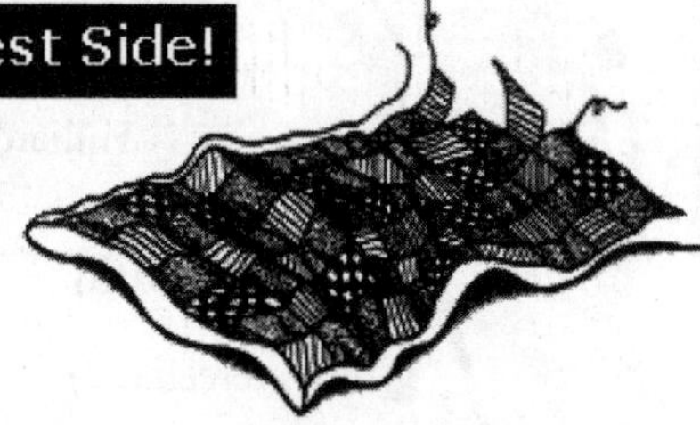

Cincinnati, OH #2

Victorian Quilt Shop

Mon - Thur 10 - 8
Fri & Sat 10 - 5

8556 Beechmont Ave. 45255
(513) 474-9355
Est: 1998 3800 sq.ft.

We stock 5500 bolts of cotton fabric, including Hoffman, Moda, P&B, Thimbleberries, Bali, Maywood, RJR, Benartex, Kona Bay, etc.
We offer supplies, books, stencils, notions, classes, discounts, gift items, specialty threads, glass beads, and imported heirloom fabrics, laces & supplies, & gift certificates.

Five Mile Rd. | Eight Mile Rd. | I-275 | Victorian Quilt Shop | Beechmont Mall | 8556 | Ohio Pike | Beechmont Ave. | Exit 65 | Rt. 125

Cincinnati, OH #3

Mon - Sat 9:30 - 5:30
Wed til 8:30
Sun 1 - 4

Creative Cottage
Quilting & Cross Stitch

6934 Miami Ave. 45243 in "Madeira"
(513) 271-2028
15 min. from downtown Cincinnati
Owner: Marie Tsacalis Est: 1988 3300 sq.ft.

Quilting - Large selection of books, patterns, stencils& tools. Fabric - 1500+ bolts of exciting cotton plus large selection of flannels. Cross Stitch supplies too.

Montgomery | Exit 12 | I-71 | Exit 11(N. Bound Only) | Miami Ave. | Euclid Rd. | to down-town | Kenwood Rd. | 6934 | Creative Cottage

Sharonville, OH #4

Mon - Sat 10 - 5
Tues & Thur til 6

Aunt Ruth's Scrapbasket

11096 Reading Rd. 45241
(513) 733-0006 Fax: (513) 733-0466
auntruthscrapbasket@fuse.net
www.auntruthsscrapbasket.com
Owner: Ruth Roy Est: 2002 2000 Bolts
We carry a wide variety of 100% quilters cottons. Featuring Batiks and Brights.
Friendly Atmosphere.

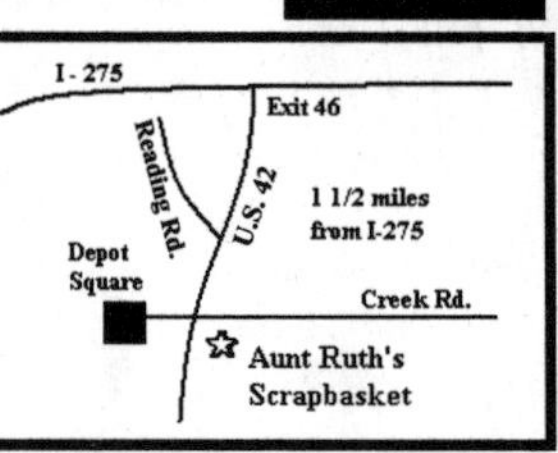

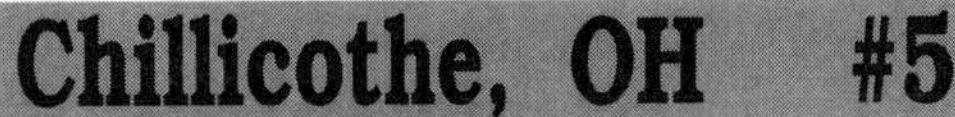

Creations SEWCLEVER Quilt Shop

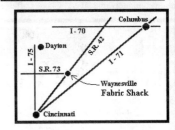

192 S. Paint St.
Chillicothe, Oh 45601
(740) 775-1957 or
Toll Free 1-888-SEW-CLVR
Fax: (740) 773-2390
E-Mail: Sewclevr@bright.net

Creations SewClever is a friendly, full-line quilt shop found in a beautiful 1800's Greek Revival home in the historic district of downtown Chillicothe, OH. Call, write, or e-mail us for class schedules, or a free quarterly newsletter.

- Machine Quilting Services
- Janome Sewing Machines
- Kits
- Fine Fabrics
- Classes

MON-SAT 10AM-5PM
THURS 10AM-8PM

www.creationssewclever.com

Fabric Shack

Mon - Sat 10 - 5
Thur til 8 Sun 12 - 5

Waynesville, OH #6

99 S. Marvin Ln. & Miami St. 45068
(877) 666-4245 or (513) 897-0092 Fax: (513) 897-7175
info@fabricshack.com www.fabricshack.com
Owner: Maxine Young Est: 1986 3000 sq.ft. 10,000+ Bolts

Columbus
I-70
Dayton
I-75
S.R. 42
I-71
S.R. 73
Waynesville Fabric Shack
Cincinnati

The ultimate quilt shop . . .
All the fabrics, colors, designers, the biggest in the midwest . . .
Notions, patterns, and books too!
Exclusive online supplier for Mountain Mist patterns and supplies.

Leggett & Platt. INCORPORATED

Mountain Mist

Recently Leggett & Platt, Inc. purchased the Mountain Mist product line and brand name. Due to this acquisition, the retail mail order service offered by Stearns Technical Textiles ended. We apologize for the delay in processing your order while a new system is arranged.

We are also please to announce that Fabric Shack, a quilt shop in Waynesville, Ohio will be the fulfillment center for Mountain Mist patterns and products by mail order and through their online services. All mail order requests should be directed to:

The Fabric Shack, P.O. Box 517, Waynesville, OH 45068
(513) 897-0092 or (877) 666-4245 info @ fabricshack.com www.fabricshack.com

Order Form
Catalog

Please Print

Name ______________________
Address ____________________
City _______________________
State ____________ Zip ____________
Telephone (___)_______________

Fairfield, OH #7

Mon, Wed Fri, Sat 10 - 4
Tues 10 - 8
Sun 1 - 4

Stitches 'n Such

702 Nilles Road 45014
(513) 829-2999
Web Site: www.stitchesnsuch.com
located 5 miles north of Cincinnati

Fabric, fabric, fabric - over 3,000 bolts including homespuns, flannels, fleece, wool. Patterns, books, notions. We also carry rug hooking, yarn & cross stitching supplies.

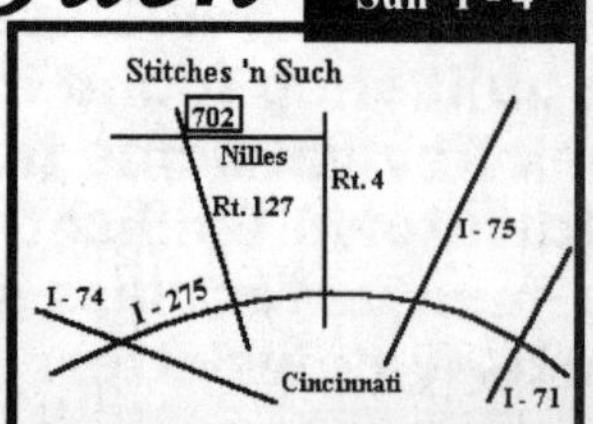

Centerville, OH #8

Mon - Thur 10 - 8
Fri & Sat 10 - 5

Sew-A-Lot

232 N. Main St. 45459
(937) 433-7474 Fax: (937) 433-0757
sewalot@erinet.com
Owner: Debbie Bernhard
Est: 1982 3500 sq.ft. 3500 Bolts

Sales & Service of Pfaff machines. Great selection of 100% cotton fabrics, patterns, books & machine threads. Classes. Historic building built in 1874

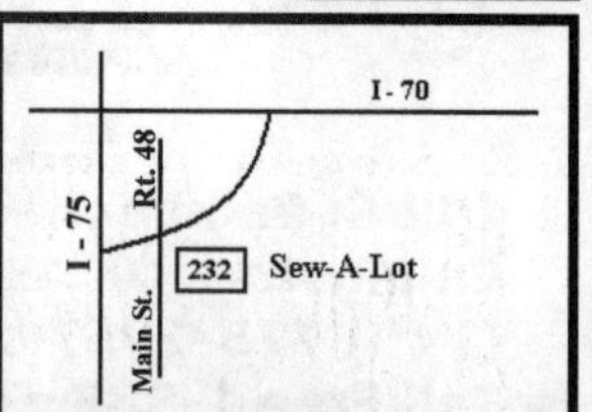

Beavercreek, OH #9

Mon - Sat 10 - 4
Mon & Thur til 8

Unique Stitches Quilt Shop
& Professional Machine Quilting

3295 Seajay Dr. Beaver Valley Shp. Ctr. 45430
(937) 429-0894 usquilts@sbcglobal.net
www.uniquestitches.com
Owner: Marian Gebele
Est: 1997 3600 sq.ft. 2000 Bolts

Visit us at our new location! We now offer more fabric, books, notions and classes! Bring your quilt in to be professionally machine quilted. We also make custom made bedspreads and pillow shams.

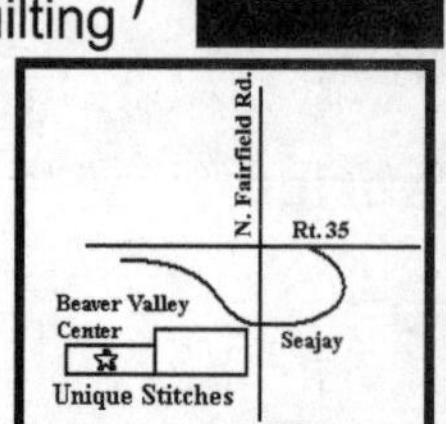

Fairborn, OH #10

Tues, Wed, Fri, & Sat 10 - 4
Mon & Thur 10 - 8

Daisy Barrel, Inc.

19 West Main Street 45324
(937) 879-0111
Web Site: www.daisybarrel.com
Owners: Marjorie, Sandy, Judy, Phyllis, & Gretchen
Est: 1972 5000 sq.ft. 4000+ Bolts

We specialize in best quality materials for the quilter, cross-stitcher, & teddy bear maker, (including mohair). Our experienced staff will be glad to help.

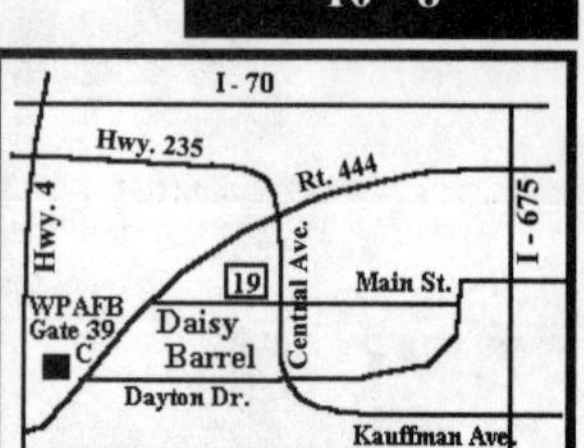

Greenville, OH #11

Mon - Fri 9:30 - 5:30
Sat 10 - 4

The Fabric Gallery

413 S. Broadway 45331
(937) 547-9126 Fax: (937) 547-9127
Est: 1999 1300+ Bolts

Quality quilting fabrics including homespuns and flannels. Also garment fabrics, patterns, notions, uniquely displayed. Classes offered.

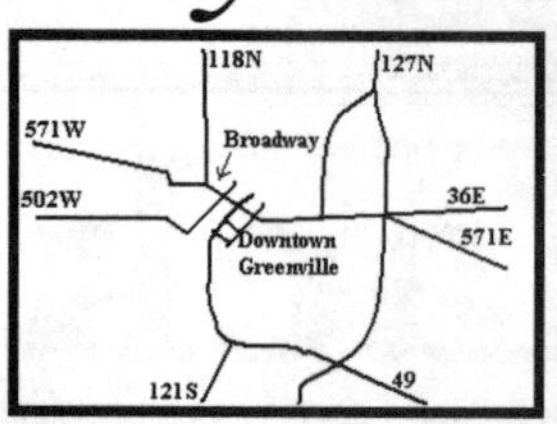

Englewood, OH #12

Mon 10 - 7
Tues - Fri 10 - 5
Sat 10 - 4

Quilters Fare Sewing Center

506 W. National Rd., P.O. Box 189 45322
(937) 836-4949 Fax: (937) 836-4707
quiltersfaresc@aol.com Est: 2003
www.quiltersfare.com 1200 Bolts
Owners: Ron & Darlene Keller

1400 sq.ft. of fabric, notions, patterns, sewing furniture (Horn), and sewing/embroidery machines. Authorized Janome, Brother & Singer Dealer.

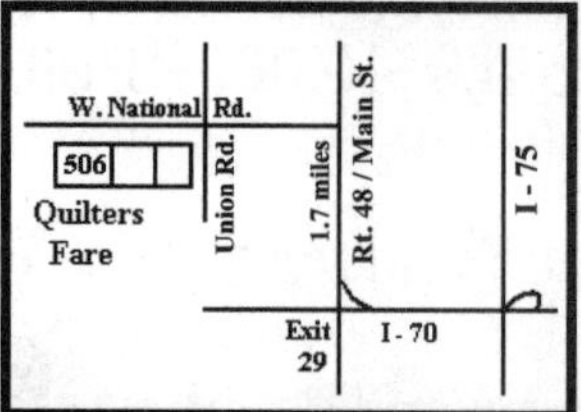

Springfield, OH #13

Tues - Sat 11 - 5
Sun & Mon By Appt.

Creative Fires, LLC

1525 Progress Dr. 45505
(937) 327-9420 Fax: (937) 327-9421
creativefires2@aol.com
Owners: Robert & Kathryn Fowler
Est: 2001 3000 sq.ft.

Authorized Bernina Dealer. Bernina Accessories, Notions, Patterns, Design Cards, Wall of Thread, Fat Quarters, Quilt Kits, Classes.

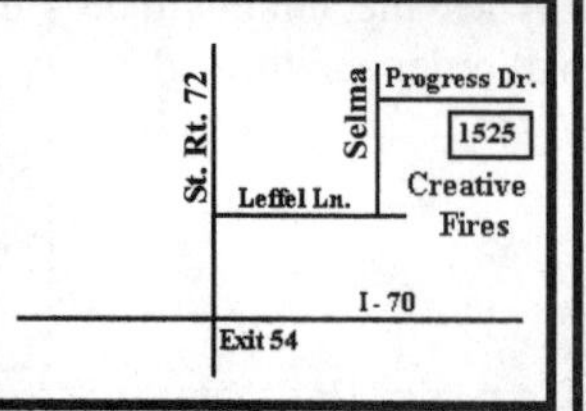

Columbus, OH #14

Picking Up The Pieces

911 City Park Avenue, Columbus, OH 43206
Phone: 614-443-9988 Fax: 614-443-9798
E-mail: quiltpati@aol.com

NOW ONE NAME FOR QUALITY!

MOTHER & DAUGHTER QUILT TEACHERS
DESIGNING FOR QUILTERS

Gay Dell-Howard is the creator of the Helyn's Hoops:
Hoop~de~Deux™, the **best** border hoop on the market!
Cinch Hoop™, the **first** patented bungee corded hoop!
Emma Sings©, The first quilters' songbook.

Pati Shambaugh is the creator of:
Quilt Patis™ as seen on Simply Quilts
and the ***Tec~Spec©*** line of patterns.

Hours: 9 AM – 6PM Monday – Saturday
Other times by chance or appointment.

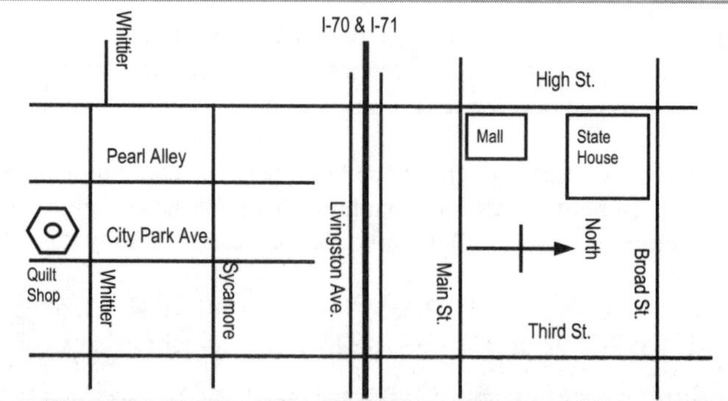

Columbus, OH #15

Est: 2003

Tues, Wed, Thur
10 am - 7 pm
Fri & Sat
10 am - 5 pm

A Different Kind of Quilt Store

6112 Boardwalk St., Columbus, OH 43229 614-841-7845
QuiltTrends@QuiltTrends.com Fax: 614-841-7846
Owners: Susan & David Sandritter

explore the art
elna usa

www.QuiltTrends.com
We offer free shipping on all internet fabric orders (except sale items)

Anheuser Busch
Schrock Rd.
N
Busch Blvd.
Very easy freeway access!
I-71
Mediterranean
QUILT Trends
Shapter
Boardwalk St.
Giant Eagle
Dublin-Granville Rd. (161)

If you like bright colors, whimsical prints, or daring patterns, then we invite you to visit QuiltTrends.

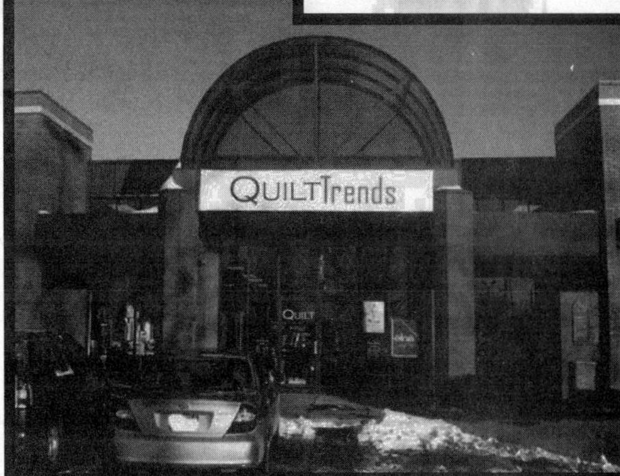

QuiltTrends is a new quilt store on the north end of Columbus, Ohio. Our mission is to supply all quilters, who desire contemporary fabrics and designs, with the appropriate fabric, notions, books, and patterns for your interest, while offering friendly and knowledgeable customer service.

- Fabrics from all major manufacturers
- Over 600 years of one-of-a-kind hand-dyed fabric
- Generous quantities of ethnic fabrics
- 2500+ Bolts in a spacious 2800 sq. ft.
- Over 700 bolts of batiks
- Art quilting classes & supplies

The Glass Thimble

3434 N. High St. 43214
(614) 267-9566 Fax: (614) 447-2440
E-Mail: baquilter@aol.com
Owners: Bev & Gary Young
Est: 1979 5800 sq.ft.

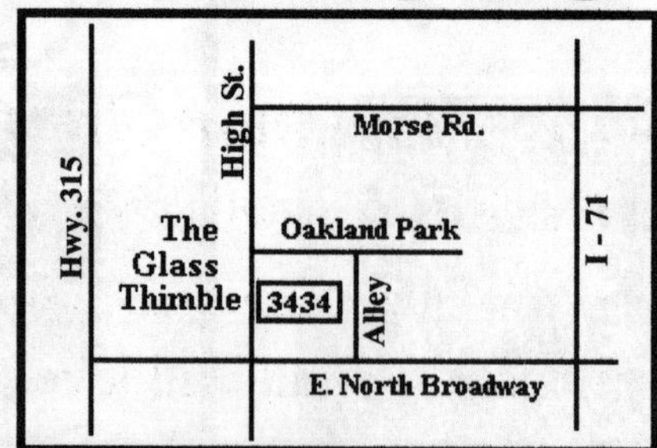

Columbus, OH #16

The Complete Quilt Shop . . . .
Over 8000 bolts of cotton fabrics,
lots of books & patterns plus
stained glass supplies.
We love quilting and it shows.

Mon - Sat
10 - 5
Tues & Thur
10 - 8

Come Shop with us On-Line: www.glassthimble.com

Quilt Beginnings

A Friendly Place to Shop

Columbus, OH #17

Bright, airy quilt shop with over 4500 bolts. Our staff loves to help with any quilt!

Mon & Wed 10-6
Tues & Thur 10-8
Fri & Sat 10-5

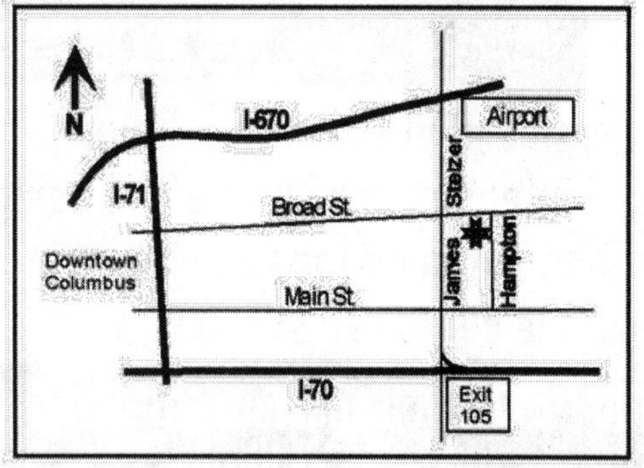

- 5 minutes from airport
- 4 miles from downtown
- New location/lots of parking
- Authorized Pfaff dealer

(614) 237-1322

3409 E. Broad St. Est. 1998 www.quiltbeginnings.com

Pataskala, OH #20

Mon - Thur 10 - 7
Fri & Sat 10 - 5

Calico Cupboard Quilt Shop

74 Oak Meadow Dr. 43062
(740) 927-2636
calicocup@aol.com
www.calico-cupboard.com
Est: 2003 1300 sq.ft. 4500 bolts
Located in Pataskala Square. We have 100% cotton, wool, flannel, homespuns, wool felt, books, patterns, notions.
Something on sale every month.

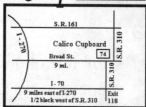

S.R. 161
I - 270
Calico Cupboard
Broad St. 74
9 mi.
S.R. 310
I - 70
9 miles east of I-270
1/2 block west of S.R. 310
Exit 118

Newark, OH #21

Mon - Sat 10 - 5:30
Wed til 8:30

Bunny's Sew Fine Fabrics

28 Price Rd. 43055
(740) 366-1433
sewfinefabrics@hotmail.com
Owner: Linda Schofield
Est: 1999 2000 sq.ft. 2500 Bolts
Full service quilt shop. Machine quilting service done in house.
Notions, books, patterns and classes.
Authorized Janome dealer.
Thimbleberries Club.

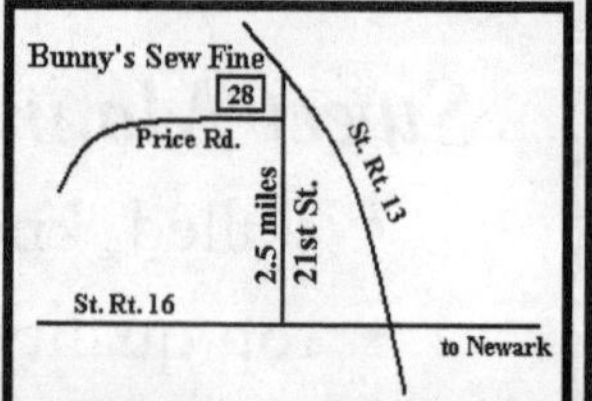

Lancaster, OH #22

Mon - Sat 10 - 5

Farmer's Country Store

540 N. High St. 43130
(740) 654-4853
www.farmerscountrystore.com
Est: 1973

Moda - Thimbleberries - RJR - Benartex
Indo US - P&B - Red Rooster - South Seas
Clothworks - Marcus Brothers - Northcott
AE Nathan - Kona Bay - David

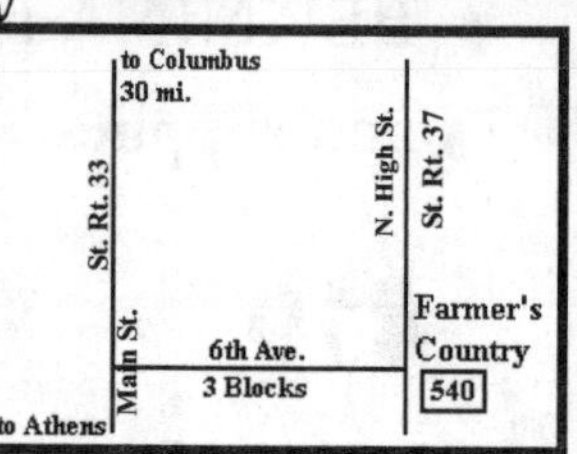

Plain City, OH #23

Mon - Sat 9 - 5

Tomorrow's Heirlooms

9872 U.S. 42 43064
(614) 873-4123 Fax: (614) 873-8304
mbeach@copper.net
Est: Mid 70's 2000 sq.ft. 2500+ bolts

A large line of quilting fabrics, notions, books, & patterns. A large selection of "Quilting Creations" templates. Finished quilts (large, small & baby). Custom quilt orders also welcome.

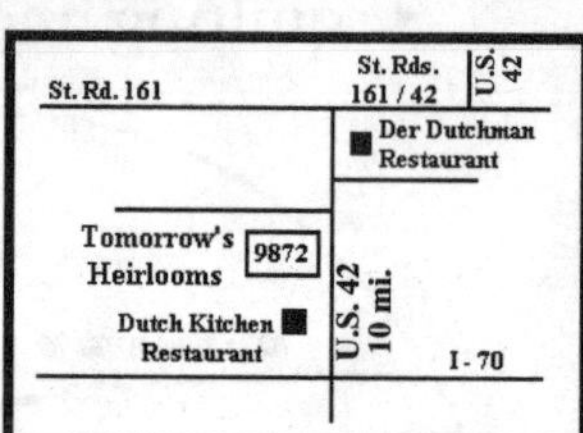

Quilt Pox Shoppe & More

Owner:
Karen Sue Weiler

Luigi's Pizza
Lattimer
3876 Quilt Pox
Chamber of Commerce
Cemetery Rd.
Rome-Hilliard
I - 270
I - 70

Hilliard, OH #24

In-house Custom Machine Quilting.
Janome Sewing Machines.
Notions.

Proverbs, 31:22 N.I.V.
She makes coverings for her bed.

Summer Hrs 6/21 - 9/30
Mon - Sat 10 - 5
Winter Hrs 10/1 - 6/20
Mon - Sat 10 - 5
Tues & Thur til 8

3876 Lattimer St. 43026
(614) 771-0657
3700 sq.ft. 3500+ Bolts
www.quiltpoxshoppe.com
Discover, Amex, Visa, MC

Bus tours: By appt. only please.
Plus: We have a child's play area for your little ones and two reclining easy chairs and color T.V. for those who are with you that have not been infected with "*Quilt Pox*" yet.

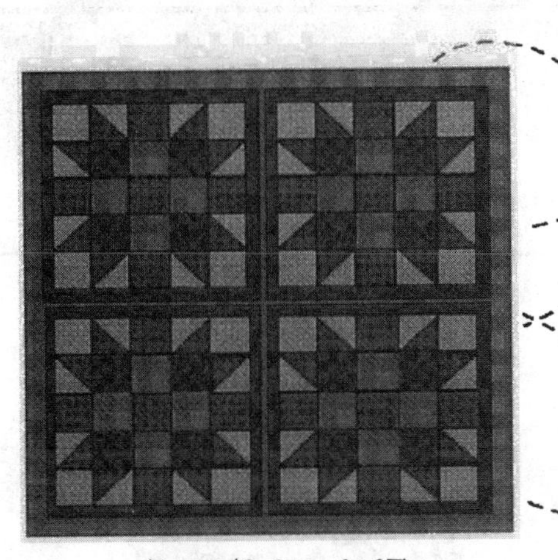

Forever In Stitches, LLC

120 N. Main Street
Bluffton, OH 45817
www.foreverinstitches.com

419-358-0656

Mon & Wed - Sat 10 - 5:30 Tues 12 - 9

Fax: 419-358-0207
RuthG@fisllc.com

Est: 2004 3000 sq.ft. 1500 bolts

Owners: Ruth & Rick Grihalva

Full service quilt shop providing 100% cotton quilting fabrics, a complete line of notions and classes along with long-arm quilting services. We provide mail order quilting services using our two Gammill long-arm machines, (one including the computerized Statler Stitcher). See our web site for details

Exit 142
OH - 103
(1.1 miles)
Main St.
Elm St.
I - 75
Forever in Stitches
120
(alley) Extra Parking in rear

Bluffton, OH #25

Findlay, OH #26

ohio farm house

Larry and Darlene Hammond, Proprietors

Monday thru Saturday
9:30 - 5:00
Open 12:00 - 4:00 Sundays in November and December
(419) 422-5031

16056 Rt. 224 E.
Findlay,
Ohio
45840

www.ohiofarmhouse.com
ofhgals@aol.com

A Quilter's Delight...
Great selection of "Fat Quarters" and Bolts and Bolts of Homespun Fabrics. Featuring the primitive look of Moda, Brannock & Patek designs, plus many Civil War reproduction fabrics. Boasting a large selection of flannels and coordinating fabrics. During your visit, browse through our offerings of primitive pieced quilts, matching bedding ensembles, pillows, clothing and much more!

S.R. 68
S.R. 12
I-75
Ohio Farm House
S.R. 224

* Woolens and Etc *
Hand-dyed and Felted Wool available
Fat Quarters, Fat Eighths, Stripped or by-the-yard
Choose from our primitive woolen rug hooking kits, cutters, dyes, project books, frames and hoops. Penny rugs and other project samples for your enjoyment.

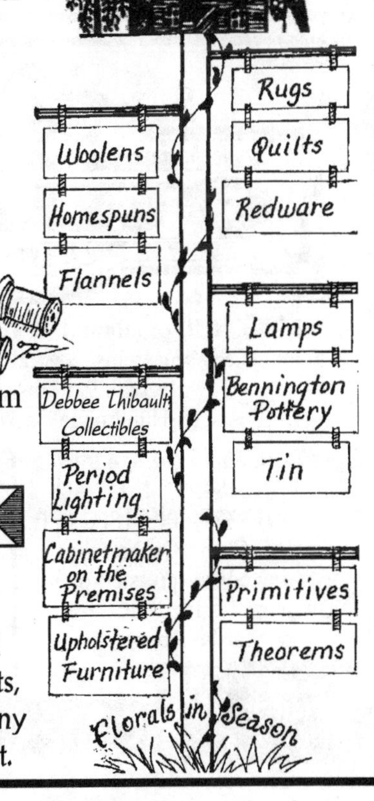

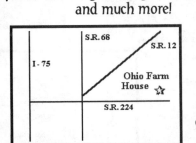

THE DOOR MOUSE

Over 15,000 bolts of cotton, patterns, and quilting supplies in a barn setting. Featuring quilts and many handcrafted memories, legends and heirlooms which capture the beauty and simplicity of rural life. Join our friendly staff for classes in the corn crib.

Mail Orders Welcome. We accept Visa/MC & Discover

5047 W. SR 12
P.O. Box 455 44815
(419) 986-5667
E-Mail:
doormouse@nwonline.net
Web Site: www.
thedoormouse.com
Owner: Mary Ann Sorg

Mon - Sat 10 - 5
Wed til 8
Last Sunday of each month 12 - 5

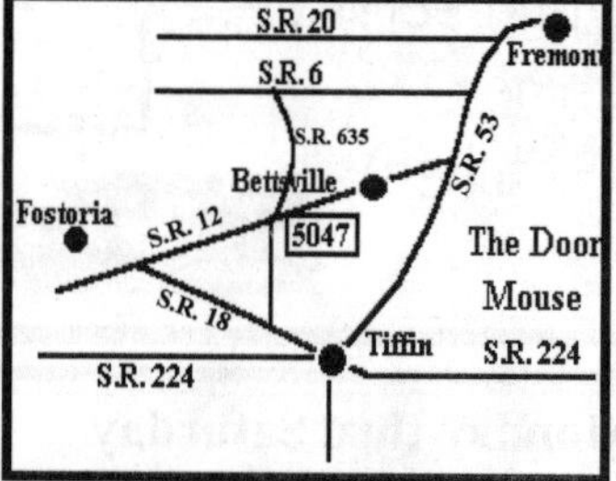

Est: 1979 3600 sq.ft.

Bettsville, OH #27

Pemberville, OH #28

Tues, Wed, Thur 10 - 3 & 6 - 9
Fri & Sat 10 - 3

Quilt Makers

208 E. Front St. 43450
(419) 287-0221
Owners: Judy Seifert & Judy Kaminski
Est: 2002 1000 sq.ft.

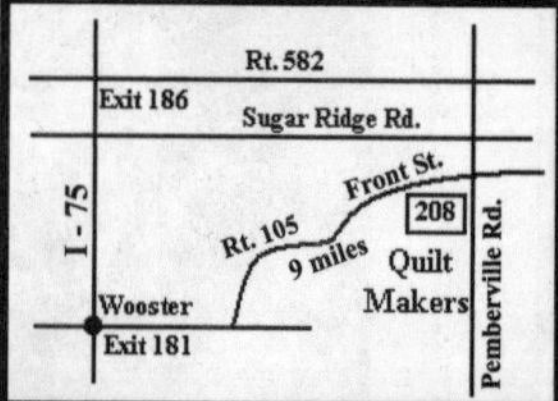

Small warm atmosphere. We cater to quilters with Quality Fabrics, Patterns, Books, Notions, and classes.

Maumee, OH #29

Mon - Sat 10 - 4
Tues eve 7 - 9

The Quilt Foundry

234 W. Wayne 43537
(419) 893-5703
Owners: Mary Beham, Margaret Okuley, Peg Sawyer, Gretchen Schultz
Est: 1981 1000 sq.ft.

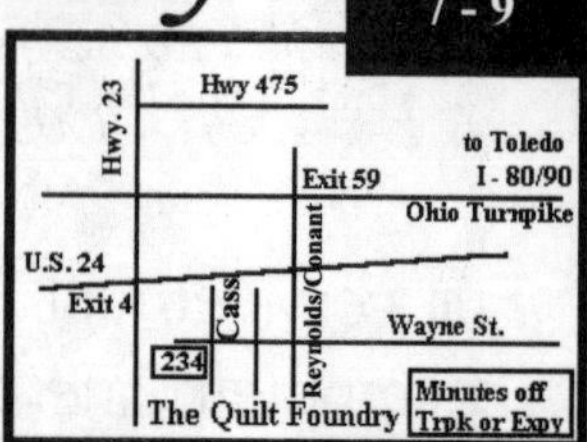

The Quilt Foundry offers friendly, personalized service in your search for wonderful fabric, supplies, books and classes.

Van Wert, OH #30

Mon - Fri 9:30 - 5
Sat 9 - 3:30

The COUNTRY CUPBOARD

229 S. Washington St. 45891
(888) 795-5751 or (419) 238-7742
sharon@thecountrycupboard.org
www.thecountrycupboard.org
Owner: Sharon K. Cox Est: 1997

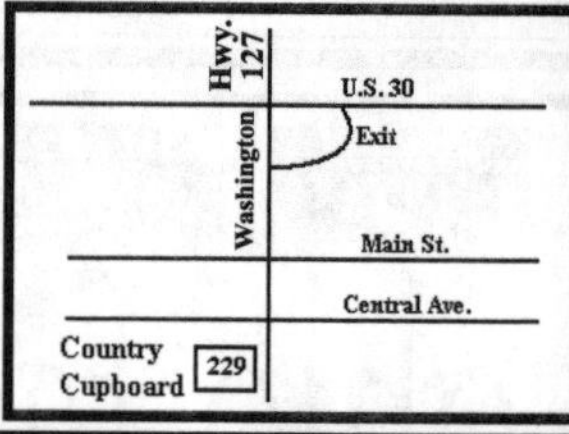

Small shop but very personable. We carry Moda - Thimbleberries and name brand fabrics. Patterns - Craft Supplies - Gifts & Classes.

2500+ Bolts of fabric, 100% cotton, large selection of flannels & homespuns, several 108" wide cotton backing. Books, Patterns and Notions. Amish Handmade Baskets, Gifts, Classes.

14707 County Rd. J 43567
(419) 337-8458 Est: 2002
Fax: (419) 337-0600 1800 sq.ft.
sales@CornerQuilts.com
www.cornerquilts.com
Owners: Kathie McClarren & Martha Bennetts

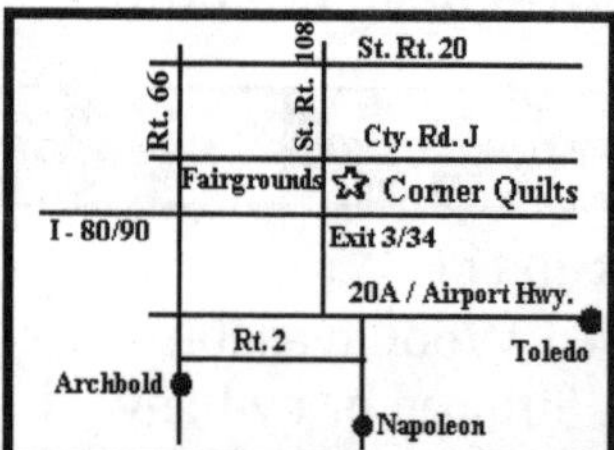

Mon - Fri 9 - 5
Thur 9 - 8
Sat 9 - 4

Wauseon, OH #31

Sylvania, OH #32

Tues - Sat 10 - 4
Tues & Thur til 7

Sonflower Quilts & Gifts

Saxon Square, 6600 Sylvania Ave. 43560
(419) 885-4438 Fax: (419) 885-4408
sonflowerquilts@sonflowerquilts.com
www.sonflowerquilts.com
Owners: Kathy Walch & Cathy Frick
Est: 2003 1000 sq.ft. 1000+ bolts

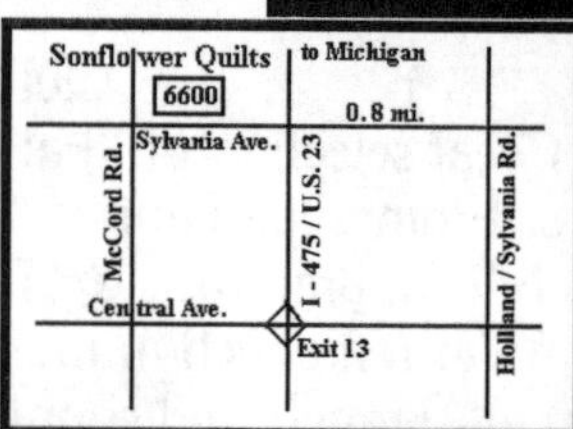

A full-service friendly quilt shop offering a wide selection of fabrics, quilting notions, patterns, and classes as well as fellowship.

Toledo, OH #33

Tues - Sat 10 - 5
Thur 10 - 8

something extra inc.
a country needlework shop
with a passion for primitive

25 years in Business

3310 Glanzman Rd. 43614
(419) 385-7299 Fax: (419) 385-8570

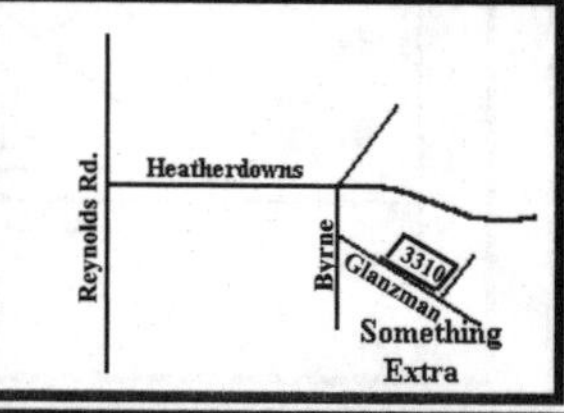

Counted cross stitch, Primitive stitch embroidery, Custom Framing, Applique & Quilting, Moda Fabrics, Wool Rug Hooking, Over-dyed wool, Antiques, Gifts, classes and so much more! MC and Visa accepted.

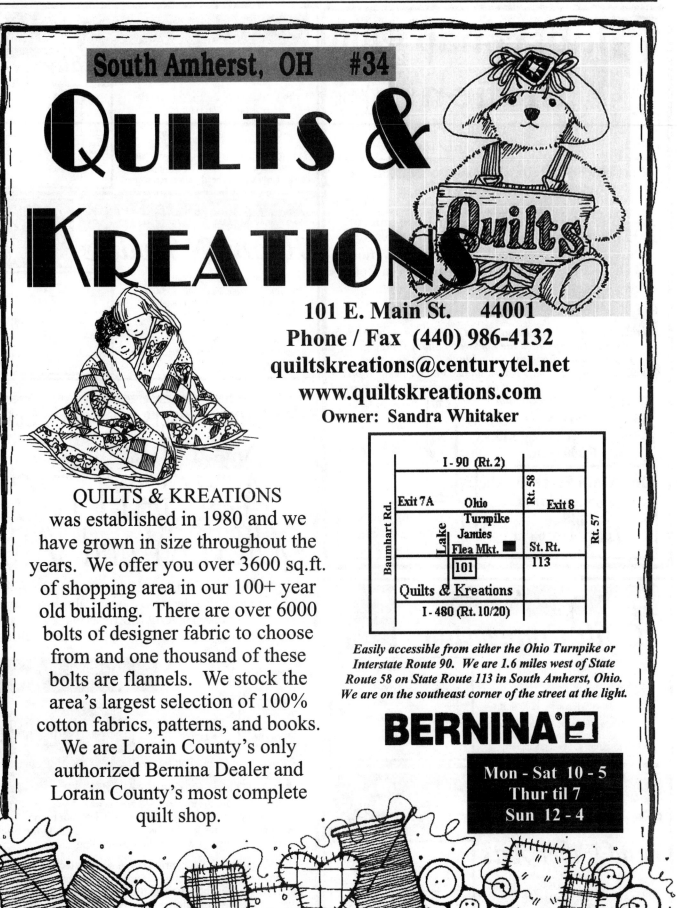

South Amherst, OH #34

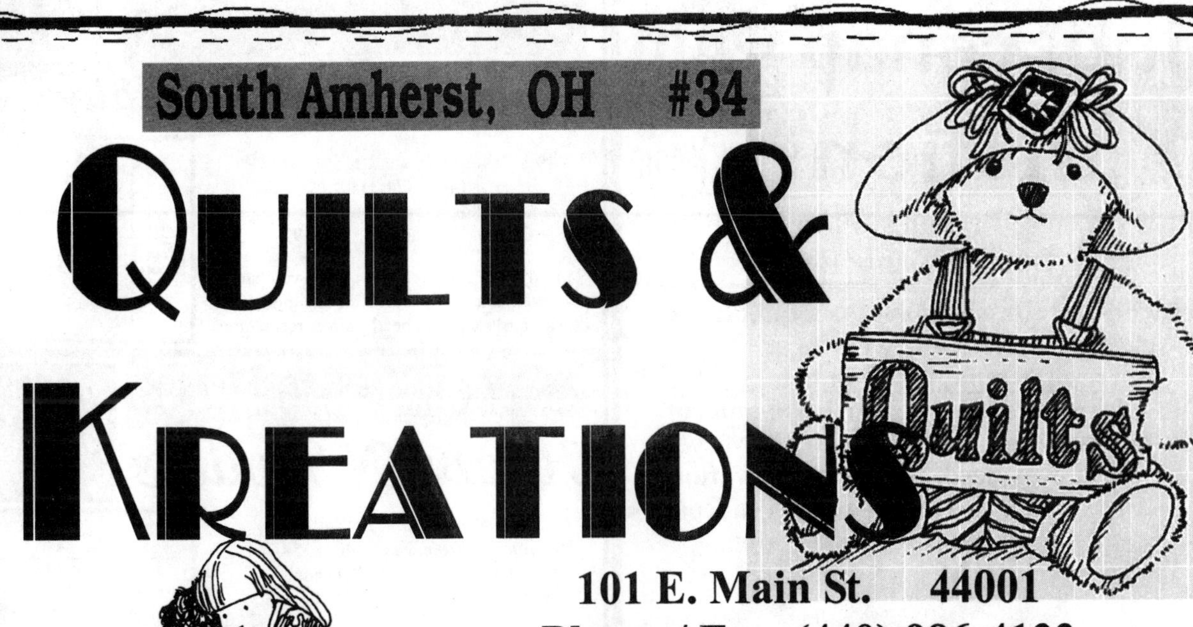

101 E. Main St. 44001
Phone / Fax (440) 986-4132
quiltskreations@centurytel.net
www.quiltskreations.com
Owner: Sandra Whitaker

QUILTS & KREATIONS was established in 1980 and we have grown in size throughout the years. We offer you over 3600 sq.ft. of shopping area in our 100+ year old building. There are over 6000 bolts of designer fabric to choose from and one thousand of these bolts are flannels. We stock the area's largest selection of 100% cotton fabrics, patterns, and books. We are Lorain County's only authorized Bernina Dealer and Lorain County's most complete quilt shop.

I-90 (Rt. 2)
Exit 7A
Ohio Turnpike
Rt. 58
Exit 8
Baumhart Rd.
Lake
Jamies Flea Mkt.
St. Rt. 113
Rt. 57
101
Quilts & Kreations
I-480 (Rt. 10/20)

Easily accessible from either the Ohio Turnpike or Interstate Route 90. We are 1.6 miles west of State Route 58 on State Route 113 in South Amherst, Ohio. We are on the southeast corner of the street at the light.

BERNINA®

Mon - Sat 10 - 5
Thur til 7
Sun 12 - 4

Gingersnap Junction Quilt Shop & Tea Room

Shop for Fabrics, Antiques, Florals, Home Décor, Boyd & Gantz Bears

Classes, Classes, Classes...Call for a quilt class schedule, or visit our website at www.gingersnapjunction.net
We offer a large selection of over 1,000 bolts of fabric, patterns and quilt books, with every accessory you'll ever need. Call for reservations and enjoy a cup of tea and lunch at GJ Tea Room

Milan, OH #35

All this is presented in a beautiful old building that was built in 1835, formerly called the Lockwood Smith Building. While you are shopping, enjoy lunch at our Tea Room, featuring tea from Daily soups, salads, quiche, desserts plus scones are the choice each day.
Lunch 11 AM - 2:30 pm

Owners: Mary & Lyn Dircks
Est: 2001 Catalog $12.95
6,000 sq.ft.

Rt. 113
Gingersnap Junction
on the Square
Rt. 250
Main St.
Rt. 113

One Main Street on the Square, Milan, OH 44846
(419) 499-9411

Stop in Tues thru Sat 9 AM - 5 PM

Oberlin, OH #36

Tues - Sat 10 - 6

ginko gallery & studio

19 S. Main St. (State Rte. 58) 44074
(440) 774-3117
ginkogallery@oberlin.net
Owner: Liz Burgess Est: 1997

Hand-dyed fabrics, original quilts, wall hangings, wearables. Fiber art studio within one block of art museum, bead shop & restaurants.

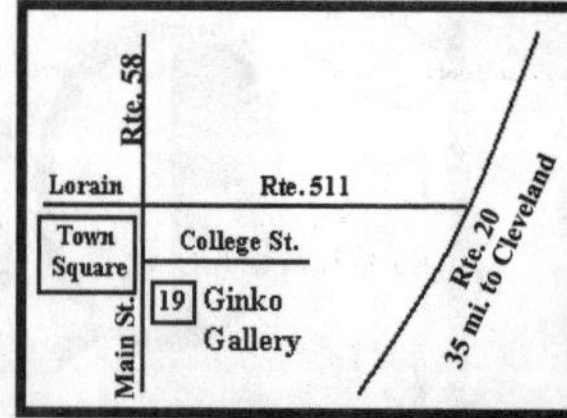

North Olmsted, OH #37

Mon, Tues, Wed 10 - 6
Thur & Fri 10 - 9
Sat 10-6 Sun 1-5

Hoops N Hollers

24888 Lorain Rd. 44070
(440) 779-4700 Fax: (440) 835-0761
www.Hoops-n-Hollers.com
Est: 1981 2500 sq.ft. 1500+ Bolts

Located in a house 1/4 mile east of Great Northern Mall. Lots of fabric, patterns, kits and thread. Largest selection of quilt books around.

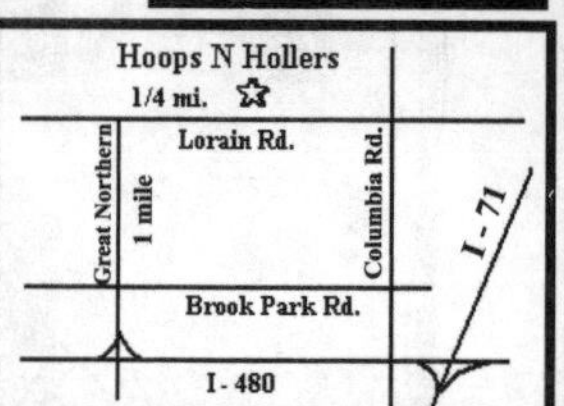

For Fabric Lovers, By Fabric Lovers

Olmsted Falls, OH #38

ABIGAYLE'S QUILTERY and YARN

8096 Columbia Rd. 44138 (440) 235-7446
shop@abigayles.com www.abigayles.com
Owners: Beverly Morris & Nancy Bryant
Est: 1999 3000+ Bolts

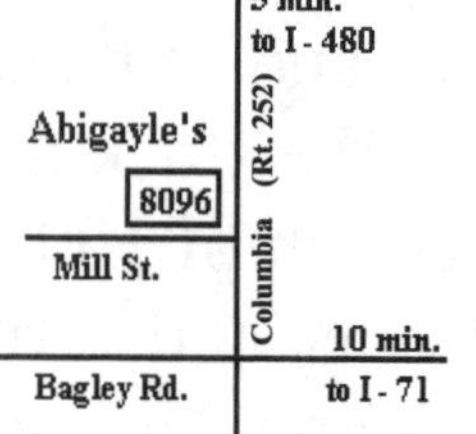

Mon - Sat 10 - 5
Thur til 8 Sun 12 - 5

Located in Grand Pacific Junction in Historic Olmsted Falls, Ohio, Abigayle's Quiltery occupies the Simmerer Homestead; a large, charming Victorian home. Step back in time & allow yourself to stroll along the brick walkways & visit the surrounding shops.

At Abigayle's we take pride in our great selection of ever-changing samples, huge class schedule, many fun and interesting clubs, both here at the shop and by mail. We host several quilt shows, feature almost constant trunk shows. Yarn, books, patterns, Pfaff sewing machines and the newest, most wonderful 100% cotton fabrics around.

Mansfield, OH #39

Mon - Thur 10 - 5:30
Fri & Sat 10 - 4

Quilt Connection

415 Park Ave. W 44906
(419) 522-2330 Est: 1980
E-Mail: quiltwthus@aol.com
Web Site: www.quiltconnectionoh.com
Owner: Janet Williams 1200 sq.ft.

Visit us for quality products & personal, friendly service!
Fabrics, Quilt & Sewing Supplies, Bernina Sewing Machines. Classes.

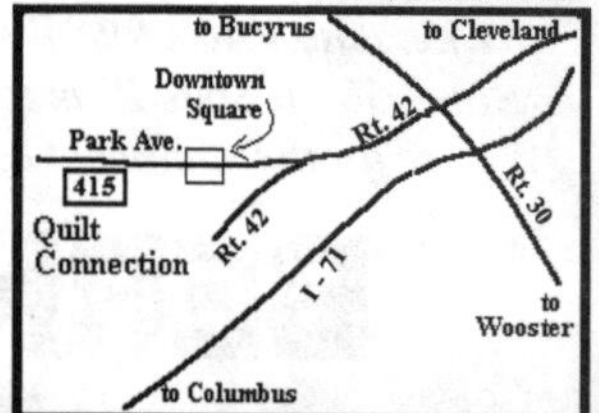

Lexington, OH #40

Tues - Fri 10 - 6
Thurs til 9
2nd Sat 10 - 4

Thistle Bee Quilt and Fiber Arts

46 W. Church St. 44904
(419) 884-0753
Est: 2003 1500 sq. ft.
100% cotton Fabrics, Notions, Books, Patterns, Classes and Fiber threads.
Rughooking and wools. High quality fabrics at great prices. Hand-dyed cottons and wools.

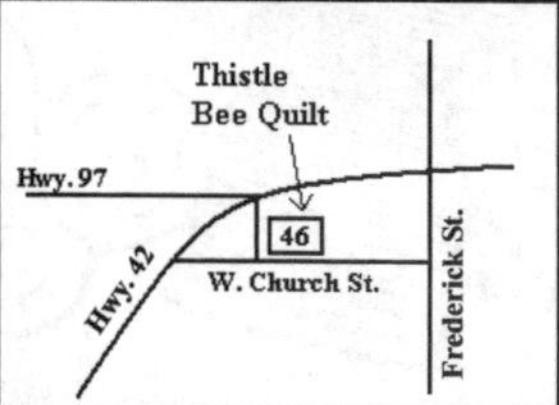

THE VILLAGE QUILTERY

FABRIC NOTIONS PATTERNS CLASSES

36966 DETROIT RD.
AVON, OH 44011
(440) 934-1764

HOURS: MON - SAT
10:00 - 5:00
THURSDAY til 8

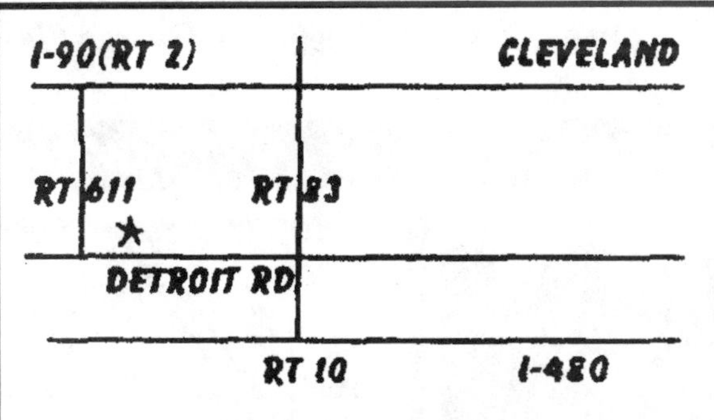

A FULL SERVICE QUILT SHOP LOCATED IN THE FRENCH CREEK DISTRICT OF AVON.
FEATURING MODA, RJR, THIMBLEBERRIES & JINNY BEYER FABRICS.

OWNER: CAROLYN KOBASHER
quilty@kellnet.com
Est: 2002 1600 sq.ft.

Avon, OH #41

Come visit our newly renovated church with 4500 square feet of the best in fabric, wool, patterns, books, notions, & more!
Friendly knowledgeable staff.
Rug Hooking supplies, hand-dyed wool, and classes.
Classes and workshops for the beginner thru the advanced.
Member of the **Northern Ohio Quilt Shop Hop**
last week of September-Call for details
Free newsletter by mail or E-mail

Fine Yarn Department

Beautiful yarns from Berroco, Plymouth, Ironstone, Brown Sheep, Trendsetter, Mountain Colors, and more!
Needles from Skacel, Brittany, Clover, and others. Great books, patterns, and kits, too!
Knowledgeable staff to help with all your knitting needs.

Medina, OH #42

378 Lafayette Rd.
(330) 764-3333
qbee@nobleknights.com
Owner: Linda McCauley
Est: 1997

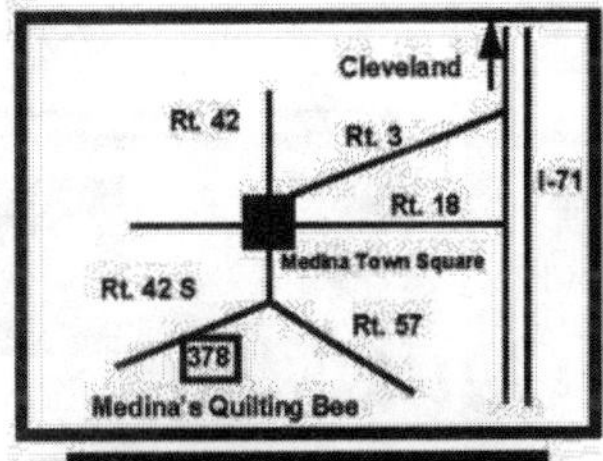

Mon-Sat 10-5
Tues & Thur. 10-7
Sun. 12-4

Located just SW of Historic downtown Medina

Bring this ad and receive 50% off any item. (maximum value $15). *Not good with other discounts*
EXPIRES May 2006

www.medinasquitingbee.com

Ashland, OH #43

Country Charm Fabrics and Sew Crazy

Est: 1975

1422 Township Road 593 44805
Country Charm—(419) 281-2341
Sew Crazy—(419) 281-9422
Owners: Cindy Doggett & George Finley

Husqvarna VIKING

Mon, Tues, Thur, Fri 10 - 5
Sat 10 - 4
Closed Sun & Wed

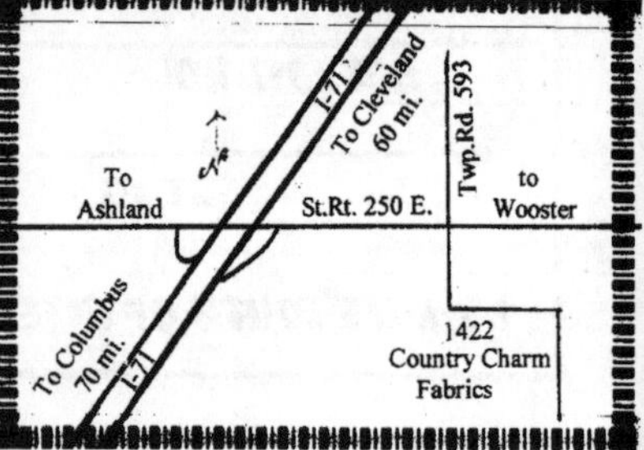

A Complete array of Quilting fabrics from the best mills in America. Notions, Quilt Frames, Classes, and all of the essentials for the Quilting Enthusiast.
Viking Dealer Sewing Machines Repair

Mount Vernon, OH #44

Mon - Sat 10 - 5

Jordan's Quilt Shop

225 S. Main 43050
(740) 393-7463 Fax: Same
penny@jordansquilt.com
www.jordansquilt.com
Est: 1986 2000 sq.ft. 1200+ Bolts

The friendly shop everyone loves. Over 1200 bolts of 100% cotton fabric, books, patterns, classes, quilts. Bernina Sewing Machines.

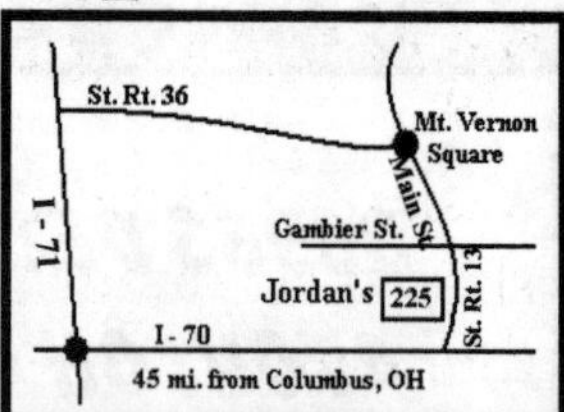

Mt. Vernon, OH #45

444 Columbus Rd. Suite E
Mt. Vernon, OH 43050
(877) 397-9450
Fax: (740) 397-9450
ppqs@ezlinknet.com
www.ppqs.com
Est: Sept. 2002
1100 sq.ft. 1000+ bolts

Tues - Fri 10 - 5
Sat 9 - 3

Come into our relaxing and friendly family run quilt shop in the heart of beautiful Knox County. We have a specially chosen selection of current and unique 100% cotton quilting fabrics, books, patterns and notions with our customers in mind. We especially enjoy hand dyes. We carry Debra Lunn, Starr Designs, Alaskan Dye Works and several local dye artists. We are also expanding our Bali section with Hoffman and other unique companies. Our services include quality quilting as well as custom made quilts and quilt racks. We offer many quilting classes and love children quilters. We are handicap accessible. We have great front door parking and a large bright shop and classroom. There is a wonderful cookie shop next door and specialty and Amish shopping nearby. We enjoy sharing ideas and helping you to create beautiful quilts - the teapot is always on!!

Jean, Carol & Sammy

JANOME
Because You Simply Love To Sew™
At Paw Patch Quilt Shop
Authorized dealer and service center

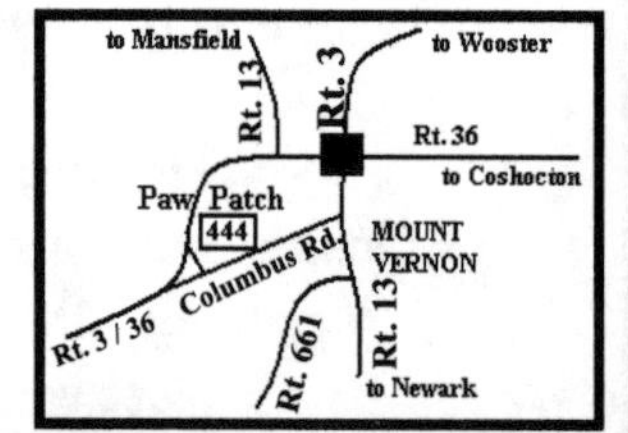

Charm, OH #46

Mon - Sat 8 - 5

Miller's Dry Goods

4500 S.R. 557 Est: 1965
Mail—Millersburg, OH 44654
(330) 893-9899
Owners: The Miller Family
Also—a whole barn full of quilts.

Over 8,000 bolts of fabric, including outlet in basement. Beautiful selection of local handmade Quilts, Wall Hangings, Rugs, Tablerunners, etc. Also Quilt books, patterns, stencils and lots of notions.

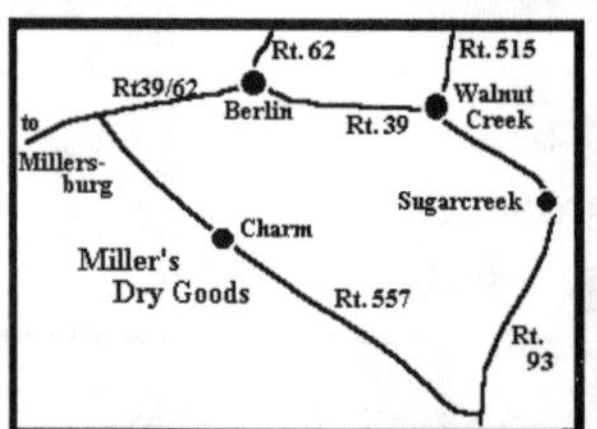

Berlin, OH #47

Mon - Sat 9 - 5

Helping Hands Quilt Shop

4818 St. Rt. 39, Main St., P.O. Box 183
(330) 893-2233 44610
Fax: (330) 893-8004 Est: 1975
www.amishheartland.com

Hundreds of handmade crafts and quilts. All your fabric and quilting supplies. Quilt museum with video and Christmas room. Two buildings.

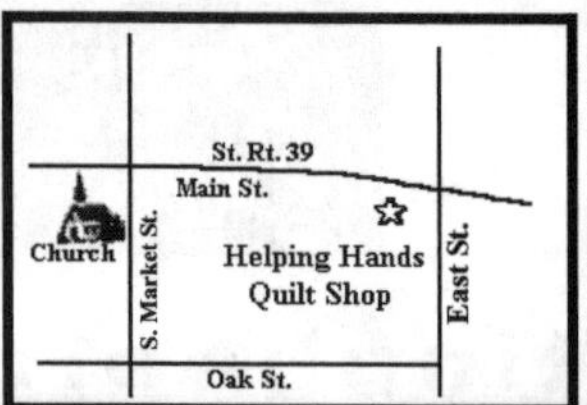

Berlin, OH #48

Mon - Sat 10 - 5

Country Craft Cupboard

P.O. Box 419, 4813 E. Main St.
(330) 893-3163 44610
Owner: Karen Lamp
Est: 1984 3500 sq.ft. 1000 Bolts

1000+ bolts of specialty fabrics, including 100% wool. Supplies for rug hooking, scrapbooking, rubber stamping, painting & more! Wonderful yarns! Hundreds of patterns & models.
In an old country Store!

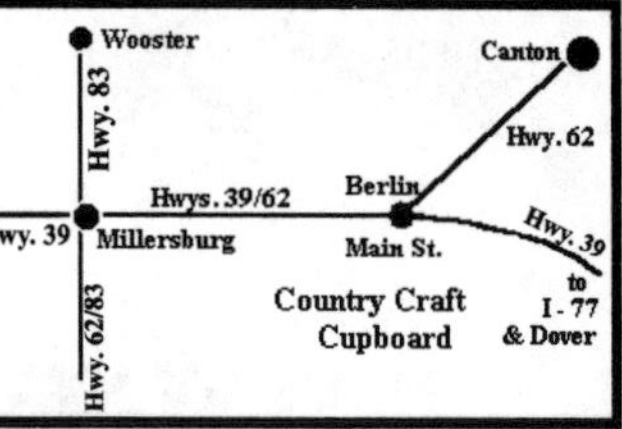

Gramma Fannie's Quilt Barn

Mon - Fri 10 - 5 Sat 10 - 6

Visit our unique shop specializing in:

- our own line of patterns & kits
- custom order quilts
- top of the line quilt fabrics
- books
- stencils.

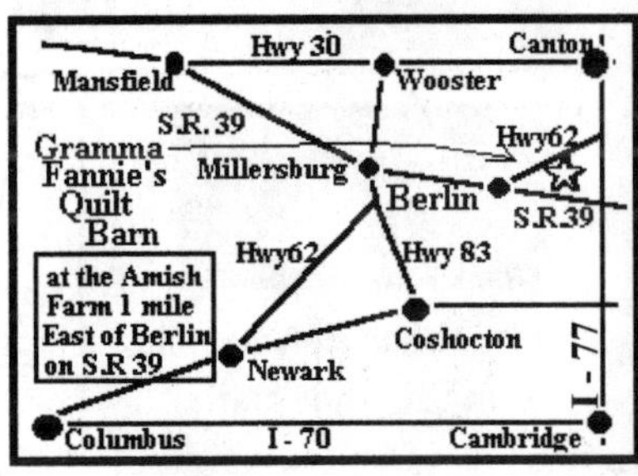

Located at Schrock's Amish Farm and Home
4363 State Route 39
P.O. Box 270
44610
(330) 893-3232
Call about our Annual Quilt Show
Est: 1991
1 mile east of Berlin

www.amish-r-us.com

Berlin, OH #49

Stone Creek, OH #50

Mon - Fri 10 - 5 Sat 10 - 4

Shirley's Quilt - Fabric Shop

4681 Stonecreek Rd. SW 43840
(330) 339-2286 Fax: (330) 308-8089
moose@tusco.net
Owner: Shirley Muhs
Est: 2003 2000 sq.ft. 1500+ Bolts

100% quality cottons & flannels, notions, books, classes. Country setting 1 1/2 miles from exit. Coffee's always on ! Also scrapbooking supplies.

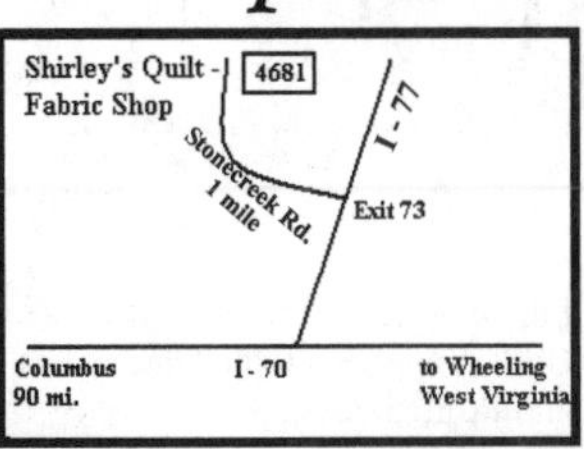

Seams Sew Simple

Enjoy your visit in this 1881 Antique Barn where you'll find a quilter's delight in the hayloft.

You'll be visually inspired as you view locally made quilts hanging from the peg fitted beams along with 1000 bolts of fabric, many books, kits, patterns, stencils and notions. Also here are many quality antiques, scrapbooking supplies and a coffee shop.

"Enter a stranger, leave a friend."

Air Conditioned • MC/Visa accepted • WE SHIP

Wilmot, OH #51

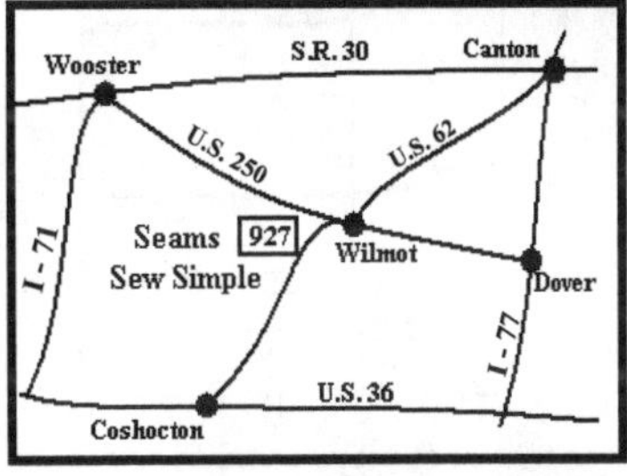

Bus Tours -- Please call ahead for special customer service and a gift. Personalized quilt tours and retreats Large or small groups.

927 U.S. 62, Wilmot, OH 44689
Ph/Fax: (330) 359-0581
seamssewsimple@wilkshire.net
Hours: Mon - Sat 9-5

Sugarcreek, OH #52

Mon - Sat 8 - 5 Fri til 8

Spector's Store

122 E. Main 44681
(330) 852-2113

Full line of Fabric and Notions, Quilt and Craft Supplies. Excellent values on Solid and Printed Fabrics.

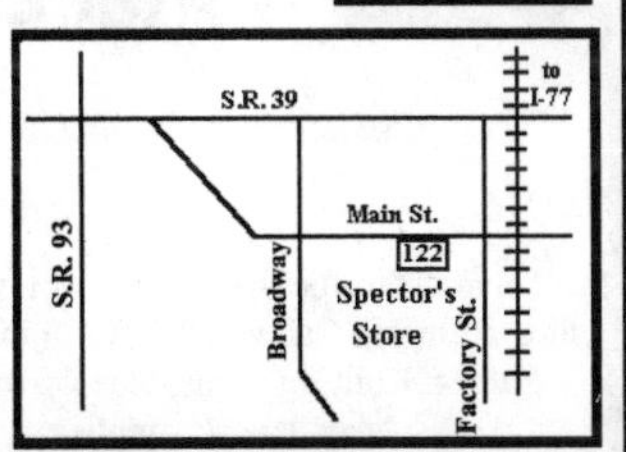

Sugarcreek, OH #53

Mon - Sat 9 - 5

Swiss Village Quilts and Crafts

113 S. Broadway P.O. Box 514 44681
(330) 852-4855
Owners: Aden & Anna Hochstetler
Est: 1982 1250 sq.ft. Free Brochure

Quality, local-made Quilts, Wallhangings and related items. Most items made locally by Amish. Special orders gladly Accepted.

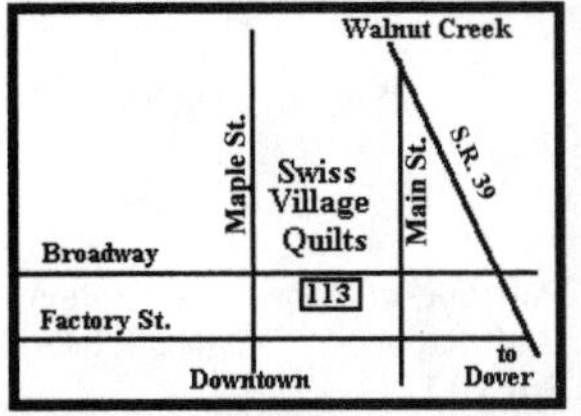

Kidron, OH #54

Mon - Sat 9:30 - 5 closed major holidays

Hearthside Quilt Shoppe

13110 Emerson Rd. Box 222 44636
(330) 857-4004 Est: 1990
hearthsidequilts@aol.com
Owners: Clifford & Lena Lehman
2400 sq.ft. Mgr. Cheryl Gerber

Amish and Swiss Mennonite Quilts, Wall Hangings made in our area. Large selection to choose from. Custom orders welcome! Free Brochure.

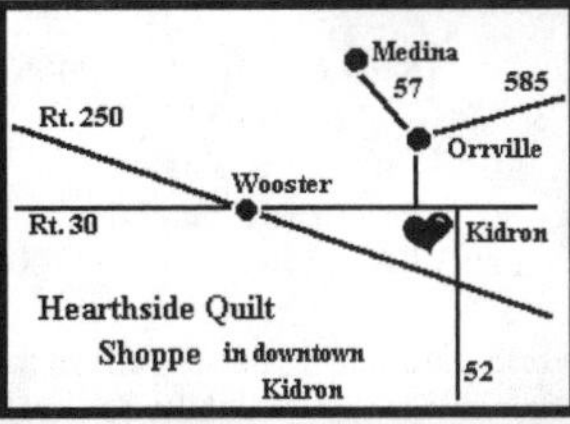

Mount Eaton, OH #55

Mon - Fri 8 - 5
Sat 8 - 3

Spector's Store

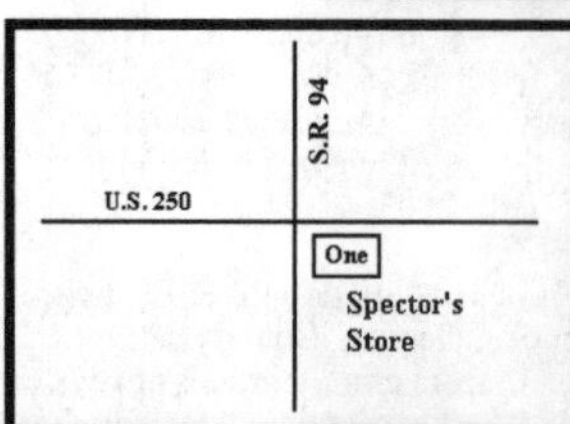

One W. Main St., P.O. Box 275 44659
(330) 359-5467

Full line of Fabric and Notions, Quilt and Craft Supplies. Excellent values on Solid and Printed Fabrics.

Hartville, OH #57

Mon - Sat 9 - 5

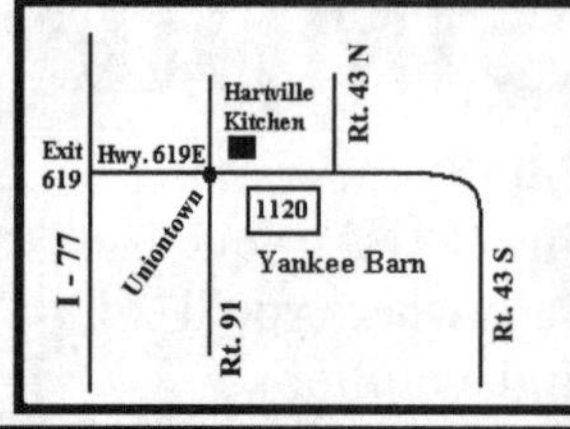

1120 W. Maple St. 44632
(330) 877-6507 Fax: (330) 877-3605
Est: 1983 12,000 sq.ft. 2500 Bolts
Located in 1850's barn in Historic Hartville. 2500+ Bolts of 100% cotton, homespun, flannels and wool. Primitive and traditional accessories.

Quilt Garden

"planting the seeds of quilting"

1664 N. Main St.,
North Canton, OH 44720
(330) 361-0158

North Canton, OH #56

Mon - Fri 10 - 5
Thurs 10 - 7
Sat 10 - 4

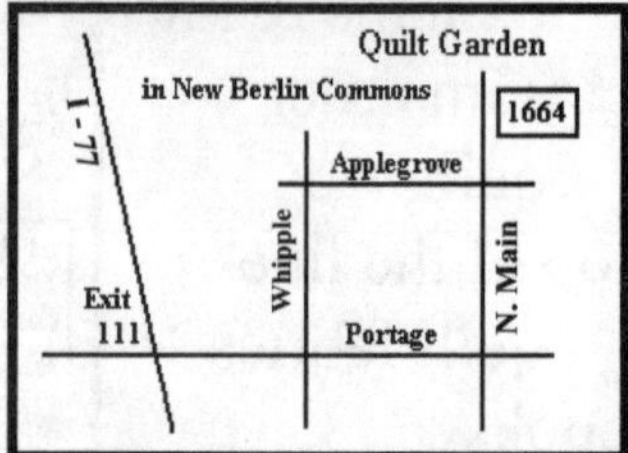

Spacious shop with friendly, knowledgeable staff.

The very latest fabrics from Moda, Hoffman, RJR, Timeless Treasures and more. Books, patterns, kits and notions. Two large classrooms for quilting and sewing classes.

A Piece In Time

Truly wonderful fabrics, Pfaff and Elna sewing machines, incredible selection of Books, Notions, Patterns...Beautiful quilts everywhere. We offer exquisite custom machine quilting, UPS your tops to us. Then our expert quilt artists will call you to discuss your preferences. We ship within the continental US. Call ahead to schedule a bus tour!

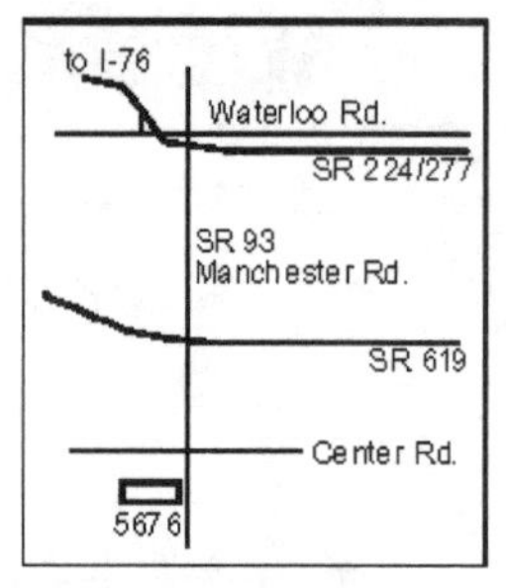

5676 Manchester Road
Akron, Ohio 44319
330-882-9626 1-800-SANDY-98
www.apieceintime.com
apieceintime@aol.com

6,000 sq ft playground for quilters!
Owner: Sandy Heminger

Open 7 Days: Mon-Thur 10-6, Fri & Sat 10-5, Sun 12-4

Akron, OH #58

Wadsworth, OH #59

Mon - Fri 10 - 6
Sat 10 - 3

The Fabric Peddler

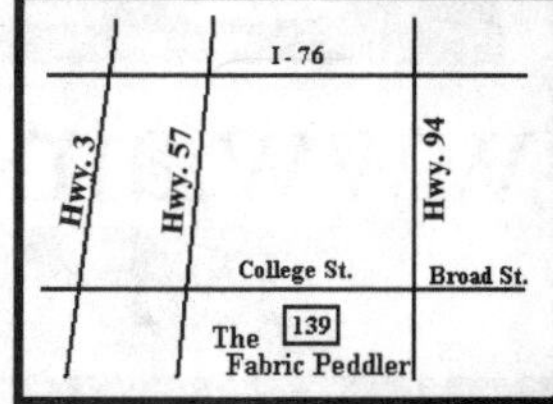

139 College St. 44281
(330) 336-1101
blanmo2001@yahoo.com
Owner: Barb Moore
Est: 1998 2000+ Bolts
Over 2000 bolts of Quality Fabric, Books, Patterns, Quilting Supplies & Cross Stitch. Participant in The Amish Country Quilt Shop Hop.

Cuyahoga Falls, OH #60

Mon - Thur 10 - 9
Fri & Sat 10 - 4

Stitch, Piece 'n Purl

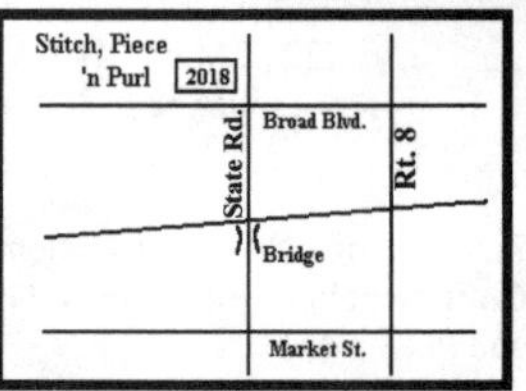

2018 State Rd. 44223
(330) 928-9097

Welcome to Northeastern Ohio's most complete shop featuring Calico, quilting supplies, quilt frames, Knitting yarns, Needlework and Needlework supplies.

Middlefield, OH #61

Mon - Fri 10 - 5
Sat 10 - 4

Iona's Quilt Shop

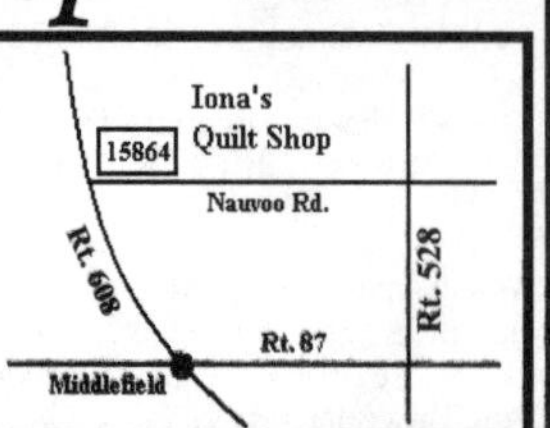

15864 Nauvoo Rd 44062
(440) 632-9410
ionaquilts@simcon.net
Owner: Iona Eden
Est: 1998 1500 sq. ft. 1100 Bolts

Fabrics, Notions, Quilts, Wallhangings, Books, Patterns, Classes, Will take Special Orders.

Middlefield, OH #62

Mon, Tues
Wed 8 - 5
Thur 8 - 6
Fri 8 - 8
Sat 8 - 2

Spector's Store

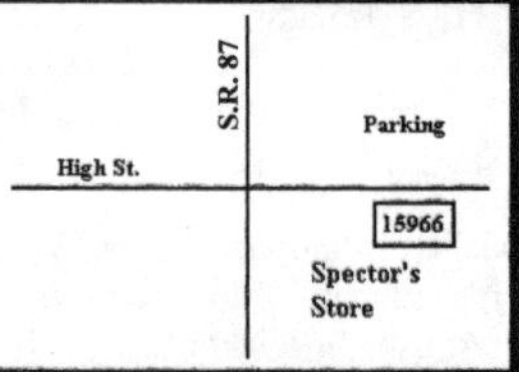

15966 E. High St. 44062
(440) 632-0104

Full line of Fabric and Notions, Quilt and Craft Supplies. Excellent values on Solid and Printed Fabrics.

Aurora, OH #65

Mon - Sat 9:30 - 5 Wed til 7

The Gathering Room

324 Aurora Commons Circle 44202
(330) 995-0838

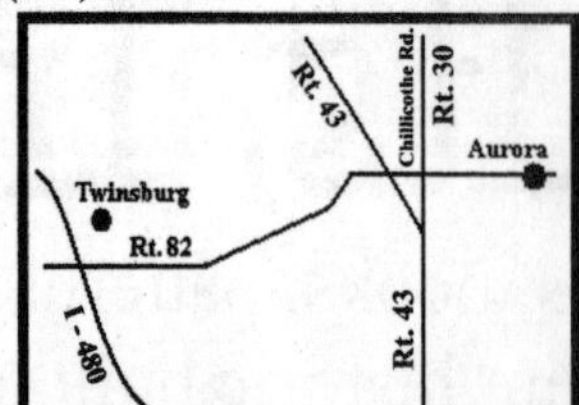

gatheringroom@adelphia.net
Owner: Nancy Bowen Fax: (330) 995-0839
100% cotton primitive & reproduction fabrics, wool, rug hooking supplies and redwork embroidery. Home of Nana's Needlework redwork embroidery patterns.

North Kingsville, OH #66

Mon - Fri 10 - 6
Sat 10 - 4:30

Quilt Depot

2736 E. Center 44068
(440) 224-3255
Owner: Leanna Rodabaugh 2000 Bolts

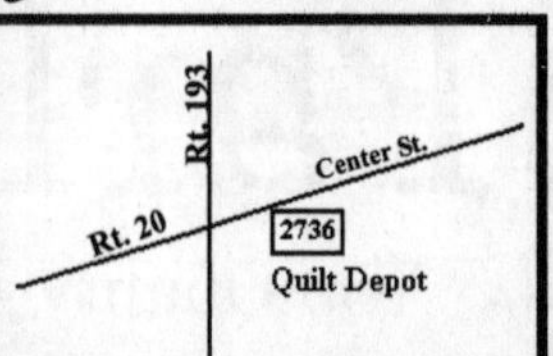

100% Cottons Books, Patterns, Notions, & Classes

Remembrances

12570 Chillicothe Rd. 44026
(440) 729-1650
Owner: Cheryl Pedersen
Est: 1984 1200 sq.ft.
Visit our Web Site At:
www.shopremembrances.com

Chesterland, OH #67

Cotton Fabrics, Notions, Books.
Classes: quilting & dollmaking.
We specialize in Redwork and Reproduction Fabrics.

Celebrating 20 Years

Mon - Sat 10 - 5

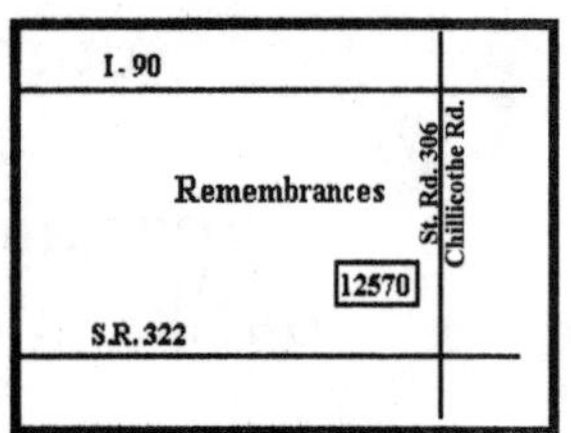

Named one of the top ten Quilt Shops by American Patchwork & Quilting Quilt Sampler for 2002

Cortland, OH #68

Tues - Fri 10 - 4:30
Sat 10 - 4

Olde Liberty Dry Goods

136 S. Bank St. 44410
(330) 638-1733
abkerner@aol.com
Owner: Betty Kerner Est: 1999

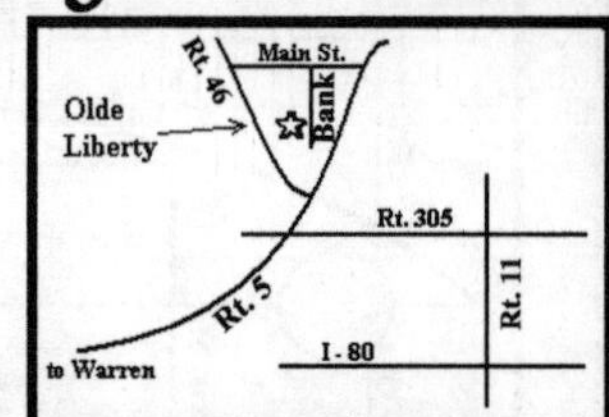

100% cotton fabrics - brushed homespuns, flannels, wool (100%) Rug hooking - Penny Rugs - Books - Patterns - many of our own designs.

Cortland, OH #69

Designers Two

284 W. Main St. 44410
Phone & Fax 330-638-3737
1-800-732-8932
Owner: Peg Viole Est: 1989

Mon - Fri 10 - 5
Sat 10 - 2

Quilting cottons to die for. The best quality, fabulous colors & prints. Lots of novelties too, even cozy flannels. Heirloom supplies, unusual notions & gadgets, fun patterns, & more! Our shop is stuffed to the brim & well worth the trip!

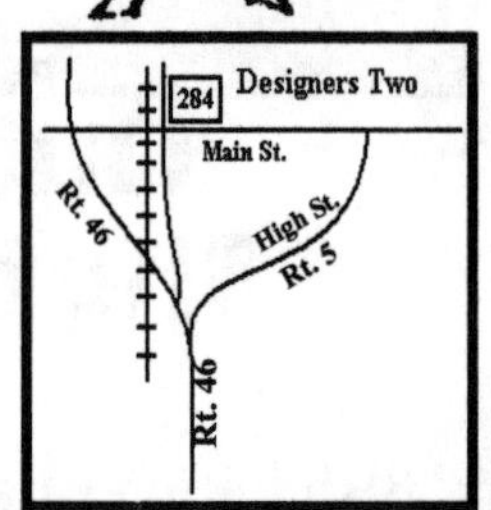

Warren, OH #70

Mon & Thurs 10 - 8
Tues, Wed, Fri 10 - 5
Sat 10 - 3

A Quilting Asylum

179 Folsom NW 44483
(330) 847-6711
qasylum@netdotcom.com
1000+ Bolts

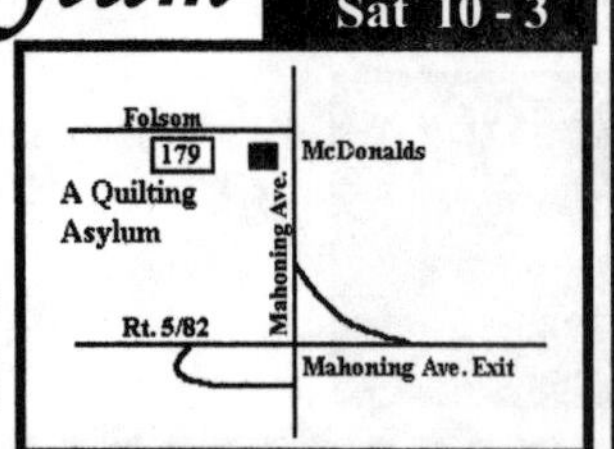

Pfaff Sewing Machines, machine quilting service, major lines of fabrics, notions, books, patterns, quilt frames, plus antiques & gift shop.

Lordstown, OH #71

Tues - Fri 10 - 6
Sat 10 - 3

Fabric Patch

8398 Tod SW (Rt. 45) 44481
(330) 824-3611
thefabricpatch@aol.com
Owner: Dorinda Clay
Est: 2000 1200 sq.ft. 1000+ Bolts

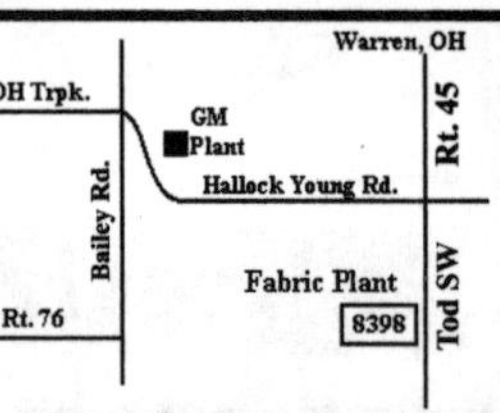

Offering fabric, books, notions, and quilt classes. Located near GM Lordstown plant, just off Ohio turnpike and Rt. 76

#72

Patches, Pretties, 'n Lace

☆ *Patches, Pretties, 'n Lace*
4550 Nelson Mosier Road
(Braceville Twp.)
Southington, OH 44470

Hours:
Wednesday thru Saturday 10 - 4
Other times by appointment
Closed Sunday, Monday & Tuesday

Phone: 330-898-2833
Fax: 330-898-2843
E-mail: **ppnl@earthlink.net**

Fabric · Classes · Quilting Supplies
Elna Sewing Systems · 2800+ Bolts of Fabrics
Shop Lit by Ott Lighting

Quilter's Quarters

8458 Market Street 44512
(330) 758-7072
Owner: Julie Maruskin
Est: 1989 900 sq.ft. 900+ Bolts

We carry quilting supplies, fabrics, tools, books and patterns.

Youngstown, OH #73

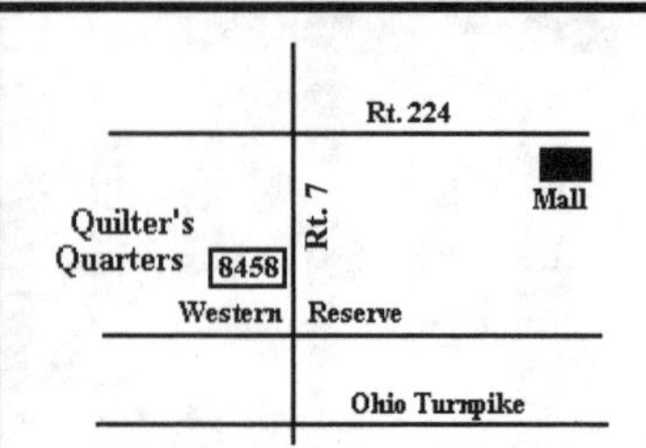

Mon - Fri 11 - 5
Sat 11 - 4
Closed Tues & Sun

Cambridge, OH #74

Mon - Sat 10 - 6

1996 E. Wheeling Ave. 43725
(740) 435-9590

Full line of top quality quilting fabrics from RJR, Mumm, Thimbleberries, Benartex, Hoffman to mention a few. Notions & Books Galore. Also available needlepoint, rubber stamping and scrapbook supplies.

Fax: (740) 432-7340
E-Mail:stitchinpost@jadeinc.com
Owners: Hallie Ray & Linda Britten
Est: 1999 2800 sq.ft.

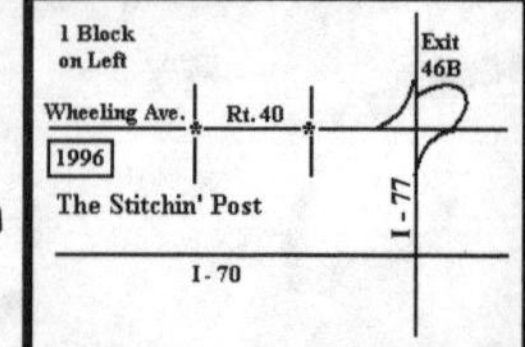

Cumberland, OH #75

Tues - Fri 11 - 5
Sat 11 - 4

Cumberland Quilt Shop

424 Main St., P.O. Box 73 43732
(740) 638-2626 Fax: (740) 962-4276
E-mail: quiltshop@msn.com
www.cumberlandquiltshop.com
Owners: Rita & Phil Lawrence

Top quality 100% cotton quilt Fabric, Books, Patterns, Notions & Classes. Custom Machine Quilting. Located in the historic Cumberland Bank Building. Est: 1996

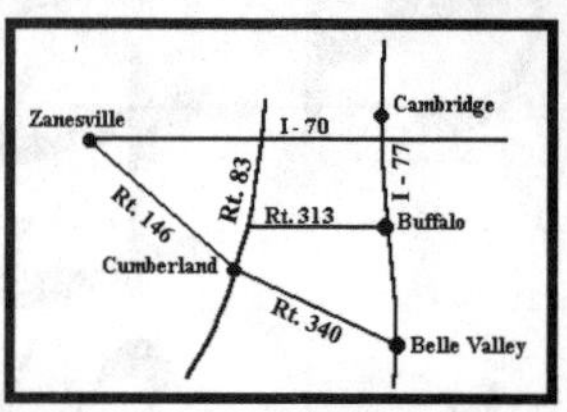

Woodsfield, OH #76

Tues - Fri 10 - 6
Sat 10 - 3

45325 State Route 78
43793
(740) 472-1714 or
(866) 472-1714
Owner: Lida Conn
Est: 2003
350 sq.ft. 150 Bolts

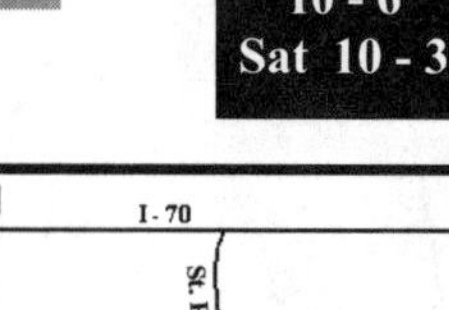

Full service independent quilt shop with designer fabric, rag dolls, crochet rugs, rag bags, finished quilts, wooden quilt racks, many gift items & gift certificates.

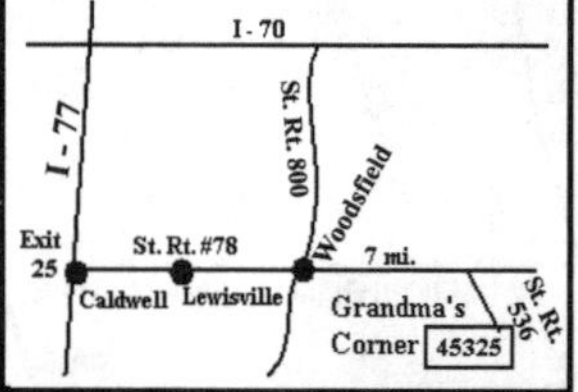

McConnelsville, OH #77

Mon - Sat 9 - 5

32 E. Main St. 43756
(740) 962-6206
Web Site: www.sewnsewohio.com
Est: 1988

Authorized Pfaff Dealer, Quilt Fabrics & Supplies

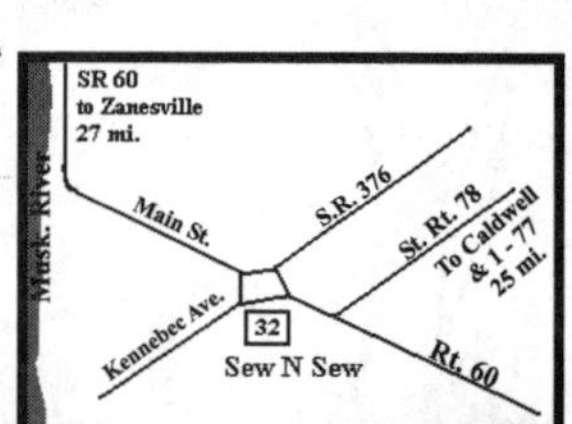

Marietta, OH #78

Mon - Sat 9 - 5
Fri til 6

Townsquare Fabrics & Quilt Shop

Second & Butler Streets 45750
(877) 373-6150 (toll free)
staff@townsquarefabrics.com
Owner: Effie Townsend Est: 1985

Cotton Fabric * Stencils * Quilting Supplies Batting * Patterns * Books * New Larger Showroom * Authorized Bernina® Dealer

Pomeroy, OH #79

Mon - Sat 9 - 5

The Fabric Shop

110 W. Main St. 45769
(740) 992-2284 Fax: (740) 992-4189
becky@thefabricshop.net
www.thefabricshop.net
Owner: Becky Anderson Est: 1959

We specialize in QUILT FABRIC, NOTIONS AND MACHINE QUILTING. Biggest quilt shop in the area. Stop by, it will be worth your trip.

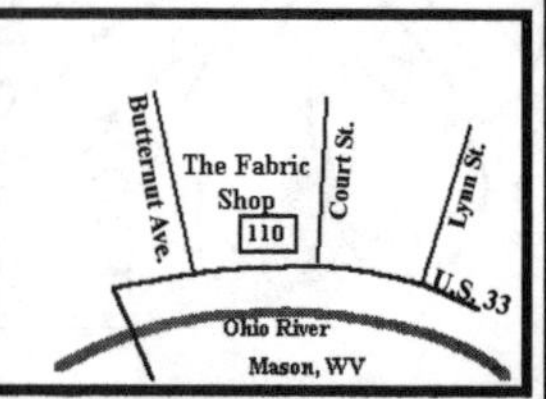

Other Shops in Ohio: *We suggest calling first*

Albany	Quilting Tree, 5264 W Clinton St	740-698-8733
Archbold	Sauder's Farm & Craft Village, 22611 State Rt. 2	419-446-2541
Athens	Dairy Barn Arts Center, 8000 Dairy Ln.	740-592-4981
Athens	Quilt Shop, 9629 Oxley Rd.	740-592-3874
Berlin	Zinck's in Berlin, 115 E. Main St., P.O. Box 153	330-893-2071
Boardman	Gay Lee's Deisgner Fabrics, 7081 West Blvd.	330-726-9396
Canfield	Heart of Dresden, P.O. Box 737	330-533-9443
Centerville	Stitching Post, 101 E. Alex Bell Rd. #176	937-436-9200
Chillecothe	The Cross Patch, 14 W. Water St.	614-774-4104
Cincinnati	St. Theresa Textile Trove, 1329 Main St.	513-333-0399
Cincinnati	Banasch's Faabrics, 2810 Highland Ave	513-731-2040
Cleveland	Quilter's Source, 6683 State Rd	440-843-2458
Columbiana	Heart of the Country, 14895 South Ave. #14	330-482-5001
Columbus	Plantation Quilts, 2363 Somersworth Dr.	614-252-5552
Dayton	Quilting Books & Patterns, 10670 Willow Brook Rd.	937-885-6189
Delta	Tender Loving Care, 219 Main St., PO Box 164	419-822-5861
Dresden	Quilt Bee, 1363 Chestnut St.	740-754-2261
Dresden	American Harvest Dry Goods, 617 Main St.	740-754-3622
Gallipolis	Maynard's Quilt Fabric & Craft, 1192 Jackson Pike	740-441-9060
Hamilton	The Holly Berry Quilt Shop, 3682 Shank Rd	513-868-0721
Hebron	Heavy Metal Quilting, 140 E. Main St., P.O. Box 53	740-929-3940
Jackson	Guhl's Country Store, 120 #C Twin Oaks Dr.	614-286-5271
Kidron	Cozy Corner Quilt Shop, 4776 Kidron Rd.	330-857-0441
Lebanon	Oh Susannah, 16 S. Broadway	513-932-8246
Lima	Country Side Stitch & Sew, 1207 North McClure Rd.	419-649-1391
Lima	Connie's Buttons, 4646 Bowsher Rd	419-999-6383
Louisville	Empty Spools, 10087 Reeder Ave.	
Loveland	Lady Bug Quilt Shoppe, 1464 Highway 28	513-575-0110
Mansfield	Bev's Fabric Shop, 466 Melody Lane	419-589-3276
Millersburg	Katie's Quilts & Wall Hangings, 7635 St. Rt. 241	
Millersport	Quilter's Retreat, 2595 Canal Dr., Box 667	740-467-2366
Minerva	Calico Grandma's, 616 Valley St.	216-868-6937
Mt. Hope	Lone Star Quilts, 7700 CR 77, Box 32	no phone
Oberlin	Olla Mae's Dry Goods, 5 S Main St	440-776-0309
Piqua	Blackberry Patchworks, 408 N Main St	937-615-0877
Portsmouth	Clara's Sewing Center & Fabric Shop, 2227 6th	614-354-1881
Portsmouth	Seams Like Yesterday, 325 Front St.	740-355-2009
Protorville	D & B Quilt Shop, 6971 St. Rt. 775	740-886-8730
Richfield	Memory Lane Quilting, 4183 W Streetsboro Rd	330-659-4916
Salineville	The Attic, 16060 Spring Valley Rd.	
Sardinia	Pieceful Place Quilt Shop, 3351 State Route 138	937-446-2181
Shiloh	Country Fabrics, 1991 Shatzer Rd.	419-896-3785
Sidney	BJ Fabrics, 1126-B Michigan St.	
Upper Arlington	Fabric Farms, 3590 Riverside Dr.	614-451-9300
Walnut Creek	The Farmer's Wife, 4952 Walnut St.	216-893-3168
Wellington	Village Quiltery, 113 E Herrick Ave	440-647-0209
West Milton	Little Creek Farm Fabrics, 3923 S Rangeline Rd	937-698-3367
Willoughby	Erie Street Quilts, 38025 Second St. #102	440-953-1340
Woodville	Quilt Nest, 400 Woodpointe Dr	419-849-3338
Worthington	Quilted Threads, 871 Troon Trl.	614-847-5857
Zanesfield	Mad River Quilt Company, 4830 Cty. Rd. 10	937-593-7758
Zanesville	The Quilt Cottage, 2316 June Pkwy.	740-453-9690
Zoar	Quilting Creations, PO Box 512	330-874-4741

Ohio Guilds:

Akron	The Cascade Quilters of Akron, 2270 Thurmont Rd., 44313	
Alliance	Sew Happy Carnation Quilters, 11693 Easton St. NE, 44601	
Archbold	Village Quilters	Meets: 1st Monday 7 p.m. at Sauder Village Quilt Shop
Ashland	Old Uniontown Quilt Guild	
Beavercreek	Miami Valley Quilt Guild, P.O. Box 340141, 45434	Meets: 2nd Tuesday 7 p.m. at Fairborn Senior Center, Fairborn
Bellefontaine	Logan Piecemakers	Meets 2nd Monday 7 p.m. at Heartland of Bellefontaine
Berlin	Chestnut Ridge Quilter's Guild, P.O. Box 183, 44610	Meets: 4th Monday @ 7pm at Chestnut Ridge Sewing Shop
Caldwell	Townsquare Quilt Lovers, P.O. Box 207, 43724	
Chillicothe	Ross County Quilt Guild, 632 Anderson Sta. Rd., 45601	
Cincinnati	Ohio Valley Quilters' Guild, P.O. Box 42078, 45242	
Circleville	Goodtime Quilters, 23400 Alkire Rd., 43113	
Columbus	Quintessential Quilters, 2136 Shoreman Rd	Meets: 2nd Thursday @ 7pm at Mountview Baptist Church
Columbus	Columbus Metropolitan Quilters	Meets: 3rd Tuesday 7:30 p.m. at Ohio School for the Deaf Multipurpose Room, 500 Morse Rd.
Conneaut	Conneaut Quilters' Guild, 7194 Pitts Rd., 44030	Meets: 3rd Monday 7 p.m.
Coshocton	Canal Quilters	Meets: 2nd Tuesday 7 p.m. at Grace Methodist Church
Cumberland	Cumberland Quilt Guild, 426 Main St., P.O. Box 73, 43732	Meets: 1st Tuesday 5 p.m. at 426 Main St.
Granville	Heart of Ohio Quilters	Meets: 3rd Tuesday 7 p.m. at St. Edwards Church
Greenville	Towne Squares Quilt ClubChestnut St., 45352	Meets: 3rd Tuesday 7:30 p.m. at Brethern Home--Brick Room
Kent	Portage Patchers Quilt Guild	
Mansfield	Mansfield Millenium Quilters	Meets: 2nd Monday 6:30 p.m. at First Congregational Church
Maumee	The Quilt Foundry Guild, 234 W. Wayne St., 43537	
Medina	Medina Honeybee Quilt Guild	Meets: 3rd Thursday at Medina County Library, 210 S. Broadway
Middlefield	Middlefield Country Quilters, 15864 Nauvoo Rd, 44062	Meets: Every Wednesday @ 6pm at Iona's Quilt Shop
Middletown	Buckeye Blossoms Quilt Guild, 11 McKinley St., 45042	
Oregon	Maumee Bay Country Quilt Guild	
Painesville	Ladies of the Parlour, 216 E. Main St., 44077	Meets: 4th Wednesday @ 7 p.m. at Key Bank Bldg.
Palestine	Towne Squares Quilt Club, Box 2, 45352	
Port Clinton	Ohio Star Quilters, 808 Jefferson St., 43452	
Portsmouth	Down By the River Quilt Guild, 319 Chillicothe St.	Meets: 1st Thursday at Homespun Treasures
Sabina	Clinton County Quilt Association, 2675 Melvin Rd., 45169	
Sylvania	Gathering of Quilters Guild, P.O. Box 631, 43560	
Westlake	North Coast Needlers, P.O. Box 450952, 44145	
Wilmington	Clinton County Quilt Assoc., P.O. Box 68, 45177	Meets: 1st Thursday 7 p.m. at Prairie View Apts, 360 Prairie Ave. (Quilt show at Corn Festival in Wilmington the weekend after Labor Day)

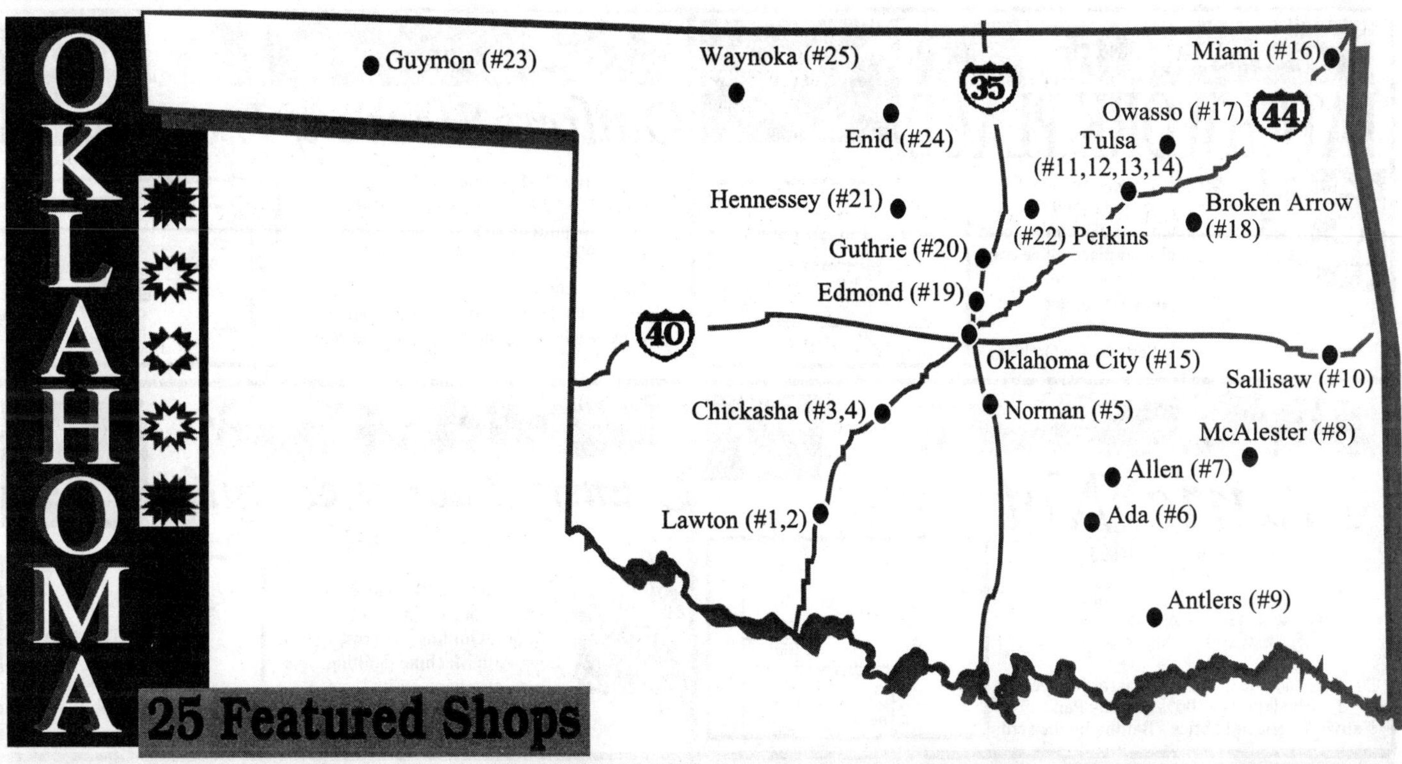

25 Featured Shops

Sharon's Quilt Shoppe

"for the love of quilting and quilters©"

We are your full-service quilt shoppe.
We carry the latest exclusive line of quality quilting fabrics, classes and a full line of quality quilting supplies, notions, books and patterns.
Flannels, Florals, Reproductions, Marbles, Batiks!

Trunk Shows... Stop by ***Sharon's Quilt Shoppe*** to see the many popular trunk shows that we have scheduled.

Mon - Fri 10 - 5:30
Sat 10 - 5

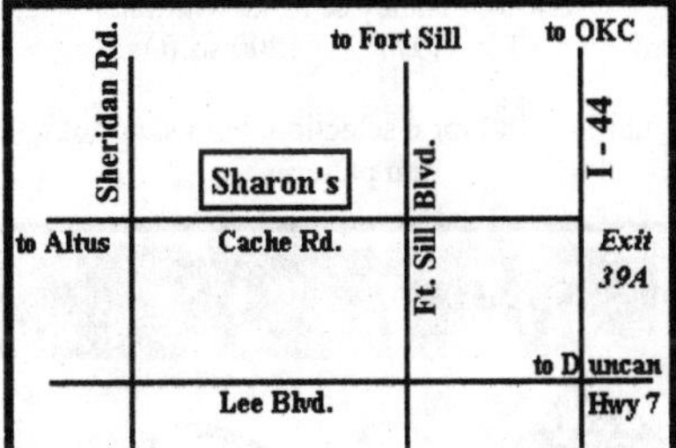

1811 NW Cache Rd.
73507
(580) 357-8458
Est: 1991 3000 sq.ft.
Sharon & Howard Boss And the Duke!
www.sharonsquiltshoppe.com

Lawton, OK #1

Lawton, OK #2

Mon - Fri 10:30 - 5
Tues & Wed til 8
Sun 1 - 5

1010 SW "E" Ave. 73501 (580) 248-9200
Owners: Carola Whicker & Bobbie Sowers

We have 1500 bolts of fabric, quilting and tapestry notions, books, patterns, a large selection of pre-worked needlepoint with coordinating thread and yarns, classes and gifts.

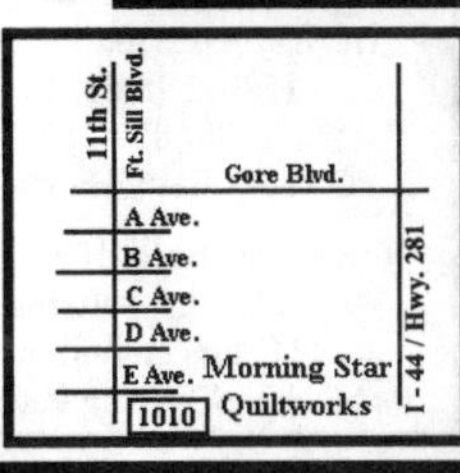

Chickasha, OK #3

Please Call Ahead for Hours

Becky's Stitch in Time

2227 Carolina 73018
(405) 224-0332 Fax: (405) 222-3983
Owner: Noel & Becky Lambert

We carry a full line of 100% cotton fabrics & flannels. Lines include P&B, Benartex, Hoffman & more.

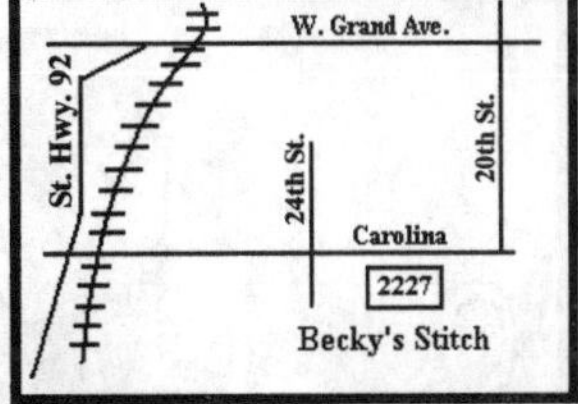

Chickasha, OK #4

Mon - Fri 10 - 5:30
Tues til 9
Sat 10 - 4

STEELMAN & Framing, Gifts & Sew Much More

410 Chickasha Ave. 73018
(405) 224-2036
framedgolf@aol.com

Owner: Wade & Phylis Steelman
Est: 1960 5000 sq.ft.
Step inside historic downtown's most unique building to experience a quilter's heaven. 1200+ bolts of quality 100% cotton fabric from top companies, supplies and notions.

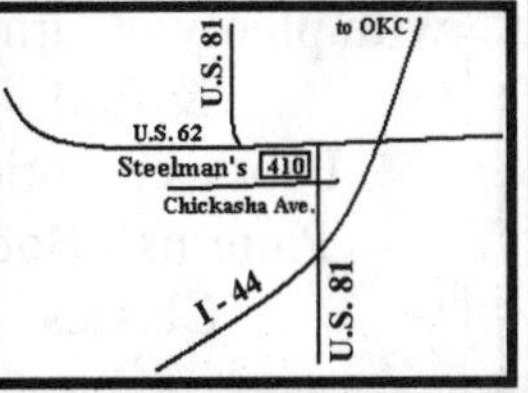

Norman, OK #5

Mon, Tues, Thur, Fri 10 - 6
Wed & Sat 10 - 4

PATCHWORK PLACE

924 24th Ave. SW 73069
(405) 321-4569
store@patchworkplaceonline.com
www.patchworkplaceonline.com
Owners: Anne Gaines &
Nancy Baysinger

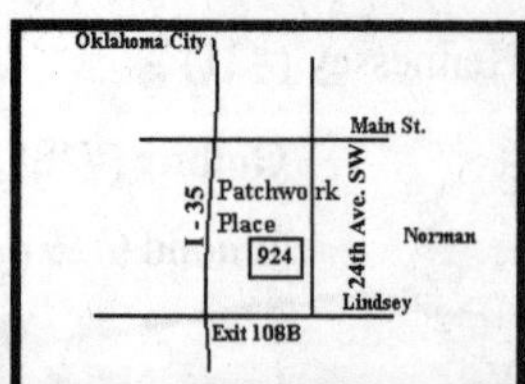

Fabrics - Books - Tools - Patterns for Quilting

Ada, OK #6

Mon - Fri 9:30 - 5
Sat 9:30 - 4

Quilters Heaven, Inc.

107 W. Main St. 74820
(580) 310-0596 Fax: (580) 310-0597
quilter@adacomp.net
Est: 1996 4000 sq.ft. 1000+ Bolts

Large selection of 100% cotton fabrics. Patterns, books, notions and gifts. Janome sewing machines, custom machine quilting. Mail orders welcome.

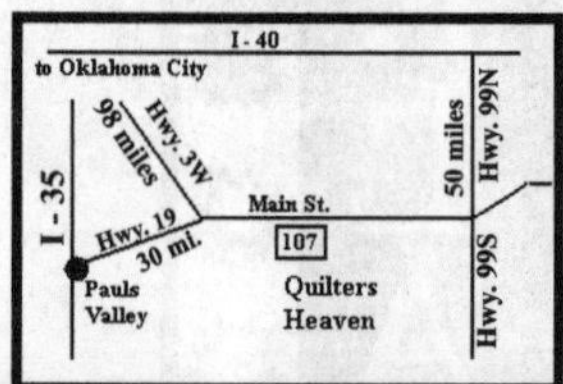

Allen, OK #7

Mon - Sat 8 - 6

Prairie Notions

701 E. Gilmore 74825
(580) 857-2831
Okie_page@hotmail.com
Owners: George & Pamala Price
Est: 2001 900 sq.ft.

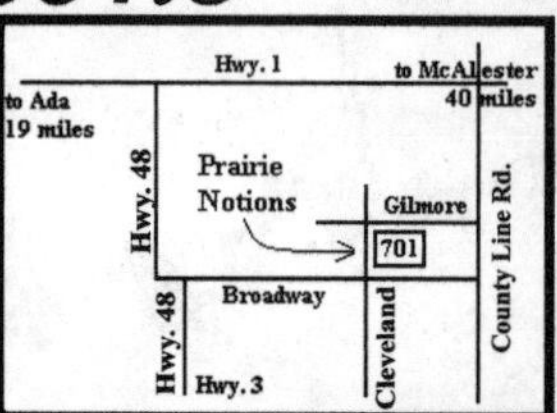

Custom Machine Quilting - Scissor Sharpening
Finished quilts - 100% of Baby Panels
Native American Fabrics - Batting by the yard

McAlester, OK #8

Mon - Sat 9 - 5:30
Wed 1 - 5:30

Country Fabrics & Quilts

5400 S. Hwy. 69 74501
(918) 423-0933
Owner: Louise Hoffman
1000+ Bolts of Quality Fabrics, Notions, Quilting Patterns, Books, Long Arm Machine Quilting. We also have quilt classes.
On Hwy. 69 3 mi. S of Wal-Mart or 1/2 mi. N of Turnpike.

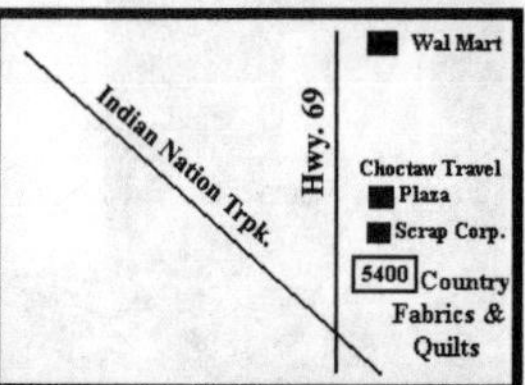

Antlers, OK #9

Mon - Fri 9 - 6
Sat 9 - 4
Evenings by Appt.

Betsy's Quilts

HC 83, Box 870, P.O. Box 947 74523
(580) 298-5821 Fax: Same
(888) 817-5821 Est: 1994
Owner: Betty Hairfield 3600 sq.ft.

Over 1000 Bolts of Name Brand Fabrics.
Books, Patterns, Notions.
Quilts & Quillows for Sale.
Machine Quilting Pattern or Outlined.

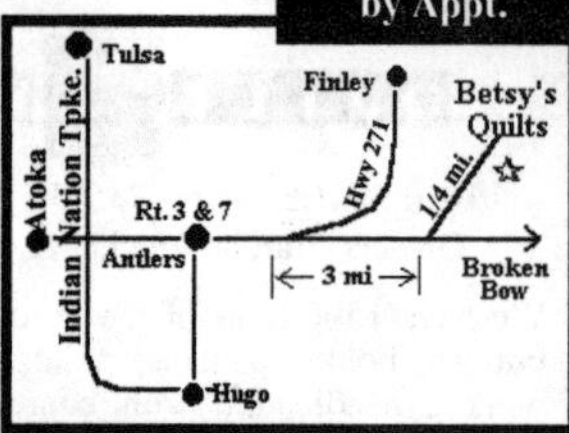

Sallisaw, OK #10

Tues - Fri 10 - 5
Sat 10 - 3

That Quilting Place

1018 W. Cherokee Ave. 74955
(918) 776-0787
Owner: Anne Bottorff

100% Cotton Fabrics, Notions, Books, Patterns, Classes, Long-arm Machine Quilting.
Look for Quilt Blocks on the Front of our Building.

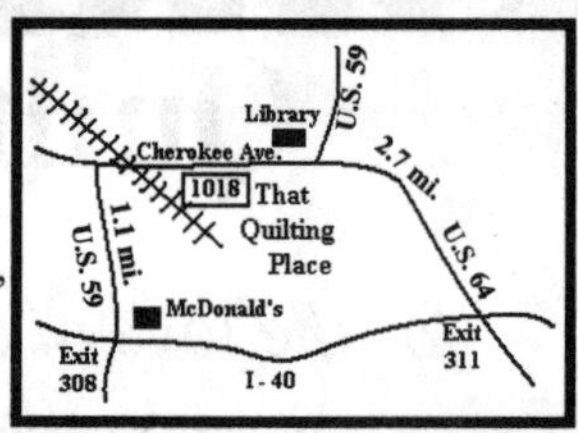

Tulsa, OK #11

Just Quilt It!, Inc.

8142 S. Harvard Ave. 74137
(918) 477-7747
info@justquiltit.com
www.justquiltit.com
Owners: Scott & Le Ann Weaver
Est: 2003 2100 sq.ft. 1500 Bolts

Tues - Thur 9:30 - 5:30
Fri & Sat 9:30 - 5 Sun 12 - 5

A full service shop
with plenty of atmosphere
& fun!
Fabrics - Notions
Patterns - Books
Classes

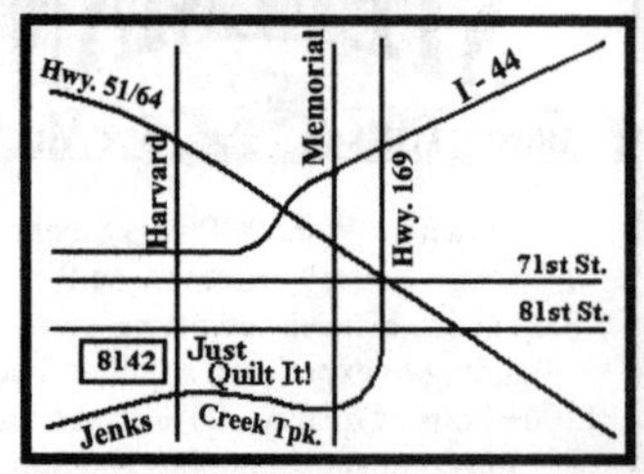

Tulsa, OK #12

Mon - Fri 10 - 5:30
Tues til 7
Sat 10 - 5

Cotton Patch

8250 East 71st St. 74133
(918) 252-1995 Fax: (981) 294-9542
www.ecottonpatch.com
Owner: Nancy & Mike Mullman
Est: 1977 1200 sq.ft.

Large quilt fabric selection, books, notions, and patterns.

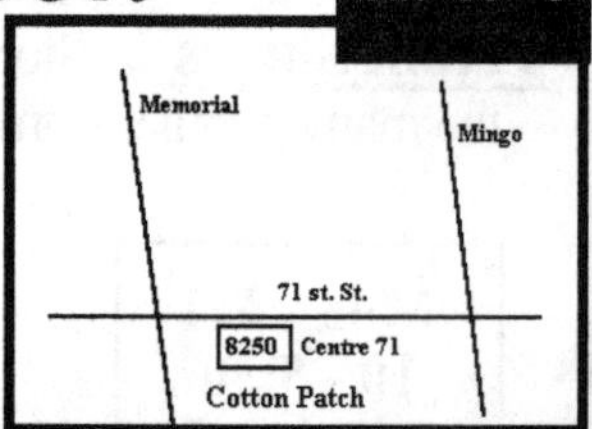

Tulsa, OK #13

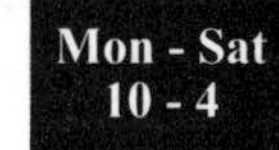

Nora's Quilts, Etc.

8130-B S. Lewis 74137-1207
Located at the Plaza
(918) 298-0271
Owner: Nora N. Cope
Est: 2001 1350 sq.ft.

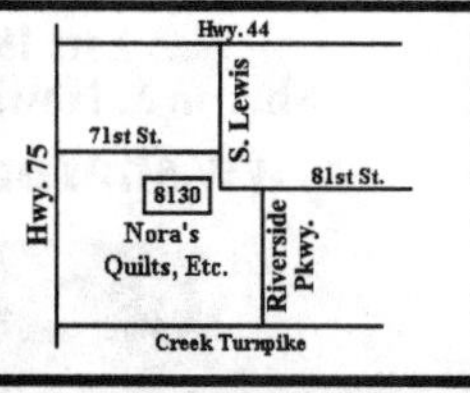

A complete Quilt Shop - Heirloom Quilts, Fabric - Classes - Notions & Books-Patterns-Rug Hooking

MATERIAL GIRLS

#14

A QUILTERS' EMPORIUM

4734 S. Peoria Avenue
Tulsa, OK 74105
(918 7[illegible]7-7525
Ellen Sonnenschein
& Kelly Spann

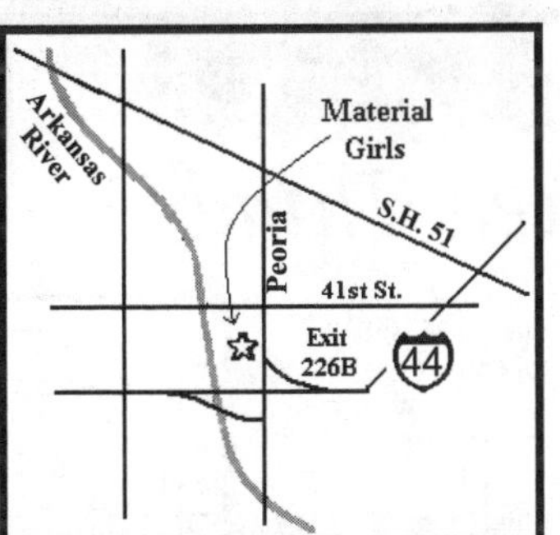

Tulsa's Largest Quilting Store!

materialgirls@materialgirlsquilts.com

MON-WED-FRI 10-5:30 TUES-THUR 10-7
SATURDAY 9-6 SUNDAY 1-4

Off I-44 go North on Peoria approx. 1/3 of a mile on the west side of Peoria.

STOP. SHOP. AND SEW

www.materialgirlsquilts.com

Oklahoma City, OK #15

Oklahoma QUILTWORKS

9323 N. Pennsylvania 73120 (405) 842-4778
Barbara Stanfield & Carole Jo Evans Est: 1988 3900 sq.ft.

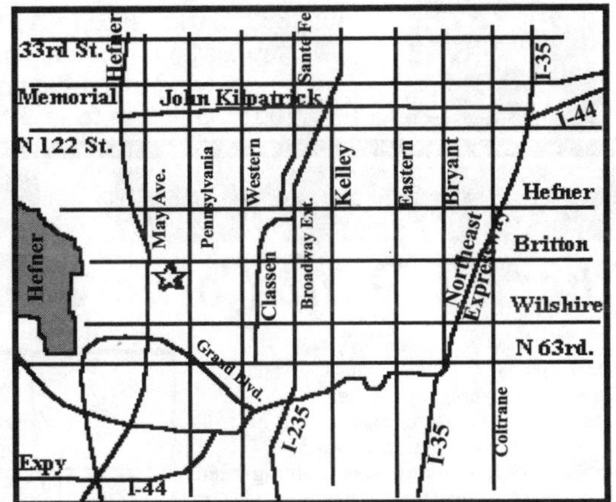

3500+ bolts of Cotton Fabric
500+ Quilting Book Titles
Notions, Patterns, Classes & Gifts

Mon - Fri 10 - 5
Thur til 8 Sat 10 - 3

Visit us on the Web at
www.okquiltworks.com
or e-mail us at: quilters@okquiltworks.com

Seay's Quilt Shop

224 "E" SW 74354
(918) 542-7896
Owners: Joyce & Ruth Seay
Est: 1997
2000 sq.ft. 2000 Bolts

Miami, OK #16

Tues - Sat 10 - 5

A Selection of all the Best Books
A Full line of Quilting Fabrics
2000 Bolts of all 100% Cotton
Complete line of Notions

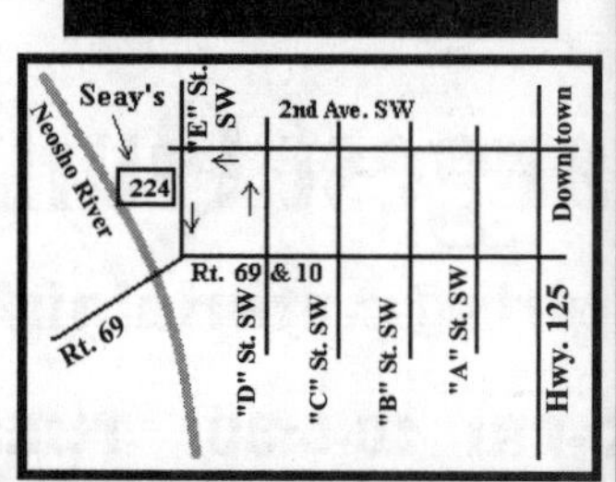

Owasso, OK #17

Mon - Fri 10 - 6
Sat 9 - 4:30

SEAMS GOOD Inc.

9100 N. Garnett Rd. Ste G 74055
(918) 272-7613 Fax: (918) 272-6915
Cg@seamsgood.com
Www.seamsgood.com
Est: 2003 2400 sq.ft. 2000 Bolts

"Start something beautiful today."
Our friendly staff has over
100 years combined experience.
100% Cotton Fabrics - Patterns - Books - Notions.

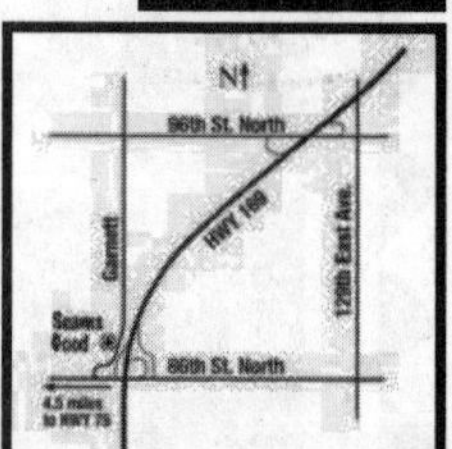

Broken Arrow, OK #18

Mon - Fri 9:30 - 5:30
Sat 10 - 4

The Quilted Thimble

825 N. Aspen 74012
(918) 259-1077 Fax: (918) 251-6852
QuiltedT@aol.com
www.QuiltedThimble.com
Owner: Marilyn Shoalmire
Est: 1998 2400 sq.ft.

Quality 100% cotton quilting fabrics, books, patterns & notions. Classes. In-shop quilting service. Warm, friendly atmosphere. Tours!

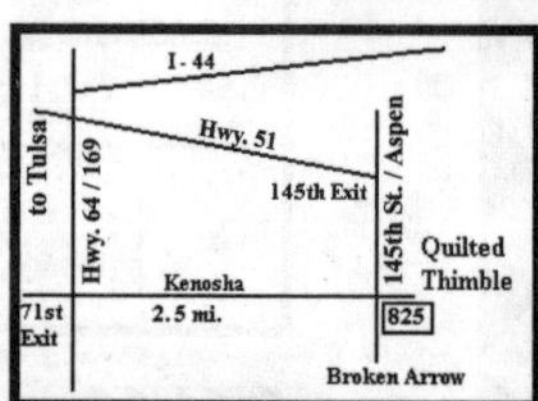

Edmond, OK #19

Mon - Sat 10 - 6
Thur til 8
1st Sun 1 - 5

My Sister's Quilt

425 S. Fretz Ave., Suite C 73003
(405) 715-1730 Fax: (405) 715-1721
Mysistersquilt@aol.com
Www.mysistersquilt.com
Owners: Myrna Douglass & Brenda Esslinger
Est: 2002 2500 sq.ft. 2000+ Bolts

Located in the Fountains. Reproductions, Asians, Novelties, Flannels, etc. Husband's corner (TV & recliners). Just off historic Rt. 66

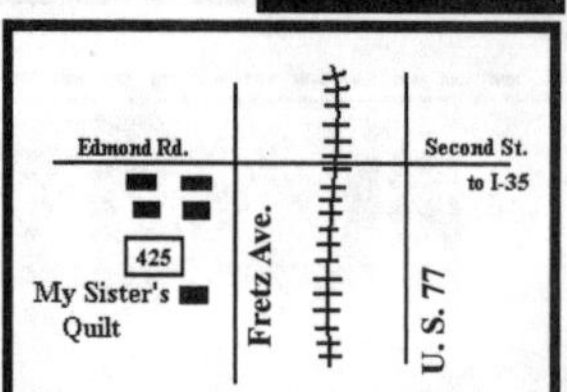

Guthrie, OK #20

Mon - Sat 10 - 6

EXTRA SPECIAL

109 S. Division St. 73044
(405) 282-1144 Est: 1991
laurah@extraspecialfabric.com
www.extraspecialfabric.com
Owner: Laurah Kilbourn 1600 Bolts

Specializing in Western fabrics, Southwest, Novelty, Calico, Faux Fur, Fleece, Barkcloth. Fashion to quilting. Clothing; Western Victorian; broomstick skirts decorated T-shirts.

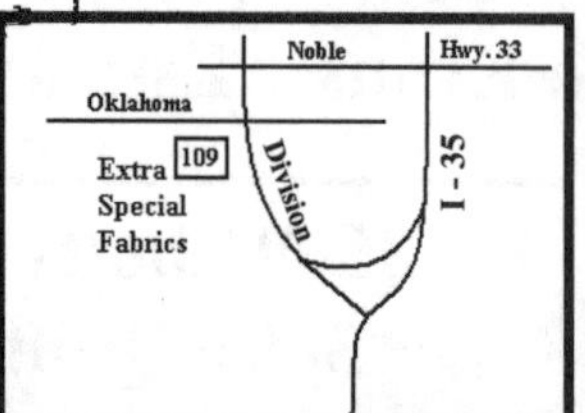

Hennessey, OK #21

Prairie Quilt

Prairie Quilt is the producer of the Oklahoma City Winter Quilt Show held the third weekend of January each year.

Show us this ad and receive 10% off any regularly priced item

Located ½ mile south of Highways 51 & 81 junction. Step back in time in this delightful shop located beside the Gardens Edge tea room. Large selection of 100% cotton fabrics, notions, books, and patterns.

Mon - Fri 9 - 5
Sat 9 - 4

101 S. Main St., Hennessey, OK 73742
(405) 853-6801 Fax: (405) 853-4548
randa@prairiequilt.com
www.prairiequilt.com
Est: 2001 5,000 sq.ft. 3,500 Bolts

Perkins, OK #22

Mon - Fri 9 - 5:30
Thur til 8
Sat 9 - 3

The Quilting Post

411 N. Main, P.O. Box 1109 74059
(405) 547-8300
Granniesew@aol.com
Owners: Darlene Leach & Joyce Rigsby
Est: 2000 Over 1500 Bolts

100% Cotton Fabrics -- Moda - Hoffman - RJR - P&B - Island Batiks, Etc.
Books. Notions. We offer lots of classes.

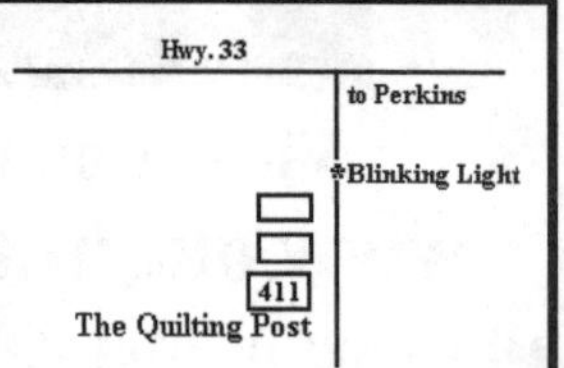

Guymon, OK #23

Mon 5 - 8
2nd Sat 10 - 5
or by Appt.

Cheryl's Quilt Corner

1608 N. Ellison 73942
(580) 338-3677 Owner: Cheryl Ashpaugh
cherylas@ptsi.net
www.cherylsquiltcorner.com
Online Store open 24 / 7

A growing shop meeting your quilting needs with a warm home atmosphere. Custom machine quilting, 100% top quality cotton fabrics, books, patterns, notions & battings. Classes by request.

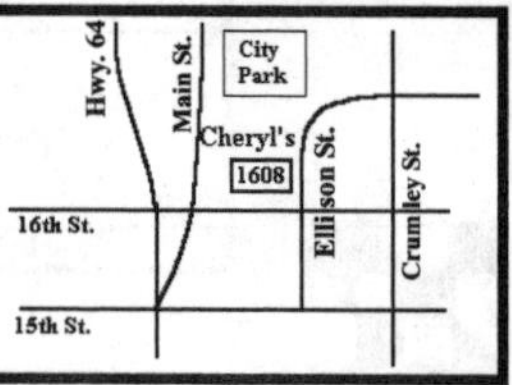

Thimbles & Threads
100% cottons notions classes books patterns
gifts, stitcheries, buttons
Husqvarna Viking
•sewing machines
•sergers
•accessories
Enid, OK #24

121 N. Grand 73701
580-234-3306

N

Visit our website: www. thimblesandthreads.com

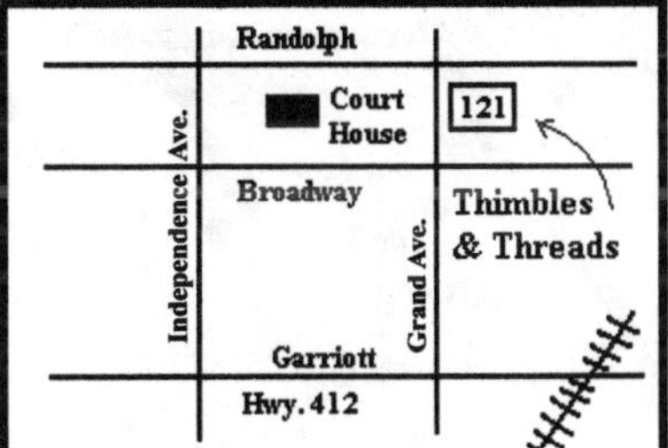

Mon - Fri 10 - 5
Sat 10 - 3

Northwest Oklahoma's Premiere Quilt Shoppe!

Connie Allen • Nadine Hayes

200 S. Main 73860
(800) 903-7762
(580) 824-0400
Fax: (580) 824-0401 Depot@Pldi.net

Tuesday - Saturday 10:00 AM - 5:00 PM

Waynoka, OK #25

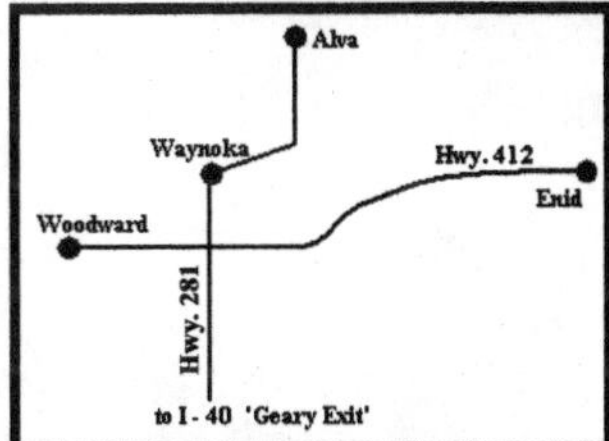

An Uptown Quilt Shop in a small town.
2,000 bolts of brand name fabrics, Patterns, supplies and notions with an "At Home" atmosphere.

Other Shops in Oklahoma: *We suggest calling first*

Broken Arrow	Creative Quilting, 10407 S. 194th East	918-455-3809
Clinton	Cindy's Quilts, P.O. Box 1212	580-323-1174
Copan	Corner Sew & So, 101 S Coney	918-532-5533
Duncan	The Fabric Zone, 815 West Main St	580-252-4984
Duncan	Deb's Sew Biz, 427 S. Hwy. 81	580-255-2843
Elk City	Donna's Quilting Rack, RR2 Box 4330	
Fairfax	Downtown Hilltop Quilting, 320 N Main St	
Fargo	Calico Gal Quilt Shop, 121 1st St.	405-698-2440
Grove	The Quilt Shop 2112 U.S. Hwy. 59 N	918-786-2046
Guthrie	Pamela Taft Quiltworks, 202 W Harrison Ave	405-282-7563
Harrah	Martin Fabric Shop, 1960 N. Church Ave.	405-454-2960
Henryetta	Tiger Mountain Quilt Barn, Box 296A Route 2	918-466-3244
Hooker	Fabric Garden, 119 Glaydas St	580-652-2883
Jenks	Victorian Charm Quilt Shoppe, 108 E. Main St.	918-298-9090
Lawton	Hilltop Fabrics, 8202 W. Lee RR #4	405-536-5776
Mangum	Busy Bee, 120 E. Lincoln St.	580-782-3805
McAlester	Bernina Sewing Center, 206 E Choctow Ave	918-426-4840
McLoud	Homestead Sewing, 801 N. St. Hwy. 102	405-964-6887
Newkirk	Rippit Quilt Shoppe, 114 1/2 S Main St	580-362-1234
Oklahoma City	Buckboard Antiques, 1411 N. May Ave.	405-943-7020
Ponca City	Linda's Creative Sewing, 111 N. 4th St.	405-762-6694
Purcell	3rd Street Fabrications, 112 S 3rd Ave	405-527-9395
Salina	Cummings Sewing, 108 Owen Walters Blvd	
Shawnee	Sue's Sewing Shoppe, 2301 North Kickapoo	405-273-4600
Skiatook	Quilted Garden, 209 E Rogers Blvd	918-396-0650
Tipton	Aunt Neva's Quilting, 400 N. Broadway	580-667-5611
Tulsa	Quilts & Handcrafts, 908 W. 24th St.	918-584-8617
Tulsa	Creative Quilting, 4905 W. 7th St.	918-599-8931
Valliant	Quilts Unlimited, 48 E. Wilson	405-933-4641

Oklahoma Guilds

Altus	Southwest Oklahoma Quilters, 1021 S. Fowler, 73521
Anadarko	Oklahoma Prairie Quilters Guild, 312 W. Colorado, 73005
Antlers	Pushmataha County Quilt Guild, P.O. Box 947, 74523
	Meets: Last Tuesday 10 a.m. at Church of Christ Annex Bldg.
Ardmore	Southern Oklahoma Quilters, 4244 S. Plainview Rd., 73401
Bartlesville	Oklahoma Quilters State Org., 74005
Bartlesville	Jubilee Quilters Guild, P.O. Box 3113, 74006
Bethany	Northside Quilters of OKC, 7500 NW 25th Terr., 73008
Blackwell	P.M. Patches & Pieces, 310 Fairview, 74631
Claremore	Country Fare Quilters Guild, 2614 SE Crestview, 74017
Clinton	Western Oklahoma Quilters Guild, 711 Frisco, 73601
	Meets: 4th Monday (except Dec.) 7:30 p.m. at Senior Citizen Center, 8th St.
El Reno	Patchwork Quilters Guild, 1528 W. Oak, 73036
Grove	Grand Lake O'Cherokees, 60451 E. 317th Ct., 74344
Guthrie	First Capital Quilters, 1206 Magnolia Ct., 73044
Guymon	Timeless Treasures Quilt Guild, Rt. 3, Box 32K, 73942
	Meets: Last Saturday 10 a.m. at Methodist Church Enrichment Center
Guymon	Panhandle Piecers Quilt Guild, 721 NW 5th, 73942
Lawton	Wichita Mountains Quilt Guild, 816 NW Ferris Ave., 73507
McAlester	Kiamichi Quilt Guild, 200 E. Adams, 74501
	Meets: at McAlester Bldg. Room 311
Muskogee	Muskogee Area Quilters Guild, 2175 S. 72nd St. E, 74403
Norman	Norman Area Quilter's Guild, 73069
	Meets: 3rd Monday @ 7pm at St. Joseph's Parish Center
Norman	Washita Valley Chumdashers, 73069
Okemah	Town & Country Quilters, Rt. 1, Box 186, 74859
Oklahoma City	Central Oklahoma Quilters, P.O. Box 23916, 73123
Perry	Cherokee Strip Quilters Guild, 1914 Lakeview Dr., 73077
Ponca City	Pioneer Area Quilters' Guild, P.O. Box 2726, 74604
Shawnee	Spinning Spools Quilt Guild, 46506 Westech Rd., 74801
Stillwater	Cimarron Valley Quilters Guild, P.O. Box 1113, 74076
Tulsa	Green Country Quilter's Guild, P.O. Box 35021, 74153
Weatherford	Western Oklahoma Quilters Guild, 122 Grandsview, 73096

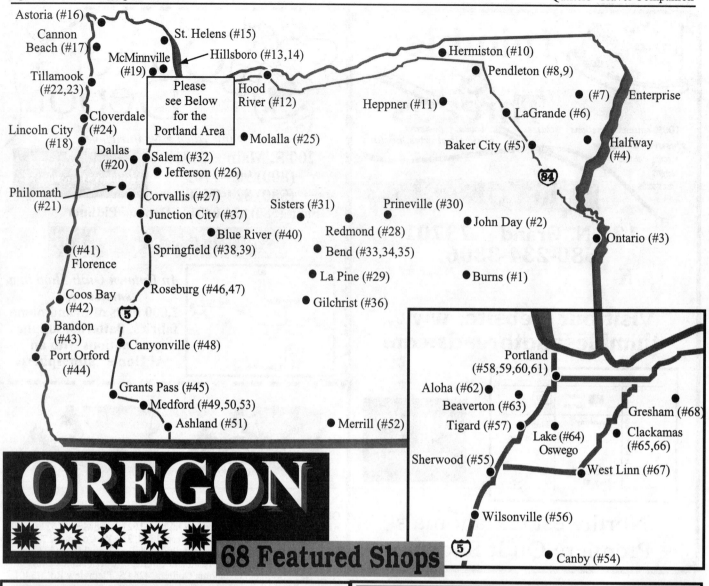

Astoria (#16)
Cannon Beach (#17)
St. Helens (#15)
McMinnville (#19)
Hillsboro (#13,14)
Tillamook (#22,23)
Please see Below for the Portland Area
Hood River (#12)
Hermiston (#10)
Pendleton (#8,9)
(#7) Enterprise
Heppner (#11)
LaGrande (#6)
Cloverdale (#24)
Lincoln City (#18)
Molalla (#25)
Baker City (#5)
Halfway (#4)
Dallas (#20)
Salem (#32)
Jefferson (#26)
84
Philomath (#21)
Corvallis (#27)
Sisters (#31)
Prineville (#30)
Junction City (#37)
John Day (#2)
Redmond (#28)
Blue River (#40)
Ontario (#3)
(#41) Florence
Springfield (#38,39)
Bend (#33,34,35)
La Pine (#29)
Burns (#1)
Roseburg (#46,47)
Coos Bay (#42)
Gilchrist (#36)
5
Bandon (#43)
Canyonville (#48)
Port Orford (#44)
Grants Pass (#45)
Medford (#49,50,53)
Ashland (#51)
Merrill (#52)

Portland (#58,59,60,61)
Aloha (#62)
Beaverton (#63)
Gresham (#68)
Tigard (#57)
Lake Oswego (#64)
Clackamas (#65,66)
Sherwood (#55)
West Linn (#67)
Wilsonville (#56)
5
Canby (#54)

OREGON

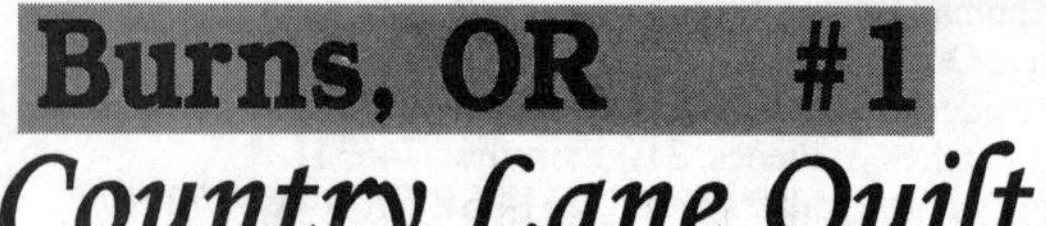

68 Featured Shops

Burns, OR #1

Mon - Sat 10 - 5

Country Lane Quilts

406 N. Broadway 97720
(541) 573-6406 Fax: (541) 573-6155
countrylanequilts@centurytel.net
Owners: Barbara Ormond & LaDonna Baron
Est: 2003 5000 sq.ft. 1400 Bolts & growing
"A Quilters oasis in the Oregon High Desert."
Large selection of Western Fabric, Janome Sewing Machines, Quilters Supplies, Books, Buttons & Patterns.

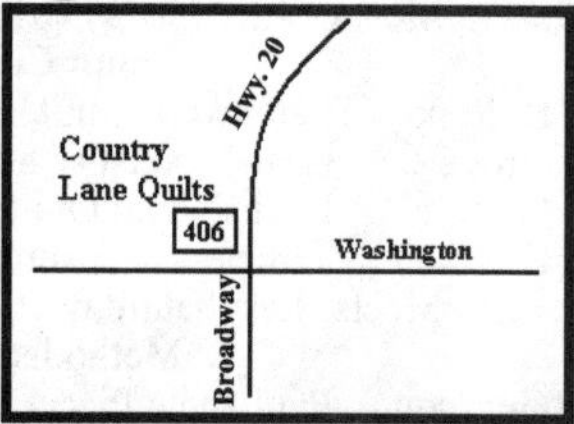

John Day, OR #2

Mon - Fri 9 - 5
Sat 9 - 1

Dee-Dee's Quilts & Fabrics

777 E. Main 97845
(541) 575-3996

A Working Quilt Shop.
Top Fabrics at low prices. R.V. Parking.
Always Helpful and Friendly.
Better then Sew Sew!

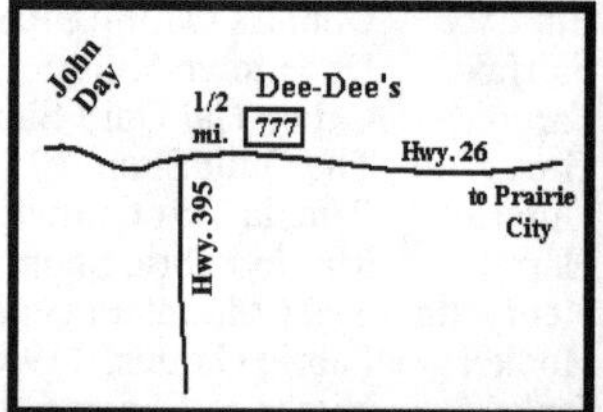

Ontario, OR #3

Mon - Fri 10 - 6
Sat 10 - 4

Nancy D's Quilt Corner

199 S. Oregon St. 97914
(541) 823-8047 Fax: (541) 823-0877
nancyds@fmtc.com
Owners: Mike & Nancy McGuire
Est: 2002 3000 sq.ft.
Only 3 minutes from the freeway, we offer quality 100% cotton fabrics, notions, books & classes. Ever expanding inventory

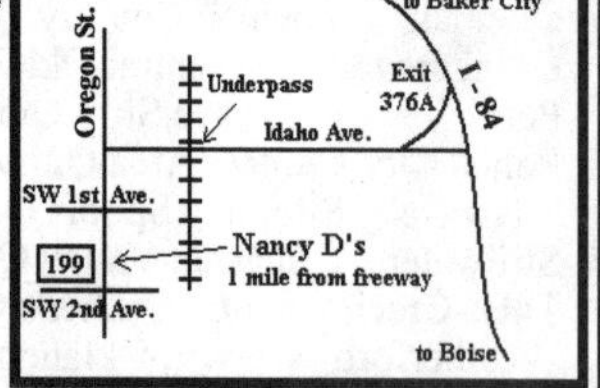

Halfway, OR #4

Mon - Sat 8 - 5

Quilts Plus

280 S. Main St., P.O. Box 626 97834
(541) 742-5040 Fax: (541) 742-5041
quiltsplus@pinetel.com
www.halfwayor.com
Owner: Roberta Bryan
Est: 1986 2400 sq.ft.
Over 2500 Bolts of Quilting Fabric - Custom Machine Quilting - Gift Shop - Espresso Bar
Antiques & Collectibles - Notions - Craft Supplies

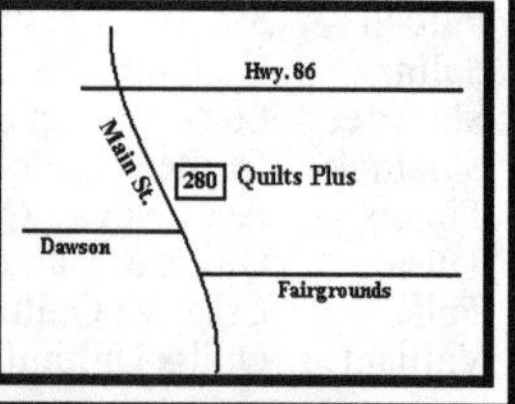

Baker City, OR #5

Kountry Quilters

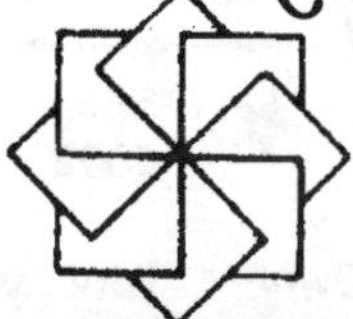

2658 10th St. 97814
(541) 523-0500
Fax: (541) 523-8565
Owner: Ruth Pedersen

Mon - Sat 10 - 5

Quilting Fabrics—
Benartex, Batiks,
Hoffman, Kaufman,
Timeless Treasures.
1800+ Bolts
Books, Patterns,
Notions, Gifts.

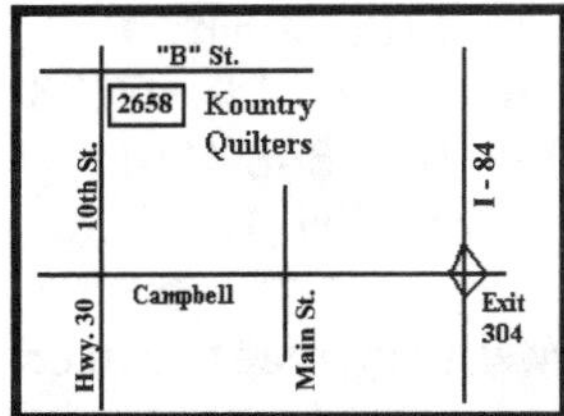

La Grande, OR #6

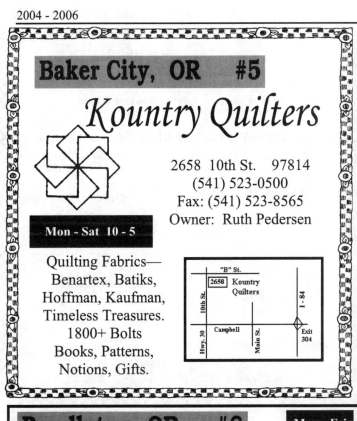

Mon - Fri 10 - 5
Sat 10 - 4

Quilt Therapy

1101A Washington 97850
(888) 663-1817 or (541) 663-1817
Fax: (541) 663-9728
Est: 2001 1600 sq.ft.
Owner: Faith Hohstadt
& Joanne Mahoney
quilttherapy@eoni.com
www.quilt_therapy.com

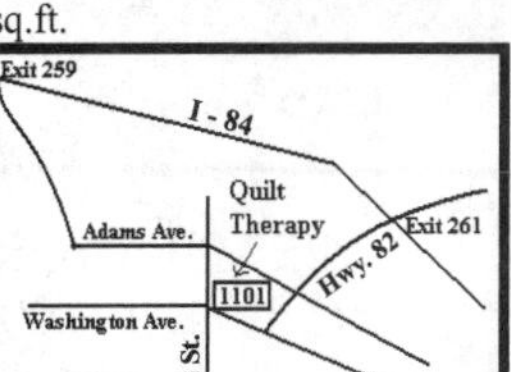

Everything for your quilting and knitting addiction! Quality fabrics, specialty yarns, notions, gifts, kits, BOM, classes and helpful advice.

Enterprise, OR #7

Wed - Sat 11 - 5

The UnCommon Thread

116 S. River #B 97828
(541) 426-3089 or (877) 434-6623
grappler@uci.net
Est: 1997

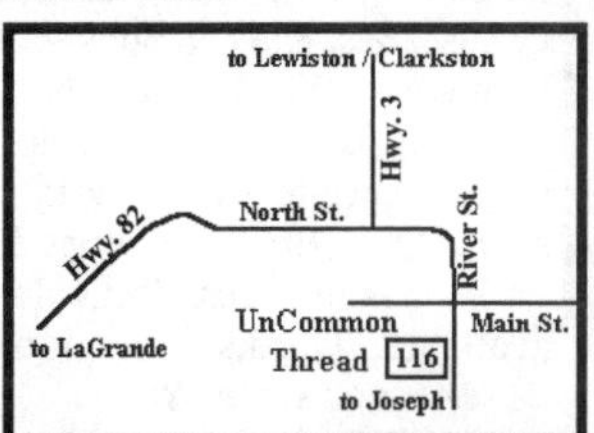

Specializing in natural fibers & friendly advice. We offer quilting fabrics, books, patterns & notions, yarn, spinning fibers & classes.

Pendleton, OR #8

Mon - Fri 10 - 6
Sat 10 - 4
Sun 12 - 4

Pendleton Quilt Works

37 SE Dorion 97801
(541) 276-9546
pendletonquiltworks@hotmail.com
Owner: Rachelle Doherty Est: 2003

New Store, New Classes, New Friends, Quality Fabrics! Color, Creativity and Customer Satisfaction. "Where you can create a Work of Art from the Heart."

Pendleton, OR #9

Mon - Fri 10 - 6
Sat 10 - 2

the Quilt House

1005 SW Frazer 97801
(541) 276-2128
Owner: Anita James
Est: 1997
2200 sq.ft.
1500+ Bolts

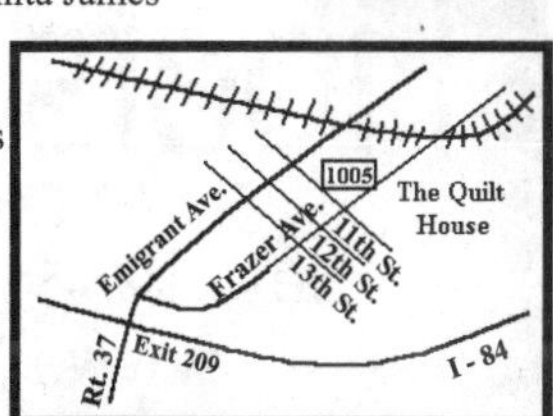

100% cotton quilting fabric. Books, Patterns, Notions and Classes. Stitchery patterns. DMC
Web Site: www.thequilthouseweb.com

Hermiston, OR #10

Mon - Sat 10 - 5:30
Thur til 8

Aunty Ida's Country Loveables Quilt Shop

435 W. Hermiston 97838
(541) 567-2726
Owner: Idamarie & Tom Martin
PC Quilter and SuperQuilter on Display! Over 1200 bolts of quality fabrics! Books, Patterns, Notions and Classes. Located inside Shirley's Sew & Vac. Pfaff and Brother Sales & Service.

Hood River, OR #12

Mon - Sat 10 - 4
Thur til 6

Every Thread Counts

1215 "C" Street 97031
(541) 386-5044
Est: 1987
Owner: Ann Zuehlke
etc@gorge.net
www.everythreadcounts.net
Quilting Supplies * Fabric
Newsletter * BOEOM * Classes
$5.00 Quilt * Monthly Clubs

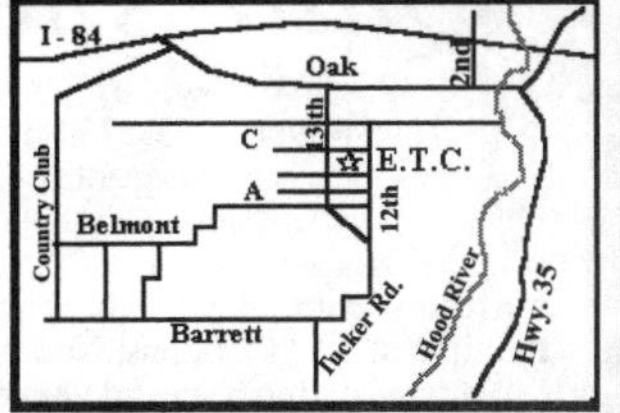

Heppner, OR #11

Quilter's Round-Up

288 N. Main St., P.O. Box 1029 97836
541-676-8282 Fax: 541-676-8036
quiltersroundup@artisanvillage.biz
www.quiltersroundup.com
Est: 2001 2500 sq.ft. 4000+ bolts

Mon - Wed 9:30 - 5:30 Thur 9:30 - 7:30
Fri 9:30 - 5:30 (til 4 Nov - Feb)
Closed Sat Sun 12 - 5

A destination shop: Incredible wide selection of topnotch quilting fabrics from the best companies. Cottons, wools, tapestries. Also American handmade baskets.

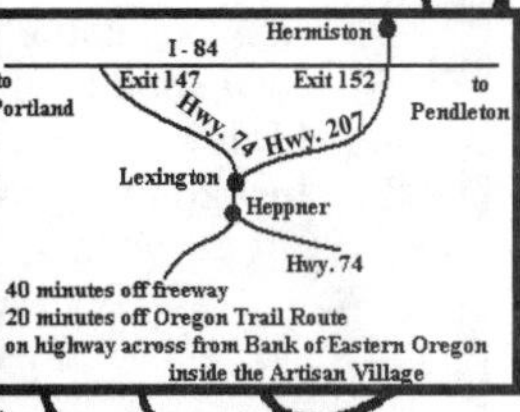

Hillsboro, OR #13

Furever Friends
Quilt Shop

2257 NE Cornell Rd. Hillsboro, Oregon 97124
(503) 640-1907 email: ffquiltshop@aol.com
www.measurebytheyard.com

Home of: "Measure-By-The-Yard"™ the Tape Measure designed by a quilter for quilters. The ONLY Tape Measure that converts inches into yards @ a glance…(order on line). We specialize in 100% cotton fabrics (over 1,800 bolts) from unique to traditional: Batiks, Reproductions, Landscapes, Kids & Bugs, Florals, Brights & Flannels… We also carry beautiful quick & easy kits featuring Watercolor style fabrics, using preprinted fusible grid in assorted sizes. Quilt Books, Notions & Patterns for your quilting needs. Individual help always available. Thanks for Quilting and letting us serve you since 1988!

Don & Nola Aman (owners)

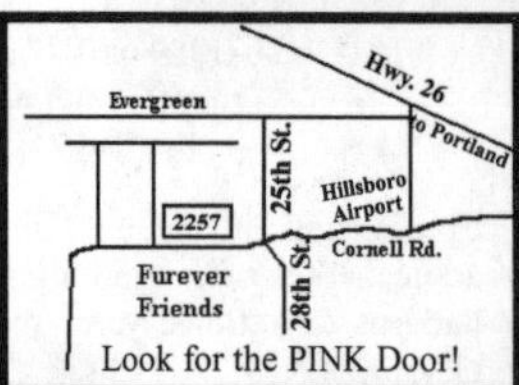

MAINSTREET CLOTH & MERCANTILE

WHERE THERE IS "ALWAYS SOMETHING NEW"!

We have a vast array of fabrics. Fine English lawns, Flannels and everything in between.

Quilt Sampler Top Ten Shop 2002

Owner: Toni Lynn
Est: 1996
3000 sq.ft.

Home of: MAINSTREET PATTERN COMPANY.
"ART FROM THE HEART"

231 E. Main St.
Hillsboro, OR 97123
503-846-1891
Mon - Fri 10 - 5:30
Sat 10 - 5
www.mainstreetcloth.com

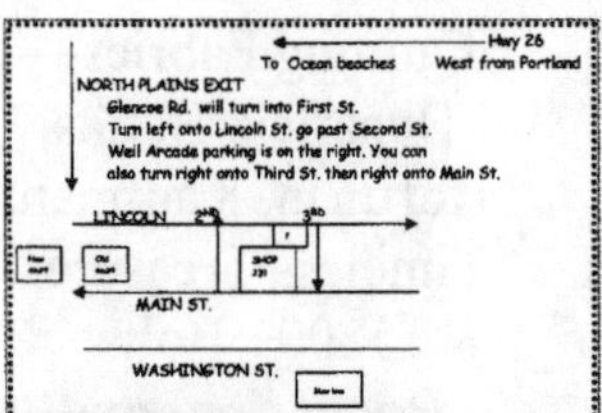

Hillsboro, OR #14

St. Helens, OR #15

Fibers & Stitches

58093 Columbia Hwy. 97053
(503) 397-5536 Fax: (503) 397-1635
www.fibersandstitches.com
Owner: Kathy Miners

Mon-Fri 9:30 - 6
Thur 9:30 - 9
Sat 9:30 - 5
Sun 11 - 4

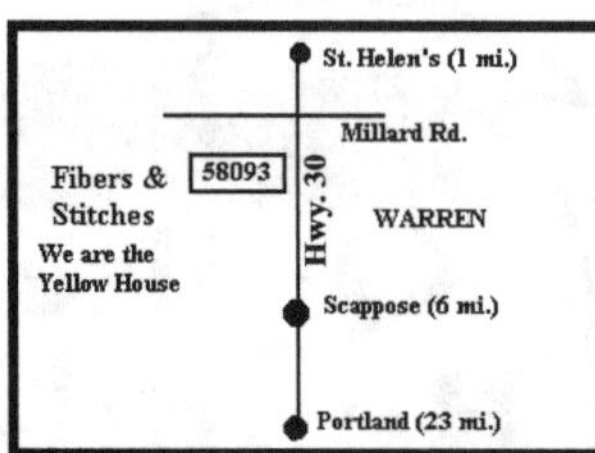

Fabric from these great companies - Moda/United Notions, Hoffman, Timeless Treasures, Maywood Studio, South Seas, Kona Bay, Seattle Bay, Island Batiks, Alexander Henry, Free Spirit, Robert Kaufman, In the Beginning, RJR, P&B.

- 2500+ bolts of fabric
- Over 200 bolts of Batik fabric
- Flannel, flannel and more flannel
- Home décor fabric and accessories.
- Class schedule posted on website
- New shop hours - Open until 9pm on Thursday's and 11am - 4pm on Sundays
- Just 20 miles from Portland.

We are in the bright yellow house, by the flashing yellow light!

Astoria, OR #16

Mon -Sat 9:30 - 5
Sun 11 - 3

Northwest Stitchin's

108 10th St. 97103
(503) 325-3300
Fax: (503) 325-9744
www.northweststitchins.com

Quality Cotton Fabrics for quilters & sewers. Wool felt and rug hooking supplies, Books, patterns, notions, classes and Thimbleberries Club.

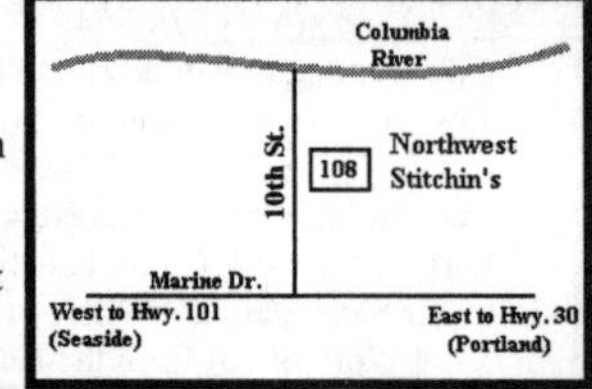

Cannon Beach, OR #17

7 Days a Week
10 - 5

Center Diamond

1065 S. Hemlock 97110
(503) 436-0833 Fax: (503) 436-2540
centerdiamond@aol.com
www.centerdiamond.com
Owner: Julie Walker
Est: 1994 1500 sq.ft. 2000+ Bolts

Over 2000 bolts of the most gorgeous 100% cotton fabrics. Books, patterns, notions & gifts. Located 1 block from the beach.

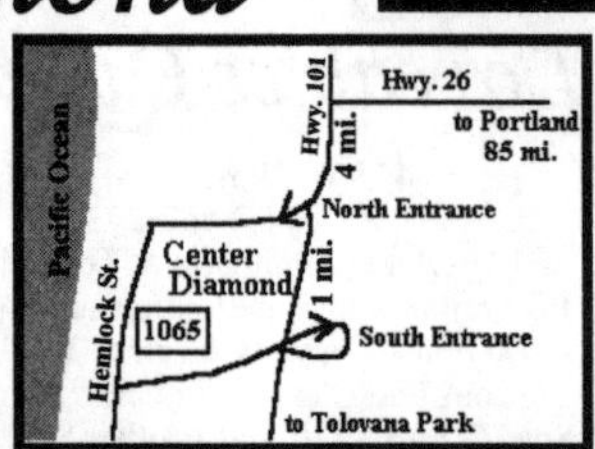

Lincoln City, OR #18

Mon - Sat 10 - 5
Sun 11 - 4

Seams Sew Right Quilt Shoppe

3203 SW Hwy. 101 97367
(541) 994-6946 Fax: (541) 994-6919
Chrisnquilts@aol.com
www.seamssewright.net
Owner: Chris Murrell Est: 2001 2200 sq.ft.
A friendly Quilt Shop in a historic mercantile. Full line of 100% Cottons, Notions, Books & Patterns on the beautiful Oregon Coast.

Eagles Lodge
to Lincoln City
SW 32nd Ave.
Seams Sew Right 3203
in the Nelsutt Mercantile
Hwy. 101
SW 33rd Ave.
to Taft

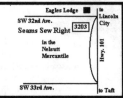

It's SEW Much Better!

203 E. 3rd St. McMinnville, OR 97128
(503) 472-4611 (800) VAC-SEWS
jack@boersmas.com
Owners: Jack & Michelle Boersma Est: 1935
Located in Historic Downtown 20,000 sq.ft. 10,000 Bolts

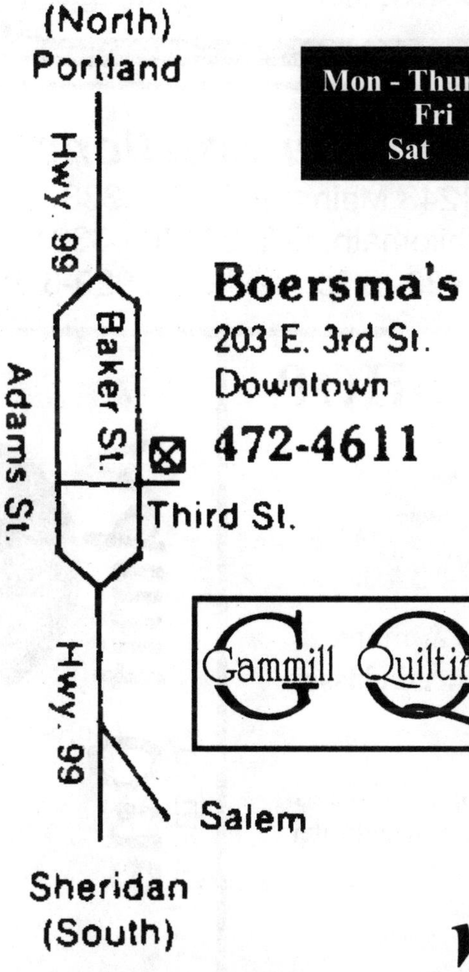

(North)
Portland
Hwy. 99
Baker St.
Adams St.
Third St.
Hwy. 99
Salem
Sheridan
(South)

Mon - Thur	8:30 - 6
Fri	8:30 - 7
Sat	9 - 5

Boersma's
203 E. 3rd St.
Downtown
472-4611

Gammill Quilting Systems

McMinnville, OR #19

- Sales & Service
- Hands-on Training
- Set-Up & Delivery
- Classes
- In-store Machine Rental

- Fine 100% Cottons
- Quilt Books
- Notions
- Classes
- Collectibles & Gift Items

Sewing Machine Sales & Service
Experienced Staff

www.boersmas.com

Rachel Greco, Owner

Grandma's Attic Sewing Emporium, Inc.

- 100% cotton fabrics for Quilting/Sewing
- Patterns, Books, Notions and More!
- Block of the Month/Fabric Clubs by Mail
- Send for FREE catalog!

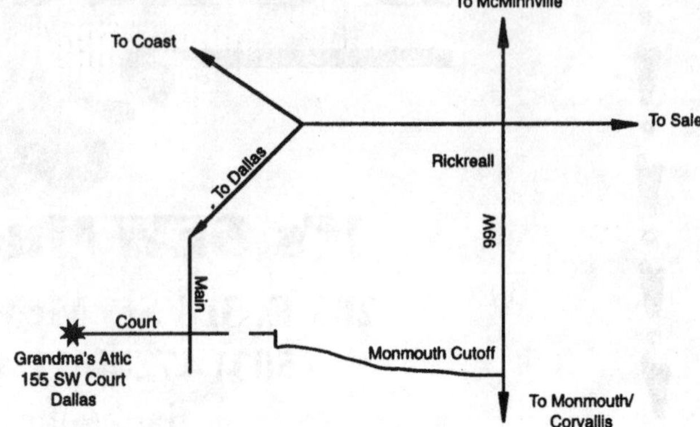

Dallas, OR #20

167 SW Court St. 97338
Est: 1995 4400 sq.ft.
3000+ Bolts

Mon - Fri
9:30 - 5:30
Sat 10 - 5
Sun 12 - 4

(503) 623-0451 Fax: (503) 623-0498
E-Mail: GrandmasAttic@compuserve.com
Web: www.GrandmasAtticQuilting.com

JanniLou Creations
1243 Main P.O. Box 333
Philomath, OR 97370-0333
(541) 929-3795; fax (541) 929-3597

QUILT SHOP

Philomath, OR #21

- Great Patterns, books, notions & more.
- Absolutely beginning to advanced classes
- Mail order catalog $1

Next time you're in Philomath, drop by to see us "on location" at the old Waucomah movie theater building.

Mon, Wed, Fri and Sat, 9:30a-5:30p
Tues & Thurs 9:30a-9:00p

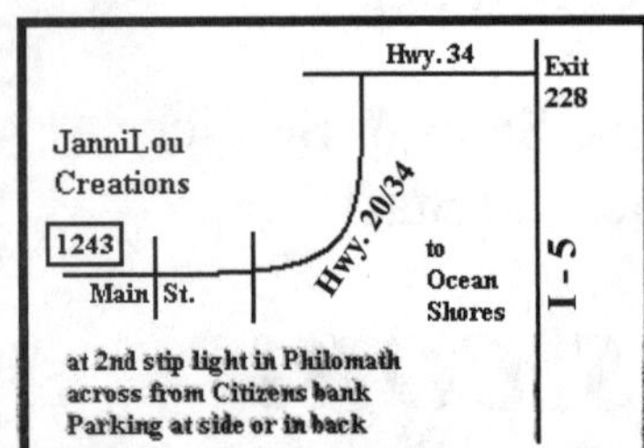

Jane's Fabric Patch

Tillamook, OR #22

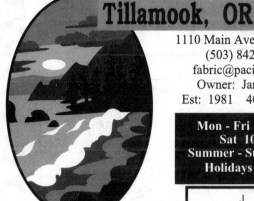

1110 Main Ave. 97141
(503) 842-9392
fabric@pacifier.com
Owner: Jane Wise
Est: 1981 4000+ Bolts

Mon - Fri 9 - 5:30
Sat 10 - 4
Summer - Sundays & Holidays 11 - 3

9th St.
Main St.
10th St.
Pacific
11th St.
Jane's Fabric Patch 1110

Coastal Retreat.
Multi-faceted Quilt shop.
Large fabric selection, creative, knowledgeable and friendly ideas and assistance.

Web Site: www.janesfabricpatch.com

Tillamook, OR #23

LATIMER QUILT & TEXTILE CENTER

Tues - Sat 10 - 4
Sun 12 - 4
Closed Sun Nov - Feb

2105 Wilson River Loop 97141
(503) 842-8622
latimertextile@oregoncoast.com
www.oregoncoast.com/latimertextile

An active textile museum, dedicated to the preservation and promotion of the textile arts...weaving, spinning, quilting, history, research, education & exhibits. Handcrafted gift items for sale.
Exhibits change every four to eight weeks.

We are located one block east of Shilo Inn off Hwy. 101

Cloverdale, OR #24

Mon - Sat 10 - 5

B J's Fabrics & Quilts

38105 Hwy. 101 S, P.O. Box 215 97112
(503) 392-6195 Est: 1997
BJsfabricsquilts@wcn.net
Owner: Barbara Lewis

Over 2000 bolts of fabric. Hwy. 101 from the North-2 miles south of Cloverdale, turn left past the 90 mile marker, then left again at the 2nd driveway. Hwy. 101 from the South-¼ mile from the Pacific City Turn-off, turn right after BJ's Fabrics & Quilts state sign, L 2nd driveway.

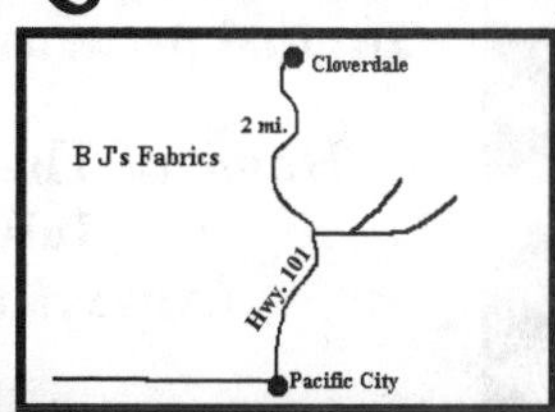

Molalla, OR #25

Tues - Fri 10 - 5
Sat 10 - 4

Cozy Quilts & Friends

538 N. Molalla Ave. 97038
(503) 829-7364
cozyquilts1@netzero.com
Owner: Ruth Derksen
Est: 2000

100% cotton fabrics, hand-dyed wools, books & patterns, notions & classes. Our customers are #1; warm, friendly customer service.

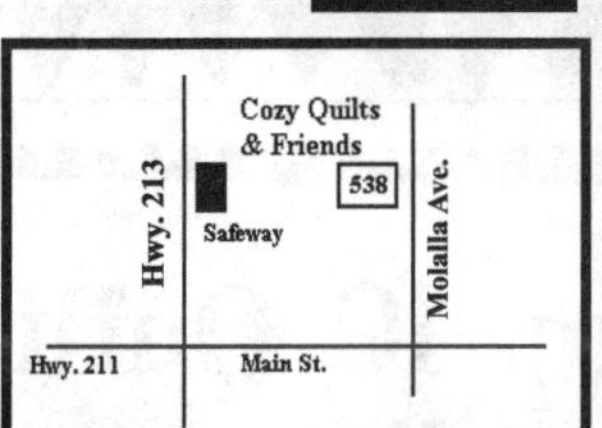

Jefferson, OR #26

Mon - Fri 9:30 - 6
Sat 10 - 5

The Grateful Thread

115 S. 2nd St.
P.O. Box 1290 97352
(541) 327-3333

Fabrics that Rock! 100% cotton prints & solids. Books, notions, classes and handcrafted items. Friendly, personal service. Open 7 day a week.

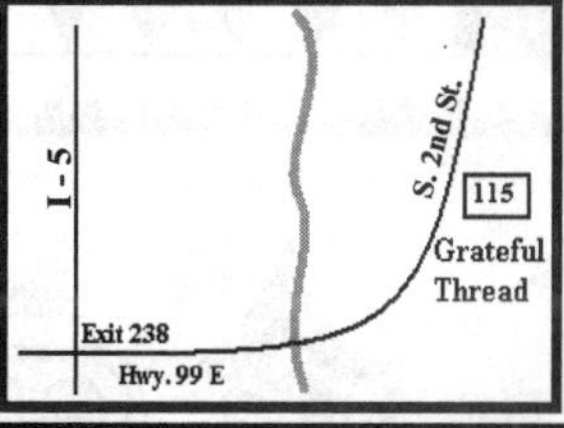

Corvallis, OR #27

Mon - Sat 9:30 - 5:30

Quiltwork Patches

212 SW 3rd St. 97333
(541) 752-4820
Owner: Jessy Yorgey
Est: 1979 2000 sq.ft. 3000 Bolts

Over 3000 bolts of fine quality fabrics, plus a large selection of Quilter's tools and books. Free Brochure

Redmond, OR #28

Mon - Fri 10 - 5:30
Sat 10 - 4

High Mountain Fabrics

1542 S. Hwy. 97 97756
(541) 548-6909
Est: 2002 2500 sq.ft. 1500+ Bolts

A Quilt Shop with 100% Cottons, Flannels, Books, Patterns & Notions.

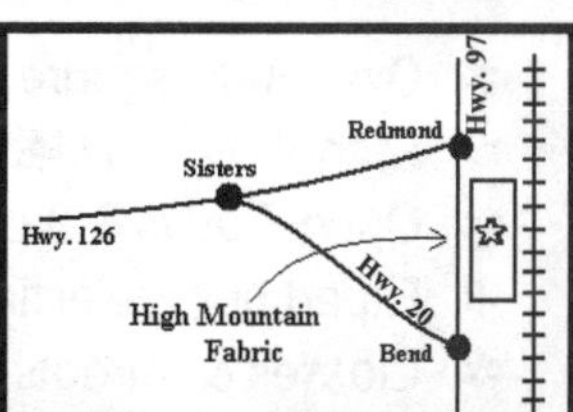

LaPine, OR #29

Mon - Fri 9 - 5
Sat 10 - 4

Dera's Fabric & Craft Supplies

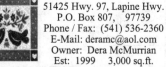

51425 Hwy. 97, Lapine Hwy.
P.O. Box 807, 97739
Phone / Fax: (541) 536-2360
E-Mail: deramc@aol.com
Owner: Dera McMurrian
Est: 1999 3,000 sq.ft.

Quilting fabrics, Notions, Books, Patterns, Yarns, Craft supplies, Floral supplies, Classes And much more.

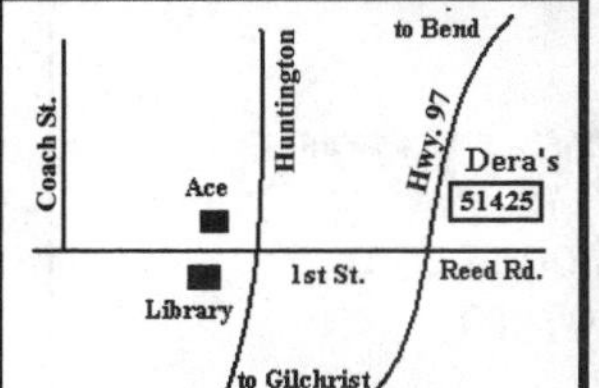

Prineville, OR #30

Mon - Fri 9:30 - 5:30
Sat 10 - 4
Open Mon-Sun July 5-11 for Sister's Show

Prairie Girls' Quilt Shop, LLC

970 NW Third St. 97754
(541) 416-2004 Fax: (541) 447-3052
prairiegirls@crestviewcable.com
www.e-prairiegirls.com
Est: 2000 2100 sq.ft. 1600 Bolts

Customer service oriented quilt shop, specializing in classic western, flannels, homespun, batiks, & 30's fabrics. Quilting supplies, books & patterns.

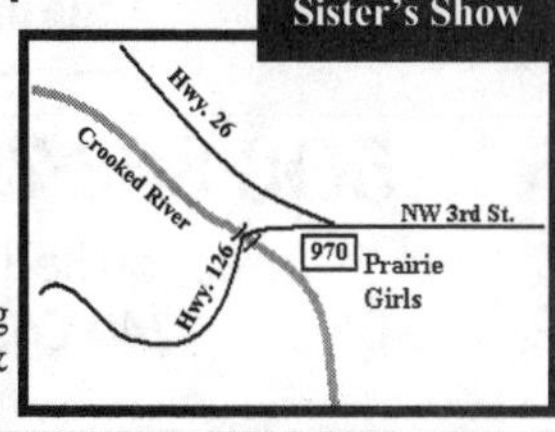

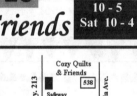

STITCHIN' POST #31

Established 1975~Jean Wells

Where originality and inspirational ideas capture the quilter:

Exclusively from the Stitchin' Post:
Valori Wells' Designer Series Swatch Club
& Fabric Finders Swatch Club

Gifts for Quilters and Gardeners
7000+ bolts of cotton fabrics
Original patterns designed by the Stitchin' Post Staff

Home of **The Sisters Outdoor Quilt Show™**
July 10, 2004 • July 9, 2005
(Always the Second Saturday in July)

Shop online or come visit one of the finest quilt shops in America.

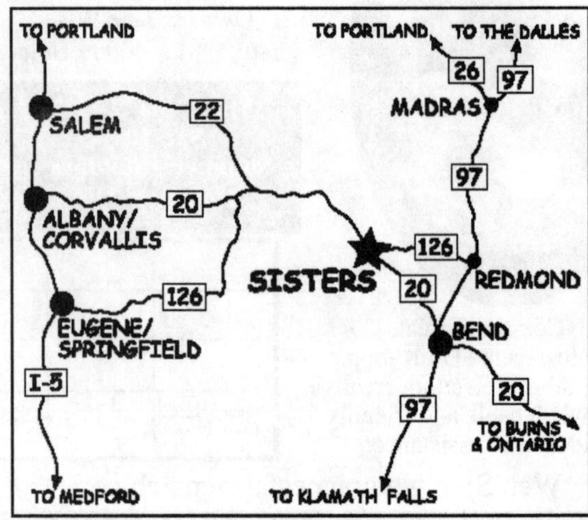

Hours:
Monday - Saturday: 9 - 5, Sunday: 10 - 5

311 W. Cascade/PO Box 280, Sisters, OR 97759 • (541)549-6061 • Fax (541) 549-1922
e-mail: stitchin@empnet.com • www.stitchinpost.com

Top 10 Quilt Shop 2003

Better Homes & Gardens' *Quilt Sampler*

Salem, OR #32

- Over 3000 square feet filled with the hottest fabric, books, patterns & more!
- Friendly & knowledgeable staff
- Open 7 days & 3 evenings for your shopping leisure
- Expert help selecting fabric. Use our carts to select from Hoffman, Moda, Bali, and more!
- Classes & retreats
- Exclusive Oregon Thimblelady thimble dealer

HOURS

Mon, Fri, Sat. 9:30 am to 5:30 pm
Tues, Wed, Thurs. 9:30 am to 8:00 pm
Sunday Noon to 5:00 pm

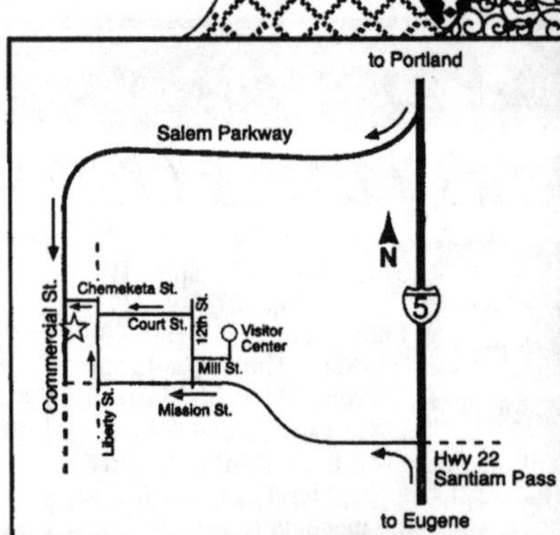

503-363-7973 or Toll Free 1-877-700-2233

web: quiltedforest.com • e-mail: sylvia@quiltedforest.com
240 Commercial Street NE • Salem Oregon 97301

Bend, OR #33

400 SE 2nd St., Ste 2 97702
541-385-7166
Fax 541-385-8741
Owners: Gail Ransdall & Sharon Lang
E-Mail: sewmanyquilts@coinet.com

You don't want to miss our shop!!

You're invited to Bend's newest quilt shop featuring a charming personality, the friendliest atmosphere and a great selection of fabrics, books, patterns, notions, antiques and unique gifts. We have a large variety of stitchery and wool felt projects ready to take and stitch. Located two blocks north of Wilson near the Old Mill District.

Mon - Sat 9:30 - 6
Sat 9:30 - 5 Sun 12 - 4

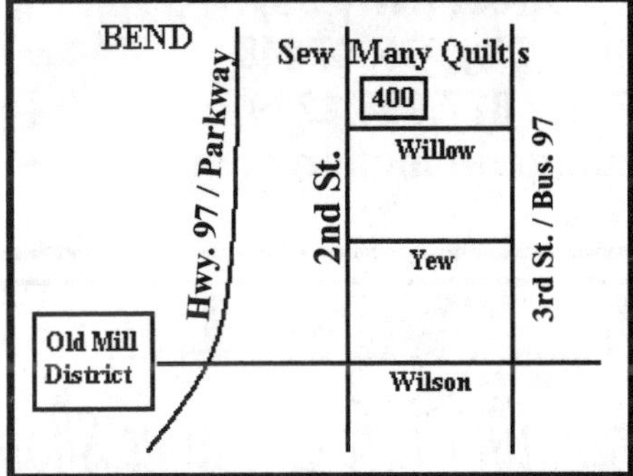

Bend, OR #34

Mon - Sat
9:30 - 5:30
Sun 12 - 4

20225 Badger Rd. 97702
(541) 383-4310 Fax: (541) 383-2484
Owner:
Barbara Schreiner
Est: 1992
5400 sq.ft. 5000 Bolts
www.bjsquiltbasket.com

Top Quality fabrics, 600 book titles, patterns, notions, classes, fat quarters, fabric packets, mail order. July Festival of Classes

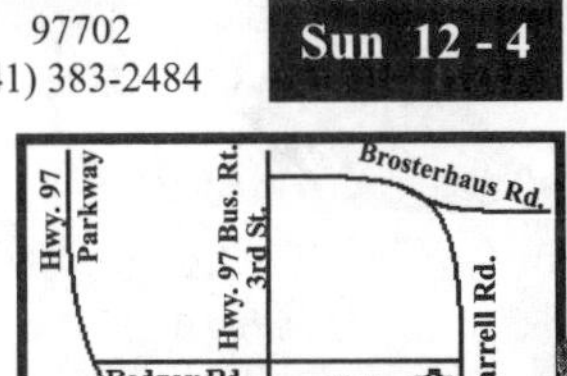
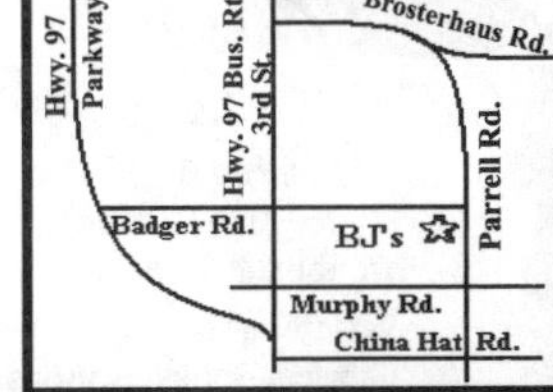

Bend, OR #35

Mon - Fri
10 - 5
Sat 10 - 4:30

1568 NW Newport Ave. 97701
(541) 382-5984
6500 square feet of fabric, mostly calico - flannel - wool. 6000-7000 bolts of fabric.

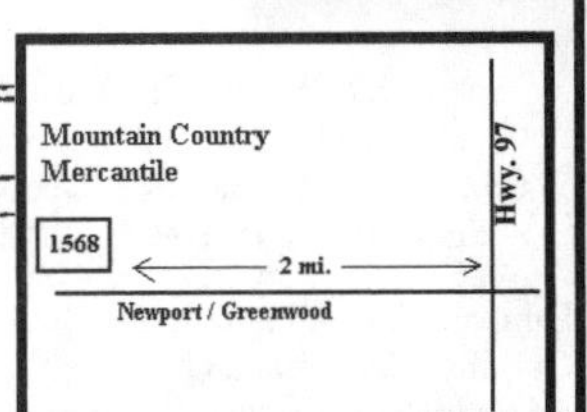

Pinetown
Quilting Adventures

P.O. Box 320, 71 Michigan Ave. 97737
(541) 433-2435 Proprietor: Cynthia Buell

Tues - Fri 10 - 5:30
Sat 12 - 4
Longer hrs in July

Always Something special to be found. Visit us on your trip to the Sister's Quilt Show. Bus Turn-around

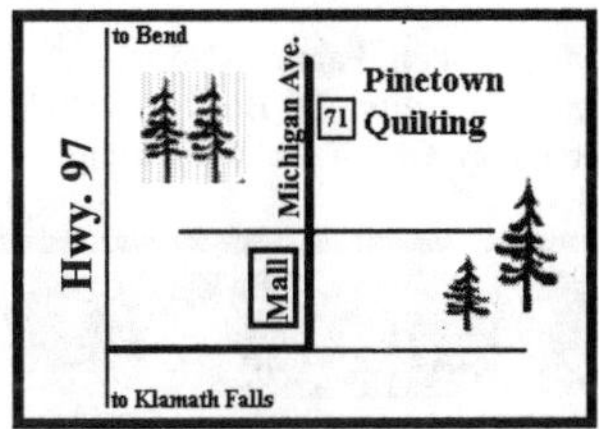

Take main entrance into Gilchrist, turn left behind mall, Go 2 blocks North

Gilchrist, OR #36

Quilter's Junction

dedicated to sharing and promoting the joy of quilting worldwide!

Mon - Fri 10 - 5 Thu til 8 Sun 1 - 5

Junction City, OR #37

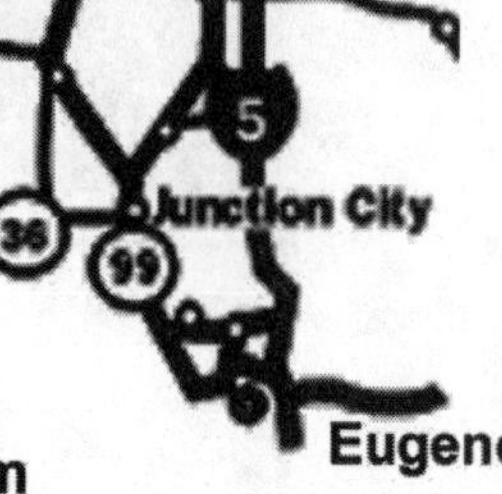

595 Ivy Street (Hwy 99)
Junction City, OR 97448
Toll Free: 877.998.2289
www.quiltersjunction.com

Springfield, OR #38

4227-C Main St. 97478
(541) 746-3256
Est: 1993 1400 sq.ft.
Owner: Kennette Blotzer
stca@somethingtocrowabout.com

Something to Crow About

Mon - Sat 10 - 5:30

Over 3,000 Bolts of Cottons, Flannels, Homespuns, Wool-felt, Wools, and Thimbleberries.
Books, Patterns, and Quilting related supplies.
Call about Thimbleberries Club and Girl Gang.

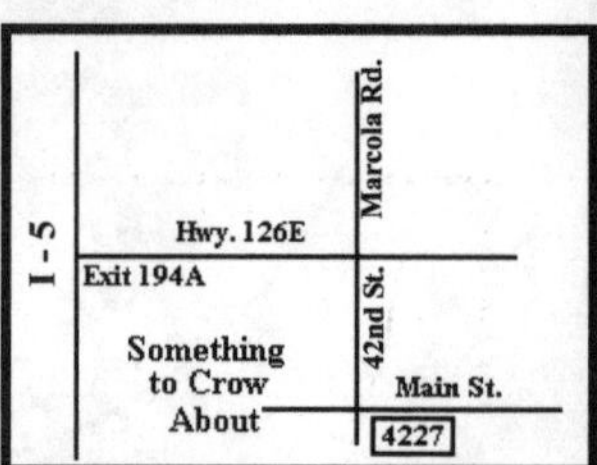

Springfield, OR #39

Mon - Fri 9:30 - 9
Sat 9:30 - 6
Sun 11 - 6

Ben Franklin Craft & Frame Shop

1028 Harlow Rd. 97477
(541) 726-2641
Fax: (541) 726-2643
Est: 1990 11,000 sq.ft.

A full service Craft store with a great fabric department featuring quality quilt fabrics, books, patterns, batting and quilting notions.

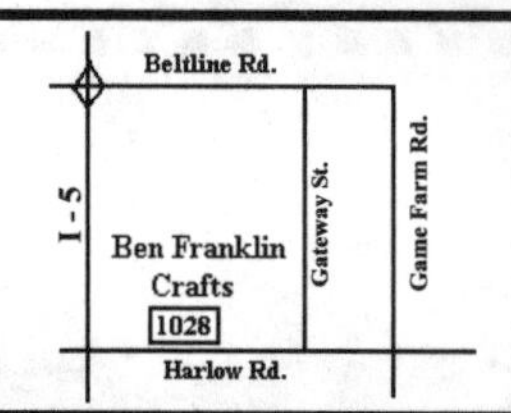

Blue River, OR #40

Wed - Sun 10 - 5

FOXFIRE FARM Quilt and Gift Shoppe

50560 McKenzie Hwy. 97413
(541) 822-1011
KKrions@aol.com
Owner: Kathie Hoffman

Fabric (Full line of Moda Marbles) Books Patterns - Notions - Classes - Block of Month - Custom Machine Quilting

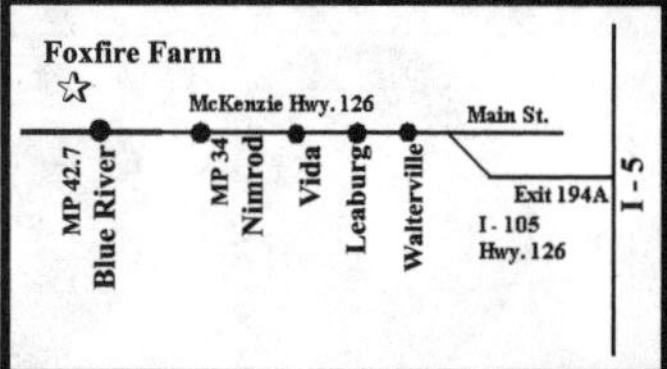

Florence, OR #41

Mon - Sat 10 - 5

Jodi's Quilts & Fabrics

5045 Hwy. 101 97439
(541) 997-3293 Fax: (541) 997-3573
E-Mail: Jodi@Presys.com
Owners: John & Jodi Ringen

100% Cotton Fabrics, Notions, Wool Felt, Great Selection of Books, Embellishments for Crazy Quilts, Friendly, Helpful Service. Classes Too.

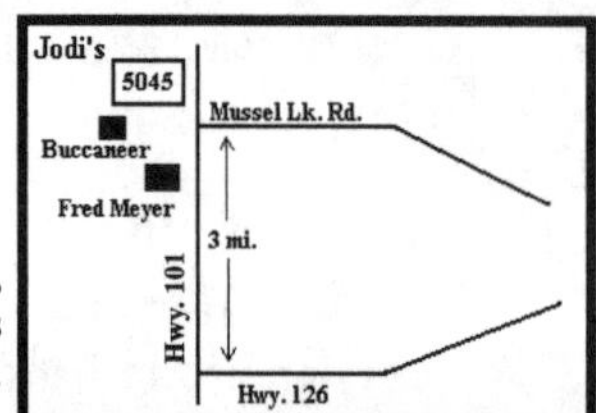

Coos Bay, OR #42

Mon - Fri 10 - 6
Sat 10 - 5

120 Central 97420
(541) 267-0749 Est: 1996
E-Mail: threads@harborside.com

Everything for the Quilter!
Fabrics, Books, Notions

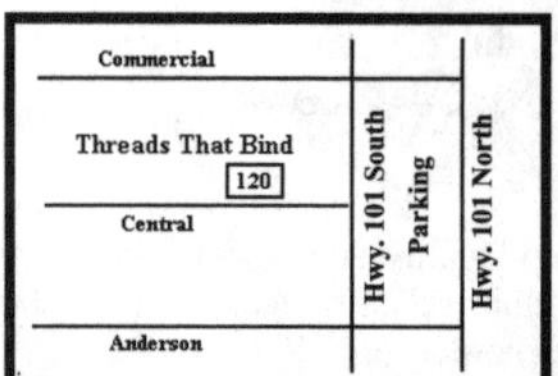

Bandon, OR #43

Mon - Sat 10 -5
Sun 12 - 4

Forget-Me-Knots

125 Baltimore Ave. 97411
(800) 347-9021
Owners: Michelle Hagglund
Est: 1988 1500 sq.ft. 3000 Bolts

A unique & charming shop specializing in quilting, dollmaking, silk ribbon embroidery. Supplies, patterns, books, classes & a large selection of 100% cottons.

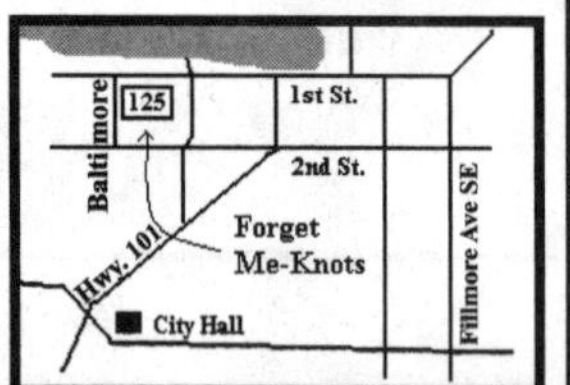

Port Orford, OR #44

Seven Days a Week 10 - 5

Quilter's Corner

335 W. 7th, P.O. Box 69
(541) 332-0502 97465
Owners: Dottie Barnes & Debbie Dorman
Est: 1994 1800 sq.ft. 3000 Bolts

Fabric, Notions, Patterns and Books. Machine Quilting, Classes and Quilts.
Friendly, Spacious and Wonderful Lighting.

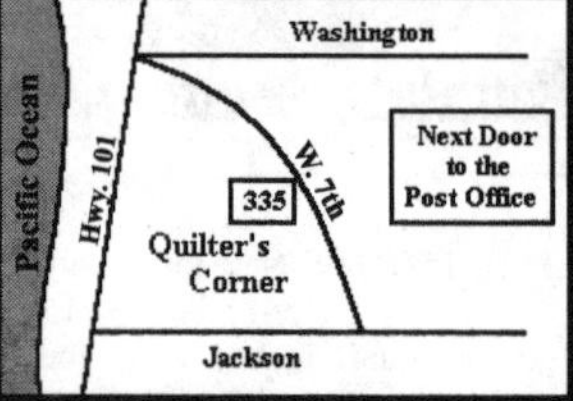

PLAZA SEWING CENTER

A QUILTER'S HAVEN

We have a full line of high quality fabrics for the quilter.
Over 3,000 prints and over 200 solids.
A great selection of quilt and craft patterns and books.
Also a great selection of aids, notions and threads.
GREAT PRICES!

Mon. - Fri. 9:30 - 6
Sat. 9:30 - 5:30
Sun. 11-5

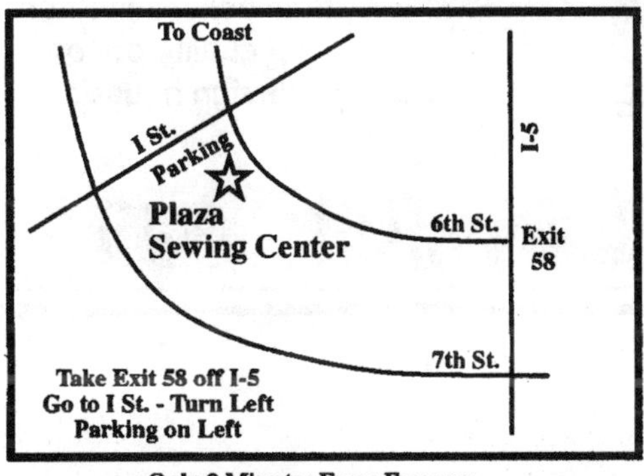

Only 8 Minutes From Freeway

311 SE 6th St. Golden Rule Plaza 97526
(541) 479-5757
Owners: Rick & Mary Chapman
Est: 1967 5000 sq. ft.

Grants Pass, OR #45

Est: 1983

Roseburg, OR #46

611 S.E. Jackson St. 97470
(541) 673-1007
cntryldy@rosenet.net

- Stop and Pet the Fabric
- Open Sisters Weekend
- Traveling - "Call", we will stay open
- Gammill Long-arm Quilting Machine Classes
- In-store Award Winning Long-arm Quilter/Instructor

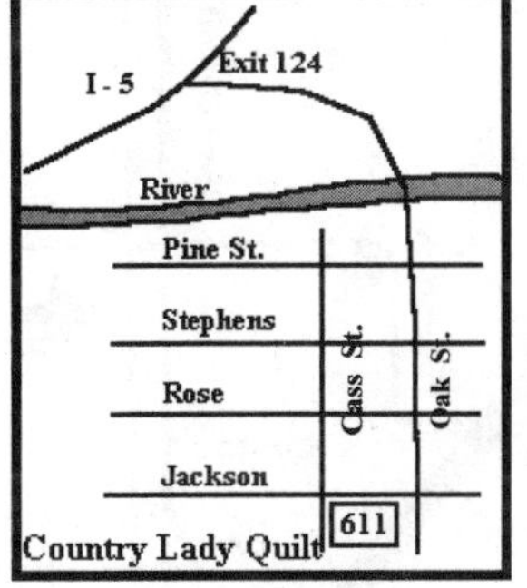

Mon - Sat
10 - 5

Owner:
Charlie Weckerle

Roseburg, OR #47

Tues - Fri 10 - 5
Sat 10 - 2

Material Possessions Fabric Shoppe

631 W. Ballf 97470
Next to Harvard Ave. Drug
(541) 229-1011 Fax: (541) 679-2031
martie@mcsi.net
www.materialpossessions.biz
Owner: Martie Clausen
Fabric, books, patterns & notions. Special orders, classes, quilting machine rental, sewing machine repair.

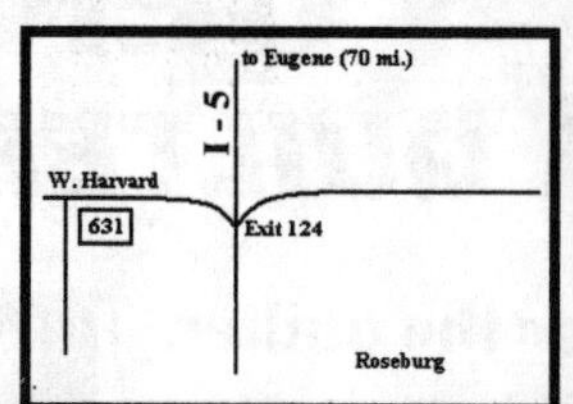

Canyonville, OR #48

Mon - Fri
10 - 5
Sat 10 - 4

J & J Fabrics

413 S. Main St., P.O. Box 549 97417
(541) 839-4319 Fax: Same
Owner: Judy Cuthbertson
Est: 1990 1840 sq.ft.

Quilters Welcome. 100% cotton fabric, flannels, books, patterns, notions. Just south of Seven Feathers Hotel & Casino Resort

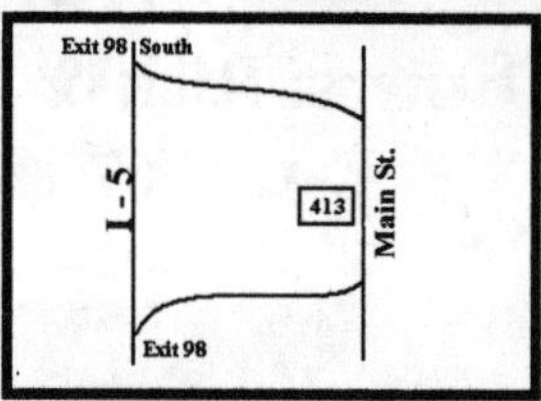

TOP STITCH

BERNINA

1596 Biddle Rd., Medford, OR
(541) 608-7722
topstitch@qwest.net

HWY 62
MORROW
I-5
EXIT
30
D.Q.
KINKO'S
TOP STITCH
PROGRESS

Mon. - Sat., 10: - 6:
Closed Sundays

Featuring unique and complete fabric collections from top quality cotton design houses.

Medford, OH #49

Medford, OR #50

Grandma Dee's

Fabrics, Quilts & Stitchery
4918 Crater Lake Avenue
Medford, OR 97504
541-608-2874

GRANDMA DEE'S

M-F 10-6, Sat 10-5, Sun 11-4

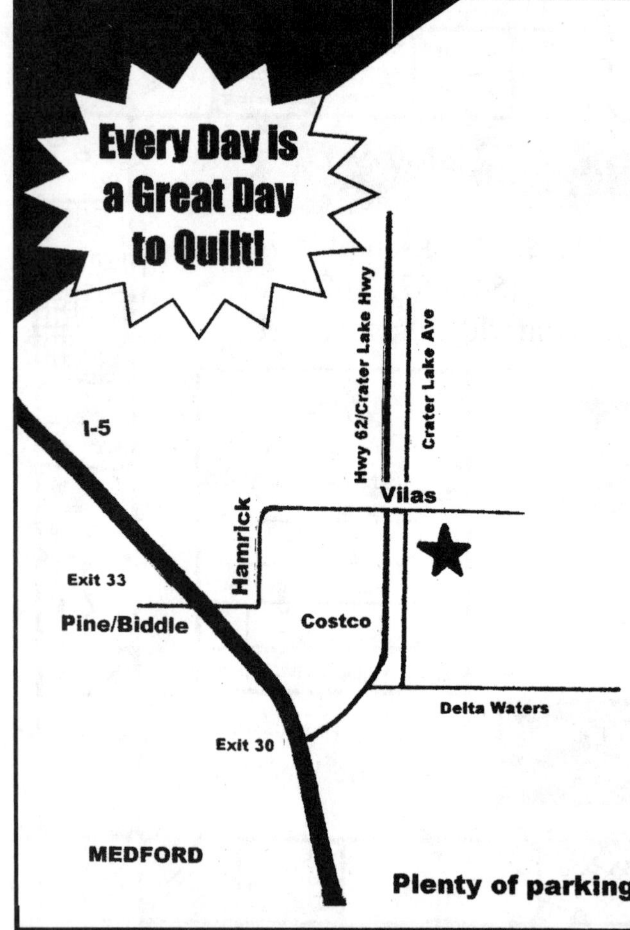

- Thousands of bolts, including batiks, flannels, orientals and much more!
- Hundreds of books and patterns
- Classes
- Expert help

Authorized Janome & Brother Dealer

Plenty of parking - RV Parking, too!

Located in beautiful Ashland Oregon.
Home of the Oregon Shakespeare Festival.

Ashland, OR #51

EVERYTHING for the Quilter . . . .
Huge selection of the finest cotton fabrics
-- Over 3000 Bolts --
Batiks, Orientals, 30's Reproductions. Theme Prints, Novelty and Flannels
Complete selection of Moda Marbles
Friendly & Knowledgeable Staff
Tax Free Shopping!

QuiltZ is an Authorized Viking Dealer

QuiltZ
293 East Main, Ashland, Oregon
(541) 488-1650 Fax (541) 488-0751
ashlandquiltz@earthlink.net

DIRECTIONS TO QUILTZ

From 1-5 North use Exit 19
From 1-5 South use Exit 11
Follow signs to Shakespeare.
QuiltZ is 2 blocks from Shakespeare Festival Theaters on Main Street

---

Est: 1996

TATER PATCH QUILTS

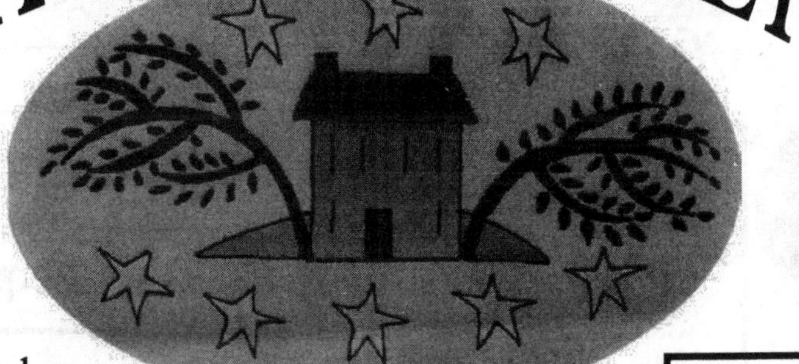

14141 Falvey Rd.
P.O. Box 298 97633
(541) 798-5955
2100 sq.ft
TaterPatchQuilts@aol.com

Mon - Fri
10 - 5
Sat 10 - 4

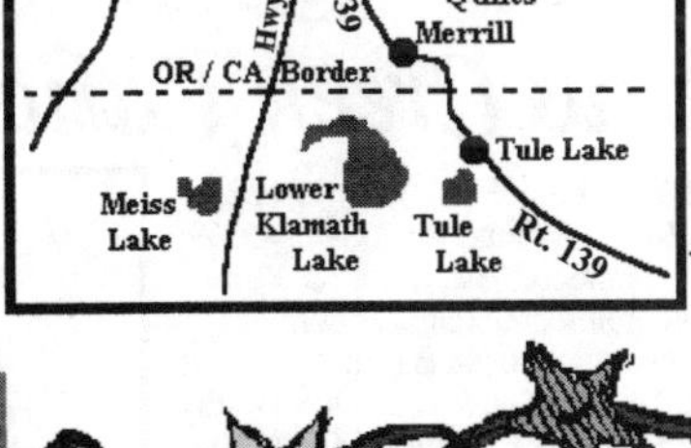

Klamath Falls
Hwy. 97
Rt. 39
Tater Patch Quilts
Merrill
OR / CA Border
Tule Lake
Meiss Lake
Lower Klamath Lake
Tule Lake
Rt. 139

Large Selection of 100% Cotton Fabrics and Flannels.
Books, Patterns, Notions and Classes.
"Quilt Treats" (mini-group quilting retreats--call for details)
"On the Road to Reno"
Parking Available for Recreational Vehicles.

Merrill, OR #52

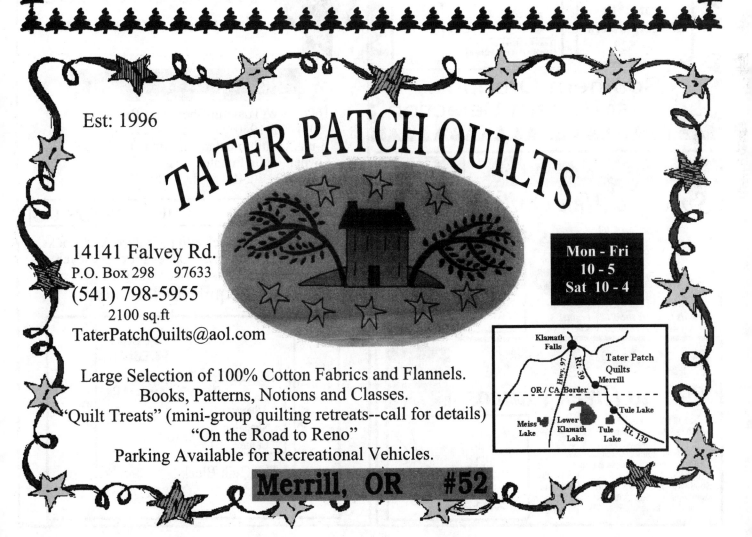

1000+ bolts of Hoffman, Kona Bay, South Seas, Maywood and Moda.

Medford, OR #53

CALICO JUNCTION

1310 - C Center Dr. 97501 (541) 770-8001
Owner: Vickie Kiser
Est: 1977 1500 sq.ft. 1000 Bolts

Mon - Sat 10 - 6 Sun 12 - 5

Fat Quarter Sale Every Sept. 25th 25 fat quarters for $25

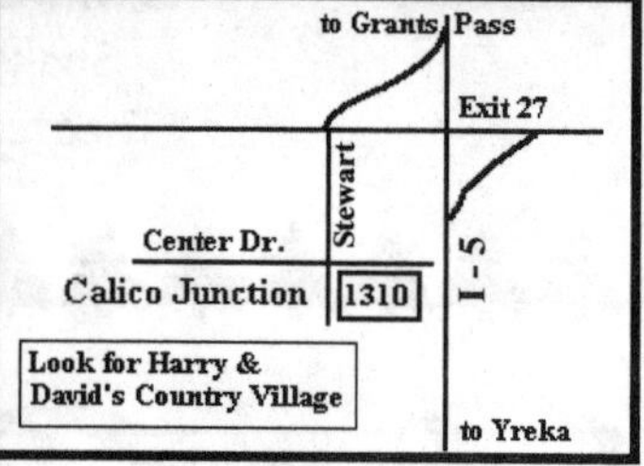

Southern Oregon's Largest Pattern Selection

Canby, OR #54

Country Dry Goods

Mon - Fri 10 - 5
Sat 10 - 4:30

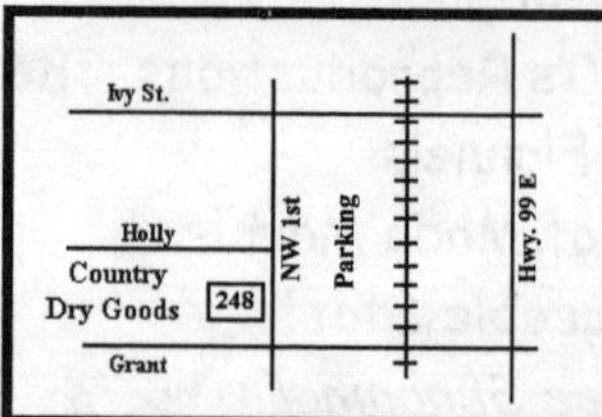

248 NW 1st Ave.
97013
(503) 263-3563
Est: 1987 2000 sq.ft.
Owner: Linda Peck

DEDICATED TO THE QUILTER AND WOULD BE QUILTER.
We carry the latest books, patterns and 100% cotton fabrics.

The Quilt Block

Everything for the Quilter...

Sherwood, OR #55

16064 SW Tualatin-Sherwood Rd. 97140
(503) 625-1040
E-mail: Quilt.block@verizon.net
Owner: Julie Fugate
Est: 1999 2400 sq.ft. 3000 Bolts

Mon - Fri 10 - 6 Sat 10 - 5 Sun 12 - 4

Colorful and varied selection of fabric, kits, books, notions and patterns. Classes for every level.
Authorized Husqvarna-Viking Dealer
www.thequiltblocknw.com

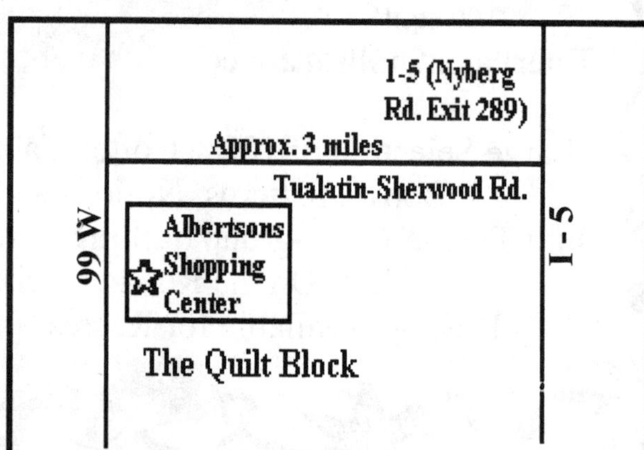

Wilsonville, OR #56

Speckled Hen Quilts

M • W • F • S 10 - 5
Tues & Thur 10 - 9
Sun 12 - 5

30789 SW Boone Ferry Rd.
Suite K 97070
(503) 570-3368
Specializing in 1800's reproduction, & 30's fabrics.

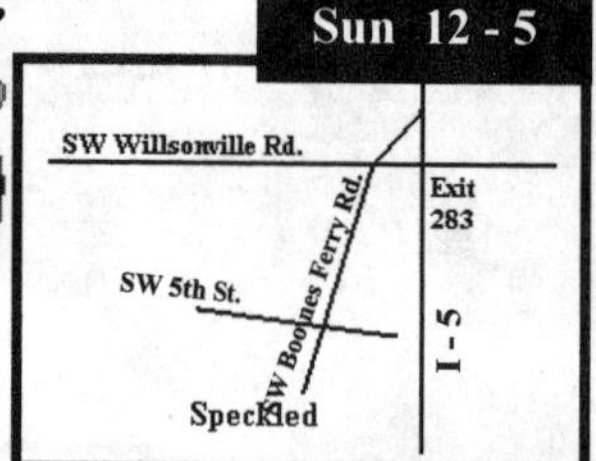

Spotted Roosters & Speckled Hens
This is where the FUN begins!
www.speckledhenquilts.net

Tigard, OR #57

Fanno Creek Calicos

Mon - Sat 9:30 - 5:30
Sun 11 - 5

12192 SW Scholls Ferry Rd. 97223
(503) 579-7977 Fax: (503) 590-4537
fannocreek@att.net
www.fannocreekcalicos.com
Owner: Susan Baxter
Est: 2000 2000 sq.ft. 1500+ Bolts

Southwest Portland's Premier Quilt Shop supplying quilters with the latest fabric, notions, books & classes. "We'll keep you in stitches."

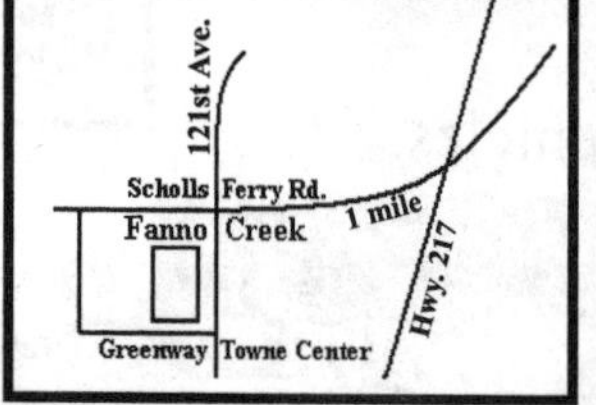

Fabric Depot

700 SE 122nd Ave, Portland, Oregon 97233
Mon - Sat: 9 AM - 9 PM Sun: 10 AM - 7 PM

1- 800 -392-3376
Ph (503) 252-9530 • Fax (503) 252-9556

1 ½ ACRES OF FIRST QUALITY FABRICS!

- A STORE IN A CLASS OF ITS OWN -

9000 Quilting Prints • 2000 Home Dec Fabrics
Extensive Fashion & Bridal Departments
Fabric Related Crafts • Notions
Many Hard-to-Find Items
Retail - Wholesale

LATEST OFFERINGS OF MORE THAN 75 MANUFACTURERS
All fabric displayed at eye level and draped for easy handling and selection

Bountiful traditional floral and background fabrics • 300+ Bali Batik Cottons • 1930's Reproduction Prints
Quilter's Flannel • Outstanding Asian, Christmas and Harvest prints • Themed Prints • Children's prints
All the Gadgets! • Large Selection of Rulers & Cutters • Quilting Kits

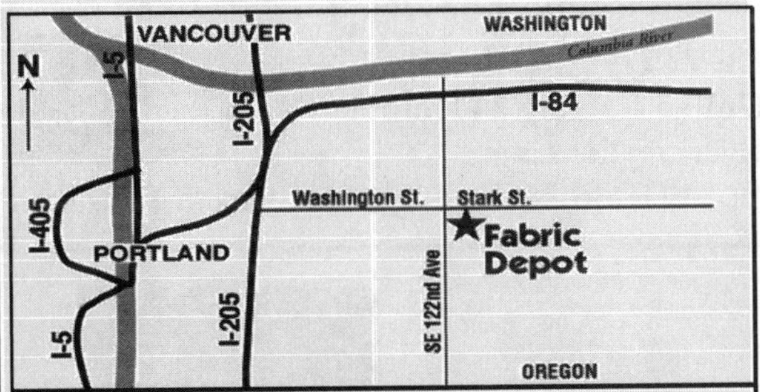

FROM I-205 N: Exit #20 (Washing. & Stark): Right on Washington. Travel 1 mile east to corner of 122nd and Stark. ***Washington becomes Stark St.***
FROM I-205 S: Exit # 21A (Glisan & Stark): Follow exit to 3rd light. Left on Washington St. Travel 1 mile east to corner of 122nd and Stark. (Washington becomes Stark)
FROM I-84 E: Exit #6 (I-205 South/ Salem). Follow exit to third light as above.
FROM I-84 W: Exit #9 (I-205 South). From I-205 S, Exit # 21A as above.

www.fabricdepot.com

30% OFF ALL FABRIC & notions every day on the web!

SPECIAL REQUESTS WELCOME

If it's not on our website, we'll find it on the floor!

info@fabricdepot.com 1-888-896-1478

Come Visit Us - Seeing is Believing
Plenty of Free Parking - Cars • Buses • RV's

Portland, OR #58

FIBERS IN MOTION

7855 SW Capitol Hwy., Portland, OR 97219
503-977-2758

Mon - Fri 10 - 6
Sat 10 - 5

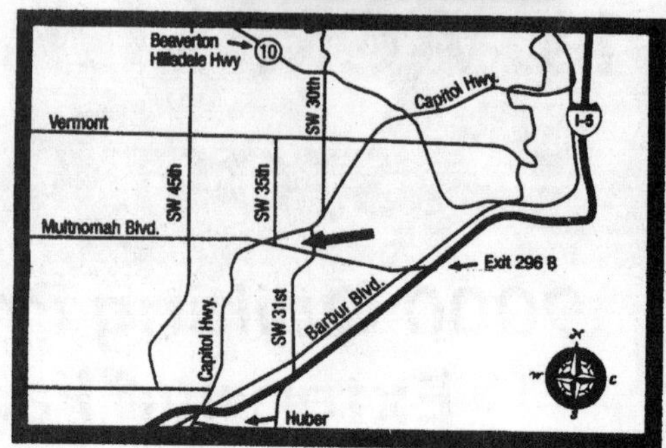

Portland, OR #59

Fax: 503-977-2762 fibersinmotion@comcast.net
Owner: LuAnn Rukke Est: 2002 1800 sq.ft.

Portland's innovative fabric store specializing in contemporary & international textiles.
Located in Historic Multnomah Village, just five minutes from Downtown Portland.
Celebrate you creativity . . . Fabrics, buttons, notions, books & gifts.
We offer classes for every skill level from beginning to advanced.
All designed to inspire the artist within!

Portland, OR #60

Tues-Sat 10 - 4
Sun 12 - 4

Patchwork Peddlers

4107 NE Tillamook
(503) 287-5987 97212
Owner: Gail Pope
Est: 1977 1200 sq.ft.

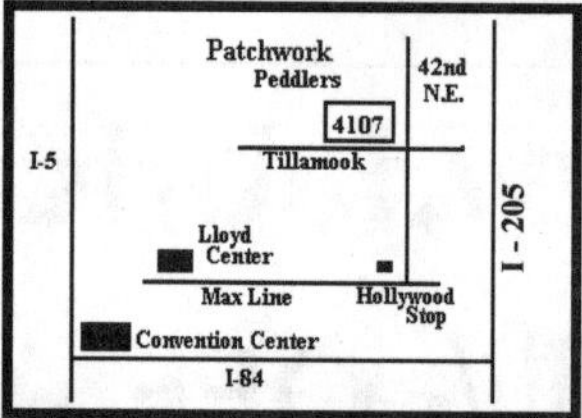

Largest selection of quilt books in the Northwest; 1200 bolts of 100% cotton fabric.

Portland, OR #61

Alyen Creations

Japanese Kimono Fabrics
Painted & Dyed Fabrics
Shop Online Catalog 24 Hours!
www.alyencreations.com

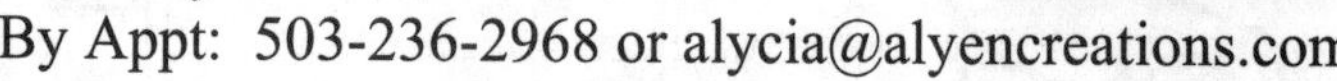
By Appt: 503-236-2968 or alycia@alyencreations.com

Website Or By Appt.

Aloha, OR #62

Mon - Fri 10 - 8
Sat 9 - 5

Sharon's Attic Quilt Shop

18365 SW T.V. Hwy. 97006
(503) 259-3475
Fax: (503) 259-3469
ssrice99@earthlink.net

Sharon Rice opened her first store on February 16th 2004. Started out with over 700 bolts of fabric. Two walls of notions, patterns and books. We also have a Gammill long-arm quilting machine.

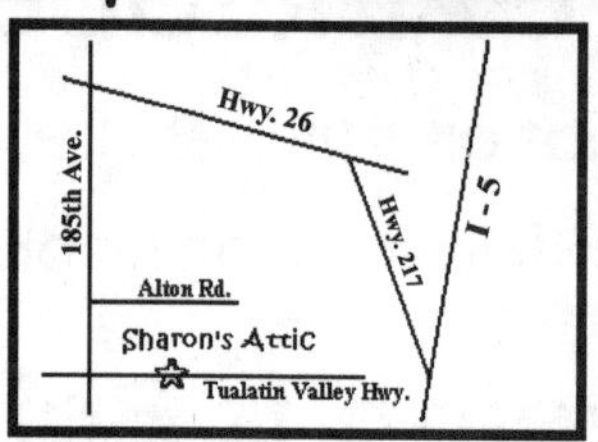

StoryQuilts.com

Where quilting is suspenseful, romantic, & full of passion. Please wear a thimble!

Large selection of 100% cotton fabrics from the finest manufacturers along with books, notions, classes, quilt kits and block of the month programs.

Mon, Wed, Fri 9:30 - 5:30
Tues & Thur 9:30 - 7:30
Sat 9:30 - 5:00 Sun 1:00 - 4:00

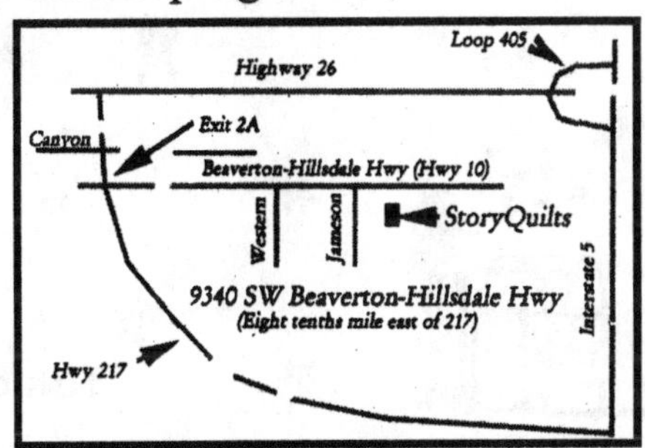

9340 SW Beaverton-Hillsdale Hwy.
503-384-0185
www.storyquilts.com
E-Mail: quilter@storyquilts.com
Fax: 503-384-0613 2650 sq.ft.

Directions: Take exit 2A from hwy. 217. Go East on Beaverton-Hillsdale (hwy. 10) approximately 0.8 miles. StoryQuilts is just East of Jameson (stop light) on the right.

Lake Oswego, OR #64

A Common Thread

Owned and operated by women who sew

Portland's #1 Bernina dealer. Authorized Janome Dealer.
Quilting and Fashion Fabrics, Books, Notions,
Patterns, Embroidery Supplies, Unusual threads.
We specialize in Customer Service.

Mon - Fri 9:30 - 6
Sat 10 - 5 Sun 12 - 5

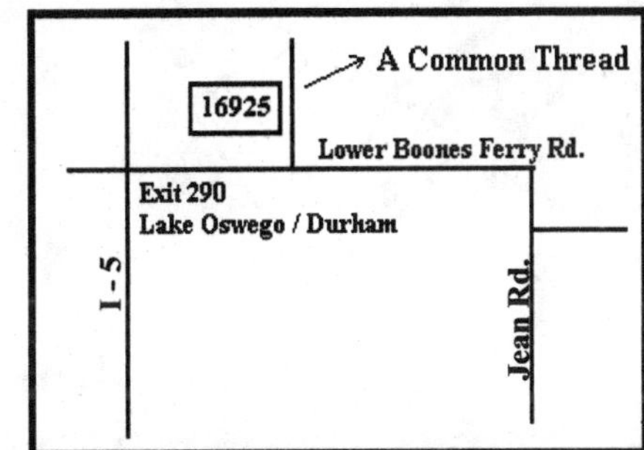

(503) 624-7440 Fax: (503) 670-9860
E-Mail: Actbernina@aol.com
Web Site: www.acommonthreadfabrics.com
Owner: Laura Dickson
Est: 1999 5200 sq.ft. 3000+ Bolts

16925 SW 65th
Lake Oswego, OR 97035
Toll Free: 1-877-915-6789

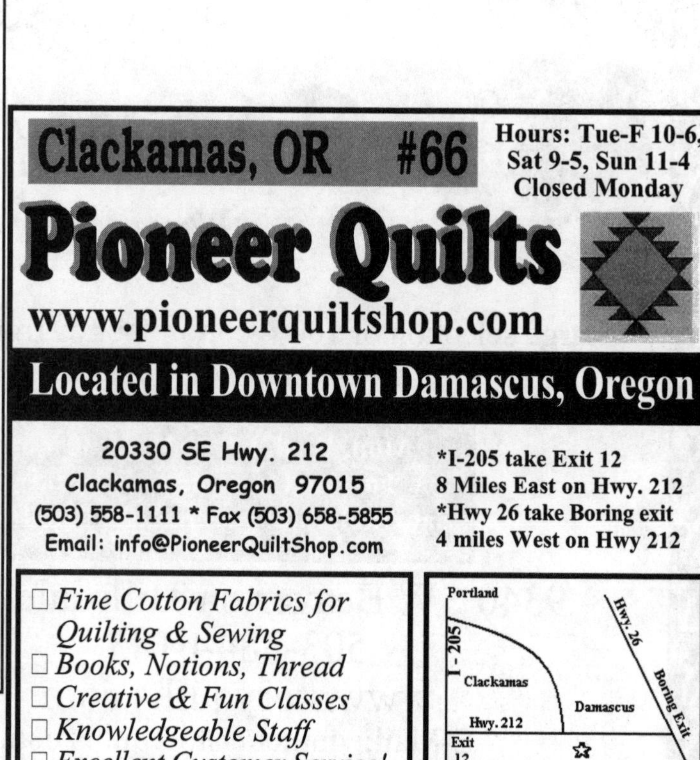

West Linn, OR #67

The Quilt Shoppe

1795 Willamette Falls Dr.
West Linn, Oregon 97068
503•722•7430

Come See Us

4500 plus bolts of fabric
We have more space for fabric, a great classroom and easy access from Stafford Rd. or Interstate 205

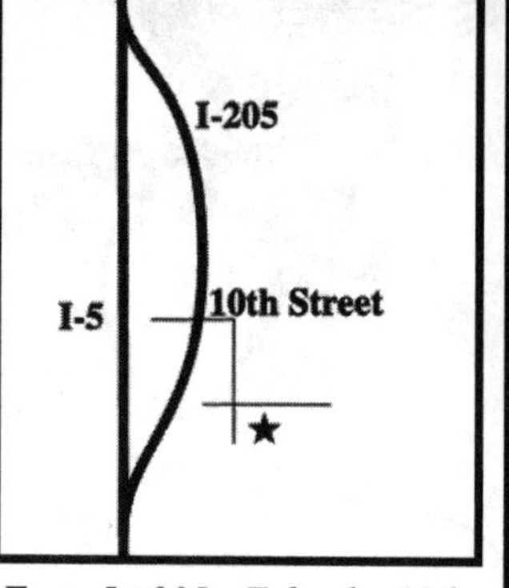

From I - 205: Take the 10th Street Exit, Go West on Willamette Falls Dr., Go three blocks, We're on the left.

Mon - Fri 9:30 - 5:30
Sat 10 - 5 Sun 11 - 5

"We pride ourselves in friendly customer service"

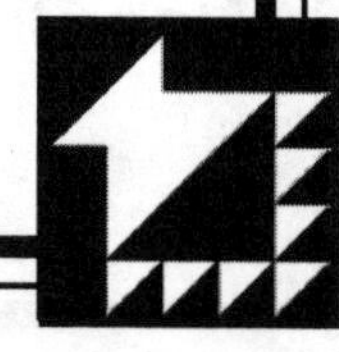

PARADISE
Quilts & Fabrics

455 N. E. Burnside - Gresham, OR 97030

503-666-1899 - email: paradisequilts@effectnet.com

Gresham, OR #68

Fabric • Notions • Patterns • Fat Quarters • Books • Classes

Machine Quilting Service Now Available....
by Award Winning Machine Quilter Dennis Dries

Come visit us in Paradise!

JoAnn Dries, Owner
Monday - Friday 10 - 5:30
Saturday - 10 - 4
Sunday - noon - 4

City	Store Name Store Address	Phone
Beaverton	Mill End Retail Store, 4955 NW Western Ave	503-646-3000
Beaverton	Sewing Center West, 11439 SW Beaverton-Hillsdale Hwy	
Bend	Amish House, 2620 NE Hwy. 20 #230	541-388-4651
Brownsville	Troyer's Stitches, 898 W. Bishop Way	541-466-5323
Burns	Foxy Fabrics, 433 N Broadway Ave	541-573-6325
Carlton	Late Bloomers Quilt Shop, 125 W. Main St.	503-852-5533
Cave Junction	Vintage Charm Quilts, 339 S Redwood	541-592-3210
Clackamas	Quilting Delights, 14863 SE Oregon Trail Dr	503-658-1600
Clackamas	Quilting Delights, 13159 SE 132nd Ave	503-698-4360
Clatskanie	Bobbin Along, 80 NE Art Steele St	503-728-3913
Coos Bay	Linda's Crafts & Quilts, 63425 Jerome Rd.	541-751-8118
Corvallis	Sewing Plus/Country Calico, 6120 S.W. Country Club Dr.	541-758-3323
Corvallis	Creative Crafts & Frames, 934 NW Kings Blvd	541-753-7316
Enterprise	The Country Quilter, 118 W. Main St.	541-426-9026
Enterprise	Savoies Specialties, 105 SW 1st	541-426-3232
Eugene	The Quilt Patch, 448 W. 3rd Ave.	541-484-1925
Eugene	27th Street Fabrics, 2710 Willamette	541-345-7221
Eugene	Paramount Sew & Vac, 1056 Green Acres	541-345-2100
Florence	Laurel Street Fabrics, 208 Laurel St.	541-997-7038
Gold Beach	Sew Like the Wind Quilt Art, 33066 Nesika Rd	541-247-8626
Grants Pass	Quilt Country, 2175 NW Vine St.	541-479-2700
Grants Pass	Home Shop, 147 SW G St	541-955-0160
Grants Pass	Jordan's, 1100 NW Regent Dr.	541-476-0214
Gresham	Craft Warehouse, 604 Eastman Pkwy.	503-661-0574
Gresham	All About A Dream, 336 N Main Ave	503-491-9336
Hermiston	Oregon Trail Quiltworks, 34025 Riverview Dr	541-667-8756
Hillsboro	Crazy 4 Quilts, 3080 SE Willow Dr	503-640-4445
Klamath Falls	Sewing Machine Center, 1414 E Main St	541-884-6949
Lake Oswego	The Pine Needle, 429 First St.	503-635-1353
Lebanon	Strawberry Patches Quilt Shop, 764 Main St.	541-258-4075
Lebanon	Whims Watercolor Quilts, 36453 Bohlken Dr	541-451-6776
Lincoln City	Quilt Shop, 545 NW Hwy 101	541-994-5455
Madras	Hatfields Dept Store, 347 5th St	541-475-6329
Medford	Fasturn Junction, 3859 S. Stage Rd	541-776-9030
Medford	Cottage Quilting, 1545 Modoc Ave	541-261-3884
Milwaukee	Mill End Store, 9701 S.E. McLoughlin Blvd.	503-786-1234
Milwaukie	Quilt & Sew Shoppe, 11123 SE 30th	
Moro	Lisa's In Stitches, 408 Main St	541-565-3400
Newberg	Itchin' to Stitch, 3809 Coffey Ln.	
Newberg	Threads and More, 602 B E. 1st	503-538-3577
Newport	The Newport Quilt & Gift Co., 644 SW Coast Hwy.	541-265-3492
Portland	Daisy Kingdom, 134 NW Davis	503-222-9033
Portland	Montavilla Sewing Center, 8326 SE Stark	503-254-7317
Portland	A Quilted Kitchen, 9938 SW Terwilliger	503-245-5158
Portland	Heart To Hand, 8407 NE Fremont Ave.	503-309-4037
Portland	Scarborough Flair, 4442 N. E. 131 Pl.	503-254-3882
Reedsport	Quilt Shop, 679 W. Alder Pl.	541-271-2616
Salem	Ruth's Quilt Tops & More, 2651 Brooks NE	503-485-5330
Salem	Heartland Quilts, 4939 Countryside NE	541-962-5374
Seaside	Montero Sisters Fabrics, 130 S Holladay	503-738-7730
Silverton	Window Box Quilts, 106 N. First St.	503-873-5015
Springfield	Jean Marie's Fabrics, 637 Main St.	541-746-0433
Stayton	Quilt-N-Stitch, 601 N 1st Ave	503-767-4240
Sublimity	Country Classics, 480 S. Center	503-769-4645
Sublimity	Needles & Thread, 246 NE Starr St.	503-769-1336
Sutherlin	Sonya's Sewing Basket, 683 W Central	541-459-6077
Sweet Home	Seamingly Creative, 1245 Main St.	541-367-8934
Talent	McQuilts, 117 N. Pacific Hwy.	541-535-2573
Tigard	Calico Corners, 9120 SW Hall Blvd.	503-624-7218
Tillamook	Sister's Quilt Shoppe, 516 Madsona Ave	503-842-4075
Toledo	Kelly's Kalico Korner, 170 N Main St	541-336-2268
West Linn	Olde Tyme Stitching, 2085 Ridgebrook Dr	503-635-1192
Wheeler	Creative Fabrics, 475 Nehalem Blvd	503-368-5900
Winston	Just-A-Stitch, 33 NE Main, PO Box 1022	541-679-4445
Yoncalla	Quilt Connections, 8542 Hayhurst Rd.	

Oregon Guilds:

Albany Beulah Rebkah Lodge #35 Quilters, 540 SE 2nd, 97321 Meets: Weekly at Hill St. Church of Christ
Albany Albany Sew & Chat Quilt Club, 1215 W. 37th, 97321 Meets: Thursday 9 a.m. at United Methodist Church
Aloha Tualatin Hills Park & Recreation Quilters, 8005 SW Grabhorn Rd., 97007
Aloha PHD 18490 SW La Paz Court, 97007 Meets: Weekly in member's home
Ashland Hands All Around, 175 N Main Meets: Wednesdays @ 10am at 1st Methodist Church
Astoria School House Quilters, 97103 Meets: 2nd & 4th Monday 7 p.m. at Astoria Middle School
Aurora The Aurora Colony Historical Society Quilters Meets: Annual quilt show early Oct. at Aurora Colony Museum
Baker City Baker City Quilters, R.R. 1, Box 27, 97814 Meets: Wednesday 8 a.m. at County Extension Office
Bay City Tillamook County Quilters, 6735 Tillamook Ave., 97107 **Bend** Mt. Bachelor Quilt Guild, 97701
Beaverton Beaverton Community Center Quilters, 14185 SW Alibhai, 97005 Meets: Thursday 9 a.m.
Bend Bend Quilters, 1665 SE Ramsey, 97702 Meets: Weekly during the day
Blodgett Summit Quilters, 20445 Marval Pl., 97326 **Brookings** Brookings Quilt Guild, P.O. Box 994, 97415
Brookings Azalea Quilt Guild, P.O. Box 994, 97415 Meets: 4th Monday 7 p.m. except Dec. and Summer at Presbyterian Church, 540 Pacific
Cave Junction Illinois Valley Quilters, 316 Terrace Drive Meets: Wednesdays @ 10am at 316 Terrace Drive
Clackamas Gladstone Chautauqua Quilters, 190 W. Gloucester, 97027 Meets: Weekly 6:30 p.m. at Senior Center
Clatskanie Castle Quilters Guild, P.O. Box 992, 97016 **Foster** Sweet Home Quilters, P.O. Box 175, 97345
Coos Bay Coos Sand N' Sea Quilters, P.O. Box 1234, 97420 Meets: 1st Thursday 7 p.m. (Sept. - June) at Gloria Dei Lutheran Church, 1290 Thompson or 3rd Wednesday 10 a.m. at First Christian Church, 2420 Sherman, North Bend
Coquille Coquille Valley Art Center Meets: 2nd & 4th Tuesday
Corvallis Quilts from Caring Hands, 889 NW Grant Ave., 97330 Meets: Weekly afternoons, at Briar Rose Quilt Shop
Estacada Garfield Skip-a-Week Quilters, P.O. Box 234, 97023 Meets: Wednesday at Garfield Grange Hall
Etna Scott Valley Quilt Guild, P.O. Box 634, 96027 Meets: 1st Thursday 1 p.m. at Etna Methodist Church
Eugene Emerald Valley Quilters, P.O. Box 70744, 97401 Meets: 3rd Thursday @ 7pm. At Masonic Center
Eugene Pioneer Quilters, 2130 Bedford Way, 97401 **Grants Pass** Rogue Valley Applique Society
Florence Rhododendron Quilt Guild, 160 Florentine Ave., 97439 Meets: 2nd & 4rth Wednesday at 10 a.m. at Church of the Nazarene Satellite
Gates North Santiam Quilters, 824 W. Central St., 97346 Meets: Thursday at Gates Church of Christ
Gold Beach Gold Beach Quilters Guild, P.O. Box 138, 97444 Meets: 3rd Thursday 7 p.m. at Curry County Fairgrounds
Grants Pass Mountain Stars, 404 Pavillian, 97526 Meets: 2nd Saturday 1 p.m. or March, June & Sept
Grants Pass Pine Tree Quilters, 128 Covey Ln., 97527 Meets: 2nd Tuesday in member's home
Hillsboro "Quilts for Warmth" Project, 2257 NE Cornell Rd., 97124 Meets: 1st & 3rd Tuesday 6 p.m. at Furever Friends Quilt Shop
Hood River Dog River Quilters, 1215 C St., 97031 Meets 1st Monday 6:30 p.m. at E.T.C. shop, works on community quilts.
Hugo Hugo Ladies Club Schoolhouse Quilters, 201 Hitching Post Rd.6 Meets: Tuesdays & Fridays @ 9am at Hugo Ladies Club Schoolhouse 6050 Hugo Road
Jacksonville Mountain Stars Quilt Guild, P.O. Box 101, 97530 Meets: 2nd Saturday of odd months 9:30 a.m. at Rogue River Community Center, 132 Broadway, Rogue River
Jacksonville Jacksonville Museum Quilters, P.O. Box 284, 97527 Meets: 9 a.m. Wednesdays & Thursdays at US Bank Bldg.
Joseph Wallowa Mountain Quilters' Guild, P.O. Box 932, 97846 Meets: 2nd Thursday at St. Katherines Parish Hall
Junction City Junction City Quilt Guild, 1225 W. 10th St., 97448 **Medford** Mountain Stars Quilters, 80 High Oak Dr., 97504
Klamath Falls Pelican Piecemakers, 1915 Carlson, 97603 Meets: Wednesdays @ 10am at Lkamath County Museum
La Grande Quilt Questers, 2006 Washington Ave., 97850 Meets: 3rd Tuesday @ 7pm at Island City City Hall
Madras Jefferson County Country Quilters, 3576 W. Franklin Ln., 97741
McMinnville McMinnville Piecemakers, 106 Kingwood St., 97128 Meets; 2nd Monday 7 p.m. at McMinnville Residential Estates
Medford The Monday Club, 4918 Crater Lake Ave Meets: 2nd & 4th Mondays @ 9:30am at Grandma Dee's Fabrics
Medford Cotton Pickers, 2617 E Barnett Rd Meets: Thursdays @ 6:30pm at Ascension Lutheran Church
Merrill The Tater Patchers, 14141 Falvey Rd, 97633 Meets: 1st Monday @ 6pm
Milwaukie Loose Threads Meets: Every Thursday 10 a.m. at Mill End Store
Monmouth Quaint Quilters, 130 Cottonwood Ct., 97361 Meets: Weekly (except summer) in member's home
Mt. Shasta Shasta Lily Quilt Guild, 312 W Alma St Meets: 1st Thursday @ 7pm at Methodist Church
Nehalem Tillamook County Quilters, 41325 N. Fork Rd., 97131 Meets: 3rd Thursday at Latimer Quilt & Textile Center
Newberg Chehalem Park & Recreation Quilters, 3300 Victoria Way #106, 97132 Meets: Every Tuesday 1 p.m. at Senior Community Center, 2nd & Howard and Thursday 7 p.m. at Vittoria Square Rec Hall, Springbrook & Vittoria Way
North Bend Coast Quilters, P.O. Box 436, 97459 **North Powder** Baker City Quilt Club, P.O. Box 89, 97867
Oakridge Uper Willamette Piecemakers, P.O. Box 1101, 97463 Meets: 1st Tuesday at the Museum
Ontario Treasure Valley Quiltmakers, P.O. Box 1198, 97914 Meets: 3rd Thursday 1 p.m. at Pilgrim Lutheran Church, 208 SW 1st Ave.
Pendleton Blue Mountain Piecemakers Quilt Guild, 3307 NE Riverside Ave., 97801 Meets: 3rd Tuesday 6:45 p.m. at First Christian, 215 N. Main
Philomath Mary's River Quilt Guild, 101 Main St, 97370 Meets: Last Thursday (except Nov. & Dec) 7:30 p.m. at Benton County History Museum, 1101 Main St.
Portland Northwest Quilters, P.O. Box 3405, 97208 Meets: 2nd Monday alternates morning and evening at Emmanuel Lutheran Church, 7810 SE 15th, annual quilt show late March at Portland State Univ.
Portland High Fiber Diet, 6920 SW 3rd Ave., 97219
Portland Heirloom Quilters, 8805 SW Woodside Dr., 97225 Meets: Thursday 9:30 a.m. at Beaverton Mill End Store
Portland Fabric Depot Quilters, 3651 SE Washington St., 97214 Meets: Wednesdays 1 p.m. at 122nd & SE Washington
Portland Columbia Stitchery Guild, P.O. Box 19645, 97280 Meets: Quarterly (Sept, Dec, Mar, June) Lakewood Ctr, 368 S. State St., Lake Oswego
Prospect Tall Tree Patchers, 428 Red Blanket Rd Meets: 2nd & 4th Fridays @ 7pm
Reedsport Coast Quilters, 97467 Meets: 1st Wednesday 10 a.m. (Sept. - May) at United Presbyterian, 2360 Longwood
Rogue River Rogue River Piecemakers, P.O. Box 550, 97537 Meets: 1st & 3rd Monday 9 a.m. at Live Oak Grange
Roseburg Umpqua Valley Quilt Guild, P.O. Box 1105, 97470 Meets: 1st & 3rd Tuesday 10 a.m. at the Umpqua Valley Arts Center, Harvard Ave.
Salem Capitol Quilters, 4211 Gardner SE, 97302 Meets: Every Other Week, day time at Mission Mill Museum
Salem Mid Valley Quilt Guild, P.O. Box 621, 97308 **Scappoose** Summerplace Quilters, 31942 Raymond Creek Rd., 97056
Shady Cove Material Girls Meets: Tuesdays Open Sew @ 9am, 2nd Tuesday Class @ 6:30 pm at Grange Building
Sisters East of the Cascade Quilters, P.O. Box 280, 97759 Meets: 4th Wednesday 7 p.m. at Stitchin Post Classroom
South Beach Oregon Coastal Quilters Guild, P.O. Box 382, 97366 Meets: 2nd Thursday Noon odd months and 6:30pm even months at Atonement Lutheran Church, 2315 N. Coast Hwy. Newport
Sublimity Sublimity Quilters, P.O. Box 36, 97385 Meets: Every Thursday 9 a.m. at St. Boniface Rectory Basement, 375 E. Church
Sunriver Sun River Quilters, P.O. Box 3219, 97707
Warren Columbia Piecemakers Guild, 58093 Columbia Hwy, 97053 Meets: 1st Wednesday 7pm at Columbia Technology Center
Wimer Covered Bridge Quilters Meets: 2nd & 4th Mondays @ 9am at Wimer Grange

Erie (#55)
Fairview (#54)
North East (#56)
Union City (#57)
Russell (#58)
Wellsboro (#33)
Canton (#32)
Honesdale (#31)
Tunkhannock (#30)
Carlton (#53)
79
Knox (#51)
Montoursville (#35)
Woolrich (#34)
(#52)
Sharpsville
Brookville (#50)
Bloomsburg (#28)
80
Mayport (#49)
Mifflinburg (#36)
Danville (#29)
Elderton (#48)
Indiana (#47)
Belleville (#37)
Effort (#17)
(#18)
Hamburg (#19)
Weissport
Bethlehem (#29)
Monaca (#44)
Allison Park (#46)
Pittsburgh (#43)
New Kensington (#42)
Roaring Spring (#38)
Martinsburg (#39)
Greensburg (#40)
Marysville (#27)
Denver (#10,11)
(#12) Kutztown
Oley (#13)
(#16) Doylestown
Finleyville (#45)
Scottdale (#41)
70
76
Carlisle (#26)
King of Prussia (#2)
Sanatoga (#14)
Chambersburg (#25)
Gettysburg (#23)
Waynesboro (#24)
Littlestown (#22)
Pottstown (#15)
Hershey (#20)
Manheim (#21)
Bird-In-Hand (#9)
Glenmoore (#3)
Chestnut Hill (#1)
New Holland (#7)
Gordonville (#8)
(#6) Chadds Ford
Intercourse (#5)
Morgantown (#4)
PENNSYLVANIA
58 Featured Shops

Chestnut Hill, PA #1

Byrne Fabrics

We specialize in natural Fibers -- wool, cotton, linen, silk
Large selection of buttons and ribbons.
Bernina and Brother authorized dealer.

Mon - Sat 10 - 6
Wed til 8 Sun 12 - 4

8434 Germantown Ave.
Philadelphia, PA 19118
215-247-3485 or 888-302-9411
byrne@brynesewing.com

Fax: 215-753-7006
Est: 1979
1500 sq.ft.
Owners:
Debbie & Mike Byrne

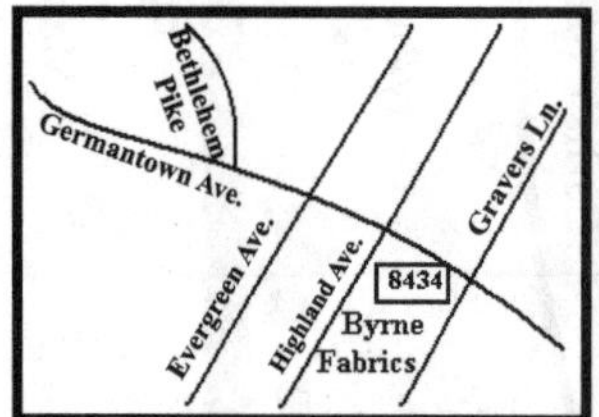

www.byrnesewing.com

King of Prussia, PA #2

Steve's Sewing, Vacuum & Quilting

Valley Forge Shopping Centre, Rte 202
156 West Dekalb 19406
(610) 768-9453 Fax: (610) 337-2622
steves@stevessewandvac.com
www.stevessewandvac.com
Owners: Steve & Karen Chubin
Est: 1992 7000 sq.ft. 2000+ Bolts

Mon - Fri 10 - 9
Sat 10 - 5 Sun 12 - 5

Sewing Machines • Sergers • Vacuums
Quilting Supplies • Fabrics • Sewing Notions
Accessories • Furniture • Lessons • Classes

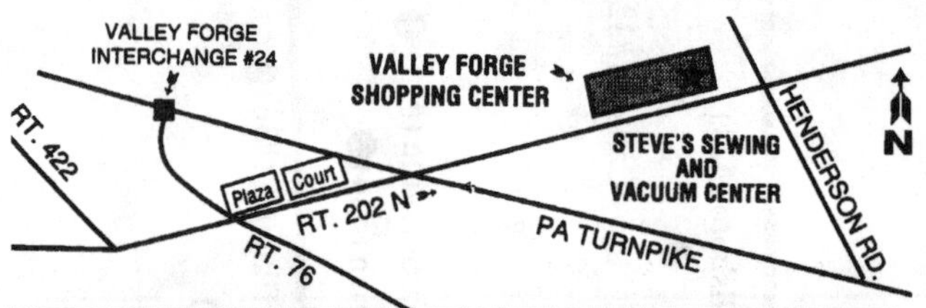

Directions: from Rt. 76 or PA Turnpike; Take Route 202 (Dekalb Pike) North past King of Prussia Plaza and Court. Turn left into Valley Forge Shopping Center (approx 1-1/2 miles). Steve's is in lower level.

SINGER baby lock BERNINA ORECK
EUREKA ROYAL DIRT DEVIL

Glenmoore, PA #3

Mon - Sat 10 - 5
Wed til 8
Sun 12 - 4

Tudor Rose Quilt Shop

Ludwig's Village, Rt. 100 & 401
(610) 458-5255
www.tudorrose.com
Owner: Jane Russell
Est: 1990 1200 sq.ft. 2000+ Bolts

100% cotton fabrics. Plus silks & wools. Everything a quilter needs plus friendly smiles, expert help.

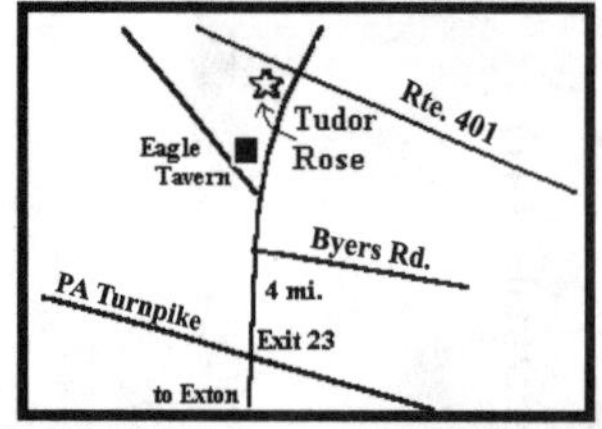

Morgantown, PA #4

Mon - Fri
9 - 9
Sat 9 - 5

Hayloft Fabrics

150 Morview Blvd. 19543
(610) 286-5045

One Stop Fabric Shop!
A huge selection of almost 7000 bolts of quilting fabric, plus loads of quilting notions and books AND the latest designer yarns.

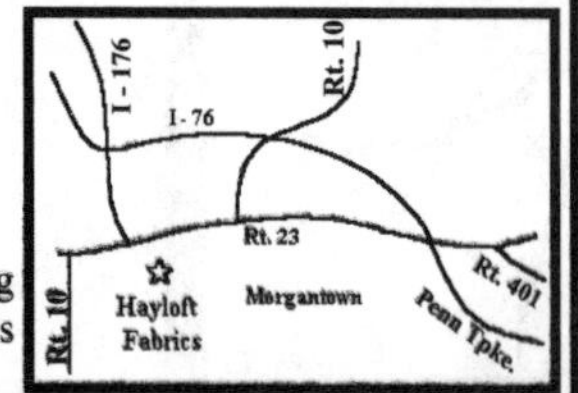

Celebrating our 39th Anniversary

Zook's Fabrics

Mon - Sat 8 - 5

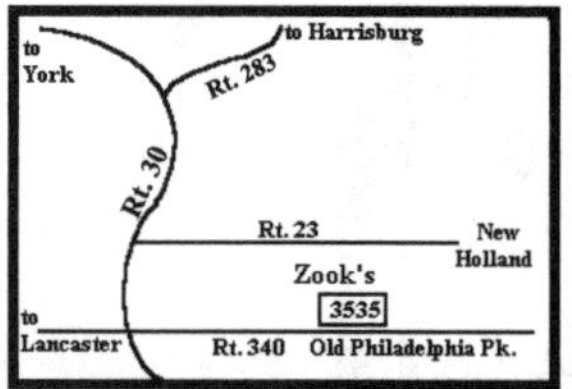

Intercourse, PA #5

3535 Old Philadelphia Pk.
17534
(717) 768-8153
Fax: Same
5000 sq.ft.

Large Selection of quilting fabric, books, patterns, quilting notions & hand made gifts. Also a large selection of sale fabric.

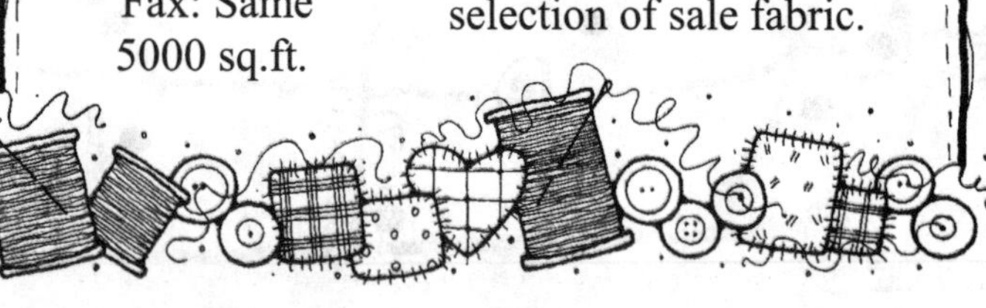

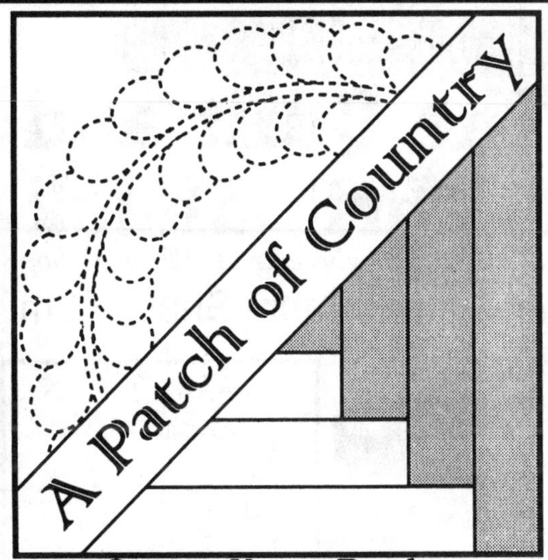

Chadds Ford, PA #6

22 Olde Ridge Village 19317
(610) 459-8993

Mon - Sat 10 - 5
Thurs til 8
Sun 12 - 5

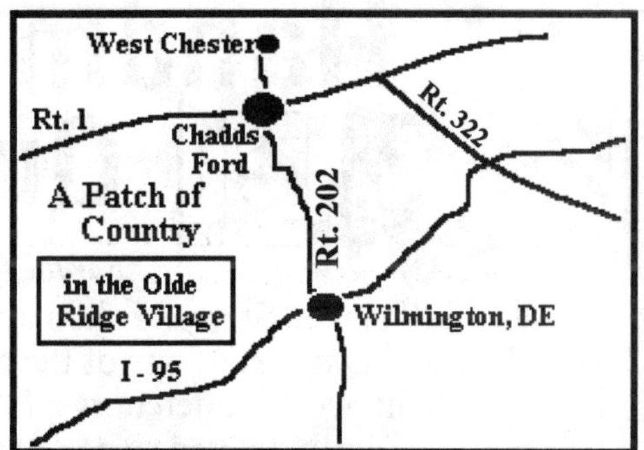

Celebrating Over 20 Years of Excellence

Owner: Karen Reed
Est: 1983 2200 sq.ft.

- **Block of the Month Programs for hand, machine or applique techniques**
- **Highest Quality Cottons & Quilter's Tools**
- **250+ Book Titles, Patterns**
- **Staffed exclusively by Friendly, Knowledgeable Quilters**
- **Special Order & Mail Order Services Available**
- **Year-round classes for all skill levels with full student support.**

Located 1 mile south of Route 1 on Route 202. Within half an hour of the New Jersey & Maryland state lines. 1 mile north of the Delaware state line. Minutes from Brandywine River Museum, Winterthur Museum, Longwood Gardens, Brandywine Battlefield State Park and Valley Forge.

- Pfaff, Janome and Brother and Singer Sewing Machines
- Amish Custom Cabinets
- Fabrics and notions including Thimbleberries
- Classes and clubs
- Grace Quilt Frames
- Friendly, helpful staff—Fast reliable service all makes and models
- Large parts inventory-many hard-to-find items
- Parking for Cars and Buggies

You can also visit us at:
www.BrubakersSewing.com
Or email at: Sewing@frontiernet.net

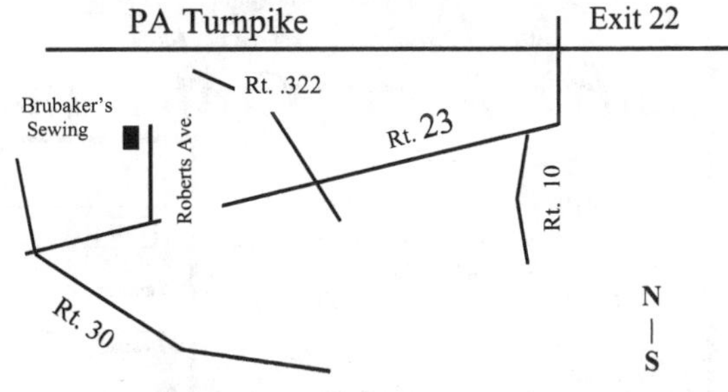

New Holland, PA #7

20 North Roberts Avenue
(12 miles from the PA Turnpike)
Just off Route 23!

1-800-466-7315

Store Hours:
Mon. thru Friday 8-5:30 Thursday 8-8
Saturday 8-3 Closed Sunday

We proudly participate in these quilt events:

Philadelphia Quilt and Embroidery Showcase
Quilters Heritage Celebration
York Quilters "Celebration of Quilts"
Quilt Odyssey
Pennsylvania National Quilt Extravaganza

From PA Turnpike, take exit 22. Follow 10 south to Main St. Turn right, this is Rt. 23. Follow Rt. 23 west into New Holland. Turn right on Roberts Avenue. Brubaker's is on the left.

From Lancaster, take Rt. 30 to Rt. 23 east Follow Rt. 23 into New Holland Turn left on Roberts Ave.

Mon - Sat
9:00 am - 6:00 pm

Esh's Quilts
Rt. 340 E
Intercourse
Rt. 30
1 miles east of Intercourse

Esh's Handmade Quilts

"For the finished product."

Quilts of all sizes. Stop and shop at our Country Store. Located just east of one of the quilt capitals of the world, Intercourse, PA.
"Family owned since 1980"
Look for the quilt sign & quilts on the front porch.
3829 Old Philadelphia Pike 17529
(717) 768-8435 Owners: Jacob & Anna Esh

Gordonville, PA #8

Bird-in-Hand, PA #9

The Quilt and Fabric Shack

A newly renovated Fabric Shop

www.TheQuiltandFabricShack.com

- 4500 Bolts of Famous Brands
- Books - Kits
- Fat Quarters
- Fleece - Flannels
- Wide Quilt Backing
- Novelty Prints
- New Closeouts at $3 yd.
- Large spacious well-lit room
- Over 300 Quilts & Wallhangings
- Quillows, hotpads, local hand-mades
- Handicap Entrance
- Buses Welcome--Call for reservation
- Visa - Mastercard - Discover

Mon- Sat
9 - 5

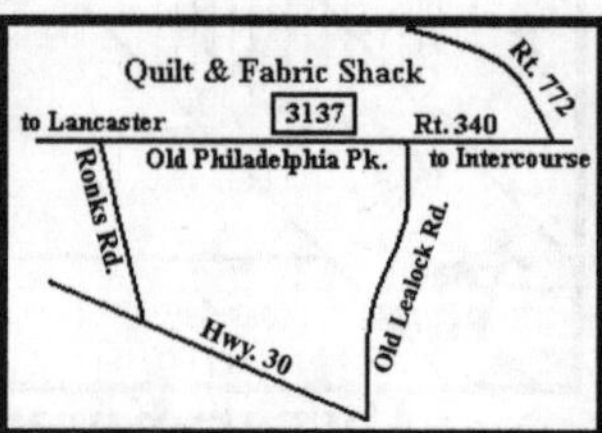

3137 Old Philadelphia Pike 17505
(717) 768-0338
Owners: Omar & Katherine Stoltzfus

Sauder's Fabrics

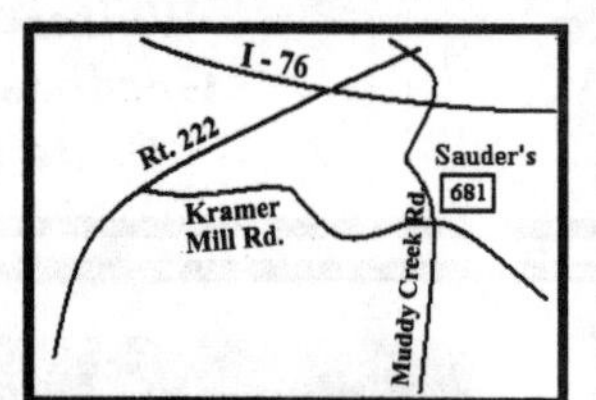

Mon - Sat 8 - 5

Denver, PA #10

681 S.
Muddycreek Rd.
P.O. Box 409
17517
(717)336-2664

Large Selection of quilting fabric, books, patterns, quilting notions & hand made gifts. Also a large selection of sale fabric.

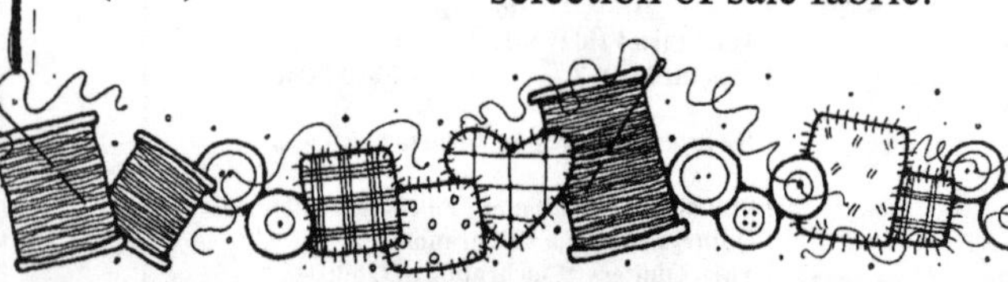

Denver, PA #11

Mon, Tues, Thur & Fri 8 - 8
Wed 8 - 5
Sat 8 - 4

Burkholder's Fabrics

2155 W. Rt. 897 17517
(717) 336-6692
www.burkholdersfabrics.com
Owners: Eugene Martin
Est: 1972 3000 sq.ft.
Sewing notions, quilt supplies, lace, fabrics, including VIP, Debbie Mumm, Springmaid, Concord, Hoffman, Peter Pan, knits & more.
We accept all major credit cards.

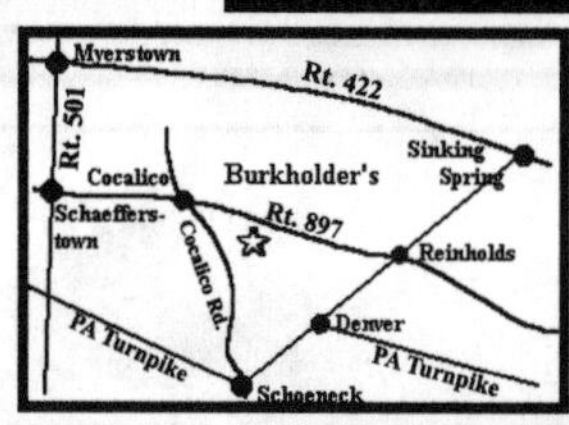

Kutztown, PA #12

Mon-Tues-Fri 9 - 5
Wed & Thur 9 - 7
Sat 9 - 4

Wooden Bridge Drygoods & Purrfect Stitches

195 Deysher Rd. 19530
W.B. (610) 683-7159 P.S. (610) 683-0266
Fax: (610) 683-7284
W.B. Anna Mae Martin & Louise Shirk
P.S. Sherry Monberger
Over 5000 bolts of 100% cotton
Fabrics, quilting supplies, notions, Kwik-Sew patterns, quilt books, quilt tops. Bernina Sewing Machines & accessories.

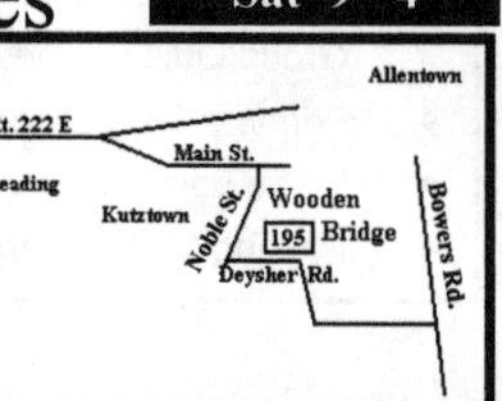

Oley, PA #13

Wed 10 - 5
Thur 10 - 8
Fri & Sat 10 - 5

Ladyfingers Sewing Studio

6375 Oley Turnpike Rd. 19547
(610) 689-0068 Fax: (610) 689-0067
gail@ladyfingerssewing.com
www.ladyfingerssewing.com Est: 1975
Owner: Gail Kessler 4000+ bolts
THE destination quilt shop in PA! Fabulous selection, great service, reasonable prices. Restored c.1860 hotel in the heart of historic, scenic Oley Valley farmland.

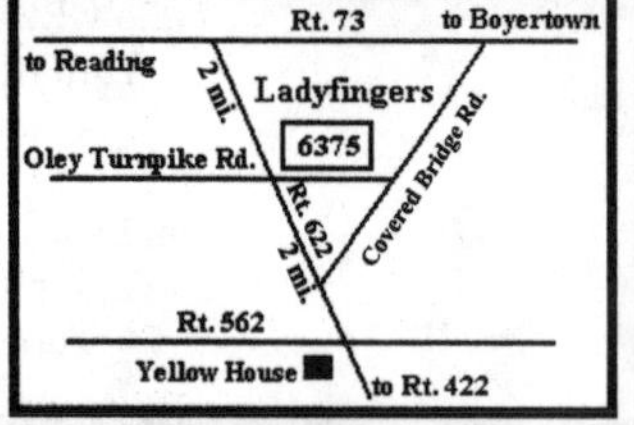

Sanatoga, PA #14

Tues & Thur 10 - 8
Wed & Fri 10 - 4
Sat 10 - 2

Sally's Sewing Center, Inc.

2228 E. High St. 19464
(610) 323-7419 Fax: Same
samsew@fast.net
www.sallysewingcenter.com
Est: 1998 1200 sq.ft. 2000 Bolts

Great selection of fabric, patterns, books and notions.
PFAFF sewing machines & sergers.

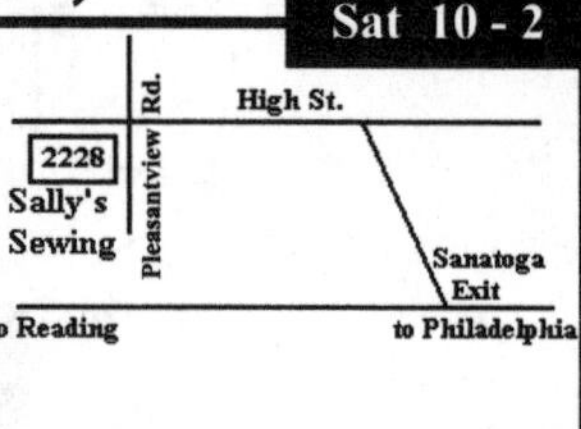

Pottstown, PA #15

Generations Quilt Shop

Wed - Sat 10 - 5
Thur 10 - 8
Sun 12 - 5

120 Shoemaker Rd. 19464
(610) 718-5505

Fax: (610) 718-5507
generationsquiltshop
@netzero.com
Est: 2001
1500 sq.ft.

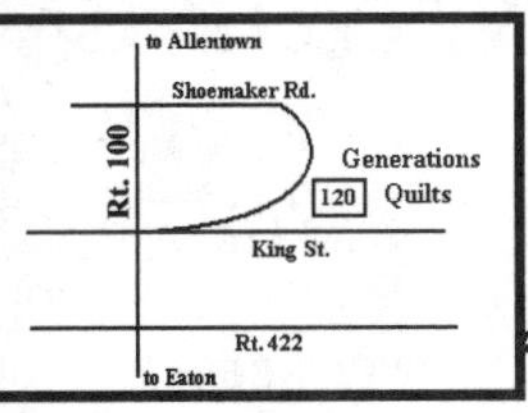

Owner: Linda Mendenhall
2000 Bolts & growing Daily

Our bright and cheery A-Frame Cottage holds Books, Patterns, Notions and a friendly staff. Our beautiful Fabrics come from all major manufacturers with an extensive collection of Flannels & Children's Fabric.

Doylestown, PA #16

Byrne Sewing Connection

We specialize in natural Fibers -- cotton, linen, silk, batiste, heirloom laces
Large selection of specialty threads.
Bernina and Brother authorized dealer.

Mon - Sat 10 - 6
T, W, Th til 8 Sun 12 - 4

422 E. Butler Ave.
New Britain, PA 18901
215-230-9411 or 888-302-9411
E-Mail: byrne@brynesewing.com

Fax: 215-230-0378
Est: 1979
4500 sq.ft.
Owners:
Debbie & Mike Byrne

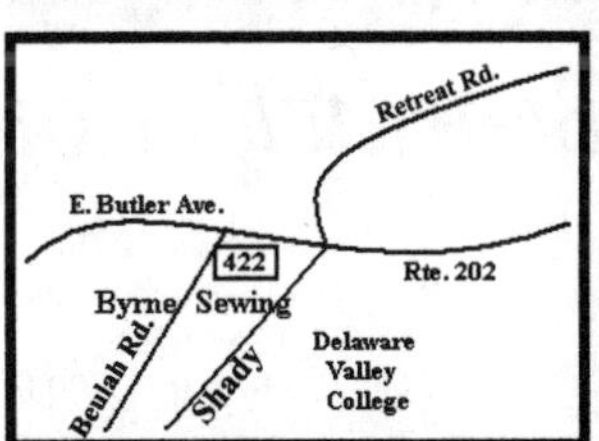

www.byrnesewing.com

Effort, PA #17

7 Days a Week
10 - 5

The Country Quilterie

Carriage House Square
R.R. #3, Box 2482, Route 115 N, 18330
(570) 620-9707
makwant@noln.com
Owner: Maryann Kwant
Est: 1989 1500 sq.ft. 2500 Bolts

Over 2500 Bolts of Quilting Fabric, Books, Notions, Supplies. Largest selection of Quilts in the Poconos. Quilted Accessories and Gifts.

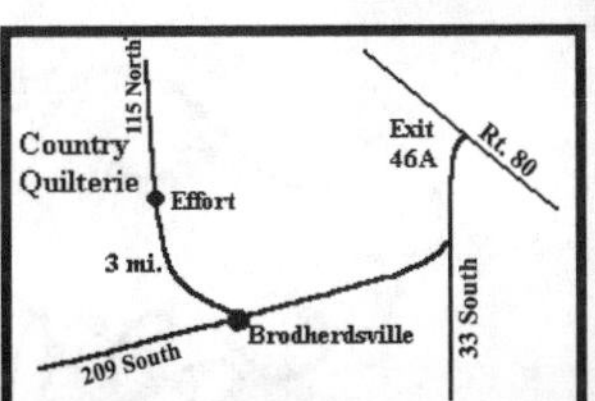

Weissport, PA #18

Mon, Wed, Thur, Sat 10 - 5
Tues 10 - 9
Sun 11 - 4

The Quiltery

410 Bridge St. 18235
(610) 377-5590 or (866) WeQuilt
www.thequiltery.org
Est: 2002 8000 sq.ft. 1000 Bolts

We are a full service quilt shop and antique Center. We carry top quality fabric, books, patterns & notions and have 20 antique dealers in our building.

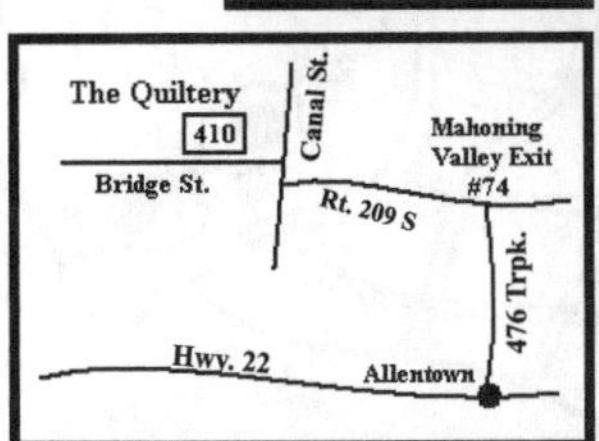

Hamburg, PA #19

260 N. 4th St. 19526
(610) 562-7173
hapsew@comcast.net
www.happysewingroom.com
Owner: Jean Boyd
Est: 1990 1000 sq.ft.

Happy Sewing Room

We offer beautiful cotton fabrics, quilting supplies, patterns, books, sewing machines, classes & most important the personal service every quilter deserves.

Tues - Fri 9:30 - 6
Sat 9:30 - 4

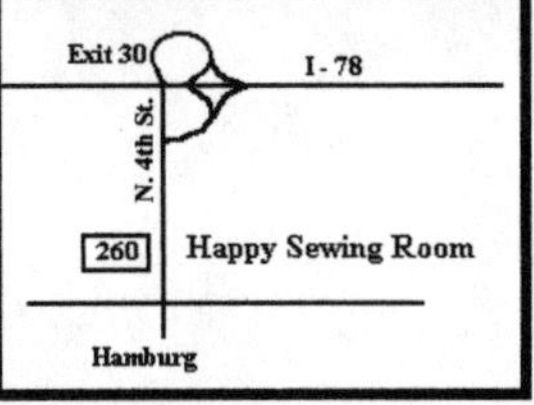

Hershey, PA #20

Tues - Fri 10 - 6
Sat 10 - 5

1034 E. Chocolate Ave. 17033
(717) 534-9900

Friendly, welcoming atmosphere. Extensive selection of fabrics: batiks, flannels, orientals, brights, contemporary, & traditional.
Wide selection of books, patterns, supplies.

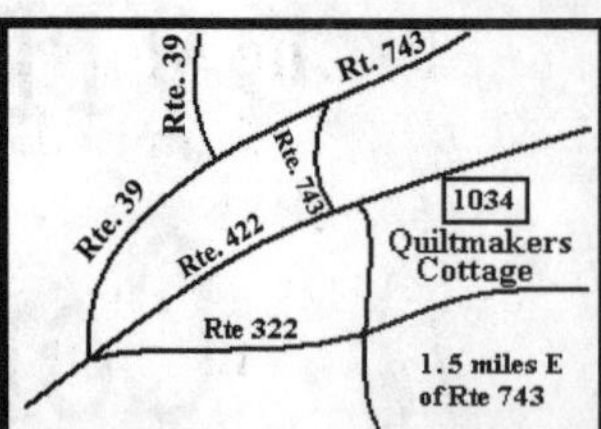

Manheim, PA #21

Mon - Sat 9 - 5
Tues & Fri til 8

Stitch & Craft

2957 Lebanon Rd. 17545
(717) 664-4230 Fax: (717) 664-4244
Brossstitchcraft@aol.com
Owner: Alice Bross

Beautiful fabric; friendly, helpful service; many classes; easy access to PA Turnpike.

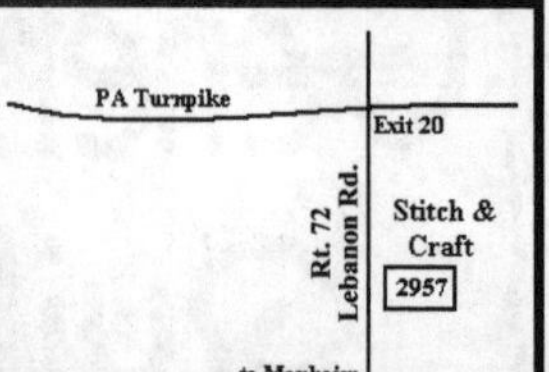

Littlestown, PA #22

Mon - Sat 9:30 - 5
Sun 1 - 5

The Quilt Patch

1897 Hanover Pike 17340
(717) 359-4121 Fax: (717) 359-8124
www.quiltpatchshoppes.com
Owners: Scott & Debra Cromer
Est: 1979 12,000 sq.ft.

RJR, Batiks, South Seas, Moda, Hoffman, Homespuns, Thimbleberries, Quilts & Supplies. Art Gallery. Gifts, Collectibles (Dept. 56, Hummel, Byer's Choice, Etc.)

Rt. 30 U.S. E
Gettysburg Square
RT 97
U.S. Rt. 15 N
Littlestown Square
Just 10 miles from Gettysburg
Hanover Pike Rt. 194 N
Light
1897
The Quilt Patch

Gettysburg, PA #23

Mon, Wed, Thur 9:30 - 6
Fri 9:30 - 8
Sat 9:30 - 5

Needle & Thread

2215 Fairfield Rd. 17325
(717) 334-4011
Owner: Darlene Grube
Est: 1985 7000 sq.ft.

FULL LINE FABRIC STORE
10,000 bolts to Choose from—Pendleton, wools, silks, cottons. Books & Patterns

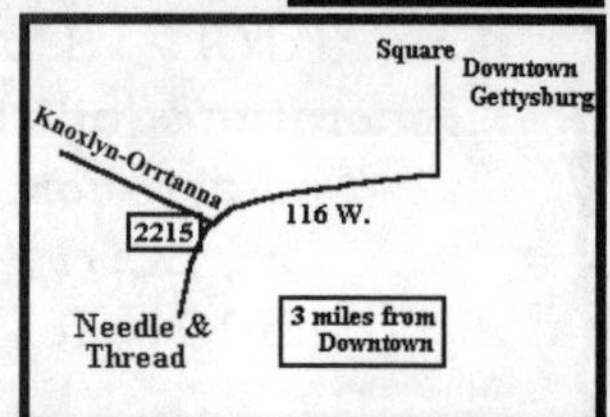

Waynesboro, PA #24

Mon & Fri 8 - 8
Tues - Thur 8 - 5
Sat 8 - 4

Benedict's Country Store

6305 Marsh Rd. 17268
Moving to New Location in Jan 2005
(717) 762-6788
Est: 1980 2200 sq.ft. 3000 Bolts

Over 3000 Bolts Fabric in stock.
Large selection Quilt Books, Patterns and Quilting Supplies.

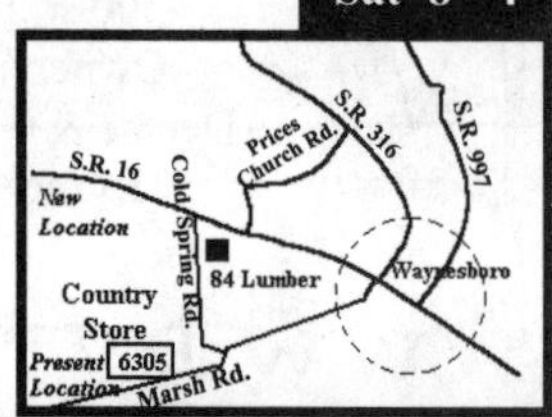

Chambersburg, PA #25

Mon - Fri 9 - 8
Sat 9 - 6

The Sew'n Place

979 Wayne Ave. 17201
(717) 263-5606
TheSewnPlace@hotmail.com
Est: 1982 1700 sq.ft. 2500 bolts

We sell Quilting Fabrics - Supplies - Books
We sell Singer - Viking - Bernina - Pfaff
We service Sewing Machines in the store also.

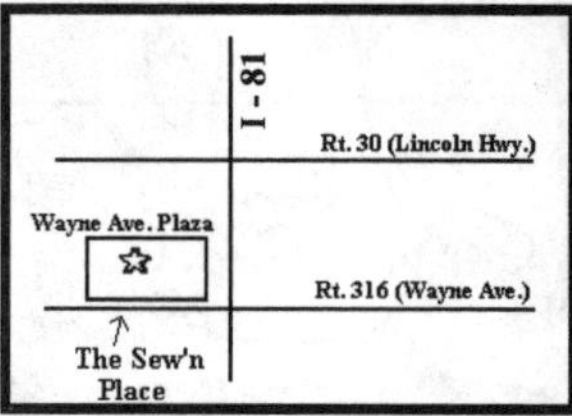

Carlisle, PA #26

Tues- Fri 9 - 4
Thurs 9 - 8
Last Sat. of Month 9 - 2
Call for Summer Hrs.

Calico Corner

341 Barnstable Road 17013
(717) 249-8644
calicoquil@aol.com
www.calicocorneronline.com
Owner: Janet Shultzabarger
Est: 1984 600+ Bolts

Personal attention to quilters needs. 100% cottons, notions, books, classes. Very reasonable prices and service with a smile.

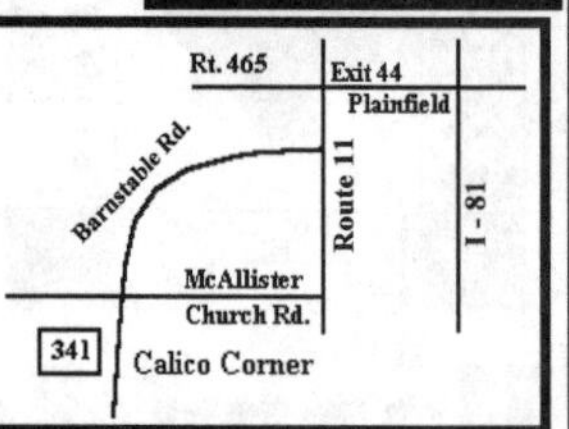

Marysville, PA #27

1975 Valley Rd.
Marysville, PA 17053
Phone / Fax: (717) 957-4225
Email: Jbac1@aol.com
Website: www.smilespinners.com
Owners: Cathy L. Queitzsch & Joel L. Bacon
Est: 2000 3000 sq.ft.

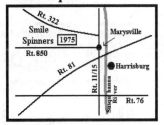

Mon 10 - 4
Tues - Thur 10 -6
Fri 10 - 8
Sat 10 - 4
Sun 1 - 4

Rt. 322 | Smile Spinners 1975 | Marysville | Rt. 850 | Rt. 81 | Rt. 11/15 | Harrisburg | Susquehanna River | Rt. 76

Located near Harrisburg, PA Just 4 mi. West of Marysville on Rt. 850

A full service Quilt Shop located in a tranquil country setting. Gorgeous 2000+ bolt collection of the finest fabrics. Hundreds of books, Notions, and Patterns. Custom machine quilting. Ever changing Quilt Show in our large Gallery.

We'll have you in stitches

Bloomsburg, PA #28

Mon - Sat 9:30 - 5 Thur til 8

Fabric Galore

58 E. Main St. 17815
(570) 784-8799

Over 1,000 bolts of fabric, hundreds of quilting books, patterns, notions, Grace frames. Horn cabinets. Janome sewing machines & sergers. Panasonic Vacuums. Free instruction with machine purchase. Long-arm quilting. Scissor sharpening. Classes & workshops for all ages.

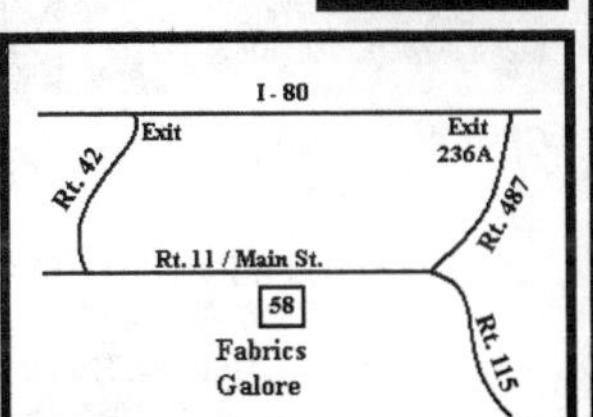

Danville, PA #29

Mon - Fri 10 - 5 Sat 10 - 4

Contrary Wife Quilt Shoppe

120 Walnut St. (Rt. 11) 17821
(570) 275-8182
Owner: Sharon Kashner
Est: 2001 1200 Bolts

Fabrics - Books - Patterns - Notions

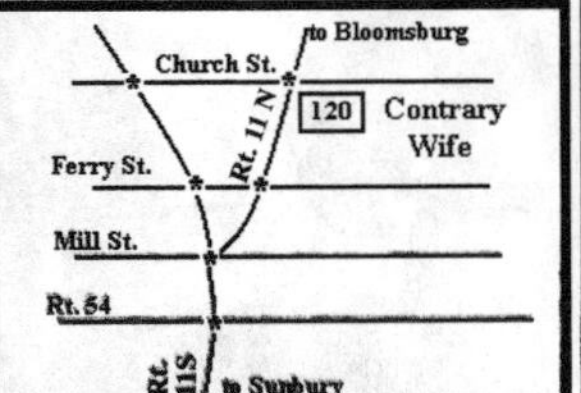

Tunkhannock, PA #30

Endless Mountains Quiltworks, inc. and Yarns
158 W. Tioga Street, Tunkhannock, PA

Tues - Sat 10 - 5
Thur 10 - 9 Sun 1 - 5

(570) 836-7575
EMQ2001@epix.net
www.emquiltworks.com
Owner: Jeannette Goeringer Kitlan
Est: 2001 1500 sq.ft.

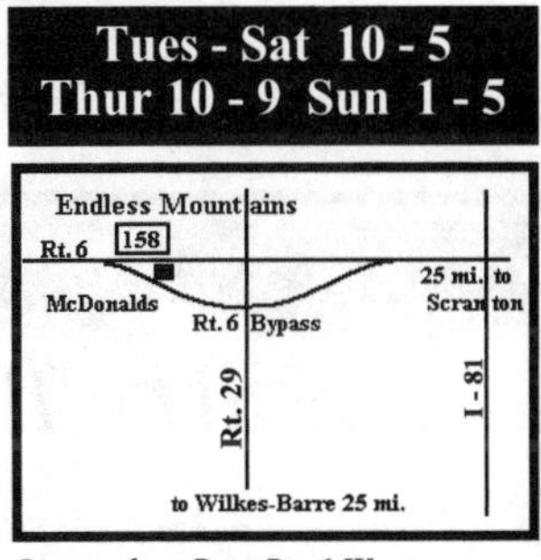

We nourish the quilter's heart, hands and soul with over 3000 bolts of beautiful cotton fabric, classes, books and fine knitting yarns, too!

Located on Bus. Rt. 6 West across from McDonald's in Tunkhannock, PA., the gateway to the Endless Mountains of northeastern PA

Honesdale, PA #31

Tues - Sat 10 - 5

The Mountain Quiltworks

R.R. #4, Box 4111 18431
(570) 253-9510
Owner: Amy R. Dunn
200+ Bolts 1100 sq.ft

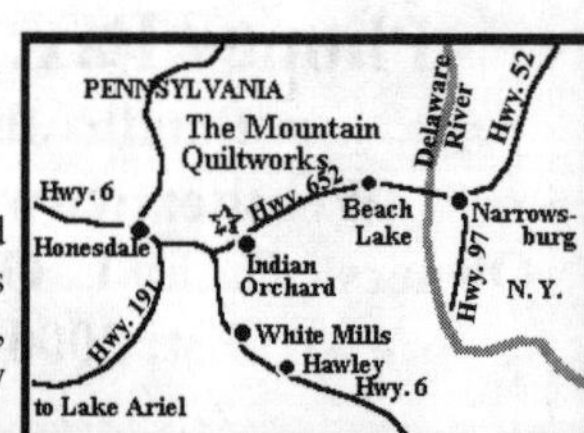

Custom Hand-Quilting our Specialty! Find everything you need to create tomorrow's heirlooms. From various source books, stencils & patterns too of course, top quality cotton fabrics.

Canton, PA #32

Tues - Sat 10 - 5

The Weathervane Quilt Shop

R.R. #2, Box 26, Rt. 14 17724
(570) 673-4944 Fax: 297-3074
nortsned@epix.net
Owner: Nancy Swatsworth
Est: 1996 3000 sq.ft.

1000+ Bolts of 100% fine cotton fabrics, books, patterns, notions. Lovely handmade gifts. Featherweight Singer Sewing machines.

Wellsboro, PA #33

29 Waln St. 16901
(570) 724-1616
Fax: (570) 723-8539
Owners: Katie Mader & Mary Ginn
Est: 2003

needlesquiltshop@yahoo.com
needlesquiltshop.com

Mon - Sat 10 - 5

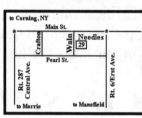

to Corning, NY
Main St.
Crafton
Waln
Needles
29
Pearl St.
Rt. 287 Central Ave.
Rt. 6/Erst Ave.
to Morris
to Mansfield

The Cozy Little Quilt Shop in the heart of Canyon Country

- Fabrics, Notions, & Accessories for the dedicated Quilter.
- Long-Arm Services on the premises.
- Full Schedule of Classes for all skill levels.
- Personalized service to aid in the making of your Treasured Heirlooms.

Woolrich, PA #34

Open Everyday

39 Boardman Dr.,
P.O. Box 130 17779
(570) 769-7401
Fax:
(570) 769-7832

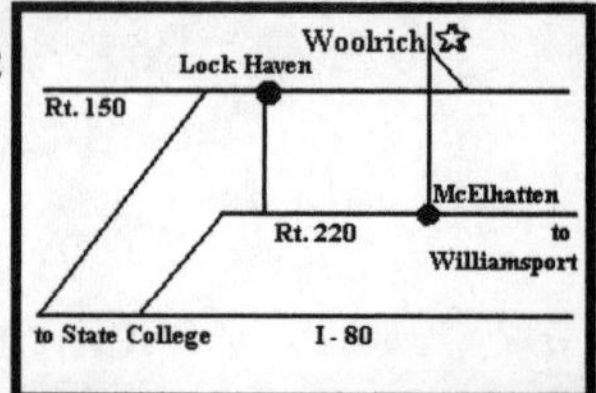

The Store for Outdoor People. Sportswear & Outerwear for Men & Women. Large Selection of Quilters Cottons, Mill End of Wool for Braiding Rugs or Making Garments.

Montoursville, PA #35

Tues, Wed, Thur 10 - 5 Fri 10 - 7 Sat 10 - 3

Our Gathering Place

936 Plaza Dr. Savoy Plaza 17754
(570) 368-1130
Owner: Chris Kroboth 4000 Bolts

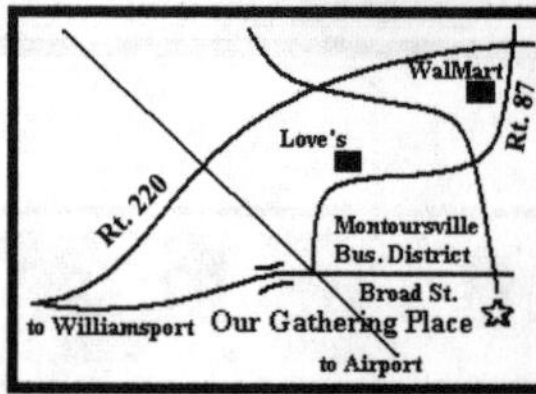

Fine cotton fabrics and quilting supplies. Many books and patterns plus classes. Come Gather, share & enjoy!
Montoursville is located about 5 mi. E of Williamsport off I - 180 / U.S. 220

Mifflinburg, PA #36

Mon, Tues, Thurs, Fri 9 - 9 Wed & Sat 9 - 5

Verna's Fabrics

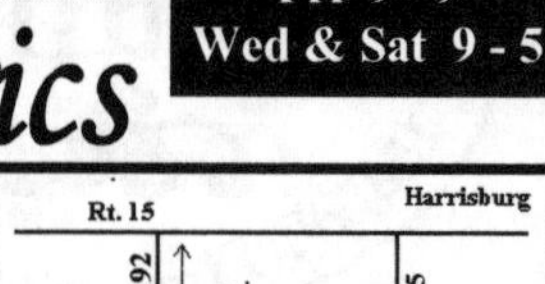

1430 Red Bank Rd. 17844
(570) 966-2350
Owner: Verna H. Duke

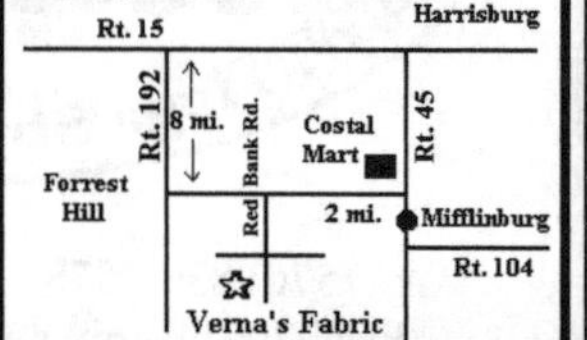

Fabrics — Books — Patterns

Belleville, PA #37

Mon - Sat 9 - 5

A.M. Buchanan Dry Goods

Newly Remodeled!

2459 S.R. 655 17004
(717) 483-6428
Owner: Anna M. Buchanan
Est: 1983 2050 sq.ft.

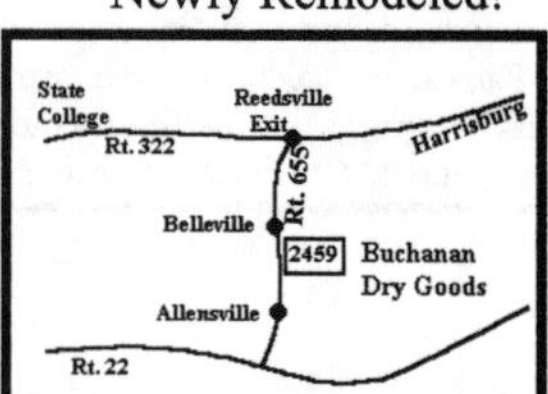

Largest selection of fabrics, patterns, books & quilting supplies in the area. Hand made Quilts, hangings, Pillows & more. Great Gifts in stock. Located 2 mi. south of Belleville on Rt. 655

Roaring Spring, PA #38

Mon - Fri 9:30 - 4:30 Saturdays May - Sept 10 - 2 Oct - Apr 10 - 4

Country Beefers

RD #1, Box 495 16673
(814) 224-4818 Est: 1981
Owners: Louann Ferraro

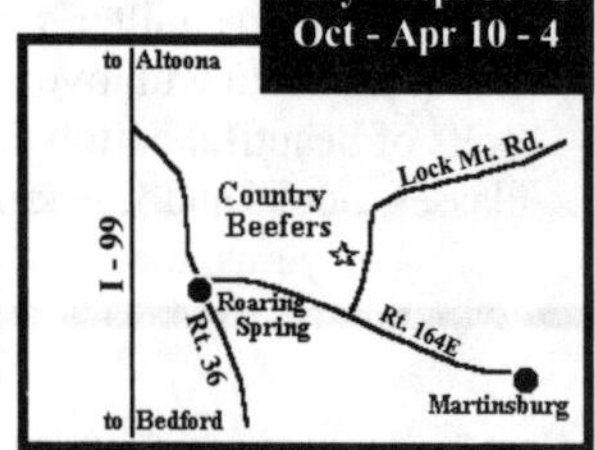

Cotton fabrics, homespuns, books, craft patterns, notions, stencils. Also locally made gift items, appliqued clothing and Yankee Candles.

Traditions LLC
QUALITY FABRIC & CLOTHING

We feature over 2000 bolts of fabrics and sewing notions as well as quilting supplies. Browse through our Jack Dempsey Needle Art, Peddler patterns, wall hangings and custom quilts. Also TreeFree greeting cards, crafted doilies, cedar chests, country aprons, handtowels, and many more thoughtful gifts. Baby Boutique plus shoes & clothing including Carhartt.

Visit our totally unique shop.

Martinsburg, PA #39

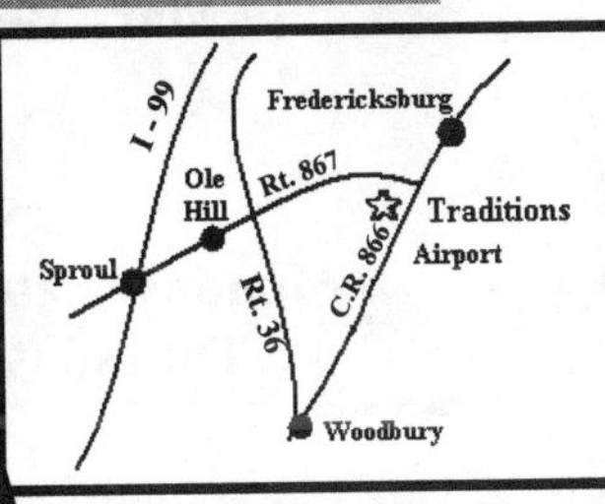

I-99 to Roaring Spring exit
Follow Rt. 36 South
Left onto 164 East
Right at light approx. 1 mi.

Reg. Hours: Mon/Thur 9 to 5; Fri 9 to 8; Sat 9 to 5
2327 Curryville Rd., Martinsburg, PA 16662
814-793-3980

The Stitch In Time Shoppe

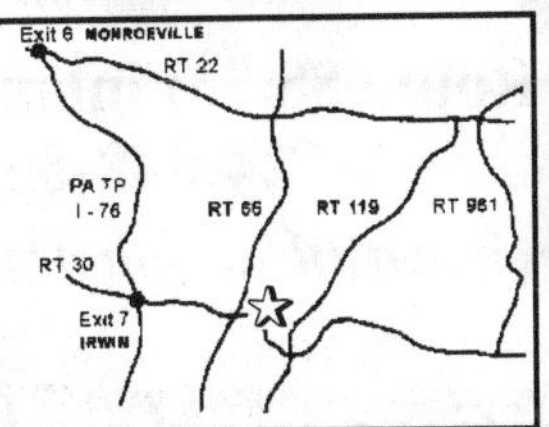

Mon - Thur 10:00 am - 6:00 pm
Fri - Sat 10:00 am - 5:00 pm
Sunday Noon - 5:00 pm
(Check for summer hours)

100% cotton quilting fabrics, name brands, classes, books and sewing machines. Located in Gabriel Brothers Plaza, Route 30, Greensburg. Approx. 5 miles east of the Irwin exit of the PA turnpike on Rt. 30.

Greensburg, PA #40

Gabriel Brothers Plaza, Suite 9C
(724) 836-0611

Scottdale, PA #41

Tues - Sat 10:30 - 5

Kate & Becca's Quilt Patch

West Overton Village, 1045 Frick Rd. 15683
(724) 887-4160
Web Site: www.quiltpatchetc.com
Owners: Kate Hepler & Becca Flack

Calico Prints, Stencils, Quilt Books, Templates, Quilt Kits. Selection of Handmade Quilts—Contemporary and Traditional. Done by craftspeople who do only the finest work. Gifts for all occasions.

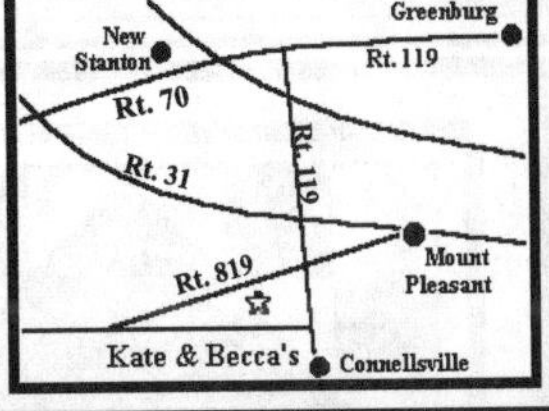

New Kensington, PA #42

Mon - Sat 10 - 5
Wed 12 - 8

L & K Cottage Quilts

3740 Milligantown Rd. 15068
(724) 334-8599 Fax: (724) 334-8270
cottagequilts@earthlink.net
www.cottagequilt.com
Owner: Laura Barnes
Est: 2001 1200 sq.ft. 2000+ Bolts
Batiks, Cottons, Wool, Flannel including 30's, Thimbleberries, Debbie Mumm. A Large Selection of Books, Patterns and Notions.

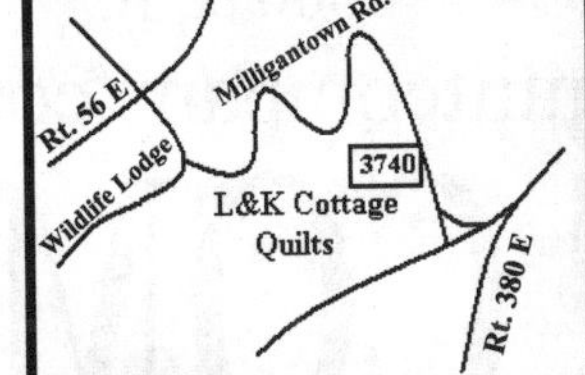

Pittsburgh, PA #43

Mon - Sat 10 - 5
Thur til 8

Piecing It Together

3458 Babcock Blvd. 15237
(412) 364-2440
E-Mail: piecngit@fyi.net
Web Site: www.fyi.net/~piecngit
Owners: Johanna Blanarik
Est: 1986 1200 sq.ft.

Complete line of quilting supplies, 100% cotton fabrics, books, notions, patterns, and classes. Lots of samples. Personal, friendly.

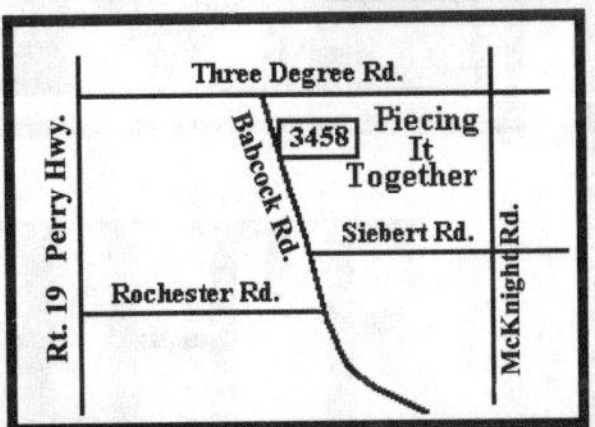

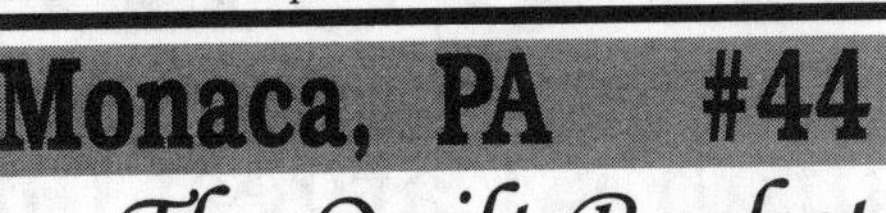

Monaca, PA #44

Mon - Sat 10 - 4

The Quilt Basket

1116 Pennsylvania 15061
(724) 775-7774
Owner: M. Maxine Holmes
Est: 1984

The Quilt Basket is a complete quilt shop offering lots of classes & all the supplies: i.e. fabrics, patterns, books, and notions.

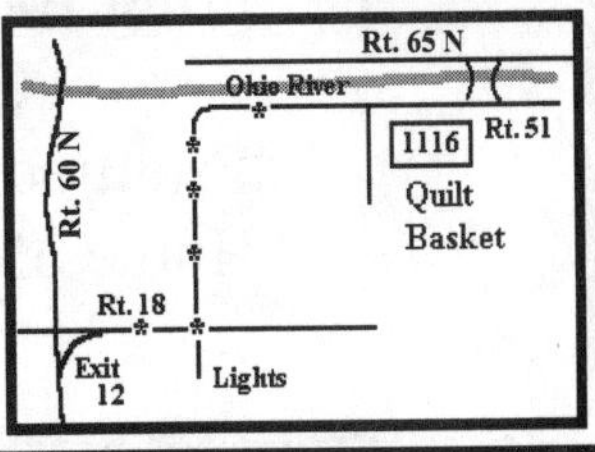

Finleyville, PA #45

Quilters Corner

6101-1 Route 88 Finleyville, PA 15332
1-724-348-8010
www.quilterscorner-pa.com

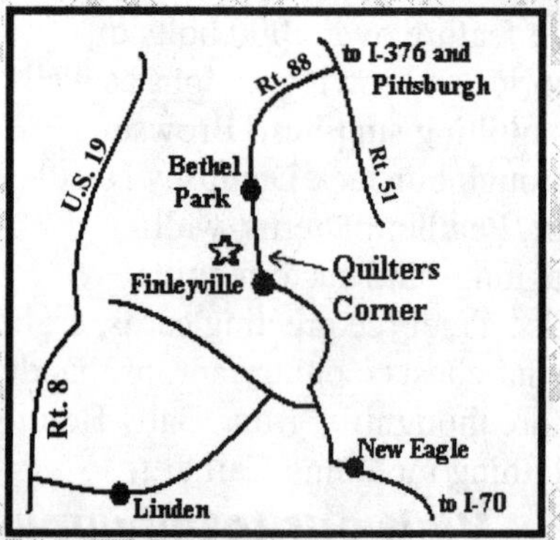

Enter the exciting world of quilting...

- *Explore our extensive selection of both traditional and contemporary cotton fabrics with over 4000 bolts to browse.*
- *Consult with our friendly, knowledgeable staff.*
- *Choose from a variety of "Block of the Month" selections.*
- *Classes for all skill levels from beginner to advanced*
- *Books, Patterns, Notions ~ We will be happy to order anything you need!*

Est: 1989 with over 3750 sq. ft.
Mary Beth Hartnett- Owner

Shop Hours:
Monday- Saturday 10:00 am-5:00 pm
Thursday evening till 9:00 pm

We are your premier quilt shop in South-Western Pennsylvania.

Allison Park, PA #46

3940 Middle Rd. 15101
(412) 487-9532
Fax: (412) 487-9581
e-mail: quilt@nauticom.net
Owner: Karen Montgomery
Est: 1994 3500 sq.ft.
www.thequiltcompany.com

Mon - Sat
9:30 - 5
Mon & Thur
til 9

THE QUILT COMPANY

Pittsburgh's Largest Quilt Shop!

Featuring 100% cottons, books, and original patterns.
Quilting Supplies & Notions.
"Featured in Quilt Sampler Magazine in 1997"
Home of The Quilt Company line of patterns
& BlockWatchers Club

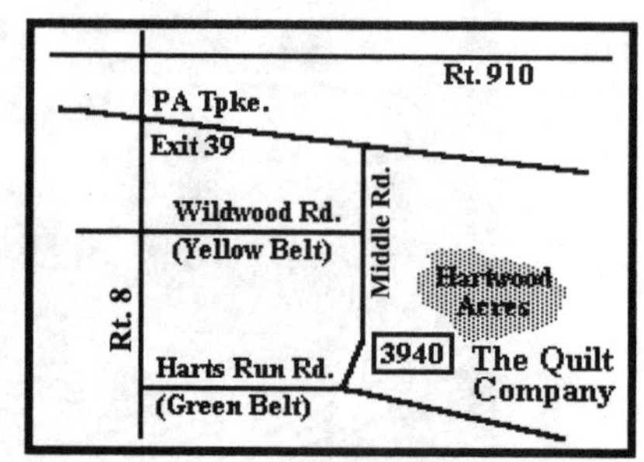

Indiana, PA #47

Daffodil Cottage Quilt Shop

533 Philadelphia St.
Indiana, PA 15701
(724) 465-4990

Mon 10 - 8
Tues - Sat 10 - 5

1400+ bolts of fabric, stencils, and books. We pride ourselves on quality customer service. We tailor our classes to suit individual needs.

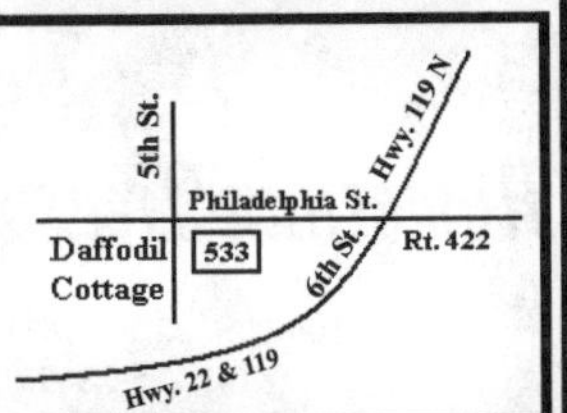

Elderton, PA #48

Judys' Sewing Center

M, T, TH, F 10 - 5
Wed 12 - 8
Sat 10 - 3

Rte. 422, P.O. Box 178 15736
(724) 354-3360 Fax: (724) 354-3145
E-Mail: judyssew@ptdprolog.net
Web Site: www.judyssew.com
Owners: Judy Hicks & Judy Kimmel
Est: 2000 1700 sq.ft.
2000+ Bolts 100% Cotton Fabric. Heirloom Supplies. Books, Patterns, Notions, Threads, Stencils. Husqvarna Viking Sales-Service. Friendly Service. Fun Classes.

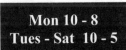

12 mi. to Kittanning
Rte. 422
Saltwork St.
Elderton
Rte. 210 N
10 mi. to Indiana
Shelocta
Judys' Sewing Center
Rte. 210 S
Rte. 56

Mayport, PA #49

MAYPORT COTTONS

& Quilt Shop

Mon & Fri 10 - 5
Tues & Thur 10 - 8
Sat 10 - 3

68 Paradise Rd. 16240
(814) 365-2212
Owner: Patty Toy Est: 1999

1000+ bolts of beautiful 100% cottons, mettler thread, lots of books, patterns, & notions. Full variety of classes.

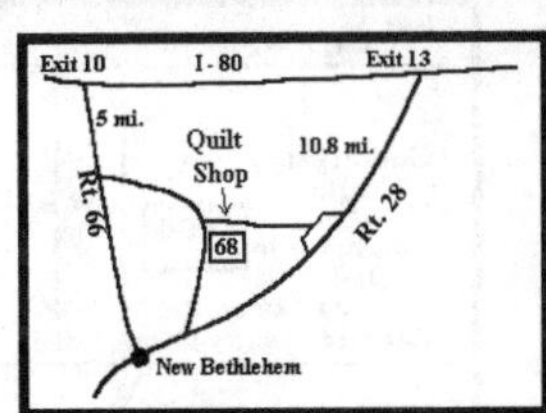

#50

HEIRLOOM Quilting and Antiques

Heirloom Quilting and Antiques
1.5 Miles North
I-80
Exit 78
Route 36

PFAFF MACHINES & ACCESSORIES

2000+ BOLTS FABRIC • BOOKS • NOTIONS

Quilting / Sewing Classes - FUN

HOURS:
Mon-Sat 10 am - 6 pm
www.heirloomquilting.com

(814) 849-USEW (8739)
Durfee Burtner, Proprietor
1225 RT. 36 BROOKVILLE, PA 15825
1.5 MILES N. OF 1-80, EXIT 78

Knox, PA #51

Countryside Crafts & Countryside Quilts

Est: 1987

Owners:
Jolinda Tharan (Crafts)
& Sally Byers (Quilts)
6361 Canoe Ripple Rd.
Knox, PA 16232
Exit 7 from I - 80
(814) 797-2434

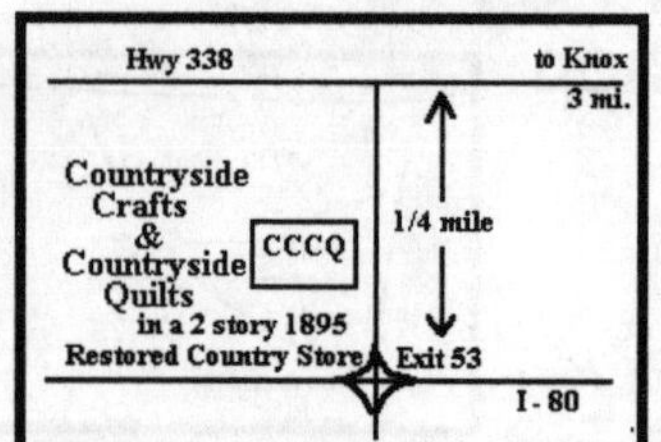

Mon - Sat 10 - 4:30

In the heart of Clarion County.
We are the area's Largest and Most Unique Country gift, craft and Quilting supply shop.
With 100% Cottons, Books, Quilting Patterns and the area's largest supply of craft patterns.
Homespuns and flannels.
Handmade Country Clothing. Free Newsletter.

Sharpsville, PA #52

Shaffer's Countryside Quilting

Wed 12 - 7
Thur & Fri 10 - 5
Sat 10 - 3

2741 Winner Rd. 16150
(724) 962-9394
judyquilts@hotsheet.com Est: 1998
Owner: Judy Shaffer 2000 bolts

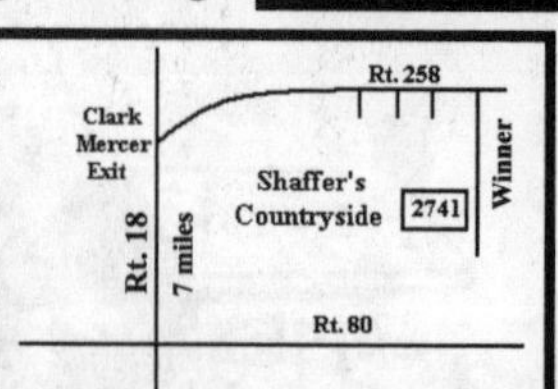

Best quality cotton fabrics - Moda, RJR, P&B, and more. Knowledgeable, friendly staff, special orders welcome. Visa and Mastercard.

Carlton, PA #53

Homespun Treasures Quilt Shoppe

Mon - Sat
9:30 - 5

509 U.S. 322 16311
(814) 425-2889
quiltLov@Certainty.net
Owner: Gail M. Baker

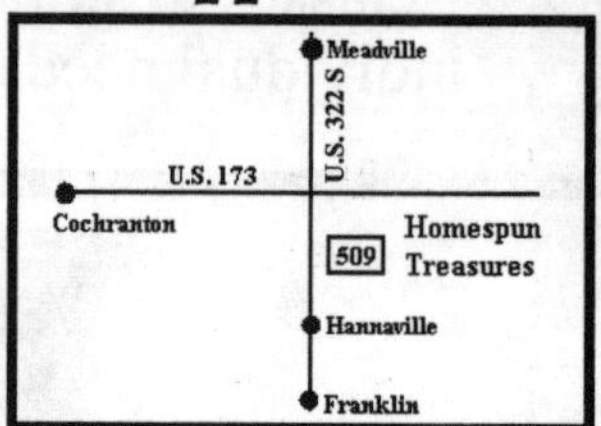

Located between Meadville & Franklin, PA. Large selection of Fabric & Books & Notions. Classes Available. Always looking to see your work. Bring it in and share.

Fairview, PA #54

International Fabric Collection

7870 W. Ridge Road, P.O. Box 72, Fairview, PA 16415
info@intfab.com 2500 sq.ft.
www.intfab.com
Owner: Dorothy Brown Est: 1987

Cottons from Africa, Alexander Henry, Australia, France, Germany, Guatemala, Holland, Italy, Japan, Kona Bay, Liberty Fabric, Dupioni Silks, Sashiko Supplies, Unusual Books and Patterns.

Open most days from 10 am to 3 pm
and always on Thursday.
Please call 800-462-3891 to check hours.

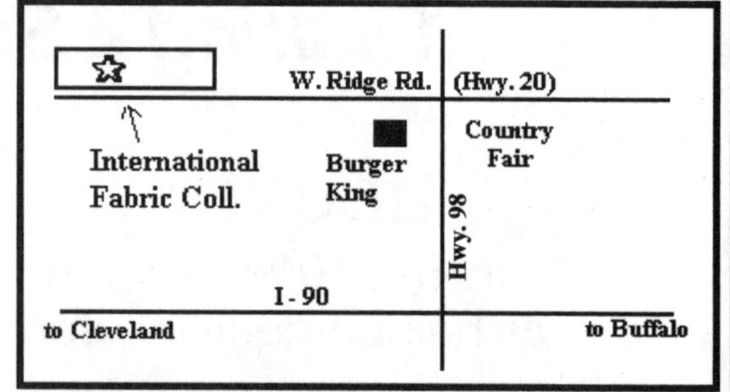

Erie, PA #55

2421 West 26th St., Erie, PA 16506
814-836-8227 First turn west of I - 79
Web Site: www.millcreekvac.com
Est: 1998 4800 sq.ft. 4000+ Bolts

"Just to see the Marvelous Samples ... It's Worth the Trip!"

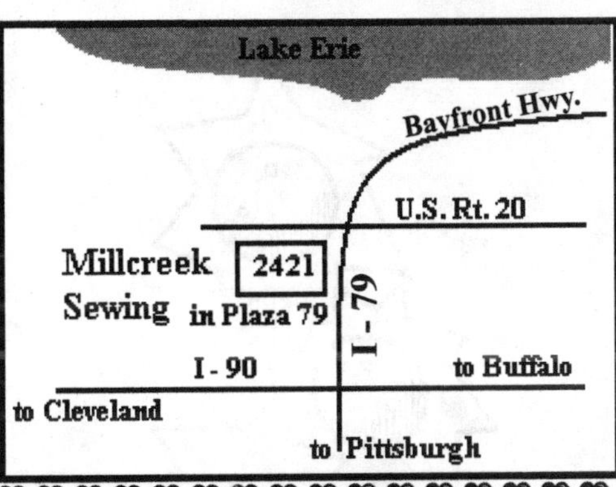

Tri State Leader in Batiks and Flannels

Hundreds of Books and Patterns
Friendly, Knowledgeable Staff

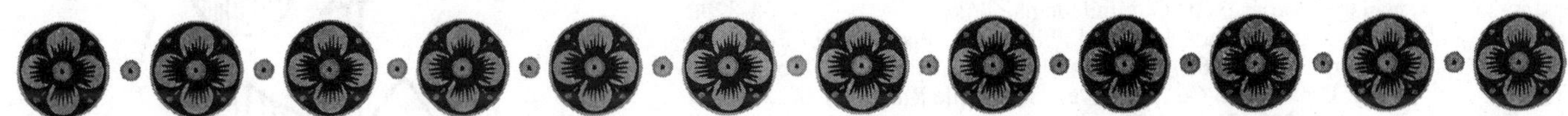

North East, PA #56

CALICO PATCH Quilt Shop

107 Clay St. #3 16428
(814) 725-2275 or (877) 260-1000
calpatchqs@aol.com
www.calicopatchquiltshop.com

Mon - Fri 10 - 5
Sat 10 - 4

Owner: Joy Reich
Est: 1998
1600 sq.ft.
1400+ Bolts

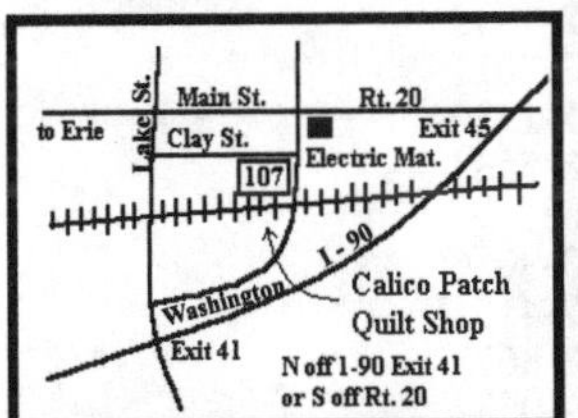

Books - Notions - Classes and the largest selection of Thimbleberries Fabric in the Tri-state area.
Mail Order - Guild discount.

Union City, PA #57

Tues - Sat 10 - 5

The Sewing Loft

10 N. Main St. 16438
(814) 438-9007 or (877) 9SEWING
Owners: Judy Heintz, Juanita Johnson, Jean Grzejka, & Kathy Hamilton

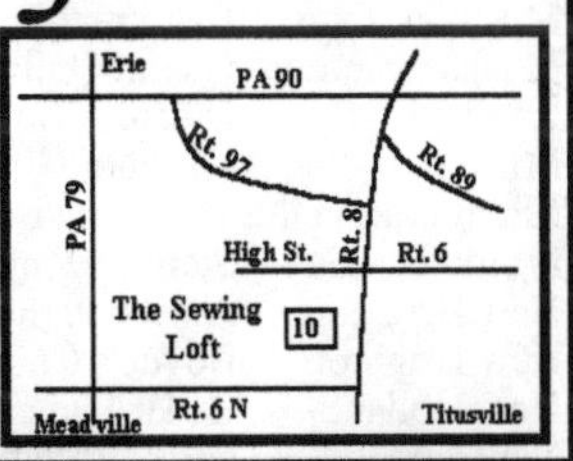

Over 800 bolts of 100% cotton from top designers. Samples, classes, friendly service and the coffee is always on.

Russell, PA #58

Mon 11 - 2
Tues -Sat 10 - 5
Fri til 7
Sun 11 - 2

The Ivy Vine Quilt Shop

Cable Hollow Rd. 16345
(814) 757-1480 Fax: (814) 757-7776
www.ivyvine.com Est: 2000
Owner: Lynn Eckman 3200 sq.ft. 4000+ bolts
Visit our beautiful, 100 year old building full of fabric for quilters. Beautiful rural setting. Notions, books, patterns, helpful and experienced quilters to answer your sewing questions. Batiks, flannels, homespuns and quilters cottons. Also long-arm quilting on site

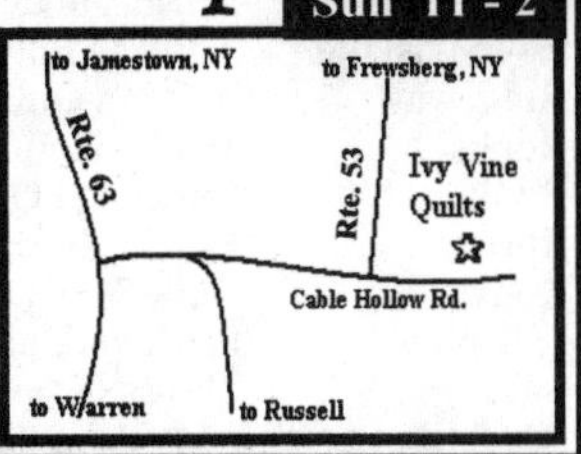

Other Shops in Pennsylvania: *We suggest calling first*

Allentown	Tucker Yarn Co., 950 Hamilton Mall	610-434-1846
Allentown	Julie's Sewing Basket, 1870 Briarcliff Ter.	610-434-7600
Allentown	L & M Fabrics, 4713 W. Tilghman St.	610-530-1601
Allentown	Springtown Textile Co., 950 E Hamilton	610-439-8811
Altoona	R Quilt Shop, 2700 Windwood Rd.	814-942-2606
Bellevue	The Quilted Cottage, 690 Lincoln Ave.	412-734-5141
Bensalem	Quilting Circle, 2631 Street Rd	215-638-1006
Bethlehem	Fabric Mart of Bethlehem. 2485 Willow Park Rd.	610-866-3400
Bethlehem	Schlosser Quality Quilt Frames, 25 Club Ave.	610-758-8488
Bethlehem	Creative Quilting Workshop, 415 High St.	610-868-0376
Bird in Hand	Fisher's Hand Made Quilts, 2713-A Old Philadelphia	717-392-5440
Bird in Hand	Quilt Barn, 207 N. Harvest Rd.	717-656-9495
Bird in Hand	Sylvia Petersheim Quilts, 2544 Old Philadelphia Pike	717-392-6404
Blandon	Greenery - Quilted Cat, 8477 Allentown PK	610-916-1595
Bloomsburg	Quilt in Time, 3214 Old Berwick Rd	570-784-3557
Camp Hill	Country Patchwork, 1603 Carlisle Rd.	717-761-2586
Canton	Four Hands Fabric Shop, 158 N. Center St.	570-673-5280
Carmichaels	Joy's Quilting, 566 Inwood Ave	724-966-7715
Clarks-Summit	Carriage Barn Antiques, 1550 Fairview Rd.	717-587-5405
Clifton Heights	Hayes Sewing Machine Co., 9 E. Baltimore Pike	610-259-5959
Connoquenessing	Added Touch, 1366 Evans City Rd., P.O. Box 137	412-789-7019
Corry	My Sewing Room, 109 N. Center St.	814-664-9424
Covington	Williams Quilt N Craft Supplies, 1 Main St.	570-659-5079
Curwensville	Quilters Stash, 308 Thompson St	814-236-0377
Dallas	Back Mountain Quiltworks, 52 Mill St.	717-675-4018
Doylestown	Sew Smart Fabrics, 53 W. State St.	215-345-7990
Drums	Labors of Love Designs, 61 Pamela Dr	570-788-5954
DuBois	Stitches Etc., 602 W. DuBois Ave. #5	814-371-9665
East Earl	Family Farm Quilts, 1352 Main St	717-354-0054
Elkland	Golden Thimble, 114 W. Main St.	814-258-5677
Forty Fort	Touch of Eyelet, 1006 Wyoming Ave.	570-283-3048
Frederick	Quilted Heirlooms, 2015 Hoffmansville Rd.	610-754-1980
Gilbert	Ladybutton Fabrics, PO Box 495	610-681-5162
Gillett	My Hands To Thee, RD 1 Box 1535	717-596-3773
Gipsy Village	Variety Store, 33 Main St.	814-845-7503
Glenside	Granny's Sewing Den, 243 Keswick Ave.	215-885-4959
Goodville	Obie's Country Store, 1585 Main St., P.O. Box 69	717-445-4616
Intercourse	Christy's Quilt Shoppe, 14 Center St #C	717-768-0044
Intercourse	Village Quilts, 3519 Old Philadelphia Pike	717-768-0783
Intercourse	Nancy's Corner, 3503 Old Philadelphia Pike	717-768-8790
Intercourse	The Country Market, 3504 Old Philadelphia Pike	717-768-8058
Jennerstown	My Front Porch, 1654 E. Pitt St.	814-629-5414
Kutztown	Sugar Creek Quilt Co., 2753 New Smithville Rd.	610-285-0368
Lancaster	Es Quilts, 2224 Hobson Rd	717-509-7587
Landenburg	Gail Bush, 8 Springer Way	610-255-0548
Lebanon	Tom's Quilts, 15 E. High St.	717-279-6262
Lebanon	Martin's Fabric Barn, 2799 E Cumberland St	717-274-5359
Lititz	Weaver's Dry Goods, 108 W. Brubaker Valley Rd.	717-627-1724
Loysville	Wise Dry Goods, RT 1 Box 274-C	717-789-4308
Mansfield	Lucia's Fabric & Craft Shop, Rte. 15 S	717-662-7024
Marion Center	Regina's Quilting Studiio, 1218 Richmond Rd	724-397-9227
Mechanicsburg	Ben Franklin Crafts, 4880 Carlisle Pike	717-975-0490
Mechanicsburg	Quaint Quilts, 500 Cocklin St.	717-766-7166
Midland	Create A Stitch, 17 7th St.	724-643-4833
Milford	Haybarn Gift & Quilting Shop, 167 Arbutus Ln.	
Montgomeryville	The Country Quilt Shop, P.O. Box 828	215-855-5554
Montoursville	Stere Sewing Machine Center1116 S. Broad St.	717-368-8819
New Brighton	Amy Baughman's Sewing, 472 Constitution Blvd.	724-846-8140
New Brighton	Boyde's Country Stitch, 81 E. Inman Dr.	412-846-4175
New Holland	Cedar Lane Dry Goods, 204 Orlan Rd.	717-354-0030
New Hope	Glorious Patchwork, 6777 Upper York Rd	215-862-3134
New Wilmington	The Quilting Bee, 126 S. Market St.	724-946-8566
Northampton	Dave Iron's Antiques, 223 Covered Bridge Rd.	610-262-9335
Philadelphia	A&J Fabrics, 752 S. 4th St.	215-592-7011
Pittston	Edelstein's Fabrics, R.R. 141 South Main	717-655-1930
Punxsutawney	Lydia's Quilt Shop, R.D.7, Box 113	814-938-5533
Rebersburg	Brush Valley Dry Goods, Star Route, Box 33	no phone
Reynoldsville	Quilter's Edge, 441 E Main St	814-653-9076
Ridgeway	Jo Rae's Quilt, 16 S Mill Ave	814-772-4155
Ronks	M&N Hand Made Quilts, 3582 W Newport Rd	717-768-8672
Ronks	Dutchland Quilt Patch, 2851A Lincoln Hwy. E	717-687-0534
Ronks	Family Farm Quilt, 3511 W. Newport Rd.	717-768-8375
Ronks	Quilt Shop at Millers, 2811 Lincoln Hwy E	717-687-8480
Saltsburg	Patchwork at Heart, 219 Point St.	412-639-8441
Sayre	Mary's General Store, 927 W. Lockhart	717-888-2320
Stroudsburg	Fox Glove Gallery, 805 Scott St	570-424-3220
Trafford	The Quilter's Shop, 329 Cavitt Ave.	412-856-6088
Trafford	Quilting Needle, 418 Cavitt Ave.	412-380-8003
Tyrone	Positively Heaven Quilt ShopOld Rte 220	814-684-5780
Volant	Quilted Collectibles, Main St.	412-533-3863
Warren	Sew Necessary, 209 Liberty St.	814-723-3188
Wellsboro	Gammie's Attic, RD 6, Box 128	717-724-6151
Wellsboro	Finishing Threads, 33 Waln St	570-724-7878
Willow Grove	Yours, Mine & Ours Sewing, 219 Easton	215-659-3347
Wyoming	Quilts to Treasure, 886 Shoemaker Ave.	570-693-1299

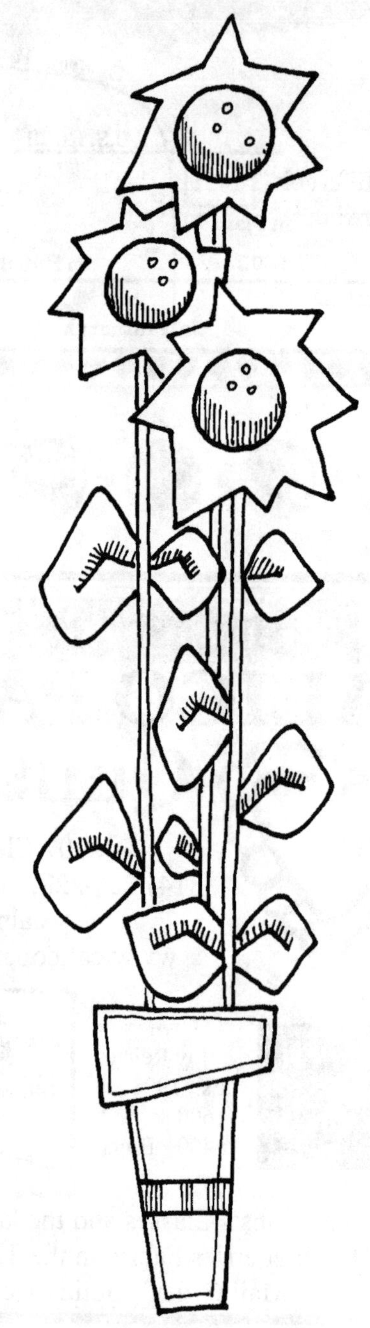

Pennsylvania Guilds:

Altoona	Pieceful Patchers	Meets: 2nd & 4th Tuesday 7:30p.m. at Hillcrest Apts., Hollidaysburg
Audubon	Keystone Quilters, 806 Mill Grove Dr., 19403	
Beaver	Beaver Valley Piecemakers, 302 Windy Ghoul Estates, 15009	
Beaver Falls	Beaver Valley Piecemakers, P.O. Box 1725, 15010	Meets: 1st Wednesday 7 p.m. at Mt. Olive Lutheran Church
Bethlehem	Colonial Quilters' Guild, P.O. Box 4033, 18018	
Boalsburg	Centre Pieces, P.O. Box 657, 16827	
Canton	Scrap of Time Quilters, 43 N. Center St., 17724	Meets: 1st and 3rd Wednesday at Canton Ecumenical Parish
Carlisle	LeTort Quilters, P.O. Box 372, 17013	Meets: 1st Sun 2 p.m. & 3rd Mon 7 p.m. The Tree of Life Church 5 OK St.
Carlton	Country Charms Quilt Guild, 509 U.S. 322	Meets: 1st & 3rd Wed 6:30 p.m. at Homespun Treasures Quilt Shoppe
Charleroi	Mon Valley Quilters, 15120	
Churchill	Quilt Company East	
Clarkstown	Susquehanna Valley Quilters Guild	Meets: 2nd & 4th Thursday at Messiah Lutheran Church
Concordville	Brandywine Valley Quilters, P.O. Box 953, 19331	
Corry	Corry Cut-Ups, 109 N. Center St., 16407	Meets: 2nd Tuesday 10 a.m. at My Sewing Room
Dover	Mid-Appalachian Quilters	
East Stroudsburg	Pocono Mountain Qulter's Guild, P.O. Box 1465, 18301	Meets: 2nd Wednesday (Sept-June) 7 p.m. at Stroudsburg High School Cafeteria
Fairview	Hands All Around, 1420 Lord Rd., 16415	Meets: 4th Monday 7 p.m. at Wayside Presbyterian Church
Gettysburg	Stitch-in-Peace Quilt Guild	Meets: 4th Monday at 1 p.m. & 7 p.m. at Gettysburg Quilting Center
Great Bend	Sisters Choice Quilt Guild Randolph Rd., 18821	
Harborcreek	Hands all Around Erie Quilt Guild	
Hollidaysburg	Calico Quilters	Meets: 1st Tuesday 7 p.m. at Hillcrest Apts., Hollidaysburg
Indiana	Pine Tree Quilters, 271 Phila St., 15701	Meets: 1st Monday at Harriets Quilt Shop
Johnstown	Log House Quilt Guild, P.O. Box 5351, 15904	
Kutztown	Heart and Home Quilters Guild	Meets: 3rd Wednesday 7 p.m. St. Pauls United Church of Christ, 47 S. Whiteoak
Lebanon	Lebanon Quilt Guild	Meets: 1st Monday 7:30 p.m. at Cornwall Manor
Lenhartsville	Heart & Home Quilters Guild, 24 Schock Rd., 19534	
Ligonier	Ligonier Quilters, 15658	Meets: at Ligonier Town Hall
Ligonier	Laurel Mountain Quilters, 15658	Meets: At Ligonier Town Hall
Mayport	Nimble Thimble Quilters	Meets: Wednesday mornings 10 a.m. at Shannondale Grange
Montomeryville	Quilt Study Group, 515 Stump Rd, 18936	Meets: Last Tuesday 10am at 515 Stump Rd
Newton	Newtown Quilters Guild	
North East	North East Crazy Quilters Guild, 16428	Meets: 2nd Monday @ 7pm at Presbyterian Church
Pittsburgh	Three Rivers Quilters	
Pittsburgh	Keystone Quilters, 5540 Beverly Pl., 15206	
Portersville	Tri-County Quilters Guild, P.O. Box 318, 16051	
Saltsburg	Loyal Hannahs Quilt Guild, 512 Chestnut St., 15681	
Schuylkill Haven	Schuylkill County Quilters Guild, P.O. Box 85, 17972	Meets: 3rd Monday 6:30 p.m. at First United Methodist Church, 420 Saylor St.
Scranton	Pennsylvania Quilters Association, 825 N. Webster Ave., 18510	
Southwestern	Piece and Happiness Quilt Guild	
St. Marys	New City Quilters, 15857	
Wellsboro	Mountain Laurel Quilt Guild, 134 Main St., 16901	Meets: 3rd Monday 7 p.m. at Gmeiner Art & Cultural Center
Williamsport	Tiadaghton Quilt Guild	Meets: 2nd and 4th Wednesday 7 p.m. at New Covenant United Church
Wyomissing	Berks Quilters Guild, P.O. Box 6942, 19610	Meets: 3rd Tuesday 6:30 p.m. at GPU, Rt. 183, just north of the Reading Airport

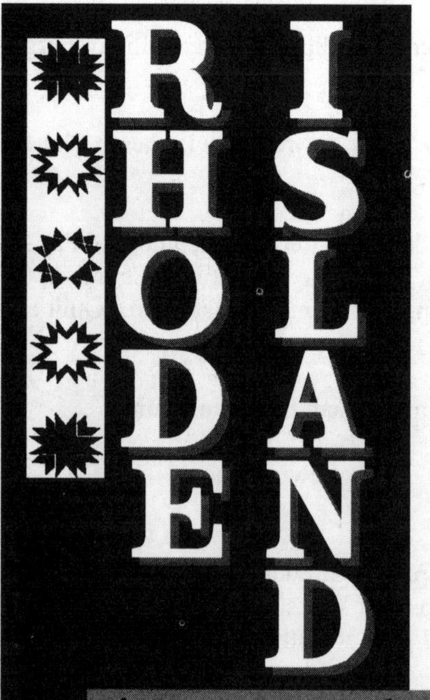

5 Featured Shops

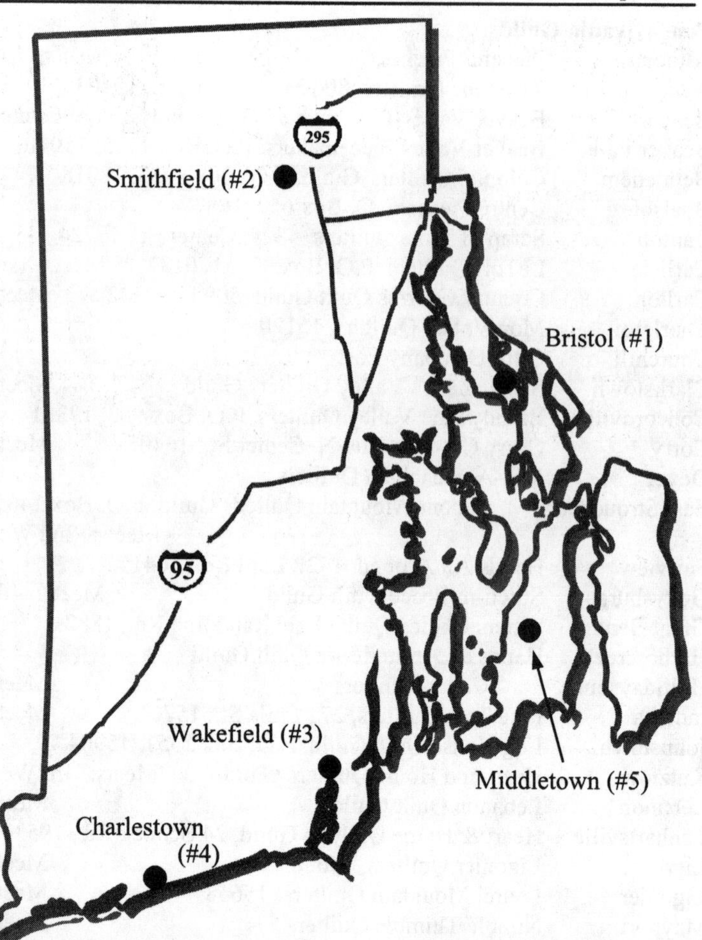

Bristol, RI #1

Tues - Sat
10 - 5

Est: 1998

Just Quilts

576 Metacom Ave.
Bristol, RI 02809
(401) 254-1240
www.justquilting.com

We offer friendly service and carry 1000+ bolts of fine quality cotton fabrics and quilting supplies.

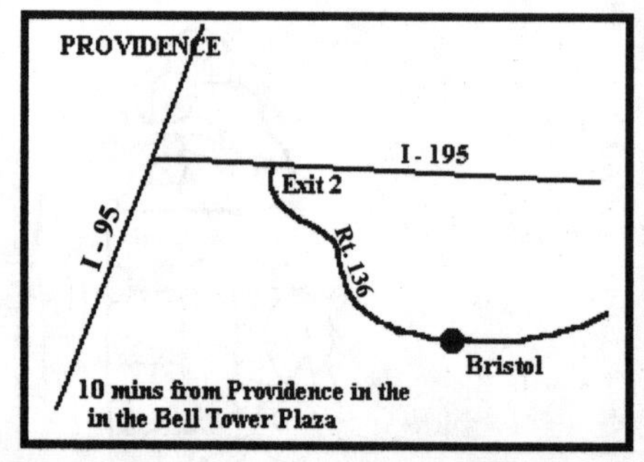

Smithfield, RI #2

Tues - Sat 10 - 5 Wed til 8

Quilter's Market

20 Cedar Swamp Rd. 02917
(401) 233-3949
Owner: Lynda Young

Over 1200 bolts of 100% cotton fabric. Books, Patterns and Notions totally devoted to Quilting. Classes and Private Lessons.

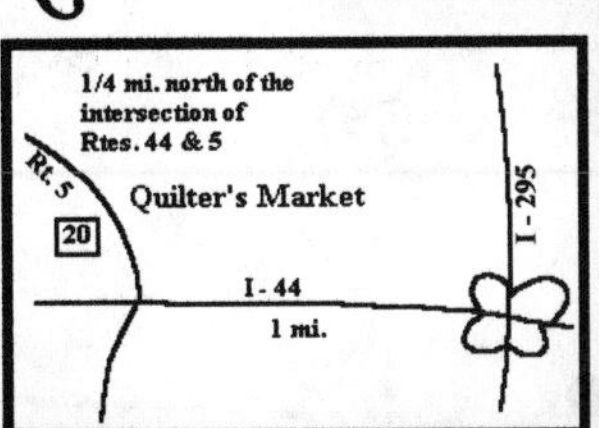

Charlestown, RI #4

Mon - Sat 9 - 5

QUILTS AND MORE

5000A S. County Tr. (Rt. 2) 02813
(401) 364-3711 Fax: Same
BJCRI@aol.com Est: 2003
Owner: Betty Combs 750 sq.ft.
We offer Fabric, Notions, Books, Patterns, Beads, Quilts and Quilted Clothing on Consignment. We are easy to find on the corner of Route 1 and Route 2. In the "Country Barn" Complex.

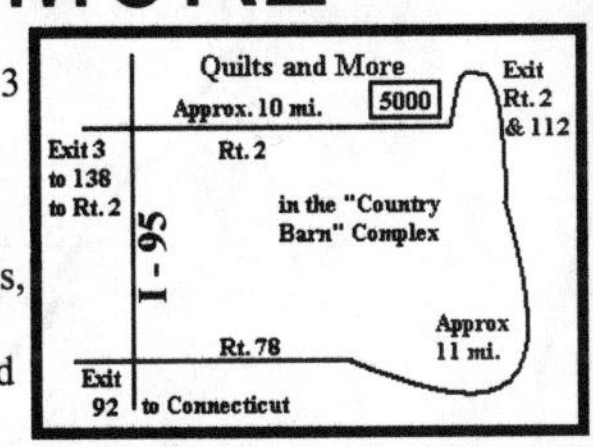

Wakefield, RI #3

Folk Art Quilts

344 Main St. 02879 (401) 789-5985
Owners: Evie Cherms & Mary Loftes

Tues - Sat 10 - 5

2500+ bolts of quality 100% cotton fabrics by Moda, Benartex, Westminster Fibers, P&B, Robert Kaufman, Thimbleberries and many others. Quilting supplies, notions, patterns and books. Classes available.

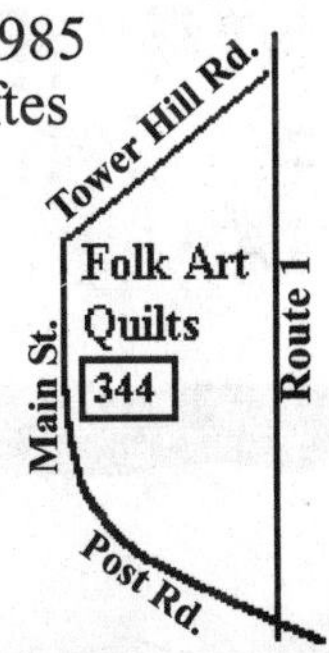

Middletown, RI #5

**Mon - Wed 11 - 5
Fri & Sat 11 - 4
Sun 12 - at least 3
Closed Thursday**

747 Aquidneck Ave. 02842
(401) 846-2127 or (800) 736-4364

Quilt Artisan

Owners: Linda Hilliard
Est: 1984 2000 sq.ft.
Rhode Island's largest selection of Quilting Fabrics. Hoffman, Henry's etc. Books, Sterling Thimbles, Classes & Workshops, Quilts & Gifts

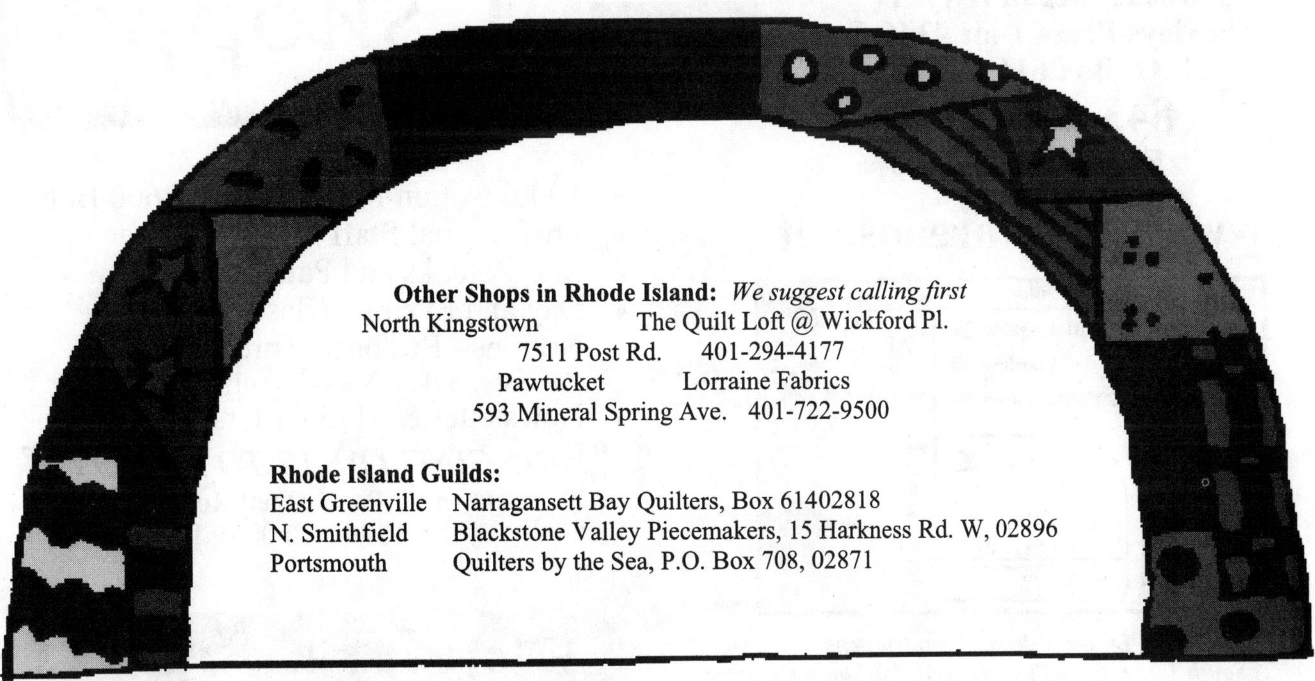

Other Shops in Rhode Island: *We suggest calling first*

North Kingstown The Quilt Loft @ Wickford Pl.
7511 Post Rd. 401-294-4177

Pawtucket Lorraine Fabrics
593 Mineral Spring Ave. 401-722-9500

Rhode Island Guilds:

East Greenville Narragansett Bay Quilters, Box 61402818
N. Smithfield Blackstone Valley Piecemakers, 15 Harkness Rd. W, 02896
Portsmouth Quilters by the Sea, P.O. Box 708, 02871

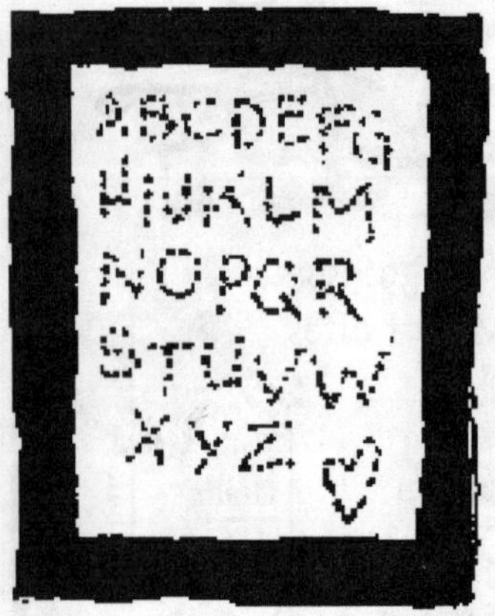

ABCDEFG
HIJKLM
NOPQR
STUVW
XYZ

85
Central (#9)
(#8)
Greenville
77
26
Little Mountain (#7)
Columbia (#10)
(#11)
Cayce
20
95
Myrtle Beach (#2)
Pawleys Island (#1)
Summerville
(#3)
Bluffton (#6)
Charleston (#4)
Beaufort (#5)

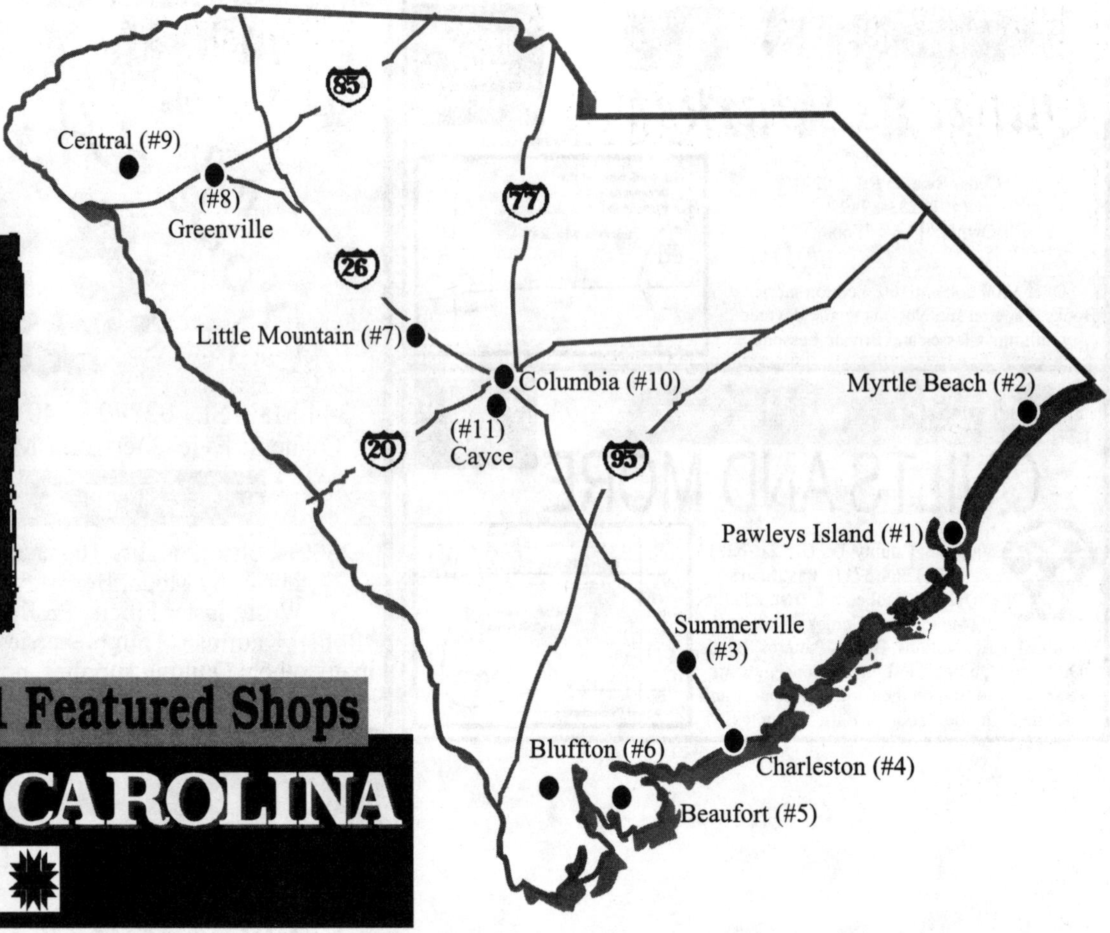

11 Featured Shops

SOUTH CAROLINA

Island Threads

A Quilt Shoppe

10225 Ocean Hwy. 17
Pawleys Plaza Unit #346-348
P.O. Box 616 29585
843-235-3725
Fax: 843-235-3723

Mon - Sat
10 - 5

www.islandthreads.net

Waverly Rd.
to Pawley's Island
McDonalds
Hardees
CVS Pharmacy
5 lights South of Brookgreen Gardens
Frank's Restaurant
Bank
Island Threads
Ocean Hwy. 17
Atlantic Ocean

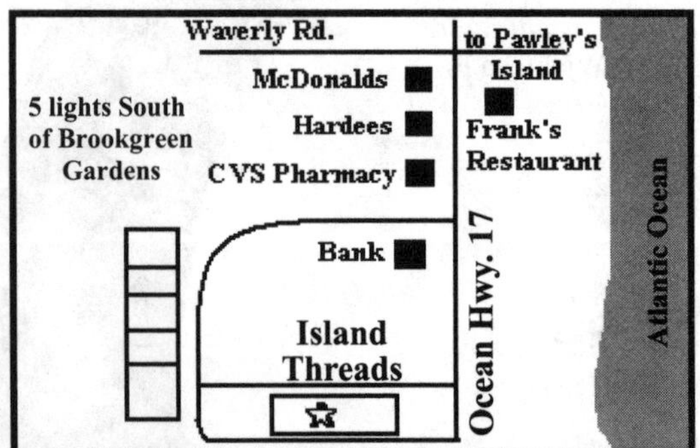

From North 5th Lt. from Brookgreen Gardens
South 1st Lt. from Pawleys Island @ South Causeway

- 100% Cotton Fabrics - over 2600 Bolts
- Professional Staff for Assistance
- Many Books and Patterns
- Day and Evening Classes
- Notions - Buttons - Threads (Cotty, Sylco, Mettler, Sulky)
- Newsletter & Mail Orders

"BRINGING IDEAS TO REALITY"

Owners: Pat & Rhett Roman
Est: 1998 2600 sq.ft.

Pawleys Island, SC #1

Myrtle Beach, SC #2

Mon - Sat
9 - 5:30

Sewin' in the Carolinas

3246 Waccamaw Blvd. 29579
(843) 236-8901
www.sewinginmyrtlebeach.com
"A Quilt Shop with all the Fixins"
Sales & Service - Fabric, Patterns, Notions
Classes, Sewing Machines, Embroidery
Machines, Embroidery Software. Only
authorized Pfaff Dealer on the Grand Strand.
Friendly Staff to Assist You. Over 2000 bolts.

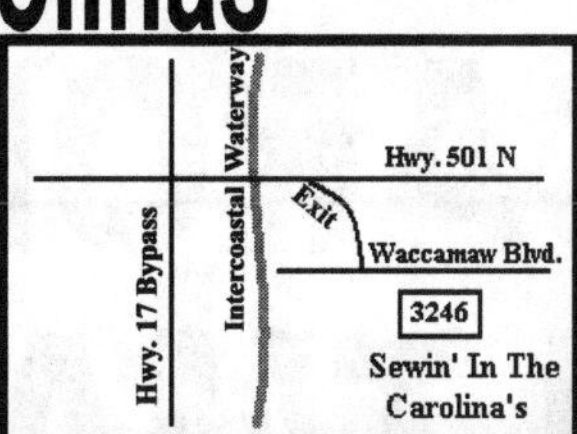

Summerville, SC #3

Mon - Fri
10 - 5:30
Sat 10 - 5

People, Places, & Quilts

129 West Richardson Ave. 29483
In Cauthen's old Hardware Store
(843) 871-8872 Free Newsletter
E-Mail: email@ppquilts.com
Web Site: www.ppquilts.com
Owner: Diane F. Wilson Est: 1990

A full service quilt shop with folk art ~ specializing in reproduction fabrics. Selected by Better Homes & Gardens Quilt Sampler as one of the top 10 shops in America.

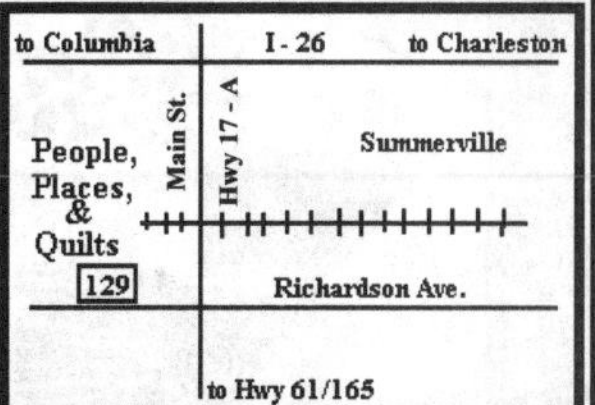

Charleston, SC #4

Mon - Sat
10 - 5

People, Places, & Quilts

1 Henrietta St. 29403
In Historic Downtown Charleston
(843) 937-9333 Free Newsletter
E-Mail: email@ppquilts.com
Web Site: www.ppquilts.com

A full service quilt shop with folk art ~ specializing in reproduction fabrics. Selected by Better Homes & Gardens Quilt Sampler as one of the top 10 shops in America.

1 block off Marion Square within walking distance of the Museum, Visitors Center and Aquarium

Creative Stitches

60 B Robert Smalls Pkwy. Beaufort, SC 29906
843-524-1892 Fax: (843) 770-9922
cstitches@hargray.com
Est: 2000 1500 sq.ft. 1500 bolts

Mon - Fri 10 - 6 Sat 10 - 5

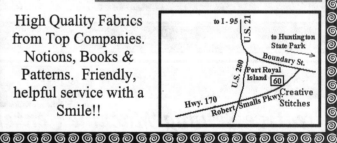

Beaufort, SC #5

High Quality Fabrics from Top Companies. Notions, Books & Patterns. Friendly, helpful service with a Smile!!

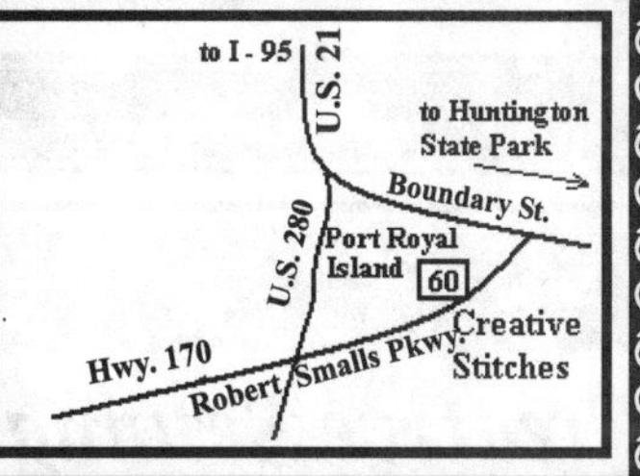

Bluffton, SC #6

Mon - Sat
11 - 5

Belfair Towne Village 103 Towne Dr. 29910
(843) 815-7878
E-Mail: crossstitchjunct@aol.com

Cross Stitch Junction

Owners:
Geri Rihn &
Cheryl Walter
Est: 2000
1400 sq.ft.

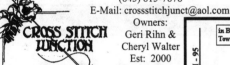

"Quilting and Cross Stitch Boutique"
Reproduction Samplers & Designer Charts.
Classes · Finest Cottons · Exquisite Linens
Specialty Threads · Supplies · 2000+ Bolts

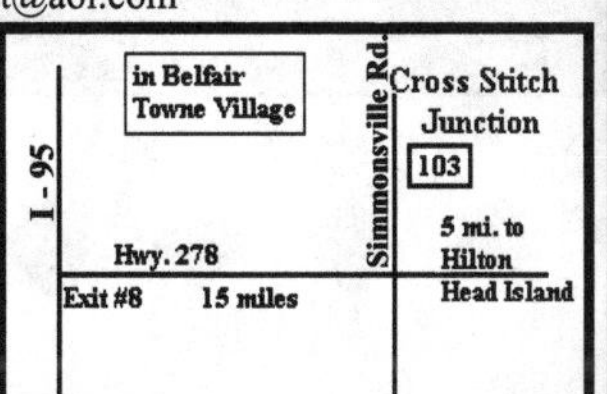

Little Mountain, SC #7

Little Mountain Quilt Shop

834 Main St., Little Mountain 29075
In Historical District
(803) 932-0504 Fax: (803) 932-0975
kathryn.gertz@worldnet.att.net
Owner: Kathryn M. Gertz

Mon - Fri 9:30 - 5 Sat 10 - 4

Wonderful selection of 100% Cotton Fabrics.
Huge selection of Books - Notions - Patterns - Classes.
Friendly, Country Atmosphere

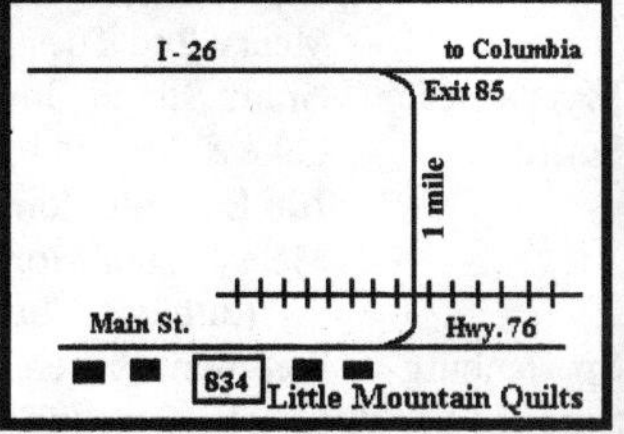

Greenville, SC #8

Mon - Fri
10:00 - 5:45
Sat 10 - 4

Viking Says Sew'n Quilt

1266 Woodruff Rd. 29607
In Shops of Merovan
(864) 286-9507
www.heirloomsandcomforts.net
Est: 2001 1400 sq.ft. 1200+ Bolts

Greenville's most complete quilt shop--Fabrics - Books - Patterns - Notions - Classes - Machines - Heirloom Sewing - Easy on/off I-85 & I-385 Husqvarna/Viking Dealer

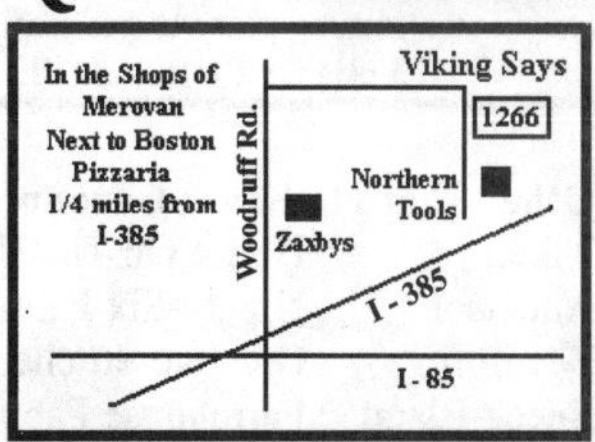

Central, SC #9

Mon - Fri
9:30 - 5:30
Sat 9 - 4

Heirlooms & Comforts

104 Madden Bridge Rd. 29630
(864) 639-9507
Web Site: www.heirloomsandcomforts.net
Est: 1984 2000 sq.ft. 1800 Bolts

Upstate's most complete quilt shop--Fabrics - Books - Patterns - Notions - Classes - Machines - Heirlooms Sewing - In a friendly atmosphere. Husqvarna/Viking Dealer.

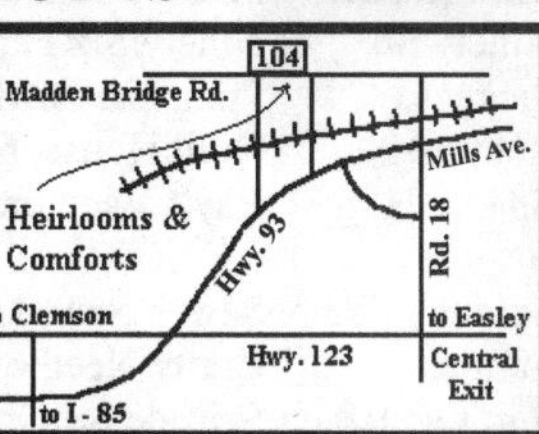

For all your quilting needs . . . and wants.

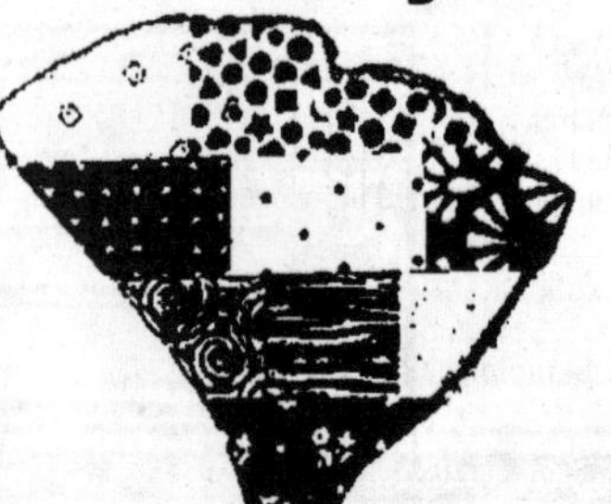

CAROLINA QUILTMAKER

Always the newest in books and fabrics. Custom machine quilting service.
Bring us your antique or new tops for quilting. Customer service our specialty.

Tues 10 - 7 Wed - Sat 10 - 5

2716 Devine St. 29205 (803) 931-0900
Owners: Ellen Simon & Leonard Damond
Est: 1996 1500 sq.ft. 1000 Bolts

Columbia, SC #10

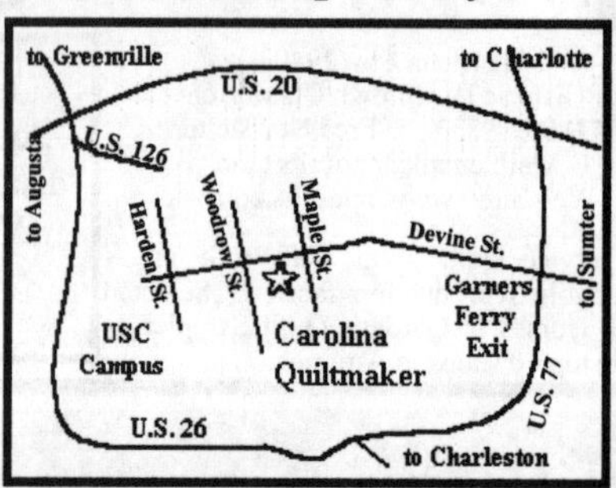

We are about 6 miles from the Garners Ferry Exit off U.S. 77

Cayce, SC #11

Mon - Fri 9 - 6
Sat 9 - 3

Creative Sewing Machine Center

986 Knox Abbott Dr. 29033
(803) 936-1251 Fax: (803) 936-1973
sewcreate@sc.rr.com
www.creative-sewing-machine-center.com
Est: 2001 3500 sq.ft.
100% Cottons, Notions, Patterns, Books, Samples, Classes. 6 brands of machines, a welcoming place to get inspired.
Let's GET CREATIVE!

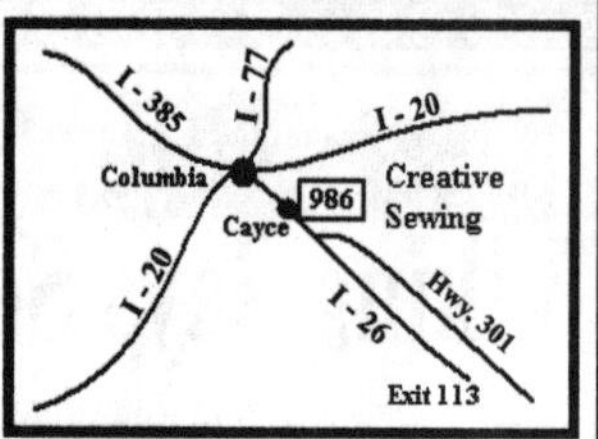

Other Shops in South Carolina: *We suggest calling first*

Aiken	House On The Hill, 1818 Huckleberry Dr	803-649-3372
Anderson	Ninety-Six Fabrics, 910 Bypass 28 S, PO Box 1546	
Beaufort	Creative Stitches, 60 B Robert Smalls	803-524-1892
Beech Island	Farmhouse Fabrics, 270 Church Rd	803-827-1801
Charleston	The Dressing Room, 427 Kind Street	843-723-7888
Charleston	Margiotta's Sewing Machine, 874 Orleans	803-766-3621
Florence	Needle Niche, 518 W. Palmetto St.	843-678-9373
Greenville	Classic Keepsakes, 626 Congaree Rd.	864-288-0273
Greer	Around the Block, 214 Pelam St	864-877-2066
Mt. Pleasant	Fashion Fabrics, 320 W Coleman Blvd	843-884-5266
Ninety Six	Ninety Six Fabrics, 301 E Main St	864-543-3363
Pickens	Pumpkin Town Quilts, 3414 Hwy 11	864-836-4822
Reevesville	Quilt House, 6841 Johnston Ave.	803-563-3890
Spartanburg	Ray's Vacuum & Sewing, 410 W Blackstock Rd	864-574-6001
Summerville	Sew 'n Sew, 1107 N. Main St.	843-971-7822
Sumter	Crafty Needle Shop, 600 Bultman Dr. #1B	803-775-9393
Surfside Beach	Seaside Stitching, 1510 Hwy 17N	843-477-1611

South Carolina Guilds:

Charleston Cobblestone Quilters Guild, P.O. Box 42864, Northbridge Station, 29407
Meets: 2nd Thursday at Lutheran Church of the Redeemer

Columbia Devine Quilters, P.O. Box 25604, 29224
Meets: 1st Monday 6:30 p.m. at Shandon Presbyterian Church, 607 Woodrow St.

Columbia Greater Columbia Quilters
Meets: 3rd Tuesday 10 a.m., 2nd Tuesday 9:30 a.m. and last Thursday 7 p.m. at McGregor Presbyterian Church, 6505 St. Andrews

Columbia Logan Lap Quilters, P.O. Box 7034, 29201
Meets: 3rd Tuesday 9:30 a.m. and 1st Tuesday 6:30 p.m. and 3rd Tuesday 6 p.m. at St. Andrews Recreation Center, 920 Beatty Rd.

Fountain Inn Mauldin Quilt Guild, 36 Green Meadow Cir., 29644

Greenville Foothills Piecemakers, P.O. Box 26482, 29616
Meets: 1st Thursday 7 p.m. at Grace Baptist Church of Taylors

Hilton Head Island Palmetto Quilt Guild
Meets: 3rd Thursday 12:30 pm at Quality Inn

Mauldin Nimble Thimbles, P.O. Box 756, 29662
Meets: 2nd Tuesday 7 p.m. at Messiah Lutheran Church

Myrtle Beach Grand Strand Quilters, Oak Street

Seneca Lake & Mountain Quilters Guild
106 Emerald Pointe Dr. 29672
Meets: First Monday 7 p.m. at Eternal Shepherd Lutheran Church, 200 Carson Rd.

Spartanburg Piedmont Piecers, 29307

Surfside Beach Coastal Carolina

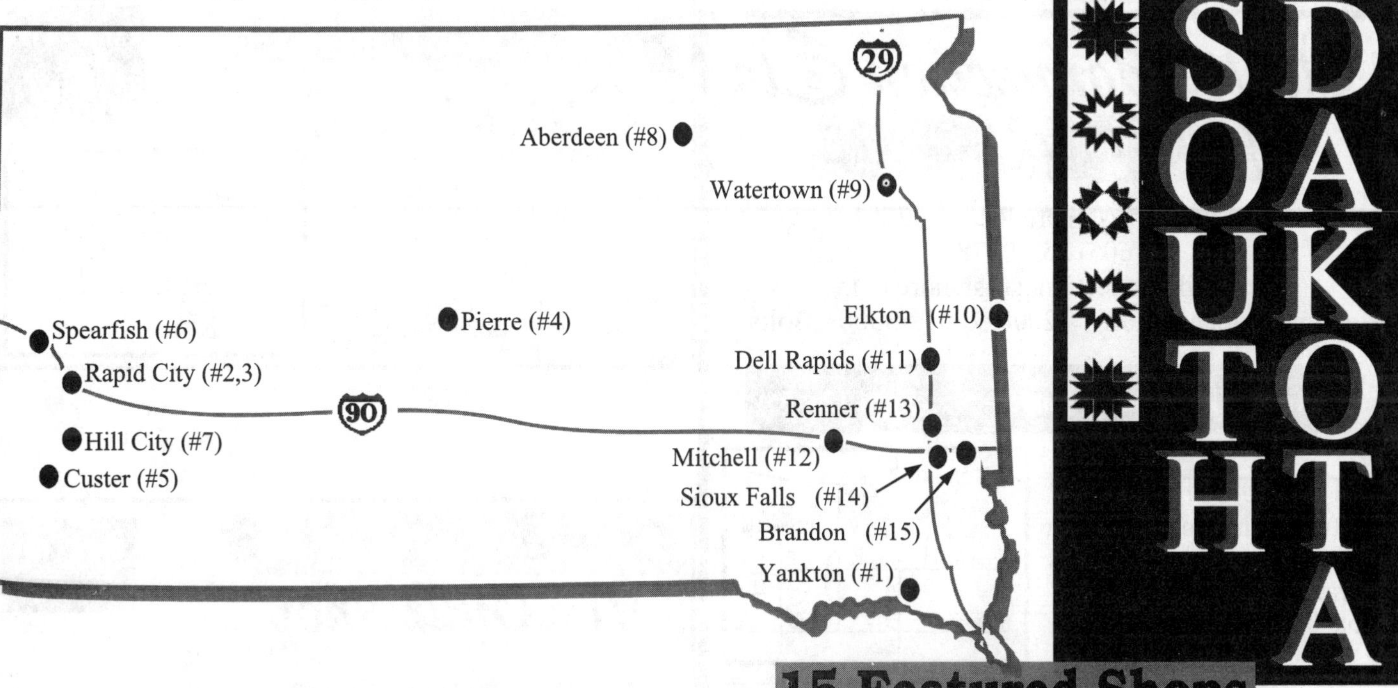

SOUTH DAKOTA

15 Featured Shops

Yankton, SD #1

Four Seasons Fabric

909 Broadway #4 57078
(605) 665-3406
Visit Us On-Line at:
www.fourseasonsfabrics.com
info@fourseasonsfabrics.com
Owners: Misty & Jon Nockels

A great array of cottons, books, patterns, notions and other quilting goodies plus apparel fabrics and super classes! Machine Embroidery Supplies

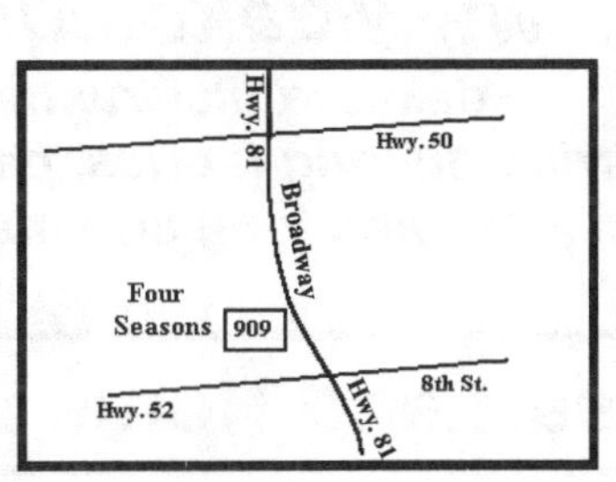

Mon - Fri 10 - 5:30
Thur til 8
Sat 10 - 5

Nothing Sews Like A Bernina. Nothing.
BERNINA®
Authorized Bernina Dealer

When Visiting the Black Hills Come Visit Us!
We are Located 25 Miles from Mt. Rushmore

Thimble Cottage

Quilt Shop and Boutique

1201 Mt. Rushmore Rd. Rapid City 57701
(605) 341-6569 www.thimblecottage.com

OPEN
Mon. - Fri.
9:00 - 5:00
Saturday
10:00 - 4:00

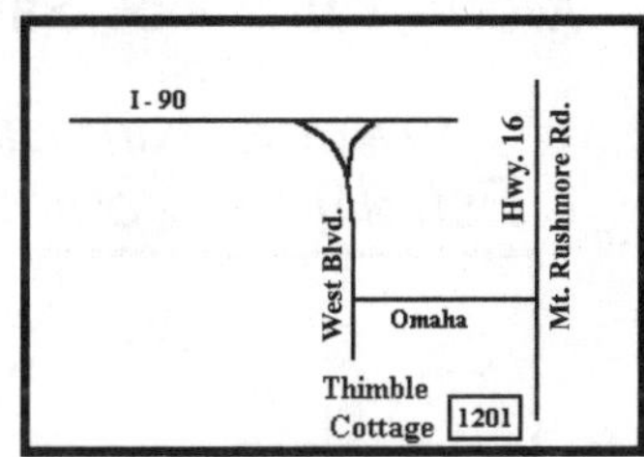

Filled with the Best Quilting Fabrics, Books, Notions, Gifts and Patterns Including Pearl Louise Design Originals!

Rapid City, SD #2

Quilt Connection Etc.

Rapid City, SD #3

318 Mt. Rushmore Rd. 57701
(605) 355-0178
myquiltconnection@rushmore.com
Owner: Joan Schaff 2000 sq.ft. 3000+ Bolts

Mon - Fri 9 - 8 Sat 9 - 5 Sun 12 - 5

"THE FUN SHOP"
featuring the finest quilting fabrics, books, and notions available. Viking sewing machines and accessories.

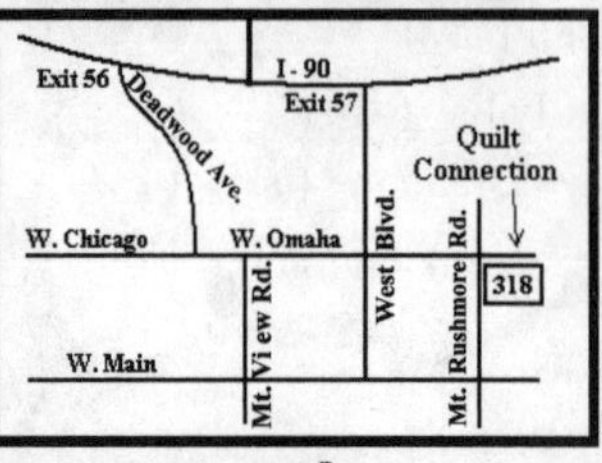

Pierre, SD #4

Quilt Yard

Mon - Fri 9:30 - 5 Sat 9:30 - 4

209 W. Dakota, Suite 101 57501
(605) 945-1195
Owner: Nancy Galinat

100% Cotton, Books and Patterns. Classes.
Moda, RJR, Benartex, SSI, P&B

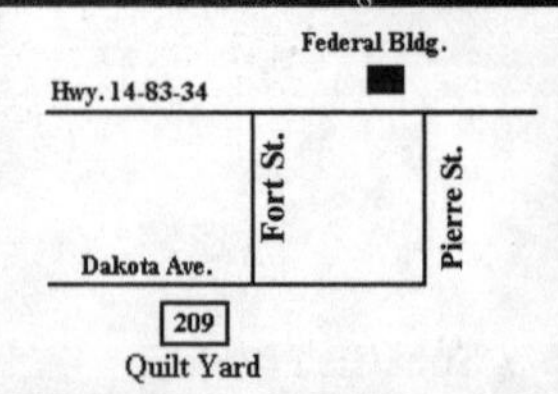

Custer, SD #5

The Quilt Shop

Mon - Sat 9 - 5

325 Mt. Rushmore Rd. 57730
(605) 673-3606

Quilting fabric and supplies.
Next to the Dairy Queen.

Dakota Quilt Company

1004 Main St.
Spearfish, SD 57783
(605) 642-2939
or (877) 642-2939

Store Hours:
Mon - Fri 9 - 5 Sat 9 - 4

Owner: Kim Ellis
Est: 1998 2500 sq.ft.

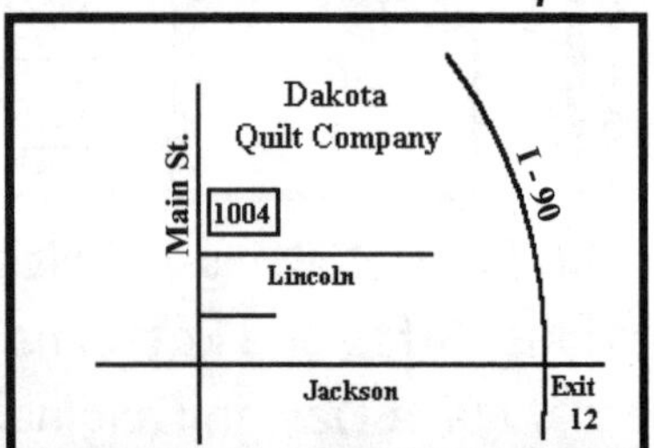

Spearfish, SD #6

Heart and Hand Quilt Shop

...where hearts and hands come together to create lifetime friendships and heirlooms.

www.dakotaquilt.com

dakotaquilt@rushmore.com

Featuring quilting fabrics, patterns, books, kits, classes and long arm machine quilting.

Heart and Home Decorating

A house is built with boards and beams...
A home is made with love and dreams.
Our designer will guide you through the process of color, texture, scale, placement and selection to help piece together your very own "Quilted" home. Let us make your house a home.

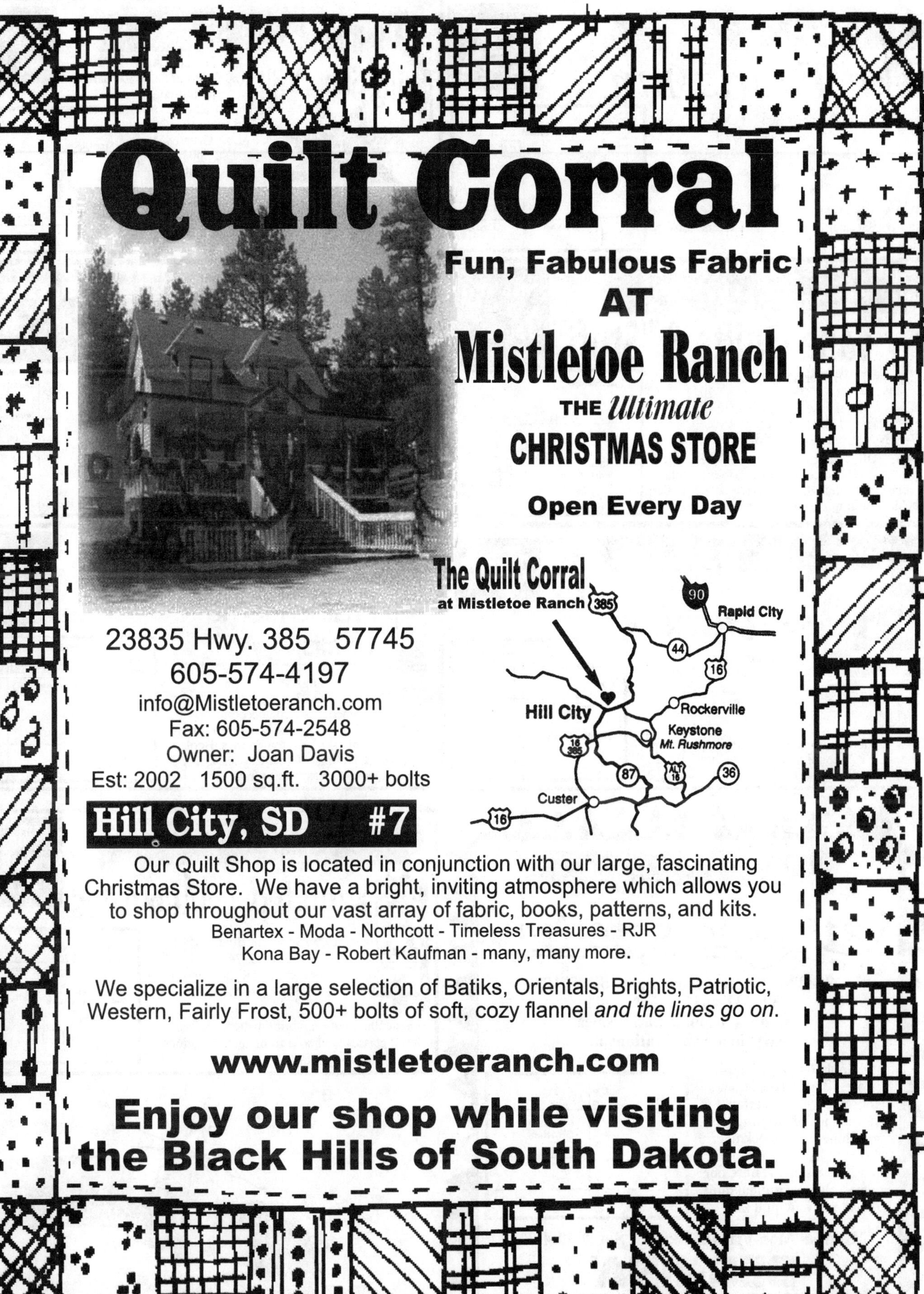
Quilt Corral
Fun, Fabulous Fabric
AT
Mistletoe Ranch
THE Ultimate
CHRISTMAS STORE
Open Every Day
The Quilt Corral
at Mistletoe Ranch
385
90
Rapid City
44
16
Hill City
Rockerville
Keystone
Mt. Rushmore
16 385
87
ALT 16
36
Custer
16
23835 Hwy. 385 57745
605-574-4197
info@Mistletoeranch.com
Fax: 605-574-2548
Owner: Joan Davis
Est: 2002 1500 sq.ft. 3000+ bolts
Hill City, SD #7
Our Quilt Shop is located in conjunction with our large, fascinating Christmas Store. We have a bright, inviting atmosphere which allows you to shop throughout our vast array of fabric, books, patterns, and kits.
Benartex - Moda - Northcott - Timeless Treasures - RJR
Kona Bay - Robert Kaufman - many, many more.
We specialize in a large selection of Batiks, Orientals, Brights, Patriotic, Western, Fairly Frost, 500+ bolts of soft, cozy flannel and the lines go on.
www.mistletoeranch.com
Enjoy our shop while visiting the Black Hills of South Dakota.

Aberdeen, SD #8

Mon - Sat 9 - 5:30 Sat 9 - 4

The Fabric Bin

inside Sander's Sew -N- Vac
111 & 113 S. Main 57401
(605) 225-4203 Fax: (605) 225-6707
E-Mail: sewvac@mdex.net
Est: 1945 5000 sq.ft.

Offering Pfaff and Janome Sewing Machine Sales & Service. Classes, notions and quality cotton fabrics.

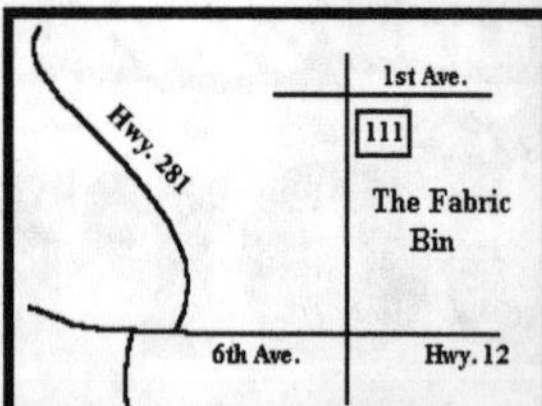

Watertown, SD #9

Mon - Fri 9 - 5:30 Sat 9 - 4

201 E. Kemp Ave. 57201
(605) 886-2653 Fax: Same
risingstar@iw.net
Owners:
Orville &
Lois Grund
Est: 2003
1000 bolts

Newest quilt shop in South Dakota. All fabric 100% cotton.

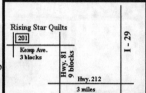

Rising Star Quilts
201
Kemp Ave. 3 blocks
Hwy. 81 9 blocks
I - 29
Hwy. 212 3 miles

Elkton, SD #10

Mon - Fri 9 - 5 Thur til 9 Sat 9 - 4

Ivy Lane Quilts & "Stuff"

502 E. North Dr. 57026
(605) 542-2051 Fax: (605) 542-2052
E-Mail: ivylane@itctel.com
Owners: Linda Louder & Bev Lytle.
Free Newsletter Est: 1998 2000 sq.ft.

Moda, RJR, Benartex, Hoffman, SSI, P&B, Kona Bay. Outstanding books, patterns, notions & class offerings. Authorized Pfaff dealer, machine quilting. 1st in customer service.

Dell Rapids, SD #11

Tues - Fri 10 - 5 Sat 9 - 2 Oct - March Wed til 7

Always Your Design

434 E. 4th, P.O. Box 144 57022
(605) 428-4545 Fax: Same
Owners: Diane Bunkers
& Deb Mergen
Alwaysydesign@siouxvalley.net
www.Alwaysyourdesign.com

2-Friendly sisters in an 1904 Quarry Rock building. 1400+ Bolts, 3500+ Fat quarters, Flannels, Cottons, Reproductions, Homespuns, Batiks, & notions.

I - 29
Always Your Design
under the green canopy
Exit 98
E. 4th 434
3 miles

Mitchell, SD #12

Mon - Sat 9 - 5:30

The Pin Cushion

320 North Main Street
(605) 996-0947 Fax: (605) 996-0017
E-Mail: pincushion@santel.net
Owner: Carma Popp
Est: 1987 2000 sq.ft.

100% cottons, Books, and Patterns. Classes. Friendly, helpful staff. Authorized Pfaff Dealer

PFAFF

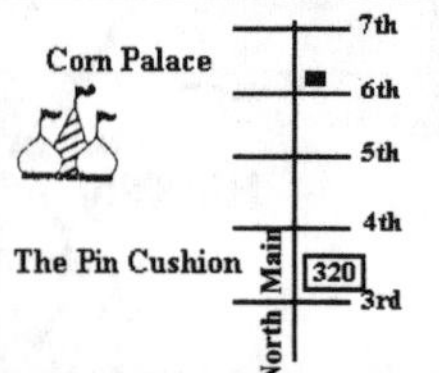

Renner, SD #13

Mon - Fri 10 - 5 Thur til 8 Sat 10 - 4

25795 475th Ave. 57055
(605) 274-6863 Est: 2003
prairiehomequilts@alliancecom.net
Owner: Susie Dorris & Donna Bowar
1000+ bolts of 100% Cotton Fabrics, Books, Patterns & Notions. Great Classes. Gifts. Machine Quilting. Easy access from I-90 or I-29

Renner/ Crooks Exit
Prairie Home Quilts 25795
475th Ave.
Cliff Ave./Hwy. 15
I - 29
I - 90
Cliff Ave. Exit

Sioux Falls, SD #14

Heirloom Creations

3800 S. Western, Sioux Falls, SD 57105
605-332-4435 Est: 1989
info@heirloomcreations.net
www.heirloomcreations.net

Sioux Falls' largest quilt store, Bernina dealer and embroidery headquarters for all brands of embroidery machines. We stock over 4,000 bolts of cotton fabric and flannels and feature our own exclusive original quilt patterns and quilt kits.

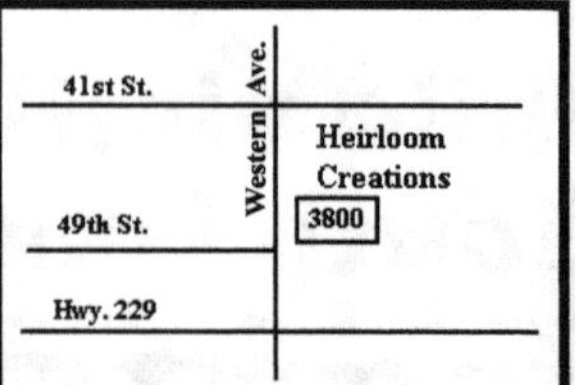

Hours: Mon-Fri 9:30-6:00, Sat 9:30-4:00

BERNINA®

Brandon, SD #15

Mon - Fri 9:30 - 5 Sat 9:30 - 3

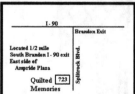

Quilted Memories

723 N. Splitrock Blvd. 57005
(605) 582-7411
Owner: Jeff & Twyla Voldseth
Est: 1997 3000+ Bolts

Great 100% cotton fabrics, patterns & books, lot of classes to choose from, quality notions, gifts. Right off I - 90 Interstate.

I - 90
Brandon Exit
Located 1/2 mile South Brandon I - 90 exit East side of Ampride Plaza
Splitrock Blvd.
Quilted Memories 723

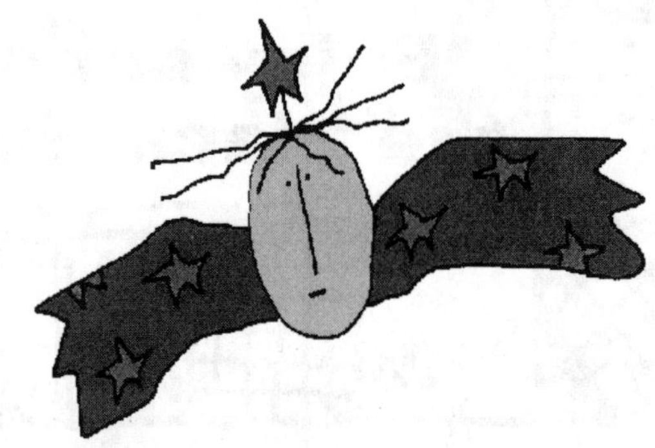

Other Shops in South Dakota: *We suggest calling first*

Belle Fourche	South Dakota Quilter, RR 1 Box 706	
Gregory	Quilt Stitchery, 515 Main St.	605-835-9050
Hartford	Sewing Treasures, 305 Colton Rd.	605-528-7140
Madison	Fabric Patch, 225 N Eagan Ave	605-256-0462
Newell	Quilting in the Country, R.R. #1	605-456-2822
Pierre	Bears Den Quilts, 3451 Bond Pl.	605-224-4423
Prairie City	Strictly Country, 103 S. Main St.	605-866-4484
Renner	Country Lane Quilting Studio, 25797 Country Lane	605-543-5253
Stickney	Needle Nook, Main St.	605-732-4310
Trent	Olive's Mercantile, R.R. #1, Box 31	605-428-4147
Watertown	Klein's, 112 E Kemp	605-886-6499
Winner	The Sewing B, 225 S. Main St.	605-842-0802

South Dakota Guilds:

Aberdeen	Candle Light Quilters	Meets: 4th Thursday @ 7PM at Holy Cross Lutheran Church
Belle Fouche	Northern Hills Quilters Guild, R.R. #1, Box 248, 57717	
Belvidere	Happy Scrappers, P.O. Box 165, 57521	Meets: at Fellowship Hall
Clearfield	South Dakota Quilters' Guild, HCR 88, Box 6A	
Custer	Custer Piecemakers Quilting Guild, Rt. 1, Box 85C, 57730	Meets: 1st Thursday--Annual Quilt Show during Gold Discovery Days (Late July)
Mitchell	Heartland Quilters Guild, P.O. Box 195	
Onida	South Dakota Quilters Guild, P.O. Box 526, 57564	
Pierre	Stately Stitchers, 1606 Hilltop Dr., 57501	
Rapid City	Black Hills Quilters Guild, P.O. Box 2495	
Sioux Falls	Sioux Falls Quilt Guild, 3400 E 49th St, 57103	Meets: 2nd Thursday @ 6:30pm at Southern Hills United Methodist
Badlands	Quilters Guild, P.O. Box 3666, 57790	
Yankton	Dakota Prairie Quilters Guild	Meets: 4th Monday 7 p.m. at Public Library, 515 Walnut St.

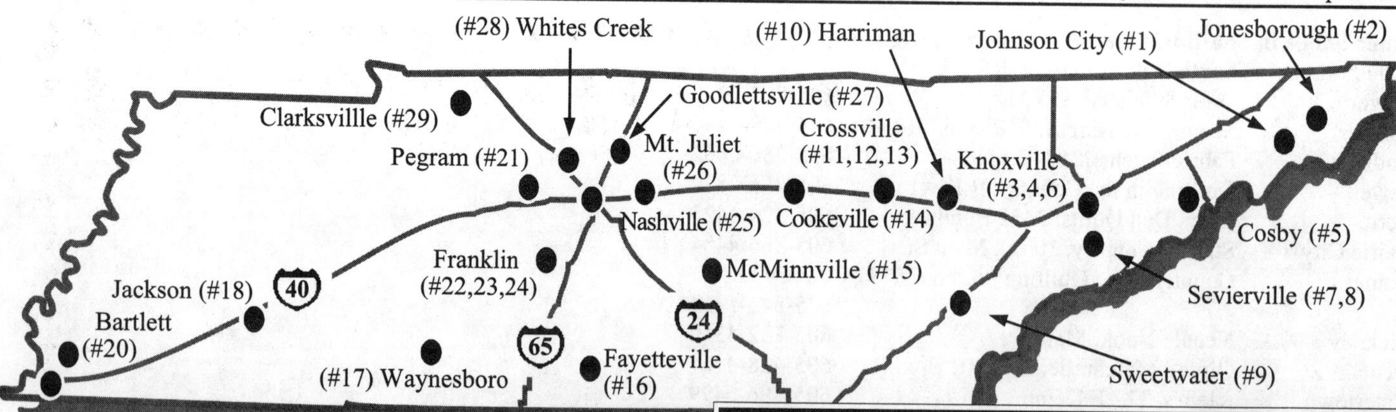

TENNESSEE

29 Featured Shops

somewhere sewing

Mon, Thur, Fri 10 - 6
Tues 10 - 8 Wed 12 - 5 Sat 9 - 4

"A Quilters Paradise."

Experience 6000 bolts of quality cottons starting at $6.99. Books, Notions, Sewing/Embroidery Machines. Classes Available.

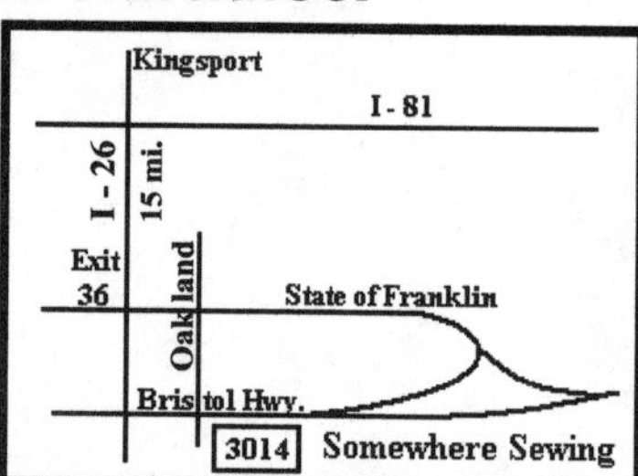

3014 Bristol Hwy. 37601
423-926-1417 or 866-558-9739
www.somewheresewing.com
somewheresewing@aol.com Est: 2000
Owner: Debi Moffitt 6000 sq.ft. 6000 Bolts

Johnson City, TN #1

Sewing Bee

112 E. Jackson Blvd., Hwy. 11-E 37659
(423) 753-7399 Est: 1994

Jonesborough, TN #2

Located in Tennessee's Oldest Town

Tues - Fri 10 - 5
Sat 10 - 3

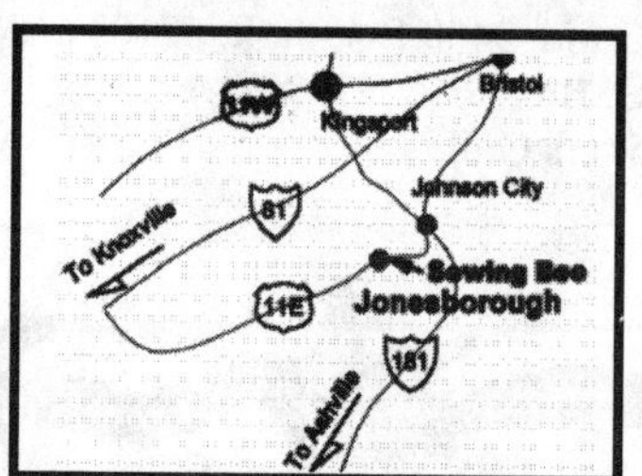

Quilting Fabrics and Notions.
Authorized Pfaff dealer.
Books, patterns & gift items.

Authorized Pfaff Dealer

Knoxville, TN #3

Mon - Sat 10 - 6

Cloth 'n Craft

4954 Clinton Hwy. Clinton Plaza 97312
(865) 689-6010 Fax: (865) 463-8675
tnpbyrne@cs.com
Est: 1997

Over 2000 bolts in 3000 sq.ft. store. RJR, Debbie Mumm, Kugat, Marcus, Concord, VIP, & Springs. Notions & Crafts. Discount Pricing.

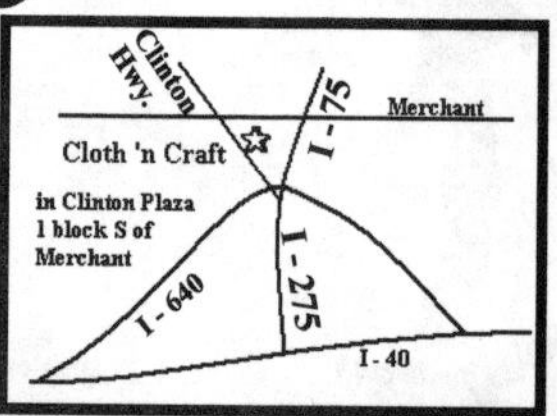

Knoxville, TN #4

Mon 10 - 5
Tues - Sat 10 - 7
Sun 1 - 5

Mammaw's Thimble

Fabric & Quilt Shop

6500 Papermill Dr. #101 37919
(865) 588-8818 Est: 2002
mammawsthimble@wmconnect.com
Owners: Vivian Ann Wright & James Hodge
Over 3500 Bolts of Quilt Shop Only 100% Cottons, Books, Patterns, Notions. Friednly, knowledgeable Service. "Country" Atmosphere.

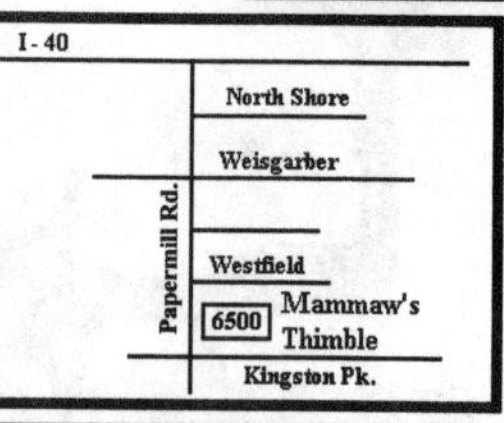

ONE OF TENNESSEE'S LARGEST SHOPS

Cosby, TN #5

Holloway's Country Home

3892 Cosby Highway
(Scenic Hwy. 321)
(just 19 miles from Gatlinburg)
(423) 487-3866
jamahol@mindspring.com
www.hollowaysquilts.com
Owners: Maria & John Holloway

Full line quilt shop featuring American made quilts, wall hangings and wearable art. Fabric - Notions - Kits.

Daily 9:00 - 5:00
March 1 to Dec. 15
Closed Sundays
Winter Hours Vary
Please Call Ahead

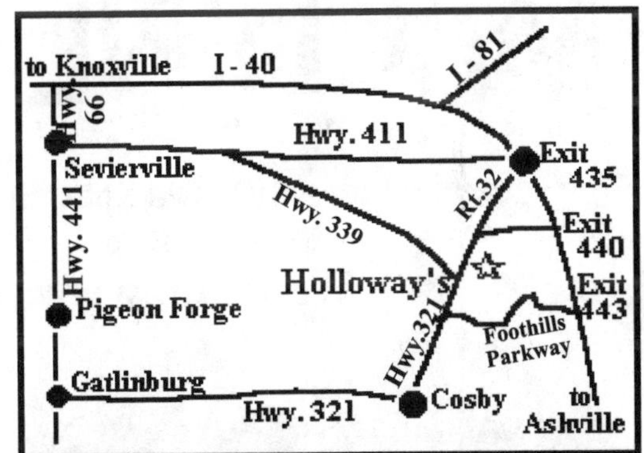

HAND QUILTED WITH AMERICAN PRIDE

Uniquely designed quilts, wall hangings.

THE LARGEST SELECTION OF FINE VINTAGE QUILTS IN THE AREA!

If you are a collector of American Quilts or other American hand crafts, visit us in our historical log building in the quiet country atmosphere of the small Tennessee community of Cosby.

Our house next door is a quilters overnight getaway. We can accommodate up to twelve quilters. We have a large sewing room and all the comforts of home.

Call or email us about our Quilt Retreats

GET AWAY TO THE PEACEFUL SMOKY MOUNTAINS AND QUILT - QUILT - QUILT

Gina's BERNINA Sewing Center

Knoxville, TN #6

Specializing in quilting & heirloom sewing. We have over 3000 bolts of top quality brands including Robert Kaufman, Hoffman, P&B, Bali, In the Beginning, Free Spirit, Moda, RJR, etc. Gina's has been a full service sewing store for over 20 years. We would love to assist you in all of your sewing needs.

Call for our extensive class schedule.

Gina's is the place for all your Bernina needs.

10816 Kingston Pike
Knoxville, TN 37922
(865) 966-5941 or
Toll free 1-877-236-1291

Join us on the web at ginasbernina.com

Directions: We are just 5 minutes from the interstate. Coming from **I-40/75** take the Lovell Road **exit #374**. **Go South to Kingston Pike** (approximately 1 mile) and **take a right**. (Landmark= Walgreens on your right at this intersection). **Go 3/10's of a mile and we will be on your left in Farragut Square**. Our building is right after a nursery that changes names every few months (currently Saplings) So don't count on the name but it hasn't disappeared completely yet!
Follow these directions & you'll make it!

Store Hours
Monday-Friday 9:30-5:00
Saturday 9:30-4:00

Sevierville, TN #7

MACHINE QUILTIN' BY IVA

1020 Old Knoxville Hwy. 37862
(865) 428-8008 Fax: (865) 908-8483
Web Site: www.IvasQuilts.com

Mon - Fri
9 - 5:30
Sat 10 - 4:30

CUSTOM QUILTING

Bring your quilt top by for pricing or call with size of top. Quilting also available for bedspreads, comforters and shams. Quilting priced according to size of top.

Hobbs Heirloom, Hobbs Cotton and Warm & Natural Batting in Stock for all your quilting needs. Large assortment of patterns and books for both quilting and clothing. Assortment of Quilting & Sewing Notions.

FABRIC FOR ALL SEWING NEEDS

Debbie Mumm • Peter Pan
Springmaid • K.P. Kids
Northcott • Maywood
Mission Valley • Benartex • P&B
Fabri-Quilt • Cute As A Button
Moda • Jinny Beyer • RJR
Thimble Berries • Alaska Dieworks
Kona Bay • Hoffman • Bali
Large Assortment of Homespuns
Over 3500 Bolts of the Best

SEWING & QUILTING NOTIONS

Threads • Sulky Embroidery/Bobbin/
Sliver Metler Metrosene • Metler Quilting
Pearl Cotton • Thimbles
Hand Sewing/Machine Needles
Buttons • Rotary Cutters
Cutting Mats • Replacement Blades

the CHERRY PIT QUILT SHOP next to Virgil's in Historic Downtown Sevierville TN

About Our Quilt Shop

- **Models** hang on the 1930's red brick walls.
- 100% cotton **fabric** from major fabric manufacturers and designers. **You'll feel our quality**.
- Check out our clothing, wallhangings and quilt **kits**.
- Need a new quilt project? Browse through our many **books and patterns**.
- Extensive **Block of the Month** program available to fit all lifestyles. We ship. See BOMs on web site.
- 3600 sq. ft. **show rooms**.

Sevierville, TN #8

115 Bruce Street
Sevierville, TN 37862

"In historic Downtown Sevierville"

OPEN
Mon.-Fri.
9:30 - 5:00
Sat.
9:00 - 1:00
Phone
865-453-4062

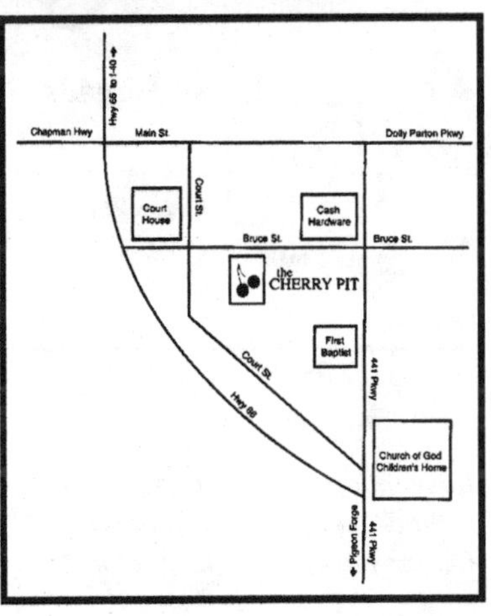

tcherryp@bellsouth.net Browse our 50 item site: www.quiltingatthecherrypit.com

Sweetwater, TN #9

Stitches from the Heart

Fine Fabrics for Quilting

111 N. Main St. Sweetwater, TN 37874
(423) 351-7008
www. Stitches-fromtheheart.com
Fax: (423) 351-7030 stitches111@earthlink.net
Owners: Sherri Martinez and Chris Duncan 2000+ Bolts

Mon - Fri 10 - 4
Sat 10 - 3

Nestled in the heart of Sweetwater's historic district, discover a treasure trove of quality fabrics, patterns, kits, notions and books. Come and experience the genuine warmth of an old fashioned quilt shoppe, where new ideas embrace the rich heritage and art of quilt making. We carry only the highest quality 100% cotton fabrics, threads, and the best in battings. Whether you're searching for a new project or looking for that perfect fabric to include in your latest 'work in progress', Stitches from the Heart has something for you!

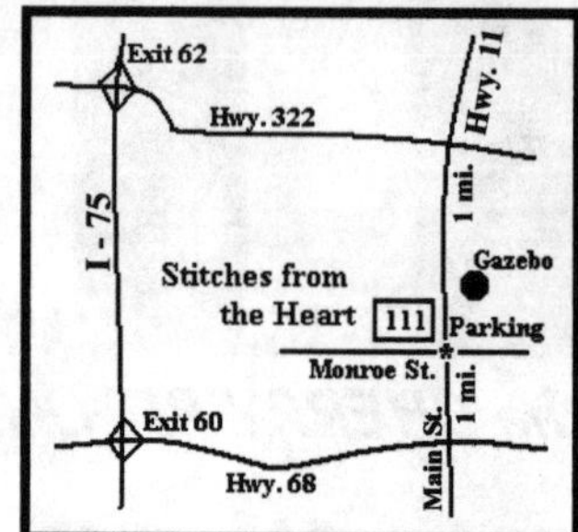

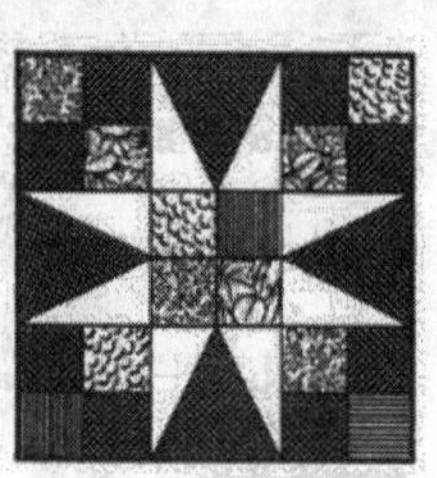

Loose Threads

1211 S. Roane St. #5,
Harriman, TN 37748
865-882-5588
Fax: 425-944-6547
loosethreadstn@earthlink.net
Est: 2003 1200 sq.ft.

Loose Threads
Roane Plaza
Hwy. 27
1/2 mile
I - 40
Exit 347

Easy on/off I-40, exit 347
2 Block North (Hwy. 27) on Right.
On the back left hand side of Roane Plaza

Mon 10 - 5
Tues , Wed, Fri 10 - 6
Thur 10 - 7 Sat 10 - 4

Fabric & Quilting Supplies, etc.etc.etc.

Come visit us and our ever-growing FIRST quality 100% cotton prints, including Batiks & Flannels. Plus Wool for applique & rug hooking.

Books, Patterns, Threads, Notions -- Sale Rack

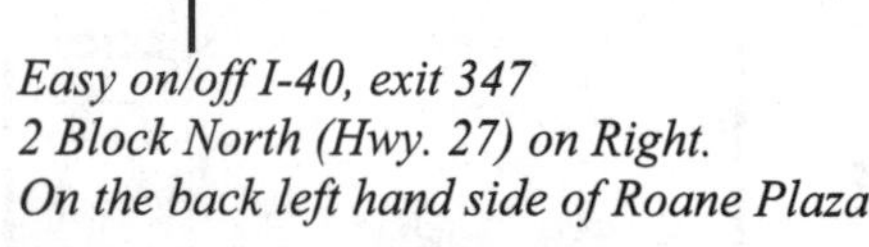

4351 Hwy. 127 North
Crossville, TN 38571
931-707-7724
blessings4u@frontiernet.net
Owners: Robert & Julia Ranney
Est: 2004 2250 sq. ft.

- Large selection of quality 100% cotton quilting fabric and growing.
- Featuring the Newest Patterns & Books
- Large selection of quilting and sewing notions
- Friendly knowledgeable Staff
- Comfortable classroom

Classes for all skill levels

Mon - Tues & Thur - Fri 9:30-5:00
- Wed & Sat
- 9:00-3:00

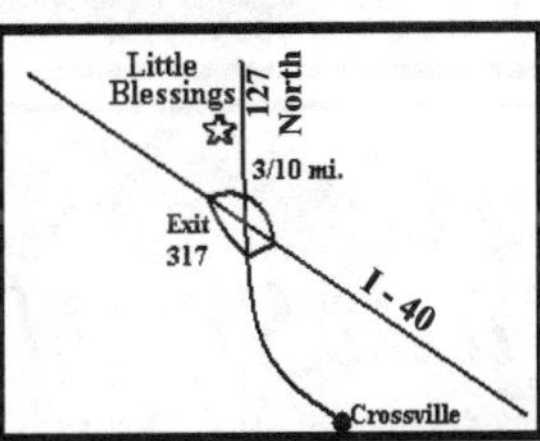

Crossville, TN #11

Crossville, TN #12

Yoder's Quilting Lodge

Est: 1999

Quilters Retreats

Two Night Min. Groups of 8-10. Check website for available dates. Less than 8 is 20% more per person. Includes continental Breakfast, Lunch & Dinner. 5 Bedrooms - 5 Baths. Large Work area, cutting mats, irons & rulers.

2526 Highland Lane
Crossville, TN 38555
(931) 484-1714
yoder@yoderquilt.com
www.yoderquilt.com
Owners: Loretta & Paul Yoder

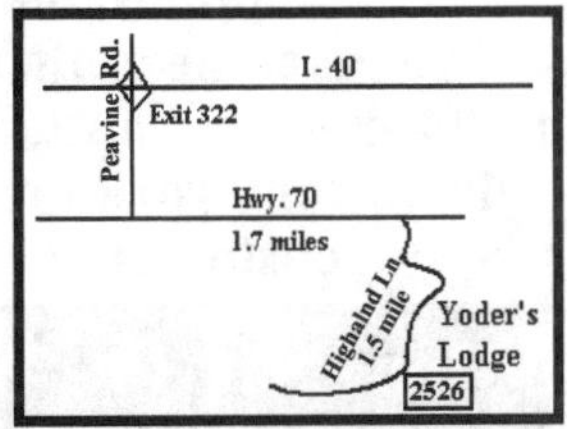

Crossville, TN #13

Mon - Fri 10 - 5
Thur til 7
Sat 10 - 3

PieceTime - Quilters' Mercantile

738 Webb Ave. 38555
(931) 727-0546
piecetime@frontiernet.net
Owner: Carolyn Linkous
Est: 2004 1100 sq.ft.
A cozy shop filled with fine fabrics, notions, books, patterns, and classes for the dedicated quilter.

Exit 320 | I-40 | Genesis Rd. | ~2 mi. | PieceTime | 738 | 1 block | Webb Ave. | U.S.127 Main St.

McMinnville, TN #15

Tues - Sat 9:30 - 4:30

Barn Loft Quilts

686 Abe Curtis Rd. 37110
(931) 939-3796
quilter@blomand.net
www.barnloftquilts.com
Owner: Angie Higgins
Est: 2004 # of bolts growing weekly
The Largest selection of Nineteenth Century fabric, books and patterns in the area!
"Try It Before You Buy It' program.

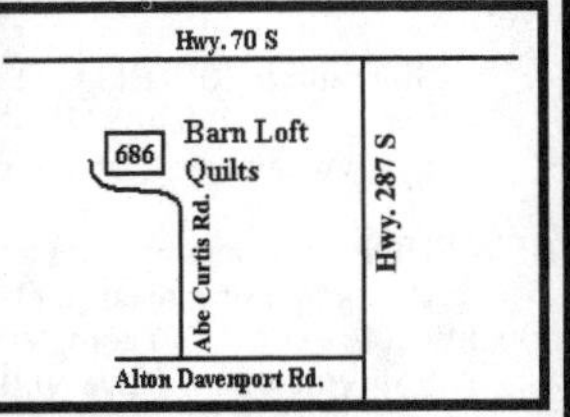

Glenda's Fabrics & the Quilter

735 S. Jefferson Ave. (931) 528-2734
"A Premier Quilt Shop"
glendasfabrics@charter.net
www.glendasfabrics.com

Cookeville, TN #14

9 AM - 5 PM Mon. - Sat

Glenda's is conveniently located 3/4 miles north of I-40 (Exit I-40 at Exit 287—Jefferson Ave.) Glenda's Fabrics is in the Jefferson Square Shopping Plaza.

Largest Selection of 100% cotton Quilting Fabrics & Supplies in Middle Tennessee

Featuring: Kaufman - Hoffman - Benartex - RJR
Timeless Treasures - Maywood - Debbie Mumm
Aunt Gracie - Moda marbles, dots & stars
In The Beginning - Hand Painted BATIKS
Books - Templates - Notions - Grace Quilting Machines
Quilting frames & Hoops

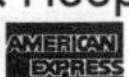

Fayetteville, TN #16

103 East Market St. (On the Square)
Fayetteville, TN 37334
(931) 433-1886
bhook@tnweb.com
www.hookedonquilting.com
Owner: Betty C. Hook
Est: 1998 3800 sq.ft. 2500 Bolts

Hooked On Quilting

We cater to quilters and those who love quilts. 100% cottons from well known manufacturers, notions, books and patterns.

We machine quilt, sell quilts--new and antique and do custom work for our customers.

Mon - Sat 10 - 4:30

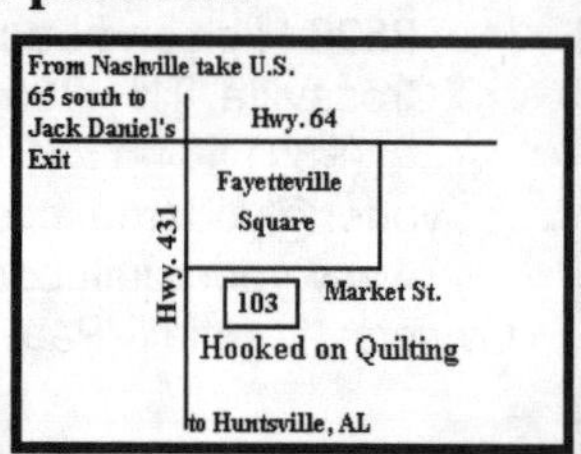

Custom Quilts,
Quilt Repair,
Long Arm Quilting,
Quilts For Sale,
Quilt Kits

Thur, Fri & Sat 11 - 5

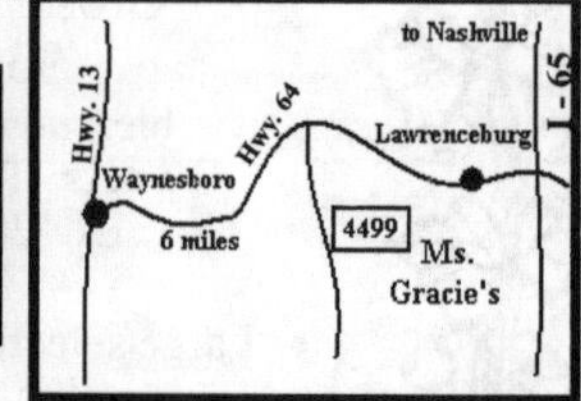

4499 S. 48 38485
(931) 722-7840
msgracie@tds.net www.msgracies.com

Waynesboro, TN #17

Jackson, TN #18

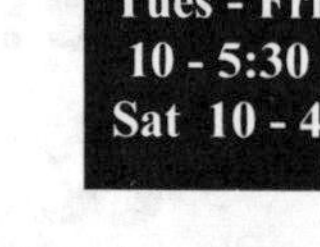

24-D Federal Dr. 38305
(731) 661-9669
Fax: (731) 661-9610
Owner: Pam Cole
Est: 2001
2350 sq.ft.

Friendly happy people work and shop here. Cherry Lane isn't a street, it's a destination for all quilt lovers. Right off I - 40! Authorized Janome Dealer.
info@cherrylanequilts.com
www.cherrylanequilts.com

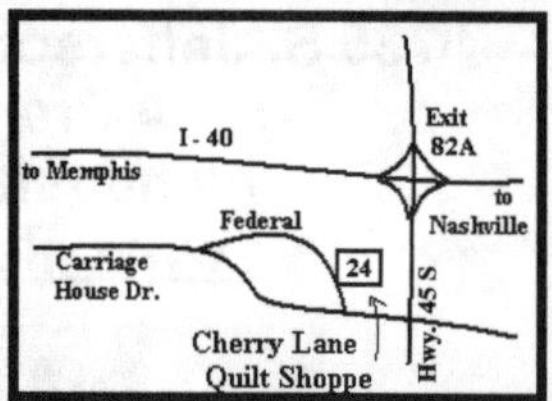

Cordova, TN #19

Mon - Sat 10 - 6

QuiltSmiths

8553 Macon Rd. #102 38018
(901) 624-9985 Fax: (901) 624-9974
E-Mail: qltsmith@bellsouth.net
Web Site: www.QuiltSmiths.com
Owners: Michael & Rita Smith
Est: 1999 1550 sq.ft. 2500 Bolts
Best lines of fabric. Large selection of batiks, children's prints, 1930's prints, Moda, Hoffman, Kona Bay-all your favorites! Classes, notions, friendly service.

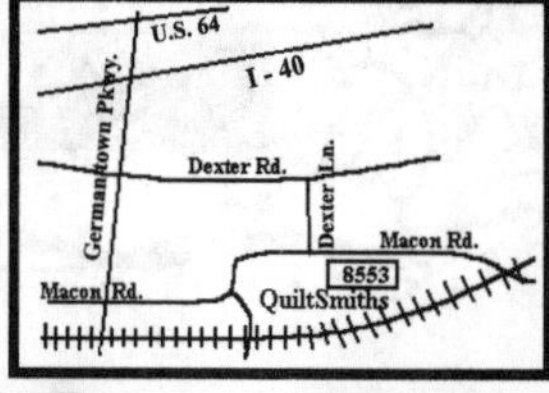

Klassy Katz

QUILTING & CLOTHING FABRIC

Tues - Fri 10 - 5
Sat 10 - 4:30

Come shop in a friendly atmosphere.
Lots of samples throughout the store.
Over 2000 bolts of name brand cottons.

2958 Elmore Park Blvd.
Bartlett, TN 38134
(901) 213-0099
klassykatz@earthlink.net
www.klassykatzquilts.com
Owner: Toni Katz
Est: 2001 1500 sq.ft.
Minutes from I - 40

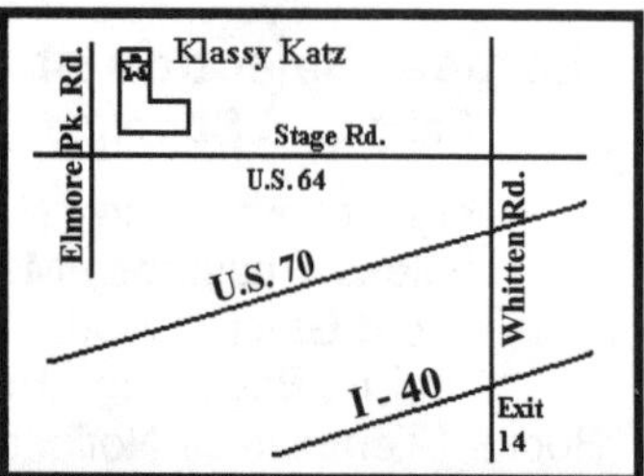

Bernina Dealership

Bartlett, TN #20

Pegram, TN #21

Mon - Sat 9 - 5

Harpeth Clock & Quilt Co.

462 Hwy. 70 37143
(615) 646-0938 Fax: (615) 646-5702
www.harpethclock.com

100% cotton Fabrics, Notions, Books, Patterns, & Battings. Quilts for sale. Quilters on site to help you. Just 20 min. W of Nashville

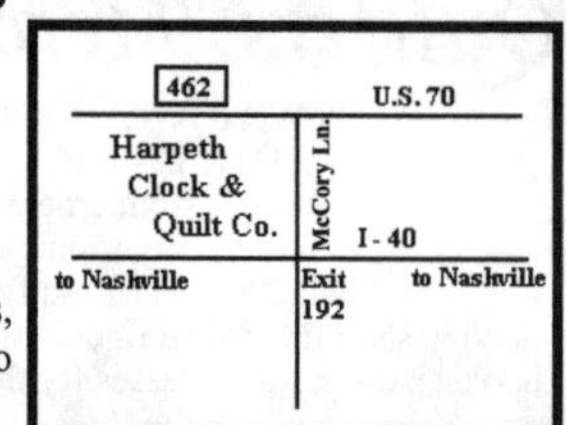

Franklin, TN #22

Mon - Sat 10 - 5

Fabric Stash

230 Franklin Rd. Bldg. 12 37065
(615) 830-8338
www.factoryatfranklin.com

NEW SHOP - Located in The Factory, we have everything a quilter needs including High Quality 100% cottons to complete your Stash!
"cause you gotta have your Stash"

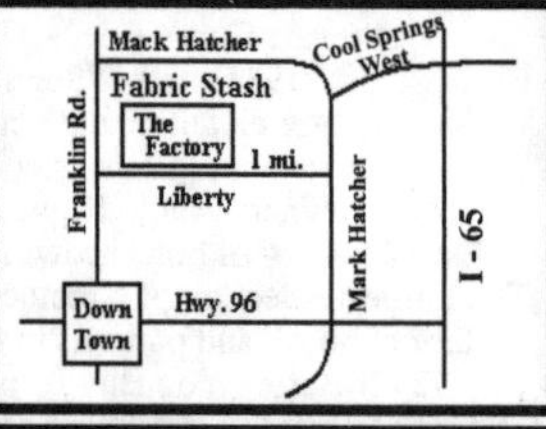

Franklin, TN #23

Opening Sept. 2004
Tues - Sat 10 - 4

The Quilting Squares

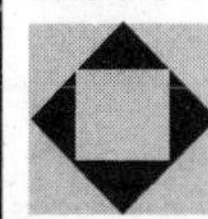

103 Confederate Dr. #2 37064
(615) 794-4769 Fax: Same
www.thequiltingsquares.com
Est: 2003 1000 sq.ft.

A gathering place for quilters to enjoy the art of quiltmaking. Fabrics, notions, books & kits. We are vendors at quilt shows specializing in the Square in a Square® technique. Workshops/lectures available.

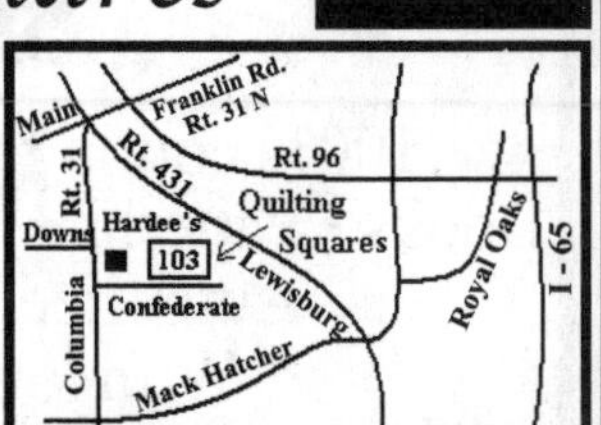

Franklin, TN #24

Mon - Sat 9:30 - 5

Stitchers Garden

413 Main St. 37064
(615) 790-0603
E-Mail: myra@stitchersgarden.com
Web Site: www.stitchersgarden.com
Owner: Myra Nickolaus
Est: 1988 3000 sq.ft.

Middle Tennessee's Most Complete Quilting Shop! Over 8000 bolts of all cotton fabrics, complete Jinny Beyer palette, Q-Snap frames, stencils, books, templates, patterns, and classes.

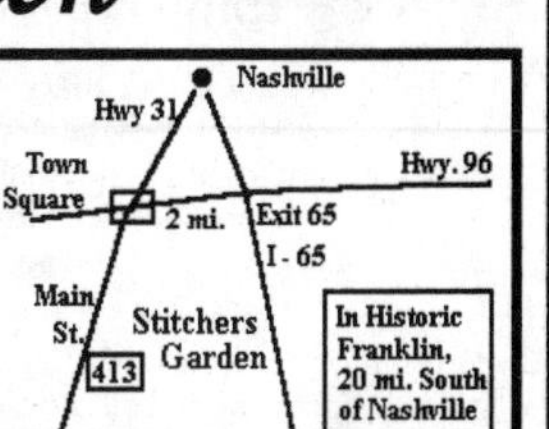

Nashville, TN #25

Mon - Fri 10 - 4:30
Sat 10 - 3

Sew Much More

Specialty Quilt Shop

195 Thompson Ln. 37211
(615) 332-7970
sewmuchmore@juno.com
Est: 1994 1400 sq.ft. 2000+ Bolts

Friendly, courteous staff. Great selection of fabrics, notions, books, patterns and Janome machines. Classes to fit your schedule all set in a quaint little old house.

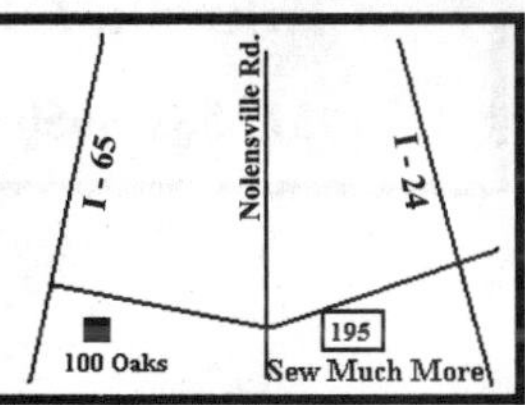

Mt. Juliet, TN #26

Mon - Sat 10 - 6

Mt. Juliet Quilt & Things

1251 N. Mt. Juliet Rd. 37122
(615) 773-1042 Fax: (615) 773-0819
sulurene@aol.com
www.quiltandthings.com
Owner: Su Lu Rene Smith & Robert Smith
Est: 2003 3000 sq.ft. 1000+ Bolts

Long-arm & hand quilting - Notions - Books
Patterns - 100% cottons - Flannel & Batiks
30"s reproductions - Classes - Hand dyes &
Painted Fabrics - Elna Dealer

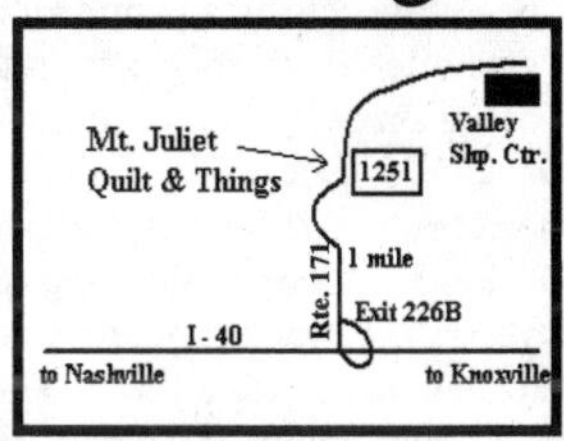

Goodlettsville, TN #27

Quilter's Attic

126 N. Main St. 37072
(14 Miles North of
Downtown Nashville)

(615) 859-5603

Established 1987

Mon - Fri 9 - 4
Thurs til 8 Sat 10 - 4

One stop shopping for quilters and bear makers...
Classes, fabric, books, patterns and notions...
Set in the midst of an antique community...
4500 sq.ft. Over 3000 Bolts
Owners: Fran Sargent, Connie Stowers & Betsy Ross

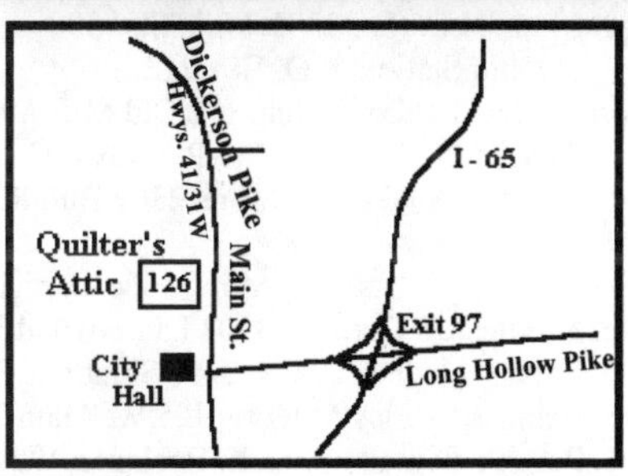

Easy Access From I - 65

Whites Creek, TN #28

Tues - Fri 10 - 5
Sat 10 - 4

4409 Whites Creek Pike 37189
(615) 299-0304
www.thesewingbugandquiltshoppe.com
Owner: Vickie Dalton
Est: 2001 1200 sq. ft.

Quilt Shoppe is in historic Jesse James Building. Just 10 min. from Opryland Hotel. Check out our website for pictures and better driving directions.

Clarksville, TN #29

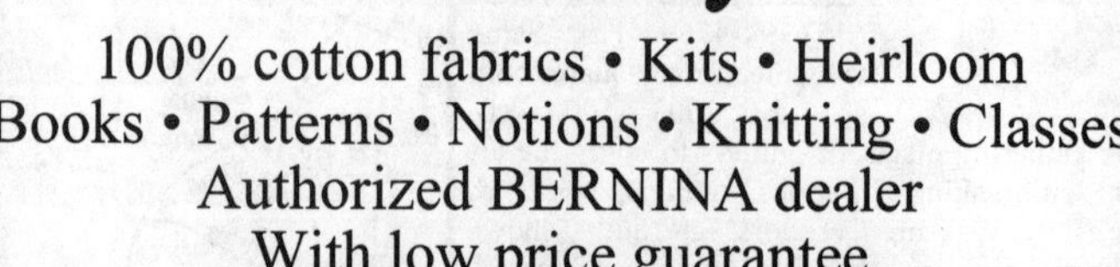

100% cotton fabrics • Kits • Heirloom
Books • Patterns • Notions • Knitting • Classes
Authorized BERNINA dealer
With low price guarantee

Mon - Fri 10 - 5 Sat 10 - 4

Visit us at www.countryquilting.com and receive a free pattern with every purchase!

1953 Madison Street
Clarksville, TN 37043

(931) 551-3650

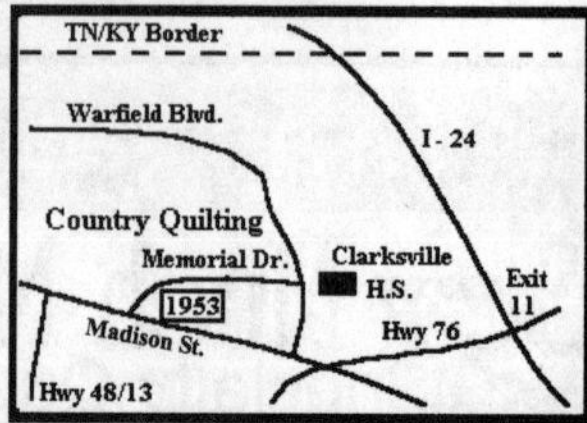

BERNINA

Other Shops in Tennessee: *We suggest calling first*

Athens	The Cotton Patch Quilt Shop, 154 County Rd. 653	423-745-1914
Cleveland	Bettys Quilt Shop, 110 Keith St SW #2	423-559-2458
Cleveland	Karen's Korner, 447 Durkee Rd SE	423-479-4325
Clinton	Sew Unique Fabric Store, 403 Hillcrest St	865-457-5070
Columbia	Anna's Quilters Shop, 119 Nashville Hwy	931-490-6800
Cookeville	Country Patchworks, 283 S. Lowe Ave.	931-526-7276
Cookeville	Parrott's Fabric House, 396 Short St.	931-526-1788
Corssville	Fairyland Fabrics, 3315 Lantana Rd.	931-788-2453
Covington	All Things Fabric, 105 Mueller Brass Rs #F	901-475-3911
Decatur	Decatur Quilting, 856 Goodfield Rd.	423-334-2949
Decatur	The Sewing Connection, 167 Dogwood Cir	
Decherd	Country Quilting & Stitchery, 101 Noles St.	931-968-0048
Dyersburg	Sew Many Ideas Sewing, 100 D Comm. Park	731-286-4721
Elizabethtown	Ida's Place, 874 Gap Creek Rd.	423-542-0999
Gatlinburg	Quilts & Such, 625 Pkwy.	865-430-9340
Gatlinburg	Victorian Eye, 611 Parkway #C3	865-436-0805
Gatlinburg	Quilt Tree, 805 Parkway	865-436-4333
Grimsley	Susan's Quilt Shop, 5300 S. York Hwy.	931-863-3446
Harrogate	Cosby's Fabric & Crafts, 662 Patterson Rd.	423-869-5599
Jackson	The Fabric Source, 1090 U.S. Highway 45 Byp	901-668-1877
Johnson City	CMQ Outlet Center, 1600 E. Jackson St.	423-753-9220
Jonesborough	Tennessee Quilts, 123 E. Main St.	423-753-6644
Knoxville	Martha's Quilting Loft, 4401 Felty Dr	865-688-2582
Knoxville	Grainery, 12010 Prater Ln.	865-675-5153
Manchester	Finishing Touch, 114 W Fort St	931-728-8828
Maryville	Dorothy's, 433 Lee Lambert Rd.	423-983-4969
McMinnville	B & J Quilt Shop, 1202 Sparta St.	931-473-8141
Memphis	Cloth Connections, 3764 Summer Ave.	901-458-7129
Mountain City	Donnelly House, 3142 Hwy 91 N	423-727-9005
Murfreesboro	Quilting Squares, 119 Regina Ct	615-848-1737
Murfreesboro	Quilt Connection, 1011 #A Memorial Blvd.	615-867-0210
Murfreesboro	LadyBug Quilts, 111 E. MTCS Rd.	615-217-7018
Murfreesboro	Bee Quilting, 3710 Maple Ln	615-890-1260
Murfreesboro	AAA Silver Threads, 1447 Kensington Dr.	615-890-7551
Nashville	Dancing Needles, 2717 Lebanon Rd	615-885-0898
Nashville	B Quilted, 2435 Cabin Hill Rd.	615-883-5143
Nashville	Textile Fabric Stores, 4051 Hillsboro Rd	615-297-5346
Oak Ridge	The Quilting Corner, 333 E. Main St. #504	865-483-7778
Oak Ridge	Cloth 'N Craft, 333 E. Main St. #508	865-425-0486
Pegram	Stitchin Station, P.O. Box 212	615-797-9477
Pigeon Forge	The Pattern Hutch, 172 Old Mill Ave.	866-728-8376
Pikeville	Fabric House Main St. PO Box 607	423-447-6195
Powell	Elizabeth's Quilts & More, 2302 Bull Run Valley Rd.	865-947-5766
Red Boiling Springs	Quilts & More, 3606 Carthage Rd.	615-699-3776
Sevierville	Needlecraft Cottage, 3103 Laurelwood Way	423-428-7044
Sevierville	Edith's Cloth & Crafts, 2267 Shinbone Rd.	
Smithville	Becky's Fabrics & More, 105 W. Main St.	615-597-8521
Sparta	Peggy's Sew-Shop, 16 E. Bockman Way	931-836-2888
Sparta	Aunt Bonnie's Quilts, 138 Scott Town Rd.	931-738-4750
Tullahoma	Alley Cat Quilt Shop, 117 Wall St	931-393-3870
Winchester	Hammer's Dept. Store, 102 1st Ave South	931-967-2886

Tennessee Guilds:

Athens Heritage Quilt Guild
Meets: 1st Tuesday 7 p.m. at Heritage Museum
Chattanooga Chattanooga Quilters Guild, 808 Windy Hill Dr., 37421
Clarksville Country Quilter's Guild, 37043
Meets: 1st Monday @ 7pm at St. Bethlehem Christian Church
Cleveland Cherokee Blossom Quilt Guild, 2815 N. Ocoee St., 37311
Meets: 4th Tuesday 6:30 p.m. at N. Cleveland Baptist Church
Cookeville Glenda's Fabrics, 735 S. Jefferson Ave., 38501
This shop offers several clubs (Bernina, Artista, & Machine Embroidery) call ahead for information
Cordova Pickin' Up The Pieces Quilt Guild
2000 N. Germantown Pkwy, 38018
Meets: 4th Tuesday @ 6:30 at St. Luke Lutheran Church
Crab Orchard Tennessee Valley Quilters Assoc., 37723
Dickson SewDelightFul Quilt Guild, 37055
Meets: 3rd Monday @ 6pm at Walnut Street Church of Christ
Englewood Heritage Quilters, 121 Valley Lane, 37329
Johnson City Blue Ridge Quilters Guild, 5 White Oak St., 37604
Knoxville Smoky Mountain Quilters of Tennessee
Meets: 2rd Monday at 7 p.m. at Cokesbury Methodist Church
McDonald Cherokee Blossom, 1430 Brymer Ck. Rd. SW, 37353
Memphis Boll Weevil Quilt Guild, 253 Brierview, 38120
Memphis Memphis Cotton Patchers Quilt Guild, 561 S. Prescott, 38117
Meets: 1st & 3rd & 5th Thursdays 10 a.m. at Buntyn Presbyterian Church
Memphis Millington Quilt Guild, 9130 Ellen Dvies Rd., 38133
Memphis Uncommon Threads, 38133
Meets: 4th Tuesday 6:30 p.m. at Germantown Presbyterian Church
Millington Picking Up The Pieces
Meets: 4th Tuesday @ 6:30pm at St. Lukes Lutheran Church 2000 Germantown Pkwy.
Murfressboro Heirloom Quilters, 1918 Battleground Dr., 37129
Nashville Music City Quilters Guild, P.O. Box 140876, 37214
Sycamore Stitchers
Meets: 2nd Thursday 9:15 a.m. at Sycamore Shoals State Park

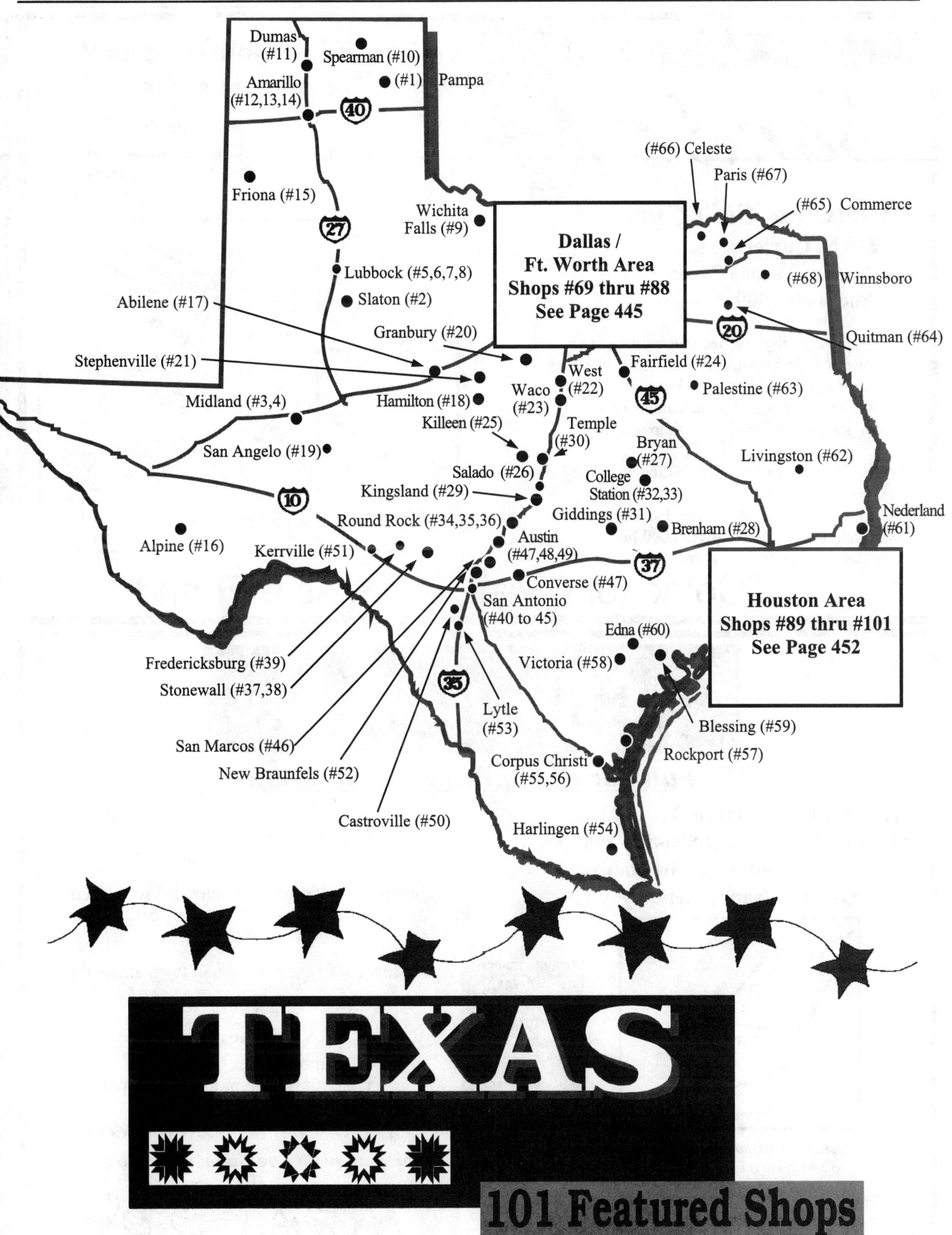

Dumas (#11)
Spearman (#10)
Amarillo (#12,13,14)
(#1) Pampa
40
Friona (#15)
27
Wichita Falls (#9)
Lubbock (#5,6,7,8)
Slaton (#2)
Abilene (#17)
Granbury (#20)
Stephenville (#21)
Midland (#3,4)
Hamilton (#18)
San Angelo (#19)
Killeen (#25)
Waco (#23)
West (#22)
Temple (#30)
Dallas / Ft. Worth Area Shops #69 thru #88 See Page 445
(#66) Celeste
Paris (#67)
(#65) Commerce
(#68) Winnsboro
20
Quitman (#64)
Fairfield (#24)
45
Palestine (#63)
Bryan (#27)
Livingston (#62)
Salado (#26)
College Station (#32,33)
Kingsland (#29)
10
Giddings (#31)
Brenham (#28)
Nederland (#61)
Round Rock (#34,35,36)
Alpine (#16)
Kerrville (#51)
Austin (#47,48,49)
37
Converse (#47)
San Antonio (#40 to 45)
Houston Area Shops #89 thru #101 See Page 452
Edna (#60)
Victoria (#58)
Fredericksburg (#39)
Stonewall (#37,38)
35
Lytle (#53)
Blessing (#59)
San Marcos (#46)
Corpus Christi (#55,56)
Rockport (#57)
New Braunfels (#52)
Castroville (#50)
Harlingen (#54)

TEXAS

101 Featured Shops

Pampa, TX #1

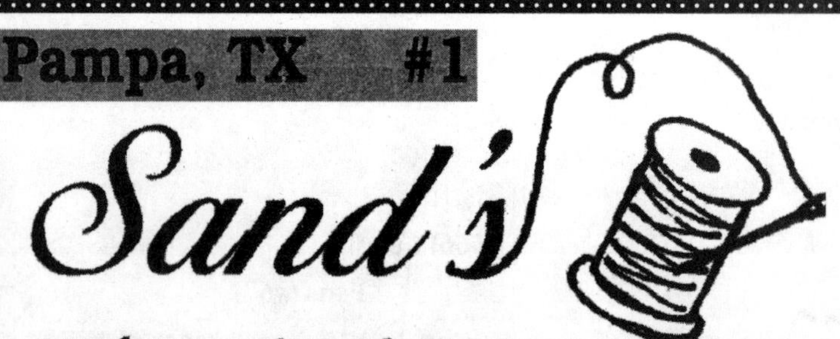

The Largest Quilt Shop in the Texas Panhandle

Established 1959
Owner: Janie Morris
Monday - Saturday
9:30 - 5:30

Fabric and Quilt Corner

225 N. Cuyler
Pampa, Texas 79065
(806) 669-7909

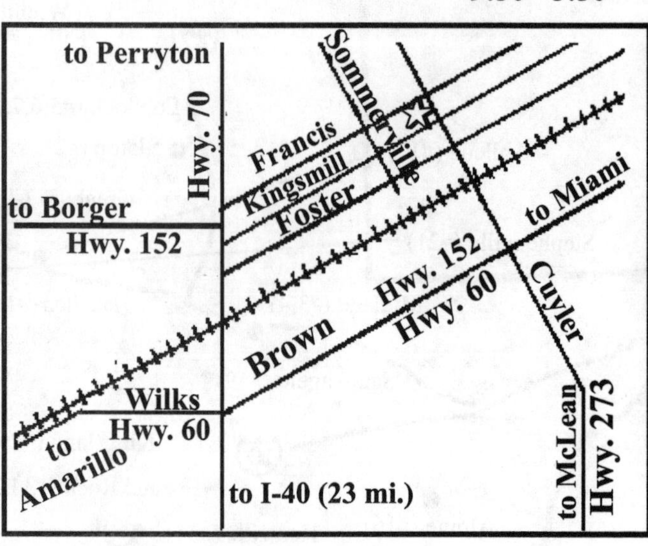

We have everything you need for quilting or sewing. We have threads, buttons, notions, patterns, books, quilting supplies and battings. We also have fashion fabrics, bridal fabrics, laces & trims. We have quilting classes, kits, BOM, and lots of shop samples.

Authorized Dealer of Brother & Elna Sewing Machines

Oh! Did I mention that we have Fabric! We have oodles and gobs of fabric **(over 6000 bolts)**, and more **flannel** than the law allows.

"Come for a visit, leave as a Friend"

Full service, premier quilt shop

121 South 9th, Slaton, TX 79364
806-828-3222 Fax: 806-828-3990
Sew-much-fun@excite.com
Owner: Nancy Hendley

Bakery
U.S. 84
121
Quilts-n More
9th St.
Division
FM - 41

Take 1st Slaton Exit off Hwy. 84. Follow to downtown and make a U-turn at 2nd traffic light.

Tues & Thur
11 - 9
Tues - Fri
11 - 7
Sat 11 - 3

1000+ bolts of outstanding 100% cotton fabrics
300+ quality quilt reference books
150+ unique pattern titles

Specializing in a wide array of color and reproduction; plus a tremendous selection of supplies, batiks, batting, gadgets and quilting tools.

An uptown quilt shop in a small town atmosphere.

Where Brights Are Neutrals!

Mystery Quilt 2nd Saturday 2-4 pm.
Thimbleberries Quilt Club
4th Saturday 2-4 pm, lock-in 5-9 pm

Also Visit *Quilts to Treasure*
Home of quality heirloom machine quilting.

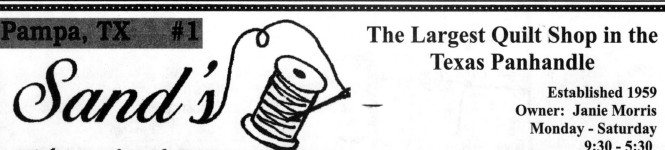

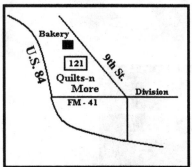

Lubbock, TX #6

Mon - Fri 10 - 5
Thur til 7
Sat 10 - 3

Quilter's Front Porch

3501 50th St., Suite 124 79413
(806) 687-6264
Est: 2003 2800 sq.ft.

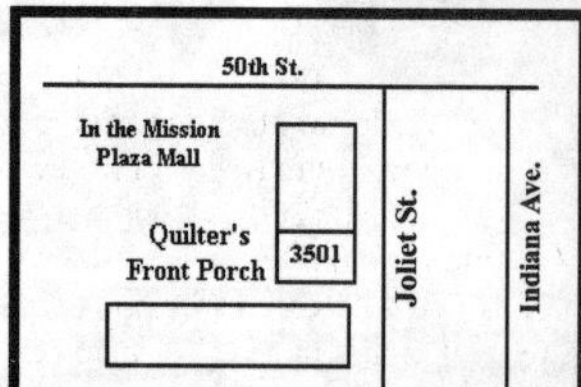

We carry fabrics, books, patterns, notions and kits. We have a variety of classes and clubs offered monthly.

Lubbock, TX #7

Mon - Fri 10 - 5
Sat 10 - 4

The Quilt Shop II

6405 Indiana Ave. 79413
(In the KK's Courtyard Mall)
(806) 793-2485
Owner: Lunann Burke
Est 1979

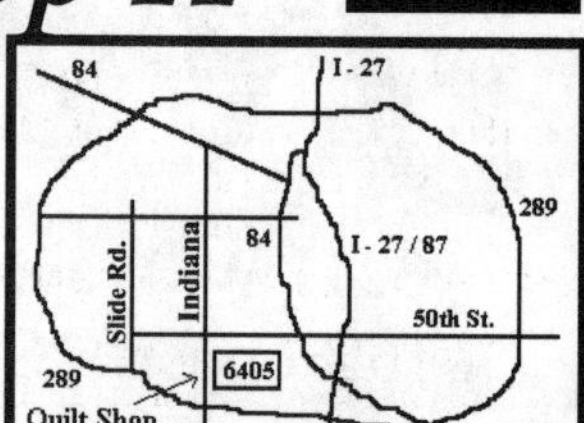

We have 1500 bolts of cotton, books, supplies & classes. Appraisals by appointment.

Lubbock, TX #8

Mon - Fri 10 - 6
Sat 10 - 5

BERNINA® Sewing Studio

4601 S. Loop 289 #14 79424
(806) 792-3863 Fax: (806) 792-1454
Berninasewingstudio@msn.com
Owners: Howard & Vicki Tracy
Est: 1981 5000 sq.ft.

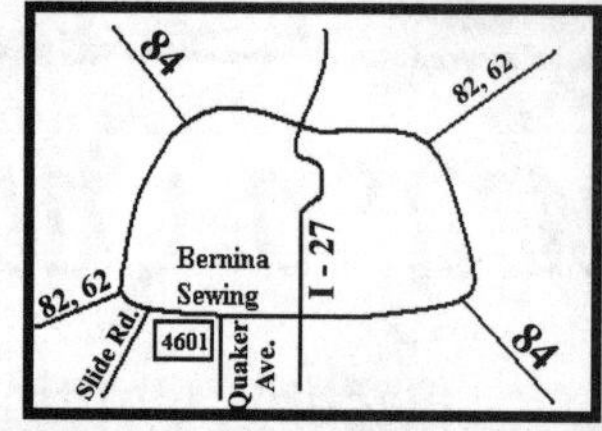

Promoting the art of sewing by providing: Quality equipment and products Great classes and service in a creative, positive atmosphere.

Wichita Falls, TX #9

Stitchers' Corner

900 Van Buren St., Wichita Falls 76301
940-767-4944 Fax: 940-767-4706
E-mail: scquilt@wf.net

Tues - Fri 10 - 5
Sat 10 - 3

"Texas friendly" full service quilt shop. We have a large selection of 100% cotton fabrics, books, notions and patterns.
PFAFF sales & service.
Cross Stitch Too!

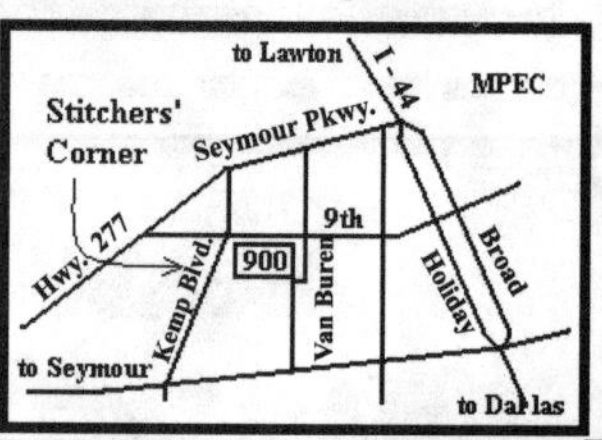

Spearman, TX #10

Mon - Fri 9:30 - 5:30
Sat 9:30 - 5

Jo's This N' That

214 Main 79081
(806) 659-3999
Owner: Joan Farr

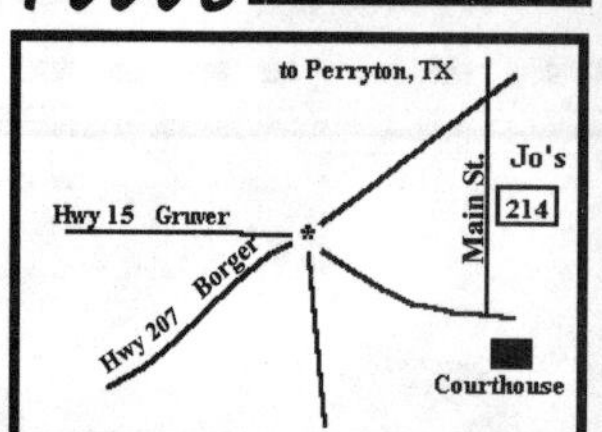

We are a Traditional Quilt Shop.
Also machine Quilting & Monogramming.

Dumas, TX #11

Mon - Fri 10 - 6
Sat 10 - 4

Down Home Quilts

102 E. 7th, Suite A 79029
(806) 934-4041 Fax: (806) 934-4042
downhomequilts@nts-online.net
Onwers: Carol Gillingham & Helen King
Est: 2001 1800 sq.ft. 1100 Bolts

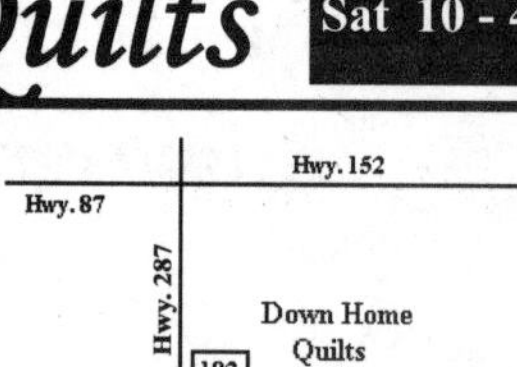

Quilt kits for those on the go. Fabric, batting & notions for those planning their own. And Custom Quilting to help you finish your project.

Amarillo, TX #12

Mon - Sat 10 - 5

Old 66 Quilts & More

3614 W. 6th Ave. 79106
(806) 373-7777
aliceama@arn.net
www.old66quilts.com
Owner: Alice Grant
Est: 1996 7500 sq.ft. 2000 Bolts

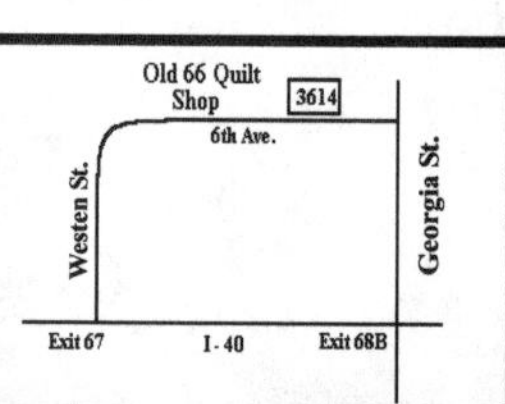

Quilt Shop located on Historic Route 66. Quilting supplies, fabric, notions, books and long arm quilting supplies. Route 66 Fabric.

Amarillo, TX #13

Mon - Sat 9 - 5:30

Sisters' Scraps Quilt Shop

600 S. Maryland 79106
(877) 727-8458
(806) 372-0660
Est: 2003

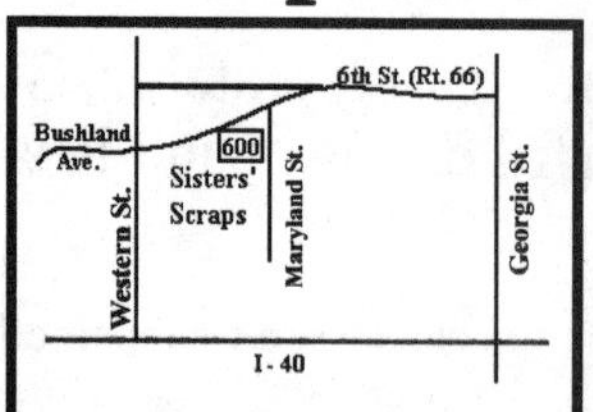

Located in an Historic two-story home on Route 66, we offer beautiful quilting fabric, wool, stitcheries, and great, friendly service.

Amarillo, TX #14

Mon - Sat 9:30 - 5:30

Get the Red Carpet Treatment at

R & R Quilts and More

4332 Teckla Blvd. 79109-5422
(806) 359-6235
rrquilts@amaonline.com
www.rrquilts.com

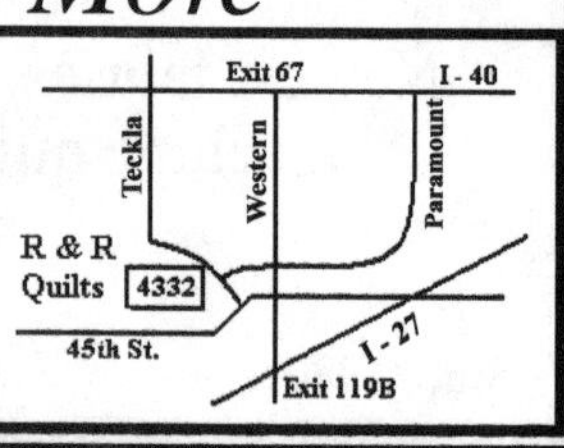

Over 4500 Bolts of 100% cotton fabrics. Classes, Supplies, Books and Patterns.

Friona, TX #15

Everyday 8 - 5

Malouf's Fabrics

503 W. 11th St. (Hwy. 60) 79035
(806) 250-3575 Fax: (806) 250-5093
material@wtrt.net
Owner: Jiselle Malouf Hand
Est: 1959 Over 1 million yards of fabric

Our fabric store is listed in the Panhandle Tourism brochure as "Best In The West". All types of fabric. Come and Enjoy!

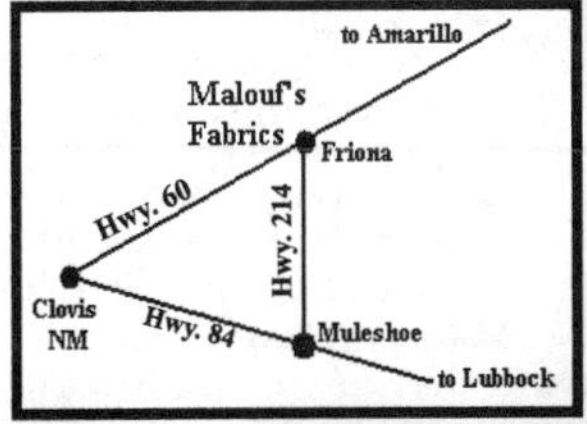

Alpine, TX #16

Tues - Fri 10 - 5
Sat 10 - 2

A Stitch In Time

2305 FM1703 (Hwy. 90 W) 79831
(432) 837-0950
Alpineqltmkr@yahoo.com
www.wtexasastitchintime.com
Est: 2002 4000+ sq.ft.

A Stitch in Time has all of your quilting needs. We offer classes and carry gifts with the quilter in mind. We also have antiques, imports & Fiestaware.

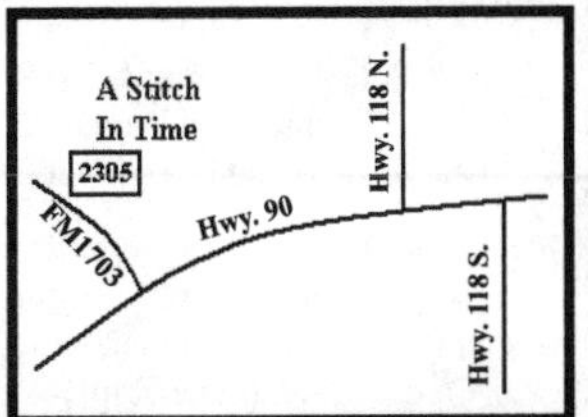

Abilene, TX #17

Mon - Fri 9:30 - 5:30
Sat 10 - 4

Patchwork Garden Quilt Shop

3301 S. 14th, Suite 31 79605
(325) 698-5544 Fax: (325) 698-6468
edjd@bitstreet.com Est: 2002

We offer a selection of fabrics including Moda, Hoffman, Maywood, RJR, and Benartex: as well as a wide selection of books, notions, and patterns. Original Home of Briar Rose Designs.

Hamilton, TX #18

Tues - Fri 9 - 5
Sat 10 - 3

One More Stitch

108 E. Henry St. 76531
(254) 386-8874
E-Mail:
onemorestitch@htcomp.net
Est: 2001 1700 sq.ft.

Quilt Fabric - Batting - Notions - Classes
We do Custom Quilting on Gammill Long-arm

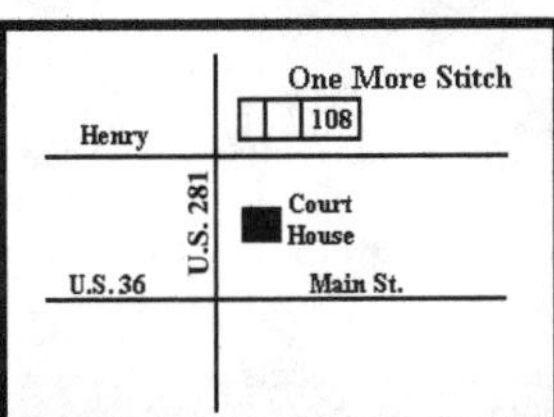

The Quilt Connection

Come visit the friendliest quilt shop in West Texas! We offer a large selection of 100% cotton fabrics from all of your favorite brands, as well as books, patterns and notions. We are a full service Gold Standard Bernina sewing machine dealer.

Fax: (325) 942-6768
quiltconnection@aol.com
Janet Moran & Angie Stripe
Est: 1997 2500 sq.ft.

Mon - Fri 10 - 5
Sat 9 - 5

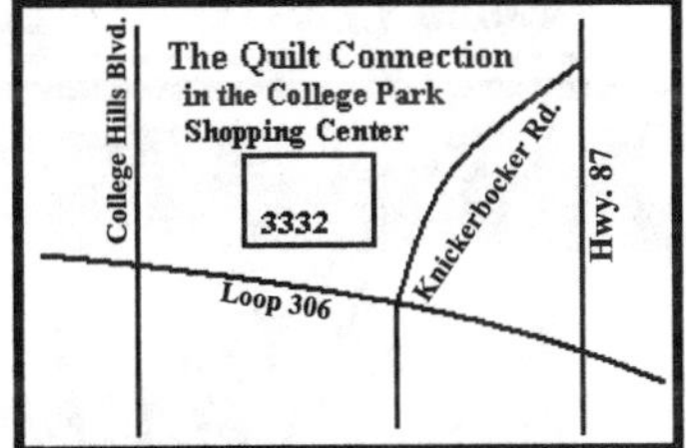

3332 W. Loop 306, San Angelo, TX 76904
(325) 223-8334

San Angelo, TX #19

Granbury, TX #20

Houston St. Mercantile

126 N. Houston St. 76048
(817) 279-0425
Owner: Glenda Westbrook
Website Coming Soon!

Mon - Fri 10 - 5
Sat 10 - 6
Sun 12 - 5

Houston St. Mercantile

offers a delight to quilters with its fantastic selection of quality fabrics, (over 3,000 Bolts) patterns, books, and classes. All major credit cards accepted.

Also of interest is

The Quilt Inn of Granbury,

a quaint and historic Bed and Breakfast especially for quilt retreats.
For information call owner, Glenda Westbrook
817-279-0425, email-houstonstmerc@itexas.net

Stephenville, TX #21

Mon - Sat 9 - 6

The Flying Needle

1495 W. South Loop
76401 Est: 1971
(254) 965-7577 or (877) FNEEDLE
Theflyingneeedle@ht.comp
www.Theflyingneedle.net

2300+ Bolts of Cotton from Dozens of Manufacturers, Notions New and Old, Hundreds of Books, Patterns and Supplies.

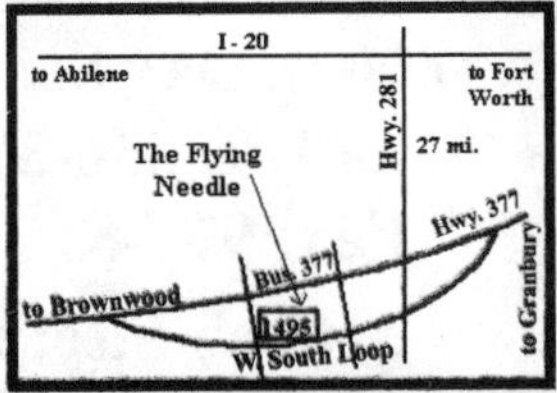

West, TX #22

Tues - Sat 9 - 5

Tex-Czech Crafts & Quilting

111 S. Main St. 76691
(254) 826-0100 Fax: (254) 829-0691
Rschiemenz@aol.com
Est: 2001 1000 sq.ft. 200+ Bolts

Machine quilting, 30's reproduction fabric, Aunt Grace's collections, quilt tops, locally made crafts, candles, & much more! Worth the Trip!!

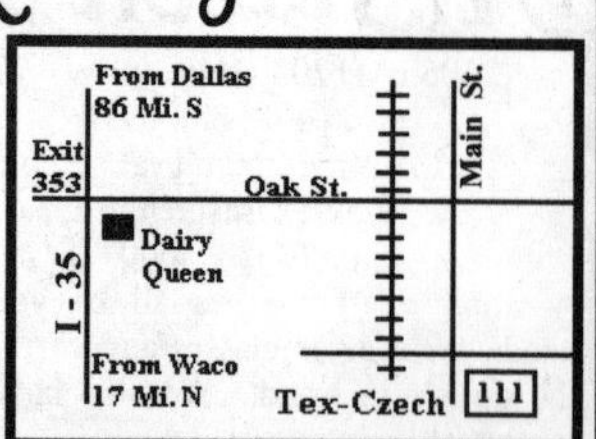

Waco, TX #23

Mon - Fri 10 - 5:30
Sat 10 - 4

Nancy's Quilt Block

1412 N. Valley Mills Dr. #228 76710
(254) 776-4989
NANQUBLOCK@prodigy.net

Good selection of quality 100% cotton fabrics, books, patterns & notions. Authorized Dealer of PFAFF Sewing Machines. Classes available. Friendly Service. "To God be the Glory."

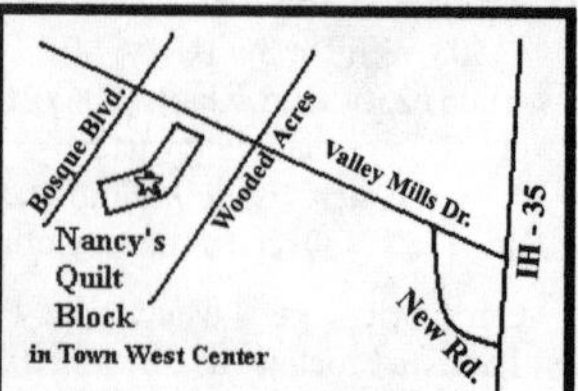

Fairfield, TX #24

Tues - Fri 10 - 5
Sat 10 - 3

Cotton Cottage

221 E. Commerce 75840
(903) 389-6528
beeqp@aol.com
Owner: Pam Beene Est: 1996

100% Cotton fabric, notions, books, patterns. Catering to Quilters & Creative Clothing. Classes and Friendly Service. Husqvarna Viking Dealer.

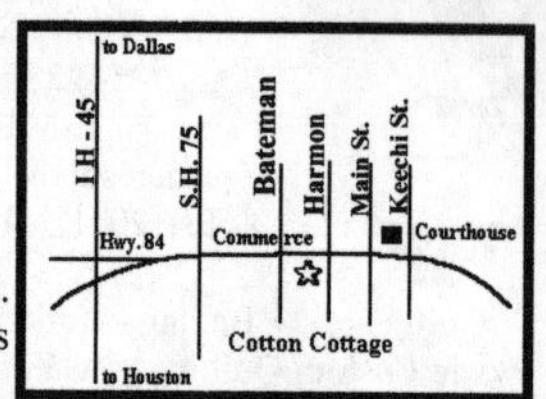

Killeen, TX #25

Mon - Fri 9:30 - 5:30
Sat 9:30 - 4:30

Quiltin' Country

4904 W. Stan Schlueter 76549
(254) 554-3700
Redbirdbluebird@aol.com
Owner: Gayle S. King
Est: 2003 2000 sq.ft.

Beautiful 100% cotton fabrics, friendly clerks, spacious showroom, books & patterns, notions, classes. Machine quilting available.

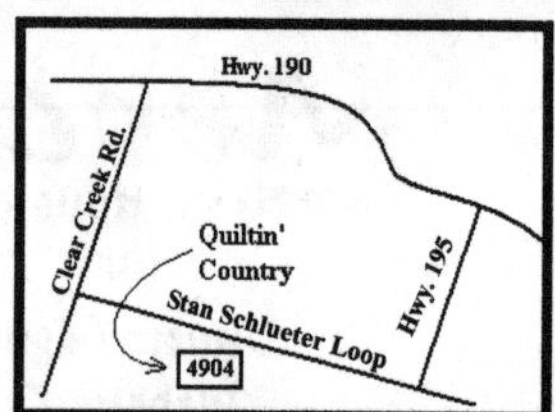

The Sewing Basket

560 N. Main Street Salado, TX 76571
1-877-244-0450 or (254) 947-5423
Www.TheSewingBasket.com
Open Mon-Fri 10-5 & Sat 10-5:30
Closed Sundays

Quality fabric, quilting supplies & Classes, sewing notions, Books, patterns, Pfaff machines, And sew much more!

#26 PFAFF

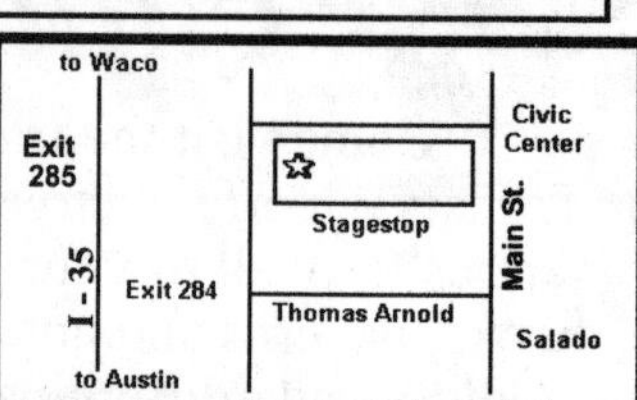

Come Visit Our New Location on Main Street!

Texana Quilting Company

3211 S. Texas Avenue
Bryan, TX 77802
979-775-1681
www.texanaquiltingcompany.com

Open Mon - Fri 9:30 til 5:30
Late Weds til 9, Sat 9:30 - 3:30
Closed Sunday

The best little quilt shop in Texas!

★ Knowledgeable friendly staff ★ Latest Fabrics ★
★ Inspiration ★ Advice ★ Instruction ★
★ Gifts ★ Books ★ Notions ★
★ Extensive collection of maroon fabrics ★
★ Licensed Aggie Quilt Maker ★

Located 1.3 miles north of Texas A&M University. From Hwy 6, turn west on University Drive. Turn north on Texas Avenue. We're on the east side of the street, just past the Sulphur Springs stop light!

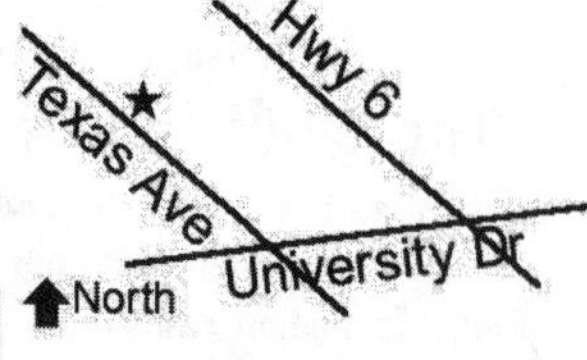

Bryan, TX #27

Brenham, TX #28

Stitch Haven

For Those Who Love Quilting Needlework and Fine Fabrics

Tues - Fri 10 - 5:30
Sat 10 - 3

Featuring Cotton Fabrics and Supplies for Quilting, Wearable Art, Smocking, and Embroidery

1600 S. Day St. 77833
(979) 836-3200
Fax: 979-836-3355

Web Site: www.stitchhaven.com

BARB'S QUILT NOOK, ETC

PO BOX 868 / 120 DAN ST KINGSLAND, TEXAS 78639
PH (915) 388-5225 FAX (915) 388-3999
TOLL FREE 1-800-762-7096
EMAIL barbsew@moment.net WEB www.barbsquilts.com

Kingsland, TX #29

"WHERE FRIENDS MEET FRIENDS"

EST. 2001 - 3600 SQ FT - OVER 2000 BOLTS OF FABRIC

QUILT SHOWS -- RETREATS -- SHOW VENDOR

Mon - Fri 9 - 5
Thur 9 - 6
Sat 9 - 4

ALL YOUR QUILTING NEEDS!

QUALITY COTTON FABRICS BY TOP MANUFACTURERS

BOOKS & END OF BOLT SALE 20% OFF EVERYDAY!
PATTERNS -- NOTIONS -- CLASSES

ALL CREDIT CARDS & CHECKS ACCEPTED

COME ENJOY THE BEAUTIFUL TEXAS HILL COUNTRY!
WE WOULD LOVE TO MEET YOU!

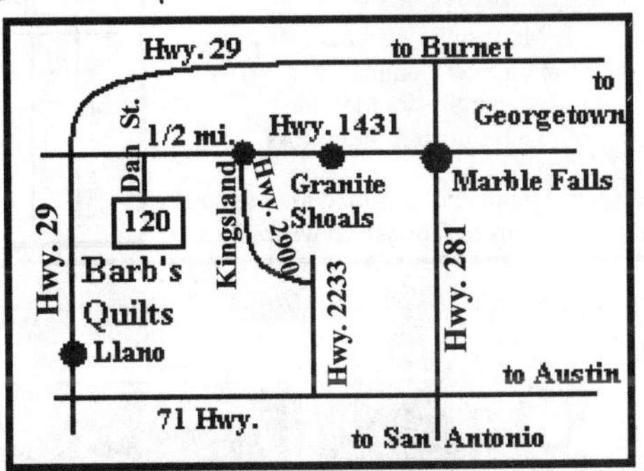

A Stitch in Time

in the historic Governors Ferguson Home

518 North 7th • Temple, Texas 76501
Owner: Karen Summers, Licensed Pullen/Viking Instructor
254.774.9990 • e-mail: astitchintime@sbcglobal.net
Monday - Friday 9:30 am - 5:30 pm • Saturday 9 am - 5 pm
Open Late Thursday - 7 pm
www.astitchintimequiltshop.com

We offer creative inspiration and:

- Moda
- Timeless Treasures
- Elna Sewing Machines
- Jinny Beyer
- Hoffman
- Red Rooster
- RJR
- P & B
- Andover

Come recharge your creative batteries in a restored former Texas Governors' home. See the latest fabrics & patterns, find unique jewelry, learn a new skill, or just relax with a cup of coffee.

You will also find everything for Heirloom Sewing:

- silks
- batiste
- nelona
- french laces
- linens
- heirloom cotton

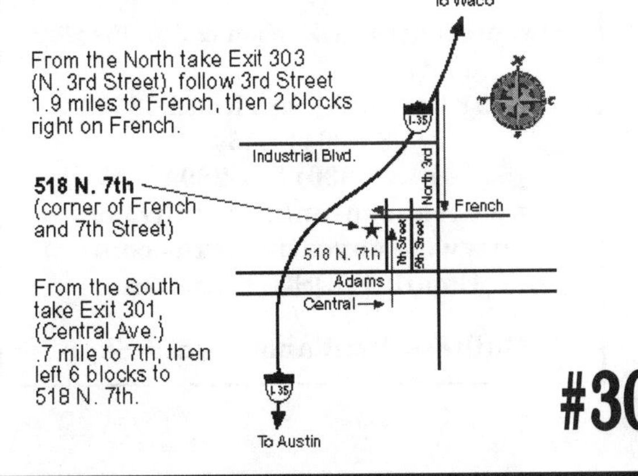

#30

Giddings, TX #31

Mon - Fri 9 - 6 Sat 10 - 3

979 N. Leon 78942
(979) 542-2782
2fisches@tconline.net
Est: 2003

Machine Quilting
Embroidery &
Fabric
"A Place Where
Friends Gather!"

Hwy. 2440 | Waco | 979 | All Around The Block | E. Independence | Hwy. 77 | N. Grimes | N. Leon | P.O. | Hwy. 290 | to Austin | to Houston

College Station, TX #32

Mon - Sat 10 - 6

Pruitt's Fabric and Quilt Shop

318 George Bush Dr. 77840
(409) 693-9357 Fax: (409) 696-6264
www.aggielandfabric.com Est: 1946

Everything A Quilter Needs
Large selection of vibrant colored cottons (5000+ Bolts), quilting books, patterns, & supplies, plus Silk, Wool, Linen, Velvet, Ultra Suede, Bridal Laces and Trims. Special Orders Welcome.

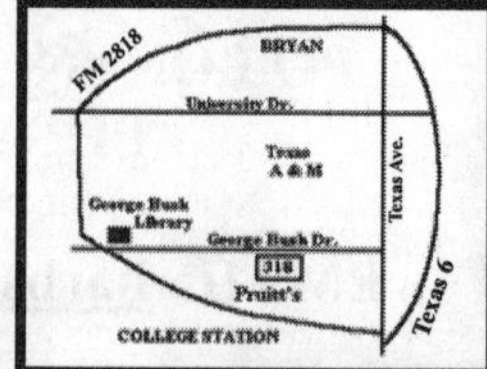

College Station, TX #33

By Appt. Only

Dyeing To Be Different

14 Ranchero Rd. 77845
(979) 776-8632
E-Mail: smjjd@myriad.net
Web Site: Coming Soon
Owners: Sandra Melville,
Connie Currin & Judy Ross

We specialize in one-of-a-kind assorted and custom hand-dyed fabrics and wearable art.

Harvey Rd. | Hwy. 30 | Dyeing To Be Different | 14 | Ranchero Rd. | Earl Rudder Frwy. W | Appomattox Dr. | Linda Lane

Round Rock, TX #34

Mon - Fri 9 - 6 Sat 9 - 5

Austin Sewing Machines

2000 S. IH 35, Suite C-1 78681
(512) 310-7349
Fax: (512) 310-7465
E-Mail: oldbob@texas.net
Web Site: austinsewing.com
Est: 1953 2800 sq.ft.

Over 2,000 Bolts of Current Fabrics.
Husqvarna Viking & PFAFF Sewing Machines, also Janome Sales & Service -- also vacuums

Austin Sewing in the Skyridge Plaza next to Walgreens | 2000 | IH 35 | Hesters Crossing | Exit 251 | to Austin

Stonewall, TX #37

The Best Little Ole' Texas Hill Country Quilt Shop

Hours:
Mon—Sat
10:00—4:30

Full line of Fabrics, Notions, Books & Patterns

Specializing in Fabrics & Patterns for Cats - Chickens - Cowboys

Est: 1999 - 2000 sq. ft. - over 2000 bolts

Owners: Lorraine Zensen & Jim Fridley

1621 Lower Albert Road 78671
830-644-2554
Fax: (830) 644-2894
www.vonzensenburgquilts.com
www.sleepycatinntexas.com
Email: VZQSCI@ktc.com

Quilters' B&B above Quilt Shop

Round Rock, TX #35

Evenings & Weekends By Appointment

Kim's Quilts

2403 Meadow Brook Dr. 78664
(512) 248-8858
E-Mail: kim@kims-quilts.com
Web Site: www.kims-quilts.com
Owner: Kim Jones Est: 1998

Custom quilt studio. Excellent quality, affordable prices. Hand-tied * 100% cotton fabric * hypo-allergenic batting. See quilts, books, fabric & crafts in stock on my website.

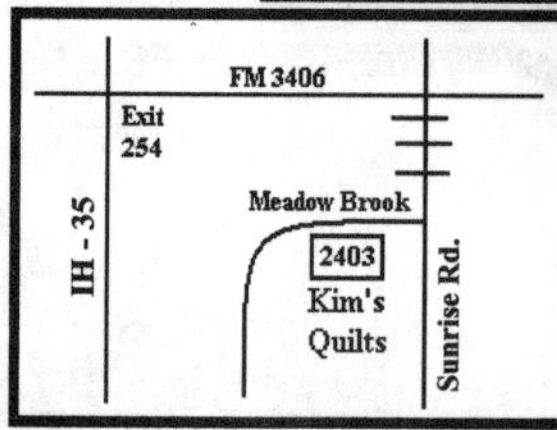

Round Rock, TX #36

Tues - Sat 10 - 5

Mini Stitches

208 W. Bagdad Ave. #7 78664
Corner of Brown & Bagdad
(512) 255-8545
Owner: Carol Kussmaul Est: 1994

Fulfill your creative destiny with our select fabrics, patterns, classes, and personalized assistance. Silk Ribbon also available.

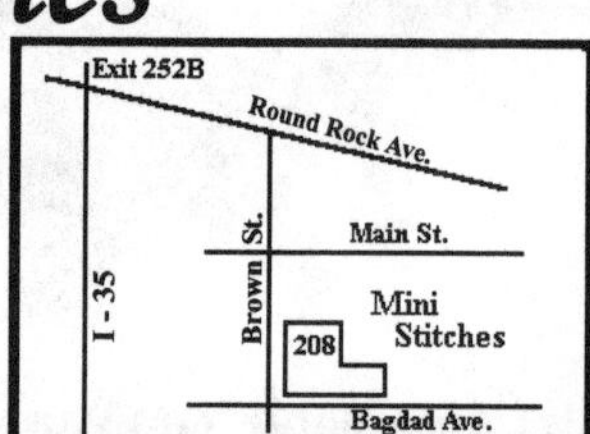

Stonewall, TX #38

Quilters' B & B

1621 Lower Albert Rd. 78671
(830) 644-2554
Fax:
(830) 644-2894

VZQSCI@ktc.com
www.sleepycatinntexas.com
Owners: Lorraine Zensen & Jim Fridley

Plan your next retreat with us! Quilters' B&B Above Von Zensenburg Quilts
"Where only the cats are in charge"

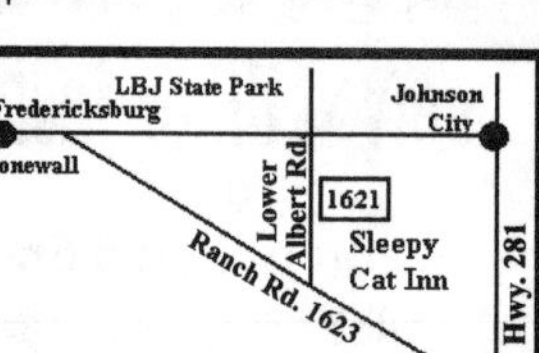
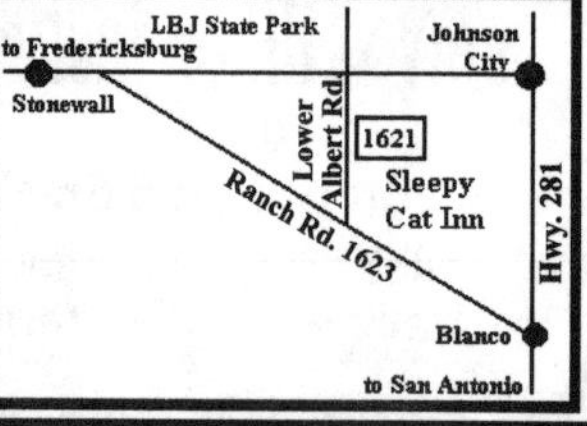

Fredericksburg, TX #39

Mon - Sat 10 - 5:30

Pocketful of Poseys

311 East Highway St. 78624
(830) 990-4140 or (877) 427-6739
Fax: (830) 990-8221
E-Mail: Claurent@KTC.com
Web Site: www.geocities.com/pocketfulofposeys
Owner: Cynthia Laurent-Conner
Est: 1999 3600 sq.ft. 1500+ Bolts

Full line of Quilting Fabrics & Notions, Books & Patterns, Threads & Buttons plus more. Located in the hill country.

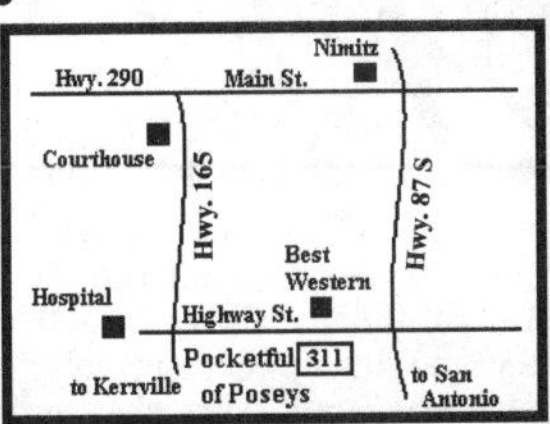

San Antonio, TX #40

Sew Special Quilts - Bernina

The Market at Leon Springs
24165 IH 10 West #421, 78257
(800) 891-8279 or (210) 698-6076
Owner: Laurie Mangold
Est: 1987 2600 sq.ft. 1800 Bolts

Open 7 Days A Week

A full service shop for all of your quilting and wearable needs. Staffed by a helpful, friendly group of crazy ladies. Come see our unique "Quilt Block Floor".

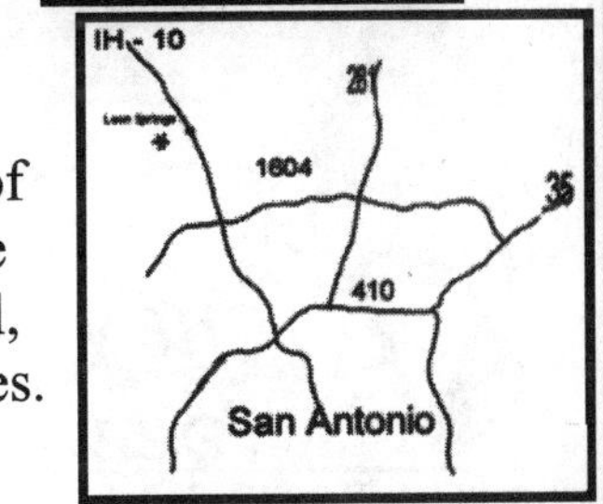

Exit 550 from Boerne
Exit 551 from San Antonio

Creative Sewing Center- Bernina

11777 West Ave. at Blanco Rd. 78216
(210) 344-0791 or toll free 877-331-7862
berninasat@aol.com Terry & Vince Soll

Mon - Sat 9:30 - 6:00
Sun Noon - 5

Come visit us when you are in the San Antonio area. Bus tours welcome and handicap parking right in front. There are 8000 square feet filled with beautiful quilting and natural fiber fabrics from unusual novelty prints to the complete color range of Moda Marbles. Large selection of rulers, quilting accessories and books. We carry the largest selection of threads in the area—from machine embellishment to quilting & fiber arts. Heirloom lace, trims and fabrics including floral batiste.

Sales, service and machine instruction for Bernina and Brother Pacesetter. Machines from $199.00 to the most exciting embroidery machines and software on the market today. We have a large selection of sewing machine notions, accessories and cabinets.

www.sewsanantonio.com

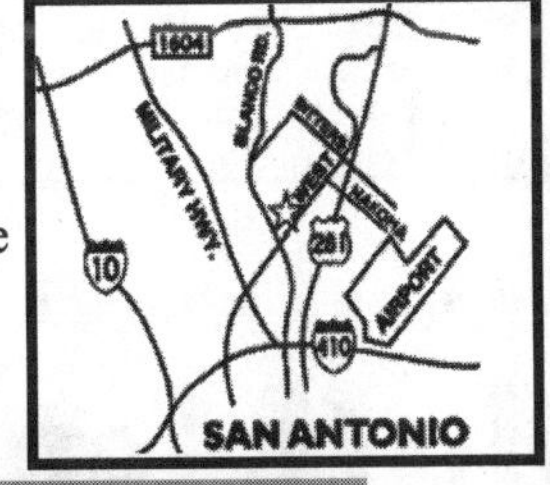

San Antonio, TX #41

San Antonio, TX #42

Mon - Sat 10 - 6
Sun 12 - 6

Plain Jane's

555 Bitters Rd. 78216
(210) 496-5436
www.plainjanesfolkart.com

Specializing in Country Primitive Folk Art and Hand did Stuff. Patterns, quilts, Samplers, dolls.

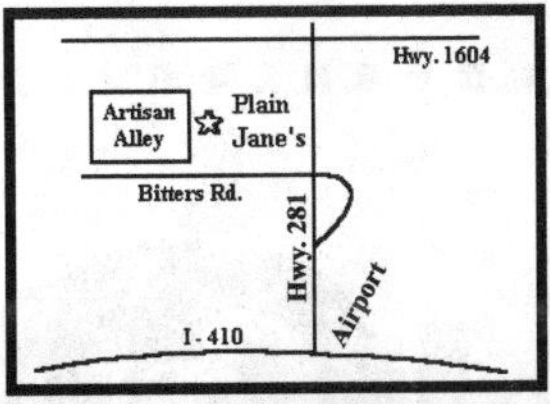

San Antonio, TX #43

Mon - Fri 9:30 - 5:30
Sat 9:30 - 3

Seventh Heaven

6706 N. New Braunfels 78209
(210) 822-9980
Owner: Dixie Bradbury & Shelby Bonner
quilts@seventhheavenquiltshop.com
seventhheavenquiltshop.com
Est: 1990 3600 sq.ft. 2000+ Bolts

Heavenly delight 100% Cotton Fabrics, Supplies. Thimbleberries, RJR, P&B, and Moda. Patterns, Books and more. Elna & Singer Sewing Machines.

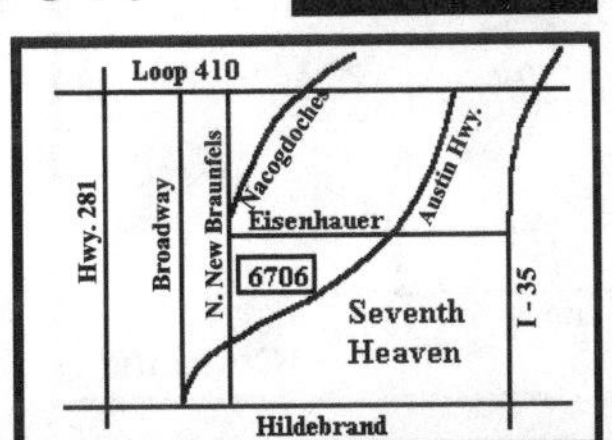

San Antonio, TX #44

Tue - Sat 10 - 5
Tue & Thur til 7

Las Colchas

110 Ogden St. 78212
(210) 223-2405
Quilts@LasColchas.com
www.LasColchas.com

100% Cotton Fabrics - checks, plaids, Homespuns. Supplies & Classes Patterns, Books, Kits. Year Round Christmas Room all in a cozy Victorian House.

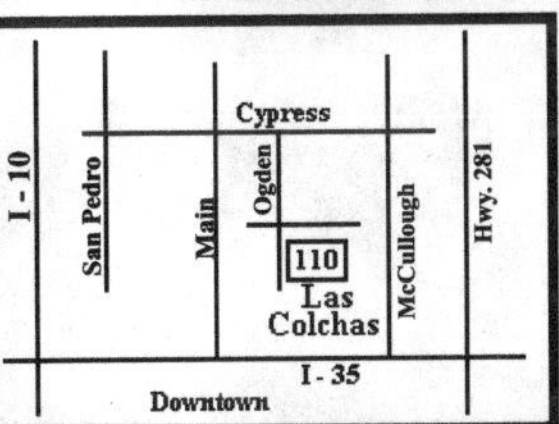

San Antonio, TX #45

Mon - Fri 10 - 7
Sat 9 - 4

6816 Huebner Rd. 78238
(210) 520-4833 Fax: (210) 520-6216

Featuring 2000+ cotton and flannel fabrics from Kaufman - Hoffman - Benartex - RJR Timeless Treasures - Moda - FabriQuilt Anover - Michael Miller - Cranston Marcus Brothers. Books, Patterns & Quilting Supplies.

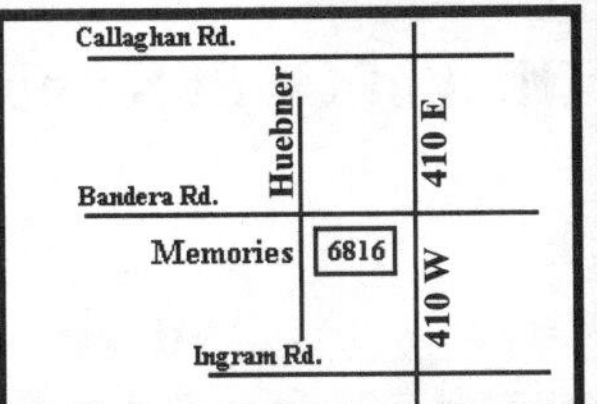

San Marcos, TX #46

Mon - Fri 10 - 5:30
Sat 10 - 5
Sun 10 - 4

Gifted Quilter, Inc.

1917 Dutton Dr., Suite D 78666
(512) 754-3467
info@giftedquilter.com
giftedquilter.com

"A Quiltmaker's Haven!"

Great selection of high quality cotton fabrics, books, patterns, notions & classes. Mosey in for a dose of our Texas Hospitality!

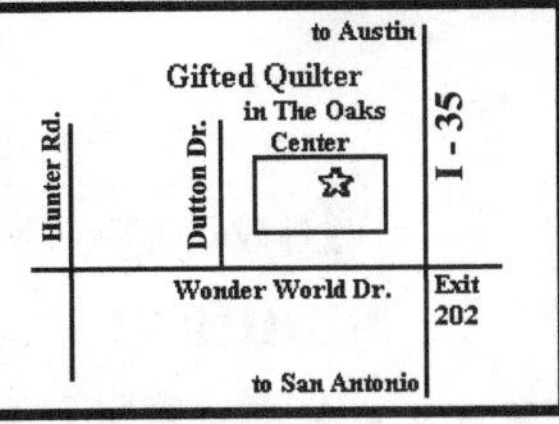

Mon - Sat
10 - 5
Thur til 8

The Quilt Store, Inc.

2700 W. Anderson, #301 78757
(512) 453-1145
www.quiltstore.com

More than 5,000 bolts of 100% cotton fabric plus much more.

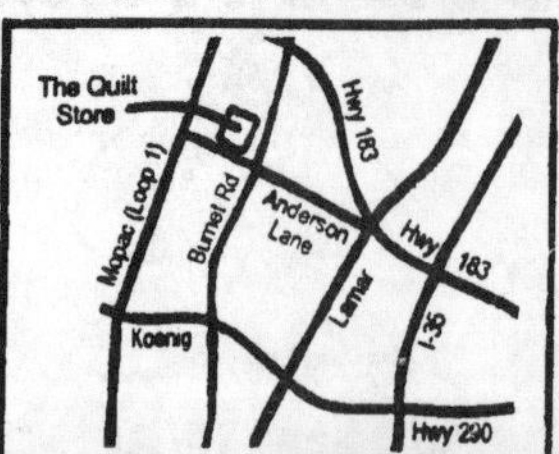

Austin, TX #48

Mon - Sat
9 - 6

Ginger's Needlearts, Quilts & Framing

5322 Cameron Rd. 78723
(512) 454-5344
or (800) 982-8444

Fax: (512) 454-1489
Est: 1985 4000 sq.ft. 3000+ Bolts

Since our buying philosophy is, "When in doubt, buy it all.", our shop is packed with cross stitch and quilting.

Mon - Sat
9 - 5
Tues til 8
Sun 12 - 5

10401 Anderson Mill Rd. #107 78750
(512) 257-1269
www.honeybeequiltstore.com

A most charming quilt store, founded by three sisters to serve your every quilting need! We have over 2,500 bolts of fabric!

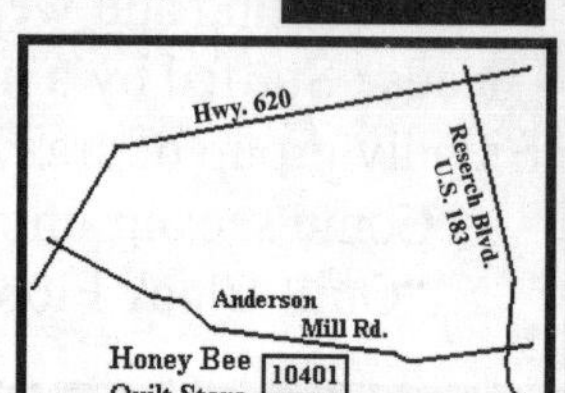

Castroville, TX #50

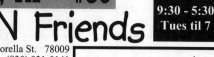

Mon - Sat
9:30 - 5:30
Tues til 7

Fabric 'N Friends

1103 Fiorella St. 78009
(830) 931-0141
Fax: (830) 931-0142
fabricnfriends@msn.com
Owner: Jeanne M. Stephens
Est: 2003 2000 sq.ft. 2000+ Bolts

Friendly Service providing top quality cotton fabrics - batiks, homespuns, brights, western, 30's and great prints. Patterns, books, notions & classes too.

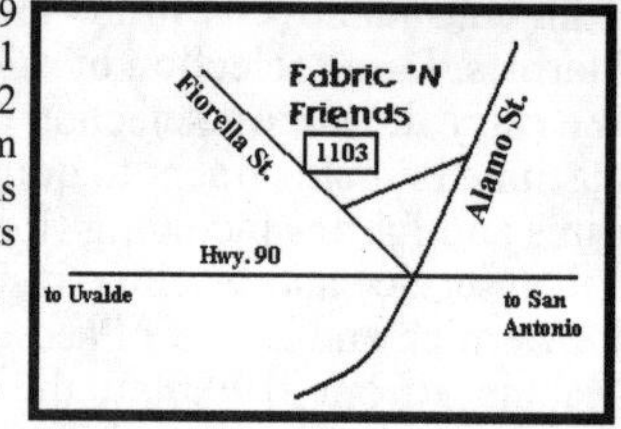

CREATIONS

Great Stuff for the Quilter and Sewing Enthusiast

Kerrville, TX #51

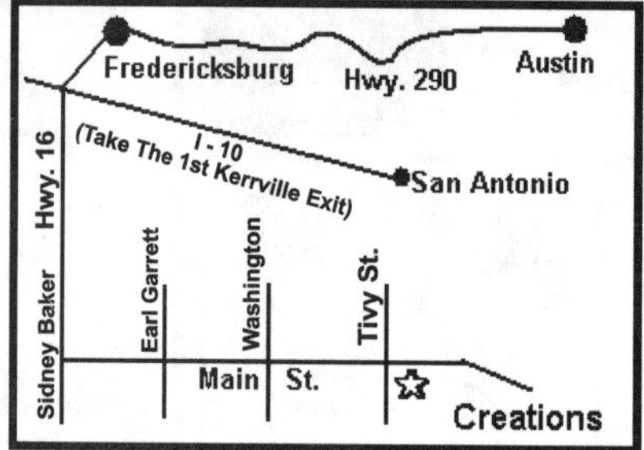

CREATIONS
1013 E. MAIN
KERRVILLE
830-896-8088
Est: 1978

Beautiful fabrics and great displays set in a turn of the century home. You'll find gifts and accessories as well as cottons, linens, Bali rayons and home dec fabrics. Enjoy a cup of coffee or frozen cappuccino while wandering through the spacious rooms. Take an on-line tour of the store at: www.creations-online.com

Featured in the 1996 edition of Quilt Sampler.

Monday--Saturday: 9:30--5:30
Sunday: 12:30--4:00

e-mail: creation@ktc.com

The QUILT HAUS

Fabulous selection of over 2500 bolts of 100% cotton quilting fabrics.
Books, patterns, wearable, notions, kits, gifts and ELNA sewing machines.
Friendly, expert staff. Classes for all levels.

471-A Main Plaza 78130
(830) 620-1382
www.quilthaus.com
Owner: Deanne Quill

Mon - Sat
9:30 - 5:30
Sun 12 - 4

We're bustin' our seams! We're moving to a more spacious location in 2004. Call or visit our website for directions.

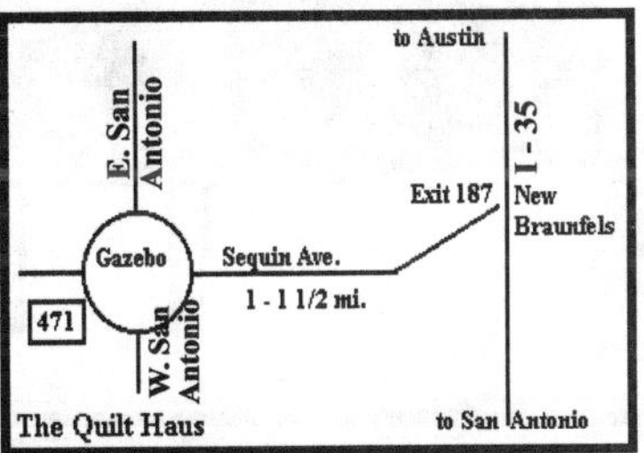

New Braunfels, TX #52

Lytle, TX #53

Mon - Sat
9 - 6

Kalico & Keepsakes

14945 Main St., P.O. Box 329 78052
(830) 772-4721
Owner: Dee Cromer
Est: 1997 2300 sq.ft.

Full line quality Fabric and Notions.
Classes — day, night and Saturdays.
Professional finishing on Gammill Machine.
Our Customers are soon Friends.

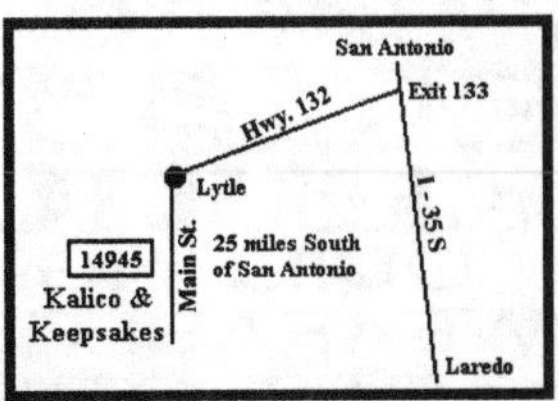

Harlingen, TX #54

Mon - Sat
9:30 - 5:30

SCAIEFS FABRICS

810 S. Dixieland Rd. 78552
(956) 425-4082 or (800) 221-1-SEW
scaiefs@aol.com
www.sew2000.com/scaiefsfabrics
Est: 1978

Home of Bernina. New Home of Janome
A fabulous assortment of good quilting cottons - color sorted. Plus threads, cutters, mats, templates, patterns, books, and sewing machine accessories.

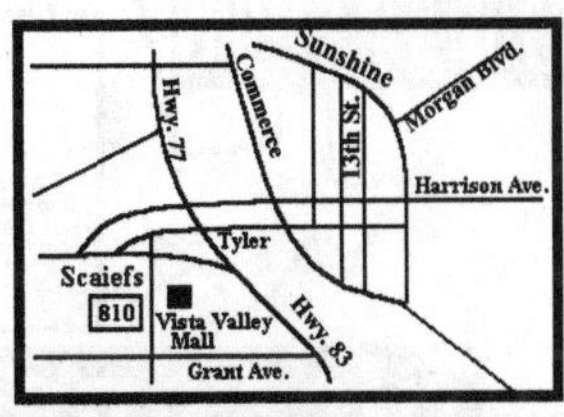

Corpus Christi, TX #55

Tues - Fri
10 - 5
Sat 10 - 4

11229 Leopard St. 78410
(361) 241-8155 Fax: (361) 241-8199
divinequilters@aol.com
Owners: Lari Ainsworth & Dubby Pemberton
Est: 2001 1400+ sq.ft. 1500+ Bolts

Quaint little store boasting of 1500+ bolts of 100% cottons, books and notions. Batiks, flannels, 30's reproductions, fleece, and novelty prints abound. Classes offered from the beginner to the advanced. Machine quilting available.

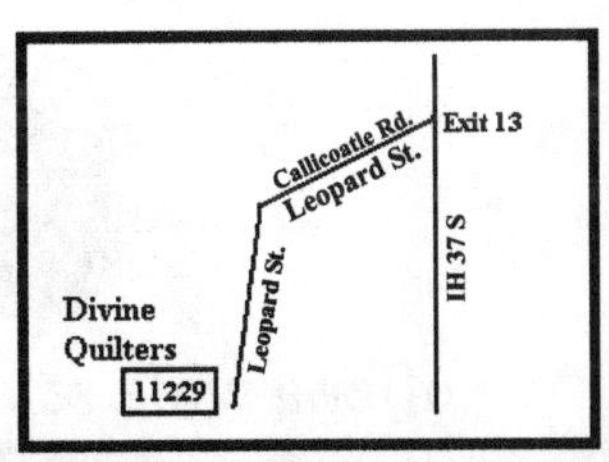

Corpus Christi, TX #56

Mon - Fri
10 - 6
Sat 10 - 5

The Quilt Cottage

5433 S. Staples 78411
(361) 985-0908
www.thequiltcottage.com
Owner: Lynda Butler
Est: 1994 1600 sq.ft.

A very warm & friendly shop. We have over 2000 bolts all cotton fabric. Loads of Books, Patterns, Notions, Classes, etc.
Professional Machine Quilting

Staples
5433
The Quilt Cottage
S.P.I.D.
Bonner
Holly
Everhart

Rockport, TX #57

Mon - Fri
10 - 5
Sat 10 - 4

Golden Needles & Quilts

701 N. Allen 78382
(361) 729-7873 Fax: Same
KTSTAN@aol.com
www.quiltscapes.com
Owner: Kay Stanley
Est: 1989 2800 sq.ft. 3000+ Bolts

Original Blocks of the Month & Patterns.
100% cotton fabrics, books, notions.
Janome Sewing Machines.

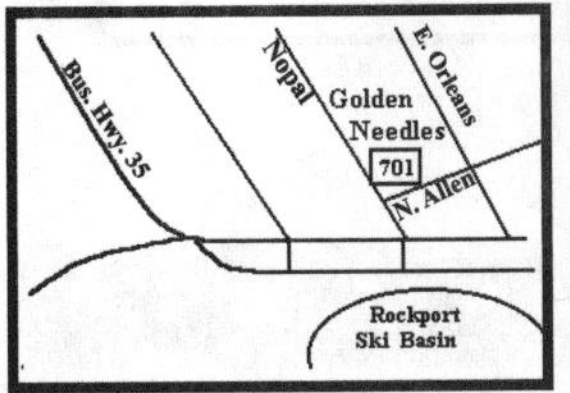

Victoria, TX #58

Mon - Fri 10 - 5
Sat 10 - 2
Summer
Mon - Fri 10 - 4

Quilters Patch

205 North Star, Suite Q 77904
(361) 578-0380 or (866) 578-0380
qpatch@tisd.net
www.quilterspatch.com
Owners: Karen Leach & Sherry Ware
Est: 1995 2000 sq.ft. 4000 Bolts

Bolts of Cotton Fabric, Hoffman, Moda, RJR, Aunt Graces, Andover, Maywood, Hi-Fashion, Batiks, P&B, & Kona Bay. Located off Hwy. 77

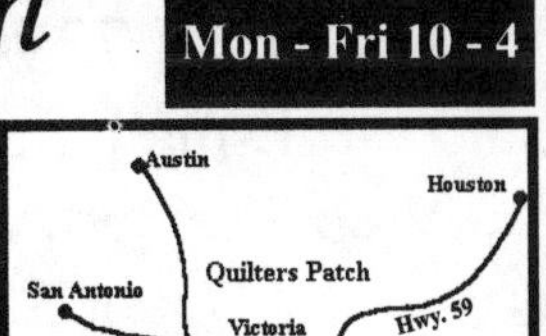
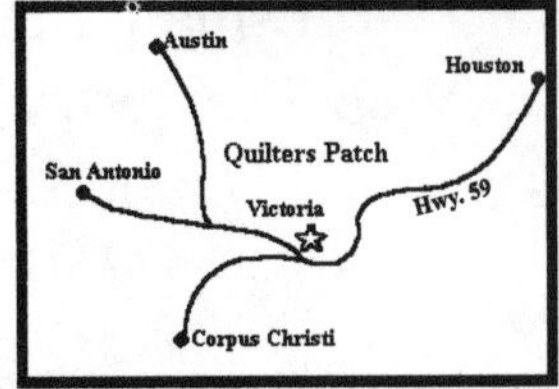

Edna, TX #60

By Appt. Only

The Scrappy Quilter

7429 C.R. 283 77957
(361) 781-0542
Rachael Gotcher

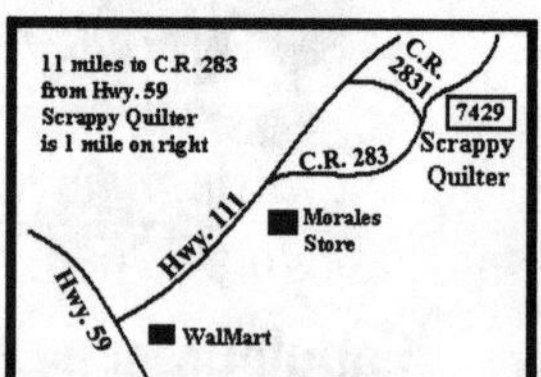

I am a machine quilter and also I make custom quilts. I do custom quilting and also have several edge-to-edge patterns available. Sorry no fabrics.

THE FABRIC STORE

We offer a wide selection of quality quilting, fashion and name decorator fabrics, along with patterns, notions & classes. Come see us--We love to sew and quilt as much as you do!

1605 South Hwy. 69,
Nederland, TX 77627
(409) 729-5288 Fax: Same
E-mail: thefabricstore@exp.net
Web Site: www.thefabricstoreonline.com
Over 5,000 bolts of fabric
3500 sq.ft.

Mon - Fri
10 - 5:30
Sat 9:30 - 5

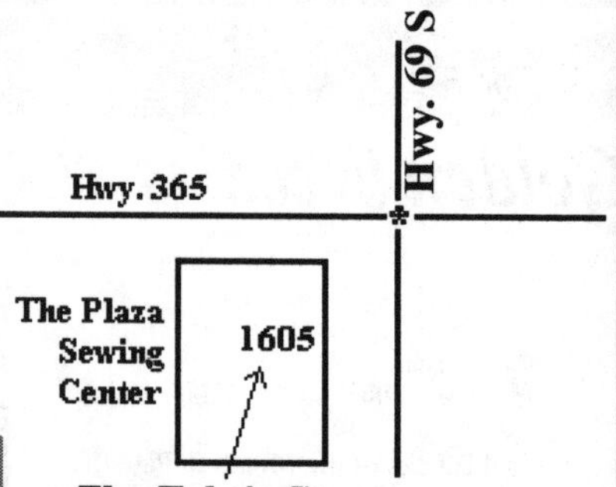

Hwy. 365
Hwy. 69 S
The Plaza Sewing Center
1605
The Fabric Store

Nederland, TX #61

Jean's Corner

712 N. Jackson 77351
(936) 327-8817
Fax: (936) 327-6411
jyarbrough@livingston.net
Owner: Jean Yarbrough

Mon - Fri 9 - 5
Sat 9 - 1

Brand name 100% cotton Fabrics
Books - Notions
Janome Sewing Machines
2,000 Bolts of Fabric

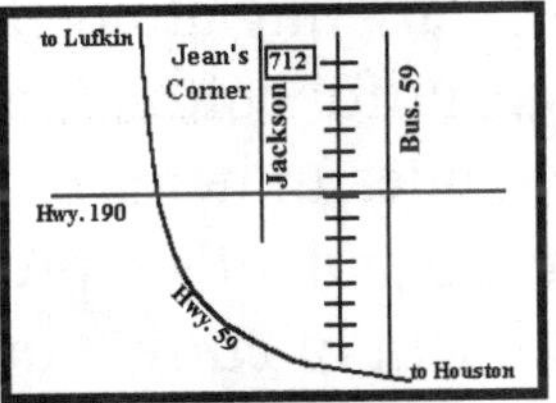

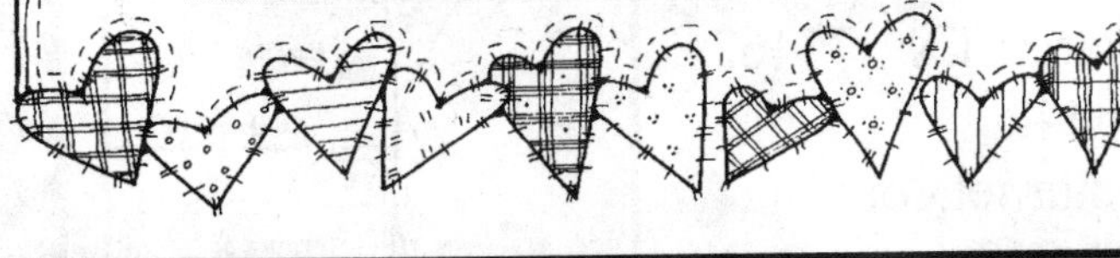

Palestine, TX #63

Tues - Fri 9 - 5
Sat 9 - 1

Grimes Sewing Center

619 W. Oak St. 75801
(903) 729-2889
Est: 1991 2600 sq.ft. 2000+ Bolts

Fabrics, Quilting Supplies, Patterns, Books, Notions, Classes

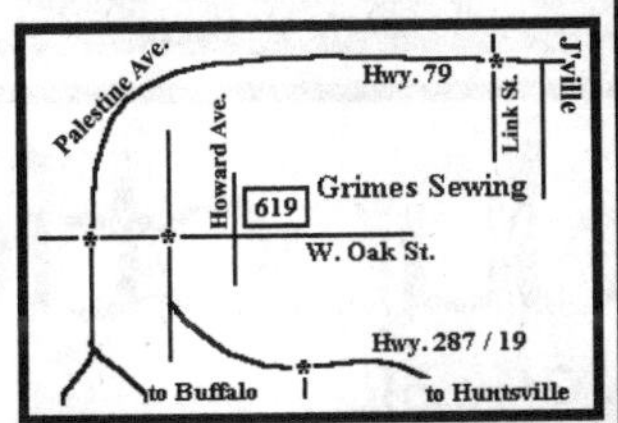

Commerce, TX #65

Mon - Sat 9:30 - 5:30
Tues til 8

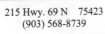

Quilts on the Square

1223 Washington St. 75428
(903) 886-2299
www.quiltsonthesquare.com
quilts@neto.com
Owner: Anne Swartz
Est: 2000

100% Cotton Fabric
Books, Patterns, Lots of Notions
Third Saturday Sampler
Great Classes - all levels

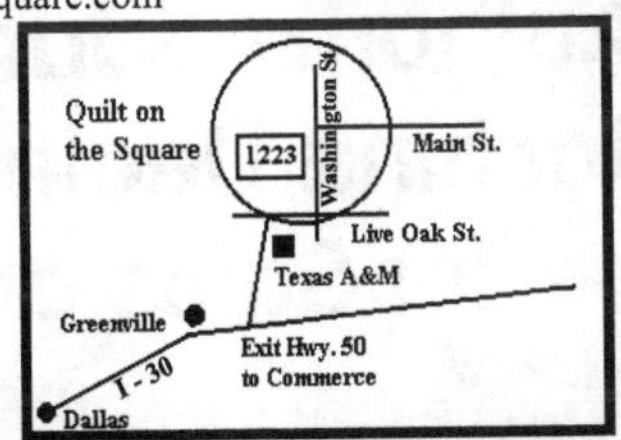

Celeste, TX #66

Tues - Fri 9 - 6
Sat 9 - 1

215 Hwy. 69 N 75423
(903) 568-8739

quiltmercantile215@msn.com
Owners: Vickey Dees & Jennifer Tenney
Est: 2002 3000 sq.ft. 1800 Bolts
Step back in time visiting our early 1900's rustic building with a twenty foot high tin ceiling located 15 miles north of Greenville.

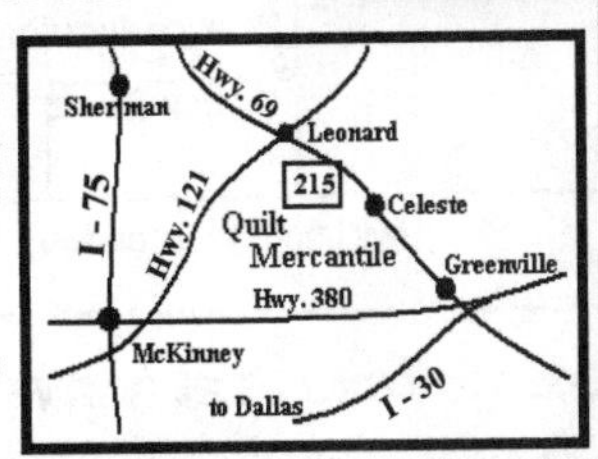

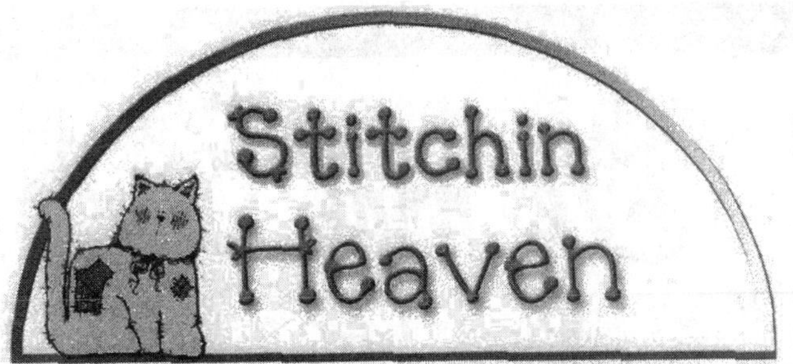

Quitman, TX #64

Located in Beautiful East Texas!
Featured shop in Quilt Sampler 2000

Over 3000 bolts of quality cotton fabrics in this 4200 square foot "Quilter's Paradise"
The very latest in quilting tools and supplies
A complete library of books & patterns

Free Full-Color Newsletter

Home of "Camp Quilt S'more"

A sewing retreat held once each quarter.
Two nights of uninterrupted sewing and fun!

"The Bunkhouse"

Rent our 2200 square foot log cabin built especially for quilters for your next small group retreat!

Visit our website www.stitchinheaven.com
For a complete listing of happenings in the shop and an incredible on-line shopping experience!
Be sure and register for our "Hot Flashes" - our on-line newsletter!

Owner: Debby Luttrell
502 E. Goode PO Box 1914
Quitman, Texas 75783
Email: info@stitchinheaven.com
Toll free: 800 841-3901
Fax: 903 763-3117

100% Satisfaction Guaranteed!
Be sure and plan to visit when you are in the area!
It's worth the drive!

A full service shop with a bright, inviting atmosphere to enjoy a huge (over 6000 bolts) selection of beautiful cotton fabrics, notions, books, patterns, kits and all the wonderful items that quilters love.
We specialize in flannels, orientals and 30's reproduction prints while still offering a full compliment of current quilting fabrics.

Paris, TX #67

2400 Stillhouse Rd., Paris, TX 75462
(903) 784-6342
sewmuchmore@1starnet.com
Fax: (903) 784-0694
Authorized Bernina & Babylock Dealer
www.sewmuchmorequilt@1starnet.com

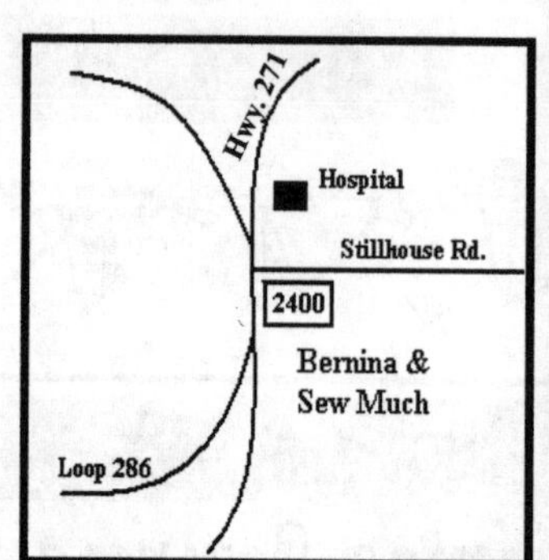

Calico Junction

107 East Elm Street
Winnsboro, TX 75494
(903)342-3399

Mon-Sat
9:30-5:00

Winnsboro, TX #68

Authorized Janome Sewing Machine Dealer in East Texas for Sales and Service

5000 sq feet of fabrics, quilts & antiques

Sewing Notions * Patterns * Classes * Gifts * Antiques * Cappucino * Quilts * Sewing Machines * Custom Quilting

The friendliest and most helpful shop in East Texas!

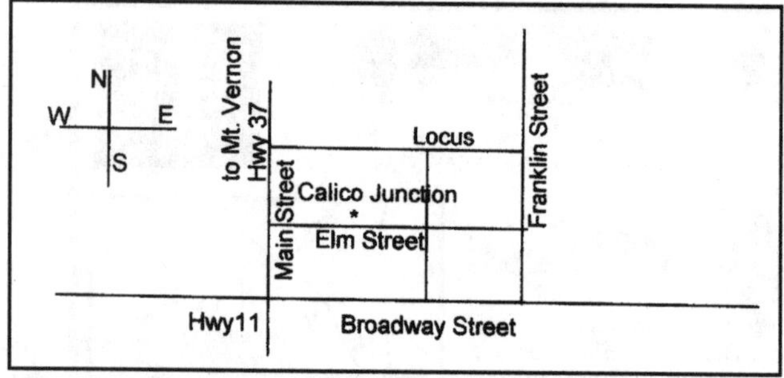

When your'e planning a trip to East Texas, call and we'll send you our newsletter!

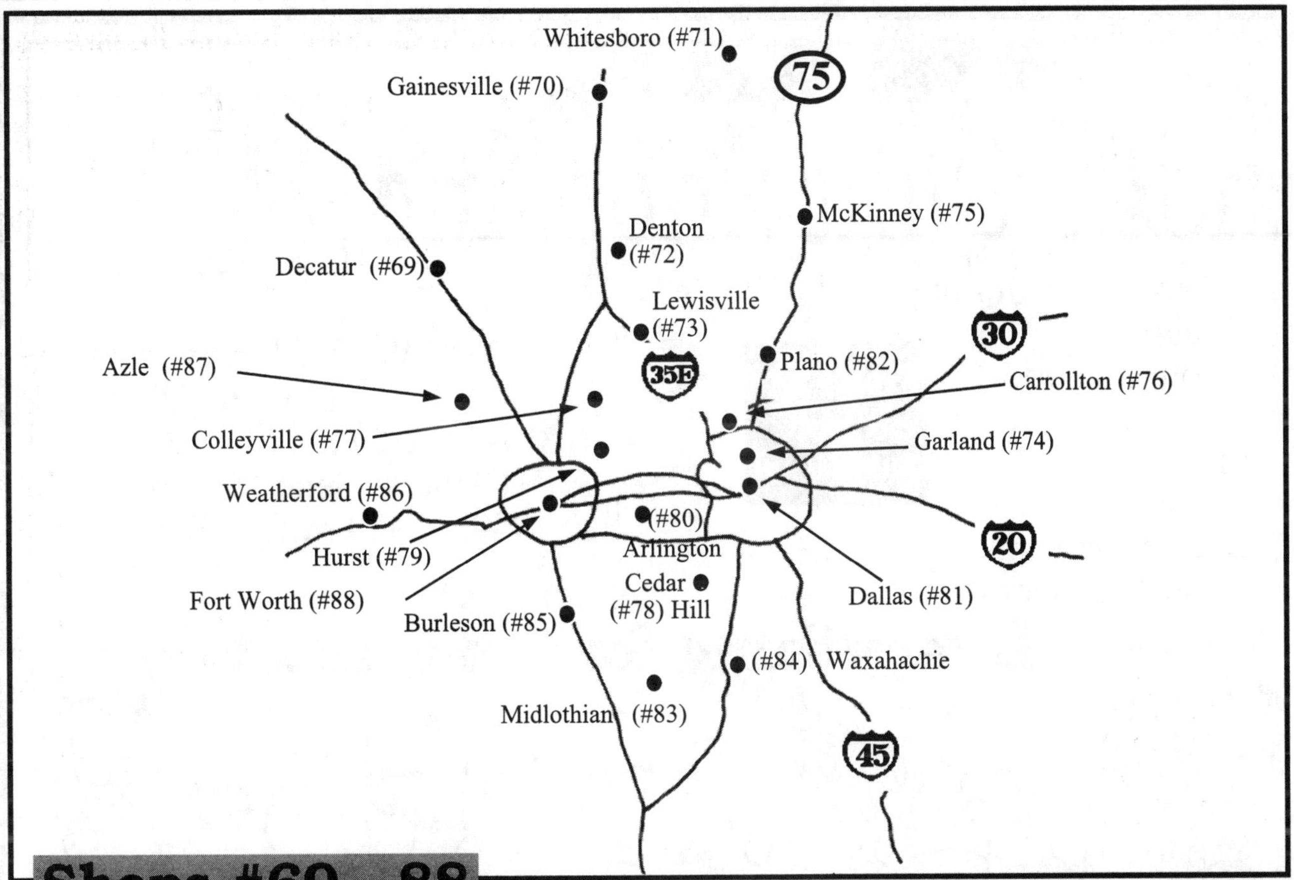

Whitesboro (#71)
Gainesville (#70)
75
McKinney (#75)
Denton (#72)
Decatur (#69)
Lewisville (#73)
Azle (#87)
35E
Plano (#82)
30
Carrollton (#76)
Colleyville (#77)
Garland (#74)
Weatherford (#86)
(#80) Arlington
20
Hurst (#79)
Cedar (#78) Hill
Dallas (#81)
Fort Worth (#88)
Burleson (#85)
(#84) Waxahachie
Midlothian (#83)
45

Shops #69 - 88

20 Featured Shops

Dallas / Fort Worth Area

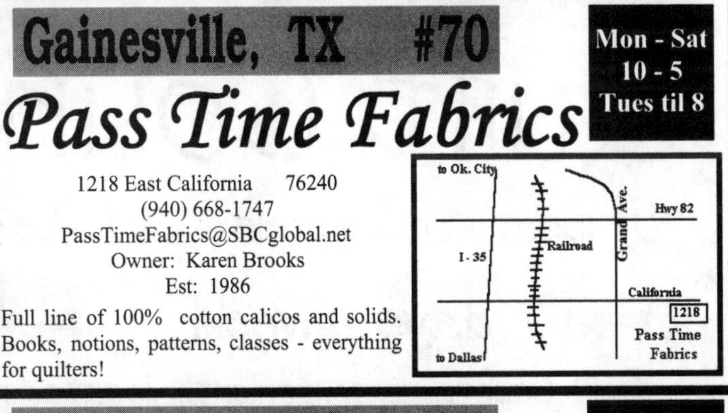

Whitesboro, TX #71

Mon - Fri 10 - 5
Sat 10 - 4

Kaleidoscope Quilt Shop

114 E. Main St. 76273
(903) 564-4681
donnasluder@msn.com
Owner: Donna Sluder
Est: 2001 2000 sq.ft. 1200+ Bolts
We are a quaint shop located in an early 1900's building. We have a very knowledgeable and friendly staff. Lots of 100% cotton fabrics, books, notions & classes.

Denton, TX #72

Linda's Quilt Shop, Inc.

- Custom Machine Quilting
- Quilt Classes
- 100% Cotton Fabric
- Notions
- Patterns
- Books
- A-1 long arm machine sales & service.

Mon - Fri 10 - 5
Sat 10 - 4

2317 W. University Dr. #C-9
Denton, TX 76201
(940) 387-7912 Fax: (940) 323-0450
Owners: Gene & Linda Cagle
Est: 1999 2000 sq.ft. 3000+ Bolts

to Oklahoma
University Dr. (U.S. 380)
1/2 mi.
2317
Linda's Quilt Shop
I-35
Bell Ave.
to Fort Worth
to Dallas

Everything for the Quilter!

Quilt Country

701 South Stemmons #260 ~ Lewisville, Texas 75067

North I-35
1171
Fox Ave.
Hwy. 121
South I-35

Open 7 days a week!

Lewisville, TX #73

Quilt Country is conveniently located right on I-35 E, exit 451. We have a wide variety of fabrics including batiks, plaids, traditional, 30's, novelty prints, bright fun fabrics, and flannels year 'round. We also have many original patterns, and kitted projects. Our tall ceilings provide space to hang lots of models to inspire you!

Monday - Saturday 10:00AM - 5:00PM ~ Sunday 1:00PM - 5:00PM

8000 bolts ~ 5000 sq. ft. ~ established 1995

972-436-7022 ~ fax-972-436-6065 www.quiltcountry.com

Suzy's Quilt Shop

111 N. 6th Street, Garland, Texas 75040 972-272-8180
Website: www.suzysquilts.com Email: suzysquilts@aol.com

Owner: Suzanne Cook
Est 1989 4200 sq ft.

Garland, TX #74

Now On Line Shopping

Store Hours:
Mon-Fri 9:30 am -5:00 pm
Saturday 9:30 am -4:00 pm

Mondays Are Fun
Every Monday Is
Sit-n-Sew
Bring Your Project
Bring A Friend

Original Designed Patterns

Classes Are Fun!
See our Class Schedule on our Website:
www.suzysquilts.com.
Color Pictures of each class.
Sign up by phone.
Plan your trips to be here for one of our classes.

You are the heart of our business.

Clubs
Thimbleberries, 20-30's, Appliqué Lovers, Tea Party, Floss & Chocolate, Dear Jane, Scrap Swap, and Redwork/ Embroidery, &Fat (hind) Quarter.

"The road to Suzy's is never long."

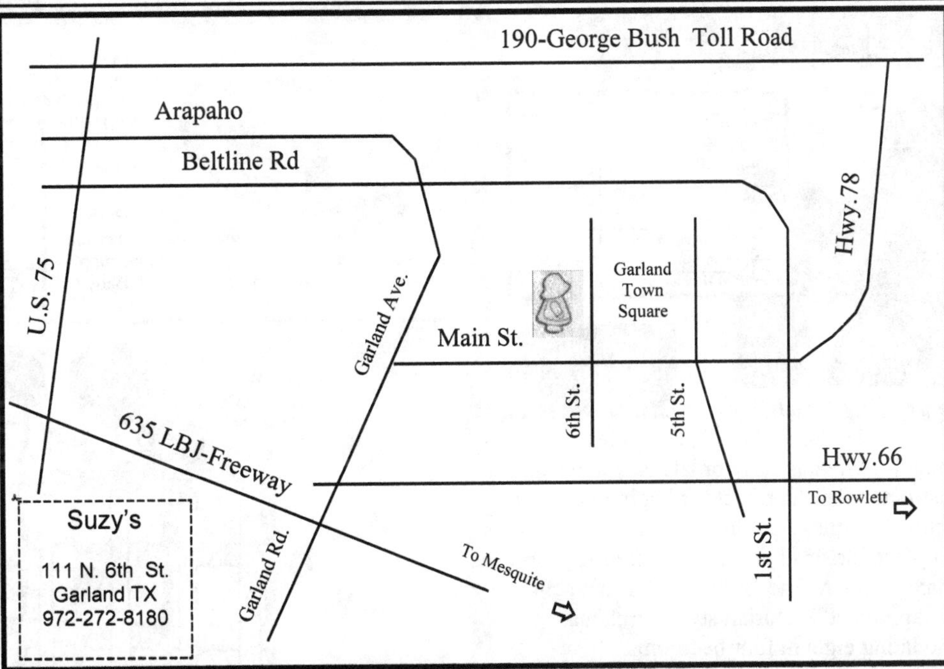

Kits 1st Sat. Samplers Gifts Lots of Samples

Patterns Supplies Books Fabrics Classes Clubs

McKinney, TX #75

Mon - Sat 10 - 5

The Quilt Asylum

405-A N. McDonald St. 75069
(972) 562-2686 Fax: (972) 562-6431
thequiltasylum@aol.com
Owners: Susan and Russell Allen
Est: 2000 2300 sq. ft. 3000 Bolts

McKinney's newest quilt shop featuring batiks, brights, novelties plus books, patterns, notions, and kits.

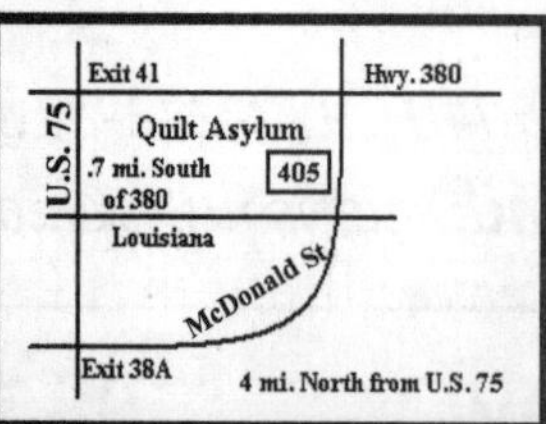

Colleyville, TX #77

Mon & Thur 9 - 6 Tues, Wed, & Fri 9 - 5 Sat 10 - 4

Quilter's Dream

6409 Colleyville Blvd. 76034
(817) 481-7105
Owner: Beverly Ingram

We are known for our knowledgeable, friendly staff and large selection of beautiful 100% cotton fabrics, books & notions.

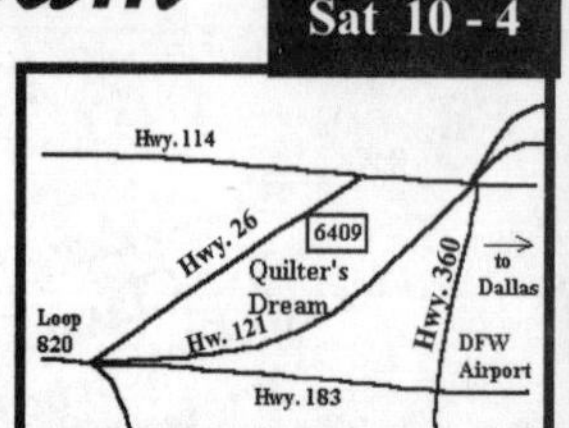

fabrics books patterns notions

Carrollton, TX #76

The Old Craft Store

1110 W. Main Street 75006
(972) 242-9111 Fax: (972) 245-0407
www.theoldcraftstorequilting.com
Owner: Melba Hamrick
Est: 1971 3000 sq.ft.
2500 Bolts

Mon - Sat 10 - 5 Thurs til 7

classes for all Levels us post office

rug hooking redwork embroidery

buyer's club thimbleberries club

1890 House
A Quilters Retreat

398 S. Broad St.
(866) 249-1890 or (972) 291-0472
Mailing: 445 East F.M. 1382, Suite 3-189, 75104
info@1890quilters.com www.1890quilters.com

Cedar Hill, TX #78

Reservations Only

"A Place for Expressing Creativity"

Only minutes from Dallas/Ft. Worth Metroplex. Set your own schedules-work as early or late as you wish. Bring your own instructor-Finish projects or begin new ones without the usual interruptions of our hectic lives. We offer that difficult to find place for small groups of friends to work, play, create and relax together. The 1890 House is a recently restored, nicely appointed Victorian style farmhouse accommodating eight in four bedrooms.

Hurst, TX #79

Mon - Fri 10 - 6:30 Sat 10 - 5

Quilter's Stash

848 W. Pipeline Rd. 76053
(817) 595-1778
bill@quiltersstash.com
www.quiltersstash.com
Owner: Bill Moore
Est: 1999 6000+ Bolts

Best Quality 100% Cotton Fabrics, Books, Notions, Patterns and Classes. Gift Certificates Available.

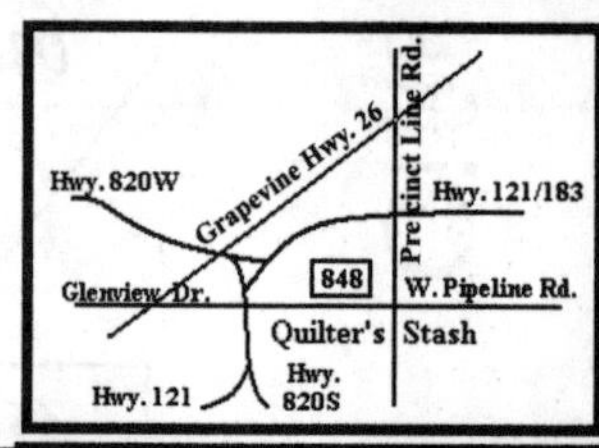

Arlington, TX #80

Mon - Sat 10 - 5:30

Embroidery & Sewing Place

740 SW Green Oaks Blvd. #204
(817) 467-8585 76017
Fax: (817) 466-3276
Owners: Kellie & Charles Rushing
Est: 1999
1800 Bolts

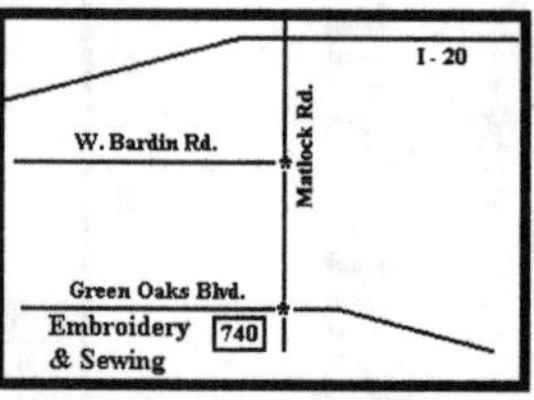

embroiderysewingplace@comcast.net

ESP is 3100 sq.ft. of quilting & heirloom supplies and fabric as well as the full line of Babylock and Bernina sewing machines and sergers.

Est: 2000

Quilts 'n More

Midlothian, TX #83

3000+ bolts of 100% cotton fabrics, notions, books, patterns, classes and long-arm quilting.

Mon - Fri 10 - 6
Sat 10 - 4

211 W. Ave. "F", Midlothian, TX 76065
(972) 723-8669
quiltsnmore2000@yahoo.com
Owners: Kathleen Allen & Jean McKinney

Waxahachie, TX #84

Mon - Fri 9:30 - 5
Sat 9:30 - 4:30

Common Threads Quilting

113 N. College St. 75165
(972) 935-0510 Fax: (972) 938-2271
commonthreads@sbcglobal.net Est: 2002
www.commonthreadsquilting.com
Owner: Denice Lipscomb 1800 sq.ft.
Specializing in 19th and 20th Century Reproduction Fabrics. Large selection of Traditional Florals. Victorian building just off the Square.

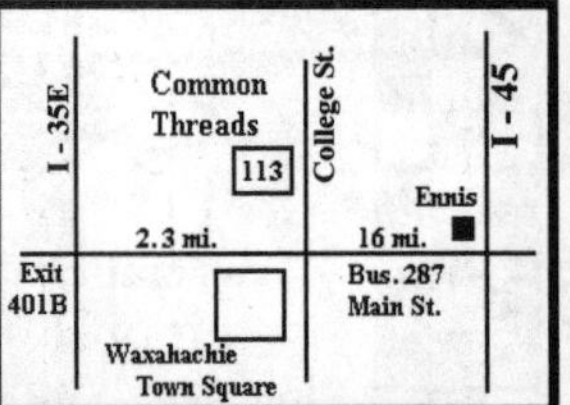

Burleson, TX #85

Mon - Fri 10 - 5
Sat 10 - 3

Country Stitches Quilt Shop

426 SW Wilshire Blvd. 76028
(817) 426-5981
www.countrystitchesquiltshop.com
3000 sq.ft. 3600 Bolts

We carry only 100% High Quality Cotton Fabrics, Books, and Notions. Come see our Large Selection of Reproduction Fabrics.

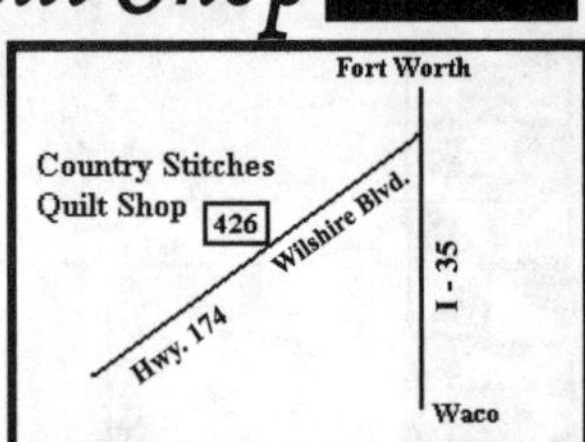

Weatherford, TX #86

Tues - Sat 10 - 5:30

Peachtree Quilts

133 N. Waco St. 76086
(817) 599-4114
Owner: Linda Payne
Est: 1994 1800+ Bolts

Specializing in Batiks and Designer fabrics

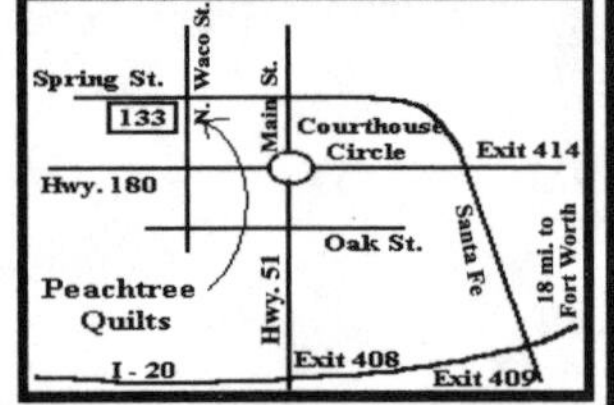

Azle, TX #87

Tues - Fri 10 - 5
Sat 10 - 3

Quilts & Stuff

900 NW Parkway 76020
(817) 270-0452
Q-S.inc@juno.com
Owner: Anna Waghalter
Est: 1996 1300 sq.ft.

"At Home" take your shoes off atmosphere.
Cotton Fabrics, Notions, Quilt Books, Patterns, Fabric Kits, Classes.

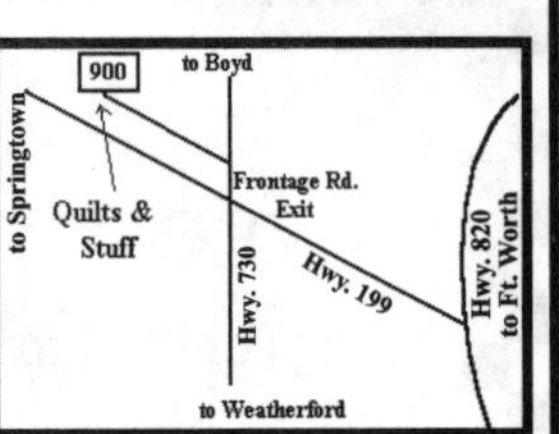

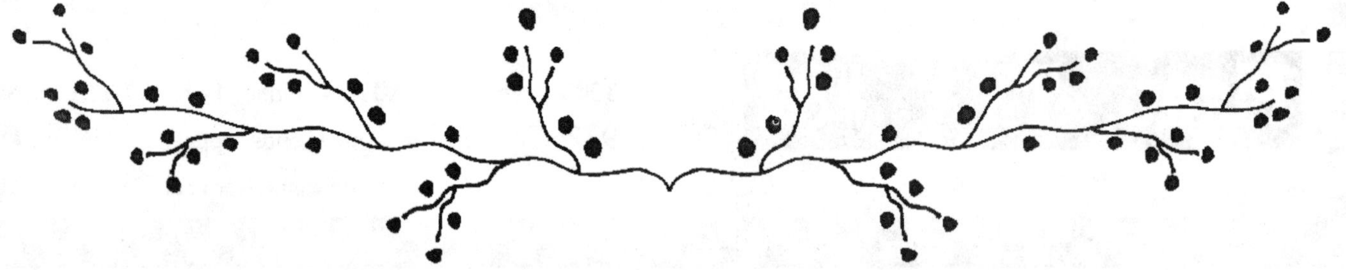

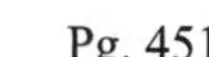

Cabbage Rose

Quilting, Knitting and Gifts

Over 8,000 fabrics in stock,
5,000 sq. ft. of quilting paradise.

- A complete line of quilting and knitting supplies
- including books, notions, patterns, gifts and classes.
- Fabrics range from Batiks, Westerns, Pastels, Reproductions and Brights
- Loads & Loads of Wonderful Samples.
- Great Assortment of Robyn Pandolph Fabrics & Patterns.
- Veda Wilhite original Blocks of the Month.
- Located near Fort Worth's Cultural District.

"Come spend the day with us."

Exit 11
Arlington
30
35W
Montgomery St.
Locke Ave.
Lovell Ave.
Rosedale St.
W. Vickery Blvd.
University Dr.

3526 W. Vickery Blvd.
Fort Worth, TX 76107
(817) 377-3993
Est: 1997
crquilts@flash.net
Owner: Karen O'Neill

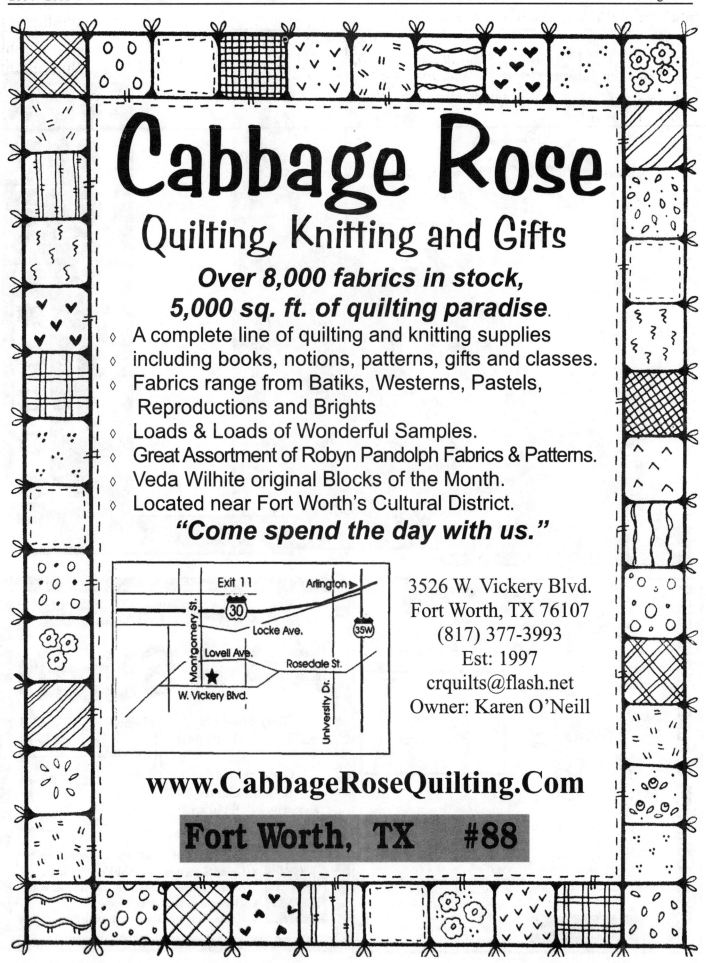

www.CabbageRoseQuilting.Com

Fort Worth, TX #88

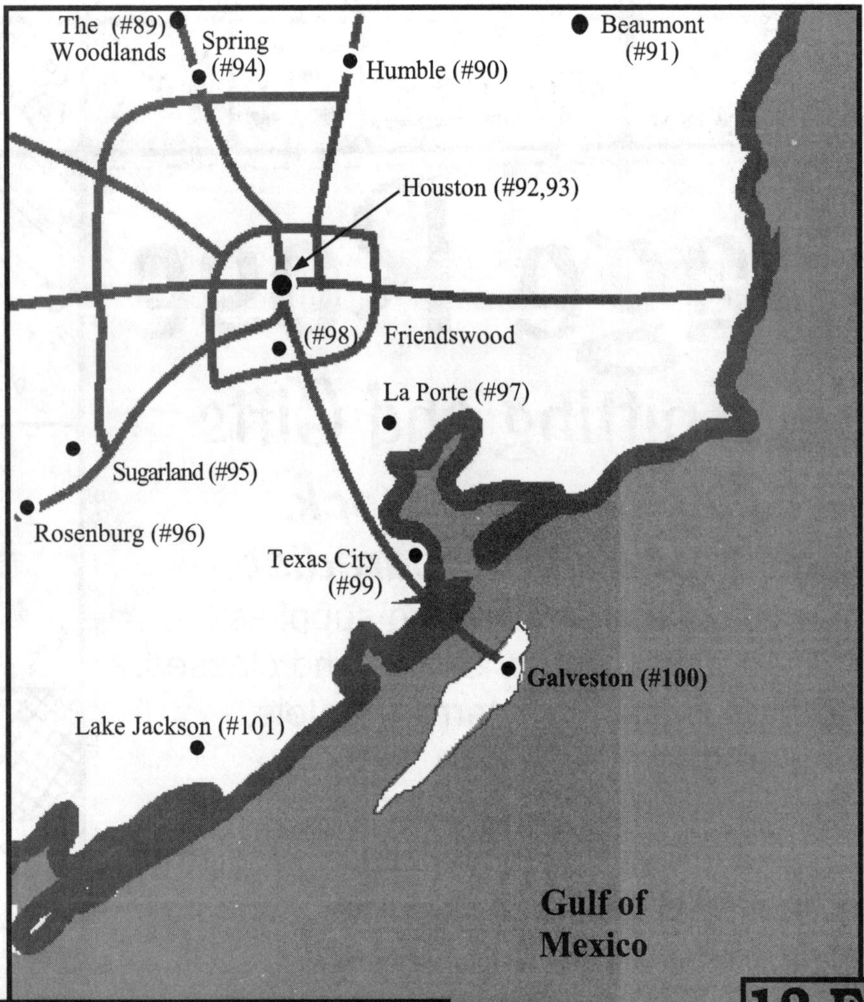

The (#89) Woodlands
Spring (#94)
Humble (#90)
Beaumont (#91)
Houston (#92,93)
(#98) Friendswood
La Porte (#97)
Sugarland (#95)
Rosenburg (#96)
Texas City (#99)
Galveston (#100)
Lake Jackson (#101)
Gulf of Mexico

HOUSTON AREA

Shops # 89 - 101

13 Featured Shops

The Woodlands, TX #89

Largest Selection of Fabric in Houston

Plain & Fancy

27118 I-45 N
Oak Ridge North, TX
77385
"The Woodlands"
(281) 367-1021
Fax: (281) 367-1172

Mon - Sat 9 - 5

From Houston:
Exit Woodlands Parkway. Stay on the feeder for approx. 2 miles. We are in Woodridge Plaza just past the bowling alley

From Conroe:
Exit Woodlands Parkway. Take the Oak Ridge / Robinson Road exit off the feeder. This will take you up over the freeway. Immediately loop back down on the feeder going north. We are in Woodridge Plaza just past the bowling alley.

Humble, TX #90

It's A Stitch

(281) 446-4999
9574 FM 1960 Bypass
77338
Owners: Judy & John Curtis
Est: 1992 8350 sq.ft.

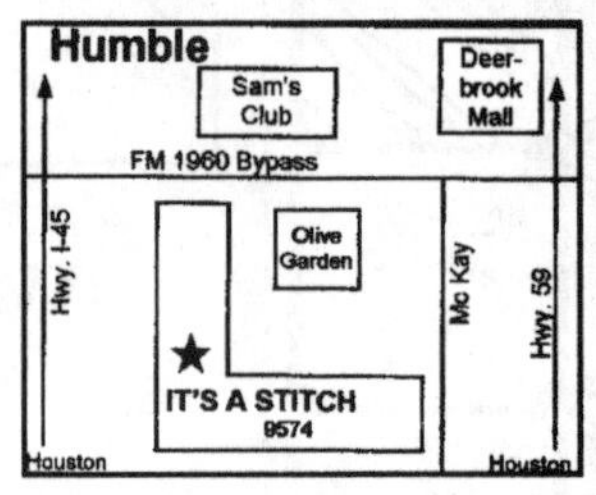

Mon - Fri 10 - 5:30
Sat 10 - 5
Sun 12 - 5

- Over 6,000 Bolts of 100% Cotton Fabric
- Great Selection of Wool Felt, Notions, Books, Patterns, Stencils, Batting & Kits
- #1 Bernina Dealer in Texas
- Koala, Horn & Roberts Furniture

Beaumont, TX #91

The Piecemaker

Mon - Fri 10 - 5
Tues til 6 Sat 10 - 3

3865 Calder Ave. 77706
(409) 835-4736
Owner: Noel Ann McCord

Fabrics — 100% Cottons
Patterns, Books, Notions.
Silk Ribbon,
Cross-Stitch and
Needlepoint Supplies.

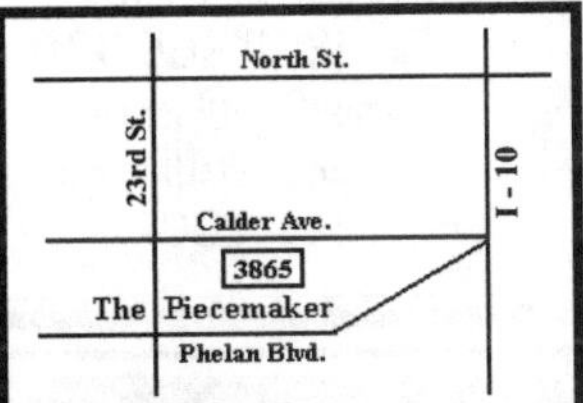

Now Offering:
M & M Quilting Service
Custom Quilting
Gammill Machine
Brochure Available

Located Inside the **Piecemaker**
(409) 833-9256

The Bay Area's Oldest Quilt Shop Since 1978

Houston, TX #92

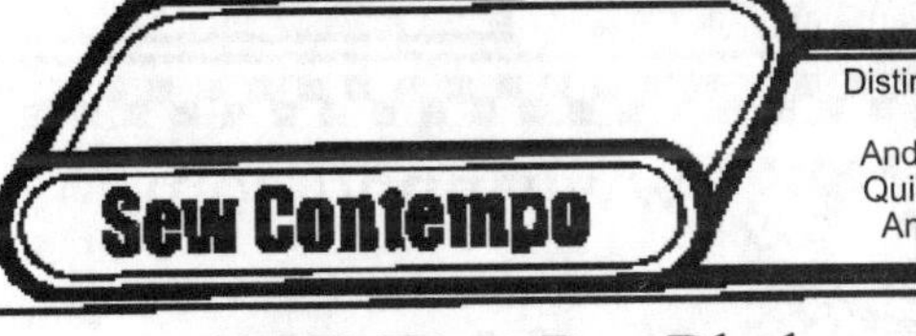

18203 Egret Bay Blvd.
Houston, TX 77058
(281) 333-5322
sewcontempo@ghg.net
5000 sq.ft. 3000+ Bolts

Mon - Fri 9:30 - 6
Thur 9:30 - 8 Sat 9:30 - 5:30

www.sewcontempo.com

- Quilting Classes and Supplies
- Over 3000 Bolts of Quality Fabrics
- Great Batik Selection
- Fabrics from quality manufacturers - Moda, Hoffman, Benartex, Alexander Henry, Robert Kaufman and many more!
- Heirloom Sewing Supplies and Classes
- Complete Source for Embroidery Machine Supplies and Classes
- Bernina - Brother - Viking - Elna - New Home Sewing Machines Authorized Dealer

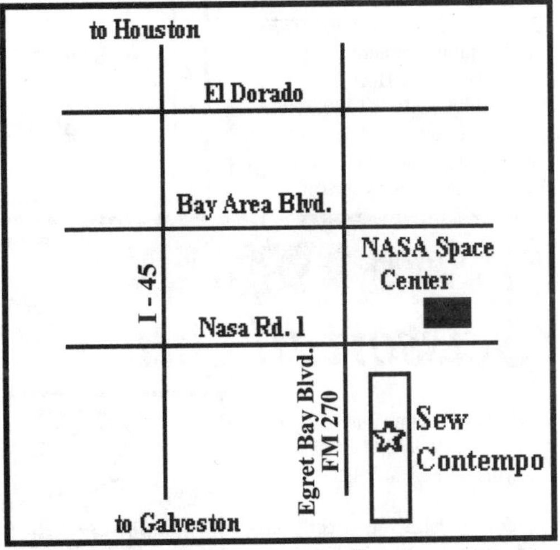

5 minutes from Johnson Space Center (NASA) and 30 minutes from Galveston

Houston, TX #93

Tues - Sat
10 - 3

Turkey Ridge Primitives

17218 Bamwood 77090
(281) 440-0775
Turkey Ridgeprim@aol.com
www.turkeyridgeprimitives.com
Owner: Rosemary Watson
Est: 2002 1500 sq.ft. 1000 bolts
Primitive quilt shop, rughooking supplies, classes, reproduction fabrics, flannels and homespuns, doll and stitchery patterns.
Only primitive shop in Houston.

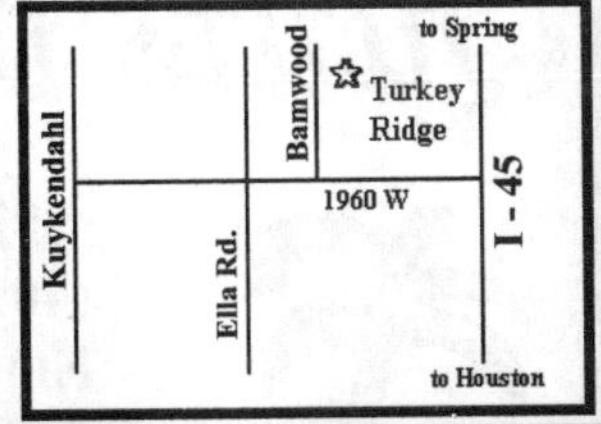

Spring, TX #94

Tues - Sat
9:30 - 6
Sun 12 - 5

Juliene's Quilt Shop

1416 Spring Cypress Rd. 77373
(281) 355-9820 (800) 976-0633
julienes@sbcglobal.net
www.JPQuilts.com
Est: 1993 2500 sq. ft. 3000 Bolts
A full service quilt shop. Fabrics, Patterns, Notions, Gifts, Classes. Authorized Dealer of Husqvarna Viking sewing machines, Software, sales and service and education. Machine quilting services.

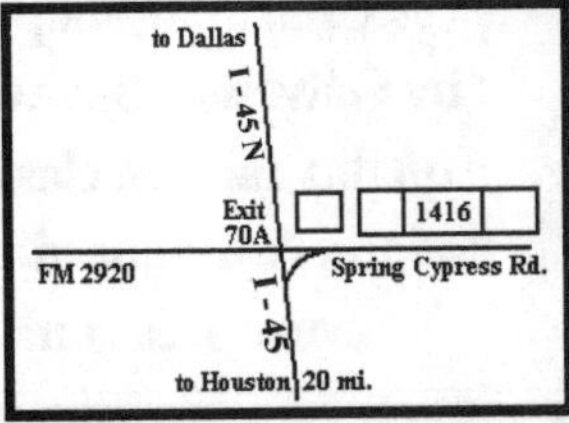

Sugar Land, TX #95

Mon - Sat 10 - 5 Thurs til 6

"Putting all the pieces together at . . ."

11581-C Hwy. 6 S
77478
(281) 491-0016

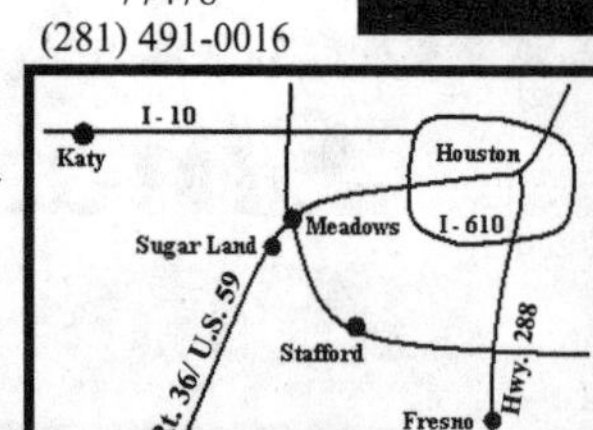

www.quiltersemporium.com
Owner: Rose Ann Cook
Fabric, kits, patterns, books, gifts, antiques, consignments, BOMs, retreats, cruises, and classes for all skill levels.

Rosenburg, TX #96

My First Stitch Quilt Shop

Wed - Sat 10 - 5 Sun 1 - 5

Located in the Historic Vogelsang Building built in 1910. 1,000 Sq. Ft. of 2,000+ bolts. Large line of Thimbleberries & 1930's Reproduction fabrics. Notions, books & patterns.
Shop for the fabrics you need or want, look for antiques, then take a break & eat lunch at Martha's Cupboard.

1903 Avenue G 77471
(281) 344-1602
Fax: (281) 565-9311
swong311@aol.com
www.myfirststitch.com
Est: 2002

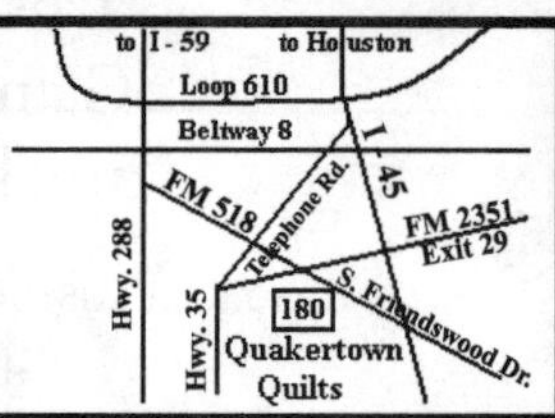

www.ppnq.com

Est: 1986

Mon - Fri 10 - 5
Thurs til 7 Sat 10 - 4

Painted Pony 'n Quilts

10,000+ top name quilting fabrics in contemporary, country, plaid and reproduction styles. Notions, Gifts, Janome/New Home Dealer. Friendly, knowledgeable staff to assist in all areas. Samples on display.
Gammill Machine Quilting offered on the premises.
International mail-order for: BOM's, Fabrics, Books, Patterns, Kits. Tour shop for the Houston Int. Festival.

1015 S. Broadway
77571
(281) 471-5735
Fax: (281) 471-1713
ppnqstaff@ppnq.com
Owner: Sherrie S. Thomas
Expanded to 8600 sq. ft.

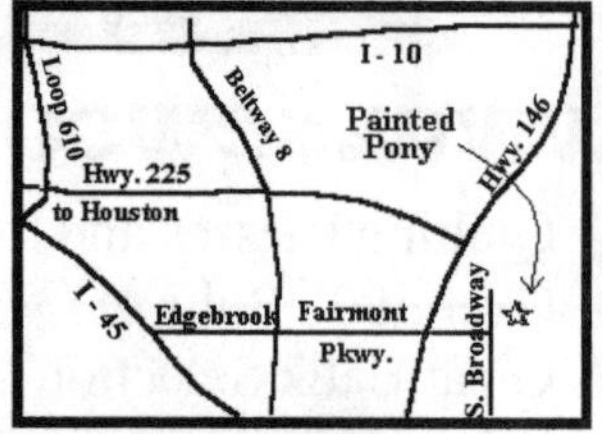

La Porte, TX #97

Friendswood, TX #98

Mon - Fri 10 - 5:30 Sat 10 - 4

Quakertown Quilts

180 S. Friendswood Dr. 77546
(888) 464-7845
www.QuakertownOnline.com
(281) 996-1756 Fax: (281) 648-9090
Owner: Pat Forke Est: 1988 5000 sq.ft.
Complete Quilt Shop. 3000+ bolts of cotton fabric. Books, Patterns, Notions & Gift Items Blocks of the Month. Wholesale inquiries welcome.

to I - 59
to Houston
Loop 610
Beltway 8
I - 45
FM 518
Telephone Rd.
FM 2351
Exit 29
Hwy. 288
Hwy. 35
180
S. Friendswood Dr.
Quakertown Quilts

Texas City, TX #99

Mon - Sat 10 - 5:30

Cactus Quilts

1811 6th St. N 77590
(409) 965-9778 Fax: (409) 965-9779
cactusquilts@aol.com
Owner: Carla Hoff
Est: 2002 2000 sq.ft. 1200 bolts
1200 bolts of 100% cotton fabrics, notions, books & patterns. Smiles always here and they are free. Come see for yourself.

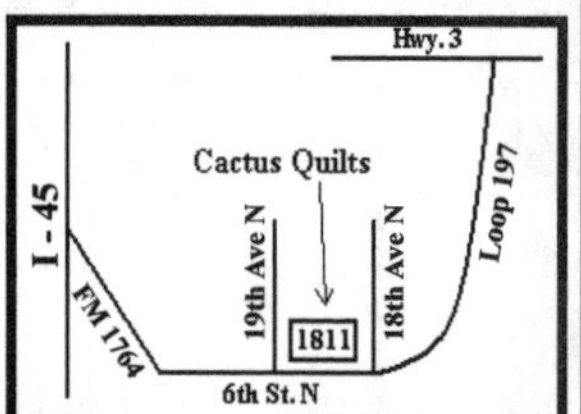

Galveston, TX #100

Quilts by the Bay

5923 Stewart Rd. 77551
(409) 740-9296 Est: 1991
Email: qbtb@comwerx.net
Owner: Patricia Stephenson
3500 sq.ft. 4000 Bolts

Mon - Sat 10 - 5:30 Sun 12:30 - 5

Charming shop by Galveston Bay with top quality fabrics, classes, notions, & unique gifts for every occasion.

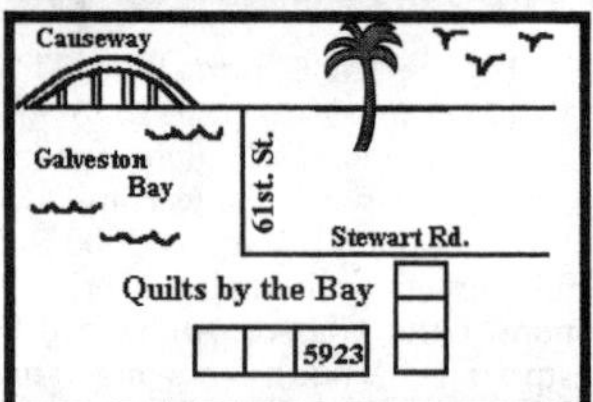

Lake Jackson, TX #101

Mon - Sat 10 - 5

Scissortail Quilts

217 Parking Way 77566
(979) 297-8595
Owner: June Hatfield

Friendly clerks will help you select from the latest and greatest quilt fabric, notions, books and classes. Fun atmosphere.
Bernina Sewing & Service Center

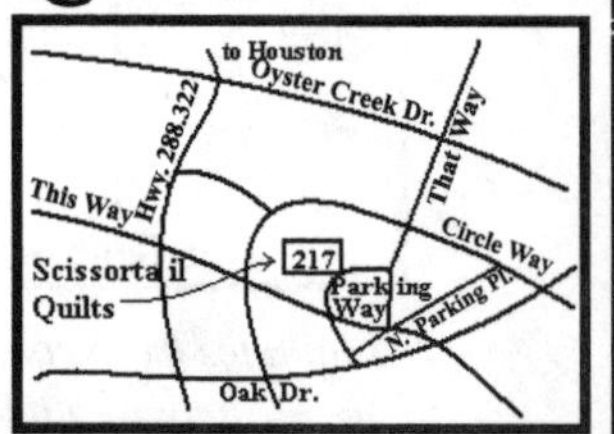

Other Shops in Texas: *We suggest calling first*

Abilene	Alton's Sewing Maching Co., 929 Butternut St	915-698-4770
Abilene	Linda's Treasury, 7500 Cty. Rd. 203	915-529-3328
Abilene	Cornerstone Quilting, 1425 Sylvan Dr.	325-692-6317
Allen	Rock Pile Quilters, 701 Victorian Dr.	972-396-8160
Amarillo	Quilting Friends, 91 N. Fairmont St.	806-373-8379
Argyle	The Pepper Tree, 6835 FM 1830	940-241-2469
Arlington	Abram House Quilt Shop, 1210 W. Abram St.	817-277-4749
Arlington	Dee's Quilts Supplies, 2720 Trail Oak Ct.	817-496-4854
Aubrey	Fruit Jar Junction, 5848 Harmony Ranch Rd.	940-365-3158
Austin	Quilts & Patchwork, 4024 Travis Country Cir.	512-892-4101
Austin	Quilts 'N Things 8210 Briarwood Ln.	512-451-7073
Azle	Eagle Mountain Products, 1157 SE Parkway	817-237-0881
Bay City	Threads, Quilts & Creations, 1728 6th St.	979-245-5347
Belton	Kay's Quilts, 1668 Jamie	254-933-7140
Boerne	Tea Rose Quilts, 101 S. Main St. #A	830-249-0639
Bowie	Bowie Sewing Center, 217 N. Smythe St.	940-872-6220
Brownwood	Quilted Heart, 503 E. Anderson St.	915-646-2331
Burkburnett	Red River Quilting, 539 Charlotte Ave	940-569-7350
Carrollton	Pierson's Fine Quilts, 1020 W Main St	972-242-1507
Cedar Park	B J's Quilts & Things, 3404 Shenondoah Dr.	512-258-2852
Cedar Park	Hill Country Quilts, 117 N. Winecup Trl.	512-331-1241
Childress	Arbor Rose Quilts & Gifts, 611 Avenue F NW	940-937-2797
Cisco	Bunk House Quilting, 418 Cty. Rd. #119	254-442-2205
Clarendon	Millie B's Country Corner, 200 S Goodnight	806-874-0549
Colleyville	Blue Frog Quilts, 3809 Oakbrier Ln.	817-514-1515
Comanche	Quilts & Tops, 605 E. Central Ave.	915-356-2047
Conroe	Quilt 'N Time Sisters, 17641 Linda Ln.	409-231-3322
Converse	General Store/Quilt Studio, 305 S. Sequin Rd.	210-659-7278
Corpus Christi	Hanging by a Thread, 1817 S Alameda	361-887-9005
Corpus Christi	My Scraps, 6618 Opengate Dr.	361-993-8552
Corsicana	Beiry Quilting & Crafts, 1602 Cherry Ave	903-872-1578
Corsicana	Quilters Nest, 1021 W 2nd Ave	903-875-1212
Dallas	The Copper Lamp, 5500 Greenville Ave.	214-521-3711
Dallas	Berina Sewing Center, 12801 Midway Rd	972-247-5103
Demas	Charlee's Wuilting, 104 Country Cluf Ter	806-935-8619
Denton	The Stitching Post, 2318 San Jacinto #104	940-483-9077
Dripping Springs	Peacemakers, 301 Mercer St.	512-858-0272
Duncanville	Seasoned Stitches, 527 Wren Ave	972-283-3730
Edgewood	Bobo's Cupboard, 507 Laura Dr.	903-896-1600
El Paso	Bernina of El Paso, 1809 Trawood Dr.	915-599-1909
Fair Oaks Ranch	Sew Special Quilts, 28255 Steeplechase	210-698-0458
Floresville	Center Point Sensations, 680 Cty. Rd. 312	830-393-6978
Fort Stockton	Sue's Quilt Studios, 1800 W. 7th St.	915-336-8432
Fort Stockton	Sue's Quilt Shop, 121 N. Main St.	915-336-8664
Fort Worth	Cherrie's Quilt Shop, 4320 Wichita St.	817-531-0074
Fort Worth	Busy Bee Quilting, 14 Legend Rd.	817-763-8777
Fredericksburg	Fredericksburg Rugs, 231 Rock Creek	800-331-5213
Fredericksburg	Hill Country Collectibles, 249 E. Main	830-990-9289
Fredericksburg	Material Things, 237 E Main	830-997-6426
Fredericksburg	Sandy Jenkins Designs, 203 E Austin St	830-997-8944
Fredericksburg	Tea Rose Quilts & Gifts, 128 E Main	830-997-6572
Fredericksburg	Tea Rose Quilts & Gifts, 339 E Main St	830-997-2749
Freeport	Broad Street Market, 120 West Broad St.	979-233-6900
Fritch	Kwiltwerks, 505 W. Broadway	806-857-8572
Garland	Quilting Friends, 318 Saddlebrook Dr.	972-496-3753
Georgetown	Sew & Quilt, 502 San Gabriel Blvd	512-863-9201
Granbury	In Stitches, 4909 Fall Creek Hwy. #6	817-326-6444
Grapevine	Bluebonnet Quilting, 2713 Newcastle Dr	817-251-1813
Groesbeck	Quilt Patch, 212 Nashua St	254-729-8742
Haarlingen	Eye of the Needle, 1414 Maple Ct	956-245-9059
Hallettsville	Country Quilters, 107 N Texana St	361-798-9917
Harlingen	Picket Fence Quilts, 2815 S. 77 Sunshine Strip	956-412-2668
Hewitt	Wrapped in Quilts, 935 Vail Highlands	254-666-5226
Hilltop Lakes	Esther's Quilts & Things, P.O. Box 1271	936-855-2088
Houston	High Fashion Fabric Center, 3101 Louisiana	713-528-7299
Houston	Front Porch Quilts, 5050 FM 1960 W. #127	281-444-2882
Houston	Buttons 'n' Bows, 14086 Memorial Dr	281-496-0170
Houston	Cottontail Quilts, 14781 Memorial Dr.	713-899-3884
Houston	Teacups & Lace, 18014 River sage Dr	281-347-3770
Huntington	Mrs. B Quilt Patch Pond, 110 N. Hwy. 69	409-876-3234
Huntsville	Granny's Quilting Shack, 123 A Hall Ranch Rd	
Huntsville	Fabric Carousel, 1101 12th St.	409-295-8322
Irving	Hobbit's Hollow Quilts, 4021 W. Northgate	972-259-1415
Jefferson	Quilter's Corner, 1102 FM 2208	903-665-3385
Jewett	Kountry Klutter, 322 N. Main St.	903-626-6562
Joshua	Sandy's Quilt Shop, 301 B 12th St.	817-558-2882
Katy	My Secret Shelf, 902 East Ave	291-394-1311
Keene	Quilt N Stitches, 615 Lewis Ln.	817-645-9860
Keller	Stitchin' Sisters Bernina, 830 Keller Pkwy.	817-379-1299
Keller	Grandma's Quilts, 111 W. Vine St.	817-431-1348
Keller	Sew Creative, 945 Tealwood Dr.	817-788-2407
Keller	Old Town Quilts, 105 S Main St	817-379-4433
Keller	Quiltingly Yours, 1613 Lost Lake Dr	817-577-5640
Kerrville	Jasmine Heirlooms, 229 Earl Garrett St.	830-257-5440
Kerrville	Sewing Circle, 1810 Junction Hwy	830-895-5600
Killeen	Carol's Creations, 601 S 2nd St	254-628-8788
Kountze	Jae's, 7616 Old Honey Island Rd.	409-246-4462
Kress	Granny's Quilts, 603 Ripley Ave	806-684-2240
La Grange	The Quilters Cottage, 239 N. Madison	979-968-8804
League City	The Fabric Hut, 2214 Fair Pointe Dr.	713-477-7531
Livingston	Christie's Quilting Magic, 7220 Hwy 190 W	936-967-2709
Lockney	The Old Blue Quilt Box, 200 S. Main St.	806-652-2183
Longview	Peaceful Things, 116 W. Tyler St.	903-984-1720
Longview	Sharman's Sewing Center, 1017 McCann Rd.	903-753-8014
Lubbock	Quilt Emporium & Mercantile, 9208 Wayne	806-798-7648
Lufkin	Country Quilting & More, 1200 S. 1st. St.	409-639-1503
Magnolia	Quilter's Mercantile, 6311 FM 1488 Rd	281-252-3550
McKinney	Quilting Room, 2418 Sherbrooke Ln.	972-569-3936
Memphis	Greene Dry Goods, 109 S. Sixth St.	806-259-2912
Monahans	Ye Olde Quilt Shoppe, P.O. Box 1183	915-943-5855
Munday	Prairie Stitches, 111 N. Munday Ave.	940-422-5444
Natalia	Rose Cottage Quilting, 260 Cty. Rd. 6715	830-665-5053
NcKinney	Linda's Eletric Quilters, 4964 Hwy 75N	972-542-4000
New Braunfels	Grandby's Quilts, 161 S Sequin Ave	830-620-7813
North Richland Hills	Sue's Creations, 6900 Glenwood	817-577-1042
Odessa	Betty's Bobbin Box, 2740 N Grandview	915-550-0093
Odessa	Heavens Quilting, 1301 McKinney Ave.	915-580-8919
Olney	Grannie's Quilt Box, 811 N Ave. E	940-564-2846
Pampa	Kriss Kross Quilting, 119 Western St.	806-665-8410
Plano	Quilt Shack, 1709 Canadian Trl	972-517-2145
Plano	Bernina Sewing Of Plano, 2400 K Ave	972-567-9227
Plano	Mama J's, 2701 W 15th Ste 648	214-679-3128
Plano	Pieceful Patchwork, 3417 Parkhaven Dr.	972-964-9678
Plano	Pickin Cotton Quilts, 3117 Pinehurst Dr.	972-867-3607
Plano	Xignature Ltd., 2109 Eveing Sun Dr.	972-596-7479
Portland	Stitches Sewing Center, 801 Houston St.	361-643-1739
Princeton	Seams to Me, 1914 Cty. Rd. 900	972-734-0323
Randolph	The Quilt Cottage, P.O. Box 58	
Richardson	The Fabric Affair, 339 Dal-Rich Village	972-234-1937
Richardson	Canyon Creek Quilting, 310 Arborcrest Dr.	972-699-8750
Richardson	Kay Fabrics, 518 W. Arapaho Rd.	972-234-5111
Roanoke	Seams Like Yesterday, 14 Colonial Ct.	817-430-0004
Rockwall	Texaz Quiltworks, 2845 Ridge Rd	972-771-9952
Rockwall	Catlin Sisters Quilting, 2205 Chisholm	972-722-5408
Round Rock	Color With Quilts, 1813 Provident Ln	512-244-3883
Salado	Three Dogs on a Quilt, 101 Salado Plaza Dr	254-947-9070
San Angelo	Angelo Sewing Center, 5030 Knickerbocker	915-942-9780
San Antonio	Grandby's Quilts, 2519 E. Bitters Rd.	210-490-7813
San Antonio	Amish Quilt Conn., 2219 Fawn Mist Ln.	210-492-3882
San Antonio	All To Pieces, 18911 Surreywood	210-479-8969
San Antonio	Herman's Heirlooms, 7731 Apple Grn.	210-509-4578
Santa Anna	Quilters Patch, 705 Wallis Ave.	915-348-3771
Sequim	Betsy Rose Quilt Shop Etc., 114 N. River St.	830-372-0965
Sequin	Quilting Gin, 286 Gin Spur	830-303-5765
Sherman	Mary's Quilt Shop, 1520 Texoma Pkwy	903-893-6277
Spearman	Country Stitches, 512 S. Townsend St.	806-659-2080
Spring	The Hen House, 17822 Asphodel	281-257-3231
Spring	The Needle Nest, 2219 Sawdust Rd.	281-292-3153
Sugar Land	Astrid's Creations, 1823 Cheyenne River Cir.	281-265-6429
Sunrise Beach	Patches, 103 Sunrise Dr.	
Sunset Valley	C & C Sew & Vac, 5400 Brodie Ln.	512-899-3233
Taylor	Morning Glory Products, 302 Highland Dr.	512-352-6311
Temple	Quilting Corner, 1401 S 31st	254-773-8331
Tyler	Ann's Sewing Center, 322 E. SELoop 323	903-581-4926
Tyler	Granny's Needle Haus, 6004 S. Broadway Ave.	903-561-4637
Tyler	Sharman's Sewing Center, 6005 S Broadway	903-581-5470
Van Alstyne	Quilt Basket School, PO Box 1430	903-482-5947
Van Alstyne	Madole Lane Treasures 268 Madole	903-482-6314
Waxahachie	Waxahachie Emporium, 116 N Collage	972-938-2262
Webster	Fabrics Etcetera, 571 W. Bay Area Blvd.	281-338-1904
Whitney	Francie's Personally Yours, 5120 FM 933 N	254-694-4950
Wichita Falls	A Stitch In Time, 4708 K Mart Dr #G	940-691-5575

Texas Guilds:

Allen	Allen Quilt Guild	Meets: 3rd Thursday at First United Methodist Church, Hwy. 5
Amarillo	High Plains Quilters Guild, 2433 I-40 West, 79109	
Amarillo	New Horizons Quilt Guild, 4224 S. Van Buren, 79110	Meets: 1st Thursday 7 p.m. at Amarillo Federated Women's Bldg., East Room
Arlington	Arlington Guild	Meets: 2nd Tuesday 7 p.m. at Vandergriff Convention Center, 2800 S. Center St.
Austin	Austin Area Quilt Guild, P.O. Box 5757, 78763	Meets: 1st Monday 7 p.m. at Faith Lutheran Church, 6600 Woodrow
Azle	Happy Scrappers Quilt Guild, 76020	Meets: 3rd Monday @ 7pm at West Parkway Baptist Church, 900 NW Parkway
Bay City	Memory Makers Quilt Guild, 1840 7th St., 77414	Meets: Last Wednesday at Matagorda County Fairgrounds
Beaumont	Golden Triangle Quilt Guild	
Bowie	Busy Bee Quilt Club, R.R. 2, Box 297, 76230	
Brenham	Freindship Quilt Guild, 309 Giddings Ln., 77833	Meets: 3rd Thursday at Fellowship Baptish Church, 2000 FM 389
Bryan	Brazos Bluebonnet Quilt Guild, 3211 S. Texas Ave, 77802	Meets: 2nd Tuesday @ 7pm at Brazos Center
Cleburne	Cleburne Area Quilters Guild, P.O. Box 1072, 76031	Meets: 2nd Monday 7 p.m. at Ascension Lutheran Church, 205 S. Ridgeway
College Station	Brazos Bluebonnet Quilt Guild, P.O. Box 9497, 77842	Meets: 2nd Tuesday 7 p.m. at Brazos Center, Bryan
Corpus Christi	Coastal Bend Quilt & Needlework Guild, P.O. Box 181074, 78480	Meets: 2nd Thursday 10 a.m. at Ethel Eyerly Community Center
Dallas	Quilters Guild of Dallas, 15775 N. Hillcrest, 75248	Meets: 1st Thursday 7 p.m. Congregation Shearith Isreal, Kaplan Hall, 9401 Douglas
Dayton	Dayton Quilt Guild, Inc., P.O. Box 231, 77535	
Denton	Denton Quilt Guild, 400 E. Hickory St.	Meets: 3rd Thursday 7 p.m. at Visual Arts Center
Dublin	Town & Country Quilt Club, Rt. 4, Box 104 HV, 76446	Meets: 1st Saturday 1 p.m. at The Flying Needle, Stephenville
Dumas	Piecemakers of Dumas, P.O. Box 435	Meets: Wednesdays 10 a.m. at Down Home Quilts
Fairfield	Freestone Quilt Guild, 75840	Meets: 1st Monday 6:30 p.m. at Fairfield Harmony Presbyterian Church
Fort Worth	Trinity Valley Quilters' Guild	Meets: 3rd Friday 9:30 am at Central Christian Church, 3205 Hamilton St.
Fredericksburg	Vereins Quilt Guild of Fredericksburg, P.O. Box 1362, 78624	Meets: 3rd Saturday 9 a.m. at 95 Frederick Rd.
Gainesville	Common Threads Quilt Guild, PO Box 293, 76241	Meets: 2nd Monday @ 7pm at Waley Methodist Church
Giddings	Happy Hearts & Hands Quilt Guild, P.O. Box 1348, 78942	Meets: 1st Tuesday 6:30 p.m. at NBC Bank Community Room
Granbury	Granbury Quilt Guild	Meets: 3rd Monday 7 p.m. at First Baptish Church, 1851 Weatherford Hwy.
Grand Prairie	Grand Prairie	Meets: 1st Monday 7:30 p.m. at First Presbyterian Church of Grand Prairie, 310 SW 3rd St.
Harlingen	Frontera Quilt Guild, 2008 Martha	Meets: 2nd Monday @ 6:30 pm at Hoeard Hohnson's Hotel
Hewitt	Homespun Quilter's Guild, P.O. Box 2228, 76643	Meets: 4th Monday 7 p.m. Harrison Senior Citizen's Center, 1716 N. 42nd St., Waco
Houston	Quilt Guild of Greater Houston, P.O. Box 79035, Memorial Park Station, 77279-9035	
Houston	Bay Area Quilt Guild 1094 Scarsdale, P.O. Box M237 77089	Meets: Evening--3rd Wednesday 7 p.m. at J D Bruce Student Building (Second Floor), San Jacinto College South, 13735 Beamer Rd. Daytime-- 3rd Thursday 10 a.m. at M.U.D. Building, 11610 Sageyork
Houston	The West Houston Quilt Guild, 17731 Mossy Ridge Ln., 77095	Meets: 3rd Wednesday 7 p.m. at Bear Creek Ext. Center, 2 Abercrombie
Irving	Irving Quilt Guild	Meets: 3rd Thursday 7 p.m. at First Baptist Church, 403 S. Main St.
Jefferson	Jefferson Quilt Guild	Meets: 3rd Tuesday at 10-12 at Quilters Corner
Johnson City	Johnson City Quilter's Guild	Meets: 4th Thursday 7 p.m. at Good Shepherd Catholic Church, CR 213
Keller	Bear Creek Quilt Guild 223 S. Pearson Ln.	Meets: 3rd Tuesday 7 p.m. at St. Martin-in-the-Fields Episcopal Church
Kerens	Piecemakers Quilt Guild, 101 Hulan Dr., 76144	Meets: 1st Monday 10 a.m. at Church of Christ Fellowship Hall, Corsicana
Kerrville	Hill Country Quilt Guild, P.O. box 293177, 78029	Meets: 3rd Monday 9:30 a.m. at Church of Christ Fellowship Hall, 505 Sidney Bakert.
Killeen	Crossroads to Texas, P.O. Box 10543	Meets: 2nd and 4th Monday at 7 p.m. at 1st United Methodist Church, 507 N. 8th St.
La Grange	Colorado Valley Quilt Guild, P.O. Box 165, 78945	Meets: 4th Tuesday 10 a.m. (odd months) 7 p.m. (even months) at First United Methodist Church, 1215 Von Minden
Lake Jackson	Plantation Quilt Guild, 102 Yaupon	Meets: 2nd Tuesday 9:15 p.m. at First Presbyterian Church
Lampasas	Keystone Square Quilters, 410 E. 3rd St., 76550	Meets: Every Wednesday 10 a.m. at M.J.'s Fabrics
Lampasas	Lampasas Quilt Guild, 303 South Western, 76550	
Lewisville	Land O' Lakes Quilt Guild	Meets: 1st Monday 7 p.m. at Garden Ridge Church of Christ, Main & Garden Ridge
Mesquite	Mesquite Quilt Guild, P.O. Box 850137, 75185	Meets: Day and evening meetings at Rutherford Community Center, 900 Rutherford
Midlothian	Creative Quilters Guild of Ellis County, PO Box 301, 76065	Meets: 4th Monday @ 7pm at St. Paul's Episcopal Church, Wazahachie
Nassau Bay	Lakeview Quilters Guild, P.O. Box 580365, 77258	Meets: 3rd Monday 7 p.m. at St. Paul's Catholic Church, 18223 Point Lookout
Natalia	Medina County Quilters Guild	
New Braunfels	New Braunfels Area Quilt Guild, P.O. Box 310828, 78131	Meets: 3rd Saturday, 9:30 a.m. at New Braunfels Christian Church
Pampa	Panhandle Piecemakers Quilters Guild	Meets: 4th Thursday 6:30 p.m. at various locations
Paris	Red River Valley Quilt Guild, 2400 Stillhouse Road, 75462	Meets: 2nd Saturday @ 10am at Bernina & Sew Much More
Plano	Quilters Guild of Plano, P.O. Box 260216, 75026	Meets: 2nd Thursday 7:30 p.m. at Pitman Church of Christ, 1815 W. 15th St.
Port Lavaca	Calhoun County Quilting Guild, P.O. Box 352, 77979	Meets: 1st Wednesday
San Antonio	Alamo Heritage Quilter's Guild, P.O. Box 7, 81134	
San Antonio	Greater San Antonio QG, P.O. Box 65124, 78265	Meets: 2nd Saturday
Sunrise Beach Village	Marble Falls Quilt Club, 120 Inspiration Point, 78643	Meets: 2nd Wednesday 10am at Marble Falls Library
Temple	Wildflower Quilt Guild, 3011 N. 3rd.	Meets: 3rd Tuesday at 6:30 p.m. at Cultural Activity Center
Tyler East	Texas Quilt Guild, P.O. Box 130773, 75713	Meets: 2nd Thursday at 9:30 a.m. at Trinity Lutheran Church, 2001 Hunter St.
Victoria	Quilt Guild of Greater Victoria, Box 3164, 77903	Meets: 4th Thursday 9 a.m. at Grace Presbyterian Church
Waco	Homespun Quilters' Guild, PO Box 22073, 76702	Meets: 3rd Monday @ 6:30 at Central United Methodist Church
Weatherford	Quilter's Guild of Parker County, 1225 Holland Lake Rd, 76086	Meets: 3rd Thursday 6:30 p.m. Senior Center, 1225 Holland Lake
Weslaco	Rio Grande Quilt Guild, P.O. Box 32, 78599	Meets: 2nd Saturday 10 a.m. at First Christian Church
Wichita Falls	Red River Quilters' Guild, P.O. Box 9484, 76307	Meets: 1st Monday at 7 p.m. at Church of Christ

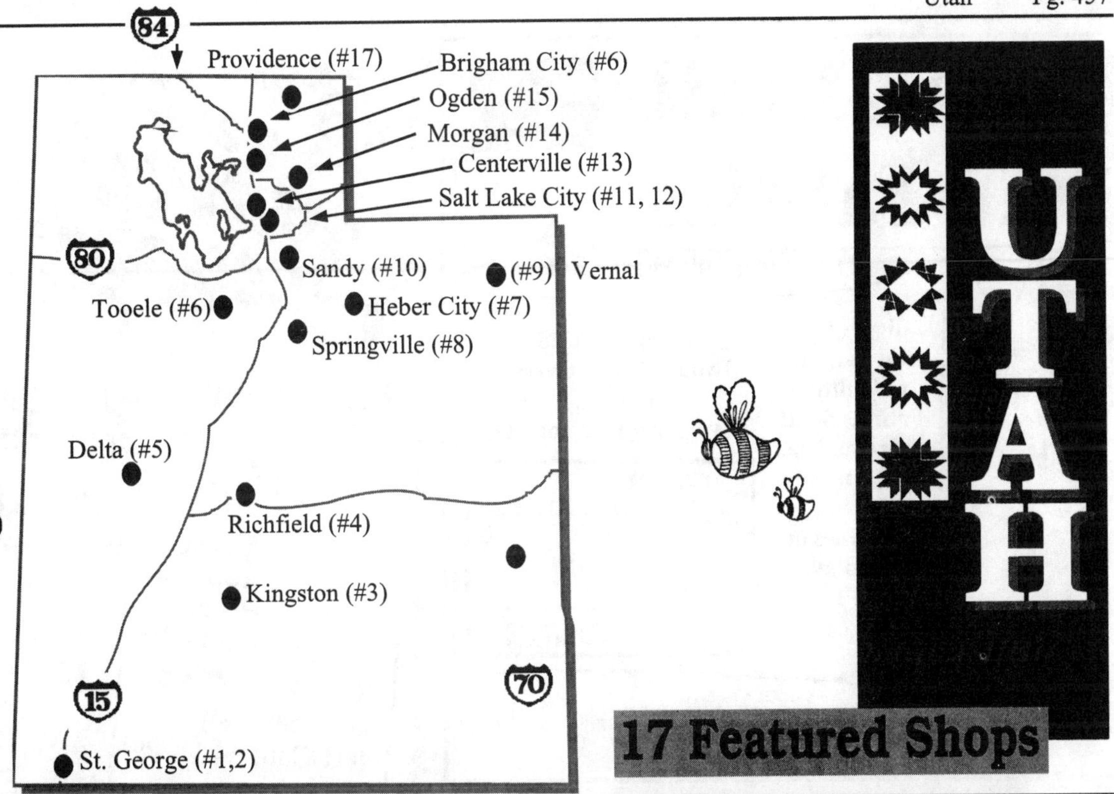

17 Featured Shops

St. George, UT #1

Mon - Sat 10 - 5:30

Sew Suite, Inc.

43 N 700 E 84770
(435) 673-9117 Fax: (435) 673-5931
Est: 1996 3000 sq.ft. 3500 Bolts

Come and visit the "sweetest" quilt shop in color country. We are a complete quilting resource shop. (There's plenty of great golfing as well.)

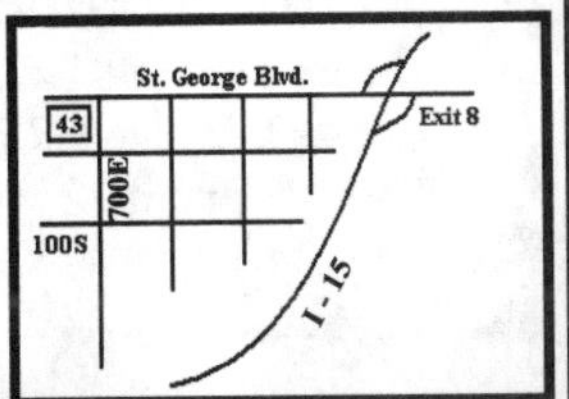

St. George, UT #2

Mon - Fri 10 - 5:30 Sat 10 - 4:30

Lazy Daisy Cottage

46 N 100 W 84770
(435) 673-5659 Fax: (435) 673-5513
Owner: Dana Brooks
Est: 2003 2100 sq.ft. 1800 Bolts

Stop by our cozy historical home which is filled with fabrics, patterns, notions and a large variety of homespun cottage gifts.

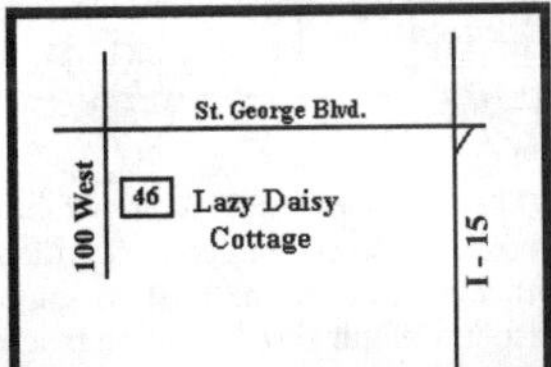

Richfield, UT #4

Mon - Sat 9 - 6

MARCIA'S

25 N. Main St. 84701
(435) 896-8354
Est: 1989

Central Utah's largest fabric shop. We cater to quilters. Custom hand quilting and edging.
Gifts - Fabric - Quilting - Classes

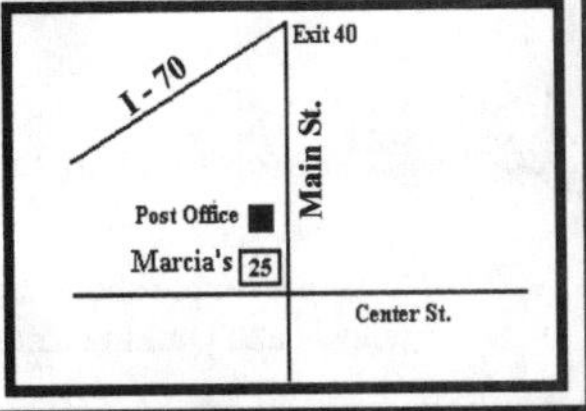

Kingston, UT #3

Imaginique

98 W. Main St.,
P.O. Box 362,
Kingston, UT 84743
435-577-2204
or 577-2203
www.imaginique.com
imaginique01@netscape.net

"We Dye for You"

Specializing in Unique Hand Dyed Quilt Fabrics

By Appt. Only

- 100% Cotton
- 100% Cotton Sateen
- Pima Cotton
- Denim Blocks and Panels for Cowboy Quilts
- Quality 100% Cotton Bandana Quilts and Kits
- Hand Dyed Felted Wool
- Hand Dyed Cotton Apparel

Imaginique is a working Studio located in the small town of Kingston, in South Central Utah. We are just two miles East of Hwy. 89 on State Road 62.

We dye on the premises and have a small show room for you to peruse to find your treasures.

Piute County

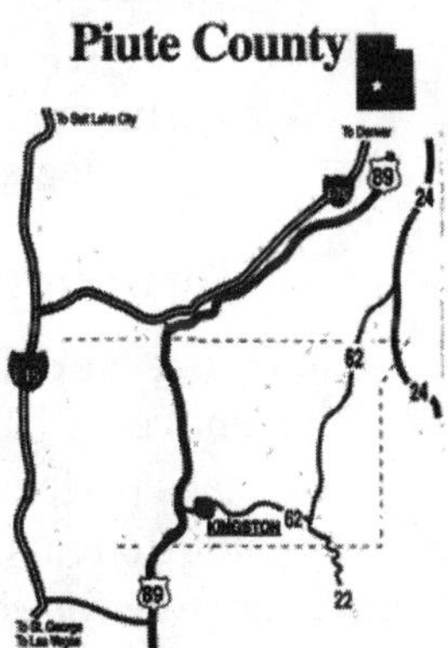

Mom's Crafts and Fabrics

Mon - Sat 10 - 6

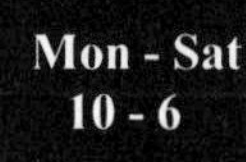

313 South 100 West 84624

Biggest and Best Selection of Quilting Fabrics South of Provo, Utah. 100 Antique Sewing Machines on Display. Est: 1973 4800 sq.ft.

(435) 864-3325
Owner: Peggy Overson
E-Mail:
poverson@xmission.com

Delta City Park
Hwy. 6 & 50
Delta's Main St.
to Reno
100 West
300 South
313 Mom's Crafts and Fabrics

Delta, UT #5

#6

Fabric
Books
Notions
Fat Quarters

289 N Main - Tooele, UT 84074
435-833-0370
Toll Free 1-866-283-1045
www.sewsweet.net

Shop Hours
Tuesday thru Friday
10:00am - 7:00pm
Saturday
10:00am - 5:00pm
closed
Sunday & Monday

Owners:
Marta & Melissa
Est: 2001
2,500 Bolts
quilters@sewsweet.net

Just 35 miles west of Salt Lake City

From the Salt Lake area, take I-80 west and take exit 99. This is SR 36 and will become Tooele's Main Street in about 12 miles. We are located in a strip mall, behind Jim's Family Restaurant on the west side of Main.

Heber City, UT #7

Heber Cotton Company

350 S. Main St.
Heber City, Utah 84032

(435) 654-5013

Summer Hours:
Mon - Thur 10 - 6 Fri & Sat 10 - 5

Brights, Bali's and Retro Fabrics give us a unique flavor
Wonderful staff and classes will help your projects be wonderful too!

And, across our shared driveway

The House Next Door
This renovated 1920's Cottage is perfect for Quilt Retreats.
Call our store for details.

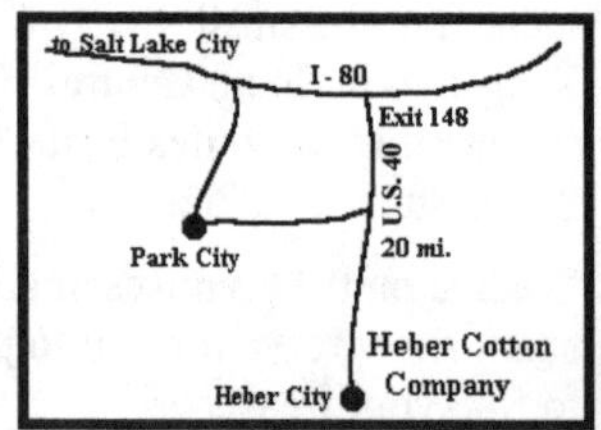

Springville, UT #8

Mon - Fri 10 - 6 Sat 9 - 5

303 E 400 S 84663 (801) 491-3551
Fax: (801) 491-7256
cornwquilts@aol.com

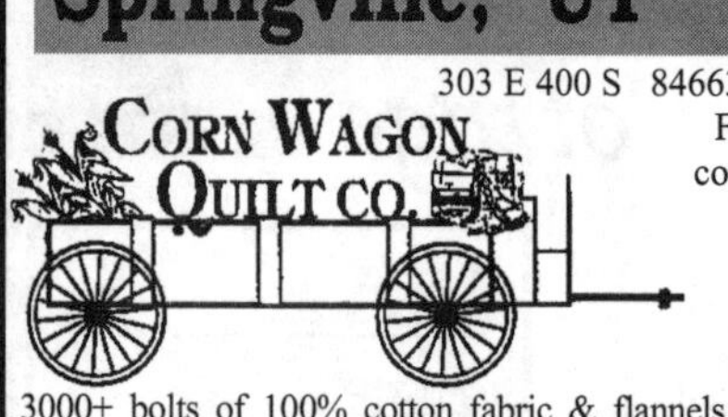

3000+ bolts of 100% cotton fabric & flannels, books, patterns, notions, & stitchery supplies. Stitchery frames and custom framing. Beautiful displays of our shop's custom machine quilting.
Owner: Marsha Harward Est: 1999

I-15
Main St.
Corn Wagon Quilt Co.
303
4th St.
Exit 263
Art Museum

Vernal, UT #9

Mon - Fri 11 - 5:30 Sat 11 - 4:30

Quilted Hens

38 South 600 West
84078
(435) 789-2411

We have a simple abundance of Flannels and Quilting Cottons.

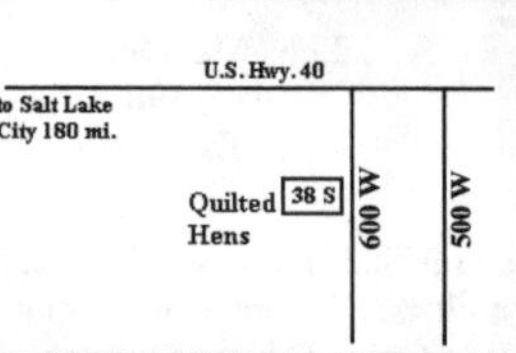

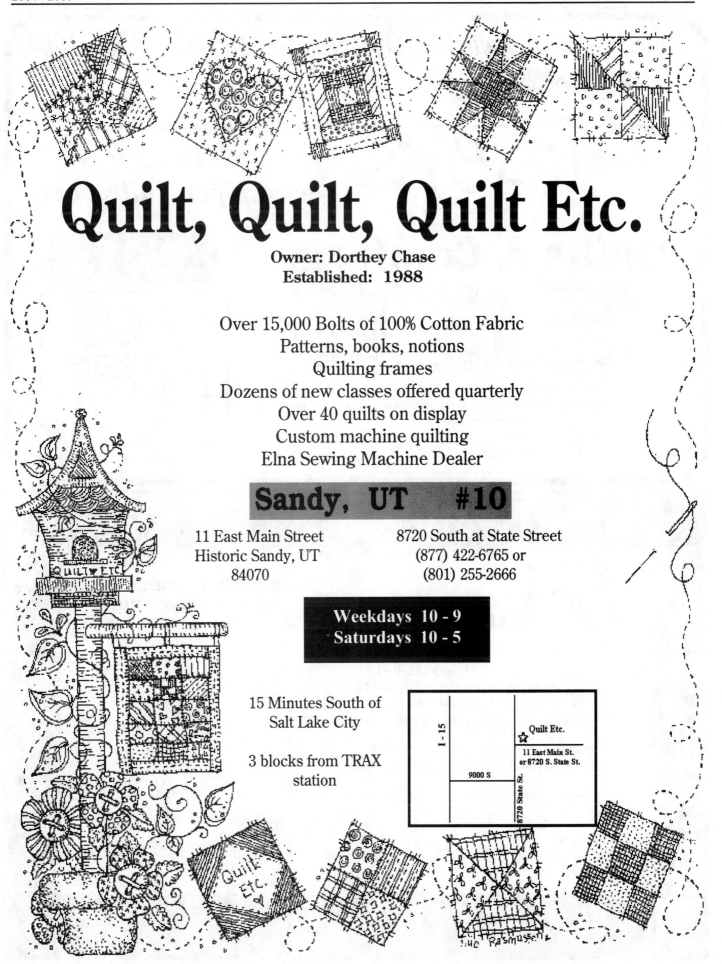

Quilt, Quilt, Quilt Etc.

Owner: Dorthey Chase
Established: 1988

Over 15,000 Bolts of 100% Cotton Fabric
Patterns, books, notions
Quilting frames
Dozens of new classes offered quarterly
Over 40 quilts on display
Custom machine quilting
Elna Sewing Machine Dealer

Sandy, UT #10

11 East Main Street
Historic Sandy, UT
84070

8720 South at State Street
(877) 422-6765 or
(801) 255-2666

Weekdays 10 - 9
Saturdays 10 - 5

15 Minutes South of
Salt Lake City

3 blocks from TRAX
station

I - 15
Quilt Etc.
11 East Main St.
or 8720 S. State St.
9000 S
8720 State St.

American Patchwork & Quilting Top 10 Quilt Shop 2004

Salt Lake City, UT #11

Pipers

1944 South 1100 East 84106
(801) 484-5890
Fax: (801) 484-5890
info@pipersquilts.com
Est: 1998 3500 sq. ft. 1500 Bolts.

www.pipersquilts.com

Quilts & Comforts

Mon - Thur 10 - 9
Fri & Sat 10 - 6

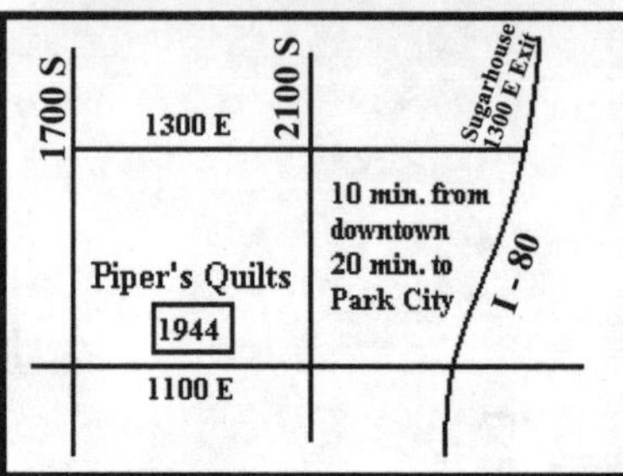

Located in Historic Sugarhouse's oldest home.
An amazing array of fabrics: featuring Moda & Alexander Henry.
We specialize in kits!!!
Complimentary classes! We love beginners.
Fine Hand Applique & Hand Quilting

Across from the Sugarhouse Post Office
5 Minutes from downtown Salt Lake City

#12

Elaine's Quilt Block

6970 South 3000 East
Salt Lake City, UT 84121
801-947-9100 10-8 M-TH, 10-6 F,S
www.elainesquiltblock.com
(801) 947-9100

LOCATED AT THE BASE OF UTAH'S SCENIC WASATCH MOUNTAINS

Full-service shop including Instruction, Machine Quilting and Hemstitching

Come visit our unique 19th century style building with 6,100 square feet of floor space

Discover over 2,500 bolts of fabric including:

- Orientals
- Batiks
- Brushed Plaids
- Country
- Chenille
- Baby Flannels
- Civil War Collection
- All Moda lines

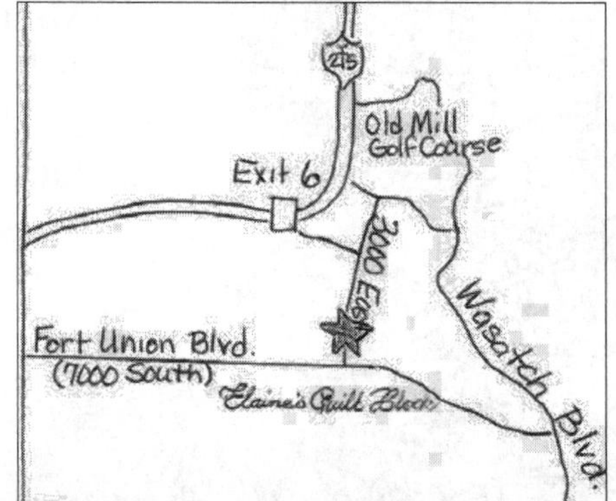

Centerville, UT #13

Mon - Fri 10 - 6 Sat 10 - 5

Threads of Time: Fabric for Quilts

158 W. Parrish Lane 84014
(801) 298-5077 Fax: (801) 298-8780
CherylS@quiltedweb.com
www.quiltedweb.com
Owner: Cheryl Styler Est: 1999 4000 sq. ft.

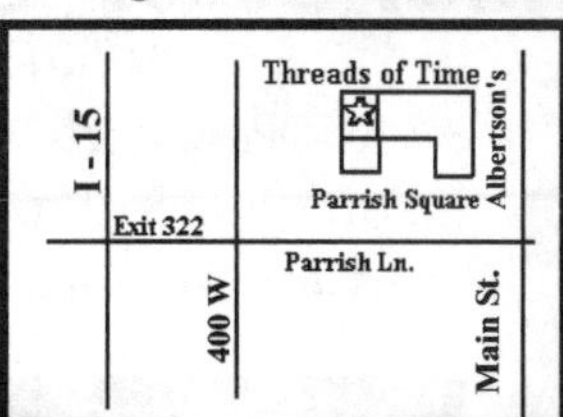

More bolts of fabric than we care to count! Everything that a Quilter could dream of! Books, Patterns, Notions & a huge selection of quality cotton Fabrics. Fun, knowledgeable Staff!

Morgan, UT #14

Tues - Thur 10 - 5:30 Fri & Sat 10 - 4

GQuilts.com

Gwendolyn's Fabrics

117 N. Commercial St. 84050
(801) 829-4001 gwen@gquilts.com
www.gquilts.com
Owner: Gwen Henley
Est: 1997 2000 sq.ft.

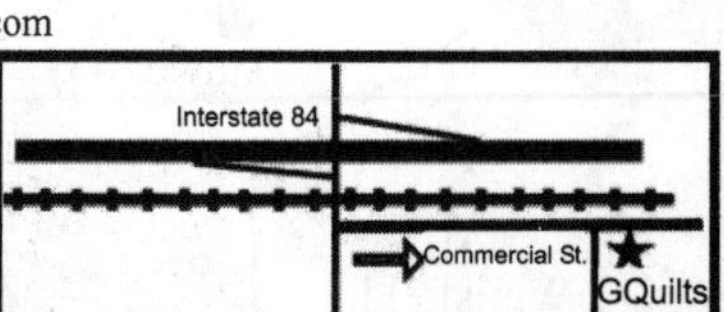

Fabrics, Machine Quilting, Hemstitching, Lots of flannels, notions, White sewing machines.

Ogden, UT #15

Mon - Sat 10 - 6

Gardiners Sew & Quilt

3789 Wall Ave. 84405
(801) 394-4466
Owners: Curt & Irene Gardiner
Est: 1975 3000 sq.ft.

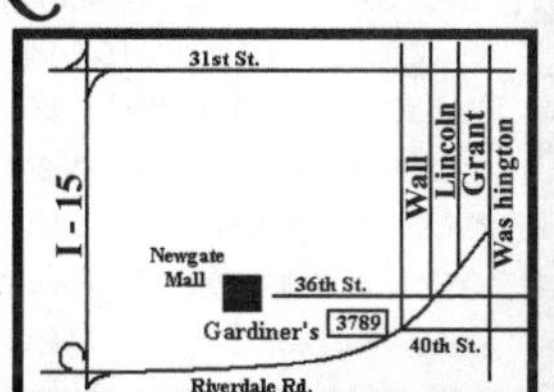

- Northern Utah's Premier Quilt Shop -
5000+ bolts of 100% cotton, Largest selection of Flannels, Notions, Books, Patterns, Hemstitching, expert machine quilting and classes.

Brigham City, UT #16

Mon - Sat 10 - 6

Village Dry Goods

96 S. Main 84302
(435) 723-1315
www.villagedrygoods.com
Owners: RoLayne & Rosa

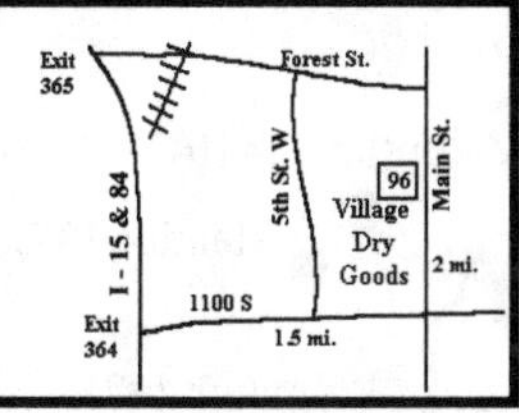

On Historic Main Street. Specializing in quilt fabric, tons of kits, stitchery, and Block of the Months.

Providence, UT #17

Mon - Sat 10 - 6

Red Rooster

Quilts & Treasures

517 W 100 N, Suite 101 84332
(435) 787-8857
redroosterquilts@hotmail.com
Owners: Debi Booth & Kaye Neilson
Est: 2003 2500 sq.ft.

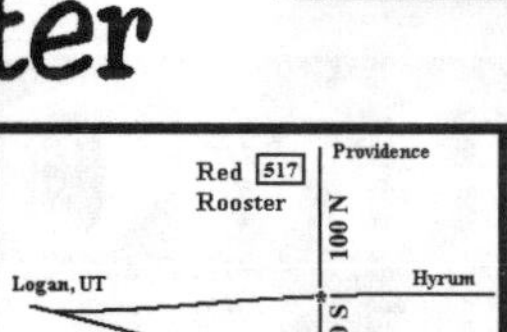

"We have something to Crow about"
A unique assortment of 100% cotton fabrics, over dyed wools, notions, books, classes, gifts and fun!

Other Shops in Utah: *We suggest calling first*

Beaver Patches & Pieces, 86 N Main St 435-438-6173
Bountiful Quilter's Haven, 846 S. Main St. 801-292-1846
Bountiful Brooks Fabrics, 220 North Main 801-295-2940
Cedar City The Quilters' Nook, 535 S. Main 435-867-4834
Centerville Handi Quilter 322 E 500 N 801-292-7988
Clearfield Sew N Save, 1475 South State 801-825-2177
Draper Thimbles & Threads, 12215 S. 900 E. 801-576-0390
Kaysville Vonda's Quilt Frames, 99 N. Angel St. 801-543-1876
Layton Nimble Thimble Quilt Shop, 1868 N Hill Field Dr 801-773-4950
Logan Needles N Neighbors, 128 S. 1170 E 801-753-6589
Logan Bernina Fabric Center, 138 N. Main St. 435-752-4186
Logan Stylish Fabrics, 138 N Main 435-752-6077
Logan Quilter's Courtyard, 825 W 200 S 435-792-4185
Logan Threads & Things, 1045 N Main 801-752-6077
Mendon Quilters' Courtyard, 87 W 300 N 435-755-7065
Monticello L J Quilting Bee, 220 W. N Creek 435-587-3368
Murray The Cotton Shop, 6100 S State 801-266-6942
Orem Thread Count, 48 N Geneva Rd 801-221-5459
Orem Fabric Mill, 414 E 1400 S 801-225-3123
Orem Creative Quiltworks, 848 W 260 S 801-319-4422
Orem The Stitching Corner, 631 E 1700 S 801-426-6900
Orem American Quilting, 843 S State St 801-802-7841
Panguitch Snowed in Quilt Shop, 190 N. Main 435-676-8666
Providence The Quilt House, 135 S. 100 E 801-752-5429
Provo Fabric Mill, 90 W. Center St. 801-375-4818
Riverdale Fibers & Twigs, 4555 S 700 W 801-627-6475
Riverton Loving Stitches, P.O. Box 1489
Riverton J J Quilts, 2075 W 12130 S 801-253-9747
Roy Marlene's Quilts, 3118 W 5200 S 801-825-0547
Roy The Quilter's Basket, 4684 S 3600 W 888-703-7031
Salt Lake City Ana's 4 Queens, 1899 S Redwood 801-973-1175
Salt Lake City Mormon Handicraft, 15 W South Temple St. 801-355-2141
Salt Lake City Gentler Times, 4880 S. Highland 801-277-9233
Salt Lake City Quilter's Patch, 2370 S. 3600 W. 801-973-6117
Sandy The Cotton Shop, 9441 S 700 E 801-572-1412
Sandy Creative Quilting, 2463 Glaciet Ridge 801-942-3237
Sandy Quilted Keepsakes, 1897 Falcon Way 801-571-9671
Sandy Sew Many Quilts 2440 Vail Cir 801-943-3462
Spanish Fork Quilted Memories, 130 E 400 S 801-798-8272
Sunset Nuttalls' Bernina, 2465 N. Main St. 801-544-5911
Tremonton La Rue's Quilts, 145 W. Main 435-257-0801
Tremonton Miller's Buttons & Bolts, 25 W. Main St. 435-257-5604
Vernal Dinaland Quiltworks, 2280 S 2000 E 435-789-6426
West Jordan Stawberry Creek Designs, 5478 Aristada Ave
West Jordan Village Quilt Shop, 1100 W 7800 801-566-1846
West Jordan The Stitching Corner, 1550 W. 7800 S. 801-566-1400
West Valley City Quilt Shop, 3601 S 2700 W 801-966-7915

Utah Guilds:

Brigham City Heritage Quilters, 33 S. Main, 84302
Meets: 1st Saturday 9 a.m. at Village Dry Goods
Delta Piece in the Valley, 647 E. Bristlecone, 84624
Meets: 2nd Thursday 7 p.m. Heartspun Treasures Quilt Shop
Ogden Ogden Quilt Guild, 340 N. Washington Blvd., 84404
Provo Utah Valley Quilt Guild, 270 West 500 North
Meets: 3rd Wednesday 1:30pm at Provo Eldred Center
Richfield Cove View Quilters, 379 Pahvont, 84701
Meets: 2nd Monday 10 a.m. at Richfield Senior Citizen Center, 890 N 300 W
Roy Roy Pioneer Quilters, 4232 S. 2275 West, 84067
Salt Lake City Utah Quilt Guild, P.O. Box 17032, 84117
St. George Dixie Quilt Guild, P.O. Box 507, 84771
Tooele Tooele County Quilters, 432 S. 300 W, 84074
Meets: 3rd Tuesday @ 9:30am at Tooele Cty Health Building

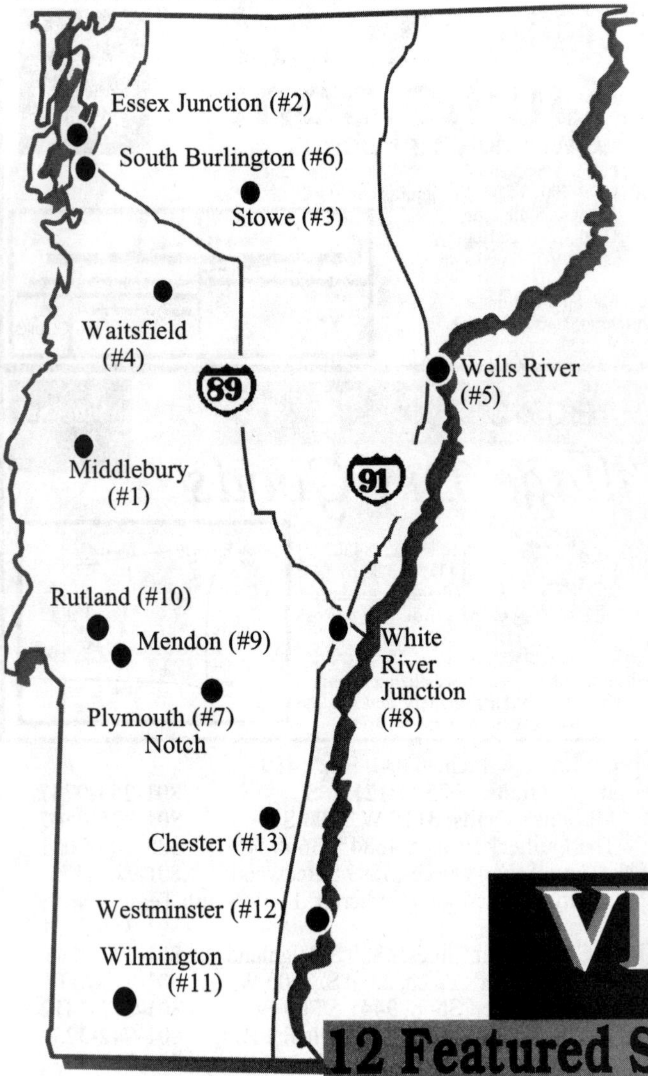

Essex Junction (#2)
South Burlington (#6)
Stowe (#3)
Waitsfield (#4)
Wells River (#5)
89
91
Middlebury (#1)
Rutland (#10)
Mendon (#9)
White River Junction (#8)
Plymouth (#7) Notch
Chester (#13)
Westminster (#12)
Wilmington (#11)

Middlebury, VT #1

Thread Connections

"Where Friends Meet"

18 Creek Rd. #1B 05753 Est: 2000
(802) 388-9400 Fax: (802) 388-9413
threadco@msn.com Owner: Rita Glidden

Mon - Fri 11 - 5
Sat 9:30 - 5

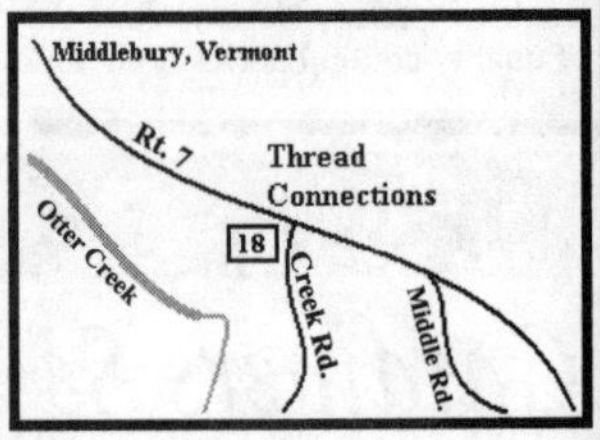

Middlebury, Vermont
Rt. 7
Thread Connections
Otter Creek
18
Creek Rd.
Middle Rd.

We have 1500+ high quality bolts of Quilting Fabrics in stock from the top manufacturers. Our line includes 100% Cottons, Batiks, 1930's prints, and many more. We stock over 4000 Fat Quarters to choose from. Stop by and look at our large selection of books and notions. Sign up for one of our Quilt classes to fit every skill level. One day classes can be arranged, give us a call! We will ship your purchases anywhere. Gift Cards are available. Our friendly staff look forward to helping you with your Quilting needs.

VERMONT

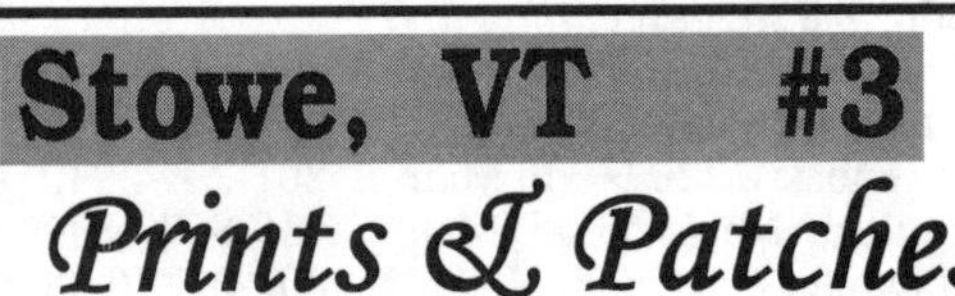

12 Featured Shops

Essex Junction, VT #2

Mon 10 - 5
Tues - Thur 10 - 7
Fri 10 - 9
Sat 10-5 Sun 12-4

Yankee Pride

9 Main St. 05452
(802) 872-9300
Est: 1981 2500 Bolts

All the top brands of fabrics, the newest books and notions, classes. Friendly, knowledgeable service.

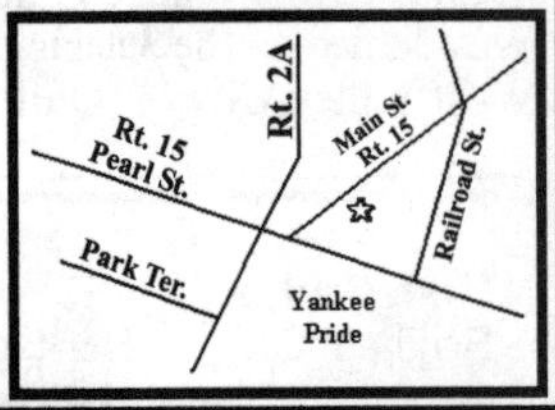

Rt. 15 Pearl St.
Rt. 2A
Main St. Rt. 15
Railroad St.
Park Ter.
Yankee Pride

Stowe, VT #3

Mon - Sat
10 - 5

Prints & Patches

Main St., P.O. Box 1205 05672
(802) 253-8643
quilts@stowe.nu
www.quiltsvermont.com
Owner: Mary Johnson
Est: 1979 800 sq.ft.

Come on into our Retail shop in Stowe.
FABRIC - YARNS - QUILTS

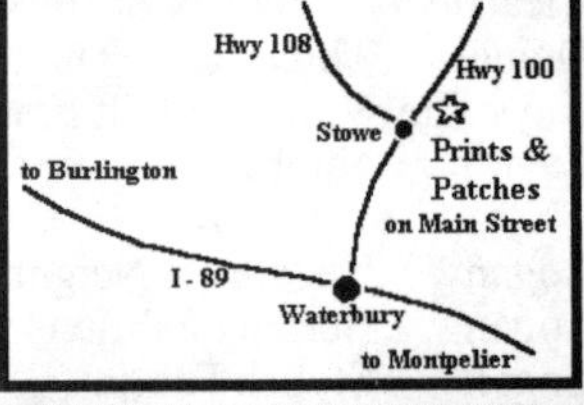

Waitsfield, VT #4

Mon - Sat
10 - 5

Cabin Fever Quilts

The Old Church Route 100
P.O. Box 443 05673
(802) 496-2287 Owner: Vee Lowell
Est: 1976 1200 Sq.ft.

Cabin Fever Quilts offers large display of hand quilted, machine quilted and hand tied quilts. Custom orders are our specialty. Fabrics, quilting supplies, quilt kits and much more.

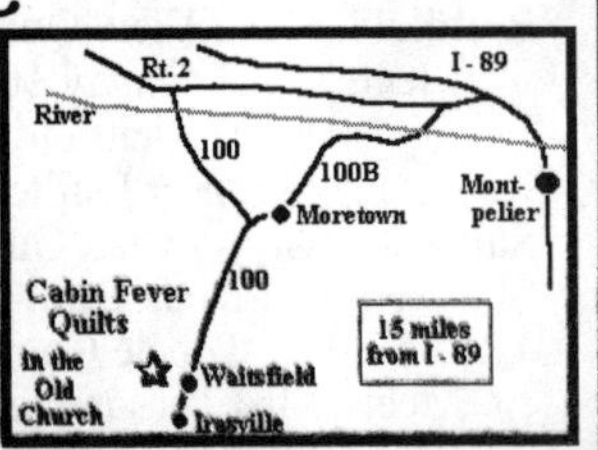

Wells River, VT #5

Mon - Sat
9:30 - 5
Sun 10 - 3

Catamount Quilt Studio & Shoppee

11 Water St., P.O. Box 7 05081
(802) 757-2200 Est: 2003
catquilt99@hotmail.com
www.CatamountQuiltShoppee.com
Owners: Bill & Mary Schilke

Wonderful closeout Cotton Fabrics at discount prices. Custom hand guided machine quilting services, books, notions, gifts & more. Consignment Crafts.

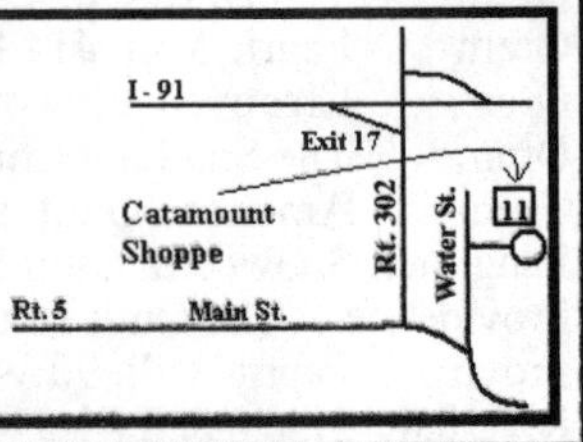

Quilter's Courtyard

A haven for quilters, quilt lovers, and friends.

shop hours

monday - friday 10am-9pm
saturday 9am-9pm
sunday noon-5pm

shop online

www.quilterscourtyard.com

Beth Cousins
Owner

4 Market Street, Suite 4
South Burlington, VT 05403
802.863.4656

Nothing Sews Like A Bernina. Nothing.
BERNINA®
Authorized Bernina dealer for sales and service

see our new location in St. Paul, Minnesota!

Visit our beautiful courtyard, just brimming with delightful treasures!

- A spectacular selection of contemporary and traditional fabrics.
- Exquisite fabrics and trim imported from Japan, Australia, England, and Switzerland.
- Extensive collection of the latest books, notions, and patterns.
- Specialty thread and floss collections for hand and machine embroidery.
- Huge selection of yarn and knitting supplies.
- Personalized weekend getaways for your group or guild.
- Many uniquely wonderful gifts.
- Tour groups welcome.
- Visit us in St Paul, Minnesota as well!

South Burlington, VT #6

Plymouth Notch, VT #7

Daily Late May - mid Oct 9:30 - 5

President Calvin Coolidge State Historic Site

Plymouth Notch Historic District
(802) 672-3773 Est: 1956
P.O. Box 247 05056
11 Museum Buildings

Several late 19th Century Quilts on Permanent exhibition. Including one pieced by Calvin Coolidge when he was 10 years old. (Tumbling Blocks)

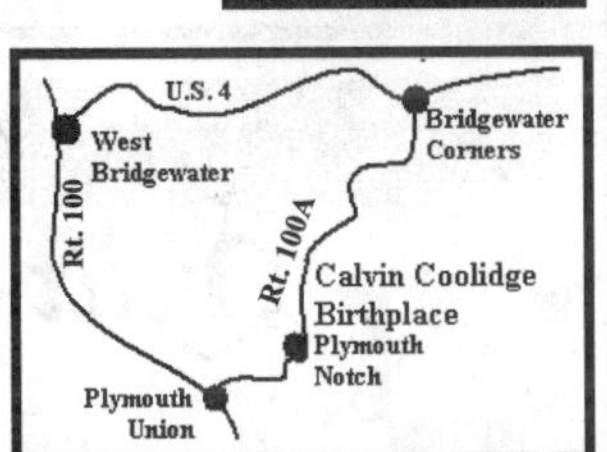

White River Junction, VT #8

**Mon - Fri 9:30 - 6
Sat 9 - 4**

Country Quilters Emporium

1011 N. Main St. The Junction Marketplace 05001
(802) 295-1375 Fax: (802) 295-1398
cqemporium@aol.com
www.countryquilters.com
Owners: Buzz & Nancy Barr
Est: 2000 4000 sq.ft. 2500 Bolts

Over 2000 bolts of 100% cotton. Area's Largest Selection of Quilting Books & Supplies. Specializing in Sales & Service of Bernina.

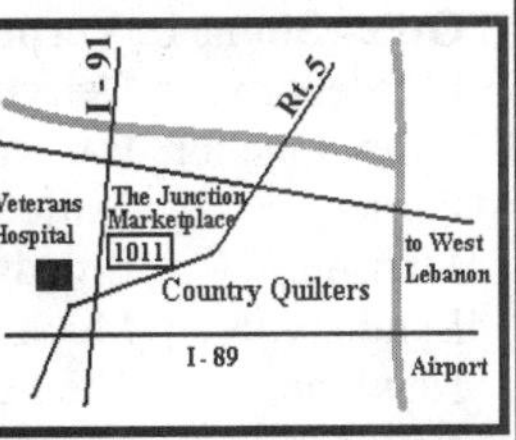

Mendon, VT #9

1 Route 4 East, Mendon, VT 05701
(802) 773-5628
Fax: (802) 773-5641
pbahnson@yahoo.com
Est: 2000 2500 sq.ft. 1500 Bolts

Quilt Fabric, Patterns, Notions, Books & Quilt Classes

"It is my pleasure to provide you with the best of customer service in an environment which delights your senses."
Peggy Bahnson - Owner

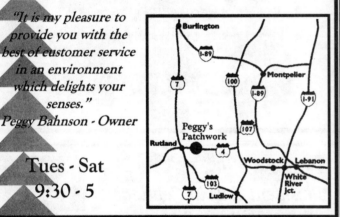

Tues - Sat
9:30 - 5

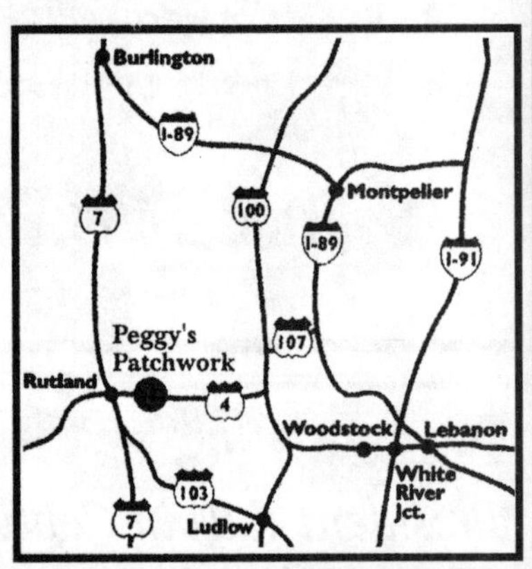

Rutland, VT #10

Mon - Sat 9:30 - 5
Sun 12 - 5

Country Quilt & Fabric

4 U.S. Rt. 4 (Rt. 4E) Mendon, VT 05701
(802) 773-3470
Quilters12@aol.com
Owners: Pat & Lynne Benard
Est: 1982 1400 sq.ft.

4000+ bolts of 100% cotton fabrics -- Hoffman, South Seas, P&B, RJR, plus Notions, Books & Patterns
Custom Orders too.

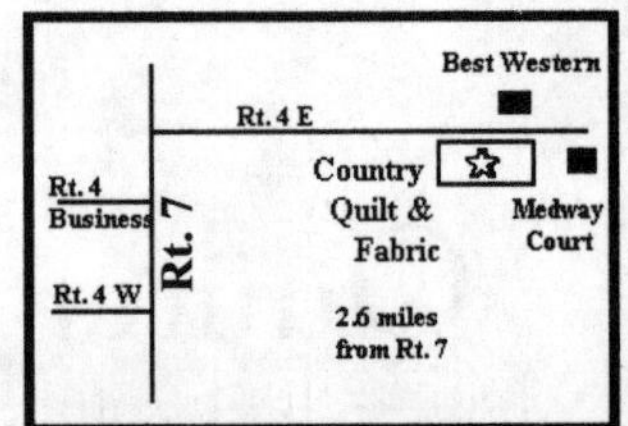

Wilmington, VT #11

Norton House

A Quilter's Paradise !

Over 3000 100% Cotton Fabrics.
The most beautiful fabric at the best prices!

Our Fabric Sale Attic is stuffed with 100% top quality cottons specially priced at 20 to 50% off.

Books - Notions - Patterns - Quilting Classes
Vermont Made Quilts - Needlework Kits - Toys - Gifts

BERNINA & elna Sewing Machines

Open 7 Days a Week, 9 - 5, all year

30 W. Main St., P.O. Box 579 05363
(802) 464-7213
norquilt@sover.net
Owner: Suzanne Wells Wurzberger
Est: 1967 2000 sq.ft.
Shop our online store: www.norquilt.com

W. Main St. | Route 100 | Route 9 | 30 | Norton House

Westminster, VT #12

M, T, Th, F 12 - 4
Sat 10 - 4
or by Appt.

Quilt-a-way

540 Back Westminster Rd.
(802) 722-4743 05159
Owner: Carol Coski
3200 sq.ft. 8000+ bolts. 1800+ bolts of Batiks.

"She who dies with the most fabric wins!" Every day is a sale day & we discount everything we sell.

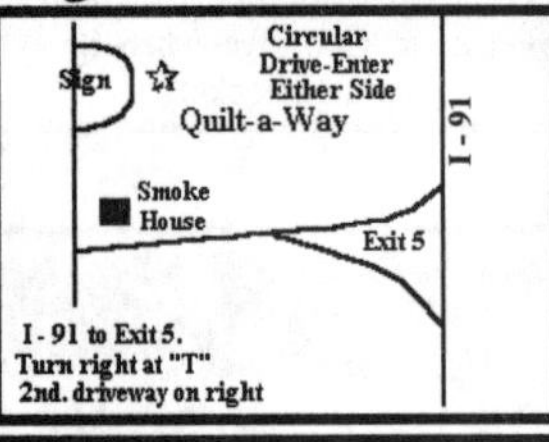

Other Shops in Vermont: *We suggest calling first*

Brattleboro	Delectaable Mountain Cloth, 125 Main St	802-257-4456
Essex Junction	Backcountry Threads, 169 Brigham Hill Rd.	802-872-7855
Fairlee	Fairlee Village Quilt Shop, 446 US Rte 5N	802-333-3566
Johnson	Broadwoven Fabric Mill, R.R. # 2 #1035	802-635-7880
Lyndonville	Moonlight Inn Vermont, 801 Center St., P.O. Box 1325	802-626-0780
Newfane	The Log Cabin Quilting Shop, R.R. #1, Box 925	802-365-7974
Newfane	Newfane Country Store, 598 Rte. 30, P.O. Box 56	802-365-7916
North Clarendon	Quilt Barn of Vermont, 1943 East St.	802-775-0988
Richford	Pinnacle Peddler, 5 Main St	802-848-3886
Wilmington	Quilt & Fiber Arts Loft at Adams Farm, 15 Higley Hill Rd.	802-464-3762

Country Treasures

Chester, VT #13

FABRIC - QUILTS - GIFTS – FOLK ART & BOOKS

P.O. Box 994
12 Common St.
Chester, VT 05143

Phone: (802)875-4377
ww.vermontquilting.com
Email: sue@vermontquilting.com

Store Hours:
Monday-Saturday 10AM-5PM
Sunday, 12PM-4PM
*Closed in April

Country Treasures is one of the premier quilt shops in New England

Over **6,000** bolts of fabric including an entire room of flannels and brushed homespuns.

Established in 1990, Country Treasures is 3000 sq. ft.

Fat quarter bundles done in complete lines or color coordinated are favorites with our customers.

– Large selection of books and patterns – Quilt classes to fit every skill level –
– Gift Department – Will ship anywhere –

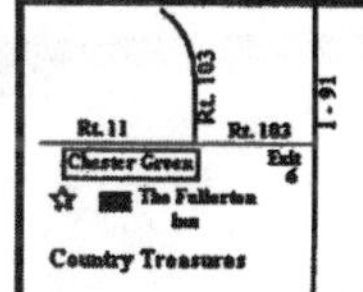

Annual Fabric Sale:

Anniversary Sale– Starting the last week of June through July

Vermont Guilds:

Bradford Oxbee Quilter's Guild, P.O. Box 148, 05033
Champlain Valley Quilt Guild, 05482
Meets: 1st Tuesday 7 p.m. at Essex Alliance Church, Essex Junction
Fairfax Green Mt. Quilters State Guild, P.O. Box 56, 05454
Hartland Heart of the Land Quilter's Guild, Box 332, 05048
Meets: 4th Wednesday @ 7 p.m. at Hearland Rec. Center
Mendon Maple Leaf Quilter's Guild, P.O. Box 7400, 05701
Montgomery Center Montgomery Quilting Circle, PO Box 517, 05471
Meets: 1st Thursday @ 6:30 pm at St. Isidore's Parish Hall
S. Strafford Northern Lights Quilt Guild, c/o 169 Alger Brook Rd., 05070
Meets: 7 p.m. Second Wednesday at Methodist Church, Lebanon, NH

VIRGINIA

38 Featured Shops

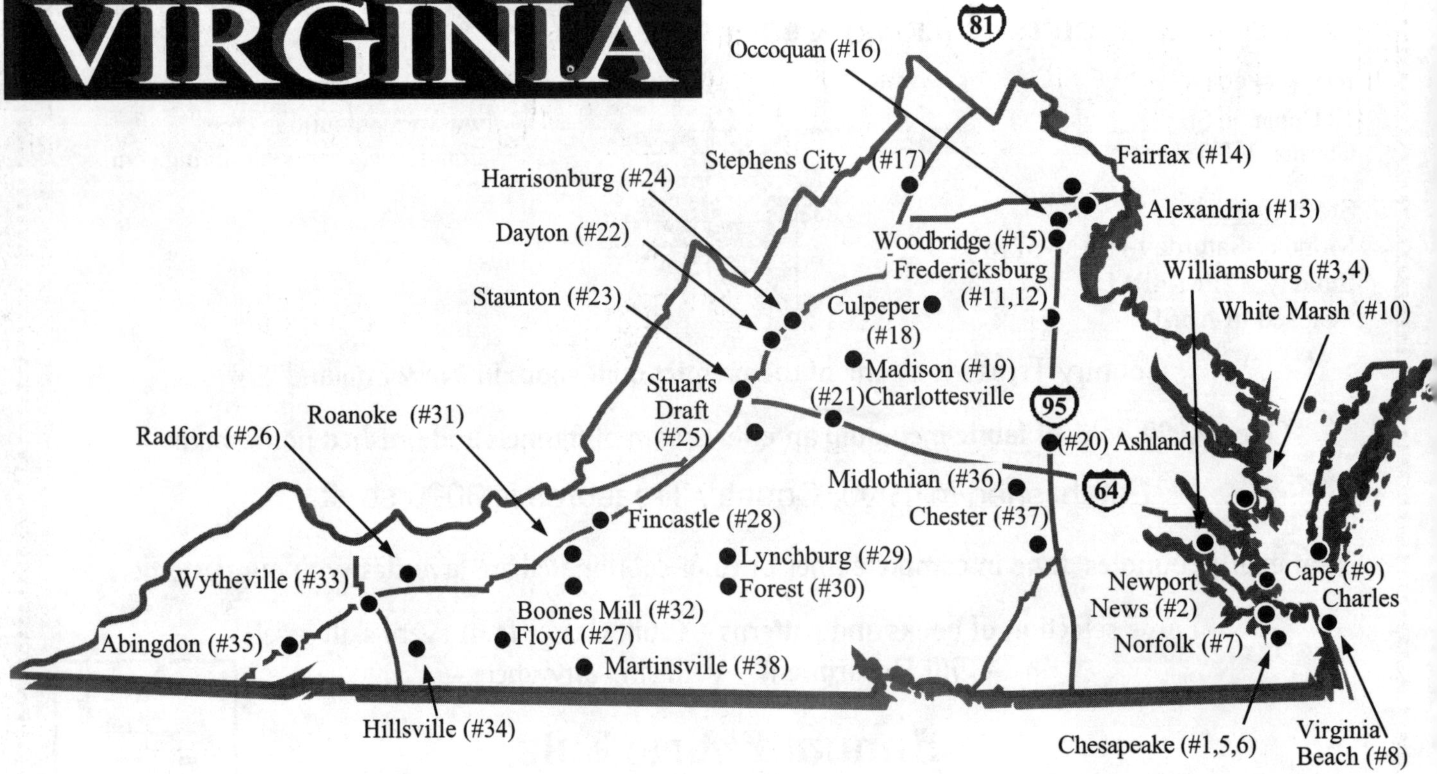

81
Occoquan (#16)
Stephens City (#17)
Fairfax (#14)
Alexandria (#13)
Harrisonburg (#24)
Woodbridge (#15)
Dayton (#22)
Fredericksburg (#11,12)
Williamsburg (#3,4)
Staunton (#23)
Culpeper (#18)
White Marsh (#10)
Madison (#19)
Stuarts Draft (#25)
(#21)Charlottesville
95
Roanoke (#31)
Radford (#26)
(#20) Ashland
Midlothian (#36)
64
Chester (#37)
Fincastle (#28)
Lynchburg (#29)
Cape Charles (#9)
Wytheville (#33)
Forest (#30)
Newport News (#2)
Boones Mill (#32)
Floyd (#27)
Norfolk (#7)
Abingdon (#35)
Martinsville (#38)
Hillsville (#34)
Chesapeake (#1,5,6)
Virginia Beach (#8)

Spooling Around

Chesapeake, VA #1

801 Volvo Pkwy. #138 23320 (757) 436-4664

www.SpoolingAround.com

"No such thing as a stranger, just Friends we haven't met yet." That's how we look at things here.

Come in for a fine selection of 100% cotton fabrics, books, patterns, and notions. Classes for beginners to advanced. Custom machine quilting on our shop Gammill.

This is your "Full-Service" Quilt Shop

Spooling Around

Mon - Fri 10 - 6
Sat 10 - 5 Sun 12 - 5

Fax: (757) 436-6667
Susan@SpoolingAround.com
Owner: Susan Crowder Cyr
Est: 1999 3200 sq.ft. 3000 Bolts

I - 64
Greenbrier Pkwy.
Greenbrier Mall
Volvo Pkwy
Spooling Around
Food Lion

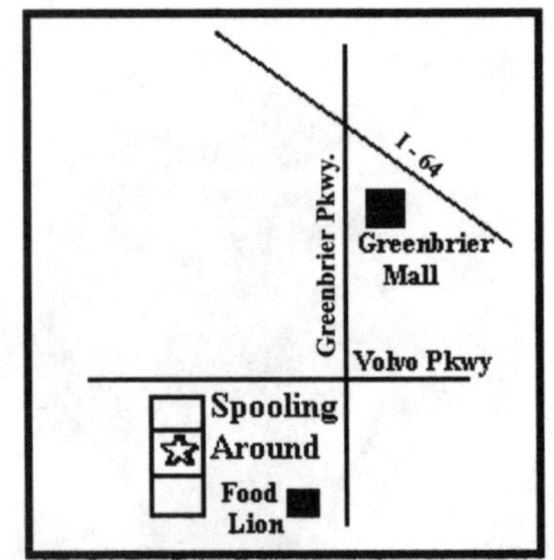

Needlecraft Corner

aka "Sherry's Shop"

Featuring Your Favorite 100% Cotton Fabrics

Home of "Granny Nanny's Quilting Gadgets" foundation piecing patterns, needlework kits, fibers, books and accessories.

Williamsburg, VA #4

7521 Richmond Rd. 23188
(757) 564-3354
Fax: (757) 564-8453
needlecraft@wsac.com
Est: 1977
Owner: Jack Barnett

Everyday 9:30 - 5

One mile from I - 64 at exit 231A

Chesapeake, VA #5

Mon - Fri 10 - 7
Sat 10 - 6
Sun 12 - 5

Sis 'N Me Quilt Shoppe

4107 Portsmouth Blvd. #114
(757) 686-2050 23321
www.sisnme.com
Owner: Carole King
Est: 1987 4400 sq.ft

Tidewater's Largest Quilt Shop. Fabrics, Books, Notions, Patterns, Stencils, Classes, Block-A-Months. Large Oriental department.

Chesapeake, VA #6

Mon - Sat 9:30 - 5

The Quilting Bee

701 N. Battlefield Blvd. Suite S 23320
(757) 547-2552 Fax: (757) 547-2622
info@quilting.com
Est: 2002 1600 sq.ft.
Located blocks from Interstate. A full line of quilting fabrics, notions and classes.
Visit us online at www.quilting-bee.com.

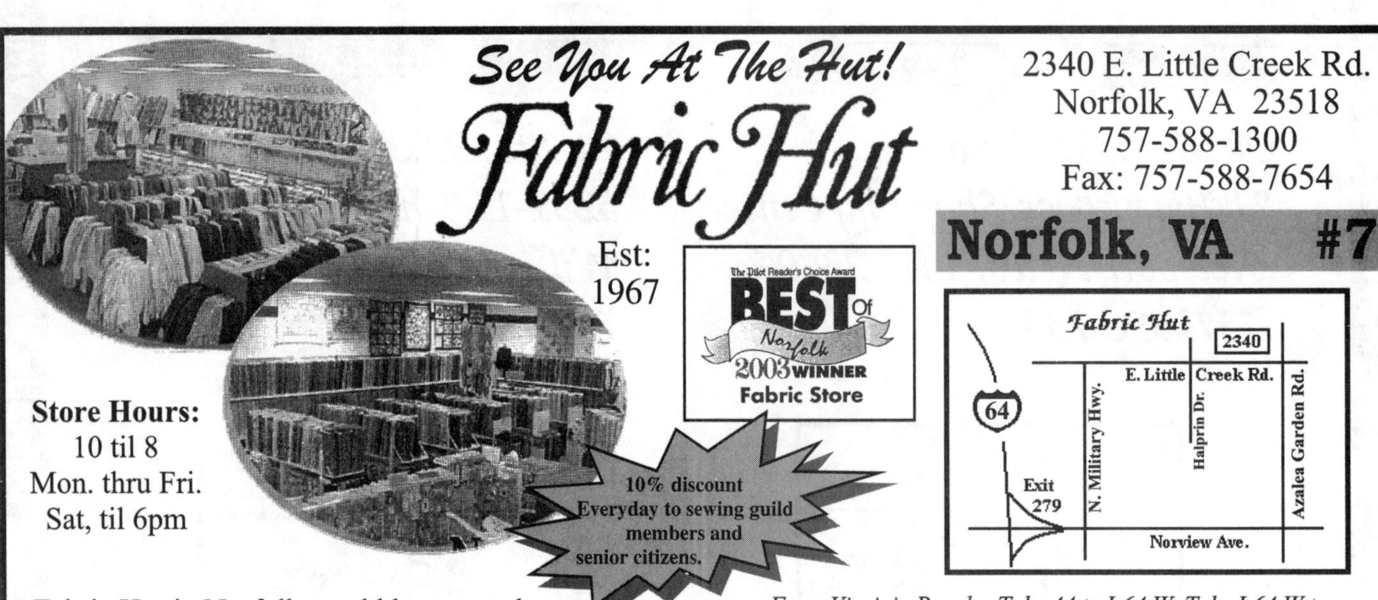

See You At The Hut!

Fabric Hut

Est: 1967

2340 E. Little Creek Rd.
Norfolk, VA 23518
757-588-1300
Fax: 757-588-7654

Norfolk, VA #7

Store Hours:
10 til 8
Mon. thru Fri.
Sat, til 6pm

10% discount Everyday to sewing guild members and senior citizens.

Fabric Hut in Norfolk would love to welcome you to our Big 14,000 sq. foot Store, full of some of the most beautiful fabrics from around the world. See our complete collection of Bridal Fabrics and Trims, Apparel and Evening Wear Fabrics, Designer Fabrics, Buttons & Trims, and Notions. Also, see our large quilt department with approximately 6,000 bolts from some of the best known companies. Come see our new Home Dec fabrics and trims.

Visit us also at: **www.fabrichut.com**

From Virginia Beach: Take 44 to I-64 W. Take I-64 W to Exit 279B. Turn LEFT onto Military Hwy. Turn RIGHT onto E. Little Creek Rd. Fabric Hut is 1 mile on left hand side in Roosevelt Gardens Shopping Center.

From Hampton, Newport New, Williamsburg: Take I-64 E to Norfolk, Take exit 279. Turn LEFT onto Military Hwy. Turn RIGHT onto E. Little Creek Rd.. Fabric Hut is 1 mile on left hand side in Roosevelt Garden Shopping Center.

From Portsmouth: Take downtown tunnel to I-264. Take I-264 to I-64 W. Take I-64 W to Exit 279B. Turn LEFT onto Military Hwy. Turn RIGHT onto E. Little Creek Rd. Fabric Hut is 1 mile on left hand side in Roosevelt Garden Shopping Center.

Virginia Beach, VA #8

Mon - Sat 10 - 5:30
Thur til 8
Sun 12 - 4

What's Your Stitch 'N Stuff, Inc.

5350 Kempsriver Dr. #104 23464
(757) 523-2711
Owners: Holly Erdei-Zuber & Irene Erdei
Over 2000 bolts!

100% Cotton Fabrics, Books, Patterns, Notions, Primitive Rug Hooking, Penny Rugs & Wool Applique.
PLUS ALWAYS FRIENDLY SERVICE!

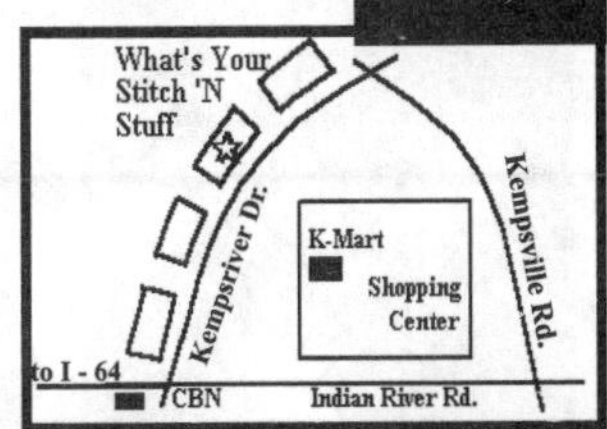

Cape Charles, VA #9

Mon - Sat 10 - 5

Quilts & More Fabric Outlet

27376 Lankford Hwy 23310
(757) 331-3642
Owner: Henrietta Morris
Est: 1990 3900 sq. ft.

Quilting, curtain, upholstery and clothing fabrics, also leather. Sewing supplies & notions. Much more at reasonable prices.

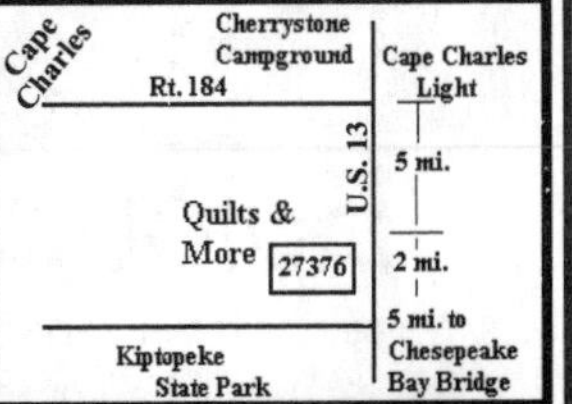

White Marsh, VA #10

Tues - Sat 10 - 6
Sun 12 - 5

Love2Quilt & More

4904 George Washington Mem. Hwy. 23183
(804) 695-2700 Fax: (804) 695-2616
love2quilt@inna.net
www.love2quilt.com
Owners: Diane & Thomas
Est: 2001 2000 sq.ft. 2000+ Bolts

Stop in to see Thomas (the cat), he "Loves" company. He caters to all Quilters, with lovely Quilt Fabrics, Books, Notions and Doo-Dads. He loves kids.

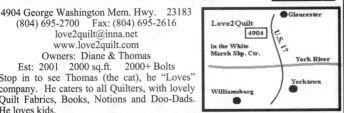

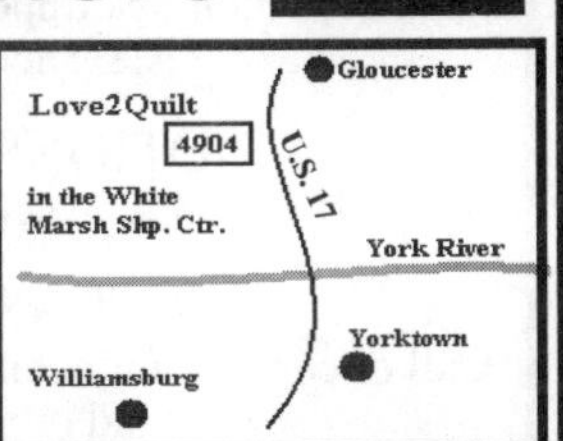

Fredericksburg, VA #11

Mon - Sat 10 - 5 or by Appt.

Quilter's Heaven

4622 Harrison Rd.. 22408
(540) 898-7302
Owners: Janice Fletcher
Est: 1998

Over 1500 Bolts, Books, Patterns & Notions.
Friendly Southern Hospitality.

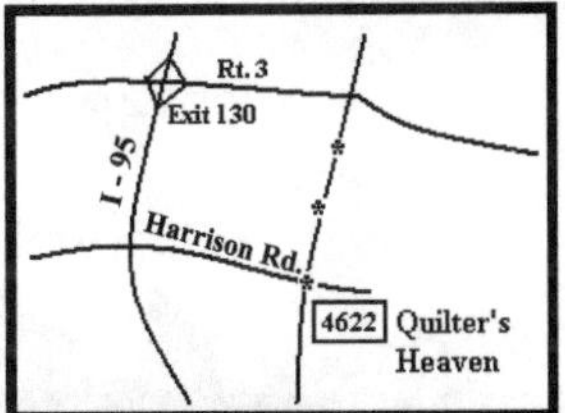

Fredericksburg, VA #12

Mon - Sat 10 - 5

Summit Sewing Center

3940 Plank Rd., Suite M 22407
(540) 548-2377 Fax: (540) 548-2910
summitsewing@aol.com
www.summitsewing.com
Est: 1999 2500 sq.ft. 2500+ bolts
Authorized Bernina & Janome Dealer
Authorized Horn Cabinet Dealer. Classes: Machine Guiding, Quilting, Wearable Art, Designer Software.

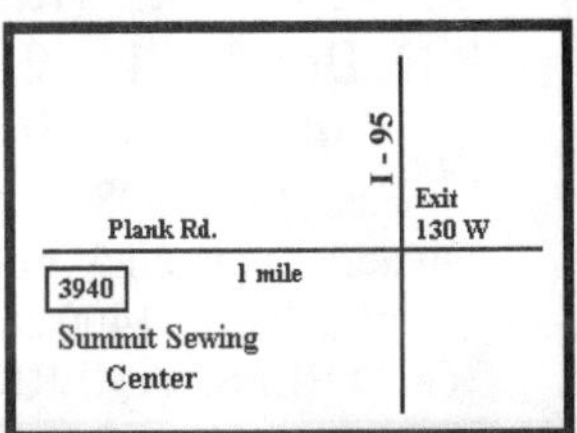

Alexandria, VA #13

Tues - Sat 11 - 5
Sun 1 - 5

Rocky Road to Kansas

215 South Union Street 22314
(703) 683-0116 Est: 1980
Owner: Dixie Kaufman

Large selection antique/vintage Quilts. Tops, Patches, Feedsacks. Quilt Related Items. Gifts and accessories. Vera Bradley Bags.

Visitors Center
Torpedo Factory Art Center
King St.
Fairfax St.
Lee St.
Union St.
Potomac River
Prince St.
Rocky Road to Kansas
215
Duke St.
In "The Carriage House" second floor

Woodbridge, VA #15

Please Call Ahead

Quilting Dreams by Belmont Bay

Opening Fall 2005
Harbor Side Street 22191
(571) 217-7546
Owner: Judith Taylor

Unique Quilt Shop for all Your Creative Fabric Needs.

2,500 bolts of 100% Cotton Quilting Fabrics, Quilting Supplies, Notions, Patterns and Books. Classes

The Quilt Patch

Bernina of Northern Virginia

(703) 273-6937
10381 Main St.
Fairfax VA
22030

www.quiltpatchva.com

Monday - Saturday 10 am - 5pm
Thursday 10 am - 8 pm

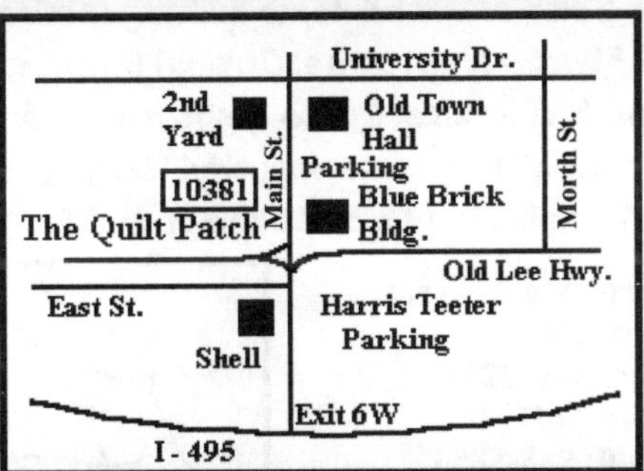

Fairfax, VA #14

Occoquan, VA #16

Epicurean Crafts

We specialize in carrying fabric lines representing Teresa Kogut, Nancy Halvorsen, Mary Engelbreit, Sandy Gervais, Memes Quilts, and Robyn Pandolph. We stock a variety of stitchery and quilt patterns, books, hand-dyed wools, quilt & rug kits, and specialty threads. We teach quilt & rug-hooking & scrapbook classes!

www.epicureancrafts.com
305 Mill Street, Occoquan, VA
(703) 490-0777

M-F 11-4:30
Sat 11-6 Sun 11:30-5:30

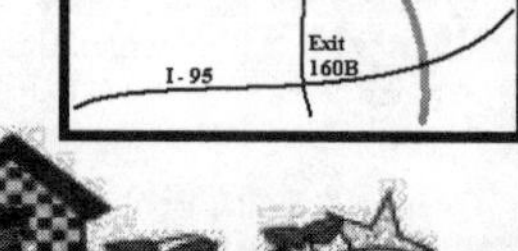

Learn the soothing therapy of creating a work of art. By hand or machine, a quilt is a future heirloom.

Stephen's City, VA #17

Shenandoah Quilt Patch

1000+ BOLTS OF FABRIC
Hoffman, Moda, Kona Bay, Maywood, Timeless Treasures, Batiks, South Sea Imports, RJR, Thimbleberries, Jinny Beyer, Alexander Henry and many more.

NOTIONS, BOOKS, PATTERNS
Large selection of quilting stencils

!!CLASSES AVAILABLE!!
Call or come in for details and times. Beginner classes available for hand or machine piecing and quilting.

10% discount to all current guild members.

Long Arm Quilting Available

Tues - Fri 10 - 4 Thurs til 6 Sat 10 - 2

5279 Main St. (Rt. 11)
P.O. Box 1284 22655
(540) 868-2150
Fax: (540) 868-2151
Owner: Yvonne E. Orndorff
Est: 2000 1400 sq.ft.
GOD BLESS AMERICA!

to Winchester
5279
Shenandoah Quilt Patch
2 1/2 Blocks North
Fairfax Pike
Hwy. 81
Exit 307
Hwy. 11
to Strasburg

Culpeper, VA #18

Tues & Thurs 7 - 9
Wed & Fri 10 - 2
Sat 9 - 4

Early Times Workshop

604 S. Main St., Suite 112 22701
(540) 829-7200
E-Mail: etwmwm@aol.com
Owner: Marty Moon Est: 1983

Specialty items for Special Needleworkers -- Quilting, Cross Stitch, Canvas work -- Books -- Classes
Hard-to-find notions and fibers -- Fabric
Personal Attention

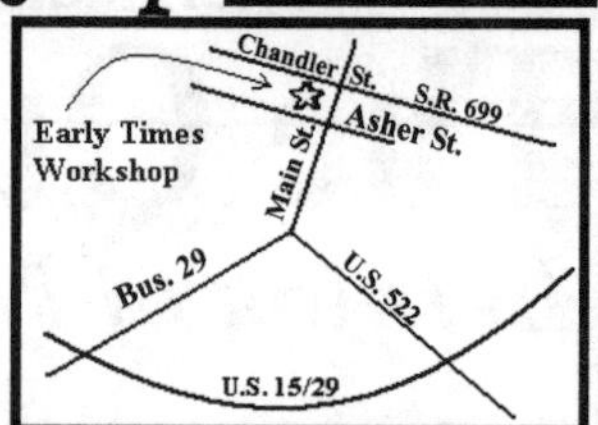

Madison, VA #19

MON--SAT 10-5 CLOSED SUN

That Little Quilt Shop

Established 1978

2000 + Bolts of Brand name quilting fabrics, hundreds of books & patterns. Original B.O.M.s, Redwork patterns & quilt kits. Quilts & gift items for sale. Classes for all levels in a beautiful 150 year old church 70 miles south of Washington D.C.

212 North Main Street
P.O. Box 274
Madison, VA 22727
(540) 948-4147
Fax: (540) 948-5853
Quiltshopmadison@aol.com
Owner: Gay Kulenguski

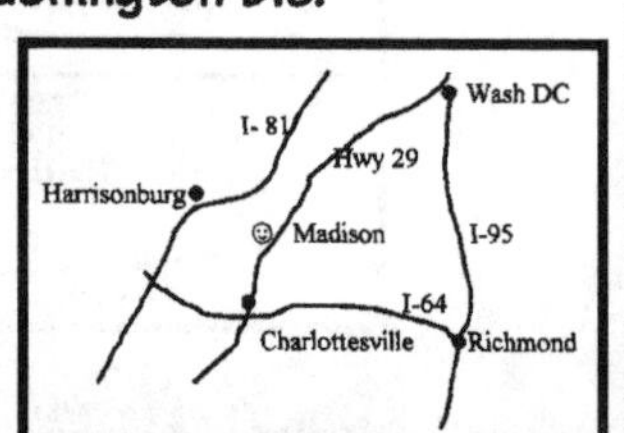

THE QUILT MAN

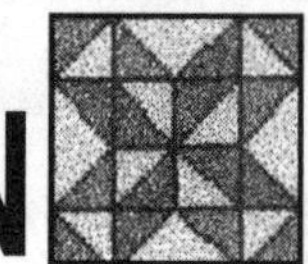

425 England St. 23005
804-798-6077
thequiltman1@aol.com
Est: 2002
1150 sq.ft. 2000+ bolts

Store Hours:
9:00 - 6:00 Mon - Fri
9:00 - 7:00 Thursday
9:00 - 4:00 Saturday
Closed on Sundays

Guild Discount -- Gift Certificates -- Frequent Buyer's Card

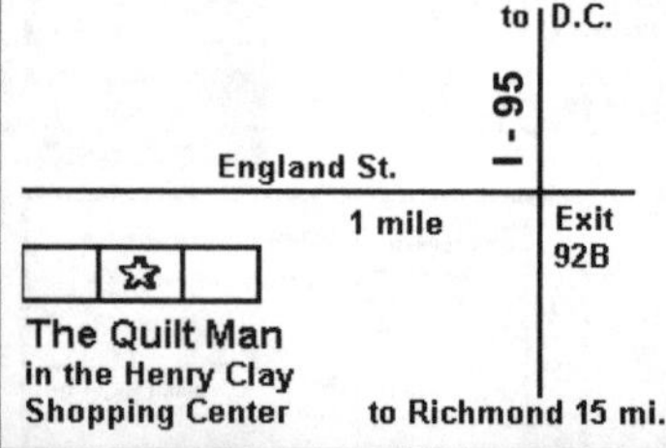

Quality Quilting Fabric, including Orientals, Batiks and 30's Reproductions, Books & Notions, Classes, Quilting Services Represented.

Ashland, VA #20

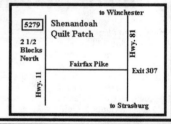

Charlottesville, VA #21

COTTONWOOD

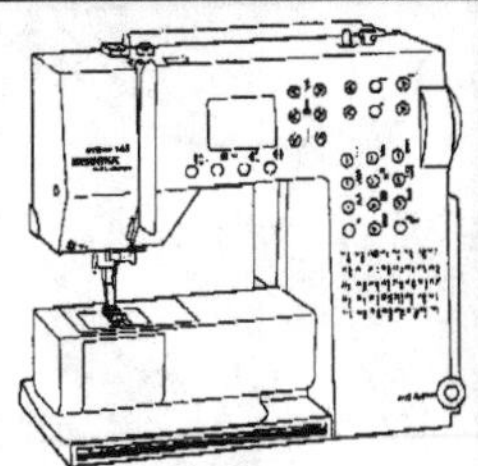

Meadowbrook Shopping Centre
2039 Barracks Road, Charlottesville, VA 22903
(434) 244-9975 fax: (434) 244-5072
E-Mail: mary@cottonwoodquiltsshop.com
Web Site: www.cottonwoodquiltshop.com
Est: 1995 1500 sq.ft.

Come visit our shop in **Charlottesville.**
Over 1800 Bolts of Quilting Cottons, Batiks,
Homespun Plaids, Flannels, Wools and Velvets
Books, Patterns, Supplies
Jasmine Quilt Frames
Gail Wilson Designs - Kits for Dolls, Angels, Santas and more
BERNINA Sewing and Embroidery Machines, Sergers
Embroidery Software, Service
Classes for Quilting, Rug Hooking,
Redwork and Primitive Stitchery

Shop Hours:
Mon - Sat 10:00 - 6:00 pm; Wed 10:00 - 8:00 pm
Sun 12:00 0 4:00 pm, September 1 - March 31
Closed Sunday, April 1 - August 31

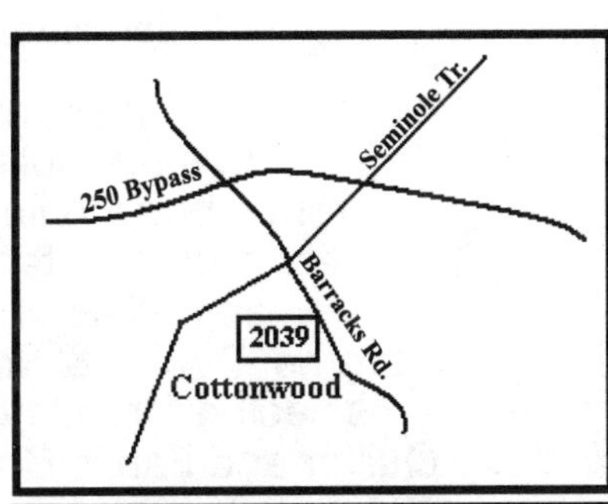

COTTONWOOD is located at the southeast corner of Emmet Street (Rt. 29) and Barracks Road in the Meadowbrook Shopping Centre.

Dayton, VA #22

HOURS: Mon--Wed 9-5
Thur--Sat 9-6
Closed Major Holidays

- **A Full Service Shop** offering the best of what quilters need
- **9,000 Sq. Ft.** Showroom, Classroom, Office & Service Area
- **Knowledgeable Staff** with over 600 years combined experience
- **Major Brands** of quality fabrics, notions, books, & patterns
- **A Full Line** of Bernina® sewing machines, sergers, embroidery machine, software and accessories

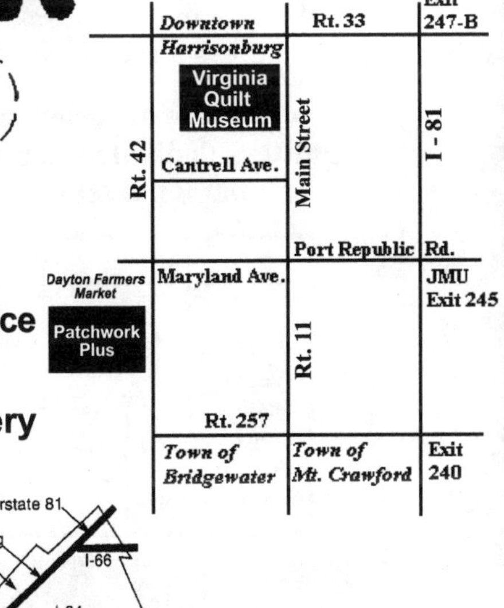

17 Killdeer Lane (off Rt. 42), Dayton, VA
(on the hill above Dayton Farmers Market)
Phone 540-879-2505
Toll Free 1-877-674-4821
E-mail: patchwrk@shentel.net

Rachel's QUILT PATCH

Enjoy a unique shop
in Historic Downtown Staunton
at the Train Station

Our shop features
100% cotton fabric collections
from top of the line
designers and manufacturers,
as well as
Patterns, Books, & Notions
selected for today's
Quilter and Fabric Crafter.

*Ask us about
ongoing classes for
quilters and crafters.
Custom made dinner napkins
and ties are available.*

40 Middlebrook Ave. 24401
(540) 886-7728
Owner: Rachel W. N. Brown
www.rachelsquiltpatch.com

Hours
Mon. Wed. Fri. & Sat.
10:00 a.m.- 5:00 p.m.
Tues. & Thurs.
10:00 a.m.- 8:00 p.m.

**We are experienced
quilters dedicated to offering
personal service.**

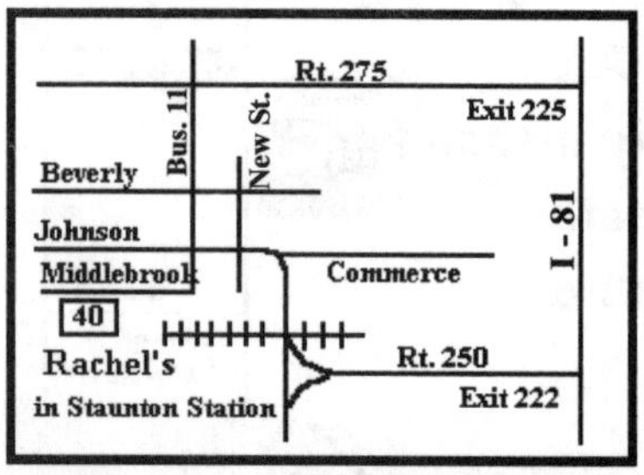

Rt. 275
Exit 225
Bus. 11
New St.
Beverly
Johnson
Middlebrook
Commerce
I - 81
40
Rachel's
in Staunton Station
Rt. 250
Exit 222

Staunton, VA #23

Harrisonburg, VA #24

Mon - Thur 9 - 5
Fri 9 - 6
Sat 9 - 4

60 W. Market St. 22801
(540) 434-5663
belle@ragtimefabrics.com
Owner:
Laura "Belle" Stemper
Est: 2003 4800 sq.ft.

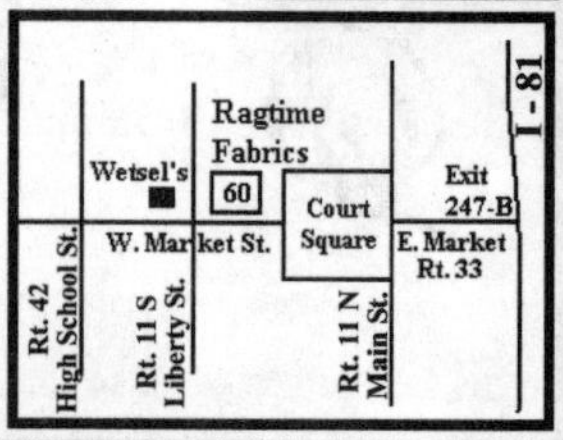

www.ragtimefabrics.com
A pennyworth fabric store for your priceless projects and heirlooms. Fabrics and trims for apparel, home decorations, costuming and handmade creations. Husqvarna/Viking Dealer.

Ragtime Fabrics
I - 81
Wetsel's
60
Court Square
Exit 247-B
W. Market St.
E. Market Rt. 33
Rt. 42 High School St.
Rt. 11 S Liberty St.
Rt. 11 N Main St.

"A Community Sewing Together"

2421 Stuarts Draft Hwy. 24477
540-324-0548 Fax: 540-324-0549
valleyfabrics@opexonline.com
Est: 2001 2500 sq.ft.

Stuarts Draft, VA #25

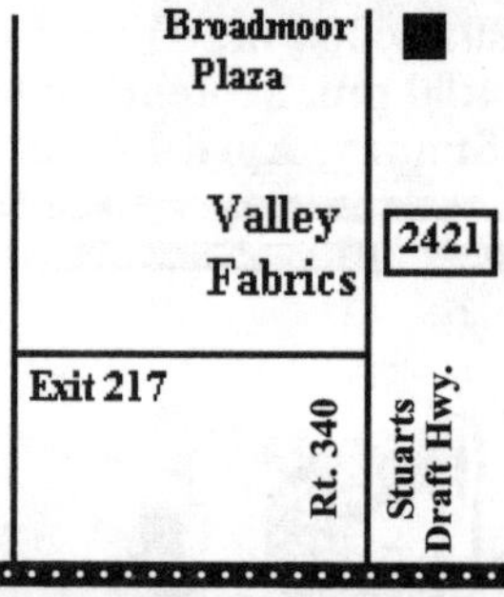

Broadmoor Plaza
I - 81
Valley Fabrics
2421
Exit 217
Rt. 340
Stuarts Draft Hwy.

We carry a full line of quilting and apparel fabrics, notions and upholstery.

Mon - Sat 9:30 - 5

Radford, VA #26

Mon - Sat 9 - 5:30
Thur til 8

92 & 94 Harvey St. 24141
(540) 639-1138
sewoften@aol.com
Est: 1981
3600 sq.ft.
2000+ Bolts
Web Site: www.sewbiz.com

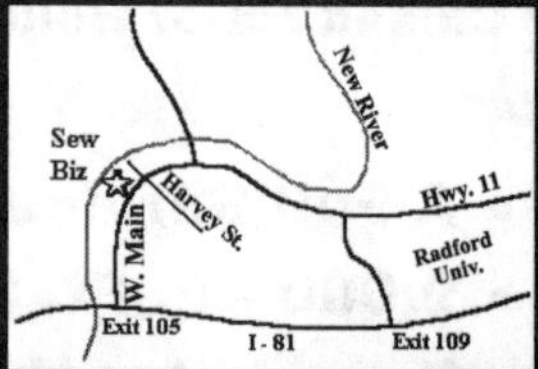

Two floors of beautiful fabrics for quilting and apparel. Historic building (1889). Extensive selection of books, patterns, tools, accessories for Bernina & Elna.

Floyd, VA #27

Mon - Sat 9 - 5:30

Schoolhouse Fabrics

"A Sewing Paradise"

220 N. Locust St. 24091 Est: 1971
(540) 745-4561 Fax: (540) 745-4168
Located in old School House built in 1911.
3 floors with 12 rooms filled with fabrics, patterns & books, notions, quilting frames, etc.

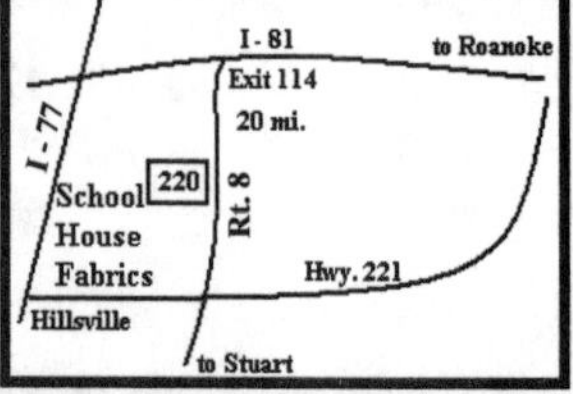

Old Trinity Schoolhouse Quilt Shop

QUILT SHOP

Broad Selection of Quilt Fabrics
(3500+ Bolts)
Including: Orientals, Batiks, Jinny Beyer,
Thimbleberries, Moda & many others.
Specialty:
Reproduction Fabrics (1780-1930)
Books:
Many with Historical Focus

Notions, Block of the Months,
Kits, and Classes

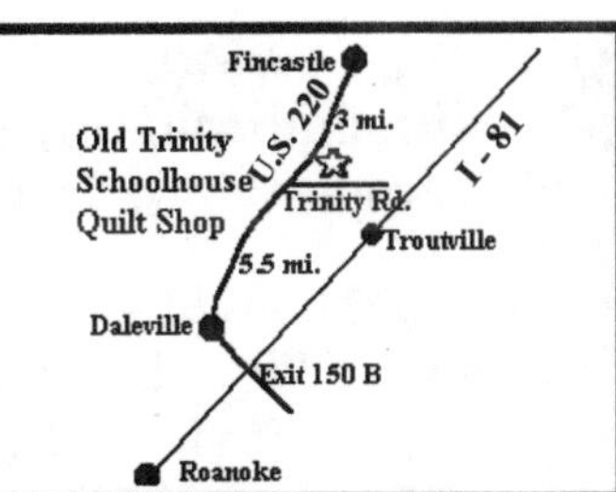

3200 Trinity Road, P.O. Box 189, Fincastle, VA 24090
Corner U.S. 220 and Trinity Rd. (540) 992-1233

Fincastle, VA #28

Mon - Sat 9 - 6

www.TrinityQuilts.com
Owners: Carolyn and Stan Nelson

Quilted Expressions Quilted Expressions

Lynchburg, VA #29

QUILTED EXPRESSIONS
& Sewing Possessions

3622 Old Forest Rd. 24501
(434) 385-6765
Mon.-Sat.:10am – 5pm, **Thurs:** 10am – 7pm

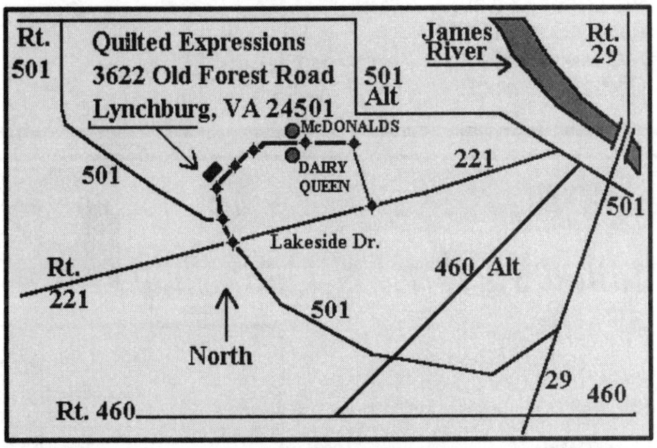

Rt. 501
Quilted Expressions
3622 Old Forest Road
Lynchburg, VA 24501
James River
Rt. 29
501 Alt
McDONALDS
DAIRY QUEEN
221
501
501
Lakeside Dr.
Rt. 221
460 Alt
501
North
29
460
Rt. 460

Internet: **www.quiltedexpressions.com**
Email: **info@quiltedexpressions.com**
Owners: **Roberta & Buddy Whitt**, Opened: 1992

More than **4000 bolts** of Top Quality 100% Cotton Fabrics, such as Batiks, Moda, Benartex, Thimbeberries. We also carry a wide range of Civil War and 30's prints. QE carries all the popular notions, patterns and books. We offer a variety of classes for quilting, sewing, heirloom and machine embroidery, from beginner to advanced. Join our friendly and courteous staff for all your quilting needs. Call for information on our fun birthday parties for you and your quilting friends.

Mail Order inquiries invited. We offer several kits with patterns and fabric included. Check out our website for more info.

Quilt Guilds/Clubs welcome - Please call ahead for us to prepare a special event for you.

Authorized Pfaff & Bernina Dealer
**** Sales and Service ****

Quilted Expressions Quilted Expressions

Stop by the Studio...

QUILT & SEW STUDIO

Quilting, Sewing, Machine Embroidery, Heirloom Sewing, Smocking

- Over 2,000 bolts of top-quality fabric
- Great selection of batiks and bright colors
- Notions, incl. the full line of Sulky & Mettler threads
- Viking Sewing and Embroidery Machines
- Large selection of multi-format embroidery designs
- Sewing cabinets and sewing chairs

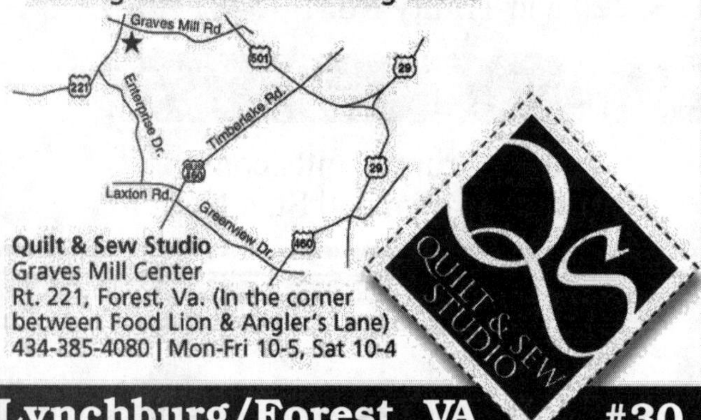

Quilt & Sew Studio
Graves Mill Center
Rt. 221, Forest, Va. (In the corner between Food Lion & Angler's Lane)
434-385-4080 | Mon-Fri 10-5, Sat 10-4

Lynchburg/Forest, VA #30

Roanoke, VA #31

Wed - Sat 10 - 5

Turkey Tracks Quilt Shop

6342-A Peters Creek Rd. 24019
(877) 599-0808
Web Site: www.turkeytracksquilts.com

Primitive/folk art quilting, cross stitch & rug hooking supplies. I-81 exit 143 to I-581, then Exit 2N onto Peters Creek Rd., then 1.5 miles on left.

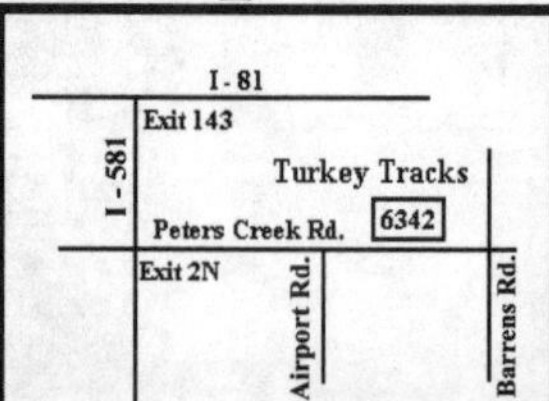

Boones Mill, VA #32

Tues - Sat 9:30 - 5:30

Boone's Country Store

2699 Jubal Early Hwy. 24065
(540) 721-2478
Owners: Randy & Elva Boone
Est: 1975 3588 sq.ft

Old Fashioned Quality -- Up to date Values. Calicoes, broad cloth, sheetings, quilting supplies, books, gifts. Homemade breads, pies, cakes & sweet rolls. 9 miles from Boones Mill.

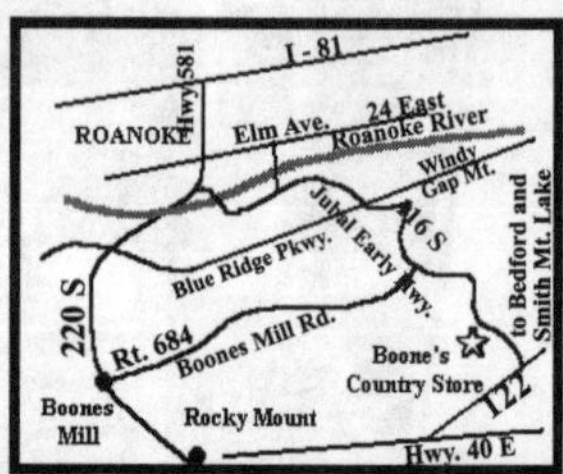

Wytheville, VA #33

Mon - Sat 10 - 5:30

Batiks Etcetera &

Sew What Fabrics

460 East Main Street, Wytheville, VA 24382
276-228-6400 or 800-228-4573 Fax: 276-228-9597
Owner: Carol C. Britt www.batiks.com info@batiks.com
Est: 1982 4200 sq.ft. 8000 bolts

The most complete retail source for batik fabrics! Batiks Etcetera & Sew What Fabrics is located in an 1840's home in old town Wytheville, VA Gourmet cottons, Indonesian, Malaysian & Indian batiks, flannel, specialty threads, notions, books and lively classes are available with expert, friendly assistance. Automatic shipment and swatch services are available. Check out our secure web site. Come have a ball!

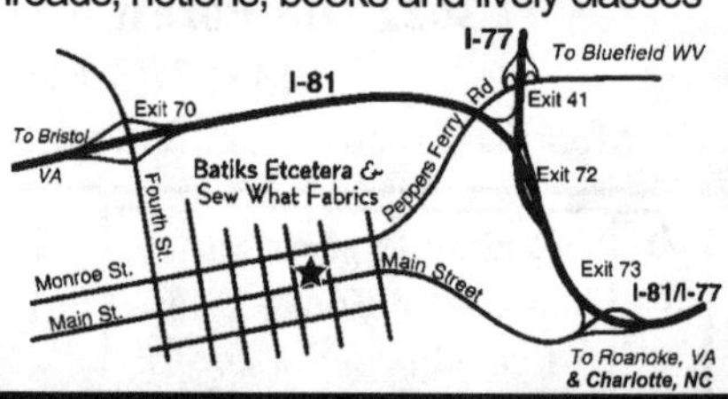

Hillsville, VA #34

Mountain Plains Fabrics

4505 Fancy Gap Hwy.
Hillsville, VA 24343
(276) 728-7517
www.mtnplainsfabrics.com

Quilting Fabric & Supplies * Quilt Frames
Buttons * Polyfoam * Lace * Drapery
Upholstery Material * Vinyl * Pillow Tops

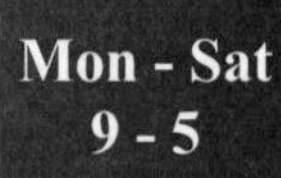

Mon - Sat 9 - 5

Est: 1960
8000 sq.ft. 2500 Bolts

Abingdon, VA #35

Mon - Fri 9:30 - 5:30
Sat 9:30 - 5

Jeannine's Fabrics & Quilt Shop

414 W. Main St. 24210
(276) 628-9586
Owners: Jeannine & Gene Widener
Est: 1968 3000 sq.ft. 1000+ Bolts

Full Line Quilting Supplies including 100% cotton from RJR, P&B, Hoffman, Springs, VIP, Concord, Fabri-Quilt.
Books, Patterns, Rulers, Stencils.

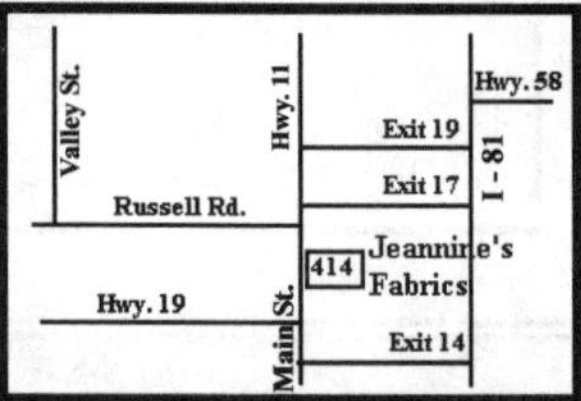

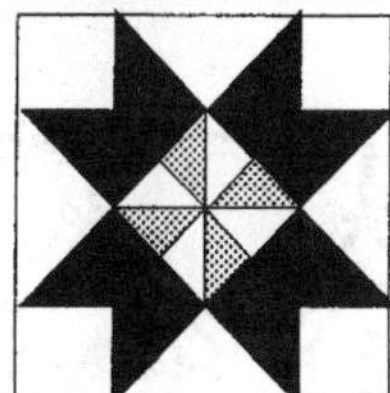

QUILTER'S CORNER

Richmond Area's Largest Quilt Shop

1318 Sycamore Square
(804) 794-1990
email: QuiltersCornerVA@aol.com

Owners: Sheddy & Bill Reese

Richmond's premiere quilt shop. We carry a wide selection of 100% cotton fabric plus everything for all your quilting needs.

Mon-Sat 10-5	**Est: 1998**
Thu til 7	**2400+ sq.ft.**
Sun 1-4	**3000+ Bolts**

Sycamore Square is a delightful shopping village with many unique shops and restaurants.

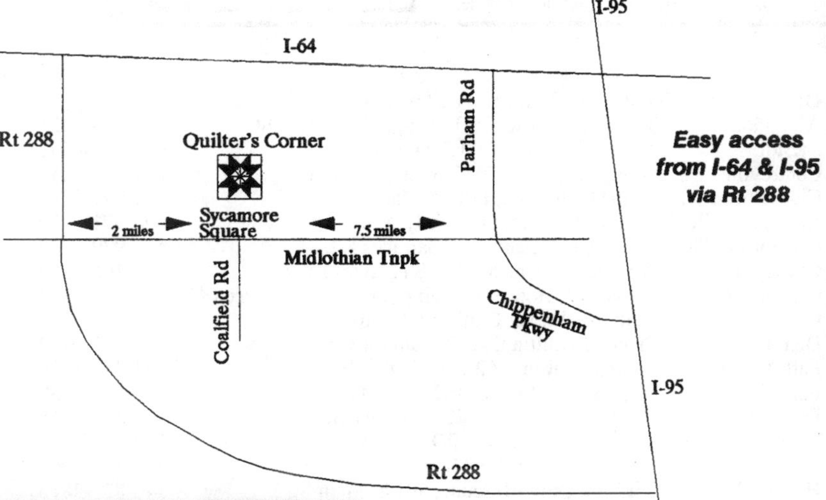

Easy access from I-64 & I-95 via Rt 288

Midlothian, VA #36

#37 The Busy Bea

Est: 1976

Bea & Cathy Chase

11934 Centre St., Chester, Va.

(804) 748-4951

Mon.-Fri., 8:30-6:00
Sat., 8:30-4:00
Closed Sun.

Fax: **(804) 748-2126**
Email: **cathy.bea.chase @worldnet.att.net**

Mettler Threads

3,000 bolts of 100% cotton fabric, Notions, books & assorted supplies

elna

Elna Sewing Machines

Quilting Frames

Horn

Sewing Cabinets

Cathy is a certified teacher in Eleanor Burns..."QUILT IN A DAY" Techniques

Pre-Beginner to Post-Grad Classes

Just South of Richmond I-95: Take the Chester (61B) Exit, Rt. 10 West. Start counting traffic lights. Turn RIGHT at light #6 (approximately 2 miles). We are the 2nd business on left.

I-295: Take the Chester (15B) exit. Rt. 10 West. Start counting traffic lights. Turn RIGHT at light #10 (approximately 6 miles). We are the 2nd business on left.

From Western Part of State: Follow I-64 East to I-95 South to Chester, then follow I-95 directions.

Martinsville, VA #38

Mon - Fri 8:30 - 5
Sat 10 - 2

The Sewing Studio, Inc.

1310 S. Memorial Blvd. 24112
(276) 632-5700 Fax: Same
jfeeny@sitestar.net
www.thesewingstudio.com
Owner: Brenda S. Feeny
Est: 1992 5000 sq.ft. 1700+ Bolts

Large selection of fabric, books & notions.
BabyLock dealer. Sales - Service. Classes.

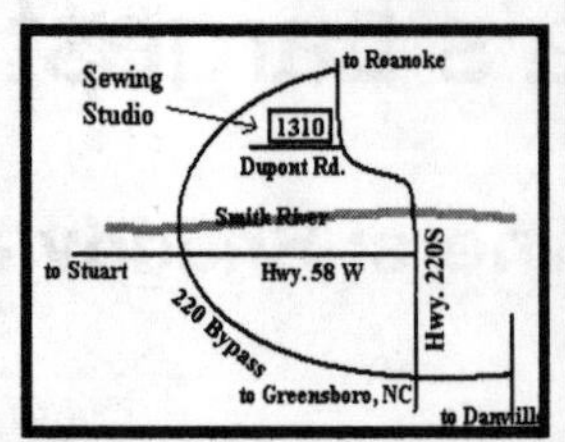

Other Shops in Virginia: *We suggest calling first*

Abingdon	The Cave House Craft Shop, 279 E. Main St.	540-628-7721
Bristol	The Quilt Shop, 2000 Euclid Ave.	540-466-8552
Centreville	G Street Fabrics, 5077 Westfields Blvd.	703-818-8090
Charlottesville	Quilts Unlimited, 118 W. Main St.	434-979-0025
Charlottesville	Cottage Clothes, 946 Grady Ave	804-971-7119
Charlottesville	Quilts Unlimited, 2128 Barracks Rd.	434-979-8110
Chesapeake	A Different Touch, 1107 S Military Hwy	757-366-8830
Clarksville	Patchwork House, 315 Virginia Ave. P.O. Box 1477	804-374-5942
Council	Betty's Fabric & Crafts HC4, Box 57	
Danville	Pieceful Quilting, 4062 Franklin Trpk.	434-835-0440
Falls Church	G Street Fabrics, 6250 Arlington Blvd.	703-241-1700
Falls Church	Appalachian Spring, 102 W. Jefferson St.	703-533-0930
Fredericksburg	Quilts 'N' Treasures, 721 Caroline St.	540-371-8166
Fredericksburg	The Virginia Quilter, PO Box 83	540-548-3207
Gainesville	Quilting Cellar, 4198 Stepney Dr.	703-354-2061
Harrisonburg	Virginia Quilt Museum , 301 S. Main St.	540-433-3818
Hot Springs	Quilts Unlimited, Cottage Row	540-839-5955
Kilmarnock	The Briar Patch, 81 N. Main St., P.O. Box 2040	804-435-9065
Leesburg	Loudoun Quilt Shop, 26 S King St	703-777-0720
Mechanicsville	Quilt Shack, 8107 Mechanicsville Tpke.	804-559-1992
Mechanicsville	Millstone Quilts, 4348 Fox Hunter Ln	804-781-0768
Middletown	The Quilt Shop, Belle Grove Plantation, Rte. 11	540-869-2028
Newport News	Colonial Quilt Works, 171 Little John Pl.	757-872-0538
Oaktown	Merryvale, 11416 Vale Rd	703-264-8959
Occoquan	Treasures from the Heart, 304 Mill St	703-481-5091
Roanoke	Creative Quilting, 2825 Brambleton Ave SW	540-772-2757
Rocky Mount	Fabric Mill Outlet, 453 S. Main St.	540-483-2822
Salem	Quilt Sand Crafts, 1306 Roanoke Blvd.	540-387-0339
Vienna	Vienna Quilt Shop, 396 Maple Ave. E	703-281-4091
Virginia Beach	Nimble Thimble, 2245 W Great Neck Rd	757-481-1725
Williamsburg	Quilts Unlimited, 440A W. Duke of Gloucester St.	757-253-8700

Virginia Guilds:

Abingdon	Wolf Hills Quilters, P.O. Box 1584 24212	Meets: 2nd Saturday 10 a.m. at Abingdon United Methodist Church
Appomattox	Courthouse Quilters, PO Box 11	Meets: 4th Monday 6:30pm at Everything Beautiful Quilt Shop
Charlottesville	Moonlighters	Meets: 2nd & 4th Wednesday 7pm at Cottonwood Quilt Shop
Charlottesville	Crozet Quilters	Meets: 2nd & 4th Monday 10am at Meadows in Crozet
Charlottesville	Courthouse Steps	Meets: 1st & 3rd Tuesday 1pm at Cottonwood Quilt Shop
Charlottesville	Tuesday Morning	Meets: Every Tuesday 10am at Aldersgate United Methodist Church
Deltaville	Stingray Stitchers, HCR - 1, Box 321-A 23043	Meets: 1st Monday 7 p.m. at Deltaville Public Library
Dry Fork	White Oak Mountain Quilters	
Fredericksburg	Virginia Star Quilters Guild 22402	
Harrisonburg	Shenandoah Valley Quilters Guild, P.O. Box 913, 22801	Meets: 3rd Saturday 9 a.m. at Highlands Bldg., Sunnyside Presbyterian
Heathsville	Tavern Quilt Guild	Meets: 1st Tuesday 10 a.m. at Historical Society Building
Keezletown	Shenandoah Valley Quilters Guild	
Lynchburg	The Virginia Reel Quilters	
Madison	Madison County Quilters Guild, P.O. Box 452, 22727	
Martinsville	Virginia Foothills Quilt Guild, Starling Ave., 24112	Meets: 2nd Tuesday 6:30 p.m. at Piedmont Arts Association, Starling Ave.
Newport News	Peninsula Piecemakers Quilt Guild, P.O. Box 1295, 23601	Meets: 2nd Friday 10am at Yorkminster Presbyt. Church - 2nd Tuesday 7pm Northhampton Comm Center, Hampton VA
Norfolk	Tidewater Quilters Guild	Meets: 1st Monday 7 p.m. at Azalea Baptist Church, Little Creek Rd.
Richmond	Richmond Quilter's Guild	
Roanoke	Star Quilters Guild, P.O. Box 5276 24012	
Roanoke	Blue Ridge Quilters, 28 Avery Rd. 24012	Meets: 2nd Tuesday 7 p.m. at Blue Ridge Library
Rocky Mount	Lake Quilters Guild	Meets: 4th Tuesday 3 p.m. at Halesford Baptist Church
Virginia Beach	Tidewater Quilters Guild, P.O. Box 62635 23462	
Woodbridge	Cabin Branch Quilters, P.O. Box 1547 22193	
Yorktown	Colonial Piecemakers, 201 Yorkview Rd. 23692	

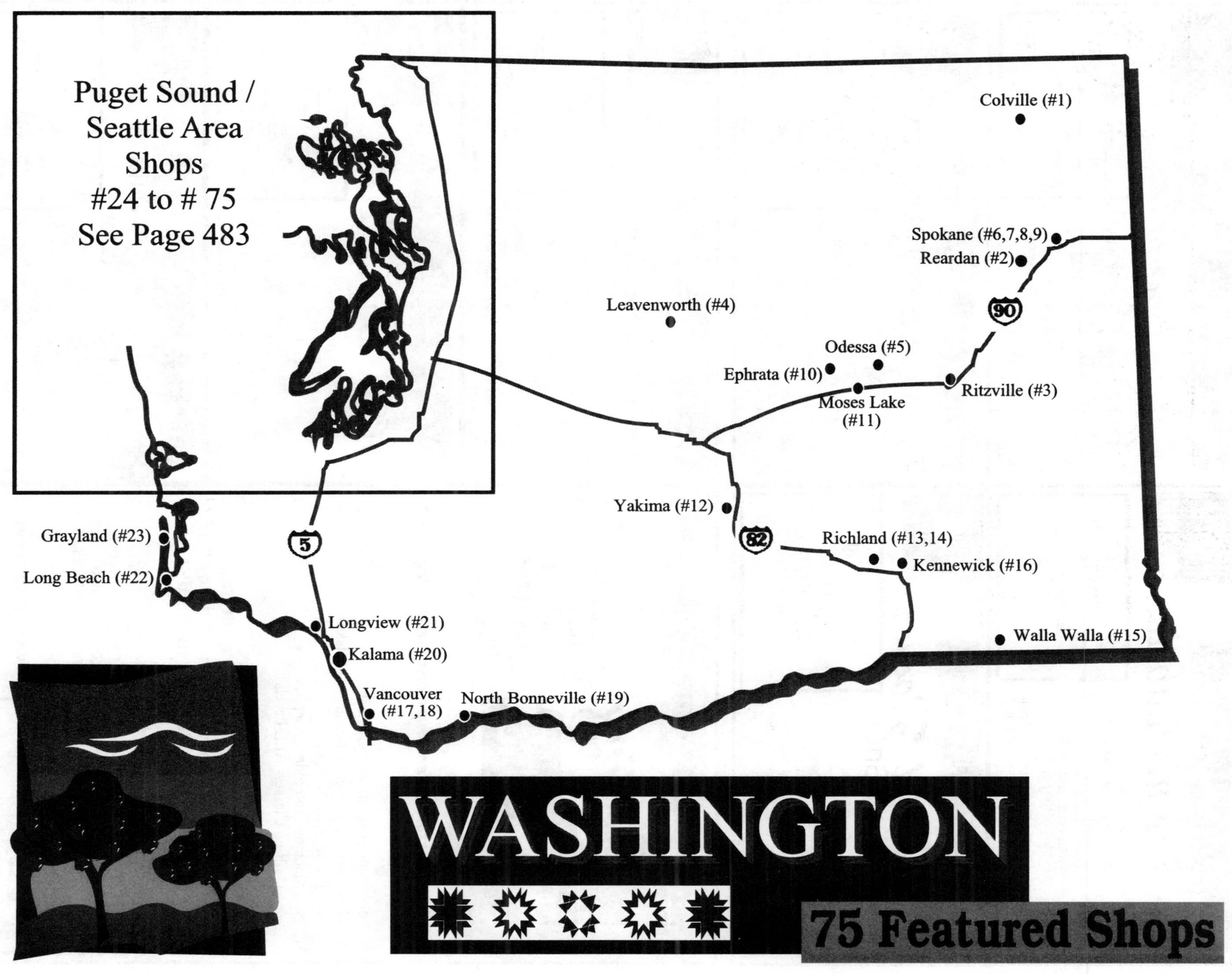
Puget Sound / Seattle Area Shops #24 to # 75 See Page 483
Colville (#1)
Spokane (#6,7,8,9)
Reardan (#2)
90
Leavenworth (#4)
Odessa (#5)
Ephrata (#10)
Moses Lake (#11)
Ritzville (#3)
Yakima (#12)
82
Richland (#13,14)
Kennewick (#16)
Walla Walla (#15)
Grayland (#23)
Long Beach (#22)
5
Longview (#21)
Kalama (#20)
Vancouver (#17,18)
North Bonneville (#19)
WASHINGTON
75 Featured Shops

Colville, WA #1

Mon - Sat 9 - 5:30

E - Z Knit Fabrics

165 N. Main 99114
(509) 684-2644 Fax: (509) 684-6659
ezknit.com
www.ezknit.com
Owners: Vickie Black & Helen West
Est: 1969 3000 sq.ft.

3 stores in one — Beads — Fabrics — Yarn
One of the largest selections of fabric in Washington.

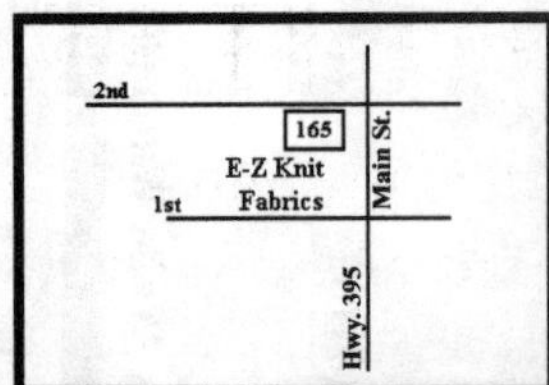

Reardan, WA #2

Tues - Sat 10 - 5

28848 Tramm Rd. N
99029
(509) 796-2188

www.buggybarnquilts.com
Owners: Pam Soliday & Janet Nesbitt

Unique Quilt Shop in the Country. Featured Shop in *Patchwork & Quilting* May 2002

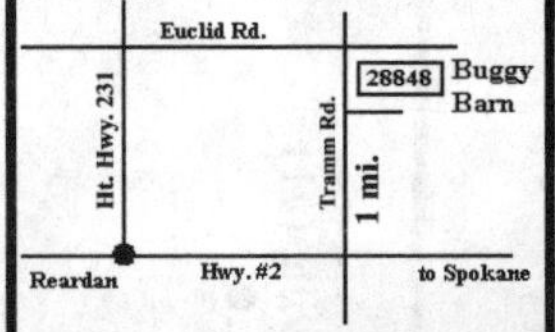

Ritzville, WA #3

Mon - Fri 10 - 5
Sat 10 - 4

Wild Flowers
Quilt Shop

201 E. Main St. 99169
(509) 659-4450
wildflowers@ritzville.com
Owner: Ami Danekas Est: 2003

More than a Quilt Shop! Great customer service. Antiques, gifts, fabrics, notions, patterns. Espresso. All of this in a lovely old Victorian Home in downtown Ritzville.

1 miles off of
I - 90 in
Downtown
Ritzville

Leavenworth, WA #4

All Year 9 a.m. to 6 p.m.

Dee's Country Accents

917 Commercial St. 98826
(800) 253-8990
E-Mail: info@quiltersheaven.com
Web Site: www.quiltersheaven.com
Owners: Dee & Al Howie
Est: 1987 1500 Bolts

Incredible Fabrics, Largest selection in the Pacific Northwest of Quilt Books and Patterns. PLUS a Bed & Breakfast decorated with quilts and antiques.

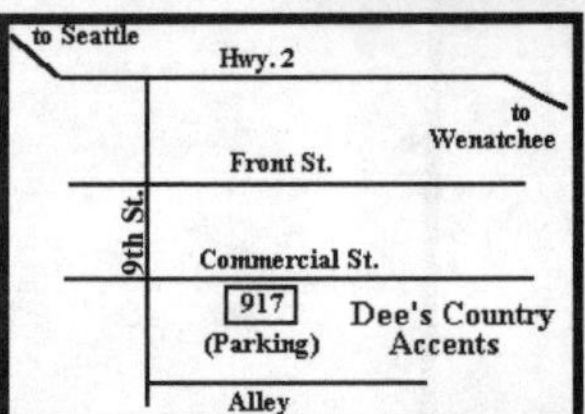

Spokane, WA #6

Store Hours
M-F 10:00-8:00
Sat 10:00-5:30
Sun 12:00-5:00

"Where lasting friendships are pieced together"

- Authorized BERNINA Dealer
- Machine Service & Repair – All Makes
- Fabric, Kits, Notions
- Machine Embroidery Supplies
- Quilting Classes- ALL Levels

1998 Award Winning Quilt Shop
"American Patchwork and Quilting"
The 10 Best Quilt Shops in the USA

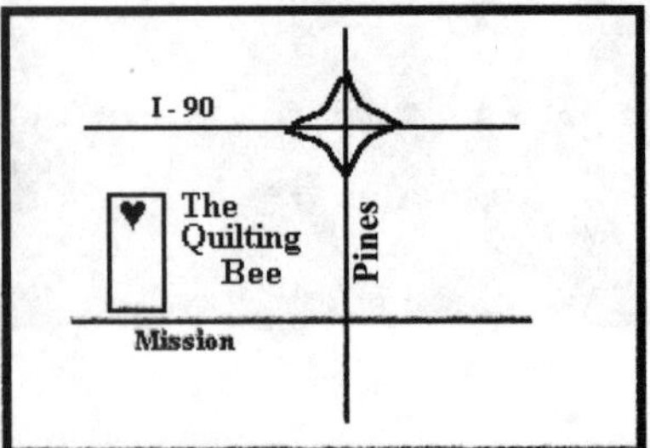

12117 E. Mission
Spokane, WA 99206
Phone 1-888-928-6037

www.quiltingbeespokane.com

Odessa, WA #5

Mon - Fri 10 - 5
Sat 10 - 4

the Quilt Crossing

4 W. First Ave., P.O. Box 206 99159
(509) 982-2194 Fax: (509) 982-2623
schmidtinsurance@odessaoffice.com
Owner: Lois Fisher

100% Cotton Fabrics, Patterns, Books, Stencils & Notions. Cross stitch & silk Ribbon embroidery supplies. Classes, "Sew Much Fun" quilt-ins. Free Newsletter.

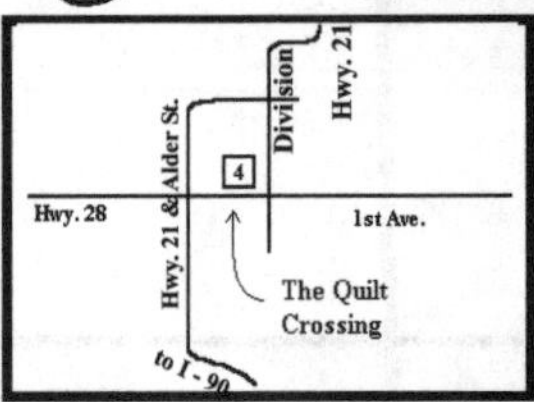

Spokane, WA #7

Mon - Thur 9 - 7
Fri & Sat 9 - 6

Sew E-Z, Too

603 W. Garland 99205
(877) 417-4694 or (509) 325-6644
www.ezknit.com
Owner: Vickie Black
Est: 1997

Designer Fabrics and More.
Large selection quality cottons, books, patterns.

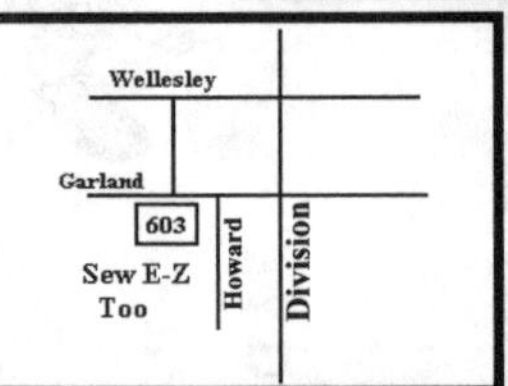

Spokane, WA #8

Mon - Sat 9:30 - 5:30

Kaleidoscope Quilting
& Home Decor

1011 E. 2nd Ave. #3 99202
(509) 456-7375 Fax: (509) 444-7333
quilting@kquilting.com
www.kquilting.com
Est: 2000 3500 sq.ft. 2000 Bolts

Just off I - 90, near downtown Spokane. Fabric, Notions, Patterns, Books, Classes, Completed Quilts, Wall Hangings, Kits, Racks, Gifts, Home Décor.

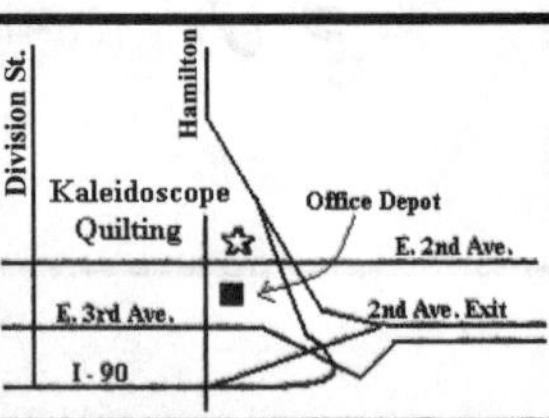

Spokane's

QUALITY SHOP FOR QUILTERS

Mon - Fri 10 - 8
Sat 10 - 6
Sun 11 - 5

Great fabric, Books, patterns and notions.
We provide mail order service anywhere.
Warm, friendly service in a bright & sunny shop.

(509) 484-4808

7454 N. Division 99208

Fax #: (509) 484-4918
pcq@pcqspokane.com
www.pcqspokane.com

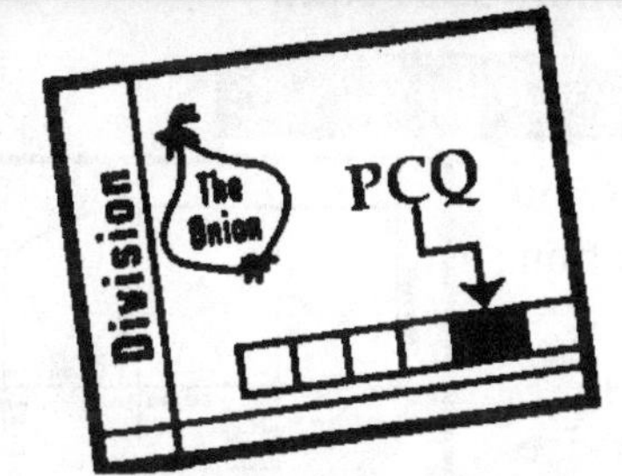

Owner: Sandy McCauley
Est: 1995 4000 sq.ft.
5000 Bolts

Spokane, WA #9

Quality Fabric & Notions for Quilting & Fabric Crafts

The Fabric Patch

11th Ave.
Basin St.
"C" St.
10th Ave.
220
The Fabric Patch
9th Ave.

Ephrata, WA #10

220 Tenth Ave. SW, Ephrata, WA 98823
509-754-8280
www.fabricpatch.net
rang@crcwnet.com Est: 1999 2500 sq.ft.
Owners: Cindi & Brianna Rang

3500+ bolts of 100% cotton in Batiks, flannels, novelties and more. 900+ book titles. Complete line of notions and hundreds of patterns. Extensive classroom schedule. Finished samples for sale.

We own two 14 foot Gammill long arm machines that are available for customer use. (Reservations are required) Machine quilt your quilt top in a few hours, or send it in for us to complete.

Columbia Basin Quiltworks

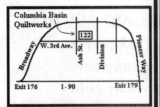

AUTHORIZED BERNINA SALES & SERVICE. A FRIENDLY QUILT STORE WITH 100'S OF BOOKS & PATTERNS PLUS UNFINISHED FURNITURE. LOCATED IN DOWNTOWN MOSES LAKE.

Mon - Fri 10 - 5:30
Sat 10 - 5

122 W. 3rd Ave. 98837
(509) 764-2238
sew2000.com/cbquiltworks
bernina@cbquiltworks.com
Owner: Connie Lindell
Est: 1998
4500 sq.ft. 2500+ Bolts

Columbia Basin Quiltworks
122
W. 3rd Ave.
Broadway
Ash St.
Division
Pioneer Way
Exit 176
I-90
Exit 179

Moses Lake, WA #11

Yakima, WA #12

BERNINA
Sewing Center & Firehouse Fabrics

103 S. 7th Ave. 98902
(509) 248-0078 Fax: (509) 248-0348
E-Mail: bernina@wolfenet.com
Owners: Brad & Sue McMillan
Est: 1968 3500 sq.ft.

Mon - Fri 9 - 5:30 Sat 9 - 5

Over 2500 Bolts of Quilt Fabric. Large Selection of Books, Patterns, Notions, Classes. Bernina Sales & Service.

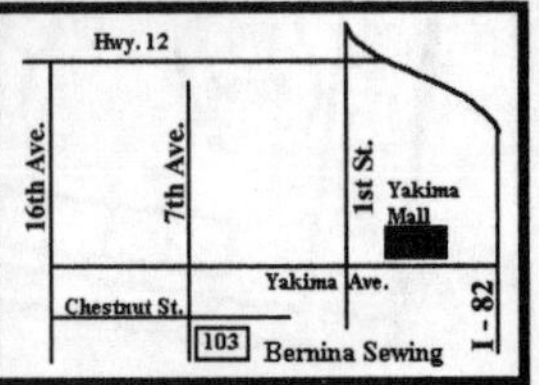

Village Quiltworks

Richland, WA #13

QUEENSGATE VILLAGE
1950 Keene Road, Suite B, Richland, WA 99352
(509) 628-0652
Est: 2001 3000 sq.ft. Over 2000 bolts

Web Site:
www.villagequiltworks.com

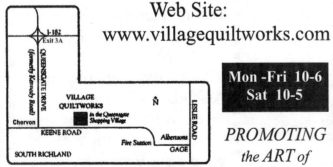

I-182
Exit 3A
QUEENSGATE DRIVE (formerly Kennedy Road)
VILLAGE QUILTWORKS in the Queensgate Shopping Village
N
LESLIE ROAD
Chervon
KEENE ROAD
Fire Station
Albertsons
GAGE
SOUTH RICHLAND

Mon -Fri 10-6
Sat 10-5

PROMOTING the ART of QUILTING

Village Quiltworks is a full service quilt shop located in a charming walk-through shopping village.

OFFERING
Unique fabrics • Large selection of batting • Classes • Machine quilting service • Friendly & helpful staff

Richland, WA #14

Quiltmania!!

1442 Jadwin Ave. #C
99352
(509) 946-PINS (7467)
Owner: Debi Merhar
Est: 1991 2000 Bolts

Mon - Thur 10 - 9
Fri & Sat 10 - 5

Classes, Notions, Fabric. Over 600 book titles to choose from.
Quilts for Sale.

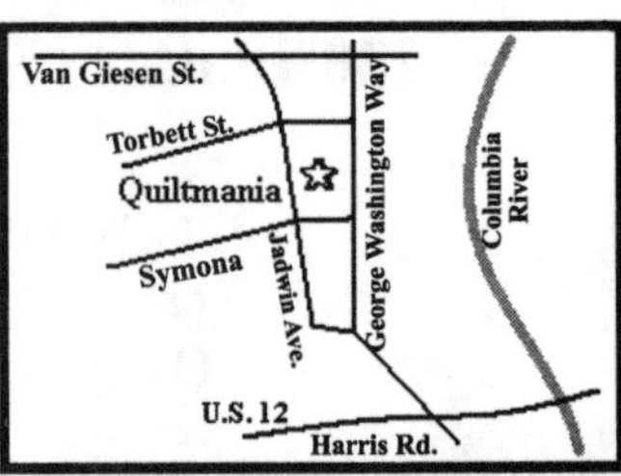

Walla Walla, WA #15

FabriCity (a quilt shop)

Mon - Fri 10 - 5:30
Sat 10 - 4
Summer til 5

47 E. Main St. 99362
(509) 526-5564
Est: 1998 1200 sq.ft.

Our specialty is Quilting in all aspects: fabrics, books, patterns and most importantly; friendly, knowledgeable service.

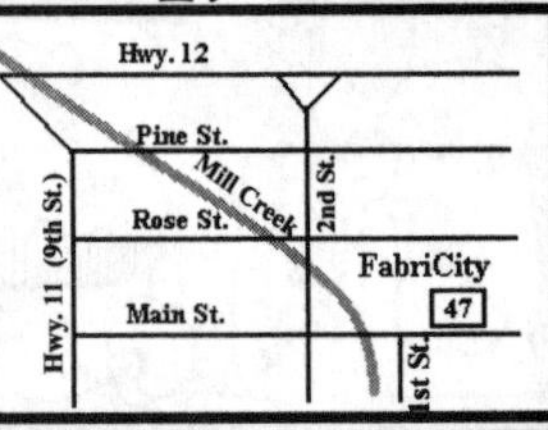

Est: 1991

Kennewick, WA #16

5215 W. Clearwater #106
Marineland Village 99336
(509) 735-6080
Owners: Terry Burkhart
& Barbara Ward
Mon - Fri 10 - 5:30
Sat 10 - 5

Pieceable Dry Goods

"A Country Quilt Store"
Selected by American Patchwork & Quilting magazine as one of the Top 10 Quilt Shops for 1998.

As you step into our cozy country quilt store you'll be inspired by numerous samples and country displays. The courteous and professional staff will help you create your quilt from our large selection of over 2000 bolts of fabric. Specializing in the "Country" look, from Romantic florals to primitive folk art. You'll love our great homespun plaids and extensive selection of primitive stitchery, quit patterns, historical books, wool felt and wool rug hooking.

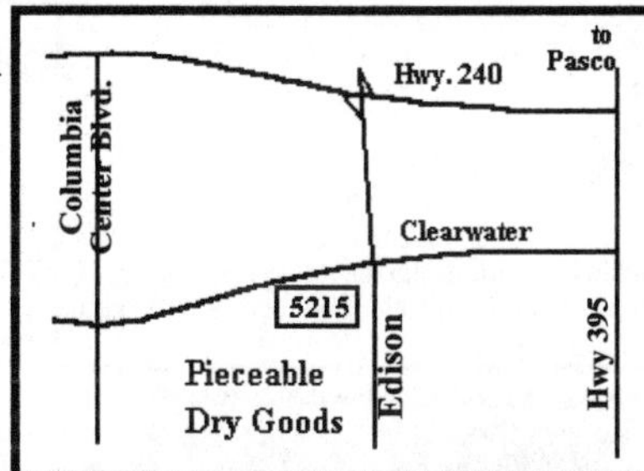

Country Living Quilts

A series of nap-size quilt kits designed by the staff of Pieceable Dry Goods. These quilts capture that primitive antique scrap look we love. Each quilt reminds you of a treasure found in a family trunk or in an antique shop. We add a few new ones each year.

No matter what your age...It's time to start quilting!

Connecting  Threads

 **You've enjoyed our catalog, now see our store!** 

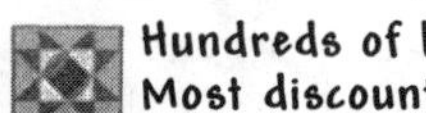
Hundreds of books! Most discounted 20%

Hundreds of Tools!

Latest fabric collections All 100% cotton!

Exculsive Quilt Kits with Free Patterns included!

Great Bargains! Catalog fabric overstocks arrive daily!

Open 10 am - 6 pm Monday - Friday, 10 am - 5 pm Saturday

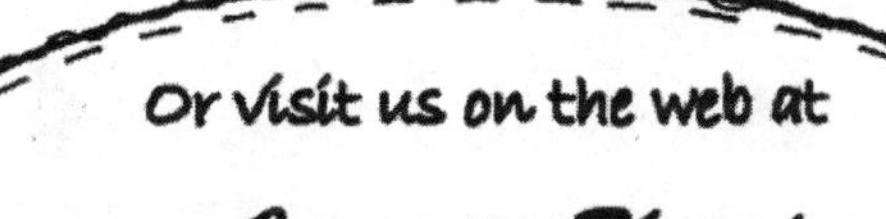

Or visit us on the web at
www.ConnectingThreads.com

View the inside pages of hundreds of books and patterns before you buy. Check out every fabric in stock and compare colors and values with 4 different views on our design table. Choose from thousands of tools, notions and supplies. Free pattern downloads!

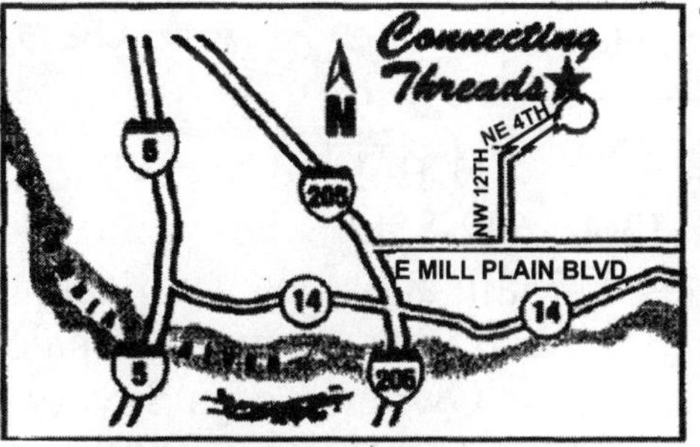

Conveniently located just 10 minutes from the Portland Airport, 20 minutes from downtown Portland.

13118 NE 4th Street
Vancouver, WA 98684
360-260-8900 • 800-574-6454
Call for a free catalog!

Vancouver, WA #17

Vancouver, WA #18

Mon - Fri 9 - 5:30 Sat 9 - 5

Quilt-n-Stitch

808 SE Chkalov Dr. #3 98683
(888) 800-8791 fax: (360) 896-4722
www.quilt-n-stitch.com
Owner: Betty Markee Est: 2000

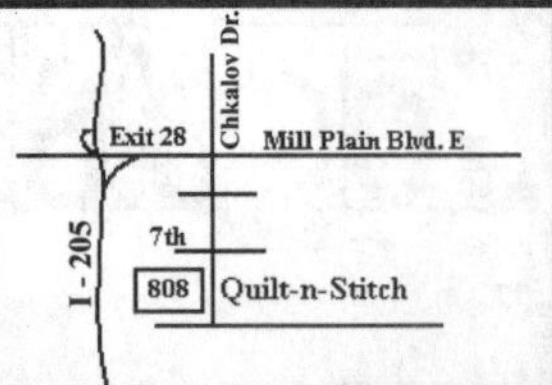

A full line of quilting fabric and supplies. Unique kits and patterns designed by our staff. Fun and friendly group.

North Bonneville, WA #19

Tues - Sat 10 - 6

Quilters Landing

72 Cascade Mall Dr. 98639
(509) 427-7581 Fax: (509) 427-7641
E-Mail: ottoslanding@yahoo.com
Web Site: www.quilters-landing.com
Owner: Linda Otto Est: 2001

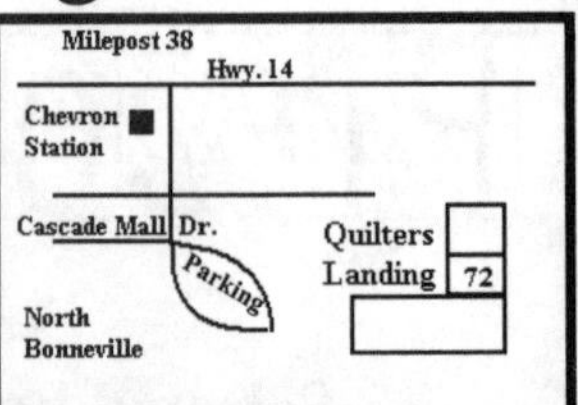

Fabrics, Notions, Books, Patterns, Gifts
All in a park like setting in the Columbia River Gorge--Classes, Friendly Service.

Kalama, WA #20

Mon - Sat 10 - 5

THE NINE PATCH

384 N. 1st St. 98625
(360) 673-1725 Fax: (360) 673-1739
E-Mail: theninepatch@kalama.com
Web Site: www.TheNinePatch.net
Owners: Jackie Jamison & LeeAnn Hadaller
Est: 2001 1600 sq.ft.

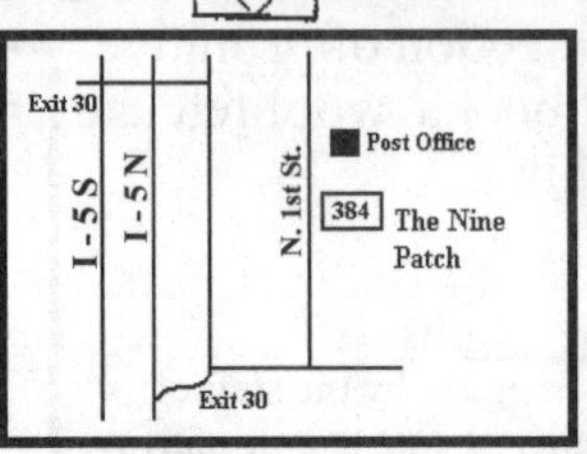

Our shop has successfully joined the established 'Antique District' and we carry all the fabrics and notions needed to get you started quilting.

A charming 1930's cottage filled to the brim with over 1,500 bolts of traditional fabrics and quilts. Established in 1996.

2035 9th Ave. Longview, WA 98632
360-636-5631 www.mommamadeit.com

Directions: From I-5 take Exit #39.
Follow the signs to Hwy 4 West (Ocean Beaches)
At Taco Time turn left on 9th Ave.
2nd little house on the right.

Hours:
Mon. – Thur. 10 – 6
Fri. 10 – 5 Sat. 10 – 4

Longview, WA #21

Long Beach, WA #22

7 Days a Week 10 - 5:30

A full line of quilting fabrics & notions including over 300 bolts of 1930's reproductions & our own line of 30's patterns.

We make our own fudge.

111 Bolstad Ave. 98631
(360) 642-8585 Fax: (360) 642-8948
E-Mail: annalena@willapabay.org
Web Site: www.annalena.com
Owner: Karen Snyder
Est: 1998 6000 sq.ft. 3000 Bolts

We're at the end of the Lewis & Clark Trail! Come see why we're worth the trip!

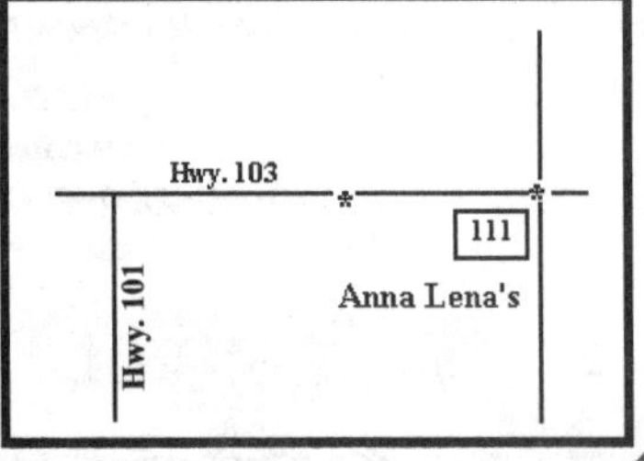

Grayland, WA #23

Est: 1999

Quilt Harbor

2172 St. Rt. 105, P.O. Box 771 98547
Toll Free (877) 676-3300
(360) 267-3300 Fax: (360) 267-0129
E-Mail: quiltharbor@olynet.com
Web Site: www.quilt-harbor.com
Owner: Elizabeth McElliott

Mon - Sat 10 - 5 Sun 12 - 4 Summer Sun 10 - 4

1200 sq.ft. of over 2000 bolts of 100% cotton Fabrics, Notions, Books & Patterns. Coffee's always on. Copy & Fax Service. Authorized Bernina & Elna Dealer Sales & Service.

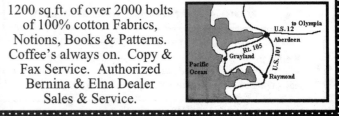

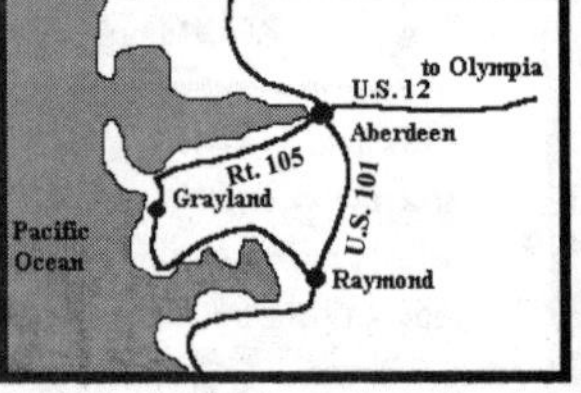

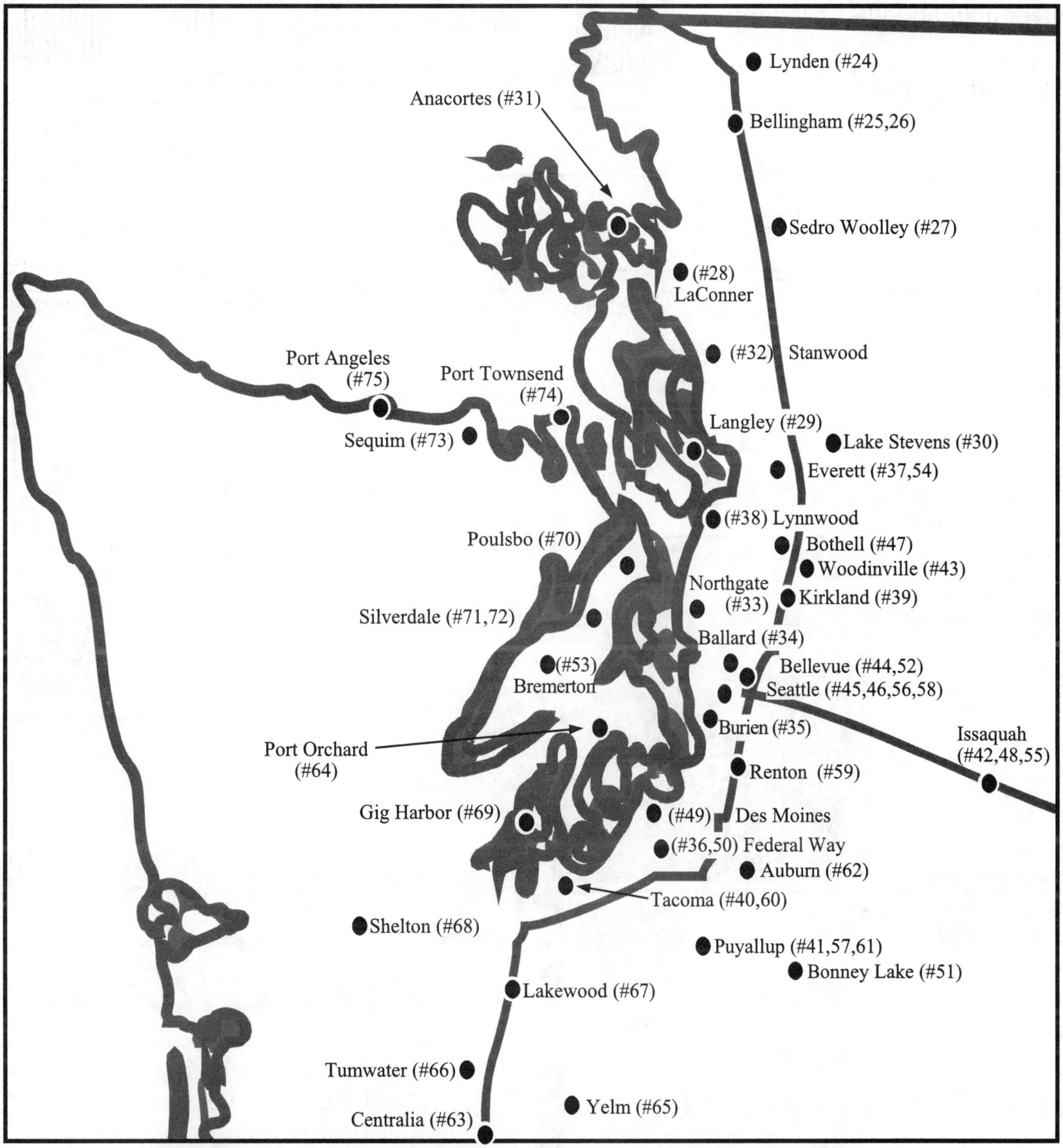

Lynden (#24)
Anacortes (#31)
Bellingham (#25,26)
Sedro Woolley (#27)
(#28)
LaConner
Port Angeles
(#75)
Port Townsend
(#74)
(#32) Stanwood
Langley (#29)
Sequim (#73)
Lake Stevens (#30)
Everett (#37,54)
(#38) Lynnwood
Poulsbo (#70)
Bothell (#47)
Woodinville (#43)
Northgate
(#33)
Kirkland (#39)
Silverdale (#71,72)
Ballard (#34)
(#53)
Bremerton
Bellevue (#44,52)
Seattle (#45,46,56,58)
Burien (#35)
Issaquah
(#42,48,55)
Port Orchard
(#64)
Renton (#59)
Gig Harbor (#69)
(#49) Des Moines
(#36,50) Federal Way
Auburn (#62)
Tacoma (#40,60)
Shelton (#68)
Puyallup (#41,57,61)
Bonney Lake (#51)
Lakewood (#67)
Tumwater (#66)
Yelm (#65)
Centralia (#63)

52 Featured Shops

SEATTLE AREA

Shops #24 - 75

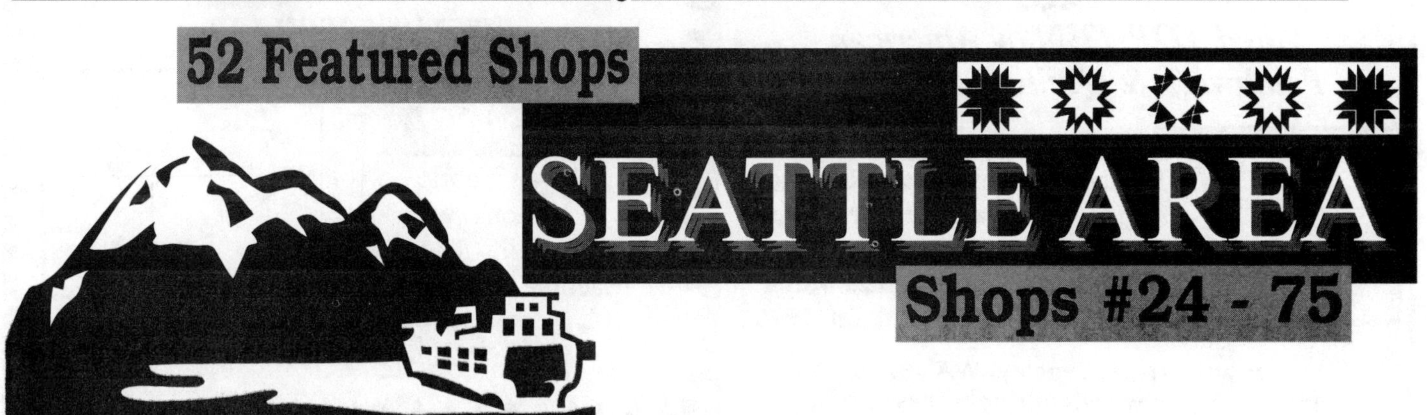

Lynden, WA #24

Wed - Sat 10 - 5

Folktales

1888 Kok Rd. 98264
(360) 354-0855
folktales@netzero.net
Owner: Linda Kroon
Est: 1995 1000+ bolts

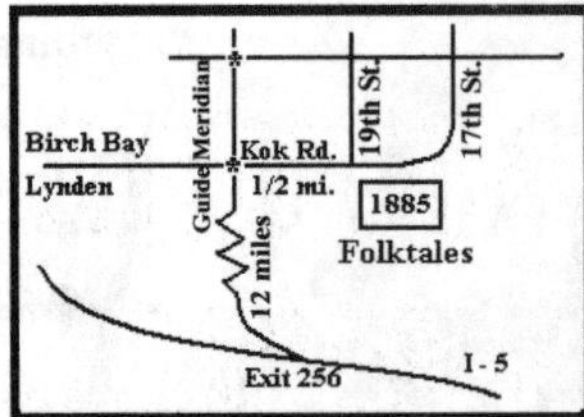

A little shop full of big ideas. Homespuns, flannels, cottons, woolfelt. Patterns for quilting, stitcheries, wood, & dollmaking.

Bellingham, WA #25

Mon - Sat 10 - 6

Fabric Expressions

1633 Birchwood Ave. 98225
(360) 671-5277
fabex@johncarol.com
www.fabricexpressions.net
Est: 1997 1800 sq.ft.

- 2500+ bolts of quality quilting cottons
- Large selection of fashion fabrics
- Books, patterns, notions

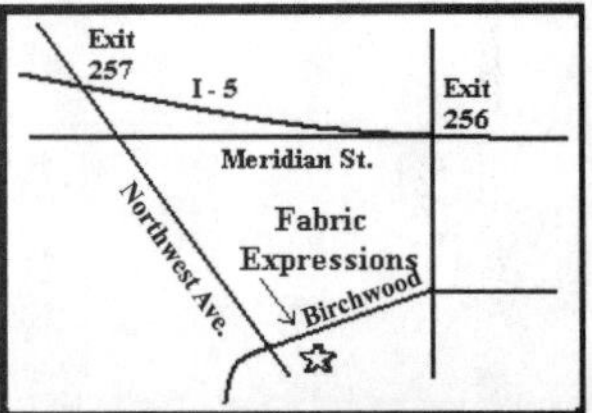

BELLINGHAM'S
NEWEST QUILT SHOP!
WITH A **HUGE** CUSTOM CLASSROOM!

QUILTS

#26

Quality Quilting Fabrics, Notions, Books & Patterns

GREAT FABRIC VALUES

1844 N State Street
Bellingham WA 98225

- I-5 N - exit 254. Left on Iowa, left on State
- I-5 S - exit 254. Veer right, left on State.

360•714•0070

STORE HOURS:
Monday - Saturday
10am - 6pm

Sedro Woolley, WA #27

Mon - Fri 9:30 - 5:30
Sat 9:30 - 5

Cascade Fabrics

824 Metcalf 98284
(360) 855-0323
Owner: Paul Kelley
Est: 1978 3000 sq.ft.

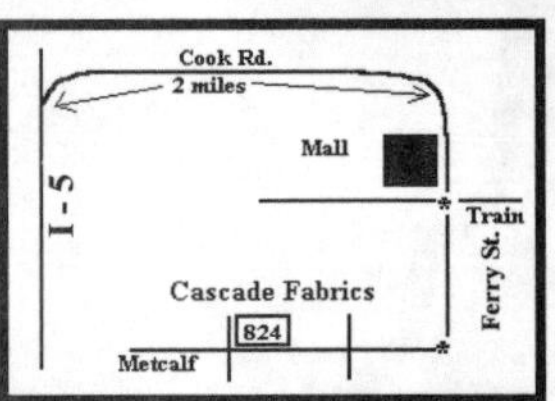

Quilting Supplies and Books, Classes. Experienced Staff. 20% off all quilting cotton always. Additional non-quilting fabrics also.

LaConner, WA #28

Wed - Sat 11 - 4
Sun 12 - 4

La Conner Quilt Museum

703 S. 2nd St.,
P.O. Box 1270 98257
(360) 466-4288 Fax: Same
Director: Rita Hupy
E-mail: lacquiltm@aol.com
www.laconnerquilts.com

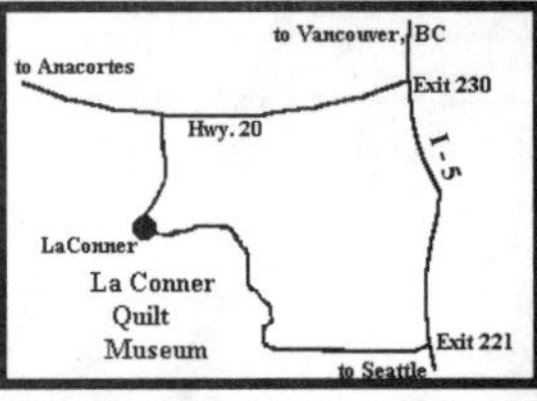

One of only 10 Quilt Museums in the U.S.A. Five shows a year from around the country and the world. Memberships Available.

Langley, WA #29

Mon - Sat 10 - 5
Sun 12 - 5

QUILTING•BY•THE•SEA

Voted TOP TEN by American Patchwork & Quilting Magazine

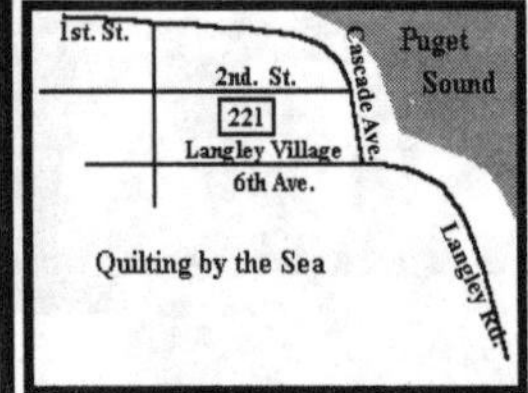

A complete quilting shop - fabrics, books, patterns, supplies and gifts. We are a place where friends gather to share ideas and be inspired. Retreat space with a view of Puget Sound. Est. 1995

221 2nd Street, Langley, WA 98260
360.221.8171 • www.quiltingbythesea.com

Twin Quilts INC.

1805A 124th Ave. NE, P.O. Box 1414
Lake Stevens, WA 98258
425-334-8803 Fax: 425-334-8872
twin.quilts@verizon.net 1700 sq.ft.
www.twinquilts.com

Mon - Fri 9:30 - 6:30
Sat 9:30 - 5

Classes • Fabric
Notions
Finished Quilts for Sale
Machine Quilting

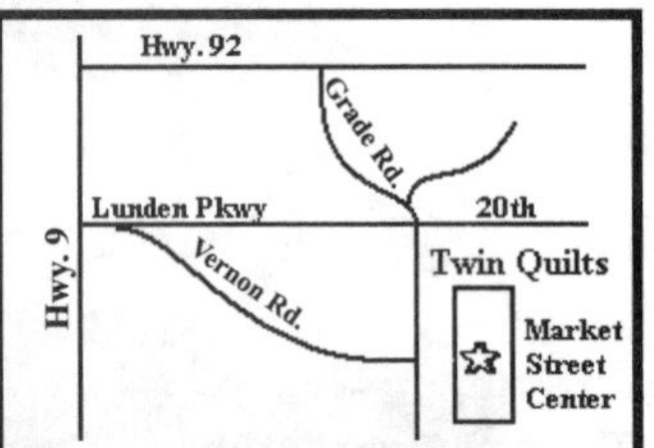

Lake Stevens, WA #30

"Your next quilt starts here"

the Quilt Shop

Anacortes, WA #31

Mon - Sat
9:30 - 5:30
Sun 11 - 4

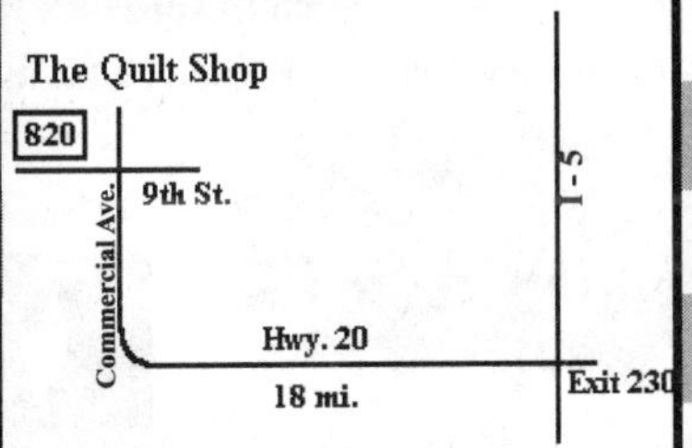

820 Commercial Ave. 98221 (360) 293-2146
Owners: Cathy Berk & Mary Gillman 3000+ Bolts

Everything for the Quilter!
Fabrics, patterns, books, notions & classes.

Stanwood, WA #32

Cotton Pickins'

Choose from a wonderful selection of notions, books, patterns, kits and special gifts. Featuring quality 100% cotton quilting fabrics, homespuns and flannels from Hoffman, Moda, South Seas, Bali, RJR, Thimbleberries, Benartex and More!

Mon - Sat 10 - 5:30

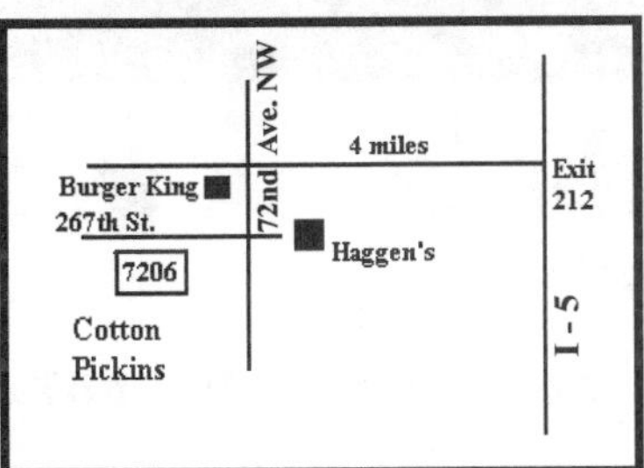

7206 267th St. NW, Suite 102
Stanwood, WA 98292
360-629-4771
email: CottonPickins@aol.com
Owner: Kathy Blank
Fax: 360-629-7530
Est: 2000 3000 Bolts

www.QuiltingwithCottonPickins.com

Gold Standard Quilting Table

Get professional quilting results at home for all quilts from small to king size!

- Lightweight, high-strength aircraft grade aluminum construction
- Can be configured for quilting widths from 47" to 105" (King Size)
- Handle mounted sewing machine speed control & on/off switch
- Can be comfortably operated while seated or standing
- Pattern shelf with handy stylus for perfect sewn patterns
- Optional kit allows creation of 3 additional widths: 18", 76" or 134" (King Size Bedspread)

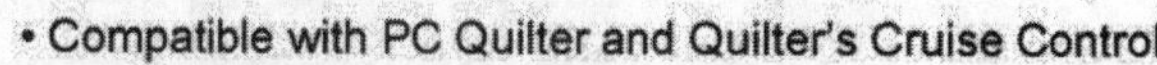

- Compatible with PC Quilter and Quilter's Cruise Control

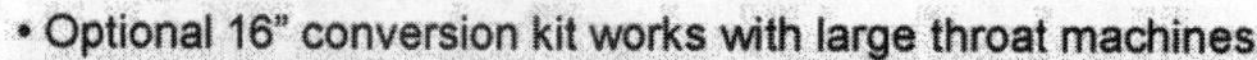

- Optional 16" conversion kit works with large throat machines

FREE **Delivery** with this Ad

Our Special Package Includes the...

PQ 1500 High Speed Quilting Machine
Type II Laser pointer and instructional video

Includes 105" Set Up

Visit one our friendly locations today

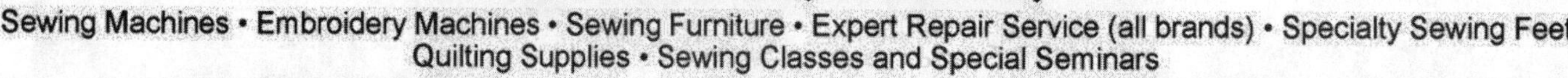

Sewing Machines • Embroidery Machines • Sewing Furniture • Expert Repair Service (all brands) • Specialty Sewing Feet
Quilting Supplies • Sewing Classes and Special Seminars

Visit **www.qualitysewing.com** to subscribe to our free magazine or sewing update via email

"Sewing Fun Starts Here" • ***Quality Sewing & Vacuum Centers*** • www.qualitysewing.com

10 Western Washington Locations

#33	Seattle/Northgate	842 NE Northgate Way	206/363-1634
#34	Seattle/Ballard	1428 NW 56th St	206/782-9400
#35	Seattle/Burien	10859 1st Ave S	206/244-5555
#36	Kent/Federal Wa	27045 Pacific Hwy S	253/946-5865
#37	Everett	10121 Evergreen Way	425/290-8000 800/488-0458
#38	Lynnwood	19800 44th Ave W Inside Jo-Ann Fabrics	425/775-6612
#39	Kirkland	13501 100th Ave NE	425/821-1747 800/526-5717
#40	Tacoma	I-5 & S 38th St	253/471-3899 800/447-7913
#41	Puyallup	111 N Meridian	253/841-4288 800/266-8842
#42	Issaquah	1440 NW Gilman Blvd	425/392-9868 800/253-8022

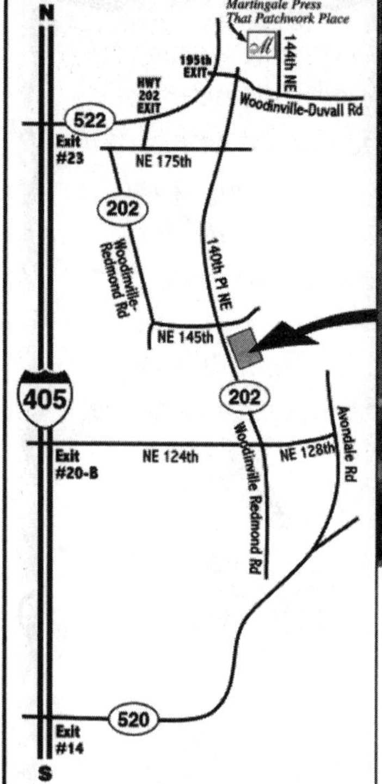

Located in the heart of wine country in Historic Woodinville, Washington

gathering fabric #43

Fabric and Accessories to the Quilt Maker and Textile Artisan!

14450 Woodinville Redmond Road NE • Woodinville, WA 98072
425-402-9034

www.gatheringfabric.com

Regular Shop Hours: Mon-Fri 10 am - 5:30 pm • Sat 10 am - 5 pm • Closed Sunday

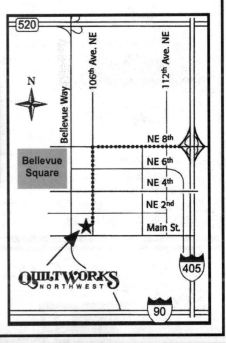

Seattle, WA #46

Mon - Sat 10 - 6
Sun 11 - 5

Undercover Quilts from the U.S.A.

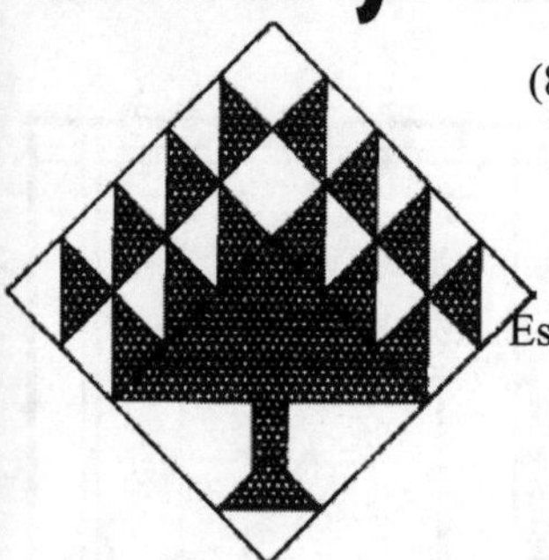

1411 1st Ave. #106 98101
(800) 469-6511 or (206) 622-6382
Fax: (206) 622-6382
quilts@serv.net
Owner: Linda Hitchcock
www.undercoverquilts.com
Est: 1990 1000 sq.ft. 2000 Bolts
Inside the South Arcade Bldg.

Largest Selection of American Made New and Antique Quilts in the Pacific Northwest! Fabrics, Books, Supplies, gifts, antique tops, and blocks.

Pike Place Market
Pike
Undercover Quilts Inside the South Arcade Bldg. 1411
Union
Seattle Art Museum
1st. Ave.
University

From North I - 5 take Exit 165B
From South I - 5 take Exit 165

Bothell, WA #47

Mon - Sat 10 - 6
Sun 11 - 5

Keepsake Cottage Fabrics

817 238th St. SE. 98021
(425) 486-3483
Owners: Delberta Murray & Julie Stewart
Est: 1985 1000 sq.ft.

Quilting Fabrics, patterns and notions. In the heart of Bothell's Country Village.

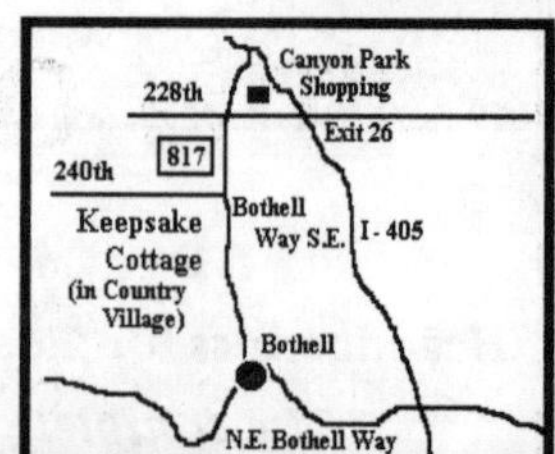

Issaquah, WA #48

The Loft

1480 N.W. Gilman Blvd. #2
98027
(425) 392-5877
Est: 1975

Exit 15
I - 90
St. Rt. 900
Front St.
The Loft
1480
N. W. Gilman Blvd.

Mon - Fri 10 - 6
Sat 10 - 5
Sun 12 - 5

Lose yourself for a few minutes or a few hours browsing in our inspiration filled shop. The walls are hung with quilts galore. Our shelves are filled with the latest in fabrics. Bundles and kits abound. Our book collection is huge and we are proud to feature pattern by northwest artists! Located just off the freeway for easy access, parking for large vehicles is available! We look forward to meeting you!

Carriage Country Quilts

Driving Directions: Exit I-5 at exit #149. Head west on the Kent-Des Moines Road. Continue as the road curves and eventually becomes Marine View Dr. S. As you enter downtown Des Moines. We are in a gray house, between the Shell Gas Station and Washington Mutual Bank.

#49

22214 Marine View Drive S.
Des Moines, Washington 98198
Phone: 206-878-9414
email: info@carriagecountryquilts.com
www.carriagecountryquilts.com

Hours: Mon-Fri 10-7 ♥ Sat 10-5 ♥ Sun 12-4

Federal Way, WA #50

Sues Rags Quilt Shop

1520 S. Dash Point Rd., Federal Way, WA 98003
(253) 941-5076 or Toll Free (888) 844-7247
Website: www.suesrags.com
E-mail: suesrags@aol.com

Regular Store Hours:

Monday-Friday	10 am-6 pm
Saturday	10 am-5 pm
Sunday	Closed

Books Available by Susan Dissmore, owner:
Clever Quarters,
Clever Quilt Encore
& Clever Quilts

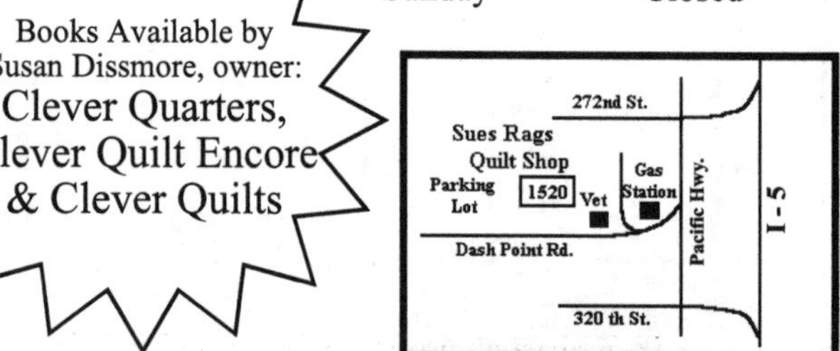

Bonney Lake, WA #51

Mon - Fri 9 - 8
Sat 9 - 6
Sun 10 - 6

Quilters Cottage

inside Ben Franklin Crafts

21121 Hwy. 410 98390
(253) 862-6822 2500+ Bolts

Fine 100% Cotton Quilting Fabrics. Great Selection - Notions, Books, Patterns, Craft Supplies & Classes. Expert Service by our Friendly Knowledgeable Staff

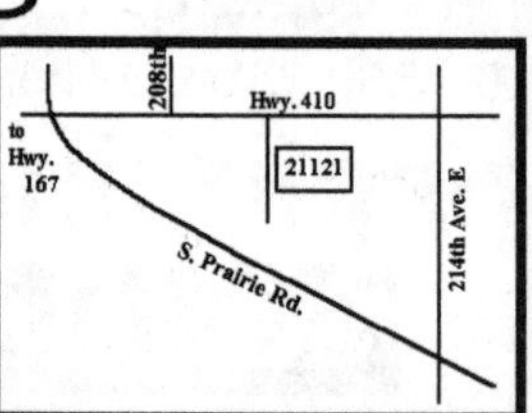

We'd like to invite you to visit "The Quilt Shop" at Pacific Fabrics & Crafts

We are a group of family-owned, full service fabric stores dedicated to serving the needs of quilters, sewers, and crafters in the Pacific Northwest.

We carry an ever-growing, ever-changing collection of quilting fabrics from all the top companies, plus patterns, books, notions, and classes for all levels.

We're open from 9am-9pm Monday through Friday, 9am-6pm on Saturday and 11am-6pm on Sunday.

1645-140th Ave. N.E.
Bellevue, WA 98005
(425) 747-3551

Bremerton, WA #53

4214 Wheaton Way
Bremerton, WA 98310
(360) 479-4214

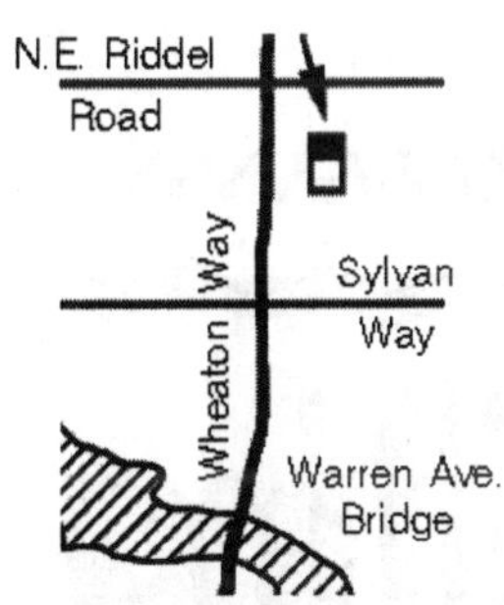

Everett, WA #54

10203 Evergreen Way
Everett, WA 98204
(425) 353-8866

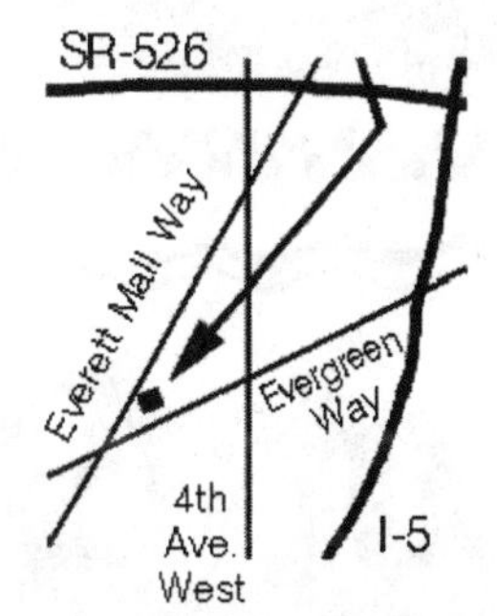

Issaquah, WA #55

6000 East Lake
Sammamish Parkway
S.E., Suite B
Issaquah, WA 98029
(425) 392-6696

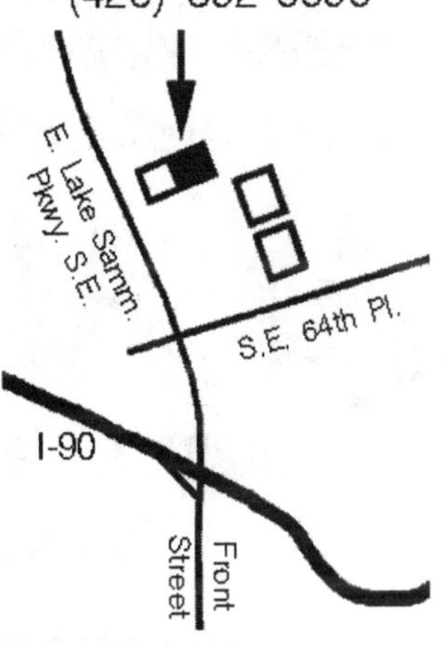

Seattle, WA #56

2230 4th Avenue S.
Seattle, WA 98134
(206) 628-6237

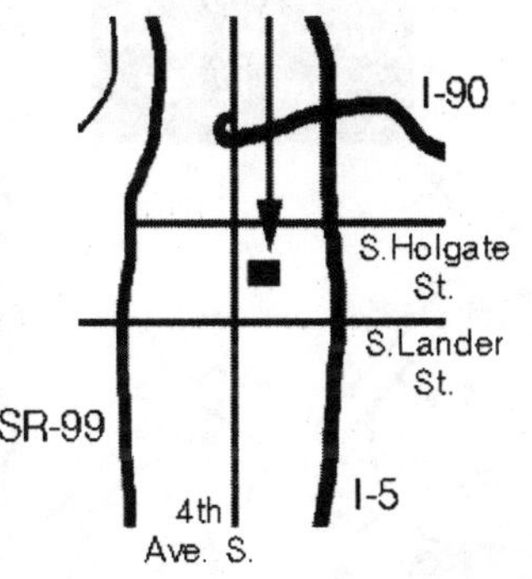

Puyallup, WA #57

3715 S. Meridian
Puyallup, WA 98373
(253) 770-1095

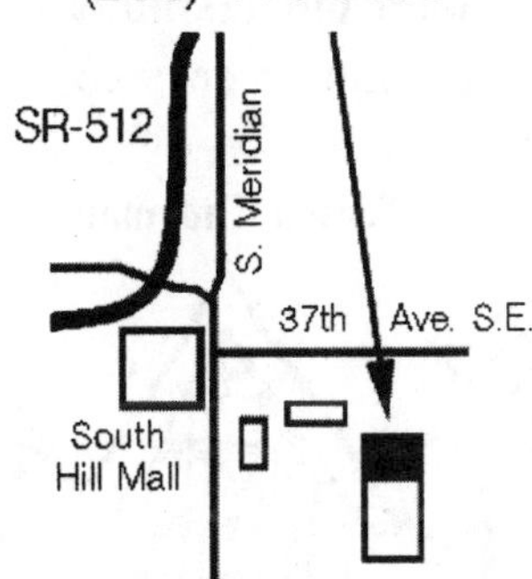

Seattle, WA #58

838 N.E. Northgate Way
Seattle, WA 98125
(206) 362-0111

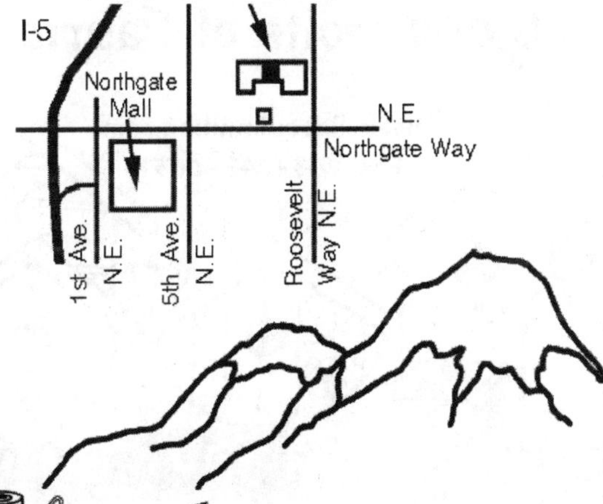

Visit our web site at www.pacificfabrics.com

Pacific Fabrics & Crafts
at Home in the Northwest since 1917

Pieces

Quality Fabrics & Quilting

364 Renton Center Way SW #59
Renton, WA 98055
(425) 271-7160
Toll Free: (888) 271-7160
mail@piecesquiltshop.com
piecesquiltshop.com
Est: 1996
3500+ Bolts

Mon, Wed, Fri 10 - 7
Tues & Thur 10 - 8:30
Sat 10 - 5
Sun 11 - 5

Mail Orders.

Quarterly Newsletter.

Specializing in a wide array of color!
Batiks, Collections & Unique Prints !
Classes & Kits year round !

Renton, WA #59

All About Quilting

1613 E. 31st St. 98404
(253) 274-0336
www.allaboutquilting.com
Over 6,000 Bolts of Fabric

Full line of notions, largest selection of flannel in the area. Good old fashioned customer service.

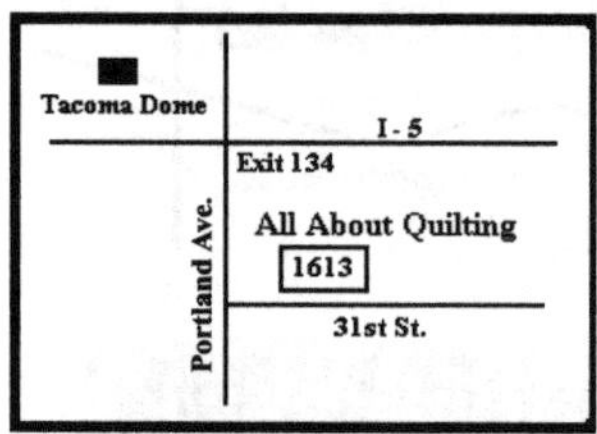

Located 2 Blocks off of I-5
Exit 134 North Bound
Exit 135 South Bound

Mon - Sat 10 - 6
Sun 12 - 5

Est: 1998
2400 sq.ft.

Shop@allaboutquilting.com
Fax: 253-248-0037

Teresa Thormar

Tacoma, WA #60

Serving Quilters for 24 years!

The Quilt Barn

1206 E. Main Puyallup, WA 98372

(253) 845-1532 or 1-800-988-BARN

www.quiltbarn.com or email QuiltBarn@aol.com

Regular Business Hours:

Tues., Wed., Fri. 10-7 p.m. Thurs. 10-9 p.m.

Sat. 10-6 p.m. Sun. 12-5 p.m. Closed Mon.

OWNER: Pamela Hewitt 2500 sq. ft.

Puyallup, WA #61

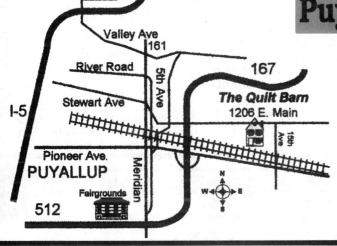

- Fine 100% Cotton Quilting Fabrics
- 4,000 bolt selection
- Complete Quilting supplies and notions
- Large selection of Books and Patterns
- Friendly and knowledgeable staff
- Day and Evening Classes
- Open 6 days a week
- Thimbleberries Quilt Club 2004
- Web Site and Mail Order services

Call for our catalog or details about Classes.

Fife
Valley Ave
161
River Road
167
5th Ave
Stewart Ave
The Quilt Barn
1206 E. Main
I-5
15th Ave
Pioneer Ave.
PUYALLUP
Meridian
Fairgrounds
512
N W E S

Auburn, WA #62

CALICO CAT
and Bernina Too

201 N. Auburn Way 98002

(800) 908-0885 or (253) 939-0885

Owner: Mary Stanton Est:1992

fabric@Thecalicocat.com 5000 sq.ft.

www.thecalicocat.com

Mon - Fri: 10 - 7
Sat: 10 - 5 Sun: 12- 5

Over 2800 fine cotton fabrics extensive book collection, notions, patterns, classes, free newsletter and patterns. Bernina Sewing machines and sergers accessories and classes technician on site for service and repair.

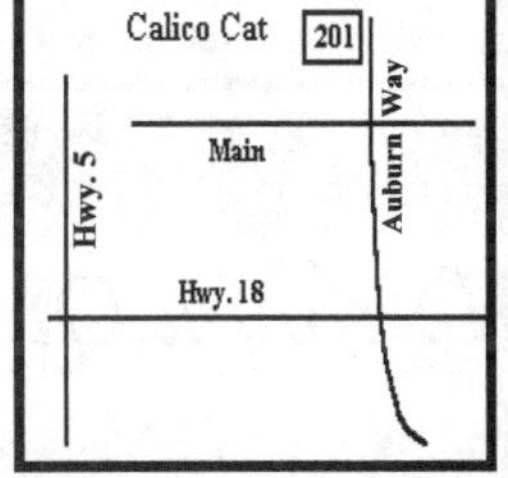

Wheel-Chair Accessible

Centralia, WA #63

Mon - Fri 10 - 5
Sat 10 - 4

Quilters Junction

1131 Mellen St. 98531
(888) 553-7865 or
(360) 807-1255

quilters@quik.com

Located in a large house built in 1916. Take Exit 81 (Mellen St. Exit) off I - 5, and go one block east. Only house with quilts hanging on the porch. Fabrics, Patterns, Books & Notions.

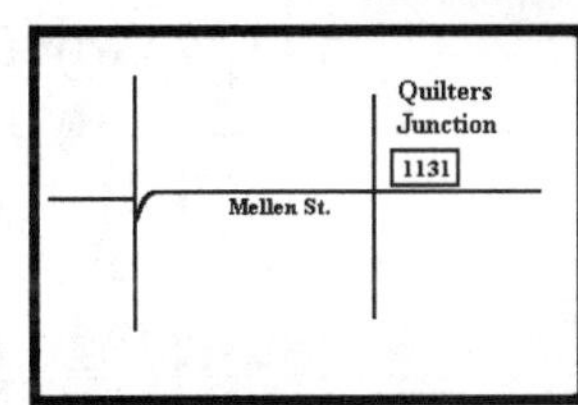

Port Orchard, WA #64

Mon - Fri 10 - 8
Sat 10 - 6
Sun 12 - 5

Rochelle's Fine Fabric & Quilting

1700 Mile Hill Drive #200C
South Kitsap Mall: Upper Level
(360) 895-1515 98366
rochelle@oz.net
Owner: Rochelle Savage
Est: 1981 5500 sq.ft.

A complete collection of cotton solids & prints from all the best manufacturers. A large selection of books & notions. Classes too!

Rochelle's is located between Gig Harbor and Bremerton. From Tacoma on Hwy. 16 pass the Gig Harbor exits, 20 minutes, take Tremont St./Port Orchard Exit. Go Rt (east) toward Pt. Orchard. Travel 1.4 miles then go left on Bethel. Travel 1 mile and go right on Mile Hill Rd. 1 Block on your right is the So. Kitsap Mall. We are on the Upper level!!

GEE-GEE'S Quilts
Crafts & Gifts

100% Cotton Fabrics, 8000+ bolts,
over 600 Quilting Books,
Over 200 Patterns, stencils,
notions, craft supplies, and yarns.
Plus Collectible Gifts,
TY Beanies & Finished Quilts.
Machine Quilting Available.

Mon - Fri 9 - 6
Sat 9 - 5
Sun 11 - 4

601 Yelm Ave. W 98597
(360) 458-5616
geegees@ywave.com
www.geegeesquilting.com
Est: 1978 6000 sq.ft.

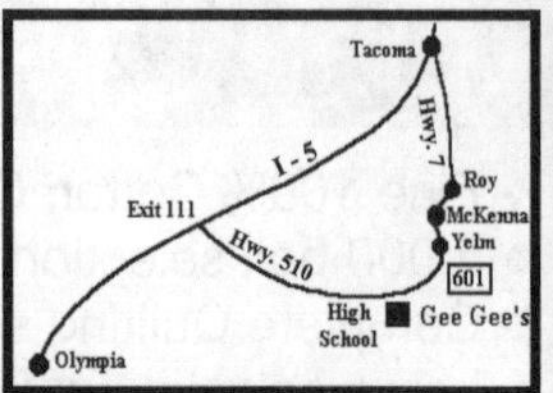

Yelm, WA #65

Tumwater, WA #66

QUILTER'S QUARTERS
BEST SEWING CENTER
100 Ruby St. SE, 98501-4546
360-236-0596
Owners: Julie and Joan Bonin
Est: 1998 2700 sq. ft.
"Your Full Service Quilting Headquarters"

Offering the finest and latest in quality
- 100% Cotton Fabric
- Books and Patterns
- Quilting Supplies and Notions
- Classes at all levels
- Authorized Bernina, Elna and Balylock Dealership

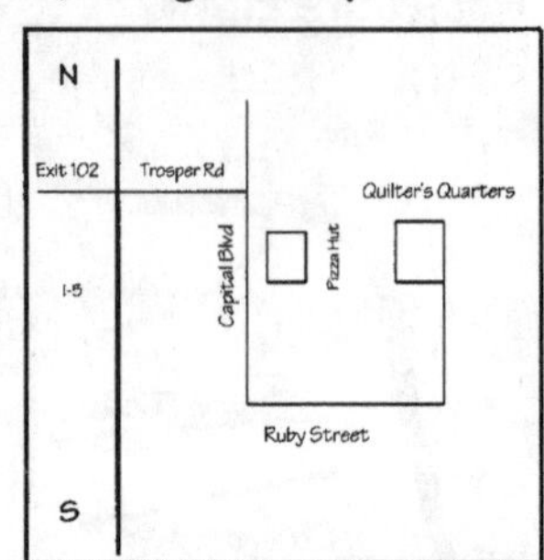

Store Hours: Mon - Fri 10-6

Take exit 102 Trosper Rd.
Turn right on Capital Blvd.
Then left on Ruby

The Quilted Dragon
11124 Gravelly Lake Drive SW
Lakewood, WA 98499
Phone: (253) 582-7455
E-Mail: quilted-dragon@juno.com

Lakewood, WA #67

Quilting & Wearable Art with an Asian Flair

Specializing in Oriental, Asian, African and Batik Fabrics, Sashiko Supplies, Unique Beads, Buttons & Embellishments, Clothing & Quilting Patterns, Kimono and Vintage Silks

On-Line Catalogue:
www.quilted-dragon.com

Mon - Fri 10 - 6
Sat 10 - 5
Sun Noon - 4

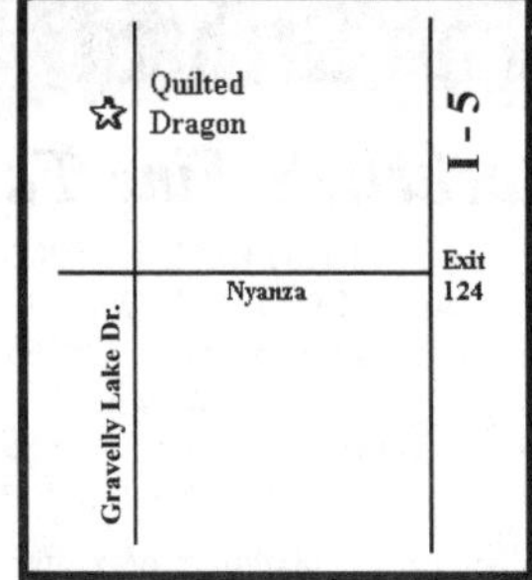

Take the Gravelly Lake Exit 124 Off I-5

Shelton, WA #68

Mon - Sat 10 - 5:30

Sue's Stitch in Time
927 W. Railroad Ave. 98584
(360) 427-6164
suesstitch@netzero.net
Owner: Sue Bennett
Est: 2000 3400 sq.ft. 2500 Bolts

Beautiful, new, well-lit store offering thousands of bolts of fabrics with professional & enthusiastic customer service

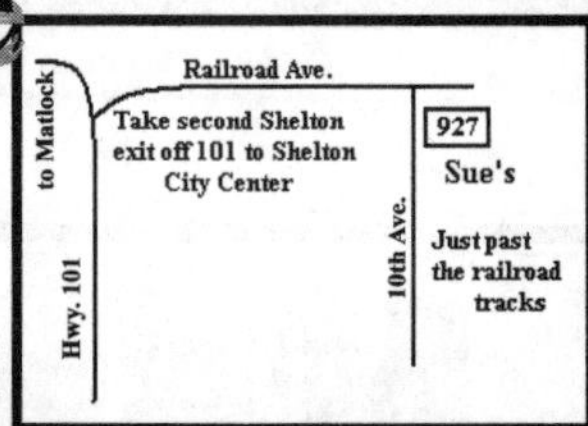

Gig Harbor, WA #69

Mon - Sat 10 - 5
Sun 12 - 5

HARBOR QUILT
3607 Hunt St. NW 98335
(253) 858-5414 or (800) 743-9995
Fax: (253) 858-5416
pgvin@harbornet.com
www.harborquilt.com
Owner: Patti Vincent Est: 1999

2000+ bolts of 100% cotton, books, notions, everything for quilting. Batiks, flannels, plaids, 30's reproductions and novelties. Enlarging soon to sell finished quilts.

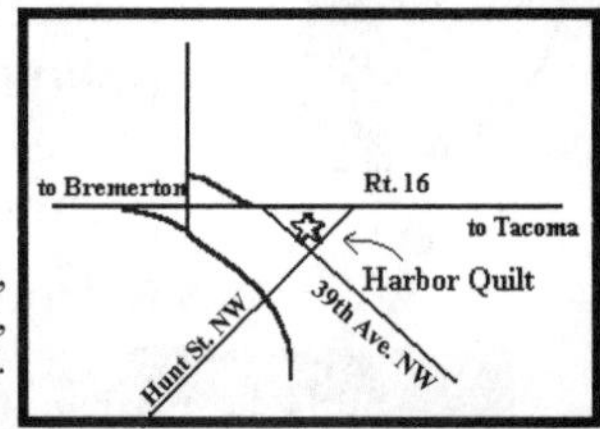

Poulsbo, WA #70

Mon - Sat 10 - 5:30
Sun 11 - 4

Heirloom Quilts & Fabric
18833 B. Front St., P.O. Box 1957 98370
(360) 697-2222 Fax: (360) 697-4495
Est: 1986 4000 sq.ft. 3000 Bolts

100% cotton fabric, books, notions, everything for quilting. Batiks, flannels, plaids, 30's reproductions and novelties. Longarm quilting available.

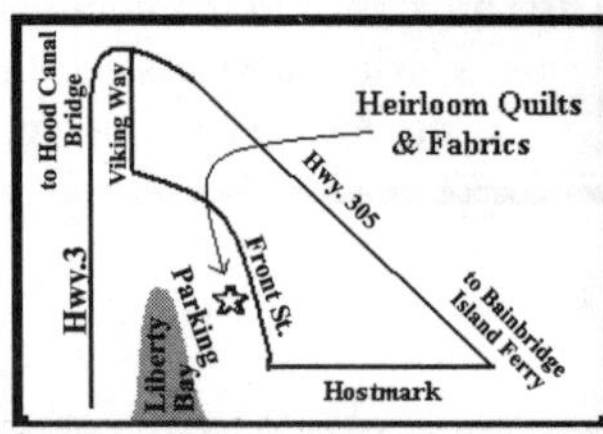

Come in and see our great selection or take a class!

2600 sq.ft. store with over 1200 bolts of 100% cotton fabric

Notions, books and patterns

Fabric includes Batiks, Flannels, 30s, Thimble-berries and more!

Large comfortable class-room with lots of classes

#71

Quilting 4 Friends • (360) 337-7707
3726 NW Plaza Rd., Suite 106 • Silverdale
www.quilting4friends.com

Directions: From Hwy. 3 take the Kitsap Mall/303 exit. Turn south on Clear Creek/Kitsap Mall Blvd. Go to NW Plaza and turn right. We are on your right in the shopping center with Tony Roma's.

Hours: Mon.-Fri. 10-8 • Sat. 9-6 • Sun. 12-5

Silverdale, WA #72

materialGIRLS QUILT SHOP

Ross Plaza, 10404 NW Silverdale Way
P.O. Box 3750, Silverdale, WA 98383
360-692-0286
materialgirls@donobi.net
www.silverdalequiltshop.com

Mon - Sat 10 - 6 Thur 10 - 8

Fine Quilting Fabrics, Longarm Quilting Machine Let us do it or rent it out yourself. Bernina Sewing Machines & Accessories, Patterns, Books, & More!!!

Sequim, WA #73

The Stitching Heron

The Premier Quilt Shop on Washington's North Olympic Peninsula

Visit us in sunny Sequim!

- Hoffman, Moda, P&B, Kona Bay, batiks, silk and more!
- Unique selection of thread & notions
- **Chocolate & Dessert shop on site**
- Open Mon. – Sat, 10-5, Sun., 11 – 4
- Visit area lavender farms, hike in the Olympic National Park, visit Victoria, BC and Vancouver Island
- Our web site has great travel links!

Directions: Located in downtown Sequim under the navy blue awning. From Hwy 101, take Sequim Ave. Exit, go through light at Washington Street, turn right into public parking lot and park behind our shop.

126 E. Washington Street
Sequim, WA 98382
(360) 582-1230
www.thestitchingheron.com

Quilter's Cove

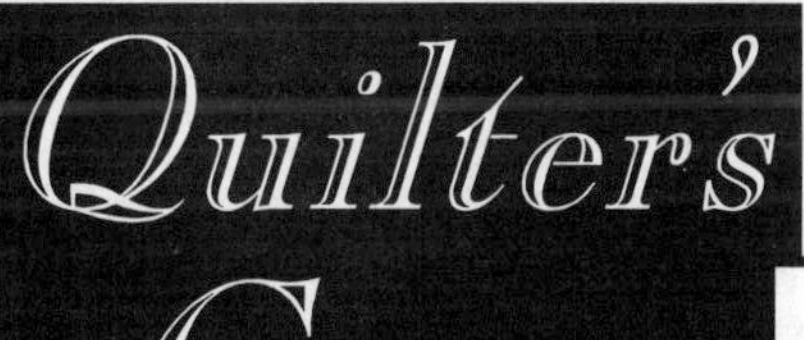

1010 Water St. 98368
(360) 385-4254

Quilterscove@aol.com

Mon - Sat 10 - 5:30 Sun 11 - 5

Best Selection of Books. Large Selection of 100% cotton fabrics. Complete line of notions, patterns & classes. Gifts for the Quilter.

Port Townsend, WA #74

Port Angeles, WA #75

Mon - Sat 10 - 5

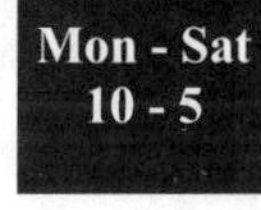

QUILTED STRAIT

111 N. Oak St. 98362
Phone / Fax: (360) 457-4733
quiltedstrait@olypen.com
www.quiltedstrait.com
Owner: Kris Cornell
Est: 2001 1500 sq.ft.

Come see our extensive collection of flannels, hand dyed wools and batiks. Over 2000 bolts of fabric as well as notions, books and patterns.

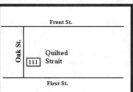

Other Shops in Washington: *We suggest calling first*

Anacortes Fabrics Plus, 608 Commercial Ave 360-293-7641
Arlington Eagle Springs Mercantile, 13403 233rd St NE 360-403-3059
Arlington Arlington Fabrics, N 401 Olympic Ave 360-435-4949
Arlington Bunny Patch, 24613 27th Ave. NE 360-435-8414
Arlington Aunt Mary's Quilt Shop, 3323 169th Pl NE #D 360-657-1116
Bainbridge Isle Quilt or Dye Quilting Shop, 15473 Sunrise Dr NE 206-780-5324
Battle Ground Quilted Memories, 23513 NE 229th St. 360-687-9393
Battle Ground Cottons, 7702 NE 179th 360-573-6084
Battle Ground Cottons, 316 E. Main St. 360-666-0366
Bellevue Block Butter, Inc, 1004 141st PL NE 425-644-4242
Bellingham Lynda's Quilting & Needle Art, 5021 Northwest Dr
Bremerton Thread Connection, 1710 15th St. 360-479-2651
Bridgeport Cottage Quilting, 1020 Columbia 509-686-2213
Camano Island Over the Rainbow, 740 Michael Way 360-387-2366
Camas Seed Lady Quilts, 4824 NW 38th Ave. 360-833-9604
Castle Rock The Quilt Nest, 4 Cowlitz Ave. W 360-274-4663
Centralia Crafts Galore, 1724 S. Gold 360-339-0200
Chehalis Quilts Sew Easy, 1286 NW Maryland Ave. 360-740-1769
Chehalis Sisters, 476 N. Market Blvd. 360-748-9747
Chelan Needle Nook, P.O. Box 1529 509-682-5513
Danville Fabric Sandwich, 19097 Hwy 21 N 250-442-2998
Davenport Cottonwood Quilts, 537 Morgan St. 509-725-0700
Dayton Hawthorne Gallery, 245 E. Main 509-382-3137
Deer Park Bobbin Along, 831 S. Main, P.O. Box 1128 509-276-1914
Duvall The Quilter's Garden, 15726 Main St. NE 525-844-1621
East Wenatchee Studio Q, 100 11th St NE 509-884-5666
Eastsound Poppies, 294 "A" St., P.O. Box 1075 360-376-2686
Elk Cedar Mountain Design, P.O. Box 315 208-448-4737
Ellensburg Sew Much More, 411 N. Pine St. 509-933-3030
Ellensburg Moser's Clothing Store, 118 E. 4th Ave. 509-925-1272
Ellensburg Mom's Fabrics & Crafts, 203 W. 9th Ave. 509-933-1520
Evans Wumpkin Quilt Shop, 1072 A Williams Lake 509-684-3838
Everett Quilt with EASE, 3122 Broadway 425-259-6579
Forks Chinook Pharmacy & Variety, 11 S Forks Ave 360-374-2294
Freeland Island Fabrics, 1609 E Main St 360-331-4435
Friday Harbor Patchwork Passion, 425 Argyle St. 360-378-6025
Issaquah Tilton's Treasures, 4611 NE 243rd Ct. 425-961-0015
Kelso Ad's Fabrics, 300 S. 10th Ave. 360-636-1060
Kennewick Crafts Warehouse, 7411 W Canal Dr #A 509-783-9663
Kent Northwest Craft & Décor, 10432 Kent-Kangley 253-856-3401
Kettle Falls Red Rooster, 475 S. Meyers St. 509-738-4418
Longview Longview Sewing & Vac, 945 Washington 800-930-2628
Longview Park Place Quilting, 510 17th Ave 360-636-0946
Lopez Island Enchanted Needle, 9 Old Post Rd #B 360-468-2777
Lynden Calico Country, 1722 Front St. 360-354-4832
Lynnwood The Calico Basket, 4114 198th St. SW 425-774-6446
Lynnwood Calico Basket, 4114 198th St. 425-774-6446
Maple Valley Perfect Points Quilting, 23745 - 225th Way SE #103 425-413-7845
Marysville The Quilting Place, 1515 3rd St 360-659-8455
Metaline Falls Sweet Creek Creations, E 219 5th Ave. 509-446-2429
Morton Sugar-n-Spice, 680 Airport Way 360-496-6629
Moses Lake LaFaun Quilts, 7516 Dick Rd. NE 509-762-5614
Moxee Common Thread Quilting, 240 Meadowlark Ln. 509-248-3878
Moxee Spoolin Around, 541 E Duffield Rd 509-453-0610
Mt. Vernon Calico Creations, 400 S. 1st. St. 360-336-3241
Mukilteo Peacock & Periwinkle, 11924 Cyrus Way 425-493-8040
Newport The Pin Cushion, 306 S. Washington Ave. 509-447-5913
Olympia Needles Quilt Shop, 420 Steele St SE 360-264-7090
Olympia TLC Creations, 8825 Johnson Point Rd NE 360-923-0988
Omak Needlelyn Time, 9 N. Main St. 509-826-1198
Pomeroy Rather-Be's Quilting Shop, 382 Highway 12 509-843-6162
Port Orchard Christina's Heritage, 2516 SE Bethel Rd. 360-895-1034
Port Roberts Quilted Canoe, 145 Tyee Drive 877-845-3288
Port Townsend Northwest Quilt Co, 1011 Water St 360-344-3636
Poulsbo Bird House Quilts, 91 NW Beaver Rdg. 360-779-4618
Prosser The Sewing Basket, 1108 Wine Country Rd. 509-786-7367
Prosser Quilters Garden, 1205 Meade Ave 509-786-2766
Pullman Quilted Heart, 134 N. Grand Ave. 509-334-7544
Renton Material Me, 1308 Dayton Ave NE 425-227-9212
Richland Perks Sewing, 621 The Parkway 509-943-1149
Sea Beck The Dancing Needle, 18503 Morgan Narsh Ln 360-830-0366
Seattle Nancy's Sewing Basket, 2221 Queen Anne N 206-282-9112
Seattle Creative Quilting, 900 NW 80th St. 206-297-8270
Seattle Quilt Haus, 3511 NE 196th St. 206-362-0719
Snohomish Clearview Triangle, 8311 180th St. SE 360-668-4151
Snohomish The Speckled Hen, 915 1st St Ste A 360-568-9758
Spokane Simply Kits Quilt Shop, 11417 E Spraque 509-891-6624
Spokane Cotton & Co. Quilt Shoppe, 2923 N Argonne 509-891-7858
Spokane This N' That, 9826 N. Andrew St. 509-467-9496
Spokane Valley Briar Patch, 13608 E Nora Ave 509-924-9478
Stanwood Flair Fabric Design, 550 N. Hawk Ridge Pl 360-387-4034
Sunnyside Quilts & More, Mid-Valley Mall A3 509-837-4134
Suquamish Quilts & Gifts, 19298 Park Blvd NE 360-779-7781
Tacoma Trains, Fabrics, Etc., 1315 S 23rd 253-779-0219
Tacoma Bart's Quilting, 5612 35th Ave CT E 253-922-9584
Union Gap The Threaded Needle, 2640 Main St 509-469-3838
Valleyford Dana's Country Quilting, 11017 E. Connor 509-891-9234
Vancouver The Quilter, 8080 East Mill Plain 360-696-2880
Vancouver Quilting Etc., 13202 NE 3rd Ave. 360-573-6758
Walla Walla Suzanne's Quilt Shop, 425 B St. 509-526-9398
Wanatchee JC's Stitching Post, 1601 N Wenatchee 509-667-0525
Woodinville Gathering Fabric, 14450 Woodinville Red 425-402-9034
Yakima Fiddlesticks, 1601 Summitview 509-452-7718
Yakima Ann's Quilts and Things, 3504 Ahtanum Rd 509-965-2313
Yakima Country Quilter, 551 Windy Ln 509-966-9130
Yakima Double Bobbin, 4202 Garden Park Way 509-966-5327
Yakima Cozy Cottage Quilts, 4111 Englewood Ave. 509-972-8558
Yelm Quilts by Flo, 13242 Rocking S. Lane SE 360-458-6667

Washington Guilds:

Anacortes Fidalgo Island Quilters, P.O. Box 1302, 98221 — Meets: 1st & 3rd Monday 12:30 p.m. and 7 p.m. at United Methodist Church
Anacortes Northwest Quilting Connection, 906 35th St., 98221
Bellingham Evergreen Quilters , P.O. Box 5344, 98227 — Meets: 1st & 3rd Thursday 10 a.m. at Garden St. Methodist Church
Bellingham Moonlight Quilters, 98226 — Meets: 2nd Monday 6:30 p.m.
Burlington Cascade Quilters, 1273 Eagle Dr., 98233 — Meets: 2nd Monday (Sept - June) 2 p.m. at Conway Fire Hall
Camano Island Camano Island Quilters — Meets: 1st Wednesday 10 a.m. (Sept. - June) at Country Club Fire Station, 1326 S. Elger Bay Rd. 1st Thursday 6:30 p.m. at Stanwood Library
Centralia S.W. Washington Rainy Daze Quilt Guild, P.O. Box 13, 98531 — Meets: 2nd Tuesday 6:30 p.m. at Fords Prairie Grange
Chehalis Country Quilters, 975 NW Pennsylvania Ave., 98532 — Meets: Weekly in member's home
Chimicum Cabin Fever Quilt Club, P.O. Box 207, 98325 — Meets: Mondays at Tri-Area Community Center
Colfax Whitman Samplers Guild, 114 N. Main, 99111 — Meets: 2nd Monday 7 p.m. at Becky's Fabrics
Colville Colville Piecemakers, 1496 Q Hwy. 20 E, 99114 — Meets: 3rd Tuesday 6:30 p.m. at Lutheran Church, 295 E. Dominion
Colville Quilters II, 129 E. Elm, 99114 — Meets: 4th Monday 1 p.m. at Free Methodist Church, E. 1st & S. Elm
Cosmopolis Pieceful Discoverers Quilt Guild, 1439 4th — Meets: 2nd & 4th Tuesday 7 p.m.
Dayton Blue Mountain Quilters, 245 E. Main, 99328 — Meets: 4th Monday 7:30 p.m. at Methodist Church
Deer Park Fat Quarter Quilters, W 2024 Antler Rd., 99006
Eatonville Mountain Quilters, 39615 Meridan E., 98328
Everett Quilt by Degree Club, 3122 Broadway, 98201 — Meets: Last Friday 7 p.m. at Quilt with EASE
Fairfield Rock Creek Quilters
Fairfield Fairfield Quilt Guild, Rt. #1, Box 134A, 99205
Federal Way Crazy Quilters of Federal Way, 615 SW 346th St., 98023 — Meets: 2nd & 4th Thursday 6 p.m. at Faith Baptist Church, 5714 - 20th St. NE, Tacoma
Gig Harbor Peninsula Lutheran Church Women Quilters, 6509 38th Ave. NW, 98335
Gig Harbor One Block Short, 8711 92nd St. NW, 98332
Graham Mountain Valley Guild, 24809 50th Ave. E, 98338
Grandview Horizon Quilters Ltd. of Yakima Valley, P.O. Box 202, 98930 — Meets: 2nd Tuesday 9:30 a.m. at Immanuel Lutheran Church, 300 S. Euclid
Grays Harbor Pieceful Discovers Quilt Club, 42 Panhandle Rd., 98550 — Meets: Twice a month Tuesdays 6:30 p.m. (Except Nov. & Dec) at Cosmopolis School
Greenbank Quilters on the Rock, 1188 E. Sherwood Ln., 98253
Hoodsport Ladies of the Lake, P.O. Box 36, 98548

Hoquaim	Pieceful Discovers Quilt Guild	
Issaquah	Issaquah Quilters Guild, P.O. Box 337, 98029	Meets: 2nd Friday 10 a.m. at Our Savior Lutheran Church
Kalama	Quacky Quilters, 417 Modrow Rd., 98625	
Kenmore	Quilts From the Heart, P.O. Box 82133, 98028	Service organization making quilts for "at risk" children.
Kennewick	Tri City Quilters, 7807 W. 12th Ave., 99338	
Kennewick	Kennewick Senior Center Quilters, 500 S. Auburn, 99336	
Kent	Covington Quilters, 26503 168th Pl. SE, 98042	
Kent	Evergreen Piecemakers, P.O. Box 5817, 98064	Meets: 2nd & 4th Monday at First Christian Church
LakeBay	Narrows Connection Quiltmakers1604 A St. KPN, 98349	
Lamont	Cheney Country Quilters, Rt. #2, Box 70, 99017	Meets: Mondays 1 p.m. at Ben Franklin store, Cheney
Langley	Crazy Quilters, 2845 E. St., Hwy. 525, 98260	Meets: Weekly 10 a.m. at Bayview Senior Services
Leavenworth	Piece Full Quilters, 917 Commercial St., 98826	Meets: Mondays 6 p.m. at Mrs. Anderson's Lodging House
Long Beach	Peninsula Quilt Guild, Box 12621, 98931	Meets: 2nd Monday 1 p.m. at Peninsula Church Center
Longview	Chatty Quilters, 250 Niemi Rd., 98632	Meets: 2nd & 4th Wednesday 10 a.m. (except Dec)
Longview	Calico Quilter, 4723 Olympia Way, 98632	Meets: Weekly in member's home
Lopez Island	Enchanted Quilters, Rt. #2, Box 3030, 98261	Meets: 2nd Tuesday, Lopez Senior Center
Lynden	Sew and Sews, 825 Fern Dr., 98264	Meets: 3rd Friday at 825 Fern Dr.
Lynden	Pieceable Quilters, 830 E. Wiser Lake Rd., 98264	Meets: 1st Tuesday 7 p.m. at the Fabric Cottage
Lynnwood	Quilters Anonymous, P.O. Box 322, 98046	Meets: 2nd Wednesday 10 a.m. and the Tuesday night before 7 p.m. at Church of Christ
Milton	Quilters Les Complete, P.O. Box 594, 98354	
Moses Lake	Basin Piecemakers, 5103 Viking Rd., 98837	Meets: 4th Tuesday 7 p.m. at Immanuel Lutheran Church
Mt. Vernon	Cascade Quilters, 1302 E. Kincaid St., 98273	
Naches	Apple Valley Piecemakers, 98937	Meets: 3rd Monday 7 p.m. at Naches Fire Hall
Newport	Pend O'Reille Quilters, 306 S. Washington, 99156	
Ocean Shores	Sea Gal Quilters, P.O. Box 1022, 98569	Meets: 4th Wednesday 1 p.m. at Centerbury Inn, 634 Ocean Shores Blvd.
Odessa	Fronen Stepdecker Odessa Quilt Club, P.O. Box 705, 99159	Meets: Every Monday @ 7 pm at Odessa Museum "Barn"
Olympia	Quiltmakers of Olympia, P.O. Box 7751, 98507	
Orcas Island	Creative Quilters of Orcas Island, P.O. Box 264, 98245	
Port Angeles	Crazy Quilters, 727 S. Alder St., 98362	Meets: 2nd & 4th Tuesday 1 p.m. at member's home
Port Angeles	Court House Quilters, 305 W. 3rd, 98362	
Port Orchard	Port Orchard Quilters Guild, P.O. Box 842, 98366	
Port Orchard	West Sound Quilt Guild, 1860 SE Van Skiver Rd, 98367	Meets: 1st Wednesday 7 p.m. at Givens Community Center on Sidney
Port Townsend	Cabin Fever Quilters, 581 Pinecrest Dr., 98368	
Poulsbo	Kitsap Quilters, P.O. Box 2787, 98370	Meets: 4th Tuesday 7 p.m. (3rd Tues. in Nov & Dec) at St. Charles Episcopal Church
Pullman	Patchin People, 405 SE Grant, 99163	Meets: Monthly 1:30 p.m. at Rec Hall Statesman Condo
Puyallup	Tacoma Quilters, 2028 Historic Way, 98371	
Puyallup	Puyallup Valley Quilters, P.O. Box 1421, 98371	
Rainier	Rainier Chapel Women's Quilters, 13902 Finian Rd. SE, 98576	
Raymond	Willapa Harbor Quilters, Rt. #3, Box 39A, 98577	Meets: Tuesdays 11 a.m. & Thursdays 7 p.m. at First Baptist Church, 9th & Duryea
Reardan	The Country Samples Quilts Club, Rt. #1, Box 15E, 99029	
Redmond	Block Party Quilters, P.O. Box 932, 98073	Meets: 1st Thursday 7 p.m. at Eastside Catholic High School, 11650 SE 60th, Bellevue
Renton	Cedar River Quilters	Meets: 3rd Wednesday 6:30 p.m. at Lutheran Church, South 2nd & Whitworth
Richland	South Eastern Washington Quilters, P.O. Box 1201, 99352	Meets: 1st Tuesday 7 p.m. at Benton Co. PUD
Richland	Tri City Quilters, P.O. Box 215, 99352	Meets: 2nd Monday 7 p.m. at PUD, Kennewick & 3rd. Monday 10 a.m. at Central United Church, Richland
Ritzville	Peace by Piece Ritzville Quilter Guild, 107 W. Main, 99169	Meets: 2nd Monday night at Zion Congregational Church
Roy	Eatonville Quilt Club, 32425 S.R. 507, 98580	
Seattle	Contemporary Quilt Assoc., P.O. Box 95685, 98145	Meets: 2nd Saturday 10:30 a.m. at University Unitarian Church, 6556 35th Ave. NE
Seattle	The Y's Piecemakers, 7740 17th Ave. SW, 98106	
Seattle	Seattle Quilt Troupe, 6203 Vassar Ave. NE, 98115	
Seattle	Big Pretty Girls	
Seattle	Pacific Northwest Needle Arts Guild, 4649 Sunnyside Ave. N, 98103	Three general meetings each year and approx. mine workshops
Seattle	Around the Sound Quilters Guild, 350 N. 190th St. #418-C, 98133	
Seattle	Pacific Northwest Quilters, P.O. Box 22073, 98122	
Seattle	Northwest Association of Quilt Artists, 8361 30th Ave. NW, 98117	
Seattle	Riverton Park United Methodist Women, 98168	
Sequim	Sunbonnet Sue Quilt Club, P.O. Box 211, 98382	Meets: Wednesdays at Masonic Hall
Shelton	Christmastown quilters, E. 200 Tramac Pl., 98584	Meets: 2nd Thursday 7 p.m. at Mason General Hospital
Shoreline	Wednesday Friendship Quilters, 19342 1st NW, 98177	
Snohomish	Q.U.I.L.T. Connectin, P.O. Box 61, 98291	Meets: 2nd Thursday in member's home
Snohomish	Busy Bee Quilters, P.O. Box 26, 98291	Meets: 3rd Thursday 6:30 p.m. at St. Michaels Catholic Church, 1512 Pine Ave.
South Colby	West Sound Quilt Guild, P.O. Box 4306, 98384	
Spokane	Spokane Valley Quilters Guild, P.O. Box 13516, 99213	Meets: 1st Tuesday evenings (Feb, March, June, Sept, Oct, Dec) at Valley Senior Center
Spokane	Rock Creek Quilters, Rt. #1, Box 158, 99012	
Spokane	Washington State Quilters, P.O. Box 7117, 99207	Meets: 3rd Thursday Jan, April, July & Sept 1 p.m. & 7 p.m. at Mukigawa Ft. Wright Institute
Stanwood	Northwest Quilting Connection, 1641 County Line Rd., 98292	Meets: 1st or 2nd Saturday (Jan, March, May, Sept, Nov) in various locations
Steilacoom	Piecemakers, 405 Isaac Pincus St., 98388	
Steilacoom	Steady Stitchers, 83 Chapman Loom, 98388	Meets: Tuesdays 9 a.m. in member's home
Sultan	Fat Quarters, 821 4th St., 98294	Meets: 1st Wednesday in member's home
Sunnyside	Lower Valley Quilters of Sunnyside, 5881 Hwy. 241, 98944	Meets: Monthly in member's home
Tacoma	Narrows Connection Quiltmakers	
Tacoma	Mt. Tahoma Quilt Guild, 871 S. 142nd St., 98444	
Tacoma	Needle Arts Guild of Puget Sound, P.O. Box 99093	
Tacoma	Comforters, 98408	Meets: 4th Thursday at South End Community Center
Tacoma	PM Patchers, 1239 E. 54th St., 98404	
Tacoma	Titlow Lodge Quilters, 8425 6th Ave., 98465	
Toledo	Cowlitz Prairie Crazy Quilters, P.O. Box 56, 98591	
Vancouver	Clark County Quilters, P.O. Box 5857, 98668	Meets: 2nd Thursday (Sept - June) 6:30 p.m. at Church of Christ, 800 NE Andersen Rd.
Vancouver	Ongoing Quilters of Marshall Center, 13316 SE McGillivray, 98684	
Vashon	Vashon Island Quilters, P.O. Box 1132, 98070	
Vashon Island	Needle & I Night, 13714 SW 240th St., 98070	Meets: 2nd Monday 7 p.m. at Shoreline Center, 18560 1st Ave. NE, Seattle
Wenatchee	New Kids on the Block Quilters 407 N. Western Ave., 98801	
Wenatchee	North Central Washington Quilters, P.O. Box 2715, 98807	Meets: last Wednesday 7 p.m. at Wenatchee Museum, 127 S. Mission St.
Westport	South Beach Quilter's Guild, P.O. Box 1315, 98595	
White Salmon	White Salmon Quilters, 161 Tunnel Rd., 98672	
Yakima	Yakima Valley Quilter's Guild, P.O. Box 10771, 98909	Meets: 1st & 3rd Wednesday evenings at New Senior Center
Yakima	Yakima Valley Museum Quilters, 2105 Tieton Ave., 98902	Meets: Thursdays 9 a.m. at the museum
Yelm	Prairie Points Quilt Guild	

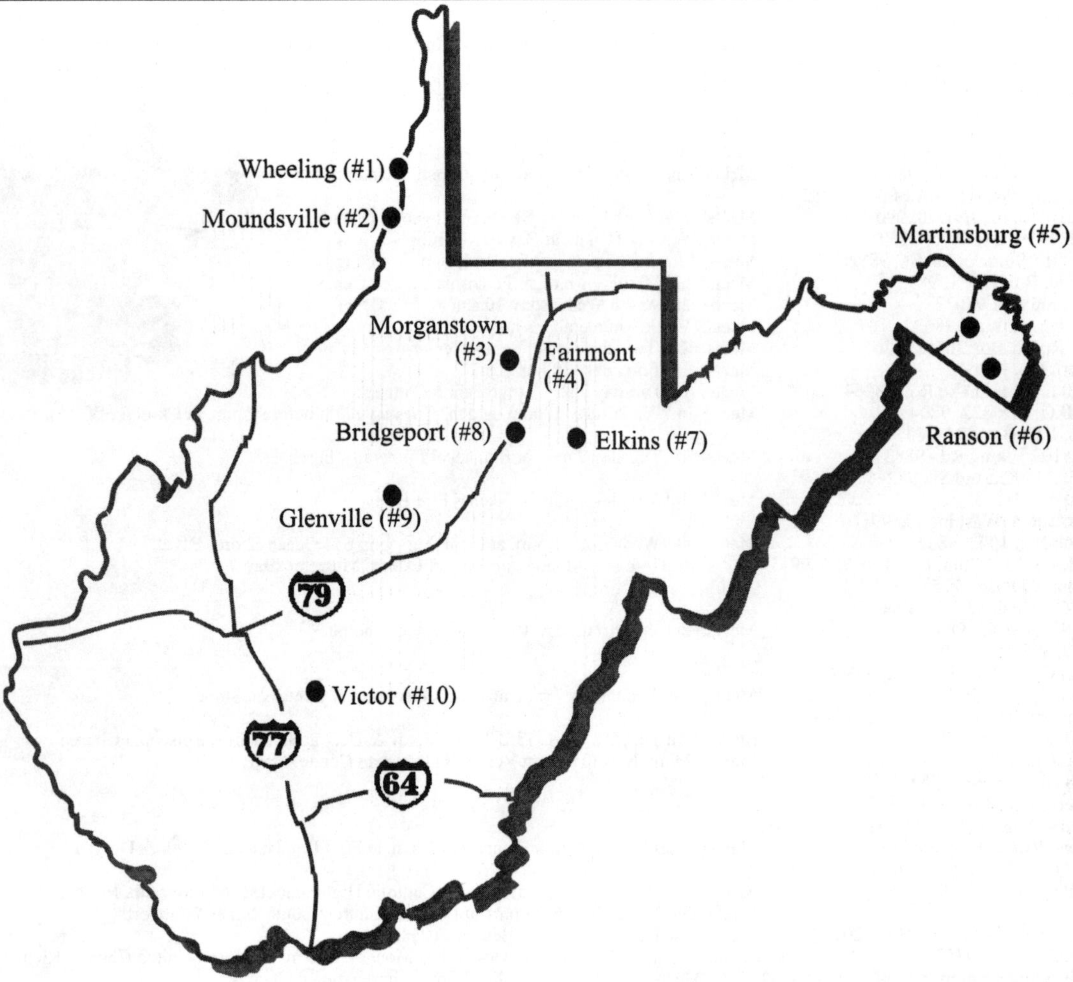

Wheeling (#1)
Moundsville (#2)
Morganstown (#3)
Fairmont (#4)
Martinsburg (#5)
Ranson (#6)
Elkins (#7)
Bridgeport (#8)
Glenville (#9)
Victor (#10)
79
77
64

WEST VIRGINIA

10 Featured Shops

Wheeling, WV #1

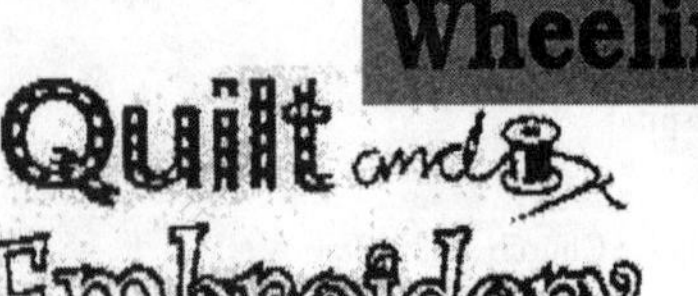

We are Wheeling's only complete fabric and quilting supply shop.

"Come take a stroll down"
FABRIC ROW
1st quality 100% cotton fabrics
Kona Moda P&B RJR
Thimbleberries Batik's Wools
Custom Embroidery

That Patchwork Place & C&P Books

PFAFF SEWING MACHINE DEALER

Cross Stitch Supplies Too

Our friendly, courteous and knowledgeable staff are ready to help with any of your creative ideas.

35 GC & P Road
Wheeling, WV 26003
(304) 233-8299
Fax: (304) 233-9331
Owner: Leslie McGlumphy
lmcglumphy@aol.com

Mon - Fri 10 - 5
Sat 10 - 3

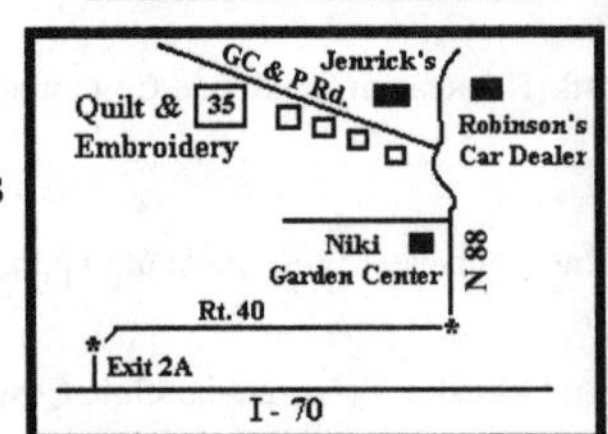

Follow the signs to Oglabay Resort. Simply turn left at Jim Robinson's Ford - we are only 100 yards off of RT88 on GC &P Rd.

Moundsville, WV #2

Mon - Fri 10 - 5
Sat 10 - 3

Theresa's Fabrics

264 Jefferson Ave. 26041
(304) 845-4330
Theresasfabrics@cs.com
Owner: Theresa M. Gouldsberry
Est: 1986 5500 sq.ft. 3000+ Bolts

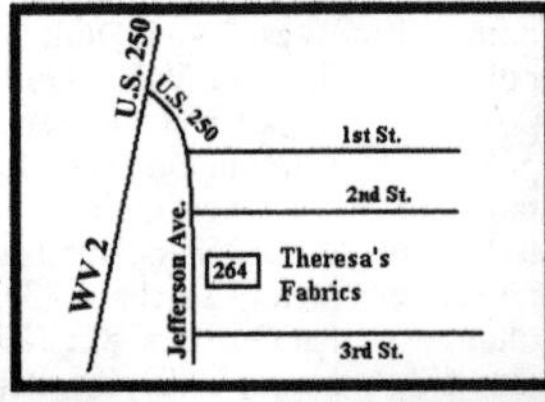

Located in historic Moundsville. We arry over 3000 bolts of fabrics, books, notions, everything for quilting.

Morgantown, WV #3

Mon - Fri 10 - 6
Sat 10 - 5

The Sew Inn, Ltd.

120 High St. 26505
(304) 296-6802
Owner: Virginia Showers
Est: 1973 1500 sq.ft. 3000 Bolts

Wonderful collection of quilting cottons, books, notions & classes. Bridal & Special occasion fabrics. Knowledgeable & Friendly service. Authorized Viking Dealer. Participant in "Mountain Quilt Quest"

Easy Access from I - 79 or I - 68. Located downtown across from The Hotel Morgan.

Fairmont, WV #4

Sew Chic

- Over 2500 bolts of designer cottons
- Complete line of quilting supplies, books, patterns, and notions
- Huge thread assortment
- Free newsletter on-line or by request
- Year round classes
- Mail orders welcome

Authorized dealer of BERNINA and PFAFF

Mon - Fri 10 - 6
Sat 10 - 2

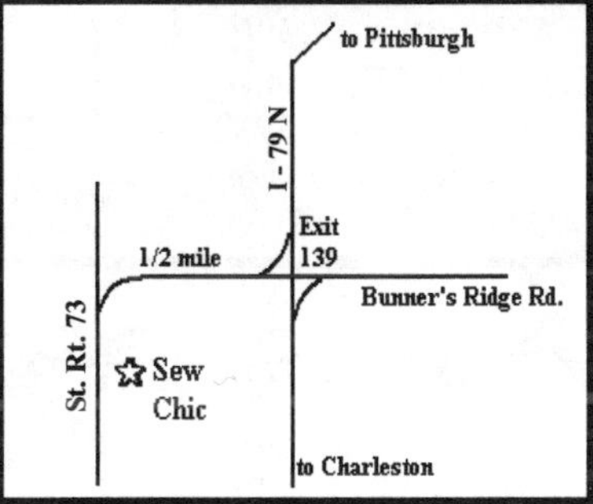

Rt. 3, Box 339 Fairmont, WV 26554
(877) 366-4135 or (304) 366-4135
Participant in Mountain Quilt Quest
(Shop hop held 2nd Thurs, Fri, Sat in June)
www.sewchic.com
Owner: Sue Henderson Est: 1996

Martinsburg, WV #5

Tues - Fri 10 - 5
Sat 10 - 3

NUTMEG LODGE
318 Wilson St. 25401
(304) 262-6633
nbradley67@msn.com
Owner: Barbara Bradley

A complete Quilt Shop featuring 2500+ bolts of 100% cotton fabric, books, patterns, notions galore. Warm, cozy atmosphere. Pleasant, Friendly Staff!

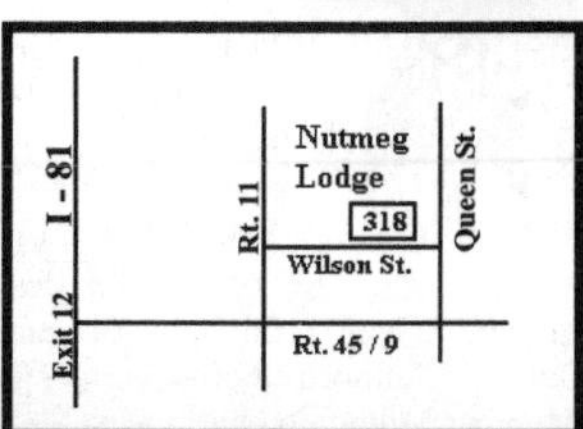

Ranson, WV #6

Quilts 'N Such

101 S. Mildred St. Ranson, WV 25438
Ph: 304-724-9018 Fax: 304-724-9019
E-Mail: info@quilts-n-such.com
www.quilts-n-such.com
Owner: Gayle Schild

Mon – Sat 10 – 5
Wed 12 - 6

Quality Quilting FABRIC, BATTING, WOOL FELT, DMC, PATTERNS, NOTIONS, ...and all the finishing touches in a warm and inspiring atmosphere

Helping you build your family heirlooms - one block at a

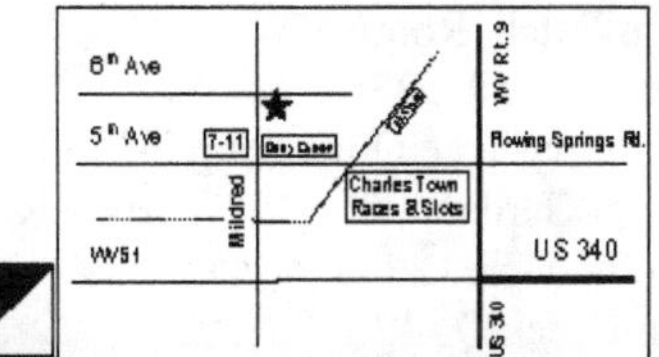

Ranson is next to Charles Town WV

15 Miles East of Martinsburg WV / I-81 on WV Route 9

8 Miles West of Harpers Ferry WV on US 340

Elkins, WV #7

Mon - Sat 9 - 5
Fri til 7

Elkins Sewing Center

300 Davis Ave. 26241
(304) 636-9480 or (800) 229-9480
Fax: (304) 636-9486 Est: 1982
E-Mail: SueESC@aol.com 4000 sq.ft.
Owners: Sue & Jim Pifer Free Catalog

Quilting fabrics, books & notions Specialty threads and trims. Cross stitch supplies. Classes. Viking sewing machines and sergers.

Bridgeport, WV #8

The Pine Tree Quilt Shop

Mon - Fri 9:30 - 5
Sat 9:30 - 4

132 Thompson Dr. 26330
(304) 842-3200
pinetreequiltsho@ma.rr.com
Owner: Kerri E. Smith
Est: 1987 1200 sq.ft.

A quilt shop to satisfy the desires of any quilter. Over 1100 bolts of quality quilting fabrics. Authorized Husqvarna Viking Dealer. Member Mountain Quilt Quest Shop Hop.

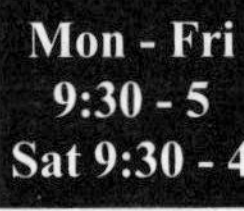

Glenville, WV #9

The Crafter's Patch

Tues - Sat 9 - 5

Main and Morris Sts. 26351
(304) 462-4010
Owner: Sadie Kelble
Est: 1994 1500 sq.ft. 500 Bolts

The Best 100% Cotton Quilt Fabrics. P&B, Benartex, RJR, South Seas. Quilting and Sewing Notions. Year round classes. Helpful information when needed. Member of the WV Quilt Shop Hop.

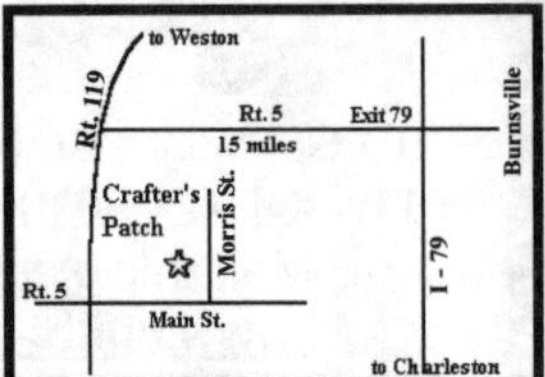

Victor, WV #10

QUILTS & MORE

- Quality Fabrics From Top Designers and Manufacturers
- Books, Patterns, Notions, Thread
- Custom Quilts, New and Collectible Quilts
- Custom Pre-Cut Quilts
- Antiques and Collectible Consignment Shop
- Home of Emma & Estella's Pattern Company

Member of the Annual WV Quilt Shop Hop

Mon - Sat 10 - 5
Dec 1st to March 31st
Mon - Sat 10 - 4

HC.65, Box 51
Victor, WV 25938
(304) 658-3606
Fax: (304) 574-3910
Wvquilter1@aol.com
Owner: Debra Davis

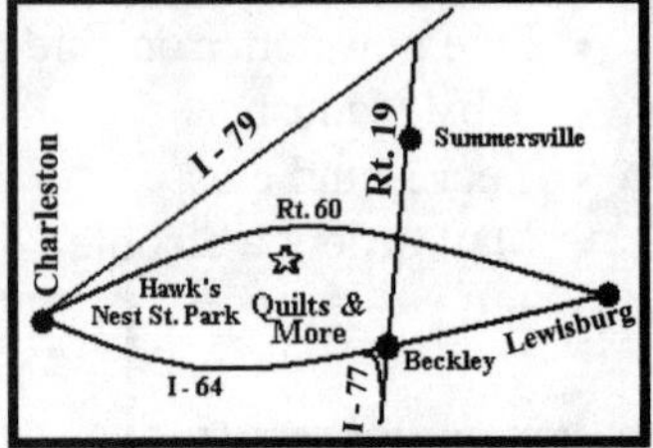

From Rt. 19 go 2½ miles West on Rt. 60 or 3½ miles East of Hawks Nest State Park on Rt. 60

Other Shops in West Virginia: *We suggest calling first*

Clarksburg	Clarksburg Sewing Center, P.O. Box 353A Route 2	304-622-8112
Farmington	Cotton Patch, Route 250 N.	304-825-6225
Huntington	Quilts & Crafts, 2887 5th Ave.	304-736-2778
Huntington	The Cherry Tree Quilt Shop, 6306 E. Pea Ridge	304-736-8086
Hurricane	Quilters Garden, 3006 Mt. Vernon Rd. #1000	304-760-1111
Hurricane	Quilts & More, 2943 Putnam Ave.	
Malden	Cabin Creek Quilts, 4208 Malden Dr.	304-925-9499
Peterstown	Shannon's Quilts, 687 Hansbarger Rd	304-753-5345
Reedsville	Eleanor's Quilt Shop, Rt. 7 E., Kanes Creek	304-864-5762
Rippon	Gunny Sack, Rt. 340 S	304-725-3080
Summersville	Quilt Shoppe, 508 Main St. #A	304-872-0959
Winfield	Fern's Fabric and Quilt Shoppe, 6130 St. Rt. 34	304-757-3047

West Virginia Guilds

Beckley Hands All Around Meets: 1st Monday at United Methodist Temple
Beckley Penthouse Quilters Meets: Every Monday & Thursday at Earhart Dodge Bldg.
Bridgeport Millennium Quilters, 26330 Meets: 4th Monday @ 6:30pm at Maplewood Retirement Condos
Elkins Log Cabin Quilters Meets: 1st Thursday at Elkins Manor
Elkview Mountain Quilters c/o Mary Burdette, 104 Greenberry Dr., 25071
Fayetteville Nimble Thimbles Meets: 3rd Tuesday at American Legion Bldg.
Glenville Thimbles & Thread Quilt Guild, Main & Morris St., 26351
Meets: 3rd Thursday 10 a.m. at Trinity Methodist Church
Hurricane Quilt Lovers Guild c/o Edna Ross, Rt. 4, Box 386, 25526
Morgantown Country Roads Quilt Guild, 120 High St. 26505
Meets: 2nd Thursday 7 p.m. at South Middle School
Pleasant Valley Mountain Heritage Quilters Guild Meets: 2nd Friday at YWCA
Princeton Mercer Co. Quilting Bee c/o Margaret Meador, Rt. 6, Box 109, 24740
South Charleston West Virginia Quilters Inc, P.O. Box 18016, 25302
South Charleston Kanawha Valley Quilters, P.O. Box 8252, 25303
South Charleston Moon & Stars Quilt Guild, P.O. Box 18040, 25303
St. Marys Pleasants County Quilt Club, 116 Lafayette Ave., 26170
Meets: 1st & 3rd Wednesday @ 10am at Zepora's Quilt Shop

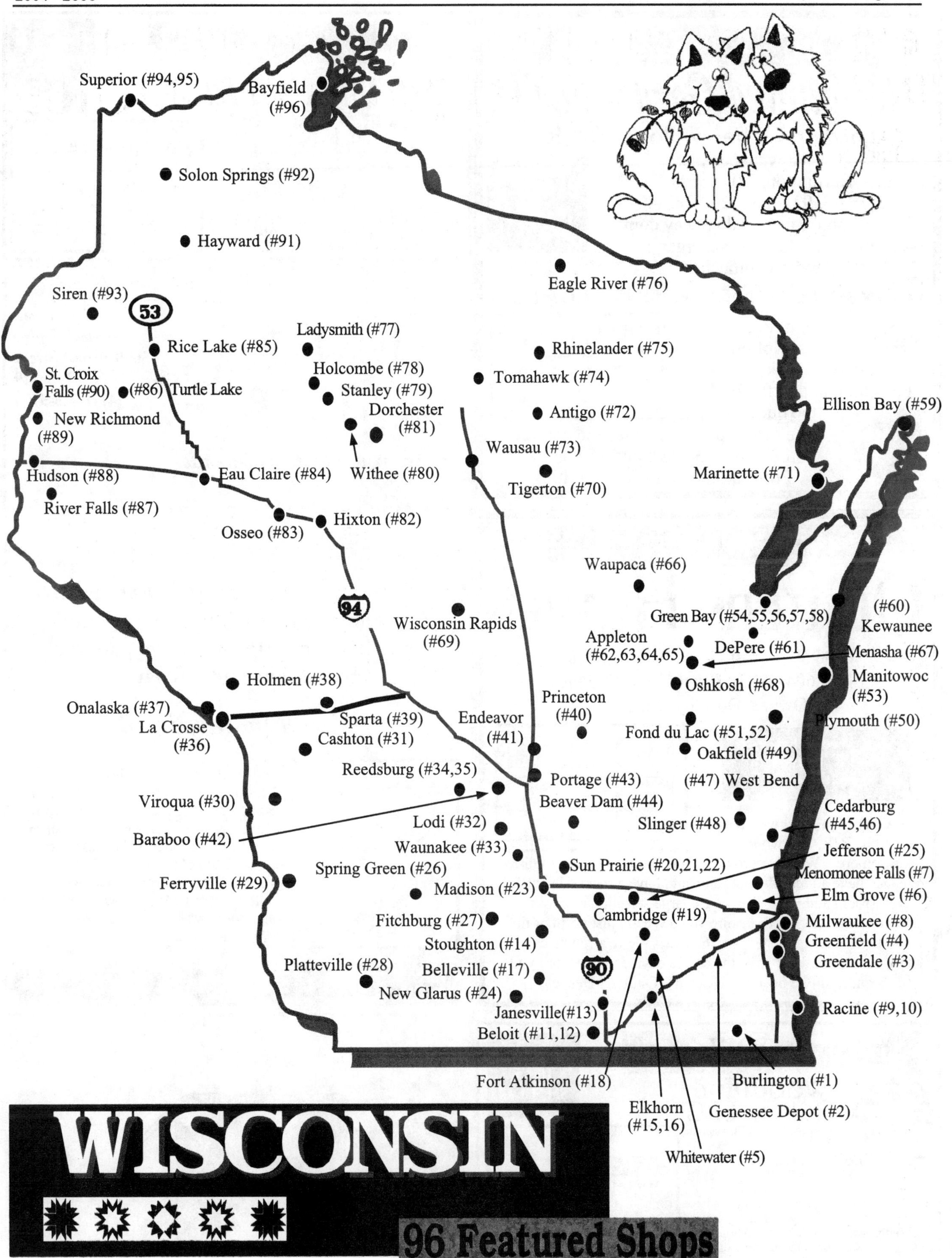
Superior (#94,95)
Bayfield (#96)
Solon Springs (#92)
Hayward (#91)
Eagle River (#76)
Siren (#93)
53
Ladysmith (#77)
Rice Lake (#85)
Rhinelander (#75)
Holcombe (#78)
Tomahawk (#74)
St. Croix Falls (#90)
(#86) Turtle Lake
Stanley (#79)
Dorchester (#81)
Antigo (#72)
Ellison Bay (#59)
New Richmond (#89)
Wausau (#73)
Hudson (#88)
Eau Claire (#84)
Withee (#80)
Marinette (#71)
Tigerton (#70)
River Falls (#87)
Osseo (#83)
Hixton (#82)
Waupaca (#66)
94
Wisconsin Rapids (#69)
Green Bay (#54,55,56,57,58)
(#60) Kewaunee
Appleton (#62,63,64,65)
DePere (#61)
Menasha (#67)
Holmen (#38)
Oshkosh (#68)
Manitowoc (#53)
Onalaska (#37)
Princeton (#40)
La Crosse (#36)
Sparta (#39)
Endeavor (#41)
Plymouth (#50)
Cashton (#31)
Fond du Lac (#51,52)
Oakfield (#49)
Reedsburg (#34,35)
Portage (#43)
(#47) West Bend
Viroqua (#30)
Beaver Dam (#44)
Cedarburg (#45,46)
Lodi (#32)
Slinger (#48)
Baraboo (#42)
Waunakee (#33)
Jefferson (#25)
Spring Green (#26)
Sun Prairie (#20,21,22)
Menomonee Falls (#7)
Ferryville (#29)
Madison (#23)
Elm Grove (#6)
Cambridge (#19)
Fitchburg (#27)
Milwaukee (#8)
Greenfield (#4)
Stoughton (#14)
Greendale (#3)
Platteville (#28)
Belleville (#17)
90
New Glarus (#24)
Janesville(#13)
Racine (#9,10)
Beloit (#11,12)
Fort Atkinson (#18)
Burlington (#1)
Elkhorn (#15,16)
Genessee Depot (#2)
Whitewater (#5)
WISCONSIN
96 Featured Shops

Burlington, WI #1

The Quilted Garden, LTD.

Formerly Liberty House Quilts

925 Milwaukee Ave.
Burlington, WI 53105
262-763-7393 Fax: 262-763-8090
libertyhousequilts@direcway.com
Owners: Mary Shinabargar & Dawn Schumacher

www.thelibertyhouse.com

Mon - Fri 10 - 5
Wed til 8
Sat 9 - 4

Specializing in Fine Fabrics, Wools, Notions, Patterns, Books, Furniture, and Gifts for the quilter.

We offer opening sewing and classes.
Thimbleberries Club and $5 Sampler.
Professional Long Arm Quilting

The Quilted Garden
Lynch Chevrolet
Milwaukee Ave.
925
Hwy. 36
Hwy. 83
Hwy. 20

Genessee Depot, WI #2

Pamella's Place

Mon - Fri 9:30 - 6
Tues til 8
Sat 9:30 - 4

S 42 W 31230 St. Rd. 83 53127
(262) 968-3821
E-Mail: sewing@centurytel.net
Web Site: www.pamellasplace.com
Owner: Pamella Gray
Est: 1987 3200 sq.ft. 2500 Bolts

Bernina sewing machines.
Inspiring Quilting & Fashion fabrics.
Creating Sewing Excitement!

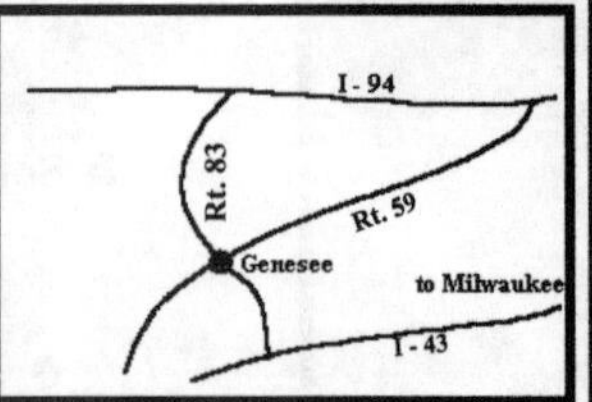

Greendale, WI #3

the Quilting Bee Inc.

Where your creativity blooms!

Located in Historic Greendale Village
5690 Broad Street
Greendale, WI 53129
(414) 423-9774

Come visit our bright, cheerful shop in Historic Greendale Village! (We're only minutes away from downtown Milwaukee.) We have a *fabulous* supply Of quilting fabrics (we carry the entire Jinny Beyer palette), exclusive patterns, books, kits and giftware!

You'll be inspired!

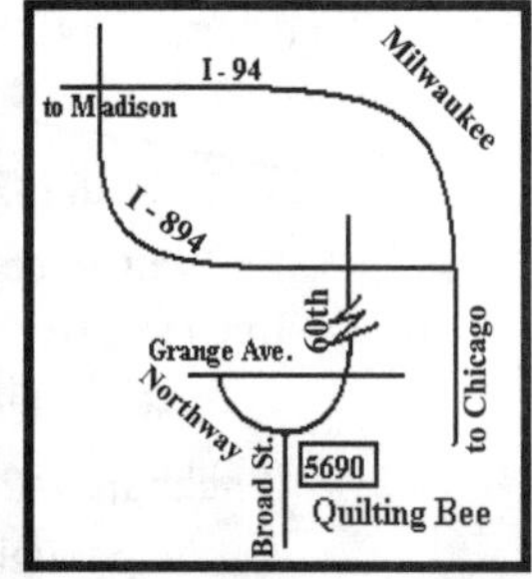

M,T,W,F............9:30am to 6:00pm
Thurs...............9:30am to 9:00pm
Sat...................9:30am to 5:00pm
Sun.................... Noon to 4:00pm

From I-94 outside of Milwaukee, take I-894 to the 60th St. Exit. Turn south. Follow through Grange Ave. where 60th St. turns into Northway. At stop sign turn Left onto Broad Street.. We're across from the Library.

Greenfield, WI #4

Quilters Heaven

6633 W. Forest Home Ave. 53220
(414) 604-9193 Fax: (414) 327-0496
Owner: Dorothy Dorger

Mon, Wed & Fri 9 - 6
Tues & Thur 9 - 8
Sat 9 - 4

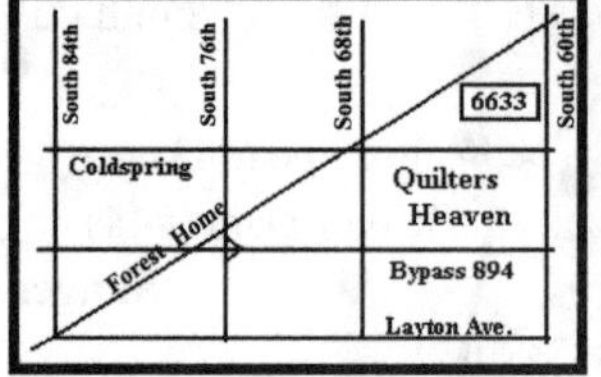

Established in 1999 with Moda, Benartex, RJR, Maywood, South Seas & more. We have grown to 4000 bolts of yummy fabric. We also have a great flannel room and have a second beautiful classroom addition. We have a large selection of books, patterns and samples to inspire you. (We are just north of the 894 bypass using the 60th or 76th exit) We're a fun place to shop, so step in, we'll have the coffee on and you can tell your friends you've been to "Heaven" (Quilter's Heaven)

Whitewater, WI #5

Woodland Quilts, LLC

"Over the River & Through the Woods to Woodland Quilts."

Mon - Fri 10 - 5
Sat 10 - 4

135 W. Main St. 53190
(262) 473-2978
woodland@sbcglobal.net
www.woodlandquilts.com
Owner: Cheryl Kehm

A friendly Quilt Shop offering fabrics, kits, patterns, books and classes for all ages, beginner to advanced. Kids' classes too!

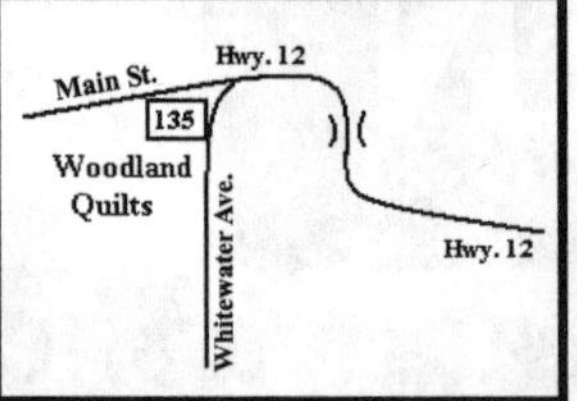

Elm Grove, WI #6

Patched Works, Inc.

In a Western Suburb of Milwaukee
13330 Watertown Plank Rd., Elm Grove, WI 53122
(262) 786-1523
Owner: Trudie Hughes
Est: 1978 6000 sq.ft.

Owned by a Master Fabricaholic

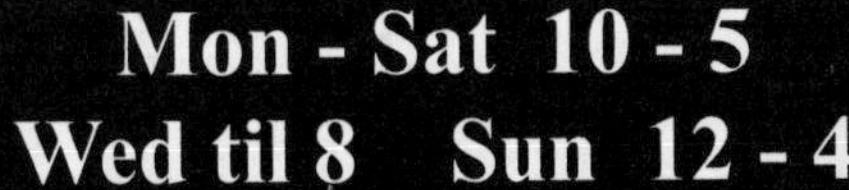

Long Arm Quilting
Service Available
Short Turn Around

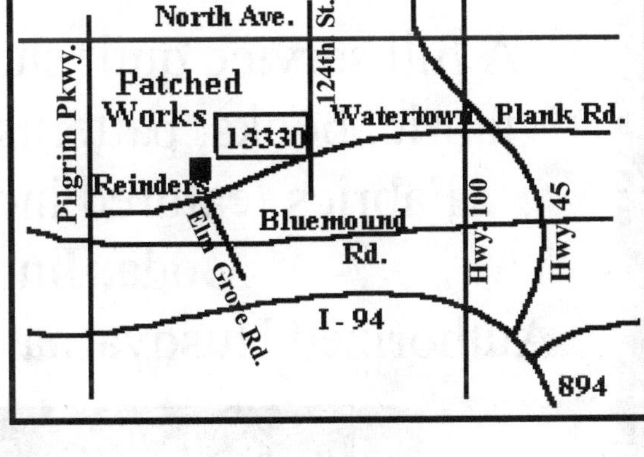

8000 bolts of Cotton Fabric
Hundreds of Books &
Patterns for the Quiltmaker

Menomonee Falls, WI #7

The Quilted Basket, Inc.

N88 W16599 Main St. 53051
(262) 251-8791
tawanke@execpc.com
www.thequiltedbasket.com
Owner: Ann & Tom Wanke

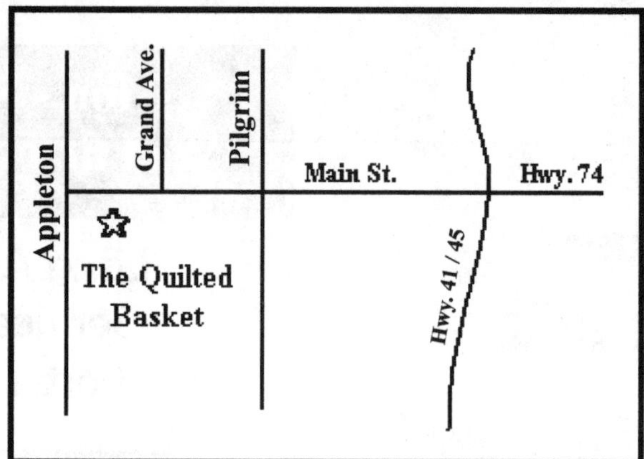

A full service quilt shop featuring over 4000 bolts of fabric, books, patterns, notions and hand dyed wool. Fabrics featured include reproductions, thirties, Moda, Jinny Beyer and more.
Authorized Husqvarna Viking Sewing Machine Dealer.

Mon & Fri 9 - 5 Tues, Wed, Thur 9 - 8
Sat 9 - 4 Sun 11 - 4

Directions to The Cutting Table

From West: Take I-94 East to I-794 East (Port of Milwaukee) over the Hoan Bridge. Take first exit "Port of Milwaukee". Turn left on Carferry Dr. (to Lincoln Memorial Drive). Turn Right on Lincoln Memorial Drive and follow it around to stop light. (Lincoln Memorial Drive turns into Russell Ave.) Stay to the right, through the stop light, ahead two blocks, to Delaware Ave. Shop on your right.

From North: Take 43 South to I-794 East (Port of Milwaukee). Follow directions above.

From South: Take 43 North. Exit Lincoln/Becher Sts. Take Becher Avenue east to Russell. (Becher changes name to Bay Street at Kinnickinnic Ave.) Go left (east) on Russell 2 blocks to Delaware Ave. The Cutting Table is on the corner of Russell and Delaware Avenues.

The shop is south of downtown and 4 blocks west of beautiful Lake Michigan

www.cuttingtable.com

THE CUTTING TABLE®

Fabric

quilting cottons, fashion, bridal, heirloom, wool and home dec

Classes

all types and levels

Machine Quilting Service

2 quilting machines on site

Books · Notions · Patterns · Buttons · Trim

Full-Service Bridal Department

Exquisite Silks, Satins, and Laces · Special Orders Welcome

Bridal Consultant Available Upon Request

AUTHORIZED ELNA DEALER

.... You will be impressed! ....

7000 square feet of inspiration for quilters, seamstresses, rug hookers, heirloom sewers, and home decorators. We welcome you to visit us!

HOURS: M, W 9:30am-8pm T, TH, F 9:30am-6pm
SAT 9:30am-4pm — SUN 12pm-4pm

2499 S. Delaware Ave.
Milwaukee, WI 53207
414-744-3747

Milwaukee, WI #8

Complete Quilt & Cross-Stitch Shop

Two stories of Wonderful Fabrics, Graphs, Patterns and Gifts with a friendly, knowledgeable staff to help.

Mon, Wed, Fri	10:00 a.m. - 5:00 p.m.
Tues, Thurs	10:00 a.m. - 8:00 p.m.
Saturday	10:00 a.m. - 4:00 p.m.
Sunday	11:00 a.m. - 4:00 p.m.

Calico, Canvas & Colors

Racine, WI #9

3305 Washington Ave. 53405
(262) 632-4224

Look for our newly published books and patterns by *Calico Printworks* (that's us!)

We'd love to have you visit us - in person or on our new web site!
We also have a new toll-free telephone number to make ordering easier.

(888) 3CALICO — (888) 322-5426

Fax: (262) 632-2457 E-Mail: calicocc@execpc.com

Est: 1979 3000 sq.ft

Web Site: www.calicocanvasandcolors.com.

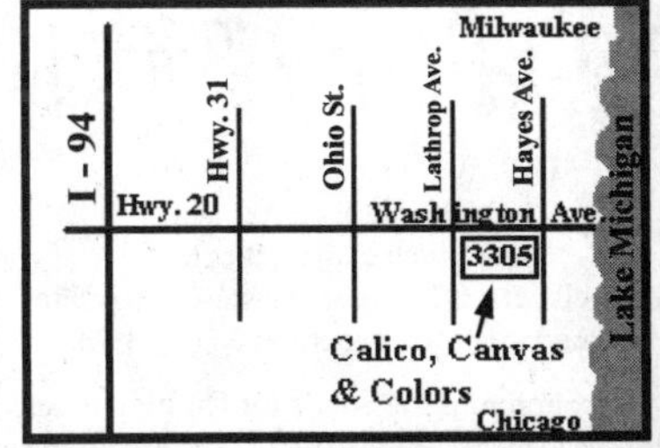

Racine, WI #10

Hours by Appt. Only

Quilters' Studio, LLC.

5640 Tracy Circle 53402
(262) 681-2000
Pat@QuiltersStudiollc.com
www.quiltersstudioLLC.com
Owner: Pat Barry Est: 2002

Call For Directions

Learn to use our Gammill plus Long-arm Quilting Machines
Then finish your quilt yourself. Classes, Rentals, No Fabric.

Beloit, WI #11

Mon - Fri 10 - 5:30 Sat 10 - 4

Attic Quilts

314 State St. 53511
(608) 364-4037 Fax: (608) 368-2913
smquilts@aol.com Est: 1997
www.atticquilts.com 3000 sq.ft.
Owner: Sally McFerren 2700 Bolts

Books, Patterns, Notions, lots of gadgets. 100% Cotton Fabrics: RJR Hoffman, Benartex, Moda, South Seas, Kona Bay, Clothworks, Thimbleberries, Plaids, Flannels.

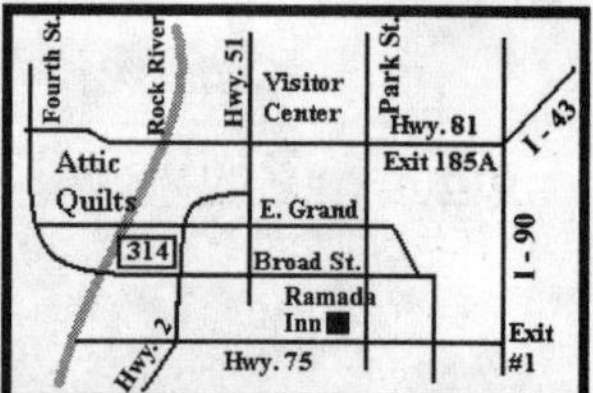

Beloit, WI #12

Schoolhouse Quilts

5618 Luther Valley Rd. (Hwy 13)
Beloit WI 53545 608-879-9990
www.ILove2quilt.com

Visit Our Online Quilt Show

Tue - Sat 10 - 5 Sun 12 - 4
Call ahead for Winter Hours

You will feel as if you have stepped back in time when you visit our charming 1800's schoolhouse. We offer the finest quilting fabrics, books & notions as well as those hard to find items for crazy quilting. Hand-dyed wool & velvet, beads, satin, French wire & silk ribbon. We also have many gifts and antiques. Come Visit Us Soon!

Janesville, WI #13

Est: 2003
1500 sq.ft.
1200 Bolts

3000 Milton Ave. #109, Janesville, WI 53545
Phone/Fax (608) 756-9850
lifesastitch@sbcglobal.net Owner: Patricia Riley

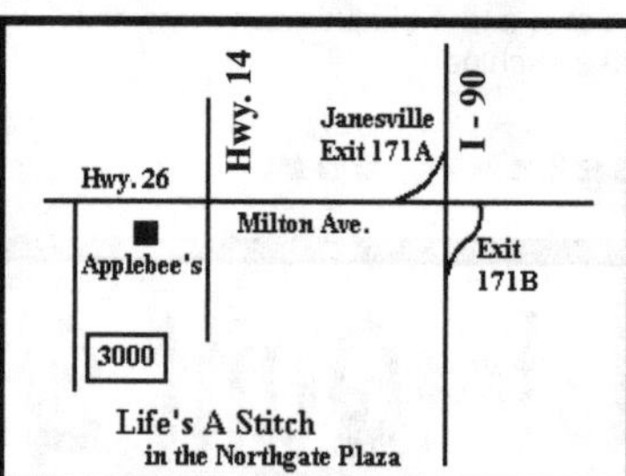

Located 2 blocks west of I-90 off Hwy. 26 (Milton Ave.). High quality fabrics and friendly, helpful service.

Mon - Fri 9:30 - 5:30
Tues & Thur til 8
Sat 9 - 5 Sun 12 - 4

Elkhorn, WI #15

Mon - Fri 10 - 5 Sat 10 - 4

Sawdust & Stitches LLC

13 S. Wisconsin St. 53121
(262) 723-1213 Fax: Same
saw_stitch@hotmail.com
www.elknet.net/Lauds/sawdust&stitches.htm
Owner: Sharon Lauderdale Est: 1996

100% cotton prints & solids for Quilting needs. Patterns, Books, Stitchery & Painting Books. Quilting Classes & Painting classes offered.

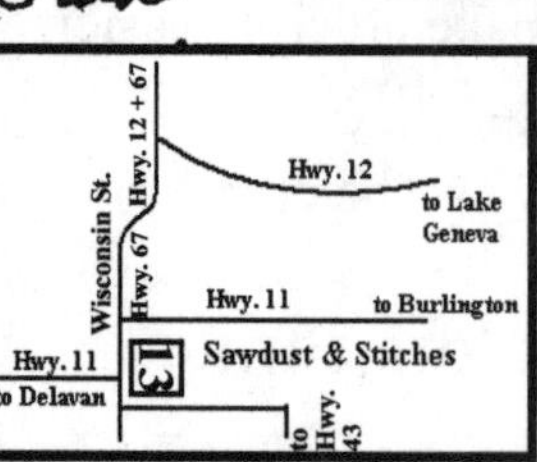

Saving Thyme

233 W. Main St., Stoughton, WI 53589
(608) 877-0075 Fax: (608) 877-0076
gstehley@inxpress.net Owner: Gloria Stehley
Est: 2000 1700 sq.ft.

Stoughton, WI #14

Located in a 4 level Victorian style shop on the river in Historic Downtown Stoughton. Houses a unique blend of quilting fabric, notions, and kits and Scandinavian Imports with local art enhancing the unique atmosphere.

Mon - Sat 10 - 5
Thur til 7
Sun (seasonal) 12 - 4

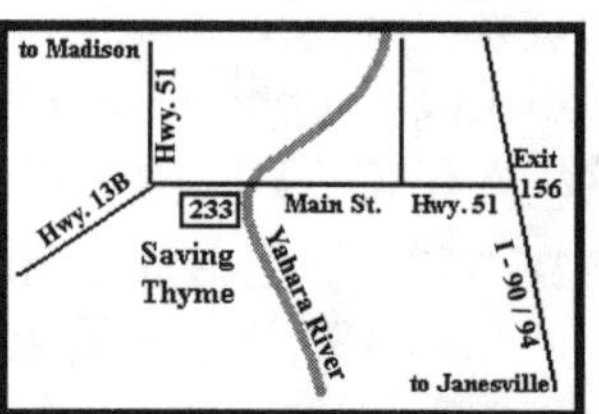

www.savingthyme.net

The Quilting Connection

Longarm Rental & Quilting Retreats

Tuesday thru Thursday or Friday thru Sunday
Longarm Training Classes - We teach you!
Longarm Rentals - Quilt your own quilts!
6 Local Quilt Shops to "Hop"!
On site overnight accommodation for 6 guests: 3 bedrooms, sitting room and a room for piecing! Our sewing room is equipped with a 5' table and chair for each guest, a cutting table, iron and ironing board. Bring your sewing machine and piece at night, then finish your quilt tops on our longarms during the day! Call Sue to book a date! Our Retreat is also available for knitting, scrapbooking, hand quilting or other crafts. If you teach or want to get a group of 6-9 friends together to do your own thing call Sue for more info.

Quilting Supplies

108" - 110" fabrics, thread, batting, stencils, patterns, PatternGrid, and the *Quick Zip System* for accurate quilt loading and advance pinning. Great on longarm or Handi-Quilter / Grace type frames!

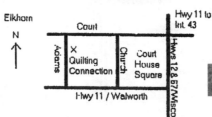

Elkhorn
N
Court
Hwy 11 to Int. 43
Adams
X Quilting Connection
Church
Court House Square
Hwys 12 & 67/Wisconsin
Hwy 11 / Walworth

APQS Representative & Trainer

American Professional Quilting Systems produce the Millennium, Liberty, Freedom and the Discovery longarm models. As an Authorized APQS Representative, we include a FREE training and supply package with each machine purchased from our shop. Mention this ad and receive a free 3 day training workshop with 2 FREE nights in our Quilting Retreat!

Elkhorn, WI #16

We are located 1 block west of the courthouse square

21 Adams Street, Elkhorn 262-723-6775

Hours: Tues. - Fri. 10 - 5: Sat. 10 - 3. www.longarmconnection.com

Belleville, WI #17

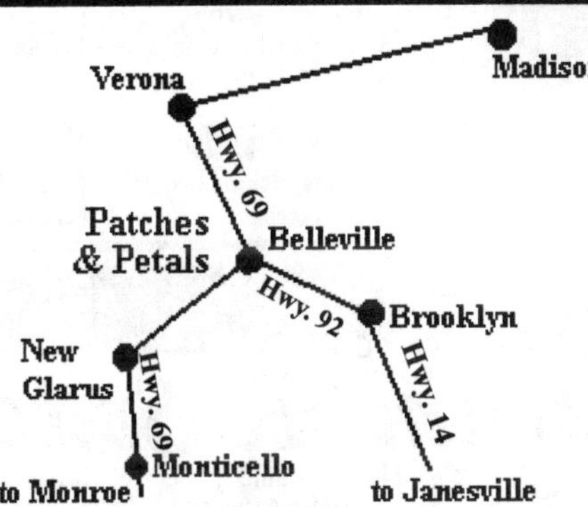

13 W. Main St. 53508
(608) 424-1516 Fax: (608) 424-1730
E-Mail: patches1@chorus.net
Est: 1999 3000 sq.ft. 4000 bolts

Patches & Petals

Warm, Friendly Service.

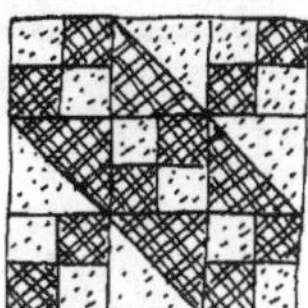

Visit us at: www.patchesandpetals.com

Unique shop featuring fine quilting fabric, books, patterns, quilting supplies, handcrafted gifts, collectibles and antiques. Great Classes.

Home of Sweet Pea Designs

Fort Atkinson, WI #18

The Quilt Patch LLC

Tues - Thur 11 - 5
Fri 10 - 4
Sat 9 - 4

W3352 Lower Hebron Rd. 53538
(262) 593-8462
thequiltpatch@compufort.com
Owners: Wayne & Jane Strunk
Est: 2003 1200 sq.ft.

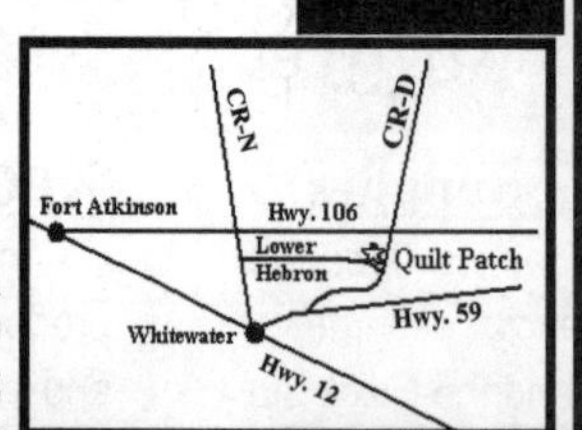

Country quilting at its best. Wonderful selection of fabrics, patterns, books, and gifts to choose from. Worth the trip. Classes and custom long arm quilting.

Sun Prairie, WI #20

Prairie Quiltworks, LLC

Mon - Fri 10 - 5
Sat 10 - 4

229 E. Main St. 53590
(608) 837-9201
Owner: Sue Alstad

Quilting fabrics and supplies. Classes.
Hand guided machine quilting.
Warm and friendly atmosphere.

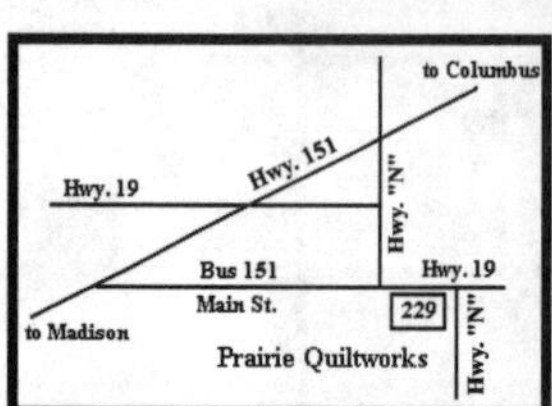

The Quilt Shop

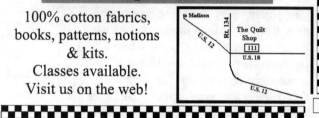

111 Hwy. 18, P.O. Box 280
53523
(608) 423-3185
thequiltsh@aol.com
Owner: Cindy Imhoff
Est: 1996
1500 sq.ft. 1000 Bolts

Annual Quilt Show "Quilts On Ice" 1st Weekend in Feb.

Mon - Fri 10 - 5
Sat 9:30 - 4

Cambridge, WI #19

100% cotton fabrics, books, patterns, notions & kits.
Classes available.
Visit us on the web!

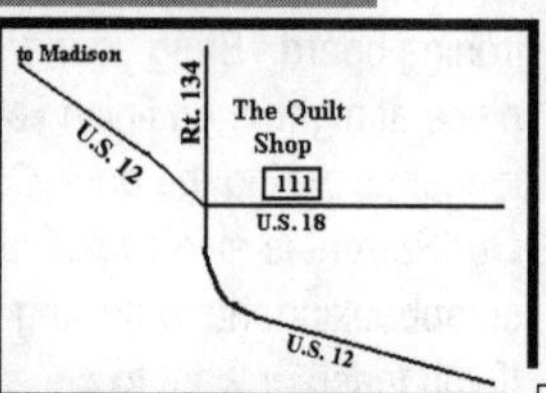

Sun Prairie, WI #21

J.J. STITCHES

Mon - Fri 9:30 - 5:30
Sat 10 - 5

221 E. Main St. 53590
(608) 837-2266
www.jjstitches.com
Est: 1975 5000 Bolts

Featured shop in Quilt Sampler 2002. Store features homespuns, tickings, and vintage replica fabrics.

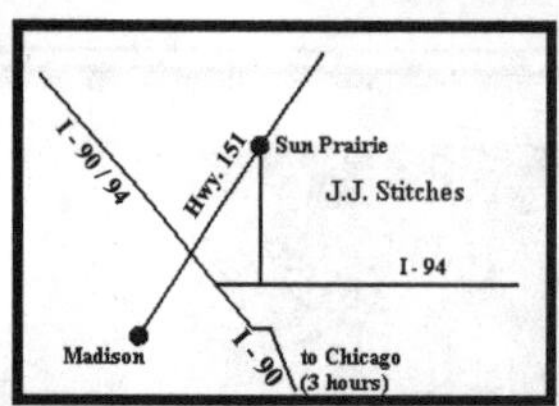

Sun Prairie, WI #22

Itchin' To Stitch

Mon - Fri 9:30 - 5
Sat 9 - 4

509 W. Main St. 53590
(608) 837-4419
Fax: Same
Est: 1983 3500 sq.ft.
7000 Bolts

7000 Bolts of the finest cottons from all major suppliers, notions, books & gifts. Flannels & Homespuns.

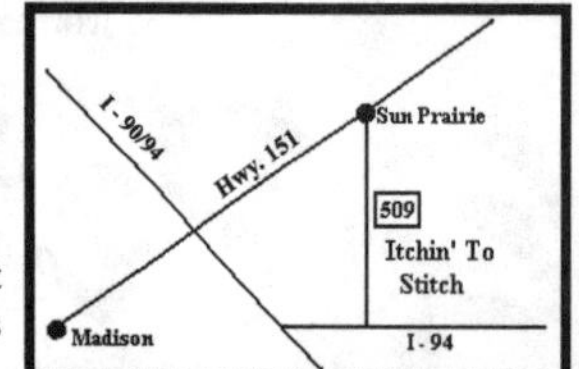

New Glarus, WI #24

Backtown Quilt Shoppe

Mon - Fri 10 - 5
Wed til 6
Sat 10 - 4

307 Second St., P.O. Box 854 53574
(608)5276416
backtownquilt@yahoo.com
Owners: Sharon Schlimgen & Teresa Steele
Est: 2000 2000 sq.ft.

Enjoy our fine fabrics, notions, patterns, books and classes in a warm home-like atmosphere. We have rug hooking supplies and yarn too. Also Machine quilting service!

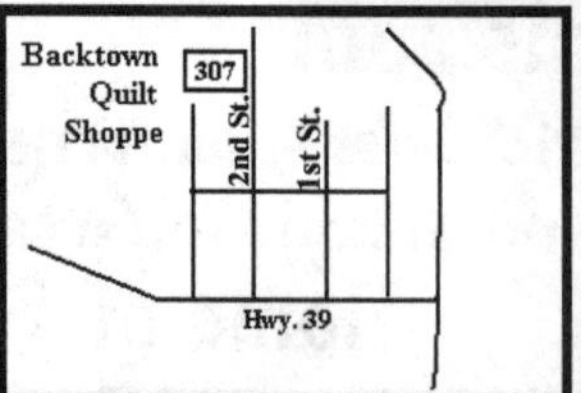

Madison, WI #23

Stitcher's Crossing

"A 2003 Top Ten Quilt Shop"

6122 Mineral Point Rd. 53705
608·232·1500 tel
608·232·1750 fax
e-mail: info@stitcherscrossing.com
Web: www.stitcherscrossing.com
Owner: Sharon Luehring
Est: 1980 4600 sq.ft.

Mon - Fri 9:30 - 6
Thur til 8:30
Sat 9:30 -5

- Great selection of fabrics, books, and patterns for counted cross stitch, quilting, and knitting
- Knowledgeable and friendly staff
- Extensive class schedule
- Bimonthly newsletter

"where country meets contemporary"

"Home of Courageous Fabric"

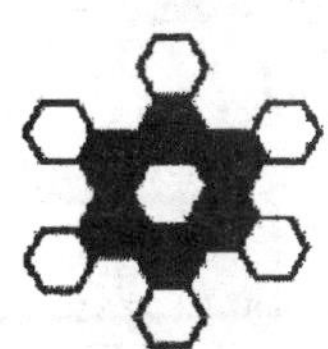

Tea and Textiles, LLC
107 S Main Street Jefferson, WI 53549-1631
On the SW corner of Hwy 26 & Hwy 18
920-674-9010 teaandtextiles@yahoo.com

Join us for a Complimentary Cup of Tea

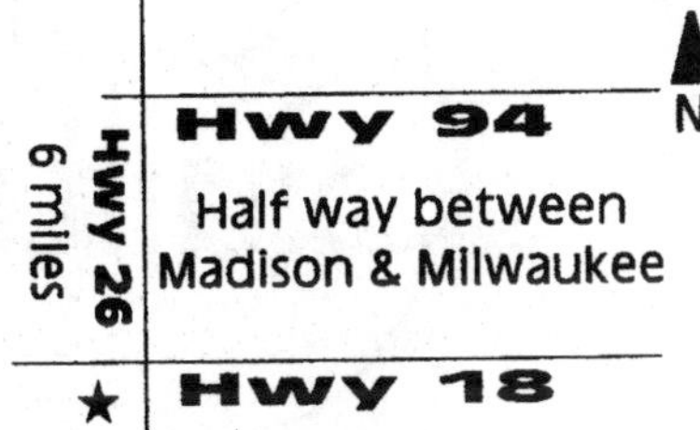

M-Th 9:00 AM - 8:00 PM
F-Sat 9:00 AM - 5:00 PM
Sun 10:00 AM - 5:00 PM

Jefferson, WI #25

3,000 Bolts of 100% Cotton Fabrics
60" - 116" wide Quilt Backings
60" Wide solid color Tundra Fleece

Software:
EQ-5, Aunt Helen's Quilt Designs
Sew Precise Paper Piecing Patterns

Books Patterns Notions Classes Ott-Lites Quilt Racks Gift Certificates
Sew and Tell - 3rd Sunday of Month Charity Sewing Days

Challenge Block of the Month

Reference Library of over 500 books
Free Use of Flannel Board for Design Play and Table for Layering and Pinning Quilts

Linus Quilt Drop-Off Site

Country Sampler

Spring Green, WI #26

www.sgcountrysampler.com
133 E. Jefferson . 53588
608 . 588 . 2510
Fax: 588 . 3528
Owner: Jeanne Horton
Est: 1983
1800 sq. ft.
2000+ Bolts
Newsletter/Catalog $6.00

Featured in Quilt Sampler® 2000

You'll find our specialty shop full of Moda designer homespuns prints, wools, unique kits and patterns.
We are also know for our counted cross-stitch samplers and hand-dyed linens. It's all about inspiration and our finishing ideas do just that.
You'll be further inspired by our reproduction furniture and Americana Collectible Folkart showcased in and around our antique décor.

Designer Workshops.
Fall Favorites Top Tour Participant.

Open Daily
Mon - Thurs 10 - 5
Friday 10 - 6
Sat 10-4:30 • Sun 12-4

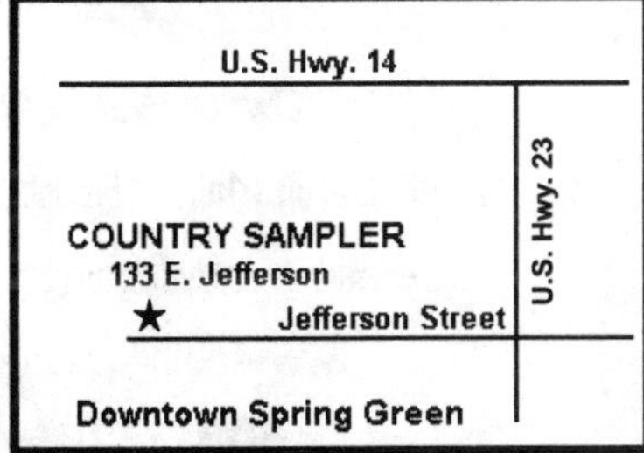

Friendly, knowledgeable Staff and Classical Music all add up to a very enjoyable shopping experience. VISIT SOON!

#27

Find yourself
Going Quilting –
free your creative spirit.

- Full service quilt shop, open 7 days a week
- 10 minutes from downtown Madison
- 5 minutes from 12/18; 15 minutes from 90/94
- 3,000 square feet
- Play area for children
- Comfortable seating area for non-quilters

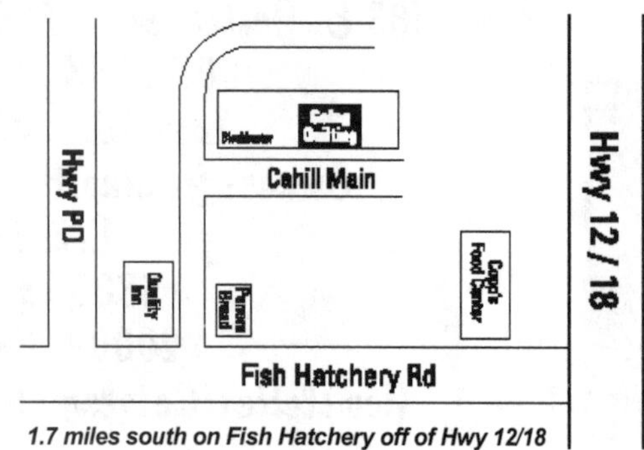

1.7 miles south on Fish Hatchery off of Hwy 12/18

Owner, Wendy Apple

2980 Cahill Main • Fitchburg, WI 53711

email: wendy@goingquilting.com

www.goingquilting.com

608-277-8458

OPEN 7 DAYS A WEEK
Mon-Fri 10-6 • Thurs 'til 8 pm • Sat 9-4 • Sun 12-4

Platteville, WI #28

Mon - Fri 10 - 6
Sat 10 - 4

Hidden Quilts LLC

915 B East Mineral St. 53818
(608) 348-3327
hiddenquiltsllc@mhtc.net
Est: 2002 1200 sq.ft. 1200 Bolts

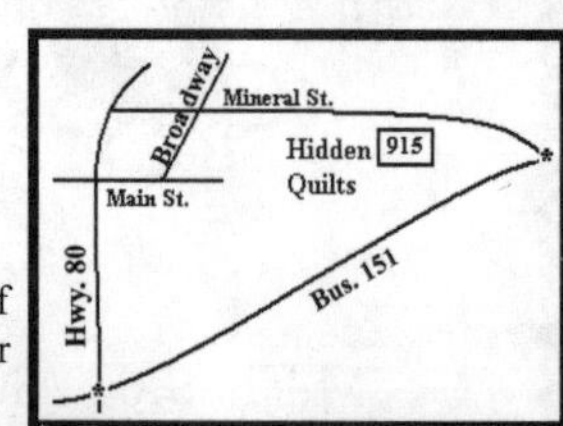

Featuring Hoffman Batiks, carrying entire line of 1895's (hand-dyed colors), Moda and other quality fabrics, patterns, books and notions.

Ferryville, WI #29

Mon - Sat 10 - 5

Olde Tyme Quilt Shoppe

62682 Rush Creek Rd. 54628
(608) 648-2081
Owner: Virginia Johnson
Est: 1986 900 sq.ft.

Virginia's original custom made Quilts--Hand dyed fabric, notions. Hand or machine quilting, outline quilting. Classes

Viroqua, WI #30

Mon - Sat 9:30 - 5
Thur til 7

Quilt Basket 'n' Creations

117 F. S. Dr. 54665
(608) 637-7002
Fax: (608) 637-8049
klswens@yahoo.com
Owner: Karen L. Swenson Est: 1999

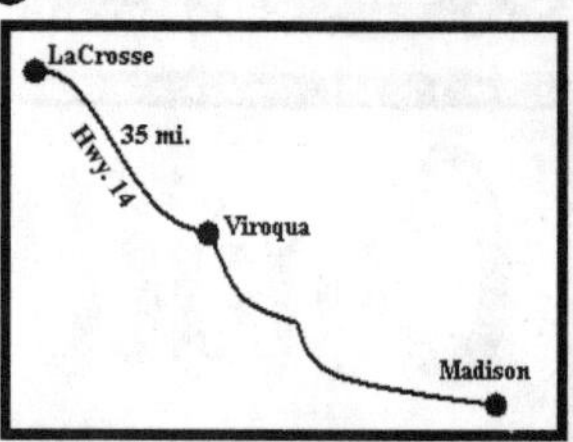

Great selection of 100% cotton fabrics, books, patterns and notions. We also offer a large selection of gifts. Bus Tours Welcome.

Cashton, WI #31

Opening Summer 2004

Inspirations at Dovetail Farm

29553 Nevada Rd. 54619
(608) 654-5727
dovetailfarm@centurytel.net
Est: 2004 400 sq.ft.

Heart of Amish Country. Kits, supplies, books, patterns for quilting, yarn arts, paper and other crafts. Antiques & wood-worked items.

Lodi, WI #32

Tues - Fri 10 - 5
Sat 9 - 2

Village Creek

123 S. Main St. 53555
(608) 592-5793

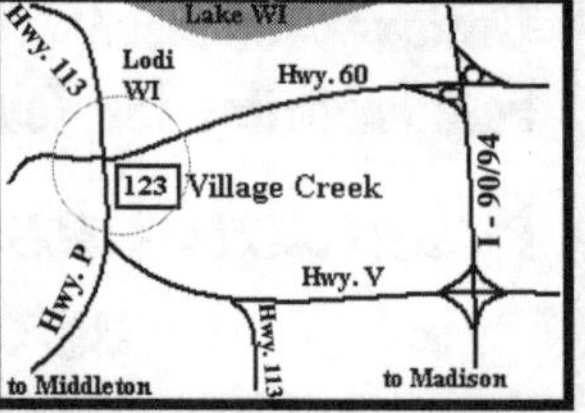

Cozy little shop in the center of downtown Lodi. 1/2 block south of 4 way stop at Hwy. 60.

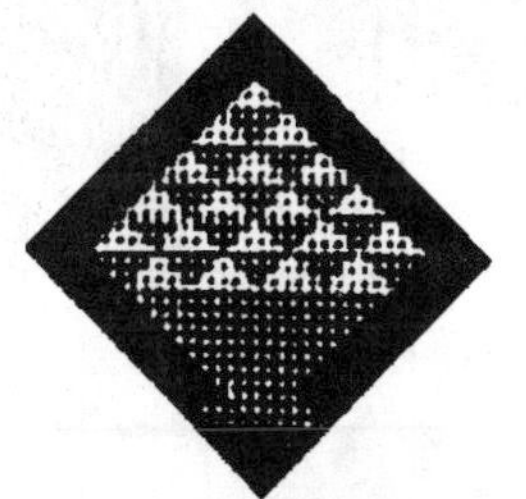

Waunakee, WI #33

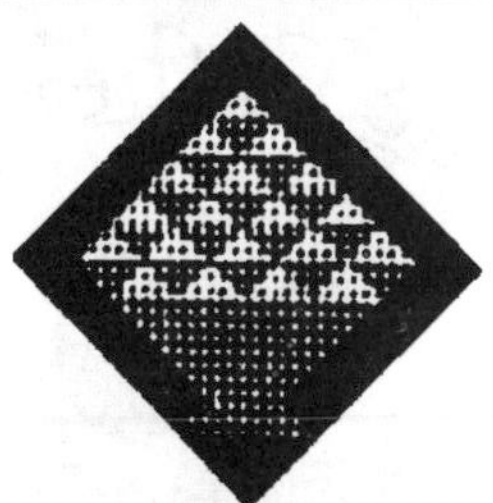

100 Baker St. 53597 (608) 849-6473
Owners: Mike & Debbie Kuehn
Website: www.millhousequilts.com
E-mail: quilts@chorus.net
Est: 1995 8000 sq.ft. Over 7000 Bolts

Mill House Quilts

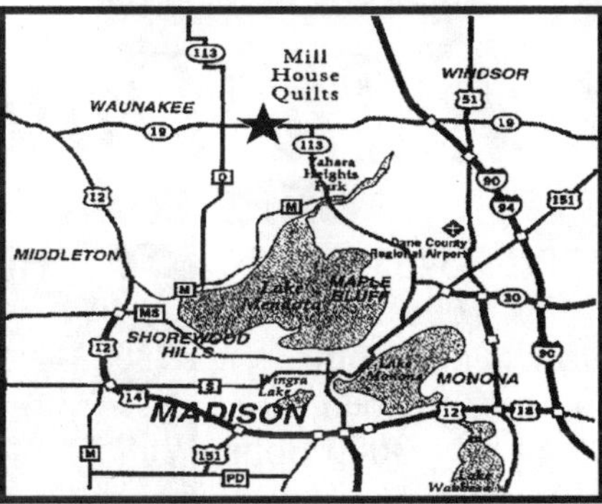

A Top 10 Shop in 2000!

A Refurbished 1875 Feed Mill featuring over 7000 bolts of fine quilting fabrics, quilting supplies, books, patterns & classes. Newsletter and mail orders available upon Request.

Mon - Sat 9 - 5
Thurs til 8

Off 90 - 94 exit Hwy. 19 West to Waunakee
Located just off Main St. in the "Heart of Waunakee"
7 miles from Madison

Reedsburg, WI #34

Quintessential Quilts

940 East Main 53959 (608) 524-8435
Est: 1989 qquilts@jvlnet.com
Please check out our sister shop in Baraboo.
www.qquilts.com

Mon - Sat 9 - 5
Thur 9 - 8
Sun 12 - 4

WISCONSIN'S BEST KEPT QUILTING SECRET!

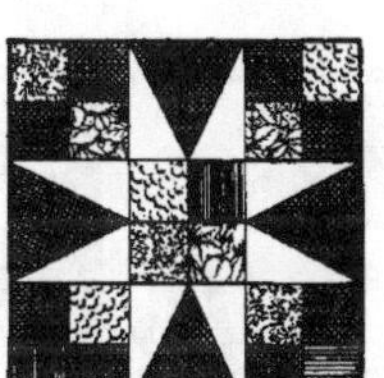

Over 12,000 bolts of fabric.
Large selection of books, patterns & notions. All your quilting needs located under one roof!
Continuous schedule of classes.
Spring & fall weekend seminars.
Mail orders and newsletter available upon request.
Authorized Husqvarna Viking Sales & Service.

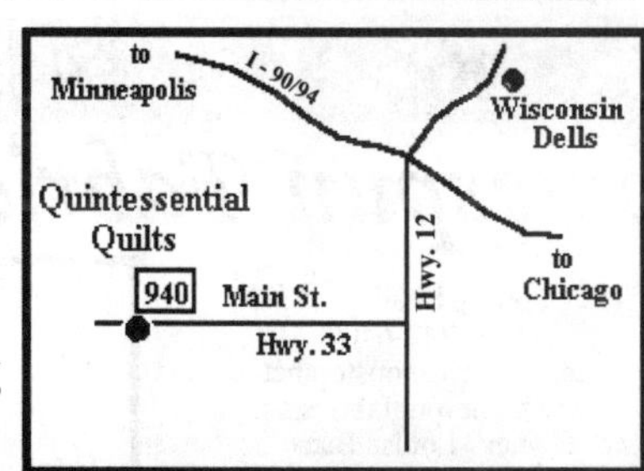

HISTORIC 1876 HOME

- Quilters, Scrapbookers, Crafters
- Accommodations for ten people
- One night, weekend or weekly
- Homemade Breakfasts
- Enjoy our large country kitchen
- Work Stations for Crafters
- Feature Classes & Workshops

A very special place for crafters to come together to create, bond, laugh & relax!

321 N. Park St.,
Reedsburg, WI
608-524-0909
gathering@mwt.net
www.gatheringreedsburg.com

Reedsburg, WI #35

La Crosse, WI #36

Tues, Wed, Thur 10 - 6
Fri, Sat, Mon 10 - 5
Sun 12 - 4

212 Main St. 54601
(608) 796-1515
Fax: (608) 784-5148
Owner: Linda Sherony
Est: 2003 2000+ Bolts

Home of an easy, versatile quilt-as-you-go method. We have a great selection of flannel and cotton fabrics.

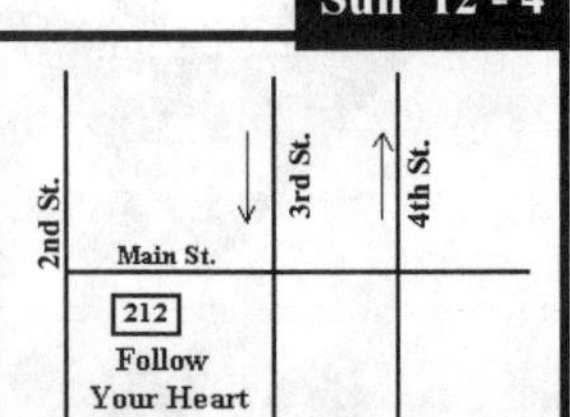

Onalaska, WI #37

A Stitch In Time

BERNINA

1258 CTH PH 54650
(608) 782-3257 Fax: (608) 782-0154
laxastitchintime@msn.com
Owner: Monica Campbell
Est: 1992 3000 sq.ft. 3000 Bolts

Mon - Sat 10 - 5
Thur til 8
Sun 12 - 4
Closed Sun Mem. Day to Labor Day

From I - 90 take exit 4 - 157 East
From 157 East turn left onto PH
Go 3/10 of a mile, shop on right.

Large selection of fabric, books, patterns, & quilting supplies. Lots of great samples.

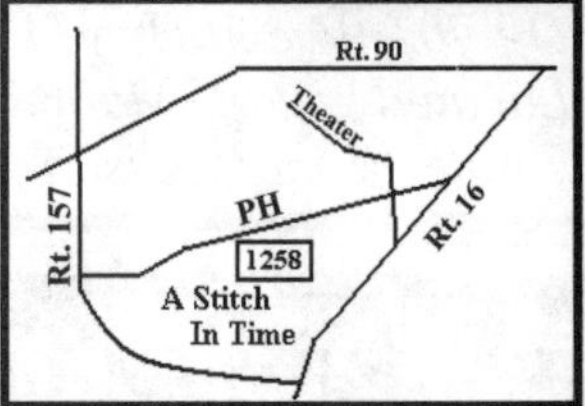

Voted one of America's top 10 Quilt Shops in 1998 Better Homes & Garden Quilt Sampler Magazine!

Holmen, WI #38

Tues - Sat 10 - 5
Sun 12 - 5

Wooden Shoe Quilts

W8154 Holland Dr. 54636
(608) 526-3135
Owner: Sharon Slimmen

Classes in and supplies for quilt making. Outlet for quilted items done by customers. Prize winning quilters to teach classes.

Sparta, WI #39

Mon - Fri 9 - 5
Sat 9 - 3

Quilt Corner, LLC

219 N. Water St. 54656
(608) 269-1083

We've got everything quilters need! Fabrics, Notions, Patterns, Books & ready-made quilts & gifts. Large Selection of 100% cotton Fabrics. One Block past Downtown.

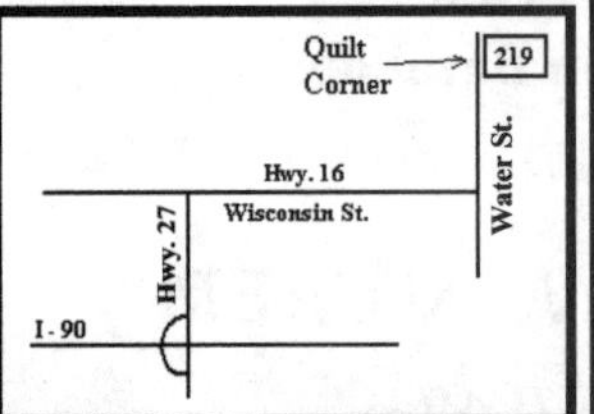

Princeton, WI #40

Mon -Fri 8:30 - 5
Sat 9 - 3

Quilts & Quilting

607 W. Main St. (920) 295-6506
P.O. Box 362 54968 Est: 1971
E-Mail: ronm@vbe.com
Owners: Sandy & Ron Mason
Machine Quilting & Kit Brochure SASE

Custom Machine Quilting Since 1971. Fabric, Notions, Books, Classes. Photos printed on Fabric. Die-Cut Quilt Top Kits—pillows to king size.

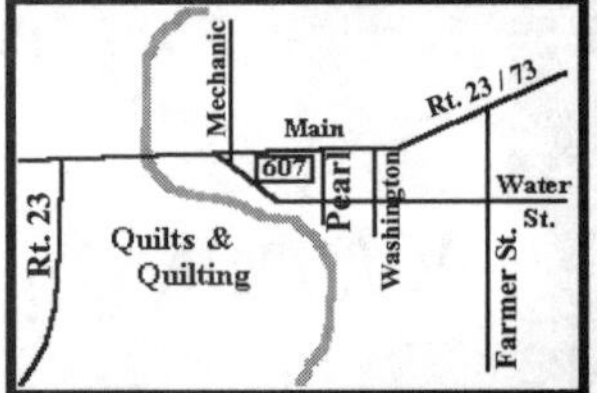

Endeavor, WI #41

Mon, Tues Thur 9:30 - 5
Fri & Sat 9:30 - 4

Homespun Fabrics

N149 County Road T 53930
(608) 742-6400
homespun@shopstop.net
www.homespunfabrics.net
Owner: Louise Back
Est: 1995 1000 Bolts
Great Selection of 100% Cotton Fabrics, Books, Notions & Patterns.
Machine Quilting.

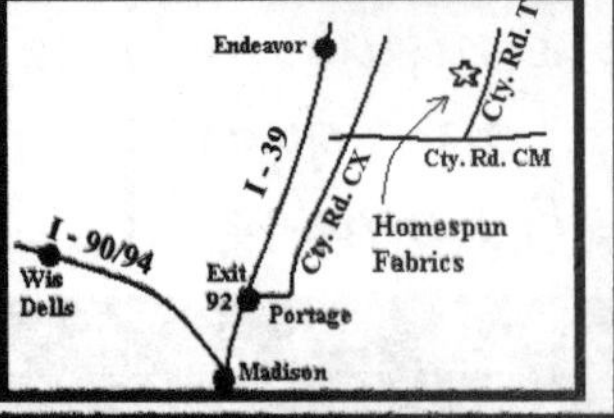

Baraboo, WI #42

Mon - Fri 10 - 5
Sat 10 - 4

Quintessential Quilts

524 Oak St. #10 53959
(608) 356-8090
qquilts@jvlnet.com Est: 2004
www.qquilts.com

Large selection of books, patterns & notions.
Continuous schedule of classes.
Authorized Husqvarna Viking Sales & Service.
Please check our main shop in Reedsburg.

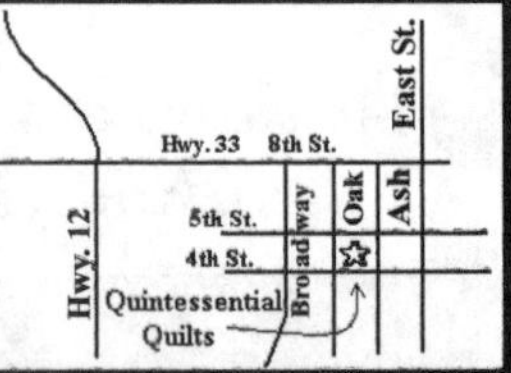

Portage, WI #43

Mon - Fri 9 - 5
Sat 9 - 2

The Gingham Goose

313 DeWitt St 53901
(608) 742-0420 Fax: (608) 742-4068
E-Mail: mgee@jvlnet.com
Owner: Mae Gee
Est: 1989 3000 sq. ft.

I - 90 / 94 | DeWitt St. | Gingham Goose 313 | St. Hwy. 33 | Portage Exit | Hwy. 51

Large assortment of 100% cotton fabrics, books, patterns, tools & finished products. Longarm quilting services available. Friendly, helpful employees.

Cedarburg, WI #45

Wed - Sat 10 - 5

Ye Olde Schoolhouse

318 Green Bay Rd. 53012
(262) 377-2770

Quilts, Reproduction and Homespun Fabric, Rughooking, Hand Dyed Wool Redware and Primitive Folkart. See our website for a tour of the shop: www.yeoldeschoolhouse.com

Cedarburg | Lakefield Rd. | Washington Ave. | Hamilton | Green Bay Rd. | 318 Ye Olde Schoolhouse | Port Washington Rd. | I - 43 | Pioneer | Green Bay Rd. | C

Grand Creations

QUILTING
Supplies & Classes

"THE QUILT SHOP" IN HISTORIC DOWNTOWN CEDARBURG

W64 N717 Washington Ave. 53012
(262) 377-8400

Virtual tour: www.grandcreations.com

Cedarburg, WI #46

- 4000 Bolts (Top Designers)
- 100's of Samples
- Specializing in Kits
- Notions
- Patterns
- Books

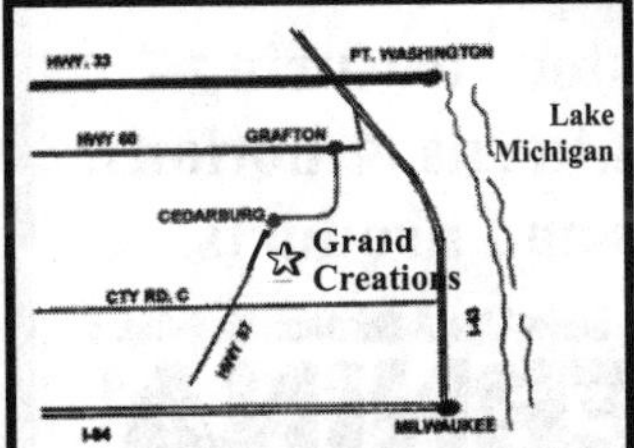

OPEN Fall & Winter
7 DAYS A WEEK
Call for Spring & Summer Hrs.

Celebrate the art of Quilting in a charming 1860's historical landmark home, truly a place of inspiration. Bus tours and groups welcome. Special programs available pending notification.

Beaver Dam, WI #44

HOMESPUN PRIMITIVES

Country Quilt Shop

112 S. Spring St., Beaver Dam, WI 53916
(920) 887-3060 Fax: (920) 887-3190
E-Mail: homespun@powerweb.net
Owner: Sandra Firari
Est: 2001 4800 sq.ft. 2000+ Bolts

Mon - Fri 9 - 5
Sat 10 - 4

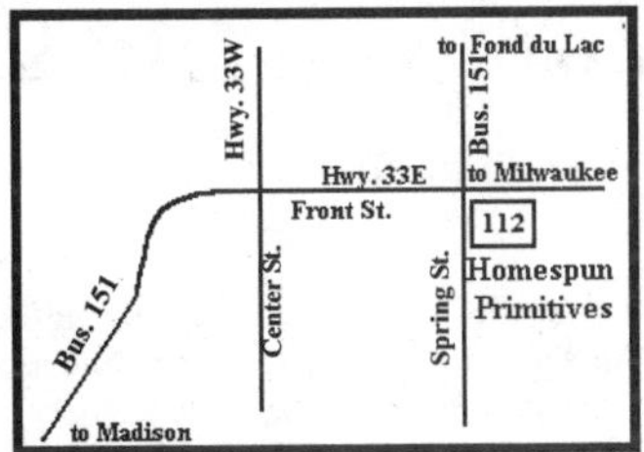

Area's newest Country Quilt Shop. Large selection of Moda designer fabrics, Thimbleberries fabrics, wools, quilting books, patterns, rug hooking, & primitive stitching. Learn from experienced Quilters. We offer a variety of Classes & Workshops, featuring all the latest and traditional quilting techniques. Something for everyone!

Royce Quilting

BERNINA® Sewing Center

West Bend, WI #47

840 S. Main 53095
(262) 338-0597

Mon - Tues 9:30 - 8
Wed, Thur, Fri 9:30 - 6
Sat 9:30 - 4 Sun 11 - 4

roycequilting@hnet.net
Owner: Jerry Quasius
Est: 1971 3000 sq.ft.

Specializing in 30's Prints and Reproduction Fabrics. 3000 Quilting Fabrics. Books, Soft Patterns, Quilting Classes.

Authorized Sales & Service Bernina Dealer for 25 Years.

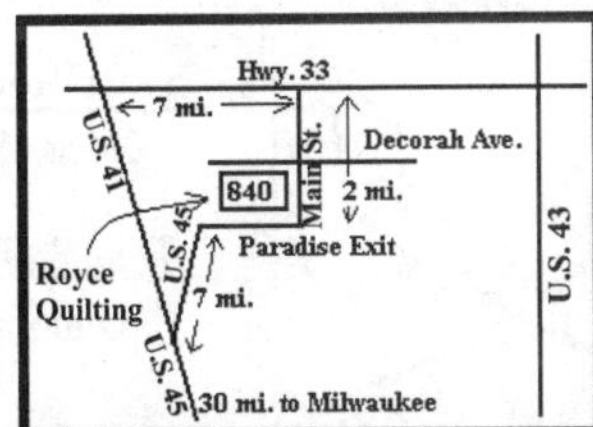

Slinger, WI #48

Mon, Wed, Fri 9 - 5
Tues & Thur 9 - 7
Sat 10 - 4

Common Threads Quilt Shop, LLC.

425 C East Washington St. 53086
(262) 644-0613
commonthread@nconnect.net
See us at: www.ctquiltshop.com
Owner: Jenifer Moegenburg
Est: 1995 2300 sq.ft. 2000 Bolts
For women who take pride in their quilting & sewing. Friendly, Expert Service by Knowledgeable Staff.
Husqvarna Viking Authorized Dealer.
Professional Quilting Service Available.

Oakfield, WI #49

Mon - Fri 10 - 5
Sat 10 - 3

Stitches 'N Tyme, LLC

203 S. Main St. 53065
(920) 583-2625
Owners: Jeff & Donna Redman
Est: 2000 1500 sq.ft. 2500+ Bolts

A full service quilt, antique, gift shop specializing in individualized customer service, long arm quilting, Certified Pfaff dealer.

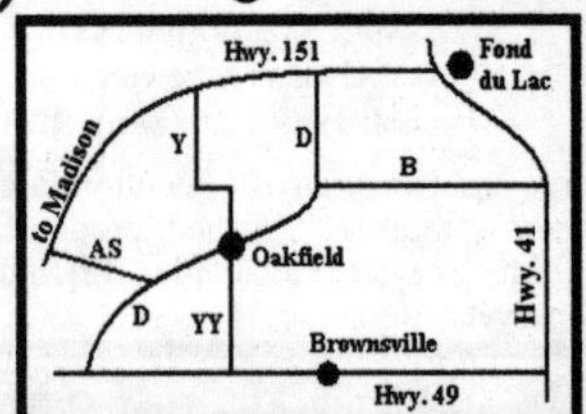

Plymouth, WI #50

Mon - Sat 9 - 5
Wed 9 - 8

The Sewing Basket

426 E. Mill St. 53073
(920) 892-4751

We cater to your creative side. Beautiful quality quilting fabrics; quilting books, patterns and notions with a wide variety of cross-stitch fabric, fibers and charts.
Long Arm Quilt Finishing Available.

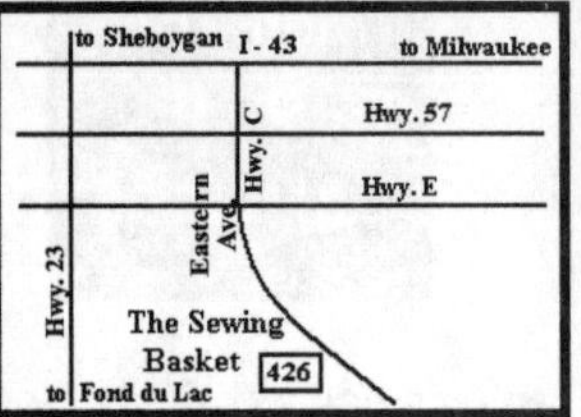

Fond du Lac, WI #51

Mon - Fri 10 - 5
Sat 10 - 2

Wool & Needle

46 N. Main St. 54935
(920) 907-1331 Fax: (920) 907-2974
www.woolandneedle.com
Owner: Kathy Geis
Est: 2000 1700 sq.ft. 1200 Bolts.
Unique "country" atmosphere. Hand dyed wool and cotton is our specialty. Moda fabrics - kits - rug hooking - silk ribbon embroidery - unique yarns & supplies.

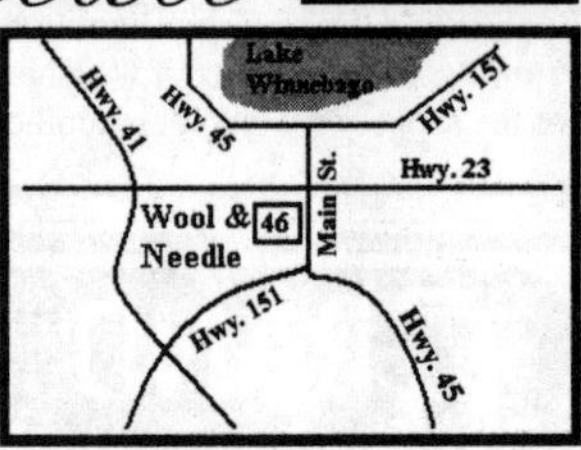

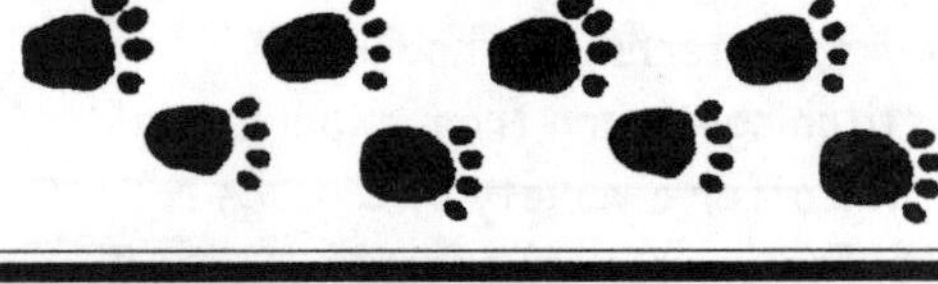

Fond du Lac Quilting & Sewing Center

Fond du Lac, WI #52

Mon - Fri 9:30 - 5
Sat 9:30 - 4

15 North Main Street 54935
(920) 921-3816 or (800) 594-9064
E-Mail: queenbee@fdlquilt.com
Owner: Cathleen Christensen

We are a full service quilting & sewing store featuring thousands of bolts of 100% cotton fabric, patterns & notions.
We carry a full line of Bernina machines and products.
Stop in to browse or take a class
Enjoy!

Nothing Sews Like A Bernina. Nothing.
BERNINA

We are the Host of two of the largest quilting events in the mid-west:
Quilter's Escape & Summer School for Quilters
Please Visit our Website at www.fdlquilt.com

Quilts n' Silks

Fabrics and Supplies

Manitowoc, WI #53

Mon - Fri 9 - 6
Sat 9 - 3

Authorized PFAFF Dealer

711 York St. 54221-2232
(800) 933-1161
(920) 686-0839 Fax: (920) 686-0876
Owner: Elaine A. Springer
Est: 1995 2400 sq.ft. 3000 Bolts
E-Mail: quiltsnsilks@lakefield.net

For all of your quilting fabrics, books, patterns, notions & quilting classes visit Quilts n' Silks!

Kona ¤ South Seas ¤ Bali
Thimbleberries ¤ RJR
Benartex ¤ P&B ¤ Hoffman
Moda ¤ Robert Kaufman

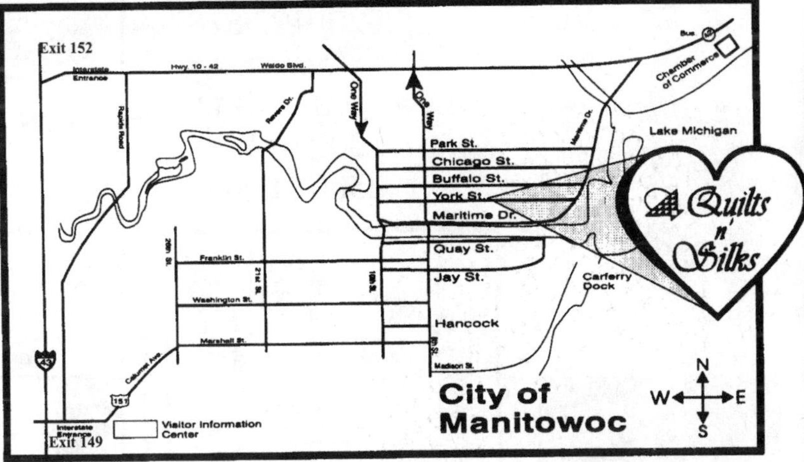

Overlooking the Wisconsin Maritime Museum in historic downtown Manitowoc. Near the Car Ferry dock.

2475 University Ave.
University Courtyard
54302
(800) 469-1495
(920) 468-1495
Owners: Nanette Guzzonato & Elaine Corson
Est: 1990
Wheelchair Accessible

Mon & Thur 9:30 - 8
Tues & Wed 9:30 - 5
Fri 9:30 - 4 Sun 11 - 4

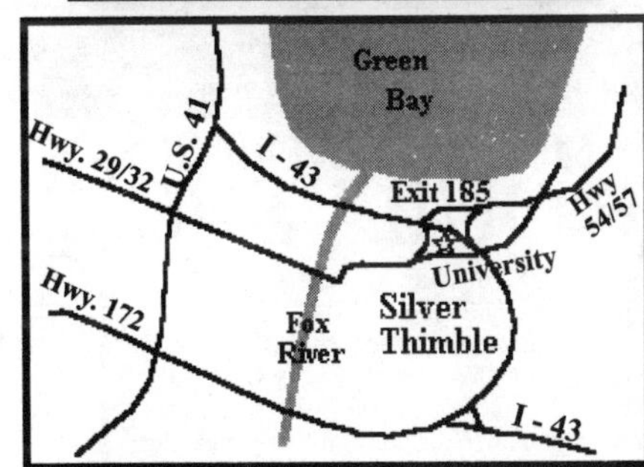

Take I - 43, exit 185, to Green Bay
Turn left at first stoplight.
Go one block & left into parking lot

Green Bay, WI #54

- Over 3000 bolts 100% cotton fabric
- Books & Patterns
- Notions
- Help selecting colors/fabrics
- Pfaff Sewing Machine Sales
- Complete line Thimbleberries fabric, books & patterns at reduced prices
- Classes
- Gifts
- Hand-dyed Wool
- Custom Sewing
- Hand-dyed Silk Ribbon
- Large Selection of Hoffman Batiks

Green Bay, WI #55

Quilter's Connection

2269 True Ln. 54304
(920) 497-8787
Owners:
Jan & Mark Ahrens
3000 sq.ft.
2500+ Bolts

Fabric? What Fabric?

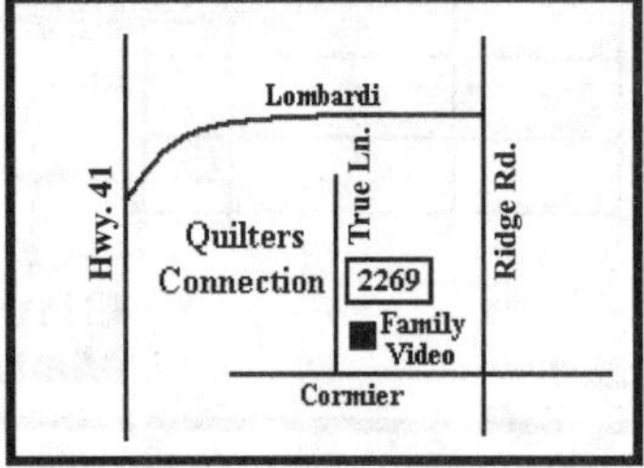

Mon & Fri 10 - 6
Tues, Wed, Thur 10 - 5

Located west of the Ridge Rd. & Cormier intersection next to Family Video

We are a full service quilt shop featuring:
Fabrics - Notions - Hand dyed wool
Books & Patterns - Classes
Custom Machine Quilting
Our friendly staff is waiting to help you.

Green Bay, WI #56

Mon - Fri 10 - 5
Sat 10 - 4

Friendship Quilts & Custom Framing

1235 S. Military Ave. 54303
(920) 490-7877 or (866) 214-6721
fqff@juno.com Est: 1998
Owners: Faith Kornowski & Julette Kusch

* Over 2000 Bolts of Quality Cotton Fabrics
* Classes, Books, Patterns & Notions
* Custom Hand-Guided Machine Quilting (member IMQA)
* Custom Framing & Framed Art

Helpful and Always Friendly Staff!

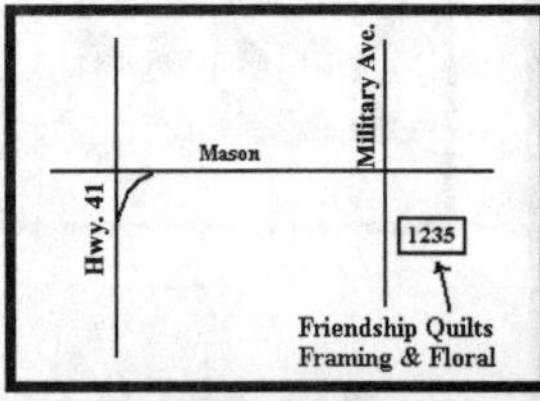

Green Bay, WI #57

Mon - Fri 10 - 6
Tues & Thur til 8
Sat 10 - 4
Sun 12 - 4

Main Street Cotton Works

1812 Main St. 54302
(920) 469-5694
Owners: Patt and Gil Nowak
Est: 1995 1000 Bolts

Located in a 50 yr. old home featuring 100% cotton fabrics, books, patterns & quilting supplies, classes and Friendly, Knowledgeable Staff

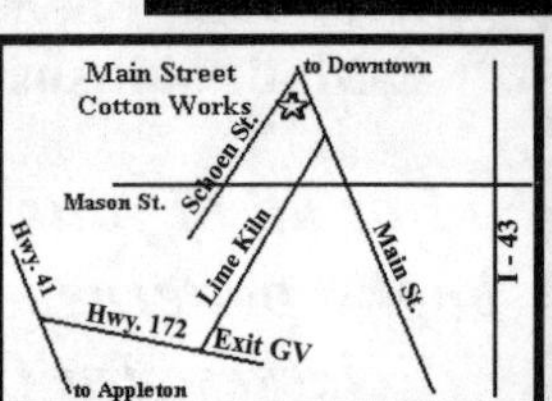

Green Bay, WI #58

Mon - Fri
9:30 - 5:30
Sat 9:30 - 4

MY FAVORITE QUILT SHOP

1550 Dousman St. 54303
(920) 965-2085 Fax: (920) 965-7224
Ibsengirls@aol.com
Owners: Cordy Wescott & Peggy Goddard
Est: 2002 1000 Bolts

We make you feel welcome as you meander through our unique shop that combines fabric with classic art. Country, vintage, 30's, batiks and Kaffe Fassett!

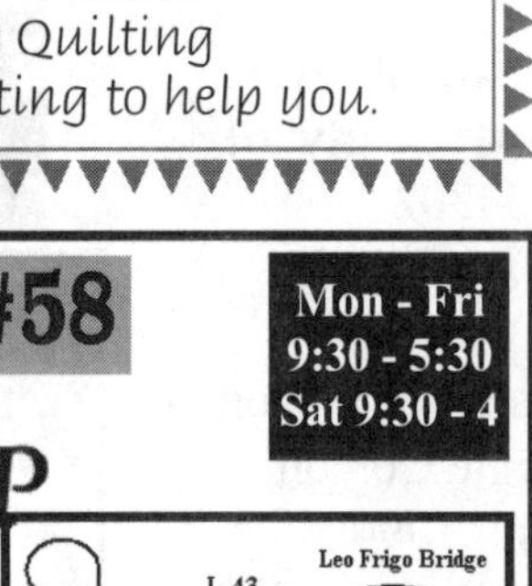

Kewaunee, WI #60

Wed - Fri 1 - 5
Sat 10 - 4

Norman General Store & Quilt Shop

E3296 Cty. Rd. G 54216
(920) 388-4580 Fax: (920) 388-0423
normanbb@itol.com
www.normangeneralstorebb.com
Owners: Anne & Jerry Sinkula
Est: 1998

Quilting Fabrics, Books, Patterns and Notions. In an Historic 1870's General Store connected to our home / Bed and Breakfast.

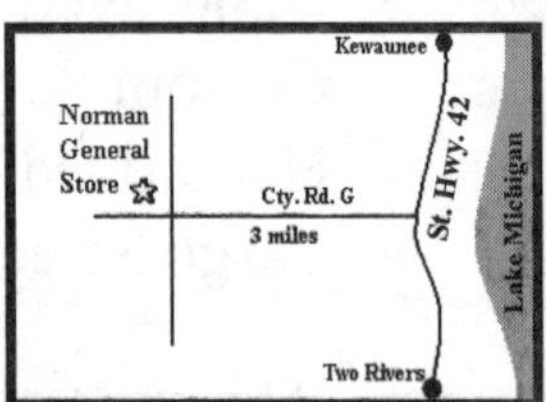

Quilter's Quest

11996 Hwy. 42
P.O. Box 346, Ellison Bay, WI 54210
(920) 854-1824 • Toll Free (866) 854-1824
quiltersquest@charterinternet.net
www.doorcountyquilts.com Linda Batley, Owner

IN BEAUTIFUL NORTHERN DOOR COUNTY

May - Oct Daily 10 - 5
Nov - April
Thurs - Sat 10 - 5

Special Hours on Request
(920) 854-6538

We are Always willing to Accommodate Special Hour Requests.

Over 2600 bolts
Specialty Notions, Books, Patterns
Gifts for Quilters & Non-Quilters
Classes - Warm, Friendly Service

Ellison Bay, WI #59

A Truly Unique
Shopping
Experience!

Life's a Stitch

- Learn, Create, Have Fun !
- Over 2500 Bolts of Current 100% Cotton Fabrics
- All your Quilting & Sewing Needs
- Repair all Brands of Sewing Machines
- Quilting Classes for all Levels
- Authorized Bernina Dealer

2 Great Locations!

Owners:
Susan & Mike Carmichael

Nothing Sews Like A Bernina. Nothing.
BERNINA®

158 E. Northland Ave.
Appleton, WI 54911
920-993-9772

Appleton, WI #62

Hours:
Mon - Fri 10 - 5
Thurs til 7
Sat 10 - 3

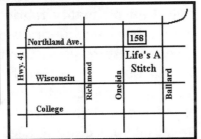

Northland Ave. 158 Life's A Stitch Hwy. 41 Wisconsin Richmond Oneida Ballard College

Located in the Lee Building
On the second floor (elevator)
124 North Broadway
DePere, WI 54115
920-338-1381

DePere, WI #61

Hours:
Wed & Fri 10 - 5
Tues & Thur 10 - 7
Sat 10 - 3

Located Just South of Green Bay

Hwy. 172 I - 43 Hwy. 41 Fox River Broadway Riverside Life's A Stitch 124 Wisconsin Webster Main George St.

Piece By Piece

1350 W. College Ave.
Appleton, WI 54914
(920) 749-1957
Piecebypiece@earthlink.net

An inviting unique shop located ½ mile west of historic downtown and 2 miles east of the Fox River Mall.

Come and visit our shop and view the 200 samples that are sure to inspire anyone. Kits are available for most samples.

We feature a large selection of quality fabrics for the quilter including florals, many kid's prints, 200 batiks, flannels, seasonal prints, Marbles, Crystals, Fairy Frost

Blocks of the Month, Classes, Books, Patterns.

Hours: Monday and Thursday 10-8
Tuesday, Wednesday, Friday 10 - 5
Saturday 10-4

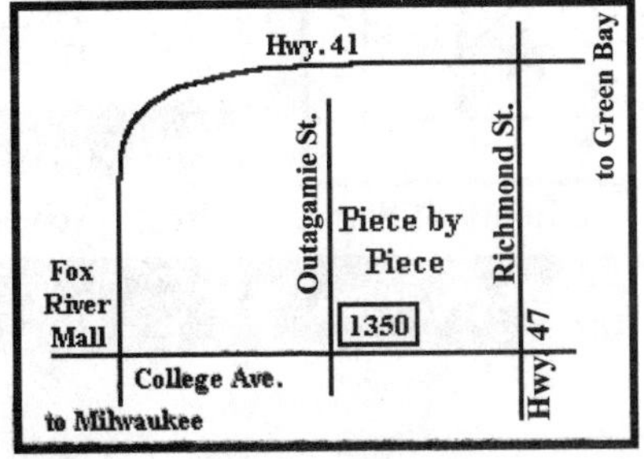

Appleton, WI #63

2306 S. Oneida St. 54915
(920) 991-9021
Www.patchworksampler.com
E-mail: info@patchworksampler.com
Owners: Rhonda Roberts & Kim Teigen
Est: 1997 4200 sq. ft. 4500+ bolts

Appleton, WI #64

Patchwork Sampler

"Your one stop shop for quilting inspiration!"

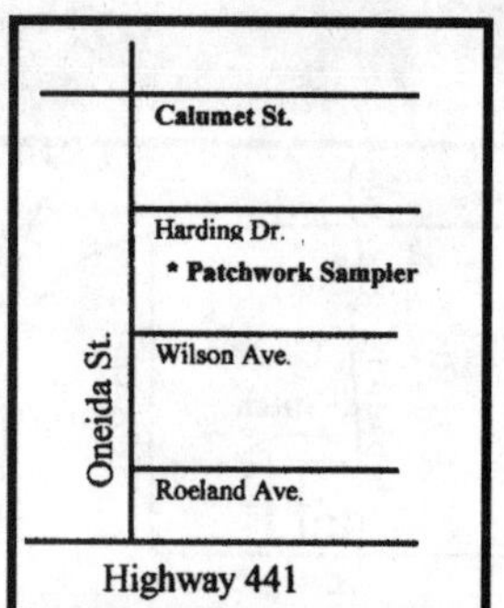

Located just 1/2 miles North of Highway 441 on Oneida Street

Mon & Fri 9:30 - 5:00
Tues - Thurs 9:30 - 8:00
Sat 9:30 - 4:00

We welcome you to our newly expanded shop. Come and browse the area's largest selection of quality fabrics, books and patterns. We have hundreds of samples on display to inspire you. Can't visit in person? Check out our website for weekly specials and upcoming events. In person or online, our friendly, knowledgeable staff is eager to meet all your quilting needs.

Mon - Fri 10 - 5
Sat 10 - 4

Quilting Fabric • Patterns Books • Notions.
Heirloom supplies • Classes Year Round
Premier Dealer for Husqvarna Viking Sewing Machines

Appleton, WI #65

1881 N. Silverspring Dr. 54915
920-830-9372
Fax: 920-830-9379
Est: 2000 2500 sq.ft. 1500 Bolts

FULTON
Sew 'n Sew
MAIN
UNION
BADGER

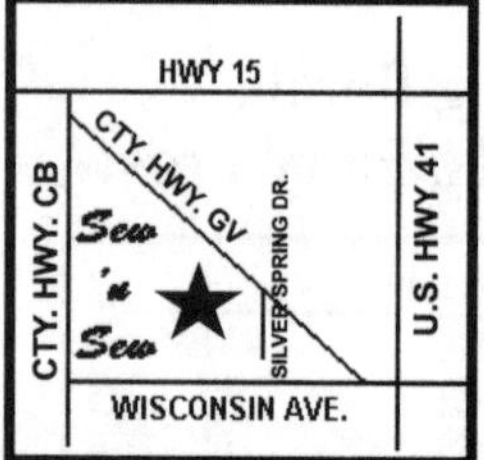

112 S. Main 54981
715-256-1071
Fax: 715-256-1198
Est: 1997 2100 sq.ft. 2000 Bolts

Waupaca, WI #66

Owners: Bonita & Samuel Welsch sewnsew@gglbbs.com

Husqvarna VIKING

Menasha, WI #67

Mon - Fri 10 - 5
Thur til 8
Sat 10 - 4

Primitive Gatherings

850 Racine St. 54952
(920) 722-7233
Lisa@backyardquilts.com
Owners: Lisa & Nick Bongean
Est: 2004 4000 sq.ft.

A new quilt shop with an old fashioned look.
We specialize in reproduction fabrics, homespuns and our own hand-dyed wool.
Lots of kits and inspiration!

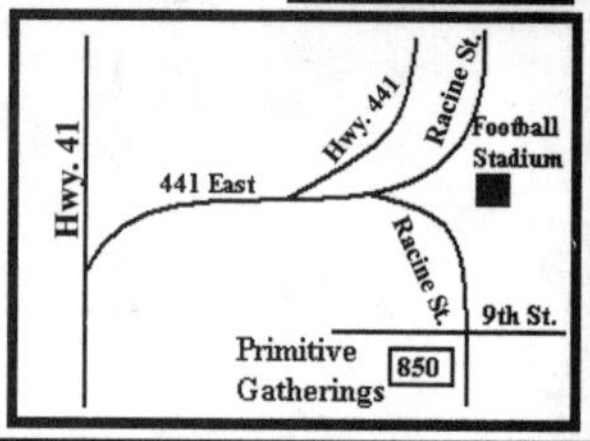

Hwy. 41
441 East
Hwy. 441
Racine St.
Football Stadium
Racine St.
9th St.
Primitive Gatherings
850

Oshkosh, WI #68

QuiltEssentials

(920) 230-3680
Owners: Susan Cammack & Mary Toll

M, W, F 9 - 6
T, TH 9 - 8
Sat 9 - 4
Sun 11 - 3

Opening Summer 2004

Wisconsin Rapids, WI #69

540 Daly Ave. 54494
(715) 424-1122
cthimble@wctc.net
Owner: Carol Prahl
Est: 1993

Mon - Fri 10 - 5
Sat 10 - 4

Over 6500 Bolts of 100% Cottons Books, Patterns, Stencils, & Quilting Notions.

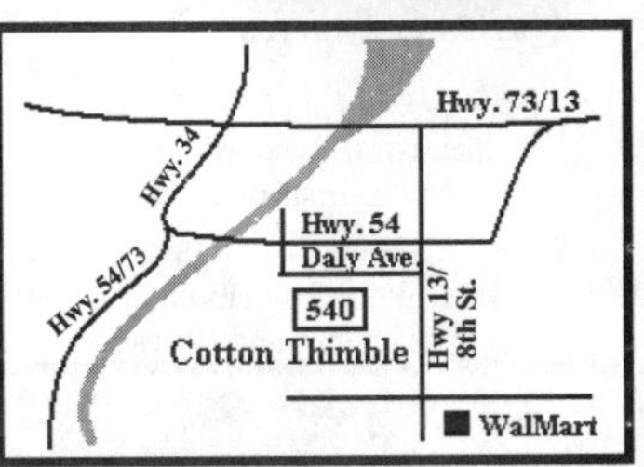

Tigerton, WI #70

Tues - Sat 9 - 6

PINERY PATCHES LLC

N 4647 Hwy. 45 54486
(715) 535-2277 Est: 2003
lkrueger@frontiernet.net 1500 sq.ft.
Owner: Linda Krueger
Fabric, patterns and books for all levels of quilting. Kits for the quilter on the go. "Coffee pot's always on!"

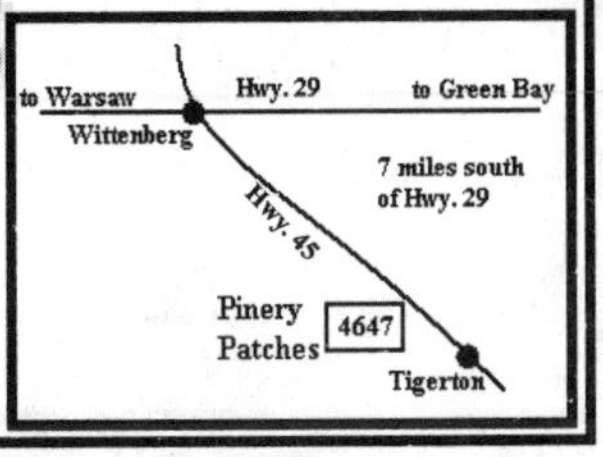

to Warsaw | Hwy. 29 | to Green Bay | Wittenberg | 7 miles south of Hwy. 29 | Hwy. 45 | Pinery Patches | 4647 | Tigerton

Marinette, WI #71

Mon - Fri 10 - 6
Sat 10 - 4

Pine St. Quilts

801 Marinette Ave. #2 54143
(715) 735-9806
Owner: Cyndie Halfmann
Est: 2002 1200+ bolts

Friendly small town Quilt Shop with Quality Fabric, Books, Patterns and Notions. Just 50 miles north of Green Bay.

Fabric & Craft Supply Shoppe, LLC

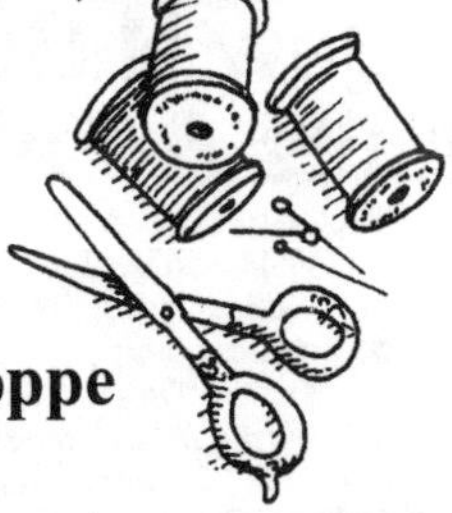

816 5th Ave., Antigo, WI 54409
(715) 623-3590
cutedge@antigopro.net

14,000 square feet of Quilt shoppe, Yarn shoppe, Counted Thread shoppe
Mon-Thur 10-6, Fri 10-5, Sat 9-4

Branch store in Wausau
3300 Rib Mountain Dr.
(715) 359-2407

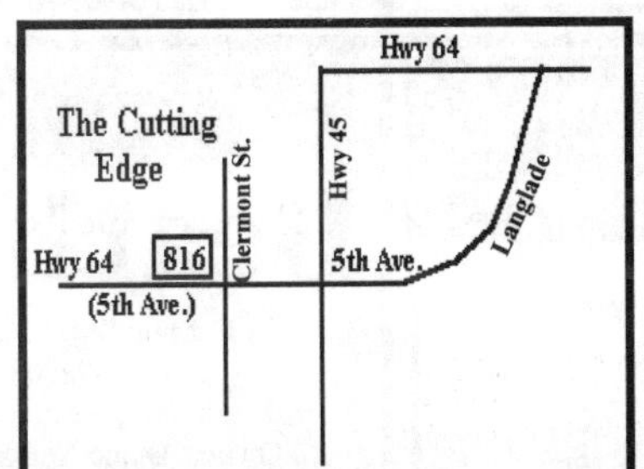

Antigo, WI #72

Owner: Marla Arndt
Est: 1990

VIKING

Wausau, WI #73

Mon - Thur 10 - 5
Fri 10 - 7
Sat 10 - 5

The Quilting Workshop

314 S. First Ave. 54401
(715) 848-5546
swanmum@dwave.net
Est: 2003 1200 sq.ft. 3000 Bolts

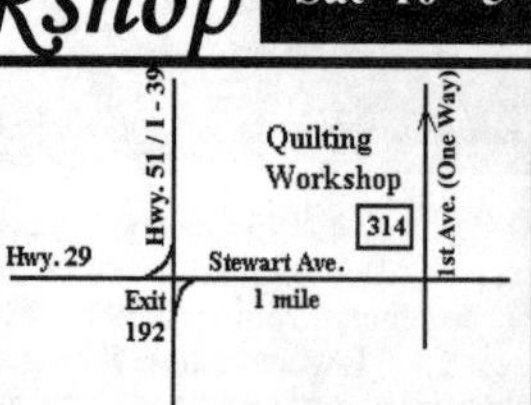

Wausau's only quilt shop! We carry quilting fabrics, supplies and wool, adjoining The Needle Workshop all in one historic building.

Tomahawk, WI #74

Between Friends Quilting & Supplies, LLC

14 W. Wisconsin Ave. 54487
(715) 453-8884 Fax: (715) 453-9026
Est: 1997

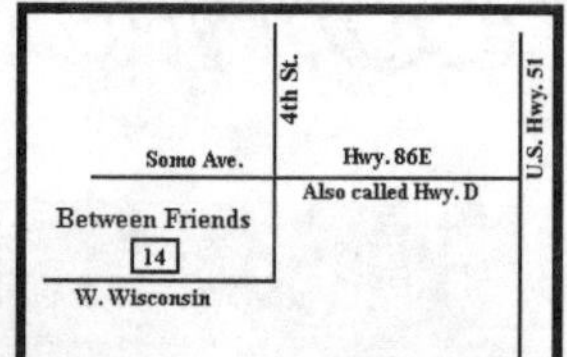

Quilting Books, Fabrics, Quilting Supplies, Thread, Floss, Ribbon Embroidery, Classes. Free Newsletter, friendly Service, Inspiration & sharing of ideas.

Rhinelander, WI #75

Mon - Sat 9 - 5

Karen's Quilt Corner

403 N. Brown St. 54501
(715) 362-1944
kuphal@nnex.net Owner: Karen Kuphal
Est: 2003 2400 sq.ft. 1500+ bolts

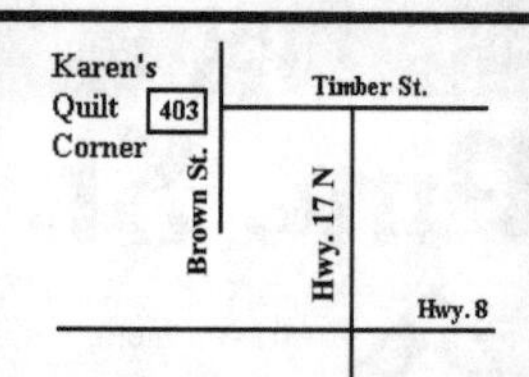

Bernina dealer, Always met with a smile, Classes - Beginner to Advanced, Batiks, flannels, 30's, Thimbleberries, Civil War, Northwoods and many more. Large selection of thread & notions.

Eagle River, WI #76

Mon - Sat 10 - 5

Heartstrings Quilts & Fabrics

220 S. Main St.,
P.O. Box 194 54521
(715) 479-2313
Owner: Lisa Wood
Est: 1995 1000 sq.ft. 1500+ Bolts
heartstr@newnorth.net
www.heartstrings.com

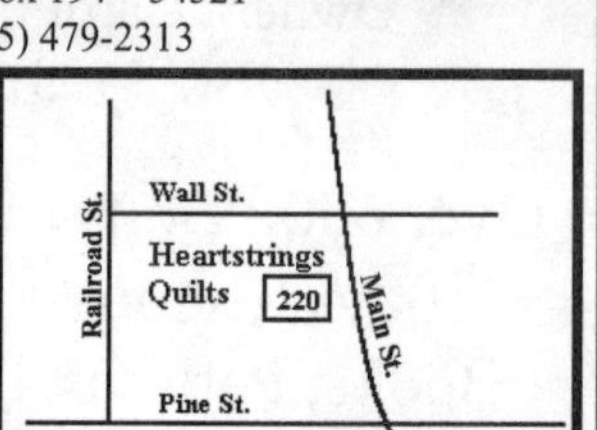

North Woods Quilting at its Best! Fabrics, Patterns, Books, Wool Rug Hooking Supplies, Viking Sewing Machines and Classes.

Ladysmith, WI #77

Mon - Sat 10 - 6

Quilter's Passion

W8198 Edgewood Ave. E 54848
(715) 532-5803 Fax: (715) 532-5806
quilters@centurytel.net
Owner: Nancy Rosolowski
Est: 2003 750+ Bolts

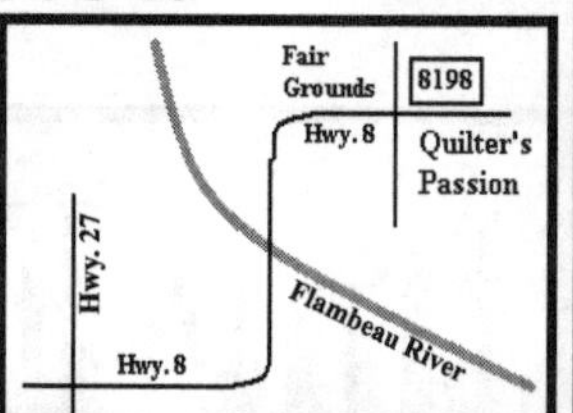

Newly opened store on Hwy. 8, offering quilting fabrics and supplies.

Holcombe, WI #78

Mon - Sat 10 - 5

Log Cabin Quilts

26353 Hwy. 27 54745
(715) 959-6888
Logcabinquilts@centurytel.net
Owner: Fern Baker Est: 2000

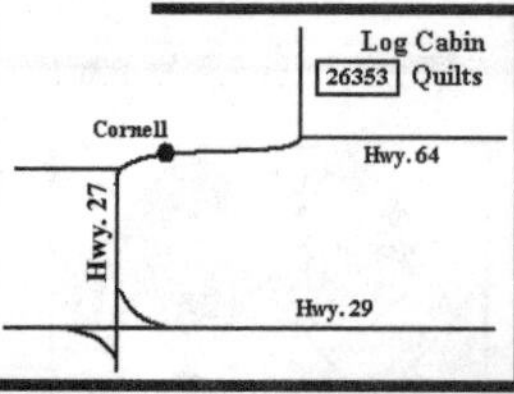

A little shop in the Northwoods. We give individual attention to your quilting desires. Fabrics and notions from top companies and always friendly service.

Stanley, WI #79

Mon - Fri 9 - 5
Evenings & Sat by Appt.

Sew N Sew Quilts & Fabrics

36360 Cty. Hwy. MM 54768
(715) 644-5563 Fax: Same
dhaas@ecol.net
www.geocities.com/piecefulpatches/
Owner: Donna Haas

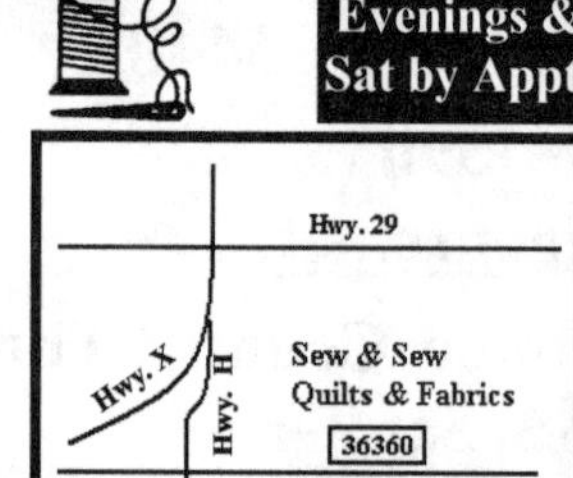

Machine Quilting, Also Home of Pieceful Patches. A Small Country Shop with a Big Atmosphere. Fabrics, Notions, Books, Stamping, Classes & Fun!

Withee, WI #80

Mon - Fri 8 - 8
Sat 8 - 4

Brubaker Sewing Center

W 7634 Oak Rd. 54498
(715) 669-3224 Fax: (715) 229-4394

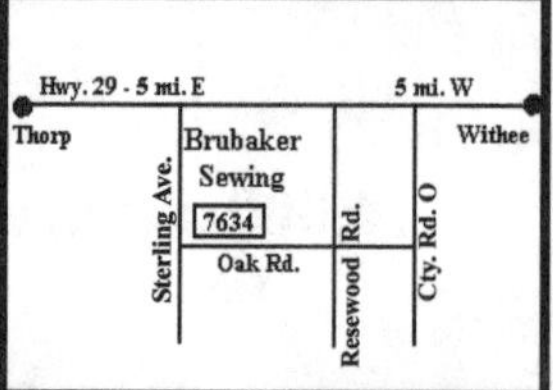

Bernina Sewing Machine Sales & Service. Over 2500 Bolts of fabric. Fabric, Quilts & Batting, Baby Supplies, Hosiery, Underwear, Childrens Shoes, Sweaters, Sewing Notions, Disposable Diapers, & Hair Accessories.

Dorchester, WI #81

Mon - Fri 9:30 - 5:30
Sat 9:30 - 4

Cow Country Fabrics & Quilts

800 E. Center Ave. 54425
(715) 654-5250
cowcountry@tds.net
cowcountryfabrics.com
Owner: Donna J. Reamer
Est: 1997 2600 sq.ft.

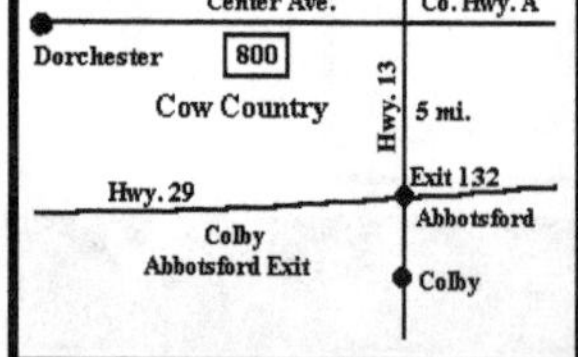

3000 bolts quality Fabrics Books, Patterns, Notions — Machine quilting services— Classes — Kits — Quilts for Sale.

Hixton, WI #82

Mon - Fri 10 - 5
Sat 10 - 4

Bearhill Quilts

125 E. Main St. 54635
(715) 964-9200
bearhill@triwest.net
Owner: Diane Nelson
Est: 2000 800 Bolts

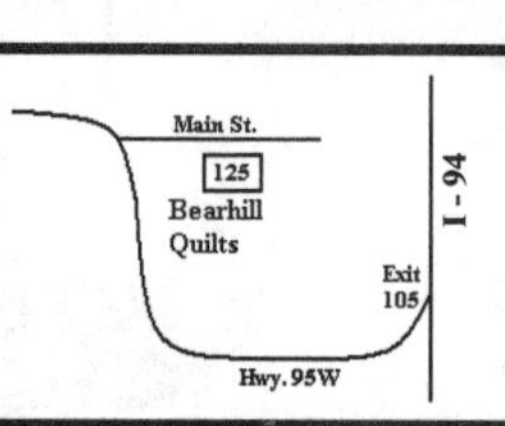

We cater to our customers. Friendly, helpful customer services.

Osseo, WI #83

13900 7th Street
P.O. Box 277
Osseo, WI 54758
(715) 597-2452
Email: quiltyard@quiltyard.com
Web: www.quiltyard.com
Est. 1996 6000 Sq. Ft. 5000 Bolts

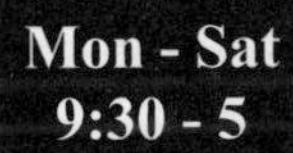

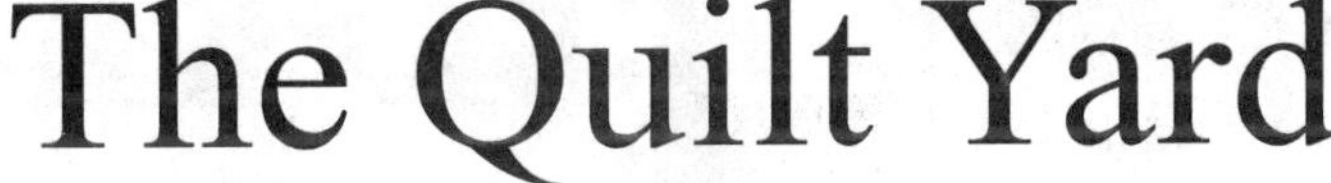

TM

Featuring a unique way to quilt by Betty Cotton called "THE COTTON THEORY"™

A fast and easy method of "Quilt first Then assemble", using the fold and finish procedure.

You will have a completed, reversible quilt with an extra dimension.

We will be more than happy to give you a demo...including 2-tone binding.

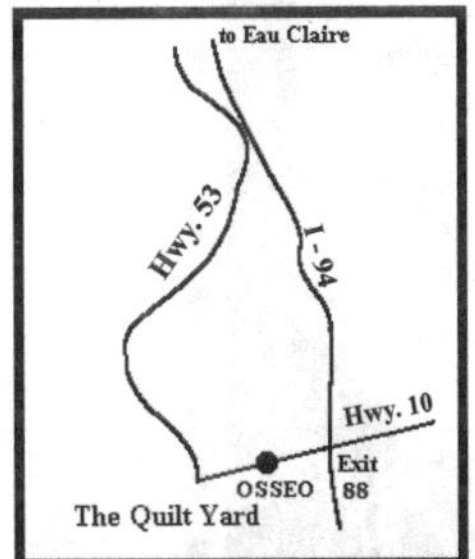

Located just off I - 94, Exit 88 (Hwy 10) At the corner of 7th St. and Hwy. 53

Looking forward to meeting you!

Bus tours and large groups always welcome

- **Large selection of designer cotton fabric**
- **Entire flannel room**
- **Notions, patterns and books**
- **100's of samples and kits available**
- **Giftware - including Heartwood Creek figurines by Enesco**
- **5-6 Special events each year**
- **Mailing list, newsletter and mail orders available.**

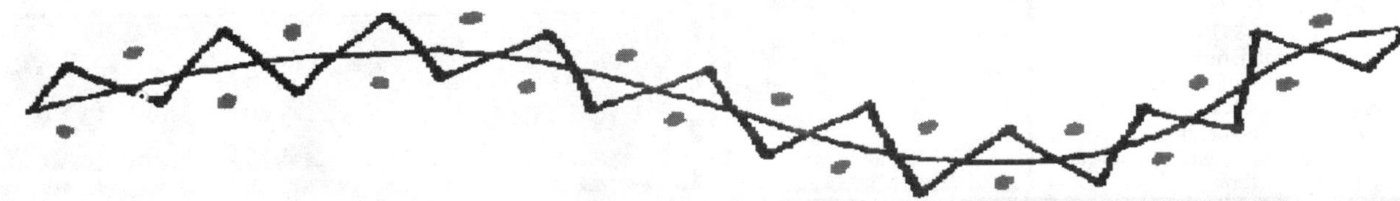

Eau Claire, WI #84

Mon - Fri 10 - 5
Sat 10 - 4

The Calico Shoppe

214 S. Barstow St. 54701
(715) 834-9990
www.calicoshoppe.com
Owner: Lynn Goelzer
Est: 1993 3000+ Bolts

Our shop is located in Eau Claire's Historic Downtown area. Our unique shop offers distinct fabrics, books, patterns, notions & classes; along with a charming gift shop, "The Purple Petunia"
Make a Quilt . . . Make a Memory!

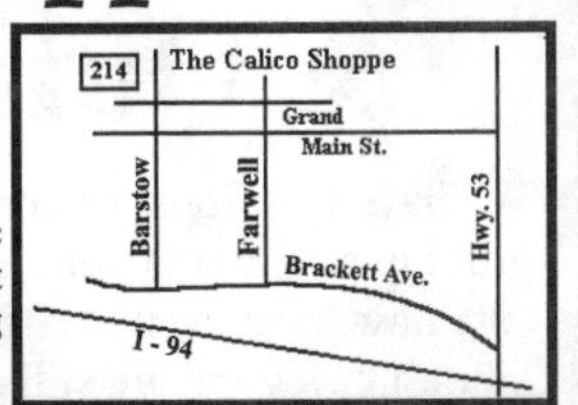

Turtle Lake, WI #86

Mon - Fri 9:30 - 5
Sat 9:30 - 3
Jan 1 - May 1
Closed Mon

P.O. Box 200 54889
612 U.S. Hwy. 8 & 63 W
(715) 986-2983

Quilting, Cross Stitch & Yarn. Books, patterns, buttons & notions. Fabrics include: cottons, flannels, polar fleece and hand-dyed wool. Visit our new kitchen & culinary dept. as well as our book loft including Christian books and Bibles.

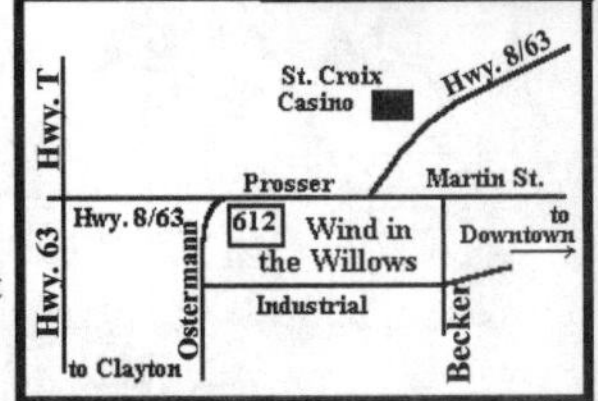

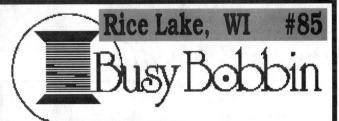

Rice Lake, WI #85

Busy Bobbin

Large selection 100% Cotton fabrics, patterns, books, and quilting notions. Classes offered.

Mon - Fri 9:30 - 5 Sat 9:30 - 3

234 N. Wilson Ave. 54868
(715) 234-1217
www.busybobbin.com
Fax: (715) 234-6326
Owner: Diann Raymond
E-Mail: diann@busybobbin.com
Est: 1981 1300 sq.ft. 3000 Bolts

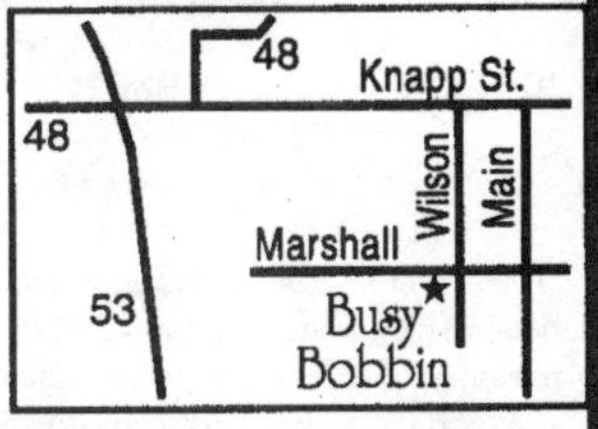

Cliff's

204 N. Main St. River Falls, WI

Tina's Quilt Shop

❖ Quilting Fabric, Batting and Threads ❖
❖Quilting Books & Patterns, Classes and Supplies ❖
❖ Loads of Fleece and Needles ❖
❖ Friendly, professional help ❖

River Falls, WI #87

Mon - Sat 10 - 5 Est: 1997

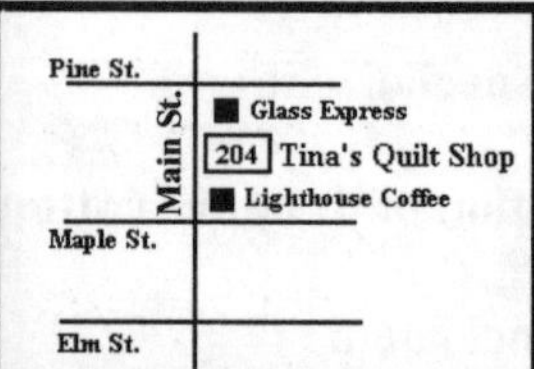

Authorized Janome Sewing Machine Dealer. Sewing Machine Repair--All makes. 1200 sq. feet with over 2500 bolts of 100% cotton fabrics. If we don't have it, we'll order.

715-425-5133

Tina's

Hudson, WI #88

A large selection of bright contemporary fabrics; specializing in the largest selection of batiks in the Twin Cities area.
Pfaff Sewing Machines and Sergers. PFAFF®

A Time To Sew

596 Outpost Circle 54016
(715) 377-0098 Fax: (715) 377-0104
atimetosew@direcway.com
Est: 2001 3032 sq.ft. 2400 bolts

www.atimetosew.com

Mon - Wed 9 - 6
Thur 9 - 8
Fri - Sat 9 - 5
Sun 12 - 5

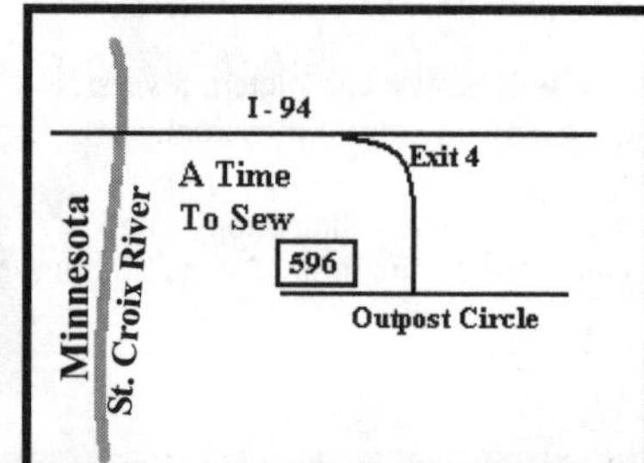

Specializing in Brights & Batiks

New Richmond, WI #89

Mon - Fri 10 - 5
Sat 9 - 3
Sun 1 - 4

Traditions

122 S. Knowles Ave.
P.O. Box 26 54017
(715) 246-9910
traditio@frontiernet.net
www.traditionsquiltshop.com
Owners: Anna Dzik & Mary Jensen
600+ bolts of fabric, patterns, books, notions, quilting stencils, cross stitch, online newsletter, classes & Brown Sheep Yarn

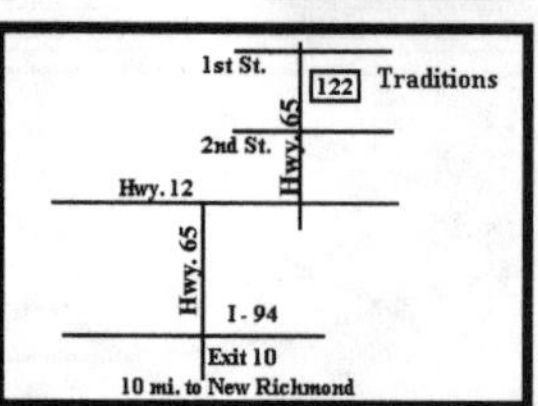

St. Croix Falls, WI #90

Mon - Sat 9:30 - 5:30

Pins 'N' Needles

126 N. Washington 54024
(715) 483-5728
Owner: Mary E. Anderson
Est: 2000 2800 sq.ft.

Over 1500 bolts of fabric along with books, patterns, and notions. Friendly people waiting to help you. Come see us!

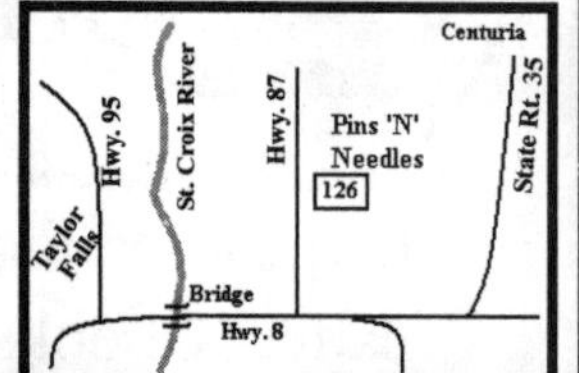

Hayward, WI #91

River's Edge Antiques & Quilt Loft, Ltd.

We have two floors of quality antiques in addition to our Quilt Loft. We now have over 1400 bolts of Cotton fabrics and are still growing. We have Books, Patterns, Notions and many Gift Items. We also offer a wide assortment of classes.

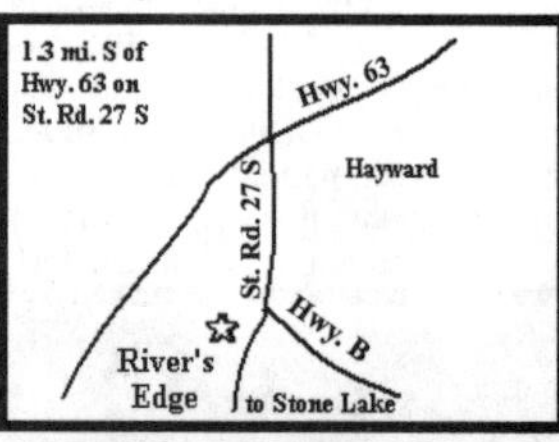

Mon - Sat 10 - 5 Sun. 12 - 4

10103 State Road 27
Hayward, WI 54843
(715) 634-0706
riveredg@cheqnet.net

Solon Springs, WI #92

Mon - Sat 10 - 5

The Little Gift House

9234 E. Main St., P.O. Box 297 54873
(715) 378-4170
Est: 1974 2000 sq.ft.

100% cotton fabrics. Large selection of flanels, batiks, plaids, and novelties. Books & notions. Classes year round. Great gifts. Good Customer Service is our goal.

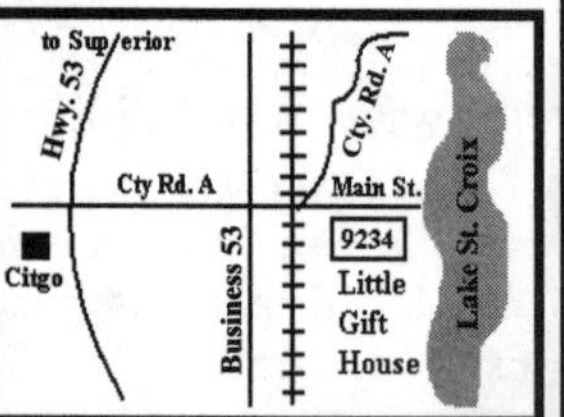

Bear Den Quilt Co.

Siren, WI #93

24665 State Road 35-70, Suite C
Siren, WI 54872
715-349-2250
Fax: 715-349-8939
Owner: Karen Miller
www.beardenquiltco.com

Hours :

Summer (May 1 - Oct 31)
Mon - Thur 9:30 - 5 PM
Fridays 9:30 - 6 PM
Saturday 9:30 - 4 PM
Sunday Noon - 4 PM

Winter (Nov 1 - April 30)
Mon - Fri 10 - 5 PM
Saturday 10 - 4 PM
Open Evenings during classes

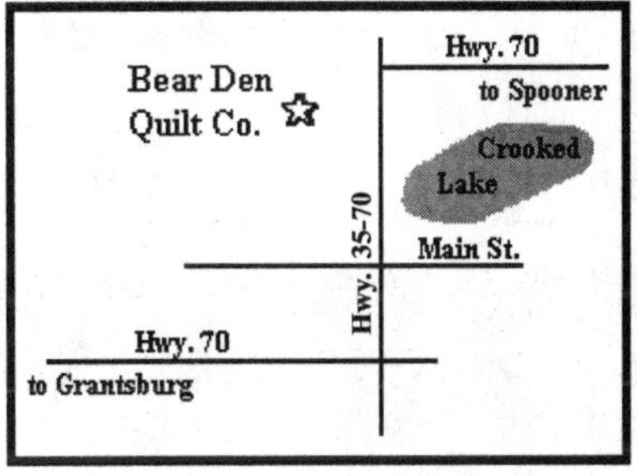

Travel 1.5 miles north of Siren's Main Street on Highway 35-70 and we are on the left-hand side of the highway. Look for the blue Quilt Shop sign.

While visiting beautiful Northwestern Wisconsin don't miss a stop at the area's newest Quilt Shop. You will find over 3,000 bolts of 100% cotton quilting fabric and walls filled with samples in full view. Surely you will be inspired for your next quilt project. Our shop is well lit and we are known for our friendly atmosphere and personal service. We specialize in the "Northwoods" look and have extensive selections in flannels and batiks along with the latest books, patterns and notions. Don't miss our fat quarter aisle, it's been called "Fat Quarter Heaven". You will also find many unique gift items and fabric packs for the discerning quilter. We host quilt retreats twice a year and offer classes year around.

Superior, WI #94

Tues 12 - 5
Wed & Thur 10 - 6
Fri 10 - 5 Sat 9 - 1
Call for Summer Hrs.

The Country Schoolhouse

2104 E. 5th St. 54880
(715) 394-9782
CtrySchlhs@aol.com
Owner: Marsha Bergren Est: 2001

Specializing in "Up North" fabrics. Lots of flannels. Civil War Reproductions. Moda, South Sea Imports, Thimbleberries, RJR are major lines. *"...where quilting is fun"*

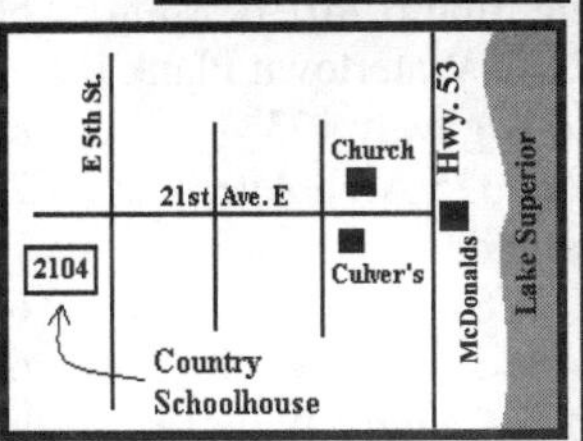

Superior, WI #95

Mon - Fri
9:30 - 5
Thur til 8
Sat 10 - 4

Fabric Works

1320 Tower Ave. 54880
(715) 392-7060
Owner: Barb Engelking
Est: 1991

Over 2000 Bolts of 100% Cotton Fabric. Quilting Books, Patterns and Supplies.

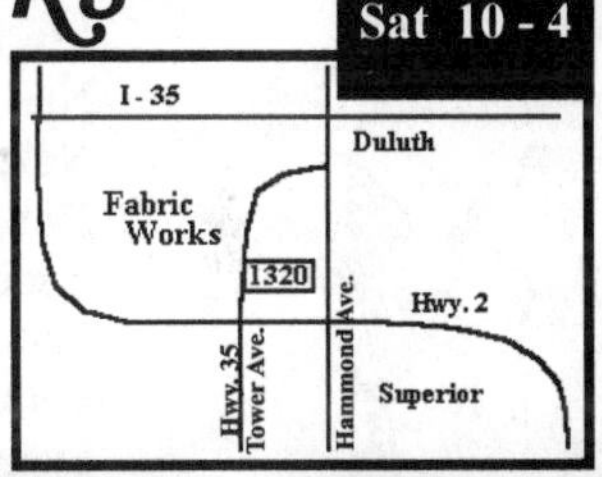

Bayfield, WI #96

Mon - Sat
10 - 6
Nov-May
Closed Mon

Bayfield Quilt Company

84460 Hwy. 13, P.O. Box 1575 54814
(715) 779-3095 Fax: (715) 779-3059
barb@bayfieldquilt.com
www.bayfieldquilt.com
Owners: Barb and Bruce Hoekstra
Est: 2003 650 sq.ft. 1250 bolts

The BEST little Quilt Shop on the Bayfield Peninsula; actually, we are the *only* quilt shop on the Bayfield Peninsula.

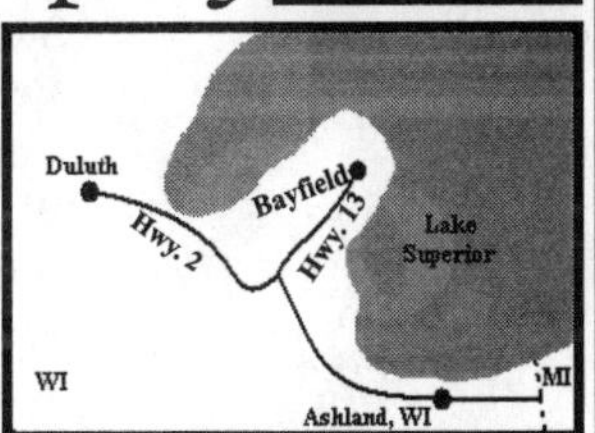

Other Shops in Wisconsin: *We suggest calling first*

Amery	Rita's Needles, 906 Wisconsin Ln.	715-268-9524
Arcadia	Kountry Krafts, 102 W Main St	608-323-3770
Beaver Dam	Nancy's Notions, 333 Beichl Ave.	920-887-7321
Brookfield	Bigsby's Sewing Center, 2435 N 124th St	262-785-1177
Butternut	Pioneer Quilt Shop, 126 E. Main St.	715-769-3284
Cedarburg	Cedarburg Woolen Mill, W. 62 N. 580 Washington	414-377-0345
Clayton	Pine Cone Quilting, 318 7th Ave.	715-948-2111
Cornell	Uncommon Creations, 311 Main St	715-239-1030
Deer Park	Sew Country Quilt & Craft, 194 135th St	715-269-5684
Delavan	The Stitchery, N2482 County Road O	262-728-6318
Elmwood	Simple Pleasures, 125 E. Race Ave.	715-639-6201
Genoa City	Quilted Corner, 201 Freeman St	262-279-0928
Grafton	Rasbery Hill Patchworks, 2277 Edgewood Dr	414-377-9116
Green Bay	Door County Quiltworks, 1043 S. Quincy St.	
Green Bay	A Quilter's Dream, 1298 Velp Ave	920-490-1282
Green Bay	A Quilter's Dream, 4505 Pine Ln	920-434-1969
Hayward	Granma's Workshop, 15981 W Carol Dr	715-634-2754
Hazelhurst	The Quilt Cottage, 6823 Hwy. 51 S	715-358-7074
Herbster	Cabin Fever Quilt Co., P.O. Box 6	715-774-3309
Iola	Come Back in Quilt Shop, 175 N Main St	715-445-5700
La Crosse	Carol's Corne, 731 10th St. N	608-784-7860
Lake Geneva	The Last Stitch, 1350 Hwy H North	262-742-3214
Lake Geneva	Churchhouse Quilt Studio, 1100 Park Row	262-249-7858
Madison	Walcott Sewing, 4522 E Washington Ave #6	608-249-5151
Marinette	Quilt Stitcher, 2456 Elm St	715-735-3099
Marshfield	Quilters Garden, 302 S Maple Ave	715-384-3465
Medford	Treasure Chest Gifts, 345 N. 8th St.	715-748-6860
Menasha	Mystical Threads, 220 Main St.	920-725-3350
Middleton	Quilted Creations, 6771 University Ave.	608-831-5072
Mt. Horeb	She Seams Together Quilting Studio, 401 E. Main	608-437-7290
Nashotah	Natural Options, N44 W 32646 Watertown Plank Rd	
Nekoosa	Mitches Stitches, 4891 State Highway 173	847-622-8399
New Richmond	Bear Paw Quilting Studio, 2325 Arch Ave.	715-246-5854
Osceolo	Quilting Bee, 215 1/2 N. Cascade	715-294-2722
Platteville	Quiltyme, 5832 State Rd 80 & 81	608-348-6271
Potosi	Quilt Spot , 446 Hwy 61S	608-763-2646
Sister Bay	Easy Stitchin' Needle Art, 326 Country Walk Ln	920-854-2840
Spencer	After Hours Creations, 212 S. Pacific	
Spring Green	Sew 'N Sew, 122 N. Lexington	608-588-2273
Stetsonville	Betty White's Fabrics, 109 Mink Ave.	715-678-2294
Stevens Point	The Sampler House, 1129 Main St.	715-341-5540
Stockholm	Amish Country, 119 Spring St.	715-442-2015
Stone Lake	Jan McKichan, 16719 W. Sissabagama Rd.	715-865-6406
Verona	She Seams Together Quilting, 307 Edward St.	608-848-4119
Verona	Maple Springs Farm, 1828 Highway PB	608-845-9482
Watertown	Country Corner Quilt Shop, 210 S Water St	920-206-0939
Waukesha	Just A Little Bit Country, N 4 W 22496 Blue Mound	262-542-8050
Waukesha	Genesee Woolen Mill, S 40 W 28178 Hwy. 59	414-521-2121
Waukeshaw	Treasures of Tomorrow, 1700 E. Racine Ave	262-549-9701
Waupaca	Nichols Creek Quilt Studio, 201 N. Main St.	715-258-5183
Webster	Aunt Thelma's Antiques, 26632 Lakeland Ave N	
West Bend	Gingerbread Junction, Ltd., 310 N. Main St.	262-335-3935

Wisconsin Guilds:

Amherst	Tomorrow's Quilters, 54406	
Appleton	Darting Needles, P.O. Box	Meets: 3rd Monday 7 p.m. at First United Methodist Church
Augusta	Augusta Quilt Addicts, 54722	Meets: Mondays at 1 p.m. at Augusta Senior Center
Baraboo	Baraboo Quilters, 901 Moore Street #15, 53913	
Beaver Dam	Phi Beta Cabin Quilter's Sorority, W 8834 Niblick Rd., 53916	Meets: 2nd Wednesday 6:30 p.m. at Trinity Methodist Church
Boyceville	Heart in Hands Quilt Guild, Box 12A, 54725	
Brookfield	Lake Country Quilters, 1385 Countryside Lane, 53045	
Brookfield	Piecemaker's , 1165 Parkmoor Drive, 53005	
Burlington	Chocolaate City Quilters, PO Box 557	Meets: 2nd Monday @ 6:30 pm at Burlington High School
Cambridge	Fort Atkinson Piecemakers, 163 Hoopen Road, 53523	
Cedarsburg	Cedar Creek Quilters, 1654 Summit Drive, 53012	
Dorchester	Blossoms & Bees Quilt Club, P.O. Box 266, 54425	Meets: 1st Tuesday 1 p.m. at Cow Country Fabrics
Dorchester	Stetsonville Stitchers Quilt Club, P.O. Box 266, 54425	Meets: 1st Tuesday 7 p.m. at Cow Country Fabrics
Eagle	Old World Quilters, 304 Larkin Street, 53119	
Eagle River	Cranberry Country Quilt Guild, P.O. Box 194, 54521	Meets: 3rd Monday 10 a.m. at Prince of Peace Church
Eau Claire	Clear Water Quilters, 2112 Rudolph Rd.	
Ephraim	Trillium Quilt Guild, PO Box 293, 54211	Meets: 2nd & 4th Thursday @ 9:30 pm at Meadows of Scandia Village
Fall Creek	A Piece at a Time, 440 W. Washington Ave., 54742	Meets: 4th Monday at 7 p.m. at Faith Evangelical Church
Fontana	Village Quilters of Harvard, 53125	
Fort Atkinson	Piecemakers Quilt Guild, 510 Grove Street, 53538	
Frederic	Mixed Sampler Quilt Club, Box 133, 54837	
Germantown	Menomonee Falls Quilters, W. 154 N. 11666 Daniels, 53022	
Gillett	Essentially Yours Quilt Guild, 121 E. Main St., 54124	Meets: 2nd Saturday 9 a.m. at Diann's Essentials
Grafton	Heritage Quilters, 203 Beech, 53024	
Green Bay	Evergreen Quilters, PO Box 783, 54305	
Holmen	La Crosse Area Quilters, W. 8154 Holland Drive, 54636	Meets: 4th Tuesday 7 p.m. at Onalaska Community Center
Hudson	Hudson Heritage Quilters, 874 Willow Ridge, 54016	
Jackson	It's a Stitch Quilt Club, 3280 Highway P, 53037	
Janesville	Rock Valley Quilters Guild, PO Box 904, 53547	Meets: 3rd Tuesday @ 7pm at New Life Assembly of God Church
Kenosha	Southport Quilter's Guild, PO Box 1523, 53141	
Lodi	Prairie Sampler Quilt Club, N2173 Smith Park Rd., 53555	Meets: 3rd Tuesday at Sauk City Library
Madison	Mad City Quilters, 157 Nautilus Drive, 53705	
Madison	Twilight Quilters Guild, 9 Leyton Circle, 53713	
Manitowoc	A Patch of Lakeshore, 1696 Skyline Dr., 54220	Meets: 2nd Thursday 6:45 p.m. at St. Mary's Home
Marinette	Northwoods Quilters, P.O. Box 595, 54143	
Menasha	Darting Needles Quilt Guild, PO Box 603, 54952	Meets: 3rd Monday @ 7 pm at United Methodist Church, Appleton
Mequon	Covered Bridge Quilters, 13907 N. Port Washington Rd., 53092	
Milwaukee	Orchard Inn Quilters, 5510 W. Calumet Road, 53223	
Milwaukee	West Suburban Quilters Guild, 2621 N. 65th Street, 53213	
Milwaukee	Wisconsin's Quilter's Inc., PO Box 83144, 53223	
Milwaukee	Stitch it or Stuff it Quilters, 6551 N. 66th Street, 53223	
Milwaukee	North Shore Quilters Guild, PO Box 17263, 53217	
Minocqua	Ladies of the Lake, P.O. Box 481, 54548	
Monroe	Courthouse Quilters	Meets: 4th Monday @ 6:30 pm at Pleasant View Auditorium
Montello	Evergreen Quilters, Box 426, 53949	
Montello	Calico Capers Quilt Guild, RR 1 Gem Avenue, 53949	
Mukwonago	Crazy Quilters, S 70 W 32864 Oak Pl., 53149	Meets: 2nd Wednesday 7 p.m. at First Congregational Church
Muskego	Log Cabin Quilter's	Meets: 2nd Tuesday @ 7 pm at Muskego Library
Neshkoro	Pine Tree Needlers, N 9028 W Silver Spring Dr ,54960	Meets: 4th Wednesday @ 12:30 pm at Mountain View Community Center
New Richmond	Willow River Piecemakers, P.O. Box 26, 54017	Meets: 2nd Thursday 7 p.m. at St. Lukes Lutheran Church
Oak Creek	Wandering Foot Quilters, 8620 S. Howell Avenue, 53154	
Oshkosh	Lake Side Quilters, 1350 Menominee Drive, 54901	Meets: 3rd Wednesday 6:30 p.m. at Marion Manor
Plum City	Plum Creek Quilters, W 601 210th Ave., 54761	
Racine	Lighthouse Quilters, PO Box 124, 53403	
Reedsburg	Cornerstone Quilt Guild, 337 K Street, 53959	
Reedsburg	Around the Block Quilters, 940 E. Main, 53959	
Rhinelander	Rhinelander Northwoods Quilters, 49 Lake Creek Road, 54501	Meets: 1st Tuesday at 7 p.m. at Senior Center
Richland Center	Friendship Quilter's Guild, 587 N. Park Street, 53581	Meets: 4th Monday 7 p.m. at Schmidt Woodland Hills
Sayner	Ladies of the Lake Quilters, 9200 Longs Road, 54560	
Shawano	Shawano Area Quilters, 225 S. Main, 54166	
Sheboygan	Sheboygan County Quilter's Guild, 53083	Meets: 2nd Wednesday @ 1 pm Jan, Mar, May, July, Sept, Nov and 7 pm Feb, Apr, June, Aug, Oct, Dec. at Ebenezer United Church of Christ, 3215 Saemann Ave
Slinger	Ties That Bind Quilt Guild, 425 E. Washington St., 53086	Meets: 3rd Wednesday 7 p.m. at Common Threads Quilt Shop
Solon Springs	Ladies of the Lake, 9291 E. County Rd. A, 54873	Meets: Every Thursday 9:30 a.m. at Village Hall Downstairs
Spooner	Wild Rivers Quilting Guild, Box 1065, 54801	
Stevens Point	Bernina Club, 1129 Main, 54481	Meets: 1st Wednesday 10 a.m. & 6:30 p.m. at The Sampler House
Stevens Point	Star Point Quilters Guild, P.O. Box 607, 54481	
Stoughton	Stoughton Piecemakers, 233 West Main Street, 53589	Meets: 1st Thursday @ 7 pm at United Methodist Church
Sun Prairie	Prairie Heritage Quilters, PO Box 253, 53590	
Superior	Casda Quilts, 2231 Catlin Avenue, 54880	
Superior	Scrap Happy Quilters, 7622 Hughitt, 54880	Meets: 2nd Thursday 6:00 at Darrow Rd. Church
Tomahawk	Four Rivers Quilt Guild, 54487	Meets: 2nd & 4th Wednesday 9 a.m. at River Valley State Bank
Tomahawk	Tomahawk Stitchers Guild, 54487	Meets: 3rd Monday 7 p.m. at United Methodist Church
Viroqua	Vernon County Piecemakers, 117 FS Drive, 54665	Meets: 3rd Tuesday @ 7 pm at Vernon Memorial Hospital
Wales	Patched Lives Quilt Guild, 500 Pebble Creek Pass, 53183	Meets: 2nd Wednesday 7 p.m. at Brandybrook School
Washburn	North Woods Quilters, 709 W. Third Street, 54891	
Wausau	Pine Tree Quilters Guild, P.O. Box 692, 54402	Meets: 2nd Tuesday at 7 p.m. & 4th Tuesday 10 am at Cedar Creek Community Room
Wautoma	Pine Tree Needlers, 54982	
West Bend	Kettle Moraine Quilt Club, 53095	Meets: 2nd Tuesday @ 9:30 am at Fifth Avenue Methodist Church
Whitewater	Stone Mill Quilters, 53190	Meets: 3rd Wednesday @ 6:30 pm at Congregation Church
Williams Bay	Scrappers Quilt Guild, Hwy 67	Meets: 3rd Tuesday 7 pm at Lions Field House
Wisconsin Dells	Dells Country Quilters, #530 Highway 23 E., 53965	

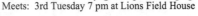

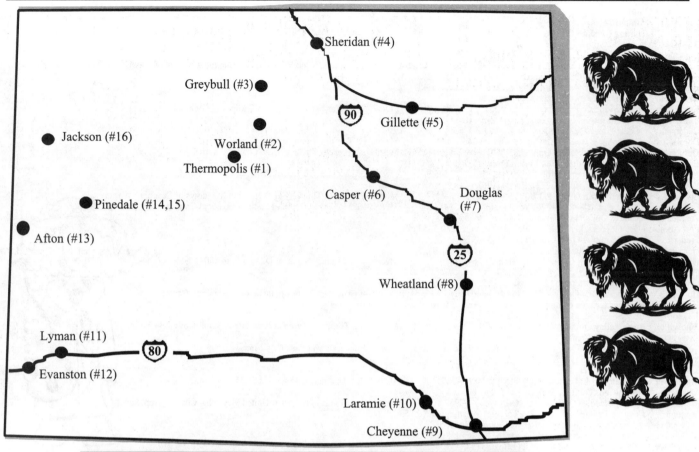

Sheridan (#4)
Greybull (#3)
Gillette (#5)
Jackson (#16)
Worland (#2)
Thermopolis (#1)
Casper (#6)
Douglas (#7)
Pinedale (#14,15)
Afton (#13)
Wheatland (#8)
Lyman (#11)
Evanston (#12)
Laramie (#10)
Cheyenne (#9)
90
25
80

WYOMING

16 Featured Shops

Thermopolis, WY #1

Mon - Sat 9 - 5:30
Sun 12 - 4

Keeping You In Stitches

524 Broadway 82443
(307) 864-9490
Owners: Karen & Dennis Sinclair
3000 sq.ft. 3000+ Bolts

We pride ourselves on being the region's favorite quilt shop! Stop in for some quilting inspiration, fabric, patterns, books & more.

to Worland
Hwy. 20 N
Keeping You In Stitches
524
to Cody
The one & only stoplight
Broadway
Horse Statue
to Shoshoni

Worland, WY #2

Mon - Sat 9 - 5:30

Hansen's Fabric

734 Big Horn Ave.
82401
(307) 347-4895

Quilting Cottons & much, much more! Quilt books, notions, patterns etc. PLUS—guaranteed, experienced sewing machine service.

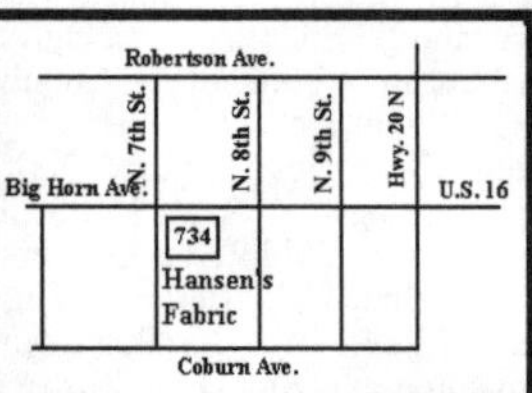

Greybull, WY #3

Mon - Sat 9 - 5

Big Horn Quilts

529 Greybull Ave. 82426
(877) 586-9150
or (307) 765-2604

julie@bighornquilts.com
www.bighornquilts.com
Owners: David & Julie Owens
Est: 1998 8000 Bolts Full Online Catalog

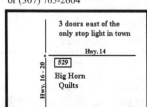

3 doors east of the only stop light in town
Hwy. 14
529
Big Horn Quilts
Hwy. 16 - 20

Sheridan, WY #4

Mon - Fri 10 - 5
Sat 10 - 4

Treasured Stitches

28 N. Main 82801
(307) 674-0558
Owners: Josephine Schreibeis & Rita Baker
Est: 1996

Top quality Fabrics, Patterns, Books, Quilter's Notions, and Supplies. Classes. Silk Flowers and some finished crafts.

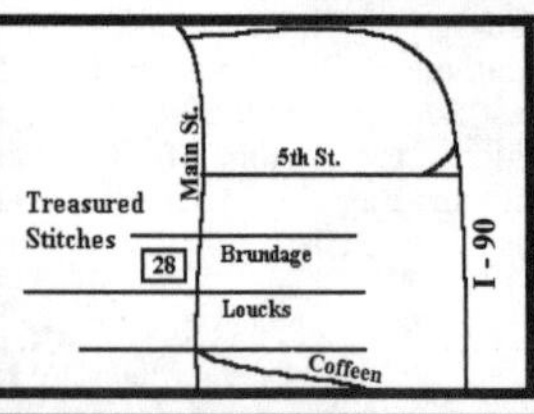

Gillette, WY #5

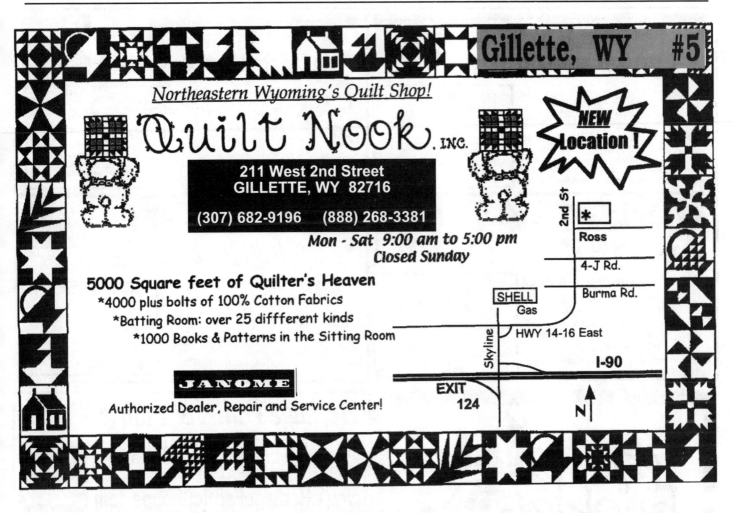

Northeastern Wyoming's Quilt Shop!

Quilt Nook, INC.

NEW Location !

211 West 2nd Street
GILLETTE, WY 82716

(307) 682-9196 (888) 268-3381

Mon - Sat 9:00 am to 5:00 pm
Closed Sunday

5000 Square feet of Quilter's Heaven

*4000 plus bolts of 100% Cotton Fabrics
*Batting Room: over 25 diffferent kinds
*1000 Books & Patterns in the Sitting Room

JANOME

Authorized Dealer, Repair and Service Center!

2nd St
Ross
4-J Rd.
Burma Rd.
SHELL Gas
HWY 14-16 East
Skyline
I-90
EXIT 124
N

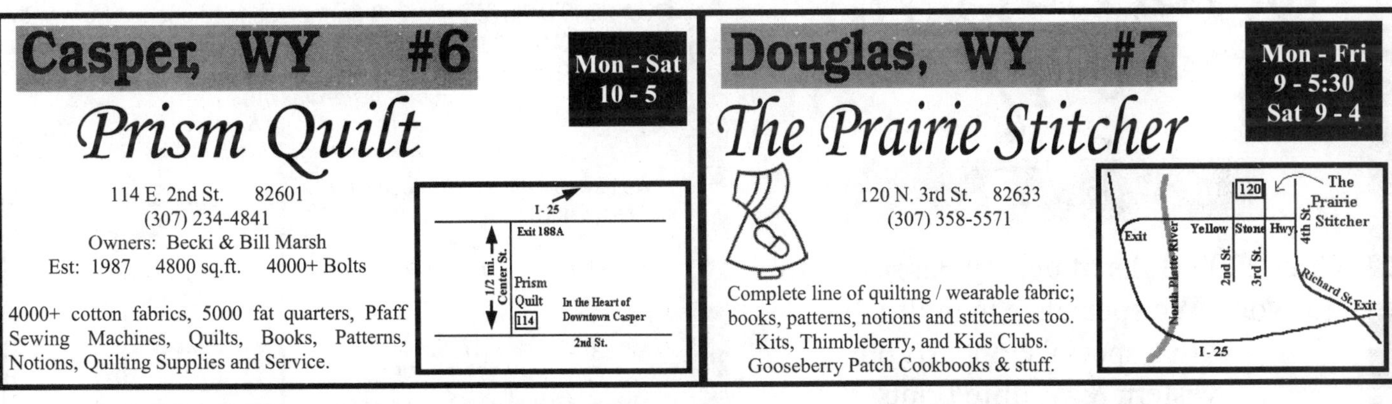

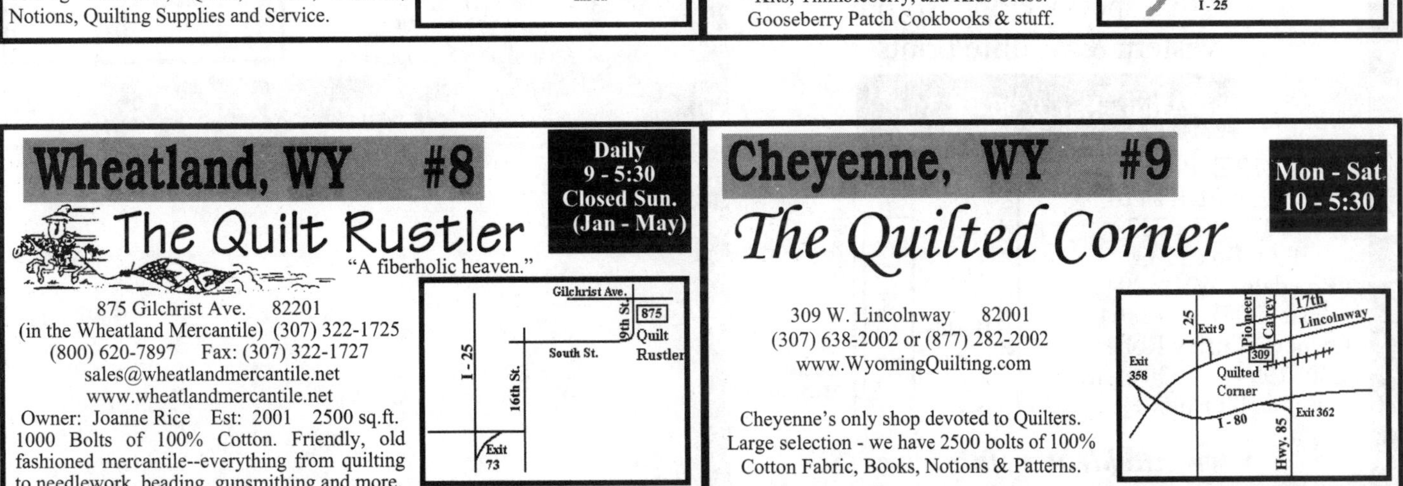

Laramie, WY #10

Mon - Sat 10 - 5:30

QuiltEssentials

314 S. 2nd St. 82070
(307) 742-6156
quiltessentials@qwest.net
www.quiltessentials.org
Owners: Cynthia Deveraux & Rose McNerney
Est: 2002 3100 sq.ft. 2500 Bolts

A full line of Fabrics, Books, Notions and Gift Items. Located in Historic Downtown Laramie.

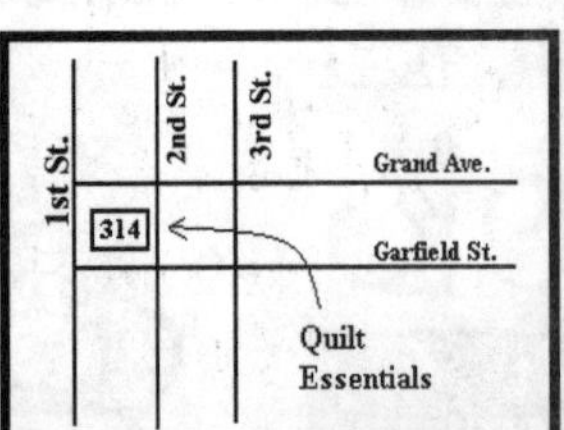

Lyman, WY #11

Valley Fabric Shop

102 Mountain Meadow St.
(Urie) 82937
(307) 786-2653
Fax: (307) 786-2655
Est: 1979 2,000+ Bolts

Wyoming's best kept secret. Quilting Fabrics, flannels, books, notions & patterns. Our sample displays are worth the visit. Terrific Service.

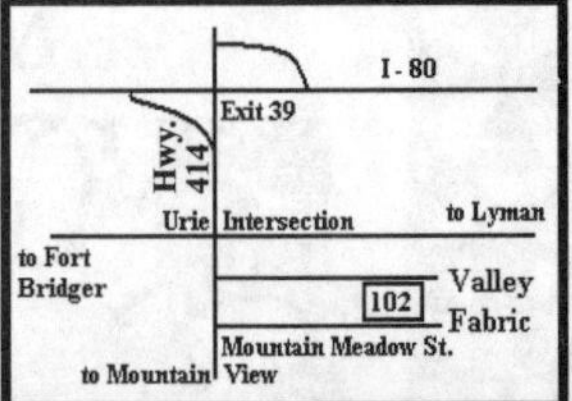

Evanston, WY #12

Tues - Fri 9 - 5
Sat 9 - 2

R&V High Country Fabrics

528 County Rd., #7, P.O. Box 1956 82931
(307) 789-7300 Fax: Same
Montoyarv@allwest.net Est: 2001
Owner: Vickie J. Montoya 1000 Bolts
We cater to Quilters!
Quality Fabrics (Moda - Robin Pandolph) and much more. Quilting supplies and notions.

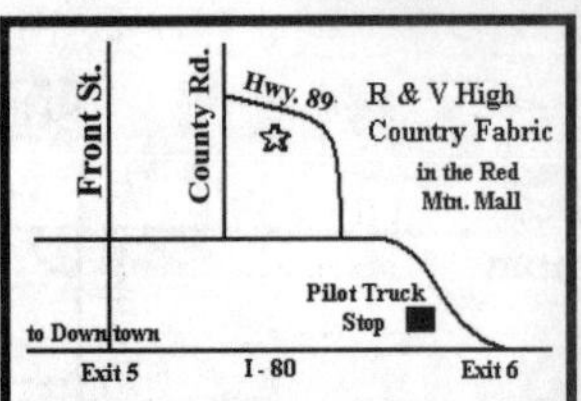

Afton, WY #13

Mon - Sat 10 - 5:30

The Cottage

425 S. Washington, P.O. Box 252 83110
(307) 885-2522
thecottage@silverstar.com
Owner: Marie Wilkes
Est: 2003 1200 sq.ft.

Beautiful fabrics - 100% cottons - Flannels
Notions - Patterns - Books - Quilts - Gifts
Warmth & Friendship. Just north of the Elkhorn Arch on Hwy. 89

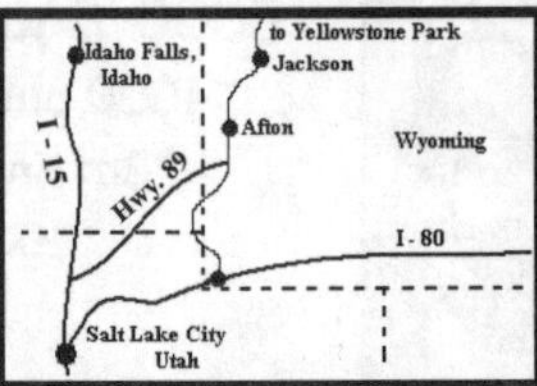

the huckleberry patch

Pinedale, WY #14

Over 2000 Bolts of quality Fabric waiting for you! We specialize in quilt fabrics -- with a special emphasis on western & wildlife prints.

Mon - Sat 9:00 - 5:30

219 E. Pine
Summit Mall #116
(307) 367-6727
P.O. Box 1733,
Pinedale, WY 82941
Fax: (307) 367-2864
Owner: Shirley Roberts
Est: 1994 1500 sq.ft.
2500 Bolts

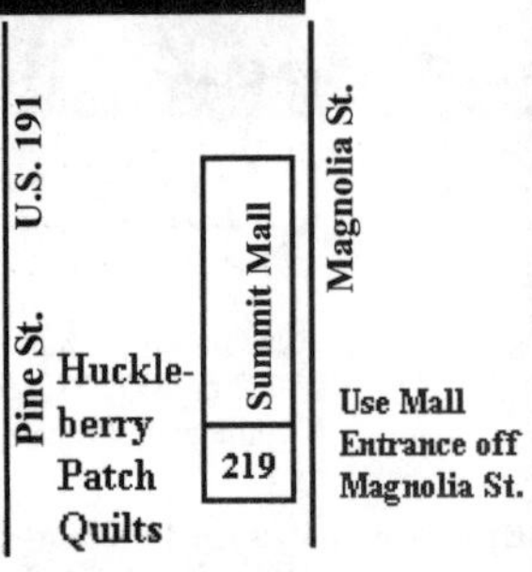

www.huckleberryfabrics.com

Heritage Quilts & Fabric Shoppe

THE AREA'S FRIENDLIEST QUILT SHOP & QUILTERS RETREAT FACILITY

www.HeritageFabricShoppe.com

Mon - Sat 9 - 5:30
Summer Sun 12 - 5

Over 2000 bolts of cottons & flannel fabric to choose from with books, patterns, notions & distinctive gifts. Classes Offered. Authorized Husqvarna-VIKING dealer

Quilt programs by:
McKenna Ryan of Pine Needles
Thimbleberries Quilt Club 2004

We have everything you need for a successful quilt retreat. Sleeps up to 12 people. Located in the heart of the Wind River Mountains, Pinedale is your Basecamp for Adventure!
21 East Pine St.,
P.O. Box 1517 82941
(307) 367-7397 (SEWS)
sue@HeritageFabricShoppe.com

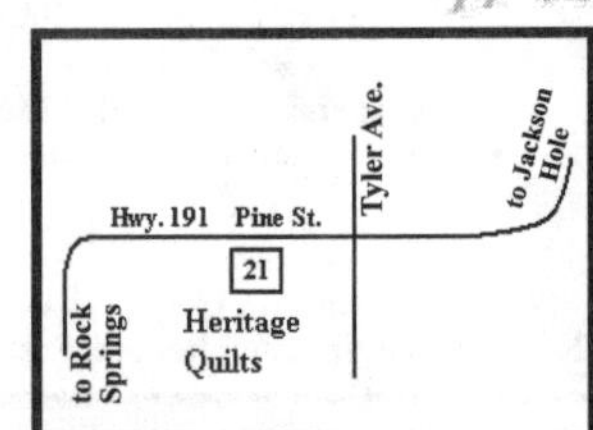

Pinedale, WY #15

Other Shops in Wyoming: *We suggest calling first*

Buffalo	D.J. Variety Store, Hwy. 16 W, 5 W. Fort	307-684-2518
Casper	Patchwork Palace, 1241 East 18th Street	307-265-1021
Casper	Quilts & Things, 2113 E. 12th St.	307-266-5894
Casper	Wyoming Sewing Center, 2635 E. 2nd St.	307-234-4581
Clearmont	The Best Kept Secret, 1617 New York	307-758-4456
Douglas	Above the Cellar, 132 N. 2nd St.	307-358-2206
Douglas	Sheila's Fabrics, 515 S. 4th St.	307-358-5333
Gillette	Quilt Trail, P.O. Box 4175	307-686-0676
Green River	A Little Country Character, 1740 Uinta Dr.	307-875-7172
Laramie	Stitch Garden, PO Box 402	307-742-8083
Lovell	Mayes Fabrics, 435 Oregon Ave.	307-548-7715
Marbleton	Fantasy Fabrics 112 Maxwell Ave.	307-276-3610
Riverton	Quilted Treasures Studio, 1006 E. Jackson Ave.	307-856-9727
Riverton	Hazel's Quiltworks, 118 W Pershing Ave	307-856-3899
Rock Springs	Country Fabrics, 426 S. Main St	307-382-2897
Story	Chickadee Charms Designs, 27 Loucks	307-683-2902

Wyoming Guilds:

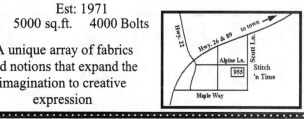

Basin	Loose Threads, P.O. Box 740, 82410 Meets: 3rd Monday @ 7 pm, call 307-765-2604 for location
Cheyenne	Cheyenne Heritage Quilters, P.O. Box 21194 82003-7023 Meets: 1st & 3rd Monday @ 7 pm at Creative Ministries 600 East Carlson
Douglas	Purple Sage Quilt Guild, 1954 E Richards St Suite #6, 82633 Meets: 1st Thursday 7:30 p.m. Senior Center
Gillette	Northeast Wyoming Quilt Guild, P.O. Box 661 82718 Meets: 2nd & 4th Monday @ 9 am at 1st Presbyterian Church
Greybull	Tuesday Nighters, 529 Greybull Ave, 82426 Meets: Every Tuesday @ 6:30 pm at Big Horn Quilts, ignore 'closed' sign
Jackson	Jackson Hole Quilt Guild, P.O. Box 11412 83002 Meets: 1st Monday 7 p.m. at Grand Teton National Park Maintenance Bldg. in Moose, WY
Moorcroft	Moorcroft Busy Bobbins, 82721 Meets: 1st, 3rd & 4th Tuesday @ 9 am at St. Patricks Catholic Church
Powell	Paintbrush Piecers Quilt Guild, P.O. Box 258 82435
Worland	Cottonwood Quilters, 911 Howell Ave, 82401 Meets: 2nd Monday @ 7 pm at St. Mary Magdalen Catholic Church

Bahamas

1 Featured Shop

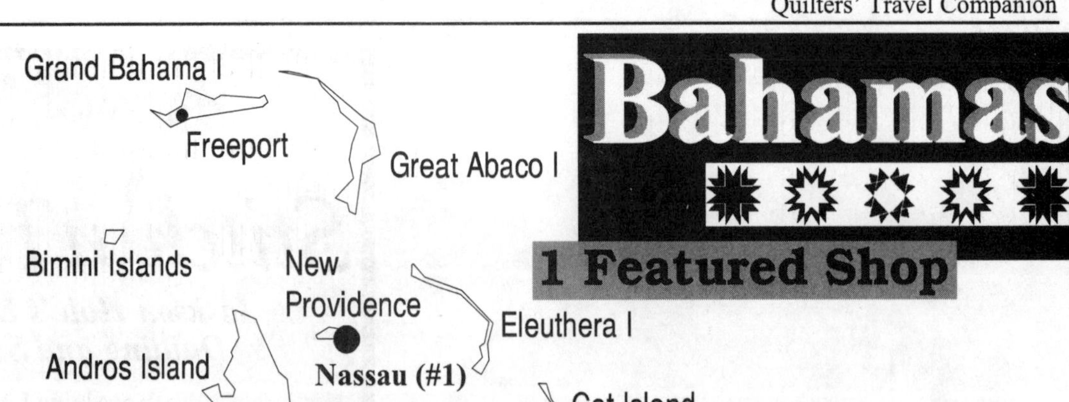

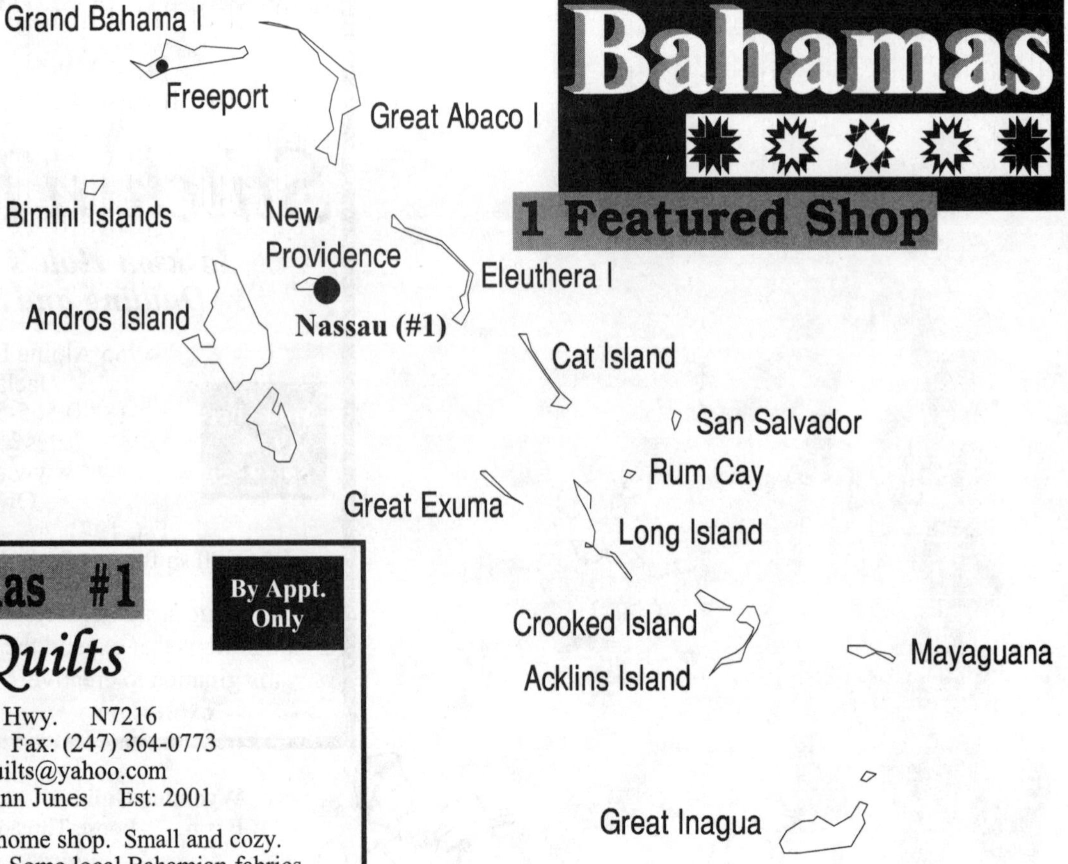

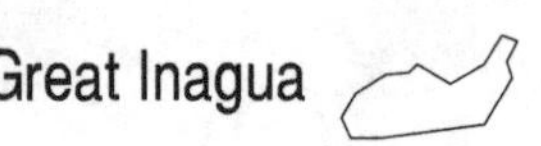

Nassau, Bahamas #1

By Appt. Only

Silk Cotton Quilts

#3 Winton Hwy. N7216
(242) 824-1073 Fax: (247) 364-0773
silkcottonquilts@yahoo.com
Owner: Mary Ann Junes Est: 2001

Silk Cotton Quilts is a home shop. Small and cozy. Approximately 300 bolts. Some local Bahamian fabrics. Please call for directions.

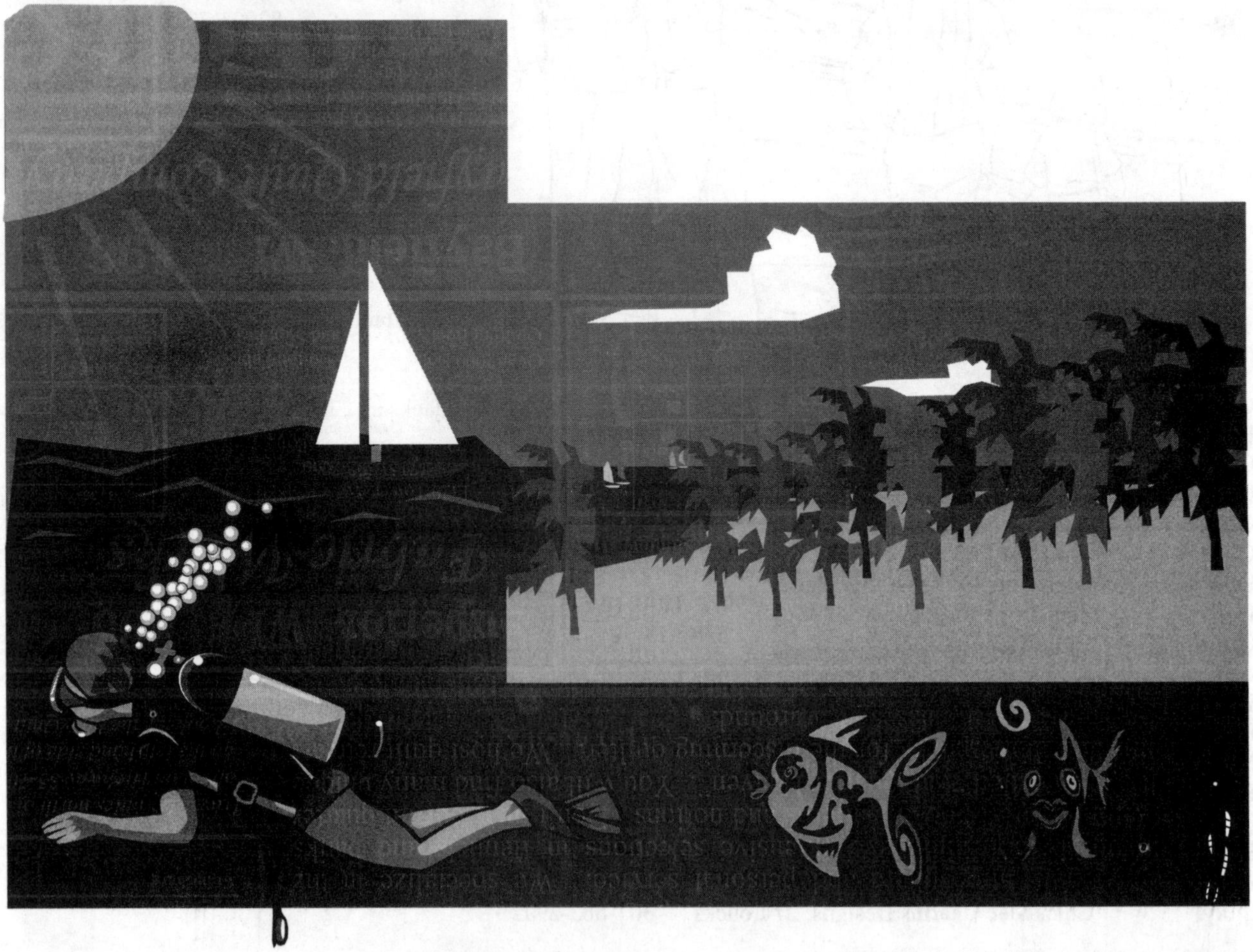

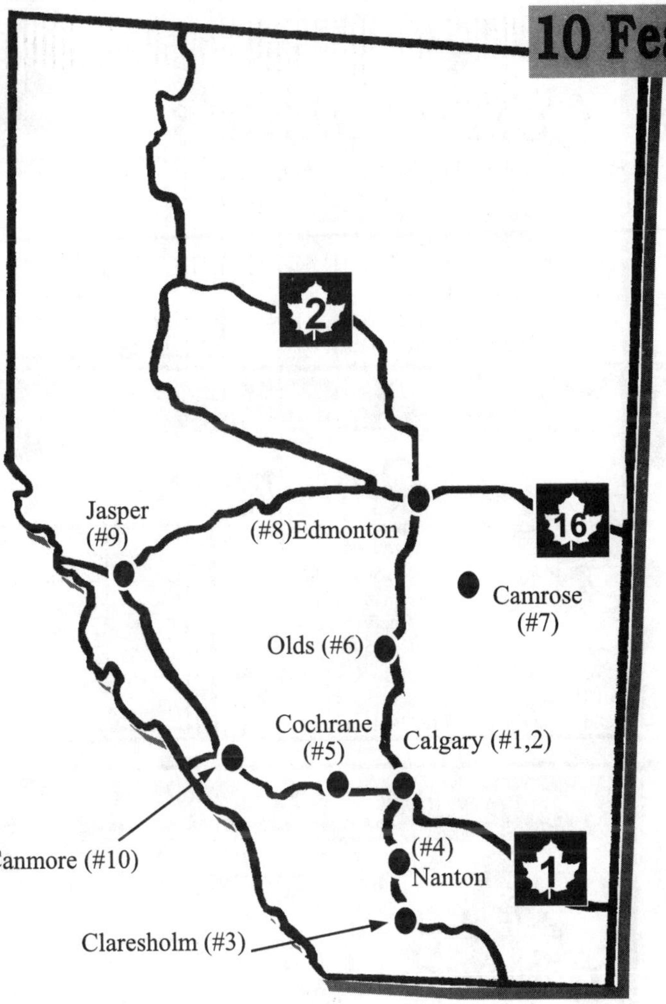

10 Featured Shops

Jasper (#9)
(#8)Edmonton
Camrose (#7)
Olds (#6)
Cochrane (#5)
Calgary (#1,2)
Canmore (#10)
(#4) Nanton
Claresholm (#3)
2
16
1

ALBERTA CANADA

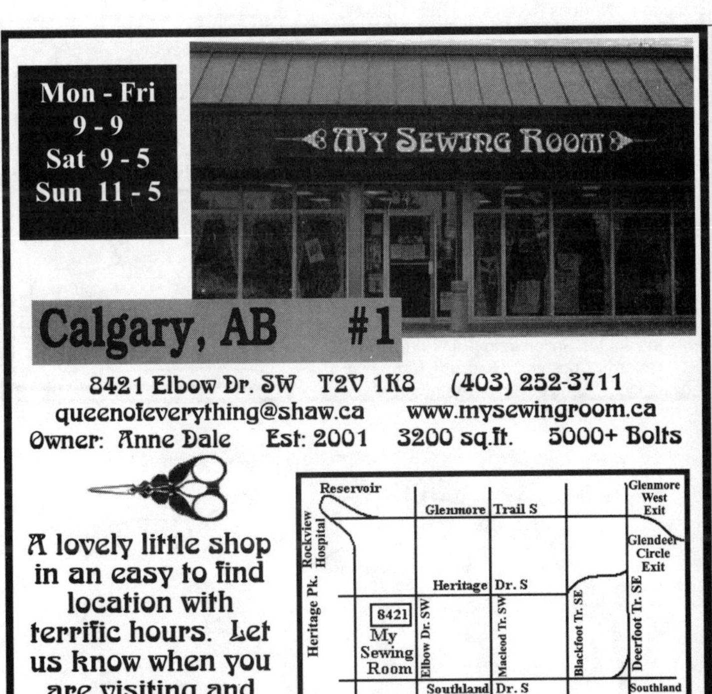

Mon - Fri 9 - 9
Sat 9 - 5
Sun 11 - 5
My Sewing Room
Calgary, AB #1
8421 Elbow Dr. SW T2V 1K8 (403) 252-3711
queenofeverything@shaw.ca www.mysewingroom.ca
Owner: Anne Dale Est: 2001 3200 sq.ft. 5000+ Bolts
A lovely little shop in an easy to find location with terrific hours. Let us know when you are visiting and where you found out about us.
Reservoir
Glenmore Trail S
Glenmore West Exit
Rockview Hospital
Glendeer Circle Exit
Heritage Dr. S
Heritage Pk.
8421 My Sewing Room
Elbow Dr. SW
Macleod Tr. SW
Blackfoot Tr. SE
Deerfoot Tr. SE
Southland Dr. S
Southland West Exit

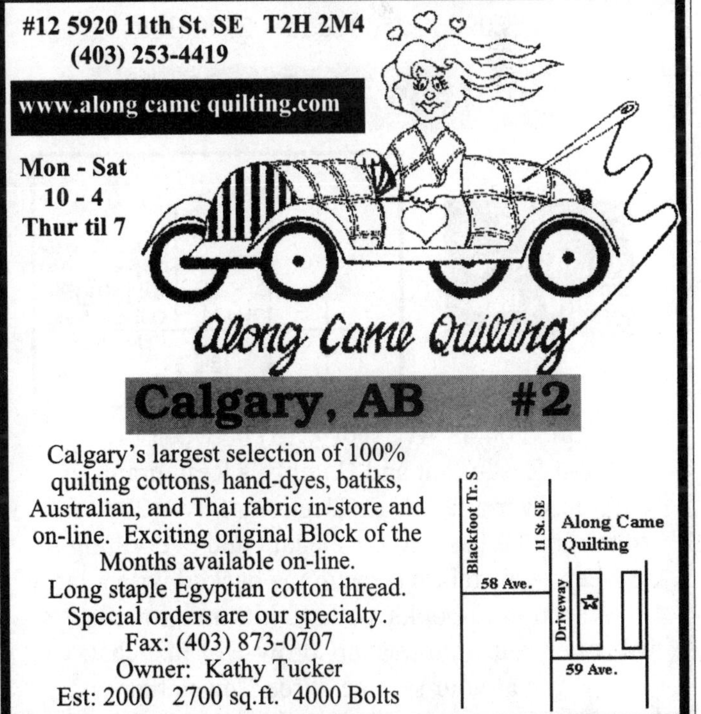

#12 5920 11th St. SE T2H 2M4
(403) 253-4419
www.along came quilting.com
Mon - Sat 10 - 4
Thur til 7
Along Came Quilting
Calgary, AB #2
Calgary's largest selection of 100% quilting cottons, hand-dyes, batiks, Australian, and Thai fabric in-store and on-line. Exciting original Block of the Months available on-line.
Long staple Egyptian cotton thread.
Special orders are our specialty.
Fax: (403) 873-0707
Owner: Kathy Tucker
Est: 2000 2700 sq.ft. 4000 Bolts
Blackfoot Tr. S
11 St. SE
Along Came Quilting
58 Ave.
Driveway
59 Ave.

Claresholm, AB #3

Mon - Sat 12 - 5:30

Wood Lily Floral & Quilting

4721 1st St. W, P.O. Box 1137 T0L 0T0
(403) 625-3349
Owner: Constance H. McNair
Est: 1998 300 sq.ft. 250 Bolts
The smallest, cutest quilt shop in the west. In an old red victorian house, stocked with quilting goodies for quilters!
Also Cross Stitch and Unique Gift Items.

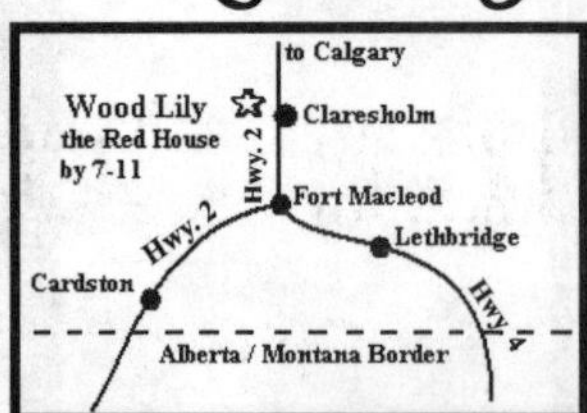

Nanton, AB #4

**Mon - Fri 9:30 - 5:30
Sat 9:30 - 5**

Cottonwoods

2109 - 20 St., P.O. Box 1021 T0L 1R0
(403) 646-2086 Fax: (403) 646-2398
cotwoods@telusplanet.net
www.cottonwoodsquilts.com
Est: 1998 5000 sq.ft. 1200 Bolts
Quilting fabrics, classes, books, notions & patterns. Quilts for Sale.
Authorized Pfaff Dealer.

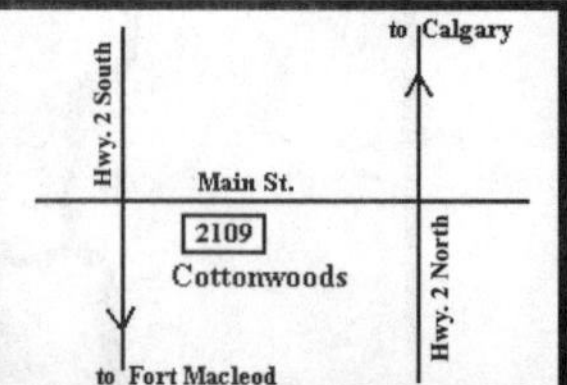

Cochrane, AB #5

Mon - Sat 10 - 5:30

420 First St. W, Box 1047 T4C 1B1
(403) 932-1500 Owner: Corlienne Pennell
addies@telusplanet.net
www.addiesmaterialgoods.com
A unique turn of the century style Quilt Shop. 100% cotton fabrics, books, patterns & workshops.

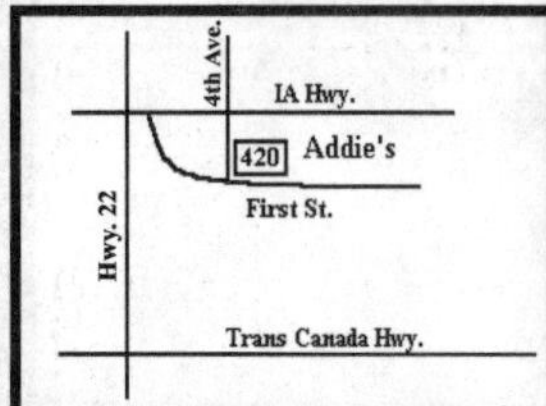

Olds, AB #6

Mon - Sat 10 - 5

The Quilting Bee

5026 51 Street T4H 1P7
(403) 507-8825
Fax: (403) 507-8826
quiltbee@telusplanet.net
Owner: Cheryl Naglis
Est: 2000 2500 sq. ft.
Located in downtown Olds. Large selection of 100% cottons, notions, books and stitchery. Old fashioned prices and hospitality!

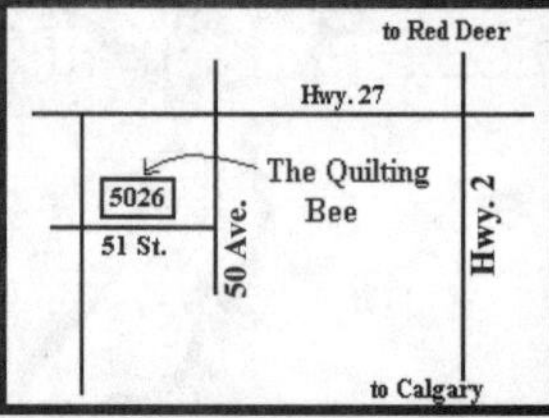

Quilting from the Heart

Fabric ♥ Books ♥ Patterns ♥ Classes

5710 - 48th Ave. T4V 0K1
(877) 679-5492 Fax: (780) 672-5419
info@quiltingfromtheheart.ab.ca
www.quiltingfromtheheart.ab.ca
Est: 2000 2500 sq.ft. 2700 Bolts

Camrose, AB #7

Mon - Sat 9:30 - 5:30 Thurs til 8

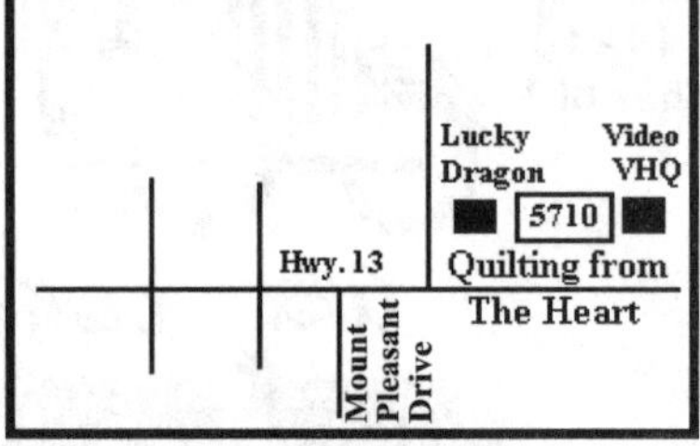

Located on 48 Ave (Hwy. 13) between Lucky Dragon Restaurant and Humpty's Restaurant, you will discover a fantastic selection of over 2700 fabrics from the basic to the elegant and everything in between. Our fabric selection is backed with a large selection of books, pattern, kits and notions. Whether you want to shop, browse or just chat, we are at your service. Free Newsletter

Edmonton, AB #8

**Mon - Fri 9 - 8
Sat 9 - 5
Sun 12 - 5**

Earthly Goods

5848 111th St. T6H 3G1
Lendrum Shopping Center
(780) 433-7179 Fax: (780) 430-0817
Est: 1985
Owner: Sandy Bowhay
4000 sq.ft.
2000 Bolts
info@earthlygoodsquilting.com
www.earthlygoodsquilting.com
Featured in Quilt Sampler Magazine.
Everything you need for quilting including Cottons, Notions & Books. Great Classes.

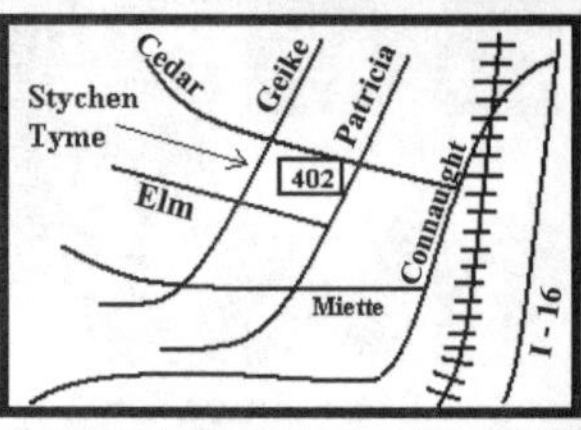

Jasper, AB #9

**Summer Daily 10 - 8
Winter Closed Monday**

Stychen Tyme Quilt & Yarn Shop

402 Patricia St.,
P.O. Box 2230 T0E 1E0
(780) 852-7490 or (866) 852-7490
Fax: (780) 852-7491 Est: 2000
www.stychentyme.com 1000 sq.ft.
Owner: Romy Quackenbush 2000 Bolts
Large selection of fabric, yarn and cross-stitch available. Specializing in "Lodge" and "Nordic" designs. Featuring Canadian designers. Stitch a Rocky Mountain Memory.

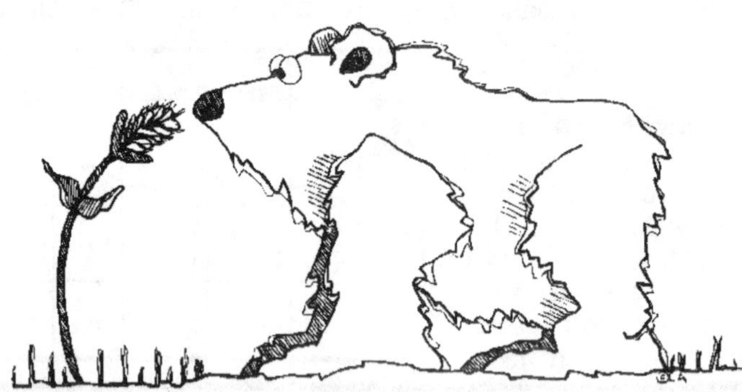

Other Shops in Alberta: *We suggest calling first*

Beaver Lodge Around the Block, 1040 1St. Ave. 780-354-3423
Boyle Crystal's Crafts, 5021 - 3rd St.
Brooks Family Fabrics, 106 - 2nd St. W, Box 862 403-362-2948
Calgary The Quilter's Cabin, 1150-012100 Macleod SE 403-278-4433
Calgary Freckles Quilt Shop, Ltd., 13A-728 Northmount Drive NW 403-270-2104
Calgary Ant Hill, 148 10th St. NW 403-283-8989
Calgary Traditional Pastimes, 7 Parkdale Cres. NW 403-286-9421
Calgary The Fabric Cottage, 16 Crowfoot Terr. NW 403-241-3070
Cardston Imagination Unlimited, 257 Main St. 403-653-2633
Carstairs Custom Woollen Mill, R.R. # 1 403-337-2221
Cold Lake Quilted Gems, 5214 50 Ave. 780-594-5200
Crooked Creek Country Stitches Quilts, R.R. #1 780-957-2446
Daysland Rug Rats and The Fabric Patch, 5009-50 St. 780-374-2549
Drayton Valley Material Matters, 5119 51st St. 403-542-3233
Edmonton Quilter's Dream, 10732 - 124 St. 403-452-1133
Edmonton The Notion Place, 4748 - 99th St.
Edmonton C & M Cottons & More, 5640 104 St. 780-431-9816
Edmonton The Quilter's Palette, 522 Carse Ln.
Fort Kent Donna's Quilting, Box 26
Grande Prairie Cotton Candy Crafts & Quilts, #7 11500 100 Street 708-532-2202
Grande Prairie Patchwork Cottage, 10209 - 102nd St. 708-539-1245
Grimshaw Cabin Crafts, Main St. 780-332-1160
High River Chinook Fabrics, Box 5482
Innisfail Fabric Fantasy, 5018 50th St., PO Box 1645 403-227-4618
Killam Tatters, 5007 - 50th St.
Lac La Biche Cottage Crafts & Creations, Box 1888 780-623-9477
Lacombe Wildflower Creations, 5025 50 Ave 403-782-4141
Lamont L.A. Sewing Centre, 5028 50 Ave. 780-895-2599
Lethbridge Village Crafts, 227 - 2nd Ave. N 403-320-1817
Lethbridge Thistle Down Quilts, 200 4 Ave. S 403-329-1551
Lethbridge Fanny's Fabrics, 1245 2nd Ave. S 403-329-3355
Linden Jo-Al Styles & Fabrics, 113 Central Ave. 403-546-3882
Lloydminster Patchwork Junction, 5732 44th St. 403-875-5935
Mayerthorpe Behind the Seams, P.O. Box 843 403-786-2660
Mayerthorpe Kountry Krafts, 5015 50 Street 780-786-2821
Mayerthrope Katherin Kountry Krafts, P.O. Box 1109 403-786-2821
Medicine Hat Quilt Art, 520A 4th Ave. SE 403-528-4515
Milk River Stitch in Time, 207 Main St. NW
Mundare The Chicken Coop, 5103 50th St. 780-764-3727
Nanton Fabrique Boutique, 2119 20 St 403-646-2106
Okotoks Old Country Store, 64 N. Railway St.
Okotoks Rainbow End, 2 Elma St. W
Okotoks Patchwork Plus, 1100 Village Ln. Bay 6 403-938-6107
Olds The Stitchery, Box 6, Site 1, R.R. #2 403-556-6221
Oyen The Country Fabric Shop, 513 - 2 St. E 403-664-2220
Red Deer Cotton Threads Quilt Co., 5020 Gaetz 403-346-4005
Rocky Mountain House The Fabric Centre, 5116 50 St. 403-845-3740
Standard Cotton & Candy Country Store, 818 The Broadway 403-644-3895
Stettler Stettler Fabric Place, 4909 B 50 St. 403-742-6145
Strathmore Darlene's Fabrics, Box 10, Site 3, R.R. #1 403-934-5370
Strathmore Country Creations, P.O. Box 2142 403-934-4054
Vegreville McFabrics & More, Box 668
White Court Sew Right, 5106 50th St. 403-778-5717

Alberta Guilds:

Barrhead Barrhead Country Quilts, 5514-60 Ave., T7N 1E1 Meets: Tuesday 7 p.m. at Barrhead Catholic Church
Beisiker Alberta Handicrafts Guild, Beisiker Branch, Box 59, T0M 0G0
Blue Ridge Country Quilters, Box 37, T0E 0B0 Meets: 2nd Monday 7 p.m. at Anselmo Hall
Botha Heartland Quilters' Guild, Box 218,T0C 0N0
Calgary Piecemakers Guild of Calgary, 42 Hampstead Circle NW, T3A 5P1 Meets: 3rd Monday (Sept - June) at St. Peters Anglican Church
Calgary Stitch-In Witches, 5003 Balhart Rd. NW,T3A 1C1 Meets: 2nd Tuesday 7 p.m. in member's home
Calgary Stitch-In Time, 89 Flavelle Rd. SE,T2H 1E8
Calgary St. Stephens Quilt Group, 1312 - 106th Ave. SW, T2W 0B7 Meets: Wednesdays 9:30 a.m. at St. Stephen's Church
Calgary St. Cyprian Quilters, 927 Ranch Estates Pl. NW, T3G 1M5 Meets: Mondays 9:30 a.m. in member's home
Calgary Springbank Quilters, Box 18, Site 18, RR #12, T3E 6W3 Meets: Every other Thursday 1 p.m. in member's home
Calgary Prairie Wind Quilters, 856 Lake Twintree SE, T2J 2W3 Meets: 2nd Wednesday 11:30 a.m. in a members home
Calgary Newcomers Club, 171 Woodsman Lane SW, T2W 4Z5
Calgary Calgary Guild of Needle & Fibre Arts, Box 52146, Edmonton Tr. RPO, T2E 8K9 Meets: 2nd Wednesday (Sept - June) 7 p.m. at the Scandinavian Centre, 738 - 20th Ave. NW, Calgary
Calgary Bow River Quilters, 2188 Brownsea Dr. NW, T2N 3G9 Meets: 1st Friday (except July & Aug) 9:30 a.m. 2188 Brownsea NW, Calgary
Calgary Handicrafts Guild, Calgary Branch, P.O. Box 34085, T3C 2W0 Meets: Mon. 9 a.m. Rossacarrock Comm. Hall, 1406-40th St. SW, Calgary
Calgary Sew & Sew Quilters, 4623 - 26th Ave NE, T1Y 2R9 Meets: Tuesdays 7 p.m. in member's home
Canmore Mountain Cabin Quilters, Box 2868, T0L 0M0
Cochrane Big Hill Quilters, 50 Glenwood Pl, T0L 0W3
Dalmead Alberta Handicrafts Guild, Dalmead Branch, Box 312, T0J 0V0
Drayton Valley Hearts & Hands Quilters Guild, Box 6321, T0E 0M0
Edmonton Edmonton District Quilt Guild, Box 68004, 70 Bonnie Doon Mall P.O.,T6E 4N6 Meets: at the Provincial Museum
Edmonton Alberta Handicrafts Guild, Edmonton Branch, 75 sunset Blvd. St. Albert, T8N 0P2
Edmonton Quilter's Co-Op, 1016 - 46th St., T6L 5V8
Edmonton Southeast Quilters Guild, 10519 - 52nd St., T6A 2G7
Edmonton Quilt Guild, 9104 - 116th St., T6G 1P9
High River Alberta Handicraft Guild, High River Branch, Box 5733, T1V 1T3 Meets: Fridays 9 a.m. the Cultural Centre, 251 9th Ave. W, High River
Hinton Rocky Mountain Quilters Guild, 111 Tamarack Ave., T7V 1C6
Lacombe Central Alberta Quilters Guild, Box 5462, T4L 1X2 Meets: 1st Monday at Lacombe Jr. High Home Ec Room
Lacombe Lacombe Quilters, Box 2577, T0C 1S0
Lethbridge Centennial Quilters Guild, 811 - 5th Ave. S, T1J 0V2 Meets: 4th Tuesday (except Dec, July & Aug), at the Bowman Arts Center, 811 0 5th Ave. S
Lloydminster Log Cabin Quilters Guild, 5301 - 23rd St., T9V 2P9
Medicine Hat Medicine Hat Quilters, 45 - 1st St., T1A 6G9
Millarville Country Lane Quilters, Box 89, T0L 1K0 Meets: 1st Tuesday (Sept - June) at Millarville Church House
Mundare Kalyna Country Quilters Guild, 5103 - 50 St. Meets: 3rd Friday 6:30 p.m. at The Chicken Coop
Okotoks Chinook Country Quilters, 32 Downey Rd., T0L 1T2
Pincher Creek Lebel House Quilters Guild, Box 2434, T0K 1W0 Meets: 3rd Thursday at Lebel House
Redwood Meadows High Country Quilters, 6 Wolf Court, T3Z 1A3 Meets: 2nd Wednesday 7:30 p.m. at Redwood House
Rimbey Rimbey & District Quilters, P.O. Box 1131, T0C 2J0
St. Albert St. Albert Quilters Guild, 94 Finch Crescent, T8N 1Y6
Stony Plain Stony Plain Quilters, Box 866, T0E 2G0

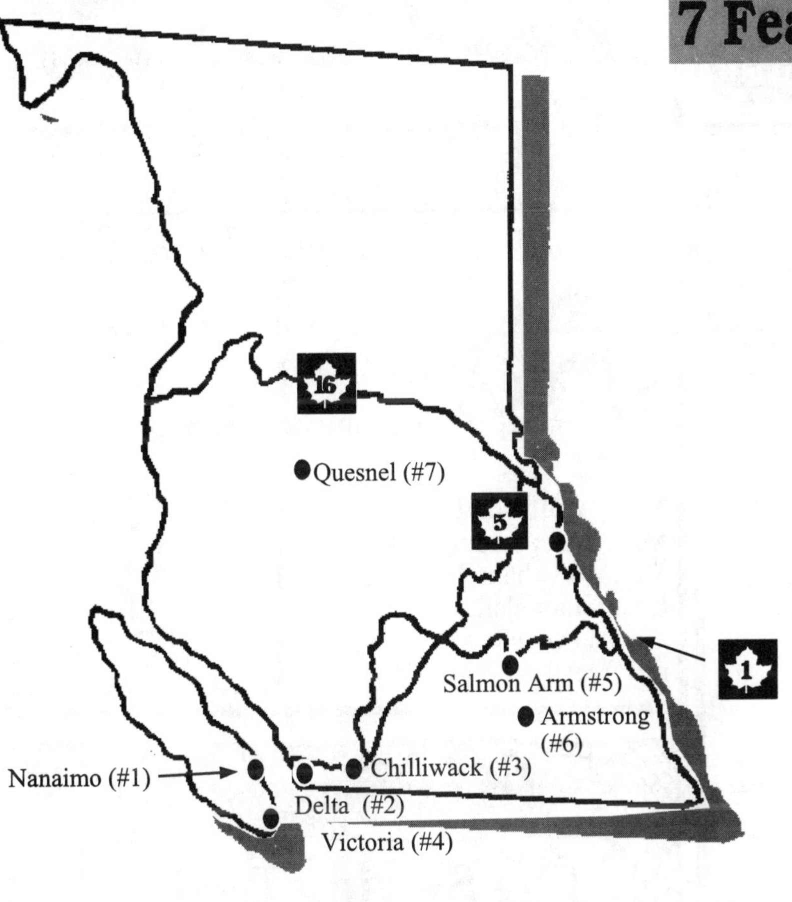

7 Featured Shops

Delta, BC #2

Mon - Sat 10 - 6 Thurs til 8

The Quilted Bear

4869 Delta Street V4K 2T9
(604) 940-7051 Fax: (604) 940-7052
E-Mail: quiltedbear@mail.com
Owner: Lily Gledstone & Jenny Hutt
Est: 2001 720 bolts.

Specializing in that wonderful primitive look! We have reproduction fabrics, folk art stitchery & primitive patterns for dolls.

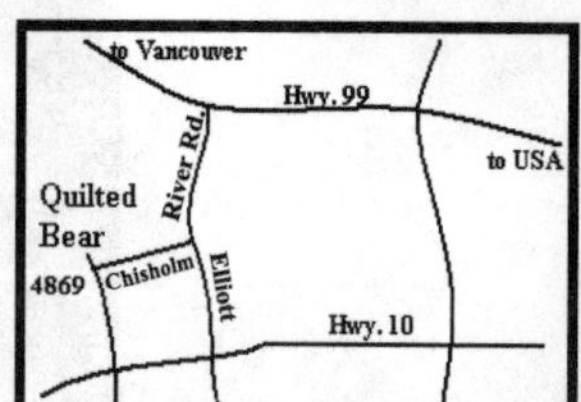

Chilliwack, BC #3

Mon - Sat 9 - 5

Hamels Fabrics

B-45923 Airport Rd. V2P 1A3
(604) 792-3231

Quality Cotton Fabrics.
Books and Quilting Notions.
Thimbleberries B.O.M.

Many Quilts on Display.
Mail Order through our Web Site: www.hamelsfabrics.com
Email: hamelsfabrics@shawcable.com
toll free: 1-877-774-2635

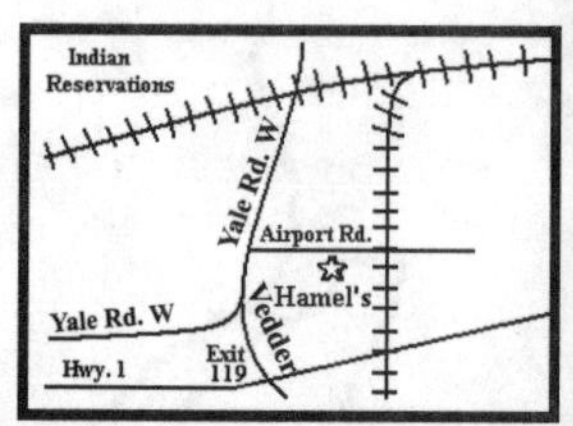

Victoria, BC #4

Discover our beautiful 19th century shop in historic Market Square, in the heart of Victoria's Old Town. You'll be delighted with the fabulous selection of quality cotton fabrics, books, patterns, threads and notions. Feast your eyes on a wealth of inspiring quilts handmade by local artists.

517 Pandora Ave.
Victoria BC
383-4023

shop@satin-moon.com

Ask our friendly staff about the best places to eat and things to do in our lovely city and have a wonderful time.

We honor all Quilter's Guilds. Show your quilt card to receive 10% off regular priced fabrics!

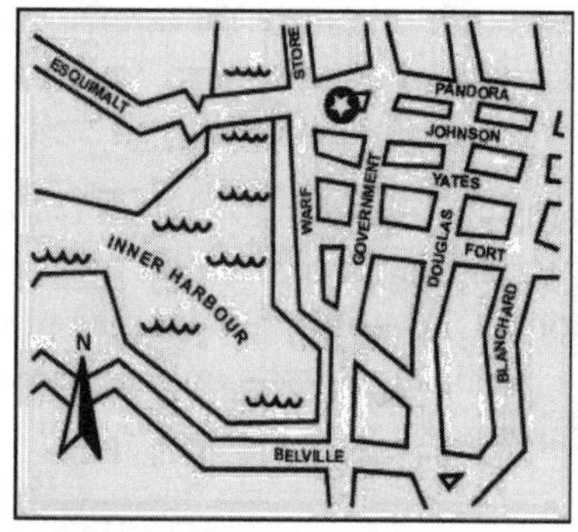

Monday - Saturday 9:30 - 5:30 Sunday 11 - 5

www.satinmoon.com

Salmon Arm, BC #5

The Sewing Basket Quilts & Crafts

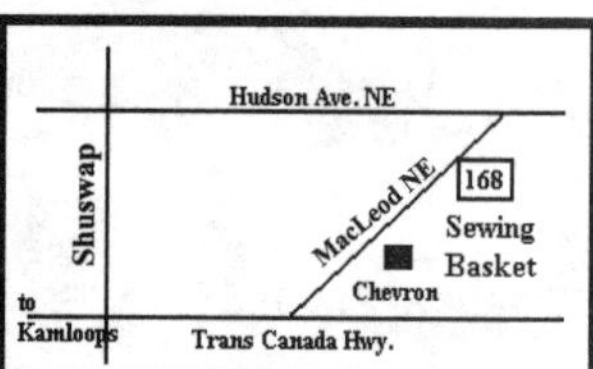

We're a ***"One Stop Shop"*** with
*A Huge Selection of Quilting Fabrics
*All the latest Notions & Books
*Great Selection of Quilting Kits
*Fun Informative Classes and the Most Fabulous Displays

A Big City Selection with a Small Town Friendly Atmosphere. It's worth a special trip and the Prices are great too.

168 MacLeod, P.O. 327, V1E 4N2
Located behind the Chevron Station
(250) 832-3937
Watch for our website: www.SewingBasket.ca

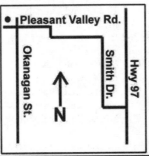

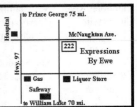

Other Shops in British Columbia: *We suggest calling first*

100 Mill House	Lillian's Fabric & Quilting, 172 S. Birch Ave.	250-395-2625
Ashcroft	Alice's Sewing Shop, 417 Railway	250-453-2356
Burnaby	Quilter's Haven, #9 - 5901 E. Broadway	604-320-0333
Burns Lake	Anna's Fabrics & Craft, 312 Hwy. 16	250-692-7890
Campbell River	Sew 'N' Sew Fabrics, 58 C Adams Rd.	250-923-6065
Campbell River	Calico & Cross Stitch, 910 Island Hwy.	250-287-8898
Cherryville	Cherry Ridge Crafts, 648 N Fork Rd, RR #1	250-547-2257
Coquitlam	Quilted Treasures, 140 1140 Austin Ave.	604-936-4778
Cranbrook	Shannon's Fabrics Ltd., 16 12th Ave. N	250-426-7877
Creston	Quiltview Corner, Box 610 115-20th Ave S	250-428-4891
Fort Langley	Pat's Quilting & Designs, 9217 Glover Rd.	604-882-9411
Fort Nelson	Fabric Fun, 4903 51 Ave W, Box 857	250-774-6468
Fort Saint James	Heart N' Sole Quilts, 241 2nd Ave W.	250-996-8395
Fort St. John	Sew It Yourself Shop, 10040 102nd St.	250-847-1395
Hagensbourg	Crafty Lady Gifts & Hobbies, PO Box 114	250-982-2358
Invermere	Stober's, 729 12th St.	250-342-9313
Kamloops	Katja's Quilt Shoppe, #101 1150 Hillside Dr.	250-851-0324
Kelowna	The Country Schoolhouse, 3070 Benvoulin Rd.	250-861-5487
Kitimat	Pine Needle Fabrics, 317 Cit Centre	250-639-9300
Langford	Cloth Castle, 786 Goldstream Ave Hwy 1A	250-478-2112
Madeira Park	The Quilted Path & Country Pleasures, 4982 Gonzales	604-883-2274
Nakusp	The Secret Workshop, 208 Broadway St.	250-265-9966
Nelson	Shannon's Fabrics Ltd., 560 Baker St.	250-352-6104
New Hazelton	Fabrics & More, 4409 10th Ave.	250-842-5028
North Vancouver	The Cloth Shop, 3068 Highland Blvd.	604-990-1325
Prince George	Prince George Sewing Center, 1210 5th Ave.	250-563-1533
Prince George	Kathy's Quilt Shop, 126-4488 Hwy. 16 W	250-964-8229
Richmond	Fabricana Imports, 4811 Hazelbridge Way	604-273-5316
Sechelt	Sew Easy, Trail Bay Centre	604-885-2725
Smithers	Fabrications, Queen St.	250-847-3250
Smithers	The Cloth Cupboard, 3773 3rd Ave.	250-847-1395
South Surrey	Creations III Fabrics, 13979 16th Ave	604-531-9311
Squamish	Nothing Finer, 38036 Cleveland Ave.	604-892-6366
Surrey	Wineberry Fabrics, 105, 6351 - 152nd St	604-597-1388
Taylor	Windy Willow Fabrics, Collins Rd. Mile 30	250-789-9248
Terrace	Cotton Pick n' Quilt Patch, 101-3239 Kalem	250-638-1335
Trail	Allan's Sewing Center, 1268 Pine Ave.	250-368-8485
Vancouver	The Cloth Shop, 4415 W 10th Ave.	604-224-1325
Vanderhoof	The Stitchery, 173 W. Stewart	250-567-4260
Vernon	Definitely Country Treasures, 2801-28th St.	545-9327
Victoria	Capitol Iron, 1900 Store St	250-385-9703
Williams Lake	E & E Sewing Centre, 65 S 1st Ave.	250-392-4055

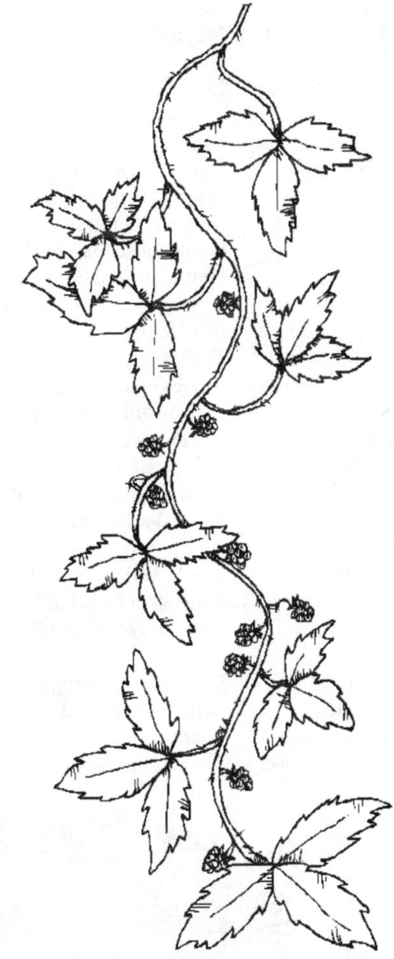

British Columbia Guilds:

Blubber Bay	Timberline Quilters Guild, Box 194, V8A 1S9	Meets: Thursday eve at Villa Soccer Center, Timberlane Park
Brentwood	Piecemakers, 1019 Marchant Rd., V5O 1A0	
Burns Lake	North Star Quilter's Guild, Box 476, V0J 1E0	
Campbell River	Campbell River Friendship Quilter's Guild	
Campbell River	Nell Hamilton Quilters, 1854 South Island Hwy., V9N 1B8	
Cherryville	Cherryville Quilting Guild, 648 N. Fork Rd., V0E 2G0	Meets: 1st & 3rd Wednesday 9 a.m. at 648 N. Fork Rd.
Chetwynd	Quintessential Quilters, P.O. Box 1454 ,V0C 1J0	
Chilliwack	Chilliwack Quilters Guild, P.O. Box 618	Meets: 3rd Tuesday 7 p.m. at Christ Luthern Church, 9460 Challes St.
Comox	The Schoolhouse Quilter's Guild, P.O. Box 1507, V9N 8A2	
Coquitlam	Como Lake Quilters Guild, 2345 Huron Dr., V3J 1A6	
Coquitlam	Pacific Spirit Quilter's Guild, #53 2905 Norman Ave., Z3C 4H9	Meets: 3rd Friday 7 p.m. at New Vista Care Home, 7550 Rosewood, Burnaby
Courtenay	Schoolhouse Quilter's Guild	
Creston	Creston Valley Quilters Guild, P.O. Box 2178, V0B 1G0	
Duncan	Heritage Quilters, 355 Dogwood Pl, V9I 1M3	Meets: Mondays 10 a.m. and Thursdays 8 p.m. at Girl Guide Hall, 321 Cairnsmore
Fernie	Fernie Quilter's Guild, Box 2577, V0B 1M0	Meets: 2nd & 4th Tuesday at Fernie Arts Station
Fort St. John	Fort St. John Quilters, P.O. Box 6474, V1J 4H9	Meets: 2nd & 4th Mon (except July, Aug & Dec.) North Peace Cultural Centre
Fruitvale	Beaver Valley Quilters, Box 1079, V0G 1L0	
Gibsons	Sunshine Coast Quilters Guild, R.R. #4, S-18A C27, V0N 1V0	Meets: Saturday every other month from Sept. at Davis Bay School
Golden	Mountain Magic Quilters, Box 2414, V0H 1Z0	
Grand Forks	Grand Forks Quilt Connection, P.O. Box 1708, V0H 1H0	Meets: 2nd Thursday 7 p.m. at Grand Forks Art Gallery
Kamloops	Sagebrush Quilters Guild, Box 392, V2B 5K9	Meets: 2nd & 4th Mondays 7:30 p.m. at Hal Rogers Centre
Kamloops	River Valley Quilters	Meets: 1st & 3rd Mondays 10 a.m. at Japanese Cultural Centre
Kamloops	Calico Quilters, 253 Beach Ave., V2B 1C4	
Kelowna	St. Pius X Quilters, 679 Clifton Rd., V1V 1A7	
Kelowna	Orchard Valley Quilters Guild, P.O. Box 585 Stn A, V1Y 7P2	Meets: Tuesday 9 a.m. (Sept to mid-Dec & Jan to mid-May) at Kelowna Curling Club
Kitimat	Kitimat Quilters' Guild, 35 Dease St., V8C 2M2	
Kitwanga	Kitwanga Patchwork Partners, Box 147, V0J 2A0	Meets: 7 p.m. Monday (Sept - June) at K.E.S. School Home Ec Room
Madeira Park	Pender Harbour Piecemakers, Site 2 Camp 28 R.R. #1, V0N 2H0	
Maple Ridge	Ridge Meadows Quilters, 12073 Rothsay St., R.R. #4, V2X 8X8	
Marysville	Marysville Quilters, 612 - 305th St., V0B 1Z0	
Mayne Island	Mayne Island Quilters Guild, 397 Neil Rd., R.R. #1, V0N 2J0	
Merritt	Nicola Valley Quilter's Guild, Box 938, V0K 2B0	
N. Vancouver	Lion's Gate Quilter's Guild, P.O. Box 54194, Lonsdale West P.O., V7M 3K5	Meets: 4th Thursday 7 p.m. at Community Services Bldg, 285 Prideaux St.
N. Vancouver	Highland United Church Quilters, 3255 Edgemont Blvd., V5K 4H8	
Nanaimo	Nanaimo Quilter's Guild	
Oona River	Oona River Sewing Circle, Box 1132, V0V 1E0	
Osoyoos	Osoyoos Quilters, P.O. Box 958, V0H 1V0	Meets: 1st & 3rd Tuesday 9 a.m. at St. Christophers Anglican Church
Parksville	Quilt House Quilters Guild, P.O. Box 1177, V9P 2H2	Meets: 2nd Monday (Sept - June) at Parksville Legion Hall
Penticton	Penticton Quilters' Guild, P.O. Box 20165, V2A 8K3	Meets: 2nd & 4th Wednesday (Sept - May) at the Library Museum building, 785 Main St.
Port Alberni	Bitts & Batts, Log Cabin Quilters, 2616 - 9th Ave., V9Y 2M7	
Powel River	Timberlane Quilters' Guild, 7296 Field St., V8A 1S9	Meets: Thursday eve. at Villa Soccer Center, Timberlane Park
Prince George	Prince George Quilters Guild, 2880 - 15th Ave., V2M 1T1	Meets: Last Wednesday at Studio 2880
Salmo	Salmo Quilters Guild, Box 83, V0G 1Z0	Meets: 2nd Thursday (except July & Aug) in member's home
Salmon Arm	Shusways Quilters Guild, Box 976, V1E 4P1	Meets: 2nd & 4th Wednesday @ 10 am at Catholic Church
Sardis	Chilliwack Quilter's Guild, P.O. Box 455, V2R 1A8	Meets: 4th Wednesday 7 p.m. at Mt. Slesse Middle School, 5871 Tyson
Sidney	Calico Cats , #4 - 10110 St., V8L 3B3	
Surrey	Fraser Valley Quilters Guild, 18971 - 59th Ave., V3F 7R8	Meets: 2nd Monday 11:30 p.m. at Chamber of Commerce, Gulidford Centennial Library, Guildford
Taylor	Windy Willow Quilt Guild, P.O. Box 501, V0C 2K0	
Vancouver	Vancouver Guild of Fabric Arts, 4397 West 2, V6R 1K4	
Vancouver	Vancouver Quilters Guild, 4085 W. 35th Ave., V6N 2P4	Meets: 1st Wednesday 7:30 p.m. (Sept - June) at St. Marys Anglican Church, 2490 W 37th Ave. (Larch)
Vernon	Silver Star Quilting Squares, Box 1853, V1T 8C3	Meets: 1st & 3rd Thursdays 9 a.m. at St. Johns Lutheran Church
Victoria	Ceilidh Quilters, 3205 Kenya Pl, V8P 3T9	
Victoria	Victoria Quilters' Guild, P.O. Box 6453, Stn C, V8P 5M4	
Williams Lake	Cariboo Piecemakers, Box 6065, V2G 3W2	

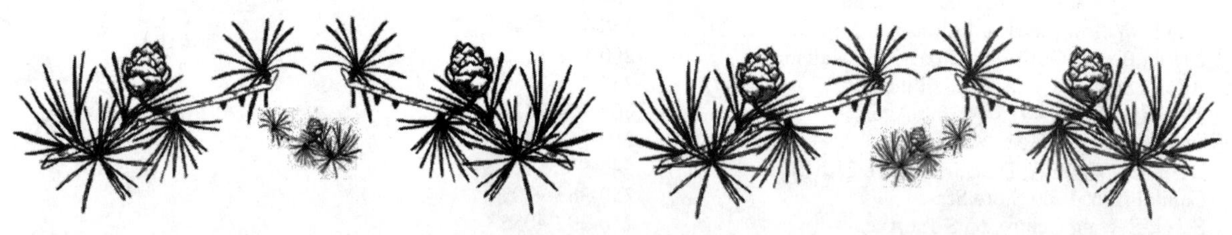

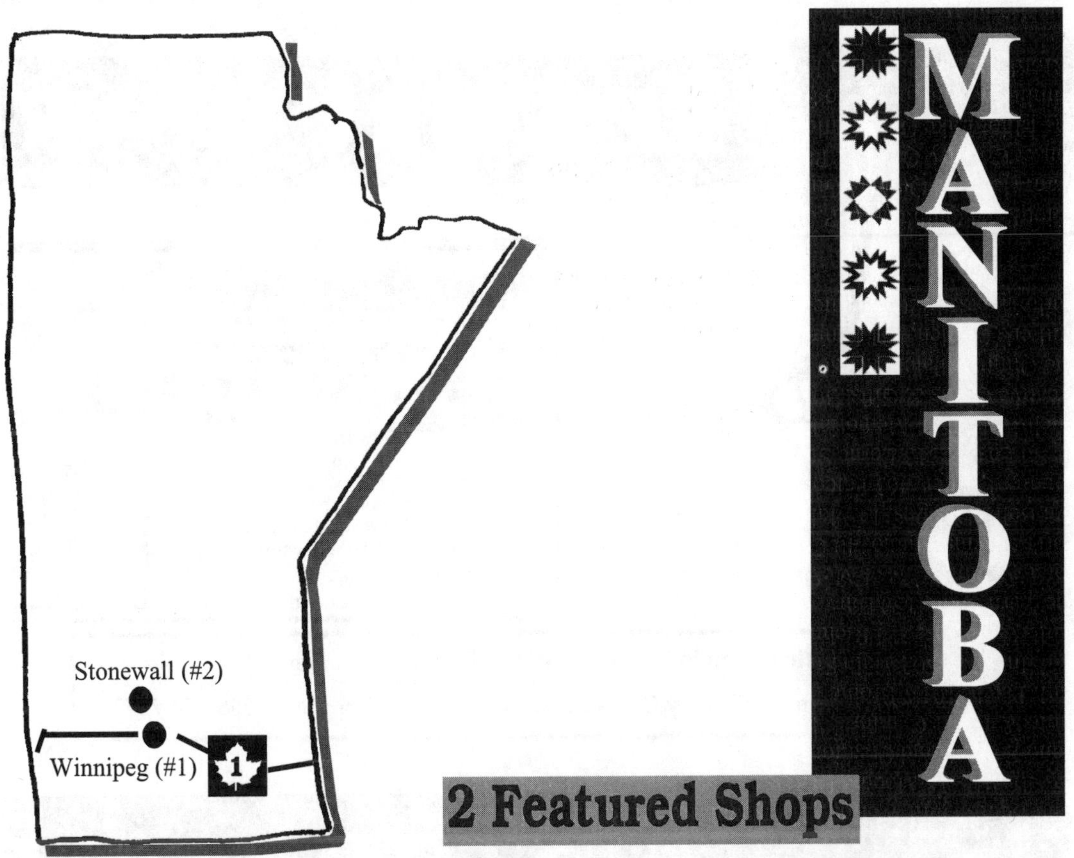

Winnipeg, MB #1

Mon - Sat 10 - 5 Thur til 7

The Quilting Bee

1014 St. Mary's Rd. R2M 3S6
(204) 254-7870 or (888) 518-3300
Fax: (204) 254-7895
Owners: Maria & Gwyneth Ball
3000 Bolts Free Newsletter

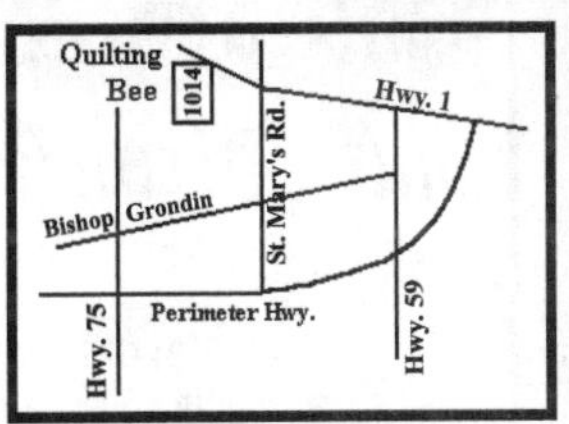

Biggest and friendliest shop in Manitoba. Wonderful selection of fabrics, notions, books, patterns and classes. Blocks-of-the-Month Avail

Stonewall, MB #2

QUILTER'S COTTAGE

277 Main St.
P.O. Box 1220
Stonewall, MB R0C 2Z0
(204) 467-2453
Fax: (204) 467-7561
Owner: Stacy Thiessen
Est: 2001 1100 sq.ft.
3000 Bolts

Mon - Fri 10 - 6 Thur 10 - 8 Sat 10 - 5

Quaint old cottage located on Main Street We specialize in friendly atmosphere and customer service. Great selection of top of the line fabrics, patterns, gifts and notions. Classes for all levels of Quilters.

Quilter's Cottage
Hwy. 67
277
Main St.
5 km
Hwy. 236
15 mi. N of Perimeter
Hwy. 7 22 km
Perimeter Hwy.
Rt. 90
Winnipeg

Other Shops in Manitoba: *We suggest calling first*

Melita Prairie Patchwork, 53 Front St. 204-522-3540
Winnipeg Croft House Quilt Shop, 1846 Portage Ave. 204-888-3370

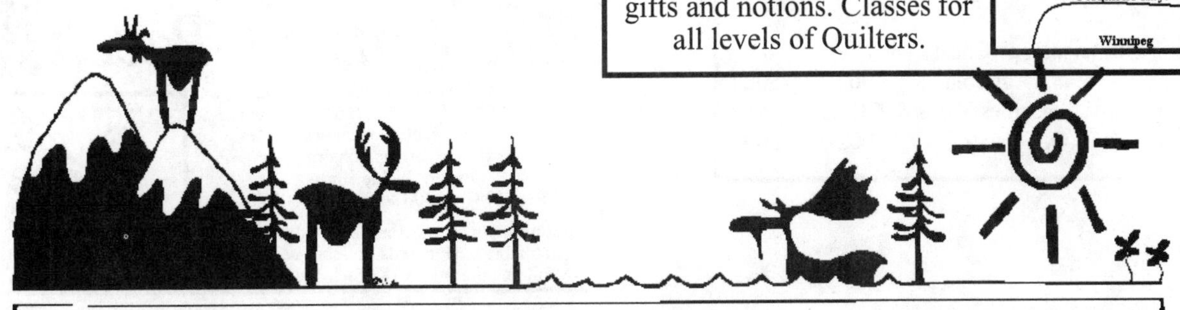

1 Featured Shop NEW BRUNSWICK

Moncton, NB #1

Mon - Thur 10 - 5
Fri 10 - 8
Sat 10 - 4

The Covered Bridge Quiltery Ltd.

"In Riverview"
630 Pinewood Rd. E1B 5M7
(506) 386-2888 Fax: (506) 386-2800
E-Mail: alj@nbnet.nb.ca
Web Site: www.thequiltery.com
Owner: Martha Davidson

100% Cotton Fabric, Books, Patterns & Notions, Hangers; Classes; Blocks-of-the-Month Kits.

Trans Canada Hwy.
to St. John
Berry Mills Rd.
Wheeler Blvd.
Hwy. 15
to Shediac
Moncton
Main St.
Mall
Sobey's
Hwy. 114
Coverdale Rd.
Whitepine Rd.
630
to Fundy Park
Pinewood Rd.
Covered Bridge

Another Shop in New Brunswick: *We suggest calling first*

Fredericton Country Crafts and Curtains 334 York St. 506-454-2572

2 Featured Shops NOVA SCOTIA

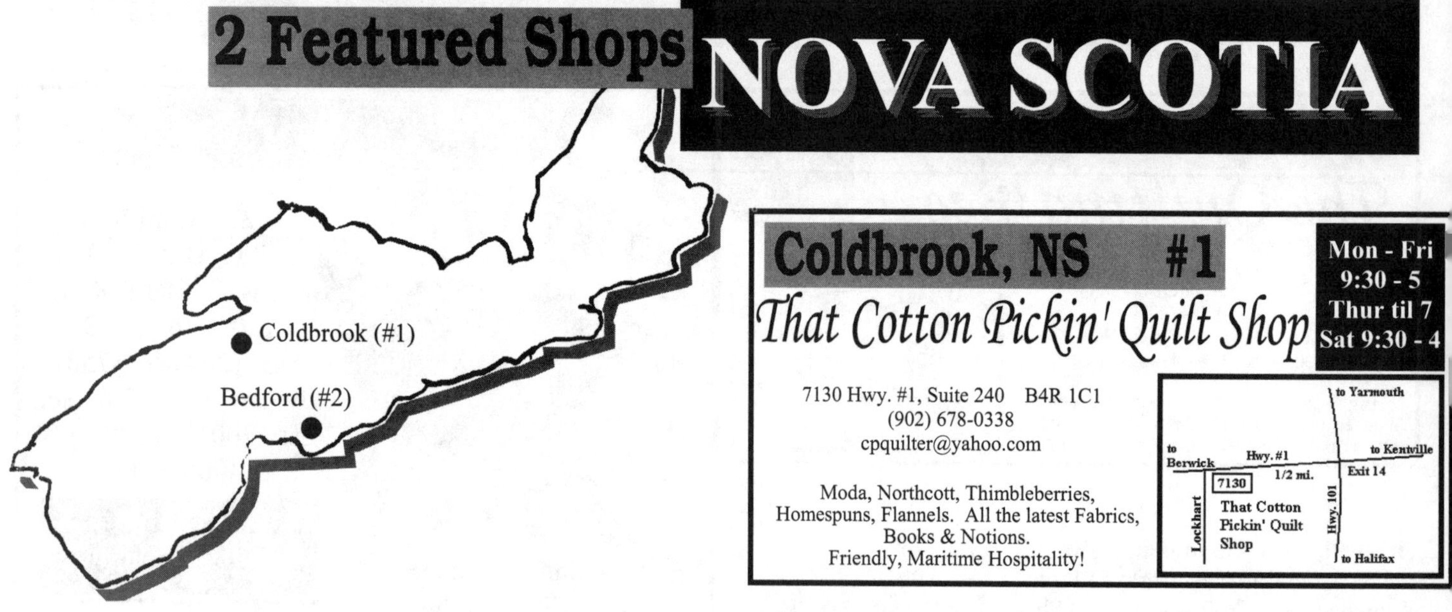

Coldbrook, NS #1

Mon - Fri 9:30 - 5
Thur til 7
Sat 9:30 - 4

That Cotton Pickin' Quilt Shop

7130 Hwy. #1, Suite 240 B4R 1C1
(902) 678-0338
cpquilter@yahoo.com

Moda, Northcott, Thimbleberries, Homespuns, Flannels. All the latest Fabrics, Books & Notions.
Friendly, Maritime Hospitality!

to Yarmouth
to Berwick
Hwy. #1
to Kentville
1/2 mi.
Exit 14
7130
That Cotton Pickin' Quilt Shop
Lockhart
Hwy. 101
to Halifax

Other Shops in Nova Scotia:
We suggest calling first

Halifax Quilter's Hope Chest
2483 Agricola St. 902-425-5002
Victoria County, Lorraines Yarns & Crafts
P.O. Box 49 902-336-2605

Bedford, NS #2

Mon - Sat 10 - 5
Thurs & Fri til 9

1746 Bedford Hwy. B4A 1G2
(902) 832-0155 Fax: (902) 832-0066
staff@cottonpatch.org
www.cottonpatch.org
Owner: Jackie Harris
Est: 1981 2400 sq.ft. 2000 Bolts

Quilting supplies including 2000 bolts of 100% cotton fabrics. Hundreds of books & patterns. A full line of notions. Knowledgeable staff.

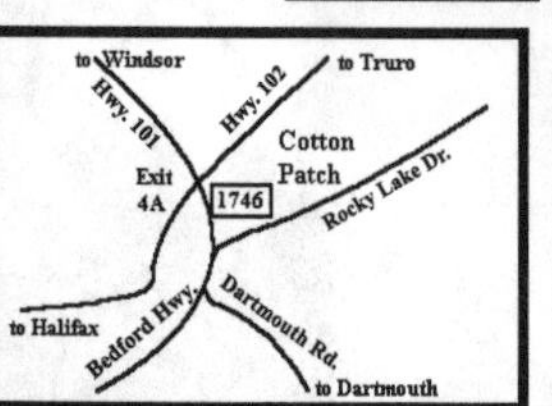

23 Featured Shops
ONTARIO
Dryden (#23)
11
Fort Frances (#22)
Sault Ste. Marie (#21)
Ottawa (#20)
Orillia (#18)
Uxbridge (#19)
401
Linwood (#16)
Midland (#17)
Georgetown (#8)
Kincardine (#15)
Kitchener (#13)
Milton (#9)
Goderich (#5)
Toronto (#7)
Shakespeare (#14)
Oakville (#6)
St. Catharines (#10)
Ailsa Craig (#3)
London (#4)
Fonthill (#12)
Windsor (#1)
Grimsby (#11)
Exeter (#2)

2 Great Shops

QUILTS and CALICOS

We feature a wide array of 100% cotton fabrics, the latest quilting notions, books, patterns and batting. Authorized dealers for Husqvarna Viking sewing machines and sergers. Classes for all skill levels offered year round. In short, your one stop quilt shops. We ship anywhere. Bear making supplies available. 10% off for all Guild Members at all times (with proof of membership) or with this ad.

Exeter, ON #2

Unique quilt shop located in a restored century old building

392 Main St., P.O. Box 42
Exeter, Ontario N0M 1S6
(888) 305-0949
(519) 235-4084
Fax: (519) 235-4967
Est: 1993 4000 Bolts

Mon - Fri 9 - 5:30
Sat 9 - 5

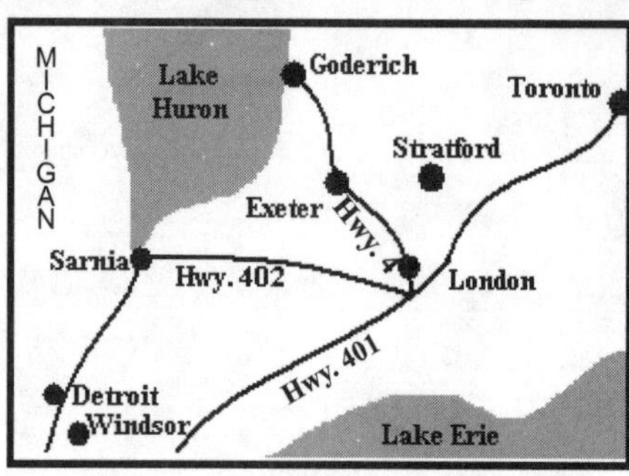

quiltscalicos@on.aibn.com
Owner: Linda Bartlett

Windsor, ON #1

Located in Windsor's first plaza

2425 Dougall Ave., Dorwin Plaza
Windsor, Ontario N8X 1T3
(888) 233-2533
(519) 250-7885
Fax: (519) 250-5129
2000 Bolts

Mon - Sat 10 - 5

www.quilts-calicos.on.ca

Cotton-By-Post Quilt Shoppe

135 Main St. N0M 1A0
Toll Free: (888) 884-4496
(519) 293-3499 Fax: (519) 293-9306
suzanne@cotton-by-post.com
www.cotton-by-post.com

The Largest Quilt Shop in Southwestern Ontario

Mon - Sat 9 - 5

Owner: Suzanne Agnew
Est: 1995 On-line Catalogue
Classes available for all skill levels.

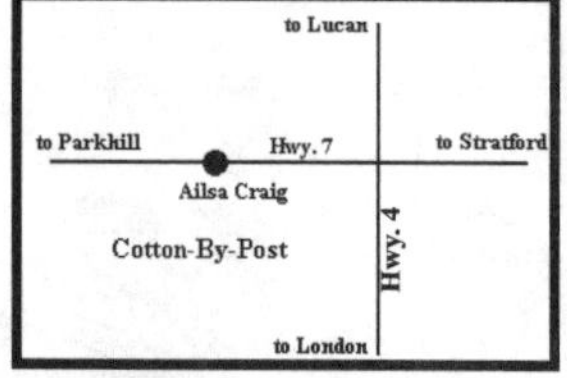

Ailsa Craig, ON #3

London, ON #4

Mon - Thur 10 - 5
Fri 10 - 8
Sat 10 - 5

Quilt Works of London

699 Wilkins St. N6C 5C8
(519) 668-7470
info@quiltworks.ca www.quiltworks.ca
Owner: Petra Uhlenbrauck
A great selection of fine quality 100% cottons, including Batiks, Thimbleberries, Moda, Reproductions, Kits & more. Classes, notions, books, & patterns.

Commissioners Rd. E
Upper Queen St.
Wilkins St.
699
Quilt Works
Southdale Rd. E
Wellington Rd. S
Bradley Ave.
Ernest
Hwy. 401

Goderich, ON #5

Mon - Sat 10 - 5:30

Quilters by the Square

32 West St. N7A 2K3
(519) 524-4333

A wide variety of 100% Cotton Fabrics, Quilting Books, Patterns, Notions, DMC floss, Bear Supplies & Classes available. Visit our friendly knowledgeable staff.

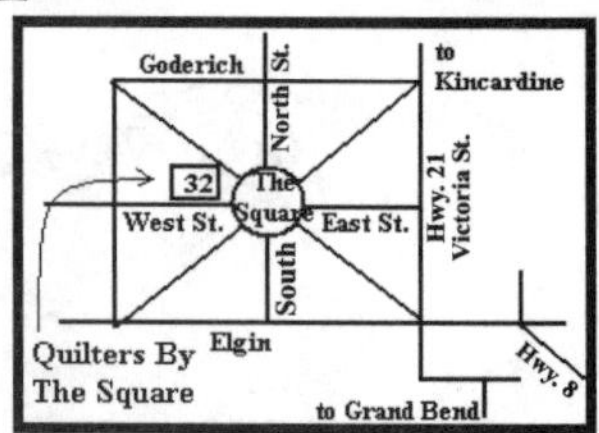

THE QUILT SHOP WITH A DIFFERENCE!

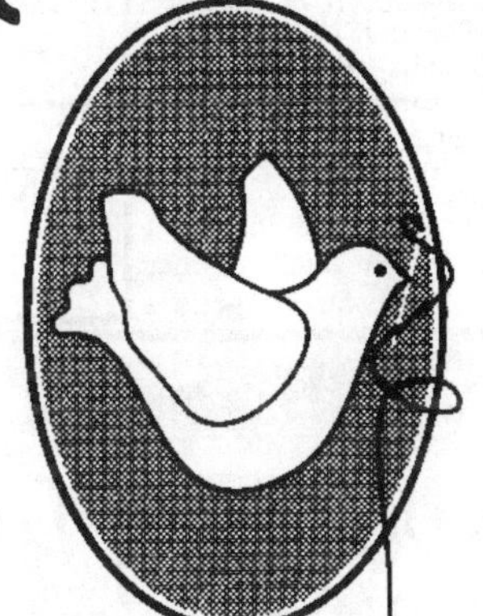

VISIT US AT
222 Lakeshore Rd. E L6J 1H6
(905) 844-1793
Owner: Jill Pettit

Mon - Sat
10 - 5:30
Fri til 8

Oakville, ON #6

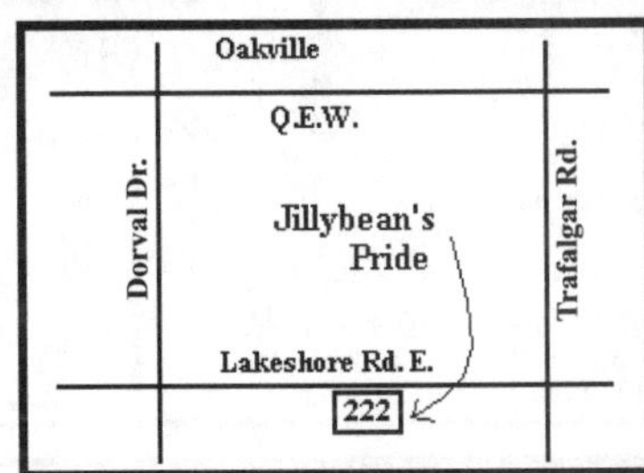

JILLYBEAN'S PRIDE

info@jillybeans.com
www.jillybeans.com
Secure on-line Shopping

Fabric, Books, Patterns, Notions, Classes, Kits, Block of the Month Clubs, Mail Order, Free Newsletter, Exclusive Quilt Designs. Quilt Expeditions, Correspondence Courses.

Quilters' Quarters

Toronto, ON #7

Close to downtown hotels, easy to get to by public transit or car.
Antique shops, restaurants, specialty shops
and gift shops also along the street.

Mon - Fri 10 - 6
Sat 10 - 5:30

595 Mt. Pleasant Rd. M4S 2M5
(416) 487-1047 Est: 1990
(800) 561-5132 (Canada & U.S.)
Owner: Connie Archambault
connie@quiltersquarters.com

Lots of 100% cotton fabrics from traditional to dramatic. Plus books, patterns, classes, & notions.

Free Smiles !

Georgetown, ON #8

Mon - Sat 9:30 - 5:30 Sun 12 - 5

The Hobby Horse

12707 9th Line L7G 4S8
(905) 877-9292 or (800) 565-5366
info@thehobbyhorse.on.ca
www.thehobbyhorse.on.ca
Owner: Gail Spence
Est: 1982 Block of the Month Programs

We're filled to the brim with bolts of cotton fabrics, quilting supplies, patterns, books, kits and much more. Come Visit Our Store.

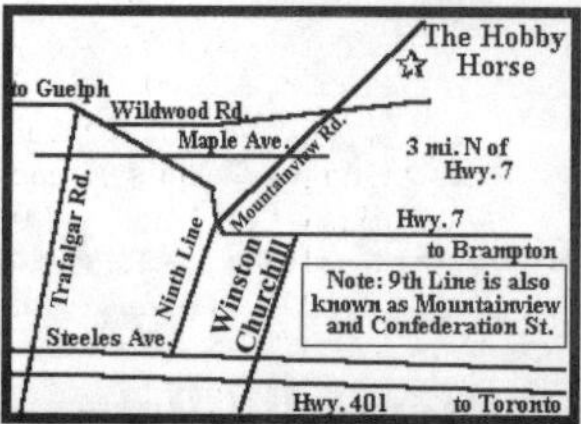

Milton, ON #9

Mon - Fri 10 - 6 Sat 10 - 4

The Quilter's Basket, Inc.

264 Bronte St. S, Unit #1 L9T 5A3
(905) 878-7333 Fax: (905) 878-5090
E-Mail: info@quilters-basket.com
Web Site: www.quilters-basket.com
Owner: Dagmar Scherer
Est: 2000 2300 sq.ft. 2500+ Bolts

Bright, Beautiful Store. Over 2500 Bolts from Top Supplies. We custom quilt on our Gammill. Year Round classes for all Ages.

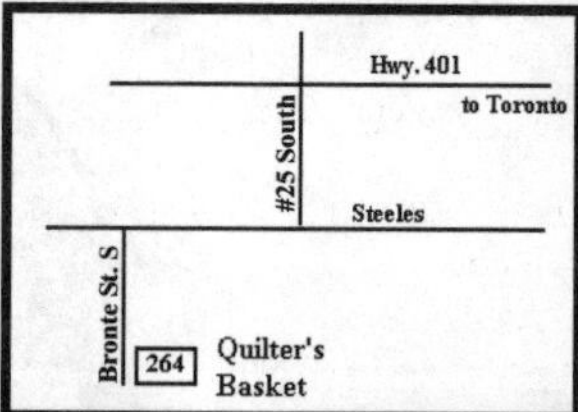

St. Catharines, ON #10

Mon - Sat 9:30 - 5:30 Thur til 8:30

Gone to Pieces

1931 Fourth Ave. L2R 6P9
(905) 684-0402
Fax: (905) 684-0605
nenigh@niagra.com
www.gonetopieces.ca
Est: 2002 700 sq.ft. 1200+ bolts

Within Niagara's Wine Country, Gone to Pieces is a friendly, country shop specializing in quality 100% cottons. Also you will find a wide selection of books, patterns, notions & quilting classes.

Lake Ontario
to Toronto QEW to St. Catharines
Jordan Rd. Gone to Pieces 1931 9th St. 7th St. 4th Ave.

Grimsby, ON #11

Mon - Fri 9 - 5:30 Sat 9 - 5

Patchworks "Plus"

32 Main St. W L3M 1R4
(905) 945-3855 Fax: (905) 945-6282
patchworksplus@yahoo.ca
ca.geocities.com/patchworksplus
Owner: Barb Tomlinson
Est: 1987 2200 sq.ft. 1000 Bolts

The largest quilt shop in the heart of Niagara's wine country. Great selection of fabrics, notions, books and patterns.

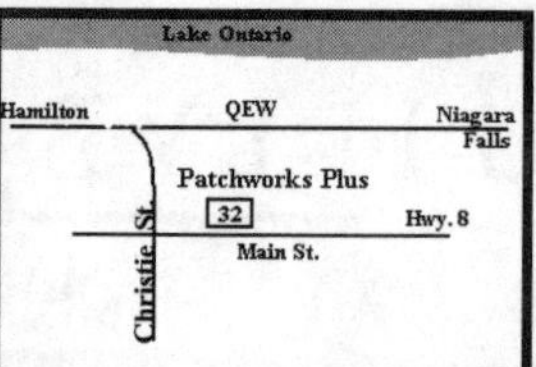

Quilters Paradise

Bring this ad in and receive 20% off selected items

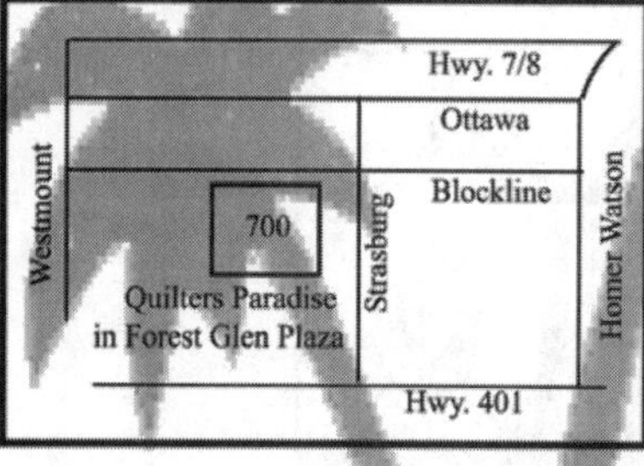

Forest Glen Plaza
700 Strasburg Road
Kitchener, Ontario
N2E 2M2

- the only Quilting specialty store in Kitchener - Waterloo!
- 100% cotton fabrics and flannels, patterns, notions, tools and more
- you can also visit us and shop online from anywhere!

www.quiltersparadise.com
email: info@quiltersparadise.com

Hours: Mon., Tues., Wed., & Fri. 10:00am to 5:00pm
Thurs. 10:00am to 8:00pm
Saturday 9:00am to 5:00pm

Phone: (519) 579-5618 Brother sewing machine dealer.
Toll Free: 1-888-687-0450

Kitchener, ON #13

Fonthill, ON #12

Mon - Sat 9:30 - 5

The Quilting Bee

121 Hwy. 20 L0S 1E0
(905) 892-7926 Fax: (905) 892-7928
kellycorfe@hotmail.com
Owner: Kelly Corfe Est: 2003

Located in Fonthill across from McDonalds. A large selection of Superior Quality 100% cotton Fabrics, Notions & Patterns.

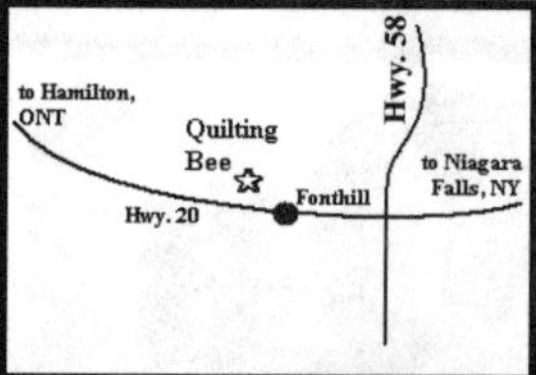

Shakespeare, ON #14

Mon - Sat 10 - 5:30 Sun 12 - 5

3991 Perth Rd. #107 N0B 2P0
(519) 625-8435 (888) 457-7077
Owner: Heather Stock
1200 sq.ft.
2000 Bolts
Est: 1986

Your place to find a timeless and elegant quilt for your home or choose the supplies to make a family heirloom. Lots of Shops for Everyone To Enjoy in Canada's Antique Capital
Waterloo County Quilt Festival Participant

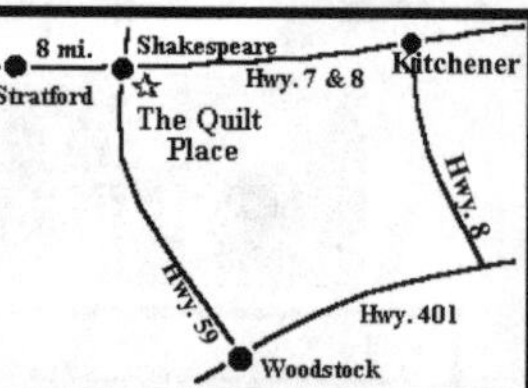

Kincardine, ON #15

Open Mon, Wed, Fri & Sat All Day Long

Retail Dry Goods

R.R. #5, #396 - SDRD 30 Greenock
No Phone N2Z 2X6
Owners: Lloyd & Laura Kuepfer

Large selection of Fabric "over 2500 bolts." Books, Stencils, Threads, Notions, Cross stitch & Floss. Finished Quilts and Quilt Tops. Also visit our second location 3½ mi. west of Linwood.

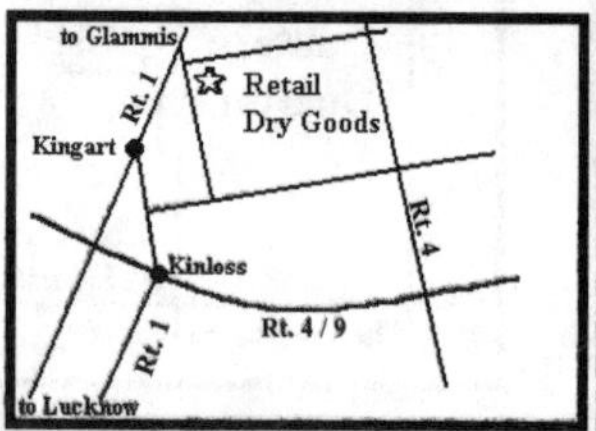

Linwood, ON #16

Open Mon, Wed, Fri 8 - 5 Sat by Chance

Retail Dry Goods

7546 Rd. 116, R R #1 N0B 2A0
No Phone
Owners: Allan & Janette Kuepfer

* Broadcloths
* Prints
* Quilt Tops
* Flanelette
* Panels
* Fleeces

Only 20 min. from St. Jacobs

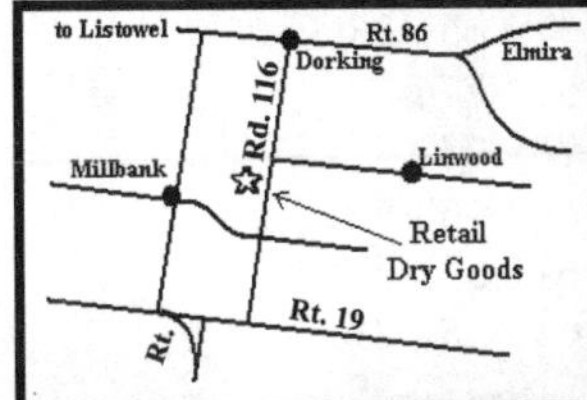

Midland, ON #17

Tues - Sat 9:30 - 5 Open 7 days July & Aug.

Notions & Sew-Lutions

Fabric & Quilt Shoppe

Unit 2 - 559 Bay St. W L4R 1L4
(705) 526-(8739) - USEW
Fax: (705) 526-8799 Est: 2000
sewlutions@bellnet.ca
www.geogianbayquiltshoppe.com
Owner: Betty-Lou Adam 4000 Bolts
Quilt shoppe overlooking beautiful Georgian Bay. Specializing in 100% fine cotton quilting fabrics. Extensive notions, books, & patterns. BOM's, kits, workshop & mail order. Brother Machines.

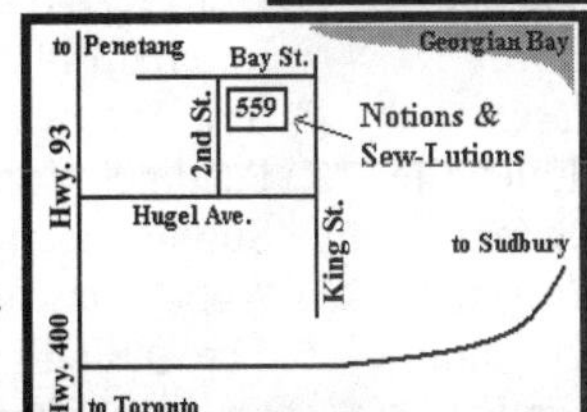

Orillia, ON #18

Mon - Sat 9 - 5

thimbles & things

1282 Brodie Dr. L3V 6H4
(705) 326-9357
thimbles@bconnex.net
www.thimblesandthings.com
Owners: Sue & Tony Polera
Est: 1999 2500+ Bolts

We stock a wide selection of 100% cotton fabrics - moda, thimbleberries, balis, flannels & more! Samples on display! Pfaff dealership.

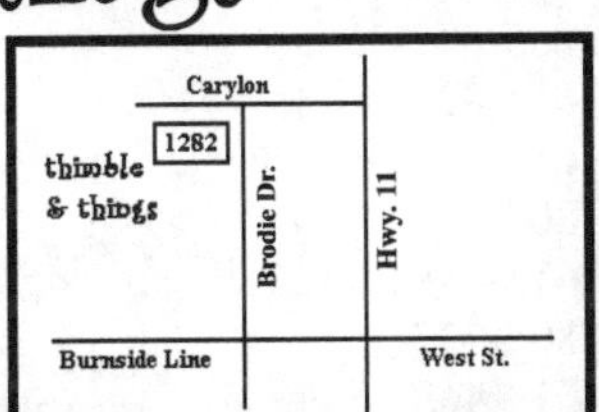

Uxbridge, ON #19

QUILTERS CUPBOARD

202 Brock St. E., Uxbridge ON
905-862-0666

Located 45 min. N.E. of Toronto, we are found in a white house, nestled in the trees at the East end of town. Every corner is filled with samples, kits, patterns and 2500+ bolts of Modas, Batiks, Thimbleberries, Homespuns, Brights and Flannels.
Plus a warm staff to greet you!

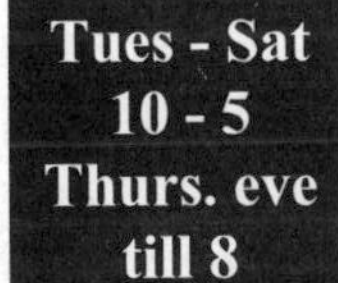

Come Visit Us!
www.quilterscupboard.ca
Sue Carmichael - Wendy Brumwell

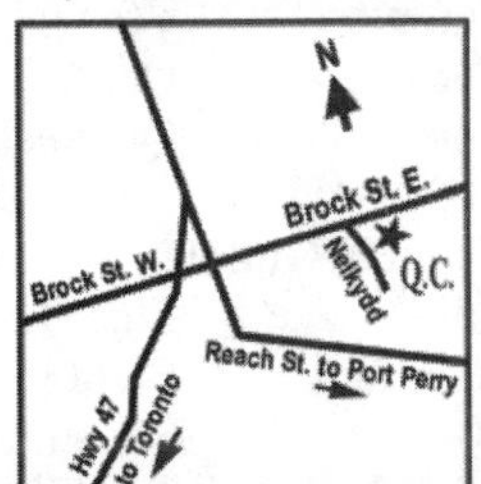

Ottawa, ON #20

1797 Kilborn Ave. at Virginia Dr.
K1H 6N1
(613) 521-9839
Owner:
Sandra Evans
Est: 1987

Mon - Sat 10 - 5

- Charming All inclusive Quilt Shop.
- Ottawa's Loveliest Fabrics.
- Best Patterns, Books and Supplies.
- Fine Needlearts and Gifts.
- Centrally Located in Pretty Residential Area.

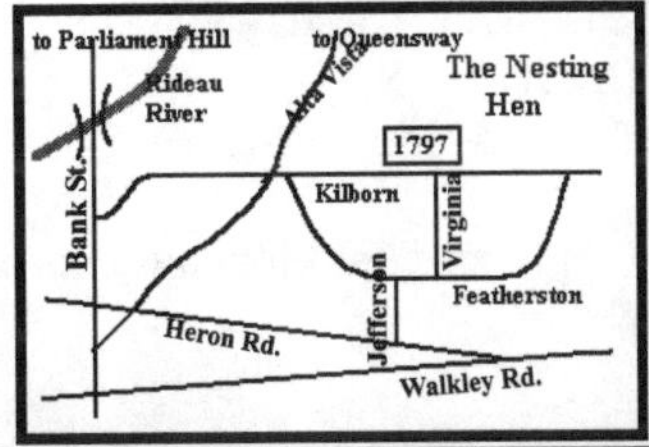

Sault Ste. Marie, ON #21

Mon - Fri 10 - 5:30 Sat 10 - 4

Life's A Stitch

516 Queen St. E P6A 2A1
(705) 254-3339 Fax: (705) 254-3358
robyn.thompson@lifesastitch.com
www.lifesastitch.ca
Est: 1997

Husqvarna Viking Sewing Machines, Quilting Fabrics and Notions, Patterns, Books, and Accessories.

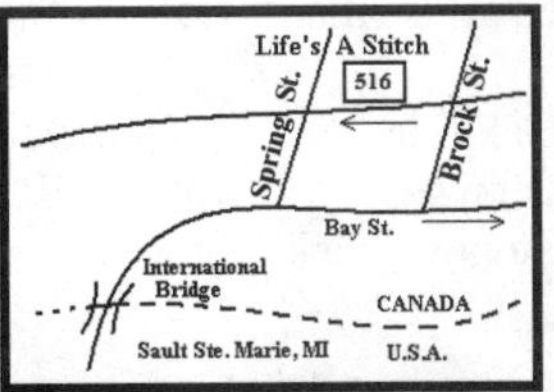

Fort Frances, ON #22

Mon - Fri 10 - 5 Sat 10 - 3

330 Scott Street P9A 1G9
(807) 274-6665
Fax: (807) 274-3168
www.crazyladiesfabrics.com
Owner: Phyllis Johnson
Est: 1998 1400 sq. ft. 1000 Bolts.
Located on the U.S.-Canada border in NW Ontario. Carrying the most popular cottons and cotton flannels from top companies.

Dryden, ON #23

Mon - Fri 9:30 - 5:30 Sat 9:30 - 5

Salavich's Serge 'n Sew

Your "One Stop Quilt Shop"
The Quilt Shop on the Highway in Dryden, ON (807) 223-4362
3 - 439 Government St P8N 2P4

Husqvarna Viking Sales & Service.
100% Cotton ~ Gifts & Novelties
Books, Patterns & Magazines ~ Notions
100% Cotton, Silk & Specialty Threads
Classes & Workshops

ed@salavichs.com
www.salavichs.com

Other Shops in Ontario: *we suggest calling first*

Bancroft	Country Quilts & Fabrics, 227 Hastings St. N	613-332-2540
Barrie	Simcoe County Quilt Shoppe, 74 Cedar Pointe Dr.	705-734-1441
Burlington	The Quilter's Cupboard, 2501 Guelph Line #11	905-332-6640
Cookstown	Quilt & Wool Shoppe, 25 Queen St.	705-458-9233
Elmira	Reichard's Dry Goods, 3 Arthur St. S	519-669-3307
Essex	Sew & Sew, 183 Talbot St. S	519-776-5363
Huntsville	Pastimes Hobby Centre, 3 Main St. W	705-789-3343
Kenora	Subtle Creations, 26 Peter St. W	807-468-6650
Kingston	Abbey Dawn Quilts, 1619 Abbey Dawn Rd.	613-542-6247
Kingston	The Quilter's Choice, 650 Progress Ave.	613-384-8932
London	Quilters' Supply, 1634 Hyde Park Rd.	519-472-3907
Minesing	Quilters Shop, R.R. #1, Box 77	705-739-6875
Navuan	Aunt Beth's Quilt World, 3217 Navan Rd., R.R. #2	613-837-6222
Nepean	Sew for It!, 418 Moodie Dr.	613-820-2201
Newton	E and E Cloth and Creations, 41 Main St.	519-595-8569
North Bay	Quilts & Other Comforts, 151 Main St. W	705-476-7811
Oakville	Quilt Patch, 101A Bronte Rd.	905-847-5105
Osgoode Village	Julee's, 5502 Main St.	613-826-1243
Ottawa	Quilts & Seams, 175 Richmond Rd.	613-725-5113
Red Lake	The Yarn Shop, 150 Harvey St.	807-727-2564
Richmond	Country Quilter, 3444 McBean, P.O. Box 968	613-838-5541
Sioux Lookout	Dori's Sewing Studio, 40 Curtis St.	807-737-3674
St. George	Lyn Bell's Designs, 14 Main St. S	519-448-3739
Sudbury	Country Quilter, 463 Falconbridge Rd. #10	705-524-6235
Sudbury	It's So Easy, 1313 Lorne St. #4	705-675-1788
Thunder Bay	Patchworks, 574 Memorial Ave	807-345-6111
Tiverton	Creative Quilts & Gifts, 3006 Hwy. 21, R.R. #1	
Toronto	The Quilting Patch Inc, 86 Dearham Wood	416-281-5561
Toronto	Quilter's Garden, 931 Kingston Rd.	416-693-1616
Toronto	Quiltmakers, 1720 Avenue Rd.	416-784-5953

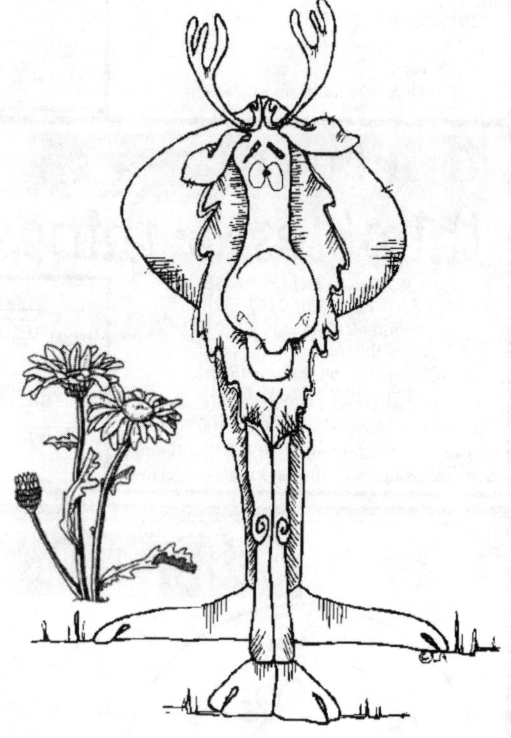

Ontario Guilds:

Elliot Lake	Elliot Lake Quilt Guild, P.O. Box 411, P5A 2J8	Meets: Every Tuesday 7 p.m. at Moose Lodge, 25 Oakland Blvd.
Brantford	Brant Heritage Quilters Guild, P.O. Box 23047, N3T 6K4	
Dryden	Sunset Country Quilters, P8N 3L8	Meets: 3rd Tuesday at Masonic Hall
Elliot Lake	The Elliot Lake Quilt Guild, P.O. Box 411, P5A 2J8	Meets: Every Tuesday (Sept. to June) 7 p.m. at the Moose Lodge
Hamilton	Hamilton Quilt Guild, c/o 8259 - 20 Rd., L9B 1P9	
Ingersoll	Oxford Quilter Guild 345 Hall St., Box 384, N5C 3V3	Meets: 1st Wednesday 7 p.m. and 1st Thursday 9:30 a.m. at Ingersoll Creative Arts Center
Kenora	Lake of the Woods Quilter's Guild	Meets: 2nd Thursday 7 p.m. at Beaver Brae High School
Kincardine	Kincardine Sunset Quilter's Guild	Meets: 2nd Wednesday 9:30 a.m. at St. Anthony's Church
Kirkton	Huron-Perth Quilter's Guild, Hwy. 23, N0K 1K0	Meets: 2nd Tuesday 9:30 a.m. at Kirkton Community Centre
Merrickville	Calgary Silver Thimble Quilters Guild, 1013 Heritage Dr., K0G 1N0	Meets: 1st & 3rd Wednesdays 7:30 p.m. at silver Springs Comm. Centre, 5720 Silver Ridge Dr. NW, Calgary
Oakville	Halton Quilters Guild, Box 171, L6J 4Z5	
Ottawa	Ottawa Valley Quilt Guild, 1439 Prince of Wales Dr.	Meets: 1st Monday (Sept-May) at Notre Dame High School
Stoney Creek	Stoney Creek Quilt Guild, c/o 22 Pembroke St., L8J 1N8	

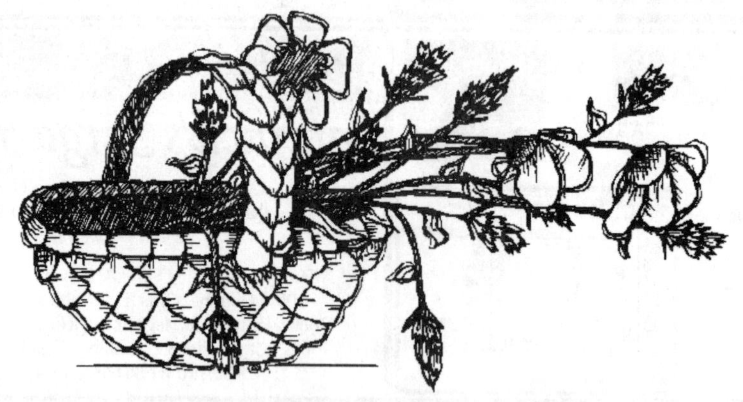

Saskatoon, SK #1

Homespun Craft Emporium, Inc.

16 - 1724 Quebec Ave. S7K 1V9
(306) 652-3585 Fax: (306) 384-9191
homespun86@hotmail.com Est: 1986
Owners: Peggy Grandberg & Sarah Sanduliak

The one stop shop for all your Quilting Supplies. 3000 Bolts of 100% Cotton Fabric, Books, Notions, & Tools. Authorized Bernina Sewing Machine Dealer, Sales & Service.

Circle Dr. E
Homespun Craft
Idylewyld Dr. N
39th St.
38th St.
Quebec Ave
1724
in Canadiana Centre
Warman Rd.
33rd St. E
2nd Ave.

Kindersley, SK #2

Mon - Sat
9 - 5:30
Thur til 8

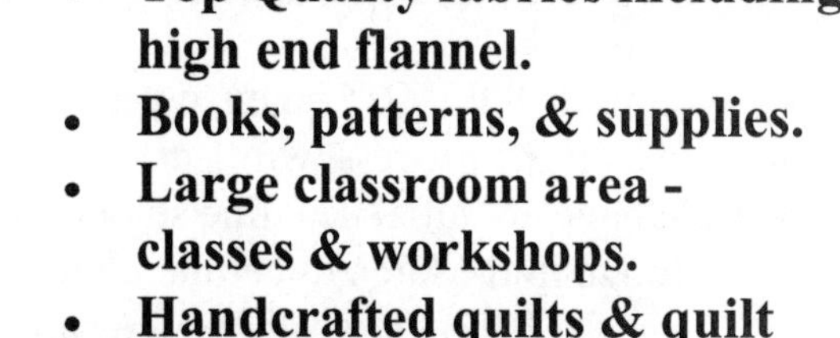

100 Main St., Box 1524 S0L 1S0
(306) 463-4505 Fax: (306) 463-4435
take.care@sasktel.net
Owner: Veronica Longmuir BSH. Ec. Est: 1979

6,000 sq. ft. of beautiful fabrics & displays
A Quilter's Gallery. Over 3000 bolts of cottons, plus 60 baby panels, fashion fabrics & More.
Pfaff, Janome & Babylock machines & sergers.

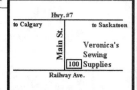

Hwy. #7
to Calgary
to Saskatoon
Main St.
Veronica's Sewing Supplies
100
Railway Ave.

Swift Current, SK #3

Quilts 'N Treasures LTD.

- **Top Quality fabrics including high end flannel.**
- **Books, patterns, & supplies.**
- **Large classroom area - classes & workshops.**
- **Handcrafted quilts & quilt products - a wide variety of methods**

#10 Hillside Plaza 1081 Central Ave. N
Swift Current, SK S9H 4Z2
(306) 773-2412
Est: 2002 2500 sq.ft.
1500 bolts including 400+ bolts of flannels
quiltsntreasures@sasktel.net
www.geocities.com/quilts_treasures

"We Keep You In Stitches"

Tuesday - Friday 10 - 5:30
Saturday 10 - 3:30

Another Shops in Saskatchewan: We suggest calling first

Moose Jaw	Prairie Quilters Loft, 116 Main St. N 2nd Level	306-693-7140
Spirit Wood	Thoughts & Things, 332 First St. E. Box 97	306-883-3800

Saskatchewan Guilds:

Moose Jaw — Moose Jaw Prairie Hearts Quilt Guild, Box 484, S6H 4P1
Meets: 1st & 3rd Thursday (Sept. to May) 7 p.m. at Diversified Services, 11 Wood Lily Dr.

Saskatoon — Saskatoon Quilters' Guild, Box 8801, S7K 6S6 Meets: 2nd & 4th Mondays 7:30 p.m. at Emmanuel Baptist

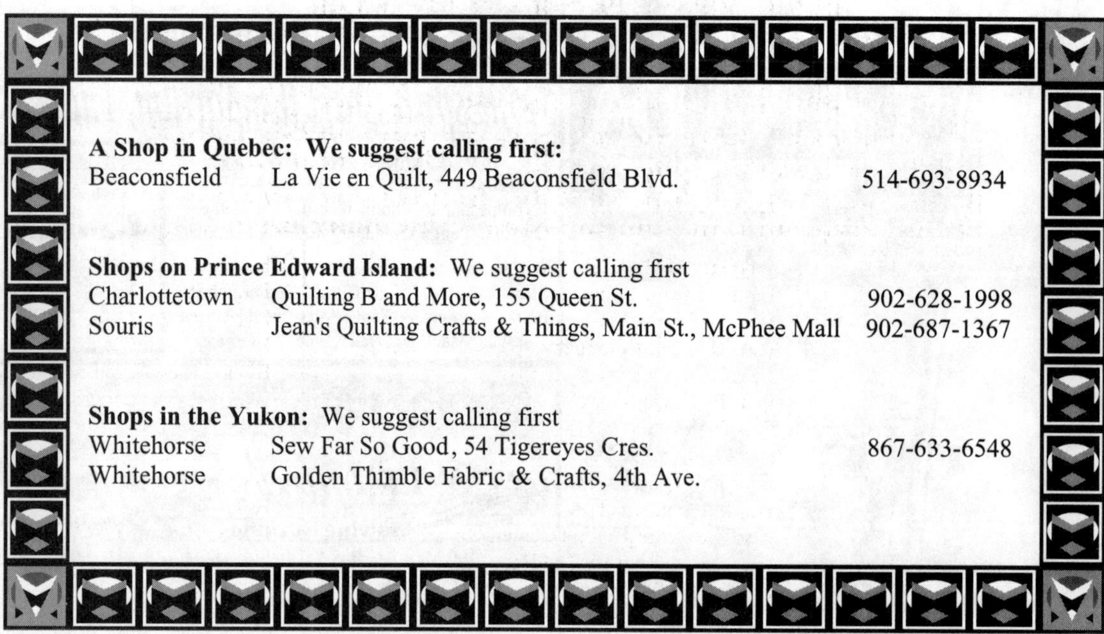

A Shop in Quebec: We suggest calling first:

Beaconsfield	La Vie en Quilt, 449 Beaconsfield Blvd.	514-693-8934

Shops on Prince Edward Island: We suggest calling first

Charlottetown	Quilting B and More, 155 Queen St.	902-628-1998
Souris	Jean's Quilting Crafts & Things, Main St., McPhee Mall	902-687-1367

Shops in the Yukon: We suggest calling first

Whitehorse	Sew Far So Good, 54 Tigereyes Cres.	867-633-6548
Whitehorse	Golden Thimble Fabric & Crafts, 4th Ave.	

Publishing Schedule of the *Quilters' Travel Companion*

- We publish the *QTC* in even years.
- We start the process with a mailing in early January.
- We have an initial deadline sometime in early February, but continue to work with shops through mid-March to get them into the book.
- After the February deadline, we call all the previous 'featured shops' that we did not hear back from through the mailing. This is a very hard part of the process, but it is our intention not to leave anyone out that would like to be in the book.
- We start the layout process for the book early in March and after many revisions and late nights we send it to the printer around the first of April
- The printer then needs two months to print thousands of copies of the book and they are then shipped back to us and we spend a back breaking week getting all the orders out to the shops across the country.

In general, the sooner we can get any information about shops or guilds, the easier and more efficient it makes our work.

Between editions we offer the "Up-To-Date" newsletter and ads on our website to get names of new shops out to the public.

If you own a shop or know of one we should be sure to include in future editions of this guide, please drop us a note, call (719) 685-5041, or visit our website at www.chalet-publishing.com.

Also if you have any suggestions for other information we could include that would be helpful when you're traveling, we'd appreciate hearing them.

We welcome wholesale inquiries.

An Alphabetical listing of featured shops by name